COUSINS
ON
THE LAW OF
MORTGAGES

AUSTRALIA
LBC Information Services
Sydney

CANADA and USA
Carswell
Toronto

NEW ZEALAND
Brooker's
Auckland

SINGAPORE and MALAYSIA
Sweet & Maxwell Asia
Singapore and Kuala Lumpur

PROPERTY AND CONVEYANCING LIBRARY

COUSINS

ON

THE LAW OF MORTGAGES

SECOND EDITION

by

EDWARD F. COUSINS B.A., LL.M.
Bencher of Lincoln's Inn
Deputy Chancery Master
Barrister of Gray's Inn and King's Inns, Dublin

with

IAN CLARKE, LL.B.
Barrister of Lincoln's Inn

Contributors

MICHELLE STEVENS-HOARE, LL.B., LL.M. (Property)
Barrister of Middle Temple
Member of the Civil Procedure Rules Committee

and

EDWARD ROWNTREE BA (OXON)
Barrister of Lincoln's Inn

LONDON
SWEET & MAXWELL
2001

Published in 2001 by
Sweet & Maxwell Limited of
100 Avenue Rd, London NW3.
Computerset by Interactive Sciences Ltd, Gloucester.
Printed in England by
Clays Ltd, St Ives plc

British Library Cataloguing in Publication Data
Cousins, Edward F.
The law of mortgages.
1. England. Mortgages. Law
I. Title
344.2064'364

ISBN 0–421–529504

ISBN 0-421-52950-4

9 780421 529502 >

PREFACE

The decision to publish this book was prompted by a perceived continuing and unfulfilled demand for a new practitioner's text on the law of mortgages.

Initially, it was envisaged that this project would involve the publication of a third edition of that valuable and now unobtainable work, *Waldock on the Law of Mortgages* (1949), the first edition of which having been written by Professor Hanbury and Mr Waldock and published in 1939. But, at an early stage of this venture, owing to the considerable developments which have occurred in the field of mortgages since the publication of the second edition of Waldock, it was found necessary to revise, reconstruct and rewrite substantial sections of this work.

It is in these circumstances that the *Law of Mortgages* was conceived, written, and now finally published, with all due acknowledgment to those remaining parts based upon (and hopefully, without any detraction from) the second edition of Waldock. It is my desire that this work will provide a useful and concise guide to practitioners and academics in the field of mortgages. I have attempted to set out the law as at June 30, 1989.

Finally, my thanks are due to colleagues and friends for their kindly criticisms and suggestions. I must also extend my thanks to my wife and children for their forbearance, large sections of this book having been written whilst on holiday in France and Spain during the Summers of 1987 and 1988.

Preface to the Second Edition

The first edition of this work was published in late 1989. As the preface to that edition stated, the decision to publish was prompted by the unfulfilled demand for a new practitioners' text. That original decision has been vindicated in two ways. First, the sales of the work since publication have been very healthy. Secondly, there has been a strong demand from practitioners for the text to be updated to reflect the wide changes in both statute law and case law that has occurred since 1989.

It is in these circumstances that the second edition has been published with all due acknowledgment to the hard work put in by Ian Clarke, Michelle Stevens-Hoare and Edward Rowntree.

Unfortunately it has not proved possible in this work to treat fully the provisions of the Financial Services and Markets Act 2000 as to mortgage regulation. The scope of the regulatory regime has still not been finalised in subordinate legislation and guidance and many provisions of the Act are still not yet in force.

The thrust of the Act is that no unauthorised person will be able to carry out any regulated activity. Authorised persons will only be able to carry out regulated activities for which they have been granted permission. A "regulated activity" is one which is regulated by the Financial Services Authority under the Act.

It is currently anticipated that the FSA's regime of mortgage regulation will come into effect no later than August 31, 2002. This date is referred to as "N3" in the latest Consultation Paper (CP98) published in June 2001 entitled "The Draft Mortgage Sourcebook, including Policy Statement on CP70". This is to be nine months after the 2000 Act (including Part II) finally comes into force. That date is referred to as "N2" in the Consultation Paper and is to be no later than November 30, 2001. The date for response to this Consultation Paper is September 14, 2001.

Thus, any detailed treatment of the Act and its subordinate legislation and guidance at this stage will be premature.

I must also extend my thanks to Peter Kennealy, Thomas Bourke and the other members of staff and the *stagières* at the European University Institute, San Domenico di Fiesole, Firenze, for all their help and assistance provided to me earlier this year. I spent happy times in the Library of the EUI revising this work having accompanied my wife whilst she held a Visiting Fellowship at the Institute.

11 Stone Buildings
Lincoln's Inn

July 2001

CONTENTS

TABLE OF CASES

TABLE OF STATUTES

TABLE OF STATUTORY INSTRUMENTS

CHAPTER 1

THE NATURE OF A MORTGAGE

INTRODUCTION

There have been many attempts, both judicial and academic, to describe a **1–01** mortgage. Two of the most famous attest to the difficulty of carrying out that task in a satisfactory manner. Lord Macnaghten was moved to say, in the case of *Samuel v. Jarrah Timber and Wood Paving Corporation*[1] that no-one, by the light of nature, ever understood an English mortgage of real estate; while Maitland described it as "one long *suppressio veri* and *suggestio falsi*".[2]

Although the essence of a mortgage transaction is the charging of property as security for performance of an obligation, the transaction had for centuries been carried out by conveying an estate in land to the lender, thereby giving rise to the difficulty. These two facts were recognised by Lindley M.R. when he formulated his well-known description of a mortgage in the case of *Santley v. Wilde*.[3] This was a case where the mortgage had been taken not merely as security for the loan but, additionally, as security for a one-third share of future profits, thus serving to demonstrate that mortgages can be raised to secure the performance of obligations other than the payment of debts.

The purpose of security is to afford to the obligee some additional means of **1–02** enforcing the performance of the obligation by, or extracting the money equivalent from, the obligor. Thus a lender is often unwilling to rely solely on the borrower's personal credit, and requires a greater certainty of repayment than the mere possibility of enforcing the claim in an action of debt. The borrower can meet this requirement by offering personal security or suretyship. In that case a third party (the surety or guarantor) undertakes to answer for the borrower's default by way of a personal commitment, and the lender has an action in debt against him should the borrower default. The surety may also reinforce his undertaking by giving a real security.

---

[1] [1904] A.C. 323 at 326.
[2] Maitland, *Equity* (2nd ed., 1969), p. 182. In 1991, and following the publication of its Working Paper (No. 99) on Land Mortgages in 1986, the Law Commission has made wide-ranging recommendations for the simplification of the law of mortgages. The major recommendation is that the present system should be abolished and replaced by a simple concept, namely the formal land mortgage and the informal land mortgage. This Report *Transfer of Land — Land Mortgages* ((1991) Law. Com. No. 204, HC 5) states that the law is complicated and has achieved " . . . a state of artificiality and complexity that is now difficult to defend" (para. 2.1). Unfortunately the Government has rejected such proposals on the basis that there is considered to be insufficient support for the proposals (see the Press Notice from the Lord Chancellor's Department issued on March 19 1998). In due course the Law Commission may reconsider these recommendations.
[3] [1899] 2 Ch. 474 and see *post* paras 18–16 *et seq.*; 18–22.

Real security is obtained when property is appropriated specifically to the satisfaction of a particular debt, so that that debt is a primary charge on the property. The lender whose right is protected by a real security is entitled to take that security for the discharge of his own secured debt, even to the extent of exhausting it entirely and withdrawing it altogether from the pool of the borrower's assets available to the general creditor.[4] If, as is usual, the lender takes a personal covenant from the borrower to repay and the security is insufficient to discharge the debt he can seek to recover the balance and prove in the borrower's bankruptcy for such purpose.[5]

1–03   By giving real security, the borrower has a property with which he cannot deal freely because it is incumbered. However, he can release the property from its incumbrance by discharging his obligation to the lender whatever the nature of the right which the lender acquired. This right to redeem is part of the borrower's equity of redemption. A mortgage deed generally contains a stipulation that the borrower shall repay on a fixed date which is, say, six months from the execution of the deed. The result, at law, of the borrower's failure to comply with this stipulation is that the property becomes vested in the lender. However in equity the borrower will be allowed to redeem the property after his default.[6] This arises even though the parties may have made time of the essence of the contract. This right to redeem will subsist until the lender has exercised such powers as he may have to destroy the borrower's equity of redemption by statute, foreclosure, sale or release.[7] The borrower's right[8] to redeem can also become statute-barred[8] if the mortgage is a mortgage of real property or of a mixed fund[9] but not if it is a mortgage of personal property only.

In spite of judicial reluctance to accept it, there is a well established principle that the borrower will not be permitted to surrender to the lender his right to redeem, by any term of the mortgage contract[10]; though he may enter into a separate contract to give the lender a collateral advantage.[11]

The Substance of the Transaction

1–04   In equity, it is a matter of substance, not of form, whether a transaction creates a security or transfers absolute ownership. If the true purpose of the transaction is to create a security, it will not assist the lender to disguise it as a conditional sale or a conveyance.[12] It is possible to demonstrate the sham nature of a written agreement masking its true nature by providing extrinsic evidence to that effect,

---

[4] *White v. Simmons* (1871) L.R. 6 Ch.App. 555.
[5] *Re London, Windsor and Greenwich Hotels Co. (Quartermaine's Case)* [1892] 1 Ch. 639. *Re Bonacino, ex p. Discount Banking Co.* (1894) 1 Mans. 59.
[6] *Seton v. Slade, Hunter v. Seton* (1802) 7 Ves. 265.
[7] *Weld v. Petre* [1929] 1 Ch. 33 at 43.
[8] Limitation Act 1980, s.17. In order to rely on that section, the mortgagee must be in possession in his character as mortgagee: *Hyde v. Dallaway* (1843) 2 H. 528. See *post* para. 22–23.
[9] *i.e.* a mortgage of real property and a life policy, see *Charter v. Watson* [1899] 1 Ch. 175.
[10] *Samuel v. Jarrah Timber and Wood Paving Corporation* [1904] A.C. 323, *per* Lord Halsbury L.C. See generally *post*, para. 18–01 *et seq.*
[11] *Kreglinger v. New Patagonia Meat and Cold Storage Co.* [1914] A.C. 25; *cf. Noakes v. Rice* [1902] A.C. 24 and *Bradley v. Carritt* [1903] A.C. 253.
[12] *England v. Codrington* (1758) 1 Ed. 169; *Re Duke of Marlborough* [1894] 2 Ch. 133; *cf. Barnhart v. Greenshields* (1853) 9 Moo. P.C.C. 18; *Re Kent and Sussex Sawmills* [1947] Ch. 177.

such evidence being admissible in court. It is necessary to look at the agreement as a whole as there is no one clear touchstone.[13] Where an agreement was intended only to create a security, that fact may be proved afterwards by parol evidence even though it contradicts the plain language of a deed.[14] Thus, where a conveyance of property was accompanied by a parol agreement for the defeasance of the deed on payment of a sum of money, it was held to be a fraud, in equity, for the grantee to refuse to give up the deed in return for the payment being made.[15] Nor is it conclusive in the lender's favour that the borrower makes two separate agreements, one to give security and one to purchase the mortgaged property. The court will declare the latter void if it appears that there was only one transaction.[16]

MORTGAGE SECURITY

A mortgage has been described as "a conveyance of land or an assignment of **1–05** chattels as a security for the payment of a debt or the discharge of some other obligation for which it is given."[17] This description brings out the essential features of a mortgage: the provision of *security* by a *transfer of property rights*. Although mortgages are most commonly raised to secure a money debt, they may also be granted to secure other obligations.

The mortgage transaction consists of a transfer of the legal or equitable title to property from the borrower, to the lender, to be held by the lender until all his claims under the mortgage are satisfied. The borrower's right is to have the title restored to him on fulfilment of his obligation to the lender even if he does not do so until after the contractual date for that fulfilment.

Although in certain circumstances the lender may assume possession of the property, his security does not depend on being in possession. If he wishes to apply the rents and profits to the satisfaction of the mortgage debt, his remedy is to appoint a receiver.[18] He cannot derive any personal profit from being in possession. Indeed, he is accountable to the borrower not only for the profits which he does make but also for those which he reasonably ought to have made.[19]

In order to protect both his own interests and those of persons who may deal **1–06** with the borrower subsequent to the giving of security, the lender should ensure to the best of his ability that the borrower is not able to represent himself as being the owner of the property free from incumbrances. This means either taking the

---

[13] See *Snook v. London and West Riding Investments Ltd* [1967] 2 Q.B. 786; *Welsh Development Agency v. Export Finance Co. Ltd* [1992] B.C.L.C. 148; *Lloyds and Scottish Finance Ltd v. Cyril Lord Carpet Sales Ltd* [1992] B.C.L.C. 609.

[14] *Lincoln v. Wright* (1859) 4 De G. & J. 16; *Walker v. Walker* (1740) 2 ATK 98; *Lord Irnham v. Child* (1791) Bro. C92.

[15] *Re Duke of Marlborough* [1894] 2 Ch. 133. See also *England v. Codrington* (1758) 1Eden 169; *Williams v. Owen* 5 My & Cr 303 at 306; *Douglas v. Culverwell* (1862) 4 De G.F. & J. 20; *Barton v. Bank of New South Wales* (1890) 15 App. Cas. 379; *United Dominion Trust Ltd v. Beech, Savan, Tabner, and Thompson* [1972] 1 Lloyd's Rep. 546.

[16] *Lewis v. Love (Frank)* [1961] 1 W.L.R. 261 where separate options to purchase were held to be void (P. V. Baker): *cf. Reeve v. Lisle* [1902] A.C. 461. See para. 18–07.

[17] *Santley v. Wilde* [1899] 2 Ch. 474 *per* Lindley M.R.

[18] L.P.A. 1925, s.109.

[19] *White v. City of London Brewery* (1889) 42 Ch.D. 237; *Shepherd v. Spansheath* (1988) E.G.C.S. 35.

documents of title in addition to the conveyance,[20] or registering his mortgage in whatever way is appropriate.

The lender's ultimate remedy is the destruction of the borrower's equity of redemption. This he can achieve by sale without the intervention of the court if there is an express or statutory power of sale but not otherwise. This can also be achieved by foreclosure. This can be decreed only by the court which has the power to order sale instead.[21]

OTHER FORMS OF SECURITY

1. Possessory securities: pledge and lien

1-07 A *pledge* (or *pawn*)[22] of chattels is effected either by actual[23] or constructive delivery, the latter being by delivery of documents.[24] It is a form of bailment. The creditor's rights arise through his *possession* under the contract of pledge. The right of the lender, or pledgee, is to retain the chattel until a proper tender of the amount due is made.[25] It is not a right of *ownership*. As against the borrower, or pledgor, he may deny him possession. If the debt remains unsatisfied, he may after a reasonable time sell the chattel. However, the borrower's right to redeem subsists until the chattel is sold.[26]

The lender thus has a special property in the chattel.[27] It is to be distinguished from a mortgage of chattels as unlike a mortgagee, the lender is not at law the owner of it and therefore can never foreclose.[28] Foreclosure is the destruction of the equity to redeem property which at law is the property of the lender and is therefore unavailable to a pledgee.[29] On the other hand, if a third party wrongfully removes the pledged chattel from keeping, it is the lender who has the right to sue in conversion, since that arises from ownership and possession, or from possession alone, or from the immediate right to possession. Whilst the chattel is in pledge, the borrower has none of these remedies.

If the lender returns the chattel to the borrower before he has discharged the debt, the lender loses his special property[30] in the chattel unless there is a

---

[20] Since the enactment of the Law of Property (Miscellaneous Provisions) Act 1989, s.2, a deposit of title deeds can no longer be construed as an act of part performance of the contract to create a legal mortgage. See para. 5–07 *et seq.*

[21] L.P.A. 1925, s.91. See *post* para. 16–103.

[22] These are interchangeable terms. However, special rules apply to "pawning" goods in, *e.g.* pawnbrokers where advances are made to the pledgor. Such transactions may be governed by the Consumer Credit Act 1974 as regulated consumer credit agreements, see s.6(2), (3) ss.114–121 (as amended), see *post* para. 14–01 *et seq.*

[23] *Re Morritt, ex p. Official Receiver* (1886) 18 Q.B.D. 222.

[24] *Official Assignee of Madras v. Mercantile Bank of India Ltd* [1935] A.C. 53.

[25] *Halliday v. Holgate* (1868) L.R. 3 Ex. 299; *Yungmann v. Briesemann* (1892) 67 L.T. 642.

[26] *Carter v. Wake* (1877) 4 Ch.D. 605.

[27] *Donald v. Suckling* (1866) L.R. 1 Q.B.D. 585.

[28] *Carter v. Wake* (1877) 4 Ch.D. 605. *Re Cosslett (Contractors) Ltd* [1988] Ch. 495 at 508 *per* Millett L.J.

[29] *Donald v.* Suckling (1866) L.R. 1 Q.B.D. 585.

[30] The term "special property" was criticised by Lord Mersey in *The Odessa* [1916] 1 A.C. 145 at 158–159. Here it was stated that the pawnee's right to sell in truth created no property right whatsoever. He preferred the term "special interest". See also *Mathew v. TM Sutton Ltd* [1994] 1 W.L.R. 1455 at 1461 *per* Chadwick J.

particular temporary purpose for the return. The lender is thereby relegated to the status of an unsecured creditor.[31]

A *possessory lien* gives the lender even less of a right against the borrower **1–08** than a pledge. The right is a right to detain the chattel until a debt is satisfied.[32] There is, in general, no right to realise the security by sale,[33] though such a right can exist in special cases.

If the lender is in possession of the borrower's chattels under any of the following circumstances, he has, provided that his possession remains continuous, a lien on the chattels until his debt is satisfied. These occur if:

(1) he has, expended labour, skill or money on them[34];
(2) he is compellable by law to receive, or to perform services in respect of them[35];
(3) he has saved them from loss or capture at sea.[36]

Such liens arise by operation of law[37] and are known as common law liens. They secure only the particular debt which accrues to the lender by reason of his dealings with the chattels in his possession.

A similar right can be created by express contract or can arise by implication **1–09** from trade or business usage.[38] Frequently such contractual liens, as they are generally termed, extend to cover the general balance between debtor and creditor, so that the indebtedness is not necessarily related to the chattel detained. Thus a solicitor's lien on papers which come into his possession in the course of business,[39] or a factor's lien on chattels,[40] gives each the right to detain against the general balance of his account. Whether the lien arises at common law, by contract or by implication, the rights under it depend on possession. Thus if the lender returns the chattels to the borrower, or contracts on terms that the borrower may temporarily resume possession, or the lender hands the chattels to a third party with the intent to abandon possession, his lien is lost. As with a pledge, there is an exception to this rule where, for some specific and temporary purpose, he delivers the chattels to the borrower or to a third party.[41]

2. Non-possessory securities: equitable lien

Like a lien at common law, an equitable lien can arise in respect of both real and **1–10** personal property.[42] However, unlike a common law lien, an equitable lien does

---

[31] *Reeves v. Capper* (1838) 5 Bing.N.C. 136; *North Western Bank v. Poynter, Son and Macdonalds* [1895] A.C. 56.
[32] *Lickbarrow v. Mason* (1787) 2 T.R. 63.
[33] *Smart v. Sandars* (1848) 5 C.B. 895; *Re Hamlet International plc* [1988] 2 B.C.L.C. 164.
[34] *Chase v. Westmore* (1816) 5 M. & S. 180.
[35] *Robins & Co. v. Gray* [1895] 2 Q.B. 501; *Marsh v. Commissioner of Police* [1945] K.B. 43.
[36] *Hartfort v. Jones* (1699) 1 Ld.Ray. 393.
[37] *Gladstone v. Birley* (1817) 2 Mer. 401.
[38] *Rushforth v. Hadfield* (1805) 7 East. 224.
[39] *Ex p. Sterling* (1809) 16 Ves. 258.
[40] *Kruger v. Wilcox* (1755) Amb. 252.
[41] *Reeves v. Capper* (1838) 5 Bing.N.C. 136.
[42] *Re Stucley* [1906] 1 Ch. 67; *Barker v. Stickney* [1919] 1 K.B. 121.

not depend on possession of the property which is subject to the lien.[43] It is a type of equitable charge arising by operation of law arising irrespective of the parties' intentions,[44] except where its retention would be manifestly inconsistent with the terms of the agreement between the parties or the true nature of the transaction.[45] It also falls within the definition of "mortgage" for the purposes of the Law of Property Act 1925.[46] Further, the holder of an equitable lien has the power to realise his security by judicial sale[47] or the appointment of a receiver. This means that the holder of the equitable lien is treated in equity as a secured creditor of the purchaser and can apply to the court for a declaration of his interest and for an order of sale of the land. His debt will be satisfied from the proceeds of sale together with the costs of proceedings. If the holder of the lien is paid off by a third party that party can claim the benefit of the lien by subrogation. However subrogation may be displaced by a specific charge.[48] It is exceptional for the holder of a common law lien to have the power of sale.

The contrast is well illustrated by reference to the position of a vendor under a specifically enforceable contract for the sale of land. Thus, at common law the vendor would have a lien on the land or the deeds for the unpaid purchase money until he had conveyed the land to the purchaser or let him into possession of it, or handed over the deeds.

The equitable lien, however, persists irrespective of possession, so long as any part of the purchase money remains unpaid. It does not appear to depend upon a specifically enforceable contract to purchase the legal estate. It is liable to be defeated by a *bona fide* purchaser for value if it is not protected, as a general equitable charge in the case of unregistered land (as a class c(iii) land charge), or by notice or caution if the land is registered. The vendor's common law lien depending on his possession is an overriding interest if the land is registered, and thus does not require to be so protected.

A purchaser also has an equitable lien for his deposit[49] and costs of investigating title should he lawfully rescind the contract.[50] The lien arises by operation of law. It does not depend upon a specifically enforceable contract to purchase the legal estate, and often will arise where there is no specifically enforceable agreement.[51] It operates as an equitable charge and the holder is in equity a secured creditor of the vendor and can apply to the court for a declaration of his interest and for an order of sale of the land.[52] The lien can be protected in the same manner as the unpaid vendor's lien. However, if the purchase goes off through the purchaser's fault, the lien is lost.[53]

---

[43] *Goode v. Burton* (1847) 1 Ex. 189; *Wrout v. Dawes* (1858) 25 Beav. 369.
[44] *Re Beirnstein* [1925] Ch. 12 at 17–18; *Re Birmingham, (dec'd)* [1959] Ch. 523 at 529.
[45] *Barclays Bank plc v. Estates and Commercial Ltd* [1997] 1 W.L.R. 415 at 420–421.
[46] s.205(xvi).
[47] *Neate v. Duke of Marlborough* (1838) 3 Myl. & Cr. 407.
[48] *Coptic Ltd v. Bailey* [1972] Ch. 446; *Orakpo v. Manson Investments Ltd* [1978] A.C. 95; but see *Bank of Ireland Finance Ltd v. DJ Daley Ltd* [1978] I.R. 83.
[49] *Whitbread & Co. v. Watt* [1902] 1 Ch. 835; but *cf. Combe v. Swaythling* [1947] Ch. 625 (no lien where deposit paid to stakeholder).
[50] *Kitton v. Hewett* (1904) W.N. 21; *Re Furneaux & Aird's Contract* (1906) W.N. 215; where the contract goes off because the vendor's title is defective, the lien extends to costs of proceedings to enforce specific performance, or of a vendor and purchaser summons. (see n. 59 *ante*.)
[51] *Chattey v. Farndale Holdings Inc.* [1998] 75 P. & C.R. 298 at 305–307.
[52] *Lyus v. Prowsa Developments Ltd* [1982] 1 W.L.R. 1044 at 1046–1047; *Chattey v. Farndale Holdings Inc.* [1998] 75 P. & C.R. 298 at 318.
[53] *Dinn v. Grant* (1852) 5 De G. & Sm. 451.

3. **Non-possessory securities: the equitable charge**

An equitable charge arises where specified property is appropriated to the **1–11**
discharge of an obligation without any right of ownership being transferred to the
chargee. In many ways an equitable chargee is in the same position as the holder
of an equitable lien. He is in the position of a secured creditor.[54] His interest is
liable to be defeated if it is not protected in the appropriate manner. Since he has
no title, he cannot foreclose or go into possession.[55] Judicial and academic
indifference to strictness of terminology has led to the two terms being treated as
largely interchangeable, and the most obvious distinction between them is that a
lien arises by operation of law and a charge by act of parties. This, however,
makes little, if any, difference to the remedies available.[56]

4. **Distress**

This is the least effective form of real security. The creditor does not get **1–12**
ownership or possession or the rights of a chargee, and the class of transaction in
which it affords the creditor protection in a bankruptcy is very limited. Most
commonly it is exercised by a landlord, whose power of distress entitles him to
take and eventually sell chattels brought by the tenant onto the demised premises
to satisfy a claim for rent. A licence to seize and sell annexed to a contract of
pledge is also valid, since it is not caught by section 9 of the Bills of Sale Act
1882.[57] However, in general, a licence to seize chattels given by contract
expressly to secure a debt is a bill of sale for the purposes of that Act and is void
because it cannot be made in the form required.[58]

MORTGAGE AND CHARGE

The essential feature of distinction between a mortgage and a charge is that a **1–13**
mortgage is a security accompanied by a transfer of property rights, whilst a
charge is an appropriation of property to the satisfaction of an obligation without
any such transfer of title. The chargee only has certain rights over the property
charged.[59] It therefore, should follow as a matter of principle that a mortgagee,
but not a chargee, should have the right to foreclose or to go into possession,
while both should have the right to appoint a receiver or to realise the security by
sale.

The distinction, nevertheless, is clouded not only by the judicial indifference **1–14**
referred to above, but also by the draftsmen of the 1925 property legislation. In
the definition section of the Law of Property Act[60] a mortgage is described as

---

[54] *National Provincial and Union Bank of England v. Charnley* [1924] 1 K.B. 431 at 445, 446.
[55] *Tennant v. Trenchard* (1869) L.R. 4 Ch. 537.
[56] *Goode v. Burton* (1847) 1 Ex. 189; *Re Richardson, Shillito v. Hobson* (1885) 30 Ch.D. 396, *per* Fry
L.J. at 403.
[57] *Re Townsend* (1886) 16 Q.B.D. 532.
[58] *ibid.*
[59] See *Jones v. Woodward* (1917) 116 L.T. 378 at 379; *London County and Westminster Bank Ltd v.
Tompkins* [1918] 1 K.B. 515.
[60] LPA 1925, s.205(1)(xvi).

including "a charge or lien on any property for securing money or money's worth" whereas a mortgagee includes "a chargee by way of legal mortgage" but not the holder of a lien or an equitable chargee.[61] Further, whilst section 90 of the Act deals with orders for sale in reference to equitable mortgages, the section is actually entitled "Realisation of equitable charges by the court."

This confusion also reflects reality when looked at from the point of view of the borrower. The lender has, *at law*, rights which differ according to whether he is a mortgagee or a chargee. As Harman J. said in *Four-Maids Ltd* v. *Dudley Marshall (Properties) Ltd*[62]:

> "The right of the mortgagee to possession in the absence of some contract has nothing to do with default on the part of the mortgagor. The mortgagee may go into possession before the ink is dry on the mortgage unless there is something . . . whereby he has contracted himself out of that right."

A chargee has no such right against the chargor, as he is never owner of the property at law. That same circumstance prevents him destroying the chargor's equity of redemption by foreclosure which is a right confined to a mortgagee.

1–15   The borrower, however, may find himself put in the same position, in practice, *vis-à-vis* the lender, whatever the lender's status. If he cannot discharge the obligation, his right to redeem is as effectively destroyed by sale as by foreclosure. He loses possession as a result either of the appointment of a receiver or the making of a possession order.

The similarity in the borrower's position, whether his lender is a mortgagee or a chargee, is reflected by the statutory provision created by the LPA 1925 allowing a legal mortgage to be created by means of a charge by deed expressed to be by way of legal mortgage.[63] In practice, therefore, a legal charge is no different from a legal mortgage. Although the document is described as a charge, the lender, regardless of his lack of title, has all the powers of a legal mortgagee[64]: foreclosure, sale, possession, and the appointment of a receiver are all available to him.

Mortgages and Statutory Charges

1–16   There are species of charges which are subsumed under the generic head of "statutory charges". They are to be distinguished from mortgages in that they are imposed by statute on land, whereas mortgages arise out of the consensual act of the parties. The nature and effect of a statutory charge depend on the terms of the particular statute.

The following are some examples of statutory charges imposed on land:

> (1) charges made in favour of local authorities relating to the expense of executing works required to render houses fit for human habitation and to put houses into repair[65];

---

[61] *ibid.*
[62] [1957] Ch. 317 at 320.
[63] LPA 1925, s.85.
[64] *ibid.* s.87.
[65] See the Housing Act 1985, ss.189, 190, 193, Sched. 10, para. 7.

(2) charges made in favour of local authorities relating to the expense of rendering houses fit for multiple occupation, or remedying neglect of management[66];

(3) charges upon premises of frontagers in favour of local authorities for expenses incurred by them in making up private streets[67];

(4) charging orders on land by way of equitable execution[68];

(5) charges in favour of landlords of business premises in respect of compensation for or the cost of improvements[69];

(6) charges in favour of landlords or tenants of agricultural holdings in respect of compensation payable[70];

(7) charges to secure the repayment of discounts given by local authorities to public sector tenants on the purchase of a house or flat in the event of early disposal of the property.[71]

CHARGE AND TRUST

A charge is created by the appropriation of specific property for the discharge of **1–17** a debt or other obligation, there having been no change in ownership of the property either at law or in equity. It confers on the chargee the right to apply to the court for an order for sale or the appointment of a receiver. The chargor has a right to redeem.[72] It does not confer the right to possession.[73] In the case of a trust there occurs the disposition of a beneficial interest in property to beneficiary or beneficiaries under the trust who are thereby entitled to the trust property.

STATUTORY LEGAL CHARGES

This is a special form of charge by way of a legal mortgage and certain covenants are implied.[74]

---

[66] See *ibid.* ss.352, 372, 375, Sched. 10, para. 7.
[67] See the Highways Act 1980, ss.203, 212.
[68] See the Charging Orders Act 1979, *post* paras 5–19, 5–20.
[69] See the Landlord and Tenant Act 1927, s.12, Sched. 1.
[70] See the Agricultural Holdings Act 1986, ss.85–87, and see para. 10–05.
[71] See the Housing Act 1985, ss.36, 156; the Housing Act 1988, s.79, Sched. 11 paras 1, 2; the Housing Act 1996, s.11.
[72] *Carreras Rothmans Ltd v. Freeman Mathews Treasure Ltd* [1985] Ch. 207.
[73] *Re Bond Worth Ltd* [1980] Ch. 228 at 248, *per* Slade J.; *Carreras Rothmans Ltd v. Freeman Mathews Treasure Ltd* [1985] Ch. 207; *Tatung (UK) Ltd v. Galex Telesure Ltd* (1989) 5 B.C.C. 325; *Compaq Computer Ltd v. Abercon Group Ltd* [1993] B.C.L.C. 602; [1991] BCC 484; and *Modelboard Ltd v. Outer Box Ltd* [1993] B.C.L.C. 623; [1992] B.C.C. 945, and see *post* para. 5–03 *et seq.*
[74] See *post* para. 3–34.

CHAPTER 2

HISTORY OF THE LAW OF MORTGAGE[1]

COMMON LAW

The practice of giving rights over land as security for debt is of great antiquity. **2–01** Until the end of the twelfth century the transaction was by way of lease by the mortgagor to the mortgagee, and was either a *vivum vadium* (live pledge, "vifgage") or a *mortuum vadium* (dead pledge, "mortgage" *i.e.* mort (dead), gage (pledge)). This depended on whether the income from the land was, or was not, used in the discharge of the debt. In default of repayment either on the appointed day or, following an order of the court, after a reasonable time, the mortgagee took the fee simple.[2] The Roman law of mortgages went through a similar evolution to that in England. By Justinian's time the use of hypothecation was almost universal. In England a mortgage is in substance if not in form a hypothecation and the charge by way of legal mortgage is in the process of ousting the mortgage. This development completes the formal evolution.

Such transactions were not wholly satisfactory to the mortgagee since the *seisina ut de vadio* which he acquired was not protected by law, and it was also doubtful whether a term of years could be enlarged into a fee simple. Mortgages of freehold land were therefore made by conveyance of the fee simple, subject to the mortgagor's right to re-enter and determine the mortgagee's estate if the money were repaid on the named date. This was very onerous for the mortgagor, who would lose the land and yet remain liable for the debt if he did not repay it on the due date.

The usual form of the mortgage by reconveyance did not remain fixed, and by **2–02** the beginning of the seventeenth century had developed into something resembling the modern pre-1926 form. It consisted of a conveyance of the fee simple with a covenant to reconvey if the money was paid on the due date. Mortgages by granting leases still existed, but their main use was for the purpose of raising portions terms. The effect of the mortgage, at common law, was not changed as a result of the change in form. The mortgagor still lost his land and remained liable for the debt if he failed to pay on the due date, unless the mortgage provided otherwise. An alternative form was a conveyance subject to a condition that the conveyance would be avoided if the debt was repaid on the due date.

---

[1] For fuller treatments of the subject, see Pollock and Maitland, *The History of English Law* (2nd ed., 1911), Vol. 2, p. 119; Holdsworth, *History of English Law*; and the preface to Turner, *Equity of Redemption* (1931).

[2] The usury laws influenced the development of the forms of mortgage as a means of securing the lending of money. Lending at a fixed rate of interest to a borrower was rendered illegal by such laws and methods were developed to avoid the restrictions—hence the concept of the borrower granting a lease over his property in favour of the lender.

The important substantial, as distinct from formal, development was that the proprietary right of the creditor arose, not by virtue of a lease and the operation of a condition precedent, but by virtue of a grant and the operation of a condition subsequent. Although the mortgagee still went into possession under the later form, his protection was no longer based on that possession but on the title derived from the grant. The form underwent an apparently minor alteration in that the reconveyance was no longer, in general, made on condition that the mortgagor was entitled to re-enter on discharging the debt, but, rather, subject to a proviso[3] that the mortgagee would reconvey the fee simple if the debt was paid on the due date. The advantage of this form was that proof of title depended on the reconveyance rather than on the date of payment of the money.

2–03   Thus the modern pre-1926 form of mortgage was by way of conveyance of the fee simple to the mortgagee, defeasible by a condition subsequent on a date fixed by the parties. The mortgagee enjoyed the following advantages:

(1) Absolute priority, in the absence of fraud, misrepresentation or gross negligence, over all later incumbrancers, by virtue of his legal title which gave him a right *in rem*.
(2) The right to custody of the title deeds.
(3) The power to convey the legal estate to a purchaser, in exercising his express or statutory power of sale, without applying to the court.
(4) The right to protect his security by going into possession.
(5) The right to apply to the court for a decree of foreclosure which, if granted, would destroy the mortgagor's equity of redemption and immediately vest the fee simple in him.

Similarly, leaseholds could be mortgaged by way of assignment of the term with a covenant to reassign. This, however, was not a popular form of mortgage because it created privity of estate between the landlord and the mortgagee.[4] The mortgagee thus became liable on all such covenants in the lease as ran with the land, including the obligation to pay rent. Consequently, the alternative method, whereby the mortgagor granted a sub-lease, one day shorter than the lease, with a proviso for cesser on redemption, was generally adopted. This became one of the two methods for the mortgage of leaseholds permitted by the 1925 legislation. As a sub-tenant, the mortgagee would not be in privity of estate with the landlord and would not be liable on the covenants in the lease.[5]

2–04   However, this method of creating mortgages of leaseholds led to two difficulties, both of which arose from the retention of a nominal reversion by the mortgagor. The mortgagee was not entitled to custody of the title deeds, nor could he, on exercising his power of sale, vest the whole of the mortgagor's lease in the purchaser. These were overcome by providing, in the mortgage deed, that the mortgagor declared himself a trustee of the nominal reversion for the mortgagee. Usually there was a clause permitting the mortgagee to appoint new trustees in place of the mortgagor. In this way the mortgagor could be compelled

---

[3] As a result of *Cromwel's Case* (1601) 2 Co.Rep. 69(b) which decided that "proviso" makes a condition, the proviso for reconveyance subjected the mortgagee's estate to a condition subsequent.
[4] Under the doctrine in *Spencer's Case* (1583) 5 Co.Rep. 16.
[5] *Bonner v. Tottenham and Edmonton Permanent Investment Building Society* [1899] 1 Q.B. 161.

to assign his reversion to a purchaser, without the need for the court to order an assignment. The mortgagee, therefore, had effective control of the nominal reversion.[6]

THE INFLUENCE OF EQUITY

The development of the law of mortgages was also affected by the laws relating **2–05** to loans made at interest. Originally, as stated above,[7] loans at interest were illegal. However, from the sixteenth century onwards, maximum rates were fixed by the Usury Acts, with the result that the Court of Chancery took the view that a mortgage should be a security only.[8] It would no longer permit the mortgagee to profit from the fee simple, and would confine his benefit to the interest permitted by statute. Occupation, likewise, would yield no advantage to the mortgagee (except in the case of the now obsolete Welsh mortgage[9]) since he would be liable to the mortgagor for a full rent should he go into possession. Thus arose the modern type of mortgage under which the mortgagor remains in possession of the land and the conveyance of the fee simple is by way of security only.

The courts of equity, which had for many years relieved the mortgagor against forfeiture in special cases, at length established the rule that the mortgagor must be permitted to redeem his fee simple even though he did not pay on the due date.[10] The mortgagee had vested in him, as soon as the mortgage was made, an equitable interest whose measure was the difference between the value of the land and the amount of the debt, and one which he could enforce against anyone except a bona fide purchaser for value from the mortgagor without notice.

In addition to the contractual right to redeem at common law, which would rarely be exercised, the mortgagor obtained an equitable right to redeem which could not be exercised until the contractual date for redemption was past.[11] This right could be exercised only if the courts of equity thought it proper. Inequitable conduct on the part of the mortgagor would bar his right to redeem.

1. The equity of redemption

The equity of redemption is an interest which the mortgagor can convey, devise, **2–06** entail, lease, mortgage or settle.[12] If the mortgagor dies intestate it will devolve subject to the intestacy rules.[13] It has been held that the equity of redemption in leasehold premises subject to a mortgage can pass to the Crown as *bona vacantia* where the mortgagor company has been dissolved.[14]

[6] *London and County Bank v. Goddard* [1897] 1 Ch. 642.
[7] See n. 2, *ante*.
[8] *Thornborough v. Baker* (1675) 3 Swans. 628; (1676) 1 Ch.Ca. 283.
[9] Coote, *Mortgages*, Chap. III.
[10] *Emanuel College, Cambridge v. Evans* (1625) 1 Rep.Ch. 18.
[11] *Brown v. Cole* (1845) 14 Sim. 427.
[12] *Pawlett v. Att.-Gen.* (1667) Hard. 465 at 469; *Fawcett v. Lowther* (1751) 2 Ves.Sen. 300.
[13] Administration of Estate Act 1925, ss.1, 3(1).
[14] *Re Wells* [1933] Ch. 29.

Prior to 1926, second and subsequent mortgages of freeholds would usually have been mortgages of the equity of redemption, since the legal fee simple would normally have been held by the first mortgagee. Until the enactment of the Conveyancing Act 1881, this led to the inconvenient situation whereby, on the mortgagee's death, the realty, that is, the legal estate, devolved on his devisee or heir who held it on trust for the persons entitled to the mortgage money, whilst the right to the money lent, being personalty, passed to the mortgagee's personal representatives. This complication was one of the factors which kept the mortgage by lease in being during the late nineteenth century.

As with subsequent mortgages of freeholds by conveyance, so subsequent mortgages of leaseholds by assignment were normally dealings with the equity of redemption. Subsequent mortgages of leaseholds made by sub-lease, however, did not involve any such dealing. Instead, further sub-leases were granted, each longer, usually by one day, than the sub-lease immediately before. Such mortgages, unlike subsequent mortgages by assignment, were legal, not equitable.

2. **Destruction of the equity of redemption**

2–07   Since an unfettered right to redeem would have nullified the intended effect of the mortgage transaction, that is, to enable the mortgagee to recover his capital, it was necessary to limit that right. The courts achieved this by a decree of forfeiture,[15] for which the mortgagee had to apply. The effect of such a decree was to destroy the equity of redemption,[16] including, of course, the right to redeem. The court, however, guarded against oppressive foreclosures by ordering a sale when the property was much more valuable than the debt, and the mortgagee then received only the balance due to him.[17]

The equity of redemption is likewise destroyed if the mortgagee, acting under his statutory power, makes a binding contract of sale of the mortgaged property,[18] and the exercise of an express power of sale has the same effect.

Whilst the equity of redemption cannot be defeated by a stipulation in the mortgage that it will be extinguished if the debt is not paid by a specified date, it is open to the mortgagor to agree to release his equity of redemption by means of a separate and independent transaction subsequent to the mortgage.[19] Transactions have, however, been set aside as clogging the equity of redemption where such a provision was part of the mortgage deed or contemporaneous with it.[20]

Finally, the mortgagor is barred from bringing an action to redeem any mortgaged land of which the mortgagee has been in possession for 12 years,[21] unless during that period the mortgagee in possession either receives a payment of principal or interest, or signs an acknowledgment of the mortgagor's title. An

---

[15] *How v. Vigures* (1628) 1 Rep.Ch. 32.
[16] Subject to rights to reopen the foreclosure; see *Thornhill v. Manning* (1851) 1 Sim.(N.S.) 451; *Coombe v. Stewart* (1851) 13 Beav. 111 and *Lancashire & Yorkshire Reversionary Interest Co. v. Crowe* (1970) 114 S.J. 435.
[17] *Rhymney Valley District Council v. Pontygwindy Housing Association Ltd* (1976) 73 L.S. Gaz. 405.
[18] *Waring v. London and Manchester Assurance Co.* [1935] Ch. 310; *Property and Bloodstock Ltd v. Emerton* [1968] Ch. 94; *Duke v. Robson* [1973] 1 W.L.R. 267; and see *post*, p. 237.
[19] *Reeve v. Lisle* [1902] A.C. 461 and see para. 18–07.
[20] *Fairclough v. Swan Brewery Co. Ltd* [1912] A.C. 562.
[21] Limitation Act 1980, ss.16, 17. See *post*, para. 22–23 *et seq.*

acknowledgment signed after the lapse of the 12 year period is of no effect if no payment has been received during the period.

LAW OF PROPERTY ACT 1925

1. **Transitional provisions**[22]

The 1925 legislation abolished two forms of mortgage: it was no longer possible **2–08** to create legal mortgages of freeholds by conveyance of the fee simple, or legal mortgages of leaseholds by assignment.

The transitional provisions which are contained in the Law of Property Act 1925, Schedule 1, Parts VII and VIII, include saving clauses which state that the subsisting rights of the parties are not to be affected by changes in mortgage forms.[23] In particular they expressly prescribe that a mortgagee of a legal estate made before January 1, 1926, and not protected by a deposit of title deeds or by registration of a land charge should not obtain any benefit by reason of its conversion into a legal mortgage, against a bona fide purchaser without notice, but was to retain, as against him, the status of an equitable interest.[24] It was therefore advisable to register pre-1926 mortgages which were not protected by a deposit of title deeds.

The effect of the provisions of Part VII on pre-1926 legal mortgages of freeholds is that:

(1) A first mortgage became a lease for 3,000 years without impeachment of waste, but subject to a provision for cesser on redemption corresponding to the right of redemption subsisting on January 1, 1926.[25]

(2) Second and subsequent mortgages were similarly converted into leases for one, two or more days longer than the term vested in the first mortgagee.[26]

(3) The legal fee simple was vested in the mortgagor or in the tenant for life, statutory owner, trustee for sale, personal representative or other person of full age who, if all money owing on the security of the mortgage or mortgages had been discharged on January 1, 1926, would have been entitled to have the fee simple conveyed to him.[27]

(4) A sub-mortgage was converted into a lease for a term less by one day than the mortgage from which it was derived.[28]

---

[22] These transitional provisions relating to freehold and leasehold mortgages in existence at January 1, 1926 are now of historical interest only as there can be few remaining mortgages that have not now been redeemed.

[23] LPA 1925, s.39 provides for the effecting of the transition from the law prior to the commencement of the LPA 1922, to the law enacted by that Act (as amended), by means of the provisions in Sched. 1.

[24] LPA 1925, Sched. 1, Pt. VII, para. 6 does not apply to mortgages or charges registered or protected under the Land Registration Act 1925.

[25] *ibid.* para. 1.

[26] *ibid.* para. 2.

[27] LPA 1925, Sched. 1, Pt. VII, para. 3.

[28] *ibid.* para. 4.

2–09   The corresponding provisions in respect of leaseholds are contained in Part VIII of Schedule 1 and affect pre-1926 mortgages as follows:

> (1) A first mortgage by assignment of a lease was converted into a sublease for a term of ten days less than the principal lease subject to a provision for cesser corresponding to the existing right of redemption.[29]
>
> (2) Second and subsequent mortgages were similarly converted into subleases for terms at least one day less than the principal lease.[30]
>
> (3) The provision as to the vesting of the principal lease corresponds to that for vesting of the legal fee simple, the person in whom it is to be vested being the person who would have been entitled to have the term assigned or surrendered to him.[31]
>
> (4) A sub-mortgage was converted into a lease for a term less by one day than that of the mortgage from which it was derived.[32]
>
> (5) The provisions of the Law of Property Act 1922, Schedule 15, paragraphs 2 and 5, which converted perpetually renewable leases to terms of 200 years and the Law of Property Act 1925, section 149(6) which converted leases for lives or marriages into terms of 90 years determinable after the death or marriage of the original lessee; apply to mortgage terms, with certain variations provided by the Law of Property Act 1925, Schedule 1, Part VIII, section 6.

2. Legal mortgages

(a) *Mortgages of Freeholds*

2–10   Under the 1925 legislation legal mortgages of freeholds may now be created only by[33];

> (1) A demise for a term of years absolute, subject to a provision for cesser on redemption; or
>
> (2) A charge by deed expressed to be by way of legal mortgage.

As a consequence, legal mortgages can only be vested by deed.

(i) *Demise for a term of years absolute*

By the first method, a long term, generally 3,000 years, is granted. The provision for cesser is that the term shall cease when the loan is repaid, but since on repayment the term becomes a satisfied term and ceases automatically, the provision is superfluous.[34]

---

[29] *ibid.* Pt. VIII, para. 1.
[30] *ibid.* para. 2.
[31] *ibid.* para. 3.
[32] *ibid.* para. 4.
[33] *ibid.* s.85(1).
[34] See *Knightsbridge Estates Trust v. Byrne* [1939] Ch. 441 at 461; aff'd [1940] A.C. 613.

Although the mortgagor now retains the legal estate, and is thus owner of the property both at law and in equity, the mortgagee does not suffer any disadvantage. The mortgagor can create successive legal mortgages, by granting a series of leases each one day longer than the preceding lease.[35] The substantial rights of the mortgagees will be their interests in the equity of redemption, not their nominal rights as reversioners.

Unlike a mortgagee by reconveyance, a mortgagee by demise before 1926 had **2–11** no right to the title deeds, a fact which made mortgages by lease unpopular. However, the 1925 legislation provides expressly that a mortgagee by demise should have the same right to the title deeds as if he had the fee simple.[36]

A purported conveyance of the fee simple by way of first mortgage now operates as a demise for 3,000 years without impeachment of waste, subject to cesser on redemption.[37] Each subsequent mortgage takes effect as a similar term one day longer than that granted to the immediately prior mortgagee.[38]

(ii) *Charge by way of legal mortgage*

The second method does *not* create a term in the mortgagee, but he is given the same powers, protection and remedies as if he had a term of 3,000 years without impeachment of waste. In order to have effect at law, the charge must be by deed and be expressed to be by way of legal mortgage,[39] although it is not necessary to use the phrase as one complete expression. The distinction between a mortgage and a charge has therefore ceased to have any real relevance. Although the chargee does not in fact have a legal term of years vested in him in the charged property, the effect is that he is as fully protected as if he had such.[40] The chargee is therefore empowered to create tenancies and enforce covenants.[41] The legal charge is in effect a mortgage and the terminology is somewhat of a misnomer and confusing to the public. The legal charge is generally considered to be more readily intelligible than the ordinary form of mortgage[42] which has in the past attracted much academic and judicial criticism.[43] It also provides a convenient method of mortgaging freeholds and leaseholds together.

Because the charge creates no sub-lease in favour of the mortgagee, it is **2–12** generally thought that it does not amount to a breach of covenant against subletting.[44] However, if, as is usual, the covenant also prohibits parting with

---

[35] A second legal mortgage for a term of the same length as, or shorter than, the first is still valid since it is binding on the lessor by estoppel. *Neale v. Mackenzie* (1836) 1 M. & W. 747.

[36] LPA 1925, s.85(1).

[37] *ibid.* s.85(2)(*a*).

[38] *ibid.* s.85(2)(*b*).

[39] *ibid.* s.87(1).

[40] See *Grand Junction Co. Ltd v. Bates* [1954] 2 Q.B. 160; *Weg Motors v. Hales* [1962] Ch. 49 at 74; *Cumberland Court (Brighton) Ltd v. Taylor* [1964] 29.

[41] See *Regent Oil Co. Ltd v. J. A. Gregory (Hatch End)* [1966] Ch. 402.

[42] *ibid.* Sched. 4 provides statutory forms of mortgage and transfer, but they are not commonly used nowadays.

[43] *Samuel v. Jarrah Timber and Wood Paving Corporation* [1904] A.C. 323, *per* Lord Macnaghten at 326; *Salt v. Marquess of Northampton* [1892] A.C. 1, *per* Lord Bramwell at 18; Maitland, *Equity* (2nd ed., 1949). p. 182.

[44] *Gentle v. Faulkner* [1900] 2 Q.B. 267; *Grand Junction Co. Ltd v. Bates* [1954] 2 Q.B. 160. If a licence is required by the lease, it shall not unreasonably be withheld; LPA 1925, s.86(1). Similarly a covenant against assignment is not hindered by the mention of a legal charge. However, normally there is inserted into the lease a covenant against charging.

possession, there will be a breach if the mortgagee enforces his right to possession.

(b) *Mortgages of Leaseholds*

Mortgages of leaseholds can be created only in two ways[45]:

  (1) by sub-demise for a term of years absolute subject to cesser on redemption, the term being at least one day shorter than that vested in the mortgagor;
  (2) by charge by deed expressed to be by way of legal mortgage.

(iii) *Sub-Demise for a Term of Years Absolute*

Because the sub-term is shorter than the original term, the mortgage will not operate as an assignment, and mortgages of leaseholds by assignment are not permitted by the 1925 legislation. It is, in fact, usual to make the sub-term ten days shorter than the original term, so that subsequent mortgages can be accommodated.[46] However, the rule has been preserved that a subsequent lease can take effect in reversion on a lease of the same or greater length.[47] Consequently all the subsequent mortgages could be secured by terms of the same length and would take effect according to whatever rules determine their respective priorities.

A post-1925 purported mortgage by assignment of a lease takes effect as a sub-demise for a term of years absolute subject to cesser on redemption. A first or only mortgagee takes a sub-term ten days shorter than the original term and each subsequent mortgage takes a term one day longer than the immediately prior mortgage term, if this is possible.[48] The sub-term must, however, always be at least one day shorter than the original term.

(iv) *Charge by way of legal mortgage*

The position with regard to leaseholds is identical to that of freeholds in that the chargee is not in fact granted a term of years. He is similarly protected as the chargee of a freehold interest and is given the same rights and remedies as if he had a sub term one day shorter than the term vested in the mortgagor.[49]

3. Equitable Mortgages

For the position as to equitable mortgages of equitable and legal interests see *post* Chapter 5.[50]

---

[45] *ibid.* s.86(1).
[46] Although they can all be of the same length; *Neale v. Mackenzie* (1836) 1 M. & W. 747.
[47] LPA 1925, s.149(5); enacting the common law rule in *Re Moore & Hulm's Contract* [1912] Ch. 105.
[48] LPA 1925, s.86(2).
[49] LPA 1925, s.87(1).
[50] See *post* p. 45 *et seq.*

CHAPTER 3

LEGAL MORTAGES OF LAND

LEGAL MORTGAGES BY DEMISE

1. Freehold land

Both first and subsequent legal mortgages may be created by demise, but **3–01** subsequent mortgages are no longer automatically equitable as was the case before the 1925 legislation. There is no necessity for the subsequent mortgage terms to be longer than the principal term, since at law the creation of a lease does not prevent the creation of a subsequent lease for a concurrent or even a shorter term. The subsequent lease is binding on the parties by estoppel.[1]

The transitional provisions of the 1925 legislation caused subsequent mortgages to take effect for terms longer by one, two or more days than the principal mortgage term. The Law of Property Act 1925, section 85(2) causes a purported second or subsequent mortgage by conveyance of the fee simple, including an absolute conveyance with the deed of defeasance on redemption, to operate similarly.

The device of causing mortgages to operate as leases with a nominal reversion on the mortgagor is a conveyancing device to keep equities off the title, in accordance with the general principles underlying the 1925 legislation. However, it was seen to be necessary to remove various uncertainties as to the positions of the parties to the mortgage. This was effected in the case of mortgages of freehold land, by sections 85 and 88 of the Law of Property Act 1925. These sections provide as follows:

   (i) A first mortgagee has the same right to documents of title as if his security included the fee simple (section 85(1));

  (ii) On a sale by a mortgagee under a power of sale, the conveyance to the purchaser operates to vest in him the whole of the mortgagor's estate, including the nominal reversion (section 88(1));

 (iii) The mortgagor's nominal reversion will be vested in the mortgagee on a foreclosure order by the court which also terminates his equity of redemption. Such vesting also occurs when his equity of redemption becomes barred by lapse of time (section 88(2), (3));

---

[1] Species of land mortgage are exempted from the provisions of the Consumer Credit Act 1974, see *post* para. 14–01 *et seq*. The Unfair Contract Terms Act 1977 does not apply to contracts for the disposition of interests in land, see s.1(2), Sched. 1, para. 1(b), but see Unfair Terms in Consumer Contracts Regulations 1999, S.I. 1999 No. 2083, *post* para. 3–37 *et seq*.

(iv) Section 88(5) operates to extend the provisions of section 88(1), (2), (3) to a sub-mortgagee so as to enable him to acquire the nominal reversions of both his immediate mortgagor and the original mortgagor;

(v) On discharge of a mortgage debt, the mortgage term becomes a satisfied term and ceases automatically (section 116). This applies equally to sub-mortgages since section 5 restates the provisions of the Satisfied Terms Act 1845 so that they apply to underleases.

3–02   The replacement of the mortgage by conveyance with the mortgage by demise saves the mortgagor the cost of two conveyances. Further, because of the provisions respecting satisfied terms, it is unnecessary to terminate the mortgage term by an express surrender. Normally, a properly executed receipt for the mortgage money is sufficient to put an end to the term.

The possibility of a series of legal mortgages of the same land altered the old rule whereby a legal mortgage automatically gave the mortgagee priority. This was lost only by his own fraud, misrepresentation or gross negligence. Priority against subsequent purchasers by registration of the mortgage as a land charge. Formerly priority could also be secured by deposit of title deeds.[2] A mortgage of freehold land can be granted by deed expressed to be by way of statutory mortgage. This is in a prescribed form modified as the circumstances require to suit the particular loan.[3] This is a special form of charge by way of legal mortgage and certain covenants are implied.

2. Leasehold land

3–03   In practice, the 1925 legislation did not bring about substantial changes in the way in which leaseholds were mortgaged because mortgages by assignment, which were converted into mortgages by sub-demise as a result of that legislation, were in any case rare. This state of affairs arose from the operation of the rule in *Spencer's Case*,[4–5] whereby the burden of a covenant which touched and concerned the land affected an assignee of a term.

By section 86(1) of the Law of Property Act 1925, the proper form of the mortgage is for the mortgagor of the land to make an underlease, for a term shorter than that of the lease, the subject-matter of the mortgage. Although an underlease for a concurrent term would be valid, the first mortgagee's term is made shorter, usually by 10 days, so as to leave room for further legal mortgages of the same lease, each of which would be for a term one day longer than the term of the immediately prior mortgage. Section 86(2) puts this on a statutory basis in respect of successive mortgages of leases which purport to be created by assignment. Sections 86(1) and 89(1), (2), (3), (5) of the Law of Property Act 1925

---

[2] For the position as to deposit of title deeds and the effect of section 2 of the Law of Property (Miscellaneous Provisions) Act 1989, see *post* para. 5–10 *et seq.*

[3] See s.117(1), Sched. 4, Form 1; Form 4 is a combined form for statutory transfer and mortgage; and see *post* para. 3–43.

[4–5] (1583) 5 Co. Rep. 16.

make the same provisions in favour of a mortgagee or sub-mortgagee of lease-hold land as are made by the corresponding subsections of sections 85 and 88 regarding freehold land.

A mortgage of leasehold land can similarly be granted by deed expressed to be by way of statutory mortgage. This is in a prescribed form modified as the circumstances require to suit the particular loan.[6] The same applies to a mortgage of freehold land.[7]

Section 86(3) of the 1925 Act provides that sub-mortgages shall be made in the same way as other mortgages of leaseholds. If one person has advanced money on the security of a lease and wishes to raise money on the mortgaged property without calling in the mortgage, he can submortgage the property to another by creating a mortgage term in the form of an underlease 10 days shorter than the lease.

3. Contents of a deed of mortgage by demise

(a) *Generally*

Mortgages by demise are becoming increasingly rare, especially in the case of residential lending where mortgagees tend to lend on *pro forma* documentation. However as such mortgages do continue to be granted in the commercial field it is necessary to have some regard to their contents. **3–04**

Certain matters must be included in a deed of mortgage by demise as a matter of formality and do not require detailed consideration here. These include the date of the mortgage, a statement of the parties and a recital of the loan agreement. Further, the Law of Property Act 1925 grants to the mortgagee by deed certain statutory powers that obviate the need for these to be created by express covenants. These are: the power to grant leases while in possession (section 99(2)); to realise a security by sale (sections 101(1), 103); and to appoint a receiver (sections 101(1)(iii), 109).

(b) *Testatum*

This states that the mortgagee has paid to the mortgagor the sum agreed to be lent, and that the mortgagor acknowledges its receipt. The receipt is not, as between the parties, conclusive as to the amount paid,[8] and it is open to the mortgagor to show that a smaller amount was actually advanced and to claim redemption on payment of that amount. Section 67(1) provides that a receipt for consideration money or securities in the body of a deed shall be a sufficient discharge for the same to the person paying or delivering the same, without any further receipt for the same being endorsed on the deed. **3–05**

---

[6] See s.117(1), Sched. 4, Form 1; Form 4 is a combined form for statutory transfer and mortgage.
[7] See *post* para. 3–43.
[8] *Mainland v. Upjohn* (1889) 41 Ch. D. 126.

Whereas the receipt may be inconclusive as between the parties to the deed, they themselves are estopped from denying its truth as against third parties.[9] The fact that one party to the deed is solicitor to the other does not fix a third party with any constructive notice or put him on inquiry. However, where a solicitor takes a security from a client and the deed does not express the real nature of the transaction, extrinsic evidence is required to prove the amount of the debt and the bona fides of the transaction.[10]

(c) Covenant for repayment

(i) The Express Covenant to Pay

3–06   This is an express covenant by the mortgagor to pay the principal, together with interest at a stated rate. The mortgagor's personal obligation to repay is a speciality debt[11] and therefore is like the remedies against the land, subject to a 12 year limitation period.[12] The six year period appropriate to actions founded on simple contracts applies to the personal remedy on a simple contract debt charged on land in a document not under seal. It also applies to a simple contract debt which is merely recited in a deed and in which there is no express or implied promise to repay. The limitation period runs not from the date of the instrument but from the date of breach of the covenant.

It is usual to stipulate that the principal be repaid on a date shortly after the execution of the deed. The date fixed is normally six months from the date of the deed. Usually the mortgagor does not provide for the mortgagor to repay prior to the date fixed for repayment.[13] A loan made subject to the bank's standard banking terms and conditions does not thereby result in it being repayable on demand.[14]

3–07   Unless the mortgage otherwise provides, the statutory powers of sale and appointment of a receiver do not arise until this date is past and usually after a demand has been made. Further, there is normally a distinct covenant for payment of interest if the principal sum remains unpaid after the due date. If this is included the dates of payment and the rate of interest should be stated. It is unclear whether this is necessary as it has been held that where there is a covenant to pay principal and interest the covenant is to pay two distinct sums of money and can be enforced by two separate actions notwithstanding that the obligations are contained in the same instrument.[15]

In most modern mortgages the amount repayable is greater than the principal sum advanced. The reason for this is that interest (either compound or simple) is

---

[9] *Powell v. Browne* (1907) 97 L.T. 854; *Bickerton v. Walker* [1885] 31 Ch. D. 151; and see LPA 1925, ss.68(1), 205(1)(xxi) for the effect of a receipt in favour of a purchaser.

[10] *Lewes v. Morgan* (1817) 5 Price 42; *Bateman v. Hunt* [1904] 2 K.B. 530.

[11] *Sutton v. Sutton* (1882) 22 Ch. D. 511.

[12] Limitation Act 1980, s.20(1). See para. 22–29 *et seq.*

[13] Under the provisions of the Consumer Credit Act 1974, ss.67—73 (as amended) certain types of mortgages can be rescinded. These are known as cancellable regulated agreements and see chapter 14 *post* para. 14–01 *et seq.*

[14] *Cryne v. Barclays Bank* [1987] B.C.L.C. 548.

[15] *Dickenson v. Harrison* (1817) 4 Price 282.

usually added to the principal sum lent and the repayments made by the mortgagor are calculated over the term of the mortgage. The advance can also be index linked so that the principal sum increases parallel with inflation.[16] Premiums and bonuses can also be added thereby increasing the amount repayable by the mortgagor. However, such aspects can give rise to consideration of collateral benefits and penalties1[17]; the provisions of consumer law relating to extortionate credit bargains under the Consumer Credit Act 1974; and unfair contract terms.[18]

(ii) *Punctual Payment*

A covenant to secure punctual payment is often inserted. This is expressed to be **3–08** for the payment of a higher rate of interest, reducible on punctual payment, to the agreed rate. A written agreement specifying the rate of interest can be varied by a parol agreement made for good consideration to reduce the rate.[19] If the covenant to secure punctual payment is made in a form whereby the agreed rate of interest is to be increased if payment is not made punctually, it will be unenforceable as a penalty.[20] Covenants to secure punctual payment are strictly construed. If the payment is not made on the specified day, the mortgagee is entitled to demand the full rate. The fact that on one occasion he has accepted the reduced rate when payment was made late does not estop him from demanding the full rate in respect of a subsequent delayed payment.[21] Unless the covenant so stipulates, one late payment by the mortgagor will not deprive him of the benefit of the covenant in respect of future payments made punctually.[22]

(iii) *Payment by Instalments*

It is not necessary to stipulate that the principal be repaid on one fixed date. The **3–09** principal may be made repayable by instalments, with a stipulation that its repayment shall not be otherwise enforced provided that the instalments and interest are duly paid. Where repayment of the principal by instalments is agreed, the parties are assumed to intend that, on default of regular payment of instalments, the whole debt shall become immediately payable. This may be provided for by one of the following covenants:

---

[16] See *post* para. 14–10 *et seq.*; and see *Cityland and Property (Holdings) Ltd v. Dabrah* [1968] Ch. 166; *Multiservice Bookbinding Ltd v. Marden* [1979] Ch. 84; *Nationwide Building Society v. Registrar of Friendly Societies* [1983] 1 W.L.R.

[17] *Lordsvale Finance plc v. Bank of Zambia* [1996] Q.B. 752, and see *post* para. 18–13 *et seq.*

[18] For extortionate credit bargains, see *post* para. 14–08 *et seq.* For unfair contract terms and the Unfair Terms in Consumer Contracts Regulations 1999, S.I. 1999 No. 2083, in particular regulations 5(1), 6, and see *post* p. 29 *et seq.* The Unfair Contract Terms Act 1977 does not apply to contracts for the disposition of interests in land, see s.1(2), Sched. 1, para. 1(b).

[19] *Lord Milton v. Edgworth* (1773) 5 Bro. P.C. 313.

[20] *Holles v. Wyse* (1693) 2 Vern. 389; *Strode v. Parker* (1694) 2 Vern. 316; *Lordsvale Finance plc v. Bank of Zambia* [1996] Q.B. 752.

[21] *Maclaine v. Gatty* [1921] 1 A.C. 376.

[22] *Stanhope v. Manners* (1763) 2 E.D.E.N. 197.

(a) to pay the principal sum on a given date, with a proviso that if the sum is to be paid by the instalments stipulated, the lender will not require payment otherwise;

(b) to pay in instalments with a proviso that if default is made in the payment of any instalment, the whole debt is to become immediately payable. Such a proviso is binding and will not be relieved against as a penalty.[23]

(iv) *Payment on Demand*

3–10   It is also possible to stipulate simply that the principal be repayable on demand or immediately after notice, in which case it is implied that the mortgagor has a reasonable time in which to comply with the demand.[24] The mortgage may, in such a case, provide that a demand is deemed to have been duly made once certain formalities have been observed.

(v) *Implied Covenant to Pay*

3–11   However, the promise to pay may be implied in the absence of an express covenant to pay.[25] It depends upon the construction of the particular agreement,[26] as does the implication whether the promise to pay takes effect as a simple contract to repay the principal and interest giving rise to a six year period of limitation or as a covenant to repay a speciality debt, in which case the 12 year period applies.[27] In the case of a third party charge where the mortgagor's property was security for the loan and the covenant repay was by the third party the presumption was rebutted.[28]

(d) *Covenants for Title*

(i) *Covenants implied by demise as beneficial owner prior to 1st July 1995*[29]

3–12   By demising the property as beneficial owner, the mortgagor gave the covenants implied by section 76 of the Law of Property Act 1925 in the mortgagee's favour.

---

[23] *Sterne v. Beck* (1863) 1 De. G.J. and Sm. 595; *Wallington v. Mutual Society* (1880) 5 App. Cas. 685; *Cityland Property (Holdings Ltd) Dabrah* [1968] Ch. 166.

[24] See *Cripps (Pharmaceuticals) Ltd v. Wickenden* [1973] 1 W.L.R. 944; *Williams & Glyn's Bank Ltd v. Barnes* [1981] Com. L.R. 205; *Bank of Baroda v. Panessar* [1987] Ch. 335; *Cryne v. Barclays Bank* [1987] B.C.L.C. 548; *Lloyds Bank plc v. Jeffrey Lampert* [1999] Lloyds Rep. Bank 136.

[25] *Sutton v. Sutton* (1882) 22 Ch. D. 511 at 515 *per* Jessel M.R.; *King v. King* (1735) 3 P. Wm.; *Ezekiel v. Orakpo* [1997] 1 W.L.R. 340 at 346.

[26] *National Provincial Bank Ltd v. Liddiard* [1941] Ch. 158; *Tam Wing Chuen v. Bank of Credit and Commerce Hong Kong Ltd* [1996] 2 B.C.L.C. 69; *Re Bank of Credit and Commerce International SA (No. 8)* [1998] A.C. 214.

[27] *Sutton v. Sutton* (1882) 22 Ch. D. 511 at 516, and see *post* para. 22–29 *et seq.*

[28] *Fairmile Portfolio Management Ltd v. Davies Arnold Cooper* [1998] E.G.L.S. 149.

[29] This is the commencement date of ss.1 and 2 of the Law of Property (Miscellaneous Provisions) Act 1994.

These are set out *in extenso* in Schedule 2, Parts III and IV. The following comprises a summary:

(a) Full power to convey and, in the case of a leasehold property, that the lease is in full force, unforfeited, unsurrendered, has not become void or voidable, and that all covenants and conditions have been observed, and in the case of a mortgage of a leasehold property to indemnify the mortgagee for future rents and covenants;

(b) Quiet enjoyment if entry is made on default;

(c) Freedom from incumbrances other than those to which the mortgage is expressly made subject;

(d) Further assurance.[30]

Section 7 provides that the benefit of the covenants runs with the estate or interest of the disponee. They are therefore capable of being enforced by any person in whom that estate or interest is (in whole or in part) for the time being vested. The burden of the covenant on the part of the disponer is absolute and his liability is therefore more extensive than under the covenants implied under section 76 of the 1925 Act.

(ii) *Title Guarantee post 1st July 1995*

Of considerable importance to the law of mortgages is the effect of the provisions of Law of Property (Miscellaneous Provisions) Act 1994 on title guarantee. This followed the recommendations of the Law Commission[31] and was enacted to remedy a perceived series of defects in the law as existing at the time.   **3–13**

Under the 1994 Act covenants for title may be implied into any instrument effecting or purporting to effect a disposition of property and expressed to be made with full or limited title guarantee. A disposition includes a mortgage or charge or lease.[32] Such covenants will only be implied if the disposition is expressed to be made with full or limited title guarantee. It is a matter of negotiation for the parties and does not arise out of the disponer's capacity. Often the instrument making the disposition may extend the operation of the implied covenants.[33] Section 8(3) further provides that where the disposition is expressed to be made at the direction of a person the implied covenants apply to him as if he were the person making the disposition. Such instances arise where a nominee conveys at the direction of the beneficial owner, or a vendor conveys to a third party at the direction of the purchaser.

---

[30] Section 76 is repealed as regards dispositions made after July 1, 1995. See the Law of Property (Miscellaneous Provisions) Act 1994 (Commencement No. 2) Order 1995, S.I. 1995, No. 1317 Certain transitional provisions exist for mortgages granted after that date pursuant to mortgages made before that date, see *ibid.* ss.11 to 12.

[31] (1991) Law Com. No. 199.

[32] "Instrument" includes an instrument which is not a deed; "disposition" includes the creation of a term of years; and "property" includes a thing in action, and any interest in real or personal property: s.1(4).

[33] *ibid.* s.8(1).

(a) *Full Title Guarantee*

3–14   The covenants implied[34] are that the disponer has:

> (i) the right to dispose of the property as he purports to do (with the concurrence of any other mortgagor)[35];
>
> (ii) that he will at his own cost do all that he reasonably can do to give the mortgagee the title he purports to give[36];
>
> (iii) that the property is free from all charges and incumbrances and free from all rights exercisable by third parties other than those of which the disponer does not and could not reasonably be expected to know[37]; and
>
> (iv) in the case of leasehold land that the lease is subsisting at the time of the disposition and that there are no subsisting breaches of any condition or tenant's obligations which would render the lease liable to forfeiture.[38]
>
> (v) In addition in the case where the disposition is a mortgage of a leasehold interest or in the case where the property is subject to a rentcharge, the mortgagor further impliedly covenants that he will fully and promptly observe and perform all obligations (in addition to the above covenants) under the lease imposed on him in his capacity as tenant or (as the case may be) imposed by the owner of any rentcharge.[39] The covenants set out above (i), (iii) and (iv) do not impose liability on the disponer in respect of any matter to which the mortgage is made subject[40] or for anything which is within the actual knowledge of the mortgagee or which is a necessary consequence of facts within his actual knowledge.[41]

(b) *Limited Title Guarantee*

3–15   Where a disposition is made with limited title guarantee the position is identical. The disponer impliedly enter into the same covenants in so far as they are applicable save for one important qualification. The disponer does *not* enter into (iii) above.[42] Instead a covenant is implied that he has not, since the last disposition or value, created any charge or incumbrance or granted any third party rights which are subsisting at the time that the disposition is made, or allowed the property to become charged or incumbered in that way, and that he is not aware that anyone else has done so.[43–44]

---

[34] *ibid.* s.1(2).
[35] *ibid.* s.2(1).
[36] *ibid.*
[37] *ibid.* s.3(1). There are also certain statutory charges for which the mortgagor is not liable, *e.g.* council tax, *ibid.* s.3(2).
[38] *ibid.* s.4(1).
[39] *ibid.* s.5.
[40] *ibid.* s.6(1).
[41] *ibid.* s.6(1).
[42] *ibid.* s.1(2)(b).
[43–44] *ibid.* s.3(3).

(a) *The habendum*

This states the length of the term, that the lease is granted without impeachment **3–16** of waste, and that there is a proviso for cesser on redemption.

(b) *Proviso for cesser on redemption*

This normally states that if the mortgagor on a given day pays to the mortgagee **3–17** the mortgage debt and interest, the mortgage term shall cease. An alternative proviso is that the mortgagee will, at any time thereafter and at the mortgagor's request and cost, surrender the term to the mortgagor or at his direction. A mortgagor cannot usually claim to be allowed to redeem before the day specified in the contract for payment of the principal, though he may do so if, before that date, the mortgagee has taken steps to recover payment. In the case of a legal charge a similar proviso is used to the effect that on payment on the date set for re-payment the mortgage will discharge the security.

Where there is a stipulation in a mortgage that the principal loan is not to be called in for a given period, there is usually a corresponding stipulation preventing the mortgagor from repaying or redeeming the mortgage, without the mortgagee's consent, until the period has expired. However, the second stipulation if standing by itself may be held invalid as a clog on the equity of redemption, at any rate where the mortgagor is precluded from redeeming for an unreasonable length of time.

(c) *Covenants to repair and insure*[45]

A mortgagee by deed has, by section 108(1) of the Law of Property Act 1925 a **3–18** limited statutory power to insure the premises for loss or damage by fire to the extent specified in the mortgage deed or, if no amount is specified, up to two-thirds of the amount required to reinstate the property in the event of its total destruction. The power is exercisable as soon as the mortgage is made.[46] This enables the mortgagee to protect his security.

This power is excluded in the circumstances set out in section 108(2). These are the following:

   (i) where there is a declaration in the mortgage deed that no insurance is required;

  (ii) where the insurance is kept up by or on behalf of the mortgagor in accordance with the mortgage deed. This the usual position;

 (iii) where the mortgage deed is silent on the question of insurance and the insurance is kept up by or on behalf of the mortgagor, with the consent of the mortgagee, to the amount authorised by the section.

By section 101(1)(ii), the premiums paid are a charge on the mortgaged property with the same priority and bearing the same rate of interest as the mortgage

---

[45] See further *post* para. 19–01 *et seq.*
[46] s.101(1)(ii).

money. The premiums are a charge and cannot be recovered from the mortgagor as a debt, hence the mortgagor in practice has to covenant to insure, and breach of that covenant causes the mortgagee's power of sale to become exercisable.

The mortgagee has no right to the policy monies if the mortgagor further insures on his own account independent of the mortgage security, and, dependant upon the term of the insurance policy, the mortgagee may receive less than anticipated. This position would arise in the circumstances where the mortgagee's insurance contained a clause limiting his liability in the event that the mortgage security was the subject of any other insurance.[47] However, in the case where the mortgagor insures having covenanted to do so, on the true construction of the covenant as a matter of law the covenant operates to grant to the mortgagee a charge over the proceeds. This position arises even if the insurance is taken out in the name of the mortgagor.[48]

Although a mortgagor is not obliged by statute to keep the mortgaged property in repair it is usual for him to covenant to do so.[49] Formerly, if the mortgage was a controlled mortgage[50] and the mortgagor failed to keep the property in a proper state of repair (measured by the general condition of the property at the date of the mortgage and not requiring that anything be done other than preserving that condition[51]) he lost his protection against the mortgagee's right to foreclose, sell or otherwise enforce his security.

(d) *Restriction on mortgagor's statutory powers of leasing*[52]

3–19 These powers, which are conferred by section 99 of the Law of Property Act 1925, can be restricted or excluded by agreement[53] except in respect of mortgages of agricultural land[54] or where such exclusion or restriction would operate to prevent the carrying out of an order to grant a new tenancy of business premises.[55] The usual form of covenant is one not to grant a lease without the written consent of the mortgagee. However, this does not prevent the mortgagor creating a lease which, as between himself and the tenant, is binding by estoppel. Such leases are not validated against the mortgagee.[56]

(e) *Mortgagees' right to consolidate*

3–20 Section 93(1) of the Law of Property Act 1925, provides that a mortgagor seeking to redeem any one mortgage is entitled to do so without paying any

---

[47] *Halifax Building Society v. Keighley* [1931] 2 K.B. 248; and see *Re Doherty* [1925] 2 I.R. 246.
[48] *Colonial Mutual General Insurance Co. Ltd v. ANZ Banking Insurance Group (New Zealand) Ltd* [1995] 1 W.L.R. 1140.
[49] But the mortgagee does have the right to have the security preserved from deterioration, see *post* para. 16–19 *et seq.*
[50] The provisions of the Rents Acts relating to controlled mortgages were repealed by the Housing Act 1980, s.152, and Sched. 26.
[51] *Woodfield v. Bond* [1922] 2 Ch. 40.
[52] See further *post* para. 19–83 *et seq.*
[53] *Iron Traders Employers' Insurance Association Ltd v. Union Land and House Investors Ltd* [1937] Ch. 313; *Dudley and District Benefit Building Society v. Emerson* [1949] Ch. 707; *Rust v. Goodale* [1957] Ch. 33.
[54] See Agricultural Holdings Act 1986, s.100, Sched. 14, para. 12(1), (2).
[55] Landlord and Tenant Act 1954, s.36(4).
[56] *ibid.* s.152.

moneys due under any separate mortgage made by him, or by any other person through whom he claims, on property other than that comprised in the mortgage which he seeks to redeem. However, this subject to the proviso that no contrary intention is expressed in any one of the mortgage deeds and that at least one mortgage was made after 1881. It is therefore usual for the mortgage deed to contain a clause excluding the operation of section 93, although the restriction can equally well be excluded by a clause expressly preserving the mortgagee's right to consolidate.

(f) *Covenant against registration of title*

The mortgagor usually covenants that no one shall be registered as owner of the **3–21** mortgaged property, under the Land Registration Act 1925, without the mortgagee's consent.

(g) *Attornment clause*

There is some doubt as to whether such a clause now has any value.[57] It was at **3–22** one time usual for the mortgagor to attorn tenant: (i) at a nominal yearly rent; or (ii) at a rent reserved equivalent to the amount of interest payable annually; or (iii) at a full rack rent.

The reason for creating the landlord-tenant relationship was to give the mortgagee the rights of a landlord as well as his right *qua* mortgagee; and in case (ii) above, to provide the right of distress as an additional security. Although such a clause would not confer the right of distress unless registered as a bill of sale,[58] its invalidity as a bill of sale does not destroy the landlord-tenant relationship.[59] Nor does it invalidate the mortgage.[60]

It is possible for a mortgagor to attorn tenant to a second mortgagee although he has already attorned tenant to the first mortgagee[61] and while the first mortgagee's rights under the mortgages are unaffected by the second attornment, that second attornment is valid by estoppel.

It has also been held that such a clause enables a mortgagee to enforce covenants given by a mortgagor's successor in title by virtue of the doctrine of privity of estate.[62] It was further held in the same case, that such a clause in a charge by way of legal mortgage created, not a tenancy at will, but a tenancy during the continuance of the security. This continued so long as the property was occupied by the mortgagor or persons deriving title under him, and subject to the

---

[57] *Steyning and Littlehampton Building Society v. Wilson* [1951] Ch. 1018. In this case such clauses were described as being "entirely obsolete" (*per* Danckwerts J.); *cf. Regent Oil Co. Ltd v. J.A. Gregory (Hatch End) Ltd* [1966] Ch. 402. See also *post* para. 16–24.

[58] *Re Willis, ex parte Kennedy* (1888) 21 Q.B.D. 384.

[59] *Mumford v. Collier* (1890) 25 Q.B.D. 279; *Kemp v. Lester* [1896] 2 Q.B. 162.

[60] *Re Burdett* (1888) 21 Q.B. 162.

[61] *Re Kitchin, ex partePunnett* (1880) 16 Ch. D. 226, CA.

[62] *Regent Oil Co. Ltd v. J.A. Gregory (Hatch End)* [1966] Ch. 402. In this case it was also held that such a clause was effective to create a legal estate in a legal charge as it was in a legal mortgage; and see n. 57, *ante*.

mortgagee's right to determine the tenancy on giving the requisite period of notice.

Where the clause requires that notice be given for determination of the tenancy, the mortgagee may not re-enter until that notice has been given.[63] In the case where the clause does not require notice to be given, commencement of possession proceedings operates as a determination[64] and thereafter no tenancy exists. In such circumstances Rent Act protection is not available and no statutory tenancy comes into existence.[65] It has also been held that an attornment clause does not of itself create an agricultural tenancy for the purposes of the Agricultural Holdings Act 1948. Thus a notice to determine the tenancy created is not subject to the restrictions on the service of a notice to quit contained in that Act.[66]

On the other hand it has been held that section 16 of the Rent Act 1957 (now section 5 of the Protection from Eviction Act 1977 (as amended)) might apply where the rent reserved by the attornment clause was a full rack rent or where the mortgagor was required to reside on the premises.[67] It is therefore advisable, in order to safeguard against such protection being available to the mortgagor, for the clause to be in a form enabling the mortgagee to take possession without notice.

UNFAIR TERMS IN CONSUMER CONTRACTS REGULATIONS 1994 AND 1999[68]

3–23   As the result of the E.C. Directive on Unfair Terms in Consumer Contracts[69] the Unfair Terms in Consumer Contracts Regulations 1994 were made.[70] These regulations came into force on July 1, 1995. However, as these regulations were not considered to reflect the Directive closely enough they were revoked and replaced by the Unfair Terms in Consumer Contracts Regulations 1999 (the "UTCCR")[71] which came into force on October 1, 1999. These regulations have the force of statute and apply to contracts made between a seller or supplier and the consumer. It is not proposed to set out in detail the effect of UTCCR, but they undoubtedly will have a wide ranging effect on mortgages granted by the consumer/mortgagor to a mortgagee advancing sums secured over residential property. The regulations provide that:

(1) a consumer may challenge a term in a contract on the basis that it is "unfair"[72] within the UTCCR and therefore void; and

---

[63] *Hinkley and Country Building Society v. Henny* [1953] 1 W.L.R. 352.
[64] *Woolwich Equitable Building Society v. Preston* [1938] Ch. 129; *Portman Building Society v. Young* [1951] 1 All E.R. 191.
[65] *Portman Building Society v. Young* [1951] 1 All E.R. 191.
[66] *Steyning and Littlehampton Building Society v. Wilson* [1951] Ch. 1018.
[67] See *Alliance Building Society v. Pinwell* [1958] Ch. 788, applied in *Peckham Mutual Building Society v. Registe* (1981) 42 P. & C.R. 186. See further *post* para. 16–24 and see *Bolton Building Society v. Cobb* [1996] 1 W.L.R. 1.
[68] See generally Wurtzburg and Mills, *Building Society Law*, (15th ed., 1989–1997), paras 5.04ff.
[69] 93/13 E.E.C. [1993] O.J. L95/29.
[70] S.I. 1994, No. 3159.
[71] S.I. 1999, No. 2083.
[72] The meaning of "unfair term" is to be found in regulation 5(1).

(2) the Director General of Fair Trading ("OFT") and "qualifying bodies" may seek injunctions against a business relying on unfair terms.

There is very little reported case law on the UTCCR and some doubts have been raised that a contract for the creation or transfer of an interest in land would fall within the scope of the Regulations. The OFT takes the view that the Regulations do apply to such contracts.[73] The UTCCR will not affect "core terms" which relate to the definition of the the the main subject matter of the contract or to the adequacy or remuneration as against the goods or services supplied in exchange. However, a term will only be a "core term" if it is set out in plain intelligible language, is not ambiguous and has been adequately drawn to the mortgagor's attention. A mortgagor's obligation to re-pay the principal of a mortgage loan is generally considered to be a core term. The UTCCR may affect "ancillary terms". These are terms that neither define the main subject matter of the contract nor concern the adequacy of remuneration for the lending services.

As to a registered charge over registered land in England and Wales it is likely that the power to transfer is excluded from the UTCCR on the grounds that it is a term incorporated to reflect a "mandatory" statutory provision of the United Kingdom, namely section 33 of the Land Registration Act 1925. This gives the proprietor of the charge power to transfer the charge to any person in the prescribed manner.

As to a mortgage or charge over unregistered land in England and Wales, it is **3–24** likely that the power to transfer is also excluded from the UTCCR on the grounds that it is a term incorporated to reflect a mandatory statutory provision of the United Kingdom, namely section 114 of the Law of Property Act 1925. This provides for the transfer of the right to sue for the mortgage monies and to transfer other benefits of the mortgage.

The matter is not free from doubt by reason of explanatory wording in recital 13 to the Council Directive on Unfair Terms in Consumer Contracts (93/13/EEC):

(1) recital 13 refers to statutory provisions that "directly or indirectly determine the terms of consumer contracts". However, it is unclear whether section 114 indirectly determines the terms of consumer contracts as it relates to a contract between a transferor and a transferee of a mortgage and not a contract between a lender and a borrower;

(2) recital 13 extends the meaning of "mandatory" in article 1(2) of that Directive so that it "also covers rules which . . . apply between the contracting parties provided that no other arrangements have been established", and section 114 applies unless contracted out. However, it is unclear whether a recital is capable of extending to the body of a Directive.

If the power to transfer is not excluded from the UTCCR, then the power is to be assessed for "fairness". Paragraph 1(p) of Schedule 2 to the UTCCR applies

---

[73] *Unfair Contract Terms, a case report bulletin issued by the Office of Fair Trading*, Issue No. 8, December 1999, para. 1.6; *contra* the position with regard to land mortgages and the Unfair Contract Terms Act 1977 . By virtue of the provisions of s.1(2) , Sched. 1 para. 1(b) that Act does not apply to contracts for the disposition of an interest in land.

to a power to transfer that "may serve to reduce the guarantees for the consumer, without the latter's agreement".

It is likely that a term imposing an early redemption charge is an ancillary term, being: (1) a fee for an option to repay early, where the mortgagor chooses to repay early; (2) or damages for breach, where the mortgagor is required to repay early for breach under an acceleration provision; (3) or a fee for a contingency, where the mortgagor is required to repay early on some other event under an acceleration provision.

Paragraph 1(e) of Schedule 2 to the UTCCR applies to a penalty for breach. The general principles of fairness apply to a penalty whether or not for breach. It is likely that the term imposing an early redemption charge is unfair if it exceeds a genuine pre-estimate of loss caused by early repayment.

3–25   The view of the OFT seems to be that a modest early redemption charge may be fair to recover administration costs, and that a substantial early redemption charge may be fair to recover costs of fixed, capped or discounted mortgage loans in the early years of the mortgage term. The OFT issued Guidance for Lenders and Borrowers in November 1997 (OFT 192). This contains guidance (in relation to early redemption charges). Research Paper 18 was published in November 1999 which contains further guidance on this subject.

It is also likely that the terms setting the initial interest rate in a mortgage is a core term but that the right to change the interest rate is an ancillary term. Paragraph 1 of Schedule 2 to the UTCCR lists terms that can be unfair. Paragraph 1(j) of Schedule 2 specifically applies to variation of interest rates without a valid reason being specified in the contract. Paragraph 2(b) of Schedule 2 to the UTCCR provides that paragraph 1(j) of Schedule 2 is without hindrance to terms under which a lender reserves the right to alter the rate of interest provided that the lender is required to inform the borrower and that the borrower is free to dissolve the contract immediately.

Nevertheless even if valid reasons are stated in the contract, those valid reasons will not necessarily make fair what would otherwise be unfair (and this appears to be the view of the OFT). Paragraph 1 of Schedule 2 sets out a list of terms that can be unfair (but are not automatically unfair), but paragraph 2 does not provide a list of terms that are automatically fair.

3–26   The OFT in February 2000 issued OFT 297 a guidance note for mortgage lenders on the way that the UTCCR apply to interest variation terms in contracts for mortgage products. This guidance note states the shared views of the OFT and the Consumers' Association (which also has power to enforce the UTCCR). The guidance note is not exhaustive nor is it definitive as decisions as to fairness are for the courts. It should be noted that the guidance contained in the guidance note applies just as much to the failure to reduce interest rates as it does to increases in interest rates.

Section 2 of the guidance note provides:

> "2.1 Specifically, unrestricted interest variation terms in mortgage products are considered unfair where consumers are 'locked in' by a require-ment to pay an early repayment charge on a mortgage.
> 2.2 Unrestricted rights to vary interest rates may also be unfair where consumers are 'locked in' by other terms or circumstances.

2.3 A term which provides that interest shall be fixed for a period, but then becomes variable, may therefore be open to objection."

The guidance note does not give any assistance as to what constitutes an "unrestricted" interest variation term. It would seem that a variation in interest rates below the maximum pledge level that reflects fluctuations in the Bank of England base rate would be more likely than not to be considered fair by the courts provided that downward movement in those linked rates were similarly reflected
Paragraphs 3 and 4 of the guidance notes provide: **3–27**

"3.1 An interest variation term may not give rise to concern

    (a) where customers are able to end the contract freely (in particular, there is nothing amounting to a penalty to prevent them doing so) and immediately (*i.e.*, without becoming subject to the variation);

    (b) where a term does not confer freedom to vary rates at will, for instance where movements in interest rates are linked to an external rate—outside the control of the lender or deposit-taker.

3.2 A term reserving the right to vary an interest rate for stated reasons does not satisfy the requirement of the Regulations unless it is drafted so that it cannot permit the rate to be moved in such a way as to leave 'locked in' consumers in a less advantageous position than new customers or those who are free move accounts.

3.3 The following are examples of such approaches. However, fairness cannot be guaranteed solely by modelling a term on one of these examples since the fairness of the whole transaction needs to be taken into account when assessing the fairness of any particular term.

    (a) *Changes which are agreed in advance*
       Specific changes agreed in advance with the customer (examples include an agreement to increase the interest rate on a mortgage by a specified amount on a specified date).

    (b) *Changes which are applicable across the board*
       Reserving the right for the lender to make a change in interest rates that is being applied to its customer accounts generally—assuming that these include accounts being actively marketed and used by consumers who are free to close them without penalty.

    (c) *An explicit link to an external rate, or index, or openly marketed rate*
       Lenders will explain low rates are explicitly linked to an external rate, or index or openly marketed rate. If the linkage does not provide for precise and immediate tracking, *i.e.*, where rate changes may be rolled up or lag behind market rates, consumers will be told the maximum margin of difference, and the time limits within which changes will be made, at the outset.

(d) *A floor or cap with reference to an external rate, or index or openly marketed rate*
The same principles as in (c) apply to terms that allow some discretion to vary interest rates, subject to a cap or floor that is linked to an external rate, or index or openly marketed rate.
The linkage to an external rate mentioned in (c) and (d) above may be chosen by the lender but not controlled by them"

4. Where lenders do not effectively limit their discretion to change rates as described above or in other ways, they will need to release the consumer from the lock in. For example in the case of increases in mortgage rates, the lender shall

   (i) notify each affected customer in writing at least 30 days before the change in rate; and
   (ii) "during the next three months, the customer may repay the whole loan without having to pay an early repayment charge."

If a term is unfair then it is not binding on the consumer. It is not possible to substitute a fair term for the unfair term. If the unfair term purports to require the mortgagor to make payment, then he will not be liable to make the payment or, to the extent that he has made the payment, he will have, as against the mortgagee or any assignee of the mortgagee a claim for restitution of the amount or a right to set off the amount of such claim against the amounts owing by the morgagor under the relevant advance.

CHARGE BY WAY OF LEGAL MORTGAGE

3–28   The Law of Property Act 1925 provides that legal mortgages of both freeholds (section 85(1)) and leaseholds (section 86(1)) may be effected by a charge by deed expressed to be by way of legal mortgage. Section 87(1) provides that a chargee by deed expressed to be by way of legal mortgage shall have the same protection, powers and remedies as if he were a mortgagee by demise or sub-demise.

By section 205(1)(xvi), "mortgage" includes any charge or lien on any property for securing money or money's worth, and "mortgagee" includes a chargee by way of legal mortgage. Nevertheless, a deed of charge does not convey any proprietary right to the chargee, so the mortgagor retains the full title instead of being left with only the nominal reversion. The charge, instead of demising the property merely states that the borrower (with full or limited title guarantee) charges it by way of legal mortgage with the payment of the principal, interest and any other money secured by the charge. In addition, the charge differs substantially from a mortgage by demise in that it contains no proviso for redemption.

The words (with full or limited title guarantee) inserted into the charge fix the mortgagor with the same implied covenants as if the mortgage were by demise.[74]

It has been suggested that it is uncertain whether the chargee can foreclose in the absence of a proviso for redemption or discharge. Foreclosure has been

---

[74] See *ante* para. 1–13 *et seq.*

judicially described as the removal, by the court, of a stop put by the court itself on the mortgagee's title,[75] which would otherwise be absolute by reason of a breach of condition on the part of the mortgagor. A legal chargee, however, has no title from which a stop can be removed. Apparently, not even an express proviso for redemption could confer on him the right to foreclose. Sometimes a provision is inserted into the deed that, for the purposes of the charge, the legal right to redemption is to cease after the contract date.

It seems, however, that the words of sections 88(2) and 89(2) of the Law of Property Act 1925 clearly mean that a legal chargee has the right to foreclose although there is no mortgage term. The only matter left uncertain is the event upon which that right arises. The provisions referred to above have the effect of fixing that date in accordance with the interpretation that the right arises as soon as the borrower is in default.

Statutory Legal Charges

There is a special form of charge by way of legal mortgage of freehold and   **3–29**
leasehold land expressed to be a statutory mortgage.[76] This charge states the names of the parties, the sum lent, the rate of interest, the receipt of the money by the mortgagor, and the fact that the mortgagor charges the named property with the principal and interest.

A mortgage when made in statutory form implies the following covenants:

(a) That the mortgagor will on the day stated pay to the mortgagee the stated mortgage debt with interest meanwhile at the stated rate; and thereafter will continue to pay interest at that rate, so long as the debt or any part of it remains unpaid, in half-yearly instalments, and this whether or not a judgment has been obtained under the mortgage;

(b) That if the mortgagor on the stated day pays to the mortgagee the mortgage debt and interest due, the mortgagee shall at the borrower's request and cost at any time thereafter discharge the mortgaged property or transfer the benefit of the mortgage as the mortgagor may direct.

Discharge and Transfer of Legal Mortgages of Land

For discharge of legal mortgages of unregistered and registered land, see Chapter   **3–30**
22.[77] For transfer of mortgages of unregistered and registered land, see Chapter 21.[78]

---

[75] *Carter v. Wake* (1877) 4 Ch. D. 605.
[76] *ibid.* s.117(1), Sched. 4 Form 1. Form 2 applies where a mortgagor does not join; Form 3 applies where a covenantor joins; and Form 4 is a combined form for statutory transfer and mortgage; and Form 5 sets out a receipt on discharge of the statutory charge.
[77] See *post* para. 22–01 *et seq.*
[78] See *post* para. 21–01.

CHAPTER 4

MORTGAGES OF REGISTERED LAND

COMPULSORY REGISTRATION OF LAND

There has been provision since the 1925 legislation for voluntary registration of **4–01** land in England and Wales.[1] However, on December 1, 1990 the whole of England and Wales became the subject of compulsory registration of land.[2] The dispositions relating to unregistered land requiring registration have since been the subject of wide extension under the provisions of the Land Registration Act 1997[3] which came into effect on April 1, 1998.[4] Fee incentives have also been brought into force so as to encourage voluntary first registrations.[5] The effect of these changes means that unregistered mortgages of unregistered land will exponentially decrease in importance.

One of the categories of disposition which are now required to be registered is where there is a legal mortgage of a freehold or of a lease having more than 21 years to run at the date of the mortgage. In certain cases there is a requirement to register the estate the subject of the mortgage. If the owner of an unregistered freehold grants a first legal mortgage over that interest the freehold title is then subject to compulsory registration within the specified period.[6] It is the owner of the mortgaged property, or his successor or assign, and not the mortgagee, who must apply for registration within two months beginning with the date of disposition.[7] There is a power accorded to the registrar to extend the period if he is satisfied that there is good reason for doing so. In such circumstances it is the extended period which applies.[8] During the period or extended period the disposition is effective according to its terms to transfer or grant a legal estate or to create a legal mortgage.[9] However, the disposition becomes void as regards the transfer or creation of a legal mortgage once the period has elapsed. It takes effect as if it were a contract to grant the mortgage for valuable consideration.[10]

---

[1] See the LRA 1925, ss.4 and 8.

[2] S.I. 1989, No. 1347.

[3] In a joint publication from the Law Commission and HM Land Registry (1995) Law. Com. No. 235 certain recommendations as to land registration were made. These were implemented in the 1997 Act.

[4] 1997 Act, s.1. This section has substituted and inserted new sections into the Land Registration Act 1925, ss.123 and 123A, and see S.I. 1997, No. 3036.

[5] See the LRA 1925, s.145(3), and (3A), as substituted by the LRA 1997, s.3, and see S.I. 1998, No. 3199.

[6] 1925 Act, s.123(2).

[7] LRA 1925, s.123A(2). The registrar will accept an application if made by the mortgagee, *ibid.* s.123A(10)(b); LRR 1925, r. 73(1).

[8] *ibid.* s.123A (3).

[9] *ibid.* s.123A (4).

[10] *ibid.* s.123A (5)(a).

4–02   In reality the registrar may grant an extension of the period within which the application for registration can be made even if the disposition has become void for non-registration. If the registrar is prepared to grant an extension the disposition "revives" and it is effective to create a legal mortgage for the duration of·the extended period.[11] In the somewhat unlikely event that the registrar refuses to grant an extension, the disposition has to be replicated at the expense of the mortgagor who failed, in the first case, to apply for his interest to be registered.[12] Any such replicated disposition must itself comply with the requirements set out above.[13]

It has been held that for the statutory sanction to apply there must be something more than a misdescription or omission in the description of the land which is the subject of the disposition.[14] However, it must be stressed that there remains a serious danger for the mortgagee if there is a failure to comply with these provisions. If the mortgage (constituting a notional estate contract) is not registered as a land charge[15] and the mortgagee is not in possession it will not bind a purchaser of the legal estate for money or money's worth. Any such purchaser will take free from it if a disposition of the legal estate is made during the period of non-registration.

CREATION OF MORTGAGES AND RIGHTS OF PARTIES TO THE MORTGAGE

1. **Creation**

4–03   The Law of Property Act 1925, sections 85(3) and 86(3), apply the provisions of that Act as regards the creation of mortgages over land registered under the Land Registration Act 1925. Section 205(1)(xxii) of the Law of Property Act 1925, states that "registered land" has the same meaning as in the Land Registration Act 1925: that is, land or any estate in land the title to which is registered under the Land Registration Act 1925, or any enactment replaced by it. Registered land includes any easement, privilege, right or benefit appendant or appurtenant to it.[16] A "registered charge" includes a mortgage or incumbrance registered as a charge under the Land Registration Act 1925.[17]

There are two ways in which a mortgage of registered land may be created, namely the registered charge and the unregistered mortgage.[18]

2. **The Registered Charge**

4–04   By section 25(1) (as amended) of the Land Registration Act 1925, the proprietor of any registered land may by deed:

---

[11] *ibid.* s.123A (6).
[12] *ibid.* s.123A (8), (9).
[13] *ibid.* s.123 (7).
[14] See *Proctor v. Kidman* (1985) P. & C.R. 67 at 72.
[15] Land Charges Act 1972, s.4(6).
[16] LRA 1925, s.3(xxiv).
[17] LRA 1925, s.3(xxiii).
[18] Formerly there was a third, that is a mortgage created by deposit of the title deeds, *i.e.* the land certificate. This has now become obsolete, see *post* para. 5–06.

"(a) charge the registered land with the payment at an appointed time of any principal sum of money with or without interest;

(b) charge the registered land in favour of a building society under the Building Societies Act 1986,[19] in accordance with the rules of that society."

(a) *Form of Registered Charge*

Rule 139 of the Land Registration Rules 1925 formerly provided the general **4–05** form of wording for the creation of legal charges as set out in Schedule I as Form 45. However, a new rule has now been substituted for that rule and Form 45 has been revoked.[20] Charges to secure annuities or further advances could be made as in Forms 46 and 47 respectively and combined with Form 45. Again these forms have been revoked.[21] In fact, Form 45 was not often used by reasons of the provisions contained in section 25(2) of the Land Registration Act 1925.

By that subsection, a charge may be in *any form* provided that:

(1) the registered land comprised in the charge is described by reference to the register or in any other manner sufficient to enable the registrar to identify the same without reference to any other document;

(2) the charge does not refer to any other interest or charge affecting the land which

    (a) would have priority over the same and is not registered or protected on the register

    (b) is not an overriding interest."

Further, the Land Registration Act 1925, section 25(3), invalidates any provision in a charge which purports to:

(1) take away from the proprietor the power of transferring it by registered disposition or of requiring its cessation to be noted on the register; or

(2) affect any registered land or charge other than that in respect of which the charge is to be expressly registered.

By section 26(1) of the Land Registration Act 1925, it is provided that the charge shall be completed by the registrar entering on the register the person in whose favour the charge is made as the proprietor of such charge, and the particulars of the charge.

Section 63(1) of the Land Registration Act 1925 further provides that, on the **4–06** registration of a charge, a charge certificate shall be prepared, and must be delivered either to the proprietor or, if he so prefers, deposited in the registry. By

---

[19] In the Land Registration Act 1925, the Acts referred to are the Building Societies Acts 1874 to 1894. The reference to the Building Societies Act 1986 was inserted by the Building Societies Act 1986, s.120; Sched. 18, para. 2.

[20] Substituted by the Land Registration (Charges) Rules 1990, r. 2. Paragraphs (2) and (3) of that rule were in turn substituted by the LRR 1997, r. 2(1); Sched. 1, para. 32; and see r. 3.

[21] LRR 1997, r. 3.

section 63(4), the preparation, issue, indorsement and deposit in the registrary of the certificate shall be effected without cost to the proprietor.

Rule 262 (as amended) of the Land Registration Rules 1925 deals with the form of the charge certificate. It must certify that the charge has been registered and must contain:

(a) either the original or an office copy of the charge;
(b) a description (if no description is contained in the charge) of the land affected;
(c) the name and address of the proprietor of the charge;
(d) a list of the prior incumbrances, if any, appearing on the register.

It must have the Land Registry seal affixed and may contain such further particulars as the Registrar shall think fit, and notes of subsequent dealings shall be entered on the charge certificate, or if more convenient, a new certificate shall be issued. The Registrar also issues a charge certificate to the chargee, while the chargor is required to deposit the land certificate at the Registry, where it remains until the charge is cancelled.

4–07   Section 29 of the Land Registration Act 1925 provides that, subject to any entry to the contrary on the register, registered charges on the same land shall rank, as between themselves, according to the order in which they are entered on the register, and not according to the order in which they are created.[22]

Subject to any contrary intention contained in the charge and unless made or taking effect by demise or sub-demise a registered charge takes effect as a legal mortgage. This is so even if the words "by way of legal mortgage" are not used.[23] The proprietor of the registered charge has all the powers conferred on the owner of a legal mortgage and is able to exercise the same, subject to any contrary entry on the register.[24]

The Land Registration Act 1925, section 31(1), gives the proprietor of a charge the power, by deed, in the prescribed manner, to alter the terms of the charge. However, this can only be effected with the consent of the proprietor of the registered land and the proprietors of all registered charges, if any, of equal or inferior priority, affected by the alteration. By section 31(3), the alteration is completed by the registrar entering it in the register.

3. The Unregistered Mortgage

4–08   Subject to a notice to the contrary being entered on the register, the proprietor of any registered land may mortgage by deed or otherwise the land or any part of it in any manner which would have been permissable if the land had not been registered, and (subject to the considerations set out below) to like effect.[25] Such

---

[22] For tacking of mortgages, see para. 20–42 *et seq*. Section 94 of the LPA does not apply to registered land. Further advances in the case of registered land may be tacked in the circumstances set out in LRA, s.30(1), (3), and see LRR, r.139A.

[23] LRA 1925, s.27(1), and see *ibid*. s.3(i). See also *Cityland and Property (Holdings) Ltd v. Dabrah* [1968] Ch. 166.

[24] LRA 1925, s.34(1).

[25] LRA, s.106(1), (4), as substituted by the Administration of Justice Act 1977, s.26(1) and see *post* paras 4–16—4–18.

a mortgage only takes effect in equity as a minor interest and is capable of being overriden by a registered disposition for valuable consideration unless duly protected by entry on the register by a notice or caution.[26]

4. Equitable Charge

An equitable charge can also be created over registered land similar to a general **4–09** equitable charge in the case of unregistered land. Such a charge takes effect as a minor interest and can be protected by notice or caution.[27]

5. Liens[28]

Section 66 of the Land Registration Act 1925 provides an alternative method of **4–10** creating a security in registered land. Prior to April 3, 1995 it was a common method of securing a loan by creating a lien by deposit of the land certificate with the mortgagee. The section provides as follows:

> "The proprietor of any registered land or charge may, subject to the overriding interests, if any, to any entry to the contrary on the register, and to any estates, interests, charges, or rights registered or protected on the register at the date of the deposit, create a lien on the registered land or charge by deposit of the land certificate or charge certificate; and such lien shall, subject as aforesaid, be equivalent to a lien created in the case of unregistered land by the deposit of documents of title or of the mortgage deed by an owner entitled for his own benefit to the registered estate, or a mortgagee beneficially entitled to the mortgage, as the case may be."

Rules 239 and 240 of the Land Registration Rules 1925 formerly provided two methods of creating a mortgage by deposit of the land certificate. Rule 239 provided a formal method. Rule 240 set out the procedure for creating a mortgage by way of notice of intended deposit. The notice did not have to be in any specified form, but rule 241 provided that certain particulars had to be given. Rule 242(1) provided that both operated as cautions under the Land Registration Act 1925, section 54.

However, resultant upon changes in the law following the enactment of the **4–11** Law of Property (Miscellaneous Provisions) Act 1989, s.2,[29] and changes introduced into the Land Registration Rules 1925,[30] the efficacy of liens created or notices of deposit entered have now to be considered in the background of the

---

[26] LRA, s.106(2), as substituted by the Administration of Justice Act 1977, s.26(1) and see *post* paras 4–16 to 4–18.

[27] LRA, ss.49(1)(c), 59(2).

[28] See also para. 20–34.

[29] See Chapter 5, *post* p. 48 *et seq.*

[30] By the LRR 1995, r.4(1), 4(4), S.I. 1995, No. 140. These revoked r.240 to 243, and substituted a new r.240. These changes were brought about as a result of the decision in *United Bank of Kuwait v. Sahib* [1997] Ch. 107.

three distinct periods.[31] These are (1) prior to September 27, 1989[32]; (2) between September 27, 1989 and April 2, 1995; (3) post April 2, 1995.

As to the first period it was possible to create liens by deposit of the land certificate or charge certificate. Such a lien was a contract to create a charge protected by a notice of deposit.[33] As to the second period a deposit made in such a manner was valid only if there was compliance with the formal requirements section 2 of the Law of Property (Miscellaneous Provisions) Act 1989.[34] As regards the third period it is no longer possible to protect a lien by notice of deposit or intended deposit. The lien can only now be protected by a notice which should be registered by the equitable mortgagee or chargee in the Charges Register of the title. The mortgagee will be only able to exercise his power of sale once the charge has been registered.

Rule 141(2) of the Land Registration Rules 1925 confers on the proprietor of a charge, while in possession, or after a receiver has been appointed, or on such receiver's behalf, the same powers as are conferred by sections 99 and 100 of the Law of Property Act 1925, as extended by the instrument of charge or any instrument varying the terms thereof; but subject to any contrary intention expressed, a note of which shall, under an application to be made for that purpose, be entered in the register.

6. Implied Covenants

4–12   Where a registered charge is created on any land section 28(1) of the Land Registration Act 1925 provides that two covenants shall be implied on the part of the chargor at the time of creation of the charge, unless there is an entry on the register negativing such implication.

They are:

(a) a covenant with the proprietor for the time being of the charge to pay the principal sum charged, and interest, if any, thereon, at the appointed time and rate; and

(b) a covenant, if the principal sum or any part thereof is unpaid at the appointed time, to pay interest half-yearly at the appointed rate as well after as before any judgment is obtained in respect of the charge on so much of the principal sum as for the time being remains unpaid.

An additional implied covenant is provided, in the case of leasehold land, by section 28(2) of the Land Registration Act 1925. That is to pay the rent and observe the covenants and conditions contained in the lease, and to indemnify the

---

[31] For a fuller treatment of this subject see Ruoff and Roper, *Registered Conveyancing* (2000), Chapter 25, Liens, paras 25.01 ff.

[32] This was the date when Law of Property (Miscellaneous Provisions) Act 1989, s.2 came into force. See *post* para. 5–07 *et seq.* and in particular para. 5–16. for a summary of these provisions.

[33] *Birch v. Ellames* (1794) 2 Anst. 427 at 431; *Carter v. Wake* (1877) 4 Ch. D. 605 at 606; *Re Wallis & Simmonds (Builders) Ltd* [1974] 1 W.L.R. 391 at 395; *Swiss Bank Corporation v. Lloyds Bank Ltd* [1982] A.C. 584 at 594—595; *Thames Guaranty v. Campbell* [1985] Q.B. 210 at 232, 233; *Re Alton Corporation* [1985] B.C.L.C. 27 at 33.

[34] See *United Bank of Kuwait v. Sahib* [1997] Ch. 107.

chargee against all proceedings or claims arising out of breaches of the covenants or conditions. If the mortgagee desires to enter and perform the covenant himself, he will have to stipulate for the power to do so, as section 28(2) does not confer that power on him.

The completion by registration of an instrument of charge negativing or modifying the provisions of section 28 (and/or sections 29 and 34) is deemed to be a sufficient negative or contrary entry on the register.[35] It is important for trustees, fiduciary owners and tenants for life of settled land to make such entries in order to avoid personal liability to pay the mortgage debt.

Covenants for title will also be implied on the part of the chargor who is expressed to charge with full or limited title guarantee under the Law of Property (Miscellaneous Provisions) Act 1994. They may be modified or extended.[36]

7. **Transfer of Registered Charges**

Section 33 of the Land Registration Act 1925 contains the provisions governing the transfer of registered charges. A registered charge of registered land must be in the prescribed form and completed by entry on the register in the name of the new proprietor.[37]   **4–13**

8. **Sub Charges**

Where there is a registered charge granted over registered land the proprietor of that charge may create a sub-charge in the same form and manner as a registered charge.[38] Rules 163 to 166 of the Land Registration Rules 1925 deal with the powers of the proprietor of a charge or sub-charge and dispositions of sub-charges and the formalities of registration. Rule 163(2) provides that the proprietor of the sub-charge has the powers as the proprietor of the principal charge. Section 106 of the Land Registration Act 1925 provides that the proprietor of registered land may also sub-mortgage the charge by deed or otherwise, in any way that would have been permissible to do so had the land not been registered.   **4–14**

PROTECTION OF THE MORTGAGEE

Mortgages may be created by transactions either on or off the land register. A registered charge is one the title to which has been examined by the registrar and its protection derives from the entry on the charges register. Securities off the register may be protected by one of the methods discussed below, but they are not entered on the charges register and no certificate is issued in respect of them.   **4–15**

---

[35] LRR, r.140. See *Fairmile Portfolio Management Ltd v. Davies Arnold Cooper* [1998] 42 L.S. Gaz. R. 34.
[36] ss.1, 8(1) and see *ante* para. 3–26 *et seq.*
[37] See *post* para. 21–11.
[38] See LRA 1925, s.86(1), (3).

Advances made by a lender on the security of registered land should be protected in the case of a legal charge by the completion of the substantive registration of the lender as the registered proprietor of the charge.[39] A legal estate does not exist until registration of the charge.[40] A registered charge cannot constitute an overriding interest as it is entered on the register itself, nor is it a minor interest as it is created by registered disposition.[41]

Subject to any entry to the contrary on the register it has always been possible for the registered proprietor of land to mortgage the land or any part thereof in any manner which would have been permissable if the land had not been registered and with like effect. Thus it has always been possible for the registered proprietor to make an unregistered dealing with registered land or a disposition off the record. A mortgage so created can be protected by an appropriate entry in the register but it cannot be completed by registration so as to take effect as a registered disposition.[42–43]

4–16   The law relating to the protection of mortgages of registered land was substantially amended by section 26 of the Administration of Justice Act 1977, which substituted a new section 106 into the Land Registration Act 1925 for that originally inserted. It is now no longer possible to protect a mortgage on the register by a special form of mortgage caution. This was a rarely used procedure in any event. That new section is as follows:

"106.—(1) The proprietor of any registered land may, subject to any entry to the contrary on the register, mortgage, by deed or otherwise, the land or any part of it in any manner which would have been permissible if the land had not been registered and, subject to this section, with the like effect.

(2) Unless and until the mortgage becomes a registered charge—

(a)   it shall take effect only in equity, and
(b)   it shall be capable of being overridden as a minor interest unless protected as provided by subsection (3) below.

(3) A mortgage which is not a registered charge may be protected on the register by—

(a)   a notice under section 49 of this Act
(b)   any other such notice as may be prescribed, or
(c)   a caution under section 54 of this Act."

Thus unless and until a mortgage becomes a registered charge it takes effect only in equity and is capable of being overridden as a minor interest unless it has been protected by entry on the register as provided.[44] In the case of a mortgage which is not a registered charge such protection includes the registration of a notice or caution.[45]

---

[39] LRA, s.26(1).
[40] *Grace Rymer Investments Ltd v. Waite* [1958] Ch 831; *E. S. Schwab & Co. Ltd v. McCarthy* (1975) 31 P. & C.R. 196.
[41] LRA, s.3(xvi), (xv).
[42–43] LRA 1925, s.106(1).
[44] LRA, s.106(2), as substituted by the Administration of Justice Act 1977, s.26(1).
[45] LRA, s.106(3), as substituted *ibid*; see LRA, s.49(1)(c) (for a notice), s.54 (for a caution).

Section 101(1) of the Land Registration Act 1925 deals with the power of any **4–17** person, whether the proprietor or not, having a sufficient interest in or power over registered land, to dispose of it, or create interests or rights in it. By section 101(2), all such interests or rights take effect as minor interests and are capable of being overridden by registered dispositions for valuable consideration. Section 101(3) deals with the protection of minor interests, which are expressed to take effect only in equity. This can be achieved by entry in the register of such notices, cautions, inhibitions and restrictions as the Act or rules made thereunder provide.

The former section 106 of the Land Registration Act 1925 provided a special form of caution for the protection of a mortgage by deed. As from August 29, 1977,[46] the Chief Land Registrar may arrange for the conversion of any mortgage, protected by a mortgage caution entered on the register before that date, into a registered charge. Rule 227 of the Land Registration Rules 1925 provides that on registration of a mortgage as a charge, all cautions relating to it shall be cancelled.

The relevant Land Registration Rules underwent some revision in the light of the 1977 Act. The Land Registration Rules 1977[47] revoked rule 223 of the 1925 Rules (this provided for the special form of mortgage caution); substituted a new rule 228 (sub-mortgage cautions protecting sub-mortgages); but left rules 224 to 227 unaltered. These refer to the withdrawal of mortgage cautions, any dealings with land affected by such cautions, the registration of the mortgage as a charge, and the effect of such registration. It also added a new rule 228A. This deals with sub-mortgages of registered charges.[48]

Section 64 makes provision for production of certificates to the registrar and the noting of certificates. Sub-section (1) provides that as long as a land certificate or charge certificate is outstanding, it shall be produced to the registrar. Sub-section (2) provides that a note of every such entry or transmission shall be officially entered on the certificate, and gives the registrar the same powers of compelling the production of certificates as the Act gives him in respect of other documents.

Section 65 provides that the land certificate must be deposited at the Land **4–18** Registry for as long as the registered charge exists. The charge certificate is issued to the chargee as his certificate of title.[49]

In order for the mortgagee to avoid the possibility of losing his security as a result of temporarily giving up the certificate, he should produce it to the registrar himself. Rule 244 of the Land Registration Rules 1925 provides that if, while a notice of deposit or intended deposit is on the register, the certificate is left at the Registry for any purpose, it shall be dealt with, notwithstanding the notice, and shall be returned to the person leaving it or as he may in writing direct.

If a notice of deposit is entered on the register under the substituted rule 239 of the Land Registration Rules 1925 the mortgagee has the additional protection conferred on a cautioner by section 55(1) of the Land Registration Act 1925. He will be entitled to notice of any intended disposition or entry on the register and will have 14 days in which to appear and to apply that the caution be continued.

---

[46] The date when section 26 of the Administration of Justice Act 1977 came into force.
[47] r.3; S.I. 1977, No. 2089.
[48] r.4.
[49] LRR 1925, r.262.

The caution also entitles the mortgagee to notice of any application for a new certificate and thus prevents his being prejudiced by such an application based on a false representation to the effect that the original has been lost or destroyed.

1. Transfer and Discharge of Legal Mortgages of Registered Land

4–19 When registered land is subject to a registered charge the proprietor of the charge has an exclusive right to transfer it in the prescribed manner.[50] The procedure for discharge of registered charges and the procedure for doing so has been altered by the provisions of the Land Registration Rules 1999 and 2000.[51]

---

[50] LRA, s.25(3), s.33(1). It shall be in Form TR3 or TR4 as the case may require, see LRR 1925, r.153 as substituted by LRR 1999, r.2(1), Sched. 1, para. 14; and see *post* para. 2–11.

[51] In Forms DS1 or DS3, LRR 1925 r.151, as substituted and amended by LRR 1999, r.2(1), Sched. 1 para. 13; and LRR 2000, r.2(1), Sched. 1, para. 1; and see *post* para. 22–07 *et seq.*

CHAPTER 5

EQUITABLE MORTGAGES OF LAND

Equitable mortgages and charges can arise in a number of different ways. **5–01**
Principally there exist equitable mortgages and charges of equitable interests of
land, and equitable mortgages and charges of legal interests of land. Within these
categories various forms of mortgage or charge can be created, such as:

(1) an equitable mortgage or charge of an equitable interest in land[1];
(2) an equitable mortgage or charge of a legal interest in land[2];
(3) a specifically enforceable agreement to create a legal mortgage[3];
(4) a mortgage which fails to comply with the formalities for a legal
    mortgage, either deliberately or accidentally[4];
(5) a charging order made under the Charging Orders Act 1979[5];
(6) a purchaser's lien to secure his deposit[6];
(7) an unpaid vendor's lien.[7]

EQUITABLE MORTGAGES OF EQUITABLE INTERESTS OF LAND

1. Creation

The provisions of the 1925 legislation did not alter the substantive law relating **5–02**
to equitable mortgages created over equitable interests in land. These mortgages
are by definition equitable as the mortgagor only holds an equitable interest. The
procedure for the creation of such mortgages is by conveyance or assignment of
the whole equitable interest as security for the advance with a proviso for
reconveyance or re-assignment on payment. There is no necessity for a deed.
However, the creation of an equitable mortgage over an equitable interest in land
subsisting at the time of the disposition is governed by the provisions of section
53(1)(c) of the Law of Property Act 1925. It must be in writing, signed by or on
behalf of the mortgagor, and not merely evidenced in writing.[8]

---

[1] See *post* paras 5–02, 5–03.
[2] See *post* paras 5–04, 5–18.
[3] See *post* para. 5–05.
[4] Deliberately created informal legal mortgages were utilised in former times to avoid stamp duty
and land registration fees. Previously, such a mortgage usually took the form of a mortgage by
deposit. This can no longer occur, see *post*, paras 5–14 to 5–16.
[5] See paras 5–19 to 5–20.
[6] See para. 1–11.
[7] See para. 1–11.
[8] *ibid.* s.205(1)(ii),(xx); equitable mortgages of personalty are also governed by the same provision.
It has been doubted that the provisions of s.53(1)(c) apply to mortgages of equitable interests which
have come into existence through an implied or resulting trust.

Thus, provided that there is such a written document where it is intended to create an equitable mortgage over a subsisting equitable interest and the meaning is plain no particular form of words is necessary.[9] However, it is advantageous for the equitable mortgage to have been created by deed so as to give rise to the mortgagee's statutory power of sale or to appoint a receiver.[10] An example of an equitable mortgage over an equitable interest occurs when beneficiaries hold under a trust of land and wish to mortgage their interest. The beneficiaries must effect the same by conveyance and re-conveyance in writing. Another example that can arise is where one of two joint holders of a legal estate purports to create a legal mortgage by pretending to be solely entitled or by forging or obtaining by improper means the co-owner's signature.

The overreaching provisions usually apply where there has been a conveyance of the legal estate subject to a mortgage of an equitable interest under a trust for land. The proceeds of sale are utilised to satisfy the mortgage advance.[11]

EQUITABLE CHARGES OF EQUITABLE INTERESTS

5–03 An equitable charge over an equitable interest is again essentially equitable as the chargor only holds an equitable interest. An equitable charge of an equitable (or legal interest) in land is created when a particular asset is expressly or constructively made liable or specifically appropriated in satisfaction of a particular debt or other obligation owed by the chargor or a third party entitling the chargee to seek to discharge that liability from that asset. It creates a transmissible interest in the land but without any transfer of title or possession (either actually or notionally) to the chargee in law or in equity.[12]

The creation of an equitable charge over an equitable interest is again governed by the provisions of section 53(1)(c) of the Law of Property Act 1925. However, the creation of an equitable charge over a *legal* interest in land will need to conform to the provisions of section 53(1)(a). No special wording is required for its creation provided that the parties demonstrate the appropriate intention that the asset should form the subject matter of the security.[13] Again, it is advantageous for the equitable charge to have been created by deed so as to

---

[9] *ibid.* s.53(1)(c); and see *William Brandt's Sons & Co. v. Dunlop Rubber Co. Ltd* [1905] A.C. 454 at 462. If the equitable mortgage is preceded by a contract for its disposition consensually made between the parties then the provisions of section 2 of the Law of Property (Miscellaneous Provisions) Act 1989 will apply, see *post*, para. 5–07 *et seq.*

[10] *ibid.* s.10(1).

[11] LPA, s.2(1)(iii), and see *City of London Building Society v. Flegg* [1988] A.C. 54 at 83 and 91.

[12] *London County and Westminster Bank v. Tompkins* [1918] I K.B. 515 at 528; *Re Cosslett (Contractors) Ltd* [1998] Ch. 495 at 507–508, *per* Millett L.J.; *Carreras Rothmans Ltd v. Freeman Mathews Treasure Ltd* [1985] Ch. 207 at 227. See also *Swiss Bank Corpn v. Lloyds Bank Ltd* [1982] A.C. 584, aff'd [1982] A.C. 584 at 595; *Re Charge Card Services Ltd* [1987] Ch. 150, aff'd [1989] Ch. 497; *Re Bank of Credit and Commerce International SA (No. 8)* [1998] A.C. 214; *Bland v. Ingram Estates Ltd* (2001) 24 E.G. 163.

[13] *Cradock v. Scottish Provident Institution* (1893) 69 L.T. 380, aff'd (1894) 70 L.T. 718; *National Provincial and Union Bank of England v. Charnley* [1924] 1 K.B. 431 at 440 and 445–456, and 459–460; *Mathews v. Goodday* (1861) 31 L.J. Ch. 282. If the equitable charge is preceded (unusually) by a contract for its disposition consensually made between the parties then the provisions of section 2(1) of the Law of Property (Miscellaneous Provisions) Act 1989 will apply, see *post* para. 5–07 *et seq.* For a recent unreported case on the provisions of s.2(3) of the 1989 Act and s.53(1)(a) of the 1925 Act, see *De Serville v. Agree Ltd*, April 26, 2001.

give rise to the chargee's statutory power of sale.[14] The equitable chargee by deed is in exactly the same position as the equitable mortgagee in relation to sale or the appointment of a receiver out of court as the statutory definition of a mortgage extends to a charge.[15] Examples of equitable charges arise where a voluntary settlement or will charges land with the payment of money.[16] It is also possible for an equitable mortgage or charge to arise by operation of law where one of two joint owners enters into a mortgage having forged the signature of the other co-owner.[17] Another instance can arise where a person holding a beneficial interest in land purports to mortgage or charge the legal estate when he has no capacity to do so.

EQUITABLE MORTGAGES AND CHARGES OF LEGAL INTERESTS OF LAND[18]

The security created by a contract to grant a legal mortgage has confusingly been **5–04** described, both judicially and academically, as an equitable mortgage or an equitable charge. However, there is an important distinction between the two the basis of which rests on the right of the party to whom the security is given to seek a decree of specific performance.[19] The distinction between an equitable mortgage and equitable charge is therefore of importance when dealing with the respective remedies available to the parties.[20]

1. Arising from contract

Equitable securities in legal estates are either executory contracts to grant legal **5–05** mortgages,[21] or charges[22] in the strict sense. Whilst a mortgage is a conveyance of property subject to a right of redemption, a charge is not a conveyance but gives the chargee certain rights over the property charged (see paragraph 5–03 *ante*). An equitable mortgage of a legal interest creates an equitable interest in the land but does not convey any *legal* estate or interest to the creditor.[23]

A typical contract creating an equitable charge over a legal interest arises where one party enters into a written contract to charge his realty with the

---

[14] LPA, s.101(1).

[15] s.205(1)(xvi); and see *ante* paras 1–13 to 1–15.

[16] *Re Lloyd, Lloyd v. Lloyd* [1903] 1 Ch. 385 at 404; *Re Owen* [1894] 3 Ch. 220. An equitable charge carries no right of foreclosure nor possession; the remedy is only by sale or mortgage of such interest, or the appointment of a receiver, see *post* para. 16–27.

[17] *First National Securities Ltd v. Hegarty* [1985] 1 Q.B. 850; and see LPA, ss63(1), 53(1)(a).

[18] Equitable mortgages of legal interests of personalty, see *post* 12–02.

[19] *Central Trust and Safe Deposit Co. v. Snider* [1916] A.C. 266; referring to *Freemont v. Dedire* (1718) 1 P. Wms. 428.

[20] *post* para. 16–21 *et seq.*

[21] *London County and Westminster Bank v. Tompkins* [1918] 1 K.B. 515.

[22] There have been many attempts to define "charge"; see *Re Sharland, Kemp v. Rozey (No. 2)* (1896) 74 L.T. 64; *National Provincial and Union Bank of England v. Charnley* [1924] 1 K.B. 431; *cf. Thomas v. Rose* [1968] 1 W.L.R. 1797.

[23] See s.205(1)(x) (amended by the Trusts of Land and Appointment of Trustees Act 1996, s.25(2), Sched. 4.

payment of a sum of money to another,[24] but only conferring on the creditor an equitable interest in the land charged. Such a contract does not amount to an agreement to grant a legal mortgage. However, the provisions of section 2 of the Law of Property (Miscellaneous Provisions) Act 1989 will apply as it is a contract for the sale or a disposition of an interest in land.[25] It may take priority over a subsequently acquired legal estate if duly registered.[26]

The essential difference, therefore, is that the equitable mortgage gives rise to a specifically enforceable agreement to create a legal mortgage enforceable under the court's equitable jurisdiction.[27] An order can then be made vesting a legal term of years in the mortgagee. An alternative is for the mortgagee to apply to the court for an order for foreclosure. An action for specific performance does not arise in the case of an equitable charge as there is no express or implied agreement to execute a legal mortgage. The remedy is for an order for sale.[28]

2. Deposit of title deeds

5–06   Formerly a mere deposit of title deeds was effective to create an equitable mortgage over a legal interest in the land constituting an act of part performance. This is no longer the case since the enactment of section 2 of the Law of Property (Miscellaneous Provisions) Act 1989 and the abrogation of the doctrine of part performance.[29]

EQUITABLE MORTGAGES OF LEGAL INTERESTS IN LAND POST-1989

5–07   The position relating to the validity of equitable mortgages has undergone transformation since September 27, 1989. This is the date when section 2 of the Law of Property (Miscellaneous Provisions) Act 1989 came into force. A contract to create a legal or equitable mortgage or charge over a legal or equitable interest can now be made only in accordance with the requirements of section 2(1) of the 1989 Act.

This has inevitably affected the creation of valid equitable mortgages by deposit of title deeds. In the case of registered land it has affected the creation of

---

[24] *Montagu v. Earl of Sandwich* (1886) 32 Ch. D. 525; but the express contract to give a charge was construed as a contract to give a mortgage, so the security was enforceable by foreclosure. See also *Craddock v. Scottish Provident Institution* (1893) 69 L.T. 380, aff'd (1894) 70 L.T. 718, where an annuity was secured by a deed appointing a receiver of rents and profits. Romer J. held this deed to be a good equitable charge, but decreed foreclosure, not sale. See also *National Provincial and Union Bank of England v. Charnley* [1924] 1 K.B. 431 at 440, 445 and 459.

[25] See *post* para. 5–07 *et seq.* and see *United Bank of Kuwait plc v. Sahib* [1995] 2 W.L.R. 94, aff'd on different grounds [1997] Ch. 107.

[26] As a Class C (iii) land charge (general equitable charge), see the land Charges Act 1972, s.2(1), (4)(iii) (as amended).

[27] *Swiss Bank Corpn v. Lloyds Bank Ltd* [1982] A.C. 584, aff'd [1982] A.C. 584; *Downsview Nominees Ltd v. First City Corpn Ltd* [1993] A.C. 295 at 311.

[28] *Mathews v. Goodday* (1861) 31 L.J. Ch. 282.

[29] See *post* para. 5–07 *et seq.* and see *United Bank of Kuwait plc v. Sahib* [1997] Ch. 107; aff'd on different grounds [1997] Ch. 107; and see *post* para. 5–11 *et seq.* for the position prior to the 1989 Act.

liens by deposit of the land certificate with the mortgagee.[30] Prior to the enactment of the 1989 Act such mortgages had for 200 years been taken as demonstrating a contract to create a legal mortgage, the deposit itself being construed as an act of part performance of that contract.[31] Since September 27, 1989 any contract for the sale or other disposition of an interest in land is not valid unless made in writing signed by both parties incorporating all the terms expressly agreed by the parties (section 2(1)). The word "disposition" includes a mortgage.[32]

The requirement that a contract for the sale of land or other disposition of an interest in land be made in writing signed by the parties and containing all the agreed terms enacted by the section is not retrospective.[33] There will therefore remain many cases where pre-Act law still continues to govern the transaction. Consequently, it will continue to remain necessary to have regard to the law prior to the enactment of the 1989 Act.[34]

1. The case for change

Section 2 of the 1989 Act followed the recommendations of the Law Commission in its Report (No. 164). This dealt with formalities for contracts for the sale of land, and considered the defects of the then existing law. This is more fully set out in Working Paper (1985, No. 92). It concluded that, in view of the potential for injustice and the complex and uncertain state of the relevant law it required reform (particularly having regard to the doctrine of part performance and the provisions of the Law of Property Act 1925, s.40). Five proposals were considered. Part IV is devoted to the preferred scheme, which requires (with three exceptions) all contracts for the sale land to be in writing signed by both parties. Part III of the Report deals with the reasons for rejection of the other four proposals. The legislative response to the Law Commission's recommendations are contained in section 2 of the 1989 Act, and section 40 of the Law of Property Act 1925 was repealed.

5–08

The Law Commission recognised that the law relating to mortgages would be affected. Paragraph 4.3 of the Report states that contracts to grant leases or mortgages, or options to purchase would be included, as well as contracts for sale. Paragraph 4.12 is concerned with the third of the three exceptions, namely, contracts made on a recognised investment exchange. A contract to sell a debenture is a contract within section 40 of the Law of Property Act 1925.[35] The Commission took the view that by the same reasoning, other forms of investment involving interests in land, and perhaps unit trusts making such investments, would fall within the old section 40 and therefore proposed new provisions. They concluded that debentures or other investments were not closely enough connected with the land to require such contracts to be subjected to the proposed

---

[30] See *post* para. 5–14 *et seq.*
[31] *ibid.*
[32] By virtue of the Law of Property Act 1925, s.205(1)(ii) (expressly incorporated into the 1989 Act by s.2(6)).
[33] See section 2(7) of the 1989 Act.
[34] See *post* para. 5–11 *et seq.*
[35] *Driver v. Broad* [1893] 1 Q.B. 744.

formalities. Section 2(5)(c) excepts contracts regulated under the Financial Services Act 1986 from the requirements of the new Act.

5–09   Inherent in the recommendation that contracts should be made in writing is the consequence that the doctrine of part performance should no longer affect contracts concerning land. The Commission accepted, as one of the principles underlying its recommendations, that any reform should not increase the risk of injustice. The view expressed in Part V of the Report is that the tortious and restitutionary remedies available at law, and the equitable doctrines of promissory and proprietary estoppel, will be adequate to ensure that justice is done between the parties in cases where formalities have not been observed.[36]

Regrettably, the Law Commission did not advert to the effect of their recommendations on the law relating to the creation of equitable mortgages. Following the enactment of section 2 of the 1989 Act there was some continuing debate as to whether a mortgage created by deposit of title deeds survived the enactment of section 2. The justification for this was (following the case of *Russel v. Russel*)[37] that an equitable mortgage could be created by the deposit of title deeds with the relevant intention to do so, this constituting the act of part performance of the agreement to create a mortgage.

However, in the preface to the first edition of this work it was stated that it appeared inevitable that a deposit of title deeds, unaccompanied by a memorandum in writing, could no longer create an equitable mortgage. This suggestion was made despite the accepted doctrine following the case of *Russel v. Russel*. This interpretation has now been vindicated by the judgment in the case of *United Bank of Kuwait Plc v. Sahib* at first instance.[38] At first instance Chadwick J. held, *inter alia*, that as a mortgage by deposit of title deeds was contract-based such a mortgage could not survive the enactment of section 2. Chadwick J. had no hesitation in rejecting the submission that the charge created by deposit of title deeds was to be seen as a *sui generis* type of equitable mortgage or charge rather than an agreement to create an equitable mortgage.[39]

Questions will no doubt continue to arise in relation to the equitable principle that equity treats as done that which ought to be done. Even though a contract for the grant of an equitable mortgage may comply with the provisions of section 2 of the 1989 Act it still may not be capable of specific performance. Such an example could arise where the loan monies have not actually been advanced.[40]

2. The current legal position

5–10   An equitable mortgage of land gives rise to a specifically enforceable agreement to create a legal mortgage enforceable under the court's equitable jurisdiction.[41]

---

[36] See paras 3.23–3.26 in Appendix D of Working Paper 92, and section 1.9 of the Report.

[37] (1783) 1 Bro. C.C. 269.

[38] [1995] 2 W.L.R. 94. It was subsequently affirmed (on other grounds) in the Court of Appeal [1997] Ch. 107.

[39] For the distinction between an equitable mortgage and an equitable charge and the provisions of section 53(1)(a), (c) of the Law of Property Act 1925. See *ante* paras 5–02, 5–03 and 5–10 *et seq.*

[40] See, *e.g. Sichel v. Mosenthal* (1862) 30 Beav. 37.

[41] See para. 5–05 *ante*; *Swiss Bank Corpn v. Lloyds Bank Ltd* [1982] A.C. 584, aff'd [1982] A.C. 584.

However, such an agreement made since September 27, 1989 must conform with the provisions of the Law of Property (Miscellaneous Provisions) Act 1989. Since then a mortgage of or charge over land or any interest in land only can be made in writing and only by incorporating all the terms which the parties have expressly agreed[42] in one document or, where contracts are exchanged, in each.[43] The terms may be incorporated in a document either by being set out in it or by reference to some other documents.[44] The document incorporating the terms or, where contracts are exchanged, one of the documents incorporating them (but not necessarily the same document) must be signed by or on behalf of each party to the contract.[45] The requirements of the Act also apply to the variation of a material term of such an agreement.[46]

A collateral contract is not itself an agreement for the disposition of an interest in land.[47] In such circumstances no enforceable equitable mortgage can be created in the case of a facility letter or a mortgage deed signed only by one party.[48] Further it has been held that a unilateral contract whereby a person who enters into a contract to sell land if the purchaser performs certain acts falls within the meaning of some "other disposition" of an interest in land. It therefore would constitute an agreement to dispose of an interest in land within the provisions of the Act.[49]

EQUITABLE MORTGAGES OF LEGAL INTERESTS IN LAND PRE 1989

It is still necessary to have regard to the position prior to the provisions of the **5–11** Law of Property (Miscellaneous Provisions Act 1989 coming into force. Legal disputes still involve dispositions made before that date. Equitable mortgages created prior to that date still remain valid and the pre-September 1989 Act still governs the position.

Agreements to give security in land are dispositions of interests in land. In the case of equitable mortgages of legal interests they were formerly, therefore, subject to the evidential requirements of the Law of Property Act 1925, section 40, and the doctrine of part performance. No specified words needed be used in order to create such agreements.[50] It was sufficient that the instrument manifested an intention to give security and in consequence, equitable mortgages have been held to be created by many types of instrument. These include the following:

---

[42] An agreement reached in correspondence does not suffice: see *Commission for the New Towns v. Cooper (GB) Ltd* [1995] Ch. 259.

[43] The Law of Property (Miscellaneous Provisions) Act 1989, s.2(1), (6), (s.2(6) has been amended by the Trusts of Land and Appointment of Trustees Act 1996, s.25(2), Sched. 4.

[44] *ibid.* s.2(2). As to incorporation by reference to some other document see *Firstpost Homes Ltd v. Johnson* [1995] 1 W.L.R. 1567.

[45] *ibid.* s.2(3). It has been held that a type-written name is not a signature for the purposes of the Act, see *Firstpost Homes Ltd v. Johnson* [1995] 1 W.L.R. 1567; on appeal [1996] 1 W.L.R. 67 the petition to the House of Lords was dismissed.

[46] *McCausland v. Duncan Lawrie Ltd* [1997] 1 W.L.R. 38.

[47] *Record v. Bell* [1991] 1 W.L.R. 853.

[48] *Lloyds Bank v. Bryant* [1996] N.P.C. 31.

[49] See *Daulia Ltd v. Four Millbank Nominees Ltd* [1978] Ch. 231.

[50] *Mounsey v. Rankin* (1885) I Cab. and El. 496; *Cradock v. Scottish Provident Institution*, (1894) 70 L.T. 718.

    (i) a defective legal mortgage signed by the mortgagor or his agent[51];

    (ii) a written agreement to create a security in consideration of a debt due or advance made[52]; but not in consideration of money to be advanced, since an unperformed agreement to lend money is not, normally, specifically enforceable[53];

    (iii) an instrument charging property with a debt and containing a declaration that the debtor holds the property on trust for the creditor[54];

    (iv) an authority for a creditor to sell land and retain his debt out of the proceeds[55];

    (v) the appointment of a receiver to receive rents and pay money therefrom[56];

    (vi) a power of attorney given to a creditor, to[57]:

        (a) mortgage the debtor's land for payment of the debt
        (b) receive rents and profits and apply them in payment of principal or interest
        (c) enter up judgment in his favour[58];

    (vii) an assignment of rent.[59]

5–12   A charge given by way of indemnity against rents equitably apportioned or charged exclusively on land in exoneration of other land and against the breach or non-observance of covenants or conditions is not a general equitable charge, nor is a loan with a provision for it to be satisfied out of the proceeds of letting or selling property. Neither of these is a charge on land or incorporeal hereditaments.[60]

    Although in such cases the equitable mortgage arose out of the agreement to create a legal mortgage, the legal mortgage was not usually intended to be created, nor was it necessary that it should be.[61] Indeed, the mortgagee could have found himself in a better position by relying on his equitable rights, as a legal mortgage must identify with particularity the lands mortgaged. Whereas it was sufficient in the case of an equitable mortgage that the lands were described so that they might have been identified either at once or when the security became enforceable.[62]

---

[51] *Taylor v. Wheeler* (1706) 2 Salk. 449.

[52] *Eyre v. McDowell* (1861) 9 H.L.Cas. 619; *Parish v. Poole* (1884) 53 L.T. 35; *Capital Finance Co. v. Stokes* [1969] 1 Ch. 261.

[53] *Rogers v. Challis* (1859) 27 Beav. 175; *Larios v. Bonony y Gurety* (1873) L.R. 5 P.C. 346; *The South African Territories Ltd v. Wallington* [1898] A.C. 309. *cf.* the provision in the Companies Act 1985, s.195, making debentures specifically enforceable in respect of unpaid calls.

[54] *London and County Banking Co. v. Goddard* [1897] I Ch. 642.

[55] *Re Cook, ex parte Hodgson* (1821) I Gl. and J. 12.

[56] *Spooner v. Sandilands* (1842) I Y. & C.Ch. 390.

[57] *ibid. Re Cook, ex parte Hodgson* (1821) I Gl. and J. 12; *Abbott v. Stratten* (1846) 3 J. & Lat. 603; *Re Parkinson's Estate* (1865) 13 L.T. 26.

[58] *Cook v. Fowler* (1874) L.R. 7 H.L. 27.

[59] *Ex parte Wills* (1790) I Ves.Jun. 162.

[60] Land Charges Act 1972, s.2(4).

[61] Prior to 1971 the creation of an informal mortgage was a common method of avoiding the payment of stamp duty. The payment of stamp duty on mortgages was abolished by the Finance Act 1971, s.64.

[62] *Fremoult v. Dedie* (1918) 1 P.Wms. 429, *Montagu v. Earl of Sandwich* (1886) 32 Ch.D. 525; *Tailby v. Official Receiver* (1888) 13 A.C. 523.

Thus such a mortgage arose immediately if the mortgagor agreed to charge all   **5–13**
the realty, or all the realty and personalty, which he had at that time, or he
subsequently acquired,[63] or he would have acquired at some specified future date.
Such a mortgage was not void either for uncertainty, nor as being against public
policy, as long as the property comprised in it could have been ascertained at the
time when it is sought to enforce the charge.[64] Even if the property was
ascertainable only at a future date, the mortgage arose immediately and binds the
property when ascertained. However, where the mortgagor agreed to charge
sufficient of his property to secure a specified sum, there was initially only a
personal covenant. No security arose until some property had been appropriated
to the satisfaction of the obligation.[65] The same was true where the security was
to be raised on only one of two specified properties; or if the agreement was to
give security "on request." Specific performance would not have been be
decreed until the property is specified or the request made.[66]

With one exception, executed consideration was necessary to make the agreement specifically enforceable. That exception is provided by section 195 of the
Companies Act 1985 which makes debentures specifically enforceable in relation
to unpaid calls. It therefore followed that the mere existence of an antecedent
debt was not valuable consideration for a security given by the debtor. In order
for there to have been valuable consideration, there must have been an agreement, express or implied, to give time or some further consideration, or there
must be an actual forbearance which *ex post facto* might have become the
consideration to support the deed.[67]

Thus it has been said:

> "It is quite enough if you can infer from the surrounding circumstances that
> there was an implied request for forbearance for a time, and that forbearance
> for a reasonable time was in fact extended to the person who asked for
> it."[68]

By contrast, the cases where the existence of an antecedent[69] debt had been held
not to be good consideration for a voluntary increase of security were cases
where that voluntary increase of the security was not known to the creditor, and
could not have influenced him in the way of forbearance.

1. Arising from the deposit of title deeds

At one time, a deposit of title deeds without a memorandum created only a   **5–14**
pledge of the deeds as chattels, giving the creditor the right to detain or sell the

---

[63] *Lyde v. Mynn* (1833) 1 My. & K. 683.
[64] *Ravenshaw v. Hollier* (1835) 4 L.J. Ch. 119.
[65] *Re Clarke, Coombe v. Carter* (1887) 36 Ch.D. 348; *Re Turcan* (1889) 40 Ch.D. S; *Re Kelcey, Tyson v. Kekey* [1899] 2 Ch. 530; *Syrett v. Egerton* [1957] 1 W.L.R. 1130 (such a charge cannot create a specific lien).
[66] *Shaw v. Foster* (1872) L.R.H.L. 321.
[67] *Wigan v. English and Scottish Law Life Assurance Association* [1909] 1 Ch. 291.
[68] *Fullerton v. Provincial Bank of Ireland* [1903] A.C. 309 at 313; and see *Alliance Bank v. Broom* (1864) 2 Dr. & Sm. 289.
[69] *Glegg v. Bromley* [1912] 3 K.B. 474; Fletcher Moulton L.J.; and *cf. Holt v. Heatherfield Trust* [1942] 2 K.B. 1; *Combe v. Combe* [1951] 2 K.B. 215.

deeds as chattels, but no security over the land. Such transactions could still have been carried out prior to 1989.[70] However, the law as to this was changed in a series of cases of which *Russel v. Russel*[71] was the first. In that case, a borrower, who subsequently became bankrupt, pledged a lease to a lender as security for money advanced to him and the lender brought an action for the sale of the leasehold. The jury decided that the lease had been deposited as security for the sums advanced and a sale was directed. In subsequent cases[72] this finding of fact was elevated into the principle that a deposit of deeds entitled the depositee to a mortgage and to have his lien effectuated. This so-called lien, however, was merely an implied contractual right to retain the deeds until the debt was paid, not a separate common law lien. In consequence it could survive the avoidance of the security should that have occurred.[73]

The mere deposit of documents of title had not always been regarded as showing the intention to create an equitable mortgage. It was possible to deposit the deeds by way of pledge without the intention of binding the subject matter of the deeds.[74] Sometimes it was apparent from the nature of the transaction that the depositor had no intention of creating a mortgage (as where the deeds were deposited by mistake,[75] or so that they could have been used for the preparation of a legal mortgage,[76] or where the deposit was made by way of indemnity without any agreement for a mortgage.[77] Again where only one joint tenant agreed to create a charge over property as security and deposited title deeds with the lender, it was held that there had been no effective deposit which could give rise to a charge in the absence of comment from the other joint tenants as first trustee of the legal estate.[78]

5–15   Nevertheless there was a presumption that a deposit of title deeds to secure a debt created a charge on land,[79] the deposit being treated as a sufficient act of part performance. Further, it was held that A might have deposited deeds to his own land to secure a debt owed by B to C.[80] That presumption was rebuttable by evidence that the intention of the parties was to give the lender a right to the deeds themselves and not to give any security in the land. This reversed what had earlier been held. Some nineteenth century cases had laid down the principle that either it was for the creditor to show affirmatively that the debtor intended to give

---

[70] *Swanley Coal Co. v. Denton* [1906] 2 K.B. 873, following *Barton v. Gainer* (1858) 3 H. & N. 387, in which it was held that an owner may separate his deeds from his estate and may grant the deeds as security, without the intention of binding their subject matter; and see *Re Wallis and Simmonds (Builders) Ltd* [1974] 1 W.L.R. 391.

[71] (1783) 1 Bro.C.C. 269. It took a long time for Lord Eldon to reconcile himself to the decision, see *Ex parte Coming* (1803) 9 Ves. 115 ("Lord Thurlow was of opinion, and that is not now to be disturbed"); *Ex parte Whitbread* (1812) 19 Ves. 209; *Ex parte Wright* (1812) 19 Ves. 255.

[72] *Edge v. Worthington* (1786) 1 Cox. Eq. Cas. 211, where Lord Kenyon M.R. held that parol evidence of the purpose for which the deeds were deposited was admissible to prove the agreement.

[73] *Re Molton Finance* [1968] Ch. 325.

[74] *Re Richardson, Shillito v. Hobson* (1885) 30 Ch.D. 396.

[75] *Wardle v. Oakley* (1864) 36 Beav. 27.

[76] *Norris v. Wilkinson* (1806) 12 Ves. 192; where it was held that the deposit of deeds for the purpose of preparing a legal mortgage created neither a lien nor an equitable mortgage. Neither *Edge v. Worthington* (1786) 1 Cox. 211 nor *Ex parte Bruce* (1813) 1 Rose. 374 was cited to the court: and see *Hockley v. Bantock* (1826) 1 Russ. 141 for a directly contrary decision.

[77] *Sporle v. Whayman* (1855) 20 Beav. 607; *cf. Ex parte Coombe* (1810) 17 Ves. 369.

[78] *Thames Guaranty Ltd v. Campbell* [1985] Q.B. 210.

[79] *Bank of New South Wales v. O'Connor* (1889) 14 App. Cas. 273.

[80] *Re Wallis and Simmonds (Builders) Ltd* [1974] 1 W.L.R. 391.

a security over land or that there was no presumption at all and that evidence was required to decide what effect the depositor intended the deposit to give.[81]

It was not necessary to deposit all the title deeds in order to create an equitable mortgage by deposit. Such a mortgage had been held to have been created by depositing deeds relating to the property but not sufficient to show the depositor's title[82]; or deeds which were not complete but were material evidence of title[83]; or a single deed.[84] It was possible also to create an equitable mortgage by deposit of documents other than documents of title. Thus an equitable mortgage of a copyhold estate had been created by a deposit of a copy of the court roll.[85]

In one case the deposit of a receipt for purchase money containing a description of the property and a plan was held to be sufficient.[86] However, a deposit of a map alone was held to be merely for the purpose of identifying the land to be mortgaged, and thus insufficient to create a mortgage by deposit.[87] Where a series of mortgages was made by splitting up the title deeds and depositing some with each of the mortgagees, priority of the competing mortgages, in the absence of gross negligence by a prior mortgagee, depended on the date of their creation, that is on the date of acquisition of the documents deposited.[88]

The creation of an equitable mortgage by deposit did not require delivery to **5–16** the mortgagee himself. Delivery to his agent or trustee was sufficient, and it had been held that, where the mortgagor delivered deeds to his own solicitor to provide security for the mortgagee, the solicitor became a trustee for the mortgagee.[89] There was no sufficient delivery if the mortgagor executed a memorandum and handed over neither the deeds nor the memorandum.[90] If an equitable mortgage by deposit was created, it was, in the absence of evidence to the contrary, security for further advances as well as the original loan. All that was required was clear parol evidence of such intention.[91] It would have been pointless to insist on delivery of the deeds to the mortgagor and redelivery to the mortgagee in respect of every further advance.[92] This applied to all mortgages by deposit, whether accompanied by a memorandum or not. This was a case where parol evidence was admissible to vary the terms of a written memorandum. It must be stressed however that parol evidence, where there was a memorandum either in writing or by deed, was not admissible to show that the deposit was not for the purpose of giving security if the memorandum stated that it was.[93]

---

[81] *Chapman v. Chapman* (1851) 13 Beav. 308; *Re McMahon, McMahon v. McMahon* (1886) 55 L.T. 763, *Dixon v. Muckleston* (1872) 8 Ch.App. 155.

[82] *Dixon v. Muckleston* (1872) 8 Ch.App. 155. *Roberts v. Croft* (1857) 24 Beav. 223.

[83] *Re Daintry, ex parte Arkwright* (1864) 3 Mont.D. & De G. 129; *Lacon v. Allen* (1856) 3 Drew. 579.

[84] *Ex parte Chippendale* (1835) 1 Deac. 67.

[85] *Ex parte Warner* (1812) 19 Ves. 202.

[86] *Goodwin v. Waghorn* (1835) 4 L.J.Ch. 172.

[87] *Simmons v. Montague* [1909] 1 I.R. 87 at 95; see also *Bank of Ireland Finance v. Daly* [1978] I.R. 79.

[88] *Roberts v. Croft* (1857) 24 Beav. 223.

[89] *Lloyd v. Attwood* (1858) 3 De G. & J. 614.

[90] *Ex parte Coming* (1803) 9 Ves. 115.

[91] *Ex parte Langston* (1810) 17 Ves. 227.

[92] *Ex parte Kensington* (1813) 2 Ves. & B. 79; *Re Ablett, ex parte Lloyd* (1824) 1 Gl. & J. 389, where the original creditors were partners, an oral agreement was held effective to charge further advances on the same security although there had been changes in the composition of the partnership.

[93] *Shaw v. Foster* (1872) L.R. 5 H.L. 321.

Prior to April 3, 1995 a proprietor of registered land or of a registered charge could have created a lien on the land by deposit of the land certificate or charge certificate with the mortgage. The lien created constituted a contract to create a charge and was capable of being protected by a notice of deposit. This is no longer the position.[94] Since April 3, 1995 a notice of deposit or intended deposit can no longer be registered and a notice should be registered instead by the equitable mortgagee or chargee in the Charges Register of the title. This is possible as such person will have the land certificate or charge certificate in his possession.[95] In the case of unregistered land registration under the Land Charges Act 1972 as a Class C (iii) land charge was not and is not available in respect of a mortgage protected by a deposit of title deeds.[96] The reason for this is that the mortgagee's retention of the title deeds provides the necessary protection against adverse dealings with the legal interest. Registration is therefore unnecessary.

2. Law of Property Act 1925, s.40 and the doctrine of part performance

5–17 Except with regard to the means of establishing priority, there was no essential difference between a mortgage by deposit and a mortgage created in any other way. The presence or absence of the deeds could affect the mortgage contract in only one way, namely, to validate it in the event that there was no sufficient memorandum for the purpose of section 40 of the Law of Property Act 1925.[97] This validation was achieved by an extension of the doctrine of part performance.[98]

Under the usual application of that doctrine, the agreement would have been enforceable in favour of the depositor only, since it was the performer of the act who was normally entitled to rely on it. However, it was well settled that equitable mortgages by deposit were also enforceable in favour of the depositee. Neither the argument that an act of part performance renders the contract enforceable only for the benefit of the actor, nor the argument that it was unsound policy to dispense with the need for writing in contracts for security, prevented the development of the equitable mortgage by deposit into a permanent feature of the law of mortgages.[99]

Although there was no necessity for a memorandum it was advisable for one to be made.[1] This would avoid disputes between the parties as to the existence or extent of the security. The memorandum could have been an informal document but in practice it was usually under seal, since an equitable mortgagee by deed has the statutory power of sale and appointment of a receiver.[2] He did not have the right to possession, however, unless there is an agreement to that effect.[3]

---

[94] Land Registration Act 1925, s.66; *Thames Guaranty Ltd v. Campbell* [1985] Q.B. 210; and see *ante* paras 4–10, 4–11. Between September 27, 1989 and April 2, 1995 a deposit would have to comply with the provisions of s.2 of the LPA 1989, see *ante* para. 4–11.

[95] LRA 1925, s.2(4)(iii) (a); s.49(1), *ante* para. 4–11.

[96] Land Charges Act 1972, s.2(4)(iii).

[97] *Re Beetham, ex parte Broderick* (1887) 18 Q.B.D. 766.

[98] *Russel v. Russel* (1783) 1 Bro.C.C. 269.

[99] *Pryce v. Bury and Price* (1853) 2 Drew. 11; *Parker v. HouseJield* (1834) 2 My. & K. 419; *Carter v. Wake* (1877) 4 Ch.D. 605.

[1] *Sporle v. Whayman* (1855) 20 Beav. 607.

[2] LPA 1925, s.101.

[3] *Garfitt v. Allen* (1888) 37 Ch.D. 48; *Ocean Accident and Cuarantee Corporation v. Ilford Gas Co.* [1905] 2 K.B. 493; *Vacuum Oil Co. v. Ellis* [1914] 1 K.B. 693.

No particular form of words were prescribed but it was desirable that the **5–18** memorandum refers to the deposit of the deeds and stated that such deposit was made with the intent that the land should be equitably charged with the repayment of the moneys advanced. Since an equitable mortgagee selling the security otherwise than by judicial sale has no power to make the conveyance to a purchaser,[4] the following provisions were normally inserted when the agreement is by deed:

    (i) an appointment of the mortgagee as the mortgagor's attorney to make the conveyance on sale under the express or statutory power;

    (ii) a declaration by the mortgagor that subject to his own right of redemption he held the property on trust, to convey it as the mortgagee shall from time to time direct, together with an authorisation for the mortgagee to appoint, at any time, a new trustee in place of the mortgagor.[5]

CHARGING ORDERS

Following a High Court or County Court judgment or order, a charging order can **5–19** be made in favour of a judgment creditor pursuant to the provisions of the Charging Orders Act 1979 over a specific asset of the debtor. Such an order is made for securing the payment of any money due or to become due under the judgment or order. The power to make such an order lies within the discretion of the court.[6] This has the like effect and is enforceable in the same courts and in the same manner as an equitable charge created by the debtor by writing under his hand.[7] It is an increasingly popular method utilised by creditors for the recovery of debts owed by debtors. Its attraction is that it creates an enforceable equitable security arising out of a judgment debt.

A charging order may be made in respect of any interest (including land or under any trust) held by the debtor beneficially.[8] This power extends to land held on trust where the judgment is against the trustee, and to any interest held on a bare trust for the debtor.[9] Also a charging order may be made where land is held by two or more debtors all of whom are liable to the creditor for the same debt and who together hold the whole beneficial interest under the trust unencumbered and for their own benefit.[10] A charging order is enforceable by sale[11] or the appointment of a receiver[12] and in the same manner as an equitable charge. Since

---

[4] *Re Hodson and Howes' Contract* (1887) 35 Ch.D. 668.

[5] *London and County Banking Co. v. Goddard* [1897] 1 Ch. 642.

[6] *ibid.* s.1(1) to (5).

[7] *ibid.* s.3(4).

[8] *ibid.* s.2(1)(a)(i), (ii), s.2(2)(a). The procedure is particularly topical in relation to interests held in the matrimonial home.

[9] *ibid.* s.2(1)(b)(i), (ii).

[10] *ibid.* s.2(1)(b)(iii); and see *Clark v. Chief Land Registrar* [1993] Ch. 370. A caution registered to protect a charging order does not confer priority. The rule in *Dearle v. Hall* (1828) 3 Russ. 1 (notice to trustees) does not extend to a judgment creditor, see *United Bank of Kuwait v. Sahib* [1995] 2 W.L.R. 94; aff'd [1997] Ch. 107. Further, a charging order takes effect subject to any prior mortgages affecting the estate or interest charged, whether legal or equitable.

[11] CPR Sched. 1, RSC Ord. 88, r. 5A.

[12] CPR Sched. 1, RSC Ord. 51; the Supreme Court Act 1981, s.37; the County Courts Act 1984, s.107.

January 1, 1997, a judgment creditor holding a charging order over a beneficial interest in land may apply under section 14 of the Trusts of Land and
Appointment of Trustees Act 1996 for an order for sale of the legal
estate.[13]

5–20   The Land Charges Act 1972 and the Land Registration Act 1925 apply as to
charging orders in the same manner as they apply in relation to other orders or
writs issued or made for the purposes of enforcing judgments.[14] In the case of
registered land, a charging order may be protected by notice in the same
circumstances as unregistered land or by caution.[15] In the case of unregistered
land a charging order is capable of being registered over the legal estate as a land
charge but only if it is a writ or order affecting land.[16] A complicating feature is
that undivided shares in land are expressly excluded from the definition of land
in section 17(1) of the Land Charges Act 1972. It follows, therefore, that in the
case of *unregistered* land where land is held beneficially under a trust of land a
charging order cannot be registered under the 1972 Act when the order imposes
a charge only on the interests of the beneficiaries. Different considerations would
apply where the order imposes a charge on the estate held by the trustees. The
logic for this is that beneficial interests held under a trust of land are themselves
not registrable under section 6(1).[17] A charging order also cannot be registered as
a general equitable charge.[18]

In the case of *registered* land when the order imposes a charge only on the
interests of the beneficiaries a charging order cannot be noted in the charges
register of the registered title.[19] A caution may be lodged instead, but this is
subject to the consent of the Chief Land Registrar where the beneficial interest
is already protected by a restriction.[20] However, the registration of a caution
will confer no priority[21] and only operates as an equitable charge of a minor
interest. When a charging order imposes a charge on the legal estate in registered conveyancing protection may be effected by notice or by a caution
depending on whether or not the land certificate is produced.

A PURCHASER'S LIEN TO SECURE HIS DEPOSIT[22]

This is dealt with elsewhere.

---

[13] Prior to that date the judgment creditor was entitled to apply for such an order pursuant to the provisions of the Law of Property Act 1925, s.30, now repealed; and see *Midland Bank plc v. Pike* [1988] 2 All E.R. 434.

[14] *ibid*. s.3(2).

[15] Land Registration Act 1925, s.49(1)(g) (inserted by the Charging Orders Act 1979, s.3(3)); for a notice, see s.54(1) (as amended), and for a caution; and see s.59(1), s.65.

[16] Land Charges Act 1972, s.6(1)(a).

[17] *ibid*. s.6(1)(A) (inserted by the Trusts of Land and Appointment of Trustees Act 1996, s.25(1), Sched. 3, para. 12(3), and see *Perry v. Phoenix Assurance plc* [1988] 1 W.L.R. 940 at 945).

[18] *ibid*. s.2(4), Class C(iii) (as amended the Trusts of Land and Appointment of Trustees Act 1996, s.25(1), Sched. 3, para. 12(2).

[19] LRA, s.49(1)(g), and see *Perry v. Phoenix Assurance plc* [1988] 1 W.L.R. 940 at 945.

[20] See LRA, s.54(1) proviso (as amended).

[21] See *United Bank of Kuwait v. Sahib* [1995] 2 W.L.R. 94; aff'd [1997] Ch. 107.

[22] See *ante* para. 1–11.

An Unpaid Vendor's Lien[23]

This is dealt with elsewhere.

Transfer and Discharge of Equitable Mortgages of Land[24]

This is dealt with elsewhere.

---

[23] See *ante* para. 1–11.
[24] See *post* paras 21–22, 22–08.

CHAPTER 6

MORTGAGES OVER MISCELLANEOUS INTERESTS IN LAND

FIXTURES

In accordance with general principles of law relating to implied grant and the **6–01** maxim *"quicquid planatur solo, solo cedit"* ("whatever is attached to the land becomes part of it") fixtures affixed to the mortgaged property form part of the security.[1] This rule applies to all fixtures the subject matter of legal and equitable mortgages[2] of freehold and leasehold land[3] whether specified or not annexed to the land at the date of the mortgage or become so during its continuance.[4] Fixtures that a tenant is entitled to retain as against his landlord pass with the mortgage by the tenant of his leasehold interest.[5] Thus the exceptions as to fixtures arising in the law of landlord and tenant do not apply in the case of mortgaged property.[6] Rights of foreclosure, possession and statutory rights of sale extend to the interest in any fixtures or personal chattels affected by the mortgage.[7]

If chattels which are bailed under a hire or hire-purchase agreement, or agreed to be sold under a conditional sale agreement, become fixtures (other than trade fixtures) they become subject to the mortgage even if affixed after it was created.[8] If they are trade fixtures, the owner or creditor has no right against a prior legal mortgagee, without notice of the agreement, to sever and remove them. However, he has such a right against a subseqent equitable mortgagee with or without notice.[9] This right is displaced by the right of a legal mortgagee of the land who

---

[1] Law of Property Act 1925, s.62(1), s.205(1)(ii).

[2] *Re Lusty, ex parte Lusty v. Official Receiver* (1889) 60 L.T. 160.

[3] *Meux v. Jacobs* (1875) L.R. 7 H.L. 481; *Southport and West Lancashire Banking Co. v. Thompson* (1889) 37 Ch.D. 64.

[4] *Mather v. Fraser* (1856) 2 K. & J . 536; *Walmsley v . Milne* (1859) 7 CB (ns) 115; *Longbottom v. Berry* (1869) L.R. 5 Q.B. 123; *Holland v. Hodgson* (1872) L.R. 7 C.P. 328; *Smith v Maclure* (1884) 32 W.R. 459; *Reynolds v. Ashby & Son* 11904] A.C. 466; *Ellis v. Glover and Hobson Ltd* [1908] 1 K.B. 388; *Vaudeville Electric Cinema v. Muriset* [1923] 2 Ch. 74; *Hulme v. Brigham* [1943] I K.B. 152 (a case where free-standing printing machines were held not to be fixtures despite the fact that the driving mechanism was fixed to the floor. See also *TSB Bank plc v. Botham* [1996] E.G.C.S. 149, *sub nom. Botham v. TSB Bank plc* (1996) 73 P. & C.R. D1 at D2, where it was held that items contained in a dwelling house were to be construed as fixtures.

[5] *Meux v. Jacobs* (1875) LR 7 H.L. 481.

[6] *Climie v. Wood* (1868) L.R. Exch. 257, aff'd (1869) L.R. 4 Exch. 328; *Monti v. Barnes* [1901] 1 K.B. 205.

[7] LPA 1925, ss88(4), 89(4).

[8] As to whether a chattel has become a fixture, see *Holland v. Hodgson* (1872) L.R. 7 C.P. 328; *Crossley Bros v. Lee* [1908] 1 K.B. 86.

[9] *Hobson v. Gorringe* [1897] 1 Ch. 182; *Reynolds v. Ashby and Son* [1904] A.C. 466; *Ellis v. Glover and Hobson Ltd* [1908] 1 K.B. 388.

has taken possession under his security. It is not so displaced by the right of an equitable mortgagee whose mortgage was created after the hire, hire-purchase or conditional sale agreement was entered into. This position applies even when an equitable mortgagee has appointed a receiver who has entered into possession.[10]

RENEWABLE LEASES AND ENFRANCHISEMENTS[11]

6–02   A first mortgagee takes the benefit of anything that either the mortgagor[12] or a subsequent mortgagee,[13] adds to the land to improve its value. Where a lease is renewable and either the mortgagor or the mortgagee renews it, the renewed lease becomes part of the mortgage security.[14]

If an option to purchase the freehold reversion, being part of the security, is exercised by the mortgagee, he is not entitled to retain the benefit of it. On redemption the mortgagor is entitled to get back the whole of his security. Thus on payment of principal, interest, costs and the purchase price of the reversion the mortgagor is entitled to a conveyance of the freehold.[15]

The freehold estate acquired by a tenant under the Leasehold Reform Acts 1967 and 1979[16] does not merge with his leasehold estate if the lease is mortgaged, since merger cannot occur when the charge and the land are owned by different persons. Unless the parties agree otherwise, the leasehold interest and not the freehold interest will continue to be the mortgage security. A mortgage term cannot be enfranchised.[17] If the mortgagor acquires an extended tenancy under the 1967 Act,[18] the extended lease forms part of the security.[19] Further,[20] the mortgagee who was entitled to possession of the title deeds relating to the original lease has the same right in respect of those relative to the extended lease.

MORTGAGES OF LEASEHOLDS AND RELIEF FROM FORFEITURE

6–03   If a mortgagor defaults on a lease subject to a legal mortgage and the lease is forfeited then any derivative interests determine with the lease. A mortgage is such a derivative interest.[21] The mortgagor still continues to remain liable on his

---

[10] *ibid.* See also *post* para. 12–13.
[11] See also *post* para. 6–02.
[12] *Re Kitchin, ex parte Punnett* (1880) 16 Ch.D. 226.
[13] See *Maxwell v. Ashe* (1752) 1 Bro. C.C. 444n; *Moody v. Matthews* (1802) 7 Ves 174; *Sims v. Helling* (1851) 21 L.J.Ch. 76; *Hughes v. Howard* (1858) 25 Beav. 575; *Landowners West of England & South Wales Land Drainage and Inclosure Co. v. Ashford* (1880) 16 Ch.D. 411.
[14] *Re Biss, Biss v. Biss* [1903] 2 Ch. 40; *Rakestraw v. Brewer* (1729) 2P Wms 511; *Leigh v. Burnett* (1885) 29 Ch.D. 231.
[15] *Nelson v. Hannam* [1943] Ch. 59.
[16] The 1967 Act, ss8 to 13, as amended by the 1979 Act.
[17] *Re Fairview, Church Street, Bromyard* [1974] 1 W.L.R. 579.
[18] *ibid.* ss14 to 16.
[19] See also the Leasehold Reform, Housing and Urban Development Act 1993, s.58(4), as regards the right of a tenant to the grant of a new lease of a flat. If the existing lease is subject to a mortgage the new lease takes effect subject to the mortgage in substitution for the existing lease.
[20] By the 1967 Act, s.14(6).
[21] *G. W. Ry v. Smith* (1876) 2 Ch.D. 235 at 253; *Viscount Chelsea v. Hutchinson* [1994] 2 E.G.L.R. 61.

personal covenant despite forfeiture of the lease. However, the court is empowered to grant relief from forfeiture on an application being made to it by the mortgagee. This can occur in one of two ways and the court exercises a discretion as to whether to grant relief at all and, if so, under which form.[22] Either the court can grant a new lease to the mortgagee or make a retrospective vesting of the lease in him.[23]

Section 146(4) of the 1925 Act[24] provides that where a lessor is proceeding by action or otherwise to enforce a right of re-entry or forfeiture under any covenant, proviso, or stipulation in a lease, or for non-payment of rent, an underlessee (which includes a mortgagee) may apply for relief from forfeiture either in the lessor's action (if any) or in any action brought by such person for that purpose. In effect the mortgagee has the same rights as, and stands in the shoes of, the lessee under the lease. For such a right to arise the mortgage must be by sub-demise or legal charge.[25] It has been held that for the purposes of the sub-section mortgagee also includes an equitable chargee holding under a charging order.[26]

In such circumstances the court can make a vesting order by virtue of the provisions of section 146(4) of the Law of Property Act 1925. This vests the whole term of the lease or any less term the property comprised in the lease or any part thereof in the mortgagee upon such conditions as to the execution of any deed or other document, payment of rent, costs, expenses, damages, compensation, giving security or otherwise as the court in the circumstances of each case may think fit. Various conditions can be imposed by the court which include making good any subsisting breaches[27] or performing the covenants of the existing lease. However, "in no case shall any such under-lessee be entitled to require a lease to be granted to him for any longer term than he had under his original sub-lease".[28] Such relief gives rise to the creation of a *new* lease in favour of the mortgagee and the new lease becomes the substituted security and is subject to the mortgagors' right of redemption and the rights of subsequent mortgagees for an account of the proceeds of sale of the mortgaged property by such mortgagee.[29]

---

[22] See *Escalus Properties Ltd v. Dennis* [1996] Q.B. 231.

[23] The Law of Property Act 1925 (as amended), either under s.146(4) or s.146(2). For the procedural aspects in the High Court and County Court, see *post* para. 16–21.

[24] Replacing Conveyancing Act 1892, s.4, and as amended by the Law of Property (Amendment) Act 1929, s.1.

[25] See *Re Good's Lease* [1954] 1 W.L.R. 309; *Grand Junction Co. Ltd v. Bates* [1954] 2 Q.B. 160; *Chelsea Estate Investments Trust Co. Ltd v. Marche* [1955] Ch. 328.

[26] *Ladup Ltd v. William & Glynn's Bank plc* [1985] 1 W.L.R. 851; *Croydon (Unique) Ltd v. Wright* (1999) 4 All E.R. 257. These decisions are in conflict with another decision, that of *Bland v. Ingrams Estates Ltd* (1999) EG 185.

[27] *Ewart v. Fryer* [1901] 1 Ch. 499.

[28] LPA 1925, s.146(4). An apparent conflict exists between these provisions, but it has been decided that the court will not grant a sub-lessee a term longer than his sub-lease see *Ewart v. Fryer* [1901] 1 Ch. 499 at 515, and see *Factors Sundries Ltd v. Miller* [1952] 1 All E.R. 630 at 634. It must be noted that a sub-lease can be extended by the provisions relating to security of tenure under the Rent Act 1977, see *Cadogan v. Dimovich* [1984] 1 W.L.R. 609.

[29] See *Chelsea Estates Investments Trust Co. Ltd v. Marche* [1955] Ch. 328; *Cadogan v. Dimovich* [1984] 1 W.L.R. 609; *Official Custodian for Charities v. Mackey* [1985] Ch. 168 at 164; and see also *Official Custodian for Charities v. Mackey (No. 2)* [1985] 1 W.L.R. 1308; *Hammersmith and Fulham LBC v. Tops Shop Centres Ltd* [1990] Ch. 237. For a recent case where relief under s.146(4) was refused to an equitable chargee, but allowed in a claim for *indirect* relief by the chargee based upon an implied obligation, see *Bland v. Ingram's Estate Ltd* (2001) 24 E.G. 163.

6–04   A number of aspects arise for consideration with regard to these statutory provisions. The most important of these are the following. First, the court is only able to grant relief under section 146(4) where the lessor is proceeding by action or otherwise. Formerly the ability of a mortgagee to seek and obtain relief from forfeiture ceased as soon as re-entry had been effected such as by peaceable re-entry.[30] This made peaceable re-entry attractive for landlords. However, since the decision in *Billson v. Residential Apartments Ltd*[31] the landlord is still "proceeding" despite physical re-entry. The mortgagee can continue to seek relief until such period has expired for him to seek such relief.

Secondly, pending relief being granted a sub-tenant (including a mortgagee) is to be regarded as a trespasser, in the inter-regnum period between the forfeiture of the lease and the grant of relief.[32] Thirdly, as stated above, the grant is of a new lease and is not retrospective.[33] Further, such a lease may not be on the same terms as the original lease.[34]

Thirdly, the mortgagee can also seek relief under the provisions of section 146(2) of the Law of Property Act 1925. This is on the basis of the decision in *Escalus Properties Ltd v. Dennis* which held that the provisions of relief contained in that sub-section were retrospective.[35] However, he is unable to seek relief on this ground if the head lease is forfeited for non-payment of rent or where the provisions of section 146 are excluded.[36]

6–04A   Further, of considerable importance is the effect that the Landlord and Tenant (Covenants) Act 1995 Act[37] has on a new lease created by order of the court after that date and the continued enforceability of the covenants contained in the forfeited lease granted before that date on the mortgagee of the reversion and of the lease. Where a lease was granted before January 1, 1996 the mortgagee of the security is entitled to enforce and take advantage of covenants having reference to the subject matter of the lease covenanted for by the lessee including the rights of re-entry.[38] He can also re-enter for breaches of covenant committed before the mortgage unless they had been waived or released at the time of the mortgage.[39]

---

[30] See *e.g. Pakwood Transport Ltd v. 15 Beauchamp Place Ltd* (1977) 36 P. & C.R. 112.

[31] [1992] A.C. 494.

[32] *Official Custodian for Charities v. Mackey* [1985] Ch. 168; *Viscount Chelsea v. Hutchinson* [1994] 2 E.G.L.R. 61; *Pellicano v. MEPC plc* [1994] E.G.L.R. 104.

[33] See n. 29 *ante*.

[34] *Hammersmith and Fulham LBC v. Tops Shop Centres Ltd* [1990] 2 Ch. 237.

[35] [1996] Q.B. 231. It had formerly been considered that the subsection did not operate retrospectively, see *Pellicano v. MEPC plc* [1994] E.G.L.R. 104.

[36] *i.e. ibid.,* s.146(8) and (9).

[37] As the Law Commission Working Paper No. 99, *Land Mortgages* pointed out at para. 3.74 that as a result of a principle of privity of contract this had the effect of making the mortgagee liable on the covenants of the new lease throughout the term of the lease. See also the Law Commission Working Paper No. 95, *Landlord and Tenant—Privity of Contract and Estate: duration of liability of parties to leases* (1986) where it was concluded that the principle of privity of contract should be abrogated. See also the recommendations of the Law Commission (1988) Law Com. No. 174 which eventually resulted in the enactment of the Landlord and Tenant (Covenants) Act 1995 (which implemented these recommendations and other unpublished recommendations of the Law Commission, subject to modifications). The main provisions of this Act apply to all tenancies granted after January 1, 1996.

[38] See the Law of Property Act 1925, s.141 (1), (2). The expression "mortgagee" includes a "chargee", *ibid.,* s.15(6).

[39] *ibid.,* s.141(3).

A mortgagee in possession of property subject to a lease granted before January 1, 1996 can enforce any tenant covenant of a tenancy or any right of re-entry enforceable by the mortgagor.[40] Similarly, a mortgagee in possession of the tenant's interest can enforce a "landlord's covenant"[41] against the landlord.[42]

Any tenant covenant of a tenancy, or a right of re-entry contained in a tenancy enforceable against the tenant in respect of any property demised by the tenancy is also enforceable against any mortgagee in possession of the tenant's interest.[43] Covenants which are express to be personal or unenforceable for non-registration are not enforceable against a mortgagee in possession.[44]

GOODWILL

On the principle that anything added to the property mortgaged by the mortgagor is an accretion for the mortgagor's benefit, the general principle is that the mortgagee is entitled to the goodwill which attaches to premises.[45] This includes the goodwill of a public house business[46] entitling the mortgagee to an assignment of the licence,[47] but not to the proceeds of sale of those rights.[48] It has been held in one case that the mortgage security included the business itself carried on from the premises.[49] It will, however, be otherwise if the terms of the security show that only the mortgaged property was intended to be the subject of the mortgage and not the goodwill of the business.[50] Further, the mortgagee is not entitled to benefit from goodwill arising from the mortgagor's personal reputation acquired from his expertise.[51]

6–05

COMPULSORY ACQUISITION OF LAND AND COMPENSATION

Where land subject to a mortgage is to be compulsorily acquired both the mortgagor and the mortgagee are entitled to a notice to treat. Where the acquiring authority pays a lump sum into court in respect of both interests, the court will apportion the sum between them. It is, however, usual for the acquiring authority to treat with the mortgagor for the full value, leaving him to discharge the mortgage. The exception would be if the mortgagee is in possession.

6–06

---

[40] *ibid.*, s.15(1). "tenant covenant" is defined by *ibid.*, s.28(1).
[41] *ibid.*, s.28(1).
[42] *ibid.*, s.15(3).
[43] *ibid.*, s.15(4).
[44] *ibid.*, s.15(5).
[45] *Cooper v. Metropolitan Board of Works* (1883) 25 Ch.D. 472. See also *Chissum v. Dewes* (1828) 5 Russ. 29; *King v. Midland Rly Co.* (1868) 17 W.R. 113; *Pile v. Pile, ex p Lambton* (1876) 3 Ch.D. 36; *Re Kitchin, ex parte Punnett* (1880) 16 Ch.D. 226.
[46] *Re Kitchin, ex parte Punnett* (1880) 16 Ch.D. 226.
[47] *Rutter v. Daniel* (1882) 30 W.R. 724 (on appeal 30 W.R. 801); *Re O'Brien* (1883) 11 L.R. Ir. 213; *Garrett v. St Marylebone, Middlesex Justices* (1884) 12 Q.B.D. 620.
[48] *Re Carr* [1918] 2 I.R. 448.
[49] *County of Gloucester Bank v. Rudry Merthyr Steam and House Coal Colliery Co.* [1895] 1 Ch. 629.
[50] *Whitley v. Challis* [1892] 1 Ch. 64; *Palmer v. Barclays Bank Ltd* (1971) 23 P. & C.R. 30.
[51] *Cooper v. Metropolitan Board of Works* (1883) 25 Ch.D. 472.

The mortgagee is entitled to the money paid as compensation for the licence of a mortgaged public house as part of the mortgage security.[52] There are special statutory provisions entitling the acquiring authority to redeem the mortgagee's interest in the land. It is necessary to refer to a specialist work in this field.[53]

INSURANCE MONIES AND MORTGAGE INDEMNITY POLICIES

6–07 Although a mortgagor is not obliged by statute to keep the mortgaged property in repair it is usual for him to covenant to do so.[54] All monies received on an insurance of the mortgaged property effected under the provisions of the Law of Property Act 1925, or for the maintenance of which the mortgagor is liable under the mortgage deed, must, if the mortgagee so requires, be applied by the mortgagor in making good the loss or damage in respect of which the money is received.[55]

However, the mortgagee has no right to the policy monies if the mortgagor insures on his own account.[56] In the case where the mortgagor insures having covenanted to do so, on the true construction of the covenant it operates to grant to the mortgagee a charge over the proceeds, but he is accountable to the mortgagor for any surplus. This position arises even if the insurance is taken out in the name of the mortgagor by way of a partial equitable assignment.[57]

It is usual for mortgagees to take out a mortgage indemnity policy with an insurance company. This is designed to protect the mortgagee in the event of the inability or failure by the mortgagor to make the repayments due under the mortgage, and the proceeds of sale being less than the outstanding debt on sale by the mortgagee. Despite the fact that it is the mortgagor who is debited with the premium and the policy is usually described as additional security in the general conditions applicable to the mortgage, the proceeds of such a policy belong to the mortgagee and not the mortgagor. They do not discharge any part of the debt owed by the mortgagor.[58]

INCORPOREAL HEREDITAMENTS AND OTHER RIGHTS

6–08 Incorporeal hereditaments are rights of property which are included as part of real property in English land law. However, they are to be distinguished from

---

[52] *Law Guarantee and Trust Society Ltd v. Mitcham and Cheam Brewery Co. Ltd* [1906] 2 Ch. 98; *Noakes v. Noakes & Co. Ltd* [1907] 1 Ch. 64; *Dawson v. Braime's Tadcaster Breweries Ltd* [1907] 2 Ch. 359.

[53] See, *e.g. Corfield and Carnwath* (1978), pp. 90–92.

[54] See *ante* para. 3–23, *post* para. 19–01 *et seq.*

[55] The Law of Property Act 1925, s.108(3).

[56] *Halifax Building Society v. Keighley* [1931] 2 K.B. 248; *Re Doherty* [1925] 2 I.R. 246.

[57] *Colonial Mutual General Insurance Co. Ltd v. ANZ Banking Insurance Group (New Zealand) Ltd* [1995] 1 W.L.R. 1140.

[58] *Mortgage Corpn v. McNicholas* (unreported, September 22, 1992); *Woolwich Building Society v. Brown* [1996] C.L.C. 625.

corporeal land as they are rights of an incorporeal nature and not physical objects. Examples of incorporeal rights include the following: franchises (such as markets and fairs)[59]; manorial rights; easements; profits (such as rights of common); rentcharges; annuities; advowsons; tithes; and other property of a like nature separated from the ownership of corporeal property but closely connected with it.

Although the treatment of incorporeal hereditaments as part of the realty may be historically accidental, their status forms part of law of realty. As such they constitute "land" for the purposes of the Law of Property Act 1925.[60] Further, as they lie in grant they can only be conveyed by deed. They may therefore be the subject matter of a legal mortgage whether by demise or by legal charge. The only exception is that of advowsons which no longer constitute "land" for the purposes of the Land Registration Act 1925.[61]

AGRICULTURAL MORTGAGES AND CHARGES

There are special provisions contained in the Agricultural Credits Act 1928 for **6–09** short-term credit by way of agricultural mortgages and charges in favour of a bank on farming stock.[62] However, these provisions do not exclude the applicability of the general law of mortgages and bills of sale to mortgages and charges of farms and stock in appropriate cases.[63]

MORTGAGE OF MINES AND MINERALS

In general property consisting of mines and minerals can be the subject matter of **6–10** legal mortgages and charges provided that there is in existence a legal interest in the property in question. However, owing to the wasting nature of the asset it is a common provision inserted into the mortgage deed to provide for the creation of a sinking fund or repayment of mortgage monies advance by instalments of the sum advanced. A provision is also often inserted in the mortgage deed permitting the mortgagee in the case of default by the mortgagor to enter upon the mortgaged property and work the mine and to make all proper expenditure for that purpose. In the case of any deficiency it may be charged against the property.[64]

The mortgagee's statutory power of sale includes (and subject to any contrary intention expressed in the mortgage deed) the power to sell the mortgaged property or any part of it with the exception or reservation of all or any of the

[59] See *Pease and Chitty's Law of Markets and Fairs* (6th ed., Cousins and Anthony, 1998).
[60] *ibid.*, s.1(2), 205(I)(ix).
[61] See the Patronage (Beneficies) Measure 1986, s.6; the Law of Property Act 1925, s.201(1).
[62] See chapter 10, *post* para. 10–07 *et seq.*
[63] See *post* para. 10–02.
[64] *Norton v. Cooper* (1854) 5 De. G.M. & G. 728.

mines or minerals, or to sell all or any mines and minerals apart from the surface.[65]

MORTGAGES OF SHIPS AND FREIGHT

6–11   The Merchant Shipping Act 1995 governs mortgages of ships.[66] A registered ship or share in a registered ship may be made security for the repayment of a loan or the discharge of any other obligation. The instrument creating any such security (referred to as a "mortgage") must be in the form prescribed by or approved under registration regulations. The registrar must register the mortgage executed in accordance with these provisions in the prescribed manner. It is known as a "registered mortgage".[67] Such registered mortgages must be registered in the order in which they are produced to the registrar for the purposes of registration. The rights of unregistered mortgagees are postponed to those of registered mortgagees.

Mortgages of ships which would otherwise require registration as bills of sale are exempt from the statutory provisions relating to bills of sale.[68] Until the mortgagee takes possession the ship's earnings remain the property of the mortgagor. However, there is also usually included with the mortgage of a particular vessel a collateral mortgage of the freight on board made in favour of the same mortgagee. This will include the mortgagor's interests in the policies of insurance and earnings from freight. The mortgagee should complete this security by giving notice to the persons who are liable to pay the cost of the freight[69] but otherwise it is unnecessary to comply with the statutory provisions for the security to be valid.

A registered mortgage of a ship or of a share in a ship may be transferred by an instrument made in the form prescribed by or approved under the registration regulations.[70] Whether or not the mortgage is registered under the provisions set out above, a mortgage of a ship or share in a ship made by a *company* is in any event registerable under the Companies Act 1985 within 21 days at Companies House. Otherwise it will be void against a liquidator or any creditor of the company.[71]

For a detailed analysis of mortgages of ships and the respective rights of a statutory mortgagee to freight, and the priorities between such a mortgagee and an assignee of freight it is necessary to consult a specialist work on the subject of shipping and freight.

---

[65] See the Law of Property Act 1925, s.101 (2) (ii), (4).

[66] *ibid.*, see s.313(1). See also Meeson, *Ship and Aircraft Mortgage* (1989); Palmer and McKendrick, *Interest in Goods* (1998), chap. 26, 27.

[67] *ibid.*, s.16(1), Sch. 1 para. 7(1), (2), (3), para. 14; and see the Merchant Shipping (Registration of Ships) Regulations 1993, S.I. 1993 No. 3138, reg. 57, 58.

[68] The Bills of Sale Act 1878 and the Bills of Sale Act (1878) Amendment Act 1882.

[69] *Mestaer v. Gillespie* (1805) 11 Ves. 621 at 629; *Davenport v. Whitmore* (1836) 2 My. & Cr. 177; *Gardner v. Lachlan* (1838) 4 My. & Cr. 129; *Langton v. Horton* (1842) 1 Hare 549.

[70] The Merchant Shipping Act 1995, s.16, Sch. 1 paras 11, 12; the Merchant Shipping (Registration of Ships) Regulations 1993, S.I. 1993 No. 3138, reg. 60 (as substituted).

[71] See the Companies Act 1985, ss395(1) (as amended), 396(1)(h), 399. These provisions have been repealed by Part IV of the Companies Act 1989 and are to be replaced from a day to be appointed. No such date has so far been appointed and is unlikely ever to occur.

MORTGAGES OF AIRCRAFT AND HOVERCRAFT

An aircraft or hovercraft,[72] duly registered in the register maintained under the **6–12** relevant statutory provisions[73] may be made security for a loan or other valuable consideration.[74] Similarly an aircraft or hovercraft with any store of spares for it can be the subject matter of a mortgage for a loan or other valuable consideration. Provision is also made for the voluntary registration of any such mortgage.[75]

Mortgages of registered aircraft which would otherwise require registration as bills of sale are exempt from the statutory provisions relating to bills of sale from October 1, 1972. However, mortgages of unregistered aircraft still remain subject to those Acts. Whether or not the mortgage is registered under the provisions set out above, a mortgage made by a *company* is in any event registrable under the Companies Act 1985 within 21 days at Companies House. Otherwise it will be void against a liquidator or any creditor of the company.[76]

There is no special form of transfer of a statutory mortgage of a ship or hovercraft.

---

[72] For the definition of "hovercraft" see the Hovercraft Act 1968, s.4(1). Hovercraft are classified as "aircraft" for mortgage purposes (although for most other purposes they rank as ships). The Mortgaging of Aircraft Order 1972, S.I. 1972 No. 1268 (as amended), applies to hovercraft by virtue of the Hovercraft (Application of Enactments) Order 1972, S.I. 1972 No. 971, art. 5, Sched. 2, Pt A. The Mortgaging of Aircraft Order 1972 was made under the provisions of the Civil Aviation Act 1968, s.16 (now repealed). However, it now takes effect as if it were made under the Civil Aviation Act 1982, s.86 (as amended) by virtue of the provisions of the Interpretation Act 1978, s.17(2)(b). See also the provisions of the Civil Aviation Act 1982, s.86 (as amended) which applies to hovercraft by virtue of the Interpretation Act 1978, ss17(2)(a), 23(2); and see the Hovercraft Act 1968, ss1(1)(h)(as amended), 1(3). The last hovercraft in commercial service in the United Kingdom was de-commissioned by Hoverspeed in the summer of 2000.

[73] Registered in the register maintained under the Civil Aviation Act 1982, s.60 (as amended) and the Air Navigation Order (No. 2) 1995, S.I. 1995, No. 1970, art. 3 (as amended). See the Mortgaging of Aircraft Order 1972, S.I. 1972 No. 1268, arts 2(2), 3 (as amended), see n.1, *ante*.

[74] *ibid.*, arts 4 to 14(1). A registered mortgage takes priority over an earlier unregistered mortgage, *ibid.*, art 14(2) to (5).

[75] The Bills of Sale Act 1878 and the Bills of Sale Act (1878) Amendment Act 1882, see chapter 12 *post* para. 12–05 *et seq.*, and see the Mortgaging of Aircraft Order 1972, S.I. 1972 No. 1268, art 16(1).

[76] See the Companies Act 1985, ss395(1) (as amended), (this also applies to ships 396(1)(h), 399. These provisions have been repealed by Part IV of the Companies Act 1989 and are to be replaced from a day to be appointed. No such date has so far been appointed and is unlikely ever to occur.

CHAPTER 7

SECOND AND SUBSEQUENT MORTGAGES

GENERAL

Before 1926, second and subsequent mortgages of freehold land were necessarily **7–01** equitable, as was also the case with leasehold land if the first mortgage was made by assignment. Subsequent mortgages of leasehold land could be legal if the first mortgage was made by sub-demise, each successive mortgage being by sub-demise for a term one day longer than the term of the previous mortgage.

It is now possible for second and subsequent mortgages of both freehold and leasehold land to be legal. These may be created by demise or sub-demise, as appropriate, or by charge expressed to be by way of legal mortgage. A second or subsequent mortgage, in addition to reciting the mortgagor's ownership and the agreement for the loan, should recite the state of the prior mortgage. This provides the mortgagee with a remedy under the implied covenants for title[1] given by the mortgagor in the event that the sum owing is greater than the sum recited. The demise or charge should be expressly made subject to any prior mortgage, and it is usual for the power of sale to be made exercisable on interest under a prior mortgage being in arrears for a specified number of days. There should also be a power for the subsequent mortgagee to settle and pass the accounts of prior mortgagees and a charge of the costs of so doing upon the mortgaged property.

1. The right to tack[2]

A second or subsequent mortgagee may be exposed to the risk that a prior **7–02** mortgagee will make further advances, ranking in priority to his mortgage, to the mortgagor. Before 1926, two classes of mortgagee had the right to tack further advances, namely an equitable mortgagee who acquired the legal estate, and a legal mortgagee who made a further advance. The right to tack is now regulated by section 94 of the Law of Property Act 1925. The purpose of this section was to rationalise the rules as to tacking, in particular (as is often the case in modern mortgages) for the lender to have the ease of ability to make further advances without losing his priority in relation to the subsequent advances. Subsection (1) provides as follows:

[1] See *ante* para. 3–26 *et seq.*
[2] See further para. 20–42 *et seq.*

"After the commencement of this Act, a prior mortgagee shall have a right to make further advances to rank in priority to subsequent mortgages (whether legal or equitable)—

(a) if an arrangement has been made to that effect with the subsequent mortgagees; or

(b) if he had no notice of such subsequent mortgages at the time when the further advance was made by him, or

(c) whether or not he had such notice as aforesaid, when the mortgage imposes an obligation on him to make further advances."

The subsection applies whether or not the prior mortgage was made expressly for securing further advances.

Therefore if B creates two mortgages, first in favour of L1 and then in favour of L2, on the same security, and then takes a further advance from L1, section 94(1)(a) of the Law of Property Act 1925 provides that L1 may, with the consent of L2, obtain priority for his further advance over that made by L2.

Section 94(1)(b) deals with the situation where L1 has no notice of L2's mortgage. He can, then claim priority for his further advance over L2's advance. For this purpose registration of L2's mortgage as a land charge constitutes actual notice. It is therefore essential that L1 makes a land registry search in order to ascertain whether any subsequent mortgages have been created. Of importance in *unregistered* land is the position where a mortgage is made expressly for securing either a current account or other further advances. Here, exceptionally, registration does *not* constitute notice for the purpose of depriving the prior mortgagee of his right to tack,[2a] and section 94(2) applies. This provides as follows:

"a mortgagee shall not be deemed to have notice of a mortgage merely by reason that it was registered as a land charge . . . if it was not so registered at the time when the original mortgage was created or when the last search (if any) by or on behalf of the mortgagee was made, whichever last happened."

7–03   An intending second or subsequent mortgagee, on making a search and discovering that the prior mortgage has been made expressly to secure a current account or further advances, should therefore give notice, on completion of his mortgage, to the prior mortgagee.

Another reason for giving such notice is that registration as a land charge is not notice for the purpose of section 96(2) of the Law of Property Act 1925. That section casts on a mortgagee having notice of subsequent mortgages, the duty to deliver the title deeds to the person next entitled in priority. Section 96(1) entitles the mortgagor, as long as his right to redeem subsists, to inspect and make copies of documents of title in the power or custody of the mortgagee. Section 205(1)(xvi) defines "mortgagor" as "any person . . . deriving title under the original mortgagor or entitled to redeem a mortgage according to his estate interest or right in the mortgaged property."

Section 94(1)(c) applies where L1 by the terms of the mortgage is obliged to make further advances. In that case, neither registration nor actual notice of the

---

[2a] See *ibid*. s.94(4).

existence of any subsequent mortgage deprives L1 of his right to tack; this provision reverses the pre–1926 common law rule.

2. The right to consolidate

It has also been suggested that a second mortgagee is exposed to the risk of **7–04** having an earlier and a later advance by a first mortgagee of the same property consolidated against him. The doctrine of consolidation applied originally where the mortgagor created two mortgages on different properties, in favour of the same mortgagee, but was later extended to the case where the mortgages were originally created in favour of different mortgagees but subsequently became vested in the same person. By section 93(1) of the Law of Property Act 1925, the operation of the doctrine is excluded unless a contrary intention is shown in one or more of the mortgage deeds.

There is one decision[3] in which consolidation was allowed in respect of three mortgages, the first two of the same property, the third being of that and other property. The judge expressed his unfamiliarity with the question and, while the decision has been accepted as authority for the propositions that: (i) the doctrine can be excluded by a provision in any one of the mortgage deeds; and (ii) that the right to consolidate exists where the mortgages become vested after the mortgagor's bankruptcy, it has never been subsequently cited as determining that the doctrine applies to successive mortgages of the same property. As a decision it is probably wrong.

3. Power of sale

A second or subsequent mortgagee may also be at risk of not recovering the **7–05** amount of his security in the event of a prior mortgagee exercising his power of sale. Section 105 of the Law of Property Act 1925 provides that such a mortgagee holds the purchase money on trust, after prior mortgages have been paid off, to pay:

(i) all expenses incidental to the sale;
(ii) to himself, the principal, interest and costs due under the mortgage;
(iii) the surplus, if any, to the person entitled to the mortgaged property.

These words are defined so as to include subsequent mortgagees, and the prior mortgagee is a trustee of the surplus for those subsequent mortgagees of whose incumbrances he has notice. Registration as a land charge is notice for this purpose (Law of Property Act 1925, section 198(1)).

Although it has been decided that a mortgagee who exercises his power of sale is not a trustee of that power for the mortgagor, he does owe a duty not only to act in good faith, but also to take reasonable care to obtain the true market value

---

[3] *Re Salmon, ex parte The Trustee* [1903] 1 K.B. 147; and see Megarry and Wade, *The Law of Real Property* (6th ed., 2000), para. 19–08, n. 28.

of the mortgaged property at the date at which he sells it.[4] In the case of a building society mortgagee this is enshrined as a statutory duty.[5] It therefore ought to follow that, provided a second or subsequent mortgagee makes reasonable enquiries and takes reasonable precautions to satisfy himself that there is sufficient equity in the property to secure his advance, he should not be at much risk of loss on a sale by a prior mortgagee. In practice, he often suffers loss resulting from the accumulated interest on the prior mortgage.

4. Trustees

7–06 By the Trustee Investment Act 1961, any mortgage of freehold property in England, Wales or Northern Ireland, or of any leasehold property of which the unexpired term is over 60 years, is an authorised narrower range investment requiring advice. Trustees lending money on the security of such property do not obtain the protection of section 8 of the Trustee Act 1925 unless they comply with the provisions of subsection 1 of that section. Since section 8(1)(b) of that Act requires them to show that the amount of the loan does not exceed two-thirds of the value of the property it may well be that second mortgages rarely comply with that provision. Trustees may also lend money on the security of personal property.[6]

5. Building societies

7–07 Formerly, section 32(1) of the Building Societies Act 1962 prohibited a building society from advancing money on the security of real property subject to a prior mortgage, except as provided by Schedule 5 to the Act or where the prior charge is in favour of the society. Section 32(2) fixed the directors jointly and severally with the liability for making good any loss occasioned to the society by the advance. The power of a building society to lend on second or subsequent mortgage was greatly extended by Part III of the Building Societies Act 1986. For the treatment of building society law and mortgage lending see Chapter 8.[7]

PROTECTION

1. Unregistered land

7–08 A second or subsequent legal mortgagee will not, in general, have the title deeds, since they will normally be in the possession of the first mortgagee. Section 2(4) of the Land Charges Act 1972 provides that a puisne mortgage (that is, one not "protected by a deposit of documents relating to the legal estate affected") shall

---

[4] *Cuckmere Brick Co. Ltd v. Mutual Finance Ltd* [1971] Ch. 949. See also *post*, chapter 14, pp. 231 *et seq.*
[5] s.12(2) of the Building Societies Act 1997 and see *ante* para. 8–33.
[6] s.1(1), (3) Sched. 1, Pt II, para. 13, Pt II, para. 5.
[7] *post* para. 8–01 *et seq.*

be registered as a class C(i) land charge, and, if not registered, it is void against a purchaser for value of any interest in the land. Equitable mortgages are registrable as general equitable charges, which belong to class C(iii), and failure to register has the same consequences.

2. **Registered land**

Here the method of protection depends on the way in which the first mortgage **7–09** was created. If a first charge has been registered the land certificate will have been deposited at the Registry in accordance with section 65 of the Land Registration Act 1925. A second legal mortgage can be registered and a charge certificate issued in respect of it. Section 29 of the 1925 Act provides that, subject to any entry to the contrary in the register, priorities among legal mortgages are determined by the order in which they were entered on the register and not according to the order in which they were created. Form 45 formerly contained stipulations altering the priority of charges under section 29. However, that form has now been revoked.[8]

Where the prior mortgage was created by deposit of the land certificate, that will be held by the prior mortgagee and protection will be by way of notice under the Land Registration Act 1925, section 49, if the depositee is willing to make the land certificate available, or otherwise by caution under the Land Registration Act 1925, section 54. The invariable practice of banks is to require a formal charge to be registered.

---

[8] Land Registration Rules 1925, Sched. 1. See *ante* para. 4–05.

CHAPTER 8

BUILDING SOCIETY LAW AND MORTGAGE LENDING

GENERAL BACKGROUND

The law governing building societies and its power to make advances secured on **8–01** residential property forms an elaborate code. The previous edition of this work attempted to summarise building society mortgage law as it then stood based upon changes brought about by the enactment of the Building Societies Act 1986 ("the 1986 Act"). Some of the provisions of the 1986 Act had not been brought into force by the time of publication of the previous edition in December 1989.

Since then the 1986 Act has been the subject of considerable amendment, principally by the Building Societies Act 1997 ("the 1997 Act"). In particular section 12(1) of the 1997 Act revoked Part III of the 1986 Act which regulated advances, loans and other assets. Further amendments have been made by the Financial Services and Markets Act 2000 ("the 2000 Act"). There are also a number of statutory instruments governing the powers of building societies promulgated under the 1997 Act. The result is a complex amalgam of legislative provisions. At present there are few summaries on the subject. Therefore in this revised chapter rather than concentrate solely on building society mortgages and secured lending an attempt has been made to summarise mortgage lending in the context of building society law in general. However, detailed consideration of the subject should be sought in works especially devoted to the subject.[1] Further as the provisions of the 2000 Act are not yet fully in force, the legal position relating to building societies in the context of that Act will have to be revisited.

SUMMARY OF THE NATURE AND POWERS OF A BUILDING SOCIETY

Building society loans are governed by the general law of mortgages.[2] The main **8–02** difference between building society mortgages and other mortgages is the incorporation of the society's rules into the mortgage. The mortgage usually provides that the mortgagor shall be bound by any alteration of the rules, and, while a

---

[1] See, *e.g. Wurtzburg and Mills; Building Society Law* (15th ed., 1989–1997). I am also grateful for the assistance provided by the Building Societies Association.
[2] *Provident Permanent Society v. Greenhill* (1878) 9 Ch. D. 122.

society has extensive powers to alter its rules,[3] such alteration must be one which could reasonably be considered as within the contemplation of the members of the society when the contract of membership was made.[4]

A building society is a corporate body[5] whose purpose or principal purpose is to make loans secured on residential property, as defined,[6] such loans being funded substantially by its members.[7] A building society operates within the powers conferred on it by its memorandum.[8] The memorandum must state this purpose or principal purpose.[9] These powers can include the power to hold land as part of a building societies' assets. Strict financial controls govern the structure of such assets and its subsidiaries. This is designed to ensure that the prescribed relationship between advances made by the society and secured on residential property and other assets is not breached.[10] However, failure to comply with these requirements will not affect the validity of any transaction.[11]

A building society may also have the power contained in its memorandum (if so conferred upon it) to raise funds and borrow money, such as to create a fixed charge over its property. Formerly this power could only have been exercised subject to the authorisation (either unconditionally or conditionally) of the Building Societies Commission ("the Commission").[12] A building society continues to remain restricted in relation to certain other transactions and the position remains unaltered by the provisions of the 2000 Act. It cannot act as a market maker in securities, commodities or currencies; trade in commodities or currencies; and enter into any transaction involving derivative interests.[13] Further a building society cannot create a floating charge over the whole or part of its undertaking or property,[14] and any such charge is void.[15]

8–03   The functions of the Commission are in the process of being transferred to the Financial Services Authority ("the FSA") and to the Treasury. This is to be effected by order of the Treasury following the enactment of the 2000 Act. The date set for the transfer was June 18, 2001, as announced by the Economic Secretary to the Treasury, Melanie Johnson, before the General Election. Section 336 of the 2000 Act provides for the prospective transfer and allocation of the powers of the Commission between the FSA and the Treasury. In effect the regulatory powers of the Commission will be redistributed between the FSA and

---

[3] *Rosenburg v. Northumberland Building Society* (1889) 22 Q.B.D. 373; *Wilson v. Miles Platting Building Society* (1887) 22 Q.B.D. 381, n: *Bradbury v. Wild* [1893] 1 Ch. 377. Also see Sched. 2, para. 6 to the 1986 Act.

[4] *Hole v. Garnsey* [1930] A.C. 472.

[5] 1986 Act, s.5(2)–(6).

[6] *ibid*. s.5(10) (substituted by the 1997 Act, s.1(4)).

[7] s.5(1)(a).

[8] *ibid*. s.5(5) (substituted by the 1997 Act, s.1(3)).

[9] *ibid*. s.5(8), Sched. 2, para. 2(1) (substituted by the 1997 Act, s.43, Sched. 7, para. 56(3)).

[10] *ibid*. s.6 (substituted by the 1997 Act, s.4), and s.6A (substituted by the 1997 Act, s.6).

[11] *ibid*. s.6(5)(b) (substituted by the 1997 Act, s.4).

[12] *ibid*. s.9 amended by the 1997 Act, ss.43, 46(2), Sched. 7 para. 3, Sched. 9). This section and Sched. 3 to the 1997 Act have been prospectively repealed by s.432(3) and Sched. 22 of the 2000 Act, but no Order has yet been made by the Treasury bringing the section into force. See also s.336 of the 2000 Act and Part III of Sched. 18, paras 17 and 18, for the transfer of the functions of the Commission to the Financial Services Authority and the Treasury, and see n. 10 *post*.

[13] *ibid*. s.9A(1). This is subject to certain exceptions contained in subsections (2) to (5).

[14] *ibid*. s.9B(1) (inserted by the 1997 Act, s.11).

[15] *ibid*. s.9B(2) (inserted by the 1997 Act, s.11).

the Treasury and the Commission will be abolished.[16] Such powers are also subject to the statutory requirements regarding the financial structure of a building society, where relevant.[17] However, failure to comply with these requirements will not affect the validity of any transaction.[18] Of importance to building societies (and other lenders) is the effect of the provisions contained in the Unfair Terms in Consumer Contracts Regulations 1999.[19]

The 1986 Act contemplates the dissolution of building societies by members' consent,[20] or its winding up, voluntarily or by the court.[21] The rules of a society must specify the entitlement of the members to participate in the surplus assets, in the event of dissolution by consent or winding up.[22] Section 92 of the Act provides as follows:

> "Where a building society is being wound up or dissolved by consent, a member to whom an advance has been made under a mortgage or other security, or under the rules of the society, shall not be liable to pay any amount except at the time or times and subject to the conditions set out in the mortgage or other security, or in the rules, as the case may be."

THE HISTORICAL BACKGROUND

The original purpose of building societies, as stated in the preamble to the **8–04** Building Societies Act 1836, was to enable persons of moderate means to buy small properties. In the early societies funds were derived from subscriptions but societies also raised funds by the issues of shares and by receiving deposits or loans. The earliest building societies can be traced back to the industrial revolution, when they were set up as small local organisations whose members pooled funds to allow them to purchase land and build houses. The first known building society was formed in 1775 in Birmingham and like most early societies was "terminating", meaning the business was closed after all of its members had been

---

[16] s.336(1) and (2) *inter alia*, were brought into force by S.I. 2001 No. 516 on February 25, 2001. No order has as yet been made under this section. See Part XXI of the 2000 Act (Mutual Societies), and in particular to s.336, and the provisions listed in paras 17 and 18 of Sched. 18, Part III of the 2000 Act. These are s.9 and Sched. 3 to the 1986 Act (as amended), *i.e.* initial authorisation by the Commission to grant consent to building societies to raise funds and borrow money. Those provisions have been prospectively repealed by s.432(3) and Sched. 22 of the 2000 Act, but no Order has yet been made by the Treasury bringing the section into force. Sections 334(1), (2), 335, 337 and 338(1), (2) and 339 (powers to transfer functions in relation to mutual societies) have also been brought into force by S.I. 2001 No. 516 on February 25, 2001. Schedule 22 (repeals) is not yet in force (save for the repeal of the Insurance Brokers (Registration) Act 1977 by S.I. 2001 No. 1282). Schedule 2 to the 2000 Act was also brought into force by S.I. 2001 No. 516 (regulated activities). See also *post* n. 28. Other bodies whose regulatory functions are similarly to be transferred to the FSA and the Treasury and who will eventually be replaced by order of the Treasury are the Friendly Societies Commission, the Registrar of Friendly Societies, the Building Societies Investor Protection Board and Industrial and Provident Societies and Credit Unions, see *ibid.* Part XXI, ss.334, 335, 337, and 338, Sched. 18, Pts I, II, and IV.

[17] *ibid.* ss.7, 8 (substituted by the 1997 Act, ss.8, 9).

[18] *ibid.* ss.7(5)(b), 8(4) (as substituted by the 1997 Act).

[19] This implemented the EC Directive on Unfair Terms in Consumer Contracts (93/13/EEC [1993] OJ L95/29). These regulations originally came into force on July 1, 1995. See *ante* paras 3–37 to 3–41.

[20] Building Societies Act 1986, s.86(1)(a) and s.87.

[21] *ibid.* ss.86(1)(b), 88 and 89.

[22] *ibid.* Sched. 2, para. 3(4).

housed. This changed when societies started accepting deposits from individuals who did not necessarily desire to borrow to buy a home, but simply wished to invest their money. No longer terminating, these formed the basis of the "permanent" societies existing today.

THE MODERN CONCEPT OF A BUILDING SOCIETY AND DE-MUTUALISATION

8–05   A building society is a financial institution that offers savings accounts and mortgages as its main business. In recent years following the liberalisation of their legal structure a number of building societies have diversified and now offer a range of personal financial services. This has been encouraged by legislative changes.

A building society is a corporate body in the nature of a mutual institution. Thus those who hold savings accounts, or have had advances made on the security of mortgages, are usually members of the society. Consequently they have certain rights to vote and receive information, as well as to attend and speak at meetings. Each member has one vote, regardless of the amount of money invested or borrowed or how many accounts they hold. Each building society has a board of directors who run the society and who are responsible for setting its strategy. The Board in effect act as trustees, holding the society's assets in trust for its members.

Building societies differ from banks. Banks are companies normally listed on the stock market and are therefore owned by, and are operated for, their shareholders. Societies have no external shareholders requiring dividends. Their mutual status prevents them from being companies. A mutual society is run in the interests of its members, namely the savers and borrowers. They are therefore not listed on the stock market or owned externally. The essential distinction, therefore, between a building society and bank lending institution is that the former does not have to pay dividends to its shareholders. This means that in principle the surplus or profit a society makes can be put back into the organisation to benefit its members.

8–06   There are currently 67 building societies in the United Kingdom with approximately 2,100 branches holding assets of over £160 billion. They employ over 31,000 staff serving more than 15 million savers and over two and a half million borrowers. Building societies currently account for 20 per cent of all outstanding residential mortgages but the share is increasing. Over the last two years around 28 per cent of all new mortgage lending (taking account of repayments) has come from building societies. Sixteen per cent of all personal deposits are held by the societies. The Nationwide Building Society is at present the largest in the United Kingdom in terms of assets held.[23] Building societies are currently regulated by the Commission. The Commission, along with a number of other financial regulatory bodies, are to be replaced by the FSA. Once the process has been completed societies will then come within the single regulatory regime under the 2000 Act with secondary powers being transferred to the Treasury.[24]

[23] Figures supplied by the Building Societies Association.
[24] See *ante* para. 8–03.

In April 1989, Abbey National Building Society became the first building society to convert to a bank, floating on the stock exchange and changing its status to that of a plc company. During the following decade this conversion (or de-mutualisation) was followed by the others, namely, Cheltenham & Gloucester, National & Provincial, Alliance & Leicester, Woolwich, Halifax, Northern Rock, Bristol & West, Birmingham Midshires and Bradford & Bingley. Not all of these institutions, however, floated on the stock market, or retained their independence. As part of these conversions, members received a variety of "windfalls" in the form of either cash or shares in the new company. The value of these windfalls varied. Despite high expectations many of these newly converted institutions have suffered a reduced share of the savings and mortgage markets.

Since the Abbey National de-mutualisation accounts have been opened by individuals in various societies with the purposive intent of seeking windfalls should they convert. A number of societies still continue to be challenged by "carpetbaggers" who use their rights as members to try to force a conversion to plc status. The term (first used in the American Civil War) was applied to those seeking building society windfalls in early 1996. Subsequently, some carpetbaggers have used their membership rights to try to force societies to convert by putting forward resolutions at their general meetings. Thus despite their obvious popularity and still continuing share of the lending market, many societies remain the subject of threatened attempts at de-mutualisation. In order to deter carpetbaggers and protect genuine investors, many societies have introduced a charitable assignment clause to application forms for new savings accounts. This means that, either for a specified period of time, or in some cases indefinitely, any possible windfalls the member may receive would go to a charity chosen by the building society.

Building Society law is, therefore, still of considerable relevance to a work on the law of mortgages.

1. The 1986 Act

This Act gave building societies a comprehensive new legal framework for the first time since building society legislation was first consolidated in the 1874 Act.   **8–07**

The 1986 Act sets out detailed provisions in relation to:

(1) The constitution of building societies.
(2) Limits on raising funds other than from individuals and on lending other than fully secured on land, and restrictions on powers.
(3) The powers of control of the Commission.
(4) Protection of investors and complaints and disputes.
(5) Management of building societies, accounts and audit.
(6) Mergers and transfers of business.

The 1986 Act as originally enacted was prescriptive as to the powers of building societies and the way in which they were exercised. However, an important feature of the 1986 Act also included the wide-ranging power given to the Commission and/or the Treasury to promulgate statutory instruments, subject to parliamentary approval. Since the Act came into force (many provisions came into force on January 1, 1987) the 1986 Act has been considerably amended and extended, especially as to the powers of building societies. Some of the main changes to the Act were made in 1988 shortly after its enactment.

2. The 1997 Act

8–08   In January 1994 the Government began a two stage review of the Act. As a result of the first stage of that review, a number of further changes in relation to building societies' powers were made in 1995. Some of these were by way of the then recently introduced Deregulation and Contracting Out Act 1994. In February 1995 the Government announced the results of the second stage of its review. After a lengthy consultation process, with the publication of successive drafts of the Bill in March 1996 and December 1996, a Building Societies Bill was introduced into Parliament on February 28, 1997. The Bill passed through all its parliamentary stages in March and received Royal Assent on March 21, 1997.

The 1997 Act made a large number of substantive amendments to the 1986 Act. Its main purposes were:

(1) To remove the prescriptive powers accorded to building societies and to replace them with a permissive regime with a view to developing the commercial freedom of societies and enhancing the scope for increased competition and wider choice for customers.

(2) To enhance the powers of control of the Commission.

(3) To introduce a package of measures to enhance the accountability of the boards of building societies to their members.

(4) To make changes to the provisions relating to the transfer of a building society's business to a company structure.

The provisions of the 1997 Act came into force on various dates from March 21, 1997. There were three Commencement Orders, bringing various provisions into force on May 21, June 9 and December 1, 1997.[25] The main provisions concerning building societies' powers and constitution, related powers of the Commission and a number of provisions as to accountability came into force in relation to each society separately. These came into force on the date on which alterations to each society's memorandum and rules became effective under Schedule 8 to the 1997 Act.[26] For most societies that date was during Autumn 1998. The transitional period for societies to adopt new memoranda and rules ended on April 30, 1999.[27] Where appropriate, the provisions of the 1986 Act are equivalent to those of company and banking legislation (the Companies Act 1985 and the Banking Act 1987).

---

[25] S.I. 1997 No. 1307; S.I. 1997 No. 1427; and S.I. 1997 No. 2668.
[26] See paras 1 to 10 relating to the transitional provisions and savings; s.46(1).
[27] *ibid.*

3. **The 2000 Act**

Subsequently in May 1997 the Government announced that it intended to intro-   **8–09**
duce substantial reforms to the regulation of the financial sector generally. This
included a consolidation of responsibility for regulation and supervision of
banks, building societies, insurance companies, friendly societies and investment
firms within a single body—the FSA. The proposals were set out in a consultation document, including a draft Financial Services and Markets Bill, issued by
HM Treasury on July 30, 1998. Specific proposals relevant to building societies
included:

(1) Transfer of all the functions of the Commission to the FSA.
(2) Repeal of the current different statutory authorisation criteria for banks,
    building societies, insurance companies, investment firms and other
    such organisations and their replacement by a single statutory
    process.
(3) Establishment of a single financial services and markets compensation
    scheme and a single financial services ombudsman scheme.

The Financial Services and Markets Bill received Royal Assent on June 14, 2000.
The date when the 2000 Act fully comes into force is to be not later than
November 30, 2001 ("N2") and the FSA's mortgage regulation regime will be
fully effective no later than August 31, 2002 ("N3").[28] It was originally planned
for July 2001. The thrust of the Act is that no unauthorised person will be able
to carry out any regulated activity. Authorised persons will only be able to carry
out regulated activities for which they have been granted permission.[29] The
provisions of the 1986 Act relating to the constitution, governance and principal
purpose of building societies in principle remain in place.

STRUCTURE OF THE 1986 ACT

The 1986 Act currently has nine Parts with 126 sections. In addition, there are 21   **8–10**
Schedules which provide supplementary detail for various sections. A number of
provisions have been the subject of substitutions and amendments by the 1997
Act and more recently the 2000 Act.
   The Act is structured as follows:

[28] At the date when this work went to press, ss.428, 430, and 433 of, and paragraphs 1 and 2 of
   Schedule 21 to, the 2000 Act had been brought into force on June 14, 2000 by the commencement
   section (s.431). Further, a number of statutory instruments implementing the majority of the
   sections of the Act had been made namely S.I. 2000 No. 516 (February 25, 2001); S.I. 2001 No.
   1282 (April 30, 2001); and S.I. 2001 No. 1820 (June 18, 2001). A number of other Orders had also
   been made. The most important of these for the purposes of this work is The Financial Services
   and Markets Act 2000 (Regulated Activities) Order 2001 (S.I. 2001 No. 544) prospectively made
   on February 27, 2001. Chapter XV of this Order defines "regulated mortgage contracts". However,
   by virtue of Article 2, Chapter XV of the Order is not due to come into force until nine months after
   section 19 of the Act comes into force. Section 19 forms part of Part II of the 2000 Act (ss.19 to
   30 and Sched. 2) and contains the general prohibition on carrying out a regulated activity. No order
   has yet been made bringing that section into force. Of Part II only ss.20(3), 21 and 22 of, and
   Sched. 2 to, the Act had been brought into force as at the date that this work went to press. See
   further paras 14–15 *et seq.*
[29] See ss.19 and 20, 31(1)(a), Sched. 2.

Part I The Building Societies Commission
Part II Constitution of building societies
Part IV Protection of investors
Part VI Powers of control of Commission
Part VII Management of building societies
Part VIII Accounts and audit
Part IX Complaints and disputes
Part X Dissolution, winding up, mergers, transfer of business
Part XI Miscellaneous and supplementary and conveyancing services
Part III (advances, loans and other assets) and Part V (powers to provide services) were repealed by the 1997 Act.

1. The Commission

8–11   Section 1 of the 1986 Act made provision for the Commission, consisting of between four and 10 members appointed by the Treasury. In 1987 the Commission took over responsibility for the supervision of building societies from the Registry of Friendly Societies. However, the latter organisation continued to be responsible for registration, maintaining the public file of each society and certain other matters concerning building societies and, until January 1999, for the provision of staff and services to the Commission. From January 1999 the FSA became responsible for the provision of staff and services to the Commission, in place of the Registry. The Commission continued to exercise its statutory functions, described below, until the legislation transferring those functions to the FSA comes into force.

The functions of the Commission and the FSA (once the regulatory powers have been transferred) are:

(1) To promote the protection by each building society of the investments of its shareholders and depositors
(2) To promote the financial stability of building societies generally
(3) To secure that the principal purpose of building societies remains that of making loans which are secured on residential property and are funded substantially by their members
(4) To administer the system of regulation of building societies provided for by or under the 1986 Act
(5) To advise and make recommendations to the Treasury or other government departments on any matter relating to building societies.

2. Purpose of a Building Society

8–12   Section 5(1) of the 1986 Act provides that a building society may be established under the 1986 Act if (and only if):

"Its purpose or principal purpose is that of making loans which are secured on residential property and are funded substantially by its members."

"Residential property" is defined as being land at least 40 per cent of which is normally used as, or in connection with, one or more dwellings, or which has been, is being or is to be developed or adapted for such use.[30]

The revised principal purpose, introduced by the 1997 Act, gives building societies the freedom to pursue any activities set out in their memorandum. This is subject only to compliance with the lending limit, the funding limit, the restrictions on powers and the criteria of prudent management, referred to below. In essence, it is these requirements, together with the fact that most of a building society's customers are its members, which give to building societies their essential character and differentiate them from other financial institutions.

There are two main differences between the previous and current principal purposes of the legislation. First, loans secured on tenanted residential property are now permissible. Secondly, there is no requirement for borrowers to be individuals, or members (although mortgage borrowers who are individuals would be members by definition).

3. Establishment and Constitution

A new building society can be established by 10 or more people, and the capital which they have to put into the society is a minimum of £1 million (to be held in permanent interest bearing shares (PIBS)). Schedule 2 of the 1986 Act makes provision for societies to have a memorandum setting out the purpose and powers of the society, and rules covering its internal regulation and arrangements concerning membership, meetings, resolutions, directors and other factors. This concept is similar to the memorandum and articles in the case of a limited company, the main difference being that the majority of a building society's customers are also its members. **8–13**

Most of the constitutional provisions are contained in Schedule 2. It is not intended to set out these *in extenso* in this chapter, but the main provisions are as follows:

(1) The definition of member, a ("shareholding member") is a person who holds a share (typically in the form of a savings account) in a building society; a "borrowing member" is an individual who is indebted to the society in respect of a loan which is fully secured on land or, if the rules of the society so provide, in respect of a loan which is substantially secured on land. No other category of member is permitted. Bodies corporate may no longer be borrowing members of a building society (the rights of existing corporate borrowing members at the time of coming into force of the 1997 Act are preserved by transitional provisions). See also below under "Funding" as to the prohibition on bodies corporate from becoming shareholding members (except by holding deferred shares).[31]

(2) Use of a society's name and use of business names by societies.[32]

---

[30] *ibid.* s.5(10) (substituted by the 1997 Act, s.1(4)).
[31] *ibid.* Part I, para. 5.
[32] *ibid.* paras 9, 10, 10A to 10C.

(3) Maintenance of a register of members by a society, and the right of members to have access to the register, subject to approval by the FSA.[33]

(4) Members' entitlement to receive notices of meetings, to vote, to nominate candidates to stand for election as director, to have a resolution circulated and to requisition a special meeting (a maximum qualifying shareholding or mortgage debt of £100 applies to such entitlements).[34]

(5) Shareholding and borrowing members have equal voting rights, except that shareholders and borrowers vote separately on proposals by a society to merge with another or to transfer its business to a company.[35]

4. Authorisation

8-14   Section 9 of the 1986 Act, as amended, requires a building society to be authorised by the FSA before it raises funds from members or accepts deposits of money. Schedule 3 sets out the basic requirements and procedures for the grant of authorisation. All building societies authorised on January 1, 1987 were treated as being authorised for the purposes of the 1986 Act. These provisions have been prospectively repealed by provisions of the 2000 Act.[36]

5. Funding

8-15   Section 7 of the 1986 Act provides that at least 50 per cent of the funds of a building society (or of the society's group) must be raised in the form of shares held by individual members of the society. This single funding limit replaced the two previous limits on funding—the 50 per cent limit in respect of non-retail funds and deposits and the 50 per cent limit on the amount due on deposits and loans.

Section 8 imposes restrictions on the categories of deposit accounts which an individual may hold with a building society, and prohibits a building society from accepting corporate bodies as shareholders (other than in respect of deferred shares (*i.e.* PIBS)). Funds raised from individuals must be in the form of shares with the exception only of current accounts; client or trustee accounts; qualifying time deposits; deposits at overseas branches; transferable instruments; and where the society has announced publicly that it intends to transfer its business to a company. The rights of existing individual depositors in respect of deposits made before the coming into force of the 1997 Act are preserved by transitional provisions in Schedule 8 to the 1997 Act.

A building society may not raise funds from a body corporate in the form of shares, except in the form of deferred shares (*i.e.* PIBS), but may accept deposits and loans from such bodies. The rights of existing corporate shareholders are also

---

[33] *ibid.* para. 13.
[34] *ibid.* Part III, paras 20 to 36.
[35] *ibid.* paras 27(1), 27A, and 29(1).
[36] See n. 16, *ante*.

preserved by the transitional provisions contained in Schedule 8 to the 1997 Act.

6. Restrictions on Powers

Section 9A of the 1986 Act (as amended) imposes restrictions, subject to certain **8–16** exceptions, on the powers of a building society or a subsidiary undertaking in relation to acting as a market maker in securities, commodities or currencies; trading in commodities or currencies; and entering into transactions involving derivatives. The main exceptions relate to hedging transactions entered into by the society or undertaking and certain transactions effected for customers of the society or undertaking or where the amount involved does not exceed £100,000. A society is required to do all that is reasonably practicable to secure that each of its subsidiary undertakings complies with the restrictions.

Section 9B prohibits a building society from creating a floating charge over its assets and any such charge will be void.[37] Section 104A allows the Secretary of State for Trade and Industry, by order, to provide that appropriate provisions of the Companies Act 1985 shall apply in relation to the registration of fixed charges created by building societies over their assets.

Part II of Schedule 2 includes "safe harbour" provisions, in parallel with those in the Companies Act 1985 as amended, whereby a building society's capacity is not limited by its memorandum and, in favour of persons dealing with a society in good faith, the powers of the directors to bind the society are free from any such limitation.

Section 92A requires a building society to seek the approval of members to the acquisition or establishment by the society or a subsidiary undertaking of a significant "non-core" business. This requirement applies only in the case of a business where, in the opinion of the directors, a greater part of the business relates to activities having no connection with loans secured on residential property, and where the acquisition or establishment would cost 15 per cent or more of the society's own funds (capital).

7. Investor Protection Scheme

Sections 24 to 30 of the 1986 Act contain detailed provisions for a statutory **8–17** Investor Protection Scheme and Investor Protection Board. The Scheme does not involve the collection of funds, unless a call is made on the Scheme. No such call has been necessary to date. Under the Scheme compensation payments are limited to 90 per cent of a building society's total liability to an investor subject to a maximum payment of £18,000 (or the sterling equivalent of 20,000 euros if greater). There is an overall maximum contribution to the fund of 0.3 per cent of a society's shares and deposits.

Section 32 of the 1997 Act gave the Treasury power, by order, to amalgamate the Building Societies Investor Protection Scheme and the Deposit Protection

---

[37] See nn. 13 and 14 *ante*.

Scheme under the Banking Act 1987. However, under the 2000 Act the Government has now established a single financial services and markets compensation scheme known as the Financial Services Compensation Scheme.[38]

8. Powers of Control of the Commission

8–18   Sections 36, 36A and 37 give the Commission certain powers where a building society fails to comply with the principal purpose requirement, the lending limit or the funding limit. These powers have been prospectively transferred to the FSA by the provisions of the 2000 Act.[39] The powers include a direction by the Commission for the society to submit for approval a restructuring plan to bring it within the relevant statutory requirements, a direction to the society to call a general meeting to consider converting to company status, a prohibition order where a society has failed to carry out a restructuring plan, and, ultimately, to present a petition for the winding up of the society.

Section 41 enables the Commission, if it has reason to believe that a building society's business is being or may be conducted in a way that may not adequately protect the investments of shareholders and depositors, to direct the society to make an application to renew its authorisation.

Section 42 enables the Commission to impose conditions on a building society's authorisation if it considers it expedient to do so in order to protect the investments of shareholders or depositors. In urgent cases such conditions may be imposed or varied without giving the usual notice required by Schedule 3.

Sections 42B and 42C provide that if the Commission considers it expedient to do so in order to protect the investments of shareholders or depositors of a building society, it may either direct the society to transfer all its engagements to one or more other building societies, or to transfer its business to an existing company. The Commission may also direct that a transfer may proceed by board resolution only rather than by seeking the approval of the members of the society.

8–19   Sections 43, 43A and 43B lay down the circumstances and procedures under which the Commission may revoke a building society's authorisation. Section 44 enables the Commission to grant re-authorisation to a building society in certain circumstances.

Section 45A requires the Commission to pass on information received from a supervisory authority in another European Economic Area state to other relevant United Kingdom regulatory authorities. Such information concerns any failure of a building society (doing business in that state) to comply with an obligation imposed in that state for purposes connected with the Second Banking Coordination Directive. The Commission must also consider whether to exercise its powers to impose conditions on, or revoke, the society's authorisation, and notify

---

[38] By s.337 of the 2000 Act the Building Societies Investor Protection Board has been abolished and replaced by the Financial Services Compensation Scheme established under Part XV of the Act, and the supplemental provisions contained in s.339(2), (3). These sections came into force on February 25, 2001 (S.I. 2001 No. 516). Most of the provisions contained in Part XV came into force on June 18, 2001 (S.I. 2001 No. 1820).

[39] See n. 16, *ante.*

its decision, and the action taken, to the supervisory authority concerned and all the relevant United Kingdom regulatory authorities.

Sections 46 to 49 provide for a system of appeals against decisions of the Commission to refuse to grant or renew authorisation, to revoke authorisation, to impose or vary conditions on authorisation, or the conditions themselves, to give a direction under the business restructuring power or that a building society seek a transfer to another society or to an existing company, or that an individual is not a fit and proper person to hold office in a society. The appeal is to a tribunal appointed by the Lord Chancellor and the Chancellor of the Exchequer.

Section 50 enables the Commission to control the advertising of a building society if it considers it expedient to do so to protect investors.

Sections 52, 52A and 54 give the Commission extensive powers to obtain information or documents and section 53 deals with the confidentiality of information obtained by that body.

Sections 55 to 57 give the Commission power to appoint inspectors to investigate any aspect of the business of a particular building society, or its affairs generally, or to summon a meeting of members.

9. Statement of Principles

Section 45AA required the Commission to publish a statement of the principles **8–20** in accordance with which it is acting or proposing to act in exercising its powers of control and in interpreting the criteria of prudent management in section 45. "Powers of control" are defined by reference to sections 9, 36, 36A, 37, 41, 42, 42A and 43 (see above). The Commission is required to report any material change in the principles in accordance with which it is acting or proposing to act in its annual report to Parliament under section 4. The Commission may publish a revised statement of principles, or "additional guidance" as to the exercise of its powers of control etc., at any time. On May 11, 1998 the Commission published the *Statement of Principles* which:

(1) explains the Commission's main statutory functions and their relationship to the criteria of prudent management;

(2) describes the Commission's approach to prudential supervision;

(3) outlines the Commission's system of risk-based supervision and appraisal;

(4) explains the purpose and effect of prudential notes and other guidance issued by the Commission;

(5) sets out the main principles which the Commission applies in its interpretation of the criteria of prudent management; and

(6) explains the Commission's statutory powers of control and sets out the principles in accordance with which the Commission would propose to act in using them.

Chapter 5 of the *Statement of Principles* explains that the main instruments which the Commission use to inform building societies and their boards of its expectations for their compliance with the criteria of prudent management are prudential notes and DCE letters (letters addressed "dear chief executive"), sent to all authorised building societies. Prudential notes are not intended to be comprehensive. Each board must consider what is necessary in the case of its society to protect the investments of shareholders and depositors and, in those areas not covered by the notes, how the general precepts apply to its particular circumstances.

Prudential notes aim to:

(1) develop an understanding between the Commission, building societies, auditors, other regulators, professional bodies and other interested parties of the prudential issues relevant to the business and supervision of building societies;

(2) provide a framework for supervisory dialogue between the Commission and societies, whether individually or collectively; and

(3) promote a consistent approach to the supervision of societies collectively.

The content of prudential and other guidance notes falls into three main categories:

(1) prudential requirements (mandatory);

(2) prudential guidance (evidential); and

(3) other policy and procedural guidance.

Further details of each category are given in Chapter 5 of the *Statement of Principles*.

10. **Management of Building Societies**

8–21 Section 45 sets out "criteria of prudent management" which the Commission can take account of in deciding whether to exercise its powers in relation to authorisation and directing that a building society transfer its engagements or business. The criteria are:

(1) Compliance with the principal purpose requirement, the lending limit, the funding limit and the restrictions on transactions imposed by section 9A.

(2) Maintenance of:

(a) adequate reserves and other capital resources; and

(b) own funds which amount to not less than 1 million euros.

(3) Maintenance of adequate assets in liquid form.

(4) Maintenance of a system for managing and containing risks to the net worth of the business, and risks to its net income, whether arising from fluctuations in interest or exchange rates or from other factors.

(5) Maintenance of the requisite arrangements:

(a) for assessing the adequacy of securities for loans which are to be made or acquired by the society or subsidiary undertakings of the society, and are to be substantially secured on land; and

(b) for assessing the willingness and ability of borrowers to repay such loans.

(6) Maintenance of the requisite accounting records and systems of control of business and of inspection and report.

(7) Direction and management—

(a) by a sufficient number of persons who are fit and proper to be directors or, as the case may be, officers, in their respective positions,

(b) conducted by them with prudence and integrity.

(8) Conduct of the business with adequate professional skills.

Chapter 6 of the *Statement of Principles* summarises the key requirements which the Commission considers the criteria of prudent management imply for the boards of building societies. Each criterion is dealt with in turn with a reference to the relevant "prudential notes". A full list of current prudential notes is published each year in the Commission's Annual Report. Under the provisions of the 2000 Act the prudential notes are to be replaced by rules and guidance made by the FSA.[40]

11. Directors and Other Officers

Part VII of the 1986 Act (sections 58 to 70) deals with the constitutional aspects **8–22** of the management of building societies. Section 58 requires that there shall be at least two directors, and section 59 requires that every society shall have a chief executive and a secretary (who may be the same person), with appropriate knowledge and experience.

Sections 60 and 61 of the 1986 Act set out detailed provisions for elections of directors. For all elections to the board of a building society, there must be a vote and each candidate must receive a positive endorsement from the members. Except where voting in an election is conducted by postal ballot, a society is required to send proxy forms to all members entitled to receive notice of the meeting at which the election is to be held, and the directors must be elected on a poll. A director must retire at the age of 70 (or lower if required by the society in its rules) unless he or she is specifically re-elected each year. Other directors are elected for a three year term. A society's rules may provide for a director to have a shareholding of not more than £1,000.

A nomination for a candidate for election as director may be made at any time. However, if the nomination is made after the last day of the financial year immediately preceding the election, the nomination is to be carried forward to the next election of directors after that, unless the candidate otherwise requires. The maximum number of members that a society's rules may require to join in nominating a person for election as a director of a building society varies from 10 to 50, depending on the society's total commercial assets (total assets *less* fixed assets and liquid assets). A person nominating a candidate may either be a

---

[40] See *ante* n. 28.

shareholding member or borrowing member (and must have the relevant minimum shareholding or mortgage debt). The maximum length of an election address which a candidate can require a society to distribute to its members is 500 words.

8–23   Sections 62 to 70 of the 1986 Act are concerned with dealings between a building society and its directors (and persons connected with them). Directors must declare any interest in contracts and other transactions with their society. There are limitations on substantial property transactions involving directors, on loans to directors on favourable terms, and a general prohibition on accepting commission in connection with loans. A contract may be rendered voidable at the instance of a building society where the board had gone beyond its powers in a transaction with a director. Societies are required to keep a register containing details of transactions made with directors, and they have to record income received from the society by related outside businesses of directors, including conveyancing, surveying and valuations, accountancy and insurance.

12. Accounts and Audit

8–24   Section 71 of the 1986 Act specifies the accounting records and systems of control of its business and records and of inspection and report which a building society and its subsidiary undertakings must maintain. The directors and chief executive of each society are required to report annually to the Commission expressing their opinion as to whether the requirements of section 71 have been complied with by the society.

Sections 72 to 76 of the 1986 Act set out the requirements on the directors of a building society to prepare annual accounts, an annual business statement, a directors' report and a summary financial statement. The summary financial statement is sent to members. The full annual accounts must be available on request. The form and detailed content of the annual accounts, etc., are prescribed in regulations made by the Commission. Sections 80 and 81 deal with the requirements concerning signing, issuing and submission of copies of a society's annual accounts, etc., to members and the Commission.

Section 77 (and Schedule 11) of the 1986 Act set out detailed provisions concerning appointment, qualification, resignation and removal of auditors. The auditors of a building society are required to report to the members under sections 78 and 79 on the truth and fairness of the annual accounts and other documents and whether the documents comply with the provisions of the Act.

8–25   Section 82 of the 1986 Act includes three important provisions. The first requires the auditors of a building society to report annually to the Commission on whether or not the society has complied with the requirements concerning accounting records, systems of control and of inspection and report. The second enables the auditors (or any "reporting accountant") in order to protect investors to provide information about the society's business direct to the Commission. This arises notwithstanding any obligations of confidence towards the society, where it is expedient in exceptional circumstances to do so. The third, by order made by the Treasury, requires an auditor (and certain other persons) to provide information direct to the Commission on any matter relating to the business or affairs of the society or its associated bodies of which he may become aware in his capacity as such, where he has reasonable cause to believe, as regards the society concerned:

(1) That its authorisation could be revoked.
(2) That there is or has been, or may be or may have been, a failure to satisfy any of the criteria of prudent management.
(3) That there is or has been, or may be or may have been, a contravention of, or failure to comply with, any provision of the Act.
(4) That its continuous functioning may be affected. In the case of an auditor of the society, that his opinion on the annual accounts may need to be qualified.

In the case of (2) and (3) above, a report is required if the failure or contravention concerned is likely to be of material significance for the exercise, in relation to that society, of the Commission's functions.

13. Complaints and Disputes

Sections 83, 83A and 84 (and Schedules 12 and 13) of the 1986 Act cover the **8–26** requirement on building societies and their connected undertakings to belong to an ombudsman scheme or schemes, recognised by the Commission, for the investigation of complaints (the 1986 Act uses the term "adjudicator"). A scheme must confer the right to have complaints investigated about action which has been taken in relation to a service of a kind and which is provided by societies for individuals in the ordinary course of business (rather than, as previously, in relation to prescribed matters). The grounds for complaint must include breach of the 1986 Act or any contract, unfair treatment or malad-ministration and a decision to refuse to provide a service (except a decision which is made in the legitimate exercise of commercial judgment), and where the complainant has suffered pecuniary loss or expense or inconvenience.

The persons entitled to have complaints investigated must include individuals and any partnership, club or other unincorporated body or body corporate whose turnover for its last financial year does not exceed £1 million. The adjudicator must be able to advise, mediate or conciliate and he must have access to relevant documents. The adjudicator must have regard to the rules of the society, the provisions of any code of conduct or any contract and the terms of any advertise-ment. Schemes may have a maximum compensation limit, but it must not be less than £100,000. A society must agree to be bound by decisions of the adjudicator unless it agrees to give notice to its members and the public of its reasons for not doing so.

Only one scheme has been established which meets the requirements of the Act, and so has been recognised by the Commission—the Building Societies Ombudsman Scheme—to which all building societies and their relevant con-nected undertakings belong. Under the 2000 Act, the Government intends to establish a single financial services ombudsman scheme.

Section 85 (and Schedule 14) of the 1986 Act provide for the settlement of disputes between a building society and a member or members, in their capacity as such (rather than as customers), to be dealt with by the Court or by arbitration.

14. Mergers

8–27 Sections 93 to 96 (and Schedule 16) of the 1986 Act deal with mergers of building societies. A merger may either be by way of an amalgamation (where two building societies establish a new society as their successor) or by the transfer of the engagements of one building society to another (the usual method). For a merger to be approved, more than 50 per cent of qualifying borrowing members who vote must vote in favour, as well as 75 per cent of the qualifying shareholding members who vote. Any compensation payments to directors and other officers have to be approved by separate special resolution of the society. Distributions of funds to members, above limits set in regulations made by the Commission, have to be approved by the members of the societies concerned. Detailed information about a proposed merger is required to be provided to members. A society is required to notify members of the receipt of any non-confidential proposals for a merger.

15. **Transfer of Business to a Company**

8–28 Sections 97 to 102D (and Schedule 17) of the 1986 Act deal with the transfer of a building society's business to a company. Where a society transfers to a company specially formed for the purpose (a "conversion"), more than 50 per cent of qualifying borrowing members who vote must vote in favour, and 75 per cent of qualifying shareholding members who vote must vote in favour; in addition, a minimum of 50 per cent of all qualifying shareholding members must vote. Where a society transfers to an existing company (a "takeover"), an additional requirement is that 50 per cent of all qualifying shareholding members (or the holders of 90 per cent of the shares) must vote in favour.

The terms of a transfer may include provision for a distribution of cash and/or shares to be made to members and others, and must provide for a distribution of funds to shareholding members not eligible to vote on the relevant resolution. The terms of a transfer must also require shares in the society to be converted into deposits with the successor company. This must have authorised status under the Banking Act 1987, and may be incorporated in an European Economic Area state other than the United Kingdom.

Any compensation payments to directors and other officers have to be approved by separate special resolution of the society. Any provision to increase the remuneration of directors or other officers, in consequence of a transfer, have to be approved by an ordinary resolution of the society.

8–29 Detailed information about a proposed transfer of business is required to be provided to members, although a summary may be supplied instead, with the full document available on request. A society is required to notify members of the receipt of any non-confidential proposals for the transfer of its business to a company.

Where a building society transfers to a specially formed company then no more than 15 per cent of the share capital in the company may be held by any one investor for a period of five years from the date of transfer. That protection from takeover is removed if, during that period, the successor company or a subsidiary undertaking takes over, or acquires the business of, another financial institution, or if its shareholders, holding 75 per cent of the shares, vote to waive the protection.

The provisions on transfer of a building society's business to a company have twice been amended by Acts which were introduced into Parliament as Private Members' measures:

(1) The Building Societies (Joint Account Holders) Act 1995[41] inserted a new section 102A in the 1986 Act to enable a distribution of cash or shares on a transfer to be made to certain second-named account holders.

(2) The Building Societies (Distributions) Act 1997[42] inserted new sections 102B to 102D in the 1986 Act to provide that where, on a transfer, it is proposed to make a cash or share distribution to members, a distribution must also be made in respect of certain trust accounts (where it is not reasonably practicable for any one or more of the beneficiaries to act in relation to the account because of ill-health or old age or any physical or mental incapacity or disability). The provisions extend not only to investors, but also to borrowers.

16. Statutory Instruments

The 1986 Act contains many instances of powers given to the Building Societies **8–30** Commission and/or the Treasury to make statutory instrument. These subject to Parliamentary approval, can amend, extend and supplement the provisions of the Act. Around 40 statutory instruments made under those powers have been abrogated as a result of the 1997 Act.

The main current statutory instruments made under the 1986 Act, and supplementing the Act, are as follows:

The Building Societies (Mergers) Regulations 1987 (S.I. 1987 No. 2005, as amended by S.I. 1995 No. 1874).

The Building Societies (Deferred Shares) Order 1991 (S.I. 1991 No. 701).

The Building Societies (Auditors) Order 1994 (S.I. 1994 No. 525, as amended by S.I. 1996 No. 1669).

The Building Societies (Prescribed Equitable Interests) Order 1997 (S.I. 1997 No. 2693).

The Building Societies (Transfer of Business) Regulations 1998 (S.I. 1998 No. 212).

[41] ss.1(1), 2(2).
[42] ss.1(1), 2(2).

The Building Societies (Accounts and Related Provisions) Regulations 1998 (S.I. 1998 No. 504, as amended by S.I. 1999 No. 248).
The Building Societies (Business Names) Regulations 1998 (S.I. 1998 No. 3186).
The Building Societies (Merger Notification Statement) Regulations 1999 (S.I. 1999 No. 1215).
The Building Societies (General Charge and Fees) Regulations 2000 (S.I. 2000 No. 668).
The Building Societies (Registered Transactions) Order 2001 (S.I. 2001 No. 1826).

Statutory instruments made under the European Communities Act 1972 are also relevant. The more important of which are as follows[43]:

The Banking Coordination (Second Council Directive) Regulations 1992 (S.I. 1992 No. 3218, as amended by S.I. 1993 No. 3225, S.I. 1995 No. 1217 and S.I. 1996 No. 1669).
The Credit Institutions (Protection of Depositors) Regulations 1995 (S.I. 1995 No. 1442).

LOANS SECURED ON LAND

8–31   The purpose or principal purpose of a building society is to make loans secured on residential property such loans being funded substantially by its members.[44]

Section 6 of the 1986 Act[45] provides that at least 75 per cent of the "business assets" of a building society (or of the society's group) must be loans fully secured on residential property.[46] The term "business assets" is not in fact used in section 6. They comprise total assets (or total group assets) *plus* provisions for bad and doubtful debts, *less* fixed assets, liquid assets and any long term insurance funds, and currently comprise mostly mortgage assets. The Treasury may reduce the limit by order to not less than 60 per cent. This single lending limit replaced the previous commercial asset structure requirements for building societies contained in the now repealed provisions of sections 10 and 11 of the 1986 Act.

That structure classified commercial assets into three classes. These were the following: class 1 (loans secured by first mortgage to owner-occupiers of residential property); class 2 (other loans secured on land); and class 3 (investments in subsidiaries and associates, ownership of land and property for residential development, and other assets such as unsecured loans to individuals and companies). Under the current provisions in order to count towards the 75 per cent limit, the residential property which is security for a loan may be either owner-occupied or let. Subject to the restrictions on powers referred to below, there is

---

[43] For a Table of European Legislation governing building societies, see *Wurtzburg and Mills; Building Society Law* (15th ed., 1989–1997).
[44] See paras 8–02, 8–05.
[45] As substituted by s.4 of the 1997 Act.
[46] For the definition of "residential property", see para. 8–12, *ante*.

no other statutory restriction on what categories of asset might be included in the remaining 25 per cent of "business assets".

Section 6A of the 1986 Act[47] defines "loans secured on land". The definition is primarily relevant to classification of assets (and not to powers) and to eligibility for borrowing membership. The land concerned has to be located in the United Kingdom or any other country or territory within the European Economic Area, the Channel Islands, the Isle of Man or Gibraltar. The Commission, with the consent of the Treasury, may by order extend the definition of a loan secured on land, and the application of any of the other provisions of the Act, to loans secured on land outside those countries or territories.

Section 6B defines "loans fully secured on land".[48] A loan which is secured **8–32** on residential property or other land is fully secured on the land if the principal of, and interest accrued on, the loan does not exceed the value of the security and there is no more than one prior mortgage of the land. The test of whether a loan is "fully secured" is to be satisfied "on the occasion on which" a loan is made or acquired. Provision is made for the re-classification of loans on the occurrence of certain events.

Transitional provisions in Schedule 8 to the 1997 Act provide that any existing advance which was a class 1 advance, or a class 2 advance to an individual secured by a first charge on residential property, immediately before the coming into force of section 6B, is treated as a loan which is fully secured on residential property.

Duties on Sale

Section 12(2) of the 1997 Act provides that the common law duty of a mortgagee **8–33** to take reasonable care to obtain a proper price or true market value when selling a mortgaged property in possession applies to building societies. This replaces the previous statutory duty.[49]

Redemption, Transfer and Discharge of a Building Society Mortgage

Borrowers under building society mortgages have the same right to redeem as **8–34** any other mortgagors.[50] The rules of a building society must provide for the manner in which advances are to be made and repaid, and the conditions on which the borrower may redeem the amount due from him before the end of the period for which the advance was made.[51] In the case of a "permanent" building society[52] the covenant for repayment is for the payment of an aggregate amount representing principal plus interest, by equal instalments over a stated period of

---

[47] Substituted by the 1997 Act, s.6.
[48] Substituted by the 1997 Act, s.6.
[49] And see the mortgagee's common law duty to "achieve the true market value" or the best price reasonably obtainable at the time". See also *Reliance Permanent Building Society v. Harwood-Stamper* [1944] Ch. 362.
[50] *Provident Permanent Society v. Greenhill* (1878) 9 Ch. D. 122.
[51] Sched. 2, para. 3(4) to the 1986 Act.
[52] One whose rules do not contemplate the termination of the society on any particular date.

years, together with any other sums which may become due under the rules of the society.

Where an advance is made to a member of a "terminating" society,[53] the covenant provides for the payment of subscriptions, fines and all other sums due under the rules of the society until the advanced member shall have paid the full amount due from an investing member, plus periodical sums called redemption monies, which are, in fact, interest.[54] The advance is of a sum, usually less a discount, equal to the amount to which the member would have been entitled on the termination of the society had he remained an investing member.

Whether the society is "permanent" or "terminating" , the mortgage normally contains a clause whereby default in the payment of any one instalment will render due immediately the entire amount advanced. Such a clause is not invalid as a penalty clause.[55] It is probably not vulnerable to challenge under the Unfair Terms in Consumer Regulations 1999.[56]

1. Transfer and discharge

(a) Transfer

8–35   Under the general law the mortgagee is entitled to transfer his security either absolutely or by way of sub-mortgage, with or without the mortgagor's consent. But where the mortgagee is a building society, the relation between the mortgagor, as member, and the society, prevents this unless the mortgagor consents or special provision is made.[57] A transfer, however, may be made under an amalgamation or transfer of engagements.[58]

In the absence of special provision or the consent of the mortgagor it may be that the society can only assign the mortgage debt,[59] and even if a transfer is possible the transferee may not be able to exercise the power of sale and will not be in the same position as the society for the purpose of exercising the mortgagee's rights. Thus in *Re Rumney and Smith*[60] it was held that trusts and powers for sale could be exercised only by the person authorised to do so by the instrument creating the trust or power.

(b) Discharge—unregistered land[61]

8–36   A society can discharge a mortgage by executing a reconveyance or surrender in favour of the owner of the equity of redemption or of the reversion expectant on

---

[53] One whose rules contemplate the termination of the society on a fixed date or on the occurrence of a specified event, *e.g.* that the amount of each share has reached a specified sum.
[54] *Fleming v. Self* (1854) 3 De. G.M. & G. 997.
[55] *Protector Endowment and Annuity Loan Co. v. Grice* (1880) 5 Q.B.D. 592.
[56] See *ante* paras 3–37 to 3–41.
[57] *Sun Building Society v. Western Suburban and Harrow Road Building Society* [1920] Ch. 144.
[58] ss.93, 94 and Sched. 2, Pt III of the 1986 Act.
[59] *Re Rumney and Smith* [1987] 2 Ch. 351.
[60] [1897] 2 Ch. 351.
[61] For discharge of charges over unregistered land generally see *post* para. 22–01 *et seq.*

the mortgage term or of such persons, being *sui juris*, as the owner may direct.

A receipt[62] operating as a reconveyance or release of property mortgaged to a building society may be given under section 115 of the Law of Property Act 1925. Such a receipt must:

(1) state the name of the person conveying the money;
(2) be executed[63] either by the chargee by way of legal mortgage of the person in whom the mortgaged property is vested and who is legally entitled to give a receipt for the mortgage money; and
(3) be indorsed on, annexed to or written at the foot of the mortgage.

Such a receipt operates as a release reconveyance or surrender and discharges the property from all principal and interest secured by the mortgage and all claims thereunder. If the person stated in the receipt to have paid the money is not the person entitled to the immediate equity of redemption, the receipt operates, not as a discharge, but as a transfer to him.[64]

The Law of Property Act 1925, section 115(9), provides as follows:

"The provision of this section relating to the operation of a receipt shall (in substitution for the like statutory provisions relating to receipts given by or on behalf of a building, friendly industrial or provident society) apply to the discharge of a mortgage made to any such society, provided that the receipt is executed in the manner required by the statute relating to the society . . . "

(c) *Discharge—registered land*

The discharge of a charge or incumbrance registered under the Land Registration Act 1925, is excluded from the ambit of the Law of Property Act 1925, section 115 by virtue of subsection 10 thereof.[65] The Land Registration Act 1925, section 35, however, provides that:

8–37

"(1) The registrar shall, on the requisition of the proprietor of any charge, or on due proof of the satisfaction (whole or partial) thereof, notify on the register in the prescribed manner, by cancelling or varying the original entry or otherwise, the cessation (whole or partial) of the charge, and thereupon the charge shall be deemed to have ceased (in whole or part) accordingly.

(2) On the notification on the register of the entire cessation of a registered charge whether as to the whole or part of the land affected thereby, the term or sub-term implied in or granted by the charge or by any deed or alteration so far as it affects the land to which the discharge extends, shall merge and be extinguished in the registered estate in reversion without surrender."

[62] For the form of such a receipt, see the LPA 1925, s.115(1), (5) and Sched. 3.
[63] *Simpson v. Geoghegan* (1934) W.N. 232.
[64] LPA 1925, s.115(2)(a); and see *Penn v. Bristol and West Building Society* (1995) 2 F.L.R. 938.
[65] For discharge of charges over registered land generally, see *post* para. 22–07.

The 1986 Act contemplates the dissolution of building societies by members' consent,[66] or its winding-up, voluntarily or by the court.[67] The rules of a society must specify the entitlement of the members to participate in the surplus assets, in the event of dissolution by consent or winding-up.[68] Section 92[69] of the 1986 Act provides as follows:

"Where at any time a building society is being wound up or dissolved by consent, a borrowing member shall not be liable to pay any amount other than one which, at that time, is payable under the mortgage or other security by which his indebtedness to society in respect of the loan is secured."

(d) Discharge of Registered Charges by Building Societies in respect of Un-Registered Land

8–38 The methods available to discharge a mortgage over unregistered land are (1) by statutory receipt under the 1986 Act, (2) by statutory receipt under section 115 of the Law of Property Act 1925, or (3) by reconveyance.[70]

(e) Discharge of Registered Charges by Building Societies in respect of Registered Land

8–39 When a building society is the proprietor of a registered charge discharge there is no special form of discharge as exists in the case of unregistered conveyancing.[71] However, discharge is usually effected by the execution of Form DS1 or DS3 under seal in accordance with the rules of the society.[72] The alternative method (as in the case of unregistered conveyancing) is for the Chief Land Registrar to accept a receipt in the statutory form endorsed on or annexed to the charge[73] The Chief Land Registrar is usually willing to accept other methods of authentication.[74]

A statutory receipt is a final discharge, and after it has been given no claim can be made by the society in respect of any sum secured by the mortgage.[75] The receipt can be delivered as an escrow and if that is done, the mortgagee may prove that the mortgage had not been paid off.[76]

---

[66] Building Societies Act 1986, s.86(1)(a) and s.87 (as amended).
[67] *ibid.* ss.86(1)(b), 88 and 89 (as amended).
[68] *ibid.* Sched. 2, para. 3(4).
[69] As substituted by s.43, Sched. 7, para. 40 of the 1997 Act.
[70] Law of Property Act 1925, s.115(5), Sched. 3, Form No. 2; Land Registration Rules 1925, r. 151 (as substituted); The 1986 Act, s.6C; Sched. 2A, para. 1(1) (as substituted by the 1997 Act s.7); Building Societies (Prescribed Forms of Receipt) Rules 1997, r. 2.
[71] See *ante* n. 70.
[72] The 1986 Act, Sched. 2, para. 12.
[73] Land Registration Rules 1925, r. 151 (as substituted by the Land Registration Rules 1999, r. 2(1), Sched. 1, para. 13) and 151 A, inserted by the Land Registration Rules 2000, r. 2(1), Sched. 1, paras 1, 2.
[74] *ibid.* r. 151A.
[75] Even if given under mistake; *Harvey v. Municipal Permanent Building Society* (1884) 26 Ch. D. 273; *London and County United Building Society v. Angell* (1896) 65 L.J.Q.B. 194; *contra, Farmer v. Smith* (1859) 4 H. & N. 196.
[76] *Lloyds Bank v. Bullock* [1896] 2 Ch. 192.

CHAPTER 9

LOCAL AUTHORITY MORTGAGES[1]

A local authority or county council may, subject to political and economic **9–01** restraints imposed on such authorities, advance money for the purpose of acquiring, constructing, altering, enlarging, repairing or improving houses, for acquiring buildings for conversion into houses or flats, for carrying out such conversions, or for paying off loans for such purposes. The powers of local authorities to make such advances are effectively controlled by central government by restrictions on borrowing[2] and the imposition of cash limits. Ministerial consent is required for the disposal of council dwellings, other than under the provisions governing "right to buy" or by way of letting under a secure tenancy (or what would be a secure tenancy if it did not fall within one of the prescribed statutory exceptions). Local authority capital expenditure on housing is determined through the Housing Investment Programme, which involves submissions by local authorities relating to levels of expenditure planned for their areas. One of the heads of such expenditure is lending to private persons for house purchase and improvement.

MORTGAGES OUTSIDE THE "RIGHT TO BUY" AND "RENT TO MORTGAGE" PROVISIONS[3]

There were formerly several statutes under which local authorities had power to make advances and to borrow money for the purposes set out above, but these were repealed[4] in the mid 1980s and the powers were then contained in the consolidating Act, that is, the Housing Act 1985. This Act has in part been amended by the Leasehold Reform, Housing and Urban Development Act 1993.

The first statutes under which local authorities were given such powers were the Small Dwellings Acquisition Acts 1899–1923. Under those Acts a local authority could advance money to a resident in any house in its area to enable him to acquire the ownership of the house, or to enable a person to construct a

---

[1] The law governing local authority mortgages and in particular the "rent to mortgage" provisions is complex. An appropriate work on the subject is Arden and Partington, *Housing Law* (2nd ed.), chapter 18.

[2] For the lending powers of other public authorities and the borrowing powers of local authorities, see *post*, paras 15–46 and 15–47.

[3] Such ministerial consent is granted from time to time on applications being made; see Housing Act 1985, ss.32–42, and see Leasehold Reform, Housing and Urban Development Act 1993, ss.135–137. See also Ministerial Letter of August 31, 1994, as amended by the subsequent letter of March 27, 1995.

[4] See the Housing (Consequential Provisions) Act 1985, Sched. 1.

house in which he intended to reside. The usefulness of that provision was severely restricted, since an advance could be made only if, in the opinion of the local authority, the market value of the house to be acquired did not exceed £5,000.[5]

Originally the advance could not exceed 90 per cent of the market value of the house as determined by a valuation made on behalf of the local authority[6] but later, 100 per cent advances were permitted.[7] The severity of the restriction meant, however, that most loans were made under section 43 of the Housing (Financial Provision) Act 1958.[8] Consequently, the Law Commission recommended, at paragraph 38(i) of their report on the consolidation of the Housing Acts, that the provisions of the 1899–1923 Acts should be re-enacted only to the extent that they are still required for the purposes of advances made before the commencement date of the Housing Act 1985. That recommendation was effected by section 456 of the 1985 Act.[9]

The powers formerly available to local authorities under the Housing (Financial Provisions) Act 1958[10] were preserved by section 436 of the Housing Act 1985.

Section 435(1) of the 1985 Act gives local authorities power to make loans, or to make advances to repay previous loans, for the acquisition, construction, alteration, enlargement, improvement or repair of houses, or for the conversion of buildings into houses or their acquisition for such conversion. Before making an advance the local authority must be satisfied that the resultant house will be fit for human habitation, or in the case of a house to be acquired, is or will be made fit.[11] The purpose of this provision is to assist owner-occupiers who already have loans secured by a mortgage and to whom the original lender is unwilling to make a further advance; and it applies whether or not the original lender was a local authority. Because the local authority is empowered to make a loan which is large enough to pay off the existing mortgage debt as well as to pay for improvements, the borrower is not faced with the difficulties of a second mortgage. In order to prevent the borrower from using the part of the loan not required to pay off the mortgage debt for purposes other than meeting his housing needs, it is provided[12] that no such advance shall be made unless the local authority is satisfied that the primary effect will be to meet the borrower's housing needs. Advances may be made to "any persons". "Person" is not defined in the Act but in view of the necessity for the local authority to be satisfied that housing needs are being met, it would seem that "persons" means "natural persons" and does not include bodies corporate. A local authority may, however, make loans to housing associations.[13]

---

[5] Small Dwellings Acquisition Act 1899, s.1(1); Housing Act 1949, s.44(1).
[6] Housing Act 1923, s.22(d).
[7] House Purchase and Housing Act 1959, s.3(1).
[8] Re-enacted by the Housing Act 1985, ss.435, 436.
[9] The provisions of Sched. 18 to the Housing Act 1985 have effect with respect to advances made under the Small Dwellings Acquisition Acts 1899–1923 before April 1, 1986.
[10] As amended by the Local Government Act 1974, s.37(2). The section was partly repealed by the Housing Act 1980, s.152, Sched. 25(9), Sched. 26.
[11] Housing Act 1985, s.439.
[12] ibid. s.439(3), re-enacting s.43(2A) of the Housing (Financial Provisions) Act 1958.
[13] Housing Associations Act 1985, ss.58 et seq.

The terms of advances are set out in section 436. The amount of the advance must not exceed the value of the mortgaged security in the case of a house or houses to be acquired, or in any other case, the value which it is estimated the mortgaged security will bear when the construction, conversion, alteration, enlargement, repair or improvement has been carried out.[14] The advance together with interest must be secured by a mortgage on the property.[15] The mortgage must provide for repayment of the principal either by instalments (of equal or unequal amounts) beginning on the date of the advance or a later date or at the end of a fixed period (with or without a provision allowing the authority to extend the period) or on the happening of a specific event before the end of that period and for the payment of instalments of interest[16] throughout the period beginning on the date of the advance and ending when the whole of the principal is repaid.[17] In either case, the balance outstanding is payable on demand if there is a breach of any of the conditions of the advance and the borrower may repay on any of the usual quarter days after giving a month's notice of his intention.[18]

The provisions as to local authority mortgage interest rates formerly contained in section 110(1),[19] (2) of the Housing Act 1980 are re-enacted by section 438(1) of the 1985 Act. A local authority may give assistance[20] by way of waiver or reduction of payments of property requiring repair or improvement,[21] or by making partially interest-free loans to first time buyers for the first five years of the loan[22] formerly those provisions did not apply to loans made by local authorities under section 228 of the Housing Act 1985.[23] That section cast a duty on local housing authorities to offer a loan, to be secured by a mortgage of the applicant's interest in the dwelling concerned, to a person who is liable:

(1) to incur expenditure in complying with an improvement notice served, or undertaking accepted, under Part VII of the Housing Act 1985; or
(2) to make a payment as directed by a court under section 217(5) thereof.

Advances may be made in addition to other assistance given by the local authority in respect of the same house under any other Act or any other provisions of the Housing Act 1985.[24]

---

[14] Housing Act 1985, s.436(3). There must be a valuation on behalf of the local authority. Except in cases of advances for acquiring houses, the advance may be made by instalments as the works proceed.

[15] Housing Act 1985, s.436(3).

[16] For interest, see the Housing Act 1985, s.438 and Sched. 16.

[17] This is subject to s.441 (waiver or reduction of payments in case of property requiring repair or improvement) and s.446(1)(b) (assistance for first time buyers: part of loan interest free for up to five years) s.436(5).

[18] Housing Act 1985, s.436(6).

[19] As amended by the Housing and Building Control Act 1984, s.64, Sched. 11.

[20] Housing Act 1985, s.438(1).

[21] ibid. s.441.

[22] ibid. s.446(1)(b).

[23] The exemption is conferred by s.438(3) of the Housing Act 1985 as amended by Schedule 2 to the Housing Act 1996 (Consequential Provisions) Order 1996 S.I. 1996 No. 2325, containing provisions formerly in s.110(14) of the Housing Act 1980.

[24] Housing Act 1985, s.435(4), e.g. under ss.460 et seq. of the 1985 Act (improvement and other grants).

SECURE TENANT'S RIGHTS TO MORTGAGES ASSOCIATED WITH THE RIGHT TO
BUY

1. The secure tenant's "right to buy"

9–02   A secure tenancy is a tenancy of a dwelling-house[25] which is let as a separate dwelling and in respect of which

(a) the interest of the landlord belongs to one of a specified list of authorities or bodies[26]; and

(b) the tenant[27] is an individual and occupies the dwelling-house as his only or principal home; or, where the tenancy is a joint tenancy, that each of the joint tenants is an individual and at least one of them occupies the dwelling-house as his only or principal home.[28]

A secure tenant has the right to buy, at discounted prices, either:

(a) the freehold of his dwelling-house if the landlord owns the freehold; or

(b) a long lease of it at a low rent if the landlord does not own the freehold or if the dwelling-house is a flat (whether or not the landlord owns the freehold),[29]

provided that the relevant conditions and exceptions stated in sections 118 *et seq.* of the Housing Act 1985 are satisfied.[30]

2. Introduction

9–03   Under the consolidated scheme set out in the Housing Act 1985 the secure tenant exercising a right to buy had a number of other ancillary rights that gave him

---

[25] In this context "dwelling-house" means a house or part of a house: Housing Act 1985, s.112(1). For land let together with a dwelling-house, see s.112(2).

[26] *i.e.* a local authority, a new town corporation, an urban development corporation, the Development Board of Rural Wales, a housing action trust which is a charity, or a registered housing association or certain housing co-operatives: Housing Act 1985, s.80(1), (2) as amended by the Housing Act 1986, the Housing Act 1988 and the Housing Act 1996 (Consequential Provisions) Order 1996 S.I. 1996 No. 2325.

[27] The definition of a secure tenant includes a former secure tenant whose right to buy has been preserved following disposal of the reversion to a private landlord: see Housing Act 1985, ss.171A—171H and Schedule 9A; Housing (Preservation of Right to Buy) Regulations (S.I. 1989 No. 368, as amended).

[28] Housing Act 1985, s.81.

[29] *ibid.* s.118(1) containing provisions formerly in the Housing Act 1980, s.1(1), (2), as amended, in the case of s.1(1) by the Housing and Building Control Act 1984, s.1(2). Where a secure tenancy is a joint tenancy then, whether or not each of the joint tenants occupies the dwelling-house as his only principal home, the right to buy belongs jointly to all of them or to such one or more of them as may be agreed between them; but such an agreement is not valid unless the person or at least one of the persons to whom the right to buy is to belong occupies the dwelling-house as his only or principal home: s.118(2) reinforcing provisions formerly in s.4(1) of the 1980 Act.

[30] For details of the right to buy see further, s.119 and Sched. 4 (qualifying period); s.120 and Sched. 5, as amended by the Housing and Planning Act 1986; s.121 (circumstances in which the right cannot be exercised); ss.122–125, as amended by the Housing and Planning Act 1986, s.4 (the procedure for exercising the right); ss.126–131 and Sched. 4, as amended by the Housing and Planning Act 1986, s.2 (the purchase price and discount).

access to funding from his public landlord which were abolished[31] with effect from October 11, 1993. Those rights were (subject to his financial status) the right to a mortgage,[32] the right to be granted a shared ownership lease[33] and the right to defer completion.[34]

The only such right the secure tenant exercising his right to buy now has is the right to acquire on rent to mortgage terms. This enables him effectively to use public funds to assist in purchase. That right is the right to acquire a share in the property at a price that when capitalised leaves the tenant paying mortgage interest at a rate which does not exceed his rent. If that right is exercised the tenant/owner has a residual right to buy the remainder of the property, described as the redemption of the landlord's share, at a later date. The tenant/owner actually becomes obliged to purchase the landlord's share in some circumstances.

3. **The right to acquire**

Where a secure tenant has claimed to exercise his right to buy and has established **9–04** that right while his notice claiming the right to buy if in force he also has the right to acquire on rent to mortgage terms.[35] That right enables the tenant to acquire a share of the dwelling house for a price that equates to a multiple of the rent payable when capitalised which enables him to fund the purchase by a mortgage where the interest payment does not exceed the rent that was payable. Where the right to buy is owned by a number of people jointly the right to acquire on rent to mortgage terms also belongs to them jointly.[36]

The right to acquire on rent to mortgage terms does not arise or is not exercisable in a number of circumstances. First if the right to buy is not exercisable for any reason the right to acquire on rent to mortgage terms does not arise. A tenant who is or was entitled to receive housing benefit in respect of any part of a period commencing 12 months before the day the tenant claims to exercise the right to acquire and ending on the day the conveyance or grant is executed in pursuance of that right is excluded from exercising the right. A claim for housing benefit made or treated as made on behalf of the tenant in respect of any part of the same period which has not been determined and withdrawn will result in exclusion of the right to acquire on rent to mortgage terms.

The maximum initial capital payment that a tenant can make in exercise of the right to acquire is 80 per cent of the purchase price. The minimum initial payment a tenant is required to make when exercising the right to acquire is calculated by reference to a formula. The minimum initial payment is the product of multiplying the weekly rent for the dwelling house with the multiplier currently declared by the Secretary of State. The Secretary of State also declares a maximum figure for the rent that may be used in determining the minimum

[31] Generally see *Woodfall*, vol. 4, chap. 27. The Housing Act 1985 as amended by the Leasehold Reform, Housing and Urban Development Act 1993, s.107 and s.108.
[32] Housing Act 1985, ss.132 to 135.
[33] Housing Act 1985, ss.143 to 151.
[34] Housing Act 1985, s.142.
[35] Housing Act 1985, s.143 as substituted by Leasehold Reform, Housing and Urban Development Act 1993, s.108.
[36] Housing Act 1985, s.143(3).

initial payment. Where the actual rent exceeds the declared maximum the formula is adjusted so that the minimum initial payment is the product of multiplying the declared multiplier and the difference between the actual rent and the maximum rent figure and adding the maximum rent figure.

The figures declared by the Secretary of State are set at a level that it is believed will result in a minimum initial payment which could be raised on a 25 year mortgage funded by monthly mortgage payments equal to the monthly rent payable. If the minimum initial payment exceeds the maximum the right to acquire on rent to mortgage terms is excluded.

4. **The procedure for exercising the right**

9–05   A secure tenant claiming to exercise a right to acquire on rent to mortgage terms must do so by serving on the landlord a written notice to that effect.[37] A landlord cannot serve an effective notice to complete the purchase while a notice claiming the right to acquire on rent to mortgage terms is in force.[37a] The service by a tenant of notice claiming to exercise the right to acquire on rent to mortgage terms after a notice to complete has been served by the landlord has the effect of deeming the withdrawal of the landlord's notice to complete.

Such a notice can be withdrawn at any time by a further written notice.[38] Withdrawal from the exercise of a right to acquire on rent to mortgage terms does not inhibit the continued exercise of the right to buy.[39]

After receipt of a notice claiming the right to acquire on rent to mortgage terms the landlord must serve written notice admitting or denying the right as soon as practicable.[40] The notice must admit the right and give further information or deny the right stating the reasons it is denied the tenant is entitled to claim the right. The further information the landlord must provide includes the various elements that are required to calculate the initial payment, that figure and its relationship to the purchase price under the right to buy, the landlord's share in the property if the initial minimum payment is made and the discount on that assumption and the provisions the landlord considers appropriate for the subsequent purchase of the landlord's share in the property.

The tenant is then required to serve a written notice[41] on the landlord stating either that he intends to pursue the right to buy exercising a right to acquire on rent to mortgage terms and the initial payment that he proposes to make or that he is proceeding with the right to buy but withdrawing the claim to the right to acquire on rent to mortgage terms or that both rights are withdrawn. The tenant's notice should be served within 12 weeks of the landlord's notice. There is provision for a landlord to serve notice requiring the tenant to respond within 28 days if no response has been received within the 12 week period. A failure by the tenant to respond after a service of such a notice will result in the claim to the right to acquire being deemed withdrawn.

---

[37] Housing Act 1985, s.144 (substituted by the Leasehold Reform, Housing and Urban Development Act 1993, s.109).
[37a] Housing Act 1985, s.144(3).
[38] Housing Act 1985, s.144(2).
[39] Housing Act 1985, s.144(4).
[40] Housing Act 1985, s.146.
[41] Housing Act 1985, s.146A.

Where the right to acquire on rent to mortgage terms is being pursued the landlord must serve a further notice confirming the landlord's share in the event of the initial payment proposed by the tenant and the initial discount on that assumption.[42]

5. The terms applicable to the acquisition

The terms of the conveyance or lease where the right to buy is accompanied by the right to acquire on rent to mortgage terms must follow the terms required by the right to buy provisions[43] plus provisions dealing with the redemption of the landlord's share. Where the property purchased on rent to mortgage terms was leasehold the tenant's covenants relating to service charges will be limited to a percentage that is proportionate to the percentage ownership of the property.

9–06

6. Purchase or redemption of the landlord's share

The conveyance or grant must include a covenant obliging the tenant to redeem the landlord's share immediately:

    (i) following a disposal by the tenant which is not an excluded disposal[44];

    (ii) on the expiry of a year from the death of the person or last remaining person entitled to the property purchased.

In addition, the conveyance or grant must include provisions entitling the tenant or his successors to redeem the landlord's share at any time.

The redemption of the landlord's share would necessitate the payment by the tenant of the value of that share less the amount of the discount. Tenants can opt to redeem part of the landlord's share provided the payment required to redeem the share being purchased is not less than 10 per cent of the value of the dwelling house.[45]

If at the time of the redemption of the last of the landlord's interest the secure tenant, or one of them or certain of their spouses is or was the owner within the preceding two years the purchasing tenant will have the benefit of a final discount of 20 per cent. Upon partial redemption the purchasing tenant is entitled to a proportionate discount.[46]

7. Registration of title

On the conveyance of the freehold or the grant of a lease under the right to buy or on a conveyance where the tenant under a rent to mortgage acquisition has

9–07

[42] Housing Act 1985, ss.147 and 148.
[43] Housing Act 1985, s.151.
[44] Excluded disposals are disposals between spouses, pursuant to s.24 of the Matrimonial Causes Act 1973, s.2 of the Inheritance (Provisions for Family and Dependants) Act 1975 or under a will or by intestacy—Housing Act 1985, Schedule 6A (inserted by the Leasehold Reform, Housing and Urban Development Act 1993, s.117).
[45] Housing Act 1985, Schedule 6A.
[46] Housing Act 1985, Schedule 6A.

acquired a 100 per cent. interest in the dwelling-house section 123 of the Land Registration Act 1925 (compulsory registration of title) applies even though the dwelling-house is not in an area of compulsory registration or the lease would not normally require registration.[47]

Where the landlord's title to the dwelling-house is not registered, the landlord must give the tenant a certificate or the form approved by the Chief Land Registrar stating that the landlord is entitled to convey the freehold or make the grant subject only to such incumbrances, rights and interests as are stated in the conveyance or grant or summarised in the certificate.[48] Such certificate is to be accepted by the Chief Land Registrar as sufficient evidence of the facts stated in it.[49]

8. Repayment of discount on early disposal

9–08   If a purchaser under the right to buy or the right to acquire on rent to mortgage terms disposes[50] of the dwelling-house or his share within three years of the acquisition, the purchaser must repay the discount, reduced by one third for each complete year which has elapsed since the acquisition.[51] The liability to repay is a charge on the dwelling-house, taking effect as if it had been created by deed expressed to be by way of legal mortgage[52] and having priority immediately after any legal charge securing an amount: (i) left outstanding by the tenant in exercising the right to buy; (ii) advanced to him by an approved lending institution[53] for the purpose of enabling him to exercise that right; or (iii) further advanced to him by that institution.[54]

---

[47] Housing Act 1985, s.154.

[48] *ibid.* s.154(2), (4).

[49] *ibid.* s.154(5). The landlord must indemnify him if a claim is successfully made against him under s.83 of the Land Registration Act 1925, as amended.

[50] For relevant disposals, see Housing Act 1985, s.159.

[51] Housing Act 1985, s.155 as amended by the Housing and Planning Act 1986, s.2(3); Housing Act 1988, s.140; Leasehold Reform, Housing and Urban Development Act 1993, s.120(1) and (2). For exempted disposals, see s.160.

[52] *ibid.* s.156(1). Such charge is a land charge for the purposes of s.59(2) of the Land Registration Act 1925; s.156(3).

[53] *e.g* a building society, bank, etc: see s.156(4)–(6) as amended by Housing Act 1996, Schedule 18, para. 22 and Schedule 19.

[54] Housing Act 1985, s.156(2); but the landlord may at any time by written notice served on an approved lending institution postpone the charge created by the liability to repay to a legal charge securing an amount advanced or further advanced to the tenant by that institution.

CHAPTER 10

AGRICULTURAL MORTGAGES AND CHARGES

THE HISTORICAL BACKGROUND

From about the middle of the 19th century a considerable body of legislation   **10–01**
came into existence affecting persons engaged in agriculture. This had among its
objects the improvement of the position of tenants of agricultural land and the
provision of finance for farmers over a longer period and on more favourable
terms than would have been available from the usual commercial lending institutions. Much of the legislation enacted is outside the scope of this work.

In addition to the normal commercial sources of money, the perceived need for
long-term finance was provided in Part I of the Agricultural Credits Act 1928
("the 1928 Act"). This provided for the establishment of the Agricultural Mortgage Corporation Limited which was encouraged to make loans or mortgages of
agricultural land and to make loans under the Improvement of Land Acts 1864
and 1899. Such long term loans were capable of being granted secured by
mortgages over agricultural land not exceeding two thirds of the value of the
mortgaged property. Such mortgages were repayable by yearly or half-yearly
instalments of capital and interest over a period of 60 years or on such other
terms as the corporation's memorandum or articles might have permitted. Such
mortgages were capable of being made irredeemable for the period during which
the instalments were repayable.

On September 25, 1991, Part I of the 1928 Act was repealed subject to a saving
in relation to mortgages or debentures subsisting the date when the repeal took
effect.[1] Despite its repeal Part I still has practical significance owing to the
continued existence of mortgages granted by farmers to secure such advances
prior to its repeal.

ORDINARY MORTGAGES AND CHARGES

Apart from the now repealed provisions of Part I of the 1928 Act it is possible   **10–02**
to create mortgages of farm stock and agricultural land. Such mortgages are
governed by the general law of bills of sales and of mortgages, respectively.

However, a number of points of difference between the general law and
mortgages of farm stock and agricultural land are to be noted.

---

[1] ss.1, 2, 4 repealed by the Agriculture and Forestry (Financial Provisions) Act 1991, s.1(1), (2),
Sched. Pt 1; s.3 repealed by the Trustees Investments Act 1961, s.16(2), Sched. 5. The latter was
itself repealed by the Statute Law (Repeals) Act 1974.

1. Agricultural Charges

10–03   Part II of the 1928 Act makes special provisions for short-term credit by way of charge in favour of a bank over farming stock and assets. These are known as agricultural charges.[2]

2. The Statutory Power of Leasing

10–04   Before the enactment of section 18 of the Conveyancing Act 1881 (now replaced by section 99 of the Law of Property Act 1925) neither the mortgagor nor the mortgagee alone could make a lease which would be valid against the other unless that power was expressly provided for in the mortgage deed.[3] Since its enactment it is provided that a mortgagor of land whilst in possession has the power as against every incumbrancer to make any such lease of the mortgaged land as is authorised by the section. A mortgagee has a similar power as against every prior incumbrancer.[4] Leases authorised by this section include agricultural leases for any term not exceeding 21 years, or in the case of a mortgage made after the commencement of the 1925 Act, 50 years. This is subject to any contrary intention being expressed in the mortgage deed, or otherwise in writing, and subject to the terms of the deed or of any such writing, and the provisions therein contained.[5]

Further, the Agricultural Holdings Act 1986 provides that the statutory power of leasing cannot be excluded in the case of a mortgage of agricultural land made after March 1, 1948.[6] Agricultural land is defined by section 1(4) of the Agricultural Holdings Act 1986 and means land used for agriculture which is so used for the purposes of a trade or business.[7]

Where a lease fails to comply with the terms of section 99 but was made in good faith and the lessee has entered the property pursuant to its terms, section 152(1) of the Law of Property Act 1925 provides that the lease shall take effect in equity as a contract for the grant, at the lessee's request of a valid lease of like effect as the invalid lease, subject to such variations as may be necessary in order to comply with the statutory power.[8]

3. Compensation

10–05   In the case where a sum becomes due to a tenant of an agricultural holding in respect of compensation from the landlord and the landlord fails to discharge his liability within the period of one month from the date upon which the sum

---

[2] See para. 10–07 *et seq.*
[3] *Carpenter v. Parker* (1857) 3 C.B.N.S. 206.
[4] s.99 (1), (2).
[5] See s.99 (13).
[6] s.100, Sched. 14, para. 12, the provision being originally contained in the Agricultural Holdings Act 1948, s.95, Sched. 7, para. 2.
[7] And see Agriculture Act 1947, s.109. The definition of "agriculture" includes horticulture, fruit growing, dairy farming and livestock breeding, see *ibid.* s.96(1). It is subject to a number of exclusions.
[8] See *Pawson v. Revell* [1958] 2 Q.B. 360, and s.152(6); *Rhodes v. Dalby* [1971] 1 W.L.R. 1325.

becomes due, by virtue of the provisions contained in section 85(2) of the Agricultural Holdings Act 1986 the tenant shall be entitled to obtain from the Minister an order charging the holding with payment of the amount due.

By section 2(2) of the Land Charges Act 1972 such a charge is registrable as a Class A Land Charge. Further, by section 87(6) of the Agricultural Holdings Act 1986 such a charge (or likewise a charge under section 74 of the Agricultural Holdings Act 1948)[9] shall rank *in priority* to any other charge however and whenever created or arising. Charges created under these sections rank, as between themselves, in order of their creation. However, generally the charge of a landlord of an agricultural holding for repayment of the payment of compensation by him to his tenant does not rank in priority to other charges.[10]

4. Growing Crops

A mortgagee, whether legal or equitable, who has not taken possession of the holding is not entitled to growing crops which have been removed by the mortgagor between the time of demand and the time of recovery of possession. However, he is entitled to all crops growing on the holding when he takes possession[11] unless under an express contract of tenancy between the mortgagor and the mortgagee the mortgagor can claim them as emblements.[12] Since the severance of the crops converts them into personal chattels, a mortgagee who has not taken possession before the mortgagor's bankruptcy has no right to them as against the mortgagor's trustee in bankruptcy.[13]   **10–06**

If an ordinary mortgage or charge of a holding includes a covenant that a mortgagor shall not without the consent of the mortgagee include any growing crops in an agricultural charge, a breach of that covenant would bring into operation the statutory power of sale pursuant to section 101 of the Law of Property Act 1925.[14]

AGRICULTURAL CHARGES

1. The nature and creation of an agricultural charge

Part II of the 1928 Act makes provision for agricultural short-term credits. Section 5 of that Act regulates the nature and mode of creation of agricultural charges on farming stock and assets.   **10–07**

---

[9] This section which dealt with recovery of compensation where a contract of tenancy is not binding on a mortgagee was repealed by s.10(2) and Sched. 4 to the Agricultural Holdings Act 1948 which itself was repealed by the Agricultural Holdings Act 1986, but charges created under the 1948 Act are still in existence.

[10] s.86 of the Agricultural Holdings Act 1986.

[11] *Bagnall v. Villar* (1879) 12 Ch. D. 812.

[12] *Re Skinner, ex parte Temple & Fishe* (1882) 1 Gl. and J. 216; *Bagnall v. Villar ibid.*; *Re Phillips ex parte National Mercantile Bank* (1880) 16 Ch. D. 104. This applies to an equitable mortgagee *Re Gordon ex parte Official Receiver* (1889) 61 L.T. 299.

[13] *Re Phillips ibid.*

[14] See *post* para. 16–55 *et seq.*

A farmer[15] who, as tenant or owner of an agricultural holding, cultivates the holding for profit[16] may, notwithstanding any provision in his contract of tenancy to the contrary[17] by instrument in writing create in favour of a bank an agricultural charge on all or any of his farming stock[18] and other agricultural assets[19] as security for sums on short-term credit advanced to him or paid or to be paid on his behalf under any guarantee by the bank and interest, commission and charges thereon.[20] An agricultural charge may be either a fixed charge, or a floating charge, or both a fixed and a floating charge.[21] The principal sum secured by an agricultural charge may be either a specified amount, or a fluctuating amount advanced on current account not exceeding at any one time such amount (if any) as may be specified in the charge. In the latter case the charge shall not be deemed to be redeemed by reason only of the current account having ceased to be in debit.[22] An agricultural charge may be in such form and made upon such conditions as the parties may agree and sureties may be made parties to the charge.[23]

2. Fixed charges and their effect

10–08 The property affected by a fixed charge shall be such property forming part of the farming stock and other agricultural assets belonging to the farmer at the date of the charge as may be specified in the charge. It may also include in the case of livestock any progeny borne after the date of the charge and in the case of agricultural plants any plant which may whilst the charge is in force be substituted for the plant specified in the charge.[24]

A fixed charge shall so long as the charge continues in force confers on the bank certain rights. These are the following:

---

[15] Defined as being any person (not being an incorporated company or society) who as tenant or owner of an agricultural holding cultivates the holding for profit: s.5(7).

[16] "Agriculture" and "Cultivation" shall be deemed to include horticulture, and the use of land for any purpose of husbandry, inclusive of the keeping or breeding of livestock, poultry or bees, and the growth of fruit, vegetables and the like: *ibid.*

[17] *ibid.* s.13.

[18] "Farming stock" means crops or horticultural produce, whether growing or severed from the land, and after severance whether subjected to any treatment or process of manufacture or not; livestock, including poultry and bees, and the produce and progeny thereof; any other agricultural or horticultural produce whether subjected to any treatment or process of manufacture or not; seeds and manure; agricultural vehicles, machinery and other parts; agricultural tenant's fixtures and other agricultural fixtures which a tenant is by law authorised to remove *ibid.* s.5(7).

[19] "Other agricultural assets" means a tenant's right to compensation under the Agricultural Holdings Act 1986, except under s.60(2)(b) or 62 for improvements, damage by game, disturbance or otherwise; and any other tenant right; *ibid.* s.5(7).

[20] *ibid.* s.5(1). The Bank is defined as being the Bank of England an institution authorised under the Banking Act 1987 or the Post Office, in the exercise of its powers to provide banking services: *ibid.* s.5(7) as amended by the Banking Act 1979, s.51(1), Sched. 6 paras 2, 14; the Banking Act 1987, s.108(1), Sched. 6 para. 2; and the Trustee Savings Bank Act 1985, ss.4(3), 7(3), Sched. 4. A bank that takes an assignment of farming stock and other agricultural assets does not become a tenant within the meaning of the Agricultural Holdings Act 1986, s.96(1).

[21] *ibid.* s.5(2).

[22] *ibid.* s.5(5).

[23] *ibid.* s.5(6).

[24] *ibid.* s.5(3).

(a) a right upon the happening of any event specified in the charge as being an event authorising the seizure of property subject to the charge, to take possession of any such property;

(b) where possession of any property has been so taken a right after an interval of five clear days (or such less time as may be allowed by the charge) to sell the property either by auction or, if the charge so provides, by private treaty, and either for a lump sum payment or payment by instalments;

(c) an obligation, in the event of such prior sale being exercised, the apply the proceeds of sale in or towards the discharge of the moneys and liabilities secured by the charge, and the cost of seizure and sale, and to pay the surplus (if any) of the proceeds to the farmer.[25]

In the absence of the happening of any event specified in the charge the farmer is entitled to remain in possession of the property charged and to sell it. However, a number of obligations are imposed upon him so long as the charge continues in force except to such extent that the charge otherwise provides or the bank otherwise allows. Whenever the farmer sells any of the property, or receives any money in respect of other agricultural assets comprised in the charge, or in the event of its receiving any money under a policy of insurance on any of the property comprised in the charge, or any money paid by way of compensation under the Animal Health Act 1981 or under the Plant Health Act 1967 in respect of the destruction of any livestock or crops comprised in the charge, the fixed charge imposes on the farmer the obligation forthwith to pay to the bank the amount of the proceeds of the sale or the money so received in or towards discharge of the money and liabilities secured by the charge.[26]

Thus, subject to compliance with the obligations so imposed a fixed charge shall not prevent the farmers selling any of the property subject to the charge, and neither the purchaser nor in the case of a sale by auction the auctioneer, shall be concerned to see that such obligations are complied with notwithstanding that he may be aware of the existence of a charge.[27]

Further, where any proceeds of sale are paid to a person other than the bank which should have been so paid to the bank, the bank has no right to recover such proceeds from that person unless the bank proves that such other person knew that the proceeds were paid to him in breach of such obligation. Notice of the charge does not amount to such knowledge.[28] A farmer who with intent to defraud fails to comply with the obligations as to payment owed to the bank of any money received by him or removes from the holding any property subject to the charge, is guilty of an offence and liable on summary conviction to imprisonment for a term not exceeding six months or a fine not exceeding the prescribed sum, or both, and on conviction on indictment to imprisonment for a term not exceeding three years.[29]

[25] ibid. s.5(4).
[26] ibid. s.6(2).
[27] ibid. s.6(3).
[28] ibid. s.6(4).
[29] ibid. s.11(1); Criminal Justice Act 1948, ss.1(1), (2); Criminal Law Act 1967, s.1; Magistrates' Courts Act 1980, ss.17, 32, Sched. 1 para. 20.The prescribed sum is currently £5000.

3. **Floating charges and their effect**

10–09   The property affected by a floating charge shall be the farming stock and other agricultural assets from time to time belonging to the farmer or such parts of the same as is mentioned in the charge.[30] A floating charge hovers over the assets charged but settles and fixes on no particular asset until some event has happened which converts the charge into a fixed charge. Subject to the consideration set out below an agricultural charge creating a floating charge shall have the like effect as if the charge had been created by a duly registered debenture issued by a company.[31]

Assets also not falling under the umbrella of the floating charge would include the farmer's house and furniture and other chattels not connected with the farming business. He may well have granted a separate legal charge in favour of the bank over the residential premises and such chattels. However, the charge is converted into a fixed charge over the property comprised in the charge as existing at the date of its becoming a fixed charge on the occurrence of the following events:

    (a)   upon a bankruptcy order being made against the farmer;

    (b)   upon the death of the farmer;

    (c)   upon the dissolution of the partnership in the case where the property charged is partnership property;

    (d)   upon notice in writing of that effect being given by the bank on the happening of any event which by virtue of the charge confers on the bank the right to give such notice.[32]

Further, whilst the status of charge is that of a floating charge the farmer is subject to the same obligation as under a fixed charge to pay over to the bank money received by him by way of proceeds of sale or money received in respect of other agricultural assets or under policies of insurance or by way of compensation.[33] However, it is not necessary for a farmer to comply with the above obligation to pay over such sums to the bank where the amount so received is expended by him in the purchase of farming stock which on purchase becomes subject to the floating charge.[34]

10–10   This means that whilst the charge remains a floating charge the farmer is able to pay his way by selling farming stock and using the proceeds of sale in purchasing new farming stock. He is therefore able to pay for the cost of, *e.g.* crops, seed, livestock, and plant *pro tempore* without accounting for the sums received from the sale of farming stock to the bank pursuant to his general obligation to do so.

Thus there is one essential difference between a fixed agricultural charge and a floating agricultural charge. In the case of the latter whilst the charge remains a floating charge the same obligation that the farmer would have if the charge were a fixed charge to pay over to the bank monies received by him is subject to the exception that such sums do not have to be paid over by him to the bank in

---

[30] *ibid.* s.5(4).

[31] *ibid.* s.7.

[32] *ibid.* s.7 proviso (a) as amended by the Insolvency Act 1985, s.235(1), Ch. 8 para. 6.

[33] See s.6(2) and para. 10–08 *ante.*

[34] *ibid.* s.7 proviso (b).

the case where the amounts so received are expended in the purchase of farming stock.

Having regard to these various provisions, set out above, a different regime therefore operates as to agricultural charges when compared with the provisions of the Insolvency Act 1986. The effect of the crystallisation of the floating charge in the event of, *e.g.* bankruptcy of the farmer converts that charge to a fixed charge. This means that all the farming stock and other agricultural assets including monies due for agricultural schemes and from persons having bought grain *prior to* the bankruptcy fall to be dealt with under the fixed charge. The charge is still floating at the date when the bankruptcy occurs but that event has the effect of crystallising the charge into a fixed charge.

4. **Registration of agricultural charge**

Every agricultural charge must be registered within seven clear days after its **10–11** execution. If it is not so registered it is void against any person other than the farmer. However, if it is proved that omission to register within this period was accidental or inadvertent, the High Court may extend the time for registration.[35]

Registration of an agricultural charge is effected at the Land Registry by sending by post to the Land Registrar a memorandum of the instrument creating the charge together with the prescribed particulars and fee.[36] The Land Registrar is obliged to keep at the Land Registry a register of agricultural charges in such form and containing such particulars as may be prescribed and on receipt of the memorandum he shall enter the particulars in the Register and file a memorandum.[37] The Register and memorandum are open to inspection on payment (except where the inspection is made by or on behalf of a bank) of the prescribed fee, and any person inspecting the Register or any such filed memorandum on payment of the prescribed fee may make copies or extracts therefrom.[38]

Registration of an agricultural charge may be proved by the production of a certified copy of the entry on the Register relating to the charge and the Schedule to the Act makes special provision as to official searches in the Agricultural Charges Register held at the Land Registry.[39] In favour of a purchaser or intending purchaser, as against persons interested under or in respect of an agricultural charge, the certificate, according to its tenor shall be conclusive, affirmatively or negatively, as the case may be.[40]

---

[35] *ibid.* s.9(1) and proviso.
[36] *ibid.* s.9(3).
[37] *ibid.* s.9(2), (3).
[38] *ibid.* s.9(4).
[39] Schedule paras 1 to 3, 5, added by the Land Charges Act 1972, Schedule 3 para. 7.
[40] Schedule paras 3, 4 as added by the Land Charges Act 1972. Para. 6 of the Schedule makes provision for any act of fraud or collusion or wilful negligence on the part of any officer, clerk or other person employed in the Registry who commits any such act or is a party or privy to the same. In such circumstances the offence is punishable on summary conviction with a fine not exceeding the prescribed sum or imprisonment for up to three months or both, and on conviction or indictment with imprisonment for up to two years, and as amended by the provisions of s.32(2) of the Magistrates' Courts Act 1980. At present the prescribed sum is £5000. Para. 7 of the Schedule further provides that a solicitor, or a trustee, personal representative, agent or other person in a fiduciary position shall not be answerable for any loss that might arise from error in a certificate obtained by him.

Registration of an agricultural charge is deemed to constitute actual notice of the charge and of the fact of such registration to all persons and for all purposes connected with the property comprised in the charge as from the date of registration or other prescribed date and so long as the registration continues in force.[41] However, where a charge in favour of a bank is expressly made for securing a current account or other further advances, the bank in relation to the making of further advances under the charge is not deemed to have notice of another agricultural charge by reason only that it is so registered if it was not so registered at the time when the first charge was created or when the last search by the bank was made, whichever last happened.[42]

5. Supplemental provisions as agricultural charges

10–12   Neither an agricultural charge nor a registered debenture issued by an agricultural society is deemed to be a bill of sale within the meaning of the Bills of Sale Acts 1878 and 1882.[43] Further, as to priorities between agricultural charges it is provided that such charges shall in relation to one another have priority in accordance with the times at which they are respectively registered.[44] Where an agricultural charge creating a floating charge has been made, an agricultural charge purporting to create fixed charge on, or a bill of sale comprising, any of the property subject to the floating charge is void as long as the floating charge remains in force.[45]

Further, where a farmer who is adjudged bankrupt has within three months of the presentation of the bankruptcy petition created a charge in favour of a bank operating to secure any sum owing to the bank immediately prior to the giving of the charge the amounts which would have been so secured by the charge must be reduced by the amount of the prior debt unless it is proved that the farmer immediately after the execution of the charge was solvent. However, this is without prejudice to the bank's right to enforce any other security for that sum or to claim payment thereof as an unsecured debt.[46] If growing crops are included in an agricultural charge then the rights of the bank in respect of such crops under the charge shall have priority to those of the mortgagee, whether in possession or not, and irrespective of the dates of the mortgage and charge.[47]

6. Charges on property of registered societies

10–13   A debenture issued by a society registered under the Industrial & Provident Societies Act 1965 creating in favour of a bank a floating charge on property

---

[41] *ibid.* s.9(8).
[42] *ibid.* s.9(8) proviso.
[43] *ibid.* ss.8(1), 14(1).
[44] *ibid.* s.8(2).
[45] *ibid.* s.8(3).
[46] *ibid.* s.8(5).
[47] *ibid.* s.8(6).

which is farming stock may be registered in like manner as an agricultural charge and the provision as to registration of agricultural charges apply.[48] Notice of such charges must be signed by the secretary of the society and sent to the central office established under the Friendly Societies Acts 1974 and registered there.[49]

---

[48] *ibid*. s.14(1). The text of this sub-section refers to the Industrial & Provident Societies' Acts 1893–1928 but these were repealed and replaced by the Industrial & Provident Societies' Act 1965; see ss.4, 77(3).

[49] *ibid*. s.14(1) proviso. This refers to the Friendly Societies Act 1896 but this was repealed and replaced by the Friendly Societies Act 1974; see s.116, Sched. 10 para. 2.

CHAPTER 11

MORTGAGE DEBENTURES

NATURE AND FORM OF A DEBENTURE

At common law, there is no precise definition of what constitutes "a debenture".[1] **11–01** Chitty J. stated that "a debenture means a document which either creates a debt or acknowledges it, and any document which fulfils either of these conditions is a 'debenture'".[2] Thus, in its simplest form, a debenture is an acknowledgement of debt.[3] The usual reason for issuing a debenture is to secure a loan, most frequently taken by a company but sometimes by an unincorporated association[4] or an individual and, in such circumstances, it will contain a charge on the mortgagor's property, thereby becoming a mortgage debenture. However, an ordinary mortgage of freehold property is not a debenture[5] but a floating charge over such security apparently is.[6] A memorandum of the deposit of title deeds as security for borrowings has been held not to be a debenture since it contains no acknowledgement of the debt or a covenant to pay.[7] Where the mortgagor is a company the debenture will normally contain a fixed charge on the company's land and a floating charge on its other assets.

1. Debenture Stock

Debenture stock, if issued by a company, can (unless the articles of the associa- **11–02** tion provide to the contrary) be transferred in such amounts as the transferor wishes. A debenture on the other hand, is indivisible and cannot be sub-divided in this manner. Debenture stock is thus more flexible and more likely to be held by trustees under a deed.[7a]

---

[1] See *The British India Steam Navigation Company v. IRC* (1881) 7 Q.B.D. 165 at 168 and 172; *Levy v. Abercorris Slate and Slab Company* (1887) 37 Ch.D. 260 at 264; *Knightsbridge Estates Trust Limited v. Byrne* [1940] A.C. 613 at 621; *NV Slavenburg's Bank v. Intercontinental Limited* [1980] 1 All E.R. 955 at 976.

[2] *Levy v. Abercorris Slate and Slab Company ante* at 264.

[3] *Edmonds v. Blaina Furnaces Company* (1887) 36 Ch.D. 215; *Lemon v. Austin Friars Investment Trust Limited* [1926] Ch. 1.

[4] *Wylie v. Carlyon* [1922] 1 Ch. 51.

[5] *Knightsbridge Estates Trust Limited, ante* although it can and is a debenture within the statutory definition provided by the Companies Act 1985, s.744.

[6] *National Provincial Bank of England Limited v. The United Electric Theatres Limited* [1916] 1 Ch. 132.

[7] *Topham v. Greenside Glazed Firebrick Company* (1887) 37 Ch.D. 281.

[7a] See *post* para. 11–06.

2. **Statutory meaning of "debenture"**

11–03   Section 744 of the Companies Act 1985 defines "debenture" as including "debenture stocks, bonds and any other securities of a company, whether constituting a charge on the assets of the company or not". Accordingly, the statutory definition is broader than the common law definition. Whether a borrowing or a particular document relating to any borrowing by a company constitutes a "debenture" is important since a number of provisions within the Companies Act 1985 relate to debentures.[8] By reason of section 17 of the Bills of Sale Act (1878) Amendment Act 1882 (which exempts debentures from the ambit of the Act) and Schedule 1 to the Stamp Act 1891[9] (which dealt with stamp duties on any mortgage, bond debenture or covenant except a marketable security otherwise specially charged with duty), there have been many cases on the question of whether a particular document is a debenture. From these, the following principles have emerged:

A document issued by a company which acknowledges a debt may be a debenture whether or not:

(1) it purports to be a debenture[10];
(2) it is under seal[11];
(3) it is one of a series[12];
(4) it is secured by any charge on any property of the company.[13]

3. **Form**

As with a mortgage, it is substance, not form, that determines the nature of the document. Since any document in writing, except a bank note, containing a promise to pay, is a promissory note, the distinction between debentures and promissory notes is not clear and the nature of the document may have to be decided on the basis of inferences from surrounding circumstances.[14]

It is not necessary for a debenture to be issued under the company's seal, though it is usual. It is not clear whether the holders of a debenture issued under seal have the powers of sale of a mortgagee by deed under the Law of Property Act 1925, section 101. In *Blaker* v. *Herts and Essex Waterworks Company*[15] it

---

[8] In particular s.185 (a duty of a company as to issue of certificates); s.190 (register of debenture holders); s.191 (right to inspect register); s.192 (liability of trustees of debentures); s.193 (perpetual debentures); s.194 (power to reissue redeemed debentures); s.195 (contract to subscribe the debentures); s.238 (persons entitled to receive copies of accounts and reports); s.239 (right to demand copies of accounts and reports); s.323 (prohibition on directors dealing and share options); s.324 (duty of a director to disclose shareholdings in own company); s.325 (register of directors' interest notified under s.324) and, perhaps most importantly, ss.396 and 397 which require registration of certain charges, both fixed and floating.

[9] Now repealed by the Finance Act 1999 in relation to instruments executed after September 30, 1999.

[10] *Edmonds v. Blaina Furnaces Co.* [1887] 36 Ch.D. 215; *Lemon v. Austin Friars Investment Trust Ltd.* [1926] 1 Ch. 1.

[11] *British India Steam Navigation Co. v. I.R.C.* (1881) 7 Q.B.D. 165.

[12] *Levy v. Abercorris Slate and Slab Co.* [1887] 37 Ch.D. 260.

[13] *ibid.* See also *Speyer Bros. v. I.R.C.* [1908] A.C. 92.

[14] *British India Steam Navigation Co. v. I.R.C., supra.*

[15] (1889) 41 Ch.D. 399. But see *post* para. 16.57, n. 18.

was held that they did not. However all the cases which follow that decision deal with the right to sell where the property of the company has been acquired under statutory powers for public purposes.

The debenture usually contains a covenant by the company to pay a specified sum, at some specified place, to the registered holder or to a person named. The covenant also provides that payment should be made on a specified date or on the earlier occurrence of certain events, including:

(1) default in payment of interest;
(2) making of an effective order or the passing of a resolution for the winding up of the company.

It is also usual to provide for the appointment of a receiver in the event of either occurrence. Further, a covenant to pay interest in the meantime at a specified rate is usually included.   **11–04**

A debenture need not, but usually does, embody a charge. Sometimes there is a fixed charge on the company's land, and commonly there is a floating charge on the company's undertaking and all its property, present or future. If a certain class of assets is excepted, the exception applies to those assets from time to time, not merely those in existence at the date of the debenture.[16] All debentures to secure bank and other institutional lending are expressed to be payable on demand. There is sometimes a side letter which restricts the lender from making a demand except in specified circumstances.

Although it can be a single instrument, it is often one of a series. If that is so, it will be stated in the conditions endorsed thereon or annexed thereto, which may also state that all debentures in a series are to rank *pari passu*[17] as a charge of a specified priority.

Conditions also regulate the holding of meetings of debenture-holders and the validity of resolutions passed so as to bind a dissentient minority.[18] The power to pass resolutions affecting minority rights must be exercised by the majority for the benefit of the class as a whole.

Debentures may be issued as payable to registered holder, or to bearer, or to registered holder with interest coupons payable to bearer, or to bearer but with power for the bearer to have them placed on a register and to have them withdrawn.[19] When a debenture is made payable to its bearer, interest coupons are attached. The principal is payable on presentation of the debenture and the interest on delivery of the coupons. Where it is payable to the registered holder, only he can receive the principal or interest unless the debenture is issued with coupons payable to bearer.

A bearer debenture is a negotiable instrument transferable by delivery[20] and a holder in due course obtains title to it free from equities and from defects in the title of the transferor. Thus it has been held that a holder in due course may demand payment of the principal secured by a bearer debenture which was

[16] *Imperial Paper Mills of Canada v. Quebec Bank* (1913) 83 L.J.P.C. 67.
[17] *Re Mersey Rly. Co.* [1895] 2 Ch. 287.
[18] *British American Nickel Corporation Ltd. v. O'Brien* [1927] A.C. 369.
[19] See Palmer, *Company Law* (25th ed., 1992), Chap. 13.
[20] *Edelstein v. Schuler & Co.* [1902] 2 K.B. 144.

stolen, or obtained by fraud, or for which the consideration has totally or partially failed.[21]

SECURITY OF DEBENTURES

1. **Trust deeds**

11–06 Commercial reality dictates that a debenture is secured on the assets of the company, not least because secured creditors enjoy priority in the event of an insolvent liquidation. It is usual (particularly in case of large scale borrowing from a number of individuals or the general public) to secure debentures by a security vested in trustees for the debenture holders, rather than in the debenture holders themselves. Where a loan is short term or from a bank, a declaration of trust is often dispensed with. The debenture trustee is often a trust corporation. If this is not the case and there is a legal mortgage of the company's realty, the legal estate therein may not be vested in more than four persons. The trustees are under an express duty to protect the interests of the debenture holders and the vesting of the security in them greatly simplifies any common action on the part of the debenture holders, particularly the realisation of the security. The trust deed empowers the trustees to appoint a receiver and manager, or to enter and realise the security, in the event of the debenture becoming enforceable. Typically, it will contain a covenant for the repayment of the principal on a fixed date, or on the earlier occurrence of certain events (default in payment; winding up, etc.) and to pay interest meanwhile at a specified rate. It will impose a specific charge on the company's realty and a floating charge over all the company's other assets.

The deed will also regulate how the beneficiaries behind the trust can, in certain circumstances, require the trustees to sell the mortgaged property or amend the beneficiaries' rights or a certain class of those beneficiaries. Usually a large majority is required in order for these rights to be exercised. The beneficiaries may, when casting their votes do so entirely in their own interests provided the whole scheme is fair[22]; secret agreements to acquire the majority of votes are offensive.[23] Unless the deed so provides, the court retains its right to sanction a compromise or arrangement under section 425 of the Companies Act 1985.

It should also provide for the remuneration of the trustees, who should not have any interest which conflicts with their duties as trustees; hence a debenture trustee should not be a shareholder. The remuneration is not payable in priority to the claims of stockholders, unless the trust deed expressly so provides.[24]

---

[21] *Bechuanaland Exploration Co. v. London Trading Bank* [1898] 2 Q.B. 658.
[22] *Goodfellow v. Nelson Line Limited* [1912] 2 Ch. 324.
[23] *British America Nickel Corporation v. O'Brien* [1922] A.C. 369.
[24] *Hodgson v. Accles* (1902) 51 W.R. 57.

(a) *Trustees' Liability*

By section 192(1) of the Companies Act 1985, any provision contained:

(1) in a trust deed for securing an issue of debentures;
(2) in any contract with the holder of debentures secured by a trust deed;

is void in so far as it would have the effect of exempting a trustee of the deed from, or indemnifying him against, liability for breach of trust where he fails to show the degree of care and diligence required of him as a trustee, having regard to the provisions of the trust deed conferring on him any powers, authorities or discretions.

Section 192(2) permits certain subsequent releases and the remainder of the section deprives the earlier sub-section of retrospective effect. A debenture trustee may, however, be protected by sections 30 and 61 of the Trustee Act 1925.

(b) *Stock Exchange requirements*

The Listing Rules of the London Stock Exchange require trust deeds to contain **11–07** a number of provisions designed to protect debenture holders. These principally concern a number of provisions determining voting rights.[25]

IRREDEEMABLE DEBENTURES

Unlike a mortgage, a debenture can be irredeemable or be stated to be redeem- **11–08** able on the happening of a specified event, however remote, or on the expiration of any period, however long.[26] Otherwise, the rules concerning collateral advantages and clogs on the equity of redemption are of general application.

ISSUE OF DEBENTURES

1. **The company's authority**

A company's powers of borrowing are discussed elsewhere in this work.[27] The **11–09** same considerations regulate a company's power to provide guarantees and to give security. Accordingly, with effect from February 4, 1991, a company's capacity to borrow is not affected by anything in its memorandum of association. Furthermore, those dealing with the company are not bound to enquire whether any transactions are permitted by the company's memorandum or as to any limitation on the powers of the board of directors to bind the company or authorise others to do so.[28]

---

[25] See *Palmer Company Law* (25th ed., 1992), Chap. 13, app. 2.
[26] Companies Act 1985, s.193.
[27] See paras 15–43 *et seq., post.*
[28] Companies Act 1985, s.35B.

2. **Statutory regulation with regard to debentures**

11–10   There are a number of statutory provisions which regulate the issue of debentures:

(1) Financial Services Act 1986 regulates the listing particulars and prospectuses which may be issued or made for the purpose of offering debentures, unless the Act provides that they should apply to shares only.[29]

(2) Companies Act 1985, section 194 provides that unless the company's articles provide to the contrary (or any contract entered into by the company so provides), it may re-issue any debentures previously redeemed. A resolution or other act which manifests an intention that the debentures that have been redeemed should be cancelled will preclude the section from operating.[30]

(3) Government regulations: formerly the issue of every type of debenture, whether registered or not was governed by the Exchange Control Act 1947 and the Borrowing (Control and Guarantees) Act 1946 and the regulations made under those Acts. The former Act is in abeyance and the latter Act was repealed on February 11, 1991 by the Government Trading Act 1990.

(4) Stock Exchange Requirements: if the debentures are to be listed on the stock exchange, the Listing Rules of the London Stock Exchange must be complied with.

3. **Issue at a discount**

11–11   Subject to any provision to the contrary in the company's articles or its memorandum of association, debentures may be issued at a discount.[31] The statutory provisions[32] which preclude the issue of shares at a discount have no application to debentures or debenture stock. However, the issue of discounted debentures or debenture stock cannot be used as an alternative method to circumvent the provisions precluding the issue of shares at a discount[33] by, for example, permitting the discounted debenture to be converted into shares at par.

4. **Irregular issues**

11–12   An irregular issue of debentures is capable of being ratified and, in any event, debentures so issued may be enforced as agreements to issue debentures.[34]

---

[29] See *Palmer's Company Law* (25th ed.), para. 5.401.
[30] Companies Act 1985, s.194(1).
[31] *Re Anglo-Danubian Steam Navigation and Colliery Co* (1875) L.R. 20 Eq. 339.
[32] Companies Act 1985, s.100.
[33] *Mosely v. Koffyfontein Mines Limited* [1904] 2 Ch. 108.
[34] *Re Fireproof Doors* [1916] 2 Ch 142; *cf. Re Anchor Line (Henderson Brothers) Limited* [1937] Ch. 483.

5. **Agreements to issue**

Where monies are advanced to a company upon terms that the company will **11–13** issue debentures securing the advance on the undertaking of the company or upon any specified property of the company, an equitable charge is created.[35] However, an equitable charge must be registered pursuant to section 395 of the Companies Act 1985[36] and a failure to comply with the requirements for timeous registration would have the consequences prescribed by that section.

6. **Specific performance**

A contract with a company to take up and pay for debentures of the company **11–14** may be enforced by an order for specific performance.[37] This right is lost if the company has forfeited the debentures in question.[38] Furthermore the company is unable to recover monies unpaid prior to forfeiture since the same do not constitute a debt.[39]

TRANSFER OF DEBENTURES

1. **Form and effect of transfer**

A debenture payable to bearer is transferable by delivery.[40] A debenture to a **11–15** registered holder is transferable in the manner specified therein, subject to the provisions of section 183 of the Companies Act 1985. Section 183 (1) states that:

> "it is not lawful for a company to register a transfer of shares in or debentures of the company unless a proper instrument of transfer has been delivered to it, or the transfer is an exempt transfer within the Stock Transfer Act 1982 or is in accordance with regulations made under 207 of the Companies Act 1989".

This applies notwithstanding anything in the company's articles.[41] Thus it is necessary for the transfer to be effected in writing and, in the case of fully paid registered debentures, the form prescribed by the Stock Transfer Act 1963[42] may be used. The transfer is taken or sent to the office of the company in order that the name of the transferee may be entered into the company's register of members.[43] If a company refuses to register a transfer, it must within two months

---

[35] *Levy v. Abercorris Slate Company* (1887) 37 Ch.D. 260 at 265; *Tailby v. Official Receiver* (1888) 13 App. Cas. 523.
[36] As to registration, see *post.* para. 11–26.
[37] Companies Act 1985, s.195.
[38] *Kuala Pahi Estate v. Mobury* (1914) 111 L.T.1072.
[39] *South African Territories v. Wallington* [1898] A.C. 309 at 315.
[40] *Edelstein v. Schuler & Co.* [1902] 2 K.B. 144.
[41] Companies Act 1985, s.183(1).
[42] As amended: S.I. 1996 No. 1571.
[43] Companies Act 1985, s.183(4).

after the date on which the transfer was lodged with it, send to the transferee notice of its refusal.[44] Section 184 of the Companies Act (certification of transfers) and section 185 (company's duty to issue certificates) apply.

2. Fraudulent Transfers

11–16 Where a transfer is forged and registered by the company, the company may incur a liability since the registration will not defeat the title of the true owner, who retains a right to require the company to restore his name to the register.[45] The company may, if it discovers that the transfer is a forgery, remove the name of the transferee from the register since no estoppel arises by reason of that registration.[46] However, if the company has issued a certificate to the transferee and a bona fide third party has acted in reliance thereon, the company may be liable in damages.[47]

In the event that the transfer is forged and the transfer effected by the company, the company may not be without remedy itself. A person who procures his registration by the production of a forged instrument of transfer is bound to indemnify the company from its liability to the victim of the transaction even though he acted in good faith.[48] This principle is not limited to a person acting on his own behalf; where a firm of stockbrokers innocently presented a forged transfer for registration, they were held liable to indemnify the company.[49] In order to minimise the danger attendant on the registration of transfers, some companies have adopted the practice of writing to the transferor upon receipt of the deposit of a transfer informing him of that fact and stating that it will be registered unless, by return of post or within a specified period, he objects. Whilst this course will not relieve a company of its obligation to ascertain the authenticity of any deposited transfer it does, in practice, operate as an effective safeguard.

The Nature of the Security: Fixed and Floating Charges

11–17 A debenture which simply created a specific charge over the property of the company (whether stock in trade or realty) would have the same effect as an ordinary mortgage, being immediately effective and binding on the mortgaged property in the hands of any third party taking it from the company. If the debenture were by deed, the debenture holder would have a statutory power of sale and foreclosure in respect of the property specifically charged. For obvious reasons, such a form of security taken over the assets and stock of a trading company would be commercially unacceptable. Accordingly the nature of the security bestowed by debentures has evolved into two classes, namely "fixed" and "floating" charges. The former operates as an ordinary mortgage and affects

---

[44] Companies Act 1985, s.183(5).
[45] *Davis v. Bank of England* (1824) 2 Bing. 393; *Barton v. L. & N.W. Rly* (1888) 38 Ch.D. 144 at 149.
[46] *Simm v. Anglo-American Co.* [1879] 5 Q.B.D. 188 at 214.
[47] *Bloomenthal v. Ford* [1897] A.C. 156.
[48] *Sheffield Corporation v. Barclay* [1905] A.C. 392; *Welsh v. Bank of England* [1955] Ch. 508.
[49] *Yeung v. Hong Kong & Shanghai Banking Corporation* [1980] 2 All E.R. 599.

the title to the property; the company can only deal with that property so charged in accordance with the terms of the agreement and subject to the fixed charge. A "floating" charge is one which enables the company to deal with the property subject to that charge in the ordinary course of its business and is thus able to sell or dispose of those assets free from the floating charge unless and until the floating charge crystallises upon the charged assets.[50]

For practical reasons, it is usual for the debenture to create both a fixed charge   **11–18** over the realty and other immoveable property of the company which is not required for disposal in the ordinary course of the company's trade and a floating charge over the stock-in-trade of the company, its general chattels, book debts and future property, thus maximising the lender's security and preserving the company's ability to trade. The debenture will specify in what circumstances the floating charge may become enforceable and crystallise upon those assets. The events specified usually include liquidation, default in payment of principal or interest for a stated period, or the presentation of a petition, etc. In construing whether a charge is fixed or floating, the courts will lean against treating goods required in the ordinary course of trade as being subject to a fixed charge and where there is an intention that the company should receive and deal with the property charged, it is assumed that only a floating charge is intended.[51] This is so even though the charge is expressed in words which would be sufficient to create a fixed charge.[52]

In *Re Yorkshire Woolcombers' Association*,[53] the Court of Appeal stated that the principle tests to be applied in determining whether a charge was a floating charge were as follows:

(1) Is it a charge upon all of a certain class of assets, present and future?
(2) Will those assets change in the ordinary course of the business of the company?
(3) Is it contemplated that the company will carry on business in the ordinary way with regard to the assets charged?

If the answer to these questions is in the affirmative, the charge has the necessary characteristics of a floating charge. The ability to answer one of the foregoing questions in the affirmative will not of itself convert a fixed charge into a floating charge. In *Re Cimex Tissues*,[54] a debenture expressly created a fixed charge over certain plant and machinery and then permitted the company to dispose of that plant and machinery in the ordinary course of and for the purposes of carrying on its trade in business with the consent of the lender in writing. It was held that such a feature did not turn what was stated to be a fixed charge into a floating charge. The court held that the extent to which a licence to deal with charged

---

[50] *Re Florence Land Company* (1878) 10 Ch.D. 530; *Weekly v. Silkston & Haigh Moor Coal Company* (1885) 29 Ch.D. 715; *Re Hamilton's Windsor Ironworks* (1879) 12 Ch.D. 707; *Re Colonial Trust Corporation* (1879) 15 Ch.D. 465; *Re HH Vivien & Co.* [1900] 2 Ch. 654.
[51] *Government Stock Investment Company v. Manilla Railway* [1897] A.C. 81; *Evans v. Rival Granite Quarries* [1910] 2 K.B. 979; *Illingworth v. Holdsworth* [1904] A.C. 355.
[52] *National Provincial Bank v. United Electric Theatre* [1916] 1 Ch. 132.
[53] In *Re Yorkshire Woolcombers' Association* [1903] 2 Ch. 284; affirmed *sub nom. Illingworth v. Holdsworth* [1904] A.C. 355.
[54] [1995] 1 B.C.L.C. 410.

property was incompatible with a fixed charge depends on all the circumstances of the case and in particular the scope of the licence and the nature of the charged property. The facts of the case were such that the charge was held to be fixed. Ultimately the determination of whether the charge is fixed or floating is a matter of construction of the document in question and, legal impossibility apart, there are no considerations which prevent parties to any debenture from creating whatever type of charge they chose.[55]

BOOK DEBTS

11–19   In the absence of specific definition in the debenture, the description "book debts" does not include credit balances of the company with a bank[56] and perhaps the best definition that can be made of them is that the description embraces all obligations which traders customarily enter into their books, whether or not the obligations are, as a matter of fact, entered into the books of the particular chargor.

A charge over both present and future book debts will be construed as a floating charge notwithstanding that it may be described as a fixed charge.[57] Where dealings with the book debts are subject to restrictions which negate such a finding, the contrary may prevail.[58] In *Re Brightlife Limited*[59] it was held that a restrictive clause which precluded the company from selling factoring or discounting its debts without the written permission of the debenture holder was not inconsistent with the charge being a floating charge since the company was still free to collect its debts and pay the debts into its bank account in the ordinary course of business and that once the monies were in that account they were at the free disposal of the company.[60]

In *Re New Bullas Trading Limited*[61] the debenture was expressed to create a fixed charge over book and other debts owing to the company and to require the company to pay the same when received into a designated account and thereafter only to deal with them in accordance with directions given by the debenture holder. However, in the absence of those directions, the debenture provided that the monies so paid in were to be released from a fixed charge and to be subject to a floating charge. In the absence of any instructions from the debenture holder, the charge was held to have created a fixed charge over the uncollected book debts and a floating charge over their proceeds once collected and paid into the designated account.

---

[55] *Re New Bullas Trading Limited* [1994] 1 B.C.L.C. 485.
[56] *Re Brightlife Limited* [1987] Ch. 200.
[57] *Re Pearl Maintenance Services Limited* [1995] B.C.L.C. 657.
[58] *Siebe Gorman & Co. v. Barclays Bank* [1979] 2 Lloyd's Rep. 142. Notwithstanding an identical provision in a New Zealand debenture, *Siebe Gorman* was not followed by the High Court in that jurisdiction: *Supercool Refrigeration & Air Conditioning v. Hoverd Industries Limited* [1994] 1 N.Z.L.R. 300.
[59] [1987] Ch. 200.
[60] See also *Re Double S Printers Limited (in Liquidation)* [1999] 1 B.C.L.C. 220; *Re Westmaze Limited (in Administrative Receivership)* [1999] B.C.C. 441.
[61] [1994] 1 B.C.L.C. 485.

Whilst a floating charge is a present charge (as opposed to a future one) it does not specifically affect any of the property which is subject to it until an event happens which causes it to crystallise and become a fixed charge.[62]

CRYSTALLISATION OF THE FLOATING CHARGE

A floating charge crystallises or becomes fixed in accordance with the terms of **11–20** the debenture creating it or, for example by the company going into liquidation, whether that liquidation is for the purpose of reconstruction or otherwise.[63] Common prescribed events of crystallisation include the debenture holder taking possession of the company's goods or appointing a receiver in accordance with the terms of the debenture. Crystallisation operates in order to effect an equitable assignment of the assets to the charge holder. However, unless the debenture holder actually takes the necessary steps in accordance with the terms of the debenture to crystallise the charge, the fact that the holder could crystallise the charge if he so wished does not limit the company's ability to deal with the assets subject to the floating charge[64] and to dispose of them free of any charge in the ordinary course of business.

Automatic Crystallisation

For this reason, the modern tendency is for the terms of the debenture to provide **11–21** for automatic crystallisation without any steps being required of the debenture holder in certain specified events. Such events habitually include the creation of second or subsequent charges. Despite longstanding commonwealth authority[65] it was not until relatively recently that the courts within this jurisdiction have expressly accepted that automatic crystallisation clauses are valid.[66] It would seem, with reference to the dicta in those cases, that the efficiency of an automatic crystallisation clause very much depends upon the true construction of its expressed terms.

A right of set-off which has accrued to the company's debtor prior to the crystallisation of the debenture holder's charge can be raised against any claim made by a receiver appointed under the debenture against that debtor.[67] Where the cross-claim was assigned to the debtor after the crystallisation of the charge, it affords no defence.[68] The usual rules concerning the right to set off in cases of an assignment of a chose in action apply. Similarly, where the defence comprises

---

[62] *Evans v. Rival Granite Quarries* [1910] 2 K.B. 979.
[63] *Player v. Crompton & Co.* [1914] 1 Ch. 954. The appointment of a receiver will cause crystallisation (*Re Florence Land & Public Works Co., ex parte Moor* (1878) 10 Ch.D. 530) as does the cessation of business or the company ceasing to be a going concern: *Re Woodroffes (Musical Instruments) Limited* [1986] Ch. 366.
[64] *Evans v. Rival Granite Quarries* [1910] 2 K.B. 979 at 986.
[65] *Re Manurewa Transport Limited* [1971] N.Z.L.R. 909.
[66] *Re Brightlife Limited* [1987] Ch. 200; *Re Permanent Houses (Holdings) Limited* [1988] B.C.L.C. 563 see generally *Palmer's Company Law* (25th ed.), para. 13.129 ff; *Griffiths v. Yorkshire Bank Plc* [1994] 1 W.L.R. 1427.
[67] *Rother Ironworks Limited v. Canterbury Precision Engineers Limited* [1974] Q.B. 1.
[68] *Robbie v. Witney Warehouse Co. Limited* [1963] 1 W.L.R. 1324.

a claim for damages by reason of the receiver's repudiation of a contract, the debtor cannot set those damages off against the debt.[69]

PRIORITY OF DEBENTURES

11–22   The priority of debenture holders depends on a number of factors which include:

(1) The true construction of the instrument or instruments creating the charge.

(2) The status of the debenture as part of a series of debentures which may give rise to the presumption of equality.

(3) The nature of the charge created and the order of creation. A legal charge has priority over an equitable charge and, as between equitable chargees, the first in time has priority over latter charges.

(4) The registration or non-registration of the charge pursuant to section 395 of the Companies Act 1985. A failure to comply with the registration requirements imposed by that Act renders the charge void as against creditors, administrators and liquidators of the company[70] although it remains good against the company itself.

1. Presumption Of Equality

11–23   Debentures created as part of the same series are usually expressed to rank *pari passu inter se*. In the absence of such an express statement, the courts will readily infer equality. In such circumstances, whether the equality is express or implied, an individual debenture holder will not be permitted to obtain an advantage over his co-debenture holders. Thus any judgment that a debenture holder obtains, inures for the benefit of all the debenture holders of that particular class[71] and any collateral security that he may obtain is held by him on trust for those individuals.[72]

Where a number of series of debentures creating floating charges are issued, they rank according to the date of issue unless otherwise expressly provided for.[73] Thus, having issued a series of debentures, the company is precluded from issuing a subsequent series of debentures that rank equally with the first series unless the express terms of the first series of debentures expressly or impliedly so provide.[74] If the terms of the first series merely reserves to the company a power to create subsequent mortgages, that will not suffice for this purpose.[75]

---

[69] *Business Computers Limited v. Anglo-African Leasing Limited* [1977] 1 W.L.R. 578.
[70] See *post* para. 11–27.
[71] *Bowen v. Brecon Railway* (1867) L.R. 3 Eq. 541.
[72] *Small v. Smith* (1884) 10 App. Cas. 119.
[73] *Gartside v. Silkstone Coal Co.* (1882) 21 Ch.D. 762.
[74] *ibid.*
[75] *Re Benjamin Cope & Son* [1914] 1 Ch. 800.

2. **Reissue Of Redeemed Debentures: Companies Act 1985, s. 194**

If a company reissues redeemed debentures, the person entitled to the debentures **11–24** has, and is always deemed to have had, the same priority as if the debentures had never been redeemed.[76] This is subject to provisions to the contrary in the company's articles of association or in any contract entered into by the company or any resolution of the company or any other act of the company manifesting an intention that the redeemed debentures should be cancelled.[77]

3. **Charges of Specific Property**

Where a company creates a charge on specific property, it will rank ahead of any **11–25** subsequent charge which embraces the same property by reason of the principle that where the equities are equal, the first in time shall prevail. A later fixed charge will take priority over a floating charge if the latter has not crystallised and the former is created by the company in the ordinary course of business.

Where a subsequent chargee obtains a legal mortgage, he will obtain priority over the first equitable charge.[78] Where a specific charge is assigned, the rule that the first in time prevails is displaced by the rule in *Dearle v. Hall*[79] which provides that the first assignee to give notice to the debtor is accorded priority over prior assignees provided that the assignee giving notice did not have notice of the earlier assignment.[80]

4. **Priority And Postponement Agreements**

There is no reason why a specific chargee cannot acquire or postpone the priority of that charge by agreement.

5. **Floating Charges**

A debenture which imposes a floating charge on property will be postponed to a subsequent fixed mortgage created by the company in the ordinary course of its business because the floating charge, being a floating security, will permit the company to create charges in priority to it in the ordinary course of its business. This is so whether there is a prohibition on the creation of subsequent charges within the debenture or not. If there is no prohibition, the company can always create a subsequent specific charge. If there is a prohibition, the subsequent specific chargee may obtain priority for various reasons such as the fact that he obtains the legal estate or he has a better equity.[81] The position will be otherwise

---

[76] Companies Act 1985, s.194(2).
[77] Companies Act 1985, s.194(1).
[78] *Pilcher v. Rawlins* (1872) 7 Ch. App. 259.
[79] (1828) 3 Rush 1.
[80] *Gorringe v. Irwell India Rubberworks* (1886) 34 Ch.D. 128.
[81] *Re Valletort Sanitary Steam Laundry* [1903] 2 Ch. 654.

if the subsequent specific chargee had actual knowledge or notice of the restrictive clause. In such circumstances his charge will be postponed to the prior charge.[82]

As indicated above, where there are successive floating charges, the first in time will prevail subject to express agreement to the contrary unless they are part of the same issue of debentures. It would seem that where a second floating charge crystallises prior to an earlier floating charge, the second charge will take priority over the first.[83]

6. Preferential Creditors

Sections 175 and 386 and Schedule 6 to the Insolvency Act 1986 bestow priority on preferential creditors over a debenture holder whose security was, at the time it was created, a floating charge. In addition, the costs and expenses of the winding up also enjoy that priority.[84]

Where a receiver is appointed by debenture holders whose charge was, when created, a floating charge and the company is not in the course of being wound up, its preferential debts are required to be paid out of the assets coming into the hands of the receiver in priority to the debenture holder's claim and any payments so made shall be re-couped by the debenture holder from the assets available for the payment of the company's general creditors.[85] The priority so accorded only applies to those preferential claims that have accrued prior to the crystallisation of the charge.[86]

7. Liens

If the goods upon which a bailee claims a general lien came into his possession prior to the crystallisation of the charge, a general lien will prevail over that floating charge. Moreover if they have come into his possession after the crystallisation of the charge but pursuant to a contract entered into before the charge crystallised, the lien will still prevail.[87] A lawful possessory lien is also good against the owner or secured creditor even if the bailment is in breach of the agreement whereby a special lien is created by operation of law.[88]

---

[82] See *post* para 11–28A.
[83] *Griffiths v. Yorkshire Bank Plc* [1994] 1 W.L.R. 1427; this decision was made without reference to *Re Woodroffes (Musical Instruments) Limited* [1986] Ch. 366 where it was held that a first floating charge enjoyed priority to a second floating charge which had crystallised.
[84] *Re Barleycorn Enterprises Limited* [1970] Ch. 465.
[85] Insolvency Act 1986, s.40.
[86] *Re Christonette International Limited* [1982] 1 W.L.R. 1245. The section does not apply to fixed charges (*Re Lewis Merthyr Consolidated Collieries Limited* [1929] 1 Ch. 498) or where there are fixed and floating charges and a receiver is appointed and sells under section 101 of the Law of Property Act 1925 and who has a surplus under section 105 of that Act: *Re G. L. Saunders Limited* [1986] 1 W.L.R. 215.
[87] *George Barker (Transport) Limited v. Eynon* [1974] 1 W.L.R. 462.
[88] *Tappenden v. Artus* [1964] 2 Q.B. 185.

REGISTRATION OF CHARGES

The question of the registration of company charges is governed by two sets of **11–26**
statutory provisions. The first are those which provide for all charges affecting
the property of a particular company to be kept in a register of charges at the
company's registered office. These provisions are contained in sections 406 to
408 of the Companies Act 1985 and are self-explanatory. They require the
company to keep, at its registered office, a register of all charges affecting its
property (whether fixed or floating charges) together with a brief description of
the asset or property charged, the amount of the sum so secured and the name(s)
of the person(s) entitled to the benefit of the charge. This register is open to
inspection by members and creditors without charge and by members of the
public on the payment of a modest charge.[89] The second, and by far the most
important set of provisions, are those contained in sections 395 to 405 of the
Companies Act 1985 and which require registration of certain charges at Companies House.

Registration Pursuant to section 395 of the Companies Act 1985

Section 395 of the Companies Act provides: **11–27**

"(1) Subject to provisions of this chapter [*i.e.* sections 395 to 409] a charge
created by a company registered in England and Wales and being a charge
to which the section applies is, so far as any security on the company's
property or undertaking is conferred by the charge, void against the liquidator or administrator and any creditor of the company, unless the prescribed particulars of the charge together with the instrument (if any), by
which the charge is created or evidenced, are delivered to or received by the
Registrar of Companies for registration in the manner required by this
chapter within 21 days after the date of the charge's creation.
(2) Sub-section (1) is without prejudice to any contract or obligation for
repayment of the monies secured by the charge; and when a charge becomes
void under this section, the monies secured by it immediately become
payable."

Section 396 of the Companies Act 1985[90] applies section 395 to the following
charges:

"(a)   A charge for the purpose of securing any issue of debentures,
 (b)   A charge on uncalled share capital of the company,
 (c)   A charge created or evidenced by an instrument which, if executed by
       an individual, would require registration as a bill of sale,
 (d)   A charge on land (wherever situated) or any interest in it, but not
       including a charge for any rent or other periodical sum issuing out of
       the land,

---

[89] Companies Act 1985, ss.407, 408.
[90] As amended by the Copyright, Designs and Patents Act 1988 and the Trade Marks Act 1994.

(e) A charge on book debts of the company,

(f) A floating charge on the company's undertaking or property,

(g) A charge on calls made but not paid,

(h) A charge on a ship or aircraft or any share in a ship,

(i) A charge on goodwill or on any intellectual property."

A "charge" includes a mortgage.[91] It is immaterial what form the charge takes. It can (subject to the relevant statutory provisions which regulate certain formalities depending on the nature of property over which security is given[92]) be by deed or simply in writing or created orally. The circumstances which give rise to the obligation to register are (i) its creation by a company registered in England and Wales and (ii) its nature as a charge to which section 395 applies. Thus a lien which arises by operation of law, *e.g.* a solicitor's lien or an unpaid vendor's lien is not created by the company for the purposes of the Companies Act 1985 and does not require to be registered.[93] A general lien gives a more extensive possessory right than a special lien but since the same still amounts to a possessory right, it should not fall to be treated as a charge.[94]

In determining whether a transaction gives rise to a charge which falls to be registered under the Companies Act 1985, the courts will look to substance rather than form. The hallmark of a charge or mortgage are (1) the mortgagor's right to redeem his property by paying off the mortgagee; (2) a liability on behalf of the mortgagor to indemnify the mortgagee in the event of a shortfall between the value of any security given and the amount borrowed and (3) the mortgagor's entitlement to recover any surplus left in the mortgagee's hands in the event of a sale of the property which secures the indebtedness at a price in excess of the sum borrowed.[95]

An agreement which creates an equitable interest in the security should be registered as should any agreement to create a mortgage in the future[96] since equity will look on that as done which ought to be done.

1. Rectification of the Register and extension of time for registration

11–28 The court has power to rectify the register and to extend time for the registration of a charge under section 404 of the Companies Act 1985.[97]

---

[91] Companies Act 1985, s.396(4).

[92] *e.g.* Law of Property (Miscellaneous Provisions) Act 1989, s.2.

[93] *London & Cheshire Insurance Co. Limited v. Laplagrene Property Co. Limited* [1971] Ch. 499. The point was, however, left open in *Burston Finance v. Speirway Limited* [1974] 3 All E.R. 735.

[94] A lien with a power of sale contractually attached to it was held not to be a charge in *Re Hamlet International plc* [1998] 2 B.C.L.C. 164; *cf. Re Coslett (Contractors) Limited* [1997] 4 All E.R. 114, where a site owner's power of sale of a contractor's plant was held to be security by way of charge. See also Pickin (1998) 11 Insolvency Intelligence 60.

[95] *Re Curtaindream Plc* [1990] B.C.L.C. 925.

[96] *Levy v. Abercorris Slate Co.* (1887) 37 Ch.D. 260.

[97] See generally *Palmer's Company Law* (25th ed.), para. 13.334.

2. **The effect of registration under the Companies Act 1985 on priorities**

The normal rules of priority as between legal and equitable charges continue to **11–28A** apply. A legal mortgage will prevail over an equitable one unless the legal mortgage had notice of the equitable mortgage. With regard to determining priority between competing legal mortgages and equitable mortgages *inter se*, the first in time prevails.

Registration pursuant to the Companies Act 1985 affects this position only insofar as it invalidates an unregistered charge which should otherwise be registered and insofar as it amounts to notice of any prior charge. Obviously a subsequent chargee who has searched the register and who knows of the charge has notice and is bound thereby. It has also been held that a subsequent chargee has constructive notice of matters entered on the register.[98] Historically, this has not extended to the terms of the charge[99] but in the case of floating charges which preclude the creation of subsequent fixed charges, the modern practice is to include that prohibition expressly on the register. It would appear that this would amount to constructive notice, although the point has yet to be decided.

DEBENTURES OVER LAND

Any legal or equitable charge on land is clearly registrable if created by a **11–29** company registered in England or Wales. An equitable charge by deposit of deeds is registrable[1] although not now capable of valid creation.[2] In circumstances where the charge is secured on land, the normal considerations relating to registration apply.

1. **Unregistered Land**

By section 3(7) of the Land Charges Act 1972, all land charges for securing **11–30** money, *other than floating charges*[3] created on or after January 1, 1970, must be registered, if registrable as land charges, at the Land Charges Regsitry. Floating charges can be registered only at the Companies Registry.

Further, section 198(1) of the Law of Property Act 1925[4] provides that the registration of any instrument or matter under the Land Charges Act 1972, or any enactment which it replaces, in any register kept at the Land Registry of elsewhere, "shall be deemed to constitute actual notice . . . to all persons and for all purposes connected with the land affected". It therefore follows that registration at the Land Registry is notice of fixed charges on land, but since floating charges cannot be so registered, there is no deemed actual notice of them.

---

[98] *Wilson v. Kelland* [1910] 2 Ch. 306.
[99] *ibid.*
[1] *Re Wallis and Simmonds Builders Ltd* [1974] Q.B. 94.
[2] Since it would fail to comply with Law of Property (Miscellaneous Provisions) Act 1989, s.2; *United Bank of Kuwait Plc v. Sahib* [1991] Ch. 107. See generally paras 5–07 *et seq., ante.*
[3] Described in *Government Stock and other Securities Investment Co. v. Manila Rly Co.* [1897] A.C. 81; *Evans v. Rival Granite Quarries Ltd* [1910] 2 K.B. 979, CA.
[4] As amended by the LPA 1969, ss.24(1), 25(2).

If a charge on unregistered land is registered under the Land Charges Act 1972 but not under section 395 of the Companies Act, a mortgagee takes free of it since he is a creditor for the purpose of section 395, but a purchaser other than a mortgagee is bound by it.

2. **Registered Land**

11–31 Where a company registered in England or Wales created a charge on registered land,[5] a purchaser will not be bound by the charge, even though it is registered at the Companies Registry, unless it is registered or protected on the register of title; this applies to both fixed and floating charges. If a debenture trust deed contains a specific charge capable of taking effect as a legal charge, it can be entered on the register as a registered charge. If it contains a floating charge, it can be protected by notice or caution, depending on whether the land certificate can or cannot be produced.

Prospective charges or mortgages of a company should always ascertain whether winding up procedures have commenced. Further, section 127 of the Insolvency Act 1986 provides that in a winding up by the court, any disposition of the company's property is void unless the court orders otherwise. If the land is subject to a floating charge, the charge will crystallise and although the company can convey land which is subject to a floating charge without the concurrence of the chargee, the purchaser is entitled to evidence of non-crystallisation. A certificate from either an officer of the company or, preferably, from the chargee should be obtained. By section 45(4)(b) of the Law of Property Act 1925, the purchaser must bear the expense of obtaining it. If the charge has crystallised, the chargee must join in the conveyance.

AVOIDANCE OF CHARGES[6]

11–32 Any charge created by a company at "a relevant time"[7] may fall to be challenged under the provisions of section 238 (transactions at an undervalue), section 239 (preferences) or section 245 (avoidance of floating charges) of the Insolvency Act 1986. In addition, section 244 of that Act permits the court to set aside or vary the terms of an extortionate transaction and section 423 enables the court to set aside a transaction which defraud creditors.

REMEDIES OF DEBENTURE HOLDERS

The debenture will contain provisions as to the circumstances when the borrower is in default. In such circumstances, the debenture holder can (subject to any consents required under a trust deed, if any) take steps to protect his position.

---

[5] When such a charge is created, a certificate of registration under s.395 of the Companies Act 1985 should be lodged with application. If this is not done, a note is made on the register that the charge is subject to the provisions of that section: Land Registration Rules 1925 (as amended), r. 145.

[6] A detailed discussion of this aspect is outside the scope of this work. See generally *Palmer's Company Law* (25th ed.), paras 15.447—15.455/2.

[7] For preferences and transaction at an undervalue, see Insolvency Act 1986, s.240; for the avoidance of floating charges see Insolvency Act 1986, s.245.

1. Unsecured debentures

If the debenture is not secured against any of the assets of the company, the debenture holder is confined to the usual steps that may be taken against a recalcitrant debtor: he can commence proceedings and levy execution of any judgment, petition for the administration of the company or for its winding up. If the debenture is held by trustees, they alone (subject to the terms of the trust) can commence proceedings. If they refuse, the aggrieved party will have to commence proceedings for the enforcement of the trust in question.

2. Secured debentures

A well-drafted debenture will provide expressly for the debenture holder's remedies in the event of default and usually permit the appointment of a receiver to sell the property of the company. Otherwise, the debenture holder is faced with a choice of four remedies: (1) a debenture holder's action; (2) the appointment of a receiver; (3) foreclosure or (4) the winding-up of the company.

(a) *A debenture holder's action*

Subject to compliance with the terms of the debenture, a debenture holder may **11–33** commence proceedings on his own behalf and on behalf of any other holders of the same class of debentures[8] in order to claim the repayment of monies owed or to enforce his security. If the consent of the majority is required and they decline by reason of some special interest adverse to the general interest of the class, the court will intervene and not permit them to benefit at the expense of the minority.[9] The court will regulate the conduct of the action and where a claimant has interests adverse to the other debenture holders, the court may order the substitution of the claimant with another member of the class.[10] Leave to commence such an action is necessary in the event that the winding up has commenced but this is given as of course.[11]

(b) *Receiver*

A receiver and manager can be appointed by the Court pursuant to its statutory jurisdiction[12] or pursuant to the terms of the debenture. A receiver's duty is to take possession of and protect the company's property. A receiver and manager has power to carry on the company's business.

---

[8] CPR 19.6.
[9] *Mercantile Investment & General Trust Co. v. River Plate Trust, Loan & Agency Co.* [1894] 1 Ch. 578.
[10] *Re Services Club Estate Syndicate Limited* [1930] 1 Ch. 78.
[11] *Re Joshua Stubbs Limited* [1891] 1 Ch. 475.
[12] Supreme Court Act 1981, s.37.

(c) *Foreclosure*

This remedy is occasionally available in debenture holders' actions[13] but is often seen as impracticable by reason of the fact that all debenture holders and the company must be parties to such a claim and, where the claim is by a legal mortgagee, any subsequent mortgagee must also be a party.[14] If the property has been conveyed to trustees on trust for sale, the remedy is not available.[15]

(d) *Winding-up*

The appointment of a receiver does not preclude the winding up of the company[16] and a debenture holder who seeks the winding up of the company is not bound to forsake his security.[17] A debenture holder can petition as a contingent or prospective creditor pursuant to section 124 of the Insolvency Act 1986. A debenture holder who is only a trustee cannot, it appears, petition to wind up the company.[18]

---

[13] *Sadler v. Worley* [1894] 2 Ch. 170.
[14] *Luke v. South Kensington Hotel Co.* (1879) 11 Ch.D. 121. This is so even if the subsequent mortgagee has only a floating charge: *Westminster Bank Limited v. Residential Properties Limited* [1938] Ch. 639.
[15] *Schweitzer v. Mayhew* (1863) 31 Beav. 37.
[16] *Re Borough of Portsmouth Tramways* [1892] 2 Ch. 362.
[17] *Moor v. Anglo-Italian Bank* (1879) 10 Ch.D. 681.
[18] *Re Dunderland Iron Ore Co. Limited* [1909] 1 Ch. 446.

CHAPTER 12

MORTGAGES OF PERSONALTY

MORTGAGES OF PERSONAL CHATTELS

1. Legal Mortgages

A debt may be secured on personal chattels by way of pledge, charge or **12–01** mortgage. Delivery of possession of the chattels to the lender is an essential element of a pledge. Possession may be constructive, as where a document of title to the chattel rather than the chattel itself is delivered. Pledge is a form of bailment. It does not create any rights of ownership in the goods. The pledgee acquires a so-called "special property" in the chattel. This term has been criticised on the grounds that no proprietary right vests in him. However, the term appears to be too well established to be replaced by any supposedly more accurate expression.[1]

Where security over the chattels is given by way of charge (or, as it is also termed, hypothecation) no transfer of possession occurs. The chargee obtains a right, in preference to other creditors, to apply the chattels to the satisfaction of the debt. For the purpose of so doing he has the right to trace the chattels into the hands of third parties other than those having a prior claim or purchasers of the legal title without notice of the charge. Since no transfer of ownership is brought about by the creation of a charge, the instrument creating it is not a bill of sale at common law. However, section 4 of the Bills of Sale Act 1878 defines "bill of sale" so as to include any agreement which *creates a charge or security* over personal chattels.

Where the chattel is mortgaged, however, it is by way of assignment of the legal title with a proviso, express or implied, for reassignment on redemption, and possession is irrelevant to the mortgagee's title. The legal title will pass when the parties intend it to pass and the transfer of that title requires neither delivery nor writing. A legal mortgage of chattels may be created orally or in writing, but if possession is given by way of security without any express transfer of the title, it will be for the court to determine whether the intention of the parties was to create a mortgage or a pledge.

2. Equitable Mortgages

Because the legal title to personal chattels cannot be divided, it is not possible to **12–02** create a mortgage by demise, nor can a second legal mortgage be created. All

---

[1] The term "special property" was criticised by Lord Mersey in *The Odessa* [1916] 1 A.C. 145 at 158–159. Here it was stated that the pawnee's right to sell in truth create no property right whatsoever. He preferred the term "special interest". See also *Mathew v. TM Sutton Ltd* [1994] 1 W.L.R. 1455 at 146, *per* Chadwick J.

subsequent mortgages are mortgages of the equity of redemption, and must, as dispositions of equitable interests subsisting at the time of the disposition, comply with the requirements of section 53(1)(c) of the Law of Property Act 1925, of being in writing signed by or on behalf of the mortgagor.[2] A valid mortgage of chattels may be created where the subject matter is a specified chattel, or chattels in the mortgagor's possession at the time the mortgage was made. It is also possible to create a mortgage of goods which have not yet come into existence or which have not yet been acquired by the mortgagor.

At common law, a purported transfer of goods *inter vivos*, not at the time of the transfer owned by the transferor, could be effective only where the subject matter of the transfer is either:

   (1) potential produce of property already owned by the transferor and to be conveyed by the transfer, which itself operated to pass the legal title to the produce when it came into existence; or

   (2) goods which the transferor had not yet acquired and the title to which passed to the transferee as a result of some further act of the transferor.

In equity, however, a transfer, or agreement for the transfer, of future goods, if made for value, vests the beneficial ownership of such goods in the transferee as soon as the transferor acquires them and without any new act of transfer on his part. This applies only when the goods are described sufficiently to be identifiable and any property answering that description will be affected.

FRAUDULENT TRANSACTIONS

12–03   The main reason for securing debts by way of mortgage, rather than pledging chattels, is that the debtor can retain the use and enjoyment of the mortgaged property while giving the creditor the desired security. The mortgagee's title does not depend on possession. Whilst this arrangement may be satisfactory as between the creditor and the debtor, the retention of possession of the mortgaged chattel by the debtor opens the way to fraud.

In the first place, it is open to the debtor to enter into a collusive transaction whereby he is able to represent to his unsecured creditors that chattels are encumbered and thus unavailable to satisfy his debts to them. This danger was realised long ago and the Fraudulent Conveyances Act 1571 avoided any assurance of chattels made with intent to delay, hinder or defraud creditors. Continued possession of mortgaged chattels by the mortgagor was taken as raising a presumption of fraud for the purposes of that statute. However, it now seems to be accepted that such possession, like any other surrounding circumstance, is a matter to be taken into account in deciding whether the assurance of chattels was made bona fide. The possession of chattels subject to a mortgage bill of sale by the mortgagor is, of course, entirely consistent with the mortgage contract and is, without more, insufficient to raise a presumption of fraud.

---

[2] See also *ibid.*, s.205(1)(ii). For equitable mortgages of land and the application of s.53(1)(c), see *ante*, paras 5–02, 5–03.

The relevant statutory provisions are now sections 423 to 425 of the Insolvency Act 1986, which in effect replace section 172 of the Law of Property Act 1925.[3] That section provided that, with certain exceptions, conveyances of property made with intent to defraud creditors were voidable at the instance of the person prejudiced. The provisions of the 1986 Act introduce a new set of rules governing transactions intended to defeat and delay creditors. These enable the court, where a person has entered into a transaction at an undervalue with the purpose of defeating the claims of creditors or other persons, to make orders restoring the position to what it would have been, had the transaction not been entered into, thus protecting the interests of persons prejudiced.[4]

This, however, is not the only danger associated with mortgages of chattels. A bona fide mortgage of chattels by an individual can lead to fraud, since, where the mortgagor remains in possession, there is nothing to show that the chattels are encumbered. He can thus obtain credit to which he is not entitled by falsely representing himself to be their unencumbered owner. Mortgages or charges of chattels by companies require registration.[5]

Since there are no essential documents of title to chattels (except for bills of lading and similar documents) it is difficult for the mortgagee to prevent the mortgagor from dealing with the chattels as if he were the legal owner. The legislation originally enacted to deal with this problem applied only in the case of bankruptcy. It transferred to the trustee in bankruptcy all goods in the possession, order or disposition of the bankrupt with a reputation of ownership. The provisions relating to reputed ownership formerly contained in section 38(c) of the Bankruptcy Act 1914 have been repealed.[6] The protection which that legislation afforded to general creditors was, in any case, limited, as all it did was to bring into the bankruptcy some chattels which would otherwise have been unavailable. Also, it did nothing to prevent them advancing credit on the strength of the ostensible ownership, nor did it in any way assist an execution creditor where there is no bankruptcy.

The Bills of Sale Acts

1. **The earlier legislation**

The first enactment designed to deal with the two problems mentioned above[7] **12–04** was the Bills of Sale Act 1854; the preamble provides, in part, as follows:

" . . . frauds are frequently committed upon creditors by secret bills of sale of personal chattels, whereby persons are enabled to keep up the appearance

---

[3] Repealed by the Insolvency Act 1985, s.235(3) and Sched. 10, Pt. III.

[4] These sections should be compared with ss.238–241 and ss.339–341 of the Insolvency Act 1986, which confer similar powers on the court in relation to transactions at an undervalue and preferences. See also the Consumer Credit Act 1974 and the law relating to extortionate credit bargains, *post*, para. 14–08 *et seq*. It is also necessary to note the jurisdiction of the court to set aside or vary the terms of any extortionate credit company; see Insolvency Act 1986, s.244. There are similar provisions in the case of bankrupts, see *ibid.*, s.343.

[5] Companies Act 1985, s.396(1)(c); see *ante* para. 11–27 *et seq*.

[6] Insolvency Act 1985, s.235, Sched. 10, Pt. III.

[7] Discussed in *Cookson v. Swire* (1884) 9 App.Cas. 653, *per* Lord Blackburn at 664; also see *Re Tooth, Trustee v. Tooth* [1934] I Ch. 616.

of being in good circumstances and possessed of property, and the grantees or holders of such bills of sale have the power of taking possession of the property of such persons, to the exclusion of the rest of their creditors".

The 1854 Act did not ascribe any particular meaning to the term "bill of sale", which is, at common law, a written instrument which effects a transfer of personal property.

The Act provided that every bill of sale of chattels, including mortgage bills of sale, whether absolute or conditional, whereby the grantee or holder was enabled to seize or take possession of any property comprised therein, should be registered. Want of registration would cause the bill to be avoided against the grantor's assignees in bankruptcy, against assignees for the benefit of creditors, and against execution creditors. Registration did not, however, amount to such a publication of change of ownership as would protect the grantee from the operation of the former "reputed ownership" rule in bankruptcy.[8] The 1866 Act provided that registration should be renewed every five years.

2. The current Bills of Sale legislation

(a) *Purpose*

12–05   The major Acts which now apply are the Bills of Sale Act 1878 and the Bills of Sale Act (1878) Amendment Act 1882. The Bills of Sale Acts 1890 and 1891 make some minor amendments to the main legislation. The main purpose of the 1878 Act,[9] like its predecessors, was the protection of creditors against having their rights prejudiced by secret assurances under which chattels were permitted to remain in the apparent possession of those who had in fact parted with them. It invalidated all unregistered bills of sale against execution creditors and the grantor's trustee in bankruptcy, but not between grantor and grantee.

The 1882 Act was designed to prevent the entrapment of the grantor by presenting him with an incomprehensible document to sign and thereby to protect him from having an oppressive bargain forced on him.[10] The 1882 Act changed the scope of the 1878 Act. From then on the 1878 Act applied only to bills of sale either by way of absolute assignment or those which enabled the grantee to take possession of personal chattels otherwise than as security for the payment of money. Such bills are termed "absolute" bills. The 1882 Act applies only to bills of sale given as security for loans ("security" bills). It invalidates such bills which do not conform to its provisions as between grantor and grantee, as well as between all other persons.

---

[8] *Badger and Williarns v. Shaw and Walker* (1860) 2 E. & E. 472. Partnership assets were outside the "reputed ownership" provisions, as no partner had an exclusive right to them: *Re Bainbridge, ex parte Fletcher* (1878) 8 Ch.D. 218.

[9] *Manchester, Sheffield and Lincolnshire Railway Co. v. North Central Wagon Co.* (1888) 13 App.Cas. 554, *per* Lord Herschell at 560.

[10] *ibid.*

(b) *Application and scope of the Bills of Sale Act 1878*

The 1878 Act defines "bill of sale", in section 4, as including: **12–06**

" . . . bills of sale, assignments, transfers, declarations of trust without transfer, inventories of goods with receipt thereto attached, or receipts for purchase moneys of goods, and other assurances of personal chattels, and also powers of attorney, authorities, or licenses to take possession of personal chattels as security for any debt, and also any agreement, whether intended or not to be followed by the execution of any other instrument, by which a right in equity to any personal chattels, or to any charge or security thereon, shall be conferred";

and as excluding:

" . . . assignments for the benefit of the creditors of the person making or giving the same,[11] marriage settlements,[12] transfers or assignments of any ship or vessel or any share thereof, transfers of goods in the ordinary course of business of any trade or calling, bills of sale of goods in foreign parts or at sea, bills of lading, India warrants, warehouse-keepers' certificates, warrants or orders for the delivery of goods, or any other documents used in the ordinary course of business as proof of the possession or control of goods, or authorising or purporting to authorise, either by indorsement or by delivery, the possessor of such document to transfer or receive goods thereby represented.";

and, additionally, the Bills of Sale Acts 1890 and 1891 exempt certain letters of hypothecation relating to imported goods.

Other charges exempted from the operation of the Bills of Sale Acts are:

(1) debentures issued by any mortgage, loan, or other incorporated company (Bills of Sale (1878) Amendment Act 1882, s. 17);

(2) any instrument of charge or other security issued by a company which is required to be registered in the company's register of charges;

(3) charges executed after September 14, 1967 by a society registered or deemed to be registered under the Industrial and Provident Societies Act 1965, and which has registered offices in England or Wales, provided that an application for recording the charge is made in accordance with sections 1(1) and 8(2) of the Industrial and Provident Societies Act 1965;

(4) an agricultural charge (as defined by section 5(7) of the Agricultural Credits Act 1928) created by a farmer on all or any of his farming stock

---

[11] In this exception "creditors" mean all the creditors: *General Furnishing and Upholstery Co. v. Venn* (1863) 2 H. & C. 153. It is sufficient if all the creditors have an opportunity of taking advantage of the deed by executing or assenting to it: *Boldero v. London and Westminster Loan and Discount Co.* (1879) 5 Ex.D. 47, although a time limit may be fixed within which a creditor must do so: *Hadley & Son v. Beedom* [1895] 1 Q.B. 646.

[12] Informal ante-nuptial agreements are within the exemption: *Wenman v. Lyon & Co.* [1891] 2 Q.B. 192, but post-nuptial settlements are not: *Ashton v. Blackshaw* (1870) L.R. 9 Eq. 510. Also see *Re Reis, ex parte Clough* [1904] 2 K.B. 769.

and other agricultural assets, in favour of a bank; and debentures issued
by a society registered under the Industrial and Provident Societies Act
1965, or by an agricultural marketing board, may be registered in like
manner as an agricultural charge, if secured on farming stock and
created in favour of a bank[13];

(5) mortgages of aircraft registered in the United Kingdom Nationality
Register and made on or after October 1, 1972[14];

(6) a mortgage of a ship or vessel or any share thereof.[15]

12–07 By section 3 of the 1878 Act, its operation is restricted to bills of sale by which
the grantee or holder has power, with or without notice, immediately or at any
future time, to seize or take possession of any personal chattels comprised in or
made subject to such bill of sale.

The Bills of Sale Acts deal with documents, not with transactions. Consequently, they do not apply where possession passes. Thus the Acts do not apply
to the case when a pledge or lien is effected by physical change of possession and
can be proved without reference to any document. This is so even when change
in possession is accompanied by a collateral instrument regulating the rights of
the parties as to the sale of the goods.[16] Possession can be constructive, as where
a pledgor gives a delivery order to a warehouseman; this was held to be
equivalent to actual possession by the pledgee.[17] The Acts do not require that any
transaction shall be put into writing. Such transactions can be made orally.[18]
They only require that *if* a transaction is put in writing and is of a particular
character, then it shall be registered, otherwise it shall be void.[19]

If the transaction is complete without any writing, so that the property intended
to be dealt with passes independently of the writing, the Acts do not apply to any
document merely confirming or referring to the transaction.[20] The transaction is
not invalidated because such a document is afterwards drawn up and not registered. Thus where a motor car, that was orally pledged as security for a debt
owing, was handed over to the pledgee, the transaction was not brought within
the Acts because the registration book was handed over at the same time.[21] If the
transferee's title is dependant upon a document, whether that document is a
transfer, an agreement to transfer, or a document of title made at that time as a
record of the transaction, it will be a bill of sale[22] and the Acts will apply.

(i) *What constitutes a bill of sale?*

12–08 There have been many cases in which tests have been suggested for determining
whether a document is or is not a bill of sale. Thus, a receipt will be a bill of sale
if it is a reduction into writing of the agreement between the parties as to the

---

[13] See *ante*, para. 10–07.
[14] See *ante*, para. 6–12.
[15] See *ante*, para. 6–11.
[16] *Re Hardwick, ex parte Hubbard* (1886) 17 Q.B.D. 690.
[17] *Grigg v. National Guardian Assurance Co.* [1891] 3 Ch. 206.
[18] *Reeves v. Capper* (1838) 5 Bing. N.C. 136; *Flory v. Denny* (1852) 7 Exch. 581.
[19] *United Forty Pound Loan Club v. Bexton* [1891] 1 Q.B. 25 n.
[20] *Ramsay v. Margrett* [1894] 2 Q.B. 18.
[21] *Waight v. Waight and Walker* [1952] P. 282.
[22] *Marsden v. Meadows* (1881) 7 Q.B.D. 80 at 85.

giving of the security.[23] In *Charlesworth v. Mills*[24] it was held that if a document, even though a simple receipt for purchase money, was intended by the parties to it to be part of the bargain to pass the property in the goods, it was a bill of sale. In *Ramsay v. Margrett*[25] Lopes L.J. posed the questions:

(i) Was it necessary to look at the document to prove the plaintiff's title?

(ii) Did the document transfer any property?

This test was applied in *Youngs v. Youngs*[26] where a receipt to which an inventory of goods was attached was held to have been given as an assurance of title and to be part of the bargain which transferred the property.

In *Re Townsend, ex parte Parsons*[27] it was held that a document giving a licence to take immediate possession of goods as security for a debt was a bill of sale within section 4 of the 1878 Act. However, where goods were pledged as security for a loan and delivered to the pledgee, a document signed by the pledgor, recording the transaction and regulating the pledgee's right to sell the goods, was held not to be a bill of sale since possession had already passed independently of the document.[28] The reasoning in *Charlesworth v. Mills* was also applied to documents created after goods had been reduced into possession under a common-law lien.[29]   **12–09**

Certain instruments conferring powers of distress are declared to be bills of sale by the provisions of section 6 of the 1878 Act. This was designed to confine powers of distress to their proper purpose, namely securing genuine leasehold rents. Before the Act, mortgages often contained an attornment clause whereby the mortgagor attorned tenant to the mortgagee at a rent equal to the mortgage interest, and the mortgagee was given power to distrain for arrears. Such a clause has been held not to be a bona fide lease[30] but a lease to secure money and thereby coming with the ambit of section 6 below: **12–10**

> "Every attornment instrument or agreement, not being a mining lease, whereby a power of distress is given or agreed to be given by any person to any other person by way of security for any present future or contingent debt or advance, and whereby any rent is reserved or made payable as a mode of providing for the payment of interest on such debt or advance, or otherwise for the purpose of such security only, shall be deemed to be a bill of sale, within the meaning of this Act, of any personal chattels which may be seized or taken under such power of distress.
>
> Provided, that nothing in this section shall extend to any mortgage of any estate or interest in any land tenement or hereditament which the mortgagee,

---

[23] *Newlove v. Shrewsbury* (1888) 21 Q.B.D. 41, *per* Lord Esher M.R.

[24] [1892] A.C. 231.

[25] [1894] 2 Q.B. 18.

[26] [1940] 1 K.B. 760.

[27] *Re Townsend, ex parte Parsons* (1886) 16 Q.B.D. 532.

[28] *Re Hardwick, ex parte Hubbard* (1886) 17 Q.B.D. 690. In *Wrightson v. McArthur and Hutchinsons (1919) Ltd* [1921] 2 K.B. 807, the contents of a room were constructively delivered by handing over the keys. A subsequently executed written licence to enter was held not to be a bill of sale. For attornment clauses, see *ante*, para. 3–36 and *post*, para. 16–24 *et seq*.

[29] *Great Eastern Railway Co. v. Lord's Trustee* [1909] A.C. 109.

[30] *Re Willis, ex parte Kennedy* (1888) 21 Q.B.D. 384; *cf. Green v. Marsh* [1892] 2 Q.B. 330.

being in possession, shall have demised to the mortgagor as his tenant at a fair and reasonable rent."

In summary, the section deems powers of distress conferred by way of security for debt to be bills of sale, except in respect of:

    (i) mining leases;
    (ii) leases, by mortgagees in possession, to their mortgagors at a fair and reasonable rent.[31]

Thus, a lease of a public house containing a power of distress for the price of goods sold was held to be a licence to take possession of personal chattels as security for a debt; this was deemed to be a bill of sale and was held void for want of registration.[32] Documents containing attornment clauses such as that referred to above are not altogether void. The landlord-tenant relationship created by such a clause exists for the purpose of giving the mortgagee the right to sue for possession or to enforce a proviso for re-entry for non-payment of rent. As the clause is merely "deemed" to be, rather than actually made into, a bill of sale, it will not be void for non-compliance with the statutory form.

(ii) *Definition of Personal Chattels*

12–11 In order for a document to fall within the provisions of the Bills of Sale Acts, it must not only be a bill of sale but it must also relate to personal chattels as defined by section 4 of the 1878 Act. The definition applies to both Acts. However, where a security bill comprises some personal chattels as defined together with some other property, it may be effectual with regard to that other property, although void, for non-compliance with the statutory form, as regards the personal chattels.[33] The 1878 Act defines "personal chattels," in section 4, as:

> " . . . goods, furniture, and other articles capable of complete transfer by delivery, and (when separately assigned or charged) fixtures and growing crops, but shall not include chattel interests in real estate, nor fixtures (except trade machinery as herein-after defined),[34] when assigned together with a freehold or leasehold interest in any land or building to which they are affixed, nor growing crops[35] when assigned together with any interest in

---

[31] *Re Roundwood Colliery Co. Ltd* [1897] 1 Ch. 373, CA.

[32] *Pulbrook v. Ashby & Co.* (1887) 56 L.J.Q.B. 376.

[33] *Re Burdett, ex parte Byrne* (1886) 20 Q.B.D. 310, following *Pickering v. Ilfracombe Railway Co.* (1868) L.R. 3 C.P. 235, *per* Willes J. at 250; followed in *Re North Wales Produce and Supply Society* [1922] 2 Ch. 340. The case of *Davies v. Rees* (1886) 17 Q.B.D. 408 (and affirmed *ibid.* at 499), was distinguished on the ground that it was a case where only personal chattels were mortgaged.

[34] By s.5, as machinery used in or attached to any factory or workshop, exclusive of (i) fixed motive power and its appurtenances; (ii) fixed power machinery; and (iii) steam, gas and water pipes.

[35] At common law, growing crops produced by agricultural labour (emblements, *fructus industriales*) or other growing crops (*fructus naturales*) after severance are "goods". However, s.4 makes all growing crops "personal chattels" provided they are separately assigned or charged.

the land[36] on which they grow, nor shares or interests in the stock, funds, or securities of any government, or in the capital or property of incorporated or joint stock companies, nor choses in action, nor any stock or produce upon any farm or lands which by virtue of any covenant or agreement or of the custom of the country ought not to be removed from any farm where the same are at the time of making or giving of such bill of sale."

a) *Growing Crops*

Thus a document transferring or charging those growing crops which are personal chattels within section 4 of the principal Act is registrable as a bill of sale[37] unless: **12–12**

(1) the crops are industrial growing crops assigned by a transfer made in the ordinary course of business[38] or contained in an agricultural charge;

(2) the crops are farming stock or produce which by virtue of any agreement, covenant or custom of the country *(i.e.* prevalent usage of reasonable duration in the neighbourhood where the land is situated) ought not to be removed from the farm; or

(3) the document is otherwise excluded from the definition of a bill of sale or is exempted from the Acts by some other provision.

A mortgage of growing crops (like a transfer of chattels) is a bill of sale if the mortgagee is able to realise his security in the growing crops independently from his security in the land.[39] It is only when growing crops are mortgaged incidentally in a mortgage of land and as part of the land are the Bills of Sale Acts excluded. In such circumstances they are treated as personal chattels so as to exclude the Acts.[40] Therefore, a mortgage of crops after severance is a bill of sale.[41]

b) *Fixtures*

Fixtures affixed to mortgaged land, whether affixed before or after the date of the mortgage, form part of the security in the land and pass automatically to the mortgagee as realty unless the mortgage shows a contrary intention.[42] As with **12–13**

---

[36] s.7 of the 1878 Act applies both to growing crops and fixtures and provides that they shall not be deemed to have been separately assigned or charged:

"... by reason only that they are assigned by separate words, or that power is given to sever them from the land or building to which they are affixed, or from the land on which they grow, without otherwise taking possession of or dealing with such land or building, or land, if by the same instrument any freehold or leasehold interest in the land or building to which such fixtures are affixed or in the land on which such crops grow, is also conveyed or assigned to the same persons or person."

[37] *Re Phillips, ex parte National Mercantile Bank* (1880) 16 Ch.D. 104.
[38] *Stephenson v. Thompson* [1924] 2 K.B. 240.
[39] *ibid.*
[40] *Re Gordon, ex parte Official Receiver* (1889) 61 L.T. 299.
[41] *Re Phillips, ex parte National Mercantile Bank* (1880) 16 Ch.D. 104.
[42] *Reynolds v. Ashby* [1904] A.C. 466.

growing crops, a mortgage of fixtures is a bill of sale only where the mortgagee can realise his security in the fixtures separate from that in the land.[43]

c) *Trade Machinery*

12–14 Trade machinery, as defined in section 5 of the 1878 Act, is deemed to be a personal chattel for the purposes of that Act. Any mode of disposition of it by its owner which would be a bill of sale as to any other personal chattels is deemed to be a bill of sale within the meaning of the 1878 Act. Fixed trade machinery not expressly mentioned in a mortgage of property may pass as part of the mortgaged premises. If there is no disposition of trade machinery as such, nor any power to sell separately, the mortgage is not a bill of sale.[44] If on the true construction of the instrument there is a power to sell it separately, the instrument is a bill of sale so far as the trade machinery is concerned.[45]

d) *Choses in Action*

12–15 Choses in action, shares and interests in stock are all specifically excluded from the definition of personal chattels in section 4 of the 1878 Act. This includes shares in partnership assets even though they involve the right to specific chattels.[46] A mortgage of a reversionary interest in specific chattels settled as heirlooms has been held to be outside the Act,[47] as has a mortgage of rights under a hire purchase agreement where the chattels subject to the agreement was not mentioned.[48] However, a charge on a car in a garage until sale and afterwards on the purchase money was held to be within the Act. The reason for this is that the charge is primarily on the chattel which the chose of action represents, namely, the prospective proceeds of sale.[49]

Mortgage of after-acquired goods   There is a conflict of opinion as to whether future goods can be "personal chattels" for the purposes of the Acts. Waldock[50] took the view that chattels not yet in existence or which are not yet owned by a mortgagor are outside the definition since they are not "capable of complete transfer by personal delivery".[51] In *Holroyd v. Marshall*[52] it was held that assignments of specific after-acquired property operate in equity to transfer an equitable title as soon as the assignee acquires the property. Such property is "specific" for the purpose of that doctrine if it is described by sufficiently precise

---

[43] *Re Yates* (1888) 38 Ch.D. 112. In *Small v. National Provincial Bank* [1894] 1 Ch. 686, it was held that there was an intention to mortgage fixtures as chattels separately because fixtures grouped with movable chattels were clearly not part of the land. See also *Reeves v. Barlow* (1883) 12 Q.B.D. 436. See also *Climpson v. Coles* (1889) 23 Q.B.D. 465 as to building materials brought on to land where buildings are in course of erection. See also *ante*, para. 6–01.

[44] *Re Yates* (1888) 38 Ch.D. 112.

[45] *Small v. National Provincial Bank* [1894] 1 Ch. 686.

[46] *Re Bainbridge* (1878) 8 Ch.D. 218.

[47] *Re Thynne* [1911] 1 Ch. 282.

[48] *Re Davis & Co., ex parte Rawlings* (1888) 22 Q.B.D. 193.

[49] *National Provincial and Union Bank of England v. Lindsell* [1922] 1 K.B. 21.

[50] Waldock, *Mortgages* (2nd ed., 1950), p. 87.

[51] *Brantom v. Griffits* (1877) 2 C.P.D. 212; *Thomas v. Kelly* (1888) 13 App.Cas. 506, *per* Lord Macnaghten at 518, affirming *Kelly & Co. v. Kellond* (1888) 20 Q.B.D. 569.

[52] (1862) 10 H.L.C. 191.

general words so to render the property intended to be comprised in the assignment ascertainable.[53] Regardless of the Bills of Sale Acts, assignments of after-acquired property create equitable mortgages which bind the property as soon as such property comes into the hands of the mortgagor.[54] A valid mortgage of personalty can be created even though the mortgagor does not know the exact nature of the chattels,[55] or where the personal property is not yet in existence, provided he has an actual or potential interest in the source of the property.[56] A security in an incomplete chattel may be created by way of a contract to complete the chattel and to assign both the materials appropriated for its completion and the chattel itself when finished.[57] If the view expressed by Waldock is correct, equitable mortgages of after-acquired property are outside the scope of the Acts. This has been doubted.[58]

It has been suggested[59] on three grounds that whether a chattel is "capable of complete transfer by personal delivery" depends on its physical characteristics and not on its existence or ownership at the time the security is created. Those grounds are:

(1) The Bills of Sales Act 1878 (repealing and replacing the 1854 Act) added, in section 4, the following words to the definition of a bill of sale, "any agreement . . . by which a right in equity to any personal chattels, or to any charge or security thereon, shall be conferred". The purpose of this addition was to catch agreements giving equitable rights over after-acquired property.

(2) Section 5 of the 1882 Act, which is headed "Bill of sale not to affect after-acquired property", refers to "personal chattels . . . of which the grantor was not the true owner at the time of execution of the bill of sale". Unless after-acquired property is within the definition, the section is inherently contradictory;

(3) Even were the section not self-contradictory, it could, unless after-acquired property is within the definition of "personal chattels", readily be evaded by the taking of a bill shortly before the grantor acquired the assets.

If a document which is a bill of sale within the 1878 Act fails to comply with the **12–16** provisions relating to form and registration,[60] it is void against the grantor's execution creditors, or his trustee in bankruptcy or his assignee for the benefit of creditors. However, it is void only in so far as it comprises any chattels which at

---

[53] *Tailby v. Official Receiver* (1888) 13 App.Cas. 523, HL; see also *Re Wait* [1927] 1 Ch. 606, *Syrett v. Egerton* [1957] 1 W.L.R. 1130.

[54] *Industrials Finance Syndicate Ltd v. Lind* [1915] 2 Ch. 345; mortgage of an expectancy in personalty under a will or intestacy is a valid equitable mortgage which matures when the property falls into possession.

[55] *Re Beattie, ex parte Kelsall* (1846) De G. 352.

[56] *Langton v. Horton* (1842) 1 Hare. 549.

[57] *Woods v. Russell* (1822) S.B. & Ald. 942; *Reid v. Fairbanks* (1853) 13 C.B. 692.

[58] See *Re Reis, ex parte Clough* [1904] 2 K.B. 769 at 778; Sykes, *Law of Securities* (5th ed., 1993), pp. 472 *et seq.* See also *Halsbury's Laws of England* (4th ed. reissue, 1992), Vol. 4(1), para. 616.

[59] See *Halsbury's Laws*, supra.

[60] Bills of Sale Act 1878, s.8.

the time of the execution of process, the filing of the bankruptcy petition, or of the assignment, are in his possession or apparent possession.

Goods remain in the grantor's apparent possession until something is done which clearly takes them out of his possession.[61] Where two people live in the same house, they may each be in apparent possession, but the person who has the legal title is in possession. The nature of the relationship between them is irrelevant provided the two people have the common use of the chattels.[62] However, the principle does not apply to a domestic servant living with his master. It has been held that there was no common use of the chattels in the house in such circumstances.[63] Where two persons live in the same house and one purports to make a gift to the other, the gift will be avoided against the grantor's execution creditor or trustee in bankruptcy if there is no sufficient delivery. There must be such act of delivery or change of possession as would be unequivocally referable to an intention by the donor to transfer possession and title in the chattels to the donee.[64] Failure to comply with the requirements of form or registration does not invalidate an absolute bill of sale as between the parties to it.[65]

APPLICATION AND SCOPE OF THE BILLS OF SALE (1878) AMENDMENT ACT 1882

12–17   The 1882 Act applies to bills of sale given by way of security for the payment of money. It applies where the subject-matter of the bill of sale is "personal chattels" as defined by section 4 of the 1878 Act, provided that:

(a)   those personal chattels should be capable of specific description, and should be specifically described therein[66];

(b)   at the time of the execution, the grantor should be the true owner of those personal chattels.[67]

There are exceptions to these rules for growing crops, plant and trade machinery, and fixtures.[68]

The main provisions of the 1882 Act are:

---

[61] *Re Blenkhorn, ex parte Jay* (1874) 9 Ch.App. 697; goods are still in the grantor's apparent possession although the broker's men are in her house, but no longer when the men start to pack up and load the goods into vans.

[62] *Ramsay v. Margrett* [1894] 2 Q.B. 18; *French v. Gething* [1922] 1 K.B. 236 (husband and wife); *contra Youngs v. Youngs* [1940] 1 K.B. 760, (in which see the observations by Goddard L.J. as to the application of the doctrine of *Ramsay v. Margrett, supra* to a case where a woman was living with a man as his mistress); *Antoniadi v. Smith* [1901] 2 K.B. 589 (mother-in-law and son-in-law).

[63] *Youngs v. Youngs, supra.* But *cf. Koppel v. Koppel* [1966] 1 W.L.R. 802, CA. (married man and housekeeper, where latter held to be living in house not as an ordinary paid domestic servant but as a person sharing a common establishment with the married man).

[64] *Hislop v. Hislop* [1950] W.N. 124 (gift by writing not under seal and no physical delivery of the chattels); *Re Cole (A Bankrupt), ex parte Trustees of the Property of the Bankrupt* [1964] Ch. 175, purported oral gift, no delivery).

[65] *Davis v. Goodman* (1880) 5 C.P.D. 128; *Tuck v. Southern Counties Deposit Bank* (1889) 42 Ch.D. 471.

[66] Bills of Sale Act (1878) Amendment Act (1882), s.4.

[67] *ibid.*, s.5.

[68] *ibid.*, s.6.

(1) the restriction of the grantee's right of seizure to five specified causes[69];

(2) a brief and simple form of bill of sale, setting out clearly the consideration and terms of payment, incorporating by reference the statutory grounds of seizure and specifying the property comprised in the bill, was made obligatory[70];

(3) a bill of sale not in the prescribed form was made absolutely void in regard to the personal chattels comprised in it[71];

(4) a bill of sale in the prescribed form was made absolutely void, if not registered,[72] in contrast to the 1878 Act, under which unregistered absolute bills of sale remained valid between grantor and grantee;

(5) all bills of sale given in consideration of a sum less than £30 were made absolutely void[73];

(6) section 20 of the 1878 Act was repealed in regard to security bills of sale so that registration does not take goods comprised in security bills of sale out of the possession, order or disposition of a bankrupt grantor.[74]

The application of the Acts has been set out in the following frequently cited words:

"Those statutes do not require that any transaction shall be put in writing; they only require that if a transaction be put in writing and be of a particular character, then it shall be registered, otherwise it shall be void".[75]

This principle, usually paraphrased as "the Acts strike at documents, not transactions" is reinforced by section 62(3) of the Sale of Goods Act 1979, which provides that nothing in that Act or the 1893 Act affects the enactments relating to bills of sale.

Nevertheless the courts have regard to the substance of the transaction, and the intention of the parties is material in two respects. If a document is essential to the transaction whereby the property passes, it is a bill of sale.[76] However, it is not a bill of sale if it is a mere record and is not intended to be essential, as where it is a receipt acknowledging the change in ownership.[77] Also, if a document is intended to conceal the fact that a transaction is a loan on security, it is caught by the Acts. Similarly, where a document purported to set out a hire-purchase agreement but the parties had no intention that the intending purchaser should ever become the owner of the chattels, it is also caught.[78]

---

[69] *ibid.*, s.7.
[70] *ibid.*, s.8, and see the Schedule which sets out the form.
[71] *ibid.*, s.9.
[72] *ibid.*, s.8.
[73] *ibid.*, s.12.
[74] *ibid.*, ss.3 and 15.
[75] *United Forty Pound Loan Club v. Bexton* [1891] 1 Q.B. 28 n., *per* Fry L.J.
[76] *Youngs v. Youngs* [1940] 1 K.B. 760.
[77] *Ramsay v. Margrett* [1894] 2 Q.B. 18.
[78] *Maas v. Pepper* [1905] A.C. 102; and see *Re Walden, ex parte Odell* (1878) 10 Ch.D. 76; *Re Watson* (1890) 25 Q.B.D. 27; *North Central Wagon Finance Co. v. Brailsford* [1962] 1 W.L.R. 1288; *Mercantile Credit Co. v. Hamblin* [1965] 2 Q.B. 242.

If a contract, according to the tenor of the document and the intention of the parties, is a contract of hire with an option to purchase, it is outside the Acts.[79] The provision in a hire-purchase agreement giving the owner the power to re-take possession of the property does not make the agreement into a bill of sale. It has been said that if a contract of sale is genuinely intended to operate according to its tenor, so that the hire-purchase agreement is executed by the legal owner of the property, the transaction cannot be impeached as a colourable cloak for a mortgage.[80] This is so even if the parties initially contemplated a transaction by way of bill of sale and genuinely changed their intention.[81]

1. Seizure and sale of goods

12–18   The grantee of a security bill of sale may only seize the chattels comprised herein if one of the following conditions set out in section 7 apply:

"(i) If the grantor shall make default in payment of the sum or sums of money secured by the bill at the time therein provided for payment,[82] or in the performance of any covenant or agreement contained in the bill and necessary for maintaining the security;

(ii) If the grantor becomes bankrupt,[83] or suffers the goods to be distrained for rent, rates or taxes;

(iii) If the grantor fraudulently removes or suffers the goods to be removed from the premises;

(iv) If the grantor upon demand in writing unreasonably refuses to produce his last receipts for rent, rates and taxes[84];

(v) If execution has been levied against the goods of the grantor under any judgment at law".

If even one instalment is unpaid, the grantee may seize the whole of the goods as security for the whole of the money, even though the bill of sale makes no such express provision. When the right to seize has accrued, the grantee may not remove or sell the goods until five clear days have elapsed.[85] Section 7 also

---

[79] *McEntire v. Crossley Bros. Ltd* [1895] A.C. 457. See also *Helby v. Mathews* [1895] A.C. 471, *per* Lord M'naughten at 482: *Modern Light Cars Ltd v. Seals* [1934] 1 K.B. 32; Pacific Motor Auctions Pty Ltd v. Motor Credits (Hire Finance) Ltd [1965] A.C. 867, PC; for further discussions, see A. L. Diamond, (1960) 23 M.L.R. 399 at 516 and Crossley Vaines, *Personal Property* (5th ed., 1973), pp. 371 *et seq.* and 467 *et seq.*

[80] *Yorkshire Railway Wagon Co. v. McClure* (1882) 21 Ch.D. 309, *Manchester, Sheffield and Lincolnshire Railway Co. v. North Central Wagon Co.* (1888) 13 App.Cas. 554.

[81] *Beckett v. Tower Assets Co.* [1891] 1 Q.B. 1. Each case must be determined according to the proper inference from the facts; see *Johnson v. Rees* (1915) 84 L.J.K.B. 1276.

[82] *Re Wood, ex parte Woolfe* [1894] 1 Q.B. 605.

[83] This means what it says and does not mean "commits an act of bankruptcy"; *Gilroy v. Bowey* (1888) 59 L.T. 223.

[84] What constitutes cause for seizure under this provision is dealt with in *Hammond v. Hocking* (1884) 12 Q.B.D. 291; *Barr v. Kingsford* (1887) 56 L.T. 861; *Ex parte Wickens* [1898] 1 Q.B. 543; *Re Wood, ex parte Woolfe* [1894] 1 Q.B. 605.

[85] Bills of Sale Act (1878) Amendment Act 1882, s.13. After the five days have elapsed, the court can grant relief only under the general law applicable to mortgages: *Longden v. Sheffield Deposit Bank* (1888) 24 S.J. 913.

provides that, during that period, the grantee may apply to the High Court for relief and the court, if satisfied that for any reason the cause of seizure no longer exists, can restrain the grantee from removing or selling them or make such other order as it thinks just. However, even after the five days have elapsed, the grantor can exercise his equitable right to redeem so long as the grantee has not sold the goods or foreclosed.[86]

2. Form and contents of a security bill of sale

The validity of a security bill of sale is dependent on it satisfying the conditions of sections 8 and 9 of the 1882 Act and the Schedule thereto. Section 8 states that: **12–19**

> "Every bill of sale shall be duly attested,[87] and shall be registered under the principal Act within seven clear days after the execution thereof, or if it is executed in any place out of England then within seven clear days after the time at which it would in the ordinary course of post arrive in England if posted immediately after the execution thereof; and shall truly set forth the consideration for which it was given[88] otherwise such bill of sale shall be void in respect of the personal chattels comprised therein".

Consideration, for the purpose of section 8, means, not the sum secured by the bill, but that which the grantor receives for giving it.[89] The consideration can include the cost of preparation of the bill, paid to a solicitor, if the grantor has agreed to pay it.[90] "Truly" means with substantial accuracy according to either the mercantile or legal effect of the facts.[91] A clerical error will not invalidate a bill of sale if it appears otherwise from the document what the true consideration was[92]—an approximate statement will suffice if nearly accurate.[93] If the consideration is not truly set forth, the bill is avoided whether the untrue statement was made intentionally or accidentally. In many of the cases the untrue statement involved the concealment of a bonus or expenses to be paid to the moneylender within the statement of the consideration.[94] The avoidance is in respect of the personal chattels only. So the covenant for payment remains valid as a personal

---

[86] *Johnson v. Diprose* [1893] 1 Q.B. 512.
[87] By one or more credible witnesses none of whom is a party; compare s.10 of the 1878 Act which provides that an absolute bill must be attested by a solicitor and that the attestation must state that before the bill was executed the solicitor explained its effect to the grantor.
[88] Which must not be less than £30, otherwise the bill is absolutely void—s.12 of the 1882 Act.
[89] *Ex parte Challinor* (1880) 16 Ch.D. 260; *Darlow v. Bland* [1897] 1 Q.B. 125; *Criddle v. Scott* (1895) 11 T.L.R. 222; *Henshall v. Widdison* (1923) 130 L.T. 607.
[90] *London and Provinces Discount Co. v. Jones* [1914] 1 K.B. 147.
[91] *Credit Co. v. Pott* (1880) 6 Q.B.D. 295.
[92] *Roberts v. Roberts* (1884) 13 Q.B.D. 794.
[93] *Hughes v. Little* (1886) 18 Q.B.D. 32; "£32 or thereabouts" held to be in accordance with the requirements of s.8.
[94] *Richardson v. Harris* (1889) 22 Q.B.D. 268; *Re Cowburn, ex parte Firth* (1882) 19 Ch.D. 419; *Cohen v. Higgins* (1891) 8 T.L.R. 8; *Parsons v. Equitable Investment Co. Ltd* [1916] 2 Ch. 527.

obligation even though the security is void as between the parties as well as against third parties.[95]

Section 9 of the 1882 Act provides that:

"A bill of sale made or given by way of security for the payment of money by the grantor thereof shall be void unless made in accordance with the form in the Schedule to this Act annexed."

The Schedule is as follows:

"This Indenture made   the day of   , between *A.B.* of   of the one part, and *C.D.* of of the other part, witnesseth that in consideration of the sum of £   now paid to *A.B.* by *C.D.*, the receipt of which the said *A.B.* hereby acknowledges *[or whatever else the consideration may be]*, he the said *A.B.* doth hereby assign unto *C.D.*, his executors, administrators, and assigns, all and singular the several chattels and things specifically described in the schedule hereto annexed by way of security for the payment of the sum of £   , and interest thereon at the rate of   per cent. per annum *[or whatever else may be the rate]*. And the said *A.B.* doth further agree and declare that he will duly pay to the said *C.D.* the principal sum aforesaid, together with the interest then due, by equal   payments of £   on the day of   *[or whatever else may be the stipulated times or time of payment]*. And the said *A.B.* doth also agree with the said *C.D.* that he will *[here insert terms as to insurance, payment of rent, or otherwise, which the parties may agree to for the maintenance or defeasance of the security]*.

Provided always, that the chattels hereby assigned shall not be liable to seizure or to be taken possession of by the said *C.D.* for any cause other than those specified in section seven of the Bills of Sale Act (1878) Amendment Act 1882

In witness, &c

Signed and sealed by the said *A.B.* in the presence of me *E.F. [add witness's name, address, and description]*".

12–20   A bill given by way of security which is not substantially in accordance with the above form is void, not only as between grantor and grantee in respect of the assignment of personal chattels, but it is also void as a contract of loan in respect of the personal covenant to pay principal and interest.[96] This is so even if it purports to be an absolute bill.[97] The lender can recover his money only in an action for money had and received but will then be allowed only a reasonable rate

---

[95] *Heseltine v. Simmons* [1892] 2 Q.B. 547.
[96] *Davies v. Rees* (1886) 17 Q.B.D. 408; *Smith v. Whiteman* [1909] 2 K.B. 437.
[97] *Madell v. Thomas & Co.* [1891] 1 Q.B. 230.

of interest rather than the stipulated[98] rate. Where a bill is void *in toto,* this does not mean that the security of which it forms a part is void *in toto.* If the security comprises personal chattels and also property which does not fall within that description, and it is possible to sever the security on the personal chattels from the security on the other property, then the security will be void as to the personal chattels but good as to the other property.[99] However, a bill of sale will be bad if it includes in the schedule property other than personal chattels.[1]

The phrase "in accordance with the form in the Schedule" was considered in *Re Barber, ex parte Stanford.*[2] It had already been decided that a material departure by way of addition would cause the bill to be avoided.[3] In *Re Barber, ex parte Stanford* the point to be decided was the effect of inserting the words "as beneficial owner" after "doth hereby assign". This insertion altered the legal effect of the document, since by section 7 of the Conveyancing Act 1881[4] the words incorporated a covenant for immediate possession on default, which was inconsistent with the provisions of section 7 of the 1882 Act. An invalid addition cannot be saved by a proviso that conditions not in accordance with the statutory form are to be disregarded, since this would be a departure of a kind "calculated to mislead those whom it is the object of the statute to protect".[5]

3. The characteristics of a bill of sale

There are 14 characteristics of a bill of sale, and a bill which departs from any of them is void, even if the legal effect of the bill is unaltered by the departure.[6] They are: **12–21**

    (1) the date of the bill;
    (2) the names and addresses[7] of the parties;
    (3) a statement of the consideration;
    (4) an acknowledgment of receipt if the advance is a present advance;
    (5) an assignment, by way of security, of personal chattels capable of specific description;

---

[98] *North Central Wagon & Finance Co. Ltd v. Brailsford* [1962] 1 W.L.R. 1288; *Davies v. Rees, supra.* In *Bradford Advance Co. v. Ayers* [1924] W.N. 152, 5 per cent per annum was taken as the appropriate rate of interest.

[99] *Re O'Dwyer* (1886) 19 L.R. Ir. 19, where the instrument comprised a bill of sale of personal chattels and a mortgage of freehold or leasehold property. In *Re Burdett, ex parte Byrne* (1888) 20 Q.B.D. 310, a bill of sale of personal chattels and also of trade machinery was excepted under s.5 of the Act of 1878.

[1] *Cochrane v. Entwistle* (1890) 25 Q.B.D. 116; but the mortgage will be effective as regards the other property.

[2] (1886) 17 Q.B.D. 259.

[3] *Davis v. Burton* (1883) 11 Q.B.D. 537.

[4] Now LPA 1925, s.76.

[5] *Re Barber, ex parte Stanford* (1886) 17 Q.B.D. 259.

[6] *Thomas v. Kelly* (1886) 13 App.Cas. 506.

[7] *Altree v. Altree* [1898] 2 Q.B. 267; bill invalidated by omission of address even though these could have been ascertained from another source with reasonable certainty.

    (6) securing of a fixed monetary obligation;

    (7) statement of the sum secured,[8] the rate of interest[9] and the instalments by which repayment is to be made[10];

    (8) agreed terms for maintenance[11] or defeasance of the security;

    (9) a proviso limiting the grounds of seizure to those specified in section 7 of the 1882 Act;

  (10) the description of the chattels to be in the schedule, not the body of the bill;

  (11) execution by the grantor;

  (12) attestation;

  (13) name, address and description of the attesting witness;

  (14) schedule describing the personal chattels.

Although superfluous material not altering the legal effect, such as recitals, will not avoid the bill,[12] it must not be such as to confuse the grantor or destroy the simplicity which the Act was designed to attain.

    Maintenance of the security means the preservation of the security "in as good a plight and condition as at the date of the bill of sale",[13] whilst defeasance of the security involves a provision which limits the operation of the bill or stipulates for its discharge on a stated event. The scope for imposing defeasance clauses is very limited since section 10(3) of the 1878 Act provides that any defeasance not contained in the body of the deed is deemed to be part of the bill and must be written on the same document as the bill prior to registration. If this is not done the registration is void, which invalidates the bill as far as the personal chattels are concerned, though the covenant for payment remains valid. If the bill is a security bill, the defeasance must comply with the statutory form[14] and the conclusion of any covenant for defeasance which gives the grantee a power of

---

[8] The amount ultimately payable must be certain: *Hughes v. Little* (1886) 18 Q.B.D. 32.

[9] Which must be stated as a rate though not necessarily a percentage, *Lumley v. Simmons* (1887) 34 Ch.D. 698, and not a lump sum: *Blankenstein v. Robertson* (1890) 24 Q.B.D. 543.

[10] Both the amount repayable and the times of repayment must be certain: *Attia v. Finch* (1904) 91 L.T. 70 (interest); *De Braam v. Ford* [1900] 1 Ch. 142 (principal).

[11] These include covenants:

    (i) to repair and replace; *Furber v. Cobb* (1887) 18 Q.B.D. 494;

   (ii) to insure; *Neverson v. Seymour* (1907) 97 L.T. 788; *Topley v. Crosbie* (1888) 20 Q.B.D. 350;

  (iii) not to remove the goods without consent; *Re Coton, ex parte Payne* (1887) 56 L.T. 571; *Furbes v. Cobb* (1887) 18 Q.B.D. 494;

  (iv) to pay rent, rates and taxes on the premises where the chattels are situated; *Goldstrom v. Tallerman* (1886) 18 Q.B.D. 1; and to produce receipts therefor; *Furbes v. Cobb* (1887) 18 Q.B.D. 494; *Cartwright v. Regan* [1895] 1 Q.B. 900;

   (v) to permit the grantee to pay insurance premiums, rent, rates or taxes, and to add such payments to the security, on default by the grantor on such payments; *Coldstrom v. Tallerman* (1886) 18 Q.B.D. 1; *Neverson v. Seymour* (1907) 97 L.T. 788; *Topley v. Crosbie* (1888) 20 Q.B.D. 350;

  (vi) for further assurance of title; *Re Cleaver, ex parte Rawlings* (1887) 18 Q.B.D. 489.

[12] *Roberts v. Roberts* (1884) 13 Q.B.D. 794; *Re Morritt* (1886) 18 Q.B.D. 222.

[13] *Furber v. Cobb* (1887) 18 Q.B.D. 494. However, the fact that two courts differ as to the construction of a bill does not lead to avoidance under this principle, *Edwards v. Marston* [1891] 1 Q.B. 225.

[14] *Smith v. Whiteman* [1909] 2 K.B. 437.

seizure not in accord with sections 7 or 13 of the 1882 Act avoids the bill totally.[15]

4. Registration: section 8

The section is set out *ante* at paragraph 12–19 and the provisions are the same as **12–22** for registration of an absolute bill of sale.[16] On registration a true copy of the bill and an affidavit in support thereof must be filed with the registrar of bills of sale at the central office of the Royal Courts of Justice. The true copy of the bill must be accompanied by a copy of every schedule or inventory herein referred to; the affidavit must contain statements as to the time of making the bill, its due attestation and execution, the residence and occupation of the grantor and every attesting witness.[17] The registration must be renewed every five years,[18] as failure to do so avoids it even against the grantor.[19] However, an assignment or transfer need not be registered.[20] If registration is not made within seven days the court may, on being satisfied that the omission to register was due to mistake or inadvertence, extend the time for registration[21] but there is no power to extend the time for renewal of registration.[22]

Although all original registrations are in London, section 11 of the 1882 Act[23] directs the registrar to transmit copies of the bill of sale to the registrar of the county court in whose district the chattels are situated, if either the chattels are situated, or the grantor resides, outside the London bankruptcy district. The bill is not avoided by the failure of the registrar to transmit the copy to a county court registry.[24]

A bill of sale is vacated by an entry of satisfaction in the register.[25] On the filing of an affidavit showing that the grantee covenants to satisfaction being entered, the registrar orders a memorandum of satisfaction to be endorsed on the bill. There is provision for the rectification of inadvertent errors in the register, but an order cannot be made for an affidavit to be filed correcting errors in the bill of sale or supporting affidavit.[26] Any order made for rectifying the register is made subject to rights which have already accrued to third parties.[27] Because the register is open to inspection and search[28] the grantor may find it difficult to

---

[15] *Davis v. Burton* (1883) 11 Q.B.D. 537 (covenant giving a right of seizure for failure to produce rent receipts on demand); *Barr v. Kingsford* (1887) 56 L.T. 861 (right of seizure for default in respect of a covenant not necessary for the maintenance of the security); *Lyon v. Morris* (1887) 19 Q.B.D. 139 (express power to sell and seize immediately on default).

[16] Bills of Sale Act 1878, ss.8, 22.

[17] So that third parties can make all necessary inquiries before lending the grantor money or supplying him with goods on credit; *Jones v. Harris* (1871) L.R. 7 Q.B. 157, a decision under the Bills of Sale Act 1854.

[18] Bills of Sales Act (1878) Amendment Act 1882, s.11.

[19] *Fenton v. Blythe* (1890) 25 Q.B.D. 417.

[20] *Re Parker, ex parte Turquand* (1885) 14 Q.B.D. 636; *Marshall and Snelgrove Ltd v. Gower* [1923] 1 K.B. 356.

[21] Bills of Sale Act 1878, s.14.

[22] *Re Emery, ex parte Official Receiver* (1888) 21 Q.B.D. 405.

[23] The same provision for absolute bills of sale is in s.10 of the Bills of Sale Act 1878.

[24] *Trinder v. Raynor* (1887) 56 L.J.Q.B. 422.

[25] Bills of Sale Act 1878, s.15.

[26] *Crew v. Cummings* (1888) 21 Q.B.D. 420.

[27] *ibid.* See also *Re Parsons, ex parte Furber* [1893] 2 Q.B. 1Z.

[28] Bills of Sale Act 1878, ss.12, 16; Bills of Sale Act (1878) Amendment Act 1882, s.16.

obtain further credit. Under the Bills of Sale Act 1854, registration could be avoided by giving successive bills of sale of the same property for the same debt before the seven-day period had expired. This practice was stopped (except where the court is satisfied that the subsequent bill was given bona fide for the purpose of correcting a material error in the prior bills) by providing that the subsequent bill should be absolutely void to the extent of the repetition.[29]

5. Inventory and specific description

12–23 The Bills of Sale Act 1882, s. 4 states that:

> "Every bill of sale shall have annexed thereto or written thereon a schedule containing an inventory of the personal chattels comprised in the bill of sale; and such bill of sale, save as hereinafter mentioned, shall have effect only in respect of the personal chattels specifically described in the said schedule; and shall be void, except as against the grantor, in respect of any personal chattels not so specifically described".

The effect of this provision is that if the bill has no schedule at all it is absolutely void for all purposes, not being in accordance with the statutory form.[30] If it has a schedule in which some of the chattels are not "specifically described" it is void against third parties in respect of the chattels, but it remains valid for all purposes as between grantor and grantee. Thus a bill of sale which refers in the Schedule to some specifically-described existing chattels, and some after-acquired chattels, it is void against third parties in respect of the after-acquired chattels but otherwise valid. On the other hand, if the body of the bill contains a mortgage of after-acquired chattels it is absolutely void for non-compliance with the statutory form.[31]

There must be an inventory. A general description such as "stock-in-trade" is inadequate.[32] The chattels must be described as a businessman would describe them[33] and the degree of detail will vary from case to case.[34] A more detailed description will be necessary when the chattels mortgaged are part of a fluctuating stock-in-trade. There is very little direct authority as to what constitutes a specific description, though it has been said that "specifically" involves a description which helps to separate a chattel from the rest of the things of the same class.[35]

---

[29] Bills of Sale Act 1878, s.9.
[30] *Griffin v. Union Deposit Bank* (1887) 3 T.L.R. 608.
[31] *Thomas v. Kelly* [1888] 13 A.C. 506.
[32] *Witt v. Banner* (1887) 20 Q.B.D. 114.
[33] *Roberts v. Roberts* (1884) 13 Q.B.D. 794, *per* Lindley L.J. at 806.
[34] *Davies v. Jenkins* [1900] 1 Q.B. 133; *Carpenter v. Deen* (1889) 23 Q.B.D. 566; *Hickley v. Greenwood* (1890) 25 Q.B.D. 277; *Witt v. Banner, supra; Herbert's Trustee v. Higgins* [1926] Ch. 794: *Davidson v. Carlton Bank Ltd* [1893] 1 Q.B. 82.
[35] *Witt v. Banner, supra.*

6. **True ownership: section 5**

Section 5 of the 1882 Act states that: **12–24**

> "Save as herein-after mentioned,[36] a bill of sale shall be void, except as against the grantor, in respect of any personal chattels specifically described in the schedule thereto of which the grantor was not the true owner at the time of the execution of the bill of sale."

The term "true owner" includes an equitable owner or a trustee[37] and is not limited to "beneficial owner". If an owner of chattels has previously executed a mortgage bill of sale, he still owns the equity of redemption and remains the true owner for the purposes of a second bill granted subject to the first.[38] A mortgage bill of sale by a legal owner is valid even if third parties have prior equitable interests in the chattels. If the grantor has already made an absolute sale or gift of the chattels, he has transferred both the legal and equitable title and is not the true owner; it is irrelevant that the grantee has no notice of the sale or gift.[39] A hirer under a hire-purchase agreement being merely a bailee for use is not the true owner. Thus he cannot create a valid mortgage of the chattel until he has exercised his option to purchase.[40] A person beneficially entitled to chattels is the "true owner" to the extent of his interest.[41] However, if two persons purport to assign goods jointly as grantor, the bill of sale will be valid only to the extent of the chattels which they own jointly.[42] A purported assignment "jointly and severally" of chattels, some of which belonged to the husband and some to the wife, was held absolutely void for non-compliance with the statutory form, which contemplates a single grantor.[43] But where a husband was correctly assigned as sole grantor and the wife was made a party to the bill of sale for collateral purposes, the bill was held to be valid.[44] Whenever a bill of sale is avoided as against third parties, a grantee cannot maintain title to the goods against such third parties, for example, the grantor's assignee under an assignment for the benefit of creditors, even though he has possession of the goods.[45]

7. **Bankruptcy: section 15**

By section 20 of the 1878 Act, chattels comprised in an absolute bill of sale are   **12–25**
deemed not to be within the possession order and disposition of the grantor for
the purpose of bankruptcy proceedings. However, section 15 of the 1882 Act

---

[36] Bills of Sale Act (1878) Amendment Act 1882, s.6, creating exceptions to the avoidance provisions in ss.4 and 5 in respect of growing crops, or fixtures, separately assigned, or trade machinery.
[37] *Re Sarl, ex parte Williams* [1892] 2 Q.B. 591.
[38] *Thomas v. Searles* [1891] 2 Q.B. 408; *Usher v. Martin* (1889) 24 Q.B.D. 272.
[39] *Tuck v. Southern Counties Deposit Bank* (1889) 42 Ch.D. 471.
[40] *Lewis v. Thomas* [1919] 1 K.B. 319.
[41] *Re Field, ex parte Pratt* (1890) 63 L.T. 289.
[42] *Gordon v. Goldstein* [1924] 2 K.B. 779, where a husband and wife purported to assign jointly chattels which belonged to the wife alone. The bill was held void against third parties under s.5.
[43] *Saunders v. White* [1902] 1 K.B. 472.
[44] *Brandon Hia Ltd v. Lane* [1915] 1 K.B. 250.
[45] *Newlove v. Shrewsbury* (1888) 21 Q.B.D. 41.

repealed this provision in respect of security bills and provided that the chattels comprised therein might be seized by the trustee in bankruptcy.[46] The provisions formerly contained in section 38 of the Bankruptcy Act 1914, which concerned the bankrupt's available property, are replaced by section 283 of the Insolvency Act 1986[47] which define the bankrupt's estate. Section 306 of the Insolvency Act 1986[48] provides for the vesting of the bankrupt's estate in the trustee by operation of law as soon as his appointment takes effect. Goods comprised in a security bill of sale can be distrained as for rates and taxes.[49] They are not protected against a distraining landlord,[50] who is entitled to exercise his right of distress during the five-day period provided by section 13 of the 1882 Act.[51]

8. **Priority of bills of sale**

12–26   It is possible to create successive security bills of sale because the grantor is still, after the execution of the first bill, the owner of the equity of redemption and is therefore the "true owner".[52] Where successive security bills of sale cover the same chattels in whole or in part, they rank in order of their registration.[53] An unregistered security bill of sale is void as to the security.[54] However, where a grantor gives an absolute bill of sale, it remains valid between him and the grantee irrespective of registration, so that he has no title to, and ceases to be the true owner of, the chattels comprised therein. Since, by section 5 of the 1882 Act, a bill of sale of chattels not made by the true owner is void against third parties, an earlier absolute bill of sale, registered or not, has priority over a later registered bill of sale. The doctrine of notice, therefore, is irrelevant to the question of priorities.[55]

Section 10 of the 1878 Act applies whether the security created by the bill of sale is legal or equitable. A registered agreement to create a bill of sale will therefore prevail over a later, registered bill of sale. But if the legal title to chattels is acquired in good faith by someone who has no actual notice of the bill of sale, it will prevail over a registered equitable mortgage of chattels by bill of sale.[56] Registration merely fixes priorities between competing bills of sale and is not notice to all the world. A legal mortgage of chattels created by bill of sale will not prevail against a third party who obtains title to the chattels from the mortgagor in the ordinary course of the mortgagor's business.[57] The grantee of

[46] *Re Ginger* [1897] 2 Q.B. 461; approved, *Hollinshead v. Egan* [1913] A.C. 564.
[47] Replacing s.130 of the Insolvency Act 1985, to which it corresponds.
[48] Replacing s.153 of the Insolvency Act 1985, to which it corresponds, and restating more precisely and clearly the law formerly contained in s.18(1) of the Bankruptcy Act 1914. See also *post*, para. 23–07.
[49] Bills of Sale Act (1878) Amendment Act 1882, s.14.
[50] Law of Distress Amendment Act 1908, s.4.
[51] *London and Westminster Loan and Discount Co. v. London and North Western Railway Co.* [1893] 2 Q.B. 49.
[52] *Thomas v. Searles* [1891] 2 Q.B. 408.
[53] Bills of Sale Act 1878, s.10.
[54] Bills of Sale Act (1878) Amendment Act 1882, s.8.
[55] See *Edwards v. Edwards* (1876) 2 Ch.D. 291, where the court refused to postpone the holder of a registered bill of sale to the holder of a prior unregistered bill of which he had express notice.
[56] *Joseph v. Lyons* (1884) 15 Q.B.D 280.
[57] If title is obtained otherwise than in the ordinary course of the mortgagor's business, the purchaser is postponed to the mortgagee: *Payne v. Fern* (1881) 6 Q.B.D. 620.

a bill of sale over the grantor's stock-in-trade impliedly authorises the grantor to carry on the business and bona fide purchasers of the chattels acquire a title valid against the grantee.[58] Nor does it matter that the bill of sale contains a covenant not to dispose of the chattels without consent.[59]

During the currency of the reputed ownership provisions, security bills comprising goods in trade or business were considered to be precarious securities. *Re Ginger*[60] decided that, if a mortgagee wished to remove the false reputation of ownership he must either publicise his title or, once one of the causes under section 7 has arisen, take possession before he gets notice of an act of bankruptcy. That disadvantage has been eliminated by the abolition of the reputed ownership provisions.[61]

---

[58] *National Mercantile Bank v. Hampson* (1880) 5 Q.B.D. 177.
[59] *Walker v. Clay* (1880) 49 L.J.Q.B. 560.
[60] [1948] 1 K.B. 705.
[61] By the Insolvency Act 1985, s.235, Sched. 10, Pt. III.

CHAPTER 13

MORTGAGES OF CHOSES IN ACTION

GENERAL PRINCIPLES

1. "Chose in action"

There is no precise definition of the term "chose in action,"[1] but it is generally **13–01** regarded as including all forms of personalty not held in possession and which, if wrongfully withheld, must be recovered by action.[2] In contrast, a chose in possession is a tangible thing the possession of which will pass by delivery and can be seized and sold in execution of a judgment in a personal action.

Choses in action, therefore, cover diverse forms of incorporeal personalty varying from simple contract debts to such specialised property as shares in a company, patents, copyrights and trade-marks. They also include equitable interests in a trust fund of personalty. Moreover, although they may not usually be regarded as including equitable interests in a trust fund of realty, it will be convenient to deal with those interests in this chapter, because their mortgages are governed by the same principles as choses in action. As it is not possible here to deal individually with every form of chose in action, the general principles of their mortgages are set out and then specific regard is directed to mortgages of equitable interests in trust funds, insurance policies, partnership shares and shares in a company all of which are particularly important in practice.

Mortgages of choses in action are expressly excluded from the operation of the Bills of Sale Acts.[3] They depend, in most cases, on the general law of assignment,[4] though the assignment of some choses in action is regulated by statute.[5]

---

[1] "Chose in action" is a known legal expression used to describe all personal rights of property which can only be claimed or enforced by action, and not by taking physical possession. *Torkington v. Magee* [1902] 2 K.B. 427 at 430, *per* Channell J.

[2] *British Mutoscope and Biograph Co. v. Homer* [1901] 1 Ch. 671.

[3] See the definition of "goods" in s.4 of the Bills of Sale Act 1878.

[4] For a more detailed treatment, see *Chitty on Contracts* (28th ed., 1999), Chap. 20; Bailey, (1931) 47 L.Q.R. 516; (1932) 48 L.Q.R. 248 and 547; Marshall, *Assignment of Choses in Action* (1950); Biscoe, *Credit Factoring* (1973).

[5] Bills of lading; Bills of Lading Act 1855, s.1. Policies of life assurance; Policies of Assurance Act 1867, s.1. Policies of marine assurance; Marine Insurance Act 1906, s.50(2). Shares in a company; Stock Transfer Act 1963 and Companies Act 1985, s.182(1). Negotiable instruments; Bills of Exchange Act 1882. Patent Act 1977, s.30. Copyrights; Copyright, Designs and Patents Act 1988, s.8. See also Law of Property (Miscellaneous Provisions) Act 1994, s.1(4), which provides that covenants for title (whether full or limited title guarantee) may apply to assignments of choses in action.

2. **The position at common law**

At common law, the general rule was that no debt or other chose in action could be assigned without the debtor's consent. It was said that assignments would be:

> "the occasion of multiplying contentions and suits of great oppression of the people, and the subversion of the due and equal execution of justice."[6]

This rule may have had its origin in the conceptual difficulties inherent in conceiving of the transfer of an intangible[7] but the possibility was recognised by statute in 1603.[8] At common law the Crown could both grant and receive choses in action by way of assignment,[9] and when the rules of the Law Merchant were incorporated into English law, mercantile choses in action became not only assignable but negotiable.[10] The difference is that, whereas an assignee takes subject to all defects in the assignor's title, a holder for value in due course gets a good title even though the person from whom he received it had not.

13–02 Apart from these exceptions, at common law the debtor had to be made a party to the assignment which, therefore, amounted to a novation, that is, the creation of a new contract between the assignor and the assignee. This involves the consent of all three parties that the original contract be extinguished and replaced by a new one.[11] It is thus necessary for the new contract to be supported by consideration.[12] An alternative procedure appears to be by acknowledgment,[13] whereby the creditor asks his debtors to pay some third party, and the debtor agrees to do so and informs the third party.[14] Assignment could also be made by power of attorney but this was normally revocable.[15]

3. **The position in equity**

Equity, however, freely permitted the assignment of both legal and equitable choses in action.[16] The Judicature Act 1873, introduced a general form of statutory assignment, but before 1875 mortgages of choses in action, subject to the exceptions mentioned above, could be created only by equitable assignment. The equitable rules still govern mortgages of choses in action which do not

---

[6] *Lampet's Case* (1612) 10 Co.Rep. 46 at 48(a).

[7] Holdsworth, *History of English Law*; Bailey (1931) 47 L.Q.R. 516.

[8] The statute 1 Jac. I, c. 15 permitted the assignment of the debts of a bankrupt.

[9] *Chitty on Contracts* (28th ed., 1999), para. 20–001.

[10] Milnes Holden, *The History of Negotiable Instruments in England Law* (1955).

[11] *Wilson v. Lloyd* (1873) L.R. 16 Eq. 60; *Miller's Case* (1876) 3 Ch.D. 391; *Perry v. National Provincial Bank* [1910] 1 Ch. 464; *Meek v. Port of London Authority* [1918] 2 Ch. 96.

[12] *Tatlock v. Harris* (1789) 3 Term Rep. 174; *Cuxon v. Chadley* (1824) 3 B. & C. 591; *Wharton v. Walker* (1825) 4 B. & C. 163.

[13] Davies, (1959) 75 L.Q.R. 220; Yates (1977) Conv.(N.S.) 49; Goff and Jones, *Law of Restitution* (5th ed., 1998), pp. 691–693; *Chitty on Contracts* (28th ed., 1999), para. 20–087.

[14] *Wilson v. Coupland* (1821) 5 B. & Ald. 228; *Hamilton v. Spottiswoode* (1849) 4 Ex. 200; *Griffin v. Weatherby* (1862) L.R. 3 Q.B. 753. As to whether and in what circumstances consideration is required, see *Liversidge v. Broadbent* (1859) 4 H. & N. 603; *Shamia v. Joory* [1958] 1 Q.B. 448. The criticisms made of this line of authorities by *Chitty, supra*, para. 20–08 are cogent.

[15] Marshall, *Assignment of Choses in Action* (1950), pp. 67–69.

[16] *Wood v. Griffith* (1818) 1 Swanst. 43.

comply with the statutory form and, as will be seen, *charges* of choses in action can only be created by equitable assignment. It is necessary, therefore, to consider two main methods of mortgaging choses in action: (i) by assignment in equity; and (ii) by statutory assignment.

MORTGAGE BY EQUITABLE ASSIGNMENT

Equity makes a distinction between the assignment of legal choses, such as **13–03** contract debts, and equitable choses such as legacies and trust interests. While both forms of chose in action are equally assignable, the assignee of a chose in equity may sue in his own name provided he has given notice to the holder of the fund.[17] An equitable assignment is absolute and complete without notice having been given to the debtor or fundholder, for notice does not render the title perfect,[18] and the validity of the assignment is not affected by the death or bankruptcy of the assignor before the holder of the fund receives notice. Furthermore, until the debtor receives notice, he is entitled to continue paying the original creditor[19]; and once the debtor has notice of the assignment, he cannot do anything to take away or diminish the rights of the assignee as they stood at the time of the notice.[20] Priorities between successive assignments are determined by the order in which the debtor or trustee receives notice of the assignee's title, in accordance with the rule in *Dearle v. Hall*.[21]

1. Essentials of an equitable assignment

An equitable assignment can be made by an agreement between a debtor and his creditor that a specific chose in action which is, or will be in the hands of a third person, or is due from them and belongs to the debtor, shall be applied in discharge of the debt. The form of an equitable assignment is considered below.[22]

Thus, in *Brice v. Bannister*,[23] G, who owed a debt to P, was performing work for D who was paying him by instalments. Before the work was finished, and at a time when D had paid all the instalments then due, G directed D to pay £100 to P out of moneys due, or to become due, from D to G. G gave D written notice but he refused to be bound by it and continued to pay the money to G. It was held, by a majority of the Court of Appeal, that this was a valid assignment on which P was entitled to recover from D, notwithstanding D's payments to G, subsequent to the notice.

Alternatively, an equitable assignment can be made by an order[24] given by a debtor whereby the holder of the fund is directed or authorised to pay it to the

---

[17] *Row v. Dawson* (1749) 1 Ves.Sen. 331; *Walker v. Bradford Old Bank* (1884) 12 Q.B.D. 511.

[18] *Ward v. Duncombe* [1893] A.C. 369.

[19] *Stocks v. Dobson* (1853) 4 De G. M. & G. 11.

[20] *Roxburghe v. Cox* (1881) 17 Ch.D. 520.

[21] (1823) 3 Russ. 1; see *post*, para. 13–09 *et seq.* and see also L.P.A. 1925, s.137(3) which provides that notice of an equitable assignment of trust interests is ineffective for the purpose of determining priority among competing interests unless in writing.

[22] See *post*, para. 13–13A.

[23] (1878) 3 Q.B.D. 569, CA (Bramwell, Cotton L.JJ.; Brett L.J. *dissentiente*).

[24] *Brown, Shipley & Co. v. Kough* (1885) 29 Ch.D. 848.

creditor.[25] There must be an engagement to pay the debt out of a particular fund.[26] A mere direction to pay money to a third person is not necessarily an assignment, for it may be a revocable mandate.[27] The direction itself gives the third person no right in the subject matter of the mandate and is revoked by any subsequent disposition of the property inconsistent with it.[28] Nevertheless, even in the case of an equitable chose, the assignor may for practical reasons have to be joined as a party when the assignment is not an absolute assignment of the whole debt. For, if the assignment is for part of the debt only, the assignor has to be joined in the action in order that the accounts may be correctly taken between the third parties, and that the debtor may be protected against a second action in respect of the same debt.[29] The modern practice in regard to joining an assignor is, unless the debtor waives the assignor's presence in court[30] to join him as a nominal claimant with an indemnity for costs, but, if he raises objection, to join him as a defendant.[31]

A cheque, being a bill of exchange is not an equitable assignment of the drawer's balance with his bankers.[32]

Where the assignment was absolute, the assignee could sue in his own sole name[33] before the Judicature Act 1873, and this position is unaltered. The provision for statutory assignment made by the Judicature Act 1873, section 25(6), did not "forbid or destroy equitable assignments or impair their efficacy in the slightest degree".[34]

If the assignment gives a right to payment out of a particular fund or property but does not transfer the fund or property, it is "by way of charge"[35] and so is an assignment of so much of a future debt as shall be sufficient to satisfy an uncertain future indebtedness.[36]

2. Form

13–04   Subject to section 53(1)(c) of the Law of Property Act 1925 (which provides that a disposition of an equitable interest or trust subsisting at the time of the

---

[25] *Row v. Dawson* (1849) 1 Ves. Sen. 331; *Burn v. Carvalho* (1839) 4 My. & Cr. 690; *Rodick v. Gandell* (1852) 1 De G.M. & G. 763; *Diplock v. Hammond* (1854) 5 De G.M. & G. 320; *William Brandt's Sons & Co. v. Dunlop Rubber Co.* [1905] A.C. 454; *Palmer v. Carey* [1926] A.C. 703, P.C.; *Cotton v. Heyl* [1930] 1 Ch. 510; *Re Warren* [1938] Ch. 725; *Elders Pastoral Limited v. Bank of New Zealand* [1990] 1 W.L.R. 1478.

[26] *Watson v. Duke of Wellington* (1830) 1 Russ. & M. 602; *Percival v. Dunn* (1885) 29 Ch.D. 128; *Re Gunsbourg* (1919) 88 L.J.K.B. 479.

[27] *Malcom v. Scott* (1843) 3 Hare 39; *Bell v. London and North Western Railway* (1852) 15 Beav. 548; *Re Whitting, ex p. Hall* (1879) 10 Ch.D. 615.

[28] *Morrell v. Wootten* (1852) 16 Beav. 197; *cf. London & Yorkshire Bank v. White* (1895) 11 T.L.R. 570 and *The Zigurds* [1934] A.C. 209.

[29] *Re Steel Wing Co.* [1921] 1 Ch. 349.

[30] *William Brandt's Sons v. Dunlop Rubber Co.* [1905] A.C. 454.

[31] *Bowden's Patents Syndicate v. Smith* [1904] 2 Ch. 86; see also *Weddell v. J. A. Pearce & Major* [1988] Ch. 26 as to non-joinder under the Rules of the Supreme Court.

[32] *Hopkinson v. Forster* (1874) L.R. 19 Eq. 74.

[33] *Cator v. Croydon Canal Co.* (1841) 4 Y. & C. Ex. 593; *Donaldson v. Donaldson* (1854) Kay. 711.

[34] *William Brandt's Sons & Co. v. Dunlop Rubber Co.* [1905] A.C. 454 at 461, *per* Lord Macnaghten.

[35] *Tancred v. Delagoa Bay and East Africa Rty. Co.* (1889) 23 Q.B.D. 239.

[36] *Jones v. Humphreys* [1902] 1 K.B. 10; *cf. Mercantile Bank of London v. Evans* [1899] 2 Q.B. 613.

disposition must be in writing signed by the person disposing of the same or by his agent thereunto lawfully authorised in writing or by will), an equitable assignment is not required to be made in any particular form either from the point of view of evidence of or terminology. It may be verbal[37] and couched in any language provided that the interest in the debt[38] is unmistakably made over to the assignee.[39] It is immaterial that the amount of the debt has not been ascertained at the time of the assignment.[40] Nor is an equitable assignment incomplete merely because notice has not been given to the debtor. Highly desirable though it is for an assignee to notify the debtor of his interest in order to bind the debtor not to pay out to any third party, an equitable assignment is by itself a perfect conveyance as between assignor and assignee.[41] Moreover, notice of an equitable assignment, when given, may be informal and even indirect, except in the case of trust interests, where notice must be in writing under section 137(3) of the Law of Property Act 1925.

Equitable assignments are thus virtually unrestricted by formal requirements. Mortgages of choses in action may still be created by these informal assignments operating only in equity. It is necessary only to make the nature of the transaction plain.[42] Thus in *Tailby v. Official Receiver*[43] it was said:

> "It has long been settled that future property, possibilities and expectancies are assignable in equity for value. The mode or form of assignment is absolutely immaterial provided that the intention of the parties is clear."

Conversely it may be clear that the transaction is not an assignment. In *Re Danish Bacon Co. v. Staff Pension Fund Trusts*[44] a revocable nomination which would not in any event become effective until the death of the nominator and this might never affect any property at all, was held not fairly capable of being called an assignment.

3. Parties to Proceedings

Whereas, prior to the Judicature Act 1873, an assignee of an equitable chose in action could sue in his own name provided that the assignment was absolute and notice had been given to the holder of the fund[45]; the assignee of a legal chose in action could not. This arises because equity, having exclusive control of

13–04A

---

[37] *Brown, Shipley & Co. v. Kough* (1885) 29 Ch.D. 848 at 854.

[38] Whereas there cannot be a statutory assignment of part of a debt or fund, there can be a good equitable assignment of a specified debt or fund: *Roddick v. Gandell* (1852) 1 De G.M. & G. 763; *Palmer v. Carey* [1926] A.C. 703, PC.

[39] *William Brandt's Sons Ltd v. Dunlop Rubber Co.* [1905] A.C. 454.

[40] *Crowfoot v. Gurney* (1832) 9 Bing. 372 at 376.

[41] *Gorringe v. Irwell India Rubber Works* (1886) 34 Ch.D. 128. An equitable assignment is good without notice against a trustee in bankruptcy: *Re Anderson* [1911] 1 K.B. 896, or against a judgment creditor: *Scott v. Lord Hastings* (1858) 4 K. & J. 633; and see applied in *United Bank of Kuwait v. Sahib* [1995] 2 W.L.R. 94, *Holt v. Heatherfield Trust Ltd* [1942] 2 K.B. 1.

[42] *German v. Yates* (1915) 32 T.L.R. 52.

[43] (1888) 13 App.Cas. 523 at 543 (assignment of future book debts in unspecified businesses not so vague as to be invalid).

[44] [1971] 1 W.L.R. 248.

[45] *Row v. Dawson* (1749) 1 Ves. Sim. 331.

equitable interests, can allow an assignee of an equitable chose[46] to sue directly. In the case of a legal chose,[47] he has to have the assignor nominally a party before the court in order to bind the assignor's rights in the legal chose at common law. Equity, in fact, treats the assignor of a legal chose as trustee of his rights for the assignee.

After the Judicature Act 1873 came into operation, the position was that assignments of legal choses in action not complying with the statute continued to be valid in equity[48] but both the assignor and the assignee had to be made parties to the proceedings.[49] If the assignor wishes to sue, he must join the assignee.[50]

It has been suggested that the rule requiring both the assignor and the assignee to be party to proceedings for enforcement of an equitable assignment of a legal chose in action serves a useful purpose only where the assignor has not wholly disposed of his interest, since in such cases it ensures that all parties with an interest in the chose are brought before the court. Conversely, it has also been suggested that there is no need for the rule where, although the assignment is absolute, it takes effect only as an equitable assignment because, for example, it is not in writing.[51]

MORTGAGE BY ASSIGNMENT UNDER THE LAW OF PROPERTY ACT 1925, s. 136

13–05   Section 25(6) of the Judicature Act 1873, introduced a new form of statutory assignment not limited to particular forms of choses in action. This section was, with negligible variations of language, re-enacted in section 136 of the Law of Property Act 1925, which provides as follows:

> "(1) Any absolute[52] assignment by writing[53] under the hand of the assignor (not purporting to be by way of charge only) of any debt[54] or other legal thing in action, of which express notice in writing has been given to the debtor, trustee or other person from whom the assignor would have been entitled to claim such debt or thing in action, is effectual in law (subject to equities having priority over the right of the assignee) to pass and transfer from the date of such notice—
>
> (a)   the legal right to such debt or thing in action;
> (b)   all legal and other remedies for the same; and

---

[46] A chose which could be sued for only in the Court of Chancery, *e.g.* an interest in a trust fund.

[47] A chose which could be sued for only in the common law courts, *e.g.* a contract debt.

[48] *William Brandt's Sons & Co. v. Dunlop Rubber Co.* [1905] A.C. 454.

[49] *Performing Rights Society Ltd v. London Theatre of Varieties Ltd* [1924] A.C. 1; *Williams v. Atlantic Assurance Co.* [1933] 1 K.B. 81; *Holt v. Heatherfield Trust Ltd* [1942] 2 K.B. 1.

[50] *Walter and Sullivan Ltd v. Murphy & Sons Ltd* [1955] 2 Q.B. 584.

[51] *Chitty on Contracts* (28th ed., 1999), para. 20–037.

[52] "Absolute" does not have the same meaning as in the Bills of Sale Act, where it means "not by way of security." *Lloyds Scottish Finance Limited v. Cyril Lord Carpet Sales Limited* (1992) B.C.L.C. 609.

[53] No particular form of words is necessary: *Re Westerton* [1919] 2 Ch. 104; but an intention to transfer the interest must be shown: *Curran v. Newpark Cinemas Ltd* [1951] 1 All E.R. 295; *Coulls v. Bagot's Executor and Trustee Co. Ltd* (1967) 119 C.L.R. 460.

[54] This means "the entire debt"; see *Re Steel Wing Co.* [1921] 1 Ch. 349: see *post*, para. 13–06.

(c) the power to give a good discharge for the same without the concurrence of the assignor:

Provided that, if the debtor, trustee or other person liable in respect of such debt or thing in action has notice—

(a) that the assignment is disputed by the assignor or any person claiming under him; or
(b) of any other opposing or conflicting claims to such debt or thing in action;

he may, if he thinks fit, either call upon the persons making claim thereto to interplead concerning the same, or pay the debt or other thing in action into court under the provisions of the Trustee Act 1925.

(2) This section does not affect the provisions of the Policies of Assurance Act 1867."[55]

1. "Absolute assignment"

The opening words of the section at once raise the query whether statutory assignment is available at all for the creation of mortgages, for only absolute assignments not by way of charge are within its scope. It is, however, well established that an assignment in statutory form of a whole debt to a mortgagee, with the usual proviso for redemption and reconveyance, is an absolute assignment within section 136.[56] The same is true where an assignment is made apparently out and out, but, in fact, for purposes of security and the equity of redemption is merely implied,[57] or where a whole debt is assigned for the discharge of a liability subject to a trust for the repayment of any surplus to the assignor.[58]

13–06

In *Durham Bros v. Robertson*,[59] S & Co. charged £1,080 due to them from R on completion of certain buildings as security for advances, and assigned their interest in that sum to D until the money with added interest was repaid to them. Unlike the cases cited earlier, this was held not to be an absolute assignment since the debtor would be uncertain as to whom he should pay the money unless he inquired into the state of accounts between the assignor and the assignee. The assignment is absolute only where the debtor is entitled to pay the whole debt to the assignee without further inquiry unless he is notified otherwise.

In that case, Chitty L.J. said[60]:

"The assignment of the debt was absolute: it purported to pass the entire interest of the assignor in the debt to the mortgagee, and it was not an assignment purporting to be by way of charge only. The mortgagor-assignor

---

[55] See *post*, para. 13–16.
[56] *Tancred v. Delagoa Bay and East Africa Rty. Co.* (1889) 23 Q.B.D. 239.
[57] *Hughes v. Pump House Hotel Co.* [1902] 2 K.B. 190, CA.
[58] *Comfort v. Betts* [1891] 1 Q.B. 737, CA; *Bank of Liverpool v. Holland* (1926) 43 T.L.R. 29; *Camdix International Limited v. Bank of Zambia* [1998] Q.B. 22, CA.
[59] [1898] 1 Q.B. 765, CA, applied in *Mutual General Insurance Co. Ltd v. ANZ Banking Group (New Zealand) Limited* [1995] 1 W.L.R. 1140, JCPC.
[60] *ibid.* at 772.

had a right to redeem, and on repayment of the advances a right to have the assigned debt reassigned to him. Notice of the assignment pursuant to the subsection would be given to the original debtor and he would thus know with certainty in whom the legal right to sue was vested."

The crucial point thus is whether the title of the assignee is absolute in the sense that the debtor, until he is informed to the contrary by notification, is entitled to pay the whole debt to the assignee without inquiry. The object of the section, in excepting assignments by way of charge, was to protect the debtor against repeated actions in respect of the same debt and against the risks involved in making payments dependent on the state of accounts between other parties. The assignment of an entire debt by way of mortgage is not inconsistent with this object because, for the time being, the mortgagee became *vis-à-vis* the debtor the absolute owner of the debt. Uncertainty in the state of accounts *between assignor and assignee* does not prevent an assignment from being absolute if it does not affect the obligations of the debtor. So in *Hughes v. Pump House Hotel Co.*,[61] when debts had been assigned to a bank as continuing security to cover a current account, this was held to be a perfectly good statutory assignment.

A fortiori, a determinable interest of only part of a debt cannot be the subject of a statutory assignment.[62] This was illustrated by the facts of *Jones v. Humphreys*,[63] in which a schoolmaster assigned to a moneylender so much and such part of his salary as should be necessary to pay £22 10s. or any further sums advanced. This is precisely what the statute means by a charge as distinct from an absolute assignment. Such a charge cannot be created by statutory assignment, but is good in equity as a partial assignment of the debt. The practical effect is that the enforcement of the charge entails the joining of the assignor as a party to the proceedings against the primary debtor, *i.e.* in the present case the headmaster of the school. It also now seems settled that part of a debt cannot be assigned under section 136 on the ground that such an assignment is not "absolute." Accordingly the mortgage even of a specified portion of a debt can only operate in equity.[64] This was held to be the case in *Walter and Sullivan Ltd v. J. Murphy and Sons Ltd*[65] where A owed B £1,808, B owed C £1,558 and B gave A an irrevocable authority to pay £1,558 to C. This was held to be a good equitable assignment of the £1,558 by way of charge. It was also held that B and C were necessary parties to an action against A.

This rule has arisen because conflicting decisions might arise if either the existence or the amount of the debt was in dispute[66] and also because of the burden on the debtor which would be created if the creditor was allowed to split up the debt into several causes of action.[67]

---

[61] [1902] 2 K.B. 190, CA.

[62] *Jones v. Humphreys* [1902] 1 K.B. 10.

[63] *ibid.*

[64] *Forster v. Baker* [1910] 2 K.B. 636; *Re Steel Wing Co.* [1921] 1 Ch. 349; *G. & T. Earle Ltd v. Hemsworth RDC* (1928) 44 T.L.R. 605 at 758; *Williams v. Atlantic Assurance Co.* [1933] 1 K.B. 81 at 100; though the point was not originally free from doubt: *Brice v. Bannister* (1878) 3 Q.B.D. 569; *Skipper & Tucker v. Holloway & Howard* [1910] 2 K.B. 630.

[65] [1955] 2 Q.B. 584, CA. See also *Three Rivers District Council v. Governor & The Company of the Bank of England* [1996] Q.B. 292, CA.

[66] *Re Steel Wing Co.* [1921] 1 Ch. 349 at 357.

[67] *Durham Bros. v. Robertson* [1898] 1 Q.B. 765, CA.

Statutory assignment of legal and equitable choses in action

Section 136 does not supersede the provisions of the Law Merchant or of **13–07**
particular statutes governing the assignment of special forms of property. Otherwise there appears to be little restriction on the kinds of choses in action which
are assignable under the section. The words "any debt or other *legal* thing in
action" have to be interpreted as not confined to legal choses properly so called.
They cover any right which the common law did not look on as assignable
because of it being a chose in action, but which equity dealt with as assignable.[68]
This means that equitable as well as legal choses in action are assignable under
the statute, but not rights such as contracts of personal service, which not even
equity has ever regarded as being assignable.[69]

2. **Notice**

Assignment under section 136 has two requirements of form: **13–08**

(1) The assignment itself must be in writing under the hand of the
assignor.
(2) Written notice of the assignment must be given to the debtor. As the
section does not say from whom, etc. notice is to issue, it may be given
by the assignor, the assignee or his successors in title.

The notice must be given, otherwise the assignee cannot sue in his own
name,[70] but it can be given by the assignor, the assignee or their successors in
title[71] at any time[72] before an action is brought. If there are joint debtors, notice
must be given to both.[73] It is essential not only for a statutory assignment to be
in writing, but also for the notice to be in writing. The requirement of notice in
writing must be met even if the debtor cannot read and the assignment is brought
to his attention in some other way.[74] Whereas notice of an equitable assignment
simply operates to establish the right of the assignee against third parties,
the notice of a statutory assignment is an integral part of the conveyance from the
assignor to the assignee. The assignment takes effect from the date when the
notice is received by the debtor and if no written notice is given, it takes effect
in equity only.[75]

---

[68] *Torkington v. Magee* [1902] 2 K.B. 427, rvsd. [1903] 1 K.B. 644; *King v. Victoria Insurance Co.*
[1896] A.C. 250; *Manchester Brewery v. Coombs* [1901] 2 Ch. 608; *Re Pain* [1919] 1 Ch. 38; *G.
& T. Earle Ltd v. Hemsworth R.D.C.* (1928) 44 T.L.R. 605.
[69] *Tolhurst v. Associated Portland Cement Manufacturers* [1903] A.C. 414.
[70] If the assignee does sue without having given notice, the claim is not a nullity but will be stayed
since (bar certain special circumstances) an equitable assignee cannot enter judgment without the
assignor being a party: *Weddle v. J.A. Pearce and Major* [1988] Ch. 26. See also *Deposit Protection
Board v. Dalia* [1994] 2 A.C. 367.
[71] *Bateman v. Hunt* [1904] 2 K.B. 530.
[72] *ibid.* See also *Compania Columbiana de Seguros v. Pacific Steam Navigation Co.* [1965] 1 Q.B.
101; including a time after the death of the assignor; *Walker v. Bradford Old Bank* (1884) 12 Q.B.D.
511; *Re Westerton* [1919] 2 Ch. 104 or assignee; *Bateman v. Hunt* [1904] 2 K.B. 530.
[73] *Josselson v. Borst and Gliksten* [1938] 1 K.B. 723.
[74] *Hockley and Papworth v. Goldstein* (1920) 90 L.J.K.B. 111.
[75] *Holt v. Heatherfield Trust Ltd* [1942] 2 K.B. 1.

There is no need to state a date, but if the notice purports to identify the assignment by its date and the date is wrong, it will be invalid.[76] It has been suggested that the notice will be invalid unless the amount of the debt is correctly stated,[77] but, apart from any question of validity that might arise, it is prudent, before executing the assignment, to obtain a written admission from the debtor as to the amount of the debt assigned,[78] so as to prevent any dispute, when the assignee comes to realise the security, as to how much was due when the assignment was taken. As a creditor can assign by directing his debtors to pay the assignee it would appear that a single written document could serve as both assignment and notice.[79]

Apart from the statutory requirement, the giving of notice forms an important part of the assignee's protection. First, it binds the debtor, trustee or other person from whom the assignor would have been entitled to claim the debt or thing in action, to pay it or convey it to the assignee.[80] Secondly, it gives priority over subsequent dealings between the debtor and the assignor. Whether an assignment is statutory or equitable, the assignee takes subject to equities between the debtor and the assignor which existed before the debtor received notice of the assignment.[81] Finally, it establishes priority over other assignees, since it is provided by the Law of Property Act 1925, section 137(1) that priority among successive assignees of choses in action is regulated by the dates on which the debtor received notice of the assignments.

Defective statutory assignments are considered below.[81a]

3. The rule in Dearle v. Hall

13–09   That final provision, which derives from the rule in *Dearle v. Hall*,[82] applies to all mortgages of equitable interests in property of whatever description which are held by a trustee or other person having legal control of the property. The date of the notice itself is irrelevant to any question of priority. Where the notice is posted, it apparently takes effect when received, though it might be argued that, as between competing assignees, the first to post the notice should have priority. There is no express decision on the point.[83]

Once notice of an absolute assignment has been received by the debtor he is no longer liable to the assignor but to the assignee[84] and if he disregards such

---

[76] *Stanley v. English Fibres Industries Ltd* (1899) 68 L.J.Q.B. 839; *W. F. Harrison & Co. v. Burke* [1956] 1 W.L.R. 419, CA; *Van Lynn Developments Ltd v. Pelias Construction Co. Ltd* [1969] 1 Q.B. 607, explaining the *Harrison* case at 612; see also (1956) 72 L.Q.R. 321.

[77] *W. F. Harrison & Co. v. Burke* [1956] 1 W.L.R. 419 at 421.

[78] *Matthews v. Walwyn* (1798) 4 Ves. 118.

[79] *Curran v. Newpark Cinemas* [1951] 1 All E.R. 295.

[80] In the absence of notice, payment by the debtor to the assignor or a release by the assignor will be good against the assignee: *Stocks v. Dobson* (1853) 4 De G.M. & G. 11.

[81] *Roxburghe v. Cox* (1881) 17 Ch.D. 520.

[81a] See *post*, para. 13–14.

[82] (1828) 3 Russ. 1; see also *post*, para. 20–16 and see also *Loveridge v. Cooper* (1823) 3 Russ 30. It seems that the rule originated earlier, but in the more restrictive form that the postponement of a prior assignee would occur only where the failure to give notice earlier was due to fraud or his gross negligence amounting to evidence of fraud. On this point see *Tourville v. Naish* (1734) 3 P.Wms. 307 and *Stanhope v. Verney* (1761) 2 Eden. 80.

[83] *Holt v. Heatherfield Trust Ltd* [1942] 1 K.B. 1.

[84] *Cottage Club Estates v. Woodside Estates (Amersham) Ltd* [1928] 2 K.B. 463.

a notice and pays the assignor after having received it he will be liable to make a second payment to the assignee.[85] If the debtor made such a payment under a mistake of fact or law he may be able to recover it from the assignor.[86] If, however, a debtor pays his debt to the assignor by cheque but afterwards receives a notice that the debt has been assigned, he is not compelled to stop the cheque.[87]

The rule in *Dearle v. Hall*[88] must not be confused with the provision in section 136 of the Law of Property Act 1925 that the assignee takes subject to equities existing when the assignment takes effect of which the assignee has notice.[89] "Equities" include defects in the assignor's title and certain claims which the debtor has against the assignor. Thus an assignee of a contract affected by mistake or illegality normally has no greater rights than the assignor would have had, though an exception exists in the field of life assurance. It was held in *Beresford v. Royal Insurance Co.*[90] (a case decided before the Suicide Act 1961 decriminalised suicide) that generally a life assurance policy could not be enforced by the representative of an assured who had committed suicide, since it was against public policy to allow his estate to benefit from his crime. However, where the assignment was made before the suicide, the assignee was permitted to recover, since the benefit did not go to the criminal or his estate.[91] If a debtor has the right to set aside a contract for misrepresentation, the assignee takes subject to that right, unless it is excluded or modified by statute[92] or contract.[93] The purpose of the provision that the assignee takes subject to equities is to prevent the debtor being prejudiced by the assignment. If a debtor has a claim against the assignor, it is immaterial whether the assignee knew of the claim when he took the assignment.[94] Correlatively the debtor cannot do anything to take away or diminish the rights of the assignee as they stood at the time of the notice, once he has received notice of the assignment.[95]

These two rules are illustrated by the case of *Bradford Banking Co. Ltd v. Briggs & Co. Ltd*,[96] where it was held that an assignee of shares or debentures takes them subject to all equitable claims of the company which arose before notice of the assignment; but that, after notice, the company could not create any fresh equities. The rule that an assignee takes subject to equities is often excluded in debentures.

The ability of the debtor to rely, against the assignee, on a claim against the assignor depends on the way in which it arose. He can rely on a claim arising out

---

[85] *Jones v. Farrell* (1857) 1 D. & J. 208; *Brice v. Bannister* (1878) 3 Q.B.D. 569.

[86] *Chitty on Contracts* (28th ed., 1999), p. 1038, n. 74; *ibid.* paras 30–026–30–048; *Kleinwort Benson v. Lincoln City Council* [1999] 2 A.C. 349.

[87] *Bence v. Shearman* [1898] 2 Ch. 582.

[88] (1828) 3 Russ. 1.

[89] *Ord v. White* (1840) 3 Beav. 357; *Mangles v. Dixon* (1852) 3 H.L.C. 702; *Phipps v. Lovegrove* (1873) L.R. 16 Eq. 80; *Lawrence v. Hayes* [1927] 2 K.B. 111.

[90] [1938] A.C. 586.

[91] *White v. British Empire Mutual Life Assurance Co.* (1868) L.R. 7 Eq. 394.

[92] *cf.* Bills of Exchange Act 1882, s.38(2); Marine Insurance Act 1906, s.50(2).

[93] *William Pickersgill & Sons Ltd v. London and Provincial Insurance Co.* [1912] 3 K.B. 614; *Re Agra and Masterman's Bank, ex p. Asiatic Banking Corp.* (1867) 2 Ch.App. 391; *Re Blakely Ordinance Co., ex p. New Zealand Banking Corp.* (1867) 3 Ch.App. 154.

[94] *Athenaeum Society v. Pooley* (1858) 3 D. & J. 294; *Biggerstaff v. Rowatt's Wharf Ltd* [1896] 2 Ch. 93.

[95] *Roxburghe v. Cox* (1881) 17 Ch.D. 520 at 526.

[96] (1886) 12 App.Cas. 29.

of the contract assigned,[97] whenever the claim arose.[98] If the debtor's set-off against the assignor exceeds the amount of the debt, the assignee will recover nothing; but he is not liable to the debtor for the excess.[99] Among the equities which bind the assignee is the debtor's right to rescind for misrepresentation, provided, apparently, that the right has not been lost.[1]

If the claim arises out of some transaction other than the contract assigned, it can be set up against the assignee only if it arose before notice of the assignment was given to the debtor.[2] If it neither accrued due before notice was given, nor arose out of the contract to be assigned, or a contract closely connected with it, it cannot be set off.[3]

If an assignor does not acquire a right to the subject-matter of the assignment the assignee can take nothing, for example, where an assignment was made of money to become due under a building contract which the assignor failed to perform.[4] Nor can the assignee recover more from the debtor than the assignor could have done.[5]

CONSIDERATION

13–10 Whether consideration is necessary to support an assignment is a question between the assignor and the assignee.[6] The debtor has to pay the debt and his only concern is that all parties should be before the court, so that he does not have to pay twice. He cannot refuse to pay the assignee because the assignment was gratuitous.[7]

A statutory assignment of either an equitable or a legal chose in action is valid whether or not consideration is given.[8] There are, however, three situations where the existence or non-existence of consideration is relevant. First, where the purported assignment is of some right which either does not exist or has not yet

---

[97] *Business Computers Ltd v. Anglo African Leasing Ltd* [1977] 1 W.L.R. 578, in which the authorities reviewed extend this principle to claims closely connected with the contract assigned. See also *Newfoundland Government v. Newfoundland Ry. Co.* (1888) 13 App. Cas. 199 at 213.

[98] *Graham v. Johnson* (1869) LR. 8 Eq. 36; *William Pickersgill and Sons Ltd v. London and Provincial Insurance Co.* [1912] 3 K.B. 614; *Banco Central S.A. and Trevelan Navigation Inc. v. Lingoss & Falce and B.F.I. Line*; *The Raven* [1980] 2 Lloyd's Rep. 266.

[99] *Young v. Kitchin* (1878) 3 Ex.D. 127.

[1] *Stoddart v. Union Trust Ltd* [1912] 1 K.B. 181. This decision has been criticised: see *Chitty on Contracts* (28th ed., 1999), para. 20–069, n. 58; Treitel, *Law of Contract* (10th ed., 1999), p. 636).

[2] *Stephens v. Venables* (1862) 30 Beav. 625; *cf. Watson v. Mid Wales Ry.* (1867) L.R. 2 P. 593. See also *Roxburghe v. Cox*; *Business Computers Ltd v. Anglo African Leasing Ltd*; and *Newfoundland Government v. Newfoundland Ry. Co.* (1888) 13 App.Cas 199.

[3] *Business Computers Ltd v. Anglo African Leasing Ltd* [1977] 1 W.L.R. 578 at 585; see also *Jeffryes v. Agra & Masterman's Bank* (1866) L.R. 2 Eq. 674; *Watson v. Mid Wales Ry. Co.* (1867) L.R. 2 C.P. 593; *Christie v. Taunton, Delmard, Lane & Co.* [1893] 2 Ch. 175; *Re Pinto Leite & Nephews, ex p. Desolivaes* [1929] 1 Ch. 221.

[4] *Tooth v. Hallett* (1869) L.R. 4 Ch.App. 242.

[5] *Dawson v. Great Northern and City Ry. Co.* [1905] 1 K.B. 260.

[6] *Re Rose* [1952] Ch. 499; *Letts v. I.R.C.* [1957] 1 W.L.R. 201; *Dalton (Smith's Administrative v. I.R.C.* [1958] T.R. 45.

[7] *Walker v. Bradford Old Bank* (1884) 12 Q.B.D. 511.

[8] *Harding v. Harding* (1886) 17 Q.B.D. 442; *Re Westerton* [1919] 2 Ch. 104.

been acquired by the assignor; secondly, where there is a voluntary equitable assignment; and, thirdly, where there is a defective statutory assignment.

1. **Assignment of future property**

A future chose in action cannot be the subject of an assignment, but only of an agreement to assign and such an agreement can be valid only when supported by consideration.[9] Rights which the prospective assignor has not yet acquired may fall into one of three categories. In the first are sums which are certain to become payable under an existing contract or other legal obligations and are treated as existing choses in action, even though the amounts which will be received are unascertained.[10] In the second are expectancies, as where the assignor hopes to receive sums under a contract not yet made, or to inherit from a person living at the date of the assignment.[11] The third, intermediate class comprises rights which may become due under an existing obligation but it is uncertain whether they will do so, because the obligation may terminate or is subject to a condition. Rights in the first category can be assigned without consideration; those in the second cannot. The decisions as to those in the third class are impossible to rationalise, though it seems clear that even where there is an existing chose in action capable of assignment, the proceeds of the chose may be a mere expectancy.[12]

ASSIGNMENTS OF RIGHTS OF ACTION

Prior to January 1, 1968 both maintenance[13] and champerty[14] were crimes. **13–11** However, the Criminal Law Act 1967 abolished the criminal nature of these acts and also a party's tortious liability therefor. However, the Act expressly provided that "the abolition of criminal and civil liability . . . for maintenance . . . shall not affect any rule of . . . law as to the cases in which a contract is to be treated as contrary to public policy or otherwise illegal".[15] Accordingly, it would seem that agreements which, under the law before 1968 would have been unenforceable for either maintenance or champerty remain unenforceable as a matter of public

---

[9] *Meek v. Kettlewell* (1843) 1 Ph. 342; *Tailby v. Official Receiver* (1888) 13 App.Cas. 523; *Glegg v. Bromley* [1912] 3 K.B. 474; *Cotton v. Heyl* [1930] 1 Ch. 510.

[10] *Shepherd v. Federal Commissioners of Taxation* (1965) 113 C.L.R. 385.

[11] *Meek v. Kettlewell* (1843) 1 Ph. 342; *Re Tilt* (1896) 74 L.T. 163; *Re Ellenborough* [1903] 1 Ch. 697; *cf. Kekewich v. Manning* (1851) 1 De G.M. & G. 176.

[12] See *e.g. Grovewood Holdings plc v. James Capel & Co. Ltd* [1995] Ch. 80. *Glegg v. Bromley* [1912] 3 K.B. 474 (proceeds of a defamation action being brought by the assignor); *Norman v. Federal Commissioner of Taxation* (1963) 109 C.L.R. 9 (interest payable in the future as a loan which was not for a fixed period; dividends on shares already held which may become due in the future). In the following cases the subject-matter has been held to be an existing chose in action: *Walker v. Bradford Old Bank* (1864) 12 Q.B.D. 511 (sum standing to the assignor's credit at date of his death); *Hughes v. Pump House Hotel Co.* [1902] 2 K.B. 190 (sums payable to a builder under an existing contract). See also *post*, para. 13–13.

[13] Where a person supports litigation in which he has no legitimate concern without just cause or excuse: see *Chitty on Contracts* (28th ed., 1999), para. 17–050.

[14] Which has been described as "an aggravated form of maintenance" in which an individual stipulates for a share in the proceeds of the litigation: *Giles v. Thompson* [1993] 3 All E.R. 328, CA. See *Chitty on Contracts* (28th ed., 1999), para. 17–054.

[15] Criminal Law Act 1967, s.14(2).

policy.[16] This state of affairs also affects assignments of rights of action. Generally a bare right of litigation, such as the right to damages for a wrongful act[17] is not assignable[18] on the principle that the law will not recognise any transaction savouring of maintenance or champerty.[19]

However, there is nothing unlawful in the purchase of property which the purchaser can enjoy only by defeating existing adverse claims.[20] Moreover, it has been held that rights of action (even in tort) which are incidental and subsidiary to property may be validly assigned when the property is transferred.[21] The test that the House of Lords applied in *Trendtex Trading Corporation v. Credit Suisse*[22] was that:

> "If the assignment is of a property right or interest and the cause of action is ancillary to that right or interest, or if the assignee had a genuine commercial interest in taking the assignment and enforcing it for his own benefit, [there is] no reason why the assignment should be struck down as an assignment of a bare cause of action or a savouring of maintenance".[23]

Thus in *Trendtex*, it was accepted that a creditor who had financed the transaction giving rise to the right of action had a legitimate commercial interest in it and that an assignment to him would be valid unless the object of the assignment was other than to protect that creditor's interest. Where the right of action assigned is ancillary to the transfer of property, it is in every case a question whether the purchaser's real object in acquiring an interest in the property is precisely that or the acquisition is merely ancillary to the true purpose, namely the acquisition of a right to bring an action, either alone or jointly with the vendor.[24]

Thus the purchaser of a freehold reversion may take an assignment of the right to recover damages for dilapidations from the sub-tenant.[25] A creditor may assign his debt so as to enable another to sue for it.[26] A person may buy shares in a company merely for the purpose of challenging, by legal proceedings, acts of the directors as being *ultra vires*.[27] An assignment by an assured to his insurer of his rights against a contract breaker or tortfeasor is good, the enforcement of the cause of action being legitimately supported by the insurer's interest in recouping

---

[16] See *Chitty on Contracts* (28th ed., 1999), para. 17–049.

[17] *e.g.* for assault: *May v. Lane* (1894) 64 L.J.Q.B. 236, 238, *per* Rigby L.J.

[18] *Dawson v. Great Northern City Railway Company* [1905] 1 K.B. 260 at 271, *per* Stirling L.J.; *Fitzroy v. Cave* [1905] 2 K.B. 364 at 371; *Defries v. Milnes* [1913] 1 Ch. 98; *Holt v. Heatherfield Trust Limited* [1942] 2 K.B. 1; *Laurent v. Sale & Co.* [1963] 1 W.L.R. 829.

[19] *Rees v. De Bernardy* [1896] 2 Ch. 437; *Laurent v. Sale & Co., supra*; *Grovewood Holdings Plc v. James Capel & Co. Limited* [1995] Ch. 80; *Re Oasis Merchandising Services Limited* [1998] Ch. 170; *Norglen Limited v. Reid Rains Prudential Limited* [1999] 2 A.C. 1.

[20] *Dickenson v. Burrell* (1866) L.R. 1 Eq. 337; *County Hotel & Wine Co. Limited v. London & North Western Railway Co.* [1918] 2 K.B. 251, affirmed on other grounds [1921] 1 A.C. 85; *Ellis v. Torrington* [1920] 1 K.B. 399; *Candex International Limited v. Bank of Zambia* [1998] Q.B. 22.

[21] *ibid.*

[22] [1982] A.C. 679.

[23] *per* Lord Reid at 703.

[24] *Dickenson v. Burrell* (1866) L.R. 1 Eq. 337; *Prosser v. Edmonds* (1835) 1 Y. & C. Ex. 481; *Harrington v. Long* (1833) 2 My. & Kay. 590; *Knight v. Bowyer* (1858) 2 De G. & J. 421.

[25] *Williams v. Protheroe* (1829) 5 Bing. 309; *Ellis v. Torrington* [1920] 1 K.B. 399.

[26] *Fitzroy v. Cave* [1905] 2 K.B. 364 (even though the wish of that other person to enforce debt arises from ill-feeling towards the debtor).

[27] *Bloxam v. Metropolitan Rly Co.* (1868) 3 Ch.App. 337 at 353.

the amount of loss which he has paid under the policy as a result of the act, neglect or default of the contract breaker or tortfeasor.[28]

A solicitor purchasing from his client the subject-matter of a suit is in a **13–12** different position from other purchasers. After his employment as such in the suit[29] he cannot purchase the subject-matter from his client[30] although he may lawfully take a mortgage on it to secure costs and expenses already incurred.[31]

The assignment of right in action by an assignor to another party where the object and effect of the assignment was to enable the assignee to obtain public funding for the pursuit of the claim which would not otherwise have been available to the assignor is not contrary to public policy or unlawful.[32] Presumably the same principles apply where an assignor, who would otherwise be at risk of providing security for costs pursuant to the Civil Procedure Rules assigns the cause of action to an assignee who is not at such a risk.

VOLUNTARY EQUITABLE ASSIGNMENTS

The general principle to be derived from the decided cases is that an assignment **13–13** of an existing chose in action need not be supported by consideration provided that the assignor has done everything within his power to transfer the property in the manner appropriate to its nature.[33] In many cases the law will not treat a gift as valid unless it has been made in the prescribed way. Thus a gift of a chattel must be made either by deed of gift or by delivery of the chattel with the intent that the property shall pass.[34] In *Milroy v. Lord*[35] the owner of shares in a company made a voluntary assignment of them by deed poll. This could not take effect as a gift since the legal title to the shares could be transferred only by execution of a proper instrument of transfer and registration of the transfer in the books of the company.

It was held that a voluntary settlement could not be valid and effectual unless the donor had done everything in his power which was necessary, having regard to the nature of the property comprised in the settlement, to transfer the property and render the settlement binding on him. That rule applies only to gifts which by law had to be made in a specified form.

---

[28] *Companie Columbiana de Seguros v. Pacific Steam Navigation Co.* [1965] 1 Q.B. 101.

[29] *Knight v. Bowyer* (1858) 2 De G. & J. 421, CA; *Davis v. Freethy* (1890) 24 Q.B.D. 519.

[30] *Wood v. Downes* (1811) 18 Ves. 120; *Simpson v. Lamb* (1857) 7 E. & B. 84; *Davis v. Freethy* (1890) 24 Q.B.D. 519.

[31] *Anderson v. Radcliffe* (1858) E.B. & E. 806.

[32] *Norglen Limited v. Reid Rains Provincial Limited* (1999) 2 A.C.

[33] *Kekewich v. Manning* (1851) 1 De G.M. & G. 176; *Milroy v. Lord* (1862) De F. & S. 264 *Harding v. Harding* (1886) 17 Q.B.D. 442; *Re Griffin* [1899] 1 Ch. 408; *German v. Yates* (1915) 32 T.L.R. 52; *Re Williams* [1917] 1 Ch. 1; *Holt v. Heatherfield Trust* [1942] 2 K.B. 1; *Re Rose Midland Bank Executor-Trustee Co. v. Rose* [1949] Ch. 78; *Re McArdle* [1951] Ch. 669; *Re Rose Rose v. IRC* [1952] Ch. 499; *Letts v. I.R.C.* [1957] 1 W.L.R. 201. *Brown and Root Technology Limited v. Sun Alliance and London Assurance Co. Limited* [1996] Ch. 51.

[34] *Re Breton's Estate* (1881) 17 Ch.D. 416; *Cochrane v. Moore* (1890) 25 Q.B.D. 57; *Re Cole (A Bankrupt), ex p. Trustees of the Property of the Bankrupt* [1964] Ch. 175.

[35] (1862) 4 De G.F. & J. 264; and see Turner L.J. at 274 for a statement of the rule. *cf. Antrobus v. Smith* (1805) 12 Ves. 39 where a gift of shares failed because it was made in writing not under seal, contrary to the company's articles.

1. **Form**

13–13A The only formality required for the assignment of an equitable chose in action is that it must be in writing[36]: so a voluntary settlement in writing of an equitable interest in a trust fund has been held binding on the settlor,[37] since he did not need to do anything else in order to transfer the property. Equitable assignments of legal choses in action are not required to be in writing.[38] Unless the nature of the property brings special rules into play, there are no formal requirements for the transfer of legal choses in action[39] and it is necessary only for the donor to do all within his power to effect the transfer. If that has been done, it is immaterial that further steps need to be taken by the donee[40] or by some other third party.[41]

DEFECTIVE STATUTORY ASSIGNMENTS

13–14 A statutory assignment may be ineffective as such, though it may take effect as an equitable assignment, if no written notice has been given to the debtor, or if it is not in writing, or if it is not an absolute assignment. Assignments which are conditional, or by way of charge, or are assignments of part of a debt, are not absolute and therefore defective by reason of non-compliance with section 136 of the Law of Property Act 1925.

Where the defect is want of notice, the assignment is effective although not supported by consideration.[42] Since it is not required by section 136 of the Law of Property Act 1925, that the assignor shall give the notice, he has done all within his power to transfer the property.

Where the defect is lack of writing, and the chose is equitable, the question of consideration does not arise because the assignment is void unless in writing. If it is a legal chose, want of consideration does not, by itself, invalidate the transfer. In *German v. Yates*[43] a voluntary oral assignment of a debt was held to bind the personal representatives of the assignor, and that the Judicature Act 1873[44] had not destroyed equitable assignments or impaired them in any way.[45] In that case, it was held that the assignment was a perfect gift. But the problem which may arise is whether an oral assignment was a perfect gift or merely a promise to make a gift in the future. A voluntary promise to assign an equitable interest is not an assignment, and the fact that is made by means of signed writing

---

[36] LPA 1925, s.53(1)(*c*).
[37] *Kekewich v. Manning* (1851) 1 De G.M. & G. 176.
[38] See *ante*, para. 13–03.
[39] See *Fortescue v. Barnett* (1834) 3 My. & K. 36, voluntary assignment, by deed, of a life insurance policy held binding on the assignor.
[40] *Re Paradise Motor Co. Ltd* [1968] 1 W.L.R. 1125.
[41] *Re Rose, Midland Bank Executor and Trustee Co. v. Rose* [1949] Ch. 78; see also *Re Rose, Rose v. I.R.C.* [1952] Ch. 499.
[42] *Holt v. Heatherfield Trust Ltd* [1942] 2 K.B. 1.
[43] (1915) 32 T.L.R. 52.
[44] The original provision enabling statutory assignments to be made was s.25(6) of the Judicature Act 1873.
[45] For a similar dictum see *William Brandt's Sons & Co. v. Dunlop Rubber Co.* [1905] A.C. 454 at 462.

is irrelevant. In *Re McArdle, Decd*,[46] the following words were held to be incapable of being construed as an equitable assignment:

> "in consideration of your carrying out certain alterations and improvements to the property . . . we . . . agree that the executors shall . . . repay to you from the estate when so distributed £488 in settlement of the amount."

The works referred to had been carried out and it was held that the document purported to be a contract to assign, not an assignment, and thus required consideration. Since the consideration was past, the contract was unenforceable. That case also suggests that a voluntary equitable assignment of part of a debt may be valid, but the reasoning by which that conclusion is arrived at has been criticised.[47]

Where the assignment is not absolute because it is conditional, its effectiveness depends on the condition. If this is such as to require some further act to be done by the donor, the assignment will be ineffective, being an imperfect gift.

Finally, where there is an assignment by way of charge the question of consideration will not normally arise because the assignment will nearly always be made to secure a debt and there will be consideration in the form of the assignee's advancing money or forbearance, or promising not to sue. Forbearance will amount to consideration only for a promise that is induced by it. Thus where a debtor executed a mortgage of an insurance policy in favour of his creditor, but the creditor did not know of the mortgage, it was held that his forbearance to sue for his antecedent debt was not consideration,[48] though it was said that he would have provided consideration if he had been told of the mortgage and forborne to sue on the strength of it. Forbearance may, it seems, be requested expressly[49] or impliedly.[50]

Assignments of Particular Choses in Action

1. Trust property

The 1925 property legislation provides for the mortgaging of equitable interests, in both realty and personalty, by assignment of the equitable interest subject to a proviso for reassignment on redemption. An interest in trust property was always freely assignable in equity, and the assignee could sue in his own name. If the whole interest was assigned, the assignor did not have to be made a party,[51] though his joinder was essential if he retained any interest, as where the assignment was conditional or by way of charge. The 1925 legislation did not alter this situation; it merely provided an alternative mode of assignment.

13–15

---

[46] [1951] Ch. 669.
[47] See R. E. Megarry, (1951) 67 L.Q.R. 295 for a critical commentary and also see D. M. Stone, (1951) 14 M.L.R. 356; Treitel, *Law of Contract* (10th ed., 1999), p. 634.
[48] *Wigan v. English and Scottish Law Life Assurance Society* [1909] 1 Ch. 291.
[49] *Crears v. Hunter* (1887) 19 Q.B.D. 341.
[50] *Alliance Bank v. Broom* (1864) 2 Dr. & Sm. 289.
[51] *Performing Rights Society v. London Theatre of Varieties Ltd* [1924] A.C. 1.

As between assignor and assignee the assignment is complete without notice to the trustee; notice is important for the reasons discussed earlier, which are to do with the interests of third parties.

(a) *Form*

The requirements of form arise, therefore, not from the provisions regulating statutory assignments but from section 53(1)(c) of the Law of Property Act 1925 which provides as follows:

> "A disposition of an equitable interest or trust subsisting at the time of the disposition, must be in writing, signed by the person disposing of the same, or by his agent, thereunto lawfully authorised in writing or by will."

In addition, it is usual for an assignment of trust property to be created by deed, since the assignee will then have the statutory powers conferred on a mortgagee by deed.[52] Because of the uncertain nature of limited or contingent interests in a trust property, the deed will contain various additional covenants and powers giving the assignee greater protection:

(1) Power for the assignee to protect his security by taking any proceedings, making any inquiries, giving any notices or obtaining any stop orders[53] necessary for that purpose.

(2) The assignment of a policy of life insurance or of insurance against a particular contingency, together with the assignment of the trust interest, and covenants by the assignor to pay the premiums and maintain the security.

(b) *Stop orders*

Power is given to the court, under the Civil Procedure Rules[54] to make an order prohibiting the transfer, sale, delivery out, payment or other dealing with funds paid into court or any part of such fund or the income thereof, without notice to the applicant. A person:

(1) who has a mortgage or charge on the interest of any person in funds in court; or

(2) to whom that interest has been assigned; or

(3) who is a judgment creditor of the person entitled to that interest,

may apply to the court by an application pursuant to CPR Part 23 in any existing proceedings, or, if there are none, by issuing a claim form. Stop orders have

---

[52] LPA 1925, s.101.

[53] CPR, Sched. 1. When a trust fund is paid into court, a "stop order" is equivalent to giving notice to the trustees: *Pinnock v. Bailey* (1883) 23 Ch.D. 497; *Montefiore v. Guedalla* [1903] 2 Ch. 26, CA. Express notice should be given to the trustees.

[54] CPR, Sched. 1, RSC Ord. 50, r.10.

priority, among themselves, in the order in which they were made,[55] but do not gain priority over existing incumbrancers who have given notice to the trustees before the stop order was made.[56] Express notice should also be given to the trustees.

(c) *Notice to the trustees*

While giving notice of the assignment to the trustees regulates priorities among assignees, it does not amount to taking possession of the trust interest unless the notice requires the payment of the income to be made to the assignee.[57] Until such notice is given, the trustees are entitled to continue to pay the income to the assignor and, in the interests of certainty, it is advisable to insert a declaration in the assignment to the effect that the assignor is entitled to receive the income until the assignee otherwise directs.[58]

Even if the assignee notifies the trustees that all available monies are to be paid over to him it does not necessarily follow that the trustees must do so.[59] If the amount available exceeds the debt to the assignee and the trustees have notice of other assignments, they should pay over only such a sum as will discharge the principal, interest and costs.[60] If trustees are uncertain of the amount of the debt, they may refuse to pay over anything, even to the assignee first in priority, until an account has been taken.[61] They are trustees for all interested parties and need not pay monies, even to persons apparently entitled to them, without making inquiries.

2. **Policies of life assurance**

Before the Policies of Assurance Act 1867, mortgages of such policies were   **13–16** governed by the general law of assignment. Since rights under life assurance policies are legal choses in action, the assignee could not, under the pre-1867 general law, sue in his own name, but section 1 of the 1867 Act made this possible subject to compliance with the statutory formalities. The statutory provisions do not displace the previous law, so that an equitable assignment of a life assurance policy can still be made subject to the rules governing such assignments.

(a) *Statutory requirements*

There are two separate and distinct methods of assignment pursuant to statute. The first is in accordance with section 136 of the Law of Property Act 1925.[62]

---

[55] *Greening v. Beckford* (1832) 5 Sim. 195; *Swayne v. Swayne* (1849) 11 Beav. 463.
[56] *Livesey v. Harding* (1857) 23 Beav. 141; *Re Anglesey* [1903] 2 Ch. 727.
[57] *Re Pawson's Settlement* [1917] 1 Ch. 541; though *cf. Dearle v. Hall* (1828) 3 Russ. 1 at 58, *per* Lyndhurst L.C.
[58] Key and Elphinstone, *Precedents in Conveyancing* (15th ed., 1953–54), Vol. 2, p. 23.
[59] They may do so: *Jones v. Farrell* (1857) 1 De G. & J. 208.
[60] *Re Bell* [1896] 1 Ch. 1, CA.
[61] *Hockey v. Western* [1898] 1 Ch. 350.
[62] See *ante*, paras 13–05 *et seq.* Section 136(2) provides that nothing in s.136 affects the Policies of Assurance Act 1867.

The second is under the Policies of Assurance Act 1867. An assignment under the 1867 Act must be made in writing, either by an endorsement on the policy or by a separate instrument in the form given by the Schedule to the Act[63] or to the purpose and effect thereof. It has been held that a letter to the purported assignee, requesting him to instruct his solicitor to prepare an assignment, was not a valid assignment, either in equity or by statute and in consequence, notice to the insurance company by the purported assignee, B, that he was holding the policies as security for a debt was not a valid notice of assignment.[64] Likewise, an agreement to assign on request is not an assignment,[65] and a notice of the agreement is not a notice of the assignment. Consequently, the purported assignee did not, by informing the company of the agreement, gain priority over a prior equitable assignee, A, by deposit who had not given the company notice of such deposit. Indeed, the inability of the assignor to produce the policy was held to be constructive notice to B, in the circumstances of the case, of A's rights.[66] This accords with an earlier decision that, where the equities of two assignees are otherwise equal, possession of deeds gives the better equity.[67]

The assignee has no right to sue on the policy until written notice of the date and purport of the assignment has been given to the company. The policy must specify the place or places at which such notice may be given. The company is bound, on request and on payment of the prescribed fee, to give a written acknowledgment of receipt of notice, and that acknowledgment is conclusive, against the company, of such receipt.

The assignee takes subject to equities, including the right of the company to avoid the policy if full disclosure has not been made.

(b) *Priority*

13–17 The 1867 Act provides that priorities between competing assignees are regulated by the order in which notice is given to the company,[68] but notice of a dealing not amounting to an assignment is ineffective. The provision does not apply where a subsequent assignee has notice, whether actual, constructive, or imputed, of a prior assignment,[69] as where money is lent on the security of an insurance policy which, being in the hands of a prior assignee, is not handed over. The non-delivery of the policy is constructive notice of the prior assignment.[70] The subsequent assignee will obtain priority by giving notice first if he has no notice of the prior assignee, even though he was prevented from getting notice by fraudulent concealment of the prior assignment.

---

[63] Policies of Assurance Act 1867, s.5.
[64] *Crossley v. City of Glasgow Life Assurance Co.* (1876) 4 Ch.D. 421.
[65] *Spencer v. Clarke* (1879) 9 Ch.D. 137.
[66] *Re Weniger's Policy* [1910] 2 Ch. 291.
[67] *Rice v. Rice* (1853) 2 Drew. 73.
[68] Policies of Assurance Act 1867, s.3. If a written request for an acknowledgment is made, the company must give an acknowledgment of receipt of notice, in writing, and this is conclusive against the company: Policies of Assurance Act 1867, s.6. The policy must specify the place at which notice of assignment is to be given: Policies of Assurance Act 1867, s.4.
[69] *Re Lake, ex p. Cavendish* [1903] 1 K.B. 151.
[70] *Spencer v. Clarke, supra*; *Re Weniger's Policy, supra*.

(c) *Assignment by way of mortgage*

Mortgages of life assurance policies are made by way of assignment with a proviso for re-assignment. They normally contain covenants not to allow the policy to become void and to pay premiums and produce receipts therefore to the mortgagee, with power, in default, for the mortgagee to pay the premiums himself and charge them against the policy. The cost of paying premiums so as to keep the policy on foot is allowable, whether or not the policy contains an express provision to that effect.[71] A mortgagee by deed has the statutory power of sale given by section 101 of the Law of Property Act 1925.

Since a creditor has an insurable interest in his debtor's life to the extent of the debt,[72] it is permissible for the creditor to take out a policy in his own name on the life of the debtor, instead of the debtor taking it out and assigning it to the creditor. Unless the creditor can be placed in a position whereby he can take advantage of section 1 of the Contracts (Rights of Third Parties Act) 1999,[73] the debtor should not take out a policy in the name of the creditor as the creditor, not being a party to the policy, would have no rights under it.[74] Thus where S took out a policy in his own name for the benefit of G, to mature in 17 years' time, and died five years after taking it out, it was held that G could not benefit as he was not a party to the policy and no declaration of trust in his favour had been made; nor did the Law of Property Act 1925, section 56(1) operate so as to confer any benefit on him.

(d) *Ownership of the policy*

Depending on circumstances, the policy may be the property of the debtor, **13–18** mortgaged to the creditor, or it may belong to the creditor absolutely. There are three possible arrangements to consider:

(1) The debtor takes out the policy and pays the premiums. The policy is part of the security and belongs to the debtor.

(2) The creditor takes out the policy in the debtor's name, and pays the premiums without having any agreement with the debtor to charge the premiums to him. The policy is treated as having been taken out for the creditor's own protection and belongs to him.[75] This is so even where the creditor purported, in his own accounts, to charge the debtor with the premiums but there was no agreement to do so.

(3) The creditor takes out the policy but the premiums are by agreement chargeable to the debtor. There are two possible views:

(a) the policy belongs to the debtor in equity, subject to security;

---

[71] *Gill v. Downing* (1874) L.R. 17 Eq. 316.

[72] *Morland v. Isaac* (1855) 20 Beav. 389; see also *Freme v. Brade* (1858) 2 De G. & J. 582; *Drysdale v. Piggot* (1856) 8 De G.M. & G. 546; *Bruce v. Garden* (1869) 5 Ch.App. 32.

[73] This Act applies to contracts entered into after May 11, 2000 and permits a third party to the contract to enforce it if the contract so provides or if it confers a benefit on him and (in the latter case) does not provide to the contrary. See *Chitty on Contracts* (28th ed., 1999), chap. 19.

[74] *Re Sinclair's Life Policy* [1938] Ch. 799.

[75] *Bruce v. Garden, supra.*

(b) the policy belongs to the creditor and the stipulation that the debtor pays the premiums is a bonus for the creditor.

There is a presumption in favour of (a) which can be rebutted by evidence showing that it was intended that the creditor should receive an outright bonus.[76]

Where the policy is part of the security, the debtor has a right to redeem and any stipulation purporting to take away that right is void.[77] Nor can the creditor claim the whole benefit of the policy if the debtor defaults in paying the premiums. He can only pay them himself to preserve the security and add them to the mortgage debt. He can acquire the security only by foreclosure.[78]

(e) *Suicide*

13–19 Life assurance policies are particularly hazardous in that they may be avoided by the suicide of the assured. It is contrary to public policy to allow the representatives of a wilful suicide to enforce a life policy,[79] and this rule has not been displaced by the Forfeiture Act 1982. That Act instigates the rule of public policy which may prevent a person who has unlawfully killed "another" acquiring a benefit from the death of that other and in certain circumstances provides for relief where a person has been guilty of unlawful killing. A mortgagee, being an assignee, cannot be in a better position than the representatives of the deceased assured unless the policy expressly provides for the preservation of rights of bona fide assignees for value.[80] Such provisions are not contrary to public policy, since they preserve the negotiability and hence the value to the assured, of the policy, and are frequently found in life policies.

Such a clause appeared in the policy the rights to which were in dispute in *Solicitors and General Life Assurance Society v. Lamb.*[81] L mortgaged a life policy and other securities to R and committed suicide. R relied on the clause against the insurance company to force the payment of the policy monies to him and also realised the other securities. The total exceeded the mortgage debt and the company claimed the surplus as against L's widow, advancing two arguments. They claimed that either the debt to R should be satisfied first out of the other securities, or that it should be apportioned rateably between the debt and the other securities. Both arguments were rejected, the court holding that the clause was inserted in the interests of the assured and created no equity in favour of the insurers in regard to monies payable to assignees.

The same principles were applied in *White v. British Empire Mutual Life Assurance Co.*[82] where the insurance company was the mortgagee. Other securities were also mortgaged to the company and it was held that, in the absence of

---

[76] *Salt v. Marquess of Northampton* [1892] A.C. 1 at 16.
[77] *ibid.*
[78] *Drysdale v. Piggot* (1850) 8 De G.M. & G. 546.
[79] *Beresford v. Royal Insurance Co.* [1938] A.C. 586. The principle was applied to prevent recovery on a policy of life insurance where the assured was executed for felony, although the policy did not expressly provide for this contingency: *Amicable Society v. Bolland* (1830) 4 Bligh.(N.S.) 194.
[80] *ibid.* It has not been decided whether the security is avoided if the assured assigned the policy before committing suicide: *Hardy v. Motor Insurers Bureau* [1964] 2 Q.B. 745, CA.
[81] (1864) 2 De G.J. & S. 251.
[82] (1868) L.R. 7 Eq. 394.

any contractual provision entitling the company to repay itself out of the other securities, the widow of the assured could require the company to repay itself first out of the policy monies. The consequences of this decision in *Lamb's* case can be avoided if the clause provides for the preservation of the rights only of assignees who are independent third parties.[83]

(f) *Discharge*

A legal mortgage of a life assurance policy is discharged by reassignment, either in the form of an express reassignment or by way of statutory receipt. The form of receipt under paragraph 1 of Schedule 2A[84] to the Building Societies Act 1986 is appropriate where a building society is the mortgagee, but discharge by simple receipt is satisfactory. The printed form of a mortgage of a life policy of banks and building societies and other institutional lenders usually, however, provide for an express reassignment. Notice of the discharge should be given to the insurance company.

3. **Shares in partnerships**

A share in a partnership confers the right to a share in the profits and, on dissolution, in the assets.[85] It is a hazardous security, particularly as, by section 33 of the Partnership Act 1890, a partnership may, at the option of the other partners, be dissolved if any partner suffers his share of the partnership property to be charged under the Act for his separate debt.   **13–20**

A mortgagee is not usually introduced into the partnership and by section 24(7) a partner may not, without the consent of all the other partners, introduce another partner into the firm. Unless he is so introduced, he has no right to interfere in the management of the partnership business,[86] to require accounts of partnership transactions, or to inspect partnership books.[87] He is not, however, precluded from impugning transactions made between the partners which are designed to deprive him of his rights.[88]

He is entitled, on a dissolution, to receive the mortgagor's share of the assets, and, for the purpose of ascertaining that share, to an account as from the date of dissolution.[89]

A mortgagee can enforce his security by foreclosure[90] and if the mortgage is made by deed, he has the statutory powers of sale and appointment of a receiver.

Although the mortgagee is entitled to share in the personal chattels of the partnership on dissolution, the mortgage is a mortgage of a chose in action and

---

[83] *Royal London Mutual Insurance Society v. Barrett* [1928] Ch. 411.
[84] As inserted by the Building Societies Act 1997, s.7(1).
[85] See *Lindley and Banks on Partnership* (17th ed., 1995), Chap. 25.
[86] *Re Garwood's Trusts* [1903] 1 Ch. 236.
[87] *Bonnin v. Neame* [1910] 1 Ch. 732.
[88] *Watts v. Driscoll* [1901] 1 Ch. 294.
[89] *ibid.*
[90] *Whetham v. Davey* (1885) 30 Ch.D. 574.

not a bill of sale,[91] and accordingly does not require registration. Notice of the mortgage should, however, be given to the other partners so as to establish priority as against other mortgagees and to bind them to pay over the share to the mortgagee.

4. **Stocks and shares**

13–21   Mortgages of stocks and shares are not regulated by the Bills of Sale Acts, such choses in action being outside the definition of "personal chattels" in section 4 of the Bills of Sale Act 1878. Stocks and shares had been made assignable at law before the Judicature Act 1873 provided for the legal assignment of choses in action. A company incorporated under the Companies Act 1985 may, by its articles of association regulate the transfer of its shares in any manner. By section 183(1)[92], it is not lawful for a company to register a transfer of shares in the company without a proper instrument of transfer being delivered to it unless the transfer is an exempt transfer within the Stock Transfer Act 1982; and a proper instrument of transfer is any instrument which will attract stamp duty. Transfers are therefore made for the nominal consideration of 50p.

The Stock Transfer Act 1963[93] provides that, notwithstanding anything in the articles of association of a company or any enactment or instrument relating thereto, fully paid up registered securities may be transferred by means of an instrument under hand, signed only by the transferor, whose signature need not be attested.

(a) *Legal mortgages*

Legal mortgages of shares are created by transfer with a proviso for re-transfer but it is not usual to mortgage shares in this way. Such a transaction gives the mortgagee both the rights and liabilities of a shareholder; thus he is subject to calls if the shares are not fully paid up and he may be compelled to vote in accordance with the wishes of the mortgagor[94]: on the other hand, he becomes entitled to the dividends.

(b) *Equitable mortgages*

An equitable mortgage of shares is usually created by a deposit of the share certificates with the mortgagee, together with a memorandum of deposit. While the mortgagor remains the registered owner, he must vote as the mortgagee directs.[95] It normally contains, *inter alia*, a statement that the deposit is by way of security, covenants by the mortgagor not to incur a forfeiture, to pay principal

---

[91] *Re Bainbridge* (1878) 8 Ch.D. 218.
[92] Uncertified Securities Regulations 1995, S.I. 1995 No. 3272 (as amended).
[93] ss.1 and 2.
[94] *Puddephatt v. Leith* [1916] 1 Ch. 200; *Musselwhite v. C. H. Musselwhite & Sons Ltd* [1962] Ch. 964. *Michaels v. Harley House (Marylebone) Limited* [1999] 3 W.L.R. 229, CA.
[95] *Wise v. Lansdell* [1921] 1 Ch. 420.

and interest, an undertaking by him to execute a registered transfer, a proviso for redemption, a power of sale, and a statement that the deposit is by way of security.

The deposit of the share certificates may also be accompanied by a transfer form executed by the mortgagor but with the date and the mortgagee's name left blank.[96] This allows the mortgagee to perfect his title by filling in the transfer and having it registered, provided that it is possible to transfer the shares merely by an instrument under hand.[97] Delivery of the blank transfer raises a presumption that the mortgagor has appointed the mortgagee his agent for the purpose of completing the transfer.[98] If, however, the shares are required to be transferred by deed, only an agent appointed by an instrument under seal can execute the deed,[99] and in such a case the deposit will be accompanied by a deed of mortgage containing a power of attorney authorising the mortgagee to execute a transfer of the shares to himself or a purchaser.[1]

Difficulties may arise if the mortgagor gives the mortgagee a blank transfer under seal and the mortgagee later executes it without having been given a power of attorney under seal or redelivering it to the mortgagor for re-execution by him. For in such circumstances the mortgagor has never acknowledged the deed as his own. He may be estopped from denying its validity as against a bona fide purchaser for value from the mortgagee without notice.[2] A transfer of the certificates without registration does not pass the legal title to the shares.[3] Nevertheless it is not a mere pledge but constitutes an equitable mortgage.[4] The equitable mortgagee can compel the mortgagor to execute a registered transfer of the shares and after default he is entitled to foreclose[5] or, after reasonable notice to the mortgagor, to sell the shares.[6]

(c) *Notice to company*

Notice of the deposit of share certificates should be given to the company. This **13–22** is not for the purpose of regulating priorities since by section 360 of the Companies Act 1985, no trust may be entered on the register of a company. The rule in *Dearle v. Hall*[7] does not apply to equitable mortgages of shares, priorities among which are governed by the same rules as applied to mortgages of land before 1926.

Notice to the company, although not regulating priorities, may cause the company to become aware of conflicting claims and to defer registration, even,

---

[96] *Barclay v. Prospect Mortgages Ltd* [1974] 1 W.L.R. 837.
[97] *Ortigosa v. Brown, Janson & Co.* (1878) 47 L.J.Ch. 168.
[98] *Colonial Bank v. Cady* (1890) 15 App.Cas. 267.
[99] *Powell v. London & Provincial Bank* [1893] 2 Ch. 555.
[1] *Hibblewhite v. M'Morine* (1840) 6 M. & W. 200; *Société Générale de Paris v. Walker* (1885) 11 App.Cas. 20; *Re Seymour, Fielding v. Seymour* [1913] 1 Ch. 475.
[2] *Earl of Sheffield v. London Joint Stock Bank* (1888) 13 App.Cas. 333; *Waterhouse v. Bank of Ireland* (1891) 29 L.R.Ir. 384; *London Joint Stock Bank v. Simmons* [1892] A.C. 201; *Fuller v. Glyn Mills, Currie & Co.* [1914] 2 K.B. 168.
[3] *Société Générale de Paris v. Walker, supra.*
[4] *Harrold v. Plenty* [1901] 2 Ch. 314.
[5] *ibid.*
[6] *Deverges v. Sandeman* [1902] 1 Ch. 579.
[7] (1828) 3 Russ. 1. For the rule in *Dearle v. Hall*, see *ante*, pp. 80–82 and *post*, pp. 350–353.

when appropriate, until the court has determined the rights of the conflicting parties.[8] It is doubtful whether a company is legally bound to delay so far,[9] but equally it is not bound to register a transfer which effectuates a fraud.[10] In *Ireland v. Hart*,[11] a solicitor was the registered owner of shares which he held in trust for his wife. He mortgaged them by deposit to H, who, being doubtful as to the mortgagor's financial stability, filled in his own name on the blank transfer which accompanied the deposit and applied for registration. In the meantime the directors of the company had learnt of the wife's interest. They deferred their decision and the court held that the wife's prior interest prevailed over H's later interest. It is only where the later equitable mortgagee has a "present, absolute and unconditional right" to be registered that he will gain priority; and this appears to be restricted to the case where the company has formally accepted the transfer and only a ministerial act by an officer of the company is required to complete registration.

Notice to the company will also protect an equitable mortgagee against equities raised by the company after the notice has been given to it.[12] Thus, if the company by virtue of its articles of association has a first and paramount lien or charge on every share issued for all debts due from the holder, notice to the company of an equitable mortgage will cause further advances on the security of the same shares to rank after the equitable mortgage.[13] Further if the company has actual notice that a shareholder does not own shares beneficially and makes advances to him, it does not acquire a lien on those shares for the debt.[14]

(d) *Priorities*

13–22A   Since, by these rules, a bona fide purchaser of the legal estate without notice of a prior equitable mortgage takes in priority to it, it is advisable for the equitable mortgagee to acquire the legal title by having the transfer registered. Priority in time is only displaced if a second equitable assignee takes without notice of the first equity and then becomes registered as the legal owner of the shares.[15] An equitable mortgagee who acquires that mortgage with notice of prior equity and then obtains the legal title does not obtain priority over prior equities and takes subject to them.[16] The relevant time, in respect of notice acquired by the later mortgagee, is the time when he gave value for his interest. He is not adversely affected by notice acquired between the time he gave value and the time when he acquired the legal title.[17] This not only protects him against earlier equitable mortgages but against subsequent dealings between a fraudulent mortgagor and an innocent third party. In certain instances, where the circumstances

---

[8] *Moore v. North Western Bank* [1891] 2 Ch. 599. See also *Simpson v. Molson's Bank* [1895] A.C. 270.

[9] *ibid.*

[10] *Roots v. Williamson* (1888) 38 Ch.D. 485.

[11] [1902] 1 Ch. 522.

[12] *Rainford v. James, Keith and Blackman Co.* [1905] 2 Ch. 147.

[13] *Bradford Banking Co. Ltd v. Briggs & Co. Ltd* (1886) 12 App.Cas. 29, applying *Hopkinson v. Rolt* (1861) 9 H.L.Cas 514; *Mackereth v. Wigan and Iron Co. Ltd* [1916] 2 Ch. 293.

[14] *Reardon v. Provincial Bank of Ireland* [1896] 1 I.R. 532.

[15] *Dodds v. Hills* (1865) 2 H. & M. 424.

[16] *Earl of Sheffield v. London Joint Stock Bank, supra.*

[17] *Ortigosa v. Brown, Janson & Co.* (1878) 47 L.J. Ch. 168.

are such that it would have been reasonable for an enquiry to have been made, notice may be imputed.[18] Thus, the non-production of the share certificates should put the third party on notice of a prior interest.[19] However, the court may well uphold the title of the third party if the mortgagor gives him a plausible excuse for not providing the certificates and the company registers the transfer to him. Even where the company's articles of association state that certificates must be produced before transfers are registered, the company is not bound to require their production.[20]

It has been held that a private company's lien arising out of a quasi-loan to a director had priority over a subsequent mortgage of the shares notwithstanding an agreement to postpone payment of the debt.[21]

(e) *Stop notices*

The limited effect of notice can be circumscribed by the entry of a "stop notice".   **13–23** Dealings with this security can be prevented by the service of a stop notice on the company under the Civil Procedure Rules.[22] The effect is that the person or body on whom the stop notice is served shall not register a transfer of the securities or take any other steps restrained by the stop notice until 14 days after sending the notice thereof by ordinary first class post to the person on whose behalf the stop notice was filed, but shall not by reason only of that notice refuse to register the transfer or to take any other step, after the expiry of that period. By this route, the mortgagee at last secures himself a reasonable period in which to act. A mortgagor who, by putting a stop on registration wrongfully obstructs the mortgagee in the exercise of his remedies is liable in damages for any resulting loss.[23]

(f) *Delivery of a blank form of transfer*

When a mortgagor of shares either transfers the legal title to shares to a mortgagee, or puts into his hands a blank transfer,[24] he enables the mortgagee to represent himself as being the beneficial owner of the shares. His beneficial interest is in the shares as security for the mortgage debt and if he transfers the shares he has the right only to assign the mortgage debt and his interest in the shares as security for it. The mortgagor, however, runs the risk of the mortgagee fraudulently transferring the shares to a third party, for value, without telling the transferee of his limited interest. When the mortgagee has perfected his legal title by registration of the transfer, the mortgagor can protect himself only by giving notice of his equity of redemption to the company as a result of which he may be able to intervene if the mortgagee attempts to make a fraudulent transfer.

---

[18] *Earl of Sheffield v. London Joint Stock Bank, supra.*
[19] *France v. Clark* (1884) 26 Ch.D. 257; *Fox v. Martin* (1895) L.J.Ch. 473.
[20] *Rainford v. James, Keith and Blackman Co.* [1905] 1 Ch. 296; reversed on the facts [1905] 2 Ch. 147.
[21] *Champagne Perrier-Jouet S.A. v. H.H. Finch Ltd* [1982] 1 W.L.R. 1359.
[22] CPR, Sched. 1, RSC, Ord. 50, rr.11–12.
[23] *Deverges v. Sandeman* [1902] 1 Ch. 579.
[24] See *ante*, para. 13–21.

Where the mortgagee is an equitable mortgagee, the rights of the parties will be determined by estoppel and by whether the person to whom the mortgagee transferred the shares is a bona fide purchaser for value without notice. When a mortgagor delivers share certificates and a blank transfer form, he confers on the mortgagee the right to do one of three things, namely to:

(1) complete his own legal title by filling in his name and registering himself as owner;
(2) sell the shares as mortgagee and fill in the name of the purchaser, having first given due notice to the mortgagor;
(3) assign the mortgage.

Even though the mortgagor has placed the *indicia* of title in the mortgagee's hands, he is not estopped from denying the mortgagee's right to deal with the shares in any other way.

In *France v. Clark*[25] F deposited share certificates with C, to secure a loan of £150, and also executed a blank transfer form. C then deposited both the certificates and transfer form with Q to secure his own debt to Q of £250. C died insolvent and Q then filled in his own name as transferee, sending on the transfer for registration. F gave notice to both the company and Q that he denied the validity of the transfer and it was not clear whether that notice was given before or after the registration in the name of C.

The Court of Appeal held that a transferee who takes a blank transfer and fills up the blanks in his own favour is not entitled to be treated as a bona fide purchaser for value without notice: and if he makes no inquiry he can take only the right that the mortgagee received from the mortgagor. Consequently, it was irrelevant whether the registration took place before or after the notice, as registration would give effect only to a prior valid transfer, but would not validate a document which, as between the mortgagee and his transferee, was of no effect. It was further held that the mortgagee had no authority to fill up the form for purposes foreign to the original contract, and thus Q had no title against F except as security for the £150 which F owed C. It would have been otherwise had the facts been such as to indicate that C had a general authority to deal with the shares; or if instead of shares they had been negotiable instruments such as bearer securities.

5. Debts

13–24   A mortgage of debts can be effected by a legal or equitable assignment with a proviso for redemption since public policy does not preclude such a mortgage.[26] Such a mortgage should relieve the mortgagee of any liability should the debt prove to be irrecoverable.[27]

---

[25] (1883) 22 Ch.D. 830.
[26] *Linden Gardens Trust Limited v. Lenesta Sludge Disposals Limited, St Martin's Corpn v. Sir Robert MacAlpine & Sons Limited* [1994] 1 A.C. 85, HL.
[27] *Williams v. Price* (1824) 1 Sim. & St. 581.

(a) *Future debts*

There cannot be a legal assignment of a future debt; if the same is made and supported by valuable consideration, it is treated as a contract to assign.[28] Such a contract is provable in the mortgagor's bankruptcy and from which the mortgagor is released on discharge.[29] A mortgage of "all the book debts due and owing and which may, during the continuance of the security, become due and owing" to the mortgagor is sufficient to pass the equitable interest in the book debts incurred after the assignment, whether in the business carried on by the mortgagor at the date of the assignment or in any other business.[30] Unless registered under the Bills of Sale Act 1878, such a mortgage of future debts by a person engaged in business is void as against the mortgagor's trustee in bankruptcy where the debt has not been paid before the presentation of the petition.[31]

(b) *Notice to the debtor*

Until notice is given to the debtor, the mortgage remains equitable[32] although since notice to a body of trade debtors can have adverse commercial consequences on the mortgagor, such mortgages often contain provisions that notice will not be given unless the mortgagor is in default. Provision is often made for the mortgagee to collect the debts as the mortgagor's agent. In the absence of notice, payment by the debtor to the mortgagor will be a good release for the debtor as against the mortgagee.[33]

(c) *Priority*

The priority of such mortgages is governed by the date of receipt by the debtor of notice of the mortgages.[34]

6. **Future things in action**

A mortgage of an expectancy or a future thing in action, such as a beneficiary's **13–25** interest under a discretionary trust or an expectancy under a will is unenforceable is purely voluntary.[35] The same principles apply as with future debts; the mortgage operates as a contract to assign the specified property when it falls into

---

[28] *Holyroyd v. Marshall* (1862) 10 H.L. Cas. 191.
[29] *Collyer v. Isaacs* (1881) 19 Ch. D. 342; *Wilmot v. Alton* [1897] 1 Q.B. 17; *Bank of Scotland v. Maclead* [1914] A.C. 411; *Re Collins* [1925] Ch. 556.
[30] *Tailby v. Official Receiver* (1888) 13 App.Cas. 523.
[31] Insolvency Act 1986, s.344.
[32] Law of Property Act 1925, s.136(1).
[33] *Stocks v. Dobson* (1853) 4 De G.M. & G. 11.
[34] See *ante*, paras 13–09 *et seq.* and Chap. 20.
[35] *Meek v. Kettlewell* (1843) 1 Ph. 342

the mortgagor's possession. The bankruptcy of the mortgagor, having effected a mortgage of an expectant share in the estate of a living person, has no bearing; such a mortgage operates as a good equitable charge and does not impose a mere personal liability on the mortgagor to charge the share upon it vesting in him.[36]

[36] *Re Lind, Industrial Finance Syndicate v. Lind* [1915] 2 Ch. 345.

CHAPTER 14

MORTGAGES OF LAND AND CONSUMER REGULATION[1]

APPLICATION OF THE CONSUMER CREDIT ACT 1974

1. Types of agreement

An agreement may be unregulated, partially regulated, regulated, or exempt.   **14–01**

Unregulated agreements are those which do not attract the operation of the Act at all, either because English law does not apply to them or because none of the debtors is an individual. Section 43(2)(*c*) refers to such agreements, but the Act does not define them.

Partially regulated agreements are agreements which are exempt from certain specific provisions of the Act. They include pledges of documents of title and some purchase-money arrangements secured by a mortgage of land.

Regulated agreements[2] are defined by section 189(1) as consumer credit or consumer hire agreements, other than exempt agreements.

Exempt agreements are defined in sections 189(1) and 16 of the Act and are not affected by the Act except for the provisions of sections 137 to 140, which apply to extortionate credit bargains.

2. Definitions

By section 189(1), a land mortgage includes any security charged on land.   **14–02**
Section 189(1) also defines "land" as including an interest in land, whether freehold or leasehold.

Exempt consumer credit agreements are of two types. Section 16(1) exempts land mortgages or agreements relating thereto where the creditor is a specified body, while section 16(5) empowers the Secretary of State to exempt certain other consumer credit agreements by order.[3] Section 181 provides for the amendment of monetary limits by statutory instrument.

---

[1] See also Goode, *Consumer Credit: Law and Practice* (2000). The Financial Services and Markets Act 2000 (Regulated Activities) Order 2001 (S.I. 2001 No. 544) prospectively removes from regulation under the Act both regulated mortgage contracts and qualifying credit promotions; see *post*, para. 14–15 *et seq*.

[2] s.126 of the Act provides that a land mortgage securing a regulated agreement is enforceable only by an order of the court; see *post*, p. 247.

[3] The Consumer Credit (Exempt Agreements) Order 1989, S.I. 1989 No. 869 presently in force, is further amended by S.I. 1991 No. 2844, S.I. 1993 No. 346, S.I. 1993 No. 2922, S.I. 1994 No. 2420, S.I. 1995 No. 1250, S.I. 1995 No. 2914, S.I. 1996 No. 1445, S.I. 1996 No. 3081, S.I. 1998 No. 1944 and S.I. 1999 No. 1956.

Section 8(2) defines a consumer credit agreement as a personal credit agreement by which the creditor provides the debtor with credit not exceeding £25,000.[4]

Exempt agreements are dealt with by section 16 of the Act. Section 16(1), as amended,[5] provides as follows:

"(1) This Act does not regulate a consumer credit agreement where the creditor is a local authority, [...] or a body specified, or of a description specified, in an order made by the Secretary of State, being—

(a)   an insurance company,

(b)   a friendly society,

(c)   an organisation of employers or organisation of workers,

(d)   a charity,

(e)   a land improvement company,

(f)   a body corporate named or specifically referred to in any public general Act, or

(pp) a body corporate named or specifically referred to in an order made under sections 156(4) or 447(2)(a) of the Housing Act 1985, [[section 156(4) of the Act as it has effect by virtue of section 17 of the Housing Act 1996 (right to acquire)]], section [[223 or 229 of the Housing (Scotland) Act 1987]] or Articles 154(1) or 156AA of the Housing (Northern Ireland) Order 1981 or Article 10(6A) of the Housing (Northern Ireland) Order 1983; or]

[(g) a building society]

[(h) an authorised institution or wholly-owned subsidiary (within the meaning of the Companies Act 1985) of such an institution.]"

The relevant order is the Consumer Credit (Exempt Agreements) Order[6] and the specified bodies are listed in Part I of the Schedule thereto. Provided that the creditor is a local authority, or a body specified or a description specified by that Order and the agreement falls within section 16(2) of the Act, it is an exempt agreement. Section 16(2) provides as follows:

"(2) Subsection (1) applies only where the agreement is—

(a)   a debtor-creditor-supplier agreement financing—

(i)   the purchase of land, or
(ii) the provision of dwellings on any land, and
(iii) secured by a land mortgage on that land, or

(b)   a debtor-creditor agreement secured by any land mortgage; or

(c)   a debtor-creditor-supplier agreement financing a transaction which is a linked transaction in relation to—

---

[4] Originally £15,000, this limit was raised by S.I. 1983 No. 1878 with effect from May 20, 1985 (being the date on which the Act came into force) and to £25,000 with effect from May 1, 1998: Consumer Credit (Amendment) Order 1990, S.I. 1998/996.

[5] By the Building Societies Act 1986, s.120(1), (2) and Scheds. 18, 19 Housing and Planning Act 1986, s.22; Banking Act 1987, s.88.

[6] S.I. 1989 No. 869 as amended: see n. 4 *supra*.

(i) an agreement falling within paragraph (*a*), or
(ii) an agreement falling within paragraph (*b*) financing—

(*aa*) the purchase of any land, or
(*bb*) the provision of dwellings on any land,
        and secured by a land mortgage on the land referred to in paragraph
        (*a*), or, as the case may be, the land referred to in sub-paragraph
        (ii)."

Where the creditor is a building society authorised under the Building Socie-   **14–03**
ties Act 1986, an institution authorised under the Banking Act 1987, or a wholly
owned subsidiary of such an institution, or a specified body under the Order, the
agreement is exempt provided that it falls within paragraph 2(2) of the Order. The
effect of paragraph 2(2) is to narrow the range of exempt debtor-creditor agreements; the position in regard to debtor-creditor-supplier agreements is unaltered,
as all such agreements within sections 16(2)(*a*) or (*c*) of the Act are within
paragraph 2(2). Building societies lost their automatic exemption from January 1,
1987.

As to debtor-creditor agreements, not all such agreements secured by land
mortgages are exempt agreements: the exemption applies only to the agreements
specified in sub-paragraphs (*b*) and (*c*) of paragraph 2(2), which read:

"(*b*) a debtor-creditor agreement secured by any land mortgage [to
finance]—

(i) the purchase of land; or
(ii) the provision of dwelling or business premises on any land; or
(iii) subject to paragraph (3) below, the alteration, enlarging, repair or
        improvement of a dwelling or business premises on any land;

(*c*) a debtor-creditor agreement secured by any land mortgage to refinance
any existing indebtedness of the debtor whether to the creditor or another
person, under any agreement by which the debtor was provided with credit
for any of the purposes specified in heads (i) to (iii) of sub-paragraph (*b*)
above."

For the purposes of the Act, a "building society" has the meaning given to it
by section 1 of the Building Societies Act 1962[7]; "local authority," in relation to
England, means a county, London borough, or district council, the Common
Council of the City of London, or the Council of the Isles of Scilly. In relation
to Wales, it means a county or a county borough council.[8] Debtor-creditor-
supplier and debtor-creditor agreements are defined in sections 12 and 13,
respectively. The essential difference between them is that, in a debtor-creditor
agreement there is either no supplier of goods or services, or there is no
arrangement between the supplier and the creditor. In a debtor-creditor-supplier

---

[7] The 1962 Act has been repealed by the Building Societies Act 1986, s.120(2), Sched. 19, Pt. I. By
    s.1(4) of the 1962 Act a building society was defined as a society incorporated under the 1962 Act
    "or any enactment repealed by this Act." The words in quotation marks are omitted in the
    definition in s.119 of the 1986 Act.
[8] CCA 1974, s.189(1).

agreement, the supplier is either the creditor or a party to the actual or contemplated arrangements between himself and the creditor.

It therefore follows that the exemption provided by section 16(2)(*a*) is effective when credit is extended by the vendor, or the builder, or a third party lender who has made arrangements with the vendor or builder, as the case may be, and where the advance is secured on the land purchased or to be built on. A dwelling, for the purpose of this provision, is any accommodation designed wholly or mainly for living or sleeping in, rather than for business. A debtor-creditor agreement secured by a land mortgage will be an exempt agreement under paragraph 2(2)(*b*) provided that it is to finance the purchase of land or the provision of dwelling or business premises on any land, and that the creditor is an authorised bank or building society or body specified in Part I of the Schedule.

Agreements to finance the alteration, enlarging, repair or improvement of a dwelling or business premises on any land are not necessarily exempt agreements even when the creditor is one of the specified bodies.[9] The exemption under paragraph 2(2)(*b*)(iii) may apply *either* because the creditor is a creditor under an agreement of the type specified in paragraph 2(3)(i)(*a*) or (*b*), *or* because the agreement has been made as a result of any such services as are described in section 4(3)(*e*) of the Housing Associations Act 1985 and which are certified as having been provided by one of the bodies specified in paragraph 2(3)(ii)(*a–g*).

The bodies listed[10] compromise various insurance companies, friendly societies, charities, the General Practice Finance Corporation Limited and the Agricultural Mortgage Corporation.

CANCELLATION AND WITHDRAWAL

14–04   Part V of the Act deals with the withdrawal by an intending debtor or hirer from a prospective regulated agreement, and with cancellation by a debtor or hirer of a regulated agreement already entered into. Most land mortgages are exempt agreements by virtue of section 8(2) and section 16, but even where a land mortgage is a regulated agreement, it can be excluded from the operation of Part V by a determination under section 74 of the Act (as amended by the Banking Act 1979, section 38(1)), which provides as follows:

"(1) This Part (except section 56) does not apply to:

(a) a non-commercial agreement, or
(b) a debtor-creditor agreement enabling the debtor to overdraw on a current account, or
(c) a debtor-creditor agreement to finance the making of such payments arising on, or connected with, the death of a person as may be prescribed.

---

[9] CCA 1974, s.189(1).
[10] Specified in the Sched. to the Consumer Credit (Exempt Agreements) Order 1989, S.I. 1989 No. 869, as amended.

(2) This Part (except sections 55 and 56) does not apply to a small debtor-creditor-supplier agreement for restricted-use credit.

[(2A) In the case of an agreement to which the Consumer Protection (Cancellation of Contracts Concluded away from Business Premises) Regulations 1987 apply the reference in sub-section (2) to a small agreement shall be construed as if in section 17(1)(a) and (b) '£35' were substituted for '£50'.]

(3) Subsection (1)(b) or (c) applies only where the Director so determines, and such a determination:

(a) may be made subject to such conditions as the Director thinks fit, and

(b) shall be made only if the Director is of opinion that it is not against the interests of debtors.

[3A] Notwithstanding anything in sub-section (3)(b) above, in relation to a debtor-creditor agreement under which the creditor is the Bank of England or a bank within the meaning of the Bankers' Books Evidence Act 1879, the Director shall make a determination that sub-section 1(b) applies unless he considers that it would be against the public interest to do so.]

(4) If any term of an agreement falling within sub-section [(1)(c)] or (2) is expressed in writing, regulations under section 60(1) shall apply to that term (subject to section 60(3)) as if the agreement were a regulated agreement not falling within sub-section [(1)(c)] or (2)."

A non-commercial agreement is a consumer credit agreement or a consumer hire agreement not made by the creditor or owner in the course of a business carried on by him.[11]

1. Section 58: Opportunity for withdrawal from a prospective land mortgage

Few land mortgages would, in fact, be excluded by the operation of section 74, **14–05** but they are excluded from the cancellation provisions of sections 67 to 73.[12] Instead, section 58(1) provides a special mechanism whereby the debtor or hirer under certain land mortgage transactions gets, in effect, the right to withdraw. Although the Act does not expressly give that right, the debtor or hirer is always free to withdraw until he has signed the written regulated agreement and an agreement to enter a regulated agreement is not enforceable against him. Section 58 provides that:

"(1) Before sending to the debtor or hirer, for his signature, an unexecuted agreement in a case where the prospective regulated agreement is to be secured on land (the "mortgaged land"), the creditor or owner shall give the debtor or hirer a copy of the unexecuted agreement which contains a notice

---

[11] CCA 1974, s.189(1).
[12] CCA 1974, s.67(e). Also excluded are restricted use credit agreements to finance the purchase of land and agreements for bridging loans. Such agreements are not covered by the mechanism set forth in s.58: see s.58(2).

in the prescribed form indicating the right of the debtor or hirer to withdraw from the prospective agreement, and how and when the right is exercisable, together with a copy of any other document referred to in the unexecuted agreement.[13]

(2) Subsection (1) does not apply to—

    (*a*) a restricted-use credit agreement to finance the purchase of the mortgaged land, or

    (*b*) an agreement for a bridging loan in connection with the purchase of the mortgaged land or other land."

The reason for the provisions of section 58(1) is the administrative inconvenience which is likely to arise from the registration and almost immediate de-registration of mortgages, were they cancellable. The exceptions in section 58(2) apply to certain transactions where there is a need for finance to be provided rapidly and the delay provided by section 58(1) might be prejudicial.

SIGNING THE AGREEMENT

14–06 Section 61 makes the following provision with regard to the signing of regulated agreements:

"(1) A regulated agreement is not properly executed unless—

    (*a*) a document in the prescribed form itself containing all the prescribed terms and conforming to regulations under section 60(1) is signed in the prescribed manner both by the debtor and hirer and by or on behalf of the creditor or owner, and

    (*b*) the document embodies all the terms of the agreement, other than implied terms, and

    (*c*) the document is, when presented or sent to the debtor or hirer for signature, in such a state that all its terms are readily legible."

(2) In addition, where the agreement is one to which section 58(1) applies, it is not properly executed unless—

    (*a*) the requirements of section 58(1) were complied with, and

    (*b*) the unexecuted agreement was sent, for his signature, to the debtor or hirer by post not less than seven days[14] after a copy of it was given to him under section 58(1), and

    (*c*) during the consideration period, the creditor or owner refrained from approaching the debtor or hirer (whether in person, by telephone or letter, or in any other way) except in response to a specific

---

[13] The Consumer Credit (Cancellation Notices and Copies of Documents) Regulations 1983, S.I. 1983 No. 1557 as amended by S.I. 1984 No. 1108, S.I. 1985 No. 666, S.I. 1988 No. 2047, S.I. 1989 No. 591 are partly made under s.58(1) of the Consumer Credit Act 1974.

[14] It is thought that this means seven clear days excluding both the date of delivery of the copy and the date of sending the agreement for signature: *R. v. Turner* [1910] 1 K.B. 346; *Re Hector Whaling Ltd* [1936] Ch. 208; *Carapanayoti & Co. Limited v. Comptoir Commercial Andre et Cie SA* [1972] 1 Lloyd's Rep. 139.

request made by the debtor or hirer after the beginning of the consideration period, and

    (*d*) no notice of withdrawal by the debtor or hirer was received by the creditor or owner before the sending of the unexecuted agreement.

(3) In subsection (2)(*c*), 'the consideration period' means the period beginning with the giving of the copy under section 58(1) and ending—

    (*a*) at the expiry of seven days after the day on which the unexecuted agreement is sent, for his signature, to the debtor or hirer, or

    (*b*) on its return by the debtor or hirer after signature by him

whichever first occurs.

(4) Where the debtor or hirer is a partnership or an unincorporated body of persons, subsection (1)(*a*) shall apply with the substitution for 'by the debtor of hirer' of 'by or on behalf of the debtor of hirer'."

The provisions of section 61(2) are additional to and, not in substitution for those of section 61(1), so, not only must the form and content of the agreement be as provided by section 60, but the requirements of section 58 must be met if that section applies.

AVOIDANCE OF AGREEMENTS TO ENTER FUTURE AGREEMENTS

Section 59 prevents the debtor or hirer having a prospective agreement enforced against him.

"(1) An agreement is void if, and to the extent that, it purports to bind a person to enter as debtor or hirer into a prospective regulated agreement.

(2) Regulations may exclude from the operation of sub-section (1) agreements such as are described in the regulations."[15]

WITHDRAWAL: RIGHTS AFTER WITHDRAWAL

14–07 Although the cancellation provisions of sections 67 to 73 do not apply to land mortgages, section 57(4) applies section 57(1) to non-cancellable agreements, and, by section 57(1), the rights of the parties after withdrawal are the same as those conferred by section 69 where the agreement was cancellable. Section 57 states that:

"(1) The withdrawal of a party from a prospective regulated agreement shall operate to apply this Part to the agreement, any linked transaction and any

[15] Consumer Credit (Agreements to Enter Prospective Agreements) (Exemptions) Regulations 1983 (S.I. 1983 No. 1552). Two categories are exempted: (1) consumer hire agreements and (2) restricted use credit agreements financing the purchase of goods where, in either case, the consumer requires the goods for business purposes or holds himself out as so needing them and the agreement embodies a quotation relating to the prospective regulated agreement and either there were no face to face dealings or the agreement was signed at business premises.

other thing done in anticipation of the making of the agreement as it would apply if the agreement were made and then cancelled under section 69.

(2) The giving to a party of a written or oral notice which, however expressed, indicates the intention of the other party to withdraw from a prospective regulated agreement operates as a withdrawal from it.

(3) Each of the following shall be deemed to be the agent of the creditor or owner for the purpose of receiving a notice under subsection (2)—

> (*a*) a credit-broker or supplier who is the negotiator in antecedent negotiations, and
>
> (*b*) any person who, in the course of a business carried on by him, acts on behalf of the debtor or hirer in any negotiations for the agreement.

(4) Where the agreement, if made, would not be a cancellable agreement, subsection (1) shall nevertheless apply as if the contrary were the case."

Linked transactions are defined by section 19 of the Act. Not only is the transaction and any linked transaction cancelled, but so is any offer by the debtor or hirer or his relative, to enter into a linked transaction, unless in both cases the linked transaction is exempted by regulation by virtue of section 69(5). Section 69(4) provides that cancelled agreements are to be treated as if they had never been entered into.

If the relevant agreement is a debtor-creditor-supplier agreement financing the supply of goods or doing of work in an emergency, or financing the supply of goods which have become incorporated by act of the debtor or his relative in any land or thing not itself comprised in the agreement or any linked transaction, the cancellation or withdrawal affects only those provisions that relate to the provision of credit, or require payment of an item in the total charge for credit. But the obligation of the debtor to pay for the work or supply of goods is unaffected.[16]

EXTORTIONATE CREDIT BARGAINS[17]

14–08 Statutory control over extortionate credit bargains formerly derived from the Moneylenders Act 1900, as amended by the Moneylenders Act 1927.[18] Under those enactments only loans made by persons who were moneylenders within the meaning of the earlier Act and certain pawnbroking transactions were caught.

---

[16] s.69(2).

[17] Where the mortgagor is a company which later becomes insolvent or enters administration, the court has jurisdiction to set aside or vary the terms of any extortionate credit transactions under the Insolvency Act 1986. It is similar to the jurisdiction under the Consumer Credit Act in respect of extortionate credit bargains. But it is only exercisable in respect of transactions entered into within three years before the day on which the company goes into liquidation or an administration order is made—see Insolvency Act 1986, s.244(1) or (in the case of an individual mortgagor who becomes bankrupt) not more than three years before the commencement of bankruptcy—s.343 of the Insolvency Act 1986. This definition of an "extortionate transaction" is, in the case of both provisions, the same as that employed in the Consumer Credit Act 1974. The burden to show that the transaction was not extortionate rests upon the party providing the credit: Insolvency Act 1986, ss.244(3), 343(3).

[18] Repealed by the Consumer Credit Act 1974, s.192(3) and Sched. 5.

There was a presumption under section 10(1) of the 1927 Act that any interest charge of over 48 per cent. per annum was excessive. In addition, the courts had an equitable jurisdiction to relieve against harsh and unconscionable bargains.

1. The jurisdiction in equity

The general equitable jurisdiction of the courts to set aside "harsh and uncon- **14-09** scionable" bargains was supplemented by section 1(1) of the Moneylenders Act 1900. Where a transaction was caught by this provision, the court had power to re-open it where there was evidence that the interest and other charges were excessive and that the transaction was harsh and unconscionable or otherwise such that the court of equity would give relief. Before 1900, courts of equity had set aside two classes of bargain. There the bargain was with an expectant heir,[19] the onus was on the purchaser to prove that it was fair, just and reasonable and if he failed to discharge that burden, the transaction would be set aside regardless of the relationship between the parties to the bargain. The second class of bargain with which equity would interfere arose where the court considered that the creditor had taken a grossly unfair advantage of the debtor thereby rendering the bargain unconscionable.[20] In *Samuel v. Newbold*[21-22] it was decided that these two grounds were quite distinct.

The Consumer Credit Act 1974 contains no power to re-open transactions unless the court considers that bargain extortionate. Absent the statutory jurisdiction, it may be, however, that a loan made on the credit of the borrower's expectancy (but without taking a security over it) would be set aside unless the lender could prove that the terms were fair and reasonable, *i.e.* he had paid the market price.[23] Such a loan is outside section 174 of the Law of Property Act 1925, which provides that a sale or loan on the security of a reversion is not voidable merely by reason of undervalue, but expressly preserves the jurisdiction of the court to set aside or modify unconscionable bargains.

The power of the courts of equity to set aside unconscionable bargains was reviewed in *Multiservice Bookbinding Limited v. Marden*.[24] It is clear from that judgment that courts will not set aside bargains which are improvident or contain terms which are, by normal standards, unreasonable. A bargain cannot be unfair and unconscionable unless one of the parties to it has imposed the objectionable terms in a morally reprehensible manner and thus in a way that affects his conscience. The categories of unconscionable bargains are not limited.

A bargain may be set aside where advantage is taken of a poor, ignorant or weak-minded person, or one who is for some other reason in need of special protection. In *Fry v. Lane*[25] it was held that there were three requirements to be

---

[19] *Earl of Aylesford v. Morris* (1873) L.R. 8 Ch. App. 484; *Earl of Chesterfield v. Janssen* (1750) 2 Ves.Sen. 125; *Nevill v. Snelling* (1880) 15 Ch.D. 679.
[20] See *Snell's Equity* (30th ed., 2000), para. 38-27—38-29.
[21-22] [1906] A.C. 461.
[23] *Shelly v. Nash* (1818) 3 Madd. 232.
[24] [1979] Ch. 84. Here the court refused to apply the test of "reasonableness" to an indexation clause in the mortgage made between the parties. The test was whether the bargain was "unfair and unconscionable". Held: stipulation valid and enforceable, reflecting *Tresider-Griffin v. Co-operative Insurance Society Ltd* [1956] 2 Q.B. 127. See also *Davis v. Directloans Ltd* [1986] 1 W.L.R. 823.
[25] (1888) 40 Ch.D. 312.

satisfied if a bargain was held to be unconscionable: (i) poverty and ignorance of the plaintiff; (ii) sale at an undervalue; (iii) lack of independent advice. In *Cresswell v. Potter*[26] Megarry J. explained "ignorant" as meaning "ignorant in the context of property transactions in general and conveyancing documents in particular". In *Backhouse v. Backhouse*,[27] Balcombe J. considered that a party who had executed a document under the emotional strain of an impending or actual marriage breakdown, might be relieved as being in the position of unequal bargaining power under the principle enunciated by Lord Denning M.R. in *Lloyds Bank v. Bundy*.[28] In *Samuel v. Newbold*[29] it was said that a transaction might fall within the description because of the borrower's extreme necessity and helplessness, or because of the relationship in which he stood to the lender, or because of his situation in other ways. That was a case in which the circumstances of the transaction and the "monstrous" rate of interest charged (418 per cent) were each sufficient to characterise the bargain as harsh and unconscionable.

2. **The Consumer Credit Act 1974**

14–10   These provisions apply to the agreements and transactions whenever made.[30]

The provisions of the Moneylenders Acts, which have been progressively repealed as various parts of the Consumer Credit Act 1974 have come into force, and were totally repealed on May 19, 1985, have been replaced by sections 137 to 140 of the Consumer Credit Act. Two important differences between the new and the former provisions are that the new provisions apply to all "credit bargains" as defined in section 137, *infra*, and the statutory presumption as to excessive interest rates has been abolished. Section 137 provides:

> "(1) If the court finds a credit bargain extortionate it may reopen the credit agreement so as to do justice between the parties.
>
> (2) In this section and sections 138 to 140—
>
> (*a*) 'credit agreement' means any agreement between an individual (the 'debtor') and any other person (the 'creditor') by which the creditor provides the debtor with credit of any amount, and
>
> (*b*) 'credit bargain'—
>
> > (i) where no transaction other than the credit agreement is to be taken into account in computing the total charge for credit, means the credit agreement, or
> >
> > (ii) where one or more other transactions are to be so taken into account, means the credit agreement and those other transactions, taken together."

---

[26] Reported as a note (p.255) to *Backhouse v. Backhouse* [1978] 1 W.L.R. 243.

[27] *ibid.*

[28] [1975] Q.B. 326 at 329.

[29] [1906] A.C. 461.

[30] Consumer Credit Act 1974, Sched. 3, para. 42. Articles 90 and 91 of the Financial Services and Markets Act 2000 (Regulated Activities) Order 2001 (S.I. 2001 No. 544) prospectively remove the extortionate credit provisions from the 1974 Act.

Section 138(1) defines "extortionate" whilst section 138(2) to (5) sets out the evidential matters which the court is to take into account in determining whether a credit bargain is extortionate:

> "(1) A credit bargain is extortionate if it—
>
> > (a)   requires the debtor or a relative of his to make payments (whether unconditionally, or on certain contingencies) which are grossly exorbitant, or
> >
> > (b)   otherwise grossly contravenes ordinary principles of fair dealing.
>
> (2) In determining whether a credit bargain is extortionate, regard shall be had to such evidence as is adduced concerning—
>
> > (a)   interest rates prevailing at the time it was made,
> >
> > (b)   the factors mentioned in subsections (3) to (5), and
> >
> > (c)   any other relevant considerations.
>
> (3) Factors applicable under subsection (2) in relation to the debtor[31] include—
>
> > (a)   his age, experience, business capacity and state of health; and
> >
> > (b)   the degree to which, at the time of making the credit bargain, he was under financial pressure, and the nature of that pressure.
>
> (4) Factors applicable under subsection (2) in relation to the creditor include—
>
> > (a)   the degree of risk accepted by him, having regard to the value of any security provided[32];
> >
> > (b)   his relationship to the debtor; and
> >
> > (c)   whether or not a colourable cash price was quoted for any goods or services included in the credit bargain.
>
> (5) Factors applicable under subsection (2) in relation to a linked transaction include the question how far the transaction was reasonably required for the protection of debtor or creditor, or was in the interest of the debtor."

Whether the bargain is extortionate has to be determined as at the date of the agreement.[33] If the bargain as struck is not extortionate, the borrower will not be relieved merely because its terms become more onerous in the light of subsequent events.[34]

Thus, section 138 deals with the matters to which the court shall have regard if evidence of them is adduced. It is for the party, not the court, to call the evidence, and the court cannot call for any evidence or direct a party to do so against his wishes. Further, by section 139 it is only the debtor or a surety who

---

[31] The cases of *Samuel v. Newbold* [1906] A.C. 461, *Poncione v. Higgins* (1904) 21 T.L.R. 11 and *Glaskie v. Griffin* (1914) 111 L.T. 712 contain decisions on similar factors under the old provisions.

[32] For relevant decisions see *Kruse v. Seeley* [1924] 1 Ch. 136; *Verner-Jeffreys v. Pinto* [1929] 1 Ch. 401; *Reading Trust Ltd. v. Spero* [1930] 1 K.B. 492.

[33] *Harris v. Classon* (1910) 27 T.L.R. 30.

[34] *Multiservice Bookbinding Ltd. v. Marden* [1979] Ch. 84. and see *Davies v. Directloans Ltd* [1986] 1 W.L.R. 823.

can apply to re-open the transaction. On a literal reading of section 139(1)(b), that provision would appear to preclude the court from raising the matter of its own volition. However, in *First National Bank plc v. Syed*,[35] Dillon L.J. expressly considered whether the Court of Appeal should, in a case in which the debtor was unrepresented and had not raised the issue, make an order of its own motion directing the County Court to determine whether the agreement was extortionate. On the facts of the case, the court did not do so. However, it does leave open the possibility that in different circumstances, the court could choose to raise the issue of its own motion.

14–11   Although section 138 directs the court to have regard to evidence adduced of factors applicable to the debtor and to the creditor, it does not follow that any weight will necessarily be placed on such evidence. The older decisions strongly suggest that, before the bargain can be set aside, the court must find that the creditor knew of the circumstances which made the debtor particularly vulnerable and unfairly took advantage of them. Although abnormally high interest rates may be taken as conclusive evidence of unfair dealing (and regard must be had not only to prevailing rates but also the type and nature of the agreement and the circumstances in which it was made),[36] they may on the other hand be intended genuinely to reflect the risk involved in lending. As Darling J. said in *Jackson v. Price*[37]: "If you had to lend a mutton chop to a ravenous dog, on what terms would you lend it?"

It is for the debtor to show, on the balance of probabilities, the existence of any fact on which he relies for the purpose of establishing any matter referred to in section 138(3) and, if it is relevant, the creditor's knowledge of that fact. If he fails to do so, the court will not take the matter into account; but if he succeeds, it is for the creditor by virtue of section 171(7) to show that, despite those facts, the bargain was not extortionate. In regard to section 138(4)(*c*), the 1974 Act does not provide a definition of the words a "colourable cash price" but this denotes a price artificially inflated so as to conceal the actual rate of charge.

The question whether a credit bargain is extortionate was considered in *Davies v. Directloans Ltd.*[38] In that case, it was held impermissible and unnecessary to look outside the Act at earlier authorities, in order to ascertain the meaning of the word "extortionate" in section 138(1), and that it does not necessarily mean the same as "harsh and unconscionable."[39] Outside the Act a bargain cannot be unfair and unconscionable:

> "unless one of the parties to it has imposed the objectionable terms in a morally reprehensible manner, that is to say, in a way which affects his conscience"[40]

---

[35] [1991] 2 All E.R. 250.
[36] *A. Ketley Limited v. Scott* [1981] 1 C.R. 241.
[37] (1909) 26 T.L.R. 106 at 108.
[38] [1986] 1 W.L.R. 823.
[39] *Castle Phillips Finance Co. Ltd v. Khan* [1980] C.C.L.R. 1 at 3.
[40] *per* Browne-Wilkinson J. in *Multiservice Bookbinding Ltd v. Marden* [1979] Ch. 84 at 110. This judgment was approved by the CA in *Alec Lobb (Garages) Ltd v. Total Oil (Great Britain) Ltd* [1985] 1 W.L.R. 173. In the latter case, a majority of the CA was of the view that there was no general doctrine of "reasonableness" independent of undue influence and duress. Equity controls only unconscionable and not unreasonable bargains. See *Lloyds Bank v. Bundy* [1975] Q.B. 326 at 339; *Nationwide Building Society v. Registrar of Friendly Societies* [1983] 1 W.L.R. 1226; and *Davies v. Directloans Ltd* [1986] 1 W.L.R. 823.

whereas within the Act it is not necessary or permissible to consider whether the creditor's behaviour has been morally reprehensible but only whether one or other of the conditions of section 138(1) is fulfilled. *A fortiori*, the creditor's conduct during negotiations need not be unlawful.

In determining whether a credit bargain is extortionate, section 138(2)(*a*) lays down that the prevailing rate of interest at the time the bargain was made is a factor to be considered. It was held that regard should be had to the true rate of interest, that is, the annual percentage rate of charge calculated in accordance with the Consumer Credit (Total Charge for Credit) Regulations 1980[41] even though the regulations did not apply to the loan in question. *Coldunell Limited* v. *Gallon*[42] was primarily concerned with the question whether A can avoid a transaction with B on the grounds of undue influence exerted by C, and decided that for such avoidance it must be shown that C was acting as B's agent. At first instance the transaction in that case was set aside both on that ground and on the ground that the bargain was extortionate within the definition in section 138(1)(*b*). On appeal it was held that C was not B's agent, and the burden on B of showing the bargain not to be extortionate was discharged, so far as section 138(1)(*b*) was concerned, by demonstrating that the bargain was on its face a proper commercial bargain and that B had acted in the way that an ordinary commercial lender would be expected to act. **14–12**

Section 139 is concerned with the methods by which the extortionate credit bargain may be re-opened, and is set out below, excluding sub-sections (6) and (7) which apply to Scotland and the Northern Ireland, respectively:

"(1) A credit agreement may, if the court thinks just, be reopened on the ground that the credit bargain is extortionate—[43]

(*a*) on an application for the purpose made by the debtor or any surety to the High Court, county court or sheriff court; or

(*b*) at the instance of the debtor or a surety[44] in any proceedings to which the debtor and creditor are parties, being proceedings to enforce the agreement, any security relating to it, or any linked transaction; or

(*c*) at the instance of the debtor or a surety in other proceedings in any court where the amount paid or payable under the credit agreement is relevant.

(2) In reopening the agreement, the court may, for the purpose of relieving the debtor or a surety from payment of any sum in excess of that fairly due and reasonable, by order—

(*a*) direct accounts to be taken, or (in Scotland) an accounting to be made, between any persons,

(*b*) set aside the whole or part of any obligation imposed on the debtor or surety by the credit bargain or any related agreement,

---

[41] S.I. 1980 No. 51, as amended by S.I. 1985 No. 1192, S.I. 1989 No. 596 and S.I. 1999 No. 3177.
[42] [1986] Q.B. 1184. See also *Davies v. Directloans Ltd, supra.*
[43] The onus of proof is on the creditor: s.171(7).
[44] See, however, *First National Bank v. Syed* [1991] 2 All E.R. 250.

(c)   require the creditor to repay the whole or part of any sum paid under the credit bargain or any related agreement by the debtor or a surety, whether paid to the creditor or any other person,

(d)   direct the return to the surety of any property provided for the purposes of the security, or

(e)   alter the terms of the credit agreement or any security instrument.

(3) An order may be made under subsection (2) notwithstanding that its effect is to place a burden on the creditor in respect of an advantage unfairly enjoyed by another person who is a party to a linked transaction.

(4) An order under subsection (2) shall not alter the effect of any judgment.

(5) In England and Wales, an application under subsection (1)(a) shall be brought only in the county court in the case of—

(a)   a regulated agreement, or

(b)   an agreement (not being a regulated agreement) under which the creditor provides the debtor with fixed-sum credit or running-account credit."[45]

Section 140 provides as follows:

"Where the credit agreement is not a regulated agreement, expressions used in sections 137 to 139 which, apart from this section, apply only to regulated agreements, shall be construed as nearly as may be as if the credit agreement were a regulated agreement."

Section 139 applies to agreements whenever made.[46] However, the limitation period in which a claim for relief under section 139(2) can be brought is 12 years from the date of execution of the agreement in question.[47]

In the event that the debtor is adjudged bankrupt prior to any application, both his and his trustee's right to apply under section 139(1)(a) are precluded by section 343(6) of the Insolvency Act 1986, pursuant to which any challenge would have to be made by the trustee alone.[48] The trustee would be able, however, to intervene in any proceedings brought by the creditor under section 139.

Section 139(4) would appear to preclude the court from re-opening a credit bargain on which the creditor has obtained judgment. However, a court may be persuaded to re-open the judgment on appeal or, in limited circumstances, to set it aside. In *Shireknight Limited v. Wareing*,[49] *obiter* dicta of Glidewell L.J. indicated that he considered that a mortgagee's order for possession might be set aside pursuant to an application under section 139.

---

[45] This section was amended and s.5A repealed by the High Court and County Courts Jurisdiction Order 1991, art. 2(8) with effect from July 1, 1991. Notwithstanding the reference to "High Court" in s.139(1)(a), the effect of that order is to require applications under that section to be brought in the County Court. Article 2(1)(h) of the Order confirms the County Courts' jurisdiction with regard to applications under s.139(5)(a).

[46] Consumer Credit Act 1974, Sched. 3, para. 43.

[47] *Rahman v. Sterling Credit Limited*, *The Times*, October 17, 2000.

[48] Insolvency Act 1986, s.343(2).

[49] [1999] G.C.C.R. 1677.

PROCEDURE

1. **Prior to October 15, 2001**

In relation to consumer credit claims relating to the recovery of land, regard must **14–13** be had to CPR, Schedule 2, CCR, Ord. 49, r. 4 and (with regard to the contents of the Particulars of Claim) CPR, Schedule 2, CCR, Ord. 6. In claims brought in the High Court, the claim form must contain a certificate to the effect that the claim is not one to which section 141 of the Consumer Credit Act 1974 applies.[50]

Applications under section 139 can be raised by way of defence or counter-claim regardless of the procedure adopted by the claimant. In such circum-stances, the debtor has 14 days after service of the claim form on him to give the requisite notices.[51]

Other claims for relief under the Consumer Credit Act 1974 which do not relate to the recovery of land are governed by CPR 7BPD.

2. **After October 14, 2001**

After this date, CPR Part 55 will apply.[52] Paragraph 2.5(5) of CPR 55PD requires appropriate details to show the property is not one to which section 141 of the Act applies. If the agreement is a registered agreement details of the giving of any notices required by section 76 or 87 of the Act must be provided.[53]

UNFAIR TERMS IN CONSUMER CONTRACTS REGULATIONS 1994 AND 1999

For the treatment of these Regulations see *ante* Chapter 3, Legal Mortgages of **14–14** Land.[54]

THE FINANCIAL SERVICES AND MARKETS ACT 2000

One of the purposes of The Financial Services and Markets Act 2000 ("the 2000 **14–15** Act") is to circumscribe the activities of certain persons. Once the 2000 Act is fully in force no unauthorised person will be able to carry out any regulated activity. Authorised persons will only be able to carry out regulated activities for which they have been granted permission. A "regulated activity" is one which is regulated by the Financial Services Authority (the "FSA") under the 2000 Act. The cornerstone of such regulation is contained in Part II of the 2000 Act, sections 19–30 (Regulated and Prohibited Activities).

The 2000 Act received Royal Assent on June 14, 2000. However, at the date that this work went to press of the provisions contained in Part II, only section

---

[50] CPR, Sched. 1, RSC Ord. 88, r. 3.
[51] CPR, Sched. 2, CCR Ord. 49, r. 4(15).
[52] See *post* paras 27–16 *et seq.*
[53] CPR 55PD, para. 2.5(4).
[54] See para. 3–37 *et seq.*

22 and Schedule 2 (defining "regulated activities") have been brought into force for all purposes. These provisions came into force on February 25, 2001 by virtue of Part I of The Financial Services & Markets Act 2000 (Commencement Order) 2001.[55] Two further provisions have come into force for the purpose of making orders or regulations under Part 2 of S.I. 2001 No. 516, namely section 20(3) (right of action for breach of permission) and section 21 (restrictions on financial promotion). Only two Orders have so far been made subsequent to S.I. 2001 No. 516. These are The Financial Services and Markets Act 2000 (Regulated Activities) Order 2001, (the "Regulated Activities Order")[56] and The Financial Services and Markets Act 2000 (Financial Promotions) Order 2001 (the Financial Promotions Order").[57] The Regulated Activities Order sets out the details of the scope of the FSA's regulatory regime for mortgages as contained in Chapter XV (Regulated Mortgage Contracts). Article 2 of the Regulated Activities Order (Commencement) provides that Chapter XV will come into force nine months *after* section 19 comes into force (see below). No Order has as yet been made bringing the section into force.

Section 19 of the 2000 Act imposes a prohibition to the effect that no person may carry on a regulated activity in the United Kingdom (or purport to do so) unless he is an authorised person, or an exempt person. This is referred to in the section as the "general prohibition".[58] This prohibition and the requirement for authorisation is central to the regulatory regime established by the 2000 Act. The requirement for permission is contained in section 20. The Act defines "authorised persons" in Part III (Authorisation and Exemption). Such persons are regulated by the FSA.[59] "Exempt persons" are defined in section 417(1) as persons who are exempted from the general prohibition in relation to the activity in respect of which they are exempt. There are four classes of such persons.

14–16   Once a person acquires and retains the status of an "authorised person" that person cannot be in breach of the general prohibition. Thus if such a person undertakes regulated activity for which he has not obtained permission from the FSA then he is not in breach of the general prohibition as long as he retains that status. In such circumstances he is taken to have "contravened a requirement imposed" by the FSA[60] and is therefore likely to be disciplined by that body.

However, the status of an "exempt person" is only conferred in relation to certain regulated activities. If such a person engages in activities outside those regulated activities, then they no longer have the status of an "exempt person" and will be in breach of the general prohibition contained in section 19 of the 2000 Act.

The restrictions on financial promotion are contained in section 21 of the 2000 Act. This section regulates such financial promotion made in the course of a business. It undoubtedly is designed to cover not only advertising but all other forms of promoting certain investment activities.

Section 22 of the 2000 Act defines the term "regulated activity". This determines the scope of the general prohibition contained in section 19 and the

---

[55] S.I. 2001 No. 516.
[56] S.I. 2001 No. 544.
[57] S.I. 2001 No. 1335.
[58] *ibid.* s.19(2).
[59] See s.31(2) and 417(1).
[60] See s.20(1).

regulatory framework of the FSA. It provides the Treasury with the necessary powers to define "regulated activities".[61]

The sanctions for breaching the "general prohibition" contained in section 19 are far reaching. Section 23 of the 2001 Act makes such a breach a criminal offence referred to as an "authorisation offence". The offence is one of strict liability but is subject to a "due diligence" offence as contained in subsection 3. This means that it is a defence for the defendant to demonstrate that he took "all reasonable precautions" and "exercised all due diligence" to avoid committing the offence. The onus is on the defendant to demonstrate this and the standard is objective. Further, section 24 of the 2000 Act imposes criminal liability on a person who makes a false claim to be an "authorised person" or an "exempt person". The offence arises if a person describes himself as an authorised person or as an exempt person or behaves or otherwise holds himself out which indicates (or which is reasonably likely to be understood as indicating) that he is such a person. Again, this section imposes strict liability subject to the "due diligence" defence. Section 25 provides the penalties for a person who contravenes section 21(1).

Sections 26 to 28 contain provisions directed to the enforceability of agreements. **14–17** Section 26 renders unenforceable against the other party and voidable at his instance an agreement made by a person conducting a "regulated activity" in breach of the "general prohibition". Section 27 contains provisions relating to agreements made through unauthorised persons in breach of the "general prohibition". Section 28 contains provisions which are supplemental to sections 26 and 27. These relate to the amount of compensation recoverable in the event of any breach of either of those sections and the court's discretion to uphold an agreement despite the fact that it is prima facie unenforceable and voidable. The court must be satisfied that it is "just and equitable" to enforce the agreement or to allow retention of the money or property transferred. In making that assessment the court is obliged to have regard to a factor referred to as "the issue" defined in section 28(5) namely whether the person carrying on the regulated activity concerned reasonably believed that he was not contravening the general prohibition by making the agreement.

In the case where there is an agreement between a person ("the depositor") and another person ("the deposit-taker") made in the course of the carrying on by the deposit-taker of accepting deposits in contravention of the general prohibition, then this is regulated by the provisions contained in section 29 of the 2001 Act. In such a case the depositor is able to apply to the court for an order for the return of his money if he is not otherwise entitled to recover his money immediately on demand. Again, the court has a discretion as to the making of the order.[62]

Finally, section 32 of the 2001 Act renders unenforceable against the customer and voidable at his instance certain agreements made and certain obligations undertaken in consequence of an unlawful communication in relation to which there has been a breach of the financial promotion restriction contained in section 21. The customer is also able to recover both the money (or other property) transferred by him and also is able to recover compensation for any loss suffered

---

[61] See now the Financial Services and Markets Act 2000 (Regulated Activities) Order 2001 (S.I. 2001 No. 544).

[62] This is similar to that contained in s.28(4)(a) of the 2000 Act.

as a result of any transfer. Again, the court has a discretion to allow the agreement or obligation to be enforced or money or property paid or transferred under the agreement or obligation to be retained if it is satisfied that it is just and equitable in the circumstances of the case to do so.

1. The Financial Services and Markets Act 2000 (Regulated Activities) Order and the consultative process

14–18 In November 2000 the FSA extensively consulted on mortgage regulation and the approach to be adopted.[63] The Government announced, following the consultation, that it intended to ensure that mortgage lending came within the scope of the 2000 Act. The details of the scope of the FSA's regulatory regime for mortgages was confirmed in the response by the Treasury in February 2001. This has now been prospectively achieved by Articles 61–63 contained in Chapter XV of the Regulated Activities Order. Some important changes to the scope of the regime following the consultation are reflected in the Regulated Activities Order.[64] Article 2 (Commencement) of the Regulated Activities Order provides that Chapter XV will come into force nine months *after* section 19 comes into force. No Order has as yet been made bringing section 19 into force. It is currently anticipated that FSA's mortgage regime will come into effect no later than August 31, 2002, nine months after the 2000 Act (including Part II) finally comes into force. That date is to be no later than November 30, 2001.

A summary of the key changes in the scope of the regulatory regime incorporated in the Regulated Activities Order are as follows:

(1) there are now two separate regulated activities namely, *entering* into a regulated mortgage contract and *administering* a regulated mortgage contract;

(2) the definition of a regulated mortgage contract has been altered so that there is no longer any maturity limitation;

(3) firms are now able to structure their affairs so that securitisation Special Purpose Vehicles are not required to be authorised by the FSA; and

(4) local authorities and registered social landlords (but not their wholly owned subsidiaries) are exempt from FSA authorisation for mortgage lending and mortgage administration.

14–19 Some relevant changes were also made to the final version of the Financial Promotion Order.[65] Under the final legislation the advertising of all secured lending products by firms authorised by the FSA to enter into mortgage contracts will in future need to meet the FSA's financial promotion rules. Such promotions are called "qualifying credit promotions" in the FSA rules.

The Regulated Activities Order also prospectively removes from regulation under the Consumer Credit Act 1974 both regulated mortgage contracts and qualifying credit promotions.

---

[63] CP70 "Mortgage Regulation: the FSA's High Level Approach".
[64] See S.I. 2001 No. 544, made on February 26, 2001 and approved by Parliament in March 2001.
[65] S.I. 2001 No. 1335.

Further, within the framework of the statutory objectives contained in the 2000 Act and the strategy document published by the FSA in January 2000 entitled "New Regulator for the New Millennium", the FSA has now developed a detailed policy proposal. This is contained in the latest Consultation Paper published in June 2001 entitled the "Draft Mortgage Sourcebook, including Policy Statement on CP70" ("CP98"). The date for response to this Consultation Paper is September 14, 2001.

CP98 sets out for comment both the detailed policy approach that the FSA proposed to take to the regulation of mortgage lending and administration, and also the rules and guidance that it proposes to implement to put that policy into effect. It does so in the context of responses received to CP70 and feedback on that Consultation Paper is also contained in this document.

Following receipt of responses to this consultation, the FSA expects to be in a position to make the rules and guidance relating to mortgage regulation by the end of 2001. The Government has stated that statutory regulation of mortgage lending and mortgage administration will start nine months after N2[66]—in other words, based on an N2 of November 30, 2001, no later than August 31, 2002. This date is referred to as N3 in CP98. However, the FSA is proposing to put in place transitional provisions in two areas to enable firms to comply with the regime of statutory mortgage regulation. The FSA is proposing to defer the implementation of the requirements contained in Chapter 6 relating to post-sale disclosure, and Chapter 12 relating to arrears and repossessions of the Mortgage Sourcebook. The period of proposed deferment is six months after N3, *i.e.* February 28, 2003.

2. Application of the FSA Handbook to mortgage business

CP98 explains that mortgage lenders, mortgage administrators and firms that **14–20** approve or communicate qualifying credit promotions will be subject to the FSA Handbook of rules and guidance. Section 5 of CP98 describes the requirements of the 2000 Act and the Handbook. This includes the need to comply with the threshold conditions (in Schedule 6 to the Act), the Principles for Businesses and the high level rules (covering, for example, systems and controls) in Block 1 of the Handbook.

The rules and guidance relating specifically to mortgage business will be contained in the Mortgage Sourcebook, which will be a separate volume within the Handbook. Annex B to the Consultation Paper contains the text of the Mortgage Sourcebook for consultation.

3. Regulated activity

There will be two separate regulated activities relating to mortgage regulation, as **14–21** set out in the Article 61 of the Regulated Activities Order. They are (1) entering into a regulated mortgage contract as lender; and (2) administering a regulated mortgage contract.

---

[66] N2 is the date on which the 2000 Act becomes fully effective *i.e.*, November 30, 2001.

Article 61(3)(a) defines a "regulated mortgage contract" as a contract under which:

"(i) a person ("the lender') provides credit to an individual or to trustees ("the borrower"); and

(ii) the obligation of the borrower to repay secured by a first legal mortgage on land (other than timeshare accommodation) in the United Kingdom, at least 40% of which is used, or is intended to be used, as or in connection with a dwelling by the borrower or (in the case of credit provided to trustees) by an individual who is a beneficiary of the trust, or by a regulated person."

Thus, the following conditions must all be satisfied:

(1) the borrower must be an individual or trustee;
(2) the contract must be entered into after N3;
(3) the lender must take a first charge over property in the United Kingdom; and
(4) the property must be at least 40 per cent occupied by the borrower or his immediate family.

The Treasury had previously proposed a further condition to be satisfied by a regulated mortgage contract i.e. that the original maturity was at least five years. The removal of this condition brings within the FSA's regulatory scope a significant amount of secured short-term leading. This includes lending for home improvements (including some in-store credit), lending for debt consolidation, lending to finance a business, and some specific banking products such as secured overdrafts, secured credit cards, bridging loans and loans secured by all monies charges. Each of these product types has been considered by the FSA in drawing up draft rules and guidance for consultation.

Article 61(3)(b) defines "administering" a regulated mortgage contract as meaning either or both of:

"(i) notifying the borrower of changes in interest rates or payments due under the contract, or of other matters in which the contract requires him to be notified; and

(ii) taking any necessary steps for the purpose of collecting or recovering payments due under the contract from the borrower;

but a person is not to be treated as administering a regulated mortgage contract merely because he has, or exercises, a right to take action for the purposes of enforcing the contract (or to require that such action is or is not taken) . . . "

Further, "credit" is defined by Article 61(3)(c) as including a cash loan, and any form of financial accommodation.

Finally, Article 62 of the Regulated Activities Order does not require persons who administer regulated mortgage contracts to be authorised if they make arrangements for an authorised person with permission to administer mortgage contracts to administer those contracts on their behalf. This provision was designed by the Treasury to ensure that Special Purpose Vehicles set up as part of securitisations could so organise themselves that they did not need to seek authorisation from the FSA.

Further information on the FSA's interpretation of Articles 61 and 62 of the Regulated Activities Order is provided in chapter 1 of the Mortgage Sourcebook.

4. Exemptions

In general, persons carrying on the regulated activities set out above will need to be authorised by the FSA where those activities are carried on in the United Kingdom and by way of business. However, in addition to the exemptions that apply in respect of all regulated activities (other than insurance business) The Financial Services and Markets Act 2000 (Exemption) Order 2001[67] specifically exempts the following from the requirement to be authorised to carry on mortgage lending or mortgage administration: **14–23**

(1) local authorities (paragraph 47 of the Schedule to the Exemption Order);

(2) registered social landlords in England and Wales within the meaning of Part I of the Housing Act 1996 (paragraph 48(a) of the Schedule to the Exemption Order);

(3) housing associations registered by Scottish Homes (paragraph 48(b) of the Schedule to the Exemption Order);

(4) the Housing Corporation (paragraph 48(c) of the Schedule to the Exemption Order); and

(5) Scottish Homes (paragraph 48(d) of the Schedule to the Exemption Order).

These exemptions apply only to the bodies themselves. Any subsidiary of, for example, a local authority, which undertakes mortgage business within the definition contained within the Regulated Activities Order, will need to be authorised by the FSA.

5. Financial promotion: controlled investments and the controlled activity

The Financial Promotion Order provides that the content of all promotions of specific secured loans will need to meet FSA requirements where those loans are provided by firms authorised in relation to mortgages. Such lending is referred to as "qualifying credit". An important consideration is that this is wider in scope than the requirements relating to regulated mortgage contracts. It extends, for example, to second charge loans, and also to unsecured loan facilities forming part of a regulated mortgage contract. Such a facility arises where a credit card is offered as part of a flexible mortgage.   **14–24**

---

[67] S.I. 2001/1201.

These financial promotions are known as "qualifying credit promotions". The controls on qualifying credit promotions also have relevance to unauthorised firms. Such firms will need to ensure that any such promotion has been approved by an authorised firm before issue.

Further detail on the scope of the financial promotion regime (including exemptions set out in the Finance Promotion Order) is provided in section 7 of CP98 and in chapter 3 of the accompanying draft Mortgage Sourcebook.

6. Boundary with the Consumer Credit Act 1974

14–25   Finally, Articles 90 and 91 of the Regulated Activities Order includes provisions that remove from regulation under the 1974 Act both regulated mortgage contracts and qualifying credit financial promotions. Most loans that will fall within the definition of regulated mortgage contracts are already largely exempt under the 1974 Act. The only significant impact will be removal of the Consumer Credit Act Advertising Regulations and of the extortionate credit provisions (sections 137–140 of the 1974 Act).

However, some loans that will fall within the regulated mortgage definition are also currently classified as regulated agreements under the 1974 Act. In these cases, the impact of the removal of these provisions by the Regulated Activities Order is more significant. In particular, the 1974 Act controls in respect of entering into, operation and termination of agreements will be removed and replaced by comprehensive disclosure requirements in the Mortgage Sourcebook. Any mortgages in place at N3 (August 31, 2001) which are subject to the 1974 Act will remain subject to that regime and will not be brought within the remit of the FSA.

CHAPTER 15

PARTIES TO MORTGAGES

ABSOLUTE OWNERS

1. General

Generally an absolute owner of property who is not subject to any incapacity[1] **15–01** may mortgage the property in exercise of the full powers of alienation with which he is invested.[2] Certain property however, such as the pay or half-pay of public officers such as officers in the Armed Forces[3] and civil servants[4] (if paid from national funds[5]) and of military pensions[6] and those of police officers, school teachers and firemen cannot be mortgaged.

2. Co-owners

Where land is owned by more than one person, such persons may be benefi- **15–02** cially interested in the land either jointly or as tenants in common. In such a case the legal estate in the land will be held by not more than four of the co-owners as joint tenants upon trust for the co-owners as joint tenants or tenants in common.[7]

As trustees of a trust of land the co-owners have, in relation to the land, all the powers of an absolute owner pursuant to statute[8] and thus may mortgage the land under their statutory powers. Where the same persons are both the trustees and the beneficiaries, they may mortgage by virtue of their powers as absolute owners and need not rely upon the statutory powers. A purported mortgage by one co-owner operates as a severance of any joint tenancy in equity and operates to charge or transfer (as the case may be) the sole co-owner's share.[9]

Where a legal mortgage of land is made to several persons, the legal estate vests in the mortgagees or the first four named as joint tenants upon trust. By virtue of section 111 of the Law of Property Act 1925 where the mortgage is

---

[1] See *post*, paras 15–02A *et seq.*
[2] See Coke on Littleton, 223a.
[3] *Stone v. Liddudale* (1795) 2 Anst. 533.
[4] *Lucas v. Lucas* [1943] P. 68.
[5] Payments from local funds do not come within this principle: *Re Muans* [1891] 1 Q.B. 594; *Lynch v. Subjic, The Times*, May 18, 1988.
[6] Army Act 1955, s.203; Air Force Act 1955, s. 203; Naval and Marine Pay and Pensions Act 1865, s.4.
[7] LPA 1925, ss.34, 36; Settled Land Act 1925, s.36; Trustee Act 1925, s.34 (all as amended).
[8] Trustee Act 1925, s.16(1); TLATA 1996, s.6(1).
[9] *Ahmed v. Kendrick* (1988) 56 P. & C.R. 120.

made to several mortgagees jointly or the mortgage money is expressed to belong to them on a joint account, then unless a contrary intention is expressed in the mortgage, the mortgage monies are (as between the mortgagees and the mortgagor) deemed to be and remain monies belonging to the mortgagees on joint account.[10] Thus, persons dealing in good faith with several mortgagees may assume that the mortgagees are entitled to the mortgage monies on a joint account unless a contrary intention is expressed in the instruments relating to the mortgage.[11]

3. **Persons subject to disabilities**

(a) Bankrupts

15–02A   Upon an individual party becoming bankrupt, the entirety of his estate vests, without conveyance, in the Official Receiver upon his becoming trustee.[11a] Thus a bankrupt retains no interest in his general assets at the date of the bankruptcy which he can mortgage.[11b]

(b) Minors

(i) *Borrowing powers.*

15–03

The law applicable to contracts by minors[12] is governed by the Minors' Contracts Act 1987 which applies to any contracts made by minors after June 9, 1987. Section 1 of that Act disapplies the Infants Relief Act 1874, which invalidated certain contracts made by minors and prohibited actions to enforce contracts ratified after majority. It also disapplies the Betting and Loans (Infants) Act 1892, section 5 of which invalidated contracts to repay loans advanced during minority.

Under section 1 of the 1874 Act, all contracts with minors for the repayment of money lent, or for goods supplied or to be supplied (other than contracts for "necessaries" which were binding on the minor), and all accounts stated with minors, were rendered "absolutely void." It did not, however, invalidate any contract into which a minor might enter by statute or the rules of common law or equity except those which under the existing law were voidable. The disapplication of that section will, therefore, result in the contracts in question again becoming subject to the rules of common law.

The disapplication of section 2 of the 1874 Act means that on a minor reaching the age of majority, his ratification of an otherwise unenforceable contract entered into by him as a minor is effective. However, section 2, while not abolishing the common law rules, imposed a bar on proceedings to enforce ratification (whether or not there was "new consideration") of a minor's contract,

[10] Replacing the Conveyancing Act 1881, s.61.
[11] LPA 1925, s.113(1)(*a*).
[11a] See *post* para. 23–07.
[11b] See generally Chapter 23.
[12] The Family Law Reform Act 1969 reduced the age of majority to 18 (s.1). For the alternative "minor", see s.12.

by providing that no action should be brought for that purpose. The removal of this procedural bar serves to reinstate the relevant rules of common law or equity.

Further, the 1987 Act disapplies section 5 of the Betting and Loans (Infants) **15–04** Act 1892, which rendered void any new agreements by a minor, after attaining his majority, to repay a loan made to him while a minor. It also invalidates any negotiable instrument given in connection with such an agreement. In doing so, the 1987 Act makes any such new agreement and any such negotiable agreement effective.

The effect of the 1987 Act is essentially to restore the common law position before 1874 whereby a loan to a minor could not be enforced against a minor, except in the case of necessaries, but the minor could, upon attaining his majority, ratify the contract.

Further, section 3(1) of the 1987 Act extends the power of the court, if it is just and equitable to do so, to require a minor who has acquired property under an unenforceable contract to restore it. This is the case even where there has been no fraud on the part of the minor.[13] The power will also be exercisable where the minor has, on the ground of his minority, repudiated the contract under which he acquired the property. The court's power is limited to ordering the transfer of property acquired under the contract, or property representing it.[14]

A minor cannot hold a legal estate in land, and consequently cannot be a legal **15–05** mortgagor.[15] Thus, although a minor may be a member of a building society and may give all necessary receipts[16] he cannot execute a valid mortgage to secure advances made to him by the society.[17] An equitable mortgage made by a minor is unenforceable, but a minor can ratify it upon attaining his majority.[18] Where the mortgage was made to secure monies lent for the purchase of necessaries the mortgage is voidable and not absolutely void.[19] As the disposition is voidable and not void it is binding if the minor fails to repudiate it within a reasonable time after attaining his majority.[20] Where a minor has executed such a mortgage and subsequently upon attaining full age charges the premises with a further advance

---

[13] Under the old law that power was confined to cases where the minor induced the other party to enter into the contract by fraud.

[14] According to the Law Com. Report No. 134 the words "property representing property" are to be interpreted as referring to the general principle of tracing. Thus, if the minor has sold or exchanged the goods acquired under the contract, he can be compelled to pay over the price, or hand over the goods received in exchange. But if he has consumed or otherwise "dissipated" the goods or their proceeds, he cannot be required to pay to the seller a sum equivalent to the purchase price, or to the value of the goods.

[15] LPA 1925, s.1(6). After December 31, 1996 a purported conveyance to a minor operates as a declaration of trust in the minor's favour (T.L.A.T.A 1996, Sched. 1, para. 1(2)). If the conveyance is to a minor and a person of age, it operates to vest the legal estate in the adult on trust for himself and the minor (ibid., Sched. 1, para. 1(2)). Prior to then, a conveyance to an infant gave rise to an agreement for valuable consideration to execute a settlement (LPA 1925, s. 19(1), SLA 1925, s. 27(1)) which, on January 1, 1997 became a declaration of a trust of land for the minor (TLATA 1996, Sched. 1, para. 1(4)).

[16] Building Societies Act 1986, s.5, Sched. 2, para. 5(3)(*a*); but cannot vote or hold office: *Notting-ham Permanent Benefit Building Society* v. *Thurstan* [1903] A.C. 6.

[17] *ibid.* but the Society in this case was entitled to a loan on the property for the purchase monies.

[18] *Gardner* v. *Wainfur* (1920) 89 L.J.Ch. 98.

[19] *Martin* v. *Gale* (1876) 4 Ch.D. 428 at 431; *Edwards* v. *Carter* [1893] A.C. 360.

[20] *Edwards* v. *Carter* [1893] A.C. 360.

and has confirmed the earlier mortgage, he cannot redeem without paying off the sum advanced during his infancy.[21]

Where a minor is beneficially entitled to any property, the court may direct the trustees to raise money by mortgage of the property or order them to apply the capital or income for the minor's maintenance, education or benefit.[22] Powers of management of a minor's lands may be conferred on the trustees appointed for the purpose or if there are none so appointed, then the trustees of the trust under which the minor is entitled. The specified powers do not include a power to mortgage, but the power generally to deal with the land in a proper and due course of management may comprehend such a power.[23] Personal representatives also have power of mortgaging property during the minority of a beneficiary.[24] Under the Settled Land Act 1925, a binding disposition of a minor's land may be made by the statutory owner which permits sales, exchanges, leases and mortgages on certain terms.[25]

(ii) *Lending powers.*

The repeal of the Infants Relief Act 1874 by the Minors' Contracts Act 1987 means that a contract of loan can be enforced by a minor.

(iii) *Mortgages to minors.*

15–06   Since the Law of Property Act 1925 a minor cannot be an estate owner. Thus he cannot hold a legal estate in land[26] and thus cannot be a legal mortgagee. Any attempt to grant or transfer a legal mortgage or charge to one or more persons who are all minors is not effective to pass the legal estate and in the meantime the mortgagor or transferor holds the beneficial interest in the mortgage debt, if any, on trust for the persons intended to benefit.[27] The minor's beneficial interest in the mortgage debt should be registered as an estate contract or by way of a caution. If the mortgage is made to an minor or minors together with a person or persons of full age it will operate to vest the legal estate in the person of full age as if the minors were not named but subject to the infant's beneficial interest.[28]

Where a minor is beneficially entitled to any property, the court may direct the trustees to raise money by mortgage of the property in order to apply the capital or income for the minor's maintenance, education or benefit.[29] Personal representatives also have powers of mortgaging property during the minority of a beneficiary.[30] Under the Settled Land Act 1925 a binding disposition of a minor's land may be made by the statutory owner which permits sales, exchanges, leases and mortgages on certain terms.[31]

[21] *Gardner* v. *Wainfur* (1919) 89 L.J.Ch. 98.
[22] Trustee Act 1925, s.53.
[23] Settled Land Act 1925, s.102.
[24] Administration of Estates Act 1925, ss.33 and 39 (as amended).
[25] Settled Land Act 1925, s.102.
[26] LPA 1925, s.1(6).
[27] LPA 1925, s.19(4), (6). See also s.19(1) and the Settled Land Act 1925, s.27(1).
[28] LPA 1925, s.19(5), (6) proviso.
[29] Trustee Act 1925, s.53.
[30] Administration of Estates Act 1925, ss.33 and 39.
[31] s.102.

(c) Persons suffering from mental disorder

Any deed executed by a person suffering from such mental disorder as to **15–07** render him incapable of understanding its effect when its nature and contents are explained to him is absolutely void as a matter of law even if no receiver has been appointed under section 99 of the Mental Health Act 1983.[32] Thus, a voluntary conveyance by a person suffering from a mental disorder may be set aside even against a subsequent purchaser for valuable consideration without notice.[33] But a deed executed during a lucid interval for valuable consideration is binding provided that no receiver has been appointed under section 99 and the person suffering from the mental disorder understood its nature and effect.[34] Similarly, a deed executed before the supervention of mental disorder is binding.[35]

Where, however, a receiver has been appointed under section 99 of the 1983 Act, the mentally disordered person probably cannot exercise any power of disposition, *inter vivos*, over his property even during a lucid interval, by reason of the fact that upon the making of such an order his property passes out of his control to the receiver[36] and any disposition made by him is inconsistent with that passing of control, and consequently is void.[37]

The position prior to the Mental Health Act 1959 was similar where there was a finding of insanity by inquisition[38] except that a will made during a lucid interval was valid.[39]

Under the Mental Health Act 1983, Part VII, the Lord Chancellor and nomi- **15–08** nated judges, or the Court of Protection, are invested with very wide powers of ordering or authorising dispositions and other transactions concerning the patient's property.[40] In practice, subject to appeal to a nominated judge, the jurisdiction is exercised by the master, deputy master, or a nominated officer of the Court of Protection. These powers include the power to appoint a receiver[41] who may exercise any of the powers under the 1983 Act under the direction of the court.[42] Such powers can be invoked, therefore, provided that it is for the benefit of the person suffering from the mental disorder or his family or other persons for whom he might have been expected to provide.[43] In a proper case of emergency these powers may be exercised even before the issue of incapacity has been determined.[44] One of these powers is the power to charge the patient's property.[45] The court has also authorised the loan of a patient's money upon

---

[32] See, *e.g. Price* v. *Berrington* (1849) 7 Hare 394 at 402; on appeal (1851) 3 Mac. & G. 486.

[33] *Elliott* v. *Ince* (1857) 7 De G.M. & G. 475; *Manning* v. *Gill* (1872) L.R. 13 Eq. 485.

[34] *Towart* v. *Sellers* (1817) 5 Dow.231; *Selby* v. *Jackson* (1844) 6 Beav. 192; *Jenkins* v. *Morris* (1880) 14 Ch.D. 674; *Drew* v. *Nunn* (1879) 4 Q.B.D. 661.

[35] *Affleck* v. *Affleck* (1857) 3 Sn. & G. 394.

[36] There is some doubt under the Mental Health Act 1983 as to the point at which a person loses all legal capacity. The appointment of a receiver is now more of an administrative function and the intervention by the court is of greater importance with regard to the question of control of the patient's affairs.

[37] *Re Marshall, Marshall* v. *Whateley* [1920] 1 Ch. 284.

[38] *Re Walker* [1905] 1 Ch. 160.

[39] *ibid.* at 172.

[40] ss.94(2) and 96(1)(*b*).

[41] s.99.

[42] *ibid.* s.99.

[43] *ibid.* ss.95 and 96. As to the meaning of "property" see *Re E* [1984] 1 W.L.R. 320; on appeal *Re E* [1985] 1 W.L.R. 245.

[44] *ibid.* s.98.

[45] *ibid.* s.96(1)(*b*).

mortgage.[46] However, there is no power to make a disposition which the patient could not himself have made if he were of sound mind.[47]

4. **Partners**

15–08A   An ordinary partner has an implied authority under the Partnership Act 1890[48] as an agent of the partnership and the other partners to pledge or mortgage partnership property and to give a receipt thereof. This implied authority, however, only arises when the dealing is for the purpose of raising money for the carrying on in the usual way of the partnership business and is in accordance with the partnership objects. It does not arise if the partner so acting has in fact no authority to act for the firm, and the person with whom he is dealing either knows that he has no authority, or does not know or believe him to be a partner. This authority does not arise in the case of a mortgage by deed of partnership property[49] in the absence of special authority.[50]

(a) *Mortgage of personal property*

15–08B   Provided that there is no notice of fraud or want of authority, a partner[51] may mortgage or pledge the personal property of the partnership for the ordinary purposes of the firm.[52] But such a transaction will not be binding upon the firm if made in order to secure the partner's personal debt without the knowledge and consent of the other partners.[53] The mortgagee must prove such knowledge and consent[54] or circumstances in which such knowledge and consent might reasonably be inferred. If it can be shown that the mortgagee is unaware[55] that the security is partnership property, then the transaction will not be set aside.[56] The authority to mortgage partnership property continues after dissolution for the purpose of winding up the affairs of the partnership and to complete any unfinished transactions at that date.[57]

(b) *Mortgage of real property*

15–09   Where partners hold the legal estate of the partnership property, either freehold or leasehold, as beneficial owners they are empowered to mortgage the legal

---

[46] *Re Ridgeways* (1825) Hog. 309.
[47] *Pritchard* v. *Briggs* [1980] Ch. 338 at 409.
[48] See s.5, and see *Re Bourne, Bourne* v. *Bourne* [1906] 2 Ch. 427.
[49] *Harrison* v. *Jackson* (1797) 7 Term. Rep. 207.
[50] *Steightz* v. *Egginton* (1815) Hoh. N.P. 141.
[51] A limited partner does not have power to bind the firm, see the Limited Partnerships Act 1907, s.6(1).
[52] See the Partnership Act 1890, s.5.
[53] *Re Litherland, Ex p. Howden* (1842) 2 Mont.D. & De G. 574.
[54] *Shirreff* v. *Wilks* (1800) 1 East. 48.
[55] *Snaith* v. *Burridge* (1812) 4 Taunt. 684.
[56] *Reid* v. *Hollinshead* (1825) 4 B. & C. 867.
[57] Partnership Act 1890, s.38; *Butchart* v. *Dresser* (1853) 4 De G.M. & G. 542; *Re Bourne, Bourne* v. *Bourne* [1906] 2 Ch. 427.

interest as joint tenants holding the same as statutory trustees of a trust of land.[58] However, one partner is unable to bind the other partners by executing a mortgage deed of partnership property without the concurrent and express authority under seal to do so.[59] Further, where one partner executes a mortgage deed on behalf of the partnership that partner alone may be bound, and not the firm, unless he can demonstrate that his signature was with the special authority of the firm and conditional upon the firm being bound.[60] Where, however, there is an equitable mortgage made by deposit of the title deeds, or the mortgage itself is not required to be effected by deed, the general rule set out above with regard to the implied authority vested in a partner will apply.

(c) *Lending powers of partners*

A partner has authority to lend the firm's money on mortgage when such a transaction is part of the firm's ordinary business.[61]

(d) *Mortgage of share in partnership*

A share in a partnership is a right to share in the profits and, in the event of **15–10** dissolution, to share in the division of the assets. It is, in the nature of things, a somewhat speculative form of security, but a partner may freely mortgage his share to cover his private debts. On the other hand, a partner is by statute precluded from introducing a new partner into the firm without the consent of all the existing partners.[62] The fact that a mortgagee is not normally introduced into the partnership materially increases the hazards of taking a partnership share as security for he has no voice whatever in the management of the business. His rights are set out in section 31 of the Partnership Act 1890, and are broadly as follows:

(1) During the partnership he is not entitled either to interfere in the management of the partnership business or to require accounts of partnership transactions or to inspect books. He is entitled to the profits but must accept the account of profits agreed between the partners.

(2) On dissolution, he is entitled to receive the mortgagor's share of the assets and, for the purpose of ascertaining that share, he is entitled to an account from the other partners as from the date of dissolution.

A mortgagee is thus in a very weak position in regard to maladministration of the partnership business. Section 31 does not, of course, preclude him from impugning transactions between the partners which are designed to over-reach him. It is

---

[58] LPA 1925, ss.34 and 36(1); Settled Land Act 1925, s.36(4). See also the Trustee Act 1925, ss.16, 17; L.P.A. 1925, s.28(1).

[59] *Harrison* v. *Jackson* (1797) 7 Term Rep. 207; *Steiglitz* v. *Egginton* (1815) 1 Holt N.P. 141.

[60] *Elliot* v. *Davis* (1800) 2 Bos. & P. 338; *Cumberlege* v. *Lawson* (1857) 1 C.B.(N.S.) 709.

[61] *Re Land Credit Co. of Ireland, Weikersheim's Case* (1873) 8 Ch.App. 831; but see *Niemann* v. *Niemann* (1889) 43 Ch.D. 198.

[62] Partnership Act 1890, s.24(7).

only a genuine partnership transaction with which he has no right to concern himself.[63]

It remains to observe that, as a mortgage of a partnership share is essentially a mortgage of a chose in action, it is not a bill of sale despite the fact that, on dissolution, the mortgagee is entitled to share in the personal chattels of the partnership.[64] The mortgage does not, therefore, require registration as a bill of sale. Notice of the mortgage should, however, be given to the other partners in order to bind them to pay over the share to the mortgagee and to establish his priority against other assignees as the mortgagee takes subject to the equities subsisting between the partners.[65]

5. **Married women**

15–11   A married woman is not by virtue of marriage subject to any disability and she can acquire, retain and dispose of property as if she were unmarried (a *feme sole*). The courts have a special jurisdiction over property disputes between husband and wife.

(a) *Married Women's Property Act 1882*

First, under the Married Women's Property Act 1882.[66] In any question between husband and wife as to the title to or possession of property, either party may apply in a summary manner to the court, and the judge may make such order with respect to the property in dispute as he thinks fit. Further, in matrimonial proceedings, under the Matrimonial Causes Act 1973, as amended, the court has a wide jurisdiction, *inter alia*, to make property adjustment orders.

(b) *Family Law Act 1996*

Secondly (and more importantly with regard to the law of mortgages) by virtue of the Family Law Act 1996.[67] That Act introduced the concept of "matrimonial home rights"[68] in substitution for the rights of occupation which were granted under the earlier legislation. Section 30 bestows on a non-property owning spouse[69] a statutory right to occupy the matrimonial home and the Act provides that for those rights to be a charge on the property-owning spouse's interest in the

---

[63] *Watts* v. *Driscoll* [1901] 1 Ch. 294.
[64] *Re Bainbridge* (1878) 8 Ch.D. 218.
[65] See *ante*, para. 13–20 and Chapter 13 generally.
[66] s.17, as amended by the Matrimonial Causes (Property and Maintenance) Act 1958, s.7 (extending and clarifying the power of the court to order a sale); Matrimonial Proceedings and Property Act 1970, s.39; the Law Reform (Miscellaneous Provisions) Act 1970, s.2 (extending the power of the court to engaged couples who terminate their engagement); Matrimonial and Family Proceedings Act 1984.
[67] Which came into force on October 1, 1997 and repealed the Matrimonial Homes Act 1983.
[68] FLA 1996, s.30(2).
[69] "Spouse" is not defined but does not include a former spouse unless the Court so orders: FLA 1996, s.33(5).

matrimonial home.[70] The right created lasts as long as the marriage subsists[71] although the court may order that the rights are not brought to an end by the death of the property-owning spouse or the termination of the marriage (otherwise than by death).[72]

Where section 30 bestows matrimonial property rights, the spouse without a proprietary interest has

> "(a) if in occupation, a right not to be evicted or excluded from the dwelling-house or any part of it by the other spouse except with leave of the Court given by an order under section 33;
>
> (b) if not in occupation, a right with the leave of the court so given to enter into and occupy the dwelling-house."[73]

For the purposes of determining whether a spouse has a proprietary interest, the court is to ignore the existence of any equitable interest that that spouse may have (whether in the property or in any proceeds of sale) if that spouse does not have a legal interest in the matrimonial home.[74]

(i) *Payments made by a non-owning spouse*

Section 30(3) of the Family Law Act 1996 states that any payment or tender **15–12** made or other act done by a spouse with matrimonial home rights in or towards satisfaction of any liability of the other spouse in respect of rent, mortgage payments or other outgoings affecting the dwelling-house is, whether or not it is made or done in pursuance of an order under section 40, as good as if made or done by the other spouse.

With regard to mortgages,[75] section 30(5) provides that if a spouse with matrimonial home rights is entitled to occupy a dwelling-house (or part thereof) and makes any payment in or towards satisfaction of a mortgage on that dwelling-house, the person to whom payment is made may treat it is payment by the mortgagor but that the fact that the payment has been made does not alter any claim that the paying spouse may have for an interest in the property.

The fact that the property is owned by trustees does not prevent the application of sub-sections 30(3), 30(4) and 30(5).[76]

(ii) *Registration as a charge*

Sections 31(1) and 31(2) of the Family Law Act 1996 provide that where **15–13** matrimonial home rights exist, they are a charge on the property-owning spouse's interest. Such a charge can only be registered against one property and, if more than one property is so charged, the Chief Land Registrar must cancel the first registered charge.[77] A charge has the same priority as if it were an equitable

---

[70] FLA 1996, s.31(2).
[71] FLA 1996, s.30(8).
[72] FLA 1996, s.33(5).
[73] FLA 1996, s.30(2).
[74] FLA 1996, s.30(9).
[75] FLA 1996, s.30(4) makes provision with regard to certain types of tenancy.
[76] FLA 1996, s.30(6).
[77] FLA 1996, Sched. 4, para. 2.

interest created at the latest of (a) the date on which the right was acquired; (b) the date of marriage or (c) January 1, 1968.[78]

If the charge so created is a charge on an interest of the other spouse under a trust and, apart from either of the spouses, there are no persons (living or unborn) who are or could become beneficiaries under that trust, then the rights shall also be a charge on the estate or interest of the trustees of that other spouse.[79] The charge so created has the same priority as if it were an equitable interest created (under powers overriding the trusts) on the date when it arises.[80]

A spouse who is not in occupation of the matrimonial home and who has not obtained the leave of the court to enter and occupy it can nevertheless still register a Class F charge.[81]

15–14   Where a spouse's matrimonial home rights are a charge on the estate or interest of the other spouse (or of trustees of the other spouse), an order under section 33 (occupation orders) binds the other spouse's successors-in-title save insofar as a contrary intention appears.[82] Merger by surrender of the estate charged into a larger estate will result in the superior estate remaining subject to the charge if, but for the merger, the person taking the estate or interest surrendered would be bound by the charge for so long as the estate or interest surrendered would have endured had it not been surrendered.[83]

If a spouse's matrimonial home rights are a charge on the estate of the other spouse (or of trustees of that spouse) and the estate is subject to a mortgage then, if after the date of the creation of that mortgage ("the first mortgage"), the charge is registered under section 2 of the Land Charges Act 1972, the charge is deemed to be a mortgage subsequent to the first mortgage for the purposes of section 94 of the Law of Property Act 1925 (which regulates the rights of mortgagees to make further advances ranking in priority to subsequent mortgages).[84]

A charge under section 31(2) or 31(5) of the Family Law Act 1996 is not registrable under section 2 of the Land Charges Act 1972 unless it is a charge on the legal estate.[85]

(iii) *Registered land*

15–15   If the dwelling house comprises registered land, any land charge affecting the matrimonial home is to be protected by entry of a notice on the register[86] provided the charge is against the legal estate.[87] A notice can only be registered against one property and, if more than one property is so subject, the Chief Land Registrar must cancel the first registered charge.[88] The spouse's matrimonial home rights are not overriding interests.[89] The existence of matrimonial home rights does not entitle the spouse with those rights to enter a caution against the

---

[78] FLA 1996, s.31(3).
[79] FLA 1996, s.31(4) and (5).
[80] FLA 1996, s.31(6).
[81] *Watts v. Waller* [1973] Q.B. 173.
[82] FLA 1996, s.34(1).
[83] FLA 1966, s.31(9).
[84] FLA 1996, s.31(12).
[85] FLA 1996, s.31(13).
[86] FLA 1996, s.31(10).
[87] FLA 1996, s.31(13).
[88] FLA 1996, Sched. 4, para. 2.
[89] FLA 1996, s.31(10).

property.[90] Cautions duly lodged before February 14, 1983 remain unaffected.[91] They entitle the cautioner to notice of any dealings with the land; they do not, however, entitle the cautioner to assert priority over any subsequently registered charge.[92]

(iv) *Release or postponement of matrimonial home rights*

A spouse entitled to matrimonial home rights may, in writing, release those rights **15–16** in relation to the whole or part of the property.[93] Similarly, such a spouse may postpone those rights in writing.[94] A spouse's matrimonial home rights are deemed to have been released where contract is made for the sale of an estate or interest in a dwelling house or for the grant of lease and, on completion, there is delivered to the purchaser's solicitor an application by the spouse with those rights for the cancellation of the registration of the charge or (if sooner) the lodging of such an application at the Land Registry.[95]

(v) *Dwelling houses subject to mortgages*

A spouse, cohabitant or former spouse or cohabitant does not, by virtue of any **15–17** matrimonial home rights or any rights bestowed by section 35 (former spouse with no rights to occupy) or section 36 (cohabitant or former cohabitant with no existing right to occupy) acquire any greater right to occupy the property as against a mortgagee than the property-owning spouse[96] unless those rights are a charge affecting the mortgagee on the estate or interest mortgaged.[97] Those individuals have certain rights to seek to be made parties to any possession proceedings.[98]

FIDUCIARY OWNERS

1. **Mortgages by personal representatives**

Personal representatives have always been able to raise money by mortgaging **15–18** the deceased's personal estate, which includes leasehold, for the payment of debts and funeral and testamentary expenses.

By virtue of sections 2 and 39 of the Administration of Estates Act 1925 (as amended), personal representatives now have the power to mortgage both the real and personal estate of the deceased. With regard to the deceased's real estate, by section 2 of the Act a personal representative has the same powers of

---

[90] FLA 1996, s.31(11).
[91] FLA Sched. 9, para. 14.
[92] *Clark v. Chief Land Registrar* [1994] Ch. 370, CA.
[93] FLA 1996, Sched. 4 para. 5(1).
[94] FLA 1996, Sched. 4, para. 6.
[95] FLA 1996, Sched. 4, para. 5(2).
[96] FLA 1996, s.54(2).
[97] FLA 1996, s.54(4).
[98] See *post*, para. 27–19.

disposition as a personal representative had before 1926 in respect of lease-holds.[99] With regard to both the real and personal estate of the deceased, by section 39 of the Act, personal representatives have, for the purposes of admini-stration or during the minority of any beneficiary or the subsistence of any life interest or until the period of distribution arrives, the same powers and discre-tions, which includes the power to raise money by way of mortgage or charge, whether or not by the deposit of documents, as a personal representative had before 1926 with regard to personal estate.[1] A personal representative also has all the powers conferred by law on trustees of land.[2] In the case of land the power may be exercised by the personal representatives by way of legal mortgage. Such a mortgage is not invalidated simply because the mortgagee had notice that all the debts, liabilities, funeral, testamentary and administration duties and legacies of the deceased had been provided for.[3]

In the case of a mortgage of real estate[4] all the personal representatives must concur or an order of the court must be obtained.[5] An exception arises, however, where probate is granted to one or some of two or more persons named as executors, whether or not power is reserved to the other or others to prove, when a mortgage may be made by the proving executor or executors for the time being.[6]

2. Powers of trustees of land[6a]

15–19   The Trusts of Land and Appointment of Trustees Act 1996, which came into force on January 1, 1997, applies to all trusts comprising or including land[7] with the exception of land which was settled land prior to 1997 and land which is subject to the Universities and College Estates Act 1925.[8] With effect from the date of commencement, settlements, trusts for sale and bare trusts have been abolished and replaced with trusts of land.

The trustees of a trust of land are vested with both the legal estate of the land and with the powers of management of that land. Section 6 of the Trusts of Land and Appointment of Trustees Act 1996 provides trustees of land when exercising their functions as trustees with the powers of an absolute owner of land. It further bestows upon them the power to convey land to the beneficiaries when they are absolutely entitled to it and the power to purchase land. All these powers must be exercised however, with regard to the rights of the beneficiaries under the trust

---

[99] Administration of Estates Act 1925, s.2(1). In relation to deaths after 1925, s.2 replaces with amendments the Land Transfer Act 1897, s.2(2), and the Conveyancing Act 1911, s.12.
[1] Administration of Estates Act 1925, s.39(1)(i), as amended by TLATA 1996, Sched. 1.
[2] *ibid.* s.39(1)(ii), (iii), as amended by TLATA 1996, Sched. 1.
[3] *ibid.*, s.36(8).
[4] "Real Estate" includes chattels real, and leasehold: see the Administration of Estates Act 1925, ss.3(1) and 55(1)(xix).
[5] *ibid.* ss.2(2) and 55(1)(ii).
[6] *ibid.* s.2(2). But see *Fountain Forestry Ltd.* v. *Edwards* [1975] Ch. 1.
[6a] See also *Lewin on Trusts* (17th ed., 2000), paras 37–13 *et seq.*
[7] TLATA 1996, s.1(2).
[8] TLATA 1996, s.1(3).

of land[9] and cannot be exercised in contravention of, or of any order made in pursuance of any enactment or any rule of law or equity.

Thus the trustees are not authorised to act in breach of trust. So, where the beneficiaries are all of age and the land is held by their nominees or the property is held on a constructive or resulting trust, any disposition of the trust property other than to the beneficiaries or with their concurrence will amount to a breach of trust since such trusts do not necessarily have all the incidents normally associated with the relationship between trustee and beneficiary.[10] A purchaser for money or money's worth[11] however need not be concerned with the nature of the trust upon which the land is held; if a disposition of land requires the consent of more than two persons to the exercise of any function by the trustees, the consent of any two of them is sufficient in favour of the purchaser.[12]

Similarly, where the trustees are authorised by any other statutory provision to act but subject to any restriction, limitation or condition imposed thereby, the trustees cannot exercise their powers under section 6 in order to circumvent that other statutory provision. For example, regard would have to be had to trustees' powers of investment or delegation. **15–20**

In addition, trustees powers are further circumscribed by the following factors. The power bestowed by section 6 is in relation to their "functions as trustees" (*i.e.* the exercise by them of their powers and obligations). However, those powers and obligations must be exercised in a fiduciary capacity in the best interests of the trust.[13] Furthermore, section 6 only provides the trustees with power in exercising their functions "in relation to the land" and thus in trusts comprising a mixed fund of personalty and land, it can only apply to the trustees' exercise of their functions with regard to the latter.

Trustees of land must act unanimously,[14] unless the trust instrument appointing them expressly so provides[15] or the court so orders.[16]

3. Charitable trustees[17]

Charitable trustees have all the powers of trustees of land. However, no mortgage of land held by or on trust for a charity (save for those held by an exempt charity) can be granted without an order of the court or of the Charity Commissioners unless the trustees have obtained and considered proper written advice concerning the matters set forth in section 38(3) of the Charities Act 1993 prior to granting the mortgage.[18] **15–21**

---

[9] Trustees should, so far as practicable, consult the beneficiaries who are *sui iuris* and, so far as consistent with the general interest of the trust, give effect to the wishes of the beneficiaries or the majority of the beneficiaries: T.L.A.T.A. 1996, s.11, subject to certain exceptions set forth in s.11(3).

[10] See *Berkely v. Poulett* [1977] 1 E.G.L.R. 86 and 93 and *Target Holdings Limited v. Redferns* [1996] A.C. 421 at 434 ff.

[11] TLATA 1996, s.23(1); LPA 1925, s.205(1)(xxi).

[12] TLATA 1996, s.10(1).

[13] *Cowan v. Scargill* [1985] Ch. 270 at 286; *Harries v. The Church Commissioners for England* [1992] 1 W.L.R. 1241 at 1246; *Edge v. Pensions Ombudsman* [1998] Ch. 513.

[14] *Luke v. South Kensington Hotel Company* (1879) 11 Ch. D. 121 at 125.

[15] *Re Butlin's Settlement Trusts* (1974) 118 S.J. 757.

[16] TLATA 1996, s.14.

[17] See also *Tudor on Charities* (8th ed., 1995), chaps 5 and 6.

[18] Charities Act 1993, s.38(1).

Those matters are:

> "(3) (a) whether the proposed loan is necessary in order for the charity trustees to be able to pursue the particular course of action in connection with which the loan is sought by them;
>
> (b) whether the terms of the proposed loan are reasonable having regard to the status of the charity as a prospective borrower; and
>
> (c) the ability of the charity to repay on those terms the sum proposed to be borrowed."

The written advice that the trustees must consider must be provided by a person who is reasonably believed by the trustees to be qualified to give that advice by reason of his ability in and practical experience of financial matters and who has no financial interest in the making of the loan. He may be an officer or employee of the charity or its trustees.[19]

15–22   The mortgage must contain a statement to the effect that the land is held by or on trust for a charity, whether the charity is an exempt charity and whether the mortgage is one for which general or special authority is given under section 36(9)(a) of the Act (authority by statute or scheme legally established; disposition to another charity in accordance with the trusts of that charity at less than the best price reasonably obtainable; grant of a lease otherwise than for the best rent reasonably obtainable to a beneficiary for purposes of the charity) and indicate whether the statutory restrictions apply. If they do apply, the mortgage must contain a statement that they have been complied with.[20] If the mortgage so states it is conclusively presumed in favour of a purchaser for money or money's worth (or his successors-in-title) that the facts so stated were true.[21] If the statement is omitted the mortgage is only valid in favour of the purchaser acting in good faith.[22]

Where the property of the charity to be mortgaged comprises assets other than land, the trustees' power to mortgage is governed by the instrument regulating the charity.

Save where the charitable trustees wish to transfer their assets to another charity or amend the charity's objects,[23] charitable trustees can act by a simple majority[24] and may exceed four in number in instances where the trust is of land.

4. Private trustees

15–23   In the case of trust property other than land held for non-charitable purposes, a private trustee may not mortgage trust property unless he is expressly or

---

[19] Charities Act 1993, s.38(4).

[20] *ibid.*, s.39.

[21] *ibid.*, s.39(3).

[22] *ibid.*, s.39(4).

[23] In which case the concurrence of the Charity Commissioners is required together with a two-thirds vote in favour by the charity trustees: *ibid.*, s.74.

[24] *Re Whitley* [1910] 1 Ch. 600.

impliedly authorised to do so by the instrument creating the trust,[25] or pursuant to a power conferred by statute or pursuant to a court order.[26]

Where trustees are authorised by the trust instrument, if any, creating the trust, or by law, to pay or apply capital monies subject to the trust for any purpose or in any manner, they have, and are deemed always to have had, power to raise, *inter alia*, money by way of mortgage of all or any part of the trust property for the time being in possession.[27] This power is available notwithstanding anything to the contrary in the instrument, if any, creating the trust, but it does not apply to trustees of property held for charitable purposes, or to trustees of settled land not being also statutory owners.[28] Further, trustees of land have, in relation to land, all the powers of a statutory owner.[29]

With regard to settled land, however, any powers to mortgage which are conferred upon the trustees are exercisable not by them, unless they are the statutory owners for the time being, but by the tenants for life or statutory owner by way of additional powers if conferred by the Settled Land Act 1925. By virtue of section 17 of the Trustee Act 1925, a mortgagee advancing money on a mortgage purporting to be made under any trust or power vested in trustees is not concerned to see that the money is wanted, or that no more than is wanted is raised, or otherwise as to its application. However, as the mortgage money is capital money the mortgagee must not pay it to fewer than two trustees unless the trustee is a trust corporation.[30]

(a) *Power to lend money on mortgage*

Trustees are only able to lend money on mortgage if authorised by the trust **15–24** instrument in the case of personal property, or pursuant to the statutory power to do so under the Trustee Investments Act 1961 in the case of real property (either freehold or leasehold), unless expressly prevented from doing so by the instrument creating the trust.[31] A tenant for life has no power to mortgage or charge the legal estate for his own benefit or use. If he wishes to do so he can mortgage his own beneficial interest.

---

[25] *Re Bellinger* [1898] 2 Ch. 534; *Re Suenson-Taylor's Settlement Trusts* [1974] 1 W.L.R. 1280.

[26] See the Trustee Act 1925, s.57. In the case of settled land, see the Settled Land Act 1925, s.64.

[27] Trustee Act 1925, s.16(1). "Possession" includes receipt of rents and profits or the right to receive the same, if any; *ibid*. s.68(10).

[28] *ibid*. s.16(2).

[29] L.P.A. 1925, s.28(1), and see *ante*, para. 15–19.

[30] LPA 1925, s.27(2); Law of Property (Amendment) Act 1926, s.7 and Sched. In order to avoid the difficulty of the beneficiaries having to join in giving a receipt for the mortgage monies, or to investigate whether or not the trustees were the duly appointed trustees of the trust in question (see *Re Blaiberg & Abrahams* [1899] 2 Ch. 340) it became the common practice to insert a "joint account clause" where two or more persons lent money. After 1881 such a clause is now unnecessary.

[31] Trustee Investments Act 1961, s.1(1), (3), Sched. 1, Pt. II, para. 13, Pt. IV, para. 5 which act is prospectively repealed from a date to be appointed by the Trustee Act 2000, s.40(1), (3), Sched. 2, Pt 1, para. 1(1) and Sched. 4, Pt 1. See *Lewin on Trusts* (17th ed., 2000), para. 35–157ff. See also generally *Lewin on Trusts* (17th ed., 2000), chap. 35. Under the Trustee Act 2000, s.3 a trustee will have a general power of investment which will permit the advance of monies secured on land.

LIMITED OWNERS

1. Tenants for life and statutory owners

(a) *Generally*

15–25　　　After January 1 1997, it is not possible to create a settlement for the purpose of the Settled Land Act 1925, nor is one deemed to be made.[32] Even so an important class of persons having power to raise money by way of a legal mortgage over the settled property is the tenant for life or statutory owner under settlements created before that date and thus governed by the Settled Land Act 1925 as trustees or parties interested under the settlement.[33] The requisite vesting instrument must have been made vesting the legal estate in the settled land in the tenant for life or statutory owner,[34] and the loan must be required for certain specified purposes. Where there is no tenant for life or person otherwise having, either under the Act or by the settlement, the powers of a tenant for life, then the trustees of the settlement may exercise those powers for the purposes of the Act as statutory powers.[35] A settlement includes any instrument or instruments whereby a fee simple or term of years absolute is limited in trust for an infant, or for any person contingently or where the land stands charged with family charges.[36] The tenant for life also has the power to create a settlement for the express purpose of overreaching equitable interests and powers.[37] There are two classes of purpose for which a mortgage may be made, namely, purposes paramount to the settlement, and purposes for giving effect to equitable interests under the settlement. It should be noted, however, that in the absence of a contrary provision in the settlement itself[38] a tenant for life has no power to mortgage or charge the legal estate for his own benefit or use. If he wishes to do so he can mortgage his own beneficial interest.

(b) *Mortgages paramount to equitable interests under the settlement*

15–26　　　The tenant for life or statutory owner has power by a legal mortgage[39] to raise money for certain specified purposes, namely where money is required[40] for any of the following purposes:

(1) discharging an incumbrance[41] on the settled land or parts thereof[42];

---

[32] TLATA 1996, s.2(1).

[33] See the Settled Land Act 1925, s.107.

[34] *ibid.* s.13.

[35] See the Settled Land Act 1925, ss.23, 26 and 117(1)(xxvi).

[36] *ibid.* s.1(1)(ii)(*d*), (iii).

[37] *ibid.* s.72 and the L.P.A. 1925, s.2. An estate owner also has the powers of a tenant for life; in particular the power to make overreaching conveyances under the Settled Land Act 1925, s.21.

[38] See *Re Egerton's Settled Estates* [1926] Ch. 574.

[39] Or charge by way of legal mortgage, see the Settled Land Act 1925, s.117(1)(xi).

[40] "Required" means reasonably required having regard to the circumstances, see *Re Clifford* [1902] 1 Ch. 87; *Re Bruce* [1905] 2 Ch. 372 at 376.

[41] *i.e.* of a permanent nature and not any annual sum payable only during a life or lives or during a term of years absolute or determinable, see the Settled Land Act 1925, s.71(2).

[42] This includes, *e.g.* local charges for making up streets, see *Re Smith's Settled Estate* [1901] 1 Ch. 689; *Re Pizzi* [1907] 1 Ch. 67.

(2) paying for any improvement authorised by the Act or by the settlement[43];

(3) equality of exchange;

(4) redeeming a compensation rent charge[44] in respect of the extinguishment of manorial incidents and affecting the settled land[45];

(5) satisfying any claim under the Landlord and Tenant Act 1927 for compensation for an improvement[46];

(6) paying a coast protection charge or expenses incurred in carrying out work under a works scheme under the Coast Protection Act 1949[47];

(7) paying certain expenses and making certain payments under the Landlord and Tenant Act 1954[48];

(8) paying certain sums recoverable under the Town and Country Planning Act 1990[49];

(9) paying expenses incurred by a tenant for life or statutory owner in connection with proceedings for enfranchising leaseholds or obtaining extensions of leases under the Leasehold Reform Act 1967, and paying compensation in connection with exercise of certain overriding rights of a landlord under that Act[50];

(10) paying the costs of any transaction authorised under the foregoing heads or by sections 69 or 70 of the Settled Land Act 1925.[51]

Thus, the tenant for life may raise the money so required on the security of the settled land or any part thereof, and the money so raised shall be capital money for that purpose, and may be paid or applied accordingly. For this purpose it must be paid to the trustees of the settlement.[52] As has already been noted the mortgage must be a legal mortgage, which includes a charge by way of legal mortgage, and the tenant for life or statutory owner cannot make an equitable mortgage.[53]

(c) *Overreaching effects of paramount mortgage of settled land*

A legal mortgage made by the tenant for life or statutory owner under the statutory powers is effectual to give the mortgagee a title to discharge free from **15–27**

---

[43] See the Settled Land Act 1925, s.83 and Sched. 3.

[44] Such power is conferred by the L.P.A. 1922, s.139(3); the Manorial Incidents (Extinguishment) Rules 1925 (S.R. & O. 1925 No. 810), r. 15; and also see the Manorial Incidents (Extinguishment) (Amendment) Rules 1935 (S.R. & O. 1935 No. 1241), r. 2.

[45] Settled Land Act 1925, s.71(1)(i)–(iii), (vi), (ix). Other purposes were also specified by s.71(1) namely, the raising of money by mortgage for extinguishing manorial incidents, for compensating the stewards on the extinguishment of manorial incidents and discharging expenses incurred in connection with the extinguishment for commuting any additional rents made payable on the conversion of a perpetually renewable leasehold interest into a long term and for satisfying any claims for compensation by an agent of the lessor in respect of loss of fees on conversion (see s.71(1)(iv) (v), (vii), (viii)). They are either repealed or spent by Statute Law (Repeals) Act 1969, s.1, Sched., Pt. III.

[46] Landlord and Tenant Act 1927, s.13(2) (as amended by TLATA 1996, Sched. 4).

[47] Coast Protection Act 1949, s.11(2)(a).

[48] Landlord and Tenant Act 1954, Sched. 2, para. 6.

[49] Town and Country Planning Act 1990, s.328.

[50] Leasehold Reform Act 1967, s.6(5), Sched. 2, para. 9(1).

[51] Settled Land Act 1925, s.71(1)(ix).

[52] *ibid.* s.75.

[53] *ibid.* s.72(1).

all the limitations, powers, and provisions of the settlement and from all estates, interests and charges subsisting or to arise thereunder, but subject to and with the exception of:

(1) all legal estates and charges by way of legal mortgage having priority to the settlement;

(2) all legal estates and charges by way of legal mortgage which has been conveyed or created for securing money actually raised at the date of the deed; and

(3) all leases and grants at fee-farm rents or otherwise, and all grants of easements, rights of common, or other rights or privileges which: (a) were before the date of the mortgage granted or made for value in money or money's worth, or agreed so to be, by the tenant for life or statutory owner, or by any of his predecessors in title, or any trustees for them, under the settlement, or under any statutory power, or are at that date otherwise binding on the successors in title of the tenant for life or statutory owner; and (b) are at that date protected by registration under the Land Charges Act 1925 if capable of registration thereunder.[54]

Notwithstanding registration under the Land Charges Act 1925 of an annuity within the meaning of Part II of that Act or of a limited owner's charge or a general equitable charge within the meaning of that Act, a mortgage under the Settled Land Act 1925 operates to overreach such annuity or charge.[55]

(d) Shifting incumbrances

15–28   By virtue of section 69 of the Settled Land Act 1925, where there is an incumbrance[56] affecting any part of the settled land (whether capable of being overreached on the exercise by the tenant for life of his powers under the Act or not) then *Re Knight's Settled Estates*[57] illustrates that the tenant for life, with the consent of the incumbrancer, may charge that incumbrance on any other powers of the settled land, or on all or any part of the capital money or securities representing capital money subject or to become subject to the settlement, whether already charged therewith or not, in exoneration of the first mentioned part and the tenant for life may by a legal mortgage or otherwise make provision accordingly.

(e) Variation and consolidation of securities

15–29   By section 70 where an incumbrance affects any part of the settled land, the tenant for life may, with the consent of the incumbrancer, vary the rate of interest

---

[54] *ibid.* s.72(2).

[55] *ibid.* s.72(3).

[56] Incumbrance in this section includes any annual sum payable during a life or lives or during a term of years absolute or determinable, but in any such case an additional security must be effected so as only to create a charge or security similar to the original charge or security, see s.70(2).

[57] [1918] 1 Ch. 211.

charged and any other provisions of the instrument, if any, creating the incumbrance and, with the like consent, charge that incumbrance on any part of the settled land, whether already charged therewith or not, or on all or any part of the capital money or securities representing capital money subject or to become subject to the settlement, by way of additional security, or of consolidation of securities. The tenant for life may by a legal mortgage or otherwise make provision accordingly.

(f) Costs

The court may direct that a tenant for life may also raise by a legal mortgage of the settled land or any part thereof, any costs, charges or expenses to be paid out of the property subject to the settlement.[58] The costs of the summons for leave to raise by mortgage such costs, may be added and raised.[59]

(g) Additional powers under the settlement

The settlement may confer powers to mortgage additional to or larger than those conferred by the Settled Land Act 1925,[60] but any power of mortgaging conferred on the trustees of the settlement or other persons for any purpose, whether or not provided for by the Act, is exercisable by the tenant for life or statutory owner, as if it were an additional power conferred on the tenant for life,[61] and operates as if it were conferred by the Act on the tenant for life.[62]   **15–30**

(h) Additional powers authorised by order of the court

By virtue of section 64 of the Settled Land Act 1925 the court has a statutory jurisdiction to authorise the tenant for life to effect any transaction affecting or concerning the settled land, or any part thereof, or any other land not otherwise authorised by the Act or the settlement[63] if in the opinion of the court it would be for the benefit of the settled land, or any part thereof for the persons interested under the settlement.[64] But it must be a transaction which could have been validly made by an absolute owner.[65] The transactions which may be authorised include any sale, exchange, assurance, grant, lease, surrender, re-conveyance, release,   **15–31**

---

[58] See the Settled Land Act 1925, ss.92 and 114.
[59] *Re Pizzi* [1907] 1 Ch. 67 at 71.
[60] s.109(1).
[61] Settled Land Act 1925, s.108(2).
[62] *ibid.* s.109(2).
[63] See *Re Symons* [1927] 1 Ch. 344 at 354.
[64] See *Re Cleveland Literary and Philosophical Society's Land* [1931] 2 Ch. 247.
[65] Settled Land Act 1925, s.64(1) as amended by the Settled Land and Trustee Acts (Court's General Powers) Act 1943, s.2. Certain words were repealed by the Statute Law (Repeals) Act 1969, s.1, Sched., Pt. III. By virtue of s.1 of the 1943 Act the jurisdiction of the court was extended to enable it, in particular circumstances, to make an order authorising expenses of management to be treated as a capital outgoing notwithstanding that in other circumstances the expense could not have been so treated. This provision was amended and made permanent by the Emergency Laws (Miscellaneous Provisions) Act 1953, s.9.

reservation, or other disposition; any purchase or other acquisition; any covenant, contract or option; any application of capital money and any compromise or other dealing or arrangement.[66] Thus, the court has authorised a tenant for life to raise a mortgage on the settled land to pay off his debts which had arisen from the expenses of maintaining the land.[67] Further, this jurisdiction empowers the court to sanction a proposed scheme on behalf of those who are unable to consent (for example an infant) which alters the beneficial interest under the settlement,[68] having as its object or effect to reduce liability for tax, including estate duties, which could not normally be effected under the general law prior to the enactment of the Variation of Trust Acts 1958.[69]

(i) *Tenant for life as trustee—limits on powers*

15–32   The tenant for life not only has the estate[70] vested in him on trust for himself and the other beneficiaries under the settlement but also he is in the position of a trustee in relation to the exercise of his statutory powers.[71] Thus, the tenant for life will be restrained by injunction from creating a mortgage which is prejudicial or unjust to the interests of the beneficiaries[72] and the court will treat the creation of any such mortgage as a breach of trust. Thus, a tenant for life is not entitled to attempt to preserve a heavily incumbered estate by mortgaging it if, by doing so, he prejudices the interests of existing equitable incumbrances.[73] However, provided that the tenant for life acts in good faith and has proper regard to his statutory duty under the Act in relation to the interests of all parties entitled under the settlement, the court will not normally interfere with the discretion of a tenant for life as to the exercise of those powers.[74]

If, however, a trustee fails to see that he is acting unjustly despite being honest and acting within the letter of his trust, it is the duty of the court to interfere.[75]

(j) *Payment of capital money to trustees and protection of mortgages*

15–33   Since money raised by virtue of the statutory powers is capital money it must be paid either to the trustees of the settlement, for the purposes of the Settled Land Act 1925 of whom there must be not fewer than two persons as trustees of the settlement unless the trustee is a trust corporation[76] or into court, at the option

---

[66] See the Settled Land Act 1925, ss.64(2), as amended, and s.109(1).

[67] *Re White-Popham Settled Estates* [1936] Ch. 725.

[68] See *Re Simmons* [1956] Ch. 125.

[69] See, *e.g. Chapman* v. *Chapman* [1954] A.C. 429.

[70] Settled Land Act 1925, s.16(1); and see *Re Boston's Wills Trust* [1956] Ch. 395 at 405.

[71] See the Settled Land Act 1925, s.107.

[72] *Hampden* v. *Earl of Buckinghamshire* [1893] 2 Ch. 531 at 543, 544.

[73] *ibid.*

[74] *ibid.*; and see *Re Richardson* [1900] 2 Ch. 778 at 790.

[75] *Hampden* v. *Earl of Buckinghamshire* [1893] 2 Ch. 531 at 544; *Re Gladwin's Trust* [1919] 1 Ch. 232; and see *Re Charteris, Charteris* v. *Biddulph* [1917] 2 Ch. 379 at 394. The title of the estate mortgaged by the tenant for life is not affected by this provision, but it causes the tenant for life to be personally bound as a trustee, see *Re Marquis of Ailesbury's Settled Estates* [1892] 1 Ch. 506 at 535, 536.

[76] Settled Land Act 1925, s.94.

of the tenant for life.[77] The tenant for life must also give notice to each of the trustees of the settlement of his intention to mortgage or charge the land, and, if known, to the solicitor for the trustees.[78] This, however, must be a notice of each specific transaction contemplated by the tenant for life[79] and a general notice does not suffice.[80] A mortgagee dealing in good faith with the tenant for life is not concerned to make any enquiry with regard to the giving of the notice.[81] Further, a mortgagee paying his advance to the trustees is not concerned to see that the money advanced is required for any purpose under the Act or that no more than is wanted is raised.[82]

(k) *Mortgages to give effect to equitable interests*

Further, by virtue of section 16 of the Settled Land Act 1925, the estate owner is a statutory trustee of the settled land for giving effect to the equitable interests. Thus, where: **15–34**

"(*a*) any principal sum is required to be raised on the security of the settled land, by virtue of any trust, or by reason of the exercise of an equitable power affecting the settled land, or by any person or persons who under the settlement is or are entitled or together entitled to or has to have a general power of appointment over the settled land, whether subject to any equitable charges or powers of charging subsisting under the settlement or not; or

(*b*) the settled land is subject to any equitable charge for securing money actually raised and affecting the whole estate the subject of the settlement;

the estate owner shall be bound, if so requested in writing, to create such legal estate or charge by way of legal mortgage as may be required for raising the money or giving effect to the equitable charge."[83]

It is therefore possible to raise money under this provision for portions.

But this is subject to the proviso that so long as the settlement remains subsisting, any legal estate or charge by way of legal mortgage so created shall take effect and must be expressed to take effect subject to any equitable charges or powers of charging subsisting under the settlement which have priority to the interests or powers of the person or persons by or on behalf of whom the money is required to be raised, or legal effect is required to be given to the equitable charge, unless the persons entitled to the prior charges or entitled to exercise the powers consent in writing to the same being postponed. But it is not necessary that such consent be expressed in the instrument creating such estate or charge by way of legal mortgage.[84] Further, effect may be given by means of a legal

---

[77] *ibid.* ss.75(1), 94.
[78] *ibid.* s.101(1).
[79] See *Re Ray's Settled Estates* (1884) 25 Ch.D. 464.
[80] *i.e.* under the Settled Land Act 1925, s.101(2).
[81] Settled Land Act 1925, s.101(5).
[82] Settled Land Act 1925, ss.95 and 110(1) and the Trustee Act 1925, s.17.
[83] Settled Land Act 1925, s.16(1)(iii); See also the Land Registration Act 1925, s.90; and the Land Registration Rules 1925, r. 144.
[84] Settled Land Act 1925, s.16(1)(iii) proviso; Land Registration Rules 1925, r. 156.

mortgage[85] to an agreement for a mortgage, or a charge or lien, whether or not arising by operation of law, if the agreement, charge or lien ought to have priority over the settlement.[86]

The Act also provides for the means of settling doubts as to whether any and what legal estate ought to be created under the foregoing provisions[87] by application to the court for directions and for vesting orders in case of refusal or neglect by the tenant for life, or any other difficulty.[88]

(l) *Overreaching effect of mortgage and protection of mortgagee*

15–35   Provided that the mortgage or legal charge is expressed to be made pursuant to section 16 of the Settled Land Act 1925, it takes effect in priority to all the trusts of the settlement and equitable interests and powers subsisting or to arise under the settlement except those to which it is expressly made subject, and shall so take effect whether the mortgagee or chargee has notice of any such trusts, interests or powers, and further the mortgagee or chargee shall not be concerned to see that a case has arisen to authorise the mortgage or charge or that no money than was wanted was raised.[89] But, if the deed is to take effect under the Act and to overreach the beneficial interests there is one important condition which must be observed. The mortgagee or chargee must require that any capital money payable in respect of the transaction must be paid either:

> (1) to or by the direction of all the trustees of the settlement who must be either two or more in number or a trust corporation[90]; or
>
> (2) into court.[91]

This rule applies notwithstanding anything to the contrary in the settlement.

(m) *Mortgage of land subject to family charges*

15–36   The meaning of settled land was extended by the Settled Land Act 1925[92] to include, not only the normal case of land limited in trust for any person in possession, but to various other cases where land is not vested in some person absolutely and beneficially.

Thus, land is settled land where it is subject to family charges, such as an annuity or jointure rent charge and charges for portions. In the circumstances the estate owner subject to such family charges only has the powers of a tenant for life[93] and can only create a legal mortgage free from such charges if the Settled Land Act procedure as to the appointment of trustees and the execution of a

---

[85] Which includes a legal charge, see the Settled Land Act 1925, s.117(1)(xi).
[86] Settled Land Act 1925, s.16(4).
[87] *i.e.* Under the Settled Land Act 1925, s.16.
[88] *ibid.* s.16(6), (7).
[89] *ibid.* s.16(2).
[90] *ibid.* s.18(1)(*b*), (*c*); L.P.A. 1925, s.2(1)(i).
[91] Settled Land Act 1925, s.18(1)(*b*).
[92] *ibid.* s.1(1).
[93] *ibid.* s.1(1)(v).

vesting deed are observed.[94] In a limited class of case provided by section 1 of the Law of Property (Amendment) Act 1926 (which allows settled land to be dealt with as if it were not settled) the estate owner may make a legal mortgage subject to such charges as if the land had not been settled land and without compliance with the Settled Land Act procedure.

(n) *Mortgage to tenant for life*

A mortgage or charge of the settled land may be made to the tenant for life.[95]   **15–37**
In such a case the trustees of the settlement have, in addition to their powers as trustees, all the powers of a tenant for life as to negotiating and completing the transaction.[96]

(o) *Mortgage by trustees where tenant for life has ceased to have a substantial interest*

If it is shown to the satisfaction of the court that the tenant for life: **15–38**

(1) has ceased to have a substantial interest in the land by reason of bankruptcy, assignment, incumbrance, or otherwise; and
(2) either consents to an order being made or has unreasonably refused to exercise any of the powers conferred on him by the Settled Land Act 1925;

then by virtue of section 24(1) of the Settled Land Act 1925:

"the court may, upon the application of any person interested in the settled land or the part thereof affected, make an order authorising the trustees of the settlement to exercise in the name and on behalf of the tenant for life, any of the powers . . . in relation to the settled land or the part thereof affected, either generally and in such manner and for such period as the court may think fit, or in a particular instance."

Once such an order has been made it prevents the tenant for life from exercising any of the powers affected by the order.[97] But a person dealing with the tenant for life is not affected by it unless and until it has been registered under the Land Charges Act 1972 as an order affecting land. Such an order does not vest the legal estate nor the statutory powers in the trustees who do not become the statutory owner. The order merely authorises the trustees to exercise the statutory powers on behalf of the tenant for life and in his name. Further, the provision does not apply to statutory owners and is limited to tenants for life.[98]

---

[94] *ibid.*
[95] *ibid.* s.13.
[96] *ibid.* s.68(2).
[97] Settled Land Act 1925, s.24(2), and see the Land Charges Act 1972, s.6.
[98] *Re Craven Settled Estates* [1926] Ch. 985.

(p) *Mortgage of tenant for life's beneficial interest*

15–39   It is possible for the tenant for life to mortgage his beneficial interest in the trust fund. Such an interest is necessarily equitable, but as it is an equitable thing in action within the meaning of section 136 of the Law of Property Act 1925, it is capable of legal assignment.[99] However, a mortgage of an equitable interest is normally by way of an equitable mortgage.[1]

2. **Tenants in tail**

(a) *Power of tenant in tail to mortgage*

15–40   A tenant in tail in possession will normally have the legal estate, either freehold or leasehold, in the entailed property vested in him as estate owner on the trusts of the settlement.[2] In such circumstances he has the statutory power of a tenant for life to mortgage. Where he has only an equitable interest in the land entailed, which is the usual case,[3] he has special statutory powers of disposing of his equitable interest in the entailed land[4] apart from the general powers of disposition conferred on limited owners under the Settled Land Act 1925, Part II, sections 38 to 72. The tenant in tail[5] can put an end to the settlement by barring the entail,[6] and, having done so by virtue of his legal estate becomes the absolute owner in equity by virtue of his legal estate and can mortgage. Unless the legal estate in the entailed land is vested in the tenant in tail[7] he can only mortgage the equitable interest in the land. By virtue of his special statutory powers of disposition the tenant in tail in possession may execute by deed a mortgage in the form of a conveyance of his equitable interest in fee simple or any less interest in the land.[8] If, however, the tenant in tail is not in possession, unless the mortgage is made with the consent of the protector of the settlement,[9] it will only convey to the mortgagee an equitable interest in the nature of a base fee. This is unimpeachable during the survival of the issue of the tenant in tail but is voidable upon the death of the survivor of that issue by the person next entitled in remainder on the estate tail.[10]

---

[99] *Re Pain* [1919] 1 Ch. 38; *Earle Ltd.* v. *Hemsworth R.D.C.* (1928) 44. T.L.R. 605; and see *ante*, para. 13–05 *et seq.*

[1] See *ante*, para. 13–03 *et seq.*

[2] Settled Land Act 1925, ss.4(2), 6(*b*), 7(1)–(4), 9(2), 20(1)(i), 117(1)(xxviii).

[3] See the L.P.A. 1925, s.1. (1), (3).

[4] See the Fines and Recoveries Act 1833, s.15, and the Law of Property (Amendment) Act 1924, s.9, Sched. 9, by which the Fines and Recoveries Act 1833 remains in force only as regards dealings with entailed interests as equitable interests.

[5] As to the circumstances of family charges constituting a settlement, see the Settled Land Act 1925, s.1. (1)(v) and the power of a person beneficially entitled to land subject to such family charges to convey or create a legal estate subject to the charges, see the Law of Property (Amendment) Act 1926, s.1.

[6] See the Fines and Recoveries Act 1833, s.15.

[7] See *ante*, n. 2.

[8] See the Fines and Recoveries Act 1833, ss.15, 40.

[9] *ibid.* ss.22–28, 32.

[10] *ibid.* s.34.

(b) *Extent of disentailment by mortgage*

When a tenant in tail mortgages the land entailed under his special statutory **15–41** powers pursuant to the Fines and Recoveries Act 1833,[11] generally the entail is wholly barred in equity to the extent of the interest created by the mortgage, irrespective of any intention to the contrary express or implied in the mortgage deed.[12] If the mortgage only creates an interest *pur autre vie*, a term of years, a charge unsecured by a term of years, or a greater interest, then the entail is barred only so far as is necessary to give effect to the mortgage, notwithstanding any intention express or implied to the contrary.[13]

(c) *Agreement to disentail*

The 1833 Act also provides that a disposition by a tenant in tail in contract is **15–42** of no force and that the courts are not to give effect to defective dispositions.[14] However, if it would seem that an agreement by a tenant in tail to disentail for the purpose of executing a legal mortgage may be specifically enforced against the tenant in tail himself.[15] But it cannot be specifically enforced against the issue in tail if the tenant in tail dies before conveying,[16] unless the remainder man was a party to the mortgage transaction.[17]

CORPORATIONS

1. **Borrowing powers of corporations**

(a) *Transactions after February 4, 1991*

The current position as to a company's borrowing power is that, with effect from **15–43** February 4, 1991, a company's capacity to borrow is not affected by anything in its memorandum of association[18] and, furthermore, those dealing with the company are not bound to enquire whether any transaction is permitted by the company's memorandum of association or as to any limitation on the powers of the board of directors to bind the company or authorise others to do so.[19] This change was brought about by the Companies Act 1989 and does not affect any act done by a company prior to February 4, 1991.[20] Accordingly, consideration of the "old" *ultra vires* law will remain relevant when considering transactions entered into before that date.

---

[11] s.15.
[12] See the Fines and Recoveries Act 1833, s.21.
[13] Fines and Recoveries Act 1833, s.21, proviso.
[14] *ibid.* ss.40, 47.
[15] *Bankes* v. *Small* (1887) 36 Ch.D. 716.
[16] See *Att.-Gen.* v. *Day* (1749) 1 Ves.Sen. 218 at 224; *Hinton* v. *Hinton* (1755) 2 Ves.Sen. 631 at 634.
[17] See *Pryce* v. *Bury* (1853) 2 Drew 11.
[18] Companies Act 1985, s.35(1), as amended by the Companies Act 1989 s.108(1).
[19] Companies Act 1985, s.35B.
[20] S.I. 1990 No. 2569, art. 7(1).

(b) *Transactions before February 4 1991*

15–44   The powers of a corporation to mortgage its property are limited by reference to any express or implied authorisation to do so. Thus, in the case of a company incorporated under the Companies Act 1985 (or its statutory predecessors) its express powers to mortgage are contained in the objects and purposes specified in the memorandum of association.[21] Similarly, a public utility company incorporated by a special act of Parliament has the powers conferred by the special act and the Companies Clauses Consolidation Act 1845[22] which enables such a company to raise money by way of mortgage of property subject to certain conditions.[23] Further, a corporation created by Royal Charter, prima facie, is empowered to mortgage on the basis that it has all the rights and powers possessed by an ordinary person.[24]

In the case of companies incorporated under the Companies Act for trading or commercial purposes, there is an implied power to mortgage the company's property even though the memorandum of association is silent provided that there is no positive prohibition preventing it[25] if the proposed transaction is in the ordinary course of the company's business and in the furtherance of its objects.[26] Such an implication will not be made in the case of a non-trading company which can mortgage its property only if it is expressly authorised to do so by its Memorandum of Association. A limited company by its Articles of Association usually delegates to the directors of the company the exercise of the power to mortgage.[27] If there is a limitation on the amount which can be borrowed with or without the sanction of a general meeting, it will be construed as an implied prohibition on borrowing beyond that limit.[28] In any event, the express, or implied power to borrow is limited to borrowing for authorised and legitimate purposes.[29]

In the case of any party to a transaction dealing with a company in good faith, such transaction being decided upon by the directors, the said party is not bound to inquire as to the capacity of the company to enter into it or as to any limitation on the powers of the directors under the Memorandum or Articles of Association. In other words, it must be deemed to be a transaction which is within the capacity of the company to enter, unless the contrary is proved.[30]

15–45   In the case of companies incorporated by the Companies Act 1985, it is not usually legitimate for one company to charge its property as security for the debts

---

[21] *Ashbury Railway Carriage and Iron Co.* v. *Riche* (1875) L.R. 7 H.L. 653.

[22] s.38. See also generally *Palmer's Company Law* (25th ed.).

[23] Companies Clauses Consolidation Act 1845, ss.38–55. In the case of nationalised corporations the powers of the particular body to raise money by way of mortgage are contained in the statute creating the particular body.

[24] *Jenkin* v. *Pharmaceutical Society of Great Britain* [1921] 1 Ch. 392 at 398.

[25] *Re Patent Ivory Manufacturing Co. Howard* v. *Patent Ivory Manufacturing Co.* (1888) 38 Ch.D. 156; *General Auction Estate and Monetary Co.* v. *Smith* [1891] 3 Ch. 432.

[26] *Blackburn Building Society v. Cunliffe Brooks & Co.* (1882) 22 Ch. D. 61 at 70.

[27] *Re Irish Club Co. Ltd.* [1906] W.N. 127. A company limited by guarantee cannot charge the amounts which the members have undertaken to contribute in the event of a winding up.

[28] *Re The Worcester Corn Exchange Co.* (1853) 3 De. G.M. & G. 180; *Re Bokbeck Permanent Building Society* [1912] 2 Ch. 183 at 207 *per* Cozens-Hardy M.R.

[29] *Introductions Ltd.* v. *National Provincial Bank* [1970] Ch. 199.

[30] See the European Communities Act 1972, s.9(1) as repealed by Companies Act 1985, s.35 prior to its repeal, substitution by the Companies Act 1989, s.108(1); see further *Buckley on the Companies Act* (2000).

of another company, for example, its parent or holding company. However, if it is proposed that a subsidiary company should guarantee a loan made to the holding company the Memorandum of Association of the subsidiary company can be altered so as to ensure that it has the appropriate authorisation to enter into such a transaction.

2. Registration[31]

Where a company incorporated under the Companies Act 1985 enters into a transaction whereby it charges the property of the company,[32] such a transaction shall be void against the liquidator and any creditor of the company unless the prescribed particulars of the charge together with the instrument, if any, by which the charge is created or evidenced, are delivered to or received by the registrar of companies for registration as required within 21 days after the date of its creation, but without prejudice to any contract or obligation for repayment of the money thereby secured.[33] When the charge becomes void under this section the money secured thereby shall immediately become payable.

PUBLIC AUTHORITIES

1. The borrowing power of local authorities

Local authorities have statutory powers of mortgaging, their powers being defined by the relevant Act[34] or being implied.[35] Under the Local Government and Housing Act 1972,[35] a local authority may borrow such sums as may be required for the acquisition of land, for building and for any other purpose relevant to these functions under any enactment.[36] All monies borrowed by a local authority and any interest accrued thereon is charged indifferently on all its revenues and any security created after June 1, 1934 ranks equally without priority.[36a] A person lending money to a local authority is not bound to inquire whether the authority has power to borrow and will not be prejudiced by the absence of that power.[37] Regulations[38] provide the manner in which the borrowing powers are exercisable. Local authorities may also borrow money for certain specified purposes under general Acts of Parliament.[39]

15–46

---

[31] See *ante*, para. 11–26 *et seq.*
[32] This includes a mortgage; Companies Act 1985, s.396(4).
[33] Companies Act 1985, s.395 (as substituted by Companies Act 1989, s.93). For a more detailed analysis of these provisions in particular the effect of non-registration, registration otherwise than under the Act, and rectificiation see *Buckley on the Companies Act* (2000). For mortgage debentures see *ante*, Chapter 11.
[34] Local Government and Housing Act 1989, ss.43–47.
[35] *Baroness Wenlock* v. *River Dee Co.* (1883) 36 Ch.D. 675.
[36] Local Government and Housing Act 1989, s.43(1).
[36a] *ibid.*, s.47(1).
[37] *ibid.*, s.44(6).
[38] Local Authorities (Borrowing) Regulations 1990, S.I. 1990 No. 767, as amended.
[39] See, *e.g.* Housing Act 1985, s.451.

2. Lending powers of local authorities[40]

15–47   A local authority or county council may, subject to any economic restraints imposed on such authorities, advance money for the purpose of acquiring, constructing, altering, enlarging, repairing or improving houses, for converting buildings into houses or flats, for acquiring houses for that purpose or for paying off a loan for such purposes.[41] Before making an advance the local authority must be satisfied that the resultant house will be fit for human habitation, or in the case of a house to be acquired is or will be made fit.[42] The mortgage can only be made if secured against an estate comprising either a fee simple absolute in possession or a term of years absolute for a term not less than 10 years in excess of the period fixed for repayment.[43]

3. Other public authorities

15–48   Further, other public authorities have statutory powers, where required, both to advance money on mortgage or to mortgage property. Such powers are conferred by the statutes regulating the authority in question. Thus, internal drainage boards[44] may raise money on mortgage. The Agricultural Mortgage Corporation Limited had power to make advances by way of mortgage.[45] The National Trust may also borrow money by way of mortgage of its alienable property.[46] National Health Service Trusts are prohibited from mortgaging or charging their assets.[47]

HOUSING ASSOCIATIONS

1. Housing associations[48]

15–49   By virtue of the Housing Act 1985 a Housing Association[49] is "a society, body of trustees or company established for the purpose of, or amongst whose objects or powers are included those of, providing, constructing, improving, or managing, or facilitating or encouraging the construction or improvement of houses or hostels, being a society, body of trustees or company who do not trade for profit or whose constitution or rules prohibit the issue of any capital with interest or dividend exceeding the rate for the time being prescribed by the Treasury, whether with or without differentiation as between share and loan capital."[50] A

---

[40] See further *ante*, Chap. 9.
[41] Housing Act 1985, s.435(1).
[42] Housing Act 1985, s.451.
[43] Housing Act 1985, s.436.
[44] See the Land Drainage Act 1991, s.35.
[45] See the Agricultural Credits Act 1928, ss.1, 2, now repealed by the Agriculture and Forestry (Financial Provisions) Act 1991, s.1(1), (2), Sched. Pt I.
[46] See the National Trust Act 1907, s.22.
[47] National Health Service and Community Care Act 1990, s.9, Sched. 3, para. 1(2).
[48] As to the history and the development of the various types of housing associations see (Craddock), (1959) 23 Conv. (N.S.) 3.
[49] This includes a housing society.
[50] Housing Associations Act 1985, s.1(1).

housing association may be either an industrial and provident society,[51] a company registered under the Companies Act 1985,[52] or unincorporated. It may also be a charity.[53] Its borrowing powers are determined by its legal status. It may or may not be registered under the Housing Associations Act 1985 and the land which it acquires may or may not be grant-aided.[54]

2. The Housing Corporation

The Housing Corporation[55] was established by Part I of the Housing Act 1964. **15–50** Its functions were extended by the Housing Act 1974 and are now consolidated in the Housing Associations Act 1985. It is a body corporate with perpetual succession and has a common seal. The objects of the Housing Corporation are to promote and assist the development of registered housing associations and unregistered self-build societies, to facilitate the proper performance of the functions of such associations and to publicise their aims and principles. Further, it is to establish and maintain a register of housing associations and to exercise supervision and control over them and to undertake the provision of dwellings for letting or sale and of hostels and the management of dwellings or hostels provided by the Corporation.[56] The Housing Corporation has certain borrowing powers[57] and it is also empowered to make loans to certain specified borrowers.[58] By virtue of section 9 of the 1985 Act a registered housing association may, not, *inter alia*, mortgage any land, and an unregistered association may not, *inter alia*, mortgage grant-aided land, except with the consent of the Housing Corporation.[59]

INDUSTRIAL AND PROVIDENT SOCIETIES[60]

Generally the rules of each society must provide whether it may enter into **15–51** loans or receive money on deposit from members or other persons, and if so,

---

[51] See *post* para. 15–51.
[52] See *ante* para. 15–43.
[53] See *ante* para. 15–21.
[54] See the Housing Associations Act 1985, s.9(1), Sched. 1.
[55] In Wales, the body is known as "Housing For Wales" and was created by the Housing Act 1988. It has all the functions conferred upon it by the Housing Associations Act 1985 and, from December 1988, has had vested in it all the property in Wales previously held by the Housing Corporation.
[56] *ibid.* s.75 (as amended).
[57] *ibid.* ss.92, 93 (as amended).
[58] *ibid.* s.79(1) permits loans to registered social landlords, unregistered self-build societies, subsidiaries of the Corporation and other bodies in which the Corporation has an interest.
[59] If, however, the association is a registered charity and the mortgage requires consent or an order under s.29 of the Charities Act 1960, such consent under the Housing Associations Act is not required.
[60] Building Societies are dealt with in Chap. 8. The regulatory functions of the Building Societies Commission, the Friendly Societies Commission, the Registrar of Friendly Societies, the Building Societies Investor Protection Board, the Industrial and Provident Societies and Credit Unions conferred on them by legislation are in the process of being transferred to the FSA and the Treasury. Certain provisions governing these bodies have been prospectively repealed. These bodies will eventually be replaced by order of the Treasury, see the Financial Services and Market Act 2000, Part XXI, ss.334–338, 423(3); Sched. 18, Pts I to V; Sched. 22; and see para. 8–03.

under what conditions, on what security and to what amounts.[61] Such mortgages and charges over the property of industrial and provident societies do not require registration with the Chief Registrar of Friendly Societies. A mortgagee is not bound to inquire as to the relevant authorisation for the mortgage by the society and the society's receipt is a good discharge for all monies arising from such a transaction.[62]

Fixed and floating charges may be created by industrial and provident societies on their personal chattels free from the provisions of the Bills of Sale Acts 1878 and 1882 if an application is lodged within 14 days at the central office established under the Friendly Societies Act 1896 to record the charge.[63]

A registered industrial and provident society may by its rules provide for advances of money to members on the security of real or personal property or, if the society is registered to carry on banking business, in any manner customary in the conduct of such business.[64] Further, advances can be made to members of agricultural, horticultural or forestry societies for agricultural, horticultural or forestry purposes without security.[65]

FRIENDLY SOCIETIES

15–52   Generally, provided that a registered society or branch's rules permit it to hold land and buildings, such land can be mortgaged.[66]

The trustees of a registered society or branch may, with the consent of the committee or of a majority of the members present and entitled to vote in a general meeting,[67] invest the funds of the society or branch or any part thereof, *inter alia*, upon any security expressly directed by the rules of the society or branch, not being a personal security but only as authorised by the provisions of the Friendly Societies Act 1974 with respect to loans[68] and in any investments authorised by law for investment of trust funds.[69] The Act also makes provisions for loans to members out of a separate loan fund.[70]

CLUBS

15–53   Clubs which are incorporated have powers to borrow in accordance with their Memoranda and Articles of Association and the Companies Act 1985.

The property of unincorporated clubs is usually held by trustees on behalf of the members. The trustees' powers to borrow are governed by the club's rules and/or the instrument creating the trust or by the applicable statutory provisions (*e.g.* as trustees of land) or any order of the court.

---

[61] Industrial and Provident Societies Act 1965, s.1 and Sched. 1.
[62] *ibid.* s.30(1).
[63] *ibid.* s.1.
[64] *ibid.* s.21.
[65] *ibid.* s.12.
[66] Friendly Societies Act 1974, s.53 which implies a power to borrow, and see s.23(2).
[67] Friendly Societies Act 1974, s.46(1).
[68] Friendly Societies Act 1974, ss.48 and 49.
[69] *ibid.* s.46(1)(*d*), (*e*).
[70] *ibid.* s.49.

The rules of an incorporated club or the Memorandum and Articles of Association of an incorporated club may permit the issue of debentures. Debentures issued by unincorporated clubs should not include personal chattels or furniture since, even if they were registered under the Bills of Sales Acts,[71] they would be void for non-compliance with the statutory form.[72]

---

[71] Bills of Sale Act (1878) Amendment Act 1882, s.8.
[72] *ibid.*, s.9.

CHAPTER 16

RIGHTS, DUTIES AND REMEDIES OF THE MORTGAGEE OR CHARGEE

INTRODUCTION

The essential feature of lending money by means of a mortgage is that the **16–01** mortgagee becomes a secured creditor of the mortgagor. The mortgagee's rights and remedies enable him to enforce his rights against the mortgaged property in the event of a default by the mortgagor. He will have first call on the mortgaged property on the assumption that he is the first and only mortgagee. By reason of the fact that in earlier times the mortgage contract was in essence regarded as an investment by the the mortgagee, the principles of law became established during the course of the nineteenth and the early part of the twentieth century to the effect that the mortgagee should have complete freedom to realise his security in the event of default on the part of the mortgagor. Most of the mortgagee's rights and remedies as developed are now enshrined in statutory enactments, in particular the Law of Property Act 1925.

These principles, however, must now be viewed in the light of the various **16–02** developments which have occurred in recent years which have tended to temper the strict application of the mortgagee's remedies. The reason for this is simple: since the 1930s, and more particularly since the Second World War, successive governments have placed strong emphasis on home ownership. Concomitant with this has been the growth in lending by the building societies, and latterly by the banks, who provide funds for the purchase of dwelling-houses secured by way of mortgage. Thus, the traditional rights and remedies of the mortgagee have required some readjustment in order to meet the changing role of the mortgage. Substantial restrictions have been placed on the mortgagee's ability to realise his security both by statute and by the courts in order to provide a measure of protection for a mortgagor in the occupation of his own home, the result being to "temper the wind to the shorn lamb."[1] However, the process of erosion of the mortgagee's remedies must not be exaggerated. In this context it must be remembered that although there has been an enormous growth in institutional lending for home ownership, the number of defaults is relatively small in comparison with the total, although one of the features of the recession of the late 1980s and early 1990s was that there developed a significant increase in the number of mortgage possession cases. The reason for this is not that building societies and banks necessarily fail to enforce their security (and there is some evidence that building societies in particular "hold back" in times of crisis) but more that such institutional lenders will, prior to lending, usually make extensive

[1] *Redditch Benefit Building Society v. Roberts* [1940] Ch. 415 at 420.

enquiries into the potential borrower's means in order to ensure that he or she can service the level of borrowing. Recent developments in the mortgage market place and in particular the growth of mortgages where the mortgagor's worth is either not investigated or is "self-certified" by the mortgagor may have led to an increase in the proportion of mortgagors in default.

1. Mortgagee's interest limited to the security

16–03   The mortgagor is in equity the beneficial owner of the mortgaged property until his interest is lost to him by the realisation of the security or by lapse of time. The corollary is that the mortgagee's interest in the property is solely as a security until he acquires full beneficial ownership by a decree for foreclosure absolute or by lapse of time. This principle was clearly stated in the case of *Thornborough v. Baker*[2] where Lord Nottingham held that, in a mortgage of land, if redemption took place after the death of the mortgagee, the redemption moneys must be paid to the personal representatives and not to his heir-at-law. At that date the legal title to land necessarily passed to the heir-at-law whereas the title to a contract debt passed to the personal representatives. Lord Nottingham's decision thus meant that the substance of a mortgagee's interest is not his title to the mortgage property which he holds as security but his right to the mortgage moneys. Although at law the mortgagee's title is made absolute by the passing of the contractual date for redemption, in equity it is his beneficial interest in the title which remains his security for enforcing payment of the mortgage debt. Hence, the legal title in the hands of the heir-at-law could not carry any beneficial interest in the mortgage debt which belonged to the personal representatives and in equity was held on the latter's behalf to enforce the debt. In other words, although at law his title gives to a mortgagee a right to the property, in equity his interest in the mortgage comprises his debt, his use of the title as security for the debt and nothing more.[3]

2. Mortgagee not a trustee

16–04   A mortgagee has, therefore, two titles, the title to the mortgaged property (which he holds subject to the mortgagor's equity of redemption) and his own beneficial interest in the property as a security. At first sight a mortgagee seems to be very like a trustee, for he holds a title to give effect to equitable rights vested in himself and another. However, although there is some analogy between the conceptions of mortgage and trust, a mortgagee is not a trustee.[4] It has been said repeatedly that no fiduciary relationship arises between a mortgagor and a mortgagee until the latter has been paid off.[5] Then, the mortgagee does indeed

---

[2] (1676) 1 Ch.Cas. 283.
[3] This position was altered by s.30 of the Conveyancing Act 1881, and the Land Transfer Act 1897, both of which have now been replaced as to deaths after 1925 by the Administration of Estates Act 1925, ss.1(1), 3(1)(ii). But the principle is still of importance.
[4] *Marquis of Cholmondely v. Lord Clinton* (1820) 2 J. & W. 1; and see Turner, *Equity of Redemption* (1931), Chap. 8.
[5] *Kennedy v. De Trafford* [1897] A.C. 180.

become a trustee of the legal estate, if the mortgage has been redeemed[6] and of the surplus proceeds of sale if the property has been sold under a power of sale.[7] A mortgagee is not a trustee of the power of sale, for the power of sale is given to the mortgagee for his own benefit to enable him to realise his security,[8] although such power must be exercised bona fide and with reasonable care.[9] The duty formerly imposed by statute[10] on building societies to take reasonable care to ensure that the price obtained on a sale of a mortgaged property was the best price that could reasonably be obtained has been repealed[11] and any rule of law requiring a mortgagee to take reasonable care to obtain a proper price on true market value is to have effect as if the statute imposing the duty on a building society (and its statutory predecessors) had never been enacted.[12] Thus, until a mortgagee has been satisfied, his interest in the property is essentially adverse to that of the mortgagor. This is never so between a trustee and a *cestui que trust*. The suggestion that a mortgagee acts in a fiduciary capacity was strongly attacked by Plumer M.R., in the case of *Marquis of Cholmondely v. Lord Clinton*,[13] in a passage which would seem to leave no room for further argument. Yet, in one form or another, the fallacy has reappeared from time to time, and in the later case of *Allen and Clarke v. O'Hearne & Co.*[14] the Privy Council had occasion again to deny the trusteeship of a mortgagee.

There are, in fact, several points on which the characters of mortgagee and **16–05** trustee diverge. The most conspicuous are:

(1) A legal mortgagee has, in general, an absolute right to take possession of the mortgaged property, whereas dispossession of a *cestui que trust* would be a breach of trust[15];

(2) Purchases by trustees from their beneficiaries are regarded with the utmost jealousy. However, mortgagees are free to purchase the equity of redemption as the relationship is considered to be that of vendor and purchaser. This remains so unless and until the mortgagor is able to show any fraud or oppression on the part of the mortgagee or when there is pressure and inequality of bargaining position, and the mortgagee has obtained the purchase at a nominal or insufficient price. Undervalue alone will not be sufficient to set the transaction aside[16];

---

[6] *Taylor v. Russell* [1892] A.C. 244.

[7] *Rajah Kishendatt Ram v. Rajah Mumtaz Ali Khan* (1879) L.R. 6 Ind.App. 145; *Banner v. Berridge* (1881) 18 Ch.D. 254.

[8] See *Warner v. Jacob* (1882) 20 Ch.D. 220 at 224; and see *post*, para. 16–67 *et seq.* for the various duties of the mortgagee as vendor.

[9] For power of sale see *post*, para. 16–53 *et seq.*, and see *Cuckmere Brick Co. Ltd v. Mutual Finance Ltd* [1971] Ch. 949; *Bishop v. Bonham* [1988] 1 W.L.R. 742. *Parker-Tweedale v. Dunbar Bank* [1991] Ch. 12, CA; *Downsview Nominees Ltd v. First City Corporation Ltd* [1993] A.C. 295; *AIB Finance v. Debtors* [1998] 2 All E.R. 929; *Medforth v. Blake* [1999] 3 W.L.R. 922. See *post*, para. 16–68 *et seq.*

[10] Building Societies Act 1986, s.13(7) and Sched. 4, para. 1.

[11] Building Societies Act 1997, s.12(1) with effect from December 1, 1997, S.I. 1997 No. 2668.

[12] *ibid.*, s.12(2) and see *ante*, chapter 8.

[13] (1820) 2 J. & W. 1 at 182 *et seq.*

[14] [1937] A.C. 213 at 219.

[15] *Marquis of Cholmondely v. Lord Clinton* (1820) 2 J. & W. 1, at 183.

[16] *Knight v. Marjoribanks* (1849) 2 Mac & G. 10; *Ford v. Olden* (1867), L.R. 3 Eq. 461, and see *post*, para. 16–68 *et seq.*

(3) In foreclosure proceedings the court actually assists a mortgagee to acquire the equity of redemption, whereas this is unthinkable in the case of a trustee;

(4) A mortgagee in possession may, while a trustee in possession never can, acquire a title under the statute of limitation[17];

(5) Apart from his duty to act in good faith and with reasonable care particularly with regard to the obtaining of a proper price (see above), a mortgagee can elect if and when to exercise his powers in his own interest[18] and need have little regard for the mortgagor's interest, whereas that is the whole duty of the trustee.[19] Certainly a mortgagee need not exercise his powers (even if advised to do so) notwithstanding that such an exercise would be highly advantageous to the mortgagor.[20]

(6) A mortgagee in possession is liable to account on the footing of wilful default without it being specially pleaded, whereas a special case must be made out for charging a trustee with wilful default.[21]

16–06   Thus, a mortgagee is plainly not a trustee for the mortgagor. He owes no duty to explain the security to the mortgagor,[22] although he would be wise to advise a mortgagor to seek independent legal advice. A mortgagee can, if he chooses, disregard his security and simply rely upon the personal covenant to repay.[23]

There are some restraints upon a mortgagee. He must act not only in good faith[24] but also with reasonable care[25] particularly with regard to taking reasonable care to obtain the best price.[26] It has also been said that a mortgagee owes the mortgagor a duty to act fairly.[27] The only other restraints upon the mortgagee are the equitable rules which establish and regulate the mortgagor's right of redemption. This means that as the mortgagee's interest is limited to his security, so long as any right of redemption still exists, he cannot make any personal

---

[17] cf. Re Alison, Johnson v. Mounsey (1879) 11 Ch.D. 284.

[18] Rontestone Ltd v. Minories Finance Ltd [1997] 1 E.G.L.R. 123.

[19] Davey v. Durrant, Smith v. Durrant (1857) 1 De G. & J. 535; but see post, para. 16–67 for the mortgagee's duties as vendor.

[20] Palk v. Mortgage Services Funding plc [1993] Ch. 330; China and South Sea Bank Ltd v. Tan [1990] 1 A.C. 536.

[21] Dobson v. Land (1850) 8 Hare 216 at 220.

[22] Barclays Bank v. Khana [1992] 1 W.L.R. 623; [1993] 1 F.L.R. 343, CA.

[23] Cheah Theam Swee v. Equiticorp Finance Group Ltd [1992] 1 A.C. 472.

[24] Tomlin v. Luce (1889) 43 Ch.D. 191; and see Cuckmere Brick Co. Ltd v. Mutual Finance Ltd [1971] Ch. 949; Downsview Nominees Limited v. First City Corp. Ltd [1993] A.C. 295. Examples of breach may be found in Downsview, supra: Albany Home Loans Ltd v. Massey [1997] 2 All E.R. 69; Quenell v. Maltby [1979] 1 W.L.R. 318; Sadiq v. Hussain (1997) 73 P. & C.R. D44.

[25] In Standard Chartered Bank Ltd v. Walker [1982] 1 W.L.R. 1410 and American Express International Banking Corporation v. Hurley [1985] F.L.R. 350, the liability of the mortgagee to the mortgagor's guarantor was considered to be a matter of tort. But the relationship between the mortgagee and the guarantor is a matter of contract (see Lord Scarman in Tai Hing Cotton Mill Ltd v. Liu Chong Hing Bank Ltd [1986] 1 A.C. 80 at 96; National Bank of Greece S.A. v. Pinios (No. 1) [1989] 1 All E.R. 253; Lancashire & Cheshire Association of Baptist Church Inc. v. Howard Seddon Partnership [1993] 3 All E.R. 467; Henderson v. Merrett Syndicates Ltd [1995] 2 A.C. 145 and see post, para. 16–70.

[26] Cuckmere Brick Co. Ltd v. Mutual Finance Ltd [1971] Ch. 949, in which Kennedy v. De Trafford [1897] A.C. 180 was explained. See also Holohan v. Friends Provident and Century Life Office [1966] I.R. 1; Bishop v. Bonham [1988] 1 W.L.R. 742. See post, para. 16–69.

[27] Palk v. Mortgage Services Funding plc [1993] Ch. 330; AIB Finance v. Debtors [1998] 2 All E.R. 929.

profits out of the mortgaged property beyond those which result directly from the mortgage bargain. Thus an accretion to the mortgaged property, for example by the exercise of an option to purchase, benefits the mortgagee by enlarging his security but it actually belongs to the mortgagor.[28] Similarly, any profits from the property, which are intercepted by the mortgagee after exercising his legal right to take possession, must be placed to the credit of the mortgagor. The only beneficial interest of the mortgagee in the property until foreclosure is as a security for the mortgage debt.

Part of a mortgagee's security derives directly from his title to the property or   **16–07** from rights granted by the mortgage agreement. Not all his rights are, however, expressed in the agreement because equity, in subjecting his title to the equity of redemption, at the same time provides him with rights and remedies for the protection and realisation of his security. Thus, the right to possession of the property follows from his legal title but the right to foreclose or to obtain the judicial appointment of a receiver or a judicial sale are equitable rights. The legal and equitable rights and remedies of the mortgagee, both in and out of court, make up the sum total of the mortgagee's security and will now be examined in detail.

The Exercise by the Mortgagee of his Rights and Remedies

Foreclosure, sale and the personal action on the covenant for payment may be   **16–08** termed *final* remedies arising from the nature of the security, their object being to recover capital and to obtain a final settlement from the mortgagor. Entry into possession and the appointment of a receiver, on the other hand, are not normally final remedies. It is true that a mortgagee in possession, after meeting outgoings and the mortgage interest, is entitled to apply surplus rents and profits to the discharge of the principal and a receiver appointed by the mortgagee may do the same, if so directed. In practice, however, the surplus is not usually large enough to enable the principal to be paid off except over a longer period than is acceptable to the mortgagee. Consequently entry into possession and the appointment of a receiver are essentially interim remedies employed out of court to protect the security and keep down the interest—very often as a preliminary step to the realisation of the security by foreclosure or sale.

A mortgagee's choice of remedy naturally depends on the particular circumstances both of the mortgaged property and of the debtor. If the property is worth the sum secured by the mortgage or if it is likely to increase in value with good management, foreclosure may be the best course. In other cases, if the property is let to tenants or otherwise produces appreciable income, the appointment of a receiver out of court followed by a sale may provide the simplest means of realising the mortgage. If, however, the mortgagor is in possession, there is nothing for the receiver to receive and the fact that vacant possession cannot be given is an obstacle to sale. Then recourse may be had to proceedings for possession followed by a sale out of court. A personal action on the covenant for payment is always available as an additional remedy where the security is insufficient to meet the mortgage debt and can be pursued without recourse to the

---

[28] *Nelson v. Hannam* [1943] Ch. 59.

security.[29] It has, of course, particular value where the mortgagor has other property which can be reached by a judgment.

1. Concurrent exercise of a mortgagee's rights and remedies

16–09 Once the mortgagor is in default the mortgagee is entitled to pursue all his remedies concurrently. He may simultaneously take proceedings to obtain foreclosure or sale, possession or the appointment of a receiver, delivery of the title deeds and payment on the personal covenant.[30] If, in the same claim,[31] he has any collateral securities, he may also enforce these at the same time.[32] If his mortgage empowers him to sell or to appoint a receiver out of court, he may exercise these powers despite the fact that he has already begun proceedings for foreclosure.[33] There are, however, two qualifications on the right to exercise remedies concurrently. Once an order nisi for foreclosure has been obtained, the leave of the court is necessary for a sale out of court.[34] Secondly, if a mortgagee takes proceedings for foreclosure and for payment on the personal covenant concurrently, he must do so in the *same* proceedings. As it is open to him to ask for foreclosure and for judgment on the covenant in the *same* action, the duplication of the concurrent actions will be regarded as vexatious. He may, as will be seen, take separate proceedings for foreclosure and payment *successively* but, if he does so *concurrently*, the action on the covenant will be struck out as vexatious.[35]

2. Successive exercise of remedies

16–10 A mortgagee may also pursue his remedies successively. The fact that he has enforced one remedy does not prevent him from afterwards pursuing another, unless by enforcing the first he has paid himself off. If a judgment on the covenant is only partially satisfied or, if after a sale there is a deficiency, a mortgagee may still pursue any other remedy that, in the circumstances, is open to him.[36] Even foreclosure absolute does not prevent him from bringing an action on the covenant for payment. If he does so, he reopens the foreclosure because a person cannot receive payment and keep the estate.[37] Only if he sells the estate after foreclosure are his remedies at an end. He can then no longer return the estate and has no further rights against the mortgagor.[38] A secured creditor is,

---

[29] *Cheah Theam Swee v. Equiticorp Finance Group Ltd* [1992] 1 A.C. 472.
[30] *China and South Sea Bank Ltd v. Tan* [1990] 1 A.C. 536; *Re BCCI SA (No. 8)* [1998] A.C. 214; *Cheah Theam Swee, ante*; *Cheltenham & Gloucester Building Society v. Grattidge* (1993) 25 H.L.R. 454.
[31] *Dymond v. Croft* (1876) 3 Ch.D. 512.
[32] *Lockhart v. Hardy* (1846) 9 Beav. 349; *Palmer v. Hendrie* (1859) 27 Beav. 349 at 351.
[33] *Stevens v. Theatres Ltd* [1903] 1 Ch. 857.
[34] *Stevens v. Theatres Ltd* [1903] 1 Ch. 857.
[35] *Williams v. Hunt* [1905] 1 K.B. 512.
[36] *Lockhart v. Hardy* (1846) 9 Beav. 349 at 355.
[37] *Perry v. Barker* (1806) 13 Ves. 198.
[38] *Lockhart v. Hardy* (1846) 9 Beav. 349. A bona fide purchaser without notice gets a good title, *Lloyds & Scottish Trust v. Britten* (1982) 44 P. & C.R. 249. See also *post*, para. 16–89 *et seq.*

therefore, largely outside the rule that separate proceedings must not be brought for different forms of relief claimed in respect of the same transaction.

Out of Court Rights and Liabilities of the Legal Mortgagee

1. **Right to custody of the title deeds**[39]

(a) *Registered land*

In the case of registered land, however, there are no title deeds on which the first   **16–11** legal mortgagee can take possession. In the case of a registered charge, which is the most common form of legal mortgage, being a charge by way of legal mortgage, the mortgagor deposits his land certificate[40] with the Land Registry, who then issue a "charge certificate" to the mortgagee as proprietor of the registered charge.[41] Since March 1998, any mortgage of a freehold or leasehold interest with more than 21 years to run which is supported by documents of title has triggered compulsory registration.[42] Accordingly, the rights discussed below pertaining to possession of documents of title to unregistered land are likely to be of diminishing significance.

(b) *Unregistered land*

The general rule is that muniments of title follow the legal title, so that the holder of the legal title has a prima facie right to custody of the title deeds.[43] Formerly, this meant that legal mortgagees in fee were, as against the mortgagor, entitled to the deeds,[44] but that legal mortgagees by demise including, of course, most mortgagees of leasehold interests were not entitled to custody of the mortgagor's title deeds.[45] But, mortgages of freeholds and leaseholds were required by sections 85 and 86 of the Law of Property Act 1925 to be by demise and those sections, at the same time, provided for the *first* legal mortgagee to have a right to custody of the deeds. Thus, a first legal mortgagee of a freehold interest has the same right to the deeds as if his title included the fee, whereas a first legal mortgagee of a leasehold interest has the same right to custody of the deeds as if his mortgage had been created by assignment of the lease instead of by demise. A mortgagee of a leasehold interest is therefore in a better position than he was before the Act unless he was then a mortgagee by assignment of the lease, which was unusual. An equitable mortgagee, however, not having the legal title, has no right to the deeds as against the mortgagor unless he stipulates for that right in the contract. Such a stipulation is, of course, almost invariably found in a first

---

[39] For what may comprise title deeds, see *Clayton v. Clayton* [1930] 2 Ch. 12 at 21.

[40] See s.27 of the Land Registration Act 1925, and see *ante*, chap. 4.

[41] In practice the Land Registry does not issue one; there is no question of its storing them nowadays.

[42] LRA 1925, s.123(2) as amended by LRA 1997, s.1 and see *ante*, chap. 4.

[43] As to what is meant by "title deeds" see *Clayton v. Clayton* [1930] 2 Ch. 12 at 21. The meaning is used in its widest sense, *i.e.* all documents necessary to prove title.

[44] *Smith v. Chichester* (1842) 2 Dr. & War. 393.

[45] *Wiseman & Benley v. Westland, Fisher, Benson, Davis & Stanbridge* (1826) 1 Y. & J. 117.

equitable mortgage. Thus, generally, the non-possession of the title deeds by the holder of the legal title constitutes notice to a subsequent mortgagee that the property in question is subject to a mortgage. Further, the possession of the title deeds by the first legal mortgagee will usually provide difficulties for the mortgagor in raising further finance on the security of the property or otherwise dealing with it to the disadvantage of the first legal mortgagee.

16–12   A first legal mortgagee's rights to the deeds, though absolute against the mortgagor, will not prevail against an equitable mortgagee who has already obtained the deeds and of whose incumbrance the legal mortgagee therefore has notice.[46] Nor would it prevail, even against a subsequent equitable incumbrancer in possession of the deeds, if the gross negligence of the legal mortgagee in not obtaining the deeds has induced the equitable incumbrancer to believe that there was no prior legal mortgage.[47] In other words, the right to the deeds may sometimes involve the question of competing priorities and the legal mortgagee's normal right to the custody of the deeds may sometimes be displaced.[48] It appears that a mortgagee with good title but to whom a forged copy of a genuine deed has been delivered can recover the genuine deed from a subsequent mortgagee.[49]

A mortgagee may require and recover all deeds and documents from any person (bar a mortgagee entitled in priority to him) as soon as the statutory power of sale has become exercisable. The deeds and documents to which the mortgagee is entitled are all those which a purchaser may require from him to be delivered.[50]

(c) Liability of the mortgagee in possession of deeds to produce them

16–13   Before 1882 a mortgagor could not compel his mortgagee to produce the title deeds for inspection without tendering the mortgage moneys[51] and this was so even though the deeds were required for the purpose of negotiating a loan to pay off the existing mortgage.[52] This rule still applies to any mortgages created before January 1, 1882,[53] but it is reversed with regard to later mortgages by section 96(1) of the Law of Property Act 1925.[54] This provides as follows:

> "A mortgagor, as long as his right to redeem subsists, shall be entitled from time to time, at reasonable times, on his request, and at his own cost, and on payment of the mortgagee's costs and expenses in this behalf, to inspect and make copies or abstracts of or extracts from the documents of title relating to the mortgaged property in the custody or power[55] of the mortgagee."

---

[46] It is just conceivable that the legal mortgagee might have a right to the deeds in such a case, see *Agra Bank v. Barry* (1874) L.R. 7 H.L. 135.

[47] See *post*, para. 20–05.

[48] Since the Judicature Act 1873, it is in all cases the duty of the court to give complete relief by ordering the delivery of the deeds to the incumbrancer, who has priority. *Re Cooper, Cooper v. Vesey* (1882) 20 Ch.D. 611; *Re Ingham, Jones v. Ingham* [1893] 1 Ch. 352.

[49] *Newton v. Beck* (1858) 3 H. & N. 220.

[50] Law of Property Act 1925, s.106(4).

[51] *Browne v. Lockhart* (1840) 10 Sim. 420.

[52] See Coote, *Mortgages* (9th ed., 1927), Vol. 2, p. 841.

[53] It is very unlikely that any such mortgages still exist.

[54] Replacing s.16 of the Conveyancing Act 1881.

[55] This includes documents in the mortgagee's solicitor's possession: *Bligh v. Benson* (1819) 7 Price 205.

Moreover, the section expressly forbids any contracting out of the above provision. It will also be noted that the subsection does not entitle the mortgagor to *borrow* the title deeds.

A mortgagee's liability under section 96 is not limited to producing the title deeds only for the mortgagor because "mortgagor" also includes "any person from time to time deriving title under the original mortgagor or entitled to redeem a mortgage according to his estate, interest, or right in the mortgaged property."[56] Presumably, in the case of trust property, the liability is only to produce the deeds to the trustees unless, owing to the default of the trustees, the beneficiaries are admitted to redeem in their place. In the case of settled land the primary liability is, of course, to the life-tenant who holds for all persons entitled under the settlement[57] and he is entitled to production of the title deeds. Whether a vested remainderman has a right to the production of the deeds is uncertain. He certainly had the right before 1926, when his remainder was a legal estate, and it may well be that this right still exists although his interest is now equitable only. Logically, his right should be confined to the case when he has the consent of the life-tenant to redeem, which he must obtain before he can redeem the mortgaged property.[58]

(d) *Delivery of deeds on extinguishment*

A mortgagee, whose debt has been satisfied, must at once deliver up any deeds **16–14** which are in his possession.[59] When the person redeeming is not the mortgagor, he has a right to keep the mortgage alive for his own benefit, and is entitled to the deeds. However, when it is the mortgagor who redeems, a mortgagee is not always obliged to hand over the deeds to him: on the contrary, if he has notice of puisne incumbrances, it is his duty to deliver the deeds to the incumbrancer next in priority of whom the mortgagee has notice.[60] If he does not do so he is liable to make good any loss resulting to the incumbrancer concerned. In this instance, however, contrary to the general rule that registration is notice, registration under the Land Charges Act 1972 or in a local register is *not* deemed to be equivalent to actual notice. Accordingly, there is no need to make a search at either registry before handing over the deeds although a mortgagee is bound to search the appropriate registries before he distributes any surplus after a sale.[61] Thus, a mortgagee is under no liability to persons of whose interest he has neither actual nor constructive notice, even though they have registered their incumbrances.[62] A mortgagor can recover possession of the mortgage and all other title deeds where the mortgagee's title has lapsed by effluxion of time.[63]

---

[56] LPA 1925, s.205(1)(xvi).
[57] See the Settled Land Act 1925, s.107(1).
[58] In *Halsbury's Laws of England* (4th ed., Re-issue, 1999), Vol. 32, para. 694, the view is expressed that as the vested remainderman has a right to redeem he therefore has the statutory right to production of the title deeds.
[59] See *Graham v. Seal* (1918) 88 L.J.Ch. 31.
[60] *Corbett v. National Provident Institution* (1900) 17 T.L.R. 5.
[61] See *post*, para. 16–73 *et seq.*
[62] See Law of Property (Amendment) Act 1926, s.7 and the LPA 1925 Schedule of Minor Amendments, which alters s.96(2) of the LPA 1925 to this extent. See also LPA 1969, s.16(2), Sched. 2 Pt. I; Land Charges Act 1972, s18(6).
[63] *Lewis v. Plunket* [1937] Ch. 306.

(e) *Liability for loss of deeds*

16–15 A mortgagee, whose mortgage includes the deeds, must be ready to give up the deeds when the debt is satisfied.[64] This duty arises from the fact that the deeds are part of the mortgaged property and the mortgagor is entitled to the return of the whole of his property.[65] Thus, a mortgagee's liability for loss of the deeds arises, not from breach of contract, nor from negligence as a bailee but from the breach of his duty to return the security of the mortgaged property. This being so, a mortgagor cannot fix the mortgagee with liability, except when he is offering to redeem. This somewhat questionable state of affairs arises as a result of the provisions of section 13 of the Law of Property Act 1925 which, in effect, preserves the principle of the pre-1926 law, which was that the mortgagee, being owner of the land, was also owner of the deeds and could not be liable for losing his own property.[66] During the currency of the security the mortgagor has, it is true, a right to inspect the deeds under section 96 of the Law of Property Act and presumably might be able to bring an action against the mortgagee for damages for breach of his statutory duty under that section but such damages could not include a sum for the permanent loss of the deeds.[67]

The loss of the deeds does not prevent a mortgagee from pursuing his remedies.[68] It only exposes him to an obligation to make compensation, should the mortgagor offer to redeem.[69] At one time the liability to make compensation was absolute, but now the court has jurisdiction to give relief in cases of accident. The practice appears to be as follows:

(1) When a mortgagor is prevented from redeeming by reason of the absence of the deeds, he has an absolute right to commence proceedings for redemption for the sole purpose of having an inquiry as to the loss of the deeds.[70] The object of the proceedings is to establish the fact of the loss in a way which will satisfy future purchasers from the mortgagor and the mortgagee will be made to bear the costs of the action. The offer of an indemnity is not enough; the master's inquiry is a protection to which the mortgagor is absolutely entitled.[71] The position is the same when redemption is forced upon the mortgagor in a foreclosure action.[72]

(2) If the master certifies that the loss was not due to any negligence or wilful default on the part of the mortgagee, the mortgagor is entitled only to an indemnity against future charges and expenses which may result from the absence of the deeds.[73]

---

[64] See *Schoole v. Sall* (1803) 1 Sch. & Lef. 176.

[65] See *Gilligan and Nugent v. National Bank* [1901] 2 I.R. 513.

[66] In the case of *Browning v. Handiland Group Ltd* (1976) 35 P. & C.R. 345 it was held that a mortgagee owed no duty of care in relation to the documents of title and thus the mortgagor was unable to recover the loss incurred when a projected sale failed as a result of the loss of the deeds.

[67] See *Gilligan and Nugent v. National Bank* [1901] 2 I.R. 513.

[68] *Baskett v. Skeel* (1863) 11 W.R. 1019.

[69] *Stokoe v. Robson* (1815) 19 Ves. 385.

[70] *James v. Rumsey* (1879) 11 Ch.D. 398.

[71] *Lord Midleton v. Eliot* (1847) 15 Sim. 531.

[72] *Stokoe v. Robson* (1815) 19 Ves. 385; *Shelmardine v. Harrop* (1821) 6 Madd. 39.

[73] *Shelmardine v. Harrop* (1821) 6 Madd. 39, where the mortgagee was robbed.

(3) If the loss is found to have been due to the negligence or other default of the mortgagee, the mortgagor is entitled both to an indemnity and to immediate compensation.[74] Compensation will cover the expense of procuring new copies of deeds where that is possible and of office-copies of any proceedings taken to establish the loss and, in addition, a sum by way of damages for future difficulties in proving title. This last is, however, confined to extra expense in proving title and may not include a speculative amount for possible depreciation of the market value of the estate caused by the lack of the deeds.[75]

(4) If the result of the inquiry is that the deeds are found not to be lost, but to be in the hands of a third party, the mortgagor will be directed to bring an action for their recovery, the expenses of the action to be debited to the mortgagee.[76]

(5) If a mortgagor has given notice to redeem and then been prevented from doing so owing to the loss of the deeds, interest ceases to run from that date when redemption was due to take place, even though he does not hand over his money. He cannot be expected to part with his money except in return for his whole security.[77]

RIGHT TO MAINTAIN THE SECURITY

1. **Rights with regard to title**

A mortgagee is entitled to take all steps necessary to perfect and protect his security and may debit the mortgagor with any costs or charges which he incurs thereby. Thus a legal mortgagee who discovers a defect in his title may call upon the mortgagor to remedy it if that becomes possible.[78] The rule is not, of course, confined to mortgages. "The doctrine of the Court of Chancery," said Cranworth L.C., in the case of *Smith v. Osborne*,[79] is "that if a man contracts to convey, or to mortgage, or to settle an estate, and he has not at the time of his contract a title to the estate, but he afterwards acquires such a title as enables him to perform his contract, he shall be bound to do so." On this principle an equitable mortgagee has a right to call for the execution of a legal mortgage and to charge the mortgagor with the costs of preparing it.[80] He may enforce this right, even though the mortgagor has begun proceedings for redemption.[81] Moreover, an equitable mortgagee who has begun proceedings for foreclosure may obtain an interim injunction to prevent dealings with the legal estate intended where there are grounds for believing that the mortgagor intends to do something improper with the legal estate.[82]

16–17

---

[74] *Hornby v. Matcham* (1848) 16 Sim. 325. For the form of the indemnity, see *Shelmardine, ante.*
[75] *ibid.*; *Brown v. Sewell* (1853) 11 Hare 49.
[76] *James v. Rumsey* (1879) 11 Ch.D. 398.
[77] *Lord Midleton v. Eliot* (1847) 15 Sim. 531; *James v. Rumsey* (1879) 11 Ch.D. 398.
[78] *Seabourne v. Powel* (1686) 2 Vern. 11.
[79] (1857) 6 H.L.C. 375 at 390.
[80] *National Provincial Bank of England v. Games* (1886) 31 Ch.D. 582.
[81] *Grugeon v. Gerrard* (1840) 4 Y. & C. (Ex.) 119.
[82] *London & County Banking Co. v. Lewis* (1882) 21 Ch.D. 490.

(a) *Rights with regard to title as against third parties*

16–18 A mortgagee may protect the security against third parties who impeach the mortgagor's title by claiming a title paramount; he may take any proceedings necessary to defend the mortgagor's title and may add the costs to the mortgage debt.[83] If the mortgage is equitable and a third party with inferior title proposes to dispose of the legal estate, an injunction will lie to restrain that party.[84] It is, however, necessary to distinguish carefully between cases where third parties are attacking or dealing vexatiously with the mortgagor's title and cases where the mortgagee's own title to the security is impeached by third parties. In the latter case the mortgagee must bear the cost of defending himself.[85] An unusual application of this rule occurred in the case of *Re Smith's Mortgage, Harrison v. Edwards*[86] in which a first mortgagee sold under his power of sale and realised a sufficient sum to provide something for the second mortgagee. The mortgagor, however, impeached the sale and the first mortgagee incurred costs in establishing its validity. He was not, as against the second mortgagee, allowed to add these costs to his mortgage debt, for he was defending himself rather than the title to the mortgaged property. In *Parker-Tweedale v. Dunbar (No. 2)*,[87] the Court of Appeal denied a mortgagee his costs out of the security in an action where a third party impugned the mortgagee's title to the mortgage even where the costs had been reasonably and necessarily incurred and the third party was interested in the equity of redemption.

2. Right to preserve the substance of the security

(a) *As against the mortgagor*

16–19 A mortgagee is also entitled to preserve the substance of his security. A legal mortgagee is to a large extent able to protect his security against the acts of the mortgagor by reason of his legal ownership, but every mortgagee, legal or equitable has a general right in equity, as against the mortgagor, to hold the security undiminished in value.[88] Thus, if a mortgagor is wasting the security by cutting timber,[89] or by removing fixtures included in the security,[90] he may be restrained from doing so, provided that the security is shown to be insufficient. But even when the mortgagor's acts do not amount to waste, they may be restrained if it be shown that the security is insufficient and will be prejudiced.

---

[83] *Sandon v. Hooper* (1843) 6 Beav. 246, on appeal (1844) 14 L.J.Ch. 120, L.C.
[84] *London & County Bank Co. v. Lewis* (1882) 21 Ch.D 490.
[85] *Parker v. Watkins* (1859) John 133; *Parker v. Tweedale v. Dunbar Bank plc (No. 2)* [1991] Ch. 26. But where beneficiaries seek, unsuccessfully, to impeach a mortgage by the trustees, the mortgagee is a party, the mortgagee will (apparently) be permitted his costs; *Laughton v. Laughton* (1855) 6 De G.M. & G. 30.
[86] [1931] 2 Ch. 168.
[87] [1991] Ch. 26, CA.
[88] *McMahon v. North Kent Iron Works Co.* [1891] 2 Ch. 148, where the mortgage debt was not even yet due.
[89] *Harper v. Aplin* (1886) 54 L.T. 383.
[90] *Ackroyd v. Mitchell* (1860) 3 L.T. 236; *Ellis v. Glover and Hobson, Ltd* [1908] 1 K.B. 388.

For example, mortgagors of tolls were restrained from reducing the toll fees, the security being insufficient.[91]

(i) Other causes

A mortgagee may similarly interfere to prevent depreciation of the security from **16–20** other causes. He may, for example, restrain by injunction a subsequent incumbrancer from dealing with the property to his prejudice.[92] If the mortgage comprises licensed premises, he may take part in proceedings to obtain the renewal of the licence.[93] Again, in a case where part of the mortgagee's security was taken under the Land Clauses Acts, he was entitled to be served with notices, and even to claim compensation for "injurious affection" of other lands.[94] Also, where the property is to be compulsorily acquired, the mortgagee as well as the mortgagor is entitled to be served with the notice to treat.[95] Other examples arise in the cases where a mortgagee is entitled to take possession of the property in order to prevent deterioration of his security by vandalism[96] or to prevent injury to the property,[97] or to enforce a restrictive covenant.[98]

(b) As against other persons

A mortgagee's right to take proceedings in respect of damage done to the mortgaged property by third parties largely depends on his title. If he is a legal mortgagee, or if his contract gives him a right, he may go into possession and avail himself of all possessory remedies. He may sue for trespass and, whether his mortgage is legal or equitable, the doctrine of trespass by relation back applies to enable him to sue for trespasses committed before his entry.[99] In relation to tenancies created on or after January 1, 1996, a mortgagee in possession can enforce any covenant or right of re-entry that the mortgagor could have enforced.[1] A mortgagee of goods, if he is in possession or has an immediate right to possession, may bring an action in trespass or conversion or seek the recovery of the goods under the provisions of the Torts (Interference with Goods) Act 1977.[2] However, if the mortgagee under the terms of the mortgage is not able either expressly or impliedly to obtain possession until the occurrence of a certain event, for example, a demand for payment on default, proceedings cannot be

---

[91] *Lord Crewe v. Edleston* (1857) 1 De G. & J. 93; *cf. Re Humber Ironworks Co.* (1868) 16 W.R. 667.
[92] *Legg v. Mathieson* (1860) 2 Giff. 71 where a judgment creditor had been restrained at the suit of the prior mortgagee, even before the mortgage debt had become due, from taking possession of the property under the legal right acquired by the former elegit.
[93] *e.g.* he can appeal to the Crown Court against non-renewal of the licence, see *Garrett v. St. Marylebone, Middlesex JJ.* (1884) 12 Q.B.D. 620.
[94] *R. v. Clerk of the Peace for Middlesex* [1914] 3 K.B. 259.
[95] *Cooke v. L.C.C.* [1911] 1 Ch. 604.
[96] See *Western Bank Ltd v. Shindler* [1977] Ch. 1.
[97] *Matthews v. Usher* [1900] 2 Q.B 535 at 538; *Turner v. Walsh* [1909] 2 K.B. 484 at 487.
[98] *Fairclough v. Marshall* (1878) 4 Ex.D. 37.
[99] *Ocean Accident and Guarantee Corporation v. Ilford Gas Co.* [1905] 2 K.B. 493.
[1] Landlord and Tenants (Covenants) Act 1995, ss.3–15.
[2] But for the recovery of title deeds themselves no action will lie under the 1977 Act.

commenced unless and until the event has occurred.[3] A different picture emerges, however, in the case of an equitable mortgagee. He may stipulate for a right to possession in his contract, but otherwise he can have no right to possession without first enforcing his contract for a legal mortgage.

Although a mortgagee may thus be able to protect his security against third parties, it is not often necessary for him to do so. As a rule, the protection of the property is as much in the interests of the mortgagor as of the mortgagee and action is usually taken by the mortgagor, the mortgagee only being joined as a party where that is necessary.[4] A mortgagor in possession has by virtue of his possession and of the rights given to him in equity and statute, a wide power to take proceedings in defence of the mortgaged property.[5] It is generally only when the mortgagor refuses or is unable to take action that the mortgagee will find it necessary to assert his own rights.[6]

3. Mortgagee's right to relief from forfeiture of leasehold security[7]

16–21   A mortgagee by sub-demise or a mortgagee by way of legal charge[8] is entitled to claim relief from forfeiture under section 146(4) of the Law of Property Act 1925 in the same way as if he were an under-lessee.[9] This right exists where the mortgagee simply has a specifically enforceable right to the creation of a legal charge or mortgage.[10] A mortgagee can even apply for relief pursuant to section 146(4) in circumstances where the lease has been disclaimed by a trustee in bankruptcy of the tenant.[11]

An equitable chargee is not entitled to relief under section 146(4) the Law of Property Act 1925 in circumstances where the lessor has already obtained peaceable re-entry notwithstanding that the charge is registered under the Land Charges Act 1972.[12] However, there is a conflict in the authorities in that it has been held that an equitable chargee holding under a charging order is a mortgagee for the purposes of the subsection.[13]

---

[3] *Bradley v. Copley* (1845) 1 C.B. 685; a future right to possession is not of course enough, so that a mortgagee cannot sue if he has covenanted to give the mortgagor possession until default: *ibid. cf. White v. Morris* (1852) 11 C.B. 1015, where the mortgagee was allowed to sue when he was a *trustee* to give the mortgagor possession.

[4] See *Van Gelder, Apsimon & Co. v. Sowerby Bridge United District Flour Society* (1890) 44 Ch.D. 374. But see in the case of leasehold interests the mortgagee's right to seek relief from forfeiture under the court's inherent jurisdiction or pursuant to statute, *e.g.* s.146(4) of the LPA 1925 *ante*, para. 6–03 *et seq.* and *post*, para. 16–21.

[5] See the LPA 1925, ss.98 and 141(2).

[6] *e.g.* this may arise in the case where the mortgagee wishes to seek relief from forfeiture under LPA 1925, s.146(4); see *ante*, para. 6–03 *et seq.*

[7] See generally *Woodfall, Landlord & Tenant*, paras 17.057–17.178 and see *ante*, para. 6–03 *et seq.*

[8] *Grand Junction Co. Limited v. Bates* [1954] 2 Q.B. 160; *Belgravia Insurance Co. Limited v. Meah* (1964) 1 Q.B. 436.

[9] *Chelsea Estates Investment Trust Co. v. Marche* (1955) Ch. 328.

[10] *Re Good's Lease* [1954] 1 W.L.R. 309.

[11] *Barclays Bank Plc v. Prudential Assurance* [1998] 1 E.G.L.R. 44.

[12] *Bland v. Ingrams Estates* [1999] 2 E.G.L.R. 49.

[13] *Ladup v. William and Glynn's Bank plc* [1985] 1 W.L.R. 851; *Croydon (Unique) Ltd v. Wright* [1999] 4 All E.R. 257. An equitable chargee can obtain relief in reliance on the implied obligation of the equitable chargor to preserve the charged security: *Bland v. Ingram's Estates Ltd* [2001] 24 E.G. 163.

RIGHT TO ENTER INTO POSSESSION

The legal title which he obtains by his conveyance gives to a legal mortgagee[14]   **16–22**
the immediate right to commence an action for possession of the mortgaged
security subject to any agreement to the contrary. Normally, the right arises at
once on the execution of the conveyance and is based upon the legal estate or
interest which the mortgagee acquires in the property as a result of the mortgage.[15] Once the right has arisen, the court will not by injunction restrain the
mortgagee from exercising his right.[16] This is so even if there has been no default
on the part of the mortgagor[17] or that a bill of exchange has been given for the
debt[18] or that a considerable time has elapsed, provided that the action for
possession is not statute-barred.[19] Alternatively, the mortgagee can enter into
receipt of the rent and profits by serving notice on the tenant to pay their rents to
himself instead of to the mortgagor.[20]

1. Qualifications and restrictions on the right to enter into possession

The right of the mortgagee to enter into possession of the mortgaged property[21]   **16–23**
is subject to a number of qualifications and restrictions.

> (1) As indicated above, the mortgage deed itself may contain an express
> term under which the mortgagee contracts out of his right to possession
> of the property for a given term, provided that the mortgagor maintains
> the repayments due under the mortgage. This may amount to a rede-
> mise or merely to a personal covenant by the mortgagee not to interfere
> with the mortagor's enjoyment.[22]
>
> (2) An agreement restricting the mortgagee's right may be implied into the   **16–24**
> mortgage deed to the effect that the mortgagee has surrendered his
> right to take immediate possession of the property. In the absence of an
> express term it is clear that the court will not lightly restrict the

---

[14] A chargee by way of legal mortgage has a corresponding statutory right by virtue of s.87(1) of the
LPA 1925, and see *ante*, para. 3–42.

[15] " ... before the ink is dry on the mortgage ... ", *per* Harman J. in *Four-Maids Ltd v. Dudley
Marshall (Properties) Ltd* [1957] Ch. 317 at 320; *Westminster City Council v. Haymarket Publishing Ltd* [1981] 1 W.L.R. 677 at 696. See also *Alliance Perpetual Building Society v. Belrum
Investments* [1957] 1 W.L.R. 720; *Western Bank Ltd v. Shindler* [1977] Ch. 1; *Mobil Oil Co. Ltd
v. Rawlinson* (1982) 43 P. & C.R. 221.

[16] *Marquis of Cholmondeley v. Lord Clinton* (1820) 2 J. & W. 1 at 181; this, of course, is one of the
points of difference between mortgagees and trustees. See also *London Permanent Benefit Building
Society v. De Baer* [1969] 1 Ch. 321.

[17] *Birch v. Wright* (1786) 1 T.R. 378 at 383; *Four-Maids Ltd v. Dudley Marshall (Properties) Ltd*
[1957] Ch. 317; see *Rogers v. Grazebrook* (1846) 8 Q.B. 895. But see *post*, para. 16–23 *et seq*.

[18] *Bramwell v. Eglington* (1864) 5 B. & S. 39.

[19] *Wright v. Pepin* [1954] 1 W.L.R. 635.

[20] See *post*, para. 16–26. See also *Horlock v. Smith* (1842) 6 Jur. 478; or merely not to pay the rent
to the mortgagor, *Heales v. M'Murray* (1856) 23 Beav. 401; see also *Kitchen's Trustee v. Madders
and Madders* [1949] Ch. 588. Affd. [1950] Ch. 134; *Mexborough U.D.C. v. Harrison* [1964] 1
W.L.R. 733 at 736, 737.

[21] A right which he has at common law and which is not affected by s.36 of the Administration of
Justice Act 1970 in relation to an unoccupied dwelling-house; *Ropaigealach v. Barclays Bank*
[1999] 3 W.L.R. 17.

[22] *Wilkinson v. Hall* (1837) 3 Bing. N.C. 508; *Doe d. Parsley v. Day* (1842) 2 Q.B. 147. Such
contractual restrictions are not common.

mortgagee's right and it has shown considerable reluctance to do so.[23] It would seem that the court will more readily imply such a term in circumstances where the principal moneys are repayable by instalments which is usual in building society (and bank) mortgages.[24] Once there has been a default, however, on the part of the mortgagor, a term restricting the mortgagee's right to possession, whether express or implied, ceases to operate whilst the default continues to occur. Then the mortgagee must take into account a number of the following factors before going into possession of the security:

(a) If a security is land which is already let on a lease binding on the mortgagee, either by reason of the fact that the lease was made prior to the creation of the mortgage, or it is a subsequent lease binding upon him, the mortgagee cannot physically go into possession. However, he can enter into receipt of the rents and profits by serving notice on the tenants to pay their rents to himself instead of to the mortgagor.[25]

(b) If the mortgagee desires to seek possession of the premises it is usually advisable to do so by means of court proceedings and not by physically taking possession although at common law he has the right to do so. This is especially so if the mortgage deed contains an attornment clause (for the relationship of landlord and tenant is created during the continuance of the security)[26] or if a dwelling-house is the subject of the mortgage in question. If a mortgagee attempts to re-enter premises he *may* be guilty of an offence under the Criminal Law Act 1977.[27] In the case of a dwelling-house an unlawful eviction of a residential occupier *may* also be a criminal offence pursuant to the provisions of the Protection from Eviction Act 1977.[28] However, if the premises are vacant or have been abandoned by the mortgagor and the mortgagee has reasonable cause to believe that the residential occupier has ceased to reside therein, or the mortgagor has consented to the taking of possession, then the mortgagee can take possession. Further, if there is an attornment clause it must be remembered that as the *substance* of the transaction is that of a mortgage, in relation to which the attornment clause plays an ancillary part, the tenancy is outside the protection of the Rent Act 1977, the Protection from Eviction Act 1977, the Agricultural Holdings Act 1986 and the Agricultural

---

[23] See *Esso Petroleum Co. Ltd v. Alstonbridge Properties Ltd* [1975] 1 W.L.R. 1474; *Western Bank Ltd v. Shindler* [1977] Ch. 1. See [1979] Conv. 266 (R. J. Smith).

[24] See *Birmingham Citizens Permanent Building Society v. Caunt* [1962] Ch. 883.

[25] See *post*, para. 16–26 *et seq*.

[26] See *Regent Oil Co. Ltd v. J.A. Gregory (Hatch End) Ltd* [1966] Ch. 402. See also *ante*, para. 3–36. Such clauses are now rare.

[27] *i.e.* of using violence to secure entry, see s.6 (replacing the Forcible Entry Acts 1381–1623, s.13). By virtue of s.6(2) it is no defence that the mortgagee is entitled to possession of the premises.

[28] See ss.2, 3. But there is nothing contained in the Act which affects the jurisdiction of the High Court in possession proceedings in a case where the former tenancy was not binding on the mortgagee (s.9(3)); and see *Bolton Building Society v. Cobb* [1965] 1 W.L.R. 1. See also *Midland Bank Ltd v. Monobond* [1971] E.G.D. 673 and *London Goldhawk Building Society v. Eminer* (1977) 242 E.G. 462.

Tenancies Act 1995.[29] Also, unless the attornment clause so provides, there is normally no need for the mortgagee to serve a notice to quit or a demand for possession on the mortgagor.[30]

(c) In the case of a mortgage which secures a regulated agreement under the Consumer Credit Act 1974, it is only enforceable pursuant to an order of the court.[31]

(3) Another way in which a mortgagee may find his desire to go into possession obstructed is by the fact that a receiver has already beeen appointed by the court at the instance of a third party. In such a case he cannot enter into possession unless his right to do so was specially reserved by the court in the order appointing the receiver. His proper course is, either to apply to the court for the discharge of the receiver or for leave to bring an action for the recovery of the land.[32] If the mortgagee is prevented from exercising his right by the mortgagor he may bring an action to eject the mortgagor.[33]   **16–24A**

(4) A practical factor which tends to inhibit the exercise of the mortgagee's right to possession is the strict liability to account which is placed upon a mortgagee in possession. He is liable to account strictly "on the footing of wilful default." This means that he must account not only for such sums as he actually does receive but also for all that he ought to have received had he managed the property with due diligence.[34]

(5) A mortgagee cannot obtain a possession order where the property in question is subject to an overriding interest under section 70(1) of the Land Registration Act 1925.[35] By analogy, the claim to an overriding interest by the occupiers of the mortgaged property may inhibit the mortgagee's entry into possession if the mortgagor or some other person claiming a beneficial interest in the property seeks to restrain the mortgagee from taking possession.

(6) A court will not grant an order for possession as against one joint-mortgagor if the other mortgagor is in possession and has an arguable defence,[36] *a fortiori*, if they are husband and wife.[37]

---

[29] Except possibly in the case where there was a full rack rent or the mortgagor was required to reside in the premises: see *Portman Building Society v. Young* [1951] 1 All E.R. 191; *Alliance Building Society v. Pinwill* [1958] Ch. 788; *Peckham Mutual Building Society v. Registe* (1980) 42 P. & C.R. 186 *Steyning and Littlehampton B.S. v. Wilson* [1951] Ch. 1018 and see *ante*, para. 3–36.

[30] *Hinkley Building Society v. Henny* [1953] 1 W.L.R. 352. As the status of the mortgagor in possession has been likened to that of a tenant at sufferance who can be ejected without any possession, (see further *ante*, para. 3–36), and *post*, para. 17–13 *et seq.*

[31] s.126. See also Goode, *Consumer Credit Law & Practice*, and see generally *ante* chap. 14 *et seq.* and *post*, para. 16–87.

[32] *Thomas v. Brigstocke* (1827) 4 Russ. 64.

[33] *Doe d. Roby v. Maisey* (1828) 8 B. & C. 767.

[34] *Chaplin v. Young (No. 1)* (1864) 33 Beav. 330. at 337, 338. See also *White v. City of London Brewery Co.* (1889) 42 Ch.D. 237 and *Shepherd v. Spansheath* (1988) E.G.C.S. 35; and further *post*, para. 16–31 *et seq.*

[35] See *Williams & Glyn's Bank Ltd v. Boland* [1981] A.C. 487 except where such overriding interests have been overreached. *City of London Building Society v. Flegg* [1988] A.C. 54; see *post*, para. 20–41.

[36] *Albany Home Loans Ltd v. Massey* [1997] 2 All E.R. 609.

[37] *ibid.*

(7) Reference should also be made to the court's general discretion and its specific statutory discretion to grant a stay in a possession action brought by a mortgagee.[38]

2. What amounts to possession

16–25 Where a mortgagee is in personal occupation of land or has obtained actual possession of chattels, his possession is beyond argument. But when his alleged entry into possession consists merely of some interference with the mortgaged property it may be doubtful whether or not his acts amount to a taking of possession. Nor is this an academic question, for a mortgagee by entering into possession renders himself liable to account to the mortgagor with considerable strictness for the profits which he has received while in possession.[39] Indeed, for this reason the court will not readily hold a mortgagee to be in possession, unless it is clearly established that such was his position[40] by, for example, giving tenants notice to pay rent to him.[41] In the case of *Noyes v. Pollock*[42] the Court of Appeal ruled that to be in possession a mortgagee must have so far interfered with the mortgaged property as to take over its control and management. The mortgagee's receipt of certain rents, even by cheques made out by the tenants themselves, was there held not to be enough for it was not shown that he had taken over the power of management.[43] Similarly a mortgagee does not, by foreclosing, render himself liable to account as the mortgagee in possession if the foreclosure is reopened: he must have gone on to control and manage the property, *e.g.* by giving notice that rent should be paid to him and not the mortgagor.[44] Moreover, even when a mortgagee is admittedly in possession, it must also be shown that he took possession in his capacity as mortgagee without reasonable grounds for believing himself to hold in another capacity.[45] A mortgagee who is in possession as tenant[46] to the mortgagor, or as a life-tenant,[47] or as a purchaser[48] under a sale which turns out to be invalid, cannot be called on to account as a mortgagee in possession, for his possession does not rest on his character as mortgagee. A similar position arose where possession was taken under a forfeiture and not as a mortgagee.[49] On the other hand, once a mortgagee has entered into possssion as mortgagee and taken upon himself the burden which is

---

[38] See *post*, para. 16–84 *et seq.*

[39] See *post*, para. 16–33.

[40] *Gaskell v. Gosling* [1896] 1 Q.B. 669.

[41] *Honlock v. Smith* (1842) 11 L.J. Ch. 157.

[42] (1886) 32 Ch.D. 53; but see *Mexborough Urban District Council v. Harrison* [1964] 1 W.L.R. 733 at 736, 737, where the mortgagee gave notice to the tenants not to pay rent to the mortgagor.

[43] *Contra* the positions where the mortgagee gives notice to the tenants to pay their rents to him, see *Horlock v. Smith* (1842) 11 L.J.Ch. 157. See also *Ward v. Carttar* (1865) L.R. 1 Eq. 29 where in the absence of the tenants recognising the mortgagee as landlord, the mortgagee's acts of insuring the premises were held not to amount to possession.

[44] *Re Loom, Fulford v. Reversionary Interest Society Ltd* (1910) 2 Ch.D. 230.

[45] *Parkinson v. Hanbury* (1867) L.R. 2 H.L. 1; *Gaskell v. Gosling* [1896] 1 Q.B. 609 at 691; *Page v. Linwood* (1837) 4 Cl. & Finn. 399.

[46] *Page v. Linwood* (1837) 4 Cl. & Finn. 399, *qua* tenant.

[47] *Lord Kensington v. Bouverie* (1855) 7 De G.M. & G. 156; see also *Whitbread v. Smith* (1854) 3 De G.M. & G. 727.

[48] *Parkinson v. Hanbury* (1867) L.R. 2 H.L. 1.

[49] *Blennerhassett v. Day* (1812) 2 Ball & B. 104 at 125.

imposed on all mortgagees who are in possession, he must continue to perform the duty and he cannot, when he pleases, elect to give it up. Nor, in the absence of special circumstances, will the court assist him to give it up by appointing a receiver under an express or statutory power.[50]

Where the mortgaged property has a bounded and defined area, entry on to part will be regarded as entry on the whole.[51] However, the mortgagee may limit his possession to part only so as not to render himself liable for default in respect of that part still occupied by the mortgagor.[52]

3. Rights of a mortgagee in possession

(a) *Right to receive rents and profits*

As long as the mortgagor remains in possession,[53] he is entitled to take all the profits from the security without being in any way obliged either to account for them or to apply them in discharging the mortgage interest.[54] However, equally, once the mortgagee goes into possession he is entitled to take the rents and profits by virtue of his legal or equitable ownership conferred upon him by the mortgage[55] and to account for the same.   **16–26**

On such entry into possession the mortgagee is entitled to the rents and profits in respect of any tenancies created before the mortgage or otherwise binding upon the mortgagee under an express or statutory power.[56] This may involve the requirement on the part of the mortgagee to have paid to himself all arrears of rent existing on entry into possession.[57] He may even claim an increased rent despite the fact that the agreement relating to such increase was made after the date of the mortgage.[58]

Where there is in existence a tenancy which is not binding on the mortgagee by virtue of the fact that it has been created after the mortgage and was not pursuant to any express or statutory power,[59] there is no contractual nexus between the tenant and the mortgagee, and thus the mortgagee is not entitled to demand payment of the rents as such from the tenant. However, after notice from the mortgagee the tenant should thereafter pay the rent to the mortgagee and not the mortgagor, since on recovery of possession the mortgagor would be entitled to recover the rents from the tenant as puisne profits.[60] Further, on entry by the

---

[50] *Re Prytherch, Prytherch v. Williams* (1889) 42 Ch.D. 590; *County of Gloucester Bank v. Rudry Merthyr Colliery Co.* [1895] 1 Ch. 629; but the mortgagee may relieve himself by appointing a receiver under an express or statutory power—see *Refuge Assurance Co. v. Pearlberg* [1938] Ch. 687. See also *post*, para. 16–43 as to the mortgagee's statutory power.

[51] *Low Moor Co. v. Stanley Coal Co. Ltd* (1876) 34 L.T. 186, CA.

[52] *Soar v. Dalby* (1852) 15 Beav. 156; *Simmins v. Shirley* (1877) 6 Ch.D. 173.

[53] See *ante*, para. 16–22 *et seq.*

[54] *Trent v. Hunt* (1853) 9 Exch. 14.

[55] *Cockburn v. Edwards* (1881) 18 Ch.D. 449 at 457; see LPA 1925, s.141 as amended and disapplied to *post* 1995 tenancies by the Landlord and Tenant (Covenants) Act 1995.

[56] *ibid.*

[57] *Moss v. Gallimore* (1779) 1 Doug. K.B. 279; *Rogers v. Humphreys* (1835) 4 Ad. & El. 299 at 314.

[58] *Burrowes v. Gradin* (1843) 1 Dow. & L. 213.

[59] See *ante*, para. 3–33 and *post*, para. 19–03.

[60] *Pope v. Biggs* (1829) 9 B. & C. 245 at 257; *Underhay v. Read* (1887) 20 Q.B.D. 209; and see *Rusden v. Pope* (1868) L.R. 3 Exch. 269 at 275.

mortgagee his possession relates back to the date of the mortgage and he is able to recover any accrued sums in respect of rent due within six years prior to his entry.[61] This position applies despite the fact that strictly the action for recovery of puisne profits is an action in trespass which normally requires the person claiming the sums due to have been in possession during that time.[62]

Although, generally, the mortgagee will be able to recover from the tenant the accrued rents due within six years prior to his entry or commencement of any action brought by him, he can only recover those rents which the tenant had failed to pay to the mortgagor. If the tenant had paid rent to the mortgagor in advance and before it was due, this does not constitute a good payment against the mortgagee in respect of those sums accruing due after notice of the mortgage has been given to the tenant and the tenant is liable to pay those sums over again to the mortgagee.[63]

A mortgagee's object in going into possession is to intercept the profits from the mortgaged property, and to utilise them for the discharge of his claims under the mortgage. Thus, after paying any outgoings, such as rents, rates and taxes, insurance premiums, etc., he may apply the profits to the payment of his interest on the mortgage debt, on the expense of improvements and then, if he so desires, to the reduction of the capital account.[64]

(b) *Right to enforce leasehold covenants*[65]

16–27   At common law, a mortgagee of a leasehold interest does not enjoy privity of estate with the lessor since the mortgage from which he derives title is effected by way of sub-demise or by means of a legal charge which has the same effect.[66] Consequently, the mortgagee has, in his capacity solely as mortgagee, no right to require the lessor to perform any of the covenants into which the lessor may have entered with the mortgagor.

Prior to January 1, 1996, statute permitted a mortgagee of a reversionary interest expectant on a term granted by lease could enforce and take advantage of covenants referable to the subject-matter of the lease and any rights of re-entry.[67] A mortgagee of the reversion could re-enter demised premises for breaches of covenant committed prior to the mortgage unless they had been waived or released.[68] A mortgagee in possession of leasehold premises was

---

[61] *Barnett v. Earl of Guildford* (1855) 11 Exch. 19; *Ocean Accident & Guarantee Corp. Ltd v. Ilford Gas Co.* [1905] 2 K.B. 493 at 498; and see Limitation Act 1980, s.19.

[62] See *Turner v. Cameron's Coalbrook Steam Coal Co.* (1850) 5 Exch. 932; see also *Wheeler v. Montefiore* (1841) 2 Q.B. 133.

[63] *De Nicholls v. Saunders* (1870) L.R. 5 C.P. 589; *Cook v. Guerra* (1872) L.R. 7 C.P. 132; *Lord Ashburton v. Knocton* [1915] 1 Ch. 274 at 282; *Smallmas Ltd v. Castle* [1932] I.R. 294. *Contra* the position where the tenant has paid a lump sum in satisfaction of all rents accruing during the term and no inquiry of the tenant is made by the mortgagee, he is bound by such payment. See *Green v. Rheinberg* (1911) 104 L.T. 149; *Grace Rymer Investments Ltd v. Waite* [1958] Ch. 831 at 847.

[64] *Re Knight, ex p. Isherwood* (1882) 22 Ch.D. 384; *Re Coaks, Coaks v. Bayley* [1911] Ch. 171.

[65] For a mortgagee's liability with regard to leasehold covenants, see *post*, para. 16–39.

[66] Law of Property Act 1925, ss.86 and 87.

[67] Law of Property Act 1925, s.141(1).

[68] *ibid.*, s.141(3).

entitled to the benefits of covenants by the lessor which "touch and concern" the demised premises.[69]

This position has changed[70] with regard to tenancies created on or after January 1, 1996. Thereafter, a mortgagee or chargee in possession of a leasehold interest pursuant to a mortgage or charge granted by the lessee may enforce any covenant which falls to be performed by the lessor unless it is either stated to be personal to any particular individual or would not be enforceable for want of registration.[71] A mortgagee or chargee in possession of premises subject to leasehold interest granted on or after the relevant date can enforce any covenant falling to be complied with by the lessee or any right of re-entry which is enforceable by the mortgagor.[72]

(c) *Right to carry on business*

A mortgagee in possession has full powers to manage the mortgaged property. In the case of business premises the mortgagee may carry on the business for a reasonable time with a view to its sale as a going concern and, for such purpose, he is able to use the name of the firm to do so.[73] Where there is a mortgage of a business as a going concern, the mortgagee in possession is entitled to be recouped in respect of any losses incurred without negligence in carrying it on out of the proceeds of sale.[74] If the mortgage includes the goodwill of the business of a publican, the mortgagee on taking possession is entitled to call upon the mortgagor to concur in obtaining a transfer to the mortgagee of the existing licence.[75] Once the mortgagee enters into possession of the business, he, in effect, becomes the owner of the business and stands in the mortgagor's place,[76] but he does not render himself liable on the existing contracts of the business unless they are specifically adopted so as to effect a novation. It would also seem that the fact that a mortgagee takes possession of a business does not of itself operate as a dismissal of the employees employed in that business.[77] Other contractual and statutory provisions might apply, however, and reference should be made to standard works on employment law and transfer of undertakings, *e.g.* Transfer of Undertakings (Protection of Employment) Regulations 1981.[78]

16–28

(d) *Right to emblements*[79]

A mortgagee entering into possession of agricultural land is entitled as against the mortgagor or his trustee in bankruptcy to emblements[80] and the mortgagor is

16–29

---

[69] *Spencer's Case* (1583) 5 Co. Rep. 16a; Law of Property Act 1925, s.78.
[70] See the Landlord & Tenant (Covenants) Act 1995, s.15.
[71] *ibid.*, s.15(5).
[72] *ibid.*, s.15(1).
[73] *Cook v. Thomas* (1876) 24 W.R. 427.
[74] *Bompas v. King* (1886) 33 Ch.D. 279.
[75] *Rutter v. Daniel* (1882) 30 W.R. 801.
[76] *Chaplin v. Young (No. 1)* (1864) 33 Beav. 330 at 337.
[77] *per* Fry L.J. in *Reid v. Explosives Co.* (1887) 19 Q.B.D. 264 at 267, 269.
[78] S.I. 1981 No. 1794, as amended.
[79] The growing crops of those plants which are produced by annual cultivation.
[80] *Keech v. Hall* (1778) 1 Doug. K.B. 21.

not so entitled.[81] The mortgagee on entering into possession is entitled to all the growing crops and the mortgagor, or any person claiming under him, such as his trustee in bankruptcy, may be restrained by injunction from cutting and removing crops on the mortgaged land.[82] However, if the mortgagee has not taken possession of the mortgaged property before the mortgagor's bankruptcy, and the crops had been cut or removed before the bankruptcy, such action converts the crops into personal chattels so that they belong to the mortgagor's trustee in bankruptcy.[83] Further, in the case of an agricultural holding which is occupied under a tenancy not binding on the mortgagee, then the tenant is, as against the mortgagee who takes possession, entitled to any compensation which would otherwise be due to him from the mortgagor with regard to crops, improvements, tillages or other matters connected with the holding pursuant to the provisions of the Agricultural Holdings Act 1986.[84]

(e) *Right to grant and surrender leases*[85]

16–30   This is dealt with under the section entitled "rights common to both parties."

4. **Liabilities of a mortgagee in possession**

(a) *Liability to account*

16–31   A mortgagee, by taking possession becomes the manager of the property in which the beneficial interest still belongs to the mortgagor.[86] In consequence, he has certain duties to the mortgagor. Thus, he is bound to be diligent in collecting the rents and profits and will have to give the mortgagor credit not only for the rents and profits which he actually receives, but also for the rents and profits which, but for his own gross negligence or wilful default, he might have received.[87] This basis of account applies whether the mortgaged property is tangible or intangible and it appears to extend to the mortgagee's receipt (or otherwise) of the rent and profits of land, the profits of a business[88] and the profits of selling and purchasing of stock which is mortgaged.[89] However, although a

---

[81] *Birch v. Wright* (1786) 1 Trn. Rep. 378 at 383; *Moss v. Gallimore* (1779) 1 Doug. K.B. 279 at 283.

[82] *Bagnall v. Villar* (1879) 12 Ch.D. 812.

[83] *Re Phillips, ex p. National Mercantile Bank* (1880) 16 Ch.D. 104.

[84] See Agricultural Holdings Act 1986, s.60; see also *Lloyds Bank Ltd v. Marcan* [1973] 1 W.L.R. 1387. As for tenancies created on or after September 1, 1995, see generally Part III of the Agricultural Tenancies Act 1995; Muir, Watt & Moss, *Agricultural Holdings* (14th ed., 1998), chap. 5.

[85] See *post*, chap. 19 *et seq.*

[86] See *Noyes v. Pollock* (1886) 32 Ch.D. 53.

[87] *Hughes v. Williams* (1806) 12 Ves. 493. *Parkinson v. Hanbury* (1867) L.R. 2 H.L. 1; see also *Chaplin v. Young (No. 1)* (1864) 33 Beav. 330. A mortgagee must utilise the usual means to recover any arrears of rent if those means may prove effectual; *Duke of Buckingham v. Gayer* (1684) 1 Vern. 258.

[88] *Chaplin v. Young* (1864) 33 Beav. 330 but not those which do not arise from the premises, see *White v. City of London Brewery Co.* (1889) 42 Ch.D. 237.

[89] *Langton v. Waite* (1868) L.R. 6 Eq. 165; reversed on another point on appeal (1869) 4 Ch. App. 402.

mortgagee is bound to be diligent, he is not bound to speculate with the mortgaged property and if he does, he must himself bear the losses.[90] The duty arises when the mortgagee enters into possession *qua* mortgagee[91] and not in another capacity, such as *qua* tenant.[92]

(b) *When the duty arises*

The mortgagee may enter into possession of the property in order to protect his **16–32** security,[93] in which case he is not liable to account for any notional rent where sale is contemplated within a reasonable period.[94] More frequently however, the mortgagee's object in going into possession is either to sell the property or to intercept the net rents and profits therefrom and to utilise them for the discharge of his claims under the mortgage. After paying any outgoings, he may apply the profits to the payment of his interest, and, if he so desires, to the reduction of the capital account. But a mortgagee cannot, however, be made to accept the return of his capital in instalments,[95] so that if the profits are more than sufficient to meet the interest, he need not apply the surplus in reduction of capital. He may hand over the surplus to the mortgagor, unless he has received notice from a later incumbrancer to divert it to him.[96] If, however, he retains the surplus in his own hands, as he is fully entitled to do, he will have to account for it when the final accounts are taken.[97] The question may then arise whether, by so doing, he is to be held to have gradually reduced the capital indebtedness of the mortgagor, and correspondingly his own claim for interest.

As a mortgagee cannot be made to accept payment by instalments, he cannot be compelled to account until either he attempts to realise his security or the mortgagor seeks to redeem.[98] It makes no difference that the mortgagee is in possession. He cannot be made to render periodical accounts. When the time comes for the mortgage account to be taken, the fact that the mortgagee has been in possession does considerably affect the terms of the order directing the account. The special nature of the account arises from the fact that the mortgagee has in his own interest assumed control over property which, beneficially, does not belong to him.[99]

(c) *Basis of the account*[1]

The first principle of the account is that the mortgagee is entitled to have nothing **16–33** from the property except his security. He cannot, by going into possession, make

---

[90] *Hughes v. Williams* (1806) 12 Ves. 493. See also *Shepherd v. Spansheath* (1988) E.G. C.S. 35.
[91] *Parkinson v. Hanbury* (1867) L.R. 2 H.L. 1 at 14.
[92] *Page v. Linwood* (1837) 4 Cl. & Fin 399.
[93] See, *e.g. Western Bank Ltd v. Shindler* [1977] Ch. 1.
[94] *Norwich General Trust v. Grierson* [1984] C.L.Y. 2306; see also Law Commission Working Paper No. 99: *Land Mortgages* (1986) para. 3.25.
[95] *Nelson v. Booth* (1858) 3 De G. & J. 119 at 122; *Wrigley v. Gill* [1906] 1 Ch. 165.
[96] If notice is received and the monies paid instead to the mortgagor, the mortgagee is liable to account to the subsequent incumbrance: *Bernsey v. Sewell* (1820) 1 Jac. W. 647 at 650.
[97] See generally chap. 25.
[98] See *Tasker v. Small* (1837) 3 My. & Cr. 63.
[99] *Eyre v. Hughes* (1876) 2 Ch.D. 148 at 162.
[1] See also *post*, para. 25–02 *et seq.*

a personal profit or reap any personal advantage beyond what is due to him under the mortgage. Although he may have credit for his proper expenditure, he cannot charge a commission for his own time and trouble.[2]

16–34   Secondly, he may have credit only for such expenditure on repairs and outgoings as is reasonably necessary. He may charge for reasonable improvements which permanently increase the value of the property but not for extraordinary improvements made without the consent of the mortgagor.[3] If he could charge for every improvement, he might add so considerably to the mortgagor's indebtedness as to make it impossible for him to redeem and thus "improve" him out of his property altogether.[4]

Thirdly, the mortgagee being under a duty to be diligent,[5] is accountable for rents and profits on the footing of wilful default.[6] As Jessel M.R., pointed out in *Mayer v. Murray*,[7] the case of a mortgagee in possession is the only one in which the charge of wilful default need not be raised in the pleadings. This means that the mortgagor will be credited not only with the profits which the mortgagee in fact received, but also with those which, but for his gross negligence or wilful default, he would have received.[8] A mortgagee who personally occupies the mortgaged property, will be charged a fair occupation rent.[9] For example, a brewer mortgagee, who takes possession of a public house and lets it as a tied house, will be liable to account for the additional rent the house would have commanded as a free house.[10] A mortgagee's duty does not, however, go so far as to compel him to make the most of the mortgaged property: he is not bound to speculate with it[11]; he is not even bound to make special exertions to get the highest possible rent or the largest possible profit.[12] Nor is a mortgagee bound to let the mortgaged property if this might hinder or interfere with an intended sale.[13] He is liable only for gross negligence or wilful default. The fact that the account is on the footing of wilful default need not, therefore, unduly alarm a prudent man of business. Maitland however, sets up a further objection by

---

[2] *Langstaffe v. Fenwick; Fenwick v. Langstaffe* (1805) 10 Ves. 405; *Re Wallis, ex p. Lickorish* (1890) 25 Q.B.D. 176; but he may stipulate for such payment in the mortgage contract, since now there is no objection to a collateral advantage as such: *Biggs v. Hoddinott* [1898] 2 Ch. 307.

[3] *Shepard v. Jones* (1882) 21 Ch.D. 469; see also *Scholefield v. Lockwood* (1863) 33 L.J.Ch. 106; *Tipton Green Colliery Co. v. Tipton Moat Colliery Co.* (1877) 7 Ch.D.192, and see *post*, para. 25–16.

[4] *Sandon v. Hooper* (1844) 14 L.J.Ch. 120.

[5] See *Sherwin v. Shakespear* (1854) 5 De G.M. & G. 517.

[6] *Hughes v. Williams* (1806) 12 Ves. 493; *Shepherd v. Spansheath* (1988) E.G.C.S. 35. Wilful default also means he is liable for damage to the *corpus* of the property. *National Bank of Australasia v. United Hand-in-Hand & Co.* (1879) 4 A.C. 391, PC.

[7] (1878) 8 Ch.D. 424 at 427; see also *Lord Kensington v. Bouverie* (1855) 7 De G.M. & G. 134 at 156.

[8] *Brandon v. Brandon* (1862) 10 W.R. 287; *Shepherd v. Spansheath, supra. Noyes v. Pollock* (1886) 32 Ch.D. 53.

[9] *Lord Trimleston v. Hamill* (1810) 1 Ball & B. 377 at 385; *Marriott v. Anchor Reversionary Co.* (1861) 3 De G.F. & J. 177 at 193, see also *Fyfe v. Smith* [1975] 2 N.S.W.L.R. 408; but not, of course, where the premises have no letting value, see *Marshall v. Cave* (1824) 3 L.J.(o.s.) Ch. 57; and letting value, *White v. City of London Brewery* (1889) 42 Ch.D. 237 either by reason of their physical condition or a local trading slump. See also Law Commission Working Paper No. 99, *Land Mortgages* (1986), para. 3.24. A mortgagee who lets a purchaser into possession early is not liable to account: *Shepherd v. Jones* (1882) 21 Ch.D. 469.

[10] *White v. City of London Brewery* (1889) 42 Ch.D. 237 and see *Shepherd v. Spansheath, supra.*

[11] *Hughes v. Williams* (1806) 12 Ves. 493. See also *Shepherd v. Spansheath, supra.*

[12] See *Wragg v. Denham* (1836) 2 Y & C. Ex. 117.

[13] *Downsview Nominees Ltd v. First City Corp. Ltd* [1993] A.C. 295; *China South Sea Bank Ltd v. Tan* [1990] 1 A.C. 536.

suggesting[14] that the account against a mortgagee in possession is often taken with annual rests, *i.e.* that at each half-year[15] if there was an excess of profit of receipts over interest charges, the surplus must be taken to have gone in reduction of the capital debt, so that interest is afterwards allowed only on the reduced amount. However, such an account is only ordered in exceptional circumstances.[16]

Rests

The general rule is that the account of rents and profits runs on from beginning **16–35** to end without reference to the question whether the mortgagee has at any particular time had in his hands more than sufficient to pay the interest. The reason for this is that a mortgagee is not bound to accept payment by instalments and is entitled to have the account taken as a whole. To this rule there appear to be two exceptions: *(i)* where the mortgagee has claimed the property as his own, thereby denying the mortgagor's right to redeem[17]; and *(ii)* where the interest was not in arrear when the mortgagee went into possession.[18] In the second case the mortgagee is considered to have elected to take his money in instalments, so that he must set off the excess of receipts and interest against the principal[19]: however, once he is in possession, the mere fact that afterwards the interest ceased to be in arrear will not render him liable to make rests. He cannot safely give up possession so that there is no evidence of an intention to take his money in instalments.[20] It is true that in some older cases[21] it is suggested that even when interest was in arrear at the time of entry, the mortgagee must account with rests where the annual profits greatly and notoriously exceed the interest. These cases cannot now be relied on[22] and the true principle seems to be that the court only directs an account with rests by way of penalising the mortgagee when he fails to treat the mortgage property as a security. If he enters when his interest is genuinely in arrears, such a penalty is out of place.[23] If, however, the profits do greatly exceed the interest, the mortgagee must be capable of restoring the property to the mortgagor as soon as his whole debt is satisfied. For, if afterwards he continues in possession, he will have to pay interest to the mortgagor on such further sums as he receives by way of profits.[24] He is not entitled to use the mortgagor's money Therefore, if the latter can establish that at any particular date the whole debt was paid off, an account will be taken against the mortgagee

---

[14] Maitland, *Equity* (2nd ed.), p. 187.

[15] Or at the end of each full year, as the case may be.

[16] *Wrigley v. Gill* [1905] 1 Ch. 241; *Ainsworth v. Wilding* [1905] 1 Ch. 435.

[17] *National Bank of Australasia v. United Hand-in-Hand & Co.* (1879) 4 A.C. 391; see *Wrigley v. Gill* [1905] 1 Ch. 241, P.C.; *Incorporated Society in Dublin v. Richards* (1841) 1 Dr. & W. 258.

[18] *Shephard v. Elliot* (1819) 4 Madd. 254.

[19] This presumption will not be made if, interest not being in arrear, he entered to protect the security; *Patch v. Wild* (1861) 30 Beav. 99.

[20] *Davis v. May* (1815) 19 Ves. 383; *Latter v. Dashwood* (1834) 6 Sim. 462; but if he settles an account with the mortgagor, capitalising the arrears, he must go out of possession or he will be treated as if he had entered when no rent was in arrear; *Wilson v. Cluer* (1840) 3 Beav. 136.

[21] *e.g. Uttermare v. Stevens* (1851) 17 L.T.(o.s.) 115; see also *Wilson v. Cluer* (1840) 3 Beav. 136.

[22] *Nelson v. Booth* (1858) 3 De G. & J. 119; *Wrigley v. Gill* [1905] 1 Ch. 241.

[23] *Per* Warrington J. in *Wrigley v. Gill* [1905] 1 Ch. 241 at 249.

[24] *Wilson v. Metcalfe* (1826) 1 Russ. 530.

from that date charging him compound interest on the excess of rents and profits over outgoings with annual rests.[25]

Thus although the account is taken against a mortgagee in possession with some strictness,[26] this need not deter a mortgagee from enforcing his right if the occasion arises for its exercise and if he keeps in mind that the property does not cease to be the mortgagor's. Mortgagees, particularly building societies, do in practice go into possession a great deal more frequently than is commonly supposed[27] but only as a last resort.

(d) *Liability for waste*

16–36 Prior to 1926 the mortgagee formerly held the legal estate in fee simple and was thus an absolute owner at law and so was not liable for waste. After 1925 the mortgagee holds by virtue of a term of years but, pursuant to the Law of Property Act 1925, this is normally expressed to be without impeachment of waste.[28] In equity, the mortgagee on redemption must hand back to the mortgagor the property unimpaired and he may not destroy any part of it unless the security is deficient. However, he must make good any such loss to the mortgagor in taking the accounts.[29]

Although a mortgagee will be liable for waste if he causes unnecessary injury to the property, such as cutting timber when the security is not shown to be defective,[30] it must, however, be remembered that if the mortgage is by deed and executed after 1881, section 101(1)(iv) of the Law of Property Act 1925 gives a mortgagee in possession the power to cut and sell timber and other trees ripe for cutting which were not planted or left standing for shelter or ornament. Further, the mortgagee may contract for this to be done on the terms of the contract being completed within one year. The power, however, may be varied or excluded by the mortgage deed,[31] and a felling licence may be necessary.[32] Further, even when a mortgagee in possession has no power to cut timber (*i.e.* the statutory power has been excluded) he will not be restrained by injunction from so doing unless the security is sufficient.[33] This reflects the position prior to 1926 in that the mortgagee of the fee simple might cut timber by virtue of his ownership without committing waste at law but in equity he would be restrained unless the security was insufficient or defective. All profits from the sale of timber must, of course, be brought into the account for the benefit of the mortgagor. The mortgagee may not open new mines[34] but he has the right to work mines already opened.[35] The court will not interfere if a new mine is opened provided that there is no wanton destruction.[36]

[25] *Ashworth v. Lord* (1887) 36 Ch.D. 545 at 551.
[26] For the practice in taking the accounts see *post*, para. 25–02 *et seq*.
[27] See Law Commission Working Paper No. 99, *Land Mortgages* (1986), para. 1.3.
[28] See LPA 1925, ss85(2), 86(2), 87(1), Sched. 1, Pt. VII, paras 1, 2.
[29] *Millet v. Davey* (1862) 31 Beav. 470.
[30] *Withrington v. Banks* (1725) Cas temp King 30.
[31] LPA 1925, s.101(3), (4).
[32] Felling licences are obtained from the Forestry Commission.
[33] *Millett v. Davey* (1862) 31 Beav. 470.
[34] *ibid.* at 475.
[35] *Elias v. Snowden Slate Quarries Co.* (1879) 4 App.Cas. 454.
[36] *Millett v. Davey* (1862) 31 Beav. 470 at 476.

(e) *Agricultural land*

A mortgagee in possession of such land is liable for damage occasioned by his 16–37 gross negligence with regard to cultivation of that land.[37]

(f) *Liability for repairs*

The mortgagee is bound to maintain the property in necessary repair but only so 16–38 far as the rent and profits allow him to do so.[38] He will be liable for any deterioration consequent on his neglect to perform this duty. Provided that such repairs and improvements are necessary and reasonable,[39] the cost of effecting the same will be charged to the mortgagor in the accounts.[40] If the security is leasehold property the rule is especially strict and he will be liable for a forfeiture of the lease occasioned by his breach of a repairing covenant.[41] He need not spend his own money on the upkeep of the security. Accordingly he will only be liable for neglect to effect necessary repairs to the extent of surplus rents and profits after providing for the interest to which he is entitled under the mortgage.[42] A mortgagee may construct new houses in substitution of ruinous old houses,[43] but he is not bound to expend money in rebuilding.[44] Although the mortgagee may without the mortgagor's consent make reasonable and beneficial improvements to the property[45] he cannot make excessive or permanent improvements unless he obtains the mortgagor's consent, or there is acquiescence on the part of the mortgagor after notice to him.[46] The reason for this is that the mortgagee must not improve the mortgagor out of his estate which would have the effect of preventing him from redeeming the property.

(g) *Liability under leasehold covenants*[47]

At common law, a mortgagee of a leasehold interest does not enjoy privity of 16–39 estate with the lessor since the mortgage from which he derives title is effected by way of sub-demise or by means of a legal charge which has the same effect.[48] Consequently, the mortgagee has, in his capacity solely as mortgagee, no liability

---

[37] *Wragg v. Denham* (1836) 2 Y. & C. Ex 117.
[38] But improvements and repairs not strictly necessary he does at his own risk, unless he first obtains the mortgagor's consent as these may affect the mortgagor's power to redeem, see *Sandon v. Hooper* (1844) 14 L.J.Ch. 120.
[39] *Richards v. Morgan* (1753) 4 Y. & C.Ex. 570. See also *Moore v. Painter* (1842) 6 Jur. 903; *Powell v. Trotter* (1861) 1 Drew. & Sm. 388; *Tipton Green Colliery Co. v. Tipton Moat Colliery Co.* (1877) 7 Ch. 192.
[40] *Scholefield v. Lockwood* (1863) 4 De G.J. & Sm. 22 L.C.; *Tipton Green Colliery Co. v. Tipton Moat Colliery Co.* (1877) 7 Ch.D.192.
[41] *Perry v. Walker* (1855) 3 Eq.Rep. 721.
[42] *Richards v. Morgan* (1753) 4 Y. & C.Ex. 570.
[43] *Hardy v. Reeves* (1799) 4 Ves. 466 at 480; *Newman v. Baker* (1860) 8 C.B.(N.S.) 200; *Marshall v. Cave* (1824) 3 L.J.(O.S.) Ch. 57.
[44] *Moore v. Painter* (1842) 6 Jur. 903.
[45] *Shepard v. Jones* (1882) 21 Ch.D. 469 at 479; see also *Powell v. Trotter* (1861) 1 Drew. & Sm. 388.
[46] *Sandon v. Hooper* (1844) 14 L.J.Ch. 120; *Bright v. Campbell* (1885) 54 L.J.Ch. 1077.
[47] For a mortgagee's rights with regard to leasehold covenants, see *ante*, para. 16–27.
[48] Law of Property Act 1925, ss.86 and 87.

to the lessor pursuant to the covenants contained in the mortgaged demise. This extends to the payment of rent. However, if the lessor is able to forfeit the demised property for non-compliance with any covenants in the lease, the mortgagee's rights at common law are, if he wishes to maintain his security, of limited benefit.

Prior to January 1, 1996, a mortgagee of the reversionary interest of a leasehold estate was liable under any covenants entered into by the lessor if they were referable to the subject-matter demised by the lease and if the lessor had power to bind the mortgagee.[49]

In relation to new tenancies created on or after January 1, 1996, section 15 of the Landlord and Tenant (Covenants) Act 1995 has altered the position. A covenant which must be complied with by the lessor is enforceable against any person (other than the reversioner) who is entitled to the rents and profits for the time being of the demised premises. A lessee's mortgagee can enforce such a covenant against the lessor.[50] The new obligations cut both ways: a lessor may also enforce any covenant which is enforceable against the lessee or any right of re-entry to the demised premises[51] against a mortgagee or chargee in possession pursuant to a mortgage or charge granted by the lessee unless the covenant in question is either stated to be personal to any particular individual or would not be enforceable for want of registration.[52]

(h) *Liability under freehold covenants*

16–40 The burden of a positive covenant will not bind a mortgagee. A restrictive covenant will, in the appropriate circumstances, be enforceable against the mortgagee as a successor in title of the covenantor.

RIGHT TO THE APPOINTMENT OF A RECEIVER

16–41 There are two ways in which a mortgagee may obtain the appointment of a receiver: *(i)* by himself making the appointment under a power in the mortgage contract; and *(ii)* by an application to the court for a receiver to be appointed by the court.[53] A mortgagee places a receiver in control of the mortgaged property for the same reasons as he goes into possession himself; either the security is in danger of being squandered by the mortgagor, or else he is anxious to intercept the profits and apply them to the discharge of the mortgage debt. Appointing a receiver has a great advantage over going into possession since, by this means the property can be taken out of the mortgagor's control without the mortgagee having to assume any responsibilities towards the mortgagor. There is only one minor disadvantage which is that lapse of time does not confer a title to the land in the case of a receiver.[54]

---

[49] Law of Property Act 1925, s.142(1).
[50] Landlord & Tenant (Covenants) Act 1995, s.15(3).
[51] Landlord & Tenant (Covenants) Act 1995, s.15.
[52] *ibid.*, s.15(5).
[53] See *post*, para. 16–115.
[54] *Contra* the position in the case of a mortgagee in possession.

1. **History**

Before 1860 a mortgagee had no power to appoint a receiver unless he had **16–42** expressly stipulated for it in the mortgage. Consequently, if, having no such power, he did appoint a receiver, it was equivalent to going into possession and the receiver was his agent.[55] Well-drawn mortgages, however, invariably contained such a power and also a statement that the receiver, when appointed, was to be considered the agent of the mortgagor and that the mortgagee was not liable to account strictly in the same way as if he had taken possession or the receiver had been his agent.[56] In 1860 Lord Cranworth's Act[57] made this power statutory for mortgages created by deed but the power was confined to the case of rents and profits from land. In 1881, section 19 of the Conveyancing Act widened the scope of the statutory power and this section was replaced by section 101 of the Law of Property Act 1925. All mortgages executed after 1881 are governed by provisions now contained in sections 101 and 109 of the Law of Property Act 1925.

2. **Appointment**

Under an express power   The appointment of a receiver out of court can be **16–43** made pursuant to an express power contained in the mortgage deed. The appointment may, somewhat unusually, be made at the time of the execution of the mortgage or, more commonly, at some time thereafter. In the latter instance, the appointment is made by the mortgagee by an instrument either in writing or under seal, depending upon the terms of the power bestowed by the mortgage deed. However the appointment is made, it will recite that the receiver is the mortgagor's agent.[58] It is now customary for the receiver expressly to be permitted under the terms of the mortgage deed (and under the instrument appointing him) to have and exercise a number of powers, usually (i) the power to do anything the mortgagor might do; (ii) an irrevocable power of attorney with regard to the execution of deeds and the sale of the mortgaged property; (iii) the power to apply the sums received during the receivership in a specified manner.

(a) *Appointment pursuant to statutory powers*

Section 101(1)(iii) of the Law of Property Act 1925 permits a mortgagee, when **16–44** the mortgage is made by deed to appoint a receiver of the income of the mortgaged property or any part thereof when the mortgage money has become due. Moreover, if the mortgaged property consists of an interest in income or of a rentcharge or an annual or other periodical sum that section permits the

---

[55] *Quarrell v. Beckford* (1816) 1 Madd. 269.
[56] *cf. Jefferys v. Dickson* (1866) 1 L.R. Ch.App. 183 at 190; *cf.* Rigby L.J., in *Gaskell v. Gosling* [1896] 1 Q.B. 669 at 692.
[57] Power of Trustees, Mortgagees, etc. Act 1860.
[58] *Jeffreys v. Dixon* (1866) 1 L.R. Ch.App. 183 at 190; *Gaskell v. Gosling* [1896] 1 Q.B. 669 at 692.

mortgagee (where the mortgage is made by deed) to appoint a receiver of that property or any part of it. Section 101 applies only if and as far as a contrary intention is not expressed in the mortgage deed and, in any event, has effect subject to the terms of the mortgage deed and to the provisions contained in it.[59] The statutory power is subject to the limitation that it may not be exercised until the mortgage money has become due pursuant to the terms of the mortgage.[60] Common practice is now for that statutory restriction to be removed and for the receiver's powers to be extended generally and, for example, for a power of the sale to be given to the receiver.[61] The statutory power of appointment may be exercised by the mortgagee in writing under his own hand.[62] A receiver may also be removed and a new receiver appointed by the mortgagee by writing under his hand from time to time.[63] The power to remove a receiver is exercised by a mortgagee even after he has gone into possession.[64]

3. Mortgagee's duties with regard to the appointment of a receiver

16–45   A mortgagee owes a general duty to both the mortgagor and any subsequent mortgagees to exercise his powers for the sole purpose of securing the repayment of any monies owing to him and further a duty to act in good faith.[65] The mortgagee, however, has a broad discretion if and when to appoint a receiver having regard to his own peculiar interest and may exercise his power even though the timing of the appointment of a receiver may be disadvantageous to the mortgagor or any subsequent mortgagees.[66] The distinction, however, should be drawn between an exercise by the mortgagee of his powers in good faith and those which are not so exercised; it would appear arguable that where a mortgagee appoints a receiver in order to frustrate a purpose of the mortgagor or a subsequent mortgagee or who stands by whilst a receiver acts in such a manner that the exercise of his powers amounts to an abuse of them may be guilty of bad faith.[67]

4. The agency of the receiver

16–46   A receiver appointed under the powers conferred by the Law of Property Act 1925 is deemed to be the agent of the mortgagor, who is solely responsible for the receiver's acts or defaults unless the mortgage deed otherwise provides.[68] The agency of the receiver on behalf of the mortgagor is determined by the receiver's

---

[59] Law of Property Act 1925, s.101(4).
[60] *ibid.*, s.101(1)(iii).
[61] Such power is, it would appear, an express power rather than an extension of the receiver's statutory powers: *Phoenix Properties v. Wimpole Street Nominees* [1992] B.C.L.C. 737.
[62] Law of Property Act 1925, s.109(1).
[63] Law of Property Act 1925, s.109(5).
[64] *Refuge Assurance Co. Ltd v. Pearlberg* [1938] Ch. 687, CA.
[65] *Downsview Nominees Ltd v. First City Corp. Ltd* [1993] A.C. 295.
[66] *Shanji v. Johnson Matthey Bankers Ltd* [1986] B.C.L.C. 278 (on appeal [1991] B.C.L.C. 36); *Re Potters Oils Ltd (No. 2)* [1986] 1 W.L.R. 201.
[67] *Downsview Nominees Ltd v. First City Corp. Ltd* [1993] A.C. 295.
[68] Law of Property Act 1925, s.109(2).

subsequent appointment by the court[69] but not by the mortgagor's death.[70] In circumstances where the mortgagor is dead, the receiver is able to sue in the name of the mortgagor's personal representatives on the provision of a suitable indemnity.[71]

The receiver's position as agent of the mortgagor is different from most types of ordinary agency. His appointment is made by the mortgagee in order to protect the mortgagee's position. However, having been so appointed, the receiver is able by his acts to affect the position of the mortgagor with the objective of benefiting the mortgagee. Furthermore, the mortgagor is obliged to pay the receiver's fees and other expenses but is unable to dismiss him since that is a power reserved to the mortgagee. Notwithstanding his obligation to pay nor the fact that the receiver is able to effect the position of the mortgagor, the mortgagor is unable to instruct the receiver as to how to conduct the receivership.[72] In exercising his powers, a receiver's duties to the mortgagor and anyone else interested in the equity of redemption of the property are not necessarily confined to a duty of good faith. Son when exercising his powers of management, the receiver can owe a duty to manage the mortgaged property with due diligence, subject as ever to his primary duty of advancing the mortgagee's interests in having the secured debt and the interest thereon being paid. So where a receiver decided to continue a business at the mortgaged property, his duties to the mortgagor required him to take reasonable steps to manage it profitably.[73] This duty was one imposed by equity. In *Medforth v. Blake*[74] the Vice-Chancellor made it clear that a receiver could not be in breach of his duty of good faith to the mortgagor in the absence of conduct which was otherwise dishonest, improperly motivated or contained an element of bad faith. To make good an allegation of a breach of duty of good faith, the court will require an element such as this to be demonstrated.

The receiver will be treated as an agent of the mortgagee in circumstances where the mortgagee holds the receiver out as being his agent[75] or where the mortgagee directs or interferes with the activities of the receiver.[76] Moreover, the agency of the receiver on behalf of the mortgagor determines if the mortgagor is placed into liquidation and thereafter if the receiver continues to act, he does so as principal unless the mortgagee, by his conduct, ratifies his standing as the mortgagee's agent.[77] Where a receiver is the mortgagee's agent, the mortgagee is liable for his acts and omissions according to the usual rules.[78] Although in the absence of an express exclusion in any contract between the mortgagee and the receiver, the mortgagee is entitled, under an implied term of that contract to an indemnity from the receiver in respect of any negligence on his behalf.[79]

---

[69] *Hand v. Blow* [1901] 2 Ch. 721.
[70] *Re Hale, Lilley v. Foad* [1899] Ch. 107, CA.
[71] *Fairhome and Palliser v. Kennedy* (1890) 24 L.R. I.R. 498.
[72] See generally *Gomba Holdings (U.K.) Ltd v. Minories Finance Ltd* [1988] 1 W.L.R. 1231, CA.
[73] *Medforth v. Blake* [1999] 3 W.L.R. 922, CA.
[74] [1999] 3 W.L.R. 922.
[75] *Chatsworth Properties Ltd v. Effion* [1971] 1 W.L.R. 144.
[76] *American Express International Banking Corp. v. Hurley* [1985] 3 All E.R. 564.
[77] *ibid.*
[78] *ibid.*; *Circuit Systems Ltd v. Zuken-Redac (U.K.) Ltd* [1997] 1 W.L.R. 721.
[79] *American Express International Banking Corp. v. Hurley, ante.*

A receiver is under a duty to any guarantor of the mortgagor's debt to take reasonable care to obtain the true market value of the mortgaged property when the same is being realised in the exercise of any power of sale.[80]

5. Powers of the receiver

(a) *Pursuant to statute*

16–47   A receiver has the statutory powers set forth in section 109 of the Law of Property Act 1925. These powers are the power to demand or recover all the income of which he is appointed receiver (whether by action, distress or otherwise) in the name either of the mortgagor or the mortgagee to the full extent of the estate or interest which the mortgagor could dispose of and to give effectual receipts accordingly for that income and to exercise any powers which may have been delegated to him by the mortgagee pursuant to the Law of Property Act 1925.[81] A person paying money to the receiver shall not be concerned to enquire whether any case has happened to authorise the receiver to act.[82]

(b) *Statutory powers as to insurance and the application of income*

16–48   If appointed pursuant to the mortgagee's statutory powers, the receiver shall, if so directed in writing by the mortgagee, insure the mortgaged property to the extent, if any, to which the mortgagee might have insured it and keep insured any building, effects or property comprised in the mortgage, whether fixed to the freehold or not, being of an insurable nature against loss or damage by fire out of the money received by him.[83]

Furthermore, subject to the provisions of the Law of Property Act as to the application of insurance money, the receiver shall apply all money received by him in accordance with section 109(8) of the Law of Property Act 1925. That sub-section requires the monies to be applied as follows:

"(i)   in discharge of all rents, taxes, rates and out-goings whatever affecting the mortgage property; and

(ii)   in keeping down all annual sums or other payments, and the interest on all principal sums, having priority to the mortgage in right whereof he is receiver; and

(iii) in payment of his commission, and of the premiums on fire, life or other insurance, if any, properly payable under the mortgage deed or under this act, and the cost of executing necessary or proper repairs directed in writing by the mortgagee; and

(iv)   in payment of the interest accruing due in respect of any principal money due under the mortgage; and

---

[80] *American Express International Banking Corp. v. Hurley, ante.*
[81] Law of Property Act 1925, s.109(3).
[82] *ibid.*, s.109(4).
[83] *ibid.*, s.109(7).

(v) in or towards discharge of the principal monies so directed in writing by the mortgagee;

and shall pay the residual, if any, of the money received by him to the person who, but for possession of the receiver, would have been entitled to receive the income of which he is appointed receiver, or is otherwise entitled to the mortgaged property."

The statutory powers given to the receiver with regard to the application of income may be extended by the mortgage deed so as to permit, for example, the receiver and manager of a business to pay its unsecured debts.[84] The obligations on the receiver imposed by section 109(8)(iv) and (v) are obligations which ensure for the benefit of both the mortgagor and the mortgagee and, accordingly, a mortgagor may institute proceedings against a receiver if he should fail to perform them.[85]

(c) *Express powers*

In any appointment otherwise than pursuant to statute, the receiver only has those powers which are conferred upon him by the mortgage deed or instrument effecting his appointment. The modern practice is for receivers to have extensive powers conferred on them expressly pursuant to the mortgage or charge.   **16–49**

6. **Duties of the receiver to the mortgagor and third parties**

A receiver owes the same duty in equity to the mortgagor and any subsequent mortgagees and guarantors of the mortgagor's liability as the mortgagee does; mainly to exercise his powers in good faith and for the purpose of obtaining repayment of the debt owing to the mortgagee.[86] Sight should not be lost of the fact that the primary duty of any receiver is to the mortgagee and not to the mortgagor.[87] A receiver cannot be in breach of his duty of good faith to the mortgagor in the absence of some dishonesty, improper motive or element of bad faith.[88] A receiver has been held liable for failing to operate rent reviews.[89]   **16–50**

A receiver owes a duty of care to the guarantor of the debts of the mortgagor and, unless otherwise expressly excluded in any contractual arrangement between the mortgagee and the receiver, owes the mortgagee an indemnity with regard to any acts of negligence committed by the receiver.[90]

---

[84] *Re Hail, Lilley v. Foad* [1899] 2 Ch. 107.
[85] *Leicester Permanent Building Society v. Bart Square* [1943] Ch. 308.
[86] *Downsview Nominees Ltd v. First City Corp. Ltd* [1993] A.C. 215; *American Express International Banking Corp. v. Hurley* [1985] 3 All E.R. 564; *Standard Chartered Bank v. Walker* [1982] 1 W.L.R. 1410.
[87] *Downsview Nominees Ltd v. First City Corp. Ltd, supra; Gomba Holdings (U.K.) Ltd v. Minories Finance Ltd* [1988] 1 W.L.R. 1231.
[88] *Medforth v. Blake* [1999] 3 W.L.R. 922; *Downsview Nominees Ltd v. First City Corp. Ltd, supra.*
[89] *Nike v. Lawrence* [1991] 1 E.G.L.R. 143.
[90] *American Express International Banking Corp. v. Hurley* [1985] 3 All E.R. 564.

7. **Remuneration of the receiver**

16–51 A receiver is entitled to retain out of any money received by him, for his remuneration, and in satisfaction of all costs, charges and expenses incurred by him as receiver, a commission at such rate, not exceeding 5 per cent on the gross amount of all money received, as is specified in his appointment, and if no rate is so specified then at the rate of 5 per cent on the gross amount, or at such other rate as the court thinks fit to allow, on application made by him for that purpose.[91] If a receiver is not appointed pursuant to the statutory powers, the instrument of appointment will usually specify the rate of remuneration that the receiver is entitled to be paid, failing which the receiver will have a remedy in *quantum meruit*.[92] For obvious reasons, the statutory limit on the remuneration of a receiver is usually excluded and, if necessary, the court can fix the remuneration that is due to a receiver in an account as between the mortgagor and the mortgagee.[93]

8. **Termination of the receivership**

16–52 Only the mortgagee can terminate the receivership[94] but the receivership is determined by a number of other circumstances usually outside the mortgagee's control: namely, the appointment of a receiver by a prior mortgagee and, where an administration order has been made of an incorporated mortgagor, where the administrator so requires.[95] The liquidation of an incorporated mortgagor does not determine the receiver's appointment or powers but will operate to determine his agency on behalf of the mortgagor.[96] Thereafter it would appear that the receiver would, in the absence of the mortgagee constituting him as his agent, act as principal.[97]

RIGHT TO REALISE THE SECURITY BY SALE OUT OF COURT

1. **History**

16–53 A mortgagee of stocks or shares[98] and a mortgagee of personal chattels, who is in possession,[99] have an implied power to sell their security when the mortgagor is in default, unless the contrary is stated in the mortgage. A mortgagee of land, however, has no such implied power and can only sell by virtue of an express or

---

[91] Law of Property Act 1925, s.109(6). See also *Marshall v. Cottingham* [1982] Ch. 82.
[92] *Re Vimbos Ltd* [1900] 1 Ch. 470.
[93] *Gomba Holdings (U.K.) Ltd v. Minories Finance Ltd (No. 2)* [1993] Ch. 171.
[94] *Gomba Holdings (U.K.) Ltd v. Minories Finance Ltd* [1988] 1 W.L.R. 1231.
[95] Insolvency Act 1986, s.11(2).
[96] *American Express International Banking Corp. v. Hurley* [1985] 3 All E.R. 564.
[97] *Gosling v. Gaskell* [1987] A.C. 575.
[98] *Wilson v. Tooker* (1714) 5 Bro.Parl.Cas. 193; *Lockwood v. Ewer, Child (Lady) v. Chanstilet* (1742) 2 Atk. 303; *Kemp v. Westbrook* (1749) 1 Ves. Sen. 278; *Deverges v. Sandeman, Clark & Co.* [1902] 1 Ch. 579; *Stubbs v. Slater* [1910] 1 Ch. 632.
[99] *Re Morritt, ex p. Official Receiver* (1886) 18 Q.B.D. 222.

statutory power,[1] or with the mortgagor's consent. Indeed, until the end of the eighteenth century,[2] a mortgage of land could not be realised except through the tedious and expensive medium of proceedings such as foreclosure proceedings in Chancery. Attempts were occasionally made to give the mortgagee power to sell but such attempts, perhaps owing to a doubt whether the power would infringe the rule concerning clogs on the equity of redemption, were not common. In the first years of the nineteenth century more attention was paid to the possibility of realising mortgages out of court through powers expressly given to the mortgagee.[3] The legality of powers of sale was established and, after some doubts about the need for the concurrence of the mortgagor in the sale[4] and some further experiments with trusts, express powers of sale became a regular feature of every mortgage deed.[5] The usual form of an express power permitted the mortgagee and any person subsequently entitled to the mortgage to give a good discharge for the mortgage debt and, at any stage after the monies became due, to sell the mortgaged property free of encumbrances. The power of sale was often limited in its usage by the requirement for the mortgagor to have been in default in some regard for a specified period. Since the ordinary form of these express powers adequately protected the mortgagor,[6] they were a legitimate improvement of the creditor's remedies for realising his security. At the same time the need to protect the interests of both parties necessitated the insertion of a very elaborately drawn clause until the legislature introduced a statutory power of sale satisfactory to creditors.

(a) *Lord Cranworth's Act 1860*

This Act largely failed because the power of sale contained in it was less **16–54** satisfactory to creditors than the usual express power and did not induce them to omit the express power. The Act was repealed by the Conveyancing Act, 1881 but remains in force for mortgages created between 1860 and 1882.[7] Even then it is only of importance in the exceptional case when the mortgage did not contain an express power.[8]

(b) *Power of sale under the Law of Property Act 1925*

The statutory power of sale in the Conveyancing Act 1881 was satisfactory to **16–55** creditors and led to the omission of express powers; that Act has, however, been repealed, the relevant provisions being replaced by sections 101–107 of the Law of Property Act 1925. The power of sale contained in the 1925 Act as in the 1881

---

[1] *Re Rumney and Smith* [1897] 2 Ch. 351. At common law he could, of course, transfer his mortgage but this would be subject to the mortgagor's equity of redemption and willing purchasers would be difficult to find.

[2] Holdsworth, *History of English Law*, Vol. 7, p. 160.

[3] It is significant that the delays of the Chancery courts were at their worst during this period.

[4] Set at rest in *Corder v. Morgan* (1811) 18 Ves. 344.

[5] *cf. Clarke v. Royal Panopticon* (1857) 4 Drew. 26.

[6] By requiring the mortgagor to be given six months' notice of the intention to sell.

[7] *Re Solomon and Meagher's Contract* (1889) 40 Ch.D. 508.

[8] The number of such mortgages still in existence must now be few.

Act is modelled on the express power of sale in common use before 1882, and is so adequate that the statutory power is almost invariably relied on. It is introduced into all mortgages made by deed[9] created after 1881 and an express power is only found in mortgages made by deed when there is some special reason for departing from the statutory power. There is nothing in the statutory power which inhibits or restricts the use of express powers.[10]

(i) *Scope of the power*

16–56   Section 101(1) of the Law of Property Act 1925 provides as follows:

> "A mortgagee, where the mortgage is made by deed, shall, by virtue of this Act, have the following powers, to the like extent as if they had been in terms conferred by the mortgage deed, but not further (namely):
>
>> (i) A power, when the mortgage money has become due, to sell, or to concur with any other person in selling, the mortgaged property, or any part thereof, either subject to prior charges or not, and either together or in lots by public auction or by private contract, subject to such conditions respecting title, or evidence of title, or other matter, as the mortgagee thinks fit, with power to vary any contract for sale, and to buy in at an auction, or to rescind any contract for sale, and to resell, without being answerable for any loss occasioned thereby; . . . "

This power is ample; the sale may be of the whole property or only of a part; it may be by public auction or by private contract, and the wording of the Act does not mean that the property must first have been put up for auction before the mortgagee can proceed to sell by private contract.[11] The mortgagee may vary or cancel a sale, and an ineffectual attempt to sell does not affect his power to enter into a new contract for sale.[12]

Subsection (2) carries the scope of the power still further where the deed is executed after December 31, 1911[13] by giving a mortgagee when exercising his power:

> "(i) A power to impose or reserve or make binding, as far as the law permits by covenant, condition, or otherwise, on the unsold part of the mortgaged property or any part thereof, or on the purchaser and any property sold, any restriction or reservation with respect to building on or other user of the land, or with respect to mines and minerals, or for the purpose of the more beneficial working thereof, or with respect to any other thing;

---

[9] LPA 1925, s.101(1).

[10] *The Maule* [1997] 1 W.L.R. 528.

[11] *Davey v. Durrant, Smith v. Durrant* (1857) 1 De G. & J. 535.

[12] This had already been decided by the Privy Council: *Henderson v. Astwood, Astwood v. Cubbold, Cobbold v. Astwood* [1894] A.C. 150 at 162, PC.

[13] If the mortgage was executed before that date, the mortgagee could probably not impose conditions at all but he may sell mines or minerals if he obtains the leave of the court to do so: *Re Hurst's Mortgage* (1890) 45 Ch.D. 263, *Buckley v. Howell* (1861) 29 Beav. 546.

(ii) A power to sell the mortgaged property, or any part thereof, or all or any mines and minerals apart from the surface:

(a) With or without a grant or reservation of rights of way, rights of water, easements, rights, and privileges for or connected with building or other purposes in relation to the property remaining in mortgage in any part thereof, or to any property sold; and

(b) With or without an exception or reservation of all or any of the mines and minerals in or under the mortgaged property, and with or without a grant or reservation of powers of working, easements, rights, and privileges for or connected with mining purposes in relation to the property remaining unsold or any part thereof, or to any property sold; and

(c) With or without covenants by the purchaser to expend money on the land sold."

The statutory power of sale set out in section 101 may be varied or extended by the agreement of the parties, and if so varied or extended, will take effect in its altered form just as if the alterations had been part of the provisions contained in the Act.[14] Consequently, it is not necessary to set out an express power unless the mortgagee's requirements are widely different from the statutory power. Finally, although this was already assumed from the law relating to express powers,[15] section 106(2) of the Law of Property Act 1925 distinctly states that the power of sale conferred by the Act does not affect the right of foreclosure.

(ii) *Who may exercise the power*

The statutory power may be excluded by agreement but, subject to this, it is **16–57** introduced into every "mortgage" *made by deed*, whether the mortgage is legal or equitable and whether its subject-matter is realty or personalty. It is thus given to a chargee by way of legal mortgage and to the holder of "any charge or lien on property for securing money or money's worth"[16]; it is given also to the proprietor of a registered charge unless a contrary entry has been made on the register.[17] The result is that the holder of *any* mortgage, charge,[18] or equitable lien on any kind of property is entitled to the statutory power so long as the security was created by deed. There is, however, one exception: the statutory power of sale has been held not to be incorporated in a document governed by the Bills of Sale (1878) (Amendment) Act 1882.[19] Subject to this exception, section 101 of the Law of Property Act 1925 applies alike to realty and personalty or any interest in it or any thing in action.[20] Section 102 further ensures that

[14] s.101(3).

[15] *Perry v. Keane* (1836) 6 L.J.Ch. 67; *Wade v. Hanham* (1851) 9 Hare 62.

[16] LPA 1925, s.205(1)(xvi), which defines "mortgage" to include these.

[17] Land Registration Act 1925, s.34(1) and see *Lever Finance v. Trustee of the Property of Needleman* [1956] Ch. 375.

[18] Debenture holders in a *public* company have no power of sale, but otherwise debenture holders appear to be entitled to the statutory power: *Deyes v. Wood* [1911] 1 K.B. 806. Coote, *Mortgages* (9th ed. 1927), p. 910, *contra*, following Kay J., in *Blaker v. Herts and Essex Waterworks Co.* (1889) 41 Ch.D. 399, but *Deyes v. Wood* seems to limit Kay J.'s statement.

[19] *Re Morritt, Ex p. Official Referee* (1886) 18 Q.B.D. 222; *Calvert v. Thomas* (1887) 19 Q.B.D. 204.

[20] LPA 1925, s.205(1)(xvi), (xx). It may be noted that Lord Cranworth's Act did not extend to personalty, being limited to *hereditaments*.

the mortgagee of an undivided share in land, who took his security before 1926, shall not lose his statutory or express power of sale by reason of the conversion of his interest into a share in personalty.

An express power of sale is only exercisable by the persons designated for that purpose by the instrument creating it.[21]

a) Co-mortgagees

16–58 The effect of a mortgage to several mortgagees is that, unless a contrary intention is expressed in the mortgage deed, the mortgage debt is deemed to be held upon a joint account[22]; this means that the power of sale is exercisable by the original mortgagees jointly and that, if one dies, the survivors may sell without joining his personal reprsentatives in the sale. In the case of land, if the mortgagees exceed four in number, the first four are the statutory trustees on behalf of all the mortgagees and the sale must be made through them, or, if one dies, the survivors of them.[23]

b) Transferees

16–59 The statutory power is exercisable by a transferee of the mortgage debt in the same way as by the original mortgagee, for section 106(1) provides[24]:

> "The power of sale conferred by this Act may be exercised by any person for the time being entitled to receive and give a discharge for the mortgage money."

Transferees include sub-mortgagees, who may either sell the mortgage debt only, leaving the original mortgagor's equity of redemption outstanding, or else sell, as assignees of the mortgage and destroy also the original equity of redemption. It is necessary to include a word of warning in circumstances where the power of sale is express and not statutory, since the original mortgage does not in terms extend the power of sale to assignments, the power cannot be transferred.[25] An express power should therefore either incorporate the language of section 106(1) or otherwise provide for assignment of the power.

c) Personal representatives

16–60 The personal representatives of the mortgagee and, after the necessary assents have been given, the persons beneficially interested in the mortgage moneys may exercise the statutory power of sale, by virtue of section 106(1). Again, this will not be so in the case of an express power unless provided for in the mortgage deed.[26]

---

[21] *Re Crunden and Meux's Contract* [1909] 1 Ch. 690.
[22] *ibid.*, s.111; trustees hold on a joint account. And see Trustee Act 1925, s.18.
[23] LPA 1925, s.34(2) as amended.
[24] In any case s.205(1)(xvi) states that "mortgagee" includes any person from time to time deriving title under the original mortgagee.
[25] *Re Rumney v. Smith* [1897] 2 Ch. 351.
[26] *Re Crunden and Meux's Contract* [1909] 1 Ch. 690.

2. **Conditions for the power of sale**

(a) *When the power arises*

There are three conditions which must be fulfilled before the power of sale   **16–61**
arises:

    (a)   the mortgage must be made by deed (as in the case of all legal mortgages); and

    (b)   the mortgage money must have become due—*i.e.* the legal date for redemption must have passed. In most mortgages there is inserted a legal date for redemption but, if there is no such clause and the mortgage debt is repayable by instalments, the power of sale arises as soon as any instalment is in arrear[27];

    (c)   there is no contrary intention in the mortgage deed.

(b) *When the power becomes exercisable*

Although the statutory power of sale *arises* at that time, it cannot—without   **16–62**
express variation of the statutory requirements by the parties—*be exercised*
unless at least one of the conditions set out in section 103 of the Law of Property
Act 1925 has been satisfied, namely:

    (a)   Notice requiring payment of the mortgage money[28] has been served on the mortgagor or one of two or more mortgagors, and default has been made in payment of the mortgage money, or of part thereof, for three months after such service[29]; or

    (b)   Some interest under the mortgage is in arrear[30] and unpaid for two months after becoming due[31]; or

    (c)   There has been a breach of some other provision contained in the mortgage deed[32] or in the 1925 Act,[33] or in an enactment replaced by that Act which should have been observed or performed by the mortgagor or by someone who concurred in making the mortgage.[34]

---

[27] *Payne v. Cardiff Rural District Council* [1932] 1 K.B. 241. But, if the mortgage money is not due (*i.e.* the interest is in arrear, but the principal is not) the statutory power does not arise, although the court may be able to order a sale in lieu of foreclosure pursuant to the LPA 1925, s.91(2). See *Twentieth Century Banking Corporation v. Wilkinson* [1977] Ch. 99; *Palk v. Mortgage Services Funding plc* [1993] Ch. 330.

[28] *i.e.* money or money's worth secured by mortgage—LPA 1925, s.205(1)(xvi).

[29] LPA 1925, s.103(i), and see *Barker v. Illingworth* [1908] 2 Ch. 20.

[30] It is for the mortgagee to prove affirmatively that the interest is in arrear, and it seems that a mortgagee in possession is not entitled to say that the interest is in arrear merely because he receives nothing on account of interest from the mortgagor. He must show that the interest is in arrear in spite of the receipt of rents and profits: *Cockburn v. Edwards* (1881) 18 Ch.D. 449 at 459, 463; *Wrigley v. Gill* [1905] 1 Ch. 241. Capitalisation of arrears may make this difficult to demonstrate: *Davy v. Turner* (1970) 21 P. & C.R. 967

[31] LPA 1925, s.103(ii). "Month" means calendar month: Interpretation Act 1978, ss5, 22(1), Sched. 1, Sched. 2, para. 4(1).

[32] *e.g.* breach of covenants to repair or insure; see *Braithwaite v. Winwood* [1960] 1 W.L.R. 1257.

[33] See *Public Trustee v. Lawrence* [1912] 1 Ch. 789 (failure to deliver counterpart of lease as required by s.99(8)).

[34] LPA 1925, s.103(iii).

Although the occurrence of one of these circumstances is normally a condition precedent to the exercise of the statutory power, the mortgage contract may, and usually does, exclude the restrictions. On the other hand, it has been suggested that a clause allowing for sale without any notice might be considered oppressive, and will be so considered, if there is any fiduciary relationship between the parties.[35] Where a mortgage provides for the monies to be due and payable on a specified date, the power of sale is not exercisable before that date, even if the mortgage is in arrears.[36]

(i) Form of notice

A notice under section 103 must be served on the mortgagor. The notice must be in writing.[37] "Mortgagor" includes any person deriving title under the original mortgagor.[38] Who ought to be served when there are later incumbrancers is an unsettled point; the course generally adopted is to give notice to the mortgagor himself and to the incumbrancer highest in priority.[39] The form of notice contemplated by section 103 is probably a demand for immediate payment, with a threat that if at the end of three months the money has not been paid, the power will be exercised: but a notice is just as good if it is merely a notice to pay at the end of three months from the date of the notice,[40] but he must then join in the conveyance to the purchaser.[41] Finally, although a sale cannot take effect until the expiry of the notice required by section 103, the contract of sale may be entered into before that time, the contract being conditional on the mortgagor not discharging the mortgage.[42]

(ii) Service of the notice

16–63   Section 196 of the Law of Property Act 1925 makes provision for the service of notices under the Act. The notice is sufficiently served if left at the mortgagor's last known place of abode or business or is affixed or left for him on the land or any house or building comprised in the mortgage.[43] It is sufficiently addressed if it is addressed to the mortgagor simply by that designation, without his name, or generally to the persons interested, without any name, and notwithstanding that any person to be affected by the notice is absent, under disability, unborn or unascertained.[44] It is sufficient service if the notice is simply placed through the letterbox of the mortgaged premises, even though those premises were at the time of service vacant, the tenant in person and the normal method of contact being via the tenant's solicitor.[45]

---

[35] *Miller v. Cook* (1870) L.R. 10 Eq. 641; *Cockburn v. Edwards* (1881) 18 Ch.D. 449; this will not be so if the security was not given for a fresh loan but for obtaining more time for payment: *Pooley's Trustee v. Whetham* (1886) 33 Ch.D. 111.
[36] *Twentieth Century Banking Corp. Ltd v. Wilkinson* [1977] Ch. 99.
[37] Law of Property Act 1925, s.196(1).
[38] LPA 1925, s.205(1)(xvi).
[39] Omission to give notice to an incumbrancer may expose the mortgagee to an action for damages (*Hoole v. Smith* (1881) 17 Ch.D. 434); this decision would appear to apply to the statutory power by virtue of the definition of "mortgagor" given in the text.
[40] *Barker v. Illingworth* [1908] 2 Ch. 20.
[41] *Selwyn v. Garfit* (1888) 38 Ch.D. 273.
[42] *Major v. Ward* (1847) 5 Hare 598.
[43] Law of Property Act 1925, s.196(3).
[44] LPA 1925, s.196(2).
[45] *Van Harlaam v. Kasner* (1992) 64 P. & C.R. 214.

Any notice required or authorised by the Law of Property Act to be served shall also be sufficiently served, if it is sent by post in a registered letter addressed to the mortgagor or other person to be served, by name, at the aforesaid place of abode or business, office, or counting house, and if that letter is not returned through the post-office undelivered; and that service shall be deemed to be made at the time at which the registered letter would in the ordinary course of post be delivered.[46] If the requirements of section 196 are met, the notice is served even if it is never received.[47] A notice left at the farthest place to which a member of the public or postman could obtain access, can constitute service at the mortgagor's place of abode.[48]

Section 196 applies subject to any contrary intention appearing in the deed creating the mortgage or charge.

3. **Protection of purchasers**

The importance of the distinction between the power of sale *arising* and the **16–64** power of sale being *exercisable* cannot be underestimated. If the power has not arisen the mortgagee has no statutory power of sale at all. Any sale by him in purported exercise of the statutory power will not give a good root of title and will not transfer the legal estate to a purchaser. It will, however, operate to transfer his mortgage, *i.e.* it will only be effective to transfer to the purchaser the rights of mortgagee as mortgagee. Thus, a purchaser must ascertain whether or not the power of sale has arisen. Since the question of its exercisability is a matter between the mortgagor and the mortgagee, this does not normally concern the purchaser of the legal estate.

Thus, if the power of sale has arisen, but is not exercisable, the mortgagee can give a good root of title which is not impeachable and the only recourse open to the mortgagor is a remedy in damages against the person exercising the power of sale.[49] In this regard it is necessary to consider the provisions of section 104(2) of the Law of Property Act 1925 in the light of the case law preceding this legislation. The subsection corresponds with the usual clause in an express power and provides as follows:

> "(2) Where a conveyance is made in exercise of the power of sale conferred by this Act, or any enactment replaced by this Act, the title of the purchaser shall not be impeachable on the ground:
>
> (a) that no case had arisen to authorise the sale; or
> (b) that due notice was not given; or
> (c) where the mortgage is made after the commencement of this Act, that leave of the court, when so required, was not obtained; or
> (d) whether the mortgage was made before or after such commencement, that the power was otherwise improperly or irregularly exercised;

---

[46] LPA 1925, s.196(4).
[47] *R. v. Westminster Unions Assessment Committee, ex parte Woodward & Sons* [1917] 1 K.B. 832.
[48] *Henry Smith's Charity Trustees v. Kyriakou* [1989] 2 E.G.L.R. 110, CA.
[49] See the LPA 1925, s.104(2).

and a purchaser is not, either before or on conveyance[50] concerned to see or inquire whether the case has arisen to authorise the sale, or due notice has been given, or the power is otherwise properly and regularly exercised; but any person damnified by an unauthorised, or improper, or irregular exercise of the power, shall have his remedy for damages against the person exercising the power.[51]

(3) A conveyance on sale by a mortgagee, made after the commencement of this Act, shall be deemed to have been made in exercise of the power of sale conferred by this Act unless a contrary intention appears."[52]

16–65   Thus, proof of title is simplified and all that the purchaser need do is to satisfy himself that the power of sale has arisen and he need not inquire whether it has become exercisable.[53] Further a purchaser is under no obligation to make inquiries as to the regularity of the sale and the protection given to him by the terms of the subsection enures to him as soon as the contract is signed and is not dependent on completion having been obtained.[54] The existence of the power of sale is proved by the document creating the power, *i.e.* the form of the mortgage deed itself, and the redemption date specified in it.

However, a number of authorities appear to lay down the rule that when the purchaser had actual notice of an irregularity such as a defect in the mortgagee's power to sell,[55] or of facts which make the proposed sale impossible or inconsistent with a proper exercise of the power,[56] the sale will be set aside,[57] and the purchaser's title will be impeached.[58] It has been stated that in the circumstances " . . . to uphold the title of a purchaser who had notice of impropriety or irregularity in the exercise of the power of sale would be to convert the provisions of the statute into an instrument of fraud. . . . ".[59]

Having regard to the above, several comments need to be made. First, the cases which establish the apparent qualification to the express provisions of section 104(2) are in the main decided upon express, as opposed to statutory, powers of sale, and generally precede the 1925 legislation.[60] Secondly, the only

---

[50] "Or on conveyance" was inserted to overrule the case of life interests etc.: *Life Interest and Reversionary Securities Corporation v. Hand-in-Hand Fire and Life Insurance Society* [1898] 2 Ch. 230.

[51] The reference to a remedy in damages does not create a special statutory remedy, nor does it refer to a common law action for damages. It is a reference to the mortgagor's equitable remedy to hold the mortgagee to account on the footing of wilful default—*McGinnis v. Union Bank of Australia Ltd* [1935] V.L.R. 161.

[52] This renders it unnecessary to state in the conveyance that the conveyance is made in exercise of a sale under the statutory power as this is presumed.

[53] *Bailey v. Barnes* [1894] 1 Ch. 25 at 35.

[54] s.104 expressly overrules life interests, etc.: *Life Interest and Reversionary Securities Corporation v. Hand-in-Hand Fire and Life Insurance Society* [1898] 2 Ch. 230.

[55] *Jenkins v. Jones* (1860) 2 Giff 99. *Parkinson v. Hanbury* (1867) L.R. 2 H.L. 1.

[56] *Selwyn v. Garfitt* (1888) 38 Ch.D. 273; *Bailey v. Barnes* [1894] 1 Ch. 25.

[57] *Bailey v. Barnes* [1894] 1 Ch. 25; *contra* Fisher & Lightwood, *Law of Mortgage* (10th ed., 1988), p. 387 which suggests having regard to the authority that the purchaser is liable to have the sale set aside not only if he took with actual notice of an irregularity but also if he took with constructive notice. *cf.* also *Parkinson v. Hanbury* (1860) 1 Dr. & Sm. 143.

[58] *Lord Waring v. London & Manchester Assurance Co. Ltd* [1935] Ch. 310 at 318.

[59] See *Bailey v. Barnes* [1894] 1 Ch. 25 at 30, *per* Stirling J., but note that that statement was made in relation to s.21(2) of the Conveyancing Act 1881, which is reproduced in the first part only of s.104(2).

[60] See, *e.g. Jenkins v. Jones* (1860) 2 Giff 99; *Parkinson v. Hanbury* (1867) L.R. 2 H.L. 1; *Selwyn v. Garfitt* (1888) 38 Ch.D. 273; and *Bailey v. Barnes* [1894] 1 Ch. 25.

case of importance since 1925 is that of *Lord Waring v. London & Manchester Assurance Co. Ltd*[61] in which dicta in *Bailey v. Barnes*[62] were approved *obiter.* Thirdly, there has been no reported case, as yet, in which the court has expressly had to consider the wording of section 104(2). In these circumstances it would seem that the present position is as follows: provided that the purchaser does not *actually know* of any irregularity he will obtain a good unimpeachable title and the mortgagor's remedy is in damages against the person exercising the power of sale. Further, it would seem that there is no obligation upon the purchaser to make the inquiries which a suspicious purchaser should make and that the purchaser will not have constructive notice of any irregularity or impropriety in the exercise of the power of sale which would have been revealed by such inquiries. However, the conveyance may be set aside if the purchaser takes with knowledge of any impropriety in the sale, in the sense of what would have come to his knowledge had he not shut his eyes to suspicious circumstances, rather than the usual sense related to failure to inquire, whether that knowledge be by way of actual or constructive notice.[63]

Sale

Mode of sale   The sale will in most cases be made under the provisions of **16–66** section 101 of the Law of Property Act 1925, without reference to the court.[64] This gives to the mortgagee a wide discretion as to the manner in which he exercises his power. It may be by auction or by private contract. It may be of the whole or part of the property and may be made subject to easements or restrictive covenants. It may include the grant of easements and privileges and may separate the mines and minerals from the ownership of the surface. However, the section gives no power to sell timber apart from the land[65] or trade machinery apart from the buildings containing it,[66] nor to grant an option.

The sale may be made either free of or subject to prior charges. This is important when there are successive incumbrancers; a puisne incumbrancer, who is desirous of selling, has two choices: *(i)* he may sell subject to the prior charges; or *(ii)* he may sell free of prior charges by arranging to discharge them out of the proceeds of sale. If the latter alternative is adopted he must either obtain the concurrence of the prior incumbrancers in the sale[67] or else he must make use of

---

[61] [1935] Ch. 310. *Holohan v. Friends Provident and Century Life Office* [1966] I.R. 1; *Forsyth v. Blundell* (1973) 129 C.L.R. 477. See also *Property and Bloodstock Ltd v. Emerton*; *Bush v. Property and Bloodstock Ltd* [1968] Ch. 94.

[62] [1894] 1 Ch. 25 at 30, 34, which seems to suggest that there is a different standard from that usually applied in relation to the doctrine of notice.

[63] See *Bailey v. Barnes* [1894] 1 Ch. 25 at 30, 34; *Holohan v. Friends Provident and Century Life Office* [1966] I.R. 1.

[64] There is an exception in the case where a mortgage provides that a power of sale shall be exercisable in the case of bankruptcy. In such a case leave of the court is required but it does not concern the purchaser; see LPA 1925, s.104(2). Also, in those cases where the mortgaged property is occupied by the mortgagor (in particular dwelling-houses) presumably the mortgagee will wish to have vacant possession prior to sale which will normally necessitate court proceedings.

[65] *cf. Cholmeley v. Paxton* (1825) 3 Bing. 207.

[66] *Re Yates, Batcheldor v. Yates* (1888) 38 Ch.D. 112.

[67] A complication arises in the case of registered land. The prospective purchaser can insist on the vendor/mortgagee procuring his registration of the charge (see Land Registration Act 1925, s.110(5)), but without the concurrence of the *first* mortgagee with whom the Land Certificate may have been deposited this cannot be done.

the procedure provided by section 50 of the Law of Property Act 1925, in which case he obtains leave to pay into court a sum sufficient to cover the requirements of the prior charges, plus any costs or expenses likely to be incurred.

(a) *Mortgagee as vendor*

16–67   The courts have repeatedly affirmed that a mortgagee is not a trustee for the mortgagor until his debt has been satisfied.[68] It follows that a mortgagee, in exercising his power of sale, is not a trustee of the power[69] and need merely act in good faith in order to obtain repayment.[70] The power arises by contract with the mortgagor and forms part of the mortgagee's security so that he is entitled to look after his own interests when making the sale.[71] In *Warner v. Jacob*[72] Kay J., stated the general principle at common law of the mortgagee's position thus:

> "A mortgagee is, strictly speaking not a trustee of the power of sale. It is a power given to him for his benefit, to enable him the better to realise his debt. If he exercises it bona fide for that purpose, without corruption or collusion with the purchaser, the court will not interfere, even though the sale be very disadvantageous, unless, indeed, the price is so low as in itself to be evidence of fraud."

So strong was this principle that a mortgagee has been held not to be a trustee of the power of sale, even when the mortgage is created in the form of an express trust for sale.[73]

(i) *Price*

16–68   At common law, therefore, the general rule flowing from this principle was that the duty of a mortgagee, exercising his power of sale, merely should act in good faith in the *conduct of the sale*.[74] If the sale was bona fide he need not consult the interests of the mortgagor, so that it would be no ground for setting aside a sale

---

[68] *Marquis of Cholmondely v. Lord Clinton* (1820) 2 J. & W. 1; *Taylor v. Russell* [1892] A.C 244; *Sands* to *Thompson* (1883) 22 Ch.D. 614; Turner, *Equity of Redemption* (1931), pp. 166 *et seq.*; and see *ante*, para. 16–04 *et seq.* But even if the mortgagee is not a trustee, he is bound to take reasonable care to obtain a true market value of the mortgaged property, see *Cuckmere Brick Co. Ltd v. Mutual Finance Ltd* [1971] Ch. 949; *Parker-Tweedale v. Dunbar Bank* [1991] Ch. 12, CA; *Downsview Nominees Ltd v. First City Corp. Ltd* [1993] A.C. 295; *AIB Finance v. Debtors* [1998] 2 All E.R. 929; *Medforth v. Blake* [1999] 3 W.L.R. 922 and see *post*, para. 16–68 *et seq.*

[69] *Kennedy v. De Trafford* [1897] A.C. 180; *Cuckmere Brick Co. Ltd v. Mutual Finance Ltd* [1971] Ch. 949.

[70] *Downsview Nominees Ltd v. First City Corp. Ltd* [1993] A.C. 295.

[71] *Farrar v. Farrars, Ltd* (1888) 40 Ch.D. 395 at 398, *per* Chitty, J.

[72] (1882) 20 Ch.D. 220 at 234.

[73] *Kirkwood v. Thompson* (1865) 2 De G. J. & Sm. 613; *Locking v. Parker* (1872) L.R. 8 Ch.App. 30. But this principle probably should now be qualified in the light of the *Cuckmere* case, see *post*, para. 16–69A *et seq.*

[74] *Kennedy v. De Trafford* [1897] A.C. 180. Lord Herschell, however, deprecated any attempt to define exhaustively the words "acting in good faith."

that a larger price could have been obtained if the sale had been delayed.[75] The court would not inquire into a mortgagee's motive for exercising his power,[76] provided the sale itself was fair. Neither spite nor any other indirect motive would invalidate the sale. The mortgagee was not a trustee of the power in any sense.[77] In the absence of evidence of fraud a sale would not be set aside.[78] Indeed, it was well settled that selling at an undervalue did not by itself constitute *male fides*. In *Adams v. Scott*,[79] for example, it was alleged that property sold for £12,000 was worth £20,000, but Wood V.-C., declared that mere undervalue was not enough to justify interference with the sale without proof of fraud. Where there was fraud, however, the court would grant an injunction to restrain the completion of a sale, or would set aside a completed sale.[80] If the property has reached the hands of a purchaser for value without notice of the fraud, an action for damages will lie against the mortgagee.[81]

However, at the same time, obviously the question of the price to be obtained by the mortgagee in respect of the security is of importance to the mortgagor. He is the person interested in the balance of the proceeds of sale after payment of the mortgage debt by the mortgagee exercising his power of sale (and the debt of any other mortgagee interested in the security). In short, the mortgagor's interests must not be sacrificed.

As the law developed, although proof of fraud was essential in order to set **16–69** aside a sale otherwise executed in accordance with the terms of the mortgagee's power, the mortgagee was made liable to account for his careless handling of the sale. A mortgagee was not to be regarded as a trustee, but he would be treated as a reasonable man of business. Dicta of Lord Herschell L.C.,[82] and Lindley L.J.,[83] were sometimes cited in support of the proposition that, in the absence of fraud, a mortgagee was only liable for selling at an undervalue if he wilfully or recklessly sacrifices the property of the mortgagor. This seemed to put the rule too favourably for the mortgagee, for in *Tomlin v. Luce*[84] a mortgagee was held responsible for the blunder made by an otherwise competent auctioneer whom he had employed. The Privy Council in *McHugh v. Union Bank of Canada*[85] defined the duty of a mortgagee more broadly:

> "It is his duty to behave in conducting the realisation of the mortgaged property as a reasonable man would behave in the realisation of his own property, so that the borrower may receive credit for the fair value of the property sold."

---

[75] *Davey v. Durrant, Smith v. Durrant* (1857) 1 De G. & J. 535.

[76] See *Nash v. Eads* (1880) 25 S.J. 95.

[77] *Belton v. Bass, Ratcliffe & Gretton Ltd* [1922] 2 Ch. 449; *Nash v. Eads* (1880) 25 S.J. 95; *Colson v. Williams* (1889) 58 L.J.Ch. 539.

[78] See *Warner v. Jacob* (1882) 20 Ch.D. 220; and see *ante*, para. 16–67 *et seq.*

[79] (1859) 7 W.R. 213.

[80] *Bettyes v. Maynard* (1883) 49 L.T. 389; *Haddington Island Quarry Co. Ltd v. Hudson* [1911] A.C. 727; *Lord Waring v. London and Manchester Assurance Co.* [1935] Ch. 310.

[81] *Dennedy v. De Trafford* [1896] 1 Ch. 762 at 772, CA.

[82] *Kennedy v. De Trafford* [1897] A.C. 180 at 185; this dictum does not in fact support the proposition.

[83] *Kennedy v. De Trafford* [1896] 1 Ch. 762 at 772, CA.

[84] (1889) 43 Ch.D. 191.

[85] [1913] A.C. 299 at 311, PC.

The true rule as it developed was that a mortgagee must use reasonable care to get a fair or proper price,[86] and if he did not, he would be debited in his mortgage account with the full value of the mortgaged property *at the date of the sale*.[87]

16–69A   It was not until 1971 that this rule finally received full judicial recognition in the English courts. In the case of *Cuckmere Brick Co. Ltd v. Mutual Finance Ltd*[88] the Court of Appeal held that a mortgagee at common law is under a duty to " . . . take reasonable care to obtain the true market value of the mortgaged property."[89] Thus, if a mortgagee in exercising his power of sale in respect of a plot of building land advertises the property and fails to mention that there is in existence planning permission for the erection of 100 flats, he will be accountable to the mortgagor for the difference between the proper price which could have reasonably been obtained and the price actually obtained.[90] This would seem now to place upon *any* mortgagee the same duty of care to obtain the best price reasonably obtainable as has been imposed upon building societies since 1939.

16–70   Further decisions in 1982 and 1985 held that this duty of care is also owed to the guarantor of the mortgaged debt as well as to the mortgagor[91] but not to a person beneficially entitled in the property and of whom the mortgagee had notice.[92] The mortgagee's duty of good faith is however owed to the mortgagor and anyone else interested in the equity of redemption.[93] It may be added that in a sale, otherwise bona fide, the price is none the less a fair price, although part, or even the whole of the purchase price is left on mortgage, but the mortgagee must, of course, have debited himself in the mortgage account with the full amount of the purchase price.[94]

The duty formerly imposed by statute[95] on building societies to take reasonable care to ensure that the price obtained on a sale of a mortgaged property was the best price that could reasonably be obtained has been repealed[96] and any rule of law requiring a mortgagee to take reasonable care to obtain a proper price on

---

[86] *Colson v. Williams* (1889) 58 L.J.Ch. 539; *Reliance Permanent Building Society v. Harwood-Stamper* [1944] Ch. 362.

[87] *Wolff v. Vanderzee* (1869) 20 L.T. 350; *Deverges v. Sandeman, Clarke & Co.* [1902] 1 Ch. 579; for a statement of the measure of the mortgagee's liability, see *Tomlin v. Luce* (1889) 43 Ch.D. 191.

[88] [1971] Ch. 949, explaining *Kennedy v. De Tafford* [1897] A.C. 180. See also *Holohan v. Friends Provident and Century Life Office* [1966] I.R. 1. The *Cuckmere* principle has since been applied in *Palmer v. Barclays Bank Ltd* [1971] 23 P. & C.R. 30; *Bank of Cyprus (London) Ltd v. Gill* [1980] 2 Lloyd's Rep. 51; *Standard Chartered Bank Ltd v. Walker* [1982] 1 W.L.R. 1410; *Tse Kwong Lam v. Wong Chit Sen* [1983] 1 W.L.R. 1394; *Bishop v. Bonham* [1988] 1 W.L.R. 742. See also "*The Calm C*", *Gulf and Fraser Fisherman's Union v. Calm C Fish Ltd* [1975] 1 Lloyd's Rep. 189. *Parker-Tweedale v. Dunbar Bank* [1991] Ch. 12, CA; *Downsview Nominees Ltd v. First City Corp. Ltd* [1993] A.C. 295; *AIB Finance v. Debtors* [1998] 2 All E.R. 929; *Medforth v. Blake* [1999] 3 W.L.R. 922.

[89] *Cuckmere Brick Co. Ltd v. Mutual Finance Ltd* [1971] Ch. 949 at 966, *per* Salmon L.J.

[90] *ibid.*, *per* Salmon L.J., who held that the proper price is the same as the true market value.

[91] *Standard Chartered Bank Ltd v. Walker* [1982] 1 W.L.R. 1410, CA, a case where there was a sale by a receiver under a debenture of a private company which was guaranteed by the directors personally; *American Express International Banking Corpn. v. Hurley* [1985] 3 All E.R. 564; see also *Downsview Nominees Ltd v. First City Corp. Ltd* [1993] A.C. 295.

[92] *Parker-Tweedale v. Dunbar Bank plc* [1991] Ch. 12.

[93] *Medforth v. Blake* [1999] 3 W.L.R. 922.

[94] *Davey v. Durrant, Smith v. Durrant* (1857) 1 De G. & J. 535; *Kennedy v. De Trafford* [1897] A.C. 180; *Belton v. Bass, Ratcliffe and Gretton Ltd* [1922] 2 Ch. 449.

[95] Building Societies Act 1986, s.13(7) and Sched. 4, para. 1.

[96] Building Societies Act 1997, s.12(1) with effect from December 1, 1997 (S.I. 1997 No. 2668).

true market value is to have effect as if the statute imposing the duty on a building society (and its statutory predecessors) had never been enacted.[97]

However, a number of points remain for consideration. First, now that the law has been clarified in that *any* mortgagee is required to act not only in good faith but also with reasonable care, how far does this duty extend? Having regard to the earlier cases, it appears that the mortgagee is under no duty to advertise the security, nor is he bound to sell it by auction.[98] Further, a mortgagee is under no duty to delay the sale in order to obtain a better price.[99] Again, the mere fact that a mortgagee in exercising his power of sale omits a material point of which he is ignorant (for example, planning permission) does not of itself justify a finding of negligence.[1] Also the mortgagee is not required to put the property into good repair.[2] The answer is that the mortgagee is entitled to proceed to a forced sale to realise his security irrespective of his motive for selling.[3] Provided that he acts bona fide and takes reasonable care to ensure that the price is the best reasonably obtainable *in the circumstances*, then such actions are justifiable. Once he elects to act, however, in a given way by, for example, carrying on business he must take all steps that are reasonably necessary to do so profitably.[4]

The duty of care imposed on a selling mortgagee by the *Cuckmere* principle, being essentially in the nature of an obligation implied by law, is capable, therefore, of being excluded by agreement.[5] The courts may not reject exclusion clauses where the exempting words are clear and are susceptible to one meaning only, however unreasonable. The result therefore may be[6] that where such clauses authorise the mortgagee to exercise the power of sale with absolute discretion, the power is nonetheless subject to the implicit restriction that it should be exercised properly within the limits of the general law, that is, with the exercise of reasonable care to obtain a proper price.[7]

Secondly, what of the position of the auctioneer or estate agent handling the **16–71** sale on behalf of the mortgagee? In other words, does a mortgagee discharge his duty to the mortgagor if he places the sale in the hands of a reputable agent? As yet, there has been no case directly on this point as in all the cases it is the mortgagee who has been held liable for his agent's negligence. It is clear that the mortgagee would have a claim to an indemnity from the agent.[8] It is now clear that a receiver does not owe a mortgagor any duty of care.[9] In addition, there are a number of suggestions that the mortgagor himself may have an action directly

---

[97] *ibid.*, s.12(2).
[98] *Davey v. Durrant, Smith v. Durrant* (1857) 1 De G. & J. 535 at 560; *Bank of Cyprus (London) Ltd v. Gill* [1980] 2 Lloyd's Rep. 51.
[99] *Davey v. Durrant, Smith v. Durrant, ante*, at 553; *Bank of Cyprus (London) Ltd v. Gill, ante*.
[1] *Palmer v. Barclays Bank* (1972) 23 P. & C.R. 30.
[2] *Waltham Forest London Borough Council v. Webb* (1974) 232 E.G. 461.
[3] *Farrar v. Farrars Ltd* (1888) 40 Ch.D. 395 at 398; and see *Adams v. Scott* (1859) 7 W.R. 215.
[4] *Medforth v. Blake* [1999] 3 W.L.R. 922 and see *ante*, para. 16–28 *et seq.*
[5] *Bishop v. Bonham* [1988] 1 W.L.R. 742 at 752, *per* Slade L.J. In the case of building society mortgages *exclusion* of limitability is presently *excluded* see Building Societies Act 1986, Sched 4, para. 1(2).
[6] *Photo Production Ltd v. Securicor Transport Ltd* [1980] A.C. 827 at 850, *per* Lord Diplock, cited by Slade L.J. in *Bishop v. Bonham* (*ante*); see also *George Mitchell (Chesterhall) Ltd v. Finney Lock Seeds* [1983] Q.B. 284 at 312; *Chitty on Contracts* (25th ed., 1983), Vol. 1, para. 878.
[7] *Bishop v. Bonham* [1988] 1 W.L.R. 742.
[8] *American Express International Banking Corp. v. Hurley* [1985] 3 All E.R. 564.
[9] *Downsview Nominees Ltd v. First City Corp. Ltd* [1993] A.C. 295.

against the agent for negligence,[10] but the correctness of this proposition raises some doubt in view of the fact that normally there is no duty of care owed to a third party in the case of economic loss.[11] Finally, despite the fact that the law now seems to have been clarified by the *Cuckmere* case, is it strictly correct to state that the duties owed by building society mortgagees and other mortgagees are identical having regard to the various developments set out above? It had previously been considered that building societies alone owed a special duty since the enactment of section 10 of the Building Societies Act 1939.

(a) *Identity of purchaser*

16–72 The sale must be a true sale. A mortgagee cannot sell to himself, either alone or with others, even though the price be the full value of the property sold.[12] Such a sale may restrained or be set aside or ignored.[13] It is not so much that there is the conflict between interest and duty, which prevents a trustee from acquiring the trust property, as the impossibility of the contract. A man cannot make an agreement with himself. Nor can he disguise the fact that he is both buyer and seller by employing an agent or trustee to purchase for him.[14] The same principle prevents a solicitor or other agent employed to conduct the sale from becoming a purchaser.[15] However, a sale by a mortgagee to a company of which he is a shareholder, or even director, or a sale by a mortgagee company to one of its members, is not necessarily invalid.[16] As Lindley L.J. said[17]:

> "A sale by a person to a corporation of which he is a member is not, either in form or in substance, a sale by a person to himself. To hold that it is, would be to ignore the principle which lies at the root of the legal idea of a corporate body, and that idea is that the corporate body is distinct from the persons composing it. A sale by a member of a corporation to the corporation itself is in every sense a sale valid in equity as well as at law."

At the same time, although such a sale is not a nullity, it may be impeached on the ground of fraud or other irregularity[18] and the fact that the mortgagee has a

---

[10] Cross L.J. in *Cuckmere Brick Co. Ltd v. Mutual Finance Ltd* [1971] Ch. 949 at 973; *Garland v. Rulp* (1984) 271 E.G. 106; *Piodeth v. Castle Phillips Finance Co Ltd* (1986) 279 E.G. 1355; and see (1986) *Conv.* 442 (Thompson).

[11] Liability is imposed in only a limited range of circumstances. Assistance for the mortgagor may be derived from the Lloyd's cases: see *Henderson v. Merrett Syndicates Ltd* [1995] 2 A.C. 145; *Aitken v. Stewart Wrightson Members Agency* [1995] 1 W.L.R. 1281. See generally *Clark & Lindsell on Torts* (18th ed., 2000), para. 8–12.

[12] *National Bank of Australasia v. United Hand-in-Hand and Band of Hope* (1879) 4 App. Cas. 391; see also *Martison v. Clowes* (1882) 21 Ch.D. 857.

[13] See *Williams v. Wellingborough Borough Council* [1975] 1 W.L.R. 1327 where a purported transfer to itself by the local authority was held to be void. A local authority has a statutory power to vest property in itself subject to the court's approval: Housing Act 1985, s.452 and Sched. 17.

[14] *Downes v. Grazebrook* (1817) 3 Mer. 200; *National Bank of Australasia v. United Hand-in-Hand etc., Co.* (1879) 4 A.C. 391.

[15] *Martinson v. Clowes* (1882) 21 Ch.D. 857; *Lawrence v. Galsworthy* (1857) 30 L.T.(o.s.) 112; *Hodson v. Deans* [1903] 2 Ch. 647; but not if the agent was not employed in the conduct of the sale: *Guest v. Smythe* (1870) L.R. 5 Ch.App. 551; *Nutt v. Easton* [1899] 1 Ch. 873.

[16] *Tse Kwong Lam v. Wong Chit Sen* [1983] 1 W.L.R. 1349.

[17] *Farrar v. Farrars, Ltd* (1888) 40 Ch.D. 395 at 409.

[18] *Tse Kwan Lam v. Wong Chit Sen* [1983] 1 W.L.R. 1349.

substantial interest in the company will throw upon the mortgagee and the company the burden of affirmatively proving the bona fides of the sale. In *Farrar v. Farrars Ltd*[19] this burden was discharged; in *Hodson v. Deans*[20] it was not, and the sale was accordingly upset.

The mortgagor himself may bid at an auction and become the purchaser, and in the case of co-mortgagors one may purchase from the mortgagee without the concurrence of the others. Nor can the others impeach the sale on the ground that they were not notified of the name of the purchaser, for there is no fiduciary relationship between co-mortgagors to render such a notification necessary.[21] Further, there is no objection to a purchase by a puisne incumbrancer[22] and the effect of such a purchase from a first mortgagee, exercising his power of sale, is quite different from a mere purchase of the first mortgage. The sale carried out in pursuance of a power created by the mortgagor cancels the latter's equity of redemption so that the puisne incumbrancer obtains an absolute irredeemable title.[23]

If the court orders a sale pursuant to statute[24] the mortgagee may be expressly permitted to buy.[25]

(b) *Distribution of surplus proceeds of sale*

Sale under a power of sale cancels the equitable right to redeem but it by no means destroys the equitable interest of the mortgagor *vis-à-vis* the mortgagee. Consequently, as on a sale under an express or statutory power of sale, the mortgagee becomes a trustee of the surplus proceeds of sale for the mortgagor and other interested parties.[26] In the case of an express power, he is an express trustee if the mortgage contains an express trust of the proceeds of sale[27]; otherwise he is a constructive trustee.[28] In the case of a statutory power, the Law of Property Act 1925, section 105 expressly states that the mortgagee is a trustee of the purchase-money and provides for its application in this order:

    (1) if the sale is "free from incumbrances" and there were some *prior* incumbrancers, in the discharge of their claims;

    (2) in the payment of all costs, charges or expenses properly incurred by the mortgagee, incidental to the sale and any attempted sale[29];

16–73

---

[19] (1888) 4 Ch.D. 395.

[20] [1903] 2 Ch. 647.

[21] *Kennedy v. De Trafford* [1897] A.C. 180.

[22] *Parkinson v. Hanbury* (1860) 1 Dr. & Sm. 143; affirmed (1867) L.R. 2 H.L. 1; *Rajah Kishendatt Ram v. Rajah Mumtaz Ali Khan* (1879) L.R. 6 Ind.App. 145, PC.

[23] *Shaw v. Bunny* (1865) 2 De G. J. & Sm. 468.

[24] Law of Property Act 1925, s.91(2).

[25] *Palk v. Mortgage Services Funding plc* [1993] Ch. 330.

[26] *Rajah Kishendatt Ram v. Rajah Mumtaz Ali Khan* (1879) L.R. 6 Ind.App. 145, PC.

[27] *Locking v. Parker* (1872) L.R. 8 Ch. 30; *Weld-Blundell v. Synott* [1940] 2 K.B. 107.

[28] *Banner v. Berridge* (1881) 18 Ch.D. 254, where Kay J. said that the fiduciary relationship did not arise unless a surplus was proved. *cf. Sands to Thompson* (1883) 22 Ch.D. 614; *Thorne v. Heard and Marsh* [1895] A.C. 495.

[29] Including any statute-barred interest, see *post*, para. 22–41. A mortgagee who exercises his power of sale may retain *all* arrears of interest out of the proceeds of sale as this is not recoverable by action.

(3) in discharging his own debt under the mortgage[30];

(4) the *residue* is to be paid to the person entitled to the mortgaged property, or authorised to give receipts for the proceeds of the sale (*i.e.* the next incumbrancer, or, if none, the mortgagor).[31]

When the persons interested in the equity of redemption have lost their titles under the Limitation Act 1980, the mortgagee holds the proceeds of sale free of any obligation to account to them, even if he has purported to sell under the power of sale in the mortgage.[32] However, any person still interested in the residue, whether as a puisne mortgagee or as a holder of the ultimate equity of redemption, is entitled to an account from the mortgagee as to his disbursements under the first three headings. Indeed, the mortgagee must have his accounts settled before he can get a discharge from the person with a first claim on the surplus[33]; if the latter disputes the account, the mortgagee can apply to have the account taken by the court.[34]

(c) *Destination of the residue*

16–74 The destination of the residue depends on what has happened to the equity of redemption; if there is one person solely entitled, there is no difficulty, but the equity of redemption may have been settled, incumbered, or have devolved upon several persons with partial interests.

(1) Settlement.   The money must be paid to the trustees or into court.

(2) Successive incumbrances.   The money belongs to the incumbrancers according to their priorities. Each successive incumbrancer holds the balance on trust to satisfy his own claim and to pass on the balance, if any. Accordingly, the mortgagee is liable to any incumbrancer, of whose charge he knows, if he pays over the money to the mortgagor.[35] This means, in the case of a legal mortgage of land, that he must search at the Land Registry, because registration has the same consequences as actual notice.[36] He is not, however, under such a duty to state his accounts correctly to other incumbrancers as to estop him from claiming repayment, if in error he pays over to the second mortgagee more

---

[30] This is so irrespective of any cross-claim by the mortgagor against the mortgagee—see *Samuel Keller (Holdings) Ltd v. Martin's Bank Ltd* [1971] 1 W.L.R. 43; and see *Inglis v. Commonwealth Trading Bank of Australia Ltd* (1972) 126 C.L.R. 161.

[31] The concluding words of s.105 are not accurate in that it states that the residue " . . . shall be paid to the person entitled to the mortgaged property." This literally means the *purchaser* and not any subsequent mortgagee or the mortgagor, if none. It would seem that the phrase must be construed with the following additional words inserted " . . . to the person *who immediately before the sale was* entitled to the mortgaged property." See *British General Insurance Co. Ltd v. Att.-Gen.* [1945] L.J.N.C.C.R. 113 at 115. Where the property of a company is subject to a fixed charge and sold, the residue is payable in accordance with s.105 and not to any preferential creditors notwithstanding that the charge may have been a floating charge on creation: *Re G.L. Saunders Ltd (In Liquidation)* [1986] 1 W.L.R. 215.

[32] *Young v. Clarey* [1948] Ch. 191.

[33] See *Eley v. Read* (1897) 76 L.T. 39.

[34] *Chadwick v. Heatley* (1845) 2 Coll. 137.

[35] *West London Commercial Bank v. Reliance Permanent Building Society* (1885) 29 Ch.D. 954.

[36] LPA 1925, s.198(1).

than is in fact left—after discharging his own mortgage.[37] The mortgagee, as a trustee of the money, appears to have three ways of obtaining his discharge. Either he may distribute the whole fund, paying to a puisne incumbrancer only what is due to him on his mortgage[38] or else he may pay the whole fund over to the incumbrancer next entitled and obtain a discharge from him. The latter will then hold the residue on the trusts set out in section 105 of the Law of Property Act 1925.[39] Thirdly, if in doubt as to the priorities, he may pay the money into court.[40]

(3) Several owners of the equity of redemption. Being a trustee, he must regulate his payments in accordance with the strict rights of the parties and give the beneficiaries all proper allowances.[41] In case of difficulty he may apply to the court for guidance.

Finally, if there is a surplus and the mortgagee does not distribute it, he will be charged simple interest on the balance in his hands in favour of persons interested in the equity of redemption; and it will not make any difference that there is delay in applying to have the money paid out.[42] He will not, however, be charged interest if distribution is prevented by disputes concerning priorities.[43]

4. Effect of a sale

The effect of a sale under a power of sale is to destroy the equity of redemption   **16–75**
and to constitute the mortgagee a trustee of the surplus proceeds for the persons interested according to their priorities.[44] It vests the whole of the estate of the mortgagor in the purchaser,[45] subject to any prior mortgage but free from the selling mortgagee's mortgage and all subsequent incumbrances, including the mortgagor's equity of redemption. The subsequent interests are overreached and transferred to any capital monies arising from the transaction if those are paid to the mortgagee.[46] In the case of registered land the purchaser must register his interest.[47] That the mortgagor's right to redeem is utterly gone is well illustrated by the case of *Shaw v. Bunny*,[48] where a puisne incumbrancer purchased the estate from the first mortgagee, selling under an express power. The fact that the

---

[37] *Weld-Blundell v. Synott* [1940] 2 K.B. 107.
[38] *Re Bell, Jeffrey v. Sayles* [1896] 1 Ch. 1; but, strictly, it is the right of the next incumbrancer to have the whole surplus paid over to him, and therefore his claims must be allowed on that footing, *i.e.* the first incumbrancer cannot limit him to six years' arrears of interest: *Re Thomson's Mortgage Trust, Thomson v. Bruty* [1920] 1 Ch. 508.
[39] *cf.* s.107(2) which covers such a receipt by a puisne incumbrancer.
[40] *Re Walhampton Estate* (1884) 26 Ch.D. 391; and see Trustee Act 1925, s.63 (as amended by the Administration of Justice Act 1965, s.36(4), Sched. 3).
[41] *Re Cook's Mortgage, Lawledge v. Tyndall* [1896] 1 Ch. 923.
[42] *Eley v. Read* (1897) 76 L.T. 39.
[43] *Mathison v. Clarke* (1855) 25 L.J.Ch. 29; presumably he would have to account for interest actually produced by the surplus, as, *e.g.*, if he put it to deposit.
[44] *Rajah Kishendatt Ram v. Rajah Mumtaz Ali Khan* (1879) L.R. 6 Ind. App. 145.
[45] LPA 1925, ss.88(1), 89(1), 104(1).
[46] *ibid.*, s.2(1)(iii).
[47] Land Registration Act 1925, s.19 as amended by the Land Registration Act 1986, s.4(3).
[48] (1865) 2 De G.J. & Sm. 468; *S.E. Rly. Co. (Directors, etc.) v. Jortin* (1857) 6 H.L.C. 425. (1865) 2 De G.J. & Sm. 468.

purchaser had been under an obligation to allow the mortgagor to redeem the property as to the puisne incumbrance did not prevent his purchase from conferring on him a title absolute and irredeemable. Moreover, under the equitable doctrine of conversion the destruction of the equity of redemption takes place as soon as there is a binding contract for sale (even if it is conditional), not upon completion. In *Lord Waring v. London and Manchester Assurance Co.*,[49] the court was invited to say that the mortgagor might redeem at any time before the execution of the conveyance: the result would be that a mortgagee could only give a conditional contract for sale and his ability to find a purchaser might be seriously prejudiced. However, the power to sell is a power to bind the mortgagor by sale, and the court had no hesitation in deciding that the contract by itself is enough to defeat the equity of redemption. If the mortgagee has, in exercise of his power of sale, entered into a contract for the sale of property, the mortgagor cannot stop the sale by tendering the moneys due.[50] Further a contract made by the mortgagor has no effect on the mortgagee's power of sale.[51]

The sale also has consequences for the mortgagee. He has taken steps to realise his security, and therefore the interest ceases to run as from the date of sale so that he cannot charge the mortgagor with an additional six months' interest after the sale.[52] On the other hand, sale is not like foreclosure and does not necessarily put an end to the mortgage debt. If there is a surplus after discharging the debt, the transaction is, of course, concluded, save for the distribution of the surplus. If the amount realised is less than what is due on the mortgage, the mortgagee may still sue on the personal covenant for the deficiency: the rule that a mortgagee disables himself from suing for the debt by putting it out of his power to reconvey does not apply to a sale under a power given by the mortgage.[53]

5. The conveyance: sale under express powers

16–76   A power to make conveyance on sale is not automatically attendant on a power to sell and it is therefore necessary to consider how the conveyance is made upon a sale by a mortgagee. Formerly, in the case of express powers, the power to sell in a mortgage by conveyance did carry with it the power to convey because the mortgagee was holder of the title. With mortgages of land by demise or sub-demise (the usual method of mortgaging leasehold), the mortgagor's reversion caused a difficulty which was usually got over by declaring the mortgagor a trustee of the reversion for the mortgagee.[54] Again, in equitable mortgages the mortgagee, having no legal title, had no power to convey and it was necessary to provide for this by giving the mortgagee a power of attorney to convey the property upon a sale.[55] The law is still the same for mortgagees by conveyance of personalty and for equitable mortgagees with express powers.

---

[49] [1935] Ch. 310.
[50] *ibid.,* and see *Property and Bloodstock Ltd v. Emerton, Bush v. Property & Bloodstock Ltd* [1968] Ch. 94. See also *post* para. 16–79 *et seq.*
[51] *Duke v. Robson* [1973] 1 W.L.R. 267.
[52] *cf. West v. Diprose* [1900] 1 Ch. 337.
[53] *Re McHenry, McDermott v. Boyd, Barker's Claim* [1894] 3 Ch. 290.
[54] *London and County Banking Co. v. Goddard* [1897] 1 Ch. 642.
[55] *Re Hodson and Howes' Contract* (1887) 35 Ch.D. 668 at 671, *per* North J. " . . . he can convey all he has; but he cannot convey the legal estate," and see *post,* para. 16–77A.

(a) *Freehold land*

However, after December 31, 1925 legal mortgages of land must be by demise or sub-demise, or by legal charge and whether the power to sell is express or statutory the mortgagor's reversion causes no difficulty, since section 88(1) of the Law of Property Act 1925 provides for mortgages or legal charges of the fee, that whether the mortgagee sells under express or statutory power:

> "(a) the conveyance by him shall operate to vest in the purchaser the fee simple in the land conveyed subject to any legal mortgage having priority to the mortgage in right of which the sale is made and to any money thereby secured, and thereupon;
> (b) the mortgage term or the charge by way of legal mortgage and any subsequent mortgage term or charges shall merge or be extinguished as respects the land conveyed; and such conveyance may, as respects the fee simple, be made in the name of the estate owner in whom it is vested."

(b) *Leasehold interests*

Section 89(1) of the Law of Property Act 1925 contains parallel provisions for mortgages of leasehold interests with one important difference. The mortgagor's nominal reversion expectant on the mortgagee's sub-term will vest in the purchaser upon a sale but application may be made to the court to have the reversion kept alive as a protection to the purchaser against onerous covenants in the original lease. If the purchaser acquires the whole leasehold interest formerly vested in the mortgagor, he will be in the position of an assignee and bound by the covenants under the doctrine in *Spencer's Case*.[56] Applications to the court under this section will be uncommon and there is no guidance as to what the court will consider a sufficient reason for allowing a purchaser to escape from performance of the covenants.[57] Further, where a licence to assign is required on sale by a mortgagee, such licence shall not be unreasonably refused. **16–77**

6. The conveyance: sale and statutory powers

Conveyances consequent upon the exercise of *statutory* powers, under which most sales take place, are provided for by section 104(1) of the Law of Property Act 1925, which states that the mortgagee shall have power: **16–77A**

> "by deed to convey the property sold *for such estate and interest therein as he is by the Act authorised to sell or convey or may be the subject of the mortgage*, freed from all estates, interests and rights to which the mortgage has priority, but subject to all estates, interests and rights which have priority to the mortgage." [author's emphasis]

---

[56] (1583) 5 Co.Rep. 16a.
[57] See Wostenholme & Cherry, *Conveyancing Statutes* (13th ed., 1971), Vol. 1, p. 181.

The words in italics require explanation. Under a statutory power the mortgagee has the advantage of sections 88(1) and 89(1) of the Law of Property Act 1925, so that a *legal* mortgagee of leasehold or freehold property may sell and convey a larger estate than was the subject of the mortgage, *i.e.* the mortgagor's reversion may be included; but that in all other cases the mortgagee can only convey the interest which was mortgaged to him, unless the mortgage gives him powers additional to that in the statute. This latter point causes no inconvenience to a legal mortgagee of personalty or to a mortgagee of an equitable interest by assignment. The mortgagor's whole title is transferred to them and section 104 merely confirms the right to make a conveyance of a title already vested in them. However, when the legal owner of land or personalty has created a mere equitable security by contract, the "subject-matter of the mortgage" is the *equitable* interest (*i.e.* the power over the equity of redemption) transferred to the mortgagee, and section 104 does not therefore confer[58] a power to convey the mortgagor's legal title to a purchaser.[59] This is a serious disability. It is, however, the universal practice to provide for this by giving an equitable mortgagee a power of attorney to convey on behalf of the mortgagor[60]; indeed, *ex abundanti cautela*, the mortgagor is usually in addition made a trustee of the legal title for the mortgagee. If no such precaution is taken, the conveyance cannot be made without either the mortgagor's concurrence or an application to the court.

(a) *Deeds*

16–78   Section 106(4) of the Law of Property Act 1925 provides that when the statutory power has become exercisable, the person entitled to sell may demand and recover from any person (other than someone with a prior interest in the mortgaged property) all deeds or documents relating to the title or to the property which a purchaser might be entitled to demand and recover from him. It should be noticed that this will apply to deeds in the hands of a *prior* mortgagee whose debt is discharged out of the purchase moneys or under section 50 of the Law of Property Act 1925.

(b) *Injunctions to restrain sale*

16–79   When there is evidence of fraud or some other irregularity in the sale which would justify it being set aside, an injunction will be granted by the court to restrain the sale provided that the purchaser had *actual* notice of the fraud or irregularity or of facts which make the proper exercise of the power impossible.[61]

---

[58] This narrow interpretation was doubted in *Re White Rose Cottage* [1965] Ch. 940 at 951, where it was suggested that s.104(1) gives an equitable mortgagee power to sell the legal estate. Also in Fisher & Lightwood, *Law of Mortgage* (10th ed., 1988), pp. 402, 403, approval is given to this interpretation and it is suggested that s.104 of the Law of Property Act 1925 approximates in its effect rather to Lord Cranworth's Act 1860, than to the Conveyancing Act 1881. This seems an odd way of regarding the section, since Lord Cranworth's Act *did* enable a mortgagee to convey the mortgagor's whole interest (*Re Solomon and Meagher's Contract* (1889) 40 Ch.D. 508), whereas the 1881 Act, like the 1925 Act, did not.

[59] "The mortgaged property" under the LPA 1925, s.101(1)(i).

[60] See *post*, para. 16–121.

[61] See *ante*, para. 16–56 *et seq.*; para. 16–61.

Otherwise the mortgagor will be left to his remedy in damages against the mortgagee.[62]

The court will also restrain a sale when the mortgagee is obstructing redemption by the mortgagor. Thus, if a tender of the mortgage debt has been made and declined[63] or if an offer to redeem has been made and the mortgagee has disputed the right to redeem,[64] the mortgagee will be restrained from *attempting* to exercise his power of sale.[65] Similarly if, upon application to restrain the sale, the amount claimed is paid into court by the applicant, an injunction will lie.[66] No injunction will be granted if the mortgagor merely expresses an intention to redeem,[67] nor even if he has begun an action for redemption[68] or if the mortgage debt is disputed[69]; it is only on the terms of *payment* that the power of sale will be restrained. Consequently, the court will always, when granting an injunction, insist on payment into court of the amount due as a condition of restraining the sale.[70] Even an order *nisi* for foreclosure in an action brought by the mortgagee does not necessarily put a restraint on the exercise of his power to sell out of court, but until foreclosure absolute he may sell with the leave of the court.[71] Finally, it may be noticed that in special cases, where there is a fiduciary relationship between the mortgagor and mortgagee, the court, without altogether restraining the sale, may interfere and control the rights of the parties.[72]

(c) *Implied power of sale at common law of chattels, shares and stocks*

The mortgagee of personal chattels, if in possession and the mortgagee of stocks **16–80** and shares has[73] a power of sale implied at common law. When the mortgage is by deed, the common law power is displaced by the power given by section 101 of the Law of Property Act 1925 but the implied power is still serviceable when there is no deed. If the mortgage fixes a day for payment, the implied power is exercisable immediately after default on that date. If no date is fixed, then it is exercisable after the mortgagor has been given reasonable notice to pay the debt and has defaulted.[74] It appears that in a mortgage of shares that a month's notice or even a fortnight's notice may be sufficient.[75]

---

[62] *Prichard v. Wilson* (1864) 10 Jur.(N.S.) 330. This is on the assumption that the sale is pursuant to the statutory power which contains the clause for the protection of purchasers (see *ante* para. 16–64 *et seq.*), or to a well-drawn express power containing such a clause. If the express power contains no such clause then the general doctrine of actual or constructive notice applies.

[63] Even without a tender for costs: *Jenkins v. Jones* (1860) 2 Giff. 99.

[64] *Rhodes v. Buckland* (1852) 16 Beav. 212; but not if the dispute is only as to the amount due: *Gill v. Newton* (1866) 14 L.T. 240.

[65] But note the position if there is in existence a binding contract of sale between the mortgagee and the purchaser in the absence of fraud or some other irregularity, *ante*, para. 16–75; n. 50 *et seq.*

[66] *Whitworth v. Rhodes* (1850) 20 L.J.Ch. 105.

[67] *Matthie v. Edwards* (1847) 16 L.J.Ch. 405.

[68] *Davies v. Williams* (1843) 7 Jur. 663.

[69] *Cockell v. Bacon* (1852) 16 Beav. 158.

[70] *Warner v. Jacob* (1882) 20 Ch.D. 220; *Macleod v. Jones* (1883) 24 Ch.D. 289.

[71] *Stevens v. Theatres Ltd* [1903] 1 Ch. 857.

[72] *Macleod v. Jones* (1883) 24 Ch.D. 289.

[73] See *ante*, para. 13–21 *et seq.* generally; *ante*, para. 16–53.

[74] *Deverges v. Sandeman* [1901] 1 Ch. 70 at 73, *per* Farwell, J., affirmed [1902] 1 Ch. 579.

[75] [1902] 1 Ch. 579.

RIGHTS AND REMEDIES OF THE LEGAL MORTGAGEE FOR ENFORCING THE
SECURITY IN COURT

1. Proceedings for possession

16–81   A legal mortgagee and a chargee by way of legal mortgage has the right to enter
into actual possession of the mortgage security from the moment the mortgage is
created.[76] If the security is land which is already let on leases binding the
mortgagee, he cannot, of course, go into possession physically but he can enter
into receipt of the rents and profits by serving notice on the tenants to pay their
rents to himself instead of to the mortgagor.[77] Normally, the right arises at once
on the execution of the conveyance. If, however, (as now rarely happens) the
mortgage deed contains a covenant for quiet enjoyment until default is made on
the day fixed for payment (or any similar provision) the right is suspended.[78]
Further once the right has arisen, the court will not by injunction restrain the
mortgagee from exercising his right.[79] Indeed, until 1936 it was true to say that
a legal mortgagee had an absolute right to possession which he could enforce
summarily by obtaining judgment for possession in the King's Bench Division.
Thus if it was necessary to commence proceedings for possession of the mortgaged premises instead of relying upon physical entry, the court would afford to
the mortgagee the same summary remedy which he had by virtue of his title to
enable him to enforce the security.

2. Discretion at common law and in equity

(a) *Prior to 1962*

16–82   An amendment to the Rules of Court in 1936,[80] however, materially affected the
enforcement of a mortgagee's right to possession. All proceedings by a mortgagee for payment or for possession were thenceforth assigned to the Chancery
Division[81] with the express object of excluding summary proceedings by a
mortgagee in the King's Bench Division where no regard was had to the
Chancery practice of granting equitable relief to the mortgagor in proper cases.
The reason for the amendment was that summary proceedings for possession
were usually taken against mortgagor-purchasers of small dwelling-houses and it
was desired to give the court discretion to "temper the wind to the shorn lamb."[82]
Proceedings for possession therefore had to be taken by writ or originating
summons in the Chancery Division and judgment for possession became discretionary but only by leave of the Master. Moreover, practice directions authorised

---

[76] See *ante*, para. 16–22 *et seq.*
[77] *Horlock v. Smith* (1842) 6 Jur 478; or merely not to pay the rents to the mortgagor: *Heales v.
M'Murray* (1856) 23 Beav. 401.
[78] *Wilkinson v. Hall* (1837) 3 Bing. N.C. 508; see *ante*, para. 16–61.
[79] *Marquis of Cholmondely v. Lord Clinton* (1820) 2 J. & W. 1, 181; this, of course, is one of the
points of difference between mortgagees and trustees. See also *ante*, para. 16–04 *et seq.*
[80] On the recommendation of the Supreme Court Rules Committee.
[81] Under RSC 1883, Ord. LV, rr. 5A, 5C. Now CPR, Sched. 1, RSC Ord. 88, rr. 1, 2. Also see *Norwich
Union Life Assurance Society v. Preston* [1957] 1 W.L.R. 813.
[82] *Redditch Benefit Building Society v. Roberts* [1940] Ch. 415 at 420.

Masters, when the defendant was in arrears with any instalment, to give him an opportunity of paying off the arrears by adjourning the summons if the circumstances warranted such a course. The mortgagee in the case of *Hinckley and South Leicestershire Permanent Benefit Building Society v. Freeman*[83] sought to impeach these directions as *ultra vires* on the ground that they conflicted with a mortgagee's established right to immediate possession but they were upheld by the court. The change in the procedural rules of court thus gave the court some measure of control over the mortgagee's exercise of his right to possession.

This practice, which continued for some 26 years, was terminated abruptly by the decision of Russell J. in *Birmingham Citizens' Permanent Building Society v. Caunt*[84] who declared that this jurisdiction was without legal foundation. The court had no power to order an adjournment if the mortgagee objected to such a course, save for a short period of up to 28 days and then only when the mortgagor had reasonable prospects of paying off the whole mortgage debt or otherwise satisfying the mortgagee in full.[85]

(b) *Post 1961*

The present position is somewhat obscure but this discretionary jurisdiction in the High Court would still seem to be extant. If, however, the mortgagor has no reasonable prospect of satisfying the mortgagee within a short period of time, an adjournment will be refused.[86] It should be added that the strict approach of the courts based upon commercial considerations is also exemplified in those decisions where despite the fact that the mortgagor has a cross-claim which may exceed the mortgage debt, the courts have still refused an adjournment.[87]   **16–83**

In the case of *Quennel v. Maltby*[88] the possibility of a wider equitable discretion was raised. There it was held by the Court of Appeal that a mortgagee would not be granted possession by the court if he was seeking to exercise his right for purposes other than the protection or enforcement of his security. In that case the mortgagee was seeking possession of a dwelling-house which, contrary to the terms of the mortgage with Barclays Bank, had been let to students. Thus, whilst the tenancies enjoyed the protection of the Rent Act 1977 *vis-à-vis* the mortgagor landlord, their tenancies were not binding on the mortgagee.[89] The mortgagee refused to commence possession proceedings against the tenants. The mortgagor then arranged for his wife to pay off the mortgagee and to take a transfer of the mortgage, thereby becoming the mortgagee. Possession proceedings were then commenced by her to obtain vacant possession of the premises.

---

[83] [1941] Ch. 32.

[84] [1962] Ch. 883.

[85] *Ashley Guarantee plc v. Zacaria* [1993] 1 W.L.R. 62, CA. See also now the statutory discretion, *post*, para. 16–84 *et seq.*

[86] *ibid.* See also *Robertson v. Cilia* [1956] 1 W.L.R. 1502; *Four-Maids Ltd v. Dudley Marshall (Properties) Ltd* [1957] Ch. 317; *Braithwaite v. Winwood* [1960] 1 W.L.R. 1257.

[87] See *Samuel Keller (Holdings) Ltd v. Martins Bank Ltd* [1971] 1 W.L.R. 43; *Mobil Oil v. Rawlinson* (1981) 261 E.G. 260; *Citibank Trust Ltd v. Aviyor* [1987] 1 W.L.R. 1157; *Barclays Bank plc v. Tennet* (unreported), CA (Civ. Div.) Transcript No. 242, 1984.

[88] [1979] 1 W.L.R. 318.

[89] See *Dudley and District Benefit Building Society v. Emerson* [1949] Ch. 707, *Woolwich Building Society v. Dickman* [1996] 3 All E.R. 204; *Barclays Bank plc v. Zaroovabic* [1997] Ch. 321 and *ante*, para. 3–33 and *post*, para. 19–04 *et seq.*

It was held by the court that she was acting as agent for the landlord mortgagor and thus could not assert the rights of the original mortgagee to evict tenants of the mortgagor. Lord Denning M.R. relied on a wider inherent equitable discretion of the courts to prevent a mortgagee or a transferee from him from obtaining possession of a dwelling-house contrary to the justice of the case when there was an ulterior motive, namely, to gain possession of the premises in order to resell it at a profit.[90] This approach and wider equitable discretion has received recent endorsement by the Court of Appeal.[91]

(c) *Statutory discretion*

16–84   *Under the Administration of Justice Acts 1970 and 1973*   Following the recommendations of the Payne Committee,[92] sections 36 to 38 of the Administration of Justice Act 1970 were specifically enacted in the case of mortgages of dwelling-houses in order to reverse the decision of *Birmingham Citizens' Permanent Building Society v. Caunt*.[93] Whether the action is brought in the High Court or the county court,[94] the Administration of Justice Act 1970, as amended, provides the court with certain powers to adjourn the proceedings, stay the order for possession, or postpone the date for delivery of possession.[95] Section 36 of the 1970 Act provides as follows:

"(1) Where the mortgagee under a mortgage of land which consists of or includes a dwelling-house brings an action in which he claims possession of the mortgaged property, not being an action for foreclosure in which a claim for possession of the mortgaged property is also made, the court may exercise any of the powers conferred on it by sub-section (2) below if it appears to the court that in the event of its exercising the power the mortgagor[96] is likely to be able within a reasonable period to pay any sums due under the mortgage[97] or to remedy a default consisting of a breach of any other obligation arising under or by virtue of the mortgage.

(2) The court—

    (a)   may adjourn the proceedings, or

---

[90] *Quennel v. Maltby* [1979] 1 W.L.R. 318 at 323.

[91] *Albany Home Loans Ltd v. Massey* [1997] 2 All E.R. 609.

[92] Report of the Committee on the Enforcement of Judgment Debts 1969 (Cmnd. 3908).

[93] [1962] Ch. 883. These powers are not dependent upon default by the mortgagor: see *per* Buckley L.J. and Scarman L.J. (*contra* Goff L.J.) in *Western Bank Ltd v. Schindler* [1977] Ch. 1.

[94] For the position where the county court has exclusive jurisdiction in mortgage actions, see Chap. 27.

[95] Unless the mortgage secures a regulated agreement within the meaning of the Consumer Credit Act 1974, in which case the 1974 Act applies (see *ante*, Chap. 14).

[96] By s.39(1) "mortgagee" and "mortgagor" include any person deriving title under the original mortgagee or mortgagor. Thus a tenant of a mortgagor may be able to avail himself of these powers, but *quare* the position where the tenancy has been created after the mortgage and is therefore not binding on the mortgagee.

[97] Meaning the arrears due at the date of the hearing: *Middlesbrough Trading and Mortgage Co. Ltd v. Cunningham* (1974) 28 P. & C.R. 69.

(b) on giving judgment, or making an order, for delivery of possession of the mortgaged property, or at any time before the execution[98]; of such judgment or order, may—

    (i) stay or suspend execution of the judgment or order, or

    (ii) postpone the date for delivery of possession,

for such period or periods as the court thinks reasonable.

(3) Any such adjournment, stay, suspension[99] or postponement as is referred to in sub-section (2) above may be made subject to such conditions with regard to payment by the mortgagor of any sums secured by the mortgage or the remedying of any default as the court thinks fit.

(4) The court may from time to time vary or revoke any condition imposed by virtue of this section."

Thus, the purpose of section 36 was to mitigate the severity of the legal rule that a mortgagee is entitled to possession of the mortgaged property by giving some protection to a mortgagor of a dwelling-house who had fallen into temporary financial difficulties over the payment of his instalments in allowing him a reasonable time to make good his default.[1]

Unfortunately, it soon became apparent that those cases in which it was likely that the jurisdiction would be invoked were the very cases where the whole principal sum had become due by reason of the fact that most building society mortgages contain a provision making the whole principal sum due in the case of default. The reference in section 36 to "a reasonable period to pay any sums due under the mortgage" had the effect of confining the operation of the section to relatively few cases where the mortgagor was reasonably likely to be able to pay off the whole of the sums due under the mortgage.[2]

As a result, section 8 of the Administration of Justice Act 1973 was enacted to overturn that decision. Section 8, in effect, redefines "sums due under the mortgage" as " . . . such amounts as the mortgagor would have expected to be required to pay if there has been no provision for earlier payment."

Scope of the discretion   Thus, section 8 of the 1973 Act restored what was **16–85** presumed to be the original intention of the 1970 Act, and, in effect, provides that where the mortgage entitles or permits the mortgage debt to be repaid by instalments or otherwise defers payment of the whole or any part of the sum, and there is also a term rendering the whole sum due in the event of a default, then the court may nevertheless exercise its powers pursuant to section 36 of the 1970 Act provided that the mortgagor is likely to be able to pay off the outstanding

---

[98] It would seem that these words have overruled the decision in *London Permanent Benefit Building Society v. De Baer* [1969] 1 Ch. 321. The court's powers under the section cease once a warrant has been executed: *Cheltenham & Gloucester Building Society v. Obi* [1994] C.L.Y. 3297; *National Provincial Building Society v. Ahmed* [1995] 38 E.G. 138.

[99] For enforcement of orders and suspended orders in particular, see CPR Sched. 1, RSC 88.5.9.

[1] *per* Griffiths L.J. in *Bank of Scotland v. Grimes* [1985] Q.B. 1179 at 1190.

[2] *Halifax Building Society v. Clark* [1973] Ch. 307; but *cf. First Middlesbrough Trading & Mortgage Co. Ltd v. Cunningham* (1974) 28 P. & C.R. 69 approved in *Cheltenham & Gloucester Building Society v. Norgan* [1996] 1 W.L.R. 343, CA where this case was not followed.

instalments. Clearly, by virtue of these provisions an instalment mortgage is now included within the terms of the sections where there was a six-month legal date for redemption, and also an endowment mortgage is similarly included as it is a mortgage which otherwise permits deferred repayment.[3]

The court's statutory discretion does not arise if the mortgagee has obtained possession pursuant to his common law right since the discretion provided by section 36 of the Administration of Justice Act 1970 only arises in circumstances where the mortgagee has brought an action for possession.[4]

In the case of *Habib Bank Ltd v. Tailor*[5] it was held that if the loan is not one which otherwise permits deferred repayment then the statutory discretion does *not* apply. This may have serious consequences for the mortgagor.[6] In that case the mortgagor secured an overdraft on his current account with his bank by a charge on his home the sums being repayable on demand. As the bank could therefore not sue on a supporting mortgage until such a demand had been made the court held that section 8 of the 1973 Act did not apply as it was not a mortgage which permitted deferred repayment. As a consequence any relief had to be sought under section 36 of the 1970 Act, and as we have seen, this would not be possible unless the mortgagor could demonstrate to the court that he could repay the whole of the debt within a reasonable period.

In the case of *Western Bank Limited v. Schindler*[7] a majority of the Court of Appeal was even prepared to hold that section 36 of the 1970 Act was applicable even in the absence of a default by the mortgagor.[8] This was an unusual case in that the mortgage made no provision for the payments of capital or interest until 10 years after its execution. The mortgagor, however, failed to pay the premium due on the life assurance policy and the policy lapsed. The debt was therefore inadequately secured and in the event it was held that it was not a proper case for the exercise of statutory discretion in the mortgagor's favour. But, the contrary opinion of Goff L.J. is probably to be preferred in that he was of the view that section 36 of the 1970 Act had no application in any event.

(d) *Exercising the court's discretion*

16–86   The conditions for the grant of an adjournment are strict. The court's discretionary powers are only exercisable if there is a likelihood of the mortgagor being able to pay the sums due (*i.e.* the arrears and also the current instalments) within a reasonable period, or that he will seek a speedy sale of the mortgaged property

---

[3] *Centrax Trustees Ltd v. Ross* [1979] 2 All E.R. 952; *Bank of Scotland v. Grimes* [1985] Q.B. 1179. The section also empowers the court to adjourn foreclosure actions but not to make suspended orders in such cases.

[4] *Ropaigealach v. Barclays Bank plc* [1999] 3 W.L.R. 17.

[5] [1982] 1 W.L.R. 1218.

[6] But not all mortgages in which the loan is expressed to be on demand fall within this category, see S. Tromans [1984] Conv. 91.

[7] [1977] Ch. 1.

[8] *ibid.* at 12, 13, 15, 19, 26. See also *Royal Trust Co. of Canada v. Markham* [1975] 1 W.L.R. 1416.

to discharge the arrears and the mortgage debt.[9] Thus the court should not grant an indefinite adjournment and the period must be fixed or ascertainable.[10] In any event, these powers are *not* exercisable where the mortgagor is unable to comply with the original payment schedule and pay off the arrears by reasonable instalments.[11] Thus the court has no power to order payment of instalments at a reduced level, for example, payment of interest only.

In assessing how long it would be appropriate to postpone the mortgagee's right of possession, the starting point in determining that period is (in the absence of unusual circumstances) the outstanding term of the mortgage.[12] The court should, at the outset, resolve any disputes over the apportionment of any instalments ordered to be paid by the mortgagor as between the interest accrued on the mortgage debt and the outstanding principal and ask itself whether the mortgagee's security was likely to be put at risk by the delay in possession occasioned by the court's order.[13]

In assessing whether a mortgagor is able to comply with the terms of any proposed suspended order for possession, the court is entitled to rely on the mortgagor's witness statements or those of his solicitor.[14] Whilst a counterclaim by a mortgagee cannot amount to a defence to a claim for possession *per se*, the existence and quantum of any counterclaim is relevant for the purposes of the exercise of the court's discretion pursuant to statute.[15] Since a counterclaim can also operate as a set-off to reduce the arrears due on the mortgage debt it is thus relevant in ascertaining the material level of indebtedness and the manner in which the court may exercise its discretion.[16]

In determining what is a reasonable period under section 36, the court (when considering the evidence before it) will consider the following factors[17]:

> "(a) How much can the borrower reasonably afford to pay, both now and in the future?
> (b) If the borrower has a temporary difficulty in meeting his obligations, how long is the difficulty likely to last?
> (c) What was the reason for the arrears which have accumulated?
> (d) How much remains of the original term?
> (e) What are relevant contractual terms, and what type of mortgage is it, *i.e.* when is the principal due to be repaid?

---

[9] *Royal Trust Company of Canada v. Markham* [1975] 1 W.L.R. 1416. *Mobil Oil v. Rawlinson* (1982) 43 P. & C.R. 221; *Bank of Scotland v. Grimes* [1985] Q.B. 1179; *Citibank Trust Ltd v. Aviyor* [1987] 1 W.L.R. 1157; *National & Provincial Building Society v. Lloyd* [1996] 1 All E.R. 630; *Cheltenham & Gloucester Building Society v. Krausz* [1996] 1 W.L.R. 1558; *Target Home Loans Ltd v. Clothier* [1994] 1 All E.R. 439.

[10] The usual time given for possession if no order is made under the Administration of Justice Acts 1970–1973, is 28 days after service, see *Barclays Bank v. Bird* [1954] Ch. 274 at 282, *per* Harman J.

[11] *First National Bank plc v. Sayed* [1991] 2 All E.R. 250; *National Westminster Bank plc v. Sketton* [1993] 1 W.L.R. 72; *Ashley Guarantee plc v. Zacaria* [1993] 1 W.L.R. 62.

[12] *Cheltenham & Gloucester Building Society v. Norgan* [1996] 1 W.L.R. 343.

[13] *ibid.*

[14] *Cheltenham & Gloucester Building Society v. Grant* (1994) 26 H.L.R. 703.

[15] *National Westminster Bank plc v. Skelton* [1993] 1 W.L.R. 72; *Ashleigh Guarantee Plc v. Zacaria* [1993] 1 W.L.R. 62.

[16] *cf. Household Mortgage Corp. Plc v. Pringle* (1997) 30 H.L.R. 250 where the court disregarded the counterclaim for unliquidated damages.

[17] *Cheltenham & Gloucester Building Society v. Norgan* [1996] 1 W.L.R. 343 at 357.

(f)   Is it a case where the court should exercise its powers to disregard accelerated payment provisions (section 8 of the Act of 1973)?

(g)   Is it reasonable to expect the lender, in the circumstances of the particular case, to recoup the arrears of interest (1) over the whole of the original term, or (2) within a shorter period, or even (3) within a longer period, *i.e.* by extending the repayment period? Is it reasonable to expect the lender to capitalise the interest or not?

(h)   Are there any reasons affecting the security which should influence the length of the period for repayment?

In the light of the answers above the court can proceed to exercise its overall discretion taking account also of any further factors which may arise in a particular case."

Once a reasonable period has been determined by the court and the mortgagor then fails to show that there is likelihood that he can pay off such arrears as may have accumulated within that time, the court has no jurisdiction under section 36 to suspend the possession order.[18]

The court also has the jurisdiction to postpone a possession order in circumstances where it is apparent that the mortgagors do not have the available funds to meet any of the liabilities other than by selling the mortgaged property[19] and where, on the evidence, the court is satisfied that a sale would be more readily effected if the house was occupied by the mortgagor rather than repossessed by the mortgagee.[20] It would seem that the mortgagor must adduce evidence relating to the actual marketing of his property[21] and that the mortgagor has not set too high a sale price.[22] The period of postponement that the court will grant is not necessarily confined to a very short period, and a period of up to a year has been considered to be potentially reasonable.[23] Where there has been considerable delay in attempting to sell the property or it is clear that the sale price of the property would be barely sufficient to discharge the debt secured on it, the court will order immediate possession or else only allow a particularly short postponement.[24]

If the proceeds of sale of the mortgaged property will be insufficient to redeem the mortgage, the jurisdiction under section 36 cannot arise since there will be no prospect of the mortgagor paying all the sums due under the mortgage within a reasonable time. In such circumstances the mortgagor may have to consider any remedies that he may have under section 91 of the Law of Property Act 1925.[25]

---

[18] *Town & Country Building Society v. Julien* (1992) 24 H.L.R. 312; *Abbey National Mortgages Plc v. Bernard* [1995] N.P.C. 118.

[19] See para. 16–86, n. 9.

[20] *Target Home Loans Limited v. Clothier* [1994] 1 All E.R. 439, CA.

[21] *cf. Mortgage Service Funding Plc v. Steele* (1996) 72 P. & C.R. 40, where the evidence was described as "utterly flimsy".

[22] *Royal Trust Bank of Canada v. Markham* [1975] 1 W.L.R. 1416.

[23] *National & Provincial Building Society v. Lloyd* [1996] 1 All E.R. 630.

[24] *Bristol & West Building Society v. Ellis* (1997) 73 P. & C.R. 159.

[25] See *Palk v. Mortgage Services Funding Plc* [1993] Ch. 330; *Cheltenham & Gloucester Building Society v. Krausz* [1997] 1 W.L.R. 1558 and para. 16–103 *et seq.*

It should also be added that where the mortgage falls within the provisions of section 8 of the 1973 Act, the court's discretion also extends to foreclosure actions whether or not possession is also sought in the same proceedings.[26]

(e) *Consumer Credit Act 1974*[27]

The Act has provided a complex series of safeguards in many different types of **16–87** credit transactions. Most mortgages are not included within its terms since generally it only applies where the credit provided does not exceed £25,000[28] and where the mortgagor is an "individual" and the mortgagee is not an exempt lender as defined by section 16 of the Act.[29] This definition of exempt lender includes some building societies,[30] local authorities, large assurance companies and other cases specified by ministerial order. The purpose of the Act in so far as it regulates mortgage lending, in effect, is to provide safeguards for borrowers raising finance by way of second mortgages. With regard to those transactions to which the Act does apply, however (*i.e.* "regulated agreements"), such agreements must be in the form prescribed by regulations in order to ensure that the mortgagor is aware of his rights and duties, the amount and rate of the total charge for credit, and the protection and remedies provided by the Act.[31]

The agreement must contain all the agreed terms, except implied terms and must be signed by both parties. Also, the mortgagee must supply the mortgagor with a copy of the proposed agreement seven days in advance of execution, and must not approach him in the meantime in order to give him an opportunity to withdraw. If the agreement fails to comply with the requirements of the Act, it is improperly executed and enforceable only on an order of the court.[32] If the mortgagor is in default the mortgagee must serve a default notice under the provisions of section 87 of the Act before he can recover possession of the goods or land. If the mortgagor complies in due time with the requirements of the default notice, the breach is treated as if it had never occurred.[33] The mortgage is only enforceable by order of the court.[34] The court has a wide discretion to make a "time order" under section 129(1) of the Act, under which the mortgagor is given time to pay by such instalments and at such time as the court having regard to the means of the mortgagor, considers reasonable. The court can also make a suspended order for possession under section 135 of the Act.[35]

---

[26] Administration of Justice Act 1973, s.8(3), and see *Lord Marples of Wallasey v. Holmes* (1975) 31 P. & C.R. 94.

[27] See generally chap. 14.

[28] S.I. 1998 No. 996 with effect from May 1, 1998, repealing S.I. 1983 No. 1878, applying a limit of £15,000 to transactions from May 20, 1985. Up until this date the original limit applies of £5,000.

[29] As amended by the Building Societies Act 1986, s.120(1), (2); the Housing and Planning Act 1986, s.22; the Banking Act 1987, s.88.

[30] From January 1, 1987, building societies lost their automatic exemption from the Consumer Credit Act 1974 when the major part of the Building Societies Act 1986 came into force; the Consumer Credit (Exempt Agreements) Order (No. 2), S.I. 1985 No. 757, presently in force, is further amended by S.I. 1985 No. 1736; S.I. 1985 No. 1918; S.I. 1986 No. 1105; S.I. 1986 No. 2186; S.I. 1987 No. 1578.

[31] ss.60, 61.

[32] ss.58, 61 and 65.

[33] s.89.

[34] s.126 (or, if the mortgagor consents, s.173(3)). The "court" is the county court, see s.189(1).

[35] For a fuller explanation of the terms of the Consumer Credit Act 1974, see chap 14, *ante*.

(f) *Regulated mortgages under the Rent Act 1977*[36]

16–88 Finally, mention should be made of the provisions of the Rent Act 1977 (as amended)[37] which impose special statutory restrictions on the right of a mortgagee to take possession of mortgaged premises in the case of regulated mortgages. A regulated mortgage is a legal mortgage or charge by way of legal mortgage[38] of land consisting of or including a dwelling-house which is let on or subject to a regulated tenancy which binds the mortgagee[39] and which is not exempted under section 131(2) of the Act. These mortgages are now rare as the provisions of the 1977 Act generally have no application unless the mortgage was created before the relevant date.[40] Thus these complex provisions are of limited importance and it is suggested that further reference be made to the standard works on the Rent Act 1977.[41]

FORECLOSURE OR JUDICIAL SALE

1. **Generally**

16–89 Equity, having created the equity of redemption, also provides means whereby a mortgagee may free his title from the equity. Otherwise a mortgagee would suffer a serious injustice since, even when in urgent need of his capital, he would have no means of compelling its restoration.[42] He might go into possession or appoint a receiver but even so, the rents and profits might do no more than pay him his interest. Consequently, although jealous to protect the equity of redemption, the court allows a mortgagee to destroy the equitable right to redeem *with its own assistance*. This assistance takes the form of an order either for foreclosure or for a judicial sale. By the former, a mortgagee's title is made absolute by the court, the effect of which is to transfer the legal estate from the mortgagor to the mortgagee.[43] By the latter, the security is, under the supervision of the court, sold freed from the equity of redemption. In the Republic of Ireland, foreclosure orders have never been favoured[44] and there judicial sale is the remedy for a mortgagee as well as for a chargee. In England, on the other hand, the natural remedy given by the court to a mortgagee is foreclosure, and judicial sale is available to him only as an alternative which the court may in its discretion grant

---

[36] Controlled mortgages were abolished by the Housing Act 1980, s.152 and Sched. 26.

[37] ss.131, 132, as amended by the Housing Act 1980, s.152 and Scheds 25, 26.

[38] Rent Act 1977, s.131(4).

[39] *ibid.,* s.131(1).

[40] Usually December 8, 1965, but in any event no later than August 14, 1974.

[41] See, *e.g.* Megarry, *The Rent Acts* (11th ed., 1988), Woodfall, *Law of Landlord and Tenant* (1994), vol. 3.

[42] *Campbell v. Holyland* (1877) 7 Ch.D. 166 at 171, *per* Jessel, M.R.

[43] *i.e.* by vesting the mortgagor's fee simple or term of years in the mortgagee, see LPA 1925, ss88(2), 89(2). In the case of registered land an order for foreclosure is completed by registration of the proprietor of the charge as proprietor of the land and by cancellation of the charge and all incumbrances and entries inferior thereto: Land Registration Act 1925, s.34(3). Prior to 1925 the remedy of foreclosure terminated the mortgagor's equity of redemption leaving the mortgagee with an unencumbered interest.

[44] *Re Cronin* [1914] 1 I.R. 23, 29; *Harpur v. Buchanan* [1919] 1 I.R. 1, 4; but the jurisdiction to give foreclosure, though not exercised, appears to exist: *Shea v. Moore* [1894] 1 I.R. 158 at 163, n, *per* Porter, M.R.

him in the course of proceedings for foreclosure.[45] The realisation of his security in court in one of these two ways is, historically, the primary remedy of a mortgagee. However, today a mortgagee will nearly always possess either an express or statutory power to sell out of court[46] and will not be obliged to seek the court's assistance. Further, the courts have shown a reluctance to order foreclosure. Consequently it is a remedy which now has only limited importance and it has been suggested that it should be replaced by the simple remedy to order a judicial sale as in the Republic of Ireland. On the other hand, the power of the court to order foreclosure is still of some interest, since a mortgagee may desire to retain the mortgaged property in his own hands and to obtain the balance of its value.[47]

2. **The right of foreclosure**

Notwithstanding the Law Commission's recommendation that the right to foreclosure be abolished,[48] in England and Wales the right to foreclose remains and is inherent in the nature of mortgage[49] and in no other form of security. It was for this reason that the test of a security as to whether it was a mortgage rather than a mere charge was determined by the availability to the creditor of the remedy of foreclosure. The only exceptions being *(i)* the old Welsh mortgage, in which any realisation of the security is impossible,[50] *(ii)* mortgages given by public utility companies where the impossibility of foreclosure arises not from the form of mortgage but from the property being in public use[51] and *(iii)* mortgages granted by the Crown, against which foreclosure is not available.[52] In instances where the Crown is the mortgagor, the court will simply order a sale and rely upon the Crown conveying.[53] All other mortgages, whether their subject-matter is realty or personalty[54] and whether the mortgage is legal or equitable, give rise to this remedy. Thus an equitable mortgagee of a legal estate by express contract or by deposit of title deeds may foreclose,[55] while a mortgagee of an equitable interest in property may foreclose the equitable interest leaving the legal title outstanding in a third party.[56] Similarly, a mortgagee of personal chattels[57] and of a share in a partnership,[58] and a debenture holder[59] may foreclose as may a mortgage of

16–90

---

[45] LPA 1925, s.91(2) and see *post*, para. 16–99.
[46] See *ante*, para. 16–53 *et seq*. In practice a mortgagee will only seek the remedy of foreclosure where the security is deficient but there is a prospect that the value of the property will improve.
[47] For a modern case illustrating the difficulties which can be encountered in foreclosure proceedings, see *Lloyds & Scottish Trust Ltd v. Britten* (1982) 44 P. & C.R. 249.
[48] *Transfer of Land—Land Mortgages 1991*, Law Com. No. 204, paras 7.26, 7.27.
[49] *Re Bogg* [1917] 2 Ch. 239 at 255.
[50] See *Coote on Mortgages* (9th ed., 1927), Vol. 1, Chap. III, p. 35.
[51] *Gardner v. London, Chatham and Dover Rly. Co.* (1867) 2 Ch. App. 201.
[52] *Hodge v. Attorney-General* (1839) 3 Y. & G. Ex 342.
[53] *Hancock v. Attorney-General* (1864) 10 Jur. N.S. 557; *Bartlett v. Rees* (1871) L.R. 12 Eq. 395.
[54] *General Credit and Discount Co. v. Glegg* (1883) 22 Ch.D. 549.
[55] *Pryce v. Bury* (1853) 2 Drew 41; *Frail v. Ellis* (1852) 16 Beav. 350.
[56] *cf. Slade v. Rigg* (1843) 3 Hare 35.
[57] *Kemp v. Westbrook* (1749) 1 Ves.Sen. 278.
[58] *Redmayne v. Forster* (1866) L.R. 2 Eq. 467.
[59] *Sadler v. Worley* [1894] 2 Ch. 170.

policies of insurance[60] and pensions[61] and of reversionary as well as present interests.[62] However, apart from statute, the remedy of a chargee is sale, not foreclosure.[63] A chargee with a charge by way of legal mortgage is a statutory exception to this rule because the Law of Property Act 1925[64] gives him precisely the same remedies as a legal mortgagee.

3. Court's control of the loss of the equity of redemption

16–91   Foreclosure is the prerogative only of a mortgagee because foreclosure presupposes a title in the creditor which has become absolute at law through the breach of a condition.[65] Under his contract a mortgagee's title to the property becomes absolute when the mortgagor fails to redeem in accordance with the terms of the proviso for redemption. Equity then intervenes on behalf of the mortgagor to give him a right to redeem notwithstanding that failure, and thus puts a stop on the absolute title of the mortgagee. However, there has to be a stage at which a mortgagee can finally enforce his security and the mortgagor's equitable rights brought to an end. Foreclosure, as Jessel M.R. indicated,[66] is no more than the court's removal from the mortgagee's title of the stop which the court itself has imposed. Foreclosure is therefore always an act of the court: today a mortgagee usually has power to sell his security out of court but he cannot become the beneficial owner of the security except under the authority of the court. In *Re Farnol, Eades, Irvine & Co.*[67] Warrington J. said:

> "Foreclosure as a thing which can be done by a person has no meaning. Foreclosure is done by the order of the court, not by any person. In the strict legal sense it is nothing more than the destruction of the equity of redemption which previously existed."

16–92   *Nature of mortgagor's default giving rise to foreclosure*   It follows that the right to foreclosure cannot arise until the mortgagor is in default *under the proviso for redemption*[68] and repayment has become due at law. The importance of this is that not every breach of his contract by a mortgagor will give a mortgagee the right of foreclosure: the breach must bring into effect the condition rendering the mortgagee's title absolute and therefore must concern the proviso for redemption. This is illustrated by *Williams v. Morgan*,[69] where a mortgage made in 1900 contained a covenant for the payment of the principal in 1914 (with interest half-

---

[60] *Re Kerr's Policy* (1869) L.R. 8 Eq. 331.
[61] *James v. Ellis* (1871) 19 W.R. 319.
[62] *Slade v. Rigg* (1843) 3 Hare 35.
[63] *Tennant v. Trenchard* (1869) L.R. 4 Ch. 537.
[64] LPA 1925, s.87; see also Land Registration Act 1925, s.34(1).
[65] *Bonham v. Newcomb* (1684) 1 Vern. 232 affd. (1689) 1 Vern. 233n, HL.
[66] " . . . the court simply removes the stop it has itself put on." *Per* Jessel M.R. in *Carter v. Wake* (1877) 4 Ch.D. 605 at 606. See also *Heath v. Pugh* (1882) 7 A.C. 235.
[67] [1915] 1 Ch. 22 at 24.
[68] In a mortgage of a legal estate, a proviso for redemption is not strictly necessary since by mere payment the mortgage term becomes a satisfied term: therefore a forfeiture clause would be sufficient. However, a proviso for redemption is often found in practice *Contra* bank mortgages, which are usually payable on demand and contain no such proviso.
[69] [1906] 1 Ch. 804.

yearly in the meanwhile) but the proviso for redemption permitted redemption in 1914 on payment of the capital and of such interest as might then be due and unpaid. The mortgagor defaulted in payment of interest before 1914 but Swinfen-Eady J. held that under this deed no right to foreclose could arise until 1914. The covenant for payment and the proviso for redemption were distinct stipulations, and it would have been altering the plain language of the deed to incorporate the terms of the covenant for payment into the proviso for redemption. The mortgagor's default did not, therefore, constitute a default under the proviso for redemption, so that the mortgagee was not entitled to a foreclosure.

However, this does not mean that the mortgagor's default must be in the repayment of capital. Even when the mortgagee has debarred himself from calling in the capital for a definite period of years, default in the payment of any instalment of interest will entitle him to foreclose if the proviso for redemption was made conditional on the punctual payment of interest.[70] The point is that the terms of the covenant for payment of interest must have been incorporated into the proviso for redemption. The same principle applies to a mortgagor's other covenants. Ultimately, it is a question of construction of the mortgage terms.[71] Thus, in a mortgage of leaseholds, the mortgagor's breach of his covenant to observe the terms of the lease will give rise to a right of foreclosure only if the performance of the covenant was expressly incorporated in the proviso for redemption.[72] If such a covenant and the proviso for redemption are expressed as distinct stipulations, the court will not, by construction, incorporate the covenant into the proviso for redemption.[73]

The time when foreclosure becomes available is therefore the moment the mortgagor makes default under the proviso for redemption. The default which usually calls into being the right of foreclosure is the failure to repay the principal on the date named in the contract for redemption which is usually six months after the execution of the mortgage deed. If no date is fixed or if the money is repayable on demand, then the right arises after a demand has been made and a reasonable time has been allowed for compliance with the demand.[74] As a rule, the right to foreclose and the equitable right to redeem arise simultaneously on the passing of that date without redemption. There is, however, no objection to a mortgagee precluding himself from foreclosing during any period of whatever length or on whatever terms and the mortgagor need not be under a corresponding obligation not to redeem.[75] As a mortgagee requires no protection when making the agreement, he cannot obtain relief on the ground of want of mutuality even when he has not made his agreement to forbear conditional on the punctual payment of interest.[76] Therefore he almost invariably makes forbearance conditional on such payment of interest in order that a failure to pay interest may lift

---

[70] *Burrowes v. Molloy* (1845) 2 Jo. & Lat. 521; *Edwards v. Martin* (1856) 25 L.J.Ch. 284; *Kidderminster Mutual Benefit Building Society v. Haddock* [1936] W.N. 158; *Twentieth Century Banking Corporation Ltd v. Wilkinson* [1977] Ch. 99.

[71] *Mohamedali Jaffer Karachiwalla v. Noorally Rattanshi Rajan Nanji* [1959] A.C. 518, JCPC.

[72] cf. *Seaton v. Twyford* (1870) L.R. 11 Eq. 591; if in an equitable mortgage by contract to create a legal mortgage the mortgagee agrees not to foreclose for a given period, the court will imply that this is conditional on the perfomance of covenants. *ibid.*

[73] *Turner v. Spencer* (1894) 43 W.R. 153.

[74] *Fitzgerald's Trustee v. Mellersh* [1892] 1 Ch. 385; *Balfe v. Lord* (1842) 2 Dr. & War. 480.

[75] *Ramsbottom v. Wallis* (1835) 5 L.J.Ch. 92; *Kreglinger v. New Patagonia Meat & Cold Storage Co. Ltd* [1914] A.C. 25.

[76] *Burrowes v. Molloy* (1845) 2 Jo. & Lat. 521.

the bar to foreclosure.[77] Nor will he afterwards lose his right to foreclose by accepting payment of the interest: to revive the bar he must actually *waive the breach of the condition*.[78]

If there is only an agreement to execute a mortgage, equity takes on that as done which ought to be done and permits the mortgagee to foreclose after non-payment by the mortgagor in accordance with the terms of the agreement or after demand and a reasonable time for compliance.[79]

The right to foreclose, once it has arisen, continues to be available so long as any part of the mortgage debt remains unpaid.[80]

4. **Persons entitled to seek foreclosure**

16–93   Foreclosure is available to a legal or equitable mortgagee and to the holder either of a registered charge or a charge by way of legal mortgage. The right to foreclose also belongs to persons who become entitled to the mortgage by assignment or devolution and is available to a trustee in bankruptcy.[81] Thus, in addition to an incumbrancer solely entitled, the following persons may foreclose:

(1) Express assignees of the mortgagee. The assignee's right is, however, subject to the state of the accounts between mortgagor and mortgagee at the date of the assignment and also to any equities then existing in the mortgagor's favour.[82] An assignment of the debt without the security leaves the right to foreclose in the original mortgagee.[83]

(2) Sub-mortgagees are assignees and may foreclose on the original mortgagor on similar terms.[84] They may also foreclose on incumbrances ranking below them.[85]

(3) Co-mortgagees. Each must foreclose the whole mortgage not merely his own share.[86] Co-ownership of land involves a trust of land and co-mortgagees of land ought presumably to foreclose through the trustees.

(4) Trustees. The beneficiaries must proceed through their trustees.[87]

(5) Personal representatives, before assent or transfer.[88]

---

[77] The way such an agreement is framed is to have the ordinary proviso for redemption putting the mortgagor in default after six months followed by a separate covenant not to call in the money for the period specified, the covenant being made conditional on the regular payment of interest.

[78] *Keene v. Biscoe* (1878) 8 Ch.D. 201.

[79] *Fitzgerald's Trustee v. Mellersh* [1892] 1 Ch. 385.

[80] A foreclosure decree will not, however, be made in respect of costs only: *Drought v. Redford* (1827) 1 Moll. 572.

[81] A judgment creditor who has obtained a charging order under the Charging Orders Act 1979 is in the position of an equitable mortgagee.

[82] *Withington v. Tate* (1869) L.R. 4 Ch. App. 288; *Turner v. Smith* [1901] 1 Ch. 213.

[83] *Morley v. Morley* (1858) 25 Beav. 253; he will, however, be a trustee of the security for the assignee.

[84] See *Hobart v. Abbott* (1731) 2 P.Wms. 643; *Norrish v. Marshall* (1821) 5 Madd. 475.

[85] *Rose v. Page* (1829) 2 Sim. 471; *Slade v. Rigg* (1843) 3 Hare 35.

[86] *Davenport v. James* (1847) 7 Hare 249; *Luke v. South Kensington Hotel Co.* (1879) 11 Ch.D. 121; as to the effect of decree in the case of an equitable mortgage, see *Re Continental Oxygen Co., Elias v. Continental Oxygen Co.* [1897] 1 Ch 511.

[87] *Wood v. Williams* (1819) 4 Madd. 186.

[88] Administration of Estates Act 1925, ss1, 3.

(6) Trustees in bankruptcy, in the case of the bankruptcy of a mortgagee.[89]

5. **Parties to the action**

If there are several persons beneficially interested in the mortgage moneys, they **16–94** must all be represented in the action; and in accordance with the general rule, trustees and personal representatives sufficiently represent the persons for whom they act so that none of the beneficiaries need be joined.[90] In the case of co-mortgagees *all* must be joined[91]; if they are willing to concur in the proceedings, they will be made claimants; if not, they must be made defendants.[92] If land has been mortgaged to several co-mortgagees, there will be a trust of land[93] and foreclosure must take place through the trustees. Clearly, when the money was advanced out of a joint account (as in the case of trustee-mortgagees), the personal representatives of a deceased co-mortgagee need not be joined. Moreover under section 111 of the Law of Property Act 1925 co-mortgagees are to be deemed joint tenants—subject to any statement to the contrary—both when the money is expressed to be advanced out of a joint account and when the mortgage is merely made to them jointly. Even in the rare case when a mortgage of land is not made upon a joint account, the personal representatives of a deceased co-mortgagee probably need not be joined, since foreclosure will always take place through the trustees of the land, who are necessarily joint tenants. In a mortgage of personalty, however, the fact that the money neither was, nor could be deemed to be, advanced out of a joint account would necessitate the joinder of the personal representative because personalty is not subject to the trust of land imposed by statute.[94] It may be added that in an action by debenture holders all must be before the court either as claimants or defendants[95]; this is usually achieved by a representative action under CPR 19.6.

In foreclosure actions, all persons interested in the equity of redemption *must* be before the court in order that they may be bound by the accounts. In general, beneficiaries are sufficiently represented by their trustees.[96] In foreclosure suits, however, so anxious is the court that no party shall be deprived of his opportunity to redeem that it will readily allow beneficiaries to be joined if it appears that the trustees may be unable to redeem.[97] The determination of who, in general, has a right to redeem and is entitled to be joined as defendant has already been investigated at length in connection with redemption and with the maxim, *redeem up, foreclose down.*[98] The details need not be repeated here but the general principle is that all persons must be joined who will be affected by the accounts taken in the action, so that in a foreclosure action all persons acquiring interests

---

[89] As to insolvency generally, see chap. 23.
[90] CPR, Sched. 1, RSC Ord. 15, r. 14.
[91] *Davenport v. James* (1847) 7 Hare 249.
[92] See *Luke v. South Kensington Hotel Co. Ltd* (1879) 11 Ch.D. 121.
[93] Law of Property Act 1925, s.34(2).
[94] *cf. Vickers v. Cowell* (1839) 1 Beav. 529.
[95] *Re Continental Oxygen Co., Elias v. Continental Oxygen Co.* [1897] 1 Ch. 511; *Westminster Bank Ltd v. Residential Properties Improvement Co. Ltd* [1938] Ch. 639.
[96] CPR, Sched. 1, RSC Ord. 15, r. 14.
[97] *Goldsmid v. Stonehewer* (1852) 9 Hare, Appendix XXXVIII.
[98] See para. 19–29A.

in the property *subsequent to the mortgage* must be joined.[99] Thus, a mortgagee must foreclose not only on the mortgagor but on all persons claiming through him, including puisne incumbrancers.[1] He may, however, foreclose without, at the same time, claiming to redeem *prior* incumbrancers[2]; one may not redeem up without foreclosing down, but one may foreclose down without redeeming up because prior incumbrancers will not be affected by the accounts taken in the foreclosure. On the same principle a mortgagee may foreclose on the mortgagor without at the same time redeeming his own sub-mortgage.

6. Procedure in foreclosure actions[3]

(a) *Jurisdiction*

16–95   If the amount actually advanced does not exceed the county court limit,[4] proceedings for foreclosure may be taken in the county court[5]; otherwise foreclosure proceedings must be brought in the High Court and are assigned by the Supreme Court Act 1981 to the Chancery Division.[6] The exclusive jurisdiction of a county court in relation to proceedings for possession of property compromising a dwelling-house outside Greater London[7] does not apply to an action for foreclosure or sale in which a claim for possession of the mortgaged property is also made.[8] Thus a mortgagee in a foreclosure action is under no compulsion to commence proceedings in the county court when his advance is less than £30,000. However, and importantly, the action for foreclosure or sale must be a genuine one for that relief and the claim for foreclosure or sale not merely added as a device to take the proceedings outside the county court's exclusive jurisdiction in possession proceedings.[9] Often a claim will include payment, possession of the mortgaged property, foreclosure of sale together with other relief in the same proceedings. The mere claim for foreclosure or sale, however, does not itself render the action one for foreclosure or sale. The test is to have regard to the nature of the relief which the claimant genuinely seeks. Thus a claim for possession under a mortgage is usually treated as an action for recovery of land

---

[99] A person entitled to redeem who has not been made a defendant will not be bound by the foreclosure: *Gee v. Liddell* [1913] 2 Ch. 62.
[1] See *Keith v. Butcher* (1884) 25 Ch.D. 750.
[2] *Rose v. Page* (1829) 2 Sim. 471; *Slade v. Rigg* (1843) 3 Hare 35.
[3] Procedure generally is considered in chap. 27.
[4] At present £30,000 (unless extended by agreement): see County Courts Act 1984, s.23; High Court and County Courts Jurisdiction Order 1991 (S.I. 1991 No. 724). Where the sum originally advanced exceeded the county court limit but is reduced by payment or otherwise, to below that sum, the county court would appear to have jurisdiction to hear the action—see *Shields, Whitley and District Amalgamated Model Building Society v. Richards* (1901) 84 L.T. 587.
[5] *i.e.* the court for the district in which the land or any part of it is situate CPR Sched. 2, CCR, RSC Ord. 4, r. 3; where the mortgage comprises property other than land action may be commenced in the court or the district in which the defendant resides or carries on business.
[6] s.61(1). This remains the case under CPR Part 55.
[7] See *post*, para. 27–02.
[8] See the County Courts Act 1984, ss21, 147(1) (replacing the Administration of Justice Act 1970, s.37(2)).
[9] *The Trustees of Manchester Unity Life Insurance Collecting Society v. Sadler* [1974] 1 W.L.R. 770.

within section 21 of the County Courts Act 1984 and not as an action for foreclosure within section 23.[10]

A claim for foreclosure whether in the High Court or county court, is begun by a Part 8 Claim Form.[11] Court procedure is considered elsewhere.[12]

Relief sought   A mortgagee may bring his claim for foreclosure only, so that his claim is merely that an account be taken of what is due to him on the mortgage in respect of principal, interest and costs, and that the court may foreclose the mortgage. In such a claim the court may, at the instance of any interested party, direct a sale, although the claim is for foreclosure. However, the mortgagee himself may favour a sale and then his claim is for an account and for foreclosure or sale. Furthermore, if he is a mortgagee in possession his claim for an account must refer to that fact and he should make a specific claim to be allowed such sums as have been properly expended by him on the mortgaged property. If a mortgagee is not in possession and is asking for foreclosure rather than sale, an order for possession will be necessary when the mortgagor proves obstructive. The court has jurisdiction to make an order for possession without any demand for such an order having been made in the claim form,[13] and may make the order even after the foreclosure decree has been made absolute.[14] Nevertheless, if the mortgagor is expected to prove obstructive, it is advisable to claim the order specifically, since the court will not make the order without notice where it was not asked for in the claim form.[15] Again, a mortgagee is entitled to pursue all his remedies concurrently and will frequently combine with his foreclosure action a claim for judgment on the mortgagor's personal covenant to pay the mortgage debt. Such actions must be commenced in the Chancery Division if the High Court is the appropriate forum.[16] However, it must be remembered that if a mortgagee sues on the personal covenant *after* foreclosing he reopens the foreclosure.[17]

A mortgagee who starts proceedings for foreclosure cannot bring an action on the personal covenant concurrently in the Queen's Bench Division, since it was open to him to combine this remedy with his foreclosure suit.[18] Thus, such an action will be treated as vexatious and will be stayed.[19] Further, although a mortgagee may obtain judgment for payment and foreclosure in the same action, the two claims are quite distinct. For example, a foreclosure decree gives the mortgagor six months in which to redeem but the judgment on the covenant is for immediate payment as there is no rule in equity that a sum of money immediately payable at law shall not be payable until after six months have elapsed.[20]

---

[10] *West Penwith Rural District Council v. Gunnell* [1968] 1 W.L.R. 1153.
[11] CPR 8 BPD–004.
[12] See chap. 27.
[13] *Salt v. Edgar* (1886) 54 L.T. 374.
[14] *Jenkins v. Ridgley* (1893) 41 W.R. 585.
[15] *Le Bas v. Grant* (1895) 64 L.J.Ch. 368.
[16] CPR, Sched. 1, RSC Ord. 88, r. 1.
[17] See *post*, para. 16–103 *et seq.*
[18] A claim for payment was only a "mortgage action" within CPR, Sched. 1, RSC Ord. 88, r. 1 (repealed with effect from October 15, 2001) if the claimant is relying upon the mortgage to make his claim: *National Westminster Bank v. Kitch* [1996] 1 W.L.R. 1316. Thus a claim by a bank for monies due on an ordinary account can be properly brought in the Queen's Bench Division.
[19] *Earl Poulett v. Viscount Hill* [1893] 1 Ch. 277; *Williams v. Hunt* [1905] 1 K.B. 512.
[20] *Farrer v. Lacy, Hartland & Co.* (1885) 31 Ch.D. 42; see also *Dymond v. Croft* (1876) 3 Ch.D. 512.

Where foreclosure has taken place by reason of the failure of the claimant in a mortgage action for redemption to redeem, the defendant in whose favour the foreclosure has taken place may apply in accordance with CPR Part 23 for an order for delivery to him of possession of the mortgaged property and the court may make such order thereon as it thinks fit.[21]

(a) *Matters to be proved*

16–96   The Particulars of Claim should provide particulars of all necessary terms affecting or giving rise to the relief claimed (*e.g.* that the date fixed for redemption has passed). Additional matters which require consideration are such aspects which may effect the taking of any accounts, such as whether the mortgagee has gone into possession of the mortgaged property.

7. **Order in a foreclosure action for account to be taken**

16–97   Since a mortgagor is entitled to have an account, the decree will first direct that the appropriate account be taken unless, of course, the parties have already agreed to it. Although a mortgagor has this right to an account, the court in exceptional cases will stay the taking of it unless he is prepared to give security for the costs of the account because if it is highly improbable that the mortgaged property will prove sufficient to satisfy the mortgage debt, it is unfair to the mortgagee to increase the costs of his foreclosure unnecessarily.[22] The court's direction for the account is subject to variation to meet the special circumstances of the mortgage. For example, a mortgagee in possession must account for rents and profits and there may be a claim for special allowances or expenses. The court order will also contain a direction for all necessary further accounts and inquiries which arise from the mortgagee's possession.[23] In any event, if a claim on the personal covenant has been joined with a foreclosure action it is necessary to have two distinct accounts, one for the sum recoverable on the personal covenant and one to determine what must be paid in order to redeem. The reason for this is obvious. A foreclosure decree allows six months for redemption and the foreclosure account will include an allowance of six months' additional interest. However, in an action on the personal covenant a mortgagee will obtain judgment for immediate payment of the sum due and correspondingly will not be entitled to additional interest. Again, if the mortgagee is in possession, judgment for the payment on the covenant cannot include in the amount to be paid any allowances or expenses in connection with the mortgaged property.[24] Similarly, judgment on the covenant carries with it a right only to the costs of proceedings on the covenant and the costs of a foreclosure must therefore go into the mortgage account only. Plainly, the two accounts must be taken separately.[25]

---

[21] CPR, Sched. 1, RSC Ord. 88, r. 7, prior to October 15, 2001. CPR Part 55 contains no similar provisions.

[22] *Exchange and Hop Warehouses Ltd v. Association of Land Financiers* (1886) 34 Ch.D. 195.

[23] For the details of the account, see *post*, chap. 25 generally; *ante*, para. 16–31 *et seq.*

[24] These are a charge upon the property, but are not a personal debt of the mortgagor: *Frazer v. Jones* (1846) 5 Hare 475.

[25] *Farrer v. Lacy, Hartland & Co.* (1885) 31 Ch.D. 42.

8. **Foreclosure nisi**

A foreclosure decree is granted in stages and in a normal case, redemption of the **16–98**
mortgaged property by the mortgagor is still possible until the end of a period of
six months from the date when the mortgage account is certified by the Master.
The decree is thus an order *nisi* which will be made absolute on a subsequent
application provided that in the meanwhile the right to redeem has not been
exercised. A foreclosure order absolute will never be granted in the first instance
unless the persons interested in the equity of redemption agree to that
course.[26]

(a) *Form*[27]

The order may take this form: It is directed that upon the payment of the sum
certified by the Master on a day six months after the date of this certificate and
at the time and place specified therein, the mortgagee shall give the defendant a
receipt in accordance with the provisions of section 115 of the Law of Property
Act 1925[28–29] and shall deliver up the title deeds but that in default of such
payment, the defendant shall be foreclosed. The order (unless the court otherwise
directs) requires the mortgagor to give seven days' notice of his intention to
attend and redeem and, in the absence of such notice and if the mortgagor does
attend, the order will provide for seven days' extension to the period allowed for
redemption. If the mortgagee has applied for possession, there will be added a
direction that the defendant shall deliver up possession to the claimant and, in the
case of an equitable mortgagee, there must be a special direction for the conveyance of the legal title to the mortgagee.[30]

However, as in redemption actions, there may be several parties before the
court with distinct rights to redeem, and the decree must provide in detail for the
exercise of those rights. Questions may arise as to priority and as to successive
periods for redemption because foreclosure means the destruction of the equity
of redemption of every person who acquired an interest in the property subsequently to the claimant's mortgage.[31] The determination of these questions,
however, proceeds in decrees for foreclosure on the same lines as in decrees for
redemption and the rules will not be repeated here.[32] It should be added that it is
also possible for the court to give the mortgagees successive periods of redemption, the party first entitled to redeem being allowed six months, and each of the
others successive periods of three months more[33] after which the rights of any

---

[26] *Patey v. Flint* (1879) 48 L.J.Ch. 696.
[27] Originally prescribed by Practice Direction [1955] 1 W.L.R. 36, that practice direction has been
repealed by the Chancery Division Practice Directions which are silent in this regard. It is
anticipated that the old form remains in use however.
[28–29] s.115 of the LPA 1925 is applied with qualifications by the Building Societies Act 1986, s.6c,
Sched. 2A (as inserted by the Building Societies Act 1997). See *ante*, chap. 8 and *post*, para.
22–02.
[30] *Lees v. Fisher* (1882) 22 Ch.D. 283; the order must also be preceded by a declaration of the
equitable mortgage: *Marshall v. Shrewsbury* (1875) L.R. 10 Ch. 250.
[31] See *Briscoe v. Kenrick* (1832) 1 L.J.Ch. 116.
[32] See *post*, para. 18–28 *et seq.*
[33] *Smithett v. Hesketh* (1840) 44 Ch.D. 161; *Platt v. Mendel* (1884) 27 Ch.D. 246.

mortgagee not redeeming would be extinguished.[34] In the event that a subsequent mortgagee redeems, proceedings are thereafter for foreclosure between him and the mortgagor who, in order to redeem, will have to pay that which the mortgagee has paid to redeem together with the amounts outstanding on the mortgage with the subsequent mortgagee.

In the case of dwelling-houses the court in foreclosure actions now has a statutory discretion to adjourn the proceedings, or to suspend executions of its order, or to postpone the date for delivery of possession as it thinks fit whether or not possession is sought in the same proceedings.[35]

9. Foreclosure absolute

16–99 After the order *nisi*, the accounts are taken and certified by the Master, and the Master's certificate fixes the time and place for redemption. However, a mortgagor's failure to pay on this date in accordance with the certificate does not automatically complete the mortgagee's title. The equity of redemption is not finally destroyed until a further decree, the foreclosure absolute, has been obtained making the mortgagee the sole owner both in law and in equity and free from any subsequent mortgages but subject to any prior incumbrances.[36] In consequence a foreclosure *nisi* is by itself no defence to an action for redemption.[37]

Moreover, although the mortgagor's further default entitles the mortgagee as of course to have his order *nisi* made absolute, the court will require the fact of non-payment to be strictly proved by the mortgagee by witness statement verified in accordance with CPR Part 22 or, if he chooses, by affidavit.[38] The evidence must be verified or sworn by the mortgagee (or by the person who acted on his behalf) to the effect that attendance was made at the time and place fixed by the certificate, and that the mortgagor did not appear[39]; in addition there must be a positive statement by the mortgagee himself that he has not paid. Evidence to that effect by his attorney is insufficient and even in the case of co-mortgagees an affidavit or witness statement by one on behalf of the others will not be accepted except where a mortgagee is out of the jurisdiction.[40] In any case a mortgagee, who has received rents or other profits after the decree *nisi* but before default was made, must inform the court of this and *cannot proceed* to a decree absolute: such a receipt reopens the account and a new date for redemption will be allowed.[41] If, however, the receipt of profits did not occur until *after* the mortgagor's default under the decree *nisi*, the account is not reopened and the mortgagee (upon

---

[34] In instances where there are successive subsequent mortgagees, this formula can lead to substantial delay. Accordingly the Master's order will usually only permit one period for subsequent mortgagees to redeem and will allow them to apply to determine their rights *inter se*: *Bartlett v. Rees* (1871) L.R. 12 Eq. 395; *Doble v. Manley* (1885) 28 Ch.D. 664; *Olding* (1884) Ch.D. 664.

[35] Administration of Justice Act 1973, s.8(3), and see *ante*, p. 245.

[36] See the LPA 1925, ss88(2), 89(2). Also see *Sheriff v. Sparks* (1737) Westtemp. Hard. 130.

[37] *Senhouse v. Earl* (1752) 2 Ves.Sen. 450.

[38] *Patey v. Flint* (1879) 48 L.J.Ch. 696.

[39] *Moore and Robinson's Nottinghamshire Banking Co. v. Horsfield* [1882] W.N. 43.

[40] *Barrow v. Smith* (1885) 52 L.T. 798; *Docksey v. Else* (1891) 64 L.T. 256; *Kinnaird v. Yorke* (1889) 60 L.T. 380.

[41] *Prees v. Coke* (1871) L.R. 6 Ch. 645; nor will the mortgagor be put under conditions as to payment of arrears of interest.

producing the proper evidence) may obtain an order absolute.[42] The actual
application for an order absolute should be made in accordance with CPR, Part
23. Notice of the proceedings must be served on the owner of the equity of
redemption, but, with one exception, the application may be made without notice.
The exception is the case of a deceased defendant, when the court will insist on
the presence of a properly appointed representative of the deceased.[43]

(a) *Form*

A foreclosure order absolute takes the form of a recital of the decree *nisi* and of **16–100**
the mortgagor's default thereunder, the evidence in support of the order and an
order absolutely debarring and foreclosing him from all equity of redemption in
the mortgaged property. In addition, the court will order the delivery to the
claimants of any title deeds to the property which are still in the defendant's
hand. Any deeds, which were executed subsequently to the claimant's mortgage,
and which therefore relate only to the equity of redemption, will not be included
in such an order, although their possession may be of advantage to the claimant.[44]
The effect of foreclosure absolute, it must be repeated, is merely to destroy the
equity of redemption and transfer the beneficial ownership to the mortgagee; it is
not a conveyance of the legal title. Consequently, in the case of an equitable
mortgage, if the mortgagor is obstructive, the order absolute must provide for the
transfer of the legal title to the claimant.[45] This is achieved by a declaration that
the mortgagor is a trustee for the mortgagee, followed by a vesting order in
favour of the mortgagee-beneficiary under section 44 of the Trustee Act 1925.
For the same reason an order absolute is not enough to give the claimant
possession of the mortgaged property. For some purposes a foreclosure action is
an action for the recovery of land,[46] but it is not an action for the recovery of *the
possession of land*, and is not enforceable by writ of possession under CPR,
Sched. 1, RSC Ord. 45, r. 4.[47] If, however, application is made, the court will add
an order for possession to the order absolute, whether or not the order *nisi*
directed delivery of possession, and whether or not such an order was asked for
in the statements of case.[48] Indeed, an order for possession will even be made, as
ancillary to the judgment, after decree absolute.[49]

(b) *Stamp duty*

An order for foreclosure absolute requires to be stamped as if it were a convey- **16–101**
ance upon a sale of the mortgaged property.[50] Accordingly, the evidence in

---

[42] *National Permanent Mutual Benefit Building Society v. Raper* [1892] 1 Ch. 54.
[43] *Aylward v. Lewis* [1891] 2 Ch. 81.
[44] *Greene v. Foster* (1882) 22 Ch.D. 566.
[45] *Lees v. Fisher* (1882) 22 Ch.D. 283.
[46] *Heath v. Pugh* (1881) 6 Q.B.D. 345, affirmed (1882) 7 A.C. 235.
[47] *Wood v. Wheater* (1882) 22 Ch.D. 281.
[48] *Salt v. Edgar* (1886) 54 L.T. 374; see also *Best v. Applegate* (1887) 37 Ch. 42; *Keith v. Day* (1888)
39 Ch.D. 452.
[49] *Keith v. Day* (1888) 39 Ch.D. 452; an order for possession should so describe the property that the
sheriff may identify it from the terms of the order: *Thynne v. Sarl* [1891] 2 Ch. 79.
[50] Finance Act 1898, s.6.

support of the application for an order for foreclosure absolute should contain the necessary details and the appropriate certificate for stamp duty purposes in order for the same to be included in the order absolute. If the effect of the order for foreclosure absolute is such that it vests the reversion of the interest in the mortgaged land automatically in the mortgagee, the order itself will need to be produced to the Commissioners of Inland Revenue for stamping.[51]

10. **Effect of an order absolute**

16–102 In circumstances where an estate in fee simple has been mortgaged either by the creation of a term of years absolute or by a charge by way of legal mortgage, an order for foreclosure absolute operates to vest in fee simple in the mortgagee (subject to any legal mortgage having priority to the mortgage in light of which the foreclosure was obtained and to any money thereby secured) and thereupon the mortgage term, if any, merges with the fee simple and any subsequent mortgage term or charge by way of legal mortgage which is bound by the order for foreclosure absolute is extinguished.[52] In the case of a sub-mortgage by a sub-demise out of an estate in fee simple, the same principles apply as if the sub-mortgage had itself been carved out of the fee simple so as to enlarge the principal term and extinguish the derivative term created by the sub-mortgage.[53]

Where a term of years absolute has been mortgaged by the creation of another term of years absolute limited out of it or by a charge by way of legal mortgage and an order for foreclosure absolute is obtained, the order operates (unless it provides to the contrary) to vest the leasehold reversion affected by the mortgage and any subsequent mortgage in the mortgagee subject to any legal mortgage having priority to the mortgage in the light of which the foreclosure was obtained and to any money thereby secured and thereupon the mortgage term and any subsequent mortgage term or charge by way of legal mortgage which is bound by the order shall, subject to any express provision to the contrary contained in the order, merge in such leasehold reversion or be extinguished.[54]

In the case of a sub-mortgage by sub-demise of a term limited out of a leasehold reversion, the provisions of section 89 of the Law of Property Act 1925 apply *mutatis mutandis*. The statutory vesting of the leasehold reversion in the mortgagee does not give the lessor of the mortgaged property a right to forfeit the term of years for want of licence to assign.

11. **Costs of foreclosure proceedings**

These are dealt with elsewhere.[55]

---

[51] Finance Act 1931, s.28 (as amended).
[52] LPA 1925, s.88(2).
[53] LPA 1925, s.88(5).
[54] LPA 1925, s.89(2).
[55] See *post*, para. 25–06 *et seq.*

12. **Re-opening foreclosure**

The effect of a foreclosure absolute is to constitute the mortgagee beneficial **16–103A**
owner of the property, so that he may at once deal with it as owner. The
proceedings between the parties, theoretically, are at an end and, apart from an
ancillary order for possession, the court cannot add to its decree as, for example,
by appointing a receiver.[56] Nevertheless, as Jessel M.R., pointed out,[57] the
finality of a decree absolute is nearly as illusory as the mortgage contract itself,
since the court reserves for itself a discretion to discharge the final decree if the
mortgagor makes out a special case for indulgence.[58] Of course, a decree
absolute, like any other decree, is liable to be set aside for actual fraud or
oppression by the mortgagee which will be sufficient to reopen the foreclosure.
Again, the mortgagee himself may cause the foreclosure to be opened by suing
the mortgagor or guarantor[59] on his personal covenant, for this automatically
revives the right to redeem as would a sale by the mortgagee under his power of
sale rather than *qua absolute* owner.[60] In such circumstances, the mortgagee is
liable to account for any surplus sale proceeds; the purchaser's title is not
affected.[61] Even so, there is an absolute discretion in the court to reopen the
foreclosure[62] and fix a new date for redemption, without the mortgagee having
been guilty of misconduct or having taken collateral proceedings against the
mortgagor. In truth, the court's tenderness towards a mortgagor is so extreme that
it is prepared in special circumstances to treat his property as still essentially
security, even after decree absolute and to give him a last chance of redeeming.
When the court exercises its discretion, the procedure is not immediately to
vacate the decree, but to fix a new date for redemption, notwithstanding the
decree, and to discharge the decree if redemption then takes place.[63] However,
since a mortgagor is not entitled, as of course, to an enlargement of time for
redemption before the decree absolute, *a fortiori* he must make out a special case
for the opening of foreclosure absolute.

(a) *The court's discretion*

The opening of a foreclosure is completely within the court's discretion and no   **16–103B**
precise rules have been laid down. In *Campbell v. Holyland*,[64] however, Jessel
M.R. made some valuable comments on the exercise of the discretion which
indicate clearly the grounds on which it is exercised which merit repetition in
full. He there said:

---

[56] *Heath v. Pugh* (1881) 6 Q.B.D. 345, affirmed (1882) 7 A.C. 235; *Wills v. Luff* (1888) 38 Ch.D. 197.
[57] *Campbell v. Holyland* (1877) 7 Ch.D. 166 at 171.
[58] Even possibly after sale of the property, but this would be most unusual especially if the purchaser had no notice of the circumstances.
[59] *Lloyds and Scottish Trust Ltd v. Britten* (1982) 44 P. & C.R. 249, and see *post*, para. 16–110 *et seq.*
[60] *Perry v. Barker* (1806) 13 Ves. 198; *Lockhart v. Hardy* (1846) 9 Beav. 349.
[61] *Stevens v. Theatres Ltd* [1903] 1 Ch. 857.
[62] See *Quarles v. Knight* (1820) 8 Price 630; *Eyre v. Hansom* (1840) 2 Beav. 478.
[63] *Ford v. Wastell* (1848) 6 Hare 229.
[64] (1877) 7 Ch.D. 166 at 172.

"On what terms is that judicial discretion to be exercised? It has been said by the highest authority that it is impossible to say *a priori* what are the terms. They must depend on the circumstances of each case. . . . There are certain things which are intelligible to everybody. In the first place the mortgagor must come, as it is said, promptly; that is within a reasonable time. He is not to let the mortgagee deal with the estate as his own—if it is a landed estate, the mortgagee being in possession of it and using it—and then without any special reason come and say, 'Now I will redeem.' He cannot do that; he must come within a reasonable time. What is a reasonable time? You must have regard to the nature of the property. As has been stated in more than one of the cases, where the estate is an estate in land in possession—where the mortgagee takes it in possession and deals with it and alters the property, and so on—the mortgagor must come much more quickly than where it is an estate in reversion, as to which the mortgagee can do nothing except sell it. So that you must have regard to the nature of the estate in ascertaining what is to be considered a reasonable time.

Then again was the mortgagor entitled to redeem, but by some accident unable to redeem? Did he expect to get the money from a quarter from which he might reasonably hope to obtain it, and was he disappointed at the last moment? Was it a very large sum, and did he require a considerable time to raise it elsewhere? All those things must be considered in determining what is a reasonable time.

Then an element for consideration has always been the nature of the property as regards value. For instance, if an estate were worth £50,000, and had been foreclosed for a mortgage debt of £5,000, the man who came to redeem that estate would have a longer time than where the estate was worth £5,100, and he was foreclosed for £5,000. But not only is there money value, but there may be other considerations. It may be an old family estate or a chattel, or picture, which possesses a special value for the mortgagor, but which possesses not the same value for other people; or it may be, as has happened in this instance, that the property, though a reversionary interest in the funds, is of special value to both the litigants; it may possess not merely a positive money value, but a peculiar value, having regard to the nature of title and other incidents, so that you cannot set an actual money value upon it. . . . All this must be taken into consideration."

This dictum suggests that three points will be likely to influence the court in favour of opening foreclosure: *(i)* promptness of application; *(ii)* the special value of the estate, whether monetary or otherwise; and *(iii)* the fact that the mortgagor had a reasonable expectation of redeeming, but was disappointed in his attempt to obtain the money. It may be added that there is little chance of obtaining the court's indulgence unless it can be shown at the time of the application that the security is reasonably sufficient and that there is a reasonable expectation of the money being obtained.[65] In any case, it is now the practice to make it a condition of opening a foreclosure that the mortgagor pay up immediately or within, at the most, one month, all arrears of interest and costs reported to be due.

---

[65] *Patch v. Ward* (1867) L.R. 3 Ch. 203; and see *Lancashire and Yorkshire Reversionary Interest Co. Ltd v. Crowe* (1970) 114 S.J. 435.

On failure to comply with this condition the foreclosure remains absolute.[66] Delay in applying for relief will prejudice the chance of reopening a foreclosure unless it can be explained; if the mortgagee deals with the estate or expends money on it, laches in the mortgagor will be fatal.[67]

(b) *The intervention of a purchaser*

However, mere dealing with the estate by the mortgagee will not prevent the   **16–103C** revival of the right to redeem because a purchaser of a foreclosed estate must be taken to know that a foreclosure may be reopened and if he purchases soon after the decree, the foreclosure may be reopened as against him. In *Campbell v. Holyland*[68] Jessel M.R. explained the position of a purchaser thus:

> "Then it is said that you must not interfere against purchasers . . . there are purchasers and purchasers. If the purchaser buys a freehold estate in posses-sion after the lapse of a considerable time from the order of foreclosure absolute, with no notice of any extraneous circumstances which would induce the court to interfere, I for one should decline to interfere with such a title as that; but if the purchaser bought the estate within twenty-four hours after the foreclosure absolute, and with notice of the fact that it was of much greater value than the amount of the mortgage debt, is it to be supposed that a court of equity would listen to the contention of such a purchaser that he ought not to be interfered with? He must be taken to know the general law that an order for foreclosure may be opened under proper circumstances, and under a proper exercise of discretion by the court; and if the mortgagor in that case came the week after, is it to be supposed a court of equity would so stultify itself as to say that a title so acquired would stand in the way? I am of opinion it would not."

13. Judicial sale pursuant to the Law of Property Act 1925, s.91

Both generally and in foreclosure action, the court has a jurisdiction to order a   **16–103D** sale of the property pursuant to section 91 of the Law of Property Act 1924. In a foreclosure action the court's jurisdiction to order a sale in lieu of foreclosure[69] does not depend on a sale having been asked for in the Particulars of Claim. Under section 91(2) of the Law of Property Act 1925, the court, on the request of the mortgagee or *of any interested person*[70] may direct a sale (a "judicial sale") on such terms as it thinks fit, including the deposit in court of a sum to meet the expenses of sale and to secure performance of the terms at any time prior to an order absolute.[71] The jurisdiction is entirely discretionary both as to

---

[66] See *Eyre v. Hansom* (1840) 2 Beav. 478; *Holford v. Yate* (1855) 1 K. & J. 677.
[67] See *Thornhill v. Manning* (1851) 1 Sim.(N.S.) 451.
[68] (1877) 7 Ch.D. 166 at 173.
[69] The county court's jurisdiction is limited to circumstances where, at the commencement of proceedings, the amount owing does not exceed £30,000; LPA 1925, s.91(8).
[70] *e.g.* a subsequent mortgagee or the mortgagor and see *Twentieth Century Banking Corporation v. Wilkinson* [1977] Ch. 99.
[71] *Union Bank of London v. Ingram* (1882) 20 Ch.D. 463.

making the order for sale and as to the terms of the sale. The court may order the sale notwithstanding the dissent of non-appearance of any person[72] and without allowing time for redemption.[73]

If a sale is requested, the order is not given as of course, but a special case has to be made out for the exercise of the court's discretion.[74] It is unusual for the court to order an immediate sale unless the mortgagor consents. The rule is not to direct a sale unless it will confer a benefit on one of the parties sufficient to justify the expenses of a sale.[75] Nor will a sale be ordered if it will prejudice the position of any person interested.[76] Conversely, if the mortgagee's refusal to sell the mortgaged property would cause the mortgagor prejudice, the court may order a sale in order to protect him from potential prejudice.[77]

The usual direction given is that accounts be certified and a period allowed to the mortgagor for redemption.[78] Indeed, if the statement of claim is for foreclosure only, the court will not order sale at all unless the mortgagor has been notified of the application for sale.[79] An immediate sale may be directed if the property is small and the security deficient.[80] The actual application for a sale may be made at any stage of the proceedings[81] and upon an interlocutory application,[82] the court's jurisdiction to order the sale being only terminated by decree absolute.[83]

(a) *Circumstances in which a sale may be ordered*

16–104   Usually the court will order a sale where the mortgagee is seeking to foreclose and the property is worth more than the amount secured by the mortgage and the mortgagor is unable to raise the sum required to redeem the property in order to obtain the advantage of securing the surplus sale proceeds for his own ends.[84] However, the jurisdiction to order a sale is not limited to such circumstances and may be used in order to relieve one party from the potentially prejudicial consequences of the other party's proposed course of conduct.[85] The jurisdiction may also be exercised in circumstances where foreclosure is sought by one mortgagee in circumstances where there are sufficient numbers of subsequent incumbrances so as to make the exercise of foreclosure excessively slow or burdensome.[86] An order for sale will be refused in circumstances where there is

---

[72] Which includes the mortgagee, and see *Wade v. Wilson* (1882) 22 Ch.D. 235.
[73] Or determining the priorities of interested parties: s.91(4) of the Law of Property Act 1925.
[74] *Provident Clerks' Mutual Life Assurance Association v. Lewis* (1892) 62 L.J. Ch. 89.
[75] *Lloyds Bank v. Colston* (1912) 106 L.T. 420.
[76] *Merchant Banking Co. of London v. London & Hanseatic Bank* (1886) 55 L.J. Ch. 479; *Silsby v. Holliman* [1955] Ch. 552.
[77] *Palk v. Mortgage Services Funding plc* [1993] Ch. 330; *Cheltenham & Gloucester plc v. Krausz* [1997] 1 W.L.R. 1558; *AIB Finance Limited v. Debtors* [1997] 4 All E.R. 677; *Yorkshire Bank plc v. Hall* [1999] 1 W.L.R. 1713, distinguishing *Palk*.
[78] *Green v. Biggs* (1885) 52 L.T. 680; see also *Smith v. Robinson* (1853) 1 Sm. & G. 140.
[79] See *Union Bank of London v. Ingram* (1882) 20 Ch.D. 463.
[80] *Palk v. Mortgage Services Funding Plc* [1993] Ch. 330.
[81] *Palk, ante.*
[82] *Palk, ante.*
[83] *Smithett v. Hesketh* (1890) 44 Ch.D. 161.
[84] *Gibbs v. Haydon* (1882) 30 W.R. 726.
[85] CPR, Sched. 1, RSC Ord. 31: Practice Direction (1999) PD RSC 31, para. 5.
[86] *South Western District Bank v. Turner* (1882) 31 W.R. 113.

no evidence before the court as to the value of the property[87] or where the sale would necessarily involve the disposition of property not subject to the mortgage in question.[88]

(b) *Conduct of the sale*

The conduct and conditions of sale are always within the court's discretion.[89] **16–105** The general practice is to give the conduct of the sale to the mortgagor since he is the person whose interest is to obtain the best price[90]; on the same principle, if the mortgagor declines the privilege, the conduct of the sale will be given to the incumbrancer lowest in priority in preference to the mortgagee.[91] It seems, moreover, that this course will sometimes be followed, even when the first mortgagee has objected and claimed the right to carry out the sale.[92] However, if the security is deficient, a first mortgagee's claim to be given the conduct of the sale will be allowed[93]; again, the court may prefer the first mortgagee's claim, on the ground that the expense may be saved by allowing the person in possession of the deeds to conduct the sale.[94] Thus, there is no rule that the mortgagor must conduct the sale although the general practice very much favours that course.[95] Furthermore the court will readily permit the sale to take place altogether out of the court, the proceeds of the sale being ordered to be paid into a court: but in such cases the order must be prefaced by a declaration that all interested parties are before the court.[96] The fact that a first mortgagee does not agree to the mortgagor having the conduct of the sale will effect the terms on which the order is made; the mortgagor (or the puisne incumbrancer) will usually have to deposit a sum to cover the expenses of an ineffectual attempt to sell and the court will fix a reserved price sufficient to cover the first mortgagee's claim.[97] If the first mortgagee's objection arises from the fact that he is himself anxious to exercise his powers of realising the security, the court will fix a time within which the sale must take place and, on default, the mortgagee may proceed to realise the security.[98] If no objection has been made to the sale by the first mortgagee, the mortgagor will not be made to give security for the expenses of the sale[99] but if the sale is to take place altogether out of the court, special directions will be given as to a reserved price and other conditions. A reserved price will also be

---

[87] *Oldham v. Stringer* (1884) 33 W.R. 251; but *cf. Hopkinson v. Miers* (1889) 34 S.J. 128.
[88] *Union Bank of London v. Ingram* (1882) 20 Ch.D. 463.
[89] *Woolley v. Coleman* (1882) 21 Ch.D. 169.
[90] *Davis v. Wright* (1886) 32 Ch.D. 220; *cf. Re Jordan, ex p. Harrison* (1884) 13 Q.B.D. 228.
[91] *Norman v. Beaumont* [1893] W.N. 45.
[92] *e.g. Brewer v. Square* [1892] 2 Ch. 111.
[93] *Cheltenham & Gloucester plc v. Krausz* [1997] 1 W.L.R. 1558; *Re Jordan, ex p. Harrison* (1884) 13 Q.B.D. 228; but not if a sum is deposited in court as a guarantee against loss: *Norman v. Beaumont* [1893] W.N. 45.
[94] *Hewitt v. Nanson* (1858) 28 L.J. Ch. 49.
[95] *Christy v. Van Tromp* [1886] W.N. 111; the language of Chitty J. goes further than the cases warrant.
[96] CPR Sched. 1, RSC Ord. 31, r. 2. See *Cumberland Union Banking Co. v. Maryport Hematite Iron & Steel Co.* [1892] 1 Ch. 92.
[97] *Whitbread v. Roberts* (1859) 28 L.J. Ch. 431; *Brewer v. Square* [1892] 2 Ch. 111.
[98] *ibid.*
[99] *Davies v. Wright* (1886) 32 Ch.D. 220; but the mortgagor is personally liable for the expenses.

fixed if the first mortgagee is given leave to bid at auction for the property.[1] Whoever conducts the sale acts primarily for himself and is not liable for improper activities of other parties to the action.[2] Any party who wishes to buy the property should apply to the court for permission to do so.[3]

(c) A vesting order conveying the property

16–106 In order to effect a sale of the mortgaged property, the court may, in favour of the purchaser, make a vesting order conveying the mortgaged property, or appoint a person to do so, subject or not to any encumbrance, as it thinks fit; or, in the case of an equitable mortgage, may create and vest a mortgage term in the mortgagee to enable him to carry out the sale as if the mortgage had been made by deed by way of legal mortgage.[4] Such a vesting order conveying the mortgaged property has the effect of rendering the conveyance beyond impeachment.[5] An order under this sub-section will only be made in exceptional circumstances and any applicant for such an order must provide the court with sufficient evidence upon which it may exercise its discretion.[6] An order will only be made if the court is satisfied that the prospects of the mortgagor impeaching the sale are utterly remote; that the conduct of the mortgagor, both during the application as well as before it is such as to justify the apprehension that he will not hesitate to threaten proceedings against the purchaser if that could spoil the proposed sale; and that the mortgagee's fear that the sale will be lost unless an order is obtained is not unreasonable.[7] Otherwise, the court will leave the mechanics of the sale to the mortgagee pursuant to his own power.

(d) Application of the proceeds of sale

16–107–
109 The proceeds of a judicial sale are applied in the same way and in the same order as the proceeds arising from a sale out of the court under a power of sale. The rules governing the distribution of the proceeds of sale will therefore be set out elsewhere.

ACTION ON THE PERSONAL COVENANT TO REPAY

16–110 A creditor's primary remedy to recover his money is to bring a personal action against his debtor[8] on the contract of loan, for a creditor by taking security only reinforces his personal remedy. As Maitland said,[9] a mortgagee is not the less a

---

[1] *Re Commercial bank of London* (1864) 9 L.T.(N.S.) 782.
[2] *Union Bank of London v. Munster* (1887) 37 Ch.D. 51.
[3] See *Palk, ante.*
[4] LPA 1925, s.91(7).
[5] LPA 1925, s.104(2).
[6] *Alba Bank Plc v. Mercantile Holdings Limited* [1994] Ch. 71.
[7] *ibid.*
[8] This includes a guarantor, see *Lloyds & Scottish Trust Ltd v. Britten* (1982) 44 P. & C.R. 249.
[9] *Maitland, Equity* (2nd ed.), p. 182.

creditor because he is a secured creditor. All well-drawn mortgages[10] contain an express covenant by the mortgagor to pay both principal and interest. Even when there is no such covenant, a promise to pay is implied in law from the acceptance of the loan so that a simple contract debt is created. Every mortgage, therefore, contains within itself a personal liability to repay the amount advanced,[11] which the mortgagee may enforce by an action on the contract. Whilst CPR Part 55 makes no express provision for the allocation of possession actions to the Chancery Division, the October 15, 2001 practice should be followed.

1. **Accrual and demand**

The covenant to pay normally fixes a date on which payment is to be made and thus no right of action on the personal covenant accrues to the mortgagee until non-payment on the day named, for the affirmative covenant to pay implies a negative promise by the lender not to sue before that date.[12] If, on the other hand, the principal is made payable on demand, and there is no express or implied provision for notice to be given,[13] the right to sue on the personal covenant of the mortgagor to whom the monies have been advanced arises immediately on the execution of the mortgage,[14] and it is not even necessary to make a demand before beginning the action. If the covenant is to pay the debt of another (*e.g.* secures another's overdraft with a bank) and is thus collateral to the indebtedness, a demand is necessary to found a claim.[15] In the case of an instalment mortgage, a written demand *is* necessary by reason of the alterations in the nature of the debtor's obligations from payment by instalments to the whole capital sum.[16] Any mode of service is sufficient which enables a mortgagor to realise that a demand has been made.[17] A well-drawn covenant stipulates expressly for payment of both principal and interest, so that the right to sue for interest is quite distinct from the right to sue for principal and the actions may be brought separately.[18]

16–111

---

[10] The personal liability of the mortgagor to pay is sometimes registered by the mortgage deed itself.

[11] *Sutton v. Sutton* (1882) 22 Ch.D. 511 at 515, *per* Jessel M.R.

[12] *Bolton v. Buckenham* [1891] 1 Q.B. 278; *Twentieth Century Banking Corporation Ltd v. Wilkinson* [1977] Ch. 99. But it is possible that a demand should be first made, see *Re Tewkesbury Gas Co., Tysoe v. Tewkesbury Gas Co.* [1912] 1 Ch. 1.

[13] *Esso Petroleum Co. Ltd v. Alstonbridge Properties Ltd* [1975] 1 W.L.R. 1474. If there is such a provision an actual demand in writing must be made before the right of action accrues, see *Lloyds Bank v. Margolis* [1954] 1 W.L.R. 644. See also Limitation of Actions, *post*, para. 22–27 *et seq.* It is also necessary to make a demand in writing if the covenant is merely *collateral* to the security, *e.g.* if the right is being enforced against a surety, see *Re Brown's Estate, Brown v. Brown* [1893] 2 Ch. 300 at 304.

[14] *Evans v. Jones* (1839) 5 M. & W. 295.

[15] *Lloyds Bank Ltd v. Margolis* [1954] 1 W.L.R. 644; *Habib Bank Ltd v. Tailor* [1982] 1 W.L.R. 1218.

[16] *Esso Petroleum Co. Ltd v. Alstonbridge Properties Ltd* [1975] 1 W.L.R. 1474. In practice a demand is usually made before action is commenced in any event.

[17] *Worthington & Co. Ltd v. Abbott* [1910] 1 Ch. 588.

[18] *Dickenson v. Harrison* (1817) 4 Pri. 282.

2. **Parties**

If a mortgagee assigns the mortgage debt, the assignee will be able to sue on the personal covenant. He can sue in his own name if the assignment meets the requirements of section 136 of the Law of Property Act 1925; otherwise he must join the original mortgagee.[19] On the mortgagee's death the right to sue on the covenant passes to his personal representatives and, after assent, to his legatees, provided that the latter give notice of the assent to the debtor.[20] The claim may be brought against the covenantee and any person who stands as surety to that person.[21]

3. **Loss of the right to sue**

16–112 The right to sue on the personal covenant may be lost by the mortgagee's inability to reconvey the mortgaged property. Although a mortgagor's covenant for repayment is usually absolute in form and is not expressed to be conditional on the reconveyance of the security, equity treats a mortgagor's liability to pay and a mortgagee's obligation to reconvey as reciprocal. A mortgagee will therefore be restrained from suing on the covenant if, without authority from the mortgagor, he has parted with the property mortgaged.[22] If the mortgagee is only temporarily disabled from making the reconveyance by, for example allowing his solicitor to obtain a lien on the title deeds, he is restrained from suing on the covenant until the disability has been removed by, for example, the discharge of the lien.[23] If he forecloses, he cannot afterwards sue on the personal covenant to make up the deficiency unless he still retains the mortgaged property in his hands.[24] In other words, a sale of the property after foreclosure extinguishes the mortgagor's liability for the contract debt.[25] It is for the same reason that if a mortgagee sues on the personal covenant after foreclosing, he reopens the foreclosure[26]: he cannot require the mortgagor or guarantor to repay his loan unless he is himself ready and willing to surrender the security.[27]

This rule still applies although the mortgagor has assigned his equity of redemption. A mortgagor cannot assign his personal liability, but if he is sued on the contract debt after assigning the equity of redemption he is still entitled to the reconveyance of his security.[28] Consequently, any bargain between an assignee of the equity of redemption and the mortgagee which prevents reconveyance will

---

[19] See *ante*, para. 13–05 *et seq.*

[20] Administration of Estates Act 1925, ss.1(1), 3(1)(ii), 36.

[21] *Esso Petroleum Co. Ltd v. Alstonbridge Properties Ltd* [1975] 1 W.L.R. 1474.

[22] *Walker v. Jones* (1866) L.R. 1 P.C. 50; *Palmer v. Hendrie (No. 2)* (1860) 28 Beav. 341; this principle applies equally to mortgages of personalty, though its application there may be more flexible: *Ellis & Co.'s Trustee v. Dixon-Johnson* [1925] A.C. 489.

[23] *Schoole v. Sall* (1803) 1 Sch. & Lef. 176.

[24] *Perry v. Barker* (1806) 13 Ves. 198; a puisne mortgagee does not, however, lose his right to sue on the personal covenant by consenting to a decree for foreclosure absolute in favour of a prior mortgagee: *Worthington v. Abbott* [1910] 1 Ch. 588.

[25] *Lockhart v. Hardy* (1846) 9 Beav. 349; *Gordon, Grant & Co. v. Boos* [1926] A.C. 781; see also *Lloyds and Scottish Trust Ltd v. Britten* (1982) 44 P. & C.R. 249.

[26] *Perry v. Barker* (1806) 13 Ves. 198, and see *ante*, para. 16–102A.

[27] See *Lloyds and Scottish Trust Ltd v. Britten* (1982) 44 P. & C.R. 249.

[28] *Kinnaird v. Trollope* (1888) 39 Ch.D. 636, subject, of course, to the equity of redemption. For the form of conveyance, see *Pearce v. Morris* (1869) L.R. 5 Ch.App. 227.

discharge the original mortgagor from his liability on the contract of loan.[29] On the other hand, a mortgagor surrenders his right to recover his security by authorising the mortgagee to part with it. Thus, a mortgagee does not lose his right to sue on the personal covenant if he sells the mortgaged property either with the express concurrence of the mortgagor or under an express or implied power of sale in the mortgage deed.[30] Nor does he lose his right if, when realising his security, he asks the court for a judicial sale instead of for foreclosure. Such a sale is a sale by the court and not by the mortgagee, so that although the mortgagee can no longer reconvey, he is entitled to recover any deficiency from the mortgagor by suing on the covenant.[31]

Limitation A claim by a mortgagee upon the mortgagor's personal covenant for the recovery of the principal monies advanced and secured by mortgage is lost after the expiry of a period of six years from the date upon which the mortgagee's cause of action to recover those monies accrued.[32] This period applies whether the covenant is contained in a deed or simply in a contract.[33] It would seem that the period in which a mortgagee may seek to recover any shortfall from the mortgagor following upon the sale of a mortgaged property is six years from the date upon which the right to receive the money accrued.[34] **16–113**

A claim to foreclose upon the mortgaged property cannot be brought more than 12 years from the date upon which the right to foreclose first accrued.[35] Any other claim to recover the principal monies secured by mortgage or other charge upon property by enforcing the security cannot be brought after 12 years from the date upon which the right to enforce the security accrued.[36]

Notwithstanding that the mortgage may be by deed, the limitation period for the recovery of interest due to a mortgagee is six years.[37] However, if a mortgagee brings proceedings to enforce a security and sells the mortgaged property, he is entitled in the ensuing accounts to retain and have brought in for his benefit all arrears of interest, whether statute-barred or not prior to accounting to the mortgagor for any surplus.[38] Furthermore, a mortgagor is not entitled to redeem the mortgaged property unless he tenders the entirety of the amount owed, whether principal or interest, to the mortgagee notwithstanding that a portion thereof may be statute-barred.[39] A discussion of the bases upon which any limitation period may be extended or the running of time postponed is beyond the scope of this work.

A mortgagee cannot recover more than six years' arrears of interest on a judgment debt by commencing proceedings upon the judgment or by executing

---

[29] *Palmer v. Hendrie* (1859) 27 Beav. 349.
[30] *Rudge v. Richens* (1873) L.R. 8 C.P. 358.
[31] *Gordon Grant & Co. v. Boos* [1926] A.C. 781. This is a particularly strong case, as the mortgagee had obtained leave to bid and had actually bought the mortgage property, subsequently reselling it at an enhanced value.
[32] Limitation Act 1980, s.5. See also *post*, para. 22–27.
[33] *Barnes v. Glenton* [1899] 1 Q.B. 885; *Romain v. Scuba TV Limited* [1997] Q.B. 887.
[34] Limitation Act 1980, ss6, 20(5); *Hopkinson v. Tupper* (1997), unreported; *Romain v. Scuba TV Limited, ante.*
[35] Limitation Act 1980, s.20(2).
[36] Limitation Act 1980, s.20(1).
[37] Limitation Act 1980, s.20(5).
[38] *Edmonds v. Waugh* (1866) L.R. 1 Eq. 418; *Re Marshfield* (1887) 34 Ch.D. 721; *Re Lloyd* [1983] 1 Ch. 385; *Holmes v. Cowcher* [1970] 1 W.L.R. 834; *Ezekiel v. Orakpo* [1997] 1 W.L.R. 340.
[39] *Bingle v. Coppenn* [1899] 1 Ch. 726.

the same.[40] A judgment may be executed in accordance with the Civil Procedure Rules[41] and is not subject to any statutory limitation period.[42]

4. Cause of action estoppel

16–114   A mortgagee who obtains judgment for possession of the mortgaged property and for the sums expressed to be due under the mortgage cannot bring a subsequent claim for any money due under a guarantee which is also secured by that mortgage since the latter claim is one which should properly have been raised in the proceedings for possession and for the monetary judgment previously obtained.[43] However, it would appear that if a mortgagee obtains an unopposed order for possession and payment of sums claimed to be due under the mortgage, the mortgagee is not estopped thereby from bringing a subsequent claim for payment.[44]

APPOINTMENT OF A RECEIVER BY THE COURT

16–115   Before the Judicature Act 1873, courts of equity always acted on the principle that they would never grant a receiver where the party applying for the receiver had a legal right to the possession. The effect of this principle is that an equitable mortgagee could obtain the appointment of a receiver, but a legal mortgagee could not.[45] However, section 25(8) of that Act, which is now replaced by section 37 of the Supreme Court Act 1981,[46] empowered the court to grant a receiver by interlocutory orders whenever it should appear just or convenient to do so.[47] The Court of Appeal has decided that a receiver will now be granted at the instance of a legal mortgagee in the same way as at the instance of an equitable mortgagee because, although a legal mortgagee has power to take possession, there are obvious conveniences in granting a receiver: for example, by relieving a legal mortgagee from assuming the responsibilities of a mortgagee in possession.[48] It should be added, however, that the statutory power usually renders it unnecessary to apply to the court.[49]

---

[40] Limitation Act 1980, s.24(2); see also *Lowsley v. Forbes* [1999] 1 A.C. 329.

[41] See CPR, Sched. 1, RSC Ord. 46, r. 2; *ibid.*, Sched. 2, CCR. Ord. 26, r. 5.

[42] *National Westminster Bank Plc v. Powney* [1991] Ch. 339.

[43] *Arnold v. National Westminster Bank Plc* [1991] 2 A.C. 93; *Talbot v. Berkshire County Council* [1994] Q.B. 290; *Lloyds Bank v. Hawkins* [1998] 47 E.G. 137.

[44] *UCB Bank Plc v. Chandler* (1999), unreported, CA.

[45] *Berney v. Sewell* (1820) 1 J. & W. 647; *Sollory v. Leaver* (1869) L.R. 9 Eq. 22 at 25.

[46] Although the power to appoint a receiver and manager under subs. (1) is wide, the duty of maintaining houses owned by a local authority is expressly entrusted to the local authority under the Housing Act 1957, s.111 (now repealed and replaced, with amendment by Housing Act 1985, s.21), and the court will not usurp that duty by appointing a receiver and manager: *Parker v. Camden London Borough Council* [1986] Ch. 162.

[47] See also CPR Sched. 1, RSC Ord. 30 which applies to proceedings in the High Court and county courts: CPR, Sch. 1 RSC Ord. 30, r. 11.

[48] *Anglo-Italian Bank v. Davies* (1878) 9 Ch.D. 275; *Re Pope* (1886) 17 Q.B.D. 743 at 749, *per* Cotton L.J.

[49] LPA 1925, s.101(iii); see *ante* para. 16–41 *et seq*. See also *Bank of Credit & Commerce International SA v. BRS Kumar Bros* [1994] 1 B.C.L.C. 211.

Although the court may now appoint a receiver in all cases in which such a course appears just or convenient, the principles on which this jurisdiction is exercised are well defined. The appointment of a receiver will be made with a view to preserving the *corpus* of the mortgaged property or to receive the income generated by that property in order to meet the mortgagor's liabilities to the mortgagee or to create a fund sufficient to meet that or other liabilities. Except in very special cases[50] the court will not make an appointment, unless an action is pending. If an action is pending, so that the parties are already at arm's length, it is preferable that the appointment should be made by the court in all cases, rather than that the mortgagee himself should appoint under a power.[51] It appears that a mortgagee is entitled to a receiver in any of the following cases:

(1) if the property would be in jeopardy if left in the mortgagor's possession until the hearing of the action[52];
(2) if default has been made in payment of the principal[53];
(3) if any interest is in arrear[54]; nor does it make any difference that the mortgagee has covenanted not to call in his loan until some future date.[55]

Subsequent mortgagees   When there are two or more mortgagees later mortgages may obtain the appointment of a receiver without prejudice to the rights of prior mortgagees.[56] Nevertheless, if the order appointing the receiver does not contain an express reservation of the rights of prior incumbrancers, the latter cannot interfere with the receiver without an application to the court, for the receiver is an officer of the court.[57] When a prior legal mortgagee has already gone into possession, the court will not appoint a receiver at the instance of a later incumbrancer who is not offering to redeem the legal mortgagee.[58] If a mortgagee in possession cannot assert on oath or by a witness statement verified in accordance with CPR Part 22 that there is something still due to him on his mortgage, the court will appoint a receiver at the instance of a later incumbrancer.[59]   **16–116**

1. **Nominating a receiver**

Although the selection of a receiver appointed by the court is in its discretion, a nomination by the party applying for the appointment will usually be accepted. One person will not, however, be appointed, namely, the mortgagee's solicitor, for it is his duty to check the accounts of the receiver.[60] When the mortgagee   **16–117**

[50] *e.g.* where the mortgagee is a patient under the Mental Health Act 1983.
[51] *Tillett v. Nixon* (1883) 25 Ch.D. 238.
[52] *Stevens v. Lord* (1838) 2 Jur. 92; *Re Victoria Steamboats, Ltd* [1897] 1 Ch. 158; *Re London Pressed Hinge Co. Ltd* [1905] 1 Ch. 576.
[53] *Curling v. Marquis of Townshend* (1816) 19 Ves. 628 at 633.
[54] *Strong v. Carlyle Press* [1893] 1 Ch. 268.
[55] *Burrowes v. Molloy* (1845) 2 J. & L. 521.
[56] *Berney v. Sewell* (1820) 1 J. & W. 647.
[57] *Aston v. Heron* (1834) 2 My. & K. 390.
[58] *Berney v. Sewell* (1820) 1 J. & W. 647.
[59] *Quarrell v. Beckford* (1807) 13 Ves. 377.
[60] *Re Lloyd* (1879) 12 Ch.D. 447.

himself appoints a receiver under a power, he frequently appoints his own solicitor to act as receiver.

2. Duties of a receiver

16–118 The duties of a receiver appointed by the court cannot be exhaustively discussed here,[61] but it may be observed that in some important aspects they differ substantially from those of a receiver appointed by the mortgagee. Thus, a receiver appointed by the court is not strictly an agent and is personally liable for what he does as receiver: consequently, the court almost invariably[62] requires him to give security before entering into office. Indeed, his appointment is normally incomplete until he has actually given security.[63] His duties are regulated by the terms of the order appointing him but in general he is bound to assume possession of the mortgage property, to get in the rents and profits, and to pay these, after deducting outgoings and his own salary (determined by the court), into court or according to the court's direction. Not being the mortgagor's agent, it is his duty to take possession himself and to compel tenants to attorn to himself. He must keep down outgoings, and has power to grant leases for a term not exceeding three years[64] and to do necessary repairs; for any other repairs, he should first obtain the leave of the court. If he requires any further powers not specially sanctioned by the terms of the order appointing him, he must make an application to the court. A receiver, for example, has no power to carry on a business, and, if such a power is desired, the court must be asked to appoint a receiver and manager.[65]

3. Registration of a receiver's appointment

16–119 The appointment of a receiver is capable of being entered as a caution against dealing or a creditor's notice in the case of registered land[66]; with regard to land which is unregistered, the order may be protected by the creation of a land charge.[67]

Right to Fixtures

16–119A In accordance with general principles, fixtures affixed to mortgaged land form part of the security in the land whether affixed before or after the date of the mortgage. They pass automatically to the mortgagee of the land as realty unless

---

[61] See *Halsbury's Laws of England*, Vol. 39(2), Receivers (4th ed., re-issue, 1998).

[62] CPR, Sched. 1, RSC Ord. 30, r. 2.

[63] *Edwards v. Edwards* (1876) 2 Ch.D. 291.

[64] *Daniel's Chancery Practice* (8th ed.), p. 1443. But see *Stamford Banking Co. v. Keeble* [1913] 2 Ch. 96 at 97, where it was laid down that no lease can be granted without leave of the court. The court, however, can approve the granting of any lease which it concludes is necessary for the protection of or making fruitful the mortgated property. See also *Re Cripps* [1946] Ch. 265.

[65] See *Re Manchester & Milford Rly. Co.* (1880) 14 Ch.D. 645 at 653.

[66] Land Registration Act 1925, s.59(1); see also *Clayhope Properties Ltd v. Evans* [1986] 1 W.L.R. 1223.

[67] Land Charges Act 1972, s.6(1)(b); see also *Clayhope Properties Ltd, ante.*

a contrary intention appears in the mortgage.[68] Accordingly, the special exceptions ("tenant's fixtures") which have developed in the law of Landlord and Tenant do not apply.[69]

RIGHT TO INSURE

This is dealt with elsewhere.[70]

RIGHT TO CONSOLIDATE

This is dealt with elsewhere.[71]

RIGHT TO TACK

This is dealt with elsewhere.[72]

RIGHTS, REMEDIES AND DUTIES OF EQUITABLE MORTGAGEES AND CHARGEES

1. **Equitable mortgagees**[73]

(a) *Foreclosure*

Since the equitable mortgagee has no legal estate, foreclosure is his primary **16–120** remedy. It is available whether the charge relates to land[74] or to personalty.[75] In the case of land as the mortgagee has no legal estate, the foreclosure order absolute will direct the mortgagor to convey the land in question freed from any right to redeem.[76] In the case of a chose in action the court will direct the execution by the mortgagor of a power of attorney.[77] In the case of a chose in action, it is available, for example, in the case of the deposit of the share certificates,[78] policies of insurance,[79] and of a share in a partnership.[80]

---

[68] *Reynolds v. Ashby & Son* [1904] A.C. 466.
[69] See Megarry & Wade, *The Law of Real Property* (6th ed., 2000), paras 14–316–14–326.
[70] See para. 19–01 *et seq.*
[71] Chap. 24.
[72] *ibid.*
[73] At one time equitable mortgages were in common use as a means of avoiding or mitigating the payment of stamp duty. Now that stamp duty has been abolished, legal mortgages are almost invariably used. See generally chap. 5 with regard to equitable mortgages of land.
[74] *Re Owen* [1894] 3 Ch. 220.
[75] *London & Midland Bank v. Mitchell* [1899] 2 Ch. 161; *Harrold v. Plenty* [1901] 2 Ch. 314.
[76] *James v. James* (1873) L.R. 16 Eq. 153. Foreclosure of an equity of redemption also occurs occasionally through the dismissal of an action for redemption, see *Cholmley v. Countess of Oxford* (1741) 2 Atk. 267.
[77] *James v. Ellis* (1871) 19 W.R. 319.
[78] See *Harrold v. Plenty* [1901] 2 Ch. 314.
[79] See *Re Kerr's Policy* (1869) L.R. 8 Eq. 331 at 336.
[80] See *Redmayne v. Forster* (1866) L.R. 2 Eq. 467

(b) *Sale*

16–121   The statutory power of sale[81] applies only where the mortgage was made by
deed.[82] Thus, it is usual for equitable mortgages to be made by deed. Even so,
there still may be difficulties for the reasons expressed elsewhere[83] arising from
the decision in *Re Hodson & Howes Contract*,[84] in that the mortgagee can sell
only the interest which he himself holds.[85]

Therefore, in order to avoid such difficulties, the practice has arisen of
employing either or both of two conveyancing devices which enables the mortgagee, in effect, to convey the legal estate:

(1) Power of attorney. A power of attorney is inserted into the mortgage
deed granting a power of attorney to the mortgagee or his assigns[86] to
convey the legal estate which remains vested until sale in the mortgagor. It is usual for such a power to be expressed to be irrevocable and
under section 4(1) of the Powers of Attorney Act 1971[87] this is
permissable since the power is given for value to secure a proprietary
interest of the donee of the power. Thus, neither the mortgagee nor any
purchaser from him will be affected by any act on the part of the
mortgagor or by his death.[88] Accordingly, by virtue of section 5(3) of
the 1971 Act, such persons are protected, as they are entitled to assume
that the power is incapable of revocation.[89]

(2) Declaration of trust. A clause is inserted in the mortgage deed whereby
the mortgagor declares that he holds the legal estate on trust for the
mortgagee and authorises the mortgagee to appoint himself or his
nominee as trustee in place of the mortgagor.[90] By this method the
mortgagee can vest the legal estate in himself or in a purchaser.[91]

It goes without saying that an equitable mortgagee is subject to the
same duties and restrictions on sale of the mortgaged property as a
legal mortgagee.[92]

Equitable mortgages not by deed   In the case of other equitable mortgages not
made by deed, there is no statutory power of sale out of court. However, by virtue
of section 91(2) of the Law of Property Act 1925, the court itself has the power
to order a judicial sale on the application of the mortgagee or of any interested
person and may vest a legal term of years in the mortgagee so that he can sell as
if he were a legal mortgagee.[93]

---

[81] See *ante*, para. 16–56.
[82] LPA 1925, s.101(1).
[83] See *ante*, para. 5–18.
[84] (1887) 35 Ch.D. 668.
[85] But this interpretation has been doubted in the case of *Re White Rose Cottage* [1965] Ch. 940 at
951.
[86] See Powers of Attorney Act 1971, s.11(2) and Sched. 2.
[87] As amended by the Supreme Court Act 1981, s.152(4) and Sched. 7.
[88] See Powers of Attorney Act 1971, s.11(2) and Sched. 2.
[89] See *Re White Rose Cottage* [1965] Ch. 940.
[90] See *London and County Banking Co. v. Goddard* [1897] 1 Ch. 642.
[91] Under the Trustee Act 1925, s.40.
[92] See *ante*, para. 16–67.
[93] LPA 1925, ss.90, 91(7), and see *ante*, para. 16–103 *et seq.*; *Oldham v. Stringer* (1884) 33 W.R.
251.

(c) *Possession*

(i) *Right to take possession*

The position with regard to the right of an equitable mortgagee to take possession **16–122**
of the mortgaged property is unclear. It is generally stated in the authorities
(including the second edition of Waldock, *The Law of Mortgages*) that an
equitable mortgagee has no right to take possession.[94] It is clear that the equitable
mortgagee has no right to take possession at law, for he has no legal estate. It is
also clear that an equitable mortgagee can take possession if there is an express
provision in the agreement giving him that right.[95] Thus, many agreements
contain a clause empowering the mortgagee to take possession in the event of a
default by the mortgagor. Another device is to insert into the equitable mortgage
a clause granting a power of attorney to the mortgagee making available to him
all the rights and remedies of a legal mortgagee including the right to take
possession of the mortgaged property. Further, the mortgagor may, by express
permission, give the equitable mortgagee the right to take possession.[96]

What remains unclear is whether or not an equitable mortgagee has the right **16–123**
to take possession absent any of the above factors. In Megarry & Wade, *The Law
of Real Property*[97] it is urged that in equity an equitable mortgagee should be
entitled to the same rights as if he had a legal mortgage and that there would seem
to be no reason why he should not take possession under the doctrine of *Walsh
v. Lonsdale*,[98] as the basis of an equitable mortgage is the creation of an
immediate relationship of mortgagor and mortgagee, rather than a mere contract
for a future mortgage.[99] However, it is possible that an equitable mortgage is an
interest in property which is independent of the doctrine of *Walsh v. Lonsdale*.
Further, it must be remembered that if this doctrine applies to equitable mortgages, it may produce a number of substantial difficulties with regard to the
question of priority.[1] The argument that the absence of a right to take possession
is founded on an implied term to that effect is unattractive and appears contrary
to authority.[2]

Thus, the equitable mortgagee's right to take possession is uncertain. The court
may in any event award him possession.[3] There is also some authority which
indicates that the equitable mortgagee may take possession in his own right,[4] but
the basis of the legality of such a right is uncertain. Unfortunately, the subject is
not merely academic for if there is such a right for an order for possession, the

---

[94] Coote, *Law of Mortgages* (9th ed., 1927), p. 823; Halsbury, *Laws of England* (4th ed., 1980),
Vol. 32 (re-issue, 1999), p. 291; Waldock, *The Law of Mortgages* (2nd ed., 1950) pp. 55, 235; and
see *Barclays Bank Ltd v. Bird* [1954] Ch. 274 at 280. See also the discussion in (1954) 70 L.Q.R.
161, and (1955) 71 L.Q.R. 204, where the authorities are reviewed.
[95] *Ocean Accident and Guarantee Corp. Ltd v. Ilford Gas Co.* [1905] 2 K.B. 493.
[96] *Re Postle, ex p. Bignold* (1835) 2 Mont. & A. 214.
[97] (6th ed., 2000), paras 19–087–19–090.
[98] (1882) 21 Ch.D. 9.
[99] And as indicated an action for the recovery of land will not be defeated merely for want of the legal
estate, see *General Finance Mortgage and Discount Co. v. Liberator Permanent Benefit Building
Society* (1878) 10 Ch.D. 15 at 24). *Re O'Neill* [1967] N.I. 129.
[1] See Fairest, *Mortgages* (2nd ed., 1980), p. 109.
[2] Megarry & Wade, *The Law of Real Property* (6th ed., 2000), para. 19–087, n. 43.
[3] *Barclays Bank Ltd v. Bird* [1954] Ch. 274; *Re O'Neill* [1967] N.I. 129.
[4] See Megarry and Wade, *The Law of Real Property* (5th ed., 1984), p. 952 n. 71.

statutory discretion pursuant to the provisions of the Administration of Justice Acts 1970 and 1973 would apply.[5]

(ii) *Collection of rents*

16–124 As there is no privity of estate nor tenure between an equitable mortgagee and the tenants of the mortgagor, the equitable mortgagee has no right to direct the tenants of the mortgagor to pay over their rents to himself, nor to collect such rents,[6] without an order of the court.[7] If the tenants do pay the rents to the equitable mortgagee, his receipt will not discharge them from liability. However, at the same time, the tenants cannot demand the return of the rent if payment has been made under no mistake of fact.[8] Moreover, if a prior legal mortgagee is already in possession, the equitable mortgagee can intercept the surplus rents and profits of the prior legal mortgagee by requiring them to be paid over to himself instead of to the mortgagor.[9]

(d) *Appointment of receiver*

16–125 In a proper case an equitable mortgagee can apply to the court for the judicial appointment of a receiver[10] and an equitable mortgagee has also the statutory power to appoint a receiver if the mortgage is by deed.[11] The statutory power usually renders it unnecessary to apply to the court to appoint a receiver.

EQUITABLE CHARGEES

16–126 An equitable chargee has no right to take possession.[12] Further, an equitable chargee cannot foreclose.[13] His primary remedies are to apply to the court for an order for sale or for the appointment of a receiver.[14] However, as the statutory definition of a mortgage extends to a charge,[15] an equitable chargee by deed will have the same statutory powers as an equitable mortgagee with regard to sale and the appointment of a receiver *out of court.*

---

[5] See *ante*, para. 16–84.
[6] *Re Pearson, ex p. Scott* (1838) 3 Mont. and A. 592; *Finck v. Tranter* [1905] 1 K.B. 427; *Vacuum Oil Co. Ltd v. Ellis* [1914] 1 K.B. 693.
[7] The appropriate order is for the appointment of a receiver by way of equitable execution, see *Vacuum Oil Co. Ltd v. Ellis* [1914] 1 K.B. 693 at 703.
[8] *Finck v. Tranter* [1905] 1 K.B. 427.
[9] *Parker v. Calcraft, Dunn v. Same* (1821) 6 Madd. 11.
[10] Supreme Court Act 1981, s.37; and see *ante*, para. 16–115.
[11] LPA 1925, s.101(1)(iii); and see *ante*, para. 16–41 *et seq.*
[12] *Garfitt v. Allen, Allen v. Longstaffe* (1887) 37 Ch.D. 48 at 50.
[13] *Tennant v. Trenchard* (1869) 4 Ch.App. 537; *Re Lloyd, Lloyd v. Lloyd* [1903] 1 Ch. 385 at 404.
[14] *Tennant v. Trenchard* (1869) 4 Ch.App. 537; *Re Owen* [1894] 3 Ch. 220. Sale is also the remedy for the holder of an equitable lien, see *Neate v. Duke of Marlborough* (1838) 3 My. & Cr. 407.
[15] See the LPA 1925, ss.101(1), 205(1)(xvi).

An equitable chargee may obtain relief from forfeiture of the charged lease-hold property even though he has no entitlement to possession or any legal or equitable interest in the property. The right arises from an implied obligation upon the chargor to preserve the security, which includes an obligation on the chargor to obtain relief from forfeiture.[16] Both the chargor and the chargee should be parties.[17]

[16] *Bland v. Ingram's Estates Ltd* [2001] 24 E.G. 163, CA, where the court required the chargee to make payment directly to the lessor of all outstanding rent costs.
[17] *ibid.*

CHAPTER 17

THE EQUITY OF REDEMPTION AS AN INTEREST IN PROPERTY

MORTGAGOR AS EQUITABLE OWNER

In *Kreglinger v. New Patagonia Meat Co.*[1] Lord Parker pointed out that the **17–01** equitable right to redeem which arises on failure to exercise the contractual right must be carefully distinguished from the equitable interest, which, from the first, remains in the mortgagor and is sometimes referred to as an equity of redemption. The equitable *right* to redeem does not exist until the mortgagor is in default and the mortgagee's estate has become absolute at law.[2] The equitable *interest*, on the other hand, arises simultaneously with the execution of the mortgage, since in equity the mortgage conveyance does not have the effect of transferring to the mortgagee the whole beneficial interest in the security, but separates the legal from the equitable ownership. Equity from the outset treats the mortgagor as continuing to be the owner of the property which he has conveyed away, subject only to the mortgagee's charge.[3] By like reasoning a mortgagee's interest is, in equity, not a right to the mortgaged property, but to the mortgage debt, and his beneficial interest in the security is only as a means for enforcing his right to the debt.[4] He is a mere incumbrancer.

The equity of redemption is therefore not only an equitable right but an interest in property.[5] When personal chattels are the subject-matter of the security, the mortgagor's equity is an interest in personalty similar to any other equitable interest in a fund of personalty. Similarly, when the subject-matter is land, the equity of redemption is an equitable interest in land, which before 1926 was termed an equitable estate.[6] Since a mortgagor *held* the same interest in equity as he had at law before the mortgage if he had mortgaged a legal estate in land, he retained afterwards a corresponding equitable estate. Lord Hardwicke, in *Casborne v. Scarfe*,[7] drew attention to the conception of the equity of redemption as an estate in the following well-known passage:

---

[1] [1914] A.C. 25 at 48.
[2] *Brown v. Cole* (1845) 14 Sim. 427, and see *ante*, para. 18–02 *et seq.*
[3] *Casborne v. Scarfe* (1738) 1 Atk. 603; *Finch v. Earl of Winchelsea* (1715) 1 P.Wms. 277; *cf. English Sewing Cotton Co. v. I.R.C.* (1947) 63 T.L.R. 306 at 307.
[4] *Thornborough v. Baker* (1675) 1 Ch.Cas. 283.
[5] A mortgagor has a title in equity "equitable right inherent in the land," *per* Hale C.B. in *Pawlett v. Att.-Gen.* (1667) Hard. 465 at 469. In view of s.1 of the L.P.A. 1925, it may now be safer to term it an equitable interest, or perhaps a mere equity.
[6] *Casborne v. Scarfe* (1738) 1 Atk. 603.
[7] *ibid.* at 605.

"An equity of redemption has always been considered as an estate in the land, for it may be devised, granted, or entailed with remainders, and such entail and remainders may be barred by a fine and recovery, and therefore cannot be considered as a mere right only, but such an estate whereof there may be a seisin."

In *Casborne v. Scarfe*,[8] Lord Hardwicke gave a husband an estate by the curtesy in his wife's equity of redemption,[8a] and his decision resulted in the equity of redemption being placed on the same footing as the equity of a *cestui que trust*. A mortgagor's equity of redemption is therefore not only his right to redeem but also his title to the beneficial ownership of the mortgaged property during the continuance of the mortgage. Having this equitable title he may deal with the beneficial ownership just as if he had never made a mortgage; he may sell it, settle it, create charges upon it, demise it; he may do anything he pleases with it, subject only to the mortgagee's incumbrance. Moreover, he will continue to have an equitable title to the property until his title is terminated by lapse of time, release, sale under a power of sale or by a judgment of the court.[9]

17–02 This view of the equity of redemption was reasserted in the case of *Re Sir Thomas Spencer Wells*.[10] A company mortgaged certain leaseholds by assigning to the mortgagees the residue of the terms, subject to a proviso for redemption. In 1910 a liquidator was appointed, who, believing the equities of redemption to be then valueless, neither surrendered them to the mortgagees nor made any attempt to sell them. In 1916 the company was dissolved. By 1931 the leaseholds had appreciated in value so considerably that the equities of redemption were claimed by the Crown as *bona vacantia*. Farwell J., at first instance, held[11] that whereas there was, immediately prior to the dissolution of the company, a legal entity entitled to redeem, that legal entity had ceased to exist, with the result that the leaseholds were vested in the mortgagee free of any right in any one to redeem. Such a result could be reached only by treating the equity of redemption, not as a title, but as a personal equity, and the Court of Appeal had no hesitation in reversing the decision and allowing the claim of the Crown. Lawrence L.J.[12] put the matter thus:

"In equity the mortgagor is regarded as the owner of the mortgaged land subject only to the mortgagee's charge, and the mortgagor's equity of redemption is treated as an equitable estate in the land of the same nature as other equitable estates . . . . It would be just as unconscionable for a mortgagee to set up a claim to hold the land comprised in his mortgage free from the equity of redemption as it would be for a trustee to set up a claim to retain the trust property in his hands for his own use. Consequently, the reasoning which has induced the Court to hold that a trustee cannot on failure of the trusts set up his legal title so as to defeat the Crown's claim to bona vacantia applies with equal force to a mortgagee of leaseholds

---

[8] (1738) 1 Atk. 603
[8a] Curtesy was abolished by Administration of Estates Act 1925, s.45.
[9] *cf. Weld v. Petre* [1929] 1 Ch. 33 at 42, *per* Russell J.
[10] [1933] Ch. 29.
[11] [1932] 1 Ch. 380.
[12] [1933] Ch. 29 at 52, 53.

where the mortgagor, being an individual, has died intestate without next of kin, or being a company, has been dissolved."

EQUITY OF REDEMPTION UNDER THE LAW OF PROPERTY ACT 1925

In the case of *Re Sir Thomas Spencer Wells*[13] the Court of Appeal did not refer   **17–03** to the effect of the Law of Property Act 1925 on the nature of a mortgagor's rights although some reference to the transitional provisions[14] of that Act might not have been inappropriate. For a mortgagor's position has, in the case of mortgages of legal estates, been technically changed by sections 85 and 86 of the Law of Property Act 1925 which alter the formal methods of creating such mortgages. A mortgagor now possesses not merely his equitable title but also a legal reversion. Under sections 85 and 86, mortgages of both freeholds and leaseholds are created by demise, so that a mortgagor necessarily retains for himself at least a nominal reversion. Freeholds can no longer be mortgaged by the conveyance of the fee simple. Now on mortgaging a fee simple, for example, the mortgagor possesses simultaneously a legal reversion expectant on a 3,000-year lease and an equitable interest in the 3,000-year term. It is contended in *Halsbury's Laws of England*,[15] that the equitable interest in the term is co-extensive with and therefore cannot exist at the same time as the legal reversion so suggesting something akin to a merger occurs. For this premise it is concluded that "instead of the equity of redemption constituting an equitable estate or interest, it subsists only as a right in equity to redeem the property, this right being attached to his legal freehold estate." No doubt this view of the equity of redemption avoids any conveyancing complications and corresponds with the broad policy of the 1925 legislation. It may, however, be questioned whether the statement in *Halsbury* provides a completely satisfactory explanation of the position of the equity of redemption in mortgages by demise. Certainly the equity of redemption, viewed simply as the equitable title arising from the right to pay off the mortgagee and recover the mortgaged property after the passing of the contract date, is co-extensive with the legal reversion. However, if the equitable interest in the 3,000-year lease is also to disappear by being merged in the fee, how is the mortgagor's right to the beneficial ownership of the lease before redemption to be accounted for? Even if the mortgagee takes possession under the lease, the mortgagor is in equity beneficially entitled to the profits, a fact which cannot be explained by reference to the fee simple title since this is *subject to the lease*. In other words, the equity of redemption in the lease appears to be essentially distinct from, and additional to, the nominal legal reversion. For this reason there does not seem to be a merger as such of the equitable interest in the fee[16] and the statement in *Halsbury* is thought to go too far. The view is preferred that sections 85 and 86 of the Law of Property Act 1925 are concerned only with conveyancing and do not effect any essential change in the character of the equity of redemption. It is clear that the substance of the mortgagor's rights is still his

---

[13] [1933] Ch. 29.
[14] Sched. 1, Pt. 7.
[15] Vol. 32 (re-issue, 1999), para. 503.
[16] Turner, *Equity of Redemption* (1931) pp. 186, 187. See also *Young v. Clarey* [1948] Ch. 191 at 198, where Harman J., seems to have regarded the reversion as a distinct interest.

equitable right of redemption and that his legal reversion is a nominal estate meeting the requirements of the modern system of conveyancing. At the same time, the legislature undoubtedly regarded the equity of redemption and the legal reversion as inseparable interests and the view in *Halsbury* that the equity of redemption is now attached to the legal reversion is perhaps correct. Otherwise, the two-fold nature of the mortgagor's interest might cause conveyancing complications.

DISPOSITION AND DEVOLUTION OF THE EQUITY OF REDEMPTION

1. Disposition inter vivos and by will

17–04 Since a mortgagor through the protection of equity remains substantially the owner of the property which he has mortgaged, he has as much power to deal with it as if he had never executed the conveyance though the dealings will generally be subject to the mortgagee's charge.[17] Thus, an equity of redemption may be sold, leased,[18] settled, mortgaged, assigned for the benefit of creditors or disposed of by will. Dispositions by will must, of course, be in accordance with the provisions of the Wills Act 1837 and conveyances of equities of redemption, being conveyances of equitable interests, must be in writing under section 53(1)(c) of the Law of Property Act 1925. When the subject-matter of the mortgage is land, the equity of redemption is an interest in land and thus any contract to assign it must contain all the terms of the parties' agreement and be signed by both or both must sign a copy and exchange them.[19] Moreover, in the case of land, although section 53(1)(c) only requires the conveyance of an equity of redemption to be in writing, it will usually be by deed. Since on a mortgage of freehold or leasehold property the mortgagor necessarily retains, at least, a nominal reversion which he will convey to his assignee, together with the equity of redemption.

The assignee of incumbered property generally takes it subject to the mortgagee's charge. The Law of Property Act 1925, however, provides special machinery, whereby a person selling or exchanging land which is subject to a charge, may transfer it free of the charge. Under section 50 an application may be made to the court to allow a fund to be brought into court to meet the charge, interest on it, if any, plus all necessary costs and then to have the property declared free from the incumbrance. If the application is granted, the court may make appropriate vesting orders or orders for conveyance and give directions

---

[17] Provision is made by s.50 of the LPA 1925 for the discharge of an incumbrance on the sale or exchange of land, if there is paid into court a sum sufficient to meet the mortgagee's claim.

[18] *Tarn v. Turner* (1888) 39 Ch.D. 456, CA When a mortgagor has no power to create leases binding on the mortgagee, a lease granted by him is valid on the principle of estoppel and confers on the lessee an interest in the equity of redemption sufficient to entitle him to redeem. See *post*, pp. 317, 338.

[19] Law of Property (Miscellaneous Provisions) Act 1989, s.2. Contracts entered into prior to September 27, 1989 were simply required to be evidenced by a memorandum in writing signed by the party to be charged or his lawful agent: LPA 1925, s.40. *Massey v. Johnson* (1847) 1 Exch. 241.

concerning the investment of the fund in court. The advantage of this machinery is that it enables land to be sold free of an incumbrance in cases when, by the terms of the charge, the incumbrance cannot immediately be paid off, for example, where an annual sum is charged on land or where a capital sum is due on some future date. It is true that the incumbrancer loses the security of the land, but the fund in court is not his only protection; for, if by the depreciation of its investments the fund proves insufficient, the deficiency must be made up by the vendor. The fund is thus not substituted for the charge but is a security for it, and consequently, if there is a surplus after discharging the incumbrance, the surplus belongs to the vendor.[20]

2. Settlement of equities of redemption

Since a large proportion of family estates are to some extent mortgaged, the **17–05** settlement of an equity of redemption was a common occurrence. Even before 1926 an equity of redemption in freehold land, being an equitable estate of inheritance, could be entailed[21] and the entail could be barred under the Fines and Recoveries Act 1833; the mortgaging of freehold estates did not therefore interrupt the continuity of a strict settlement. Section 130(1) of the Law of Property Act 1925 enabled an equity of redemption to be entailed whether the subject-matter of the mortgage be real or personal property. With the commencement of the Trusts of Land and Appointment of Trustees Act 1996 that ability was abolished along with the ability to create any entailed interest.

When entails or other successive interests were created in an equity of redemption, the question arose as to how far the tenant for life was obliged to keep down the interest on the mortgage debt. The general principle is that a tenant for life is bound on all paramount incumbrances to keep down the interest accruing during his period of enjoyment to the extent of the profits received by him.[22] Thus, if a tenant for life allowed the interest to get into arrear when the rents and profits were sufficient to meet it, the persons subsequently entitled could bring an action to have the arrears discharged and could enforce their right against the life tenant's personal representatives after his death.[23] Moreover, if incumbered and unincumbered property was included in the same settlement the tenant for life was bound to employ the profits from all the properties in discharging the interest on the incumbered portion.[24] Tenants in tail in possession, however, were not within the rule; although they were tenants for life for the purposes of the Settled Land Act 1925, they were not under an obligation to keep down the interest on incumbrances, because by the power of breaking the entail they always had the reversioner and the remaindermen at their mercy.[25]

---

[20] *Re Wilberforce's Trusts* [1915] 1 Ch. 94.
[21] *Casborne v. Scarfe* (1738) 1 Atk. 603.
[22] *Revel v. Watkinson* (1748) 1 Ves.Sen. 93.
[23] *Lord Kensington v. Bouverie* (1859) 7 H.L.C. 557; *Makings v. Makings* (1860) 1 De G.F. & J. 355.
[24] *Frewen v. Law Life Assurance Society* (1896) 2 Ch. 511; *Honeywood v. Honeywood* [1902] 1 Ch. 347.
[25] *Amesbury v. Brown* (1750) 1 Ves.Sen. 477; *Chaplin v. Chaplin* (1734) 3 P.Wms. 245. An infant tenant in tail cannot, of course, break the entail during his minority, and the interest must be kept down during that period: *Sergeson v. Sealey* (1742) 2 Atk. 412; *Burgess v. Mawbey* (1823) 1 T. & R. 167.

The duty of a life tenant to keep down interest on charges is not owed to the incumbrancer; it exists only between the life tenant and persons subsequently entitled.[26] Consequently, when the income from the settled property is insufficient to meet the claim for interest, and the life tenant makes up the deficiency out of his own pocket, he does not necessarily obtain a charge on the property for the amount of the deficiency. He is presumed to intend a benefit to the inheritance, unless he intimates to those next entitled his intention to reserve a charge on the property before he meets the claim for interest.[27]

3. Equity of redemption as assets for payment of debts

17–06 An equity of redemption is part of the mortgagor's assets available for the payment of his debts and therefore on his bankruptcy vests in his trustee for that purpose and, on his death, in his personal representatives. An equity of redemption may also be taken by a judgment creditor to satisfy his judgment, the process varying with the nature of the property.

When the equity of redemption arises from the mortgage of land the appropriate remedy is for the judgment creditor to register his judgment in the Register of Writs and Orders at the Land Charges Register pursuant to the Land Charges Act 1972.[28] If title to the land is registered, it should be protected by a caution.[29]

Alternatively, the judgment creditor can obtain the appointment of a receiver by way of equitable execution (which the High Court and any county court is empowered to do in appropriate circumstances in relation to land and interests therein).[30] It also relates to personal property.[31] The power may be exercised whether or not a charging order has been imposed under the Charging Orders Act 1979 and CPR Sched. 1, sc. 50 and is in addition to and not in derogation of any power of the court to appoint a receiver in proceedings by enforcing a charge created by a charging order.[32] The appointment of a receiver by way of equitable execution does *not* of itself create a charge on the property and will be void if not registered under the Land Charges Act 1972.[33]

---

[26] *Re Morley* (1869) L.R. 8 Eq. 594.

[27] *Lord Kensington v. Bouverie* (1859) 7 H.L.C. 557. *cf. Re Warwick's Settlement Trusts* [1937] Ch. 561.

[28] Power is given to the High Court and to any county court for the purpose of enforcing any judgment or order of those courts for the payment of money to any person, to impose by order a charge on any such land or interest in land of the debtor as may be specified in the order, and for securing the payment of monies due or to become due under the judgment order. Such an order may be made absolute or on conditions, see Charging Orders Act 1979, s.1(1). Formerly a mere interest under a trust for sale was not an interest in "land" for this purpose, see *Irani France Ltd v. Singh* [1971] Ch. 59. Since the Charging Orders Act 1979, the court is now empowered to make an order charging a debtor's beneficial interest under any trust including therefore a trust for land as such an interest now is (see *National Westminster Bank v. Stockman* [1981] 1 W.L.R. 67 and *First National Securities Ltd v. Hegarty* [1985] Q.B. 850). However under section 6 (as amended by the Trusts of Land and Appointment of Trustees Act 1996) no writ or order affecting an interest under a trust for land may be registered in the Register of Writs and Orders.

[29] Land Registration Act 1925, s.59(1).

[30] Supreme Court Act 1981, s.37; County Courts Act 1984, s.107; and see CPR Sched. 1, ss.30.1 and 51.2. See also pp. 217 *et seq.* for the power to appoint a receiver under the LPA 1925.

[31] *e.g.* such as stocks and shares.

[32] CPR Sched. 1, sc. 51/1–315.

[33] s.6. It will not, however, be void if an order has also been made under the Charging Orders Acts 1979 (see CPR Sched. 1, sc. 51/1–315).

When the equity of redemption is in personal chattels which have been mortgaged by a bill of sale, the chattels cannot be taken by the sheriff under a writ of *fi. fa.*, since the property in them has already passed to the holder of the bill of sale.[34] The judgment creditor may apply to the court for a sale of the chattels and will be entitled to any sum which is realised in excess of the amount due to the holder of the bill of sale. If it is doubtful whether there will be any excess, the court will not order a sale unless the creditor indemnifies the mortgagee against loss, while if it is certain that there will be no excess, an order for sale will not be granted.[35]

4. Devolution of equity of redemption on intestacy

Since a mortgagor continues in equity to be the owner of the mortgaged property, **17–07** the mortgage does not affect the devolution of the property after the mortgagor's death. Thus, before 1926, an equity of redemption in freehold belonged to the heir-at-law, while an equity of redemption in chattels real or in pure personalty belonged to the next of kin. Moreover, in the case of land, if any special custom of descent was applicable to the land as, for example, gavelkind, the custom governed the descent of an equity of redemption in the land.[36] Today, of course, succession to an equity of redemption, whether of chattels or realty, is governed by the provisions of the Administration of Estates Act 1925.[37] Consequently, on the death of a mortgagor intestate, the equity of redemption passes to his personal representatives with the rest of his property.

5. Incidence of the mortgage debt

A mortgagor's liability for the mortgage debt has two aspects—his personal **17–08** liability on the express or implied promise to pay and his incumbered property's liability to be taken by the mortgagee. Liabilities under a contract cannot be assigned without consent,[38] and consequently, if a mortgagor assigns his equity of redemption (even if the assignee undertakes personal liability[39]) the assignee does not become personally liable to pay the mortgage debt,[40] although the mortgagee may, of course, still take the property to satisfy his debt. Moreover, even though an assignment is made subject to the mortgage debt, the original mortgagor is still liable to be sued on the personal covenant[41] and thus usually takes an indemnity from his assignee to meet that contingency.[42] Of course, the

---

[34] *Scarlett v. Hanson* (1883) 12 Q.B.D. 213.

[35] *Stern v. Tegner* (1898) 1 Q.B. 37.

[36] *Fawcett v. Lowther* (1751) 2 Ves.Sen. 300.

[37] ss.45–52 as amended by the Family Law Reform Act 1987, ss.1, 18 and 33(1).

[38] See *Chitty on Contracts* (28th ed., 1999), paras 20–075—20–078.

[39] *West Bromwich Building Society v. Bullock* (1936) 80 S.J. 654.

[40] *Oxford (Earl) v. Lady Rodney* (1808) 14 Ves. 417; *Re Errington, ex p. Mason* [1894] 1 Q.B. 11.

[41] *Kinnaird v. Trollope* (1888) 39 Ch. 636; subsequent proceedings (1889) 42 Ch.D. 610.

[42] Even if he does not (see *Mills v. United Counties Bank Ltd* [1912] 1 Ch. 231), when the whole mortgaged property is assigned subject to the mortgage, such an indemnity will be implied (*Bridgman v. Daw* (1891) 40 W.R. 253) unless it is not made for value (*Re Best* [1924] 1 Ch. 42). See also Romer L.J. in *Re Mainwaring's Settlement Trusts* [1937] 1 Ch. 96 at 103.

mortgagee may consent to the assignee and not the original mortgagor taking over the liability to pay, by the assignee entering into a fresh covenant with the mortgagee.

The case is more complicated when the equity of redemption is transferred, not *inter vivos*, but on the death of the mortgagor, for his personal representatives succeed to the liability in contract,[43] whereas the incumbered property may devolve upon or be devised to beneficiaries who have not that liability. Until the law was altered by Locke King's Acts,[44] a deceased's personal estate was primarily liable to satisfy a debt charged upon land, so that an heir-at-law or a devisee was entitled to call on the personalty to exonerate lands from the debts charged upon them.[45] The rule was displaced if the deceased had signified a contrary intention[46] and, being based upon succession to the deceased's contractual liability, it only applied on the death of the original mortgagor. An assignee of an equity of redemption had not himself created the charge and was not therefore under any personal liability.[47]

(a) *The current position*

17–09   Today, however, the rule is reversed. Unless the deceased mortgagor has signified a contrary intention, the primary liability to satisfy charges upon his property is, as between persons claiming beneficially under him, upon the incumbered property. The personal estate is still, of course, liable to satisfy a mortgagee's claim in contract against the deceased, but, if called on to do so, has a right to be compensated out of the mortgaged property. This change was first effected in 1854 but the Administration of Estates Act 1925[48] extends the new rule to incumbered *personalty* as well as realty. Thus, specific personalty which has been mortgaged or pledged will not, after 1925, be entitled to exoneration at the expense of the general assets of the deceased, unless the latter has shown an intention by will, deed or other document to that effect. Under the Administration of Estates Act 1925, as under Locke King's Acts, the deceased's contrary direction in favour of exoneration must be clear and unambiguous. Thus, a general direction for the payment of debts, or even of *all* debts, out of the deceased's personal or residuary estate will not be sufficient to exonerate property mortgaged or charged[49] nor will a direction to charge all debts upon the personal or residuary estate. In fact, an intention to exonerate must be signified by words referring clearly to mortgage debts, and not to debts generally.[50] Such an intention can be shown in any document such as a letter.[51] It may be partial

---

[43] *Bartholomew v. May* (1737) 1 Atk. 487.
[44] Real Estates Charges Acts, 1854, 1867 and 1877.
[45] *Cope v. Cope* (1710) 2 Salk. 449; *Galton v. Hancock* (1742) 2 Atk. 436.
[46] *Morrow v. Bush* (1785) 1 Cox. 185; *Forrest v. Prescott* (1870) L.R. 10 Eq. 545; *Hancox v. Abbey* (1805) 11 Ves. 179.
[47] *Scott v. Beecher* (1820) 5 Madd. 96; *Butler v. Butler* (1800) 5 Ves. 534; *Earl of Ilchester v. Earl of Carnarvon* (1839) 1 Beav. 209.
[48] ss.35, 55(1)(xvii); this largely restates the old law.
[49] s.35(2).
[50] *Re Valpy* [1906] 1 Ch. 531.
[51] See *Re Campbell* [1898] 2 Ch. 206; *Re Wakefield* (1943) 87 S.J. 371, CA; *Re Birmingham* [1959] Ch. 523.

in that it applies to mortgages and not to liens[52] but it is not enough to make a specific demise of one property comprised in a mortgage and not the whole.[53]

These provisions do not in any way affect a mortgagee's right to satisfy himself, either out of the incumbered property or, by suing on the personal promise, out of the deceased mortgagor's general assets. The changed incidence of the debt does not alter the mortgagee's remedies.[54] They do not apply to a person who is given the right to purchase part of the estate by will. He is not a devisee or legatee, but a purchaser.[55]

6. **Contribution**

When several estates, held in different ownership, are subject to the same   **17–10** mortgage, any one owner, who discharges the common debt, has a right to contribution from the others pro rata according to the value of their securities. The primary equitable rule is that, where different properties are charged with the same debt, the burden shall be distributed proportionately among the various properties.[56] Thus the mortgagee may pursue his remedies against any estate he pleases but he cannot, by so doing, throw the whole liability on the owner of one estate.[57] The same rule applies when a mortgagor has mortgaged several estates to secure the same debt and then, on his death, the estates pass into the hands of several owners. Under section 35 of the Administration of Estates Act 1925, all the incumbered properties are responsible for the debt and if one owner discharges the whole liability, he has a right to contribution against the other properties.[58] The fundamental requirement for this right to contribution is that all the properties shall be subject to a common liability *of the same degree*.[59] It is not enough that a creditor has a charge on more than one property; the properties must, as between themselves, be equally liable. For example, a property specifically charged with a debt has no right to contribution from property over which the creditor has only a general lien. It is for this reason that the owner of incumbered property, who is also under a personal obligation to pay a common debt, cannot claim contribution from another whose property is subject to the same incumbrance, but who has no personal liability in respect of the debt.[60] Nor must it be forgotten that the doctrine of marshalling may have the result of throwing the primary liability for a common debt upon one only of the mortgaged estates, so that the owner of that estate, not having an equal liability, will lose his right to contribution.[61] Again, even in the case of joint mortgagees there may be no right of contribution because of the special circumstances of the mortgage; for example, of two co-mortgagors one may be acting as surety for the other so that, as between themselves, the primarily liability is upon the principal debtor.[62] In all

---

[52] *Re Beirnstein* [1925] Ch. 12.
[53] *Re Neeld* [1962] Ch. 643, overruling *Re Biss* [1956] Ch. 243.
[54] s.35(3).
[55] *Re Fison's Wills Trust* [1950] Ch. 394.
[56] *per* Tomlin J. in *Re Best* [1924] 1 Ch. 42 at 44.
[57] *Aldrich v. Cooper* (1803) 8 Ves. 382; *Johnson v. Child* (1844) 4 Hare 87.
[58] See *Carter v. Barnardiston* (1718) 1 P.Wms. 505; *Middleton v. Middleton* (1852) 15 Beav. 450.
[59] *Re Dunlop* (1882) 21 Ch.D. 583.
[60] *Re Darby's Estate* [1907] 2 Ch. 465.
[61] *Bartholomew v. May* (1737) 1 Atk. 487; and *post*, para. 24–10 *et seq.*
[62] *Marquess of Bute v. Cunynghame* (1826) 2 Russ. 275.

these cases, where the primary liability is upon one debtor or property, the others are not only bound to contribute but if they in fact discharge the debt, they have a right to be compensated.[63] This is important if a mortgagor mortgages two estates to cover the same debt and afterwards assigns one of the estates. Under the principles just stated, the primary liability is upon the assignor so that, if he does not intend to exonerate his assignee's estate, he must be careful to preserve his own right to contribution.[64] This right he will preserve if he assigns the estate *subject to the mortgage*, because by so doing he shows that the primary liability is not to be all on the property which he retains, and thus restores the fundamental rule of equity which requires the imposition of proportionate burdens on properties charged with the same debt.[65] On the other hand, the assignment of one estate subject to the mortgage does not, by itself, shift the *whole* burden of the whole mortgage to the property assigned. Only an express indemnity covering the whole mortgage debt will have that effect.[66]

MORTGAGOR'S BENEFICIAL ENJOYMENT OF THE SECURITY

17–11   The notion that the mortgagor is the real owner of the security is carried in equity as far as it can be, without actually infringing the rights vested in the mortgagee by virtue of his legal estate. The mortgagee, is not a trustee for the mortgagor, for he has an interest in the mortgaged property adverse to that of the mortgagor.[67] In equity, however, that interest is rigidly confined to a right to hold the property as a security. A mortgagor, until his equity of redemption is lost to him by foreclosure, sale under a power of sale, lapse of time or release, is entitled to the full beneficial enjoyment of the land. He is regarded as the owner of the land[68] subject to a mere incumbrance. It is true that a mortgage contract usually confers on the mortgagee a legal right to take possession of the property immediately and without regard to the state of the mortgage debt but equity treats this right as part of his security and not as a right to beneficial enjoyment. Thus, if a mortgagee does take possession of his security, he will be called on to account with strictness for his use of it and for the profits which he has taken or ought to have taken from the property.[69] For example, if the mortgagee occupies land the mortgagor is entitled to be credited with a fair occupation rent.[70] In consequence, not only is a mortgagee prevented from making any profit out of the mortgage property, but he is, by the strictness of the account, discouraged from exercising his legal right to take possession except as a measure to preserve his security.[71]

---

[63] *Re Best* [1924] 1 Ch. 42.
[64] *ibid.*
[65] *Re Mainwaring's Settlement Trusts* [1937] 1 Ch. 96.
[66] *ibid.*
[67] *Dobson v. Land* (1850) 8 Hare 216 and see *ante*, para. 16–04 *et seq.*
[68] See Lord Denning in *Westminster City Council v. Haymarket Publishing Ltd* [1981] 1 W.L.R. 677 at 680 B–C and 681 C–E.
[69] *Hughes v. Williams* (1806) 12 Ves. 493; *Shepherd v. Spansheath* (1988) E.G.C.S. 35; *Chaplin v. Young (No. 1)* (1864) 33 Beav. 330; *Parkinson v. Hanbury* (1867) L.P. 2 H.L. 1.
[70] *Marriott v. Anchor Reversionary Co.* (1861) 3 De G.F. & J. 177 at 193.
[71] It is the nature of the transaction that the mortgagor shall continue in possession. *per* Lord Selborne, *Heath v. Pugh* (1881) 6 Q.B.D. 345 at 359.

Equity stops short of restraining the mortgagee from taking possession by granting an injunction, but, if possession is taken, the mortgagor is considered as being entitled to the profits, subject only to the mortgagee's right to devote them to the satisfaction of the mortgage debt.

On the other hand, if, as generally happens, the mortgagor remains in posses-   **17–12** sion, he is entitled to take all the profits from the security without being in any way obliged either to account for them or to apply them in discharging the mortgage interest.[72] This is so even though the security is insufficient. Thus, in a case[73] where the property mortgaged was land let out on lease and the mortgagor went bankrupt, Lord Eldon refused to compel the assignee in bankruptcy to account for past rents received by him. He insisted that a mortgagor does not receive the rents for the mortgagee and that there is no instance of a mortgagor being directly called on to account for rents. Again, a mortgagor of land may cut and sell timber, and in so doing may even waste the inheritance provided that he does not thereby render the security insufficient.[74] A mortgagor in possession cannot therefore be considered a bailiff of the mortgagee. He is equitable owner of the property and as such is not liable to pay an occupation rent to the mortgagee.[75] Correspondingly, he has the ordinary liabilities of an owner and is, for example, responsible for the maintenance of dykes and sea walls.[76]

MORTGAGOR IN POSSESSION

1. **General**

Although in equity a mortgagor remains owner of the property, by the mortgage   **17–13** conveyance he parts with an estate or interest which carries with it the immediate right to possession.[77] Whilst it is true that he usually remains in occupation and that equity discourages the mortgagee from going into occupation, the fact remains that the mortgagee holds the legal title to possession, and that the court will never prevent him from insisting on his title.[78] It follows that as a mortgagee has the immediate right to possession, the mortgagor can only lawfully remain in occupation as the mortgagee's tenant and that in the absence of any special agreement the tenancy will be precarious. For unless the mortgage contract makes express provision for the mortgagor's continued possession of the property, his tenancy depends solely on his *de facto* possession and is terminable by

---

[72] *Trent v. Hunt* (1853) 9 Exch. 14; *Heath v. Pugh* (1881) 6 Q.B.D. 345 at 359, *per* Lord Selborne; affirmed (1882) 7 A.C. 235, HL.

[73] *Ex p. Wilson* (1813) 2 V. & B. 252; *cf. Colman v. Duke of St. Albans* (1796) 3 Ves. 25; *Hele v. Lord Bexley* (1855) 20 Beav. 127.

[74] *Usborne v. Usborne* (1740) 1 Dick. 75; *Hippesley v. Spencer* (1820) 5 Mad. 422; *Harper v. Aplin* (1886) 54 L.T. 383.

[75] *Yorkshire Banking Co. v. Mullan* (1887) 35 Ch.D. 125.

[76] *Reg. v. Baker* (1867) 2 Q.B. 621.

[77] Thus, under the old law a heriot could not be taken from a mortgagor because he was not seised: *Copestake v. Hoper* [1908] 2 Ch. 10.

[78] *per* Plumer, M.R., *Marquis Cholmondely v. Lord Clinton* (1817) 2 Mer. 171 at 359; *Pope v. Biggs* (1829) 9 B. & C. 245.

the mortgagee at any moment. The exact nature of this precarious tenancy is a subject of controversy, with three distinct theories being put forward: *(i)* that the mortgagor is a tenant at will[79]; *(ii)* that he is a tenant at sufferance[80]; and *(iii)* that as a tenant he is *sui generis* and cannot be assigned to any of the well-known classes.[81] The first theory has frequently been criticised[82] and can scarcely be correct because a mortgagee may bring ejectment against a mortgagor without any previous demand for possession[83] and a mortgagor, when ejected, is not entitled to emblements.[84] It is not, of course, suggested that a mortgagor is never a tenant at will of the mortgagee because he may be made such a tenant by actual agreement,[85] or by the mortgagee expressly or impliedly recognising him as a tenant. The receipt of interest by the mortgagee is, however, referable to the mortgage and is by itself no recognition of a tenancy in the mortgagor.[86] The second theory has more to recommend it because the position of a mortgagor in possession, who has not been recognised as a tenant, largely corresponds to that of a tenant at sufferance: he begins lawfully, holds over without title, may be ejected without previous demand for possession and is not entitled to emblements. Moreover, there are clear statements by Lord Ellenborough[87] and Lord Tenterden[88] that the mortgagor is at most a tenant at sufferance. On the other hand, unlike a tenant at sufferance, a mortgagor in possession, who pays his interest, will not find time running in his favour under the Limitation Act 1980,[89] although he is not thereby recognising the mortgagee as his landlord. Furthermore, statute[90] has given to a mortgagor in possession wide powers of bringing actions in respect of the mortgaged property and of granting leases without the concurrence of the mortgagee, so that his position is, in fact, rather different from that of a tenant at sufferance. In the past[91] analogies from tenancies at will or at sufferance may have influenced judges in deciding questions concerning the mortgage relationship, but today the rights, powers and interests of mortgagor and mortgagee are well settled.[92] Therefore, while recognising that the closest analogy to the possession of a mortgagor is the possession

[79] Lord Mansfield in *Keech v. Hall* (1778) 1 Doug. 21; *cf. Moss v. Gallimore* (1779) 1 Doug.K.B. 279; Fortescue, M.R., in *Leman v. Newnham* (1747) 1 Ves.Sen. 51.

[80] Lord Ellenborough, *Thunder* d. *Weaver v. Belcher* (1803) 3 East. 449 at 451; Vaughan-Williams J. in *Scobie v. Collins* [1895] 1 Q.B. 375. See Turner, *Equity of Redemption* (1931), p. 102.

[81] Parke B. in *Litchfield v. Ready* (1850) 20 L.J.(N.S.) Ex. 51 at 52; Turner, *Equity of Redemption* (1931), p. 110.

[82] *e.g.* by Buller J. in *Birch v. Wright* (1786) 1 Term. 378 at 381.

[83] *Doe* d. *Griffith v. Mayo* (1828) 7 L.J.(O.S.) K.B. 84; *Jolly v. Arbuthnot* (1859) 4 De G. & J. 224.

[84] *per* Buller J. in *Birch v. Wright* (1786) 1 Term. 378 at 387; *Christophers v. Sparke* (1820) 2 Jac. & W. 223. Even Lord Mansfield, who is chiefly responsible for the description of the mortgagor as tenant at will, was constrained by these differences to admit that he is a tenant at will only *quodam modo*: *Moss v. Gallimore* (1779) 1 Doug.K.B. 279.

[85] *e.g.* by the mortgagor attorning tenant to the mortgagee. See *ante*, p. 207.

[86] *Doe* d. *Rogers v. Cadwallader* (1831) 2 B. & Ad. 473; *Scobie v. Collins* [1895] 1 Q.B. 375.

[87] *Thunder* d. *Weaver v. Belcher* (1803) 3 East 449.

[88] *Doe* d. *Roby v. Maisey* (1828) 8 B. & C. 767; *cf.* Littledale J. in *Pope v. Biggs* (1829) 9 B. & C. 245.

[89] See *post*, para. 22–27 *et seq.*

[90] Now the L.P.A. 1925. ss.98 and 99. See *post*, para. 17–15 *et seq.*

[91] Turner, *Equity of Redemption* (1931), p. 104.

[92] Thus Buller J. in *Birch v. Wright* (1786) 1 Term. 378 at 383, said, perhaps somewhat prematurely: "A mortgagor and mortgagee are characters as well known and their rights, powers and interests are well settled, as any in the law."

of a tenant at sufferance,[93] it is sufficient to describe mortgagors as being in possession as mortgagors.[94]

A mortgagor, when his contract makes no provision for his continued occupa- **17–14** tion, holds precariously from the mortgagee, being liable to be ejected not only without notice, but without even a previous demand for possession. In fact it is then at the option of the mortgagee to treat his mortgagor in possession, either as his tenant or as a trespasser.[95] It is by no means uncommon however, for a mortgagor to stipulate in the mortgage the right to continue in possession of the security.[96] Such a stipulation will sometimes amount to a redemise of the property, sometimes only to a personal covenant by the mortgagee not to interfere with the mortgagor's enjoyment, and, if the language is not precise, it is not always easy to distinguish between a redemise and a mere covenant. The cases suggest the following propositions:

(1) If there is an *affirmative* covenant[97] for the mortgagor's enjoyment of the property and a determinate period[98] is indicated as the length of the term, the mortgage contract operates as a redemise for a term.

(2) If the agreement contains an affirmative covenant that the mortgagor shall continue in possession, or have quiet enjoyment until he makes default on the date fixed for repayment, he is a tenant for the intervening period.[99]

(3) In either case, if the mortgagor remains in occupation after the term has expired, he becomes a tenant at sufferance.[1]

(4) If the mortgagor is expressed to hold at the will and pleasure of the mortgagee, a tenancy at will is created and it may still be a tenancy at will, although a yearly rent is payable.[2] On the other hand, the tenancy may be a periodic tenancy, although the mortgagee reserves a right to determine it without notice.[3] In each case it is a question of the true intention of the parties.

(5) If there is a covenant, which is negative, for example, that the mortgagee shall not interrupt the mortgagor's possession, or which does not indicate any period for the lease, it will be a personal covenant and no demise is made thereby.[4] In such cases a mortgagor is tenant as mortgagor and his position is very like that of a tenant at sufferance.

---

[93] See I. Smith, *Leading Cases* (13th ed.), p. 594; Turner, *Equity of Redemption* (1931), Chap. 5.

[94] Turner, *Equity of Redemption* (1931), p. 110.

[95] *Partridge v. Bere* (1822) 5 B. & Ald. 604; *Hitchman v. Walton* (1838) 4 M. & W. 409; *Moss v. Gallimore* (1779) 1 Doug.K.B. 279; *Re Ind, Coope & Co. Ltd* [1911] 2 Ch. 223.

[96] This is sometimes effected by an "attornment clause," by which the mortgagor attorns tenant to the mortgagee. If there is such an attornment clause it can have certain consequences in a mortgagor's claim for possession. See *ante*, para. 3–36 and para. 16–23.

[97] *Wilkinson v. Hall* (1837) 3 Bing.N.C. 508; *Doe* d. *Parsley v. Day* (1842) 2 Q.B. 147.

[98] *Doe* d. *Roylance v. Lightfoot* (1841) 8 M. & W. 553; *Doe* d. *Parsley v. Day* (1842) 2 Q.B. 147.

[99] *Wilkinson v. Hall* (1837) 3 Bing.N.S. 508. See Coote, *Law of Mortgages* (9th ed., 1927), p. 677 (n.).

[1] *Gibbs v. Cruickshank* (1873) L.R. 8 C.P. 454.

[2] *Doe* d. *Bastow v. Cox* (1847) 11 Q.B. 122.

[3] *Re Knight, ex p. Voisey* (1882) 21 Ch.D. 442; *Re Threlfall, ex p. Queen's Benefit Building Society* (1880) 16 Ch.D. 274.

[4] *Doe* d. *Parsley v. Day* (1842) 2 Q.B. 147.

2. **Right of a mortgagor in possession to bring actions in respect of the mortgaged property**

17–15   Although the tenancy of a mortgagor is usually precarious, it is plain that when he is in possession of the mortgaged property, he will have the protection which the law always affords to a possessory title.[5] Except against the person entitled, a disseisor or a tenant at sufferance has all the remedies, legal or equitable, which the true owner has to protect his property.[6] So, too, has a mortgagor who is in personal occupation. However, when the mortgage property is let out on lease, the mortgagor is, of course, only a reversioner, though technically still in possession. As owner of the property in equity he has always had available to him equitable remedies to protect his interest.[7] Thus he may bring an action for an injunction against his lessee or against a third party to prevent an injury to the property,[8] or to enforce a restrictive covenant.[9] Legal remedies, however, at common law attach only to the legal estate and in days when mortgages were usually created by assignment, passed with the legal estate to the mortgagee.[10] A mortgagor was, indeed, allowed to recover the rents from his lease, and even distrain for them on the basis that he had an implied authority from the mortgagee[11] but that, at common law, was the limit of his rights. Having at law no estate he was unable, against third parties, to bring an action for damages for injury to the reversion[12] and having parted with the reversion to the mortgagee he was unable against his lessee to bring ejectment or any action on the covenants in the lease.[13] His course was either to induce the mortgagee to sue or to ask the court to compel the mortgagee to lend his name to the action. However, this he could do only on the terms of offering to redeem.[14]

17–16   The power of a mortgagor in possession of mortgaged land to sue in respect of the land was, however, considerably enlarged by section 25(5) of the Judicature Act 1873 and section 10 of the Conveyancing Act 1881, which are now replaced by, respectively, sections 98 and 141 of the Law of Property Act 1925 and, in relation to the enforcement of leasehold covenants in leases granted on or after January 1, 1996, section 15 of Landlord and Tenant (Covenants) Act 1995. These sections apply to all mortgages, whether made before or after January 1, 1926, and their effect is as follows. So long as the mortgagee has not given an effective[15] notice of an intention to take possession or to enter into receipt of the rent and profits, a mortgagor may, in his own name, sue for possession or for the recovery of rents and profits, and may bring an action for damages against a

---

[5] *Perry v. Clissold* [1907] A.C. 73.

[6] *Graham v. Peat* (1801) 1 East. 244; *Asher v. Whitlock* (1865) L.R. 1 Q.B. 1.

[7] *per* Channel J. in *Turner v. Walsh* [1909] 2 K.B. 484 at 487.

[8] *Van Gelder, Apsimon & Co. v. Sowerby Bridge, & United District Flour Society* (1890) 44 Ch.D. 374.

[9] *Fairclough v. Marshall* (1878) 4 Ex.D. 37; *Rogers v. Hosegood* [1900] 2 Ch. 388.

[10] *Doe d. Marriot v. Edwards* (1834) 5 B. & Ad. 1065. But if the mortgage was made *before* the lease there was no difficulty.

[11] *ibid. cf.* also *Trent v. Hunt* (1853) 9 Ex. 14.

[12] *per* Bramwell B., at Assizes, *Rumford v. Oxford, Worcester & Wolverhampton Rly Co.* (1856) 1 H. & N. 34.

[13] *Matthews v. Usher* [1900] 2 Q.B. 535. See also *Molyneux v. Richard* [1906] 1 Ch. 34.

[14] *per* Farwell L.J. in *Turner v. Walsh* [1909] 2 K.B. 484 at 495.

[15] Possession proceedings which are defective by means of a technicality are not sufficient, see *Kitchen's Trustee v. Madders and Madders* [1949] Ch. 588 affd. [1950] Ch. 134.

trespasser or against any other wrongdoer.[16] Similarly, whilst still a mortgagor in possession, he may, in his own name, enforce all covenants and conditions which are contained in leases of the mortgaged land.[17] It is immaterial whether the mortgage[18] or lease[19] was made before or after the statutory amendment. Finally, these statutory powers do not in any way prejudice a mortgagor's right to bring actions which may be vested in him independently of the Act, for example, by virtue of the possession of a legal estate.

---

[16] s.98(1).
[17] s.141(2) in relation to leases prior to 1996; Landlord and Tenant (Covenants) Act 1995, s.15 in relation to leases after 1995.
[18] s.98(3).
[19] s.141(4) in relation to leases prior to 1996; Landlord and Tenant (Covenants) Act 1995, s.15 in relation to leases after 1995.

CHAPTER 18

THE RIGHTS, DUTIES AND REMEDIES OF THE MORTGAGOR OR CHARGOR

THE RIGHT OF REDEMPTION

1. Legal right to redeem

The legal right to redeem is the right specifically reserved to the mortgagor in the **18–01** mortgage contract to recover his property upon discharging the obligations which the mortgage was created in order to secure. At law the contract is construed strictly so that a mortgagor exercising his legal right to redeem must comply punctiliously with the proviso for redemption. Thus a mortgage to secure a money loan ordinarily fixes a definite date for repayment and at law repayment must be made precisely on that date. Before the stipulated date the mortgagor has no right to redeem either at law or in equity,[1] nor has the mortgagee, in the absence of a special agreement to that effect, any right to call in his money. Even the fact that the mortgagor is in default upon other covenants not touching the proviso for redemption will not accelerate the mortgagee's right to call in his money.[2–3] After the stipulated date the mortgagor ceases at law to have any right to redeem his property.

The date for redemption usually prescribed by the mortgage contract is six months after the date of its execution. The period before which the property may be redeemed at law may, however, be shorter and indeed the mortgage may be made redeemable and repayable on demand, in which case the demand fixes the date for redemption. Normally the period is a short one because it is an advantage to the mortgagee to place the mortgagor in default as soon as possible. However, at law there is no restriction upon the parties making their own arrangements. Accordingly the date for repayment and redemption may be suspended for any period, however long, provided that the mortgage contract does not infringe the equitable rules for the protection of the equity of redemption discussed below. Broadly, the position under these rules is that there is no limit to the length of a mortgage contract if the date for redemption is fixed genuinely upon an investment basis and the contract is neither a device to render the right of redemption illusory nor otherwise a cloak for an unconscionable bargain.[4]

---

[1] *Brown v. Cole* (1845) 14 Sim. 427.
[2–3] *Williams v. Morgan* [1906] 1 Ch. 804.
[4] *Knightsbridge Estates Trust Ltd v. Byrne* [1939] Ch. 441; see *post*, para. 18–02 *et seq.* and para. 18–19 *et seq.*

2. Equitable right to redeem

18–02   The equitable right to redeem[5] is the right of a mortgagor to recover his security by discharging his obligations under the mortgage despite the time fixed by the contract for the performance of those obligations having passed and even though under the express terms of his agreement the security may be stated to be the absolute property of the mortgagee. Similarly, in the case of a charge it is the right to have the security freed from the charge although default was made at the time fixed by the contract for the performance of the obligations in respect of which the charge was given. The right to redeem in equity is therefore a right given in contradiction to the declared terms of the contract between the parties.[6] Today, however, the nature of the equitable right to redeem is so well known that when a mortgage is made in the usual form to secure a money payment on a certain day it may generally be taken to be a term of the real bargain between the parties that the property is to remain redeemable after default on the day named.[7] As Maitland said,[8] the common form of mortgage by conveyance "is one long *suppressio veri* and *suggestio falsi*".

The equitable right to redeem is thus the right to recover the mortgaged property *after* the expiry of the legal right to redeem through its non-exercise on the contract date.[9] After the passing of the contract date equity superimposes on the mortgage agreement a condition giving the mortgagor a continuing right to redeem which he may exercise at any time before the right is destroyed by foreclosure, sale, release, or lapse of time. In general, this equitable right is dependent on the mortgagor giving the mortgagee reasonable notice of his intention to redeem and on his fully performing his obligations under the mortgage. In special cases the mortgagor is absolved from giving notice[10] and sometimes may even be allowed to recover his security on giving the mortgagee less than that to which he is entitled under the provisions of the mortgage.[11]

THE CONTROL OF THE COURT

1. Excluding the right

However, in every case the terms of redemption in equity[12] are imposed on the parties *ab extra* by the settled custom of the court which regulates every

---

[5] The equitable right to redeem should be distinguished from the "equity of redemption," which has a wider meaning. See *ante*, para. 17–01.

[6] *Per* Lord Bramwell in *Salt v. Marquess of Northampton* [1892] A.C. 1 at 18.

[7] *Per* Lord Parker in *Kreglinger v. New Patagonia Meat and Cold Storage Co. Ltd* [1914] A.C. 25 at 50.

[8] *Equity* (2nd ed.), p. 182.

[9] The right can arise *before* the legal date for redemption if the mortgagee has demanded payment, *e.g.* by entering into possession of the security, see *Bovill v. Endle* [1896] 1 Ch. 648.

[10] See *post*, para. 18–25 *et seq.*

[11] *e.g.* in the case of a mortgage executed under undue influence.

[12] These terms are set out in full, *post*, para. 18–25 *et seq.*

mortgage contract. Nor can the court's control be ousted by any agreement in the mortgage itself. Lord Eldon in *Seton v. Slade*[13] said:

"I take it to be so in the case of a mortgage; that you shall not by special terms alter what this Court says are the special terms of that contract."

Accordingly, if property is transferred with the object of providing security and with the intention that it should be restored to the mortgagor, it is not competent for the parties so to frame their bargain that the mortgagee has a right under its terms to obtain an absolute title to the property overriding the equity of redemption. Thus, a person who has taken property by way of security will not be allowed to deprive the mortgagor of his equity of redemption by formulating the bargain as a conditional sale or by any similar device.[14] The jurisdiction of the court over mortgages cannot be ousted by any trick of conveyancing. Moreover, the question whether a transaction is a mortgage is one of substance, not of form, so that the court will freely admit parol evidence for the purpose of establishing that the true intention was merely to give a security, even if the parol evidence contradicts the plain terms of a deed.[15] The equity of redemption is thus an inseparable incident of a contract of mortgage. As counsel said in *Howard v. Harris*,[16] a mortgage can no more be made irredeemable than a distress for a rentcharge can be irrepleviable. The legislature has established one statutory exception to this principle: the Companies Act 1985 specifically authorises the creation of irredeemable mortgages in the form of irredeemable debentures or redeemable only on the happening of a contingency or the expiration of a period of time.[17]

Equity, therefore, interferes directly with freedom of contract between mortgagor and mortgagee. Today this interference is sometimes explained as being an illustration of the principle that equity looks to the intent rather than to the form. Historically, however, the Chancellor's intervention was the result partly of a desire to extend his jurisdiction[18] and partly of the position held by mortgages in the life of the sixteenth and seventeenth centuries. During that period mortgages were very generally securities taken by creditors from persons in circumstances of financial embarrassment such that the mortgagors were not free agents in making their contracts.[19] At first the Chancellor justified his interference either

18–03

---

[13] (1802) 7 Ves. 265 at 273.
[14] *Barnhart v. Greenshields* (1853) 9 Moo.P.C.C. 18.
[15] *England v. Codrington* (1758) 1 Eden 169; *Lincoln v. Wright* (1859) 4 De G. & J. 16. In the latter case, Turner L.J., puts this upon the general principle that in equity parol evidence will be admitted to prove a fraud. *Cf. Rochefoucauld v. Boustead* [1897] 1 Ch. 196. See also *Barton v. Bank of New South Wales* (1890) 15 App.Cas. 379; *Grangeside Properties Ltd v. Collingwoods Securities Ltd* [1964] 1 W.L.R. 139 (an assignment of a lease treated as a mortgage so as to enable the assignee–mortgagee to claim relief from forfeiture of the lease by the head-lessor).
[16] (1683) 1 Vern. 191 at 192.
[17] s.193 of the Companies Act 1985. Strictly an irredeemable debenture is not a mortgage; see *Samuel v. Jarrah Timber and Wood Paving Corporation Ltd* [1904] A.C. 323 at 330. See also *post*, paras 18–04—18–05.
[18] Turner, *Equity of Redemption* (1931), p. 42, thinks that this was the main reason for the development of the equity of redemption.
[19] "For necessitous men are not, truly speaking, free men, but, to answer a present exigency, will submit to any terms the crafty may impose on them." *per* Lord Northington in *Vernon v. Bethell* (1761) 2 Eden 110 at 113.

on the ground of protecting the mortgagor against an unscrupulous creditor or on the ground that relief should be given to a debtor who had been prevented from discharging his obligation only by reason of some mistake, accident or special hardship. At the same time and for the same reasons he was giving similar relief against penal clauses in bonds. Early in the seventeenth century, however, the Chancellor[20] decided to give relief against penal conditions in all cases even though no special ground for relief could be shown and the equity of redemption became part of the settled custom of the court.

PROTECTION OF THE RIGHT TO REDEEM

18–04   However, the protection of embarrassed mortgagors could not be achieved by the mere creation of the equitable right of redemption. As soon as the practice in equity to allow redemption after the contract date became known, mortgagees sought to defeat the intervention of equity by special provisions in the mortgage deed. These provisions were designed either to render the legal right to redeem illusory, thus preventing the equity of redemption from arising at all, or to defeat or clog the equity of redemption after it had arisen. For example, the mortgage contract might provide for an option for the mortgagee to purchase the mortgaged property, thus defeating both the legal and equitable right to redeem, or might allow redemption after the contract date only upon payment of an additional sum or upon performance of some additional obligation. Consequently, the Chancellor began to relieve mortgagors against such restrictions and fetters on the legal and equitable rights to redeem imposed by special covenants in the mortgage.

1. "Once a mortgage always a mortgage"

The protection of a mortgagor against all attempts to defeat or clog his right of redemption involved the creation of subsidiary rules of equity, invalidating the various contrivances which ingenious conveyancers devised. These rules are sometimes summed up in a maxim of equity "once a mortgage always a mortgage".[21] This means that once a contract is seen to be a mortgage no provision in the contract will be valid if it is inconsistent with the right of the mortgagor to recover his security on discharging his obligations. Provisions offending against the maxim may either touch the contractual terms of redemption thereby rendering the right to redeem illusory or they may touch only the equitable right to redeem after the passing of the contract date hampering the exercise of the right. Provisions of the latter kind are termed "clogs" on the equity of redemption. Greene M.R. in *Knightsbridge Estates v. Byrne*, emphas-

---

[20] Turner, *Equity of Redemption* (1931), p. 32, suggests that the Chancellor who took this step was none other than Lord Bacon.

[21] *Per* Lord Eldon L.C. in *Seton v. Slade* (1802) 7 Ves. 265 at 273.

ised that provisions touching the *contractual right* to redeem are not properly to be classed as clogs on the equity of redemption. However, it is evident that such provisions are in substance clogs on the equity of redemption since they tend to defeat it altogether.

Provisions infringing the equitable principle "once a mortgage always a mortgage" are invalid not merely against the mortgagor but against any person subsequently interested in the equity of redemption. For although the object of the rules against clogs on the equity of redemption is the protection of the mortgagor himself, the operation of the rules is to invalidate altogether any provisions which offend against them. The reason for this was clearly explained by Lord Tomlin in the case of *Mehrban Khan v. Makhna*[22]:

> " . . . the provisions in question, being a clog upon the equity of redemption, were void and could have no more binding force against the assign of the mortgagor than they had against the mortgagor himself. They are not provisions of general validity avoided against the mortgagor personally by reason of pressure or undue influence brought to bear on him. They are provisions which, when forming part of the actual mortgage contract, have under the general law no validity at all. If it were otherwise, an illogical result would follow. The mortgagor, if he redeemed, would escape from the burden, but, if he sold to another he would necessarily bear the burden, as the validity of the provisions as against the assign would be reflected in the price which he received."[23]

2. **Parties freedom to contract**

Formerly the court's jurisdiction to intervene in mortgage contracts was wider **18–05** than it is today owing to the existence of usury laws. The court, in mortgages securing money loans, asserted a general jurisdiction to invalidate the contractual terms of redemption if inconsistent with the policy of those laws. The economic fact that in the seventeenth and eighteenth centuries a mortgagee had an ascendancy over a mortgagor was taken into account by courts of equity as well as by the legislature, resulting in a jealous scrutiny of the terms of redemption. The usury laws were, however, repealed in 1854 and the court no longer invalidates the terms of a mortgage merely on the ground that they are exorbitant or unreasonable.

Today the parties to a mortgage are free to make what bargain they like, subject to the protection extended by the court to a mortgagor: (i) through the special equitable rules safeguarding the right to redeem; (ii) in cases of undue influence or duress at common law and under general equitable principles; (iii) in transactions falling within the provisions of the Consumer Credit Act 1974 as extortionate credit bargains or as regulated mortgages; and (iv) other instances

---

[22] (1930) 57 Ind.App. 168.
[23] *ibid.* at 172.

where the court will intervene pursuant to its statutory or equitable jurisdiction.[24]

3. Special equitable rules against clogs on the equity of redemption

18–06   The following are the special equitable rules protecting the right of redemption which permit the mortgagor to redeem regardless of the terms of the mortgage.

(a) A mortgage must be redeemable

A mortgage may not be framed with the design to render the security irredeemable.[25] It is the essence of a mortgage, in the conception of equity, that it shall be redeemable and the rule cannot be evaded by dressing up the mortgage as a conditional sale or by any other conveyancing device.[26] Equally it cannot be circumvented by a provision which, while not extinguishing the equity of redemption, has the result of making the right nugatory. Therefore in *Fairclough v. Swan Brewery Co. Ltd*[27] where the security was a lease with 210 months still to run and the mortgage was made redeemable only by 209 monthly payments, the mortgagor was permitted to disregard the instalment arrangement and to redeem at once on giving reasonable notice. In substance the leasehold security was made irredeemable by the terms of the mortgage. This rule, as previously stated,[28] no longer applies to debentures for section 193 of the Companies Act 1985 provides that debentures shall not be invalid by reason only that they are made irredeemable, or redeemable only on the happening of a contingency, however remote. Otherwise the only limitation upon the principle appears to be that where a short-lived asset, such as a lease or insurance policy, is mortgaged to secure a longer dated obligation, the fact that the property owing to its nature will not be restored to the mortgagor freed from the mortgage is not enough by itself to invalidate the mortgage contract.[29]

Accordingly, any condition in a mortgage is invalid if its effect is to vest the security absolutely in the mortgagee on any event whatsoever.[30] The mortgage must not only begin by being redeemable, it must continue so. Lord Northington said in *Vernon v. Bethell*[31]:

> "This Court as a Court of conscience is very jealous of persons taking securities for a loan and converting such securities into purchases, and therefore I take it to be an established rule that a mortgagee can never provide, at the time of making the loan, for any event or condition on which

---

[24] See *e.g.* Insolvency Act 1986, ss.244, 245; the Unfair Contract Terms in Consumer Contracts Regulations 1994, S.I. 1999, No. 2083 and see *ante*, para. 2–07 *et seq.*

[25] *Newcomb v. Bonham* (1681) 1 Vern. 7; *Re Sir Thomas Spencer Wells* [1933] Ch. 29 at 52.

[26] See *ante*, para. 1–04 *et seq.*

[27] [1912] A.C. 562.

[28] See *ante*, para. 18–02.

[29] *Knightsbridge Estates Trust Ltd v. Byrne* [1939] Ch. 441, 462; [1940] A.C. 613.

[30] *Toomes v. Conset* (1745) 3 Atk. 261.

[31] (1761) 2 Eden 110 at 113.

the equity of redemption shall be discharged and the conveyance absolute."

A condition which confines redemption to any particular person or period is therefore void. In *Howard v. Harris*[32] although the agreement only allowed redemption by the mortgagor or his heir male, yet it was held that *any* heir might redeem. Again, where life policies were mortgaged and redemption was confined to a period covering the life of the mortgagor himself it was held that his executor might redeem.[33]

(i) *Obtaining an option*

Similarly a mortgagee cannot by a stipulation in the mortgage contract obtain for himself an option on the property mortgaged. A contract cannot at once be a mortgage and a conditional sale even if the transaction is not oppressive.[34] So, too, if a mortgagor holds an option to purchase the fee or to renew a lease and assigns it to a mortgagee by way of security, the mortgagee cannot exercise the option and then claim the purchased property or new lease as against the mortgagor. In *Nelson v. Hannam*[35] the mortgage comprised an assignment of a 99 years' building lease plus the option to purchase the freehold. The mortgagee exercised the option after he had taken out a summons for foreclosure but before the decree had become absolute. The Court of Appeal held that the mortgagor was entitled—and, indeed, bound if called upon—to redeem not merely the lease but also the freehold reversion. Greene M.R. stated that if an option is an essential part of a mortgage transaction, whether as the sole security or merely as one element in the security, the mortgagee cannot retain against the mortgagor what is directly the fruit of the mortgaged property. The mortgagee may improve his security by exercising the option and may add the expense incurred in so doing to the mortgage account, but he cannot thus defeat the mortgagor's right to recover the fruit of the option. The court, in so deciding, acted on the analogy of cases dealing with mortgages of renewable leases, in which it has consistently been held that a mortgagee who exercises the right to renew must hold the renewed lease subject to the same equity of redemption as existed in relation to the original lease.[36]

18–07

(ii) *Purchase by the mortgagee*

The maxim "once a mortgage always a mortgage," does not, however, mean that a mortgagee can never purchase the mortgaged property while the relationship of mortgagor and mortgagee subsists. If the contract for the purchase of the mortgaged property is a transaction independent of the mortgage or genuinely collateral to the mortgage, the mortgagee is fully entitled either to buy it or to

---

[32] (1583) 1 Vern. 32 and 190; *cf. Spurgeon v. Collier* (1758) 1 Eden 55.
[33] *Salt v. Marquess of Northampton* [1892] A.C. 1. See also *Newcomb v. Bonham* (1681) 1 Vern. 7.
[34] *Samuel v. Jarrah Timber and Wood Paving Corporation Ltd* [1904] A.C. 323; *cf. Jennings v. Ward* (1705) 2 Vern. 520; *Price v. Perrie* (1702) Free.Ch. 258; *Re Edwards' Estate* (1861) 11 Ir.Ch.R. 367.
[35] [1943] Ch. 59.
[36] *Rakestraw v. Brewer* (1729) 2 P.W. 511; *Re Biss* [1903] 2 Ch. 40 at 62.

obtain an option for himself[37] provided that the agreement cannot be struck down as being in restraint of trade or is unfair or unconscionable.[38] Similar considerations probably apply to a right of pre-emption[39] for a mortgagee may take a release of the equity of redemption from the mortgagor without in any way being subject to the stringent rules which affect purchases by a trustee from his *cestui que trust*.[40] It makes no difference that the only consideration for the release is the discharge of the mortgage debt itself.[41] It follows *a fortiori* that the mortgagee of a lease containing no option to purchase the fee or renew the lease should on principle be entitled to purchase or obtain an option on the fee or obtain a renewal for his own account from a third party without being liable to have the new title redeemed by the mortgagor of the lease even if it wholly or partially destroys the equity of redemption.[42] An option is also plainly valid if it was obtained *before* the execution of the mortgage.[43] However, in a case where the executors of a deceased mortgagee sought to call in a loan and the mortgagor procured the transfer of the mortgage to a new mortgagee, it was held (following the principles set out in *Samuel v. Jarrah Timber and Wood Paving Corporation Ltd*[44]) that the options to purchase part of the mortgaged property imposed as a condition of the transfer by the new mortgagees were void. In effect, it was a new loan purportedly made subject to an option to purchase.[45]

(b) *Suspension of the right to redeem*

18–08   A stipulation postponing or suspending the right to redeem until some date in the future longer than the customary six months may not be framed with the design of rendering the right illusory under the rule just explained. In addition it may not be so framed as to be actually repugnant to the expressed right to redeem. Such a stipulation is otherwise valid unless it forms part of a mortgage contract which was extorted from the mortgagor oppressively, unconscionably or through undue influence in which the contract will be set aside under the general equitable principles applying to such cases discussed elsewhere.[46]

Stipulations postponing or suspending the contractual right to redeem for a period of years clearly have a tendency to defeat the equity of redemption or render it illusory and until recently the court adopted a reserved attitude towards any considerable postponement or suspension of redemption.[47] Nevertheless, in

---

[37] *Reeve v. Lisle* [1902] A.C. 461, where the option was granted to the mortgagee some 10 days after the mortgage itself.

[38] See *post*, para. 18–11 and chap. 26.

[39] *Orby v. Trigg* (1722) 9 Mod. 2.

[40] *Knight v. Marjoribanks* (1849) 2 Mac. & G. 10.

[41] *Melbourne Banking Co. v. Brougham* (1882) 7 A.C. 307.

[42] For a case where there was a lease by the claimants to an oil company and a re-lease at a higher rent by the oil company to the directors with an exclusive tie to sell the oil company's products after the grant of mortgage which was redeemed by the new arrangement, see *Alec Lobb (Garages) Ltd v. Total Oil (Great Britain) Ltd* [1985] 1 W.L.R. 173, approving *Multiservice Bookbinding Ltd v. Marden* [1979] Ch. 84. See also *Davies v. Directloans Ltd* [1986] 1 W.L.R. 823.

[43] *London and Globe Finance Corporation v. Montgomery* (1902) 18 T.L.R. 661.

[44] [1904] A.C. 323.

[45] See *Lewis v. Frank Love Ltd* [1961] 1 W.L.R. 261.

[46] See *post*, chap. 26; *cf. Cowdry v. Day* (1859) 1 Giff. 316.

[47] See *e.g. Fairclough v. Swan Brewery Co. Ltd* [1912] A.C. 562, (redemption allowed after only three years).

individual cases the court did accept postponement of the right to redeem for five years[48]; eight years[49]; 10 years[50] and 14 years.[51] In all these cases, however, the obligation to continue the mortgage was *mutual*, *i.e.* the mortgagee could not call in his money during the period when the mortgagor was precluded from redeeming. Moreover, the dicta in the cases suggested the equitable principle to be that a suspension of the right to redeem must be shown to be reasonable between the parties in the circumstances of the particular mortgage and that the mutuality of the obligation is the best evidence of reasonableness.[52] In *Morgan v. Jeffreys*[53] Joyce J. held invalid a postponement of the right to redeem for 28 years unaccompanied by a corresponding forbearance on the part of the mortgagee during the same period. Again, in *Davis v. Symons*[54] Eve J. was prepared to uphold a postponement for 20 years, but only if the covenant for postponement was genuinely mutual and the longer the period of postponement the more closely the ostensible mutuality required, he thought, to be scrutinised. In the particular case two insurance policies were mortgaged, and redemption was postponed for a period of 20 years during which the mortgagee was not to call in his money. The mortgage provided, however, that on maturity the policy moneys were to be paid over to the mortgagee and applied in the reduction of the mortgage debt. Both policies were due to mature before the end of the 20-year period, one four years and the other eight days before that time. This provision was held by the learned judge to destroy the mutuality[55] and to render the postponement of redemption invalid.

The modern position with regard to postponement or suspension

Recognition of the fact that today mortgages are normally genuine investments **18–09** and not oppressive exactions from the mortgagor had thus already caused a considerable relaxation in the court's attitude towards postponement or suspension of redemption, so that Eve J. could envisage a genuinely mutual postponement for 20 years as unobjectionable. In *Knightsbridge Estates Trust Ltd v. Byrne*[56] it led the Court of Appeal entirely to reject the view that a postponement of the contractual right to redeem is only permissible if reasonable between the parties.[57] A large estates company mortgaged freehold properties to the trustees of a friendly society to secure a loan of £310,000. The mortgagors covenanted to repay the principal and interest in 80 half-yearly instalments, combining principal and interest, redemption being thus suspended for 40 years. The mortgagees in turn covenanted that if the mortgagors made no default in respect of any of

---

[48] *Biggs v. Hoddinott* [1898] 2 Ch. 307.

[49] *Re Hones Estate* (1873) 8 I.R.Eq. 65.

[50] *Re Fortescue's Estate* (1916) 1 I.R. 268.

[51] *Williams v. Morgan* [1906] 1 Ch. 804.

[52] *e.g.* Sir Edward Burtenshaw Sugden L.C. in *Lawless v. Mansfield* (1841) 1 Dr. & W. 557 at 598.

[53] [1910] 1 Ch. 620.

[54] [1934] Ch. 442 at 448.

[55] This provision rendered part of the security irredeemable but more owing to the nature of the security than to the contrivance of the mortgagee.

[56] [1939] Ch. 441; affirmed on other grounds [1940] A.C. 613.

[57] See *e.g.* the explanation of the judgments in *Fairclough v. Swan Brewery Co. Ltd* ([1912] A.C. 565) in [1939] Ch. 441 at 460–462.

their covenants the money would only be called in by the 80 half-yearly instalments. There was thus mutuality in the covenant to continue the mortgage for 40 years and the contract was made between two powerful corporations at arm's length. The only reason why the mortgagors desired a release from their covenant was that they had miscalculated the future trend of interest rates and that money was now obtainable at easier rates than the mortgage rate. A less meritorious claim to the protection of equity it would be difficult to imagine and the court upheld the postponement for 40 years on the grounds that (i) as the covenant did not render the right to redeem illusory[58] or form part of an oppressive or unconscionable bargain[59] the court could not interfere; and (ii) the covenant was in any event reasonable between the parties. Although the court thus upheld this long suspension even upon the test of reasonableness, the main ground for their decision was that only a covenant which renders redemption illusory or alternatively forms part of an oppressive or unconscionable mortgage is bad. Greene M.R. who delivered the judgment of the court, stated roundly that the proposition that a postponement of the contractual right of redemption is only permissible for a reasonable time is ill-founded. He denied that there is any general jurisdiction to reform mortgage transactions because the court considers them unreasonable—a view which is undoubtedly correct.[60]

18–10   Although the covenant postponing redemption in the instant case was as a matter of fact mutual, by rejecting the test of reasonableness the Court of Appeal appears also to have rejected mutuality as essential to the validity of a postponement of redemption. The absence of mutuality may in a particular case be confirmatory evidence of an oppressive or unconscionable bargain but the covenant will not be invalidated unless the mortgage in its totality is found to be oppressive or unconscionable.

In the course of a discussion of the earlier authorities Greene M.R. also emphasised that a covenant suspending redemption may be invalid for actual repugnancy to the legal and equitable rights to redeem set up by the proviso for redemption. This will be so when, as in *Morgan v. Jeffreys*[61] and *Davis v. Symons*,[62] there is an express proviso for redemption after a few months followed by a stipulation binding the mortgagor not to redeem for a longer period. Neither of the two judges who decided those cases made this feature of the mortgages a ground of their decision but it was on this ground of repugnancy to the legal and equitable rights to redeem that the Court of Appeal alone thought that the decisions in the two older cases could be supported.

When *Knightsbridge Estates Trust Ltd v. Byrne*[63] came before the House of Lords, it was unanimously decided that the mortgage constituted a debenture within the meaning of the Companies Act 1929 so that the long postponement of

---

[58] *ibid.* at 456, 457.

[59] *ibid.* at 463.

[60] Subject now to the provisions of the Consumer Credit Act 1974 and the Insolvency Act 1986, the Unfair Terms in Consumer Contracts Regulations 1999. The Unfair Contract Terms Act 1977 does not apply to contracts for the disposition of an interest in land; see s.1(2), Sched. 1, para. 1(b); see *ante*, para. 3–37 *et seq.* and *post*, para. 18–14.

[61] [1910] 1 Ch. 620.

[62] [1934] Ch. 442.

[63] [1940] A.C. 613, and see now the Companies Act 1985, s.193.

redemption was in any event covered by the statutory authority to create irredeemable debentures contained in section 74 of that Act. The House of Lords vouchsafed no opinion on the correctness of the views expressed by the Court of Appeal—an omission to be regretted as the matter is of general importance to conveyancers. Although it is difficult to accept the Court of Appeal's explanation of the earlier authorities, as never having intended the word "reasonable" to denote anything more than "not unconscionable" or "not rendering the right to redeem illusory," it is considered that the principles stated by the Court of Appeal can be confidently accepted as representing the true modern doctrine of equity concerning postponement of the right to redeem. These principles are fully in accord with the opinions expressed by the House of Lords in *Kreglinger v. New Patagonia Meat and Cold Storage Co. Ltd*[64] upon the rules concerning the validity of collateral advantages.

The House of Lords in *Knightsbridge Estates Trust Ltd v. Byrne*,[65] and both the   **18–11** courts below, were unanimous in holding that the rule against perpetuities has no application to a covenant in a mortgage suspending the contractual right to redeem for more than 21 years. The result therefore is that the modern principles concerning suspension of redemption are such that provided that a covenant suspending redemption is framed genuinely on an investment basis, not as a cloak for oppression, it will be valid unless (i) it renders the right to redeem illusory, or (ii) it is directly repugnant to the contractual and equitable rights to redeem.

In many of the more recent cases there has been the added factor to be considered of a contract made in unlawful restraint of trade in which the mortgagor has been "tied" by a "solus agreement" to sell the mortgagee's products for the duration of the mortgage. In *Esso Petroleum Co. Ltd v. Harper's Garage (Stourport) Ltd*[66] it was held that a covenant by a mortgagor to sell only the mortgagee's brand of petrol for 21 years and not to redeem the mortgage which was repayable by instalments over a 21-year period before the expiry of 21 years was void as it was in unreasonable restraint of trade. The mortgage was therefore redeemable.

It seems, however, that a postponement for a shorter period may be valid (as in *Texaco Ltd v. Mulberry Filling Station*[67]). Further, if the tying provisions and the mortgage are separate and independent transactions, the restrictions being freely negotiated prior to the mortgage, the tie may well be valid provided that it is not unreasonable in duration.[68] It should also be added that in the *Esso* case[69] the House of Lords held valid a tie in respect of another garage owned by Harpers Ltd. But in this case the tie was for four-and-a-half years and no mortgage was involved.

---

[64] [1914] A.C. 25.
[65] [1940] A.C. 613.
[66] [1968] A.C. 269, following and extending the decision in *Petrofina (Great Britain) Ltd v. Martin* [1966] Ch. 146; see also *Hill v. Regent Oil Co. Ltd* [1962] E.G.D. 452 and *Regent Oil Co. Ltd v. J. A. Gregory (Hatch End) Ltd* [1966] Ch. 402 (an earlier case reported later), in which the doctrine of restraint of trade was not mentioned.
[67] [1972] 1 W.L.R. 814.
[68] *Re Petrol Filling Station, Vauxhall Bridge Road* (1968) 20 P. & C.R. 1.
[69] [1968] A.C. 269.

Further, it has been stated that the doctrine only applies to an agreement where a person is required to give up an existing freedom to trade as opposed to a position where there was no such previous right.[70]

(i) Ancillary Matters

(a) Nature of the obligation secured

In conclusion it should be noticed that sometimes the very nature of the obligation secured by a mortgage may render the security irredeemable for a considerable period without the mortgage being invalidated. Thus a mortgage may be made to secure an annuity during the life of some person or as an indemnity against contingent charges or for some other object not capable of immediate pecuniary valuation. Redemption in these cases is necessarily suspended for an uncertain period.[71]

(c) Clogs on the equity of redemption

18–12 A covenant is invalid if it imposes a penalty on the mortgagor for his failure to redeem on the contract date. Equity grants relief against penalties[72] in all kinds of contracts, but in the case of mortgages there is the added consideration that such covenants are designed, or at any rate calculated, to render redemption more difficult and are, therefore, clogs on the equity of redemption. Consequently, any additional sum expressed to be due from the mortgagor by reason of his default on the contract date is not recoverable by the mortgagee.[73] This principle does not, however, avoid a stipulation which obliges the mortgagor, when he redeems, to pay in respect of principal a sum greater than that actually advanced. This is not a penalty but a bonus or commission for making the advance. Since the repeal of the usury laws there is no objection to such a stipulation if the mortgage is not otherwise unconscionable.[74]

An analogous rule invalidates a provision whereby the rate of interest is unreasonably increased if it is not paid punctually. Such a provision can constitute a penalty and is accordingly void.[75] However, in *Lordsvale Finance Plc v. Bank of Zambia*,[76] Colman J. held that there was no reason why a contractual provision, the effect of which was to increase the interest rate that was payable under an executory contract on the default of one party, should be struck down if the increase could in the circumstances be commercially justified provided its

---

[70] See *Esso Petroleum Ltd v. Harper's Garage (Stourport) Ltd* [1968] A.C. 269 at 298, 306–309, 316–317. See also *Alec Lobb (Garages) Ltd v. Total Oil (Great Britain) Ltd* [1985] 1 W.L.R. 1735 and *contra, Cleveland Petroleum Ltd v. Dartstone Ltd* [1969] 1 W.L.R. 116. There is the somewhat questionable practice imposed by some finance houses which provides that if the mortgagor redeems within two or three years he pays three or six months additional "penalty" interest in any event and not in lieu of notice. Whether or not such a clause is a clog is yet to be decided.

[71] *Fleming v. Self* (1854) 3 De G. M. & G. 997 at 1024; *cf.* Lindley L.J. in *Secretary of State in Council of India v. British Empire Mutual Life Assurance Co.* (1892) 67 L.T. 434 at 439.

[72] See Snell's *Principles of Equity* (30th ed., 2000), para. 36–01 to 36–14.

[73] *Booth v. Salvation Army Building Association (Ltd).* (1897) 14 T.L.R. 3.

[74] *Potter v. Edwards* (1857) 26 L.J.Ch. 468; *cf. James v. Kerr* (1889) 40 Ch.D. 449 where in all the circumstances the mortgage itself was unconscionable; *Bucknell v. Vickery* (1891) 64 L.T. 701.

[75] *Holles v. Wyse* (1693) 2 Vern. 289.

[76] [1996] Q.B. 752.

dominant purpose was not to deter the other party from breach. Thus an increase in interest of one per cent per annum upon the default of the paying party was held to be unenforceable by reason of the increased credit risk of a borrower in default. Furthermore, there is no objection to a provision which stipulates for a higher rate of interest *reducible on punctual payment* to the rate agreed by the parties.[77] Nor does the rule invalidate a stipulation for compound interest. Formerly objection was taken to such stipulations on the ground of usury,[78] but after the abolition of the usury laws in 1854 and their subsequent replacement by the Moneylenders Acts 1900–1927 objection was no longer taken (unless the transactions fell within the provisions of the latter Acts which, *inter alia*, forbade the charging of compound interest in moneylending transactions).

Now, in addition to the courts' general equitable jurisdiction to interfere with a mortgage transaction where one of the terms is oppressive and unconsciona-ble[79] since the repeal of the Moneylenders Acts the courts have a statutory jurisdiction to interfere in all non-commercial extortionate credit bargains under the provisions of Consumer Credit Act 1974.[80]

(d) *Collateral advantages*

A stipulation which, being a term of a mortgage, secures to the mortgagee an **18–13** advantage outside his principal and interest is invalid if it (i) defeats or renders illusory the right to redeem under the first rule set out above; (ii) is repugnant to the right to redeem under the second rule; (iii) clogs the equity of redemption under the third rule; or (iv) forms part of a mortgage contract obtained oppres-sively or through undue influence under the rules discussed elsewhere.[81]

(i) *The position before 1854*

Before the repeal of the usury laws, equitable principles concerning collateral advantages were somewhat obscured by the existence of absolute limitations on the rate of interest which might legally be charged for a loan: for a mortgagee who insisted on an advantage additional to his interest might well appear to be evading the usury laws. At any rate, it appears that before 1854 collateral advantages were not enforceable. Thus in *Jennings v. Ward*[82] Trevor M.R. said:

> "A man shall not have interest for his money and a collateral advantage besides for the loan of it, or clog the redemption with any by-agreement."

---

[77] *Strode v. Parker* (1694) 2 Vern. 316; this provision is construed strictly against the mortgagor, so that his payments must be exactly punctual if he is to be entitled to pay the lower rate, *Maclaine v. Gatty* [1921] 1 A.C. 376.
[78] *Clarkson v. Henderson* (1880) 14 Ch.D. 348.
[79] See *post*, para. 18–23.
[80] See *ante*, para. 14–08.
[81] See *post*, para. 18–23.
[82] (1705) 2 Vern. 520 at 521.

(ii) *The modern position*

18–14   It is evident that this much quoted dictum propounds two distinct principles: (i) that a mortgagee may not obtain an advantage additional to his interest; (ii) a collateral covenant must not operate to impede redemption. If the first proposition is correct, the second is unnecessary; but there is ample authority that the first proposition is no longer law.

In *Biggs v. Hoddinott*[83] the Court of Appeal went so far as to declare that in all previous cases in which a collateral advantage had been disallowed it had been such as either to clog the equity of redemption or to render the mortgage oppressive. The court went on to decide that following the repeal of the usury laws collateral advantages are not in themselves objectionable and that they will be valid provided that: (i) they do not make the bargain harsh and unconscionable and; (ii) they do not clog the equity of redemption. As to the first test, we shall see that a mortgage is not unconscionable merely because it appears unduly favourable to the mortgagee and is therefore unreasonable as regards the mortgagor. Collateral advantages will not be considered unconscionable unless they were extorted from the mortgagor by active exploitation of his weakness through oppression or undue influence. It is the application of the second test which is here mainly discussed, namely, when a collateral advantage "clogs" the equity of redemption.

(iii) *Clogging the equity by a financial advantage*

18–15   A collateral stipulation is plainly a clog if its effect is to render the security irredeemable on any event whatever. In these cases, which have already been explained, the collateral stipulation may be repugnant not only to the equitable but also to the legal right to redeem.[84] For example, the grant of an option to purchase is inconsistent with the contractual right to redeem, as well as with the equity of redemption, when the option is exercisable before the contract date for redemption. On the other hand, it is equally evident that a collateral advantage is no clog if it ceases to affect both the security and the mortgagor the moment the legal or the equitable right to redeem is exercised. Thus in *Biggs v. Hoddinott*, a hotel was mortgaged to a brewery company with mutual covenants by mortgagor and mortgagee to continue the mortgage for five years. In addition, the mortgagor covenanted that during the five years and afterwards, whilst any money was still due on the mortgage, he would purchase from the company all the beer sold or consumed at the hotel. The court held that (i) five years was in the circumstances a reasonable period for the suspension of the contractual right to redeem; and (ii) the equity of redemption was not in any way clogged by a covenant which was to be operative only until redemption took place. This decision has received the emphatic approval of the House of Lords.[85]

---

[83] [1898] 2 Ch. 307. When considering collateral advantages which restrain trade, see *ante*, para. 8–11 and *post*, para. 18–22.

[84] *Kreglinger v. New Patagonia Meat and Cold Storage Co. Ltd* [1914] A.C. 25 at 50, *per* Lord Parker.

[85] *Noakes and Co. Ltd v. Rice* [1902] A.C. 24; *Bradley v. Carritt* [1903] A.C. 253; *Kreglinger v. New Patagonia Meat and Cold Storage Co. Ltd* [1914] A.C. 25.

(iv) *Collateral advantages secured on the property*

But what if the collateral stipulation is expressed to bind the mortgagor abso- **8–16**
lutely during a specified period while the mortgage allows for redemption before
the end of that period *i.e.* before the expiry of the period at the end of which the
collateral advantage ceases? Is the mortgagor to be bound until the end of the
named period, or do the doctrines of equity demand that he be automatically
released from the stipulation if he redeems before that time?[86] For a covenant
may be so framed that the collateral advantage is as much charged on the security
as the principal and interest itself, in which case the mortgagor, by the contract,
is not entitled to a reconveyance of his security until the end of the period during
which the collateral advantage is intended to operate. Thus in *Santley v. Wilde*[87]
the tenant of a theatre borrowed £2,000 at six per cent. on a mortgage of her lease
which still had 10 years to run. In addition she agreed to pay to the mortgagee
during the rest of the lease one-third of the net profits to be derived from any
underleases of the theatre. Moreover, she gave an express covenant that even if
she repaid the loan the mortgage should continue in existence to secure the
payment of the share of profits.

The Court of Appeal pointed out that a mortgage can be redeemed only when **18–17**
all the obligations have been discharged for which the mortgage was given; and
that in this case redemption, by the contract of the parties, could not take place
until the covenant to pay a share of the profits had been fully performed. The
covenant was a business agreement between parties at arm's length and was
upheld. Lindley M.R. in a classic passage,[88] explained the doctrine of clogs on
the equity of redemption:

> "A mortgage is a conveyance of land or an assignment of chattels as a
> security for the payment of a debt or the discharge of some other obligation
> for which it is given. This is the idea of a mortgage: and the security is
> redeemable on the payment or discharge of such debt or obligation, any
> provision to the contrary notwithstanding. . . . Any provision inserted to
> prevent redemption on payment or performance of the debt or obligation for
> which the security was given is what is meant by a clog or fetter on the
> equity of redemption, and is therefore void. It follows from this that "once
> a mortgage always a mortgage"; but I do not understand that this principle
> involves the further proposition that the amount or nature of the further debt
> or obligation, the payment or performance of which is to be secured, is a
> clog or fetter within the rule. . . . Of course, the debt or obligation may be
> impeachable for fraud, oppression or overreaching. . . . But putting such
> cases out of the question, when you get a security for a debt or obligation,
> that security can be redeemed the moment the debt or obligation is paid or
> performed, but on no other terms."

The principles stated by Lindley M.R. in the above passage have frequently
been approved, although the actual decision in *Santley v. Wilde* was strongly

---

[86] The stipulation is never void *ab initio*, unless it is actually unconscionable; it is void, if at all, only
after redemption.

[87] [1899] 2 Ch. 474.

[88] *ibid.* at 475.

criticised by Lords Macnaghten and Davey in *Noakes v. Rice*.[89] It is open to the objection that it takes no account of the fact that the mortgagor was prevented from discharging his obligations until a time when his security ceased to exist. The collateral covenant made the security irredeemable and there is thus some difficulty in reconciling the decision with that of the House of Lords in *Fairclough v. Swan Brewery Co. Ltd.*[90] Although there is no objection in principle to a mortgagee retaining a security for the performance of a collateral stipulation even *after* payment of principal and interest, the covenant, it is submitted, must not be such as to defeat or render illusory the right to redeem nor such as to be repugnant to it. In the light of later cases, the only way in which it seems possible to support the admittedly desirable decision in *Santley v. Wilde*[91] is by holding that the transaction was not in essence one of mortgage, but a partnership agreement to share in the profits of the theatre.[92]

(v) *Collateral advantage is not secured upon the property*

18–18   Normally the collateral advantage is not made a charge on the security. Although the additional stipulation is expressed to be binding until a named date redemption is allowed *before* that date on payment of principal, interest and costs, without more leaving the collateral advantage outstanding. In consequence, the performance of the collateral stipulation is not one of the terms of redemption. Thus in *Noakes v. Rice*[93]:

> "On mortgaging the lease of a public-house a mortgagor covenanted that during the whole remainder of the lease (which still had twenty-six years to run) no beer would be sold at the public-house, except beer bought from the mortgagees. The mortgage moneys, on the other hand, were made repayable on demand by either side, and there was an express proviso for reconveyance of the security on payment of principal, interest and costs."

The House of Lords decided unanimously that the collateral advantage was a clog upon redemption because it was repugnant to the mortgagor's right to recover his security *intact and unimpaired by the mortgage*. The covenant turned a free public-house into a tied house. In this case the fetter on the mortgaged property was direct but a covenant will, it seems, be just as much a clog if it indirectly impairs the enjoyment of the property not by fettering the property itself but by imposing personal obligations on the mortgagor which make it advisable (though not compulsory) for him to enjoy his property in a particular way. In *Bradley v. Carritt*[94] the defendant, who had a controlling interest in a tea company, mortgaged his shares to the claimant, who was a tea-broker, and, as part of the consideration, covenanted to use his best endeavours always thereafter to secure that the company should continue to employ the mortgagee as their broker; if the company should cease to do so he was to pay to the mortgagee the amount of commission the latter would have earned had his services been

---

[89] [1902] A.C. 24.
[90] [1912] A.C. 565.
[91] [1899] 2 Ch. 474.
[92] See Waldock, *Law of Mortgages* (2nd. ed., 1950), p. 187.
[93] [1900] 2 Ch. at 445 and [1902] A.C. 24, H.L.
[94] [1903] A.C. 253.

retained. The collateral stipulation was personal to the mortgagor and its performance was not made a charge on the security.

The mortgagor redeemed his shares and the House of Lords (Lords Lindley and Shand dissenting) decided that the collateral covenant was no longer binding since it was a clog on the equity of redemption. The difference of opinion between the majority of the court (Lords Macnaghten, Davey and Robertson) and Lords Lindley and Shand, lay not so much in the principle to be applied as in its application to the particular case.[95] Thus, Lord Macnaghten found in the covenant a contrivance calculated to impede redemption because, by making it advisable for the mortgagor to retain control of his shares after redemption, the covenant indirectly fettered his right to recover his security unimpaired by the mortgage. Lord Lindley, on the other hand, was unable to comprehend how the covenant, which was purely personal to the mortgagor and did not *bind* him to deal with the shares in any particular way, could possibly clog the equity of redemption when it was open to the mortgagor to recover his security merely by paying up principal, interest and costs.

(vi) *The modern position*

The difficulty in reconciling *Bradley v. Carritt* with the later decision of the **18–19** House of Lords in *Kreglinger v. New Patagonia Meat Co.*[96] has led some writers to treat the earlier case as no longer of any importance. But, although some of the dicta of Lords Macnaghten and Davey in *Bradley v. Carritt*[97] are disapproved by the judges in *Kreglinger v. New Patagonia Meat Co.*, the decisions in the two cases are not irreconcilable. Consequently the earlier case must, it is submitted, still be treated as laying down that a collateral covenant, which is a term of the mortgage and may endure *after* redemption, may constitute a clog on the equity although it imposes a purely personal obligation on the mortgagor.

In *Bradley v. Carritt* Lords Macnaghten and Davey both expressed the opinion that collateral advantages are only another form of interest and therefore must come to an end when the principal sum is repaid. Consequently it appeared to have been settled that in no circumstances could a collateral advantage survive redemption. In *Kreglinger*'s case, however, this reasoning was decisively rejected by a unanimous court who pointed out that it was unnecessary for the decision in *Bradley v. Carritt*.

(vii) *The test of severability*

In *Kreglinger*'s case the House of Lords refused to admit that a covenant clogged the equity of redemption merely because it was contained in a mortgage deed and by its nature might continue to impose obligations on the mortgagor after redemption. *Kreglinger*'s case appears to decide that, just as equity looks at the substance of a transaction rather than at its form to see if the transaction is really a mortgage and even admits parol evidence to explain the deed, so it will look at the intention of the parties rather than at the form of the documents to see if a

---

[95] *cf.* Lord Parker in *Kreglinger v. New Patagonia Meat Co.* [1914] A.C. 25 at 59.
[96] [1914] A.C. 25 at 59; applied in *Re Cuban Land and Development Co. (1911) Ltd* [1921] 2 Ch. 147.
[97] [1903] A.C. 253.

collateral covenant was intended to be truly a constituent element of the mortgage or an independent severable bargain linked to a mortgage in a larger business transaction but not constituting a term of the mortgage. In the latter case the collateral covenant does not touch the mortgage relationship and stands entirely outside the equitable principles protecting the right to redeem.

This principle will more easily be understood if regard is had to the case of *De Beers Consolidated Mines Ltd v. B.S.A. Co.*[98]:

De Beers, who had already lent the B.S.A. Co. £112,000 and were proposing to lend a further £100,000, contracted for the grant of a licence to work diamond mines in consideration of "the assistance rendered and to be rendered" by them to the company. The contract was not itself a mortgage but contained a provision enabling the company, in lieu of repayment, to cover the loan by issuing debenture stock and assigning an appropriate amount of stock to De Beers. The grant of the loan was not, however, conditional on the issue of the debentures. The company issued debentures and assigned to De Beers sufficient stock to cover the loan. Subsequently they redeemed the debentures and claimed that the licence was no longer binding on them.

18–20   The House of Lords had no hesitation in rejecting this claim. The licence had been obtained by a contract independent of and preliminary to the mortgage transaction. This contract did not even compel the company to grant a mortgage, but, when they did so, they could only mortgage assets which were already bound by the licence. The protection of the equity of redemption does not require the court to free a man of pre-existing obligations when he mortgages his property to the obligee. Similarly, the court in *Kreglinger*'s case[99] held that there were two independent contracts, a contract for the grant of an option and a contract of mortgage. The separation of the mortgage from the other contract was by no means so obvious as in *De Beers v. British South Africa Co.*[1]

The facts of *Kreglinger*'s case were these: the appellants, a firm of woolbrokers, consented to lend £10,000 to the respondents, a meat company, in consideration of obtaining an option on such sheep skins as the respondents might have for sale to the public. The £10,000 was lent at 6 per cent. and was secured by a floating charge on the assets of the meat company. If the latter paid the interest punctually, the appellants were not to call in their money for five years. The terms of the option[2] were that it was to extend over a period of five years, *but this period was not co-extensive with that during which the appellants were not to call in their loan.* The price to be paid for the skins was to be equal to the best price offered by any one else, while the respondents were to pay a commission of one per cent. on any skins sold to other buyers at the best market price. The respondents repaid the loan after only two years and claimed to be at once relieved of their obligation to offer their sheep skins to the appellants.

The House of Lords decided unanimously that the option continued to bind the mortgagors notwithstanding the termination of the mortgage. The construction placed upon the transaction by the court was that it contained two distinct bargains—the sale of an option and the loan of money on security—and that although these two bargains were contemporaneous and in fact formulated in the

---

[98] [1912] A.C. 52.
[99] [1914] A.C. 25.
[1] [1912] A.C. 52.
[2] Perhaps a right of pre-emption.

same deed, they were intended by the parties to be independent of each other. Thus, although the sale of the option was a condition precedent to the grant of the *loan* it was not intended to form a term *in the mortgage* but rather to be a separate contract as much outside the terms of the mortgage as the grant of the licence in *De Beers v. B.S.A. Co.*[3] In short, the collateral covenant was not repugnant to the mortgagor's right to recover his security unfettered *by the mortgage* because, in the intention of the parties, the mortgage was the grant of a security already subject[4] to the option.

(a) *Applying the test of severability*

The question whether a collateral stipulation is a condition independent of the **18–21** mortgage, not touching equitable principles concerning redemption of mortgages, or an actual term of the mortgage is, of course, a question of the intention of the parties in each case such that no one case will be a precise authority for another. *Bradley v. Carritt*[5] and *Kreglinger*'s case[6] can be reconciled on this ground although it must be admitted that the majority judges in *Bradley v. Carritt* held views widely divergent from those of the unanimous court in *Kreglinger*'s case. The earlier case represents the high-water mark of the old conception of a mortgage as an exaction from a man who is not a free agent. *Kreglinger*'s case,[7] by excluding from equitable doctrines concerning mortgages those cases where collateral covenants do not in the true intention of the parties constitute a term of the mortgage, has to this extent prevented genuine commercial bargains between equal parties at arm's length from being upset by technical doctrines framed to defeat usury and oppression.

Ultimately, it may be that the distinction to be drawn between the cases rests on the reluctance of the courts on the one hand to interfere in commercial transactions freely negotiated at arm's length (albeit unfair to one party), and the vigilance of the courts on the other hand to protect individuals who have been persuaded to enter into a disadvantageous trading transaction as a condition of the grant of the loans. However, even this interpretation does not lay at rest the difficulties of reconciling the various cases. Perhaps the view expressed by Megarry and Wade in *The Law of Real Property*[8] that the "severability" test introduced in the *Kreglinger* case "provides a convenient but indefinable rule for dealing with such cases on their merits" sums up the difficulties in the attempts to reconcile the differences.

(viii) *Restraint of trade clauses*

It should also be noted that it was not until *Esso Petroleum Co. Ltd v. Harper's* **18–22** *Garage (Stourport) Ltd*[9] that the issue of restraint of trade was raised in the "tie"

---

[3] [1912] A.C. 52.

[4] Or at any rate, made subject to the option by an independent agreement.

[5] [1903] A.C. 253.

[6] [1914] A.C. 25.

[7] *ibid.*

[8] (6th ed., 2000), para. 19–139. See also para. 3.35 Law Commission's Working Paper No. 99, "Land Mortgages".

[9] [1968] A.C. 269; and see *ante*, para. 18–11.

cases with a mortgage element. Thus neither in *Biggs v. Hoddinott*[10] nor in *Noakes v. Rice*[11] was this issue canvassed with the result that they should now perhaps be regarded as of doubtful authority on their particular facts. As a result of the *Esso* case, such covenants in mortgages will be prima facie void unless they are shown to be reasonable[12] in the light of the circumstances irrespective of whether or not they are rendered void in accordance with equitable principles.[13]

(ix) *Conclusion*

Thus if a mortgagee intends to impose the burden of a collateral advantage on the mortgagor for a specified period without also suspending redemption during that period, the deed or deeds must be so drawn that the court can reasonably infer an intention to keep the collateral advantage outside the terms of the mortgage.[14] For although the substance of the agreement is the determining factor, the language of the deeds is, of course, the best evidence of the actual intention. Viscount Haldane L.C. indeed suggested in *Kreglinger*'s case that[15]:

> "the validity of the bargain in such cases as *Bradley v. Carritt* and *Santley v. Wilde* might have been made free from serious question if the parties had chosen to seek what would have been substantially the same result in a different form."

Accordingly, it is submitted that a covenant giving a mortgagee advantages beyond his principal and interest is valid if:

(1) the covenant is truly collateral to the mortgage in the sense that the covenant, as a matter of construction, is not one of the terms of the mortgage; or

(2) the covenant, though a term of the mortgage, does not conflict with the three preceding equitable rules for the protection of the equity of redemption and does not form part of a mortgage extorted by oppression or undue influence; and

(3) the stipulation is not in restraint of trade; and

(4) it is not otherwise oppressive or unconscionable.[16]

---

[10] [1898] 2 Ch. 307.

[11] [1902] A.C. 24; nor indeed, in *Hills v. Regent Oil Co. Ltd* [1962] E.G.D. 452 and *Regent Oil Co. Ltd v. J. A. Gregory (Hatch End) Ltd* [1966] Ch. 402.

[12] A more simple test than having regard to equitable principles.

[13] It is also possible that mortgage terms could be challenged on the grounds that they infringe the competition provisions of the Treaty of Rome, *e.g.* Article 81, which deals with restrictive agreements, and Article 82, which deals with abuse of a dominant position.

[14] Although the point is not noted in the judgments, it is submitted that in *Kreglinger*'s case it would have been more difficult to construe the sale of the option as an independent bargain if the period during which the option was to be exercisable had been coincident with the period during which the mortgagees were not to call in their money.

[15] [1914] A.C. 25 at 43.

[16] See para. 18–23.

REDEMPTION OF OPPRESSIVE AND UNCONSCIONABLE MORTGAGES

Equity will permit an individual to redeem a mortgage which affects his property **18–23** and which has been obtained unconscionably or by the exercise of undue influence and, on occasions, to do so without charge. The law concerning such mortgages and other instances where a mortgagor may not be bound are discussed elsewhere.[17]

REDEMPTION IN COURT OR OUT OF COURT

1. Generally

Redemption takes place when a mortgagor, either under the terms of his covenant **18–24** or under the principles of equity, discharges the obligations imposed by the mortgage and thus becomes entitled to have his property revested in him free of the charge. Until the debt has been paid and the money accepted, however, the mortgage remains in being.[18] The mortgagor's right is to have his property returned to him contemporaneously with the due discharge of his obligations, so that it is the duty of the mortgagee at once to execute the instruments necessary to terminate the mortgage. In *Graham v. Seal*,[19] Swinfen Eady M.R. said:

> "The obligation of a mortgagee is, as against payment of what is due to him, to reconvey and deliver up the deeds of the mortgaged premises. It is like the obligation of a vendor to convey and hand over the title deeds and the conveyance as against payment of the purchase-money. It contemplates that the handing over of the conveyance and payment of the purchase-money shall be a simultaneous transaction, so that neither party is at risk for any time without either the money or the estate; so in the paying off of a mortgage a mortgagee is not entitled to insist upon payment of the mortgage money with a view to his reconveying at some future time."

Consequently, if a mortgagee has been fully satisfied and refuses to reconvey the security, he will have to pay the costs of any proceedings taken by the mortgagor to recover his property.[20] Even a valid tender of the mortgage debt is not, however, *equivalent* to payment. Although a tender may have the effect of stopping the running of interest and of throwing the risk of the costs of a redemption action on the mortgagee,[21] the mortgagor's obligations are not finally discharged until his tender has been accepted, or if not accepted, the money is set aside.[22] Thus, in the case of a mortgage with a deposit of title deeds, if the mortgagee improperly refuses a tender, an action for wrongful interference with goods under the Torts (Interference with Goods) Act 1977 will probably not lie

---

[17] See Chapter 26.
[18] *Samuel Keller (Holdings) Ltd v. Martins Bank Ltd* [1971] 1 W.L.R. 43.
[19] (1918) 88 L.J.Ch. 31 at 35.
[20] *Walker v. Jones* (1866) L.R. 1 P.C. 50.
[21] See Lindley M.R. in *Greenwood v. Sutcliffe* [1892] 1 Ch. 1 at 10; *Graham v. Seal* (1918) 88 L.J.Ch. 31.
[22] *Barratt v. Gough-Thomas (No. 3)* [1951] W.N. 309; and see *post*, para. 18–33 *et seq.*

for the deeds at the suit of the mortgagor.[23] If the mortgagor disputes the amount claimed by the mortgagee, his only remedy[24] is to bring an action for redemption.

(a) *Exercising the right*

A mortgagor exercises his right to redeem in one of two ways—either (i) out of court, by inducing the mortgagee to accept a tender of the money due under the mortgage; or (ii) by bringing the mortgagee into court in an action for redemption and afterwards complying with the court's order for the payment of the mortgage debt. He has, of course, no right whatever to redeem, either at law or in equity, until the day named in the mortgage as the date for repayment.[25] Before that date he cannot maintain an action for redemption against the mortgagee, while if he tenders to the mortgagee a sum representing principal and full interest right up to the contract date, plus costs, the latter is not bound to reconvey the security nor, indeed, to accept the money. The case is, however, different if the mortgagee by demanding payment or by taking steps to enforce payment (for example, by taking possession) himself disturbs the relation between the parties set up by the contract. The mortgagor may then redeem at once and need only tender the amount of the principal, plus interest *up to the date of the tender* and costs.[26]

2. **Notice of intention to redeem**

(a) *At Law*

18–25   A mortgagor who is redeeming on the contract date need not give notice of his intention to redeem.[27] He need only attend on the day named and tender to the mortgagee the full amount of the mortgage debt, plus costs, observing any conditions there may be as to time and place of payment. If the contract allows the mortgagor to redeem on demand he need do no more than give the mortgagee a reasonable opportunity to look up the deeds and prepare the instrument for the discharge of the mortgage.[28] Moreover, redemption may be made on demand in all cases where the mortgage contains no proviso for redemption or express covenant for payment. Equitable mortgages by deposit of title deeds do not, as a rule, fix any date either for redemption or repayment and either party may terminate the mortgage on demand.[29]

---

[23] *Bank of New South Wales v. O'Connor* (1889) 14 App. Cas. 273, where a claim for detinue was rejected. Similarly, a mortgagee cannot be held liable for negligence for loss of the deeds, see *Browning v. Handiland Group Ltd* (1978) 35 P. & C.R. 345.

[24] He is, however, advised to make a tender in order to put the responsibility for the extra costs on the mortgagee: *Greenwood v. Sutcliffe* [1892] 1 Ch. 1.

[25] *Brown v. Cole* (1845) 14 Sim. 427.

[26] *Bovill v. Endle* [1896] 1 Ch. 648.

[27] See *Crickmore v. Freeston* (1870) 40 L.J.Ch. 137.

[28] *Toms v. Wilson* (1863) 4 B. & S. 442.

[29] *Fitzgerald Trustees v. Mellersh* [1892] 1 Ch. 385.

(b) *In equity*

However if, as usually happens, the mortgagor allows the contract date for payment to pass without redeeming so that at law he is in default, it is a settled rule of equity that he must give the mortgagee six months' notice of his intention to redeem.[30] The reason for this is that the mortgagor, having lost his estate at law, will only be allowed to redeem in equity on the terms that he does equity to the mortgagee by giving the latter a reasonable opportunity to find a new investment for his money.[31] A mortgagee may, of course, agree to accept repayment at shorter notice but his right is to a clear six months' notice. Even though it may be possible to find suitable investments in less than six months, it is now settled practice that a mortgagee is entitled to that amount of notice regardless of the nature of the property mortgaged.[32] Indeed, the only exceptions to the rule are when a mortgagee either demands his money or takes proceedings (for example, foreclosure proceedings[33] or steps to enforce payment[34] (for example, by taking possession). The mortgagor may then redeem at any moment by paying up the principal, plus interest up to the date of payment and costs[35] and he is not deprived of this right even if he has previously given notice of an intention to redeem in six months' time.[36] It need scarcely be said that a mortgagor may always dispense with the giving of notice by offering to pay six months' interest in lieu of notice.[37]

3. **Failure to redeem on notice date**

Since a mortgagee is entitled to have six months' notice of the date of payment, **18–26** it follows that if the mortgagor fails to tender the amount due on the date fixed by his notice he is bound either to give a fresh notice, or its equivalent in additional interest.[38] Otherwise the mortgagee might be put to inconvenience and loss in finding a new investment. In this instance, however, there is no rigid rule that the further period of notice must be one of six months. At the most the mortgagee is entitled to a reasonable amount of further notice. Thus, in one case,[39] a mortgagee had agreed to take payment if he were given three months' notice. Notice was duly given but owing to conveyancing difficulties payment could not be made on the due date. Maugham J. held that the mortgagee was entitled in the circumstances to the benefit of only three months' further notice.

---

[30] *Shrapnell v. Blake* (1737) West. T. Hard. 166. *Smith v. Smith* [1891] 3 Ch. 550; *cf.* Maugham J. in *Cromwell Property Investment Co. v. Western and Toovey* [1934] Ch. 322 at 331, 332.

[31] *Browne v. Lockhart* (1840) 10 Sim. 420 at 424, *per* Shadwell V.-C.

[32] *Cromwell Property Investment Co. v. Toovey* [1934] Ch. 322 at 331, 332, *Centrax Trustees Ltd v. Ross* [1979] 2 All E.R. 952 at 955–956.

[33] *Hill v. Rowlands* [1897] 2 Ch. 361 at 363; or, *e.g.* giving the mortgagor notice to repay the debt so as to entitle the mortgagee to sell on default being made, *Edmondson v. Copland* [1911] 2 Ch. 301.

[34] *per* Romer J. *Smith v. Smith* [1891] 3 Ch. 550 at 552.

[35] *Bovill v. Endle* [1896] 1 Ch. 648; *Letts v. Hutchins* (1871) L.R. 13 Eq. 176; the same rule applies in the case of a bill of sale: *Ex p. Wickens* [1898] 1 Q.B. 543.

[36] *Re Alcock* (1883) 23 Ch.D. 372 at 376. Although the court would have considered the point had the mortgagee altered his financial position as a result of the mortgagors notice.

[37] *Johnson v. Evans* (1889) 61 L.T. 18.

[38] *Bartlett v. Franklin* (1867) 15 W.R. 1077; *Re Moss* (1885) 31 Ch.D. 90.

[39] *Cromwell Investment Co. v. Western and Toovey* [1934] Ch. 322.

He also pointed out that even this period of notice would not have been allowed if the mortgagor had not failed to communicate with the mortgagee for several days after the expiry of the first notice. He declared that the right to further notice is by no means automatic. If the mortgagor gives a reasonable explanation of the reason why a short delay is necessary and keeps the mortgagee advised as to when payment may be expected, redemption will be allowed on payment of principal, plus the interest due only up to the actual date of payment, plus, of course, costs. In any case, a mortgagee will not be entitled to six months' further notice where the security is a fund in court and he has been a party to an order directing payment of his debt out of that fund. By accepting the order he assents to be governed by all the contingencies to which the completion of the order may be subject.[40]

Once the contract date has passed, the mortgagor insisting on redemption must pay interest on the loan. This applies even if the mortgage makes no provision for the payment of interest, and it includes statute-barred interest.[41] If necessary, the court will fix the rate of such interest.[42] He must also pay the mortgagee's proper costs in any redemption action brought by the mortgagor including any expenses incurred by the mortgagee in protecting his security.[43]

4. Persons entitled to redeem[44]

18–27   The right to redeem is not confined to the mortgagor or even to those claiming through him. It is exercisable by any person who either has an interest in the mortgaged property[45] or is under a liability to pay the mortgage debt[46] irrespective of the size of their interest.[47] The mortgagor himself does not lose his right to redeem until he has made an absolute assignment of his equity of redemption.[48] Even then his right will revive if he is sued on the personal covenant.[49] If he assigns his equity of redemption by way of mortgage only, he does not lose his right to redeem the first mortgage, but he does alter his position to some extent, because the maxim "redeem up, foreclose down", prevents him from redeeming a prior mortgagee *by action* without at the same time redeeming all intermediate incumbrancers.[50]

Present owners of the ultimate equity of redemption have the same right to redeem as the original mortgagor whom they replace[51] even if they are statute-

---

[40] *Re Moss* (1886) 31 Ch. D. 90.
[41] See *post*, para. 22–41 *et seq.*
[42] See *Cityland and Property (Holdings) Ltd v. Dabrah* [1968] Ch. 166.
[43] See *Sinfield v. Sweet* [1967] 1 W.L.R. 1489. A mortgagor, however, is not personally liable for these expenses.
[44] A stranger has no right to redeem. But a person who is entitled to redeem the mortgage may, instead of redeeming, insist that the mortgage be transferred to a stranger who is discharging the mortgage debt; L.P.A. 1925, s.95. See *post*, pp. 379 *et seq.*
[45] *Pearce v. Morris* (1869) L.R. 5 Ch. App. 227.
[46] *Green v. Wynn* (1869) L.R. 4 Ch. App. 204.
[47] *Hunter v. Macklew* (1846) 5 Hare 238.
[48] *Moore v. Morton* (1886) W.N. 196.
[49] *Kinnaird v. Trollope* (1888) 39 Ch.D. 636.
[50] See *post*, para. 18–28 *et seq.*
[51] *Fell v. Brown* (1787) 2 Bro.C.C. 276.

barred[52] and it makes no difference whether they are purchasers for value[53] or mere volunteers.[54] If the property is only subject to one incumbrance, their right to redeem is the only right to redeem but if there are successive incumbrances the primary right to redeem the first incumbrance is in the holder of the second and so on, and it is only the ultimate equity of redemption which remains in the mortgagor or those who represent him.[55] Consequently the latter can only redeem a first mortgage after the other incumbrancers have had the opportunity of exercising their prior rights. Persons who may redeem as holders of the ultimate equity of redemption[56] are:

(1) Assignees.[57] It makes no differences that the assignee acquires only a partial or limited interest in the property.[58] For example, a lessee under a lease, which is not binding on the mortgagee, may redeem.[59]

(2) Persons taking the equity of redemption under an intestacy or under a will.[60] On the death of a mortgagor the right to redeem first belongs to his personal representatives but will pass to the persons beneficially interested when an assent has been made in their favour.

(3) Trustees of land and life tenants under the Settled Land Act 1925. On the mortgage of land subject to a trust of land or of settled property, the primary right to redeem is in either the trustees or, in the case of settled land, the estate owners. Consequently, when an equity of redemption is in settlement the beneficiaries, though they may redeem, must do so through their trustees or through the life tenant.[61] It is only when the trustees or estate owners are in collusion with the mortgagee, or otherwise refuse improperly to act, that the beneficiaries may take proceedings for redemption.[62] In any case, it must be remembered that a remainderman cannot redeem if the tenant for life objects.[63]

(4) Joint tenants and tenants in common. Each co-owner has a right to redeem provided that he discharges the whole debt and does not claim to redeem merely his own share.[64] Since 1925, however, co-ownership of land involves statutory trusts and presumably the rule that beneficiaries ought to redeem through their trustees applies. Consequently, in the case of land, a co-owner of the equity of redemption should proceed through the trustees.

---

[52] *Cotterell v. Price* [1960] 1 W.L.R. 1097.

[53] A purchaser for value, if he redeems, has no right to a conveyance of the legal estate from the mortgagee, or to delivery of the title deeds, unless he has already accepted his assignor's title: *Pearce v. Morris* (1869) L.R. 5 Ch. App. 227.

[54] *Thorne v. Thorne* (1683) 1 Vern. 182; *Howard v. Harris* (1683) 1 Vern. 191; *Rand v. Cartwright* (1664) 1 Cas. in Ch. 59.

[55] *Teevan v. Smith* (1882) 20 Ch.D. 724 at 730.

[56] Subsequent incumbrances can redeem as well but subject to particular rules: see para. 18–29.

[57] *Kinnaird v. Trollope* (1889) 58 L.J.Ch. 556.

[58] *Hunter v. Maclew* (1846) 5 Hare 238.

[59] *Tarn v. Turner* (1888) 39 Ch.D. 456.

[60] Administration of Estates Act 1925, ss.1 and 2.

[61] *Troughton v. Binkes* (1801) 6 Ves. 573; *Mills v. Jennings* (1880) 13 Ch.D. 639.

[62] *Troughton v. Binkes* (1801) 6 Ves. 573.

[63] *Prout v. Cock* (1896) 2 Ch. 808.

[64] *Marquis of Cholmondeley v. Lord Clinton* (1820) 2 J. & W. 1 at 134; *Pearce v. Morris* (1869) L.R. 5 Ch. App. 227.

(5) In the case of two properties mortgaged to secure one debt the owner of each property has an individual right to discharge the whole debt; indeed, since the mortgagee cannot be made to accept payment in instalments, if only one owner redeems he must redeem the whole mortgage and not merely his own share.[65]

(6) A surety or any person whose property is under any liability to satisfy the mortgage debt will be allowed to redeem.[66] For example, the doctrine of consolidation may render the purchaser of an equity of redemption in Blackacre liable to discharge a mortgage on Whiteacre in addition to that on Blackacre. This entitles him to redeem Whiteacre.

(7) A stranger, who has no title to the equity of redemption, *cannot* redeem; against him the mortgagee's title is absolute.[67]

(8) Creditors. General creditors of a mortgagor cannot redeem except in special circumstances, as when there is collusion between mortgagor and mortgagee.[68] Similarly, when the mortgaged property has been assigned to a trustee for the benefit of creditors, creditors who were parties to the deed must proceed through their trustee, but if the latter acts improperly they will be admitted to redeem.[69] Again, a judgment creditor, as such, has no right to redeem but will become entitled to do so if he has obtained a charging order[70] or he has obtained the appointment of a receiver by way of equitable execution provided that the order making the appointment is similarly registered.[71]

(9) Bankruptcy. Bankruptcy divests a mortgagor of his right to redeem and it passes to the trustee[72]; creditors of a bankrupt can thus only redeem through the trustee.[73] The mortgagee has the option either to prove in the bankruptcy as a secured creditor, in which case he puts a value on the security and proves for the deficiency,[74] or else to stand outside the bankruptcy and rest on his security. If he elects to do the former, the trustee may redeem at the valuation[75]; if he does the latter, the trustee can only redeem on the terms of an ordinary redemption.

(10) The Crown. If the equity of redemption is left vacant, whether by a failure of persons entitled to take on intestacy or by the dissolution of a company, the right to redeem vests in the Crown by reason of its right to *bona vacantia*. For the equity of redemption, being an estate or

---

[65] *Hall v. Heward* (1886) 32 Ch.D. 430.
[66] *Green v. Wynn* (1869) L.R. 4 Ch. App. 204.
[67] *James v. Biou* (1813) 3 Swanst. 234.
[68] *White v. Parnther* (1829) 1 Knapp 179; but see *Beckett v. Buckley* (1874) L.R. 17 Eq. 435.
[69] *Troughton v. Binkes* (1801) 6 Ves. 573.
[70] See Charging Orders Act 1979, ss.1, 2(2)(a), 3(2), (4); the Land Charges Act 1972, s.6 (as amended); and the Land Registration Act 1925, s.59(1).
[71] As to equitable execution, see Supreme Court Act 1981, s.37 and CPR, Sched. 1, RSC Ord. 51 (as amended).
[72] *Spragg v. Binkes* (1800) 5 Ves. 583; see *post*, pp. 387 *et seq.*
[73] *Troughton v. Binkes* (1801) 6 Ves. 573.
[74] The mortgagee must prove in the bankruptcy in accordance with Insolvency Act 1986, s.332. See Chapter 23.
[75] The trustee may redeem upon 28 days' notice at the mortgagee's value, subject to the mortgagee's right to revalue (Insolvency Rules 1986, rr.6115, 6.117). It is also subject to the trustees' right to sell the property if he considers that the mortgagee's value is excessive (r.6.118).

interest and not a mere personal equity, is not extinguished by a failure of persons representing the mortgagor.[76]

(11) Spouses. Where a spouse has matrimonial home rights under the Family Law Act 1996, that spouse will be entitled to redeem the mortgage as a person interested in the equity of redemption if able to do so.[77] Further the spouse is entitled to make such payments, *inter alia*, in respect of the mortgage due from the other spouse in respect of the matrimonial home.[78] Also the spouse is entitled to be made a party to any action brought by the mortgagee to enforce his security if such person is able to meet the mortgagor's liabilities under the mortgage and the court does not see any special reason against it. Further the court must be satisfied that the spouse may be expected to make such payments towards the mortgagor's liabilities which might affect the outcome of the proceedings.[79] The spouse is also entitled to be served with notice of the action if a class F land charge has been registered at the Land Charges Registry (in the case of unregistered land) or a registration of notice at the Land Registry (in respect of registered land).[80]

5. **Redemption by action**

In earlier chapters it was emphasised that once default is made under the contract **18–28** relations between mortgagor and mortgagee are strictly regulated by the practice of the court. This does not, however, mean that redemption invariably, or even usually, takes place in court. On the contrary, the parties, as a rule, agree to the accounts out of court and the mortgage is discharged by payment of the agreed sum. It is only when there is a dispute that an action is necessary. Nevertheless, it is convenient to deal first with redemption by action, since the practice in redemption suits largely controls the rights of the parties in settlements out of court.

(a) *Parties*

All persons interested in the equity of redemption are entitled to redeem and this **18–29** means that persons with very diverse interests in the mortgaged property may have such a right. The importance of this rule in actions for redemption is considerable since the general principle is that all persons with a right to redeem must be represented in the action.[81] The reason is that the mortgagee has a right to account once and for all which entails the presence of all persons who are

---

[76] *Re Sir Thomas Spencer Wells* [1933] 1 Ch. 29; Administration of Estates Act 1925, s.46 as amended. See Chapter 23.

[77] If the court is satisfied that the spouse is likely to be able to pay off the mortgage, see *Hastings and Thanet Building Society v. Goddard* [1970] 1 W.L.R. 1544.

[78] Family Law Act 1996, s.30(3).

[79] *ibid.* s.55, if a dwelling-house.

[80] A caution may no longer be lodged, s.33(11).

[81] *Fell v. Brown* (1787) 2 Bro.C.C. 276; *Johnson v. Holdsworth* (1850) 1 Sim.(N.S.) 106.

entitled to an account.[82] It follows that all persons known to have any interest in the equity of redemption must be joined as parties either personally or through their representatives. It is no excuse that the interest of an omitted person is very small.[83] The result is that if a co-mortgagor or other person with only a partial interest seeks to redeem, the remaining mortgagors or interested parties ought to be joined.[84] The only exception to the rule that interested parties ought to be joined is when a life tenant, trustees, executors, administrators or the trustee under a deed of assignment represent the persons for whom they act.[85] Even then it is in the discretion of the court to allow beneficiaries to be made parties if their rights cannot adequately be protected by the decree. It is not often necessary to allow this in redemption actions but in foreclosure actions the court will always bring in beneficiaries if there is a danger of the trustees having insufficient funds for redemption.[86] Again, all persons interested in the mortgage debt are necessary parties.[87] If there are co-mortgagees all must be joined. If the right to the mortgage money has been assigned or otherwise passed into different hands, the new owners are the proper persons to be redeemed. If there has been a sub-mortgage the original mortgagor, in bringing his action, must join the sub-mortgagee; the mortgagee may, however, redeem the sub-mortgage without adding the mortgagor. Although all persons known to be interested ought to be joined, the joinder of the parties is in the discretion of the court, which will sometimes allow the action to proceed without the representation of a party who cannot be found, provided that the mortgagee runs no risk.[88] In such a case the decree will expressly preserve the rights of the absent party.[89]

(b) "Redeem up, foreclose down"

18–29A   The rule that a mortgagee is entitled to account once and for all is of the utmost importance where there are successive incumbrances since it prevents a puisne incumbrancer from redeeming an earlier mortgagee by action without at the same time foreclosing on subsequent mortgagees and on the mortgagor.[90] The subsequent incumbrancers and the mortgagor have successive[91] rights to redeem and the accounts taken in the puisne incumbrancer's action for redemption will inevitably fix the price at which any later redemption can be effected. Therefore it is essential that in the puisne incumbrancer's action all persons with later rights to redeem should be before the court in order that they may be bound by the accounts. On the other hand, it would be onerous to the mortgagor and to the later incumbrancers to allow them to be dragged before the court merely that they

---

[82] *Palk v. Clinton* (1805) 12 Ves. 48.
[83] *Hunter v. Maclew* (1846) 5 Hare 238.
[84] *Marquis of Cholmondeley v. Lord Clinton* (1820) 2 J. & W. 1 at 134.
[85] See CPR 11.9.
[86] *Goldsmit v. Stonehewer* (1852) 9 Hare App. xxxviii.
[87] *Wetherell v. Collins* (1818) 3 Mad. 255.
[88] *Faulkner v. Daniel* (1843) 3 Hare 199.
[89] *Francis v. Harrison* (1889) 43 Ch.D. 183.
[90] *Fell v. Brown* (1787) 2 Bro.C.C. 276.
[91] The first right to redeem a first mortgage is in the second mortgagee, the next right in the third mortgagee and so on: *Teevan v. Smith* (1882) 20 Ch.D. 724.

might watch the accounts being taken.[92] Indeed, they cannot be joined for this limited purpose. It is the rule that a puisne incumbrancer who redeems an earlier mortgage by action must at the same time foreclose on all later incumbrancers and on the mortgagor. For the same reason any one who redeems an earlier mortgage, which is not the immediately preceding incumbrance, must also redeem any intermediate mortgages. If, for example, a third mortgagee redeems the first, it is obvious that the first mortgagee's account will affect the rights of the second. The latter must therefore be joined as a party and redeemed.[93] This principle applies also in foreclosure actions with this result—a mortgagee who forecloses must join all persons with interests in the security subsequent to his,[94] since his account will fix the price of redemption for them all. Foreclosure on the mortgagor means foreclosure also on intermediate mortgagees. The general result is that actions to discharge incumbrances are multiple actions, and this is commonly expressed by the maxim, *redeem up, foreclose down*. Two consequences of this principle should be noticed in relation to the right to redeem: (i) a puisne mortgagee cannot redeem an earlier mortgage in court without at the same time exposing himself to redemption by the mortgagor and later incumbrancers; (ii) there cannot be a redemption action in the absence of the mortgagor, such that a puisne mortgagee, who, by stipulating not to call in his money for a stated period, has precluded himself from bringing the mortgagor before the court, cannot during that period bring a redemption action against any prior mortgagee.[95]

(c) *Procedure*[96]

The proceedings are brought by a claim form,[97] and any person who has the right **18–30** to redeem any mortgage, whether legal or equitable, can, as of course seek redemption, reconveyance and delivery of possession.[98]

In a redemption action the claim is for an account and for redemption. If the parties wish to redeem, the statement of case or the evidence in support must expressly or by implication contain an offer to redeem, and, if the claimant makes out a case for redemption without such an offer, he will be compelled to amend his plea[99] or at any rate to give an undertaking to redeem.[1] It is only in exceptional circumstances that a mortgagor can bring the mortgagee into court without offering to redeem him[2]: namely;

---

[92] *Ramsbottom v. Wallis* (1835) 5 L.J. (N.S.) Ch. 92; *Slade v. Rigg* (1843) 3 Hare 35; *Rose v. Page* (1829) 2 Sim. 471; *Briscoe v. Kenrick* (1832) 1 L.J.Ch. 116.

[93] *Teevan v. Smith* (1882) 20 Ch.D. 724.

[94] See *ante*, para. 16–94 *et seq.*

[95] *Ramsbottom v. Wallis* (1835) 5 L.J.(N.S.) Ch. 92; there is, however, no objection to the prior mortgagee being paid off out of court; indeed, the prior mortgagee ought to accept payment in such circumstances: *Smith v. Green* (1844) 1 Coll. 555.

[96] See generally chap. 27.

[97] CPR Sched. 1, RSC Ord. 88 and CPR Part 8, Practice Direction A3. The extent to which CPR Part 55 will apply after October 15, 2001 is unclear.

[98] In general, a mortgagor has to pay the costs of a redemption action, but there are occasions when the mortgagee by his conduct renders himself liable to pay the costs.

[99] *Palk v. Lord Clinton* (1805) 12 Ves. 48.

[1] *Balfe v. Lord* (1842) 2 Dr. & W. 480.

[2] *Tasker v. Small* (1837) 3 My. & Cr. 63.

(1) if he claims a sale instead of redemption;

(2) when the proceedings are merely for the purpose of determining questions of the construction of the mortgage deed[3]; and

(3) when the mortgagee is a party to a trust deed affecting the equity of redemption, for the trust may be enforced without an offer to redeem.[4]

(4) possibly where the mortgagee is not exercising his power of sale bona fide.

Nor need the mortgagor offer to redeem if he denies the existence of the mortgage, or is asking that it be avoided. However, in such a case, if the mortgage is upheld, he cannot redeem in the same action unless he has pleaded in the alternative for redemption.[5]

6. Sale in lieu of redemption

18–31 A mortgagor in his plea may claim a sale in lieu of redemption, and this requires further explanation, since neither the mortgage contract nor the rules of equity give him this right. Section 91(1) of the Law of Property Act 1925 provides as follows:

> "Any person entitled to redeem mortgaged property may have a judgment or order for sale, instead of for redemption in an action brought by him, either for redemption alone, or for sale alone or for sale or redemption in the alternative."

The language of this subsection would appear to confer an absolute right on a claimant to apply for a sale in lieu of redemption, rather than to give a discretionary power to the court to order a sale.[6] It is submitted that the subsection must be so interpreted, although under the Conveyancing Act 1881, Kekewich J. undoubtedly treated the whole question of sale as a matter of discretion.[7] Section 91 does, on the other hand, provide that, when a person interested in the equity of redemption is a claimant asking for a sale the court may, on the application of any defendant, direct the claimant to give security for costs and may give the conduct of the sale to any defendant, with appropriate directions as to costs. Moreover, although, as we have suggested, the court may have no discretion to refuse an order for sale in lieu of redemption the terms of the order for sale are very much within its discretion. Section 91 further provides:

> "In any action, whether for foreclosure, or for redemption, or for sale, or for the raising and payment in any manner of mortgage money, the court on the request of the mortgagee, or of any person interested, either in the

---

[3] *Re Nobbs* [1896] 2 Ch. 830.
[4] *Jefferys v. Dickson* (1866) L.R. 1 Ch. 183.
[5] *Martinez v. Cooper* (1826) 2 Russ. 198; *Bagot v. Easton* (1877) 7 Ch.D. 1.
[6] *Clarke v. Pannell* (1884) 29 S.J. 147.
[7] *Brewer v. Square* [1892] 2 Ch. 111.

mortgage money or in the right of redemption, and notwithstanding that—

(a) any other person dissents; or

(b) the mortgagee or any person so interested does not appear in the action;

and without allowing any time for redemption or for payment of any mortgage money, may direct a sale of the mortgaged property on such terms as it thinks fit, including the deposit in Court of a reasonable sum fixed by the Court to meet the expenses of sale and to secure performance of the terms."

The practice in sales by the court has already been considered,[8] but here it may be said that in redemption actions the order for sale may be made at any time before the final decree for redemption and may, indeed, be made on an interlocutory application before the trial.[9]

(a) *Order*

In the ordinary case the court's order is that an account be taken of what is due **18–32** to the mortgagee in respect of his mortgage, including the costs of the redemption action and that upon the mortgagor paying to the mortgagee the amount certified by the Master to be due within six (calendar[10]) months after the date of his certificate and at a time and place to be appointed in the certificate the mortgagee shall surrender his mortgage term or give a receipt in accordance with section 115 of the Law of Property Act 1925 and deliver up the title deeds. The order further directs that if the mortgagor makes default in such payment his action is to stand dismissed with costs.[11] The order may be varied by an order for sale in lieu of redemption. It may be necessary to add an order for possession if the mortgagee has exercised his right to take possession. Again, the circumstances may make it necessary to give special directions for the account. For example, if the order for redemption is made after the mortgagee has refused a proper tender, the account must be stopped on the date of the tender and there must be alternative orders to meet the possibilities that the tender may or may not have been sufficient. Similarly, if the mortgagee is in possession, the account must be taken on the footing of wilful default and further variations in the order will be necessary if the mortgagee in possession has been charged with waste, improper management or improper sale of the security. Moreover, the account of a mortgagee in possession may sometimes be ordered with annual rests. The accounts taken between mortgagor and mortgagee are considered elsewhere in detail in connection with the mortgagee's interest.[12]

---

[8] See *ante*, para. 16–103 *et seq.*
[9] *Woolley v. Colman* (1882) 21 Ch.D. 169.
[10] CPR 2.10.
[11] See Seton, *Judgments and Orders* (7th ed.), Vol. 3, p. 1853.
[12] See *post*, para. 25–05 *et seq.*

7. **Successive redemptions**

18–33   Special directions will be necessary when there are several parties to the action with successive rights to redeem; the order must not only notice their priorities[13] but must also provide distinctly for the possibility of any party redeeming or failing to redeem. To take a simple case, if a second mortgagee is claiming to redeem the first and to foreclose on the mortgagor, the order is: on payment by the claimant of the amount due to the first mortgagee within six months of the certificate, the first mortgagee to surrender his mortgage term or give the statutory receipt—in default the claim to be dismissed with costs; if the claimant shall pay off the first mortgagee, interest to be computed on what he shall pay, and an account to be taken of what is due on the claimant's own mortgage and for his costs of the claim; and, on payment by the mortgagor within three months of the certificate of the amount reported due to the claimant, the claimant to surrender his mortgage term or give a statutory receipt to the mortgagor—in default, the mortgagor to be foreclosed. The introduction of other parties further complicates the order which, as we said, will provide for every contingency.

Two further points must be noticed in the form of the order given above: (i) when a mesne incumbrancer brings the claim for redemption and fails to redeem, not only is his action dismissed but he is made to pay the costs both of the first mortgagee and also of the mortgagor[14]; (ii) in special circumstances the mortgagor may be given a longer period to redeem.[15] The limitation of a successive period for redemption in case an intermediate incumbrancer redeems is obviously necessary since a new account has to be taken, but in the redemption of a first mortgage, when the claimant is the mortgagor or a third or later incumbrancer, the question will arise whether distinct periods are to be allotted to each party for the redemption of the *first mortgage*.

Formerly the practice was to give a period of six months to the person entitled to the first equity of redemption and further periods of three months to each later incumbrancer with an additional three months for the mortgagor. This rule applied only to incumbrancers so that a life tenant and remainderman under a settlement of the equity of redemption had only one period between them.[16] Nor did it even apply to incumbrancers when their mortgages were created on the same day,[17] or when it was plain that the security would be insufficient to give anything to the later incumbrancers.[18]

18–34   It is not, however, going too far to say that the practice of the court today is the reverse.[19] A mortgagee may be seriously inconvenienced by the delay caused by allowing successive periods for redemption and now, as a general rule, one period only of six months will be allotted to the puisne incumbrancers and the mortgagor together: if there is any ground for successive periods the incumbrancers must appear and make out a special case for such an order.[20] The

---

[13] *Jones v. Griffith* (1845) 2 Coll. 207; *Duberly v. Day* (1851) 14 Beav. 9.
[14] *Hallett v. Furze* (1885) 31 Ch.D. 312.
[15] See *Lewis v. Aberdare and Plymouth Co.* (1884) 53 L.J.Ch. 741.
[16] *Beevor v. Luck* (1867) L.R. 4 Eq. 537.
[17] *Long v. Storie* (1849) 3 De G. & Sm. 308.
[18] *Cripps v. Wood* (1882) 51 L.J.Ch. 584.
[19] *Bartlett v. Rees* (1871) L.R. 12 Eq. 395; *Smith v. Olding* (1884) 25 Ch.D. 462; *Platt v. Mendel* (1884) 27 Ch.D. 246.
[20] *Platt v. Mendel* (1884) 27 Ch.D. 246; *Doble v. Manley* (1885) 28 Ch.D. 664.

mortgagor himself cannot apply for the special order because he cannot enlarge his own time for redemption by merely dealing with the equity of redemption.[21] It follows that a special order will never be made if the puisne incumbrancers are not before the court. To make an order in such a case would be equivalent to giving judgment between co-defendants without their having asked for it.[22] Nor will a special order be made when the priorities are in dispute. The determination of the priorities will cause delay and is a question in which the first mortgagee has no interest.[23] But where, as is now usual, there is only one period of six months for all the defendants there is, of course, liberty to apply to the court in case any one of the defendants shall redeem. The court will then determine the rights of the defendants *inter se*.

If a special order for successive periods is made, the procedure is as follows. The first right to redeem is in the second mortgagee and if he defaults he is foreclosed; a further three months' interest is then added to the mortgage account and the person next entitled has an opportunity to redeem, and so on. If a puisne incumbrancer does redeem the action continues between him and later incumbrancers and the mortgagor; his own debt is added to the first mortgage debt together with an allowance of three months' interest and the person next entitled must redeem or be foreclosed, and so on.

8. Effect of the decree

The rules for payment by the mortgagor and for the execution of the necessary **18–35** instruments by the mortgagee are the same whether redemption takes place under the order of the court or by agreement and will be found dealt with fully in connection with redemption out of court. It must, however, be emphasised that *in redemption actions* payment has to be made strictly in accordance with the terms of the order. In foreclosure actions the court will readily grant an extension of time for redemption but not so when the proceedings are initiated by the mortgagor. He comes of his own volition to the court professing to have his money ready. If he has not, he cannot claim the indulgence which he receives when the mortgagee is pressing him for payment. Consequently, a failure to pay on the date specified results in the final dismissal of the action.[24] This is so even when after his default the mortgagor has made a tender of the full amount reported due with subsequent interest.[25] It is only in the rare case of a bona fide mistake, as when the court's order is misunderstood, that any enlargement may be obtained.[26]

9. Dismissal of an action

The dismissal of an action for redemption is obtained as of course upon production of the certificate of the amount due and of an evidence of attendance for

---

[21] *ibid* at 248.
[22] *Doble v. Manley* (1885) 28 Ch.D. 664.
[23] *Bartlett v. Rees* (1871) L.R. 12 Eq. 395; *General Credit and Discount Co. v. Glegg* (1883) 22 Ch.D. 549; *Lordsvale Finance plc v. Bank of Zambia* [1996] Q.B. 752.
[24] *Novosielski v. Wakefield* (1811) 17 Ves. 417.
[25] *Faulkner v. Bolton* (1835) 7 Sim. 319.
[26] *Collinson v. Jeffery* [1896] 1 Ch. 644.

payment resulting in no payment. In the case of a legal mortgage the dismissal of the action for any cause, except want of prosecution,[27] operates as a decree for foreclosure absolute against the plaintiff. As James L.J. said[28]:

> "The mortgagor, by filing the bill, admits the title of the mortgagee, and admits the mortgage debt, and the dismissal of the bill operates as a decree for foreclosure, because he cannot afterwards file another bill for the same purpose; he is not allowed thus to harass the mortgagee."

The claimant's equity of redemption is extinguished. In the case of a legal mortgage this completes the mortgagee's title. In the case of an equitable mortgage the effect is somewhat different. Although the claimant is not allowed to take subsequent proceedings for the same purpose, a mere dismissal of his action cannot complete the mortgagee's title. The mortgagee must either rely on the acquisition of a title by lapse of time under the Limitation Act 1980,[29] which is only possible if he is in possession, or else must take fresh proceedings in order to obtain a conveyance and possession. It is just possible that after 1925, even in the case of a legal mortgage, the mortgagee does not acquire the mortgagor's whole title. Although sections 89 and 90 of the Law of Property Act 1925 carefully provide that a foreclosure decree is to pass the mortgagor's legal reversion to the mortgagee, there is no similar provision for the dismissal of an action for redemption.

The dismissal of the action operates against the claimant only and therefore, in the case of successive incumbrancers if the mortgagor is the claimant, the dismissal of his action places the final equity of redemption in the last incumbrancer who becomes quasi-mortgagor.[30] If a puisne incumbrancer is the claimant and fails to redeem, he is not only foreclosed but must pay the costs of all parties including the mortgagor, whom he must, of course, have made a defendant.[31] Finally, it must be remembered that proceedings for redemption are a pending action, and therefore the dismissal will not bind an assignee for value between the date of the claim form and the dismissal unless the action has been registered as a pending action.

10. Redemption out of court

18–36   This is effected by an accord and satisfaction out of court, which usually resolves itself into a tender of the mortgage moneys and an acceptance of the tender. For the most part the conditions under which redemption may be claimed out of court are the same as those under which it is allowed in an action. Thus, the right to make a tender only arises at the same time as the right to redeem by action and the mortgagee, after default, is entitled to six months' notice, or to six months' interest in lieu of notice, unless the mortgage contract otherwise provides. Similarly, tender must be made by someone entitled to redeem, for, as we have

---

[27] *Hansard v. Hardy* (1812) 18 Ves. 455.
[28] *Marshall v. Shrewsbury* (1875) L.R. 10 Ch. 250 at 254.
[29] See *post*, para. 22–23.
[30] *Cottingham v. Shrewsbury* (1843) 3 Hare 627.
[31] *Hallett v. Furze* (1885) 31 Ch.D. 312.

seen, a mortgagee's estate is absolute against a stranger.[32] A mortgagee may, if he pleases, transfer his mortgage to a stranger but he cannot be compelled to accept payment from any one who is not entitled to bring an action for redemption.

The maxim "redeem up, foreclose down" does not apply to redemption out of court. That maxim is founded on the court's anxiety to make a complete decree which will bind all parties interested in the estate and redemption out of court is not governed by the same considerations. On the contrary, it is well established that a prior mortgagee ought to accept a proper tender of his money if it is made by any person interested in the equity of redemption and that he rejects such a tender at the peril of paying the costs of a redemption action.[33] Consequently, a puisne mortgagee or any person claiming through the mortgagor may redeem the first mortgage by payment out of court without at the same time discharging intermediate incumbrances. Of course, a satisfied mortgagee is strictly a trustee for the persons entitled to the equity of redemption such that he must be careful to preserve the rights of such other persons of whose interests he has notice. This does not, however, prevent him from being under an obligation to transfer his mortgage to the person who has redeemed him, subject to an express reservation of the rights of the other interested parties of whom he knows.[34] If several persons are claiming to redeem the first mortgagee at the same time, the right to redeem first out of court clearly belongs to the puisne incumbrancer whose charge has priority.[35] Whilst accounts which have been agreed out of court are not conclusive against third parties, they are binding on all persons interested until they are impeached. They may be impeached for error or fraud and then in a proper case the court will set aside the settled account.

(a) *Tender*

In order to be effective a tender must be made to the mortgagee himself, and not to his solicitor, or other agent,[36] unless the agent has been expressly authorised to receive payment of the money and to reconvey the estate.[37] However, under section 69 of the Law of Property Act 1925 the validity of a tender cannot be questioned if it was made to the mortgagee's solicitor,[38] who at the time produced a deed executed by the mortgagee and having attached to it a receipt for the mortgage moneys. Again, a tender on the contract date must conform strictly to any conditions as to time and place of payment which may have been fixed by the mortgage deed if it is to stop interest running.[39] If a particular hour has been appointed for payment the mortgagor may appear to make his tender at any time during the currency of the hour named, because in law a named hour is not an

18–37

---

[32] *James v. Biou* (1818) 3 Swanst. 234 at 237.
[33] *Smith v. Green* (1844) 1 Coll. 555.
[34] *Pearce v. Morris* (1869) L.R. 5 Ch. App. 227.
[35] *Teevan v. Smith* (1882) 20 Ch.D. 724.
[36] *Withington v. Tate* (1869) L.R. 4 Ch. App. 288.
[37] *Bourton v. Williams* (1870) L.R. 5 Ch. App. 655; and see *Bonham v. Maycock* (1928) 138 L.T. 736.
[38] And licensed conveyancer, see Administration of Justice Act 1985, s.34(1).
[39] *Gyles v. Hall* (1726) 2 P.Wms. 378.

individual moment of time but the whole hour.[40] For the same reason, if the mortgagee does not appear or is late, the mortgagor himself must continue to attend during the whole hour or his tender will be bad.[41] Today, when the fact that a mortgage is redeemable after default is well known, it is unusual to find a special hour or place for payment fixed by the mortgage deed. If, as usually happens, payment is not made until after the contract date, or, in any case, if no place is named for payment, the mortgagor must seek out the mortgagee and tender the money either to him personally or to his authorised agent. Tender on the mortgaged land is not sufficient, because mortgage moneys are a sum in gross and do not issue out of the land like a rent.[42] Consequently, a mortgagor will, as a rule, suggest a time and place for payment when he notifies the mortgagee of his intention to redeem. Then, if the suggested place is reasonably near the mortgagee's residence or is for other reasons convenient to the mortgagee and if the latter has made no objection, an effective tender may be made at that place.[43] A tender must, of course, be a "legal tender" in the proper currency. Except by special agreement, the mortgagor is not entitled to deduct any sum by way of set-off from the amount of principal, interest and costs.[44] Again, a tender must not be clogged with a condition[45]; for example, the tender of a sum on condition that it is accepted in full satisfaction of all claims is a bad tender even though the sum tendered turn out to be all that is due.[46] A tender may always be made under protest, the mortgagor reserving a right afterwards to dispute the mortgagee's claim.[47] Nor is a tender conditional if the mortgagor does no more than demand what he is by law entitled to. Thus a demand that a reconveyance be executed at the time of the tender does not invalidate the tender because, on payment, a mortgagor's right is to the immediate discharge of the mortgage.[48] In any case a tender, otherwise invalid, will be good if the mortgagee makes no objection except to dispute the amount of the mortgage debt.[49]

(b) *Payment to joint creditors*

18–38 Creditors who advance money on a joint mortgage are, in equity, entitled in common[50] even if the legal estate was conveyed to them as joint tenants. Consequently, although at law payment to one joint creditor discharges the debt to all,[51] in equity a receipt from one creditor does not release the debtor from the claims of the others.[52] The receipt must, therefore, be taken from all the creditors.

---

[40] *Knox v. Simmons* (1793) 4 Bro.C.C. 433.
[41] *Bernard v. Norton* (1864) 10 L.T. 183.
[42] Co.Lit. Vol. II, 210 b.
[43] Coote, *Mortgages* (9th ed., 1927), Vol. 1, p. 739; it has, indeed, been said that a tender for redemption need not always be such as would afford a defence to an action at law on the covenant: *Manning v. Burges* (1663) 1 Cas.in Ch. 29; *Webb v. Crosse* [1912] 1 Ch. 323.
[44] *Searles v. Sadgrave* (1855) 5 E. & B. 639. In general, the money must actually be produced; but see *Dickinson v. Shee* (1801) 4 Esp. 67.
[45] *Jennings and Turner v. Major* (1837) 8 C. & P. 61.
[46] *Strong v. Harvey* (1825) 3 Bing. 304 (an insurance case).
[47] *Manning v. Lunn and Thrupp* (1845) 2 C. & K. 13; *Greenwood v. Sutcliffe* [1892] 1 Ch. 1.
[48] *Rourke v. Robinson* [1911] 1 Ch. 480.
[49] *Jones v. Arthur* (1840) 8 Dowl.P.C. 442.
[50] *Vickers v. Cowell* (1839) 1 Beav. 529.
[51] *Rigden v. Vallier* (1751) 2 Ves.Sen. 252 at 258.
[52] *Husband v. Davis* (1851) 10 C.B. 645.

Formerly, a conveyancing difficulty arose when one of the creditors died. Since his interest was an interest in severalty it passed to his personal representatives[53] who must also therefore join in the receipt.[54] This would obviously be inconvenient in the case of mortgages by trustees and so it was customary to insert in the mortgage a statement that the moneys were advanced on a *joint account* (a "joint account clause") in order that on the death of one trustee the receipt of the survivors would be sufficient to release the mortgagor. Although the joint account clause is still frequently included in a joint mortgage, it is no longer necessary. Section 111 of the Law of Property Act 1925 provides that in all joint mortgages, not merely those of trustees, the moneys shall be deemed to have been advanced on a joint account unless the deed expresses a contrary intention. Consequently, in such cases, unless the mortgage contract otherwise provides payment may safely be made to the survivors (or survivor) of joint mortgagees. This enables the surviving mortgagees to overreach the beneficial interests in the mortgaged property. However it does not affect the right of the mortgagees *inter se* nor does it alter the presumptions as to a tenancy in common.

(c) *Effect of a proper tender when refused*

A mortgagee is bound to know the state of the mortgage debt so that if a proper **18–39** tender is made he rejects it at his peril.[55] By the contract and by the practice of the court whilst a mortgagee is entitled to all the costs of the mortgage, including those of redemption, he cannot be allowed to swell the costs and thereby render redemption more difficult. He will have to reimburse the mortgagor for such additional costs (usually the costs of a redemption action)[56] as the latter may be put to by the refusal of his tender. Clearly, therefore, even if it is known that a proper tender will be rejected it is of the first importance that the tender should be made and the risk of further expense placed upon the mortgagee. As Lindley L.J. said[57]:

> "What is the object of a tender? It is not necessarily to put an end to all controversy. It may have that effect and very often has, but its main object is to throw the risk of further controversy on the other party."

Apart from the question of costs, a tender may have the effect of terminating the mortgagee's right to interest. It is true that a tender by itself will not altogether stop the running of interest because tender is not equivalent to payment. A mortgagor who continues to have the use of the mortgagee's money will have to pay interest for its use.[58] But if, after tender, the mortgagor continues to keep the money set aside[59] and available for payment of the mortgage debt the

---

[53] *Matson v. Dennis* (1864) 4 De G.J. & S. 345; *Powell v. Brodhurst* [1901] 2 Ch. 160. The case would, of course, be different if one creditor was specially authorised by the others to receive payment for them all.

[54] *Petty v. Styward* (1632) 1 Rep. Ch. 31; no survivorship; *Vickers v. Cowell* (1839) 1 Beav. 529.

[55] Provided they were created after December 31, 1881.

[56] *Harmer v. Priestly* (1853) 16 Beav. 569.

[57] *Greenwood v. Sutcliffe* [1892] 1 Ch. 1 at 10.

[58] *Edmondson v. Copland* [1911] 2 Ch. 301.

[59] *ibid.* at p. 310.

running of interest is absolutely stopped as from the date of tender.[60] Presumably he need not keep the money completely idle and if, for example, he places it to deposit, he will only have to account to the mortgagee for the interest earned by the money while on deposit.[61] Even if he does not keep the money available, his tender afterwards enables him to enforce redemption without giving any further notice to the mortgagee by payment of the principal plus interest *only up to the date of payment*.[62] If the mortgagee unequivocally refuses a proposed tender, this is equivalent to a waiver by the mortgagee and a formal tender is not necessary.[63]

(d) *Effect of a proper tender when accepted*

18–40   Usually a proper tender is accepted and the mortgage thereby discharged. The mortgagee is then bound to execute such instruments as are necessary to release the security from the debt. Accordingly, he must be given a reasonable time in which to prepare and execute the deeds, especially when he is not the original mortgagee but a derivative holder of the mortgage. The cost of preparing these deeds falls on the mortgagor, as being part of the general costs of the mortgage and this is true even when the costs have been increased by complications in the title caused by the mortgagee's activities. For example, in a case where one trustee-mortgagee absconded the cost of obtaining a vesting order from the court vesting the estate in the remaining trustees was included in the general costs of the mortgage and added to the mortgage debt.[64]

---

[60] *Rourke v. Robinson* [1911] 1 Ch. 480.
[61] *Edmondson v. Copland* [1911] 2 Ch. 301, *per* Joyce J. at 310.
[62] *Edmondson v. Copland* [1911] 2 Ch. 301 at 307.
[63] *Chalikani Venkatarayanim v. Zaminder of Tun* (1922) L.R. Ind. App. 41.
[64] In the case of several incumbrances, the person *immediately* entitled to the equity of redemption, is, of course, the second incumbrancer. For discharge of mortgages, see *post*, chap. 22.

CHAPTER 19

OTHER MATTERS INCIDENTAL TO THE SECURITY

INSURANCE[1]

By virtue of section 101 of the Law of Property Act 1925[2] the mortgagee has the **19–01** statutory power to insure and keep insured the mortgaged property at the expense of the mortgagor in order to preserve his security in respect of loss or damage by fire.[3] The premiums paid for any such insurance shall be a charge on the mortgaged property carrying interest at the same rate as the mortgage debt. However, the premiums cannot be recovered from the mortgagor as a debt in the absence of any express covenant. The power is exercisable as soon as the mortgage is made.[4]

The disadvantages of the statutory power arise not only by virtue of this express restriction as to loss or damage by fire, but also from the terms of section 108(1)[5] of the Law of Property Act 1925 in that the power is limited to an insurance not exceeding the amount specified in the mortgage deed, or if no amount is so specified, two-thirds of the sum necessary to restore the mortgaged property in the event of total destruction. Further, by section 108(2) the statutory power cannot be exercised by the mortgagee:

"(i) where there is a declaration in the mortgage deed that no insurance is required;

(ii) when an insurance is kept by or on behalf of the mortgagor in accordance with the mortgage deed;

(iii) where the mortgage deed contains no stipulation respecting insurance, and an insurance is kept up by or on behalf of the mortgagor with the consent of the mortgagee to the amount to which the mortgagee is by the Act authorised to insure."

The mortgagee may require that the insurance moneys received be applied by the mortgagor in making good the loss or damage in respect of which it has been paid.[6]

---

[1] For a criticism of the limitations of the present legal position, see the Law Commission, Working Paper No. 99, *Land Mortgages*, paras 3.27, 3.28. See also para. 3–23.

[2] ss.101(1)(ii), 108, replacing (with slight variations) the Conveyancing Act 1881, ss.18(1)(ii), 23.

[3] The power may be varied or extended by the mortgage deed, and the section only applies if and so far as a contrary intention is not expressed in the deed—LPA 1925, s.101(3), (4).

[4] LPA 1925, s.101(1)(ii).

[5] *ibid.* s.108(3).

[6] *ibid.* s.101(1)(ii).

19–02   Thus, owing to the inadequacy of the statutory power it is usual for the mortgage deed to contain an express covenant on the part of the mortgagor to insure the security for a specified amount, or for the full value of the property. The covenant also usually contains an agreement by the mortgagor to produce receipts for the premiums on demand, and to repay to the mortgagee any sums paid by him in respect of those premiums.

The effect of such an express covenant on the part of the mortgagor enables the mortgagee, in the case of default by the mortgagor, to recover those sums paid by the mortgagee in respect of premiums as a debt and as a breach of the covenant by the mortgagor instead of having to add such premiums to the mortgage debt which occurs in the case of the statutory power. Breach of such a covenant is a default which at once sets up the mortgagee's statutory power of sale. Further, and without prejudice to any obligation to the contrary imposed by law or by special contract, a mortgagee may require that all money received under an insurance effected as mentioned above be applied in or towards the discharge of the mortgage money.[7] The covenant operates to grant to the mortgagee a charge over the proceeds. This position arises even if the insurance is taken out in the name of the mortgagor.[8] However, if the mortgagor has effected a further insurance which is independent of the security, the mortgagee will not be entitled to its benefit.[9] Thus, if the insurance policy contains a clause limiting the insurers' liability in the event of the security in question being the subject of any other insurance, the result may be that the amount payable to the mortgagee is diminished and the mortgagee will have no right to the benefit of the further insurance moneys.[10]

POWER TO GRANT LEASES

1. Generally

19–03   The power of a mortgagor to grant and enforce leases well illustrates the compromise between the equitable ownership of the mortgagor and the legal rights inherent in the title of the mortgagee.[11] Having parted with his legal right to possession by demise or legal charge and merely retaining the reversion subject to a long term of years[12] (together with the equity of redemption), the mortgagor might be expected to have no power to grant leases to take effect

---

[7] LPA 1925, s.108(4). In the case of loss or damage by fire and reinstatement of the mortgaged property from the insurance proceeds the position is somewhat complicated, see the Fire Prevention (Metropolis) Act 1774, s.83, the operation of which is not confined to the metropolis. It is generally assumed that the mortgagee's rights under s.108(4) or the mortgagee's contractual rights are subsumed to the rights of "any person interested" under s.83 of the 1774 Act to require the insurance company to utilise the insurance proceeds towards reinstatement of the building (see, *e.g.* Fisher & Lightwood, *Law of Mortgage* (10th ed., 1988), p. 52; but see MacGillivray and Parkington, *Insurance Law* (9th ed., 1997), paras 20–31ff). Even if this is a correct interpretation of the law in relation to fire insurance, a third party with no interest in the mortgage but who is a "person interested" under s.83 of the 1774 Act, can insist on reinstatement.

[8] *Colonial Mutual Insurance Co. Ltd v. ANZ Banking Insurance Group (New Zealand) Ltd* [1995] 1 W.L.R. 1140.

[9] See *Halifax Building Society v. Keighley* [1931] 2 K.B. 248.

[10] *ibid.*

[11] For the position with regard to leases granted *before* the mortgage, see *ante*, chap. 14.

[12] See *ante*, para. 3–01 *et seq.*

during the continuance of the mortgage.[13] However, unless he has actually been dispossessed by the mortgagee, he can create legal tenancies which are binding on himself and his lessee upon the principle of estoppel.[14] For a tenant is estopped from denying his landlord's title and a landlord from denying the validity of his lease. Consequently, the mortgagor may sue or distrain for rent.[15] Such a lease will not, however, be binding on the mortgagee, if the latter asserts his paramount title to possession.[16] That is the position even where, before completion of a purchase and associated mortgage, a purchaser of the legal estate purports to grant a lease of the land he has contracted to purchase.[17] Where a purchase and mortgage occur at the same time, for instance where a purchaser relies on a mortgage to fund all or part of the purchase price, the purchaser will only ever acquire the equality of redemption so there is no *scintilla temporis* when the estoppel affecting him can be fed by his acquisition of the legal estate and thus give rise to a tenancy binding on the mortgagee. However, where a mortgagee fails to register a mortgage of registered land a tenancy is granted in breach of the terms of the mortgage before its registration, it may have priority and bind the mortgagee, even when the contractual tenancy ends and only a statutory tenancy remains.[18]

Thus a mortgagor cannot—apart from express or statutory power (or, in the **19–04** limited circumstances explained above) grant leases which bind the mortgagee because he has conveyed away the title to possession. Further,[19] although the mortgagor may remain in possession of the mortgaged property and receive the rents and profits and sue in his own name[20] until demand by the mortgagee, it is the mortgagee who is always entitled to take possession or after an effective demand[21] to require the rent including any arrears[22] to be paid to himself.[23] This right to possession on the part of the mortgagee cannot be fettered by the mortgagor[24] and against the mortgagee the tenant has no defence,[25] even where as between tenant and mortgagor the tenant has the benefit of statutory protection.[26]

---

[13] See *ante*, para. 3–33.
[14] *Doe* d. *Marriot v. Edwards* (1834) 6 C. & P. 208; *Webb v. Austin* (1844) 7 Man. & G. 701; *Cuthbertson v. Irving* (1860) 4 H. & N. 742 at 754 (*affd.* (1860) 6 H. & N. 135); *Trent v. Hunt* (1853) 9 Exch. 14.
[15] *Trent v. Hunt* (1853) 9 Ex. 14; and see *ante*, para. 17–15.
[16] *Rogers v. Humphreys* (1835) 4 Ad. & El. 299; *Trent v. Hunt* (1853) 9 Ex. 14; unless, of course, the lease was authorised by the mortgagee; *Corbett v. Plowden* (1884) 25 Ch.D. 678; or his concurrence in the tenancy could be implied from some act or conduct on his part, *e.g.* by the acceptance of the mortgagees' tenant, see *Stroud Building Society v. Delamont* [1960] 1 W.L.R. 431, approved in *Chatsworth Properties Ltd v. Effiom* [1971] 1 W.L.R. 144. But such a tenancy binding the mortgagee will not arise merely because the mortgagee does not object, (*Re O'Rourke's Estate* (1889) 23 L.R.Ir. 497); or the mortgagee fails to evict the tenant, (*Parker v. Braithwaite* [1952] W.N. 504), even though the mortgagor was in default at the time, (*Taylor v. Ellis* [1960] Ch. 368); see also *Barclays Bank v. Kiley* [1961] 1 W.L.R. 1050.
[17] *Abbey National Building Society v. Cann* [1991] A.C. 56.
[18] *Barclays Bank plc v. Zaroovabli* [1997] Ch. 321.
[19] See *ante*, para. 17–11 *et seq.*
[20] LPA 1925, s.98, and see *ante*, para. 17–16 *et seq.*
[21] See *Kitchen's Trustee v. Madders and Madders* [1950] Ch. 134.
[22] *Moss v. Gallimore* (1779) 1 Doug. K.B. 279.
[23] *Pope v. Biggs* (1829) 9 B. & C. 245.
[24] See *Thunder* d. *Weaver v. Belcher* (1803) 3 East. 449.
[25] *Rogers v. Humphreys* (1835) 4 Ad. & El. 299; *Dudley and District Benefit Building Society v. Emerson* [1949] Ch. 707; *Rust v. Goodale* [1957] Ch. 33.
[26] *Britannia Building Society v. Earl* [1990] 1 W.L.R. 422.

The corollary to this ought to be that the mortgagee, having the legal title to possession, should be able to create legal tenancies to the full extent of the estate mortgaged to him, though, of course, the exercise of the power would mean that he took possession of the security. Equity, however, in pursuance of the principle that the mortgagee's estate belongs to him only as a security, refuses to recognise that leases granted by him are binding on the mortgagor after redemption.[27] Consequently, unless special powers of leasing are granted in the mortgage there may be difficulty in the management of the property, since during the continuance of the mortgage it is impossible for either mortgagor or mortgagee to grant an indefeasible term without the concurrence of the other. The result was that mortgage contracts frequently contained express powers to grant leases binding on both parties and this practice eventually received statutory recognition.[28]

2. Statutory power

19–05   The Law of Property Act 1925[29] makes elaborate provision for the creation of indefeasible tenancies by a mortgagor in possession and by a mortgagee who has gone into possession. Where the mortgage contract does not limit the statutory powers of leasing[30] and was itself executed after December 31, 1881,[31] the mortgagor in possession[32] or the mortgagee if he is in possession[33] or has appointed a receiver who is still acting[34] (in which case the mortgagee's powers of leasing may be delegated in writing to the receiver) is vested by section 99 with the power to grant leases[35] so that they will bind all persons.

(a) *Duration*

19–06   A lease may be granted for the following terms:

> (1) Agricultural or occupation leases for any term not exceeding 50 years.[36]

---

[27] *Franklinski v. Ball* (1864) 33 Beav. 560; and see *Chapman v. Smith* [1907] 2 Ch. 97 at 102. s.99 of the LPA 1925 empowers a mortgagee to make certain leases which will bind the mortgagor even after redemption: a lease made *ultra vires* these powers would still, however, be void against the mortgagor after redemption.

[28] Conveyancing Act 1881, s.18; and now the LPA 1925, s.99.

[29] s.99.

[30] See s.99(13) as amended by Agricultural Holdings Act 1986, s.100 Sched. 14, para. 12 and Landlord and Tenant Act 1954, s.36(4).

[31] The Conveyancing Act of that year first introduced the statutory powers; in cases where a mortgage was executed before 1822, the parties may now by agreement introduce the statutory powers in the mortgage.

[32] LPA 1925, s.99(1).

[33] *ibid.* s.99(2).

[34] *ibid.* s.99(19).

[35] The provisions of this section extend to agreements for a lease as well as to leases, and specific performance of such agreements will therefore be decreed.

[36] 21 years if the mortgage was executed before January 1, 1926. See LPA 1925, s.99(3)(i).

(2) Building leases for any term not exceeding 999 years.[37]

No power is, however, given to create mining leases.

(b) *Conditions*

All leases within the terms of the statute must comply with the following **19–07**
conditions:

(1) The lease must be limited to take effect in possession not later than 12
months after its date.[38]

(2) The lease must reserve the best rent that can reasonably be obtained,
and with certain qualifications no fine may be taken[39] though in a
building lease the rent may be nominal for the first five years.[40]

(3) The lease must contain a covenant by the lessee for the payment of
rent, and a condition of re-entry on the rent not being paid within a time
not exceeding 30 days.[41]

(4) In the case of a building lease there must be a covenant by the lessee
that within five years improvements will be effected on the land in
connection with buildings, repairs to buildings, or building
purposes.[42]

(5) A counterpart of the lease must be executed by the lessee and delivered
to the lessor.[43]

(6) Where it is the mortgagor who grants the lease, he must within one
month deliver to the mortgagee, first in priority, a counterpart of the
lease duly executed by the lessee.[44]

The provisions of the section extend to agreements for a lease.[45] Some doubt
has been raised as to whether the covenant by the lessee for the payment of rent
and the condition of re-entry in the event of rent not being paid can apply in the
case of an oral letting. In any event such a condition, if imposed, will be strictly
construed.[46]

---

[37] 99 years if the mortgage was executed before January 1, 1926. See LPA 1925, s.99(3)(ii).
[38] LPA 1925, s.99(5).
[39] *ibid.* s.99(6).
[40] *ibid.* s.99(10).
[41] *ibid.* s.99(7).
[42] *ibid.* s.99(9).
[43] *ibid.* s.99(8).
[44] *ibid.* s.99(11). The lessee is not, however, concerned to see that this provision has been complied
with. Non-compliance does not invalidate the lease although it renders the power of sale exercisable; see *Public Trustee v. Lawrence* [1912] 1 Ch. 789; and see *Rhodes v. Dalby* [1971] 1 W.L.R.
1325.
[45] LPA 1925, s.99(17), " ... as far as circumstances admit ... [the definitions of lease] ... to an
agreement, whether in writing or not, for leasing or letting."
[46] See *Pawson v. Revell* [1958] 2 Q.B. 360; *Rhodes v. Dalby* [1971] 1 W.L.R. 1325; Wolstenholme
& Cherry, *Conveyancing Statutes* (13th ed., 1971), pp. 198, 200. But even if the letting does not
comply with the statutory requirements, provided that it is made in good faith and the tenant has
taken possession it may be effective in equity at the tenant's option as a contract for a lease subject
to such variations as may be necessary to comply with the above conditions; see LPA 1925, s.152,
replacing the Leases Acts 1849, 1850.

A lease by the mortgagor of agricultural land does not cease to be such if it includes chattels and sporting rights not included in the mortgage.[47] But it will not bind the mortgagee if it commprises both the mortgaged land and other land at a single inclusive rent.[48]

(c) *Contrary agreement*

19–08 The above powers are subject to exclusion[49] or extension[50] by the mortgage agreement (which in fact frequently does modify the mortgagor's statutory power[51]) or otherwise in writing by the parties. But the statutory power cannot be excluded in any mortgage of agricultural land after March 1, 1948[52] and in the case of business premises the exclusion of the statutory power does not prevent the court from ordering the grant of a new tenancy.[53]

3. Leases not made under the statutory power

19–09 Section 99 of the Law of Property Act 1925, does not, however, take away the mortgagor's ordinary power, outside the statute, to create leases binding on himself by estoppel although not binding on the mortgagee, should the latter assert his paramount title to possession.[54] Thus, if the mortgage deed altogether excludes the statutory power to grant leases binding on the mortgagee, the mortgagor may still create leases effective between himself and his lessee.[55] The same is true if, as frequently happens, the mortgage deed merely restricts the statutory power by making its exercise subject to the previous consent of the mortgagee. Indeed, in a case where the mortgagors had covenanted not to exercise the statutory power without the previous consent of the mortgagees and had then created a yearly tenancy without their consent, Farwell J. held that the mortgagors must be assumed to have been exercising their general power to create leases by estoppel and had therefore not committed a breach of the covenant.[56]

Consequently, at the very least, a demise by a mortgagor in possession will create a lease which is effective between the parties.[57] Thus the mortgagor can

---

[47] *Brown v. Peto* [1900] 2 Q.B. 653.

[48] *King v. Bird* [1909] 1 K.B. 837.

[49] LPA 1925, s.99(13).

[50] *ibid.* s.99(14).

[51] As, for instance, by requiring the mortgagee's consent before the powers can be exercised; *Iron Trades Employers Insurance Association Ltd v. Union of Land & House Investors Ltd* [1937] 1 Ch. 313.

[52] Initially by reason of Agricultural Holdings Act 1986, s.100, Sched. 14, para. 12, since 1995 by reason of amendments to LPA 1925, s.99 made by the Agricultural Tenancies Act 1995. See also *Pawson v. Revell* [1958] 2 Q.B. 360; *Rhodes v. Dalby* [1971] 1 W.L.R. 1325.

[53] Landlord and Tenant Act 1954, s.36(4).

[54] See *ante*, p. 334.

[55] *Dudley and District Benefit Building Society v. Emerson* [1949] Ch. 707. *Rust v. Goodale* [1957] Ch. 33.

[56] *Iron Trades Employers Insurance Association Ltd v. Union of Land & House Investors Ltd* [1937] 1 Ch. 313.

[57] This appears to be so whether or not the lease discloses on its face the existence of the mortgage: *Morton v. Woods* (1869) L.R. 4 Q.B. 293.

distrain for rent and enforce the covenants and his interest will pass to his personal representatives or to assignees, so as to enable them to sue upon the covenants.[58] The lessee, on his side, may not only enforce the lease but obtains an interest in the equity of redemption which is sufficient to entitle him to redeem.[59] He cannot insist that the mortgagee shall accept him as tenant but he may, if he thinks fit, take over the mortgage by redeeming. If he does not redeem and is dispossessed by the mortgagee, his only relief against the mortgagor is an action for damages because the court will not compel a mortgagor to redeem for the purpose of giving efficacy to his lease.[60] The mortgagee's right to eject the mortgagor's lessee by estoppel is absolute, for he is asserting a title to possession paramount to that of the mortgagor himself. There is no contractual nexus of any kind between the lessee and the mortgagee so that the latter is not, for example, a landlord for the purpose of the Rent Act 1977[61] and the lessee cannot claim the protection of the Act.

Thus, it is now usual for the mortgage deed to contain a clause not only **19–10** excluding the statutory power of leasing but also a clause which makes the grant of any lease or tenancy or otherwise parting with possession of the mortgaged property a breach of the mortgagor's obligations under the lease.

The importation of such a clause will cause the power of sale to arise in the event of any breach on the part of the mortgagor.

If the mortgage permits the mortgagor to exercise the statutory power of leasing with the consent of the mortgagee, the onus is on the lessee to prove that the mortgagee gave his consent.[62] If the deed provides that the proposed lessee shall not be concerned to inquire as to such consent, the mortgagee is estopped from denying the lease was made with his consent.[63]

The result is that a mortgagor's power to grant leases will either be expressly stated by the agreement or will depend on section 99 of the Law of Property Act 1925. Leases granted in conformity with the express or statutory power will be binding on the mortgagee and, equally, on his assuming possession, the benefit of the covenants will pass to the mortgagee by virtue of section 141 of the Law of Property Act 1925[64] in relation to leases created before January 1, 1996 and, by virtue of section 15 of the Landlord and Tenants (Covenants) Act 1995, in relation to leases created after that date.[65]

POWER TO ACCEPT SURRENDER OF LEASES

Complementary to the power to grant leases is the power given by section 100 **19–11** of the Law of Property Act 1925 to the mortgagor or mortgagee to accept surrenders of leases. This power was first introduced by the Conveyancing Act

---

[58] *Cuthbertson v. Irving* (1860) 6 H. & N. 135.
[59] *Tarn v. Turner* (1888) 39 Ch.D. 456, CA.
[60] *Howe v. Hunt* (1862) 31 Beav. 420.
[61] *Dudley and District Benefit Building Society v. Emerson* [1949] Ch. 707; *Rust v. Goodale* [1957] Ch. 33. *Quaere* whether a statutory tenant can claim the protection of the Act, see dicta in *Jessamine Investment Co. Ltd v. Schwartz* [1978] Q.B. 264 at 273; and see P. W. Smith (1977) Conv. 197.
[62] *Taylor v. Ellis* [1960] Ch. 368.
[63] *Lever Finance Ltd v. Needlemans Property Trustee* [1956] Ch. 375.
[64] *Municipal Permanent Investment Building Society v. Smith* (1888) 22 Q.B.D. 70.
[65] See *ante*, para. 16–27.

1911[66] and now extends to all mortgages executed after December 31, 1911. Its purpose is to allow a mortgagee or mortgagor to accept a surrender in order to enable another lease to be granted.

The surrender may be accepted:

(1) by the mortgagee, if he is in possession[67] or has appointed a receiver who is still acting[68] (in which case the mortgagee may delegate his powers of accepting surrenders to the receiver in writing[69]);

(2) by the mortgagor, if he is in possession.[70]

For the surrender to be valid the following conditions must apply:

(a) a fresh authorised lease of the property concerned must be granted to take effect within one month of the surrender; and

(b) the new lease must be for a term not less than the unexpired term of the surrendered lease; and

(c) the rent must be at least equivalent to the rent reserved in the surrendered lease.[71]

These provisions also apply to agreements for a lease and are subject to the parties expressing a contrary intention either in the mortgage deed or otherwise in writing.[72] However, the power may be extended by an agreement in writing between the parties whether in the mortgage or not.[73] A surrender which does not comply with these conditions is void.[74]

---

[66] s.3. Prior to the 1911 Act a mortgagor who had granted a lease under his statutory powers could not accept its surrender unless the mortgagee consented.

[67] LPA 1925, s.100(2).

[68] *ibid.* s.100(13).

[69] *ibid.*

[70] *ibid.* s.100(1).

[71] *ibid.* s.100(5).

[72] *ibid.* s.100(7).

[73] *ibid.* s.100(10).

[74] *Barclays Bank v. Stasek* [1957] Ch. 28; *Rhyl U.D.C. v. Rhyl Amusements Ltd* [1959] 1 W.L.R. 465 applied in *Camden LBC v. Shortlife Community Housing Ltd* (1992) 90 L.G.R. 358.

CHAPTER 20

PRIORITY OF MORTGAGES

GENERAL RULES

1. Realty

As a mortgagor is able to obtain successive advances on the same property and **20–01** circumstances may arise in which the property is insufficient to satisfy all the securities, there is a need for rules which regulate priorities among the various mortgagees. Unlike the unsecured creditors of a bankrupt mortgagees do not share rateably if there is not sufficient to satisfy them all. The simplest way of regulating priorities is by order of creation. While this would be fair in many cases, it would not be fair when, by the misconduct of the mortgagor or an earlier mortgagee, the existence of that earlier mortgage was concealed from a later mortgagee.

For mortgages (including sub-mortgages) of realty, the basic rule of priority, ranking by order of creation (*qui prior est tempore, potior est jure*) was modified in two ways. The first is normally expressed by the phrase "where the equities are equal, the law prevails." In *Bailey v. Barnes*[1] Lindley L.J. said that equality meant "the non-existence of any circumstance which affects the conduct of one of the rival claimants, and makes it less meritorious than that of the other." The result of this is that, where a legal and an equitable mortgagee have, in that sense, equal claims to be preferred, the legal mortgagee will rank first even though his mortgage was created later.

The second modification was that any priority, whether depending on earlier creation or superiority of the legal estate, could be lost if the conduct of the mortgagor or the prior mortgagee was inequitable. Priorities of mortgages of realty, therefore, were regulated by general equitable principles, subject to the two following exceptions.

(1) The first depended on registration. Between 1703 and 1735, registers of transactions in land were set up for Yorkshire and Middlesex. The principle of the registration system was that an earlier transaction by A would be void against a later purchaser, B, unless A's deed was registered before B's. The efficacy of this system was severely reduced by the insistence of courts of equity on applying the doctrine of notice, so that B took subject to A's incumbrance if he knew of its existence, irrespective of registration. The system no longer exists since both counties are now wholly subject to compulsory registration of title.

[1] [1894] 1 Ch. 25 at 36, CA.

(2) The second exception was by means of tacking, a device whereby a later mortgagee can gain priority over an earlier mortgagee by amalgamating his debt with that owned to a still earlier mortgagee. The opportunities for this device to be used were cut down by the 1925 legislation and its operation is now regulated entirely by statute.[2]

2. Personalty

20–02 The rules regulating priorities of mortgages of personalty developed rather differently. Legal mortgages of personal chattels are the subject of consideration in chapter 6; they are only regulated by the Bills of Sale Acts 1878 and 1882. Mortgages of choses in action are governed by the general law of assignment though sub-mortgages, which are mortgages of mortgage debts and therefore choses in action are treated as interests in land and are subject to the same rules of priority as mortgages.[3]

Mortgages of equitable interests in personalty were subject to the rule in *Dearle v. Hall.*[4] In its original form the rule provided that priority depended on the order in which notice of the mortgages or other transactions was received by the owner of the legal estate or interest in the subject-matter except where the subsequent mortgagee had, at the time he lent the money, actual or constructive notice of the earlier transaction. Although the rule now applies to equitable interests in land subject to a trust of land and its proceeds of sale,[5] it did not do so before 1926.

PRIORITIES BETWEEN LEGAL AND EQUITABLE MORTGAGES OF LAND

1. Two successive legal mortgages

20–03 Legal mortgages of land before 1926 were almost invariably created by a conveyance of the fee simple with a proviso for reconveyance on redemption and thus the opportunity for any priority question to arise rarely occurred.

Successive legal mortgages could arise from the grant of successive terms of years in which case priority would normally be determined by the order of creation on the basis that the first lease would be a lease in possession, to which the second, as a lease in reversion, would be postponed.[6]

The earlier mortgagee could, as in *Jones v. Rhind,*[7] lose priority by parting with the title deeds. In that case, S mortgaged a leasehold property first to J, then to R, handing over the lease to R when he made the second mortgage. R had no

---

[2] LPA 1925, s.94.
[3] *Taylor v. London & County Banking Co.*; *London and County Banking Co. v. Nixon* [1901] 2 Ch. 231.
[4] (1828) 3 Russ. 1. See *post*, paras 20–16 to 20–22.
[5] LPA 1925, s.137 (as amended by TLATA 1996, s.25(1), Sched. 3, paras 4 and 15). See *post*, para. 20–23 *et seq.*
[6] *Ex p. Knott* (1806) 11 Ves. 609.
[7] (1869) 17 W.R. 1091; applying *Perry-Herrick v. Attwood* (1857) 2 De G. & J. 21. See also *Abbey National Building Society v. Cann* [1991] 1 A.C. 560.

notice of the first mortgage and he was held to have priority over J. In *Mason v. Rhodes*,[8] W created three mortgages, an equitable mortgage to G, followed by legal mortgages to B and then to R. R, who had no notice of B, arranged to pay off G, and received the title deeds. It was held on appeal that R had priority over M (B's trustee in liquidation) to the extent of G's security.

One source of successive legal mortgages was the portions term[9] contained in a strict settlement. The trustees of the portions term were empowered to raise money for the younger children by mortgaging a long term, usually 1,000 years. In *Hurst v. Hurst*[10] it was held that a tenant for life, who had power under the settlement to create portions terms, could not do so to the prejudice of the mortgagees with whom he had covenanted not to exercise that power, even though the portions term was not made subject to the mortgage term.

2. Legal mortgage followed by equitable mortgage

In this case the legal mortgagee has a claim to priority based both on earlier creation and the superiority of the legal estate.[11] This double protection can be lost. Usually the cases on such loss of protection are considered under the three headings of fraud, estoppel (or misrepresentation) and gross negligence in relation to the title deeds.   **20–04**

3. Estoppel

The so-called *estoppel* cases fall into two classes. First, there are those where the prior mortgagee puts into the hands of a mortgagor a document containing within it a statement that money has been received by the mortgagee. As against an innocent person who lends money on the property on the faith of that receipt he cannot deny that the money has been received.[12]

The second class involves a representation, express or implied, that the person in possession of the title-deeds is the mortgagee's agent to raise money or otherwise deal with the property. Thus where a mortgagee expressly authorises the mortgagor to raise money on the security of the property and gives him control of the title deeds, he represents to innocent third parties who advance money that the mortgagor has that authority to deal with the property which possession of the title deeds implies. He cannot, against such a third party, rely on any secret limitation of the mortgagor's apparent authority.[13]

Thus where the prior legal mortgagee returned the deeds to the mortgagor to enable him to raise a further loan he was postponed to a later equitable mortgagee who lent without notice of the earlier mortgage, even though the mortgagor

---

[8] (1885) 53 L.T. 322.
[9] See earlier editions of Megarry and Wade, *The Law of Real Property* (5th ed., 1984), pp. 413–414.
[10] (1852) 16 Beav. 372.
[11] *Peter v. Russell* (1716) 1 Eq.Cas.Abr. 321.
[12] *Bickerton v. Walker* (1885) 31 Ch.D. 151; *cf. Rice v. Rice* (1854) 2 Drew. 73.
[13] *Rimmer v. Webster* [1902] 2 Ch. 163; *Fry v. Smellie* [1912] 3 K.B. 282; *Abigail v. Lapin* [1934] A.C. 491; *Brocklesby v. Temperance Permanent Building Society* [1895] A.C. 173; *Lloyds Bank v. Cooke* [1907] 1 K.B. 794; *Edmunds v. Bushell* (1865) L.R. 1 Q.B. 97.

exceeded the limit that he was authorised to borrow.[14] This similarly arose where the mortgagor had undertaken to inform the later mortgagee of the existing mortgage, but failed to do so.[15]

Priority will not be lost where the title deeds are left with another for safe-keeping or without reference to any transaction regarding the property.[16] The pre-1926 rule as to questions of priority depending on possession of deeds is preserved.[17]

4. **Fraud and gross negligence**

20–05   The fraud and gross negligence cases are considered together. In *Peter v. Russell*[18] it was held that a prior mortgagee who deliberately assists or connives in a scheme of the mortgagor designed to defeat later incumbrancers is postponed to them. The same applies if the fraud is that of the party's solicitor provided that the solicitor–client relationship existed at the time of the fraud. In *Evans v. Bicknell*,[19] Lord Eldon held that a prior mortgagee would be postponed if his conduct in relation to the deeds displayed gross negligence that amounted to a fraudulent intention. In *Colyer v. Finch*,[20] however, it was held that in order to deprive a first mortgagee of his legal priority the party claiming by title subsequent must satisfy the court that the first mortgagee has been guilty of either fraud or gross negligence but for which he would have had the deeds in his possession.

Clarke v. Palmer[21] seems to have been decided in accordance with that principle. X, the first mortgagee, negligently failed to obtain the title deeds, after which the mortgagor further mortgaged part of the property to Y, then all of it to Z. Z knew of Y but neither of them knew of X, who was, on account of his negligence, postponed to both of them.

In reversing the authorities, two particular cases stand which are not wholly reconcilable[22]; *Northern Counties of England Fire Insurance Co. v. Whipp*[23] and *Walker v. Linom*.[24]

5. **Northern Counties**

20–06   In his analysis of the authorities in *Northern Counties of England Fire Insurance Co. v. Whipp*,[25] Fry L.J. held *Clarke v. Palmer* to have been rightly decided. He

---

[14] *Perry-Herrick v. Attwood* (1857) 2 De G. & J. 21; *Abbey National Building Society v. Cann* [1991] 1 A.C. 56.
[15] *Briggs v. Jones* (1870) L.R. 10 Eq. 92.
[16] *Shropshire Union Railways and Canal Co. v. R.* (1875) L.R. 7 H.L. 496; *Re Vernon, Ewens & Co.* (1886) 33 Ch.D. 402. *cf. Waldron v. Sloper* (1852) 1 Drew. 193.
[17] *Beddoes v. Shaw* [1937] Ch. 81; LPA 1925, s.13.
[18] (1716) 1 Eq. Cas. Abr. 321.
[19] (1801) 6 Ves. 174 at 189.
[20] (1856) 5 H.L.C. 905.
[21] (1882) 21 Ch.D. 124.
[22] See para. 20–08.
[23] (1884) 26 Ch.D. 482, CA.
[24] [1907] 2 Ch. 104.
[25] (1884) 26 Ch.D. 482, CA.

considered six types of case. In the first three, the prior legal mortgagee retains priority:

(1) Where he has a reasonable excuse for not obtaining the deeds. This has been extended in *Grierson v. National Provincial Bank of England Ltd*[26] where F, a leaseholder, deposited his lease with another bank as security for a loan and then granted a legal mortgage to G which was made expressly subject to the prior equitable mortgage. He then redeemed the equitable mortgage and deposited the lease with the defendant bank, who knew nothing of G, as security for a loan. It was held that G retained priority over the defendant bank.

(2) Where he reasonably believes that he has been given all the deeds though he has not, in fact, been given all of them. *Walker v. Linom*,[27] which is discussed later, is against this proposition.

(3) Where he has lent them to the mortgagor who has given a reasonable excuse for requiring them as in *Peter v. Russell*[28] and *Martinez v. Cooper*.[29]

In the remaining three, priority would be lost.

(4) Where the legal mortgagee has made no inquiry for the deeds, he will be postponed to a prior equitable estate or to a subsequent equitable owner who used diligence in inquiring for the deeds. In the first case, of which he cites *Worthington v. Morgan*[30] as an example, his reasoning was that the conduct of the mortgagee in making no inquiry was evidence of fraudulent intent to escape notice of a prior equity. In the second case, exemplified by *Clarke v. Palmer*,[31] he considered that a subsequent mortgagee who was misled by the mortgagor taking advantage of fraudulent conduct on the part of the legal mortgagee could, against him, take advantage of the fraudulent intent.

(5) and (6) These are the cases, already dealt with under estoppel, such as *Perry-Herrick v. Attwood*[32] and *Briggs v. Jones*,[33] where the legal mortgagee has conferred apparent authority on the mortgagor to deal with the property without restriction, although there were conditions as between mortgagee and mortgagor of which a third party would be unaware.

In arriving at his decision in *Northern Counties of England Fire Insurance Co.*   **20–07** *v. Whipp*,[34] Fry L.J. relied on *Evans v. Bicknell*[35] and cases which followed it and seems to have ignored the plain words of *Colyer v. Finch*.[36] He has used a later

[26] [1913] 2 Ch. 18.
[27] [1907] 2 Ch. 104; see para. 22–07 and *Cottey v. National Provincial Bank of England* (1904) 48 S.J. 589.
[28] 1 Eq. Cas. Abr. 321.
[29] (1826) 2 Russ. 198.
[30] (1849) 16 Sim. 547.
[31] (1882) 21 Ch.D. 124.
[32] (1857) 2 De G. & J. 21.
[33] (1870) L.R. 10 Eq. 92.
[34] (1884) 26 Ch.D. 482, CA.
[35] (1801) 6 Ves. 174.
[36] (1856) 5 H.L.C. 905, in the headnote and at 928.

passage[37] which refers to "gross negligence, so gross as to be tantamount to fraud" in order to reconcile those two cases and make fraud a requirement for postponement.

Walker v. Linom   In *Walker v. Linom*,[38] Parker J. reviewed the authorities, particularly the judgment of Fry L.J. referred to above, and concluded that the principle should be stated as follows:

> "Any conduct on the part of the holder of the legal estate in relation to the deeds which would make it inequitable for him to rely on his legal estate against a prior equitable estate of which he had no notice ought also to be sufficient to postpone him to a subsequent equitable estate the creation of which has only been rendered possible by the possession of deeds which but for such conduct would have passed into the possession of the owner of the legal estate."[39]

In that case, W conveyed land to solicitor trustees to hold on the trusts of his marriage settlements. The title-deeds, except for the conveyance to W, were handed over to the trustees who failed to discover the omission. They were found to have been negligent but not dishonest in that failure which had enabled W, using the conveyance, to mortgage the property to X, who then sold it to Y. The trustees were postponed to Y.

20–08   Although that decision is inconsistent with Fry L.J.'s judgment in *Northern Counties v. Whipp*,[40] it is suggested that Parker J.'s formulation of the principle is correct, the more so since Hall V.-C. did not find any fraudulent conduct in *Clarke v. Palmer*[41] but postponed the prior mortgagee on the grounds of his negligence.

The attempt to reconcile the decisions in the *Northern Counties* case and *Walker v. Linom*[42] on the basis that the first refers to negligence in failing to retain and the second to negligence in failing to obtain the title deeds, cannot be supported. As Waldock[43] has pointed out, it is not satisfactory to argue that by carelessly failing to keep the title-deeds the legal mortgagee could prejudice only himself and his carelessness would thus not tend to convict him of fraud. The owner of the legal estate is the one person who could not be prejudiced by misuse of the title-deeds. Normally the person prejudiced is one who enters into a transaction with the person who wrongly has them. The prejudice arises whether the deeds fall into the wrong hands by failure to retain or failure to obtain.

It may be, as Waldock suggests, that Fry L.J. was influenced by the doctrine of constructive fraud.[44] Commenting on the decision in *Ratcliffe v. Barnard*,[45] Jeune P. said in *Oliver v. Hinton*[46]:

---

[37] *ibid.* at 929.
[38] [1907] 2 Ch. 104.
[39] *ibid.* at 114.
[40] (1884) 26 Ch.D. 482.
[41] (1882) 21 Ch.D. 124.
[42] [1907] 2 Ch. 104.
[43] *Waldock on Mortgages* (2nd ed., 1950), p. 397.
[44] *ibid.*; and see *Le Lievre v. Gould* [1893] 1 Q.B. 491.
[45] (1871) 6 Ch.App. 652, CA.
[46] [1899] 2 Ch. 264 at 275.

"I think that what he [James L.J.] meant was . . . negligence so gross as
would justify the Court of Chancery in concluding that there had been fraud
in an artificial sense of the word—such gross negligence, for instance, as
omitting to make any inquiry as to the title to the property."

It is clear, also, from the judgments in *Derry v. Peek*[47] that fraud and gross
negligence are to be regarded as two different causes of action and from the
above cases that each of them constitutes a ground for postponing a prior legal
mortgagee.

6. **Equitable mortgage followed by legal mortgage**

Where the prior interest was equitable it was liable to be defeated by a bona fide   **20–09**
purchaser for value of the legal estate without notice of that prior equitable
interest.[48] A mortgagee is a purchaser for this purpose and a person who,
although not the purchaser of a legal estate, has a better title to the legal estate
than the equitable mortgagee, can also displace his priority.

The onus is on the legal mortgagee to show that he is a bona fide[49] purchaser[50]
without notice. It is not sufficient for him to show lack of actual notice; if he fails
to make such inquiries as would normally be made by a reasonably prudent man
of business he is fixed with constructive knowledge of what he would have
discovered by making them. Not only the failure to enquire for the title deeds but
also the inability of the mortgagor to produce them or to provide a reasonable
excuse for their non-production would amount to constructive notice of some
prior interest.

7. **Agents**

In addition, where he employed an agent to carry out the transaction, the   **20–10**
knowledge of prior interests which his agent obtained or should have obtained
was imputed to him so as to prevent him being a purchaser without notice.[51]
Originally this rule was applied very strictly, it being possible to impute to the
purchaser the knowledge acquired by his agent in an entirely separate transaction
on behalf of some other principal.[52] By section 3(2) of the Conveyancing Act
1882, however, the doctrine of imputed notice was restricted to cases in which
the agent's knowledge was obtained in the same transaction as that which led to
the question of notice being raised.[53] This provision is re-enacted by the Law of
Property Act 1925, section 199(1)(ii)(*b*).

---

[47] (1889) 14 App. Cas. 337.
[48] *Re Hardy, ex p. Hardy* (1832) 2 Deac. & Ch. 393.
[49] *Att.-Gen. v. Biphosphated Guano Co.* (1879) 11 Ch.D. 327.
[50] A mortgagee is a purchaser; *Pilcher v. Rawlins* (1872) L.R. 7 Ch. 259.
[51] *Sheldon v. Cox* (1764) 2 Eden. 224; *Berwick & Co. v. Price* [1905] 1 Ch. 632; *Kennedy v. Green*
    (1834) 3 My. & K. 699.
[52] *Hargreaves v. Rothwell* (1836) 1 Keen 154.
[53] *Re Cousins* (1886) 31 Ch.D. 671.

8. **The duty to enquire**

20–11 The words "ought reasonably to enquire" did not fix the purchaser with any legal duty to inquire but rather meant that he "ought, as a matter of prudence [to make the inquiries], having regard to what is usually done by men of business under similar circumstances."[54] It was generally considered that the following inquiries ought reasonably to have been made:

(1) Inspection of the land. Failure to inspect land occupied by a third party would fix the purchaser with knowledge of the third party's rights[55];

(2) Investigation of the title for the statutory period applicable to an open contract. Failure so to investigate would fix the purchaser with knowledge of all that he would have discovered by doing so, even if he had stipulated for a shorter contractual root of title[56];

(3) Examination of deeds executed within the statutory period if they actually affected the title. Failure to do so would fix a purchaser with notice of their contents.[57] If, however, the character of the deed was such that it was uncertain whether it would affect the title, he was permitted to rely on an assurance that it did not[58];

(4) Inquiry into the terms of any trust affecting the land, the existence of which he knew. Knowledge of the trust fixed him with knowledge of the interests of the beneficiaries.[59]

9. **Actual notice**

20–12 Whether the purchaser had actual notice was a fact to be established by evidence. The decided cases are, however, at variance as to whether information must be given by a person interested in the property in order to fix the purchaser with notice.[60]

10. **Doctrine of postponement by gross negligence**

20–13 In spite of the principle that a subsequent purchaser of a legal estate would be fixed with notice of a prior incumbrance if the mortgagor was unable to produce the title deeds, the courts found it necessary to develop a separate doctrine of "gross negligence" in relation to their non-production, the effect of which was (in circumstances where it applied) to amount to actual notice of the prior interest.

---

[54] *per* Lindley L.J. in *Bailey v. Barnes* [1894] 1 Ch. 25 at 35.
[55] *Hunt v. Luck* [1902] 1 Ch. 428.
[56] *Re Nisbet and Potts' Contract* [1906] 1 Ch. 386.
[57] *Bisco v. Earl of Banbury* (1676) 1 Ch.Cas. 287.
[58] *English and Scottish Mercantile Investment Trust v. Brunton* [1892] 2 Q.B. 700.
[59] *Perham v. Kempster* [1907] 1 Ch. 373.
[60] *Barnhart v. Greenshields* (1853) 9 Moo.P.C. 18 at 36; explained in *Reeves v. Pope* [1914] 2 K.B. 284; *cf. Lloyd v. Banks* (1868) L.R. 3 Ch. 488, where the court was dealing with notice under the rule in *Dearle v. Hall*. The effect of notice, to trustees, of dealings with equitable interests is regulated by the LPA 1925, s.137(3).

In *Hewitt v. Loosemore*[61] and in *Hunt v. Elmes*[62] it was said that to deprive a man of the protection of the legal estate he must have been guilty of either fraud or gross and wilful negligence. In *Oliver v. Hinton*[63] Lindley M.R. followed these authorities, holding that a purchaser for value of a legal estate, without notice of a prior equitable incumbrance, would not be permitted to assert the superiority of the legal estate if he had, himself, been guilty of such gross negligence as to render it unjust to deprive the equitable incumbrancer of his priority. An attempt to describe the requisite degree of negligence was made in *Hudston v. Viney*[64] where Eve J. said:

> "It must at least be carelessness of so aggravated a nature as to amount to the neglect of precautions which the ordinary reasonable man would have observed, and to indicate an attitude of mental indifference to obvious risks."

It is not clear why such conduct would not be held to fix the purchaser of the legal estate with constructive notice of the prior incumbrance,[65] and in view of the repeated failure of courts to give anything but the most general description of "gross negligence," one must sympathise (*pace* Lord Chelmsford) with the views of Rolfe B. in *Wilson v. Brett*[66]:

> "I said that I could see no difference between negligence and gross negligence—that it was the same thing with the addition of a vituperative epithet."

In *Oliver v. Hinton*,[67] X deposited the deeds of some property with O, then two years later purported to convey it to H. H's agent asked to see the deeds but X replied that he could not as they related also to other property. At first instance it was held that O retained priority because H had constructive notice of the prior incumbrance. The Court of Appeal affirmed the decision, but on the ground that H's agent had acted with such gross carelessness that it would be unjust to deprive O of priority.

11. **Summary**

However unnecessary the doctrine of postponement by gross negligence may be, **20–14** it is undoubtedly part of the law and the decided cases are authority for the following propositions as to when a prior equitable mortgagee[68] will be postponed:

---

[61] (1851) 9 Hare. 449.
[62] (1860) 2 De G. F. & J. 578.
[63] [1899] 2 Ch. 264.
[64] [1921] 1 Ch. 98 at 104.
[65] *Le Neve v. Le Neve* (1748) 3 Atk. 646.
[66] (1843) 11 M. & W. 113 at 116.
[67] [1899] 2 Ch. 264.
[68] *Taylor v. Russell* [1891] 1 Ch. 8 at 14–20; [1892] A.C. 244 at 262.

(1) The weight of the authorities favours the view that the degree of negligence needed to bring about a postponement is the same whether the prior mortgagee is a legal or an equitable mortgagee, though a contrary view had been expressed.[69]

(2) A prior equitable mortgagee will be postponed if:

    (a) his title depends on the deeds and he fails to acquire any of them,[70] and

    (b) he has a right to obtain them and not only fails to do so but fails to give a reasonable explanation for such failure.[71]

(3) A prior equitable mortgagee will not be postponed if:

    (a) he inquired for the deeds and was given a reasonable excuse for their non-production[72];

    (b) he received some of the deeds but reasonably believed he was receiving all of them.[73] The same applies if it was represented to him that the packet of deeds handed to him contained all the necessary deeds and he honestly believed that to be true. He would not lose priority by failure to examine them[74];

    (c) he lent the deeds to the mortgagor on a reasonable representation of his requiring them and was diligent in inquiring for them[75];

    (d) he allowed the deeds to be in the custody of someone in a fiduciary relationship to him who fraudulently or negligently parted with them.[76] But he would be postponed by estoppel[77] if the fiduciary had authority to deal with them.

If he was a second mortgagee and at the time of making the advance the deeds were in the hands of a prior mortgagee he would not be deprived of his priority by failure to give notice of his interest to the earlier incumbrance, even though that resulted in the deeds being returned to the mortgagor on discharge of the earlier mortgage. The same applied if the deeds had not come into existence at the time of the mortgage, as where the leasehold was mortgaged before the head lessor executed the lease.

---

[69] *National Provincial Bank v. Jackson* (1886) 33 Ch.D. 1, CA.

[70] See *Rice v. Rice* (1854) 2 Drew. 73 at 81 *per* Kindersley V.-C.; *Farrand v. Yorkshire Banking Co.* (1889) 40 Ch.D. 182.

[71] *Worthington v. Morgan* (1849) 16 Sim. 547; *Colyer v. Finch* (1856) 5 H.L.C. at 905; *Clarke v. Palmer* (1882) 21 Ch.D. 124.

[72] *Hewitt v. Loosemore* (1851) 9 Hare. 449 *Agra Bank v. Barry* (1874) L.R. 7 H.L. 135; *Barnett v. Weston* (1806) 12 Ves. 130; *Manners v. Mew* (1885) 29 Ch.D. 725.

[73] *Ratcliffe v. Barnard* (1871) L.R. 6 Ch. 652.

[74] *Dixon v. Muckleston* (1872) App. 8 Ch. 155; *Colyer v. Finch* (1856) 5 H.L.C. 905.

[75] *Peter v. Russell* (1716) 1 Eq. Cas. Abr. 321; *Martinez v. Cooper* (1826) 2 Russ 198; *Layard v. Maud* (1867) L.R. 4 Eq. 397.

[76] *Shropshire Union Railways and Canal Co. v. R.* (1875) L.R. 7 H.L. 496; *Re Vernon Ewens & Co.* (1886) 33 Ch.D. 402; *Re Richards* (1890) 45 Ch.D. 589; *Hill v. Peters* [1918] 2 Ch. 273. In *Carritt v. Real and Personal Advance Co.* (1889) 42 Ch.D. 263 it was held that where trustees advanced trust moneys on mortgage, the beneficiaries were not postponed to a subsequent equitable incumbrancer simply because they allowed the deeds to be taken by the trustees, who had subsequently misused them.

[77] *Rimmer v. Webster* [1902] 2 Ch. 163; see also *Heid v. Reliance Finance Corp. Pty.* (1984) 49 A.L.R. 229, High Ct. of Australia.

Where a mortgagee left deeds in the hands of his trustee with authority to deal with them, he was not protected against subsequent equitable incumbrances by setting limits on that authority.[78] However, beneficiaries who so act are protected if the trustee exceeds his apparent authority.[79]

12. Two successive equitable mortgages[80]

As with successive legal mortgages, priority normally depended on the order of **20-15** creation but with the additional condition that, for that rule to apply, the equities had to be equal. Inequitable behaviour on the part of the prior mortgagee could cause him to be postponed. Generally this consisted of misconduct in relation to the title-deeds, which has already been discussed.

PRIORITY OF MORTGAGES OF EQUITABLE INTERESTS IN PERSONALTY: DEARLE V. HALL

As between equitable interests, there is a rule that where the equities are equal the **20-16** first in time prevails. *Dearle v. Hall*[81] was a case in which a person having a beneficial interest in a fund assigned parts of that interest to D and to S respectively for valuable consideration and then, advertising the fund as unencumbered, sold his entire beneficial interest to H. H made enquiries of the trustees and, learning of no prior incumbrance, completed the purchase and gave the trustees notice to pay the dividends of the fund to him. It was held that H gained priority over the prior interests of D and S.

In so holding, Sir Thomas Plumer M.R. cited the case of *Ryall v. Rolle*.[82] There it was said that if a person had a right to possession and failed to exercise it, leaving the property in possession of another and thereby enabling him to gain a false and delusive credit, he must take the consequences. This may include loss of priority to a subsequent purchaser who does exercise his right in the appropriate way, that is, by giving notice to the owner of the legal estate or interest in the property. In affirming that decision[83] Plumer M.R. held that D and S, by neglecting to give the trustees notice of the assignments to them, could not assert the priority arising from the earlier creation of their interests, against H.

Before *Dearle v. Hall* there had never been a case in which a prior mortgagee of an equitable interest in personalty had been postponed to a subsequent mortgagee except where there was fraud on the part of the prior mortgagee.[84] Although the rule in *Dearle v. Hall* was approved by the House of Lords in

---

[78] *Perry-Herrick v. Atwood* (1857) 2 De G. & J. 21. And see *Abbey National Building Society v. Cann* [1991] 1 A.C. 56.

[79] *Capell v. Winter* [1907] 2 Ch. 376.

[80] *Rice v. Rice* (1853) 2 Drew. 73; *cf. Rimmer v. Webster* [1902] 2 Ch. 163. See also *Heid v. Reliance Finance Corp. Pty.* (1984) 49 A.L.R. 229, High Ct. of Australia.

[81] (1823) 3 Russ. 1; affirmed on appeal, *ibid.* at 55. The appeal in the similar case of *Loveridge v. Cooper* (1823) 3 Russ. 30, was heard together with that in *Dearle v. Hall.*

[82] (1750) 1 Ves.Sen. 348.

[83] *Dearle v. Hall* (1823) 3 Russ. 29.

[84] *Cooper v. Fynemore* (1814) 3 Russ. 60, a decision by Plumer V.-C.

Foster v. Cockerell[85] the reasons for its adoption were not clearly and consistently expressed and those reasons were criticised in *Ward v. Duncombe*.[86] The rule itself, however, continued to be accepted and was developed in a series of cases dealing with the nature of notice, the manner in which it was given or received and the effect of the subsequent incumbrancer's knowledge of a prior mortgage. As the rule applied to equitable interests in all forms of personalty it regulated the priorities of successive mortgages of equitable interests in land, such interests being treated as interests in personalty by virtue of the doctrine of conversion[87] prior to the abolition of that doctrine.[88] It does not apply "until a trust has been created" and this has been held to exclude its application to interests of purchasers under a contract of sale or a lease.[89]

In *Dearle v. Hall*, it was not necessary to consider what would have been the situation if H had known, at any time, of the existing interests of D and S, because he had no such knowledge, either actual or constructive. It was later decided[90] that the subsequent incumbrancer who gave notice first would gain priority provided that, at the time he advanced the money, he had no such knowledge. He was not adversely affected if he later acquired such knowledge and then gave notice, that being the very event which would cause him to give notice.[91]

1. **What amounts to notice**

20–17   Although the rule is expressed in terms of gaining priority by giving notice, it is in fact the receipt of the notice by the trustee, or other legal owner, not the giving of notice by the subsequent incumbrancer, that affords priority.[92] Thus in *Lloyd v. Banks*[93] priority was given to the earlier incumbrancer over a later incumbrancer who gave notice when the trustee's knowledge of the earlier incumbrancer had been derived from a newspaper report. Knowledge on which a reasonable man or an ordinary man of business would act in the execution of the trust, would be sufficient. Oral notice would be sufficient provided that it was clear and distinct[94]; however this does not include knowledge imparted in the course of a casual conversation.[95] It does not appear that the decision in *Lloyd v.*

---

[85] (1835) 3 Cl. and F. 456.
[86] *Ward v. Duncombe sub nom. Re Wyatt* [1892] 1 Ch. 188, CA, at 209; [1893] A.C. 369 at 392, *per* Lord Macnaghten; *B.S. Lyle Ltd v. Rosher* [1959] 1 W.L.R. 8, HL.
[87] *Lee v. Howlett* (1856) 2 K. & J. 531.
[88] TLATA 1996, s.3.
[89] *Property Discount Corporation Ltd v. Lyon Group Ltd* [1981] 1 W.L.R. 300.
[90] *Spencer v. Clarke* (1878) 9 Ch.D. 137; *Mutual Life Assurance Society v. Langley* (1886) 32 Ch.D. 460; *Re Holmes* (1885) 29 Ch.D. 786. These cases show that the later incumbrancer who gives notice first obtains priority provided he does not know of the earlier incumbrance when he advances the money; his state of knowledge when he gives notice to the trustees is immaterial.
[91] *Wortley v. Birkhead* (1754) 2 Ves.Sen. 571.
[92] *Calisher v. Forbes* (1871) 7 Ch.App. 109; *Johnstone v. Cox* (1881) 19 Ch.D. 17, CA. See also *Colonial Mutual General Insurance Co. Ltd v. AWZ Banking Group (New Zealand) Ltd* [1995] 1 W.L.R. 1140.
[93] (1868) 3 Ch. App. 488.
[94] *Browne v. Savage* (1859) 4 Drew 635; *cf. Re Worcester* (1868) 3 Ch.App. 555 where a statement of a directors' meeting was held sufficient notice.
[95] *Re Tichener* (1865) 35 Beav. 317.

Banks would apply so as to give a later incumbrancer priority over an earlier incumbrancer who had not given notice.[96] As Megarry[97] puts it, "stronger measures are needed to upset the natural order of the mortgages than are needed to maintain it".

2. To the legal owner

It was laid down in *Addison v. Cox*[98] that notice, to be effective, must be given   **20–18**
to the legal owner of the fund. Notice given to an executor or administrator who renounces probate is therefore ineffective,[99] as is notice given to a trustee before his appointment. In *Ipswich Permanent Money Club Ltd v. Arthy*,[1] this was done and held to be effective on the principle of *Lloyd v. Banks*, but it is thought that the effect would be only to preserve existing priorities rather than to prefer a later incumbrancer to one earlier who had not given notice.

Where the legal owner is a bank, notice is given when, in the ordinary course of business, it would be read. In *Calisher v. Forbes*,[2] X left notice with the bank after closing hours on one day, while Y gave notice immediately the bank opened the next day. It was held that the two notices were to be treated as having been received simultaneously, with the result that the charges ranked in order of creation.[3] Had the charges been created simultaneously, A and B would have shared the fund rateably.[4] Notice given to the solicitors of the trustees was held to be effective in *Foster v. Cockerell*[5] but later decisions held that this will be the case only where the solicitors are agents to receive notice on the trustees' behalf.[6]

3. Funds in court

Where the fund is in court, notice given to the trustees before the fund was paid   **20–19**
into court is effective and it is the duty of the trustees to inform the court of such notice.[7] A notice given to the trustees after payment into court is not effective and only a stop order[8] will gain priority.

---

[96] *Arden v. Arden* (1885) 29 Ch.D. 702.
[97] Megarry & Wade, *The Law of Real Property* (6th ed., 2000), para. 19–212.
[98] (1872) 8 Ch.App. 76.
[99] *Re Dallas* [1904] 2 Ch. 385. .
[1] [1920] 2 Ch. 257.
[2] (1871) 7 Ch.App. 109.
[3] *Boss v. Hopkinson* (1870) 18 W.R. 725. If notices bearing different dates are received on the same day, the notice dated earlier ranks first.
[4] *Re Metropolitan Rail Co., Re Tower Hill Extension Act, Re Rawlins' Estate, ex p. Kent* (1871) 19 W.R. 596.
[5] (1835) 3 Cl. & Fin. 456.
[6] *Saffron Walden Second Benefit Building Society v. Rayner* (1880) 14 Ch.D. 406; *Arden v. Arden* (1885) 29 Ch.D. 702 at 709.
[7] *Livesey v. Harding* (1856) 23 Beav. 141; *Brearcliffe v. Dorrington* (1850) 4 De G. & Sm. 122.
[8] See CPR, Sched. 1, RSC, Ord. 50.

4. **Trustees**

20–20   Where there is more than one trustee it is advisable to give notice to all, since that notice will continue to be effective even if they all retire or die without communicating the notice to their successors.[9] If notice is given to only one trustee it will be effective against all incumbrances created during his trusteeship, even after his death or retirement.[10] It will not be effective against an incumbrance created after his trusteeship has come to an end unless he has communicated that notice to at least one of the remaining trustees.[11] The creator of the earlier incumbrance will have to give a fresh notice in order to protect himself.

If the mortgagor is a trustee, his knowledge does not constitute notice so as to affect priorities. Clearly it would be in his interest to conceal his knowledge from subsequent incumbrancers.[12] Where the mortgagee is a trustee, his knowledge does constitute notice, as it is in his interest to disclose the existence of an existing incumbrance.[13]

5. **Judgment creditors**

20–21   The rule in *Dearle v. Hall* does not apply to a judgment creditor[14] or assignee in bankruptcy[15] of an incumbrancer to enable him, by giving notice, to gain a priority which he has lost by failure to do so, since they stand in his shoes and take subject to prior equities.[16] Nor can a volunteer gain priority over earlier incumbrances by giving notice,[17] although he can protect his priority against later incumbrances by doing so.

(a) *Right to tack*

It is not altogether clear whether the right to tack applies to mortgages of equitable interests in personalty. In *West v. Williams*[18] it was held that it did, where the mortgage was expressed to be made to cover further advances. In *Re Weniger's Policy*[19] it was decided that notice of further advances must be given to the trustees if the mortgage did not cover them. It has been suggested[20] that a

---

[9] *Re Wasdale, Brittin v. Partridge* [1899] 1 Ch. 163. For the complications which occur when there are two trustees and successive incumbrancers give notice to one only, see Fisher and Lightwood, *The Law of Mortgage* (10th ed., 1988) n. (a) at p. 501.

[10] *Ward v. Duncombe*, [1893] A.C. 369 at 394, *per* Lord Macnaghten.

[11] *Timson v. Ramsbottom* (1837) 2 Keen 35; criticised in *Ward v. Duncombe* [1893] A.C. 369 and followed in *Re Phillips Trusts* [1903] 1 Ch. 183. Although criticised in *Ward v. Duncombe* it was accepted by Lord Herschell in the same case, at 381, as it has been in *Meux v. Bell* (1841) 1 Hare 73; *Re Hall* (1880) 7 L.R.Ir. 180; *Re Wyatt, White v. Ellis,* [1892] 1 Ch. 188, CA.

[12] *Browne v. Savage* (1859) 4 Drew 635 at 641; *Lloyds Bank v. Pearson* [1901] 1 Ch. 865.

[13] *Newman v. Newman* (1885) 28 Ch.D. 674.

[14] *Scott v. Lord Hastings* (1858) 4 K. & J. 633, *United Bank of Kuwait v. Sahib* [1997] Ch. 107.

[15] *Re Anderson* [1911] 1 K.B. 896.

[16] *Re Atkinson* (1852) 2 De G. M. & G. 140.

[17] *Justice v. Wynne* (1860) 12 I.Ch.Rep. 289.

[18] [1899] 1 Ch. 132.

[19] [1910] 2 Ch. 291.

[20] Fisher and Lightwood, *The Law of Mortgages* (10th ed., 1988), p. 487 and note (u).

further advance should not be made without inquiring of the trustees whether notice of a subsequent incumbrance has been received.

6. Trustee's position

At any given time a trustee is entitled to pay out the capital or income of a trust **20–22** fund to those persons of whose interests he is aware. So, while notice is not essential to the validity of a mortgage (as between the mortgagor and mortgagee),[21] a mortgagee who gives notice to a trustee protects his own interests by so doing. A trustee will be presumed to have knowledge of such interests as would have been revealed to him by inspection of the documents handed over to him.[22]

He is not liable to a prior assignee of whose interest he is unaware,[23] if he pays out the fund or any part thereof to a subsequent incumbrancer of whom he is aware. He is bound only to pay out to all those of whose existence he knows.[24] If he is a successor trustee, he is not bound to make inquiry of his predecessor as to what notices he received. In *Low v. Bouverie*,[25] it was decided that a trustee was under no duty to answer enquiries from a beneficiary or a prospective mortgagee as to the extent to which the property was incumbered. If he did make such answers, he was bound only to answer to the best of his knowledge and belief and did not have to make enquiries to ascertain whether his existing knowledge was adequate.

The effect of this is somewhat to reduce the value of the rule in *Dearle v. Hall*, since a purchaser who received an honest but incorrect reply from a trustee as to the non-existence of prior incumbrances would have no remedy if these existed, unless the trustee was estopped from denying such non-existence. The purchaser's situation has, in this respect, been somewhat improved by the Law of Property Act 1925, section 137(8).

Part II: Priority According to the 1925 Legislation

General Rules

Before 1926 priorities of mortgages of interests in land depended on the date of **20–23** creation and the superiority of the legal estate, while the rule in *Dearle v. Hall* governed priorities between equitable interests in pure personalty which included interests arising under a trust for sale of land prior to their abolition in 1996.

The 1925 legislation reduced the number of legal estates and put the titles of limited owners "behind the curtain" as equitable interests. The registration system set up by the Land Charges Act 1925 was intended to provide a register of interests which would bind the legal estate in the hands of a subsequent

---

[21] *Burn v. Carvalho* (1839) 4 My. & Cr. 690; *Gorringe v. Irwell India-Rubber and Gutta-Percha Works* (1886) 34 Ch.D. 128, CA.

[22] *Hallows v. Lloyd* (1888) 39 Ch.D. 686.

[23] *Phipps v. Lovegrove* (1873) L.R. 16 Eq. 80.

[24] *Hodgson v. Hodgson* (1837) 2 Keen 704.

[25] [1891] 3 Ch. 82.

purchaser. Consequently, equitable interests which are overreached and become charges on the proceeds of sale of the land have no place in such a register. It therefore follows that the rules for determining priority must depend on whether the interest mortgaged is legal (in which case it is capable of binding the land in the hands of a subsequent purchaser) or equitable and not on whether the mortgage itself is legal or equitable.

The effect of the 1925 legislation is that priority of a mortgage of a legal estate in land depends either on possession of the title deeds or on registration, while priority of a mortgage of any equitable interest, whether in realty or personalty, is governed by the rule in *Dearle v. Hall* as altered by the Law of Property Act 1925, section 137(1).

It is worthy of note that ordinarily where there are two mortgages of the same property the mortgages may vary the order of priority without the mortgagor's consent.[26] It is of course open to a mortgagor who wishes to have secured debt, satisfied in a particular order to require a specific term in the mortgage which prevents the order of priority being changed.[27]

MORTGAGES OF LEGAL ESTATES IN UNREGISTERED LAND[28]

20–24 The Law of Property Act 1925 provides, by section 85(1), that a legal mortgage of a fee simple can be created only by a demise for a term of years absolute or by a charge by deed expressed to be by way of legal mortgage. Both these methods of creation admit the possibility of successive legal mortgages of a legal estate, in which case a system of priorities based on the superiority of the legal estate is inappropriate.

In the rare pre-1925 cases where successive legal mortgages were created by the grant of successive terms of years, priority would normally have been determined by the order of creation. This exposed a later mortgagee or purchaser who had made all reasonable inquiries to the risks that the mortgagor might fraudulently conceal a prior incumbrance. *Grierson v. National Provincial Bank of England Ltd*[29] affords a good example of the difficulties caused by fraudulent concealment. The mortgagor created an equitable mortgage by deposit followed by a legal mortgage by conveyance of the fee simple. The legal mortgagee discovered the existence of the prior equitable mortgagee but did not inform the equitable mortgagee of his own interest. When the equitable mortgage was paid off the deeds were returned to the mortgagor, who negotiated another equitable mortgage by deposit with the bank. Although there was no way in which the bank could have discovered the existence of the concealed legal mortgage, it was held that priority went in order of creation.

---

[26] *Cheah Theam Swee v. Equiticorp Finance Group Ltd* [1992] 2 W.L.R. 108.
[27] *Cheah Theam Swee, ante.* See also *Re Portbase Clothing Ltd* [1992] 3 W.L.R. 14.
[28] A mortgage of unregistered land or of a lease with more than 21 years to run and which is executed after March 1998 triggers a requirement for compulsory registration of the underlying legal estate: LRA 1925, s.123(2), 123A(1) (as substituted by the LRA 1997, s.1).
[29] [1913] 2 Ch. 18. See *ante*, para. 20–06.

1. **Protection by deposit of deeds**

Where a mortgage of a legal estate in unregistered land is protected by deposit **20–25** of title deeds, it is not capable of being registered as a land charge. Priorities between such mortgages are regulated by the pre-1926 rules. It appears that a "protected" mortgage is one which was originally protected, rather than one which has been continuously protected.[30] In the light of the Law of Property (Miscellaneous Provisions) Act 1989,[31] mortgages by deposit of deeds will no longer confer any security.

2. **Protection by registration**

Mortgages which are not protected by a deposit of title deeds and were created **20–26** after 1925 are registrable as land charges. They are of two types, "puisne mortgages" and general equitable charges. The Land Charges Act 1972, section 2(4) defines these as follows. A puisne mortgage is a legal mortgage not protected by a deposit of documents relating to the legal estate affected. A general equitable charge is any equitable charge on land which:

(1) is not included in any other class of land charge; and
(2) is not secured by a deposit of documents relating to the legal estate affected; and
(3) does not arise, or affect any interest arising, under a trust of land or a settlement.

3. **Failure to register**

The Land Charges Act 1972, section 4(5) deals with the effect of failure to **20–27** register such charges and reads as follows:

"A land charge of class B and a land charge of class C (other than an estate contract) created or arising on or after 1st January 1926 shall be void as against a purchaser of the land charged with it, or of any interest in such land, unless the land charge is registered in the appropriate register before the completion of the purchase."

The other provisions relevant to priorities between unprotected mortgages are section 13 of the Law of Property Act 1925 which reads:

"This Act shall not prejudicially affect the right or interest of any person arising out of or consequent on the possession by him of any documents relating to a legal estate in land, nor affect any question arising out of or consequent upon any omission to obtain or any other absence of possession by any person of any documents relating to a legal estate in land"

---

[30] Megarry and Wade, *The Law of Real Property* (6th ed., 2000), para. 19–219.
[31] s.2; *United Bank of Kuwait v. Sahib* [1997] Ch. 107.

and section 97 of the Law of Property Act 1925 as amended by section 18(1) and
Sched. 3, para. 1 of the Land Charges Act 1972:

> "Every mortgage affecting a legal estate in land made after the commence-
> ment of this Act, whether legal or equitable (not being a mortgage protected
> by the deposit of documents relating to the legal estate affected) shall rank
> according to the date of registration as a land charge pursuant to the Land
> Charges Act 1972."

(a) *Effect of the statutory provisions*

20–28   Priorities between unprotected mortgages are regulated by the above provisions,
and three possibilities exist:

(1) If the first mortgage is registered before the second is made, then the
first has priority over the second even if the first is equitable and the
second is legal. By section 198(1) of the Law of Property Act 1925,
registration under the Land Charges Acts of any instrument or matter
required or authorised to be registered under the Act is deemed to
constitute actual notice of the interest registered to all persons and for
all purposes connected with the land affected, as from the date of
registration or other prescribed date, and so long as the registration
continues to be in force. This prevents the subsequent legal mortgagee
from claiming to be a purchaser without notice of the prior equitable
interest.

(2) If the first mortgage is made but remains unregistered, it will be void,
by reason of section 4(5) of the Land Charges Act 1972, against a later
mortgagee. This is so regardless of the legal or equitable character of
the two mortgages.

(3) In both the above cases, the same conclusions are reached regarding
priorities whether section 4(5) of the Land Charges Act 1972 or section
97 of the Law of Property Act 1925 is applied.

(b) *Reconciling sections 44(5) and 97*

20–29   Consider, however, the following sequence of events:

(a) L mortgages Blackacre to A.
(b) L mortgages Blackacre to B.
(c) A registers.
(d) B registers.

The effect of section 4(5) of the Land Charges Act 1972 would be to make A's
mortgage void against B; thus the order of priority is B, A. On the other hand,
section 97 of the Law of Property Act 1925 provides for priority to run according
to order of registration, in which case the order is A, B. Earlier commentators

disagree as to which of these two solutions is to be adopted and there is no judicial decision on the point.[32]

The arguments advanced in favour of the first view are as follows:

(a) If A's mortgage is void against B it has no existence with respect to B and thus it is difficult to see how its subsequent registration can adversely affect B.

(b) Section 97 of the Law of Property Act 1925 refers not simply to registration, but to registration as "a land charge pursuant to the Land Charges Act." It is thus possible to interpret section 97 of the Law of Property Act 1925 as incorporating by reference the rule in section 4(5) of the Land Charges Act 1972 in which case there is no conflict.

(c) In relation to each of the five registers set up by the Land Charges Act 1972 it is provided that in respect of each type of incumbrance failure to register it makes it void against a subsequent purchaser. It is thought improbable that section 97 of the Law of Property Act 1925 was intended to destroy the symmetry of the scheme so set up by establishing a different rule for land charges.

(d) In the same way that, of two irreconcilable provisions in one Act, the later prevails, the provisions of the Land Charges Act 1925, the later statute, should prevail over those of the Law of Property Act 1925 where they conflict irreconcilably.

However, the arguments against this can be summarised as follows:

(e) The simple reading of section 97 of the Law of Property Act 1925 is that the first mortgage to be registered has priority.[33]

(f) The general opinion appears to be that, probably, priority will depend on the date of registration as mentioned in section 97 because that section deals expressly with priority of mortgages whereas the Land Charges Act 1972, section 4(5) deals with the avoidance of charges as against purchasers, and mortgagees are only brought in by reference to the Land Charges Act 1972, section 17(1).[34]

Perhaps the solution lies in adopting (b) above, according to which argument **20–30** the two statutes do not conflict, thus avoiding the unlikely conclusion that Parliament simultaneously enacted contradictory statutes, one expressly referring to the other.[35]

Insoluble problems involving three or more registrable mortgages have been discussed[36]; such problems have been solved in practice by resorting to the doctrine of subrogation. However, this solution is totally arbitrary since there is

---

[32] The problem was considered by Megarry ((1940) 7 C.L.J. 243) who, while stating that the subject is not one for dogmatism, comes down in favour of the first solution which is also adopted by Waldock (*Mortgages* (2nd ed., 1950), pp. 410 *et seq.*) and, more tentatively, by Fisher and Lightwood (*The Law of Mortgage* (10th ed., 1988), p. 509).

[33] Hargreaves, (1950) 13 M.L.R. 534. Megarry and Wade (*The Law of Real Property* (6th ed., 2000), para. 19–225) regard the argument for this interpretation as unconvincing.

[34] *Emmet on Title* (19th ed., 2000), para. 25–10.

[35] See Megarry and Wade, *The Law of Real Property* (6th ed., 2000), para. 19–226.

[36] *ibid.*; (1968) Conv.(N.S.) pp. 325 *et seq.* (W. A. Lee).

no reason for breaking into the circle in which the priorities run at one place rather than another—whatever is done, one creditor will lose a priority which he arguably has over another. It appears that the judicially favoured approach would be to take the mortgages in order of creation and begin by subrogating the latest mortgages to the earliest.[37]

No such difficulties arise where one mortgage is protected and the other is not. If only the first mortgage is protected, its priority runs from the date of its creation and it will have priority over the second, subject to the rules, discussed earlier, regarding loss of priority due to fraud or gross negligence. If only the second mortgage is protected, one of two situations can arise. Where the first mortgage is registered before the second is created, its priority ranks from the date of the registration by virtue of section 97 of the Law of Property Act 1925. Where it is not, it is void against the second mortgage for want of registration. The second mortgage takes priority from the date of its creation and therefore ranks first even if the first mortgage is subsequently registered.

4. **Mortgages of a legal estate in registered land**

20–31 The most important provision dealing with priorities among such mortgages is section 29 of the Land Registration Act 1925, which reads:

> "Subject to any entry to the contrary on the register, registered charges on the same land shall as between themselves rank according to the order in which they are entered on the register, and not according to the order in which they are created."

There is, or is deemed to be, a contrary entry on the register when:

(1) a charge contains provisions altering the normal rules as to priority;
(2) after the registration of two or more charges, a deed altering their priorities is noted on the register;
(3) a charge secures further advances. This fact will be noted in the register so as to give warning of the possible priority of any further advance;
(4) a chargee claims that a charge has priority by virtue of a statute. The fact of such claim is entered on the register. If the charge itself contains a statement about statutory priority, the registration of the charge constitutes a contrary entry.

Since, by sections 20 and 23 of the Land Registration Act 1925, the transferee of registered land or a legal estate therein takes subject only to overriding interests and to incumbrances appearing on the register, a subsequent registered charge has priority over an earlier charge not registered or protected on the register. In *De Lusignan v. Johnson*[38] it was held that a person who acquired a registered charge took free from an unprotected estate contract although he had express knowledge of its existence.

---

[37] Megarry and Wade, *The Law of Real Property* (6th ed., 2000), para. 19–226; (1961) 71 Yale L.J. 53 (G. Gilmore).
[38] (1973) 230 E.G. 499.

5. **Unregistered mortgages**

The creation and protection of unregistered mortgages of registered land is dealt **20–32**
with by section 106 of the Land Registration Act 1925, which, as substituted by
section 26(1) of the Administration of Justice Act 1977,[39] reads as follows:

"(1) The proprietor of any registered land may, subject to any entry to the
contrary on the register, mortgage by deed or otherwise, the land or any part
thereof in any manner which would have been permissible if the land had
not been registered, and with the like effect. Provided that the registered
land comprised in the mortgage is described (whether by reference to the
register or in any other manner) in such a way as is sufficient to enable the
registrar to identify the same without reference to any other documents.
(2) Unless and until the mortgage becomes a registered charge[40];

(a) it shall take effect only in equity, and
(b) it shall be capable of being overridden as a minor interest unless it
is protected as provided by sub-section (3);

(3) A mortgage which is not a registered charge may be protected on the
register by;

(a) a notice under section 49 of this Act,
(b) any such other notice as may be prescribed,
(c) a caution under section 54 of this Act.

(4) A mortgage which is not a registered charge shall devolve and may be
transferred, discharged, surrendered or otherwise dealt with by the same
instruments and in the same manner as if the land has not been
registered."

The effect of sections 101(2) and 106(4) of the Land Registration Act 1925 is **20–33**
that, until protected by notice or caution,[41] unregistered mortgages take effect
only in equity and, as minor interests, will be overridden by a disposition for
valuable consideration.[42]

There is no provision expressly regulating priorities among successive mortgages created off the register. It has been argued[43] that section 52 of the Land
Registration Act 1925 has the effect of giving priority among such mortgages in
order of their creation, but this has been doubted.[44]

---

[39] The amendment abolished the mortgage caution which was formerly the only way of protecting an
unregistered mortgage by deed. The Administration of Justice Act 1977, section 26(2) provided for
the conversion of any mortgage already protected by a mortgage caution into a registered
charge.
[40] By the Land Registration Act 1925, s.3(xiii) the term "registered charge" includes a mortgage or
incumbrance registered under that Act.
[41] See, however, *Mortgage Corporation Ltd v. Nationwide Credit Corporation Ltd* [1993] 3 W.L.R.
769.
[42] See *Clark v. Chief Land Registrar* [1994] 3 W.L.R. 593.
[43] (1977) 43 L.Q.R. 541 (R. J. Smith).
[44] Hayton, *Registered Land* (3rd ed., 1981), p. 141.

LIENS[45]

20–34   Prior to April 3, 1995 it was possible to create a lien over registered land by depositing the land certificate with a mortgagee.[46] Such a lien operated as a contract to create a charge[47] but following upon the enactment of the Law of Property (Miscellaneous Provisions) Act 1989, section 2 such a contract would only have been valid if in writing and in compliance with provisions of that section.[48] Accordingly the Land Registration Rules 1925, r. 239 was amended[49] such that it was now no longer possible to protect a lien by notice of deposit or intended deposit of the land certificate as formerly was the case. An entry which existed on the register before April 3, 1995 operates as a caution until it is cancelled.[50] Current practice demands that a lien under section 66 of the Land Registration Act 1925 is now protected by the entry of notice on the register.[51] If it is subsequently sought to exercise a power of sale, the mortgagee must obtain registration of his charge.[52]

MORTGAGES OF EQUITABLE INTERESTS

20–35   Priorities among mortgages of equitable interests in land arising under a trust are regulated by the rule in *Dearle v. Hall* as amended by sections 137 and 138 of the Law of Property Act 1925 (as amended by the Trusts of Land and Appointment of Trustees Act 1996).[53] According to that rule, priority depends on the order in which notice of the mortgages is received by the trustees. By section 137(10), the rule does not apply until a trust has been created. It is considered that this provision excludes the interest of a purchaser under a contract of sale or lease.[54] Section 137(3) provides that the notice must be in writing, whereas under the original rule, oral notice was sufficient.[55]

Section 137(2) specifies the persons to whom notice must be given, namely, the trustees of the settlement if the interest is in settled land; the trustees of the trust of land if the interest arises under such trust; and, in any other cases, the estate owner (*i.e.* the owner of the legal estate) of the land affected. Under the old law it was advisable to give notice to all the trustees[56] and the 1925 legislation does not alter this position.

---

[45] See *ante*, para. 1–07 *et seq.* and para. 5–06 *et seq.*

[46] LRA 1925, s.66; *Thames Guaranty Limited v. Campbell* [1985] Q.B. 210 at 232.

[47] *Thames Guaranty Limited, ante*; *Re Alton Corporation* [1985] B.C.L.C. 27 at 33.

[48] *United Bank of Kuwait v. Sahib* [1987] Ch. 107.

[49] And rr. 240–243 revoked by LLR 1995, S.I. 1995 No. 140, r. 4(1), 4(4) (as amended by LRR 1995, S.I. 1995 No. 140, r. 4).

[50] LLR 1925, r. 239(1) (as amended by LRR 1995, S.I. 1995 No. 140, r. 4).

[51] See Rouff & Roper, *Registered Conveyancing*, para. 25–07.

[52] *ibid.*, 28–33(4).

[53] The Land Registration Act 1925, s.102(2) formerly made provisions for priorities between certain dealings of equitable interests in registered land to be determined in accordance with the lodging of priority cautions and inhibitions in the Minor Interests Index. This subs. has now been repealed by the Land Registration Act 1986, s.5(1). Consequently, s.137(1) now determines questions of priority both in respect of registered and unregistered land. For the way in which existing entries are to be treated, see 1986 Act, s.5(2)–(4).

[54] Megarry and Wade, *The Law of Real Property* (6th ed., 2000), para. 19–233.

[55] *Browne v. Savage* (1859) 4 Drew 635; *Re Worcester* (1868) 3 Ch.App. 555.

[56] *Lloyds Bank v. Pearson* [1901] 1 Ch. 865; *Timson v. Ramsbottom* (1837) 2 Keen 35; *Re Wasdale, Brittin v. Partridge* [1899] 1 Ch. 163; *Ward v. Duncombe* [1892] 1 Ch. 188, CA.

Section 137(4) sets out the procedure to be adopted where the valid notice cannot be served either because there are no trustees or because its service would involve unreasonable cost or delay. The purchaser may require the endorsement of a memorandum on the instrument creating the trust or (where the trust is created by statute or operation of law) on the document under which the equitable interest is acquired or which evidences its devolution. Such an indorsement has the same effect as notice to the trustees.

By section 138 of the Law of Property Act 1925, a trust corporation may be nominated to receive the notice. Where this is the case, notice to the trustees is ineffective. Notice does not affect priorities until delivered to the corporation.

The Law of Property Act 1925, section 137(8), (9) brings about a change in the law relating to the duty to produce notices. In the case of *Low v. Bouverie*[57] it was held that trustees were not bound to answer inquiries by a prospective mortgagee or a beneficiary regarding the extent to which a beneficiary's share was incumbered. By section 137(8) any person interested in the equitable interest may require the trustee to produce all such notices. Section 137(9) places a corresponding liability on the estate owner.

PRIORITY BETWEEN MORTGAGEE AND BENEFICIAL OWNER

1. The decision in William & Glyn's Bank v. Boland

In the case of *Williams and Glyn's Bank v. Boland*[58] the husband was registered **20–36** as sole proprietor of the matrimonial home in which he and his wife lived and towards the purchase of which she had substantially contributed. She had not protected the equitable interest thus acquired by entering a notice, caution or restriction on the register. The husband, without her consent, mortgaged the house to the bank to secure his business indebtedness and the bank made no inquiries of her. The question which arose was whether that equitable interest constituted an overriding interest by which the mortgagee Bank was bound.

Section 70(1)(*g*) of the Land Registration Act 1925 provides that the class of overriding interests shall include:

"The rights of every person in actual occupation of the land or in receipt of the rents and profits thereof, save where enquiry is made of such person and the rights are not disclosed . . . "

Lord Wilberforce found no difficulty in concluding that a spouse, living in a house, has an actual occupation capable of conferring protection upon his or her

---

[57] [1891] 3 Ch. 82 at 99.
[58] [1981] A.C. 487, varying the decision of the Court of Appeal at [1979] Ch. 312, which allowed the appeal of Mr. and Mrs. Boland against the decision of Templeman J. at (1978) P. & C.R. 448. This appeal was heard together with *Williams and Glyn's Bank v. Brown* in which at first instance H.H. Judge Clapham applied Templeman J.'s decision, making an order for possession in favour of the Bank.

rights as an overriding interest.[59] In so concluding, he rejected arguments that the occupation, to come within the section, must be inconsistent with the rights of the vendor.[60] He then went on to consider whether such equitable interests were "minor interests" as defined by section 3(xv) of the Land Registration Act 1925. Although holding that the interests of co-owners under the statutory trusts[61] are minor interests, he considered that any such interests, if protected by actual occupation, acquired the status of an overriding interest, being, as section 70 of the Land Registration Act 1925 requires, interests subsisting in reference to land.[62]

2. **Effect of Boland**

20–37   This decision, as Lord Wilberforce recognised, had important consequences for conveyancers, which he formulated in these words[63]:

> "What is involved is a departure from an easy-going practice of dispensing with enquiries as to occupation beyond that of the vendor and accepting the risks of doing so. To substitute for this a practice of more careful enquiry as to the facts of occupation, and, if necessary, as to the rights of occupiers can not, in my view of the matter, be considered as unacceptable except at the price of overlooking the widespread development of shared interest in ownership."

The Law Commission considered that the law in this field had been left in a most unsatisfactory state.[64] The report made three recommendations, one for overcoming the conveyancing problems faced by purchasers and mortgagees,[65] and the others for protecting and establishing the interests of married co-owners in the matrimonial home.[66] As yet, that report has not been acted upon.

---

[59] *ibid.*, at p. 506. A person in actual occupation of part of land comprised in a registered disposition could enforce against the new registered proprietor any overriding interest which he had either in the land or part of the land occupied by him or in the remainder of the land comprised in the disposition in question. See *Ferrishurst Ltd v. Wallcite Ltd* [1999] Ch. 355.

[60] Disapproving *Caunce v. Caunce* [1969] 1 W.L.R. 286 and *Bird v. Syme-Thompson* [1979] 1 W.L.R. 440 at 444, and approving *Hodgson v. Marks* [1971] Ch. 892, CA, at 934 *per* Russell L.J.

[61] Defined in s.35 of LPA 1925.

[62] *Elias v. Mitchell* [1972] Ch. 652, *cf. Cedar Holdings Ltd v. Green* [1981] Ch. 129; for cases in which it was held that equitable interests other than those of tenants in common could be overriding interests if protected by actual occupation, see *Bridges v. Mees* [1957] Ch. 475; *Hodgson v. Marks* [1971] Ch. 892, CA.

[63] [1981] A.C. 487 at 508, 509.

[64] Law Commission Report No. 115, Cmnd. 8636 (1982), at paras. 2.52–2.54, *The Implications of Williams and Glyn's Bank v. Boland.*

[65] That co-ownership interests in land should be registrable at H.M. Land Registry and should be protected against purchasers and mortgagees if, and only if, they were so registered.

[66] That: (i) the interest of every married co-owner in the matrimonial home should carry with it a right to prevent any dealing being made without that co-owner's consent or a court order; and (ii) as a general rule married couples should, in the absence of agreement to the contrary, have an equal ownership of the matrimonial home.

3. **Enquiries to be made**

A problem which soon became apparent was that no guidance had been given as **20–38** to the extent and nature of the inquiries which would be necessary in order to ascertain the existence of persons in occupation and their equitable rights.

Criticism was also made of the fact that section 70(1)(g) does not limit the scope of such inquiries by reference to any concept of "reasonable inquiry"[67] The section does not specify who must make the inquiry, although it has been accepted that in most cases this could properly be done by the solicitor acting for the purchaser,[68] nor does it specify when inquiry or disclosure ought to be made. It is clear, however, that the inquiry must be made of the person whose rights would otherwise amount to an overriding interest.[69]

The difficulties facing a purchaser in making adequate inquiries have been extensively discussed.[70] In unregistered land conveyancing it had been decided in *Caunce v. Caunce*[71] that notice of the presence of the wife in the matrimonial home was not, of itself, notice of any interest that she might have. The decision came under judicial attack[72] and was not followed in *Kingsnorth Trust Ltd v. Tizard*.[73] In that case it was held that the mortgagee had not made such inquiries as ought reasonably to have been made by him and was therefore fixed with constructive notice of the wife's interest.[74] Two facts which (it was held) fixed Kingsnorth with constructive notice of the wife's interest were T's informing the surveyor that he was married but separated from his wife, who lived nearby, although he had described himself as single on the application form, and evidence of occupation by teenage children. In addition, however, the judge took the view that, in the circumstances, the pre-arranged inspection was not within the category of "such . . . inspections . . . as ought reasonably to have been made."[75]

Two decisions[76] have gone some way to restricting the effect of *Boland*, in that where it is established that a person who subsequently seeks to assert an overriding interest knew that the registered proprietor was acquiring the property with the assistance of a mortgage, an intention has been imputed to that person to the effect that their overriding interest should be postponed to the prior interest of the mortgagee.

---

[67] Law Com. Report No. 158, H.C. 267 (1987), para. 2.59 at para. 2.57, the Report recommends that all categories of overriding interest be made explicitly subject to the jurisdiction of the courts to postpone them in favour of subsequent purchasers and lenders on general grounds of fraud or estoppel.

[68] *Winkworth v. Edward Baron Development Co. Ltd* [1986] 1 W.L.R. 1512.

[69] *Hodgson v. Marks* [1971] Ch. 892; *Kling v. Keston Properties* (1985) 49 P. & C.R. 212 at 220.

[70] (1979) 95 L.Q.R. 501 (R.J. Smith); [1980] Conv. 85, 311 and 318; [1980] Conv. 361 (J. Martin); *Kling v. Keston Properties*, *supra*, at 222; (1986) 136 New L.J. 771 (P. Luxton); *Kingsnorth Finance Co. v. Tizard* [1986] 1 W.L.R. 783; K. Gray, *Elements of Land Law* (1st ed., 1987), pp. 189–92 and 852–862; *Emmet on Title* (19th ed., 2000), para. 5–200.

[71] [1969] 1 W.L.R. 286.

[72] *Williams and Glyn's Bank v. Boland* [1981] A.C. 487 at 505–506.

[73] [1986] 1 W.L.R. 783.

[74] LPA 1925, s.199(1)(ii)(*a*) and s.205(1)(xxi) ("purchaser" includes "mortgagee").

[75] [1986] 1 W.L.R. 783 at 795.

[76] *Bristol and West Building Society v. Henning* [1985] 1 W.L.R. 783 (which did not expressly consider *Boland*, *ante*); *Paddington Building Society v. Mendlesohn* [1985] 1 W.L.R. 778 (which did).

Further, in *Equity & Law Loans v. Prestidge*[77] the intention imputed to the second defendant (O) who sought to assert her prior beneficial interest was held to be the same with regard to a second mortgage (of which O was genuinely ignorant) which redeemed and replaced the first mortgage (of which O was aware) on no less favourable terms. The court held that the charge in favour of the second mortgage enjoyed priority to O's interest up to the amount for which consent was to be imputed to her in relation to the first mortgage.

Thus, *Boland* will not unduly trouble banks or building societies in such circumstances since there can be few cases in which the equitable co-owner of a property will be unaware that the acquisition is being financed at least in part by way of mortgage.

4. Time at which the interest is to be determined

20–39   In *Abbey National Building Society v. Cann*,[78] the House of Lords made clear that whilst the relevant date for determining the existence of overriding interests affecting the estate transferred or created was the date of registration of the estate (and not the date of transfer or creation of that estate), in order successfully to claim an overriding interest against a transferee or chargee of by virtue of section 70(1)(g), the person claiming that interest had to have been in occupation at the time of the creation or transfer of the legal estate. The argument that a *scintilla temporis* could somehow arise in a conveyancing transaction, thereby allowing an individual in possession prior to the registration of a charge to acquire an overriding interest which would bind the mortgagee was emphatically rejected.

In *Lloyds Bank Ltd v. Rossett*,[79] the House of Lords confirmed that where a wife claims that she has a beneficial interest in a house registered in her husband's sole name and that her interest has priority over the rights of the mortgagee under a legal charge executed without her knowledge, then in order to claim the protection afforded to overriding interests by section 70(1)(g) the wife must be in actual occupation of the house when the relevant estate is transferred or created, not the date when it is registered. In *Chhokar v. Chhokar and Parmar*,[80] it was held that the purchaser, who had bought the house at an undervalued price, and thereafter attempted to prevent the wife (who had contributed to the purchase price) acquiring an overriding interest by occupation, nevertheless took subject to that interest because she was in actual occupation at the time when registration of the purchaser's title was sought. Whilst it is clear that in the case of a first registration of title it is the date of registration which is decisive,[81] there appears to be no firm rule in the case of a transfer of an existing registered title.

---

[77] [1992] 1 W.L.R. 137 in which *Bristol and West Building Society v. Henning, ante*, was followed.
[78] [1991] 1 A.C. 56, HL.
[79] [1991] 1 A.C. 107, HL.
[80] [1984] F.L.R. 313, CA; (1984) 14 Fam.Law 269, CA.
[81] *Re Boyle's Claim* [1961] 1 W.L.R. 339. For discussion of what is actually decided by this case, see *Emmet on Title* (19th ed., 1985), para. 5–125; Megarry and Wade, *Law of Real Property* (6th ed., 2000) para. 6–049. So far as the proposition in the text is concerned, the case has been followed in *Schwab and Co. v. McCarthy* (1975) 31 P. & C.R. 196 at 204 and in *Kling v. Keston Properties* (1985) 49 P. & C.R. 212 at 218.

5. **Overreaching of interests**

It was not necessary to consider in *Boland* whether the interests of the beneficial   **20–40**
owners were overreached, as the mortgage money was paid to a sole registered
proprietor. In that case, Lord Wilberforce said[82]:

> "Undivided shares in land can only take effect in equity behind a trust for
> sale upon which the legal owner is to hold the land. Dispositions of the land,
> including mortgages, may be made under this trust and, provided there are
> at least two trustees or a trust corporation, 'overreach' the trusts. This means
> the 'purchaser' takes free from them whether or not he has notice of them,
> and the trusts are enforceable against the proceeds of sale."

6. **City of London Building Society v. Flegg**[83]

The question did arise in *City of London Building Society v. Flegg*. The registered   **20–41**
proprietors of Bleak House were a Mr and Mrs Maxwell-Brown, the daughter
and son-in-law of Mr. and Mrs. Flegg, who had contributed over half of the
purchase price, having sold their own home in order to do so and with the
intention that all four should live together. The Maxwell-Browns raised their
contribution by means of a mortgage and later, without the knowledge or consent
of the Fleggs, executed three more charges, the third being for the purpose of
discharging all the earlier charges. The Fleggs had been in occupation throughout
and no inquiries had ever been made of them as to whether they claimed any
interest in the property. The Maxwell-Browns defaulted on the mortgage repayments and the mortgagee sought possession. The House of Lords overturned a
much-criticised decision of the Court of Appeal and held that the Fleggs'
interests under the trust for sale were overreached. Lord Templeman[84] considered
that this was brought about by sections 27 and 28[85] of the Law of Property Act
1925, while Lord Oliver's more extensive analysis referred also to sections 2 and
26 of the same Act.[86] Although the decision of the House of Lords has been
welcomed,[87] the basis of it has been questioned.[88] Even so it is quite clear that
the equitable interest of a beneficiary under a trust of land may be overreached
if the mortgage is granted by not less than two trustees of that trust and the capital
monies are paid to them.[89] Thus from the mortgagee's point of view fail safe
practice dictates a refusal to deal with a sole proprietor and the appointment of
a second trustee, with all mortgage monies being paid to both. Such caution
however rarely manifests itself.

After the decision in *Boland*, institutional mortgagees in many cases sought to
protect themselves against the rights of occupiers by requiring them to sign forms

---

[82] [1981] A.C. 487 at 503.
[83] [1986] Ch. 605, CA; reversed [1988] A.C. 54, restoring the decision of the judge at first
instance.
[84] [1988] A.C. 54 at 71–72.
[85] s.28 now repealed by TLATA 1996, Sched. 4. See *ibid.*, s.6 for powers of trustees of land.
[86] *ibid.* at 80–81, 83, 90–91.
[87] See, *e.g. Emmet on Title* (19th ed., 2000) para. 5–202.
[88] [1987] Conv. 451 (W.J. Swadling); [1988] Conv. 141 (P. Sparkes); [1980] Conv. 313 (draft
Editorial Practice Note) entitled "Occupational Hazards."
[89] Reinforced in *Lloyds Bank v. Carrick* [1996] 4 All E.R. 680, CA.

of acknowledgement, consent or waiver. This device was, for a number of reasons, less effective than mortgagees would have wished. In the first place, it was inadequate to give protection against the rights of an equitable co-owner who was in constructive occupation.[90] Next, some persons may not be capable of giving a valid consent to the release of their rights.[91] Most importantly, however, an occupier who gives such a consent may seek to claim that the consent was vitiated by duress or undue influence.[92]

TACKING

20–42 Tacking has been described[93] as a special way of obtaining priority for a secured loan by amalgamating it with another secured loan of higher priority. Before 1926 there were two forms of tacking, of which one has been abolished by the 1925 legislation and the law as to the other has been amended.

1. Tabula in naufragio

20–43 The form which has been abolished[94] is the *tabula in naufragio* ("plank in the shipwreck"). The opportunity to tack in this manner occurred when a borrower B created a legal mortgage in favour of L followed by successive equitable mortgages in favour of M and N. If N then took a transfer of L's mortgage ("the plank") he would, provided he had no notice of M's mortgage when he advanced his money[95] obtain priority over M if B defaulted ("the shipwreck"). Tacking in this manner depended on the superiority of the legal estate[96]; provided the equities between M and N were equal,[97] N's possession of[98] or best right to call for the legal estate[99] upset the natural priorities which were governed by order of creation. Prior legal estates or rights to call for legal estates which were sufficient to bring the doctrine into operation included a term of years,[1] a judgment giving legal rights against the land,[2] an express declaration of trust by the owner of the legal estate in favour of the mortgagee who sought to tack[3] or a transfer of the legal estate to a trustee for such a mortgagee.[4] The right to tack was lost as soon

---

[90] See *Strand Securities v. Caswell* [1965] Ch. 958, CA, for discussion of what constitutes occupation for the purposes of s.70(1)(*g*) of Land Registration Act 1925.

[91] The Law Commission recognised this, referring in its Report No. 115, Cmnd. 8636 (1982) at para. 42(1)(*b*) to patients and minors.

[92] See chap. 26.

[93] Megarry and Wade, *The Law of Real Property* (6th ed., 2000), para. 19–243.

[94] LPA 1925, s.94(3), without afecting priority acquired before the passing of the Act.

[95] *Brace v. Duchess of Marlborough* (1728) 2 P.Wms. 491.

[96] *Bailey v. Barnes* [1894] 1 Ch. 25 at 36, *per* Lindley L.J.; "a curious example of the deference paid by equity to the legal estate."

[97] *Lacey v. Ingle* (1847) 2 Ph. 413; *Rooper v. Harrison* (1855) 2 K. & J. 86, in which it was held that, if the mortgagee subsequently parts with the legal estate, he lost the right to tack.

[98] *Wortley v. Birkhead* (1754) 2 Ves.Sen. 571.

[99] *Wilkes v. Bodington* (1707) 2 Vern. 599; *ex p. Knott* (1806) 11 Ves. 609.

[1] *Willoughby v. Willoughby* (1756) 1 Term. Rep. 763; *Maundrell v. Maundrell* (1804) 10 Ves. 246; *Cooke v. Wilton* (1860) 29 Beav. 100.

[2] *Morret v. Paske* (1740) 2 Atk. 52.

[3] *Wilmot v. Pike* (1845) 5 Hare 14.

[4] *Earl of Pomfret v. Lord Windsor* (1752) 2 Ves.Sen. 472; *Stanhope v. Earl Verney* (1761) 2 Eden 81; *Pease v. Jackson* (1868) 3 Ch.App. 576; *Crosbie-Hill v. Sayer* [1908] 1 Ch. 866.

as the mortgagee parted with the legal estate[5] and did not arise unless the legal estate and the mortgage were held in the same right.[6]

Notice acquired after the advance was made by N but before he got in the legal estate did not prevent him tacking.[7] Notice to L, the holder of the legal estate, was immaterial, so M could not prevent N tacking by giving notice to L of his mortgage.[8] This opened the possibility of L and N conspiring to cheat M.[9]

If a legal estate was held on trust for M, and N has notice of the trust, he was bound by it and could not get that estate in so as to tack.[10]

2. Tacking of further advances

The more important form of tacking was the tacking of further advances. The **20–44** mortgagor might wish to raise further sums on the property at a later date (as where he was developing a building estate) or the mortgagee might contemplate a variation in the state of the mortgagor's account and be prepared to make further advances. Where B mortgaged the property first to L, then to M, then took a further advance from L, it was possible, in certain circumstances, for L's further advance to be tacked on to the original advance, displacing M's priority.

Where L had no notice of the mortgage in favour of M, tacking was allowed provided one of two conditions was satisfied:

(1) Where L was either a legal mortgagee[11] or an equitable mortgagee with the best right to call for the legal estate.[12] As with the *tabula in naufragio*, priority resulted from the superiority of the legal estate.

(2) Where the mortgage to L expressly provided for the security to be extended to cover further advances, whether or not such further advances were obligatory. This form of tacking was independent of the legal estate. Originally it had been held that where M had notice that L's mortgage was expressed to cover further advances he took subject to L's right to tack further advances.[13] This, however, was overruled by a divided House of Lords[14] and the rule that notice of a subsequent incumbrance prevented the first mortgagee from tacking further

---

[5] *Rooper v. Harrison* (1855) 2 K. & J. 86.

[6] *Harnett v. Weston* (1806) 12 Ves. 130.

[7] *Taylor v. Russell* [1892] A.C. 244.

[8] *Peacock v. Burt* (1834) 4 L.J.Ch. 33.

[9] *West London Commercial Bank v. Reliance Permanent Building Society* (1885) 29 Ch.D. 954.

[10] *Sharples v. Adams* (1863) 32 Beav. 213; *Mumford v. Stohwasser* (1874) L.R. 18 Eq. 556; *Taylor v. London and County Banking Co.* [1901] 2 Ch. 231; *Saunders v. Dehew* (1692) 2 Vern. 271.

[11] *Wyllie v. Pollen* (1863) 3 De G.J. & S. 596.

[12] *Wilkes v. Bodington* (1707) 2 Vern. 599; *Wilmot v. Pike* (1845) 5 Hare. 14; *Taylor v. London and County Banking Co.* [1901] 2 Ch. 231; see also *McCarthy & Stone Ltd v. Hodge & Co.* [1971] 1 W.L.R. 1547.

[13] *Gordon v. Graham* (1716) 2 Eq.Cas.Abr. 598.

[14] *Hopkinson v. Rolt* (1861) 9 H.L.C. 514; see also *London & County Banking Co. Ltd v. Ratcliffe* (1881) 6 App.Cas. 722; *Bradford Banking Co. v. Briggs & Co. Ltd* (1886) 12 App.Cas. 29; *Union Bank of Scotland v. National Bank of Scotland* (1886) 12 App.Cas. 53; *Matzner v. Clyde Securities Ltd* [1975] 2 N.S.W.L.R. 293; *Central Mortgage Registry of Australia Ltd v. Donemore Pty. Ltd* [1984] 2 N.S.W.L.R. 128.

advances was applied even where the first mortgage contained a covenant to make further advances.[15] In that case, however, the creation of
M's mortgage released L from the obligation to make any further
advances, since further advances to him could no longer have the same
priority as the original mortgage.

Tacking could also take place if M agreed that further advances to L should have
priority over his mortgage. This was a matter of contract between the parties and
it was immaterial whether L was a legal or equitable mortgagee.

3. The modern position

(a) *Unregistered Land*

20–45 The law as to tacking is now set out in section 94 of the Law of Property Act
1925, which reads:

> "(1) After the commencement of this Act, a prior mortgagee shall have a
> right to make further advances to rank in priority to subsequent mortgages
> (whether legal or equitable)—
>
> > (*a*) if an arrangement has been made to that effect with the subsequent
> > mortgagees; or
> > (*b*) if he had *no notice of such subsequent mortgages* at the time when
> > the further advance was made by him; or
> > (*c*) whether or not he had such notice as aforesaid, where the mortgage
> > imposes an obligation on him to make such further advances.
>
> This subsection applies whether or not the prior mortgage was made
> expressly for securing further advances.
>
> (2) In relation to the making of further advances after the commencement
> of this Act a mortgagee shall not be deemed to have notice of a mortgage
> merely by reason that it was registered as a land charge[16] if it was not so
> registered at the time when the original mortgage was created or when the
> last search (if any) by or on behalf of the mortgagee was made, whichever
> last happened.
>
> This subsection only applies where the prior mortgage was made
> expressly for securing a current account or other further advances.
>
> (3) Save in regard to the making of further advances as aforesaid, the
> right to tack is hereby abolished:
>
> Provided that nothing in this Act shall affect any priority acquired before
> the commencement of this Act by tacking, or in respect of further advances
> made without notice of a subsequent incumbrance or by arrangement with
> the subsequent incumbrancer.

---

[15] *West v. Williams* [1899] 1 Ch. 132, CA.
[16] Repealed by LPA 1969, s.16(2), Sched. 2, Pt. 1.

(4) This section applies to mortgages of land before or after the commencement of this Act, but not to charges registered under the Land Registration Act 1925, or any enactment replaced by that Act."

Section 94(1) extends the doctrine of tacking in two ways. It makes the nature of the prior mortgage immaterial and it applies to any prior mortgagee; thus if B successively mortgages the property to L, M, N and M again, M has the right to tack subject to any provisions as to notice. Section 94(1)(a) preserves the pre-1926 position as to tacking with the consent of subsequent mortgagees. Section 94(1)(b) again preserves the pre-1926 position as laid down in *Hopkinson v. Rolt*,[17] but, by virtue of section 198 of the Law of Property Act 1925 registration of the subsequent mortgage as a land charge constitutes deemed actual notice. Section 94(1)(c) reverses the principle of *West v. Williams*[18] in that, where there is an obligation to make further advances, notice to the prior mortgagee does not affect his right to tack. Therefore, a mortgagee must make a search whenever he makes a further advance, unless the mortgage is made expressly to secure further advances or a current account. He is not affected by an unregistered mortgage unless he has actual notice of it.

20–46

Section 94(1) permits tacking of further advances to rank in priority to subsequent mortgages; thus the mortgagee who wishes to tack is bound by other intervening interests which are registered. It is suggested that the failure to give priority over such interests is a flaw in drafting.[19] Emmet[20] refers to the situation where an estate contract has been registered between dates of the original and a further advance. The mortgagee would be deemed to make the further advance with notice of the estate contract. It would therefore seem that he could be compelled to release his security in favour of the purchaser on receiving only the amount of the original advance if it was the case that the purchase price was insufficient to repay both the original and the further advance. The risk involved in not searching before making a further advance is discussed by Rowley,[21] as is the meaning of the words "for securing a current account or other further advances."[22]

Section 94(2)[23] provides an exception to the rule laid down by section 198(1) of the Law of Property Act 1925 that registration constitutes deemed actual notice. If the prior mortgage is made expressly for securing a current account or further advances, registration of a subsequent charge is not equivalent to actual notice of that charge to the prior mortgagee and he can tack against that charge provided that he had no actual notice of it at the time of the further advance. He takes, of course, subject to any charges which were registered at the time of the original advance. The reason for this exception to section 198 is to make it unnecessary for a bank to have to search the register before cashing each cheque drawn by a borrower who has a secured overdraft, although the exception applies whenever the mortgagee contemplates further advances on the same security.

---

[17] (1861) 9 H.L.C. 514.
[18] [1899] 1 Ch. 132.
[19] Maitland, *Equity* (8th ed., 1949), p. 214.
[20] *Emmet on Title* (19th ed., 2000), para. 25–108.
[21] (1958) 22 Conv.(N.S.) 44 at 56.
[22] *ibid.* at 49.
[23] As amended by the Law of Property (Amendment) Act 1926. The amendment safeguards a mortgage registered before the principal mortgage was created.

4. **Protecting a subsequent mortgagee**

20–47   Consequently, a subsequent mortgagee who wishes to protect himself from loss of priority by tacking should give notice to all prior mortgagees, in case their mortgages are in a form which allows them to tack further advances against registered incumbrances. Giving notice to the immediately prior mortgagee also fixes him with the duty to hand over the deeds when that mortgage is discharged.

5. **The position of banks**

20–48   Banks are affected by the rule in *Clayton's Case*,[24] the effect of which is that where there is an unbroken account between the parties, or "one blended fund" as in the case of a current account at a bank, in the absence of any express appropriation each payment is impliedly appropriated to the earliest debt that is not statute-barred. Thus, where a prior mortgage is made to secure a current account with a bank and notice of a subsequent mortgage is received, subsequent payments reduce the overdraft existing at the time of the notice and these improve the position of the later mortgagee.[25] The bank can avoid this result by closing the account and if it wishes opening a new account into which the mortgagor's subsequent payments are made.[26] The parties can agree to exclude the rule, which can also be displaced if an intention to exclude it appears from the circumstances.[27]

6. **Registered charges of registered land**

20–49   Section 94(4) of the Law of Property Act 1925 excludes charges on registered land under the Land Registration Act 1925. Further advances on the security of such charges are dealt with by section 30 of that Act:

> "(1) Where a registered charge is made for securing further advances, the registrar shall, before making any entry on the register which would prejudicially affect the priority of any further advance hereunder, give the proprietor of the charge, at his registered address, notice by registered post of the intended entry, and the proprietor of the charge shall not, in respect of any further advance, be affected by such entry, unless the advance is made after the date when the notice ought to have been received by registered post.
>
> (2) If, by reason of any failure on the part of the registrar or the post office in reference to the notice, the proprietor of the charge suffers loss in relation to a further advance, he shall be entitled to be indemnified under this Act in like manner as if a mistake had occurred in the register; but if the loss arises

---

[24] (1816) 1 Mer. 572.
[25] *Deeley v. Lloyds Bank* [1912] A.C. 756, HL.
[26] *Re Sherry* (1884) 25 Ch.D. 692.
[27] *Re James R. Rutherford & Sons* [1964] 1 W.L.R. 1211. For obvious reasons the rule is habitually excluded.

by reason of an omission to register or amend the address for service, no indemnity shall be payable under this Act.

(3) Where the proprietor of a charge is under an obligation noted on the register, to make a further advance, a subsequent registered charge shall take effect subject to any further advance made pursuant to the obligation."

Where the proprietor of a registered charge to secure further advances (but without obligation to do so) receives notice of any subsequent registered charge he can refuse to make any further advance. If he does make an advance, it has priority over a subsequent charge which is not registered but it has no priority over a subsequent charge which is registered before the further advance is made, unless the proprietor of the subsequent charge agrees to postpone his charge.

CHAPTER 21

TRANSFER AND DEVOLUTION OF RIGHTS UNDER THE SECURITY

Inter Vivos Transfer of the Mortgage

1. General

A mortgagee, like any other owner, has a right to alienate his interest either **21–01** absolutely or by way of sub-mortgage.[1] His interest comprises two distinct titles; his title to the mortgage debt and his title to the mortgaged property. Conceivably, therefore, he may assign the debt without the title and *vice versa*. Accordingly, before 1926 it was the practice expressly to provide both for the assignment of the debt and the conveyance of the security, and presumably this is still necessary when the transfer is not effected by deed. In the case of a deed executed after December 31, 1925, section 114(1) of the Law of Property Act 1925 provides that—subject to the expression of a contrary intention—the deed shall operate to transfer:

"(a) the right to demand, sue for, recover, and give receipts for, the mortgage money or the unpaid part thereof and the interest then due, if any, and thenceforth to become due thereon; and

(b) the benefit of all securities for the same and the benefit of and the right to sue on all covenants with the mortgagee, and the right to exercise all powers of the mortgagee[2]; and

(c) all the estate and interest in the mortgaged property then vested in the mortgagee subject to redemption or cesser, but as to such estate and interest subject to the right of redemption then subsisting."[3]

---

[1] *Re Tahiti Cotton Co., ex p. Sargent* (1874) L.R. 17 Eq. 273 at 279, *per* Jessel M.R.; but it is not yet settled whether a building society mortgage (as opposed to the mortgage debt) is transferable without either an express contract to that effect or the actual concurrence of the mortgagor and in any event the transferee may not be able to exercise the power of sale; see *Taylor v. Russell* [1892] A.C. 247 at 255. See also *Re Rumney & Smith* [1897] 2 Ch. 351; *Sun Building Society v. Western Suburban & Harrow Road Permanent Building Society* [1920] 2 Ch. 144; reversed on other grounds [1921] 2 Ch. 438. It would seem to be difficult to separate the rights arising from membership of the building society from the rights arising under the mortgage. Since the Building Societies Act 1986 a transfer of a building society mortgage may be made under an amalgamation of transfer of engagements between societies. In such circumstances a mortgagor will be bound by the rules of the amalgamated or transferee society, (see ss93(4), 94(8) both as amended by Building Societies Act 1997). It is also now possible to transfer business from a building society to a commercial company (see s.97). See also *ante*, Chap. 8.

[2] Express assignment of the benefit of covenants is therefore no longer necessary. Statutory powers are in any case exercisable by any person from time to time deriving title under the mortgagee: LPA 1925, s.204(1)(xvi).

[3] LPA 1925, s.114(1).

In short, if the transfer is by deed, then without these details being set out, the transferee[4] steps into the shoes of the mortgagee.[5] If, as is unlikely, a case should arise where the debt and the security have not been assigned together, the consequences are as follows. Where the debt alone is transferred, the assignor remains the mortgagee and is the person to exercise the powers and remedies attached to that position. He must therefore be the party joined in redemption of foreclosure proceedings but he is a trustee of the powers and remedies for his assignee and must hand over to the assignee any moneys he obtains by exercising them.[6] When the security alone is transferred, the assignee becomes entitled to hold the security until he is redeemed by payment of the debt charged thereon. Moreover, as mortgagee, he may foreclose and thus holds the beneficial interest in the debt to the extent that it can be satisfied out of the security[7] but the assignee cannot sue on the covenant.

2. Form of transfer

21–02   Section 114(1) applies equally to mortgages of realty and personalty with the exception of mortgage bills of sale. Its provisions are comprehensive and render a transfer by deed a completely effective instrument. Therefore, in practice a transfer is nearly always carried out either by deed or by the newer method of transfer, *i.e.* a receipt endorsed upon the mortgage deed, to which method section 115 of the Law of Property Act 1925 gives the same effect as a transfer by deed.[8] It is, however, necessary to consider the minimum requirements of form for an effective transfer of mortgages of land. Moreover, it will be assumed that the assignor intends to transfer the debt and the security together. If the debt only is transferred, the assignment must be in writing and notice given to the mortgagor for the purpose of enabling the assignee to sue in his own name.[9]

A legal mortgage of land or a charge by way of legal mortgage requires, strictly speaking, a deed for its transfer in every case because otherwise the legal title will not pass. A short precedent of such a deed is set out in the Schedule 3 to the Law of Property Act 1925.[10] If the security is a statutory charge by way of legal mortgage under section 117 of the Law of Property Act 1925 the transfer may be by one of the statutory deeds of transfer provided by section 118. This last section sets out for statutory transfers much the same benefits as section 114(1) contains for ordinary transfers together with an additional clause dealing with the case of a mortgagor concurring in the transfer. Again, transfers of legal charges on registered land must not only be by deed but must be in the prescribed

---

[4] "transferee" includes his personal representatives and assignees (s.114(2)).

[5] *Quaere* whether this is the position where further advances are then made by the transferee to the mortgagor after transfer in the absence of a supplement deed between the parties.

[6] *Morley v. Morley* (1858) 25 Beav. 253.

[7] *Jones v. Gibbons* (1804) 9 Ves. 407; *cf. Phillips v. Gutteridge* (1859) 4 De G. & J. 531.

[8] subs. (6); all that is necessary is that the receipt should on its face appear to have been given to a person not entitled to the immediate equity of redemption. See *post*, pp. 390 *et seq.* Such a transfer made before 1926 would not have passed the legal estate, (*Re Beachey, Heaton v. Beachy* [1904] 1 Ch. 67).

[9] LPA 1925, s.136.

[10] But its use is not compulsory and its form may be modified or varied (*i.e.* s.114(3)). See chap. 3, *ante*, and Appendix II, para. B–01.

form[11] and the name of the transferee must be entered on the register as the new proprietor of the charge.[12] The transfer of an equitable mortgage need not, of course, be by deed, although in practice it usually is so effected. However, transfers of equitable mortgages are caught by section 53 of the Law of Property Act 1925, and therefore such transfers ought always to be made by an instrument in writing. Section 53 applies equally to an equitable security by deposit of title deeds prior to the enactment of the Law of Property (Miscellaneous Provisions) Act 1989 as the deposit creates an equitable mortgage which can only be assigned by a disposition in writing under section 53.[13]

3. Subrogation

Such are the rules to which, strictly, transfers should conform. However, it is idle **21–03** to pretend that a transfer will be impossible without keeping to these rules given that equitable doctrines concerning the merger and non-merger of charges frequently allow a transfer to be effected by mere payment of the mortgage debt. The availability of subrogation as an equitable remedy to reverse or prevent unjust enrichment arises when A is enriched at the expense of B and such an enrichment is unjust.[13a] Whilst there must be no reason of policy for refusing the remedy,[14] subrogation is not based on any argument of common intention of the parties respectively enriched and deprived.[15] An intention that A should be unsecured may operate to prevent subrogation to any security.[16] Thus if a stranger discharges the mortgage debt, he will—unless he has manifested a contrary intention—be presumed to intend to keep the mortgage alive for his own benefit[17] that is to say, his legal relations with a defendant who would otherwise be unjustly enriched are regulated as if the benefit of the charge had been assigned to him. The person so discharging the debt will not, however, be treated as an assignee *vis-à-vis* someone who would not be unjustly enriched. Moreover, the presumption is a strong one because in one case it was held to apply although the person discharging the debt had actually contracted with the mortgagor to be given a new mortgage.[18] The result is that under this doctrine a transfer may be obtained by merely paying over the mortgage moneys, the effectiveness of the transfer being assured by the fact that in equity the person discharging the debt is *subrogated* to the rights of the mortgagee.[19]

If the mortgagee holds the deeds, the person paying him will obtain delivery of the deeds. On the other hand, this apparently simple method is not usually

---

[11] In either of the three forms (Nos. 2, 3 and 4) given in Schedule 4 to the LPA 1925, with variations adapted to the particular case—see LPA 1925, s.118 and Appendix II, para. B–02 *et seq.*
[12] See *ante*, pp. 35 *et seq.*
[13] *Re Richardson, Shillito v. Hobson* (1885) 30 Ch.D. 396.
[13a] *Banque Financière de la Cité v. Parc (Battersea) Ltd* [1999] 1 A.C. 221; [1998] 2 W.L.R. 475.
[14] For example, *Orakjo v. Menso Investments* [1978] A.C. 95.
[15] *Banque Financiere de la Cite v. Parc (Battersea) Ltd* [1998] 2 W.L.R. 475 *per* Lord Hoffmann at 483E–G.
[16] *Banque Financiere, ante*; *Paul Speirway Ltd* [1976] Ch. 220; *Boscaw v. Bajwa* [1996] 1 W.L.R. 328.
[17] *Chetwynd v. Allen* [1899] 1 Ch. 353.
[18] *Butler v. Rice* [1910] 2 Ch. 277 at 282, 283.
[19] See *Cracknall v. Janson* (1879) 11 Ch.D. 1; *Patten v. Bond* (1889) 60 L.T. 583; *Ghana Commercial Bank v. Chandiram* [1960] A.C. 732 at 744, 745.

employed because the transferee cannot thus obtain the legal estate and because there are strong reasons for making the mortgagor concur in a proper deed of transfer. Therefore, in the normal case, transfers are effected by deed, or by an endorsed receipt under section 115 of the Law of Property Act 1925.[20] It follows, and has been made clear[21] that the subrogated security can be enforced to recover the discharged secured debt together with interest. However, no order for possession should be made until the sums that would have been due under the subrogated security have been determined, including, if necessary, consideration of any repayments as had been made by the mortgagor being attributed to the subrogated security and any subsequent events.[22] Further, the principle that a subrogator is under a duty not to destroy or prejudice any right or remedy of the subrogatee and that he would be liable to compensate the subrogate if he did[23] applies equally where a prior encumbrancer had been paid off by a subsequent encumbrant.[24]

4. Transfers initiated by the mortgagor

21–04   Another form of transfer requires special mention, namely transfers which are not initiated by the mortgagee but are instigated by the person redeeming. It is a common occurrence for a mortgagor, who is pressed for payment, or who can obtain his money more cheaply elsewhere, to discharge the mortgage with the money of a stranger, who will require the mortgage to be transferred to him.[25] The primary rule is that a stranger has no right to redeem and cannot obtain a transfer except by contract with the mortgagee.[26] Section 95 of the Law of Property Act 1925 however, creates an exception to this rule when a stranger discharges the debt through the mortgagor. Subsection (1) provides[27] that, where a mortgagor is entitled to redeem and the mortgage debt is discharged, he may require the mortgagee, instead of reconveying or surrendering, to assign the mortgage debt and convey the mortgaged property to any third person as the mortgagor shall direct and the mortgagee is bound to assign and convey accordingly. This right is exercisable, not only by the original mortgagor, but by any person from time to time deriving title under him and by any person with any right to redeem. Mesne incumbrancers[28] are therefore entitled to call for a

---

[20] See *post*, para. 22–02 *et seq.*
[21] *Western Fronts Savings Ltd v. Rock* [1993] N.P.C. 89.
[22] *Halifax Mortgage Services Ltd v. Muirhead* [1997] N.P.C. 171, (1997) 76 P. & C.R.
[23] *MacGillary on Insurance Law* (9th ed., 1997), para. 22–55.
[24] *Faireharm Investments Ltd v. Citibank International plc, The Times*, February 20, 1998.
[25] A stranger assisting a mortgagor to pay off the first mortgagee cannot safely take a new mortgage from the mortgagor because of the danger that the mortgagor has created mesne incumbrances; in the case of land he would be safeguarded by searching the register, but even so, if he discovers an incumbrance he must have a transfer instead of a new mortgage to preserve his priority: *cf. Teevan v. Smith* (1882) 20 Ch. 724 at 728.
[26] *James v. Biou* (1819) 3 Swanst. 234.
[27] Notwithstanding any stipulation to the contrary in the mortgage.
[28] This follows from the definition of mortgagor in LPA 1925, s.205(1)(xvi). Accordingly, the right is exercisable by an equitable mortgagee or chargee or the holder of an equitable lien: see *Everitt v. Automatic Weighing Machine Co.* [1892] 3 Ch. 506.

transfer and subsection (2) expressly states that, where there are several incumbrancers, each incumbrancer and the mortgagor may call for a transfer, notwithstanding the existence of intervening incumbrances but that in case of conflict the right is exercisable according to their priorities.

5. Limitations

There are, however, two important limitations on the exercise of the right given **21–05** by section 95, the first of which is that a mortgagee in possession cannot be compelled to make a transfer unless he is brought into court for that purpose.[29] The reason for this is that a mortgagee who goes into possession will not be allowed to give up possession without the leave of the court if he makes a transfer and goes out of possession. He remains absolutely liable to account, as mortgagee in possession, for all rents and profits which have, or ought to have, been received after the transfer.[30] Even if the mortgagor were to concur in releasing him from liability this would not be sufficient when there were any mesne incumbrancers, for the latter would not be bound by the release. It is only under the direction of the court that a mortgagee in possession can safely transfer.[31] The second limitation is that a person does not qualify to exercise the right by merely tendering the mortgage moneys he must become entitled to a surrender or a reconveyance.[32] Therefore, if the mortgagee has notice that the mortgagor is not entitled to a reconveyance to himself absolutely he cannot be compelled to transfer the mortgage to the mortgagor's nominee absolutely.[33] This limitation is important in connection with mesne incumbrancers, for a prior mortgagee must give effect to the rights of any intervening mortgagees of whose mortgages he has notice[34] and, therefore, a mortgagee cannot under section 95 be compelled to transfer to a third party, when he has notice of a mesne incumbrancer whose consent has not been obtained.[35]

6. Effect of transfer

When a mortgage is transferred without the concurrence of the mortgagor the **21–06** transferee takes subject to any equity which, at the date of the transfer, the mortgagor might have asserted in taking the mortgage account for the debt, being a chose in action, can only be assigned subject to existing equities. It is true that in the transfer of a legal mortgage the transferee obtains a legal title, but it is apparent upon the face of the title that it is a security only for a debt and that the real transaction is an assignment of a debt.[36] As was said by Loughborough L.C.

[29] LPA 1925, s.95(3).
[30] *Re Prytherch, Prytherch v. Williams* (1889) 42 Ch.D. 590; and see *Hinde v. Blake* (1841) 11 L.J.Ch. 26.
[31] *Hall v. Heward* (1886) 32 Ch.D. 430.
[32] But subs. (2) expressly allows a mortgagor to call for a transfer, notwithstanding mesne incumbrances, overruling *Teevan v. Smith* (1882) 20 Ch.D. 724, to this extent; for the reasons given in the text, subs. (2) is, however, of limited application.
[33] *Alderson v. Elgey* (1884) 26 Ch.D. 567.
[34] *Corbett v. National Provident Institution* (1900) 17 T.L.R. 5.
[35] (1915) 84 L.J.Ch. 814.
[36] *Matthews v. Wallwyn* (1798) 4 Ves. 118; *Chambers v. Goldwin* (1804) 9 Ves. 254.

in *Matthews v. Wallwyn*[37] it is not consonant to the general course of equity to consider the estate as more than a security for a debt. The result is that, as a rule, a transferee's only right is to the sum actually owing by the mortgagor to the mortgagee at the date of the transfer and after allowing the mortgagor the benefit of any set-off or other equity which he had against the mortgagee.[38] For example, in *Turner v. Smith*,[39] a mortgagor put into the hands of her solicitor a sum sufficient to pay off the mortgage. The solicitor subsequently himself took a transfer of the mortgage, having concealed from his client that he had never paid it off; he then transferred it again to the defendant for value, but the mortgagor was held entitled to redeem without further payment because the transferee could be in no better position than the solicitor at the date of the assignment.

(a) *Attendant risks*

21–07 The moral of this story is that a man takes a transfer of a mortgage at his peril if he does not obtain an acknowledgment from the mortgagor of the sum actually due. Indeed, the transfer of a mortgage is an unsafe investment unless the mortgagor concurs or joins in the transfer as a party to the transaction[40] whereby he enters into a new covenant for the payment of the debt and interest. The risk is well illustrated by the case of *Parker v. Jackson*.[41] Real property was mortgaged for £700 and the mortgage then transferred to the mortgagor's solicitor. Before he took the transfer the solicitor had sold other property of his client such that he held in his hands £2,000 of his client's money. He did not appropriate the money to the discharge of the mortgage nor did he pay it over to the client. Without informing his client he transferred the mortgage again and became bankrupt. Farwell J. held that the fact that the money had not been appropriated to the mortgage debt was immaterial and that the transferee could be redeemed without payment. Although a transferee is as a rule entitled to no more than the sum actually due at the date of the transfer—plus subsequent interest—the mortgagor may sometimes estop himself from relying on his equity. For example, where a mortgage is executed containing an acknowledgment of the receipt of the sum expressed to be advanced, the mortgagor cannot afterwards claim that only a lesser sum was actually advanced, as against a transferee who acted on the faith of the receipt and was not aware of any special circumstances to put him upon inquiry.[42] This does not mean that where there is such a receipt the concurrence of the mortgagor is superfluous as there will always remain the risk that the

---

[37] *ibid.* at 126. It seems, however, that a legal estate may be a protection to a transferee if the original mortgage was voidable on equitable grounds; he will, if he is a bona fide purchaser, be able to hold the estate as a security for money due under the mortgage at the date of the transfer: *Judd v. Green* (1875) 45 L.J.Ch. 108; *Nant-y-glo and Blaina Ironworks Co. Ltd v. Tamplin* (1876) 35 L.T. 125. These decisions, both by Bacon V.-C. are criticised in *Halsbury's Laws of England* (4th ed., re-issue 1999), Vol. 32, para. 581.

[38] *Bickerton v. Walker* (1885) 31 Ch.D. 151 at 158. He cannot, in general add the costs of the transfer to the mortgage debt. The mortgagee must pay such costs himself (see *Re Radcliffe* (1856) 22 Beav. 201).

[39] [1901] 1 Ch. 213.

[40] See *Matthews v. Wallwyn* (1798) 4 Ves. 118 at 126(a). In the case of a transfer of statutory mortgage the covenant will be implied if the transferee is joined in the transfer (LPA 1925, s.118(3)).

[41] (1936) 155 L.T. 104.

[42] *Bickerton v. Walker* (1885) 31 Ch.D. 151; LPA 1925, s.68. *cf.* also *Dixon v. Winch* [1900] 1 Ch. 736, where the mortgagor's equity was lost on the ground of imputed notice.

mortgage was paid off, either in part or in full, between the date of the mortgage and that of the transfer.

There is a further danger. A debtor who has no notice of an assignment of the debt is entitled to pay it to the assignor.[43] Consequently, a transferee takes subject not only to the equities existing in favour of the mortgagor at the date of the transfer but also to any equities which arise after that date and before notice of the transfer.[44] Payments made by the mortgagor to the mortgagee after but without notice of the transfer are binding as against the transferee.[45] If the whole debt is thus discharged the mortgagor may redeem from the transferee without further payment.[46] Indeed, any agreement made for value to discharge the debt will be effective against the transferee in the absence of collusion.[47] The result is that if a transferee makes the initial mistake of not obtaining the concurrence of the mortgagor, it is vital that notice of the transfer should at once be given.

(b) *Matter transferred*

Since a transferee takes the mortgage subject to the state of the accounts at the **21–08** date of transfer he is, unless a contrary intention is expressed, entitled to arrears of interest.[48] In accordance, however, with the general rule that arrears may not be capitalised except by agreement a transferee has no right to treat the arrears as part of the principal merely because he has had to pay the aggregate sum to obtain his investment.[49] This right may be obtained if the mortgagor is made to join in the transfer and to assent to the capitalisation of the arrears because it will be assumed that his assent was given in return for forbearance by the creditor.[50] If the transfer is properly drawn it will contain such an agreement for capital-isation in express terms, although it seems that the court will also infer the agreement from the mere fact of the mortgagor's concurrence.[51]

It should also be noticed that the sum paid to the mortgagee on a transfer does **21–09** not determine the amount to which the transferee is entitled as against the mortgagor. The market value of a mortgage is not necessarily the amount due on the security because the soundness of the security and the general credit of the debtor materially affect its attractiveness as an investment.[52] Therefore, a trans-feree who purchases his mortgage at a price less than the amount of the mortgage debt may stand on his rights as assignee of the mortgagee and claim the full amount of the debt from the mortgagor.[53] This is true whether the transferee is a

---

[43] *Stocks v. Dobson* (1853) 4 De G.M. & G. 11.
[44] *Williams v. Sorrell* (1799) 4 Ves. 389.
[45] *Dixon v. Winch* [1900] 1 Ch. 736 at 742, *per* Cozens-Hardy J.
[46] *Norrish v. Marshall* (1821) 5 Madd 475; *Re Lord Southampton's Estate* (1880) 16 Ch.D. 178.
[47] In *Norrish v. Marshall (ante)* the mortgagor paid in goods, not money.
[48] *Cottrell v. Finney* (1874) 9 Ch. App. 541.
[49] *Ashenhurst v. James* (1845) 3 Atk. 270; *Matthews v. Wallwyn* (1798) 4 Ves. 118; *Halifax Mortgage Services v. Muirhead* [1997] N.P.C. 171, (1997) 76 P. & C.R. 418.
[50] *cf. Porter v. Hobbard* (1677) Freem. Ch. 30. But a mesne incumbrancer will not be bound by such an agreement, if the prior mortgagee had notice of his incumbrance: *Digby v. Craggs* (1762) Amb. 612.
[51] *Agnew v. King* [1902] 1 I.R. 471.
[52] See *Anon.* (1707) 1 Salk 155.
[53] *Davis v. Barrett* (1851) 14 Beav. 542.

stranger,[54] a mesne incumbrancer,[55] or a person otherwise beneficially interested in the estate.[56] However, the mortgagor himself and his personal representatives, who succeed to his liability on the contract for payment, cannot, of course, buy up the first mortgage at an under value and hold it against mesne incumbrancers for they have no right to keep the mortgage alive at all and it is wholly extinguished on the transfer being taken.[57] Again, in special circumstances a transferee may not be permitted to hold the mortgage as security for more than its purchase price on the ground that he is in a fiduciary relation with the mortgagor. Thus a trustee,[58] solicitor,[59] agent[60] or any other person whose position gives him special opportunities of buying up the mortgage and of knowing its real value, will hold the mortgage subject to redemption only at the price for which he bought it.[61]

7. Transfer part of mortgage debt

21–10 If the mortgagee wishes to transfer part of the mortgage debt rather than the whole, it is necessary either to execute a transfer of the whole debt and mortgaged property to a trustee for both the transfer and transferee, or for the mortgagee to execute a declaration of trust. The reason for this is that the mortgagee's powers of redemption, foreclosure or sale are indivisible and the execution of a trust deed or declaration of trust are the only methods available to accommodate this state of affairs.

8. Transfer of registered charge

21–11 In the case of the transfer of a registered charge the proprietor of such a charge may transfer it by use of the prescribed form.[62] Completion of the transfer then occurs when the registrar enters the transferee in the register as the proprietor.[63] Provided that he had no notice of any irregularity or invalidity in the original charge, a registered transferee for valuable consideration and his successors in title should not be affected thereby.[64] Once registration has been effected the term granted rests in the proprietor for the time being of the charge without any consequence or assignment.[65] But until the registration formalities have been completed the transferee of the charge does not become the proprietor. The effect

---

[54] *Phillips v. Vaughan* (1685) 1 Vern. 336.
[55] *Darcy v. Hall* (1682) 1 Vern. 49.
[56] *e.g.* a reversioner (*Davis v. Barrett* (1851) 14 Beav. 542); but a life tenant under the Settled Land Act 1925, would be in a fiduciary position.
[57] *Otter v. Lord Vaux* (1856) 6 De G.M. & G. 638; *Morrett v. Paske* (1740) 2 Atk. 52; see *post*, para. 21–16.
[58] *Darcy v. Hall* (1682) 1 Vern. 49.
[59] *Macleod v. Jones* (1883) 24 Ch.D. 289.
[60] *Carter v. Palmer* (1841) 8 Cl. & F. 657.
[61] *Hobday v. Peters (No. 1)* (1860) 28 Beav. 349. Similarly a surety: *Reed v. Norris* (1837) 2 My. & Cr. 361.
[62] Form TR3 (transfer of charge) or Form TR4 (transfer of a portfolio of charges) as prescribed by Sched. 1 to LRR 1925 as amended by LRR 1997 r. 2(2).
[63] Land Registration Act 1925, s.33(1), (2).
[64] *ibid.* s.33(3).
[65] *ibid.* s.33(4), (5).

of this is that until registration is completed the transferee cannot exercise his statutory powers, for example, the power to appoint a receiver.[66]

9. Transfers of local authority mortgages

Since the enactment[67] of section 7 of the Local Government Act 1986 a local **21–12** authority wishing to transfer any interests in land which they hold as mortgagee must obtain the prior written consent of the mortgagor.

The Act makes specific provision for the local authority to ensure that the mortgagor has the opportunity to make an informed decision whether or not to give consent. Thus the consent must specify the name of the transferee, it may be withdrawn by notice in writing at any time before the date of the transfer and it ceases to have effect if the transfer does not take place within six months after the consent is given.[68] Further, the Local Authorities (Disposal of Mortgages) Regulations 1986[69] impose requirements in the case of transfers taking place on or after September 1, 1986. In particular, the mortgagor's consent must be in the form set out in the Schedule to the Regulations and the local authority must supply the mortgagor with information specified by the Regulations. A transfer made without consent is void.[70] It is to be presumed that failure to comply with the requirements set out in section 7 and in the regulations has the same effect. There is also special provision in the case of transfers which appear on their face to be valid. Thus it is provided[71] that a transfer made following an initially valid consent is valid even if the consent has expired or been withdrawn by the date of the transfer provided that the transfer contains a certificate by the transferor that consent has not been withdrawn or ceased to have effect. In such a case, however, the mortgagor is entitled to have the transfer set aside and the mortgage re-vested in the transferor by serving notice to that effect on the local authority within six months of the transfer.

10. Sub-mortgages

A sub-mortgage is in essence a transfer of a mortgage subject to a proviso for **21–13** redemption. In other words, it is a mortgage of a mortgage and it arises when a mortgagee wishes to borrow money upon the security of a profitable mortgage and it avoids the calling in the whole of the loan. Therefore, the rules set out above apply *mutatis mutandis* to sub-mortgages.

After 1925, however, if the original mortgage was of the legal estate and created by demise, the sub-mortgage cannot be effected by assignment of the estate. It can only be created by *the transfer* of the mortgage debt, together with either a separate sub-demise of the estate or with a separate legal charge or

---

[66] *Lever Finance Ltd v. Trustee of the Property of Needleman* [1956] Ch. 375.
[67] Applying to all transfers made *after* April 1, 1986 (unless pursuant to a contract made before that date).
[68] Local Government Act 1986, s.7(1) and (2).
[69] S.I. 1986 No. 1028.
[70] Local Government Act 1986, s.7(3).
[71] *ibid.* s.7(4), (5).

equitable mortgage of the estate.[72] This means that the simple form of transfer provided by section 114 is not appropriate.[73] Otherwise the effect of the transaction is the same as if a transfer were made subject to a proviso for redemption.[74] In all other cases the sub-mortgage can be effected by a transfer of the benefit of the head mortgage by a deed under section 114.[75] Whatever its form, a sub-mortgage should contain an express covenant for payment of the monies due under the sub-mortgage and a proviso for redemption of the sub-mortgage. Further, the original mortgagor should join in the transaction or be given immediate notice of it in order to avoid the problems which can arise under cases such as *Norrish v. Marshall* and *Parker v. Jackson.*[76]

Therefore, a sub-mortgage makes the sub-mortgagee a transferee of the original mortgage subject to an equity of redemption in the mortgagee. As such, he may exercise all the powers of the original mortgagee and may sell, foreclose, dispose of the fee simple or lease under sections 88(5) or 89(5) of the Law of Property Act 1925 or otherwise realise the mortgaged property.[77]

For example: A mortgages Blackacre for £1,000 to B. Owing to arrears of interest the mortgage debt stands at £1,500 when B sub-mortgages to C for an advance of £500. A, the mortgagor, is made to concur and C thus holds a mortgage for £1,500 as security for his advance of £500.

If he subsequently wishes to realise his security, C has two choices. He may either realise his sub-mortgage alone, or the original mortgage which necessarily involves terminating the sub-mortgage as well. If he sells his sub-mortgage to X for £600 and his own account against B remains at £500, he must pay over the surplus to B whilst X becomes transferee of the mortgage. If, on the other hand, he sells Blackacre itself for £2,000, he pays himself his £500, then discharges A's debt to B, deducting £500 from B's claim, and finally hands over any surplus to A. On the same principle, he may foreclose on the mortgagee without disturbing the original mortgagor or making him a party. If he forecloses on the mortgagor, the mortgagee must be joined as a party and given an opportunity to redeem.

11. Registered land

In the case of registered land a proprietor of a registered charge may charge the mortgage debt with the payment of money in the same way as a proprietor of registered land may charge the land. Such charges are referred to as sub-

---

[72] LPA 1925, s.86(1), (3).

[73] It can, however, be used, since s.86(2) provides that an attempt to mortgage a term of years by assignment shall take effect as a sub-demise.

[74] See Key & Elphinstone, *Precedents in Conveyancing* (15th ed., 1953–54), Vol. 2, pl. 230.

[75] Some doubt has been expressed, however, as to the appropriateness of this method, see (1948) 12 Conv.(N.S.) 171 (H. Woodhouse).

[76] *Norrish v. Marshall* (1821) 5 Madd. 475; *Parker v. Jackson* (1936) 155 L.T. 104. A sub-mortgagee being in the position of a transferee, takes subject to the state of the accounts between the mortgagor and the mortgagee at the date of the sub-mortgage. If the mortgagor's concurrence is not obtained notice must be given to him to avoid the consequences of any equities arising after the date of the transfer.

[77] A sub-mortgage, which transfers the original power of sale to the sub-mortgagee, appears at the same time to deprive the original mortgagee of the power, see *Cruse v. Nowell* (1856) 25 L.J.Ch. 709.

charges.[78] This must be completed by registration[79] and thereupon the sub-chargee will be entered as proprietor of the sub-charge and be issued with a sub-charge certificate.[80] Subject to any entry to the contrary, the proprietor of the sub-charge has the same powers of disposition in relation to the land as if he had been registered as proprietor of the principal charge.[81]

INTER VIVOS TRANSFER OF EQUITY OF REDEMPTION

In the absence of any express provisions or statutory enactment to the contrary,[82] **21–14** a mortgagor can at any time transfer the mortgaged property without the mortgagee's consent. However, he remains personally liable on the covenant to pay despite such transfer.[83]

A mortgagor is only able to convey his property unincumbered if:

(1) the mortgagee consents to the transfer; or
(2) the mortgagor redeems the mortgage; or
(3) a declaration is obtained from the court by the mortgagor that the property is free from incumbrances upon sufficient money being paid into court.[84]

DEVOLUTION ON DEATH

In *Thornborough v. Baker*[85] Lord Nottingham settled conclusively that, whatever **21–15** the nature of the property mortgaged, a mortgagee's interest in his mortgage is personalty, the mortgagee's principal right being to the money and his right to the land being only a security for that money. The result was that until 1882 freehold estates in mortgage caused difficulty upon the mortgagee's intestacy, as the estate passed to the heir-at-law while the debt belonged to the personal representatives.[86] Further since the estate was in equity only a security, the heir-at-law held it on trust for the personal representatives.[87] The Conveyancing Act 1881[88] (superseded by the Land Transfer Act 1897[89]), however, provided that a mortgaged estate should pass to the personal representatives as if it were a chattel real notwithstanding any testamentary disposition to the contrary. The point is merely of historical interest, though it may arise in an occasional search on title. The

---

[78] Land Registration Act 1925, s.36; Land Registration Rules 1925, r. 163(1).
[79] Land Registration Rules 1925, r. 164(1).
[80] *ibid.* r. 166.
[81] *ibid.* r. 163(2).
[82] Under the Small Dwellings Acquisition Acts 1899 to 1923 the mortgagor was restricted from transferring the mortgaged property. These Acts have now been repealed by the Housing (Consequential Provisions) Act 1985. But the Housing Act 1985, s.456 and Sched. 18 (as amended), contain provisions applicable to existing mortgages made under the previous legislation. Most building society mortgages contain restrictions on transfer.
[83] See *ante*, para. 16–110 *et seq.*
[84] LPA 1925, s.50(1), (2); see *ante*, para. 16–66.
[85] (1675) 3 Swann. 628.
[86] *ibid.*
[87] *Re Loveridge, Drayton v. Loveridge* [1902] 2 Ch. 859.
[88] s.30.
[89] s.1(1).

Law of Property Act 1925 removes all difficulties by its initial provision that mortgages of freehold cannot be created by the conveyance of the title but must be effected through terms of years, the result being that both the security and the debt are in their own nature personalty. Furthermore, the Administration of Estates Act 1925[90] has instituted a single system of devolution upon intestacy for both realty and personalty. On the death of a mortgagee, the mortgage and the debt devolve on his personal representatives who, until the mortgage is discharged, or until they have assented in favour of the persons next entitled, may exercise all the powers of the mortgagee.[91] The basic principle in *Thornborough v. Baker*[92] is, however, still of importance. The benefit of the mortgage passes under a general bequest of personalty but not a general devise of realty,[93] whilst a specific devisee takes the mortgage as personalty. This rule is on the assumption that the equity of redemption is still subsisting. If the equity of redemption is destroyed by foreclosure or by the mortgagee having been in possession for the statutory period without acknowledging the debt, a conversion takes place and his interest acquires the nature of the property mortgaged so that in the case of freehold it becomes realty.[94]

1. Assent by personal representatives

21–16   Although a mortgage term is "an estate or interest in real estate" for the purposes of section 36(1) of the Administration of Estates Act 1925, a mortgage debt is not. Thus there is some doubt as to whether an assent by personal representatives is sufficient to pass both the legal estate and the debt. But as such a debt passes if there is a clear intention that it should,[95] it seems that no difficulty would arise in most cases.

DEVOLUTION ON INSOLVENCY

1. Insolvency of mortgagee

21–17   In the case of an individual insolvency of an individual mortgagee[96] any mortgage, like the rest of the bankrupt's estate, vests (with certain exceptions) in his trustee.[97] Thus his trustee may exercise all the mortgagee's powers and remedies including the right to sue for foreclosure.[98]

---

[90] ss1(1), 3(1).

[91] In the case of the death of one of several mortgagees, see the operation of the joint account clause in the case where two or more persons lend money.

[92] (1675) 3 Swann. 628.

[93] Even a specific devise of Blackacre will not give the devisee the beneficial interest in a mortgage held by the testator if he also held a reversionary interest in the property: the devisee will get the reversionary interest only: *Bowen v. Barlow* (1872) L.R. 8 Ch. 171.

[94] See *Garrett v. Evers* (1730) Mos. 364; *Thompson v. Grant* (1819) 4 Madd. 438; *Re Loveridge, Pearce v. Marsh* [1904] 1 Ch. 518.

[95] *Re Culverhouse* [1896] 2 Ch. 251.

[96] For a more detailed analysis of the positions of both the mortgagee and mortgagor on insolvency, see further *Muir Hunter on Persoanl Insolvency* (1987).

[97] Insolvency Act 1986, s.306.

[98] *Waddell v. Toleman* (1878) 9 Ch.D. 212.

In the case of registered land the trustee is entitled to be registered as the proprietor in the place of the bankrupt[99] but he may deal with the charge before registration.[1]

Where an incorporated mortgagee has been dissolved, all property and rights whatsoever vested in or held in trust for the company immediately before it dissolution are deemed to be *bona vacentia* and devolve to the Crown.[2]

2. Insolvency of mortgagor

The impact on the mortgagee of the insolvency of the mortgagor is considered elsewhere.[3] **21–18**

---

[99] Land Registration Act 1925, s.42.
[1] *ibid.* s.37; Land Registration Rules 1925, r. 170.
[2] Companies Act 1985, s.654.
[3] See *post* chap. 23.

CHAPTER 22

EXTINGUISHMENT OF THE SECURITY

DISCHARGE OF THE MORTGAGE OR CHARGE

The precise character of the instrument necessary to release the security depends **22–01**
on the nature of the mortgage, though the Law of Property Act 1925 has made
it largely a matter of an appropriate receipt. Prior to 1926, when mortgages of
freehold were usually made by conveyance of the legal estate, redemption
involved a deed of reconveyance executed by the mortgagee without which the
mortgagor's chain of title would be incomplete.[1] Again, in mortgages of a
leasehold estate made, as a rule, by sub-demise redemption necessitated an
express surrender of the sub-lease because the Satisfied Terms Act 1845 did not
apply to terms created out of leaseholds.[2] Equitable mortgages, on the other hand,
did not require any instrument of reconveyance because the receipt of the
mortgage moneys automatically terminated the equity.[3] Nevertheless it was in
fact quite common to have a reconveyance even in these cases. In one class of
mortgage, however, namely building society mortgages, special legislation[4] was
enacted enabling the discharge of such mortgages to be effected by a receipt
indorsed on or annexed to the mortgage deed. In these cases the receipt operates
as an automatic reconveyance of the property mortgaged.

1. Indorsed (or statutory) receipt: Law of Property Act 1925, s.115

The Law of Property Act 1925 has simplified the machinery of redemption by **22–02**
extending this principle to all mortgages of land except those of registered land.
Thus, under section 115 a receipt for the mortgage moneys indorsed on, written
at the foot of, or annexed to the mortgage instrument and executed by the
mortgagee[5] operates:

---

[1] *Webb v. Crosse* [1912] 1 Ch. 323.
[2] *Re Moore & Hulm's Contract* [1912] 2 Ch. 105.
[3] *Firth & Sons v. I.R. Commissioners* [1904] 2 K.B. 205.
[4] Building Societies Act 1986, s.13(7), Sched. 4, para. 2, re-enacting (with modifications) s.37 of the
Building Societies Act 1962 which itself consolidated earlier legislation, particularly Building
Societies Act 1874; See chapter 8.
[5] The receipt need not be under seal; all that the statute requires is that it should be executed under
the hand of the mortgagee: *Simpson v. Geoghehan* [1934] W.N. 232. The production by a solicitor
or licensed conveyancer of his client's indorsed receipt is a sufficient authority to the debtor to
make his payment to the solicitor or licensed conveyancer; see the LPA 1925, s.69 (as amended by
the Administration of Justice Act 1985, s.34(1)).

(1) in the case of a mortgage by demise or sub-demise as an automatic surrender of the term, so that the term is merged in the reversion, which is immediately expectant on the term;

(2) in other cases, as an automatic reconveyance of the mortgaged interest to the person who, immediately before the execution of the receipt, was entitled to the equity of redemption.

The result is that an indorsed receipt at once exonerates the property from the mortgage but does not alter the position of any one with an interest in the property paramount to the discharged mortgage. Thus it operates to discharge the mortgagor in respect of all claims against the mortgaged property.

In one case where the mortgagee had made an arithmetical error in calculating the redemption figure it was held that the mortgage had been validly discharged.[6]

2. Payment by persons not entitled to the immediate equity

A mortgage is not always redeemed by the person immediately entitled to the equity of redemption[7] but sometimes by a person—for example, a third or later mortgagee—who is entitled to have the charge kept alive against the second incumbrancer. In such cases, if the receipt were allowed to effect a surrender of the term or reconveyance of the security, the charge would be extinguished. Accordingly, it is provided that if the receipt clearly indicates[8] that the money was not paid by the person entitled to the immediate equity of redemption the indorsement is to operate as a *transfer* of the mortgage by deed to the person actually named as the payer.[9] Of course, if the latter does not wish to keep the charge alive his intention not to take a transfer can be stated in the receipt by means of a declaration to this effect, in which case the indorsement will have its usual effect. Section 115, in fact, takes care to preserve the law as to merger of charges intact and by subsection (3) prevents a mortgagor from making use of these provisions to redeem and keep alive a first mortgage against a later incumbrance which he himself has created. This was forbidden in *Otter* v. *Lord Vaux*[10] and subsection (3), perhaps *ex abundanti cautela*, warns that this case is still good law.

---

[6] *Erewash Borough Council v. Taylor* (1979) C.L. 1831 C.C.

[7] In the case of several incumbrances, the person *immediately* entitled to the equity of redemption is, of course, the second incumbrancer.

[8] There need not be an express statement to that effect, provided that the fact sufficiently appears: *Simpson v. Geoghehan* [1934] W.N. 232.

[9] s.115(2). See also *Cumberland Court (Brighton) Ltd.* v. *Taylor* [1964] Ch. 29 where it was held that although the receipt had operated as a transfer of the charge to the *vendor* (as the receipt was dated *after* the conveyance), there was no defect in title as there was an estoppel from the recitals in the conveyance which was "fed" on transfer and passed the interest in the property to the purchaser.

[10] (1856) 6 De G.M. & G. 638. For the rules regarding merger of charges see *post*, para. 22–10 *et seq*.

(a) *Partial redemption*

The Law of Property Act 1925 reserves for a person who redeems an absolute **22–04** right to demand a reconveyance in place of the indorsed receipt.[11] This right will not, however, be frequently exercised because a reconveyance only increases the cost of redemption. There are, however, occasions when a reconveyance is still not merely convenient but a necessity. For example, if a mortgagor is redeeming only as to part of the debt, so that only a portion of the mortgaged property is being exonerated, an indorsed receipt cannot be employed. Section 115 in terms confines the use of a receipt to occasions when *all* moneys charged upon the property under the mortgage are being repaid. In cases, therefore, of partial redemption a reconveyance is essential.

3. Use of a simple receipt: Law of Property Act 1925, ss 5–116

Although the extended use of the indorsed (or statutory) receipt has simplified **22–05** the conveyancing side of redemption, it is important to remember that in the case of mortgages of legal estates sections 5 and 116 of the Law of Property Act 1925 afford an alternative[12] means of discharging the mortgage[13] if it has been created by demise. Section 5 affirms the provisions of the Satisfied Terms Act 1845 and extends them to sub-terms created out of leaseholds. Section 116 expressly brings mortgage terms and sub-terms within the same principle so that (provided that there is written evidence) mortgages by demise or sub-demise may now be discharged by a mere payment of the mortgage debt, the term thereby being automatically merged in the reversion. Here again merger does not take place if the person making payment has a right to have the charge kept alive and he may in these circumstances obtain a transfer of the mortgage instead. However, it must be said that conveyancers in practice do not rely on such an "ordinary" receipt and prefer the statutory form, as the ordinary form is only prima facie evidence of payment.

(a) *Practice after redemption*

After redemption the title deeds should be returned to the mortgagor. If there is **22–06** another person, such as a subsequent mortgagee, with a better title the Law of Property Act 1925, section 96(2) (as amended) provides that the mortgagee whose mortgage is surrendered or otherwise extinguished is not liable on account of delivering the deeds to the person not having the best right thereto unless he has notice of the better right. It is further expressly provided that notice does not include statutory notice implied by reason of registration under the Land Charges Act 1972.

---

[11] s.115(4).

[12] And prior to the Finance Act 1971, s.64, (which abolished stamp duty on mortgages), a cheaper means of discharging the mortgage.

[13] Either a mortgage by demise or a charge by way of legal mortgage, see *Edwards v. Marshall-Lee* (1975) 235 E.G. 901.

4. **Mortgages of registered land**

22–07   Mortgages of registered land are outside section 115 of the Law of Property Act 1925 and are dealt with by section 35 of the Land Registration Act 1925. Under this Act, mortgages are discharged by a notification in the register that the charge has been cancelled and the registrar will enter this notification, either at the request of the mortgagee or upon sufficient proof that the mortgage has been paid off.[14] The effect of such a notification is to extinguish any term of years created by the mortgage. The Land Certificate will (if lodged at the Land Registry) then be redelivered to the mortgagor. Alternatively, under rule 160 of the Land Registration Rules 1925, the person paying off the charge may himself be registered as the proprietor of the charge, a step which is necessary when the charge is to be kept alive.

5. **Discharge of equitable mortgages**

22–08   The statutory method of discharge is inappropriate in the case of equitable mortgages. Although not strictly necessary, there is usually a reconveyance of the property to the mortgagor even though a simple receipt will suffice.

6. **Discharge of legal choses in action**

In the case of the discharge of a legal chose in action, a statutory receipt or reassignment is necessary.

Merger of a Mortgage or Charge

1. **Equitable doctrine of merger—a question of intention**

22–10   The purchase of an equity of redemption by the mortgagee or the redemption of a mortgage by a person entitled to redeem seems, at first sight, certain to put an end to the mortgage and such, in fact, was the result at common law.[15] In equity, however, the merger, both of charges and of estates, was purely a question of intention[16] and did not occur automatically on the union in one hand of a charge with an estate, or of a lesser estate in a greater. Indeed, so free from technicalities were the equitable rules that the intention to extinguish a charge

---

[14] A discharge should be in Form DS1 or DS3 (release of part of the land), see Land Registration Rules 1925, r. 151 and Sched. (as substituted and amended by LRR 1999, r. 2(1), Sched. 1, para. 13; LRR 2000, r. 2(1), Sched. 1, para. 1 and Appendix II, para. B–05 to B–06. An application to register a discharge in Form DS1 shall be made in Form AP1 or DS2. A like application to register a release in Form DS3 shall be made on Form AP1 (see Appendix II, para. B–07): L.RR. 1925, 1, 151(5) (as amended and substituted, *ante*).

[15] Either by analogy to the merger of estates or on the principle that a man cannot be his own debtor.

[16] *Forbes v. Moffatt* (1811) 8 Ves. 384.

might produce a merger, although the estate was outstanding in a trustee such that there would be no merger at common law.[17] Equitable principles now prevail[18] and, in any case, section 185 of the Law of Property Act 1925[19] expressly provides that "there is no merger by operation of law only of any estate the beneficial interest in which would not be deemed to be merged or extinguished in equity," while section 116 recognises that the discharge of the mortgage debt does not necessarily extinguish the mortgage.

(a) *Rationale behind the equitable principle*

The main object of keeping alive a charge which has been paid off is that it may afford a protection against subsequent incumbrances.[20] The doctrine of equity is based on the principle that a later incumbrancer has no claim to benefit gratuitously from a transaction to which he himself contributes nothing.[21] For when merger takes place the result is that a second incumbrancer is raised to the position of first incumbrancer without any effort of his own. Equity therefore does not, except in one case, consider a charge to be extinguished by the mere fact of its being paid off but makes merger a question of intention. **22–11**

The one exception is that where a mortgagor himself pays off an incumbrance he can in no circumstances set it up as a protection against a later mortgage which he has himself created.[22] Not even an express declaration of intention in the deed of discharge will avail him to keep the incumbrance alive. The reason is that a second mortgage, as between the parties, is a grant of the mortgagor's entire interest in the property, saving only the rights of the prior incumbrancer, and the mortgagor cannot derogate from his grant by holding the first mortgage against the second mortgagee.[23] This is the position even in the case where a third party provides the mortgagor with the necessary money to redeem the mortgage.[24] **22–12**

A purchaser of the equity of redemption is not, however, under this disability for the same considerations do not apply. He may pay off a charge and take a transfer of the mortgage. He can then keep it alive to protect himself against a subsequent incumbrance which he has not himself created because he has no personal contract with the subsequent incumbrancer.[25] Consequently, in the case of a purchaser of the equity of redemption the general rule applies and merger depends on intention.

---

[17] *Astley v. Milles* (1827) 1 Sim. 298, 344; *Forbes v. Moffatt* (1811) 18 Ves.Jr. 384 at 390.

[18] Supreme Court Act 1981, s.49(1), re-enacting the Judicature Act 1873, s.25(11) and the Supreme Court (Consolidation) Act 1925, s.44.

[19] Re-enacting s.25(4) of the Judicature Act 1873.

[20] See *ante*, para. 21–03 *et seq.*

[21] *cf.* Fletcher-Moulton L.J., in *Manks v. Whiteley* (1912) 1 Ch. 735 at 764.

[22] *Otter v. Lord Vaux* (1856) 6 De G.M. & G. 638.

[23] A mortgagor " . . . cannot derogate from his own bargain by setting up the mortgage so purchased against a second mortgagee." Per Lord Haldane L.C. in *Whiteley v. Delaney* [1914] A.C. 132 at 145. See also *Frazer v. Jones* (1846) 5 Hare 475.

[24] *Parkash v. Irani Finance Ltd.* [1970] Ch. 101. *Adams v. Angell* (1877) 5 Ch.D. 634; *Thorne v. Cann* (1895) A.C. 11; *Whiteley v. Delaney* [1914] A.C. 132.

[25] *Burrell v. Earl Egremont* (1844) 7 Beav. 205.

(b) *Establishing intention: presumptions*

22–13   The intention to extinguish a charge is a question of fact to be established by the evidence. There are, however, certain presumptions as to intention which are made by the court, and which decide the onus of proof.[26] The principle on which all these presumptions are based is that a person intends a charge to be kept alive or merged, according as to whether it is of advantage or of no advantage to him that the charge be kept alive.[27] The result is that:

(a)   If a life tenant or any other limited owner (not a tenant in tail)[28] acquires or pays off a charge there is a presumption against merger because merger would operate as a gift of the charge to those in remainder.[29]

(b)   If a person entitled in possession to either a fee simple or a fee tail acquires a charge on the estate, whether by devolution or by paying off the chargee, the presumption is in favour of merger unless the estate is defeasible by the operation of a condition. In general, there is no advantage in a man having a charge on his own estate, and the removal of the charge simplifies the title.

(c)   If a person entitled in remainder to a fee simple or a fee tail acquires a charge, no merger takes place until the estate comes into possession. When this occurs, the question of merger depends on the intention which the owner of the estate is presumed to have had *at the time when he acquired the charge*. Therefore, the presumption is against merger, (if he acquired the charge by paying it off himself) because he cannot have intended to benefit the inheritance at a time when it was uncertain that he would ever succeed to it.[30] On the other hand, if he acquired the charge by devolution, he is presumed to have intended it to merge in the inheritance and merger takes place when the inheritance comes into possession.[31]

22–14   The above presumptions as to the intention of a person who pays off a charge are derived from the nature of his interest in the incumbered property. All are founded on the principle that he intends what is for his own benefit and does not intend to confer gratuitous benefits on strangers. It is evident that at the time when a charge is acquired there may exist other circumstances which make it clearly beneficial for the person acquiring the charge to keep it alive. If this is so, the court presumes that he does not intend to extinguish his charge. This presumption will displace the ordinary presumption in favour of merger when an absolute owner pays off a charge on his estate. For example, the circumstance that a charge acquired by the owner of an estate has priority over other incumbrances, raises a presumption that he intends to keep it alive as a protection

---

[26] *Per* Parker J. in *Manks v. Whiteley* (1911) 2 Ch. 448 at 458.
[27] A tenant in tail is for this purpose an absolute owner because he has it in his power to become owner of the whole fee.
[28] *Burrell v. Lord Egremont* (1844) 7 Beav. 205; *Lord Gifford v. Lord Fitzhardinge* (1899) 2 Ch. 32.
[29] *Donisthorpe v. Porter* (1762) 2 Eden 162.
[30] *Horton v. Smith* (1857) 4 K. & J. 624.
[31] *Ibid.*

against the other charges.[32] This does not, as we have seen, apply to incumbrances created by the owner of the estate himself because he can never keep alive a charge against his own incumbrancers.[33] However, a purchaser of an equity of redemption may keep alive a charge, which he acquires, to protect himself against mesne incumbrances, if such was his intention at the time when he acquired the charge.[34] Similarly, a prior mortgagee, who takes a release of the equity of redemption, may keep his own charge alive against later mortgagees. In these cases, as in others, merger is a matter of intention.[35]

(c) *Toulmin v. Steere*[36]

It would, therefore, be expected that when the purchaser of an equity of redemption pays off a charge the existence of mesne incumbrances would automatically raise a presumption against merger under the general rule that the intention is to be gathered from what is advantageous to the owner of the charge. However, the decision of Sir William Grant in *Toulmin* v. *Steere*[37] suggests that if the purchaser of an equity of redemption has actual or constructive notice of mesne incumbrances when he pays off a charge on the estate the court will not presume an intention to keep alive the prior charge, so that the presumption is in favour of merger.[38] If this is correct, the intention to keep the charge on foot must be affirmatively proved, either by an express declaration to that effect in the deed of discharge, or otherwise by circumstances surrounding the transaction.[39]

The authority of *Toulmin* v. *Steere*, however, is very doubtful. It has been severely criticised by eminent judges,[40] and runs counter to the general principle on which presumptions in favour of and against merger are based. There is no good reason for denying to a purchaser of an equity of redemption the benefit of a presumed intention to keep his charge alive in circumstances when it is clearly to his advantage to do so. Knowledge of the mesne incumbrances is irrelevant because he can never be under any obligation to confer a gratuitous benefit on third parties. Indeed, notice of the puisne incumbrances only assists the presumption against merger, because it is sheer madness for the owner of an estate, who acquires a prior charge, to extinguish it when he knows of mesne incumbrances. *Toulmin* v. *Steere* was considered by the House of Lords in *Thorne* v. *Cann*,[41] in *Liquidation Estates Purchase Co.* v. *Willoughby*[42] and in *Whiteley* v. *Delaney*.[43] It is probably not going too far to say that the case has not been expressly

---

[32] *Forbes v. Moffatt* (1811) 8 Ves. 384.

[33] *Otter v. Lord Vaux* (1856) 6 De G.M. & G. 638.

[34] *Whiteley v. Delaney* [1914] A.C. 132.

[35] *Adams v. Angell* (1877) 5 Ch.D. 634.

[36] (1817) 3 Mer. 210.

[37] *ibid.*

[38] Sir William Grant's decision actually went further than this and denied that even actual intention could in such a case keep the charge alive. This part of his decision has been clearly overruled by *Adams v. Angell* (1877) 5 Ch.D. 634 and *Thorne v. Cann* (1895) A.C. 11.

[39] *Thorne v. Cann* (1895) A.C. 11.

[40] *e.g.* James L.J. in *Stevens v. Mid-Hants Rly. Co.* (1873) L.R. 8 Ch. 1064 at 1069; Lords Herschell and Macnaghten in *Thorne v. Cann* (1895) A.C. 11 at 16, 18; Fletcher-Moulton L.J. in *Manks v. Whiteley* (1912) 1 Ch. 735 at 759.

[41] [1895] A.C. 11.

[42] [1898] A.C. 321.

[43] [1914] A.C. 132, in particular at 144, 145.

overruled only because of the great reputation of the judge who decided it and the accident that, for the decision of the cases before the House of Lords, it was unnecessary to do so.[44] In *Thorne* v. *Cann* the court, in deciding that the purchaser of an equity of redemption intended to keep alive the charge which he had acquired, found indications of his intention, not only in the form of the instruments, but in the circumstances surrounding the transaction. It is difficult to believe that the existence of mesne incumbrances is not a circumstance from which such an indication of intention can be derived.[45] After this decision, and the language of Lord Haldane in *Whiteley* v. *Delaney*, it is safe to say that *Toulmin* v. *Steere* will no longer be followed, and that the existence of mesne incumbrances raises a presumption against merger in all cases.

(d) *Conclusion*

22–15   The foregoing presumptions do no more than establish the onus of proof and do not prevail when there is sufficient evidence that the actual intention was otherwise. Such evidence is usually to be found in the instrument under which the property and the benefit of the charge become united in the same hand. Thus, if it is intended to keep a charge on foot, the proper course is to insert in the instrument an express declaration to that effect, for this will usually be conclusive of the intention.[46] The form of the instrument itself may indicate the intention either to keep alive or merge the charge; for example, if the instrument is in terms a transfer of the charge, it suggests that the charge is to be kept alive; but if the instrument is merely a reconveyance of the security, the merger of the charge appears to be the intention. In neither case, however, is the form of the transaction decisive unless the surrounding circumstances point to the same conclusion.[47] Similarly, the fact that the charge is assigned to a trustee to be held for the owner of the estate is not by itself sufficient evidence of an intention to keep the charge alive. In one case, however, the circumstances point conclusively to an intention to extinguish the charge, namely, when a mortgagee takes a conveyance of the equity of redemption in consideration not only of releasing his own debt but of paying off all other incumbrances.[48]

In determining the question of merger or no merger, evidence of intention is therefore usually derived either from the language or the circumstances of the instrument by which the charge is acquired. It appears, however, that the court will allow parol evidence of intention to be given, for in *Astley* v. *Milles*[49] the solicitor, who had prepared the instruments by which a charge was acquired, was permitted to depose that the actual intention of the parties had been to keep the charge on foot. When the evidence establishes an intention to extinguish, this is decisive, since a charge, once merged, is destroyed for ever. If, on the other hand, a charge has been kept alive either by express declaration or by reason of the

---

[44] In *Liquidation Estates Purchase Co.* v. *Willoughby* and *Whiteley v. Delaney* the cases were decided on other grounds; in *Thorne v. Cann* an actual intention was established.

[45] Lindley L.J. in *Liquidation Estates Purchase Co.* v. *Willoughby*, thought that the dicta in *Thorne v. Cann* have overruled *Toulmin v. Steere* (1896) 1 Ch. 726 at 734.

[46] *Re Gibbon* [1909] 1 Ch. 367.

[47] *Hood v. Phillips* (1841) 3 Beav. 513.

[48] *Brown v. Stead* (1832) 5 Sim. 535.

[49] (1827) 1 Sim. 298 at 345.

circumstances of its acquisition, this will not be conclusive if a subsequent change of intention is proved. For example, when property is afterwards mortgaged or settled without the deeds noticing the charge, an intention to cancel the charge will be inferred.[50]

DESTRUCTION OR LOSS OF MORTGAGED PROPERTY

If the mortgaged property is lost or destroyed the benefit of the security may also be lost. This can arise for instance, in a case where a mortgaged leasehold is forfeited.[51] The mortgagor's personal liability on the covenant remains.[52]   **22–16**

DISCHARGE OR MODIFICATION BY STATUTE

1. Under the Housing Act 1985

The Housing Act 1985, Part XVII contains special provisions with regard to the discharge or modification of liabilities under a mortgage or instalment purchase agreement.[53] This part of the legislation was designed to provide for the removal by demolition or closure of unfit houses incapable of being rendered fit at reasonable expense and also to provide for slum clearance. Provision is made for the payment of compensation in such circumstances.   **22–17**

2. Under the Leasehold Reform Act 1967

The purpose of this Act is to enable tenants of dwelling-houses held on long leases who fulfil the requisite residential qualification to acquire the freehold or an extended lease provided that the premises are within the appropriate rateable value limits and the tenancy is a long tenancy at a low rent. Where the tenant gives notice of his desire to have the freehold or an extended lease, the landlord is bound (subject to the Act) to convey to him the fee simple absolute or a new tenancy for a term expiring 50 years after the existing tenancy. In such circumstances, mortgages of both the landlord's and the tenant's interest in the premises may be affected.   **22–18**

The Act therefore provides for the discharge of mortgages on the landlord's estate. A conveyance executed to give effect to the tenant's right to acquire the freehold shall as regards any charge on the landlord's estate (however created or arising) to secure the payment of money or the performance of any other obligation by the landlord or any other person, not being a charge subject to which the conveyance is required to be made or which would be overreached apart from this section, be effective by virtue of this section to discharge the house and premises from the charge and from the operation of any order made

---

[50] *Tyler v. Lake* (1831) 4 Sim. 351; *Hood v. Philipps* (1841) 3 Beav. 513.
[51] But see the L.P.A. 1925, s.146(4).
[52] See *ante*, para. 16–110 *et seq.*
[53] See further Hague, *Leasehold Enfranchisement* (3rd ed., 1999) for a detailed analysis of this area of law.

by the court for the enforcement of the charge, and to extinguish any term of years created for the purposes of the charge, and shall do so without the persons entitled to or interested in the charge or in any such order or term of years becoming parties to or executing the conveyance.[54]

Where in accordance with section 12(1) the conveyance to a tenant will be effective to discharge the house and premises from a charge to secure the payment of money then except as otherwise provided by section 12 it shall be the duty of the tenant to apply the price payable for the house and premises, in the first instance, in or towards the redemption of any such charge (and, if there are more than one, then according to their priorities).[55] If any amount payable in accordance with section 12(2) to the person entitled to the benefit of a charge is not so paid nor paid into court, in accordance with section 13 of the Act, then for the amount in question the house and premises shall remain subject to the charge and to that extent section 12(1) of the Act shall not apply.[56] Where the house and premises are discharged by section 12 of the Act from a charge (without the obligations secured by the charge being satisfied by the receipt of the whole or part of the price) the discharge of the house and premises shall not prejudice any right or remedy for the enforcement of those obligations against other property comprised in the same or any other security, nor prejudice any personal liability as principal or otherwise of the landlord or any other person.[57]

22–19   The tenant acquiring the freehold may pay into court on account of the price for the house and premises the amount, if known, of the payment to be made in respect of the charge or, if that amount is not known, the whole of the price or such less amount as the tenant thinks right in order to provide for that payment.[58] This can occur if:

(a)   for any reason difficulty arises in ascertaining how much is payable in respect of the charge; or

(b)   for any reason mentioned in section 13(2) difficulty arises in making a payment in respect of the charge.

Such difficulty is envisaged in the following cases:

(a)   because a person who is or may be entitled to receive payment cannot be found or ascertained; or

(b)   because any such person refuses or fails to make out a title, or to accept payment and give a proper discharge, or to take any steps reasonably required of him to enable the sum to be ascertained and paid; or

(c)   because a tender of the sum payable cannot, by reason of complications in the title to it or the want of two or more trustees or for other reasons, be effected, or not without incurring or involving unreasonable costs or delay.[59]

---

[54] Leasehold Reform Act 1967, s.12(1).
[55] *ibid.* s.12(2).
[56] *ibid.* s.12(2).
[57] *ibid.* s.12(6).
[58] *ibid.* s.13.
[59] *ibid.* s.13(2).

The tenant must pay the purchase price into court if before execution of the conveyance written notice is given to him:

(a) that the landlord or a person entitled to the benefit of a charge on the house and premises so requires for the purpose of protecting the rights of persons so entitled, or for reasons related to any application made or to be made under section 36 of the Act, or to the bankruptcy or winding up of the landlord; or

(b) that steps have been taken to enforce any charge on the landlord's interest in the house and premises by the bringing of proceedings in any court, or by the appointment of a receiver, or otherwise.[60]

Where payment is made into court by reason only of a notice under section 13(3) and the notice is given with reference to proceedings in a court specified in the notice other than the county court, payment shall be made into the court so specified.[61]

In certain cases the court is able to grant relief in respect of mortgages on the landlord's estate in order to avoid or mitigate any financial hardship that might otherwise be caused by the rights conferred on tenants by the Act.[62]

3. Under the Landlord and Tenant Act 1987

The Act provides for the compulsory acquisition of the landlord's interest and entitles qualifying tenants of blocks of flats to apply to the court for an acquisition order.[63] This contains provision for the discharge of mortgages on the landlord's interest, if such order is made.[64]

22–20

4. Under the Rent Act 1977

Variation of the terms of regulated mortgages.[65]

22–21

5. Under the Consumer Credit Act 1974

Refusal of enforcement orders and other aspects.[66]

22–22

---

[60] Leasehold Reform Act 1967, s.13(3).
[61] *ibid.* The court for the purposes of s.13(1) and (unless the landlord's notice specifies another court) s.13(3), is the county court, see s.20(1).
[62] *ibid.* s.36.
[63] Landlord and Tenant Act 1987, Pt. 111.
[64] *ibid.* s.32, Sched. 1. See further *Woodfall's Law of Landlord and Tenant* (1994).
[65] See *ante*, para. 16–88.
[66] See *ante*, chap. 14 and para. 16–87.

EXTINCTION OF MORTGAGE BY LAPSE OF TIME

1. Loss of the mortgagor's right to redeem by lapse of time

(a) *Land*

22–23   Where the security is land,[67] section 16 of the Limitation Act 1980 provides that when a mortgagee "has been in possession of any of the mortgaged land for a period of 12 years, no action to redeem the land of which he has been so in possession shall be brought after the end of that period by the mortgagor or any person claiming through him." This section means that time begins to run against the mortgagor at once from the mortgagee's entry into possession, whether or not the right of redemption has yet arisen.[68] It begins to run in respect of any part of which the mortgagee is in possession even though the mortgagor remains in possession of the rest of the land.[69] Formerly, the fact that the mortgagor was under a disability made no difference as actions for redemption were not actions to recover land within section 16 of the Real Property Limitation Act 1833 which made allowance for disability.[70] Section 22 of the 1939 Act, however, extended the allowance for disability to all cases where the Act imposed a limitation and therefore to actions for redemption of mortgages of land.[71] This is now incorporated into section 28 of the 1980 Act.

(b) *Acknowledgment and part payment*

22–24   By section 29(4) the running of time under the Limitation Act 1980, is stopped if the mortgagee:

"... either:
(a)   receives any sum in respect of the principal or interest of the mortgage debt; or
(b)   acknowledges the title of the mortgagor, or his equity of redemption."

The 12-year period then runs from the date of the last payment or acknowledgment. A receipt, to have this effect, must be of money paid "in respect of the principal or interest", so that the receipt of rents or proceeds of sale by a mortgagee in possession without accounting for them to the mortgagor will not stop the period from running. An acknowledgment must be in writing, signed either by the mortgagee or his agent, and must be made to the owner of the equity of redemption or his agent.[72] The actual form of the instrument is immaterial so

---

[67] "Land" is defined in s.38(1) of the Limitation Act 1980.

[68] *Re Metropolis and Counties Permanent Investment Building Society* [1911] 1 Ch. 698. However the mortgagee must have entered in the character of mortgagee: *Hyde v. Dallaway* (1843) 2 Hare 528.

[69] *Kinsman v. Rouse* (1881) 17 Ch.D. 104.

[70] *ibid.*

[71] Preston & Newsom, *Limitation of Actions* (1953), p. 219.

[72] s.30. *Cf. Wright v. Pepin* [1954] 1 W.L.R. 635, where the authority was inferred. There had been an acknowledgment by the mortgagor's solicitor which was held sufficient.

long as it contains an unequivocal recognition of the fact that the estate is mortgaged.[73]

Where there are two or more mortgagors, an acknowledgment to one is deemed to be made to all and so stops time from running against any of them.[74] However, an acknowledgment by one of two or more mortgagees does not bind the other mortgagees. Section 31 of the 1980 Act provides:

> "(3) Where two or more mortgagees are by virtue of the mortgage in possession of the mortgaged land, an acknowledgement of the mortgagor's title or of his equity of redemption by one of the mortgagees shall only bind him and his successors and shall not bind any other mortgagee or his successors.
>
> (4) Where in a case within subsection (3) above the mortgagee by whom the acknowledgement is given is entitled to a part of the mortgaged land and not to any ascertained part of the mortgage debt the mortgagor shall be entitled to redeem that part of the land on payment, with interest, of the part of the mortgage debt which bears the same proportion to the whole of the debt as the value of the part of the land bears to the whole of the mortgaged land."

The effect of this somewhat difficult language appears to be that:

(a) An acknowledgment by one mortgagee can in no case bind the other mortgagees.

(b) Where the mortgage moneys are not held by the mortgagees on a joint account an acknowledgment by one binds him and the mortgagor may redeem him as to his share thus acquiring an equitable right to his interest in the mortgage. The other mortgagees hold their shares in the mortgage free of the equity of redemption.

(c) Where the mortgage moneys are held on a joint account (*i.e.* no ascertained share) but the mortgagees have entered separately into possession of distinct parts of the mortgaged land an acknowledgment by one binds him and exposes him to redemption of the part of which he is in possession. As he is not entitled to any ascertained part of the mortgaged debt the price of redemption is worked out by attributing to him a share of the mortgage debt corresponding to the proportion of the mortgaged land which his part bears to the whole.

(d) Where the mortgage moneys are held on a joint account and the mortgagees are jointly in possession an acknowledgment by one is wholly ineffective to stop the running of the period in favour of all.[75]

Once the right of redemption has been barred by the mortgagee's continuance in possession for the statutory period, no subsequent acknowledgment can revive

---

[73] *cf. Stansfield v. Hobson* (1853) 3 De G.M. & G. 620.
[74] s.31(5).
[75] *cf. Richardson v. Younge* (1871) L.R. 6 Ch. 478.

it for section 17 of the 1980 Act expressly extinguishes the title to the equity of redemption.[76]

(c) *Personalty*

22–25   Although the 1939 Act placed foreclosure actions for mortgaged personalty on the same footing as for realty, barring them after 12 years, it did not subject actions to redeem mortgaged personalty to the limitations governing actions to redeem realty. The Law Revision Committee justified this differential treatment of realty and personalty in regard to redemption on the ground that whereas a mortgagee of land does not ordinarily take possession except by way of enforcing his security, the mortgagee of personalty may have possession of the property from the outset. It was for this reason that the Committee thought that serious practical difficulties might arise if the statutory limitations were applied to the redemption of mortgaged personalty. It had in mind particularly the case of bonds or shares deposited with a bank by way of equitable mortgage and left with the bank more or less indefinitely to cover an overdraft.[77] Consequently, the 1939 Act, like previous Statutes of Limitation, left actions to redeem personalty without any statutory limit. Moreover, it was well established under the former statutes that equity will not, by analogy, extend to personalty statutory limitations whose operation is expressly restricted to land.[78] This position remains unchanged under the 1980 Act.

2. **Laches**

22–26   Since no Statute of Limitation operates, whether directly or by analogy, to bar actions to redeem personalty, lapse of time will defeat such actions only on the general principle *æquitas vigilantibus non dormientibus succurrit* ("equity ends the vigilant and not the indolent"). The rules on which the court acts in refusing its assistance to stale demands cannot be stated with precision because in cases where no Statute of Limitation applies judges have refrained from fixing a definite period within which equitable remedies must be brought. In *Weld* v. *Petre*,[79] although counsel invited the court to say that no action to redeem personalty would be entertained after 20 years, the court refused to lay down any rigid rule. A defence based on lapse of time depends in equity primarily on the balance of justice or injustice in affording or refusing relief.[80] Under such a test each case will clearly be governed by its own special circumstances. Thus in *Erlanger* v. *New Sombrero Phosphate Co.*[81] Lord Blackburn said:

---

[76] *cf. Young v. Clarey* [1948] Ch. 191; and under the former law; *Re Alison* (1879) 11 Ch.D. 284.
[77] Fifth Interim Report (1936), Cmd. 5334, p. 15.
[78] *London & Midland Bank v. Mitchell* [1899] 2 Ch. 161; *Weld v. Petre* [1929] 1 Ch. 33. But in the case of a mixed fund of personalty and realty it was held in one case that the right to redeem personalty was barred as the equity was indivisible, see *Charter v. Watson* [1899] 1 Ch. 175.
[79] [1929] 1 Ch. 33.
[80] *Lindsay Petroleum Co. v. Hurd* (1874) L.R. 5 P.C. 221.
[81] (1878) 3 App. Cas. 1218 at 1279.

"I think, from the nature of the inquiry, it must always be a question of more or less, depending on the degree of diligence which might reasonably be required, and the degree of change which has occurred, whether the balance of justice or injustice is in favour of granting the remedy or withholding it."

The doctrine of laches thus really provides two distinct grounds on which a remedy may be refused:

(*i*) conduct by the claimant which suggests that he has waived his right; or

(*ii*) a change in the circumstances of the defendant which renders it practically unjust to enforce the remedy.

The leading case on the application of the doctrine to the right to redeem personalty is *Weld* v. *Petre*[82] in which it was held that:

(a) Mere inaction by the mortgagor, laches in the narrow sense, is not sufficient evidence of an intention to waive his rights and will not bar the right to redeem under the doctrine of laches. Thus, Russell J. at first instance[83] expressly said: "Equity should not, in my opinion, deprive mortgagors of their right to redeem if, when they assert it, the debt has been or can be repaid, the security is available and no one's position has been altered in the meanwhile. If these circumstances co-exist, the mortgagor should be allowed to redeem unless his right has been destroyed by statute, foreclosure, sale or release."

(b) Where the mortgagee (*i*) has not altered his position by expending money on the property in the reasonable belief that the property was now his own; (*ii*) has not, by reason of the delay, lost any evidence which will make it difficult for him to render his accounts; and (*iii*) has not otherwise altered his position to his prejudice, the mortgagor will be admitted to redeem.

(c) The fact that on the death of the mortgagee the mortgaged property has been included in the mortgagee's assets and estate duty paid in respect of it is not a sufficient ground for refusing relief to the mortgagor.

BARRING A MORTGAGEE'S REMEDIES UNDER THE LIMITATION ACT 1980

The limitations imposed by the Limitation Act 1980 ("the 1980 Act") on the enforcement of a mortgagee's remedies require to be considered under five main heads:

22–27

(1) Personal actions on the contract for payment;

(2) Actions to recover principal sums of money secured by mortgage or charge;

---

[82] [1929] 1 Ch. 33.
[83] *ibid.* at 42.

(3) Actions for foreclosure or possession;

(4) Actions to enforce mortgages of future interests; and

(5) Actions for the recovery of arrears of interest.

In addition the rules laid down for these actions are affected by the general provisions of the Act relating to disability, acknowledgment, part payment, fraud, concealment and mistake.

1. Personal actions on the contract for payment

22–28   When the mortgage is not under seal an action on the express or implied promise to pay the debt is one "founded on simple contract" within section 5 of the 1980 Act and, as such, is barred "after the expiration of six years from the date when the cause of action accrued", *i.e.* after the date for repayment.[84] It was, however, well settled under the old law that the barring of the personal action on the contract after six years did not preclude the subsequent enforcement of the remedies against the security. The reason was that the statute only barred the action and did not extinguish the debt.[85] The position in regard to the debt is still the same under the 1980 Act so that the remedies against the security are not touched by section 5 but fall under section 20, being barred only after 12 years.

When the mortgage is under seal the action on the covenant for payment is one "upon a specialty" within section 8 of the 1980 Act. The period of limitation is thus 12 years.[86]

2. Actions to recover principal sums of money secured by mortgage or charge

22–29   Section 20(1) of the 1980 Act provides:

"(1) No action shall be brought to recover—

(a) any principal sum of money secured by a mortgage or other charge on property (whether real or personal); or

(b) proceeds of the sale of land;

after the expiration of 12 years from the date on which the right to receive the money accrued."

Thus, quite apart from the limits imposed on contractual actions to recover the principal, the Act specifically bars any action to recover the principal by enforcing the security after the elapse of 12 years. The extension of this statutory limitation on enforcing securities to mortgages of personalty, as explained above,

---

[84] This will depend on whether the covenant gives the date for repayment and whether a demand is necessary.

[85] *London & Midland Bank v. Mitchell* [1899] 2 Ch. 161.

[86] It is not sufficient for the obligation to be merely acknowledged or evidenced by the security, it must be created or secured by it—*Re Compania de Electricidad de la Provincia de Buenos Aires Ltd.* [1980] Ch. 146.

was an innovation. The limitation of 12 years now applies to all forms of property.

The position is more difficult where the mortgage deed creating the security also contains a personal covenant to repay. By section 8(1) of the Limitation Act 1980, any action based on a speciality (being an obligation under seal) shall be subject to a 12 year period. However, section 8(2) of the Limitation Act provides that section 8(1) "shall not affect any action for which a shorter period of limitation is prescribed by any other provision" of the Limitation Act. As a result, it was previously considered that whether or not the mortgage was by deed, the limitation period applicable to any claim for repayment would be six years from accrual of the acion[87] and that the shorter simple contractual limitation period prevailed.

(a) *Securum Finance Ltd v. Ashton*[88]

However, in *Securum Finance Ltd v. Ashton*, Mr I. Hunter Q.C., sitting as a **22–30** Deputy Judge of the High Court, concluded that since an action on a simple contract is by definition not an action on a speciality, section 5 and section 8(1) of the Limitation Act should be read as being mutually exclusive. It follows from that conclusion that so long as the legal charge is under seal and contains a covenant to pay, the limitation period under section 5 could not be said to apply to that covenant and therefore any action on such covenant would fall within section 8(1) and not section 8(2) and the limitation period would be 12 years.

It would appear that the position is different with regard to interest. Section 20(5) provides for a limitation period of six years with regard to actions to recover arrears of interest or other charges, as opposed to capital, in respect of any sum secured by a mortgage or other charge.[89] It would appear in those circumstances that the distinction drawn in *Securum Finance Ltd v. Ashton* cannot be made and the six year period is applicable to the claims relating to interest even if the covenant to pay interest is contained in the mortgage deed.[90]

However, once the mortgaged property has been repossessed and sold and the claim is thus a claim for any shortfall between the monies realised and those owing, the claim is no longer an action to recover money secured by a mortgage so that section 20 and the shorter limitation period it provides for would no longer apply.[91] It also appears that even where the obligation originally arose pursuant to a speciality, following repossession any claim for the shortfall whether relating to capital or interest is in reality a claim pursuant to a simple contract and therefore subject to the six year limitation period.[92]

---

[87] *Romain v. Scuba T.B. Ltd* [1989] Q.B. 887 and *Halsbury's Laws of England* (4th ed.), Vol. 32 (Re-issue, 1999), para. 715.

[88] *Securum Finance Ltd v. Ashton* (unreported) June 10, 1999, Ch. D.—appeal on other grounds dismissed in the Court of Appeal, the limitation point having been conceded see *Securum Finance Ltd v. Ashton* [2000] 3 W.L.R. 1400.

[89] *ibid.*, s.20(5).

[90] See *Romain v. Scuba T.B. Ltd, ante.*

[91] *Global Finance Recoveries Ltd v. Jones* (unreported) December 14, 1999, Ch. D. and *Hopkinson v. Tupper* (unreported) January 1, 1997, CA; and *West Bromwich Building Society v. Layworth* (unreported, September 20, 1999, HHJ Nichol).

[92] *Hopkinson v. Tupper, ante.*

3. **Actions for (a) foreclosure or (b) possession**

(a) *Foreclosure*

22–31   Foreclosure actions, as already mentioned, are dealt with by the 1980 Act as actions to recover the property rather than to recover the debt by realising the security. Formerly, the Real Property Limitation Acts did not specify foreclosure actions as actions to recover land but it was settled in a series of decisions that land foreclosure actions, for purposes of the limitation of actions, are actions to recover land.[93] These decisions were not perhaps entirely logical because foreclosure is not, either in law or in equity, an action to recover the mortgagor's interest. It is an action to complete the mortgagee's title to an interest already vested in him by removing the stop on the title imposed by equity.[94] Moreover, a foreclosure action always invites redemption and is in substance an action to recover the amount of the debt by realising the security. The courts, however, looked primarily to the fact that in equity the mortgagor remains beneficial owner and that a foreclosure order absolute for the first time vests the beneficial ownership in the mortgagee.[95] On this basis, they decided to treat foreclosure actions as actions to recover land. They had a strong inducement to do so in that some of the provisions postponing the running of the statutory period applied, owing to the erratic policy of the Acts, to actions for the recovery of land but not to actions for the recovery of money charged on land.[96] Although the 1980 Act maintains the distinction between foreclosure and other remedies, happily the distinction has lost most of its importance owing to the rules relating to actions for the recovery of money charged on property having been assimilated to those governing actions to recover land.

(i) *Applicable period*

22–32   In the case of land[97] section 20(4), re-enacting the former law, declares that foreclosure actions are not within section 20 at all but are governed by the provisions of the Act relating to actions to recover land, in particular by section 15. The period prescribed by section 15(1) in ordinary cases is 12 years from the date on which the right of action accrued under the mortgage.[98] In the case of personalty where formerly there was no statutory limit on foreclosure actions, the Act does not carry logic to the extent of applying the provisions relating to recovery of chattels. Instead, section 20(2) simply enacts that foreclosure actions in respect of mortgaged personalty shall be barred after 12 years from the date on which the right to foreclose accrued. The general rule is thus the same both for

---

[93] *e.g. Heath v. Pugh* (1881) 6 Q.B.D. 345; *Pugh v. Heath* (1881) 7 A.C. 235; *Harlock v. Ashberry* (1882) 19 Ch.D. 539.
[94] See *ante*, para. 16–89 *et seq.*
[95] See *Heath v. Pugh* (1881) 6 Q.B.D. 345 at 360.
[96] A good example is the case of future interests discussed, *post*, para. 22–35.
[97] "Land" includes corporeal hereditaments, tithes and rentcharges and any legal or equitable estate or interest therein, including an interest in the proceeds of the sale of land held upon trust for sale, but except as provided above in this definition does not include an incorporeal hereditament, as defined by s.38(1).
[98] Sched. 1, para. 10, prescribes 30 years in the case of the Crown and spiritual or eleemosynary corporations sole.

land and personalty: foreclosure actions are barred 12 years after the right to foreclose accrued.

Accrual of the cause of action   The right to foreclose accrues when the mortga-   **22–33**
gor is in default on the proviso for redemption and the mortgagee's estate has become absolute at law.[99] Although any default which touches the terms of the proviso for redemption gives rise to the right of foreclosure, the right usually accrues on a default in the covenant to pay the mortgage moneys on the date specified. Where, however, the moneys are repayable on demand the right accrues immediately on the execution of the mortgage unless the demand has been made a condition precedent to the enforcement of the mortgage.[1] Such are the basic rules concerning the first accrual of the right of foreclosure and the date when the statutory period begins to run. The 1980 Act, however, contains several provisions which, for the purposes of the limitation of actions, suspend the accrual of the right of action of a mortgagee. The most important of these provisions, covering future interests, disabilities, acknowledgments and part payment, apply generally to all remedies and are dealt with separately below. One provision, however, affects foreclosure alone. If a mortgagee, whether of land[2] or of personalty,[3] has been in possession of the mortgaged property after the right of foreclosure has accrued the right is deemed not to have accrued until he has been dispossessed or has discontinued his possession.

A mortgagee who exercises his rights and obtains a foreclosure order absolute acquires, it was decided in *Heath v. Pugh*,[4] an entirely new title so that time only runs against his new right to eject the mortgagor as from the date of the order being made absolute.

(b) *Possession*

A mortgagee's right to take possession of the security is also a right to recover   **22–34**
the land and is barred 12 years after the right accrued. In this instance the period does normally begin to run immediately from the execution of a legal mortgage because the conveyance carries the right to possession. If, however, the mortgage provides for quiet enjoyment by the mortgagor until default, it operates as a redemise to him from the mortgagee and the period only begins to run from the date of the default.[5] As an equitable mortgage has no right to possession except by special agreement, the date when the right accrues can only be ascertained from the agreement if such an agreement exists.[6] The running of the statute against the right to enter into possession is, as with other remedies, interrupted by acknowledgment or part payment or by disability.

---

[99] See *ante*, para. 16–92.
[1] See *Re Brown's Estate* [1893] 2 Ch. 300; *Lloyds Bank v. Margolis* [1954] 1 W.L.R. 644.
[2] Limitation Act 1980, Sched. 1, para. 1.
[3] *ibid.* s.20(2).
[4] (1881) 6 Q.B.D. 345.
[5] *Wilkinson v. Hall* (1837) 3 Bing N.C. 508.
[6] *Ocean Accident & Guarantee Corp. v. Ilford Gas Co.* [1905] 2 K.B. 493.

4. **Actions to enforce mortgages of future interests**

(a) *Hugill v. Wilkinson*[7]

22–35   The distinction between actions for foreclosure of land and actions to recover money charged on land was formerly of particular importance in regard to the mortgage of future interests. Section 2 of the 1874 Act provided that the operation of the statute against actions to recover land should, in the case of a future interest, be postponed until the interest fell into possession. In *Hugill v. Wilkinson*,[8] North J. decided that foreclosure actions, being actions to recover land, also had the benefit of section 2 with the result that foreclosure of a mortgage of a remainder was not barred until 12 years after the remainder became vested in possession. There was, however, no similar provision to effect a postponement in the case of actions to recover money charged on land. Consequently, in the absence of acknowledgment, part payment or disability a mortgagee's other remedies were barred 12 years after the mortgagor's default in redeeming even though the security might not yet have fallen into possession.[9] This meant that in charges, properly so called, where foreclosure was not an available remedy, the creditor might lose his charge on a future interest altogether 12 years after his charge first became payable.[10] Moreover, owing to the particular language of section 2, its operation was confined to land in the strict sense and it did not, like other sections, extend to the proceeds of sale of land. The result, as previously mentioned, was that the unlucky mortgagee of a future interest in proceeds of sale found that his security was land for the purpose of attracting the 12 years' limit imposed on foreclosure actions for the recovery of land, but not "land" for the purpose of working a postponement under section 2.[11] On the other hand, the mortgagee of a future interest in pure personalty had nothing to worry about because to him no statute of limitations applied at all.[12]

The decision in *Hugill v. Wilkinson*[13] was a literal application of section 2 of the 1874 Act in the light of the decisions that foreclosure is an action to recover land. The principle of the case was not, however, really the same as that of section 2. Foreclosure operates between mortgagee and mortgagor where the right to foreclose arises immediately on the mortgagor's default whether the property be present or future and there is no legal obstacle to the prosecution of the action. Foreclosure, as stated, is really an action to terminate the equity of redemption. Even if it is regarded as an action to recover the mortgagor's interest, it is not, where the security is a future interest, a future right of action for the recovery of the land but an immediate right of action to recover the mortgagor's present right to future possession. The fact that foreclosure of a future interest does not vest in the mortgagee an immediate right to the rents and profits is immaterial. Foreclosure does effectively vest in him an immediate title to the

---

[7] (1888) 38 Ch.D. 480.
[8] *ibid.*
[9] *Re Owen* [1894] 3 Ch. 220.
[10] *Re Witham* [1922] 2 Ch. 413.
[11] *Re Hazeldine's Trusts* [1908] 1 Ch. 34; *Re Fox* [1913] 2 Ch. 75.
[12] See *Re Witham* [1922] 2 Ch. 413 where part of the property was personalty.
[13] (1888) 38 Ch.D. 480. For a discussion of this case see Preston & Newsom, *Limitation of Actions* (1953), pp. 110–114.

property mortgaged. This point was taken by Cozens-Hardy M.R. in *Wakefield and Barnsley Union Bank Ltd.* v. *Yates*[14]: "the object of foreclosure is to destroy the mortgagor's right to redeem and it is only as an incident that the right to receive the rents and profits arises." The Court of Appeal in that case refused to regard the fact that the mortgaged property was a reversion after a 21 years' lease as any reason for postponing the running of the statute. Yet, for purposes of the limitation of actions, leasehold reversions are treated as future interests in the same category as the remainder in *Hugill* v. *Wilkinson*. Consequently, the decision of the Court of Appeal in *Yates'* case is scarcely consistent with that of North J. in *Hugill* v. *Wilkinson*, although the latter case was referred to in *Yates'* case without disapproval.

(b) *The modern position*

On the other hand, the principle of *Hugill* v. *Wilkinson*, if open to question on technical grounds, has practical advantages. There is much to be said for a rule which does not constrain a mortgagee to realise his security before the asset to which the mortgagor looked as the means for repaying his debt has materialised. At any rate the Law Revision Committee so far approved the principle of *Hugill* v. *Wilkinson*[15] that section 18(3) of the 1939 Act incorporated it in statutory form now repeated in section 20(3) of the 1980 Act. This provides as follows: **22–36**

> "The right to receive any principal sum of money secured by a mortgage or other charge and the right to foreclose on the property subject to the mortgage or charge shall not be treated as accruing so long as the property comprises any future interest or any life insurance policy which has not matured or been determined."

The effect of this provision is that time does not run against remedies to enforce mortgages comprising any future interest until the future interest falls into possession and a life insurance policy that has not yet matured or been determined is treated as a future interest for this purpose. Section 20(3) applies to all remedies for the recovery of money charged on real or personal property and to foreclosure of mortgages of personalty. It does not, however, apply to foreclosure of mortgages of "land" which falls under section 15 and Schedule 1, which govern actions for the recovery of land.

(c) *Future interests in land*

Section 15 substantially re-enacts the provisions of the former Acts relating to the postponement of the statutory period of limitation in the case of future interests in land. But the primary rule is now contained in Schedule 1, paragraph 4 to the 1980 Act which provides: **22–37**

---

[14] [1916] 1 Ch. 452 at 458.
[15] Fifth Interim Report (1936), Cmnd. 5334, p. 14.

"The right of action to recover any land shall, in a case where—

(a) the estate or interest claimed was an estate or interest in reversion or remainder or any other future estate or interest; and

(b) no person has taken possession of the land by virtue of the estate or interest claimed;

be treated as having accrued on the date on which the estate or interest fell into possession by the determination of the preceding estate or interest."

Section 15(2) qualifies this rule in cases where the holder of a preceding estate, other than a term of years, has been dispossessed during its continuance by allowing to the person entitled to the future interest either 12 years from the dispossession or six years from the date when his own interest vested in possession, whichever is longer. Certain other points of detail are covered in the Act to which detailed reference should be made.

(i) *The effect of section 15 of the Act*

22–38   The result is that section 15 makes provision for the postponement of the operation of the statute in actions for the recovery of land comparable to the general provision for postponement in section 20(3) in regard to actions for the recovery of money charged on real and personal property. Ironically enough, it is doubtful whether the benefit of postponement under section 6 extends to actions to foreclose mortgages of future interests in land owing to the questionable authority of the decision in *Hugill* v. *Wilkinson*.[16] If the decision in *Wakefield and Barnsley Union Bank Ltd.* v. *Yates*[17] is correct, foreclosure actions are not within section 15 and Schedule 1. Further there is nothing in the 1980 Act to bring them within that section. Yet the intention plainly was that in the case of land foreclosure, actions should have the benefit of postponement no less than the actions now covered by section 20(3). The Law Revision Committee assumed that *Hugill* v. *Wilkinson* was good law and recommended its extension in the manner effected by the predecessor to section 20(3).[18]

The position in regard to foreclosure of future interests in land is, therefore, scarcely satisfactory. The courts may be inclined, in interpreting the 1980 Act, to overlook the difficulty of reconciling *Hugill* v. *Wilkinson* with *Yates' Case* and simply give foreclosure actions the benefit of postponement under section 15 on the basis of the decisions holding foreclosure actions to be actions for the recovery of land.[19] If this is not done, an arbitrary distinction will be created between foreclosure of mortgages of land and other actions to enforce mortgages of realty and personalty, a distinction which would be the precise opposite of that which the Law Revision Committee intended to remove.[20]

If *Hugill* v. *Wilkinson* is followed in applying the 1980 Act, the status of *Yates' Case* necessarily comes into question particularly in regard to the position of

---

[16] (1888) 38 Ch.D. 480; see *ante*, para. 22–35.

[17] [1916] 1 Ch. 452.

[18] *Hugill v. Wilkinson* had been mentioned without disapproval in more than one case, *e.g. Re Witham* [1922] 2 Ch. 413.

[19] As is assumed in Oughton, *Limitation of Actions* (1998).

[20] See Preston & Newsom, *Limitation of Actions* (1953), p. 113.

second mortgagees. Under the similar provisions of the earlier Acts it had been decided that:

(a) The existence of a prior mortgage, under which possession has not been taken, does not make a second mortgage a mortgage of a future interest so that it does not postpone the operation of the statute against a second mortgagee's right to foreclose.[21]

(b) The same is true, if the prior mortgagee goes into possession after the creation of the second mortgage.[22]

(c) Similarly the existence of a 21 years' lease under which possession has been taken before the execution of a mortgage does not postpone the running of the statute against the right to foreclose.[23]

All these decisions are obviously good sense. It would be absurd to postpone   **22–39** the running of the statute against a second mortgagee merely because of the existence of a prior mortgage term, even when the prior mortgagee has taken possession. A second mortgagee obtains the mortgagor's right to redeem the first mortgagee and there is nothing to stop him either from foreclosing the mortgagor or redeeming the first mortgagee whenever he chooses. What case is there for postponement? *Yates' Case* has a particular importance owing to mortgages now being made by demise and it is believed to be fundamentally sound. It certainly has to be accepted if any sense is to be made of the position of a second mortgagee. Yet, if foreclosure is regarded as an action for the recovery of land, *Yates' Case* is not easy to square with the general principles of the Limitation Acts under which a reversion upon a term of years is treated as a future interest. The courts are likely to uphold both *Yates' Case* and *Hugill* v. *Wilkinson*, but by what process of reasoning remains to be seen.

In any event, the 1980 Act seems to have created minor anomalies. Thus section 20(3) postpones the operation of the statute so long as the property mortgaged "comprises any future interest". These words can only mean that, where present and future interests are mortgaged together, section 20(3) protects the mortgagee's remedies in respect of *all* the property against the operation of the statute until the future interest falls into possession. No such provision is to be found in regard to foreclosure of mortgages of land, although a single mortgage comprising both a present interest in land and a future interest in realty or personalty is by no means impossible.

Again, section 15(3) excludes from the category of future interests estates or interests which fall into possession after an entail capable of being barred. There is no similar provision under section 20, although entails of personalty are now permissible.

5. **Actions for the recovery of arrears of interest**

So long as the right to the principal remains alive, the right to interest also   **22–40** continues, since interest is accessory to principal. But section 20(5) of the 1980 Act requires actions for the recovery of arrears of interest payable in respect of

[21] *Kibble v. Fairthorne* [1895] 1 Ch. 219.
[22] *Samuel Johnson & Sons Ltd.* v. *Brock* [1907] 2 Ch. 533.
[23] *Wakefield & Barnsley Union Bank Ltd.* v. *Yates* [1916] 1 Ch. 452.

sums secured by mortgage or charge to be brought within six years of the date when the interest became due. In other words, the maximum amount of interest recoverable in such an action is six years' arrears. The same limit is imposed on actions to recover arrears by way of damages, in cases where there is no covenant for payment of interest and the court gives interest by way of damages.[24]

There are, however, two qualifications on the general limit of six years by section 20(6) and (7) of the Act:

(a) Where a prior incumbrancer has been in possession of the property mortgaged, a subsequent incumbrancer, if he brings his action within one year of the discontinuance of the prior mortgagee's possession, may recover all interest which fell due during the period of that possession. The reason, of course, is that the prior incumbrancer's possession disables the second mortgagee from keeping down the interest of his own mortgage out of the rents and profits.[25]

(b) Where the mortgaged property comprises any future interest or life insurance policy and it is a term of the mortgage that arrears of interest shall be treated as part of the principal debt secured by the mortgage, then the interest is deemed not to be due until the right to receive the principal is deemed to accrue. This means that when the statute does not run against the mortgagee of future property until the property falls into possession, all arrears of interest accruing during the time when the property was still future are deemed to accrue only on the date when the property vested in possession. Consequently all such arrears are recoverable within six years of that date.

This is not, however, a general exception in favour of a mortgagee of future property. It is only when the mortgage provides for capitalisation of arrears of interest that the second exception operates. In other cases the six years' limit runs against the right to interest from the date when the interest was actually due whether or not the running of the statute against the right to the principal is postponed under section 20(3).

The six years' limit under section 20(5) applies to an action to recover arrears of interest, which includes an action to recover the principal with the interest thereon. On the basis of the decisions taken under the similar provision in section 42 of the Real Property Limitation Act 1833, the six years' limit would also apply to all proceedings by the mortgagee to enforce the mortgage, for it was settled that no more than six years' arrears of interest might go into the mortgagee's account in proceedings for foreclosure, judicial sale or the appointment of a receiver.[26] The 1980 Act, however, by wholly excluding foreclosure of mortgages of land from the provisions of section 20(4) appears inadvertently to have enacted that more than six years' arrears of interest may be claimed in foreclosure of land. Thus, while only six years' arrears will be allowed in

---

[24] *cf. Mellersh v. Brown* (1890) 45 Ch.D. 225.
[25] Unless the prior mortgagee pays over surplus rents and profits to the second mortgagee which rarely happens.
[26] *Sinclair v. Jackson* (1853) 17 Beav. 405; *Re Lloyd* [1903] 1 Ch. 385.

computing the mortgagor's personal debt, the full amount of the arrears will, in the case of land, be allowed in actions against the security.[27]

(a) *Arrears of interest in redemption actions*

In any event, it is well settled that the six years' limit does not apply in actions **22–41** by the mortgagor for redemption[28] and this is so even when the mortgagee has instituted proceedings for foreclosure and the mortgagor counterclaims for redemption.[29] A mortgagor who has lost his estate at law will only be allowed to redeem it in equity on the terms of discharging all his obligations under the mortgage. The mortgagor's neglect to pay the interest is just as culpable as the mortgagee's failure to enforce his rights. The rule is the same where the mortgagee has sold the security under a power of sale and the mortgagor seeks to recover the surplus proceeds of sale, for this is in essence an action for redemption. The mortgagee may thus retain out of the proceeds the full amount of the arrears.[30] The position is, however, not entirely clear when the property has been sold not in pursuance of the mortgagee's power of sale but under a paramount power outside the mortgage and the proceeds of sale have been paid into court. In *Re Stead's Mortgaged Estates*[31] the property had been sold under the Land Clauses Acts and the mortgagee petitioned to have the amount of his debt with full arrears of interest paid out to him. Malins V.-C. only allowed him six years' arrears. However, in *Re Lloyd*[32] the Court of Appeal allowed the mortgagee his full arrears when the property had been sold in an administration suit and the proceedings for payment out of court were initiated by the mortgagor. The court expressed no view as to the correctness of *Re Stead's Mortgaged Estates* and treated the mortgagor's claim as in substance one for redemption. The only observable difference between the two cases was in the party who took the first step in the proceedings for payment out. This difference can scarcely be material because in foreclosure the mortgagor's counterclaim for redemption, although made under the pressure of the mortgagee's proceedings, is outside the six years' limitation on arrears of interest. Indeed, if this is the difference between the cases, money may lie in court because neither party wishes to take the first step in the proceedings. It is therefore hoped that *Re Lloyd* will be regarded as having impliedly overruled *Re Stead's Mortgaged Estates*.

(b) *Disability*

It is not possible here to deal in detail with the rules governing the extension **22–42** of the period of limitation by reason of the disability of the person entitled to

---

[27] McGee, *Limitation Periods* (3rd ed., 1998), para. 13–062—13–068.
[28] *Elvy v. Norwood* (1852) 5 De G. & Sm. 240; *Edmunds v. Waugh* (1866) L.R. 1 Eq. 418 *Ezekiel v. Orakpo* [1997] 1 W.L.R. 340.
[29] *Dingle v. Coppen* [1899] 1 Ch. 726; *Holmes v. Cowcher* [1970] 1 W.L.R. 834 *Ezekial v. Orakpo, ante.*
[30] *Edmunds v. Waugh* (1866) L.R. 1 Eq. 418; *Holmes v. Cowcher, supra.*
[31] (1876) 2 Ch.D. 713.
[32] [1903] 1 Ch. 385.

sue.[33] The main rule laid down in section 28 is that if, on the date when the right of action accrued the person to whom it accrued was under a disability, the action may be brought within six years of the cessation of the disability. The disability must therefore subsist on the date when the right of action accrues which, in the case of a mortgagee's remedies is normally the date when the mortgagor defaults on the covenant for redemption.[34] It is not enough if the disability arises after the date fixed for redemption.[35]

Section 28(4) contains a provision with a special bearing on remedies to enforce a mortgage of land. Notwithstanding any disability, no action to recover land (including, of course, foreclosure) or to recover money charged on land may be brought more than 30 years after the right of action accrued. In other words, there is an absolute limit of 30 years even in cases of disability.

(c) Acknowledgments and part payments

22–43   The Act provides in sections 29 to 31 for the fresh accrual of actions—and thus for the extension of the statutory period—when an acknowledgment or part payment is made. It lays down slightly different rules for the remedies against the security and those in respect of the personal debt, so that the two forms of remedy have to be considered separately.

(i) Remedies against the security.

22–44   Section 29(1) to (3), which applies equally to realty and personalty, enacts that when there has accrued to a mortgagee any right of action to recover the mortgaged property, including a foreclosure action, and:

> (1) the person in possession of the land acknowledges the title of the mortgagee[36]; or
> (2) the person in possession or the person liable for the mortgage debt makes any payment in respect of the debt whether principal or interest;

the right shall be deemed to have accrued on the date of the acknowledgment or payment.

An *acknowledgment* is thus effective only when made by the person in possession or an agent on his behalf, while a *payment* is effective not only when made by the person in possession but also when made by the person liable for the

---

[33] See McGee, Limitation Periods (3rd ed., 1998) paras 19.001–19.031.

[34] See *ante*, p. 247.

[35] *Purnell v. Roche* [1927] 2 Ch. 142. In this case the remedies of a lunatic mortgagee were held not to have been saved by the disability, although interest had been paid after the disability supervened. Now, however, under s.29(3) of the 1980 Act, in a foreclosure or other action by the mortgagee, payment of principal or interest by the person in possession of the property causes the accrual of the right of action to be deemed to be postponed until the date of such payment, and facts similar to those in *Purnell v. Roche* would today give a different result.

[36] Or as agent on his behalf, see, *e.g. Wright v. Pepin* [1954] 1 W.L.R. 635.

mortgage debt. Both acknowledgments and payments, when effective, bind "all other persons in possession during the ensuing period of limitation."[37] In other words, the mortgagee's remedies against the property are protected against everybody for a further period of 12 years from the date of the acknowledgment or payment. Section 31, which establishes these rules, refers only to mortgages and mortgagees. There is no definition clause in the Act, which extends the meaning of "mortgage" to cover a charge. It is therefore arguable that acknowledgments and part payments under section 31 do not extend a chargee's remedies against the security. The argument gains point from the fact that section 20, which does cover charges, refers specifically to "a mortgage or other charge". The omission of charges[38] from the operation of section 31 can hardly have been intended and the courts may resort to the definition of mortgage in section 205(1)(xvi) of the Law of Property Act 1925, in order to avoid this result.[39]

a) *Mortgagor dispossessed by third party*

If after the execution of the mortgage a third party obtains possession and occupies the property under such conditions that time begins to run in his favour against the mortgagor, the mortgagee's rights will be unaffected so long as the mortgagor continues to make payments in respect of the debt (whether of principal or interest). In such a case the protection afforded by section 29(3) of the 1980 Act is absolute.[40] If, on the other hand, the mortgagor was already dispossessed at the date of the mortgage and time was already running against him, the execution of the mortgage does not confer on the mortgagee a new right of entry, so that subsequent payments by the mortgagor cannot prevent time from running in favour of his disseisor.[41]   **22–45**

(ii) *Remedies in respect of the personal debt.*

Subject to section 29(6), section 29(5) enacts that where any right of action has accrued to recover any debt or other liquidated pecuniary claim or any claim to the personal estate of a deceased person or to any share or interest in any such estate and the person liable or acountable for the claim acknowledges the claim or makes any payment in respect of it, the right shall be treated as having accrued on and not before the date of the acknowledgment or payment. This is subject to the provision that a payment of a part of the rent or interest due at any time shall not extend the period for claiming the remainder then due, but any payment of interest shall be treated as a payment in respect of the principal debt.[42]   **22–46**

The effect of an acknowledgment is different from that of a payment. A *payment* binds all persons liable in respect of the debt, including, of course, the

---

[37] s.31(1) and (2).
[38] A charge by way of legal mortgage is presumably in the same position as a legal mortgage by virtue of ss.88 and 89 of the L.P.A. 1925.
[39] "Mortgage" in the L.P.A. 1925, "includes any charge or lien on any property for securing money or money's worth.
[40] See *Doe d. Palmer v. Eyre* (1851) 17 Q.B.D. 366; *Ludbrook v. Ludbrook* [1901] 2 K.B. 96.
[41] *Thornton v. France* [1897] 2 Q.B. 143.
[42] Limitation Act 1980, s.29(6).

successors of the person paying.[43] But an *acknowledgment* only binds the acknowledgor and his successors, *i.e.* his personal representatives and any person on whom the liability for the debt devolves on his death or bankruptcy or by disposition of property or by the terms of a settlement or otherwise.[44]

(d) *The effect of acknowledgment or payment made after the relevant period of limitation has run*

22–47 Formerly there existed a rule of law that where the effect of the expiration of the prescribed period of limitation was merely to bar the remedy and not the right, an acknowledgment or payment could cause a right of action to accrue once again even though it was made after the expiry of the prescribed period of limitation unless the statute had extinguished the right itself. It is now provided by section 29(7) that a current period of limitation may be repeatedly extended under the section by further acknowledgments or payments but that a right of action once barred shall not be revived by any subsequent acknowledgment or payment.[45]

(e) *Extinction of title after expiration of time*

22–48 Section 17 extinguishes the title of a mortgagee of land who fails to exercise his remedies within the prescribed period and so a subsequent acknowledgment or payment does not revive his rights against the security.[46]

There is no corresponding provision which extinguishes the title of a mortgagee of personalty, so that a subsequent acknowledgment or payment appears to revive the mortgage as well as the personal debt.[47] This difference between realty and personalty in regard to the effect of acknowledgments and payments on a mortgagee's rights is to be explained more by reference to the history of the drafting of the relevant provisions than on rational grounds.

In any event, acknowledgments and payments made after the statutory period has once run may operate to revive the personal action for the mortgage debt. Section 5 bars the remedy for simple contract and section 8 in the case of specialty debts but neither extinguishes the debt. The right to the debt is therefore

---

[43] *ibid.* s.31(7).

[44] *ibid.* s.31(6)(9). s.31(6) and (7) re-enact s.25(5) and (6) of the 1939 Act but omit provisos which formerly existed to both sub-sections. Those limited the effect of an acknowledgement or payment made *after* the expiration of the period of limitation prescribed the commencement of an action to recover a debt or other liquidated pecuniary claim and were repealed by the Limitation Amendment Act 1980, ss.6(3), 13(2), and Sched. 2.

[45] This is subject to the Limitation Act 1980, s.29(6). This change came as a result of the recommendation made by the Law Reform Committee in its 21st Report (Final Report on Limitations of Actions) (Cmmd. 6923), para. 2.71.

[46] *Kibble v. Fairthorne* [1895] 1 Ch. 219. After the mortgagee's remedies have been barred against the land, the mortgagor is entitled to the return of the deeds; *Lewis v. Plunket* [1937] Ch. 306.

[47] It is true that s.3(2) extinguishes the title to chattels after an action for conversion has been barred, but this does not cover the case of mere inactivity by mortgagor and mortgagee.

revived and under section 31[48] it is revived not only against the person making the acknowledgment or payment but against his successors and all persons liable in respect of the debt, respectively, with one exception. The exception is that the revival of the debt by a limited owner under a settlement antedating the acknowledgment or payment does not bind other persons taking under that settlement.[49]

(f) Conditions of an effective acknowledgment or payment

Payment need only be proved as a fact. An acknowledgment to have the effects described above, must, however, be in writing signed by the person making it.[50]   **22–49**

The acknowledgment or payment has further to be made by the person specified in section 29, that is:

(1) in the case of an acknowledgment of the mortgage, by the person in possession;

(2) in the case of a payment keeping the mortgage alive, by the person in possession or by the person liable for the mortgage debt;

(3) in the case of an acknowledgment or payment keeping the personal debt alive, by the person liable or accountable for the debt.

The acknowledgment or payment may also be made by the agent of the person required to make it.[51]

(i) The "person in possession"

The "person in possession" for the purposes of section 29 is the person in possession of the interest mortgaged. It does not include a tenant from the mortgagor and a payment of rent by a tenant direct to the mortgagee does not bind the mortgagor unless made at the latter's express direction. A tenant is not the implied agent of the mortgagor for making acknowledgments or payments to the mortgagee.[52] On the other hand, a receiver, whether appointed by the court or by the mortgagee under a power, is in law the agent of the mortgagor and entitled to make payments on the mortgagor's behalf. Consequently, a receiver's acts do bind the mortgagor.[53]   **22–50**

---

[48] Subs. (6) and (7).

[49] cf. Gregson v. Hindley (1846) 10 Jur. 383.

[50] Limitation Act 1980, s.30(1).

[51] ibid. s.30(2). cf. Wright v. Pepin [1954] 1 W.L.R. 635 (acknowledgment by mortgagor's solicitor held to be sufficient).

[52] Harlock v. Ashberry (1882) 19 Ch.D. 539. A payment of rent made by a tenant of mortgaged property to a mortgagee in consequence of a notice by the mortgagee requiring the rent to be paid to him is not a receipt of any sum in respect of the mortgage debt and accordingly not a payment to prevent the barring by the Limitation Act of a foreclosure action.

[53] Chinnery v. Evans (1864) 11 H.L.C. 115 at 134.

(ii) *The "person liable or accountable"*

The "person liable or accountable" for the debt means a person liable or accountable in connection with the discharge of the mortgage debt. A surety[54] or a co-mortgagor[55-56] is clearly such a person, and their payments bind the mortgagor.

It is otherwise with a third party who is liable to make payments to the mortgagee in connection with the mortgaged property but not in relation to the discharge of the mortgage debt. The case of rent paid by a tenant to the mortgagee has already been mentioned above. Payments of rent at the request of the mortgagee convert him into a mortgagee in possession but do not constitute payments by the mortgagor. If an insurance policy is assigned by way of mortgage and notice is given to the insurers, the latter become liable to pay the moneys to the mortgagee. A payment under the policy is not, however, a payment in respect of the debt and does not keep the mortgagee's remedies alive against other securities comprised in the mortgage.[57] Similarly, if a beneficiary mortgages his interest in a trust fund, a payment by the trustees direct to the mortgagee in pursuance of their duty to give effect to all interests of which they have notice does not bind the mortgagor.[58]

The "person liable or accountable" is not limited to persons contractually liable to the mortgagee. It is enough if the person paying is "concerned to answer the debt."[59] In *Bradshaw v. Widdrington*[60] a father borrowed money on mortgage for the benefit of his son who executed a bond for the money in favour of his father. Payments by the son in respect of mortgage interest were held sufficient to keep the mortgage alive since, as between him and the mortgagor, he was bound to discharge the mortgage debt. There need not even be a contractual obligation for the discharge of the debt between the mortgagor and the person making payment. All that is necessary is that the person paying should, by reason of the relations between himself and the mortgagor, be entitled in law to discharge the debt.[61] Thus, when the property mortgaged is settled, a payment by any one beneficiary is sufficient to save the mortgagee's remedies against the property.[62] The rule appears to be that whenever a number of persons stand in peril of suit by a creditor so that all benefit by the discharge of the liability, a payment by one keeps the creditor's remedies alive.[63]

---

[54] *Lewin v. Wilson* (1886) 11 A.C. 639.

[55-56] *Re Earl Kingston's Estate* [1869] 3 I.R. 485.

[57] *Re Lord Clifden* [1900] 1 Ch. 774.

[58] *Re Edwards' Will Trusts* [1937] Ch. 553.

[59] *Lewin v. Wilson* (1886) 11 A.C. 639 at 644.

[60] [1902] 2 Ch. 430.

[61] *Bradshaw v. Widdrington* [1902] 2 Ch. 430 at 439, *per* Buckley, J.

[62] *Barclay v. Owen* (1889) 60 L.T. 220. A life tenant, who is also the mortgagee of the settled property, is presumed to be keeping down the interest on his own incumbrance so that the statute does not run against his mortgage: *Wynne v. Styan* (1847) 2 Ph. 303.

[63] *Re Lacey* [1907] 1 Ch. 330 at 346, *per* Farwell L.J.; also *Roddam v. Morley* (1857) 1 De G. & J. 1.

(iii) *Assignments of the equity of redemption*

Logically, the same rule should apply in assignments of the equity of redemp-   **22–51**
tion so that a payment either by the mortgagor[64] or by the assignee[65] would keep
the mortgagee's remedies alive. It has in fact been so decided in the case of an
equity of redemption assigned *free from incumbrances* when the original mortgagor is, as between himself and his assignee, bound to discharge the mortgage
debt.[66] If, however, the assignment is made *subject to incumbrances*, the position
is not free from doubt. In *Newbould* v. *Smith*[67] the Court of Appeal held that
payments by the original mortgagor would not bind the assignee. This decision
is inconsistent with the language of Westbury L.C. and Lord Cranworth in
Chinnery v. *Evans*[68] and it seems to have been doubted by the House of Lords in
Newbould v. *Smith* itself, the court finding other reasons for dismissing the
appeal. The decision, although the Court of Appeal was a strong one, is submitted to be entirely unacceptable. A mortgagee who receives regular payments
of interest from his mortgagor should not be concerned to inquire into the latter's
dealings with the equity of redemption. Any other rule would be very alarming
to mortgagees.[69]

(iv) *To whom the acknowledgment payment is to be made*

Finally, an acknowledgment or payment must be made to the person whose   **22–52**
remedies are to be kept alive, *i.e.* to the person entitled to the mortgage or to his
agent. Who is the right person to receive an acknowledgment or payment
naturally depends on the dealings with the mortgage debt and on the notices of
those dealings given to the mortgagor. If the mortgagee has died, his personal
representatives are the persons concerned to receive acknowledgments or payments.[70] Similarly, if the mortgage debt has been settled, the trustees are the right
persons to be paid. A payment direct to the proper beneficiary is regarded as paid
to him as agent for the trustees[71] and may be sufficient to prevent time from
running.

(g) *Institution of proceedings by the mortgagee*

If an action is begun by the mortgagee within the statutory period such will   **22–53**
prevent his rights from being barred even though the hearing does not take place
before time has run out.[72] It must be remembered that the institution of proceedings does not have the same effect as an acknowledgment and saves the remedies
only for that action, so that upon the discontinuance of the action the benefit of
the saving will not be available in a subsequent action.[73] On the other hand, if a

---

[64] *Bradshaw* v. *Widdrington* [1902] 2 Ch. 430.
[65] *Dibb* v. *Walker* [1893] 2 Ch. 429.
[66] *Bradshaw* v. *Widdrington, ante.*
[67] (1886) 33 Ch.D. 127, affirmed (1889) 14 A.C. 423 but on other grounds, the House of Lords
reserving their opinion on this point.
[68] (1864) 11 H.L.C. 115.
[69] *ibid.* at 139, *per* Lord Cranworth.
[70] *Barclay* v. *Owen* (1889) 60 L.T. 220.
[71] *Re Somerset* [1894] 1 Ch. 231.
[72] *Wrixon* v. *Vize* (1842) 3 Dr. & W. 104 at 123.
[73] *Pratt* v. *Hawkins* (1846) 15 M. & W. 399.

judgment for foreclosure absolute is obtained, the effect is to vest a new title in the mortgagee so that although the mortgagor may remain continuously in possession, the statutory period begins to run afresh from the decree.[74]

(h) *Fraud, concealment and mistake*

Section 32 of the 1980 Act provides that:

(1) where the action is based on the fraud of the defendant, his agent or any person through whom he claims and his agent;

(2) any fact relevant to the plaintiff's right of action has been deliberately concealed by fraud; or

(3) the action is for relief from the consequences of a mistake;

the period shall not begin to run until the plaintiff either discovered or could with reasonable diligence have discovered the fraud, concealment or mistake.

The section at the same time saves the rights of bona fide purchasers.[75]

---

[74] *Heath v. Pugh* (1881) 6 Q.B.D. 345 affirmed (1882) 7 App. Cas. 235. Unless, of course, the action is struck out.

[75] Limitation Act 1980, s.32(3) and see McGee, *Limitation Periods* (3rd ed., 1998), paras 20–001 to 20–035.

CHAPTER 23

INSOLVENCY OF THE MORTGAGOR

A mortgagee can usually face the insolvency of the mortgagor with greater **23–01** confidence than that which unsecured creditors often experience. Even so, the bankruptcy or insolvency of a mortgagor can cause difficulties for the mortgagee and in this chapter, consideration will be given to the impact of the bankruptcy or insolvency of the mortgagor on the mortgagee and his security, rights and remedies.

NON-CORPORATE MORTGAGORS

1. Individual Voluntary Arrangements

An individual voluntary arrangement may be entered into by a debtor who is **23–02** either an undischarged bankrupt or is able to petition for his own bankruptcy.[1] The details of the procedure that must be followed are beyond the scope of this work[2] but in summary, the debtor must apply to the Court for an interim order pending the approval of the IVA.[2a] The effect of such an application is to permit the court to stay any action, execution or other legal process against the property or person of the debtor.[3] Whilst any interim order has effect, no bankruptcy petition relating to the debtor may be presented or proceeded with and no other proceedings and no execution or other legal process may be commenced or continued against the debtor or his property except with leave of the Court.[4] Unless extended, an interim order remains in force for 14 days beginning with the day upon which the order is made.[5]

During the currency of the interim order, the nominee will prepare a proposal to place before the court which may, if it considers that the proposal should be placed before the debtor's creditors extend the period in which the interim order is in force to enable such a meeting to be held[6] debtor's creditors in order to secure the creditors' approval of the IVA at that meeting. The creditors may modify the proposal with the debtor's consent[7] and, if they approve the proposal (whether amended or not), it takes effect as if made by the debtor at the meeting

---

[1] Insolvency Act 1986, s.255(1)(b).
[2] Reference should be made to the specialist texts: *Muir Hunter on Personal Insolvency; Lawson, Individual Voluntary Arrangements* (2000).
[2a] *Fletcher v. Vooght* [2000] B.P.I.R. 435.
[3] Insolvency Act 1986, s.254(1).
[4] Insolvency Act 1986, s.252.
[5] IA, s.255(6).
[6] IA, s.256(5).
[7] IA, s.258(2).

and binds every person who, in accordance with the Insolvency Rules, had notice of and was entitled to vote at the meeting (whether or not he was present or represented at it) as if he were a party to the arrangement.[8] An IVA which unfairly prejudices the interests of a creditor of in which there has been some material irregularity at or in relation to the creditors' meeting may be challenged.[9] The Court may revoke or suspend any approval given to an IVA upon such an application or may give direction as to the summoning of a further meeting of the creditors.[10]

(a) *Effect of an interim order*

23–03 The terms of section 252 of the Insolvency Act 1986 are quite clear; once an interim order has been made "no other proceedings, and no execution or other legal process, may be commenced or continued against the debtor or his property except with leave of the court". Accordingly, once an order is made, a mortgagee will, during its currency, be governed by its terms and precluded from continuing or commencing any proceedings (whether for possession or otherwise) or enforcing any judgment that it may have in its favour.

(b) *The creditor's meeting*

23–04 A person who holds any security for a debt owed to him (whether by way of mortgage, charge, lien or other security) is a "secured creditor"[11] for the purposes of, *inter alia*, the provisions governing an IVA and is entitled to notice of the creditors' meeting[12] and to vote at that meeting.[13] A secured creditor is thus bound by the result of the meeting if he had notice of it.

(c) *The proposal and any modification thereto*

23–05 The creditors' meeting "shall not approve any proposal or modification which affects the right of a secured creditor of the debtor to enforce his security, except with the concurrence of the creditor concerned".[14] Thus, whilst the mortgagee may be precluded from enforcing his security during the period for which an interim order is in force, the rights and remedies that he would otherwise have pursuant to the terms of the security are preserved in the event that the IVA is approved unless he consents to their limitation. Obviously, if the IVA is not approved, his rights remain unaffected after the expiry of the interim order.

Any creditor must take care in the manner in which he conducts himself in relation to the creditors' meeting and any decision arising therefrom. In *Re*

[8] IA, s.260(2).
[9] IA, s.262.
[10] IA, s.262(4).
[11] IA, s.383(2).
[12] IA, s.257(2).
[13] IR, r. 5.17(1).
[14] IA, s.258(4).

Millwall Football Club and Athletic Co (1985) plc (in administration)[15] the administrator dismissed an employee of the company after his appointment. Subsequently a company voluntary arrangement was proposed. The terms of that arrangement were such that creditors of the company as at the date of the appointment of the administrator (*i.e.* prior to the employee's dismissal) were only to be paid a much reduced dividend. The employee voted in favour of the CVA and subsequently sought to argue that since the company's liability to him for his wrongful dismissal arose on that dismissal and thus after the administrator's appointment, he would not be bound by the reduced dividend provisions. Rimer J. rejected this argument. He held that the obligation arose from the contract of employment that was in place at the administrator's appointment and the liability for wrongful dismissal could be properly characterised as a future, prospective or contingent liability incurred prior to the administrator's appointment and thus subject to the reduced dividend provisions. More importantly (and perhaps of more general application) Rimer J. held that the creditor was estopped from denying that he was bound by the dividend provisions since both he and the administrator had proceeded right down to the creditor's meeting on the basis that he was and, on that footing, the administrator had not proposed any variation of the terms of the proposal before it was approved. An estoppel by convention had arisen.

Thus, a secured creditor may find that its rights to enforce its security may be lost by an estoppel arising from its conduct or by its "concurrence", which may (depending on the facts) amount to something less than its express consent.

(d) *Negative equity*

The provisions that prevail in a bankruptcy and which permit a secured creditor **23–06** to realise his security and prove for the balance or to re-value his security or for the security to be redeemed at the value attributed thereto by the secured creditor[16] do not apply to an IVA. A secured creditor who has notice of a proposal for an IVA and who envisages that the security may be worth less than the sum secured may wish for the express incorporation of some or all of the appropriate bankruptcy provisions in the proposal.[17] The same considerations would apply in a company voluntary arrangement.

2. Bankruptcy

Upon the making of a bankruptcy order, the bankrupt's estate vests in the trustee **23–07** in bankruptcy on his appointment or, in the case of the official receiver, on his becoming trustee. The estate vests without any conveyance, assignment or transfer.[18] The bankrupt's estate consists of, *inter alia*, "all property belonging to or vested in the bankrupt at the commencement of the bankruptcy",[19] *i.e.* the day

---

[15] [1998] 2 B.C.L.C. 272.
[16] IR, rr. 6.109, 6.116 and 6.117.
[17] See *Lawson, Individual Voluntary Arrangements* (2000), A12[12]–[16].
[18] IA, s.306.
[19] IA, s.283(1).

upon which the order is made.[20] The making of a bankruptcy order does not affect the mortgagee's right to enforce his security[21] unless the security is over goods held by way of pledge, pawn or other security and the official receiver has exercised his rights to inspect them.[22] In such circumstances, the court's permission is required to sell those goods unless a reasonable opportunity has been given for the estate to redeem them.[23]

(a) *Proof of debts*

23–08   A secured credit has, when faced with the bankruptcy of the mortgagor, a variety of options. First, he can decline to prove at all in the bankruptcy and must, in such circumstances, rely on his security alone. Secondly, he may surrender his security to the trustee and prove for his debt as an unsecured creditor.[24] Thirdly, he may realise his security and prove for the balance remaining due to him.[25] Fourthly, he may value his security and prove for the unsecured balance.

In the last instance, a trustee who is unsatisfied with the value placed upon the security by the mortgagee may either give the creditor 28 days' notice that he intends to redeem the security at the value placed on it by the creditor in his proof[26] or require the property to be sold and if the sale is by auction the trustee and the creditor may bid.[27] A secured creditor may, with the agreement of the trustee or the leave of the Court alter the value placed by him upon the security in his proof of debt unless he is the petitioning creditor and has valued the security in his petition or has voted in respect of the unsecured balance. In such instances, the leave of the court is required.[28]

(i) *Failure to disclose security*

23–09   A creditor that does not disclose in his proof that he holds security is required to surrender that security for the general benefit of the creditors unless relieved therefrom by the court on the ground that the omission was inadvertent or the result of an honest mistake.[29]

(ii) *Amount of proof*

This must be limited to what was due by way of principal and interest at the date that the bankruptcy order was made after deducting from the amount outstanding the proceeds of any sale.[30]

---

[20] IA, s.278(a).
[21] IA, s.285(4).
[22] IA, s.285(5).
[23] *ibid.*
[24] IR, r. 109(2). Such a surrender will not release a surety: *Rainbow v. Juggins* (1880) 5 QBD 422.
[25] IR, r. 109(1).
[26] IR, r. 6.117.
[27] IR, r. 6.118.
[28] IR, r. 6.115.
[29] IR, r. 6.116; *Re Maxson* [1919] 2 KB 330.
[30] *Re London, Windsor & Greenwich Hotels Company* [1892] 1 Ch 639; *Re William Hall (Contractors) Limited (In liquidation)* [1967] 1 W.L.R. 948.

(iii) *Interest:*

A secured creditor remains entitled to look to his security to meet the contractual **23–10**
rate of interest agreed with the bankrupt. However, a mortgagee cannot prove for
interest that has accrued due since the bankruptcy order was made[31] and, in the
event that he wishes to prove for interest that has accrued prior to the commencement of the bankruptcy, he can only do so if the requirements of Insolvency Rule
r. 6.113 are satisfied. A debt due under a written instrument and payable at a
certain time will attract interest at the rate specified under the Judgment Act 1838
at the date of the bankruptcy order from the time that the debt is due to the date
of the bankruptcy order. Debts that are due otherwise will only attract interest for
any period prior to the bankruptcy order if demand is made prior to the presentation of the petition and notice given that interest is payable.[32]

(b) *Sale of the mortgaged property*

When a trustee in bankruptcy applies, on behalf of the estate, for the sale of a **23–11**
property jointly owned by the bankrupt and any third party, section 335A of the
Insolvency Act 1986 applies and creates a statutory assumption that after the end
of the period of one year beginning with the first vesting of the bankrupt's estate
in a trustee, the interests of the creditors outweigh all other considerations and a
sale of the property will be ordered save other than in exceptional
circumstances.[33]

If a mortgagee wishes to cause the property to be sold, he may apply to the
court for a order directing that the property be sold[34] and, upon that application,
the court may order that the land or any part of it is sold with vacant possession
in such manner as the Court may direct.[35] If sale is by public auction, the Court
may permit the mortgagee to appear and bid on his own behalf.[36] Conduct of the
sale is generally given to the trustee unless the proceeds are unlikely to exceed
the secured debt, in which the mortgagee will be given conduct.[37]

Prior to any sale, the Court may order that all necessary accounts and inquiries
are made as to the outstanding principal, interest and costs due under the
mortgage and, if the mortgage has been in possession, the monies received by
him or on his behalf.[38] The procedure adopted in the Chancery Division with
regard to accounts and inquiries may be applied.[39]

The proceeds of the sale shall be applied in the payment of the trustees
expenses of and occasioned by the application to the court, of the sale and
attendance thereat and of any costs arising from the taking of accounts and the

---

[31] IA, s.322(2).
[32] IR, r. 6.113(2), (3).
[33] Such as ill-health: see *Re Raval* [1998] BPIR 389; *Claughton v. Charalamabous* [1998] BPIR
558.
[34] IR, r. 6.197(1).
[35] IR, r. 6.198.
[36] IR, r. 6.198(4).
[37] *Re Jordan, ex parte Harrison* (1884) 13 QBD 228.
[38] IR, r. 6.197(2).
[39] IR, r. 6.197(4); see *post*, chap. 25.

making of such inquiries as the court may have directed under Insolvency Rule, r. 6.197.[40]

(c) *Disclaimer*

23-12 A trustee in bankruptcy can disclaim onerous property, notwithstanding that he has taken possession of it, endeavoured to sell it or otherwise exercised rights of ownership in relation to it.[41] Such a disclaimer determines the rights, interests and liabilities of the bankrupt and his estate in relation to the property disclaimed.[42] Any person who suffers loss by reason of a disclaimer may prove to that extent as an unsecured creditor in the bankruptcy.[43]

Leasehold property can be disclaimed but only where a copy of the disclaimer has been served on every person claiming under the bankrupt as underlessee or mortgagee and either (1) no application is made for a vesting order before the end of 14 days beginning with day upon which the notice is served or (2) (where such an application is made) the court orders that the disclaimer is to take effect notwithstanding the application.[44]

A mortgagee may apply under section 320 of the Insolvency Act 1986 for a vesting order for the property which is sought to be disclaimed to be vested in the mortgagee without conveyance, assignment or transfer.[45] The court will make an order if it is just to do so but, in the case of leaseholds, will only make the order on terms that the mortgagee is subject to the same liabilities and obligations as the bankrupt was on the day that the petition was presented or (if it thinks fit) subject to the same liabilities and obligations as the mortgagee would have been subject to if the lease had been assigned to him on that day.[46]

CORPORATE MORTGAGORS

1. **Company Voluntary Arrangements**

23-13 The directors of a company which is not in administration or being wound up may initiate the approval of a CVA; if the company is in administration that right rests with the administrator and if it is in liquidation, the liquidator may make the proposal.[47] A nominee must be appointed to act in relation to the proposal.[48]

If the nominee is not the administrator or liquidator of the company, he must report to the Court within 28 days of being given notice of the proposal whether, in his opinion a meeting of the company's creditors should be summoned and, if so, when and where that meeting should be held.[49] A liquidator or administrator

---

[40] IR, r. 6.199.
[41] IA, s.315.
[42] IA, s.315(3).
[43] IA, s.315(5).
[44] IA, s.317(1).
[45] IA, s.320(6).
[46] IA, s.321(1).
[47] IA, s.1.
[48] IA, s.1(2).
[49] IA, s.2(2).

acting as nominee can simply summon a meeting to consider the proposal without recourse to the court.[50] At the meeting of the company's creditors, the proposal may be approved or rejected or modified.[51]

The substantive difference in procedure form that employed in IVA's is that there is no requirement for an application for and the making of an interim order. Accordingly, pending the approval of a CVA there is no stay or fetter on any creditor's rights to enforce as against the company or its property. Such a limitation is, however, a feature of administration.

When approved, the CVA has the same effect on the company and its creditors who have notice of and were entitled to vote at the creditors' meeting as an IVA has in relation to bankruptcy.[52] A CVA which unfairly prejudices the interests of a creditor or in which there has been some material irregularity at or in relation to the creditors' meeting may be challenged.[53]

(a) *The creditors' meeting*

The persons to be summoned to a creditors' meeting are every creditor of the **23–14** company of whose claim and address the person summoning the creditors' meeting is aware.[54] A "secured creditor" in relation to a company means a creditor of the company who holds in respect of his debt a security over the property of the company.[55] Every creditor who is given notice of the creditors' meeting is entitled to vote at the meeting or any adjournment of it.[56] Thus, a secured creditor is bound by the result of the creditors' meeting if he had notice of it.

(b) *The proposal and any modification thereto*

The creditors' meeting "shall not approve any proposal or modification which **23–15** affects the right of a secured creditor of the debtor to enforce his security, except with the concurrence of the creditor concerned".[57] Accordingly, subject to a secured creditor giving his approval, his rights remain unaffected by the implementation of a CVA. The *caveat* expressed above[58] arising from the decision in *Re Millwall Football Club and Athletic Co (1985) plc (in administration)*[59] is applicable.

---

[50] IA, s.3(2).
[51] IA, s.4.
[52] IA, s.5(2).
[53] IA, s.6.
[54] IA, s.3(3).
[55] IA, s.248(a).
[56] IR, r. 1.17(1).
[57] IA, s.5(2).
[58] See para. 23–05 *et seq.*
[59] [1988] 2 B.C.L.C. 272.

2. **Administration**

An application to the court for an administration order can be made by the company itself, its directors or by any of its creditors[60] and the court, if it is satisfied that (1) the company is unable to pay its debts (within the meaning ascribed to that expression by section 123 of the Insolvency Act 1986) and (2) that an order would achieve any of the specified statutory objectives, may make an administration order.[61] The statutory objectives are (1) the survival of the company and the whole or any part of its undertaking as a going concern; (2) the approval of a company voluntary arrangement; (3) the sanctioning of a scheme of compromise under section 425 of the Companies Act 1985; and (4) a more advantageous realisation of the company's assets than would be effected on a winding up. The grounds can be cumulative and grounds (1) and (4) are the most frequently relied on.

On presentation of the petition for an administration order notice must be given to any person who has appointed or may be entitled to appoint an administrative receiver[62] and, if an administrative receiver has been appointed, the court shall dismiss the petition unless it is also satisfied that the person who has appointed the administrative receiver has consented to the administration order or the security pursuant to which the administrative receiver is appointed is impeachable as a transaction at an undervalue or a preference or can be avoided under section 245 of the Insolvency Act (avoidance of floating charges).[63]

(a) *Effect of an application*

23–16 Section 10 of the Insolvency Act 1986 provides that "during the period beginning with the presentation of a petition for an administration order and ending with the making of such an order or the dismissal of the petition—

(a) no resolution may be passed or an order made for the winding up of the company;

(b) no steps may be taken to enforce any security[64] over the company's property, or to repossess goods in the company's possession under any hire-purchase agreement except with leave of the court and subject to such terms as the court may impose; and

(c) no other proceedings and no execution or other legal process may be commenced or continued, and no distress may be levied, against the company or its property except with the leave of the court and subject to such terms as aforesaid."

---

[60] IA, s.9(1).

[61] IA, s.8(1).

[62] IA, s.9(2). Defined in s.29(2) as "a receiver and manager of the whole (or substantially the whole) of a company's property appointed by or on behalf of the holders of any debentures . . . secured by a charge which, as created, was a floating charge, or by such a charge and one or more other securities".

[63] IA, s.9(3).

[64] *i.e.* "any mortgage, charge, lien or other security": IA, s.248(b).

(b) *Effect of an administration order*

If the court is satisfied that it is proper to make such an order in order to achieve **23–17** one or more of the statutory objectives, the order has the immediate effect of dismissing any extant winding up petition and causing any administrative receiver to vacate office. Furthermore, it continues the moratorium imposed upon the presentation of the petition, with some extensions, most notably the preclusion of the appointment of an administrative receiver.[65] Clearly the presentation of a petition for an administration order and any subsequent order made on that petition can have a substantial impact upon a mortgagee's rights and remedies.

(c) *Obtaining permission to by-pass the moratorium*

The court will, on an application by a secured creditor to enforce his rights, **23–18** undertake a balancing exercise between that creditor's rights and the interests of the other creditors in the light of the administrator's proposals. This balancing exercise is also undertaken with regard to section 15 of the Insolvency Act 1986 (power to deal with charged property) and thus the decided authorities under both sections 11 and 15 assist. A detailed analysis of the authorities is beyond the scope of this work[66] but Nicholls LJ. In *Re Atlantic Computer Systems plc*[67] felt bound "to make some general observations regarding cases where leave is sought to exercise existing proprietary rights, including security rights, against a company in administration". His Lordship observed:

"(1) It is in every case for the person who seeks leave to make out a case for him to be given leave.

(2) the prohibition in section 11(3)(c) and (d) is intended to assist the company, under the management of the administrator, to achieve the purpose for which the administration order was made. If granting leave to a lessor of land or the hirer of goods (a "lessor") to exercise his proprietary rights and repossess his land or goods is unlikely to impede the achievement of that purpose, leave should normally be given.

(3) In other cases when a lessor seeks possession the court has to carry out a balancing exercise, balancing the legitimate interests of the lessor and the legitimate interests of the other creditors of the company: see *per* Peter Gibson J. in *Royal Trust Bank v. Buchler* [1989] B.C.L.C. 130, 135. The metaphor employed here, for want of a better, is that of scales and weights. Lord Wilberforce adverted to the limitations of this metaphor in *Science Research Council v. Nassé* [1980] A.C. 1028, 1067. It must be kept in mind that the exercise under section 11 is not a mechanical one; each case calls for an exercise in judicial judgment, in which the court seeks to give effect to the purpose of the statutory

---

[65] See IA, s.11(3). The administrator is empowered to consent to acts of enforcement, re-possession or the commencement of proceedings &c. in addition to the Court's discretion: *ibid.*

[66] See generally, *Palmer's Company Law*, paras 14.024—14.026.2.

[67] [1992] Ch 505, 542 (CA).

provisions, having regard to the parties' interests and all the circumstances of the case. As already noted, the purpose of the prohibition is to enable or assist the company to achieve the object for which the administration order was made. The purpose of the power to give leave is to enable the court to relax the prohibition where it would be inequitable for the prohibition to apply.

(4) In carrying out the balancing exercise great importance, or weight, is normally to be given to the proprietary interests of the lessor. Sir Nicolas Browne-Wilkinson V.-C. observed in *Bristol Airport Plc. v. Powdrill* [1990] Ch. 744, 767D-E that, so far as possible, the administration procedure should not be used to prejudice those who were secured creditors when the administration order was made in lieu of a winding up order. The same is true regarding the proprietary interests of a lessor. The underlying principle here is that an administration for the benefit of unsecured creditors should not be conducted at the expense of those who have proprietary rights which they are seeking to exercise, save to the extent that this may be unavoidable and even then this will usually be acceptable only to a strictly limited extent.

(5) Thus it will normally be a sufficient ground for the grant of leave if significant loss would be caused to the lessor by a refusal. For this purpose loss comprises any kind of financial loss, direct or indirect, including loss by reason of delay, and may extend to loss which is not financial. But if substantially greater loss would be caused to others by the grant of leave, or loss which is out of all proportion to the benefit which leave would confer on the lessor, that may outweigh the loss to the lessor caused by a refusal. Our formulation was criticised in the course of the argument, and we certainly do not claim for it the status of a rule in those terms. At present we say only that it appears to us the nearest we can get to the formulation of what Parliament had in mind.

(6) In assessing these respective losses the court will have regard to matters such as: the financial position of the company, its ability to pay the rental arrears and the continuing rentals, the administrator's proposals, the period for which the administration order has already been in force and is expected to remain in force, the effect on the administration if leave were given, the effect on the applicant if leave were refused, the end result sought to be achieved by the administration, the prospects of that result being achieved, and the history of the administration so far.

(7) In considering these matters it will often be necessary to assess how probable the suggested consequences are. Thus if loss to the applicant is virtually certain if leave is refused, and loss to others a remote possibility if leave is granted, that will be a powerful factor in favour of granting leave.

(8) This is not an exhaustive list. For example, the conduct of the parties may also be a material consideration in a particular case, as it was in the *Bristol Airport* case. There leave was refused on the ground that the applicants had accepted benefits under the administration, and had only

sought to enforce their security at a later stage: indeed, they had only acquired their security as a result of the operations of the administrators. It behoves a lessor to make his position clear to the administrator at the outset of the administration and, if it should become necessary, to apply to the court promptly.

(9) The above considerations may be relevant not only to the decision whether leave should be granted or refuse, but also to a decision to impose terms if leave is granted.

(10) The above considerations will also apply to a decision on whether to impose terms as a condition for refusing leave. Section 11(3)(c) and (d) makes no provision for terms being imposed if leave is refused, but the court has power to achieve that result. It may do so directly, by giving directions to the administrator: for instance, under section 17, or in response to an application by the administrator under section 14(3), or in exercise of its control over an administrator as an officer of the court. Or it may do so indirectly, by ordering that the applicant shall have leave unless the administrator is prepared to take this or that step in the conduct of the administration. Cases where leave is refused but terms are imposed can be expected to arise frequently. For example, the permanent loss to a lessor flowing from his inability to recover his property will normally be small if the administrator is required to pay the current rent. In most cases this should be possible, since if the administration order has been rightly made the business should generally be sufficiently viable to hold down current outgoings. Such a term may therefore be a normal term to impose.

(11) The above observations are directed at a case such as the present where a lessor of land or the owner of goods is seeking to repossess his land or goods because of non-payment of rentals. A broadly similar approach will be applicable on many applications to enforce a security: for instance, an application by a mortgagee for possession of land. On such applications an important consideration will often be whether the applicant is fully secured. If he is, delay in enforcement is likely to be less prejudicial than in cases where his security is insufficient.

(12) In some cases there will be a dispute over the existence, validity or nature of the security which the applicant is seeking leave to enforce. It is not for the court on the leave application to seek to adjudicate upon that issue, unless (as in the present case, on the fixed or floating charge point) the issue raises a short point of law which it is convenient to determine without further ado. Otherwise the court needs to be satisfied only that the applicant has a seriously arguable case."

Thus it can be seen that the Court will not normally permit unsecured creditors to obtain a benefit by the administration of a company at the expense of a secured creditor save to the extent that this may be unavoidable and proportionate. Thus leave will usually be granted in circumstances where the secured creditor will experience a significant loss unless the loss that would be occasioned by the unsecured creditors would be out of all proportion to that which the secured creditor may suffer.

(d) *The administrator's power to deal with charged property*

23–19   The administrator may dispose of or otherwise exercise his powers in relation to any property of the company which is subject to a security as if that property were not subject if (when it was created) the security was a floating charge[68] and, in relation to any other security, if, on an application to the court, the court is satisfied that the administrator's proposed course of conduct would be likely to promote the purpose or purposes for which the administration order was granted.[69]

The secured creditor's position enjoys specific statutory protection, however. Where property is disposed of by the administrator without recourse to the court,[70] the secured creditor has the same priority in respect of any property of the company directly or indirectly representing the property disposed of as he would have had in respect of the property subject to the security.[71] Where the Court makes an order under section 15(2), it shall be a condition of that order that (a) the net proceeds of the disposal and (b) (where they are less than the amount as may be determined by the Court to be the net amount which would be realised on a sale of the property or goods in the open market by a willing vendor) such sums as may be required to make good the deficiency, shall be applied towards discharging the sums secured by the security.[72] Where there are two or more securities and (b) above applies, the sums mentioned in that paragraph shall be applied towards discharging the sums secured by those securities in the order of their priorities.[73]

Accordingly, it can be seen that the distinction between what was a fixed or floating charge on its creation is important.[74] In *Re A R V Aviation Limited*[75] the court emphasised the need to have proper valuation evidence before it as to the value of the security in question (the secured creditor was alleging that the administrator's valuation was only optimistic) and held that "the sums secured by the security" extended to interest and (subject to the court's discretion) the secured creditor's costs. Where the administrator seeks to challenge the security and wishes to cause the property to be sold prior to a challenge to that security being commenced, the court has no jurisdiction under section 15 to authorise sale and the retention of the proceeds in a designated account.[76]

(e) *Section 27: Protection of the interest of creditors*

23–20   Where a creditor of a company in administration considers that the company's affairs, business and property are being or have been managed by the administrator in a manner that is unfairly prejudicial to the interests of its creditors

---

[68] IA, s.15(1), (3).
[69] IA, s.15(2), (3).
[70] *i.e.* under IA, s.15(1).
[71] IA, s.15(4).
[72] IA, s.15(5).
[73] IA, s.15(6).
[74] See para. 11–17 *et seq.* It does not matter, for the purposes of section 15(1) that the charge has crystallised.
[75] (1988) 4 BCC 708.
[76] *Re Newman Shopfitters (Cleveland) Limited* [1991] B.C.L.C. 407.

or some part of those creditors (at least including himself) or that any actual or proposed act or omission of the administrator would be so prejudicial, he may apply to the court for relief.[77] The court may make such order as it thinks fit[78] although it cannot prejudice the implementation of a CVA or a compromise or scheme under section 425 of the Companies Act 1985 or (if the application was more than 28 days after the approval of any proposals or revised proposals by the creditors in the administration) the implementation of those proposals.[79]

3. **Liquidation**

(a) *Stay of proceedings*

At any time after the presentation of a winding up petition and before a winding   **23–21** up order is made, the company or any creditor or contributory may apply to the court for an order staying or restraining any proceedings against the company.[80] Unless there are special circumstances, the court will exercise its discretion to ensure an equal distribution of assets.[81]

Upon the making of a winding up order or the appointment of a provisional liquidator, no action or proceeding shall be proceeded with or commenced against the company or its property, except by leave of the court and subject to such terms as the court may impose.[82] In determining whether leave should be given, the court will undertake a balancing exercise and seek to do what is right and just in all the circumstances. A lessor has been permitted to take proceedings to re-enter demised premises where there has been a breach of covenant.[83] A mortgagee seeking to obtain possession would, it is submitted, enjoy equal rights and prospects.

(b) *Proof of debts*

Similar provisions to those which prevail in bankruptcy[84] apply in the event that   **23–22** a company is wound up[85] and accordingly, do not merit repetition.

(c) *Interest*

There are corresponding statutory provisions governing interest in a winding up[86]   **23–23** (as opposed to a bankruptcy[87]).

---

[77] IA, s.27(1).
[78] IA, s.27(2).
[79] IA, s.27(3).
[80] IA, s.126. In a voluntary winding up similar provisions apply: IA, s.112.
[81] *Bowkett v. Fuller United Electric Works Limited* [1923] 1 KB 160.
[82] IA, s.130(2).
[83] *Re Strand Hotel Co.* [1868] WN 2.
[84] See *ante*, para. 23–08.
[85] See IR, r. 4.88 (proving for the balance/whole debt due to a secured creditor) and Chapter 10 of the Insolvency Rules, rr. 4.95–4.99 (valuation of security; surrender for non-disclosure; redemption by the liquidator; test of value; realisation by the creditor).
[86] IA, s.189 and IR, r. 4.93.
[87] See *ante*, para. 23–08.

(d) *Disclaimer*

23–24 Similar powers to disclaim onerous property are given to the liquidator[88] as those that are given to the trustee in bankruptcy. A mortgagee is able to seek a vesting order in the case of a disclaimer of a leasehold property by a liquidator.[89]

4. **Dissolution**

23–25 At the conclusion of the liquidation of a limited company, it is dissolved and thus ceases to exist.[90] Dissolution can follow upon the completion of the winding up process, in which the company's assets are realised and its creditors paid, with any surplus being distributed to its contributories. Section 205 of the Insolvency Act provides for the dissolution of the company at the expiry of a period of three months after either the final meeting of creditors and the vacation of office by the liquidator or notice from the official receiver that the winding up is complete.[91]

(a) *Early dissolution*

23–26 However, a company may also be subject to early dissolution where it appears that the realisable assets of the company are insufficient to cover the expenses of the winding up and that the affairs of the company do not require further investigation.[92] Whilst the provisions of the Insolvency Act permit objection by the official receiver and any creditor or contributory to early dissolution,[93] the effect of early dissolution is that the company's assets will not be realised as they would if it were wound up and dissolved under section 202. Accordingly, those assets would, on dissolution pass as *bona vacantia*.[94]

(b) *Striking off by the Registrar*

23–27 The registrar of companies may initiate a procedure in relation to a company which he has cause to believe is no longer carrying on business or in operation which, at its conclusion, results in its dissolution.[95] Upon dissolution, the company's property passes as *bona vacantia*.[96]

The court may restore a dissolved company to the register in accordance with its statutory powers.[97]

---

[88] IA, s.178 (power to disclaim), s.179 (disclaimer of leaseholds), s.180 (land subject to a rentcharge), s.181 (powers of court (general)) and s.182 (powers of court (leasehold)).
[89] IA, s.182(3).
[90] IA, Chapter IX (ss.201–205).
[91] IA, s.205(1)(a), (b).
[92] IA, s.202(2).
[93] IA, s.203.
[94] Companies Act 1985, s.654.
[95] *ibid.*, ss652, 652A–F, 653.
[96] *ibid.*, s.654.
[97] *ibid.*, s.651 and 653.

(c) *Bona Vacantia*

On dissolution "all property and rights whatsoever vested in or held on trust for **23–28** the company immediately before its dissolution (including leasehold property, but not including property held by the company on trust for any other person) are deemed to be *bona vacantia* and accordingly belong to the Crown or to the Duchy of Lancaster or to the Duke of Cornwall for the time being (as the case may be), and vest and may be dealt with in the same manner as other *bona vacantia* accruing to the Crown or to the Duchy of Lancaster or to the Duke of Cornwall."[98]

The equity of redemption is an interest which the mortgagor can convey, devise, entail, lease, mortgage or settle[99] and thus it has been held that the equity of redemption in leasehold premises subject to a mortgage can pass as *bona vacantia* upon the dissolution of a corporate mortgagor.[1]

The Crown, the Duchy of Lancaster and the Duke of Cornwall can disclaim property that has vested as *bona vacantia*.[2] If the company is restored to the register, the property is deemed never to have vested in the Crown and any disclaimer is deemed not to have occurred.[3]

[98] *ibid.*, s.654(1).
[99] *Pawlett v. Att.-Gen.* (1667) Hard, 465, 469; *Fawcett v. Lowther* (1751) 2 Ves. Sen. 300.
[1] *Re Wells* [1933] Ch 29.
[2] Companies Act 1985, s.656, with the consequences specified in s.657.
[3] *Allied Dunbar Assurance plc v. Fowler* [1994] 2 B.C.L.C. 197.

CHAPTER 24

RIGHTS OF CONSOLIDATION AND MARSHALLING

The effect of these equitable doctrines is that, in certain circumstances, a **24–01** mortgagee is enabled to enlarge his security beyond the property which he took to secure his debt.

CONSOLIDATION

1. Right to consolidate

If a mortgagor has mortgaged two or more properties his mortgagee may have the **24–02** right to refuse to allow him to redeem one mortgage unless he redeems all of them. Whereas equity normally extends the right to redeem, the application of the maxim "he who seeks equity must do equity"[1] results, where the doctrine of consolidation comes into play, in a restriction of that right. Normally, the mortgagee will wish to exercise the right when one of the mortgaged properties depreciates in value so that by itself it is insufficient to satisfy the security; but he may do so even if each property is by itself a sufficient security for the debt.

The basis of the long-established right to consolidate is the practice of courts of equity in redemption actions. After the mortgagor is in default, he needs the assistance of equity in order to redeem and equity demands, in such a case, that he shall not be able to redeem an estate which is sufficient security for the debt while leaving the mortgagee with another estate which is not.[2] This would suggest that the mortgagee can exercise the right only when one of the properties mortgaged depreciates. It is, however, settled law that the right exists in any circumstances where the mortgagor has to assert his equitable title. Thus it applies in a forfeiture action since in such an action the mortgagor has to redeem then or not at all.[3] It applies also when the mortgagee has sold one property under his power of sale and the mortgagor is claiming to be paid the surplus remaining after the discharge of that mortgage; the effect of the doctrine is then to give the mortgagee the right to retain that surplus so as to satisfy a debt secured on another property.[4] Unlike the right to tack, the right to consolidate is independent of the possession of the legal estate.

---

[1] *Willie v. Lugg* (1761) 2 Eden 78; *White v. Hillacre* (1839) 3 Y. & C. Ex. 597; *Chesworth v. Hunt*, (1880) 5 C.P.D. 266; *Cummins v. Fletcher* (1880) 14 Ch.D. 699.
[2] *Jennings v. Jordan* (1881) 6 App.Cas. 698, H.L.; *Griffith v. Pound* (1890) 45 Ch.D. 553.
[3] *Cummins v. Fletcher* (1880) 14 Ch.D. 699; *Watts v. Symes* (1851) 1 De G. M. & G. 240.
[4] *Selby v. Pomfret* (1861) 3 De G. F. & J. 595; *Cracknall v. Janson* (1879) 11 Ch.D. 1, C.A.

2. **Exclusion of the doctrine**

24–03 The doctrine may cause difficulty to a purchaser of mortgaged property, since the mortgage may be liable to be consolidated against him although he has no means of knowing that to be the case. Consequently, the operation of the doctrine was abolished by statute for all mortgages made after December 31, 1881, except where a contrary intention is expressed in the mortgage. Section 93 of the Law of Property Act 1925 provides that:

> "(1) A mortgagor seeking to redeem any one mortgage is entitled to do so without paying any money due under any separate mortgage made by him, or by any person through whom he claims, solely on property other than that comprised in the mortgage which he seeks to redeem.
>
> This subsection applies only if and so far as a contrary intention is not expressed in the mortgage deeds or one of them.
>
> (2) This section does not apply where all the mortgages were made before 1st January, 1882.
>
> (3) Save as aforesaid nothing in this Act, in reference to mortgages, affects any right of consolidation or renders inoperative a stipulation in relation to any mortgage made before or after the commencement of this Act reserving a right to consolidate."

The intention to exclude the statutory rule may be effectively manifested either by a clause in the mortgage deed that section 93(1) is not to apply to the security or by a clause providing for the preservation of the right to consolidate.[5]

3. **Requirements for consolidation**

24–04 If either all the mortgages were made before January 1, 1882 or the parties have excluded section 93(1),[6] the mortgagee's right to consolidate can be exercised subject to the following conditions:

(1) The legal dates of redemption of all the mortgages sought to be consolidated have passed.[7]

(2) All mortgages must have been made by the same mortgagor.

(3) The security must be in existence at the time that the mortgagee claims to consolidate.

(4) At one and the same time all the mortgages must have been vested in some person and all the equities of redemption in some other person.

These conditions are now considered in turn.

---

[5] *Hughes v. Britannia Permanent Benefit Building Society* [1906] 2 Ch. 606. In *Re Salmon, ex p. the Trustee* [1903] 1 K.B. 147 it was held that a clause excluding the statute (at that time s.17 of the Conveyancing Act 1881) and contained in the first of several mortgages would preserve the right to consolidate; compare *Griffith v. Pound* (1890) 45 Ch.D. 553; a clause in a later mortgage is ineffective as to earlier mortgages.

[6] Which, in practice, most mortgagees require.

[7] *Cummins v. Fletcher* (1880) 14 Ch.D. 699.

(a) *Rule 1*

The right to consolidate is an equitable right and does not override the legal right to redeem on the contractual date: the mortgagor does not require the assistance of equity to redeem on that date.

(b) *Rule 2*

The right can come into existence only if the mortgages were originally made by the same mortgagor,[8] (with one possible exception). That exception is, where one mortgage is made by B and the other mortgage is made by persons claiming by devolution from him on his death.[9] Thus the right does not exist where one mortgage is made by B and the other jointly by A and B[10]; nor when B as beneficiary makes one and A, as B's trustee, makes the other[11]; nor when B as principal debtor makes one and A as surety makes the other[12]; nor when B makes one as security for a private debt and A and B as partners make the other as security for a partnership debt.

Various other differences between the mortgages are irrelevant to the existence **24–05** of the right to consolidate. First, it does not matter that the mortgages were originally made to different mortgagees.[13] Secondly, the right is not affected by either the nature of the mortgage or the nature of the property mortgaged, except that no right to consolidation can arise in respect of personal chattels as defined by the Bills of Sale Acts 1878.[14] Thus two legal mortgages, or two equitable mortgages,[15] or a legal and an equitable mortgage can be consolidated,[16] as can a mortgage of realty and a mortgage of personalty other than personal chattels.[17]

(c) *Rule 3*

Where a mortgagee holds two mortgages and one has ceased to exist because its subject matter has determined, as may be the case when it is a mortgage of a lease[18] or a life interest,[19] the mortgagee may not apply any surplus on the other to make good the deficiency on the one whose subject-matter has determined. As

---

[8] *Sharp v. Rickards* [1909] 1 Ch. 109.
[9] *White v. Hillacre* (1839) 3 Y. & C. Ex. 597.
[10] *Jones v. Smith* (1794) 2 Ves. Jun. 372; *Thorneycroft v. Crockett* (1848) 2 H.L.C. 239; *Cummins v. Fletcher* (1880) 14 Ch.D. 699.
[11] *Re Raggett, ex p. Williams* (1880) 16 Ch.D. 117.
[12] *Aldworth v. Robinson* (1840) 2 Beav. 287.
[13] Provided that they are united in the same mortgagee when the right to consolidation is claimed: *Pledge v. White* [1896] A.C. 187.
[14] *Chesworth v. Hunt* (1880) 5 C.P.D. 266.
[15] *Tweedale v. Tweedale* (1857) 23 Beav. 341.
[16] *Cracknall v. Janson* (1879) 11 Ch.D. 1, C.A.; *Watts v. Symes* (1851) 1 De G. M. & G. 240.
[17] *Cracknall v. Janson, supra. Tassell v. Smith* (1858) 2 De G. & J. 713 was overruled by *Jennings v. Jordan* (1881) 6 App. Cas. 698 which held that consolidation cannot occur so as to prejudice the purchaser of an equity of redemption by virtue of a mortgage created after the sale.
[18] *Re Raggett, ex p. Williams* (1880) 16 Ch.D. 117.
[19] *Re Gregson, Christison v. Bolam* (1887) 36 Ch.D. 223.

soon as it has determined, the debt is no longer secured and is a simple contract debt.

This does not apply when a security has ceased to exist because the mortgagee has realised it. The right to consolidate is not affected by realisation.[20]

This rule may be illustrated by the following examples. Consider these events and assume that all other conditions for consolidation are satisfied:

(a) B mortgages a leasehold interest in Blackacre to L for £10,000.
(b) B mortgages a freehold interest in Whiteacre to L for £40,000.
(c) L realises his security in Whiteacre for £50,000.
(d) The leasehold interest in Blackacre determines.
(e) L gives B notice to pay off the debt on Blackacre, with a view to becoming entitled to exercise his power of sale.

If the events (a), (b), (e) happen in that order, L can consolidate against B and can refuse a tender by B of the money secured against Blackacre.[21]

If the events (a), (b), (d), (c) happen in that order, L can consolidate and apply the surplus on realisation of his security in Whiteacre to the payment of the debt secured on Blackacre, since both securities were in existence when L claimed to consolidate.[22]

If the events (a), (b), (c), (d) happen in that order, the security on Blackacre no longer exists at the time L realises his security in Whiteacre. The debt formerly secured on Blackacre has now become a simple contract debt and in respect of it, L is in the same position as any other of B's unsecured creditors. If there are such creditors L cannot, against them, claim to apply the surplus from Whiteacre to the payment of the Blackacre debt.[23]

Both mortgages must be vested solely in L at the time when he wishes to exercise his right to consolidate, so, if in either of the first two rules above, the mortgage in one property was vested in L and M jointly at the time L wished to exercise the right, he would not be permitted to do so.[24]

(d) *Rule 4*

For the purposes of the first three rules, only the right to consolidate against the original mortgagor needs to be discussed. The fourth rule, however, involves consideration of the right to consolidate against an assignee of a mortgagor, as well as the right to consolidate against the original mortgagor.

4. **Consolidation against the original mortgagor**

24–06   Consider the following transactions:

(a) B mortgages Blackacre to L;

---

[20] *Selby v. Pomfret* (1861) 3 De G. F. & J. 595; *Cracknall v. Janson* (1879) 11 Ch.D. 14, C.A.
[21] *Griffith v. Pound* (1890) 45 Ch.D. 553.
[22] *Selby v. Pomfret, supra*; *Cracknell v. Janson, ante.*
[23] *Re Gregson, Christison v. Bolam* (1887) 36 Ch.D. 223; *Talbot v. Frere* (1878) 9 Ch.D. 568.
[24] *Riley v. Hall* (1898) 79 L.T. 244.

(b) B mortgages Blackacre to M;

(c) B mortgages Whiteacre to M;

(d) L buys M's mortgage on Whiteacre;

(e) K buys both mortgages;

(f) B assigns the equity of redemption in one of the properties to N.

Provided the conditions previously discussed are all satisfied, M will have the right to consolidate against B if the events (b) and (c) occur before (f), while L will have the same right if the events (a), (c) and (d), occur before (f). The equities of redemption are in B's hand throughout and whoever acquires both mortgages can consolidate against him. This applies equally if, instead of L buying M's mortgage, K buys both mortgages.

If, however, the equities are severed before both mortgages come into one hand, as in the sequences (b), (f), (c), or (a), (c), (f), (d) (or e); there can be no right to consolidate against B because B never owns both equities of redemption at the same time that either L or K owns both mortgages.[25] Subsequent transactions may, as explained below, create a right to consolidate against N.

It is for the mortgagee of the two properties to decide whether he wishes to take advantage of his right to consolidate. The mortgagor cannot compel him to do so against his will. In *Pelly v. Wathen*,[26] after the events (a), (c), B created a second mortgage of both properties in favour of P. It was held that P was entitled, if he wished, to redeem only one of the first mortgages even though he had the right to consolidate against B if he redeemed both.

The right to consolidate is not lost because the mortgagee does not choose to exercise it. If, following the events (a), (c), (e), K gives notice to B that he requires payment of the mortgage on Blackacre he can refuse a tender by B if it is insufficient to discharge both mortgages.[27]

5. Consolidation against the mortgagor's assignee or successor-in-title

The principle is that an assignee of the equity of redemption succeeds to **24–07** whatever rights the mortgagor had at the time of the assignment[28] and takes subject to the existing equities.[29] The simple example is where a person purchases the freehold or leasehold interest of the mortgagor subject to one or more mortgages. However a person acquiring the equity of redemption under a will or intestacy[30] by virtue of the mortgagor's bankruptcy[31] will be in the same position.

Consider the following transactions:

(a) B mortgages Blackacre to L;

(b) B mortgages Whiteacre to L;

---

[25] *Harter v. Coleman* (1882) 19 Ch.D. 630; *Minter v. Carr* [1894] 3 Ch. 498.

[26] (1849) 7 Hare 351; on appeal (1851) 1 De G. M. & G. 16; *cf. Re Thompson's Estates* [1912] 1 I.R. 194.

[27] *Griffith v. Pound* (1890) 45 Ch.D. 553.

[28] *Willie v. Lugg* (1761) 2 Eden 78.

[29] *Harter v. Coleman* (1882) 19 Ch.D. 630.

[30] *Harris v. Tubb* (1889) 42 Ch.D. 79.

[31] *Selby v. Pomfret* (1861) 3 De G. F. & J. 595; *Re Salmon, ex p. the Trustee* [1903] 1 K.B. 147.

   (c)   B mortgages Whiteacre to L and M;

   (d)   B mortgages Whiteacre to M;

   (e)   L buys M's mortgage;

   (f)   B assigns both equities of redemption to N;

   (g)   B assigns the equity of redemption in Blackacre to N.

In the events (a) and (b), L can consolidate against B and he will have the same right in the events (a), (c), (d), or (a), (d), (e), since B has both equities of redemption and at the same time L has both mortgages. As soon as (f) occurs, L can consolidate against N. The same is true if (g) occurs, because N takes the assignment subject to the existing right to consolidate. If N wishes to redeem Blackacre, L can force him to redeem Whiteacre at the same time though N will, if he redeems, be entitled to have Whiteacre transferred to him.[32]

(a) *Consolidation: improving the mortgagee's position.*

24–07   In the events (a), (d), (f) and (e) it would appear that there is no right to consolidate since, after the occurrence of (a) and (d) the two mortgages were in different hands. There would have been no right to consolidate against B and therefore no right to consolidate against N. On general principles, N should not be prejudiced by the subsequent transaction between L and M. It is, however, an old-established rule[33] that in such circumstances the assignee of both equities must be deemed to have taken the assignment with the knowledge that the two mortgages might come into one hand, with the result that the mortgagee would have the right to consolidate against him.[34] This leads to the possibility that a mortgagee whose security was inadequate could improve his position at the expense of the mortgagor's general creditors if the mortgagor became bankrupt. If, in the sequence of events (a), (d), (f), (f) takes place because N is B's trustee in bankruptcy, either L or M, if he thought his security to be inadequate, would be able to enlarge it by buying up the other's mortgage and consolidating against N and would be unaffected by B's bankruptcy.[35] It would be otherwise if the sequence were (a), (f), (d). There could be no consolidation of two mortgages, one created before and one after the start of the bankruptcy.

   It might be thought that the same result would occur as a result of the sequence (a), (d), (g) and (e); that is, that B assigns only one equity of redemption. If N is exposed to the risk of consolidation against himself when he buys both equities, the fact that he has bought only one should not make any difference. The decision in *Beevor v. Luck*[36] to that effect is, however, no longer considered to be good law, the practical reason being the risk that would be associated with the purchase of any equity of redemption. In this example, N when he took the equity of redemption in Blackacre would have no means of finding out from L that Whiteacre had been mortgaged to M by B and that, in consequence M, by buying

[32] *Cracknall v. Janson* (1871) 11 Ch.D. 1, C.A.; *Mutual Life Assurance Society v. Langley* (1886) 32 Ch.D. 460, C.A.

[33] *Bovey v. Skipwith* (1671) 1 Cas. in Ch. 201; *Tweedale v. Tweedale* (1857) 23 Beav. 341; *Vint v. Padget* (1858) 2 De G. & J. 611.

[34] As was decided, albeit with reluctance, in *Pledge v. White* [1896] A.C. 187.

[35] *Selby v. Pomfret* (1861) 3 De G. F. & J. 595.

[36] (1867) L.R. 4 Eq. 537.

L's mortgage, would be able to consolidate against him. As was said in *Pledge v. White*,[37] a person in the position of N can see, if he buys two properties mortgaged by the same mortgagor, that there is a risk of the mortgages coming into the same hand. However, if he buys one property, he can be aware of this risk only if B tells him that he has mortgaged other property.

Where the sequence of events is (a), (g), (d), (e) there can clearly be no consolidation, since the equities of redemption in the two properties have been severed before there is even a potential right to consolidate.[38]

(b) *Consolidation and the assignee of redemption.*

The general principle that the assignor of an equity of redemption should not be able to prejudice his assignee's position by subsequent transactions with third parties was qualified in *Jennings v. Jordan*[39] where it was suggested that the assignee might be affected by an express contractual term reserving to the assignor the right to consolidate future mortgages. That case was decided before the Conveyancing Act 1881 came into operation, and mortgage deeds did not then, as they commonly do now, contain clauses excluding the statutory prohibition on, or preserving the right of, consolidation. **24–08**

The question therefore arises whether an assignee of an equity of redemption is liable, by reason of such a contractual term, to have consolidated against him mortgages created by the assignor which were not in existence at the time of the assignment. In *Andrews v. City Permanent Building Society*[40] it was held that, while a second mortgagee would not by virtue of the equitable doctrine be liable to have mortgages consolidated against him which were not in existence when he took the second mortgage, he was so liable if the first mortgage contained an express stipulation for a right to consolidate later mortgages. The liability arises whether or not the second mortgagee has notice of the stipulation because the mortgage contract prevents him from redeeming free of that right.

The same point arose in *Hughes v. Britannia Permanent Benefit Building Society*[41] where the much-criticised Kekewich J. arrived at what is generally considered to be the right decision. He held that the second mortgagee is affected by the contractual stipulation but treated it as if it reserved the right to tack further advances and applied the rule in *Hopkinson v. Rolt*[42] that is, that a mortgagee with notice of an intervening mortgage could not tack further advances. The rule has been criticised on the ground that a paramount right to tack created by a first mortgage should not be capable of being defeated by the action of a second mortgagee in giving notice of his charge, but, whatever substance there is in that criticism, it is settled law that a second mortgagee can prevent consolidation of later mortgages against him by giving actual notice to

---

[37] [1896] A.C. 187.
[38] *Jennings v. Jordan* (1881) 6 App.Cas. 698, HL.
[39] (1881) 6 App.Cas. 698 at 702.
[40] (1881) 44 L.T. 641.
[41] [1906] 2 Ch. 606.
[42] (1861) 9 H.L.C. 514; see Megarry and Wade, *The Law of Real Property* (6th ed., 2000), para. 19–255.

the first mortgagee. Registration of the second mortgage is not notice for this purpose where a mortgage is expressly made for securing further advances.[43]

5. **Registration of the right to consolidate**

24–09   Where the land affected by the right to consolidate is registered land, the Land Registration Act 1925 and the Land Registration Rules 1925, rule 154 apply.

Section 25(3)(ii) of the Land Registration Act 1925 states that any provision contained in a charge which purports to affect any registered land or charge other than that in respect of which the charge is to be expressly registered shall be void.

Rule 154 of the Land Registration Rules 1925, is as follows:

"(1) Where a charge, whether affecting the whole or part of the land comprised in a title, reserves the right to consolidate, it shall not on that account be registered against any other land than that expressly described in it.

(2) But where the right reserved is to consolidate with a specified charge, or an application in writing is made to register the right in respect of a specified charge, the Registrar shall require the production of the land certificate[44] of all the titles affected, and, on the production thereof, shall enter in the register a notice that the specified charges are consolidated."

Since the Land Registration Act 1925, section 65, requires that, on registration of a charge or mortgage, the land certificate is to be deposited at the registry until the charge or mortgage is cancelled, it must be the charge certificate, not the land certificate, to which rule 154(2) should refer.

The right to consolidate does not depend on the entry of any notice under rule 154.

It has been suggested[45] that the right to consolidate mortgages of unregistered land is registrable as a class C (iii) land charge, but there is no direct authority in support of the suggestion and it is not easy to see how such a right can amount to a charge. It has also been suggested that in the case of registered land it may not be possible to exclude the provisions of the LRA as to the right to consolidate.[46]

MARSHALLING

1. **Principle underlying the doctrine**

24–10   If B has two creditors, L and M, and L has recourse to only one security in order to satisfy his debt, while M has recourse to more than one, M will not be

---

[43] LPA 1925, s.94(2) (as amended by the LPA 1969, s.16(2), Sched. 2, Pt. I; and the Law of Property (Amendment) Act 1926, s.7).

[44] Since s.65 of the Land Registration Act 1925 requires that, on registration of a charge or mortgage the land certificate is to be deposited at the registry until the charge or mortgage is cancelled, it must be the charge certificate, not the land certificate, to which rule 154(2) should refer.

[45] (1948) 92 S.J. 726.

[46] See Rouff & Roper, *Registered Conveyancing* para. 23–41 and see s.25(3)(iii) *ante*, para. 24–09.

permitted to satisfy his debt in a way that prejudices L.[47] Although the application of this doctrine will, like the application of the doctrine of consolidation, enlarge the creditor's security beyond that for which he contracted it is not a right which the creditor needs actively to assert since in any case where it should apply the court will automatically apply it without it being claimed as relief in any proceedings.[48]

An illustration of the doctrine is given by the following facts:

    (a) B mortgages Blackacre to M;
    (b) B mortgages Whiteacre to M;
    (c) B mortgages Whiteacre to L.

The effect of the doctrine is that L may claim, against B, that B shall satisfy M's debt out of Blackacre so far as possible leaving Whiteacre for the satisfaction of his own debt.[49] The doctrine applies to a fund of money as well as to realty and also applies whether the security is by way of mortgage, charge or lien.[50]

Suppose, in the above events, B had mortgaged the two properties to M to secure a loan of £25,000, and later mortgaged Whiteacre to L to secure a loan of £15,000, and suppose each of the two properties to be worth £20,000. If the doctrine of marshalling did not exist, then the primary rule[51] as to the satisfaction of M's debt would operate and it would be satisfied as to £12,500 out of each property, leaving only £7,500 of the equity in Whiteacre for L. Thus, although the two properties would between them be sufficient to satisfy the total debts owing to L and M, L's would be only half satisfied.

If the securities are marshalled, M's debt is satisfied as to £20,000 out of Blackacre and as to the remaining £5,000 out of Whiteacre, leaving £15,000 equity in Whiteacre to satisfy L.

(2) **Conditions for marshalling**

There are four such conditions which are now stated and discussed in turn: **24–11**

    (1) The right exists only where the prior mortgagee holds two securities (of whatever nature) which belong to the same owner.
    (2) The right exists against the common mortgagor and against all persons, other than purchasers, claiming through him.
    (3) The right is not enforced to the prejudice of third parties claiming as purchasers.
    (4) A puisne incumbrancer's right to marshall does not affect the prior mortgagee's right to realise his securities in whatever manner or order he decides.

---

[47] *Lanoy v. Duke of Athol* (1742) 2 Atk. 444; *Aldrich v. Cooper* (1803) 8 Ves. 382; *Trimmer v. Bayne (No. 2)* (1803) 9 Ves. 209, approved, *Webb v. Smith* (1885) 30 Ch.D. 192; *Averall v. Wade* (1835) L. & G. temp. Sugden 252.
[48] *Gibbs v. Ougier* (1806) 12 Ves. 413.
[49] *Lanoy v. Duke of Athol, supra*; *South v. Bloxam* (1865) 2 H. & M. 457.
[50] *Re Westzinthus* (1833) 5 B. & Ad. 817; *Re Fry* [1912] 2 Ch. 86.
[51] *i.e.* that the debt is satisfied out of the two properties rateably to their values.

(a) *Rule 1*

24–12   The two securities must originally have belonged to the same owner.[52] Thus where the two securities were a ship and its cargo and belonged to different owners, marshalling was not permitted.[53] It is not necessary for the securities to have been created at the same time or to have been given in respect of each of the same debt. However if two securities are given, one in respect of each of two debts, marshalling is not permitted unless the debts are those of the same person.[54] As with consolidation the right does not exist where one security is given by one person and the other security by the same person jointly with someone else.

If, in the example given above, M had satisfied his debt out of Whiteacre, L's right to marshall would be enforced by being subrogated to M's rights against Blackacre.[55]

(b) *Rule 2*

24–13   The right may be exercised against the common mortgagor[56] or against persons claiming the property or part of it under him unless those persons take by charge or assignment.[57] They are not subject to the right even if they are volunteers.[58]

As the right is exercisable against the common mortgagor's trustee in bankruptcy,[59] a puisne incumbrancer may be able to enlarge his security at the expense of the general creditors. The common mortgagor's judgment creditors[60] and real and personal representatives[61] are exposed to the operation of the doctrine.

The right is not lost by reason of the two funds or securities later becoming vested in different persons.[62]

(c) *Rule 3*

24–14   The court will not interfere with a mortgagee in the exercise of his remedies. Thus, if, in the example above M chooses to satisfy his debt first out of Whiteacre, L's debt will be thrown on Blackacre, of which he becomes second mortgagee, and if L pays off the unsatisfied part of M's debt, he becomes first

---

[52] *Douglas v. Cooksey* (1868) 2 I.R.Eq. 311.

[53] *The Chioggia* [1898] P. 1, distinguishing *The Edward Oliver* (1867) L.R. 1. A. & E. 379; *contra Webb v. Smith* (1885) 30 Ch.D. 192, which is considered incorrect on this point.

[54] *ex p. Kendall* (1811) 17 Ves. 514.

[55] *Mason v. Bogg* (1837) 2 My. & Cr. 443; *Wallis v. Woodyear* (1855) 2 Jur.N.S. 179; *Dolphin v. Aylward* (1870) L.R. 4 H.L. 486.

[56] *Haynes v. Forshaw* (1853) 11 Hare. 93.

[57] *Barnes v. Racster* (1842) 1 Y. & C.Ch.Cas. 401; *Flint v. Howard* [1893] 2 Ch. 54, C.A.

[58] *Dolphin v. Aylward* (1870) L.R. 4 H.L. 486; *Hales v. Cox* (1863) 32 Beav. 118.

[59] *Re Cornwall, Baldwin v. Belcher* (1842) 3 Dr. & War. 173; *Re Tristram, ex p. Hartley* (1835) 1 Deac. 288; *Re Holland, ex p. Alston* (1868) 4 Ch.App. 168; *Heyman v. Dubois* (1871) L.R. 13 Eq. 158.

[60] *Gray v. Stone and Funnell* (1893) 69 L.T. 282.

[61] *Lanoy v. Duke of Athol* (1742) 2 Atk. 444; *Flint v. Howard* [1893] 2 Ch. 54, C.A.

[62] *Lanoy v. Duke of Athol, ante.*

mortgagee.[63] If M realises both securities, he holds the aggregate proceeds on trust to pay himself first, then L.[64]

(d) *Rule 4*

The right to consolidate may, as *Pledge v. White*[65] shows, operate to the disadvantage of third parties claiming as purchasers. The right to marshall does not.[66] This can be illustrated by considering what would happen if there was a fourth event added to the series above (see para. 24–10), that is:

    (d) B mortgages Blackacre to N.

24–15

This does not affect L's right to marshall against B but if M satisfies himself primarily out of Whiteacre, which is the only property to which L can resort, L can no longer throw his debt on Blackacre.[67] It is irrelevant that N had notice of the previous transactions[68] or that he was a volunteer.[69]

There are only two cases in which L's right can affect N. In *Re Mower's Trusts*[70] it was held that N was bound by L's pre-existing right to marshall because his mortgage was expressly made subject to the payment of the two earlier mortgages. In *Stronge v. Hawkes*[71] there was an erroneous recital to the effect that the prior mortgagee had been paid off, so L thought that he was the prior mortgagee. N, taking with notice of the error and of L's consequent incorrect belief, was held to be subject to L's right to marshall.

The mere fact that N's second mortgage overrides L's right of marshalling does not altogether destroy the effect of the doctrine, as the following example shows:

    (a) B mortgages Blackacre and Whiteacre to M for £20,000;
    (b) B mortgages Whiteacre to L for £10,000;
    (c) B mortgages Blackacre to N for £10,000.

Suppose that, on realisation, each property was found to be worth £20,000. If L were allowed to marshall, the effect would be that M would satisfy his entire debt out of Blackacre, L would satisfy his out of Whiteacre, leaving £10,000 equity in Whiteacre to which N would have no recourse.

The rule does not permit this. The court preserves the right of all the incumbrancers, so far as possible, by apportioning M's charge, as between L and N, rateably between the two properties. There is no marshalling, strictly speaking; the rateable division simply prevents the loss from lying where it falls as a result

---

[63] *Manks v. Whitely* [1911] 2 Ch. 448, affd. [1914] A.C. 132; and see *Noyes v. Pollock* (1886) 32 Ch.D. 53.
[64] *South v. Bloxham* (1865) 2 Hem. & M. 457.
[65] [1896] A.C. 187, H.L.
[66] *Baglioni v. Cavalli* (1900) 83 L.T. 500.
[67] *Barnes v. Racster* (1842) 17 Y. & C.Ch.Cas. 401.
[68] *Baglioni v. Cavalli* (1900) 93 L.T. 500; *Flint v. Howard* [1893] 2 Ch. 54, C.A.; *Smyth v. Toms* [1918] 1 I.R. 338.
[69] *Dolphin v. Aylward* (1870) L.R. 4 H.L. 486.
[70] (1869) L.R. 8 Eq. 110.
[71] (1859) 4 De G. & J. 632.

of the way in which M elects to satisfy his debt. If M, in the above example, were to satisfy his debt entirely out of Whiteacre, N's debt would be satisfied out of Blackacre and L would get nothing; with the converse result if he satisfied it entirely out of Blackacre.[72]

Suppose, in the example above, M chose to satisfy his debt primarily out of Whiteacre and that Whiteacre was worth £10,000 and Blackacre £30,000. The court would treat the matter as if M had satisfied his debt rateably out of the two properties, that is, £5,000 out of Whiteacre (notionally leaving £5,000 equity) and £15,000 out of Blackacre (notionally leaving £15,000 equity). To the extent of the £5,000 which he would have had out of Whiteacre had M in fact satisfied his debt rateably, L will be subrogated to N's rights in Blackacre.[73]

As M satisfied his debt so as to leave no equity in Whiteacre and £20,000 in Blackacre, that £20,000 will go first towards the rights to which L is subrogated (£5,000) then towards the satisfaction of N's debt (£10,000) leaving a surplus of £5,000 which L is entitled to claim as against B.

EQUITY OF EXONERATION[74]

24–16   A right of exoneration, if enforced, has the effect of varying the incidence of a liability as between two or more properties. Primarily that incidence is determined by the doctrine of contribution which is based on the principle that, where two properties or funds are equally liable to pay a debt, one shall not escape because the creditor has chosen to satisfy himself entirely out of the other.[75]

If two or more properties, whether or not all owned by the same person, are mortgaged for or subject equally to one debt they will, under the doctrine of contribution, be rateably liable for it, the value of each property being reduced by the amount of any other incumbrance affecting it. Thus if Blackacre and Whiteacre are each worth £20,000, and if Blackacre is mortgaged to secure a debt of £10,000, after which Blackacre and Whiteacre are mortgaged together to secure a debt of £15,000, the value of Blackacre for the purpose of determining its rateable share of the later debt is £10,000. Since Whiteacre is otherwise unincumbered its value for that purpose is £20,000. Thus Blackacre will bear one third and Whiteacre two thirds of the later debt.

Circumstances exist, however, in which the doctrine of contribution does not apply and the person entitled to one property or fund has a right to be exonerated at the expense of the other.

Consider the following series of transactions:

(a)   B mortgages Blackacre and Whiteacre to L;
(b)   B assigns Blackacre to M;
(c)   B assigns Whiteacre to N.

---

[72] *Barnes v. Racster* (1842) 1 Y. & C.Ch.Cas. 401; *Flint v. Howard* [1893] 2 Ch. 54, C.A.; *Bugnold v. Bignold* (1843) 2 Y. & C.Ch.Cas. 377.
[73] *Cracknall v. Janson* (1879) 11 Ch.D. 1.
[74] See *post*, para. 26–43.
[75] See *Re Pittortouk (A Bankrupt)* [1985] 1 W.L.R. 58.

Suppose only events (a) and (b) occur. B as mortgagor is personally liable and therefore the property remaining in his hands (Whiteacre) is the primary fund for payment.[76] If B has paid the debt there is no equity to compel any contribution to be made out of Blackacre unless the assignment to M was expressly made subject to the prior mortgage.[77]

If, however, L has enforced payment out of Blackacre, M is entitled to be exonerated out of Whiteacre, whether the assignment to him was voluntary or for value.[78]

If events (a), (b) and (c) occur, the doctrine of contribution cannot be displaced by the above argument, neither M nor N being personally liable. The earlier assignee, M, will have a right to exoneration if:

(i) the assignment to him contains a covenant against incumbrances, or for further assurance; or

(ii) when he took the assignment it was represented to him, even orally, by B, that Blackacre was free from incumbrances,[79]

and, in either case, that the later assignee, N was not a purchaser of the legal estate in Whiteacre for value and without notice.

It would appear that M has no right of exoneration on the second of these two grounds if he himself is a volunteer.

The right of exoneration may also exist as a result of the following series of transactions:

(a) B mortgages Blackacre and Whiteacre to L;

(b) Both properties vest in A subject to B's mortgage which is paramount to A's title;

(c) A assigns Blackacre to M.

Since A did not create the mortgage, the doctrine of contribution is not displaced **24–17** by the existence of any personal liability; so if A pays off the mortgage, he is entitled to contribution from M, unless he made the assignment to M on the basis that Blackacre was free from incumbrances. In that case, M has a right to exoneration, which will enable him to marshall against Whiteacre unless and until it comes into the hands of a purchaser for value of the legal estate without notice.[80]

[76] *Re Darby's Estate, Rendall v. Darby* [1907] 2 Ch. 465.

[77] *Re Mainwaring's Settlement Trusts, Mainwaring's Trustee in Bankruptcy v. Verden* [1937] Ch. 96.

[78] *Re Best, Parker v. Best* [1924] 1 Ch. 42; *Ker v. Ker* (1869) 4 Ir.R.Eq. 15.

[79] *McCarthy v. M'Cartie* [1904] 1 I.R. 100; see *Finch v. Shaw, Colyer v. Finch* (1854) 19 Beav. 500.

[80] *Ocean Accident & Guarantee Corporation Ltd and Hewitt v. Collum* [1913] 1 I.R. 337.

CHAPTER 25

THE MORTGAGEE'S DEBT AND THE MORTGAGE ACCOUNT

LIABILITY TO ACCOUNT[1]

The mortgagee's substantial interest in the mortgaged property is his security for **25–01** recovering his debt. The extent of that debt depends primarily on the terms of the mortgage contract, but it also depends on the rules of equity. Some of those rules have already been mentioned in connection with the equity of redemption and the rights of the mortgagee; others depend on the practice of the court in actions for redemption and foreclosure.[2] Many of these rules are relevant in that they fix the terms of the mortgage account; for example, consolidation vitally affects the price of redemption. Nevertheless, to prevent repetition, only incidental reference can be made to such rules here in the course of explaining the contents of the account.

Assessment of the mortgage debt takes place either upon the discharge of the mortgage or the realisation of the security. Even a foreclosure action, in which the mortgagee asks for the cancellation of the right to redeem, necessitates an account, because the court will not decree foreclosure without first giving the mortgagor an opportunity to redeem.[3] But it must not be supposed that accounts are invariably or even usually taken in court: the respective rights of mortgagor and mortgagee are well defined, so that the account is generally agreed by the parties out of court. It is only in case of dispute that the account need be brought into court, and then the court directs the account to be taken (in the absence of any order to the contrary by a Master or district judge depending upon which curt hears the matter).[4] Moreover, a mortgagor cannot bring his mortgagee into court for the purpose of having the accounts taken unless either he is offering to redeem or he is seeking to recover surplus proceeds of sale.[5] The court directs an account only in actions for redemption, foreclosure, judicial sale, or for the recovery of moneys resulting from the exercise of a power of sale.

The liability to account is not, as is sometimes thought, a liability only of the mortgagee, but also of the mortgagor. A mortgagor will not be permitted to

---

[1] See *ante*, para. 16–31 with regard to a mortgagee's liability to account when in possession.

[2] See *ante*, para. 16–94 *et seq.* and *ante*, para. 18–28 *et seq.*

[3] Later incumbrancers, for the purpose of the account, are in the same position as the mortgagor, so that they may assert against the first mortgagee any equity which the mortgagor himself might assert: *Mainland v. Upjohn* (1889) 41 Ch.D. 126.

[4] CPR 40PD, para. 9.2.

[5] *cf. Troughton v. Binkes* (1801) 6 Ves. 573; *Tasker v. Small* (1837) 3 My. & Cr. 63.

redeem in equity except on the terms of allowing, to the mortgagee, all sums properly expended in the maintenance or defence of the mortgaged property, in addition to what is allowed him by his contract. Indeed, the account is primarily taken against the mortgagor and it is only a mortgagee in possession who has special liabilities in the account.

THE ACCOUNT

25–02   In *Re Wallis*,[6] Fry L.J. stated that a mortgagee's claim may comprise the following five items:

(1) the principal debt;
(2) the interest thereon;
(3) his costs in proceedings for redemption or foreclosure of the security;
(4) all proper costs, charges and expenses incurred by the mortgagee in relation to the mortgage debt or the mortgage security;
(5) the cost of litigation properly undertaken by the mortgagee in reference to the mortgage debt or security.

Of these items the first three (subject to any misconduct proved against the mortgagee) are automatically included in the account; the last two items will also be allowed if a case is made out for them. CPR 40 PD–005 provides that in taking any account directed by any judgment or order, all "just allowances" shall be made without any direction to that effect. It is now settled that the words "all just allowances" cover all payments to which a mortgagee is entitled under the terms of his security, *i.e.* all payments properly incurred in the enforcement of the rights given to him by the terms of his mortgage.[7] Accordingly, the costs of proceedings taken to obtain possession, or of proceedings by an equitable mortgagee to compel the execution of a legal mortgage and the costs of all necessary repairs and outgoings will be allowed to the mortgagee without the court having made any special direction in the decree. It is only when "permanent improvements" have been made by a mortgagee in possession, or extraordinary litigation has been pursued by the mortgagee in defence of the mortgage security that the facts justifying an extraordinary allowance must be specially pleaded and a special direction given as to the account.[8]

Apart from the possibility of extraordinary allowances, the account may be complicated by the mortgagee having gone into possession and the mortgagee's items on the credit side are then offset by his receipt of rents and profits.

The following are a mortgagee's allowances:

---

[6] (1890) 25 Q.B.D. 176 at 181.
[7] *Blackford v. Davis* (1869) 4 Ch. App. 304; *Wilkes v. Saunion* (1877) 7 Ch.D. 188.
[8] *Bolingbroke v. Hinde* (1884) 25 Ch.D. 795.

1. **Principal debt**

Under this heading a mortgagee is entitled not merely to the sums actually advanced, but also to any bonus, premium, or commission for which he has legitimately stipulated by way of a fee for advancing the money.[9] The bonus or other fee in the nature of a bonus is provided for in the mortgage either by the mortgagee deducting the amount of the bonus from the sum expressed to be advanced,[10] or else by a condition that the mortgagor shall only be able to redeem on payment of a sum larger than that actually advanced.[11] The former is the usual method, but the latter is employed when the security is a reversionary interest whose immediate value is small. Whichever course is adopted, the mortgagee is entitled to recover the full amount for which he contracted and where the mortgage deed states the sum advanced and includes an acknowledgement or receipt for that advance, the deed is prima facie evidence of an advance of that sum and the principal debt is proved by the production of the deed.[12] Again, where a mortgage is payable by instalments, and the instalments represent partly capital and partly interest—as in building society mortgages—commission or fines may payable on default upon a single instalment are not within the rule against penalties, and may be included in the account for principal.[13] Finally, if a bonus or other such sum is not claimed as part of the principal, it may be claimed specially as a "just allowance."[14]

(a) *Future advances*

A mortgagee not infrequently makes further advances upon the security of property already mortgaged to him and such advances, if proved, go into the account for principal due on the original mortgage—at any rate, as against the mortgagor. Whether a puisne incumbrancer is subject to the further advances depends on the law of tacking contained in section 94 of the Law of Property Act 1925.[15]   **25–03**

However, the further advance must be shown to have been in fact made upon the faith of the security[16] and (in the case of mortgages granted prior to 1971) the total amount claimed for principal must not exceed the sum for which the original mortgage was stamped.[17] Where further advances are contemplated, it is usual for the first mortgage to be taken on the understanding that it will cover future advances either up to a specified amount or to the amount indicated by the stamp. If a sum is so specified, it is a question of construction whether the sum named stands for principal only or for the total amount of the mortgage debt.[18]

---

[9] *Potter v. Edwards* (1857) 26 L.J.Ch. 468; *cf. Bradley v. Carritt* [1903] A.C. 253, *per* Lord Davey.

[10] See *Mainland v. Upjohn* (1889) 41 Ch.D. 126.

[11] *Webster v. Cook* (1867) L.R. 2 Ch. 542.

[12] *Piddock v. Brown* (1934) 3 P. Wms. 288.

[13] *General Credit and Discount Co. v. Glegg* (1883) 22 Ch.D. 549.

[14] *Bucknell v. Vickery* (1891) 64 L.T. 701.

[15] See, *ante*, para. 25–02 and *post*, para. 25–12 *et seq.*

[16] *ex p. Knott* (1806) 11 Ves. 609.

[17] In relation to mortgages prior to the abolition of stamp duty on mortgages by the Finance Act 1971, s.64.

[18] See *Blackford v. Davis* (1869) 4 Ch. App. 304.

(b) *Current accounts*

25–04   Again, the mortgage may be taken to secure not isolated advances but the general balance of an account; the burden of proving that the security is such a running security is upon the mortgagee[19] but if he establishes it, he may prove the amount due by extrinsic evidence. If the requisite evidence is not forthcoming, the mortgagor can only be charged to the extent of his own admissions.[20] Special questions arise if the account is taken between a first mortgagee, who holds the mortgagor's current account, and a puisne incumbrancer. If the latter acted wisely and gave notice to the first mortgagee, the first mortgage becomes as against him security only for the amount due at the date of the notice unless the first mortgagee is under an obligation to make those subsequent advances. Further advances by the first mortgagee will thereafter only rank as a third mortgage. Unless the first mortgagee took the precaution of closing the first account upon receipt of the notice, he may find that, as against the puisne incumbrancer, his priority for principal has been seriously reduced by the operation of the rule in *Clayton's Case*[20a] which provides that subsequent payments into the account by the mortgagor must be set against the first advances to him. Thus all fresh payments in, as against the puisne incumbrancer, reduce the amount secured by the first mortgage, while any further withdrawals add to the debt which now can only rank after the second mortgage.[21] Banks who, of course, hold many securities for current accounts, direct their officials to close the account at once on receipt of notice of a subsequent incumbrance, thus obviating this risk.

2. **Interest**

25–05   The rules as to allowance of interest may be shortly stated as follows:

(a)   Except in cases of undue influence or extortionate credit bargains under the Consumer Credit Act 1974 there is no rule to prevent a mortgagee from obtaining the agreed rate of interest, however high.[22]

(b)   Similarly, there is no objection to compound interest,[23] but it will only be allowed if it was contracted for in the mortgage.[24] Such a contract may be either express or implied from the usage of a trade or business.[25] Compound interest will also be chargeable when, though not a term of the mortgage, it has been agreed to subsequently for a fresh consideration, for example, in consideration of the mortgagee's forbearance.[26]

---

[19] *Re Boys* (1870) L.R. 10 Eq. 467.
[20] *Melland v. Gray* (1843) 2 Y. & C.C.C. 199.
[20a] (1816) 1 Mer. 572.
[21] *Deelay v. Lloyds Bank* [1912] A.C. 756, see *ante*, p. 374.
[22] See *ante*, para. 14–08 *et seq.* Bargains will not be interfered with merely because they are unreasonable (*Knightsbridge Estates v. Byme* [1939] Ch. 441 at 457) unless the provisions relating to interest could be seen as an unreasonable collateral advantage (see *Cityland and Property Holdings Ltd v. Dabrah* [1968] Ch. 166).
[23] *Clarkson v. Henderson* (1880) 14 Ch.D. 348.
[24] *Daniell v. Sinclair* (1881) 6 A.C. 181.
[25] *Fergusson v. Fyffe* (1841) 8 Cl. & F. 121; *National Bank of Greece S.A. v. Pinios (No. 1)* [1990] 1 A.C. 637, HL.
[26] *Blackburn v. Warwick* (1836) 2 Y. & C. Ex. 92.

(c) If there is no mention of interest in the mortgage, an agreement to pay interest will be implied. The rate formerly allowed was five per cent[27] (four per cent for equitable mortgages[28]). The court will undoubtedly order a more commercial rate today to be compounded at appropriate intervals.[29] The only exception to this rule is when the mortgage agreement expressly indicates that no interest is to be paid.[30] Whether the fact that the proviso for reconveyance is upon payment only of principal is such an indication now appears doubtful.[31]

(d) If the mortgage provides for payment of a stated rate down to the date named for repayment of the loan,[32] but nothing is said of interest to be paid afterwards, no agreement will be implied to continue payment of interest at the mortgage rate after default. Interest will, however, be recoverable for the period after default not strictly as mortgage interest, but by way of damages for detention of the debt,[33] pursuant to statute. The former practice was to allow the mortgage rate, if not in excess of five per cent, but to limit it to five per cent in other cases. The rate awarded today will presumably be the current High Court rate.[34] This rule applies to foreclosure and redemption, as well as to an action on the personal covenant: Fry J. in *Wallington v. Cook*[35] pointed out that foreclosure and redemption proceedings interest could not properly be awarded as damages but decided that it could be awarded by way of consideration for allowing the loan to remain unpaid. Thus equity once again follows the law.[36]

(e) A well-drawn mortgage deed provides for payment of interest at the mortgage rate after default so long as the security continues but even so, the mortgage rate will not be allowed after a judgment has been obtained upon the personal covenant. The mortgagee's personal right merges in his judgment and judgments carry interest only at the statutory rate.[37] This rule only affects actions on the personal covenant[38] and does not reduce the mortgagee's claim for interest in

[27] *Mendl v. Smith* (1943) 169 L.T. 153; and see *Wallersteiner v. Moir (No. 2)* [1975] Q.B. 373; *Bartlett v. Barclays Bank Trust Co. Ltd (No. 2)* [1980] Ch. 515; *International Military Services Ltd v. Capital and Counties plc* [1982] 1 W.L.R. 575; *Matthews v. T.M. Sutton Ltd* [1994] 1 W.L.R. 1455.

[28] *Re Kerr's Policy* (1869) L.R. 8 Eq. 331; *Re Drax* [1903] 1 Ch. 781.

[29] *Cityland and Property Holdings Ltd v. Dabrah* [1968] Ch. 166; *Wallersteiner v. Moir (No. 2)* [1975] Q.B. 373; *Matthew v. T.M. Sutton Ltd* [1994] 1 W.L.R. 1455. The practice of the commercial court is to award interest at base rate plus one per cent unless it is shown that would be unfair to one or other party; *Shearson Lehman Hutton Inc. v. Maclaine Watson & Co. Ltd (No. 2)* [1990] All E.R. 723.

[30] *Thompson v. Drew* (1855) 20 Beav. 49.

[31] *Mendl v. Smith* (1943) 169 L.T. 153.

[32] *Cook v. Fowler* (1874) L.R. 7 H.L. 27.

[33] See Supreme Court Act 1981, s.35A; County Courts Act 1984, s.69. See generally Civil Procedure (The White Book) CPR Part 7.010.

[34] *Re Roberts* (1880) 14 Ch.D. 49.

[35] (1878) 47 L.J.Ch. 508 at 510.

[36] *Re Sneyd* (1883) 25 Ch.D. 338.

[37] The rate under the Judgment Act 1838 has, since April 1, 1993, been eight per cent. In the county court, interest is not payable on judgments less than £5,000 (County Courts (Interest on Judgment Debts) Order 1991, S.I. 1991 No. 1184) or on a judgment which grants a suspended order for possession of a dwelling house (*ibid.*, at 2(B)(b)(ii)).

[38] Even to that extent it may be avoided by stipulation for the agreed rate to be paid "as well before as after any judgment."

redemption or foreclosure accounts. The fact that he obtains a personal judgment does not alter his right to retain his security and the mortgagor cannot redeem except on the terms of payment of all that he contracted for in the mortgage.[39] Where on the true construction of the covenant, it is a covenant to pay interest on principal monies remaining due on the security of the mortgage, the covenant remains enforceable after judgment.[40]

(f) A stipulation for a higher rate of interest in case the agreed rate is not punctually paid is a penalty and void unless it is commercially justifiable and provided its dominant purpose is not to deter the other party from breach.[41] Certainly a subsequent agreement for a higher rate, made in consideration of the mortgagee's further forbearance, is enforceable.[42] In any case, the higher rate is always obtainable by the simple device of drawing the covenant in the form that the higher rate is the agreed rate, but is reducible upon punctual payment.[43]

(g) In redemption actions the mortgagor must give six months' notice of his intention to redeem or else give six months' interest in lieu of notice[44]; the only exceptions are: (i) if the mortgagee refuses a proper tender,[45] or otherwise improperly obstructs redemption[46]; (ii) if the mortgagee takes steps to obtain payment[47]; (iii) where the mortgage is payable on demand.[48]

(h) Whether the mortgage is of land or of personalty, no more than six years' arrears of interest are recoverable on the covenant for payment.[49] The rule does not, however, apply in actions for redemption nor in foreclosure.[50]

(i) When a mortgagor is in arrears with his interest, the mortgagee may, as a condition of his further forbearance, require that the arrears be capitalised and added to the principal, so that they too may bear interest.[51] Such an arrangement is enforceable, provided that the mortgagor's positive assent to it is proved. Mere absence of protest is not enough, and there must at least be evidence from which the court can infer that he agreed to the proposal.[52] In any case, capitalisation of arrears will not bind a mesne incumbrancer, of whose charge the first mortgagee had notice before the capitalisation occurred. To allow the first mortgagee the advantage of capitalisation in those circumstances

---

[39] *Economic Life Assurance Society v. Usborne* [1902] A.C. 147.
[40] *Popple v. Sylvester* (1882) 22 Ch.D. 98.
[41] *Lonsdale Finance plc v. Bank of Zambia* [1996] Q.B. 752 where an increase of one per cent was permitted.
[42] See *Law v. Glenn* (1867) L.R. 2 Ch. 634.
[43] *Union Bank of London v. Ingram* (1880) 16 Ch.D. 53.
[44] *Johnson v. Evans* (1889) 61 L.T. 18.
[45] *Rourke v. Robinson* [1911] 1 Ch. 480, only if the money is kept available.
[46] *e.g.* by losing the deeds.
[47] *Bovill v. Endle* [1896] 1 Ch. 648.
[48] *Fitzgerald's Trustee v. Mellersh* [1892] 1 Ch. 385.
[49] Limitation Act 1990, s.20(5).
[50] See *ante,* para. 22–41.
[51] As to the difference between capitalisation of arrears and compound interest, see *Re Morris Mayhew v. Halton* [1922] 1 Ch. 126.
[52] *Tompson v. Leith* (1858) 4 Jur.(N.S.) 1091.

would be to allow him to tack a further charge with notice.[53] Capitalisation often takes place when a mortgage is transferred to a third party but it does not then bind the mortgagor without his concurrence.[54]

(j) If interest has been paid on an amount which subsequently is shown to be greater than that due, any overpayment of interest is not treated as a payment reducing the capital outstanding[55] but may be refunded to the mortgagor.[56] If there has been an underpayment of interest, that may be required to be made up by the mortgagor.[57]

3. Costs of proceedings for redemption or foreclosure

A mortgagee's right to his costs, charges and expenses reasonably and properly incurred in enforcing or preserving the security (including costs of litigation)[58] is an equity arising from his contract and is not therefore within the usual discretion of the court as to costs.[59] The right is not, however, contractual in the sense that the mortgagor is under a personal contract to pay the costs. Liability to pay the costs is rather part of the price which he must pay for being permitted to redeem, so that the costs are a charge upon the property but not (without special agreement) a personal debt of the mortgagor.[60] Similarly, the right to costs being an equitable right, the mortgagee may forfeit his right by misconduct.[61]   **25–06**

Misconduct by the mortgagee, when proved, puts the costs in the discretion of the court,[62] whose order may be either that he be merely deprived of his costs or else be made to pay the costs of the mortgagor as well.[63] In the latter case the costs are not paid to the mortgagor direct, but are credited to him in the mortgage account.[64] The following are the main instances upon which the court will depart from the normal rule as to costs although the court retains an overall discretion[65]:

(a) *Failure to accept a proper tender*

This may occur either because the tender is refused or the mortgagee has lost the deeds,[66] or because he is not ready with his receipt or conveyance.[67] On a proper   **25–07**

---

[53] *Digby v. Craggs* (1762) Amb. 612.
[54] *Agnew v. King* [1902] 1 I.R. 471.
[55] *Blandy v. Kimber (No. 2)* (1858) 25 Beav. 537.
[56] *Gregory v. Pilkington* (1856) 8 De G.M. & G. 616.
[57] *Universities Superannuation Sakemi Ltd v. Marks & Spencer plc* [1998] E.G.C.S. 168.
[58] *Parker-Tweedale v. Dunbar Bank plc (No. 2)* [1991] Ch. 26; *Gomba Holdings Ltd v. Minories Finance Ltd (No. 2)* [1993] Ch. 171.
[59] See *post*, para. 27–32 *et seq.* The costs are within the discretion of the court only when a charge of misconduct has been *made and proved*: *Charles v. Jones* (1886) 33 Ch.D. 80. See *Parker-Tweedale v. Dunbar Bank plc*, *ante*; *Gomba Holdings Ltd v. Minories Finance (No. 2) ante*.
[60] *Frazer v. Jones* (1846) 5 Hare 475. *Sinfield v. Sweet* [1967] 1 W.L.R. 1489.
[61] *Cottrell v. Stantton* (1872) L.R. 8 Ch. 295 at 302. See *Parker-Tweedale v. Dunbar Bank plc, ante*; *Gomba Holdings Ltd v. Minories Finance (No. 2), ante*.
[62] *Charles v. Jones* (1886) 33 Ch.D. 80.
[63] *Detillin v. Gale* (1802) 7 Ves. 583; *Kinnaird v. Trollope* (1889) 42 Ch.D. 610.
[64] *Wheaton v. Graham* (1857) 24 Beav. 483.
[65] CPR Part 44.3.
[66] *Stokoe v. Robson* (1815) 19 Ves. 385.
[67] *Rourke v. Robinson* [1911] 1 Ch. 480.

tender, a mortgagor is entitled to have his mortgage discharged and the mortgagee must pay the costs of subsequent litigation necessary to enforce that discharge.[68]

(b) *Mortgage already paid off*

25–08   If, after receiving the full amount of his debt, a mortgagee either takes proceedings for foreclosure or defends an action for redemption, he will be made to pay the costs of the proceedings.[69] On the same principle a mortgagee, who is paid off after he has instituted proceedings, must pay any costs consequent on his failure to discontinue the action.[70]

(c) *Untenable claim*

25–09   A mortgagee, who raises an untenable defence to an action for redemption, may also be deprived of his costs or even made to pay the mortgagor's costs. Nor is it a question of *male fides*.[71] If he sets up an unfounded claim to tack[72] or consolidate, or if he claims the conveyance to be absolute[73] and not by way of mortgage,[74] or otherwise denies or improperly obstructs the right to redeem,[75] he will be made responsible for the costs thus occasioned. However, he will not, it seems, be deprived of costs which would have been incurred in any event.[76] Moreover, he will not be penalised if his claim, though mistaken, was fairly open to argument.[77]

(d) *Vexatious or oppressive conduct*

25–10   If the mortgage transaction is shown to have been tainted with fraud,[78] or if the mortgagee's subsequent conduct has been unreasonable or oppressive, he may be made to pay costs. For example, if he refuses to account or obstructs the taking of an account[79]; if he fails to allow the mortgagor a reasonable opportunity of tendering the mortgage moneys[80]; if he harasses the mortgagor by bringing simultaneous actions for foreclosure and for judgment on the personal covenant

---

[68] *Graham v. Seal* (1918) 88 L.J.Ch. 31.
[69] *Barlow v. Gains* (1856) 23 Beav. 244; *National Bank of Australasia v. United Hand in Hand Co.* (1879) 4 A.C. 391; unless the mortgagor makes allegations against the mortgagee which he fails to substantiate when no order will be made.
[70] *Gregg v. Slater* (1856) 22 Beav. 314.
[71] *Credland v. Potter* (1874) 10 Ch.App. 8.
[72] *ibid.*; *Kinnaird v. Trollope* (1889) 42 Ch.D. 610.
[73] *Squire v. Pardoe* (1891) 66 L.T. 243.
[74] *England v. Codrington* (1758) 1 Ed. 169.
[75] See *Whitfield v. Parfitt* (1851) 4 De G. & Sm. 240; *Ashworth v. Lord* (1887) 36 Ch.D. 545; *Hall v. Heward* (1886) 32 Ch.D. 430; *Heath v. Chinn* [1908] W.N. 120.
[76] *Harvey v. Tebbutt* (1820) 1 J. & W. 197.
[77] *Bird v. Wenn* (1886) 33 Ch.D. 215.
[78] *Baker v. Wind* (1748) 1 Ves.Sen. 160; *Morony v. O'Dea* (1809) 1 Ball & B. 109.
[79] *Detillin v. Gale* (1802) 7 Ves. 583.
[80] *Cliff v. Wadsworth* (1843) 2 Y. & C.C.C. 598.

in separate proceedings[81]; in any of these cases he will have to pay the costs occasioned by his misconduct. On the other hand, not every mistake made by the mortgagee is oppression; for example, mere over-statement of his claim is not a sufficient ground for refusing him his costs.[82]

(e) *Improper joinder of parties*

A mortgagee is liable for all costs resulting from the wrongful joinder of parties, **25–11** whether as defendants or claimants.[83] This rule is of special importance for parties whose interest in a security is worthless owing to prior claims. A person who is made a party but disclaims before delivering any defence will be entitled to his costs after the date of disclaimer if the mortgagee insists on taking him to the hearing.[84] It is not, however, the mortgagee's duty to invite a defendant to disclaim.[85]

The general rule, it may be repeated, is that a mortgagee is entitled to his costs of action and that only misconduct can deprive him of that right. Judges have said time and again that the court is reluctant to depart from the normal rule.[86] However, the court is by no means so favourable to a mortgagee who has sold the security and retains in his hands surplus proceeds of sale. He is a trustee for the persons next entitled and if his conduct makes it necessary to bring an action to recover the money, he will be liable for the costs of the action.[87] In *Williams v. Jones*,[88] Eve J. said expressly that the general rule allowing a mortgagee his costs of action does not apply to an action for an account against a mortgagee who has exercised his power of sale.

4. **Costs, charges and expenses incurred in relation to the mortgage debt or security**

Disbursements under this heading are for the most part within the terms of the **25–12** mortgage contract as applied in equity, and will, therefore, be included in the account as "just allowances" within CPR 40PD–005. They are not a personal debt of the mortgagor, for they are only one of the equitable terms of redemption and are not covered by the covenant for payment unless expressly brought within it by the contract. There are four main grounds on which disbursements are admitted as "just allowances":

(a) *Perfecting the security*

An equitable mortgagee is entitled to specific performance and will be allowed **25–13** the costs of completing his security by the execution of a legal mortgage. These

---

[81] *Williams v. Hunt* [1905] 1 K.B. 512.
[82] *Cotterell v. Stratton* (1872) L.R. 8 Ch. 295; *Re Watts* (1882) 22 Ch.D. 5.
[83] *Pearce v. Watkins* (1852) 5 De G. & Sm. 315.
[84] *Greene v. Foster* (1882) 22 Ch.D. 566; *Ridgway v. Kynnerslly* (1865) 2 Hem. & M. 515.
[85] *Maxwell v. Wightwick* (1886) L.R. 3 Eq. 210.
[86] *e.g. Cotterell v. Stratton* (1872) L.R. 8 Ch. 295 at 302, *per* Selborne, L.C.
[87] See *Tanner v. Heard* (1857) 23 Beav. 555; *Charles v. Jones* (1887) 35 Ch.D. 544.
[88] (1911) 55 S.J. 500.

costs cover the preparation of the mortgage and the correspondence relating thereto; they do not include the investigation of title, because an equitable mortgagee only contracts to transfer such title as he himself possesses.[89] On the same principle a mortgagee has been allowed the costs of obtaining a stop order against a fund in court.[90] On the other hand, the costs of negotiating the loan and of preparing the original mortgage cannot be brought into the mortgage account without express contract. Farwell J. in *Wales v. Carr*,[91] said that such costs are a simple contract debt and a personal liability of the mortgagor, but are not part of the price fixed for redemption in equity. These costs may, however, be brought into the account by express contract,[92] indeed, it is the usual practice to deduct the amount of the initial expenses from the sum advanced.

(b) *Maintenance of property*

25–14   A mortgage is entitled to preserve his security and to add to the debt expenses incurred in so doing. A mortgagee of leaseholds may bring into the account payments for rent, ground-rents[93] or renewal fines.[94] A mortgagee of an insurance policy may pay the premiums to prevent default.[95] Where the payments are not merely to protect but to salve the security, a puisne incumbrancer who makes the payments is entitled to a charge for such payments in priority even to the first mortgagee.[96] A mortgagee's right to add fire insurance premiums to the mortgage debt will in general be provided for by section 101 of the Law of Property Act 1925, which gives that right to all mortgagees whose security is by deed, unless the mortgagor is keeping up a sufficient policy.[97] If the terms of the contract do not allow for the mortgagee insuring, it appears that any insurance policy he takes out is effected for his own benefit and that he cannot charge the premiums in the account.[98]

(c) *Management*

25–15   A mortgagee in possession is entitled to bring into the account the reasonable expenses of managing the property. He will thus be credited with the amount of any wages paid to such servants or agents as would reasonably be employed by an owner of the property[99]; and in most cases he will be allowed the salary or

---

[89] *National Provincial Bank v. Games* (1886) 31 Ch.D. 582. See *Pryce v. Bury* (1853) 2 Drew. 41.
[90] *Waddilove v. Taylor* (1848) 6 Hare 307.
[91] [1902] 1 Ch. 860.
[92] *Blackford v. Davis* (1869) 4 Ch. App. 304.
[93] *Brandon v. Brandon* (1862) 10 W.R. 287; *Shepherd v. Spansheath* (1988) E.G.C.S. 35.
[94] *Lacon v. Mertins* (1743) 3 Atk. 4; *Hamilton v. Denny* (1809) 1 Ball & B. 199.
[95] *Bellamy v. Brickenden* (1861) 2 J. & H. 137; *Gill v. Downing* (1874) L.R. 17 Eq. 316; *Re Leslie* (1883) 23 Ch.D. 552.
[96] *Angel v. Bryan* (1845) 2 Jo. & Lat. 763; but it must really have been a case of salvage: *Landowners, etc. Drainage and Inclosures Co. v. Ashford* (1880) 16 Ch.D. 411.
[97] LPA 1925, s.108(2).
[98] *Dobson v. Land* (1850) 8 Hare 216; but a mortgagee in possession may include such payments as part of his management expenses under just allowances: *Scholefield v. Lockwood* (1863) 11 W.R. 555.
[99] *Brandon v. Brandon* (1862) 10 W.R. 287; *Shepherd v. Spansheath* (1988) E.G.C.S. 35.

commission of a bailiff or other general agent employed to look after the whole property.[1]

Similarly, a mortgagee will be reimbursed expenditure incurred in running a business,[2] or working existing mines.[3] It appears also that, although as a rule he will only be allowed to balance his losses against his receipts, yet if a business is mortgaged as a going concern, losses may be made a charge upon the corpus of the mortgaged property.[4] However, a mortgagee is not, apart from express contract, allowed to make any charge for his own time and trouble.[5] He may not charge commission for collecting rents[6] or for any other business done in connection with the mortgaged property.[7] Formerly, an express contract that such commission should be allowed made no difference, because the agreement for commission was held to come within the rule against collateral advantages.[8] After the decision in *Biggs v. Hoddinott*[9] it is clear that collateral advantages are not bad as such, and so an agreement for commission is valid, provided the bargain is not otherwise unconscionable.[10] In any case, by virtue of section 58 of the Solicitors Act 1974[11] solicitor mortgagees may charge the usual professional fees for all business done in relation to the security, whether or not the mortgage contains an express stipulation to that effect.

Where the powers of management yield profits for which the mortgagee must account, he will be allowed the cost of obtaining them.[12] If the mortgage expressly permits this item of expenditure and any monies yielded by the expenditure do not exceed the costs incurred, the balance may be charged against the property[13] or permitted out of the proceeds of sale.[14]

(d) *Improvements*

A mortgagee may also include in his account sums expended on repairs, improvements and other outgoings. He has, for example, been allowed the amount of compensation payable to a tenant at the end of his tenancy.[15] Repairs and improvements require careful examination. Concerning "necessary repairs" there is no doubt: a mortgagee in possession is under a duty to execute them and will be entitled to his expenditure under the heading of just allowances.[16] With

25–16

[1] *Bank of London v. Ingram* (1880) 16 Ch.D. 53; *Leith v. Irvine* (1883) 1 My. & Cr. 277.

[2] *Bompas v. King* (1886) 33 Ch.D. 279.

[3] *County of Gloucester Bank v. Rudry, Merthyr Steam and House Colliery Co.* [1895] 1 Ch. 629; but not for working new mines: *Hughes v. Williams* (1806) 12 Ves. 493; *Shepherd v. Spansheath* (1988) E.G.C.S. 35.

[4] *Bompas v. King* (1886) 33 Ch.D. 279.

[5] *Bonithon v. Hockmore* (1685) 1 Vern. 316; *Nicholson v. Tutin* (1857) 3 K. & J. 159; *cf. Re Wallis* (1890) 25 Q.B.D. 176.

[6] *Langstaffe v. Fenwick* (1805) 10 Ves. 405.

[7] *Leith v. Irvine* (1883) 1 My. & Cr. 277.

[8] See *Chambers v. Goldwin* (1804) 9 Ves. 254.

[9] [1898] 2 Ch. 307.

[10] See *Bucknell v. Vickery* (1891) 64 L.T. 701 at 702, though the case is not absolutely in point; *Barrett v. artley* (1866) L.R. 2 Eq. 789.

[11] Formerly Mortgagees' Legal Costs Act 1985, s.3.

[12] *Bompas v. King* (1886) Ch.D. 279.

[13] *Norton v. Cooper* (1854) 5 De G.M. & G. 728.

[14] *Bompas v. King, ante*; *White v. City of London Brewery Co.* (1889) 42 Ch.D. 237.

[15] *Oxenham v. Ellis* (1854) 18 Beav. 593.

[16] *Tipton Green Colliery Co. v. Tipton Moat Colliery Co.* (1877) 7 Ch.D. 192.

regard to what may be called substantial repairs or permanent improvements these are only allowed if the value of the property has been increased.[17] In any event a special case must be made out for their allowance at the hearing, or no inquiry will be directed. Jessel M.R. in *Shepard v. Jones*,[18] stated the established practice to be that the mortgagee must plead that he has made a lasting improvement, and then, if he adduces evidence of laying out money and that the works were prima facie lasting improvements, he will be entitled to an inquiry. The older cases[19] suggest that even an admitted improvement, if substantial, will not be allowed to a mortgagee unless it was consented to by a mortgagor. The reason for this was that a mortgagee by increasing the price of redemption might prevent redemption altogether. But the Court of Appeal in *Shepard v. Jones*[20] greatly modified this doctrine, and stated the following rules:

(1) If the improvement is reasonable and produces a benefit, the mortgagor's consent is unnecessary.
(2) If the improvement is unreasonable and produces no benefit it will be allowed, if the mortgagor either expressly agreed to it or did what in law amounted to acquiescing to it.
(3) If the improvement is unreasonable and was not agreed to, it will not be allowed in any circumstances. The mortgagee cannot force the improvement on the mortgagor by merely serving a notice upon him, whatever the terms of the notice.

Finally, it must be observed that repairs and improvements are not "salvage" advances and do not entitle a mesne incumbrancer, who executes them, to priority for his expenditure over earlier mortgagees.[21]

(e) *Exercising his power of sale*

25–17 A mortgagee is entitled to claim in the account the expenses not merely of an actual sale, but also of an abortive attempt to sell.[22] In accordance with the general principle that he may not charge for his own time and trouble, he may not, if he is an auctioneer,[23] or a broker,[24] be credited with a commission on the sale, unless he has expressly contracted for such commission.[25]

---

[17] But not, apparently, if he alters the nature of the property: *Moore v. Painter* (1842) 6 Jur. 903.
[18] (1882) 21 Ch.D. 469 at 476.
[19] *e.g. Sandon v. Hooper* (1843) 6 Beav. 246.
[20] (1882) 21 Ch.D. 469.
[21] *Landowners West of England & South West Drainage and Inclosure Co. v. Ashford* (1880) 16 Ch.D. 411.
[22] *Corsellis v. Patman* (1867) L.R. 4 Eq. 156; *Farrer v. Lacy, Hartland & Co.* (1885) 31 Ch.D. 42.
[23] *Matthison v. Clarke* (1854) 3 Drew. 3.
[24] *Arnold v. Garner* (1847) 2 Ph. 231.
[25] *Biggs v. Hoddinott* [1898] 2 Ch. 307. But after redemption he cannot insist on being made auctioneer of the property when it is to be sold; the clause allowing him commission must terminate at redemption: *Browne v. Ryan* [1901] 2 I.R. 635.

5. Costs of litigation in connection with the mortgage[26]

In *Dryden v. Frost*,[27] Cottenham L.C. expressed the rule thus: **25–18**

> "This Court, in settling the account between a mortgagor and mortgagee, will give to the latter all that his contract, or the legal or equitable consequences of it entitle him to receive, and all the costs properly incurred in ascertaining or defending such rights."[28]

That does not mean, however, that the court has no jurisdiction in this regard. The modern inter-relationship between the court's discretion and the mortgagee's contractual and equitable entitlement is considered elsewhere.[29] In other words, the litigation must have been reasonable and if it is, the costs that are reasonably and properly incurred in that litigation are allowable.[29a] Usually, such costs are the mortgagee's costs of obtaining possession but the mortgagee is entitled his costs of a claim to recover the mortgage debt from the mortgagor or his surety[30] or for example, administrating the deceased mortgagor's estate if necessary to recover the debt.[31] Costs of litigation, with one exception, will not be allowed unless they have been specially pleaded and claimed at the hearing.[32] The one exception is costs of proceedings to obtain possession which are included under "just allowances."[33]

Costs may be allowed to the mortgagee whether he is claimant or defendant in the litigation. If his title is impeached by the mortgagor, he is entitled to be fully reimbursed, so that if he was successful and received costs in the action, he may still recover the difference between the taxed costs and his actual costs.[34] Similarly, if the mortgagor's title to the mortgaged property is questioned, the mortgagee may defend it and charge his full costs in the account.[35] But if his own title *qua* mortgagee is attacked by third parties, he must pay his own expenses, for the mortgagor cannot be made to bear the loss caused by the litigious activities of third parties.[36] Where a sub-mortgagee is a party to any proceedings and has, of necessity been joined, the sub-mortgagee's costs will be payable by the mortgagee who may than add them to his own debt and so recover them as against the mortgagor.[37] The mortgagee's right so to do will only arise in relation to sub-mortgagees claiming under him; the costs of parties claiming under the

---

[26] See para. 27–32 *et seq.*

[27] (1838) 3 My. & Cr. 670 at 675.

[28] The decision in this case was that litigation is not properly undertaken when an equitable mortgagee institutes an action available only to a legal mortgagee, and in another case a mortgagee was refused his costs when, in exercising his power of sale, he brought an action against the purchaser for specific performance and lost because of errors in the description of the property sold; see *Peers v. Ceeley* (1852) 15 Beav. 209.

[29] See *post*, para. 27–32 *et seq.* and *ante*, para. 25–06.

[29a] *Parker-Tweedale v. Dunbar Bank plc* (No. 2) [1991] Ch. 26

[30] *National Provincial Bank of England v. Games* (1886) 31 Ch.D. 582. It does not matter that the claim against the surety is unproductive; *Ellison v. Wright* (1827) 3 Russ. 458.

[31] *Ward v. Barton* (1841) 11 Sim. 534; but see also *Saunders v. Duncan* (1878) 7 Ch.D. 825.

[32] *Millar v. Major* (1818) Coop.temp.Cott. 550.

[33] *Wilkes v. Saunion* (1877) 7 Ch.D. 188.

[34] *Ramsden v. Langley* (1706) 2 Vern. 536. *cf.* also *Re Leighton's Conveyance* [1937] Ch. 149.

[35] *Parker-Tweedale v. Dunbar Bank plc (No. 2)* [1991] Ch. 26.

[36] *Parker-Tweedale v. Dunbar Bank plc (No. 2), ante*; see also *Gomba Holdings Ltd v. Minories Finance Ltd (No. 2)* [1993] Ch. 171.

[37] *Smith v. Chichester* (1842) 2 Dr. & War. 393.

mortgagor (*e.g.* a trustee in bankruptcy) cannot be so recovered.[38] The mortgagor entitled to the costs of an ejectment against third parties.[39] Similarly, the costs of an ejectment against the mortgagor and of a judgment on the personal covenant previously obtained may be included in the account.

Taking the Account

25–19   The general rule for taking a mortgage account is to take it as a continuous debtor and creditor account. A mortgagor, apart from express contract, is never compelled to pay interest on interest in arrear[40] so that, when the mortgagee is not in possession, there is no occasion for stopping the account. At the end of the account the amount of unpaid interest is added to the principal, and the resulting sum, plus any special allowances, is the price of redemption. Where the mortgagee is not in possession, the only possible exceptions to the rule are when the parties have themselves struck a balance at some date during the currency of the mortgage[41] or when part of the mortgaged property has previously been sold. In the latter case the proceeds are applied first in discharging the expenses of sale and any interest already accrued due at the date of the sale, and then the residue, if it was not handed over to the mortgagor, must be taken to have satisfied the principal debt *pro tanto*. Thus, in the final account interest will only be allowed, as from the date of the sale, on the diminished amount of the principal.[42]

1. **Mortgagee in possession**[43]

25–20   In most cases, the general rule applies equally to the account of a mortgagee in possession since it is only in special circumstances that the court will direct the account to be taken against the mortgagee with rests. On the other hand, a mortgagee's entry into possession always complicates the account because he must be debited with the amount of rents and profits which he actually received or which, but for his wilful default, he ought to have received. In practice, it means that the account is split into three distinct amounts:

(1) The account of principal, interest and costs.
(2) The account of the mortgagee's expenditure in managing, repairing or improving the property, plus interest on the expenditure.
(3) The account of rents, profits and other sums received by the mortgagee or which, but for his wilful default, he ought to have received.

The price of redemption is, of course, calculated by adding together the first two accounts and then deducting the third from the aggregate so obtained.[44]

---

[38] *Hunter v. Pugh* (1839) 1 Hare 307; *Clarke v. Wilmot* (1843) 1 Ph. 276.
[39] *Owen v. Crouch* (1857) 5 W.R. 545.
[40] *Parker v. Butcher* (1867) L.R. 3 Eq. 762.
[41] *cf. Wilson v. Cluer* (1840) 3 Beav. 136.
[42] *Thompson v. Hudson* (1870) L.R. 10 Eq. 497; here the mortgagee was in possession, but the reasoning of Romilly M.R. applies generally.
[43] See *ante*, para. 16–33 *et seq.*
[44] Interest is usually allowed.

Again, the continuity of the account may be interrupted either by the parties having struck a balance during the currency of the mortgage or by a sale of part of the security. In the latter case the net proceeds are appropriated first to the discharge of the interest in account number (1) and then to the reduction of the principal debt with a consequent reduction in the amount of interest due in account number (1). However, the rest in that account is not accompanied by a simultaneous rest in the other accounts. The mere fact of the sale cannot entitle the mortgagor at the date of the sale to have the amount of the rents and profits received before the sale immediately set off against the mortgage debt. In other words, without a general direction for rests throughout the account, the mortgagor has no right to have the items of account number (1) in any way affected by the state of account number (3) until the final accounts are taken.[45]

Since the account of a mortgagee in possession is in the normal case a continuous debtor and creditor account, the mortgagee will derive an indirect profit from his possession if the amount of his receipts exceeds that of the interest due. He may retain the balance and have the use of the money without debiting himself with interest upon it. If, on the other hand, the receipts are less than the interest, the mortgagor does not pay interest on the unpaid arrears of interest, and so he has the advantage.[46] The object and effect of directing the account to be taken with periodic rests is to prevent the mortgagee from deriving any advantage from an excess of receipts over interest due. Such a direction is unusual and operates to only penalise the mortgagee.[47] The procedure then is to strike a balance at the end of each year or half-year, as the case may be, and to appropriate at once the surplus receipts—after discharging the interest—to the reduction of the principal debt with a consequent reduction in the future interest due on the debt. Furthermore, if by this method of accounting it is found that the whole mortgage debt had been satisfied before the end of the account, the result is that the periodic rests make the mortgagee liable to account for the subsequent receipts with compound interest in favour of the mortgagor.[48]

2. Procedure for taking the account

An account or any necessary inquiries can obviously be ordered by the court at **25–21** trial. Such an order can also be made pursuant to CPR Part 24[49] and CPR Part 25.[50] In the former instance, where a claimant seeks an account or brings a claim which necessarily involves the taking of an account, he can apply for a summary order that all necessary accounts be taken and inquiries made. Alternatively, an order for the taking of an account or making of an inquiry can also be made by the court pursuant to its jurisdiction to order interim remedies under CPR Part 25. The court can, on application or of its own initiative (whether before or after judgment), make an order directing that any necessary account be taken or

---

[45] *Wrigley v. Gill* [1905] 1 Ch. 241; *Ainsworth v. Wilding* [1905] 1 Ch. 435.
[46] *Union Bank of London v. Ingram* (1880) 16 Ch.D. 53 at 56, *per* Jessel M.R.
[47] *Wrigley v. Gill* [1905] 1 Ch. 241; *cf. Cowens v. Francis* [1948] n. 2 L.R. 567.
[48] Seton, *Judgments and Orders* (7th ed.), Vol. 3, p. 1885.
[49] CPR 24PD–006.
[50] CPR 25BPD, para. 1.

inquiries made.[51] In either case, the procedural provisions of CPR 40PD also apply.

That Practice Direction states that the court may give directions generally as to the taking or the account and its verification or the conduct of any inquiry[52] and provides that the court may order the resolution of any issue that has arisen during the taking of the account or the making of the inquiry and may order the service of Points of Claim and Points of Defence, as appropriate.[53] Verification of an account can now be by affidavit or witness statement.[54]

CPR 40PD, paragraph 9 applies CPR, Schedule 1, RSC Ord. 44 to proceedings in the country court pursuant to a judgment or order made in the county court as well as to such proceedings in the Chancery Division of the High Court. In that Division, all accounts (whatever the time estimate) will be before the Master; inquiries, however, which are estimated to last more than two days and involve very large sums of money or strongly contested issues of fact or difficult points of law may be taken by the judge.[55]

(a) *Effect of an account having been taken*

25–22   In the absence of fraud, in which case an account may be re-opened after a substantial number of years have passed,[56] a settled account is prima facie binding on all parties to the action in which it was taken and on any other persons interested in the equity of redemption and will not, save in limited circumstances be disturbed.[57] A party wishing to challenge a settled account must either show that there are sufficient grounds to set the account aside and to establish a right for an order for a new account to be taken or, alternatively, demonstrate that certain aspects of the account are inaccurate and that he should be given liberty "to surcharge and falsify" some of the items and charges contained in that account.

As indicated, an account will only be opened altogether in the case of fraud or where, in the absence of fraud, it would be inequitable for one party to take advantage of it by reason of the manner in which the account took place or the nature of any error contained in it.[58] An account will be reopened if it contains considerable errors both in number and amount. What amounts to a sufficient degree of error to re-open an account is a question of fact but where a fiduciary relationship exists between the accounting parties, it would seem that fewer errors are sufficient in order to persuade the court to re-open the account.[59] In *Pritt v. Clay*[60] a single error of a substantial amount was held to be sufficient for the re-opening of the whole account but, in the absence of any evidence to demonstrate that that error was likely to be repeated elsewhere in the account, it

---

[51] CPR 25BPD, para. 2.
[52] CPR 40PD, para. 1.1.
[53] CPR 40PD, para. 5.
[54] CPR 40PD, para. 2.
[55] Chancery Guide, chapter 10.9 ff.
[56] *Vernon v. Vawdrey* (174) 2 Atk. 119; *Allfrey v. Allfrey* (1849) 1 Mac. & G. 87.
[57] *Newen v. Wetten* (1862) 31 Beav. 315.
[58] *Coleman v. Mellersh* (1850) 2 Nac. & G. 309; *Re. Webb* [1894] 1 Ch. 73.
[59] *Willamson v. Barbour* (1877) 9 Ch.D. 529.
[60] (1843) 6 Beav. 503.

would seem that such a single incident should give rise to leave to surcharge and falsify.[61] In order to re-open an account, clear allegations of fraud or specific error must be made and proved.[62]

If leave is given to surcharge and falsify an account, the settled account is permitted to stand but the specific errors that it has been shown to contain can be corrected. Liberty to surcharge and falsify will be given provided that at least one error is specifically charged and proved to court's satisfaction.[63] The error alleged may be either that of fact or law.[64]

If an account is admitted to contain and error and other accounts are pending between the same parties, that error can be "purged" by the setting-off in the subsequent accounts of the error that is admitted to be contained in the settled account.[65]

[61] *Gething v. Keighley* (1878) 9 Ch.D. 547.
[62] *Needler v. Deeble* (1677) 1 Cas. Ch. 299.
[63] *Parkinson v. Hanbury* (1867) L.R. 2 H.L. 1.
[64] *Roberts v. Kuffn* (1740) 2 Atk. 112.
[65] *Lawless v. Mansfield* (1841) 1 Dr. & War. 557.

CHAPTER 26

DEFENCES TO CLAIMS BY THE MORTGAGEE

The most common remedy sought by mortgagees in proceedings is an order for **26–01** sale of a dwelling-house, although that remedy may be pursued either in conjunction with a claim for repayment of the debt itself or on its own. The right to possession is a powerful tool in the mortgagee's armoury and is an entitlement recognised by the common law as arising even if the mortgagor is not in default.[1] The courts will, however, prevent the taking of possession if the exercise of that right is not genuinely being used as a means of enforcing or preserving security for the mortgagee's liability.[2] There are also statutory restrictions on the exercise of the right to possession.[3]

The vast majority of mortgagees' possession claims are undefended. Nevertheless there are a number of potential defences which are frequently encountered and, whilst not confined to possession actions, are often raised in response to a claim by a mortgagee for possession.

NO LIABILITY—DEBT DISCHARGED OR RELEASED

1. Debt Repaid

Once the debt secured by a mortgage is repaid or the liability secured by the **26–02** mortgage is satisfied, the mortgagor is entitled to seek redemption of the mortgage in order for his interest in the property to be released from the mortgagee's charge.[4] A dispute about the amount of the debt or the true amount of any repayments made or the recoverability of part or all of the debt[5] may provide a defence to the claim for possession if it can be established that the whole of the debt has been satisfied or is unenforceable. Such a defence, when coupled with a counterclaim for redemption, may result in the release of the mortgage. However, a challenge to the amount owed which merely reduces the claim but does not extinguish it will not provide an answer to a claim for possession, although it may be relevant to the immediacy and terms of the order made.[6]

---

[1] *Western Bank Ltd v. Schindler* [1977] Ch. 1. See *ante*, para. 16–22.
[2] *Quennell v. Maltby* [1979] 1 W.L.R. 318.
[3] See *ante*, para. 16–23.
[4] See *ante*, para. 18–24 *et seq.*
[5] For instance where a court exercises its powers under ss.137–140 of the Consumer Credit Act 1974, on the basis that the interest rate charged was extortionate.
[6] See s.36 of the Administration of Justice Act 1970. See *ante*, para. 16–84.

2. **The Position of Sureties**

26–03   Where a surety secures his obligations under a guarantee he gave by the provision of a mortgage, if he is able to establish that the principal debtor is not liable to repay the debt or that the guarantee was not valid as against him, he will have a defence to a claim for possession and will be entitled to seek redemption of his property from the mortgagee's charge.[7] Notwithstanding the fact that as between the primary debtor and mortgagee the debt or part of it is outstanding, a surety will also have a defence to a claim for payment or possession of any property mortgaged to secure his guarantee if he can establish that his liability under the guarantee has been released. In the absence of express provision to the contrary,[8] the personal liability of the surety under a guarantee may be released when the mortgagee/creditor, without the consent of the surety in question, grants a variation of the contract with the principal debtor or an indulgence to the principal debtor or another surety,[9] such that the surety's position is prejudiced without his agreement.[10] Accordingly the surety is, in such circumstances, released from his obligations.

An indulgence includes a material alteration of the principal contract[11] under which the debt arises, the giving of time to the principal debtor[12] or waiving of part of the liability. The release of any co-surety or alternative security, whether wholly or in part, may have the same effect of releasing a surety from his liability to pay under the guarantee and therefore entitling him to seek redemption of any mortgage obtained to secure his guarantee. In some instances, the existence or liability of co-sureties and/or other securities are effectively conditions[13] of the original contract of guarantee. In those circumstances it seems that the release of any element of the whole transaction will release the surety in question from any liability[14] without the need to establish that the change is a material alteration. The release of such a co-surety or security would be a breach of a condition and probably therefore a repudiation of the suretyship since the alteration to the surety's risk extends beyond that which was agreed. However, where the surety either did not know of the other elements of the transaction or, notwithstanding his knowledge, they were not conditions to the provision of his suretyship, it is likely that the creditors' release of other elements (even if not sufficient to secure the release of the surety) may have a more limited effect. Such a release, although not a breach of a condition of the suretyship, has the effect of increasing the potential liability of the surety and can have the effect of releasing the surety to the extent to which his position is prejudiced thereby.[15]

---

[7] *National Westminster Bank v. Skelton* [1993] 1 W.L.R. 72.

[8] Which is almost invariably included in modern agreements.

[9] *Whitcher v. Hall* (1826) 5 B. & C. 269; *Holme v. Briskill* (1877) 3 Q.B.D. 496; *National Provincial Bank of Nigeria Ltd v. Awolesi* [1964] 1 W.L.R. 1311; *West Horndon Industrial Park Ltd v. Phoenix Timber Group plc* [1995] 1 E.G.L.R. 77; *Howard de Walden Estates Ltd v. Pasta Place Ltd* [1995] 1 E.G.L.R. 79.

[10] See Chitty, *Contracts* (28th ed., 1999), paras 44–069 and 44–092/3.

[11] *Holme v. Brunskill* (1878) 3 Q.B.D. 495. See also *Egbert v. National Crown Bank* [1918] A.C. 903; *Credit Suisse v. Borough Council of Allerdale* [1995] 1 Lloyd's Rep. 315; *National Bank of Nigeria v. Awolesi* [1964] 1 W.L.R. 1311. See also Chitty, *Contracts* (28th ed., 1999) 44–080 ff.

[12] *Nisbet v. Smith* (1789) 2 Bro. C.C. 579; *Swire v. Redman* (1876) 1 Q.B.D. 536.

[13] See Chitty, *Contracts* (28th ed., 1999), para. 44–053.

[14] See Chitty, *Contracts* (28th ed., 1999), para. 44–092/3.

[15] *Carter v. White* (1883) 25 Ch.D. 666 and Chitty, *Contracts* (28th ed., 1999), para. 44–093.

3. **Counterclaim and Set-off**

A counterclaim for a sum that equals or exceeds the amount of the debt secured, **26–04** if it amounts to a set-off, can be a defence to any claim for repayment of the debt. However such a defence to the money claim does not amount to a defence to a claim for possession brought against the mortgagor or any surety of his.[16] In such cases, the counterclaim advanced by the party from whom possession is claimed should include in the counterclaim a claim for redemption of the mortgage. The entire counterclaim should then be prosecuted quickly to ensure that judgment on the counterclaim is secured, to enable the redemption of the mortgage to occur prior to the mortgagee's claim for possession being concluded. Practically this may present the mortgagor with grave difficulties.

4. **Alteration of the Mortgage Deed**

Where a mortgagee or his agent, without the knowledge or consent of the **26–05** mortgagor, alters or mutilates the mortgage instrument after execution, the mortgagee loses the right to enforce that instrument and the mortgagor is discharged.[17] An alteration of the repayment date and interest dates would be sufficient alteration for these purposes. In such circumstances the mortgagee will usually have a restitutionary claim for the money advanced but will have no claim directly against the property itself.[18]

LACK OF FORMALITIES—WRITING, REGISTRATION, ETC.

1. **Writing**

Where a purported grant of a mortgage on or after September 26, 1989 fails to **26–06** comply with the requirements of section 2 of the Law of Property (Miscellaneous Provisions) Act 1989, no mortgage will be created and, notwithstanding any oral agreement or deposit of title deeds, the creditor will have no interest in or rights over the debtor's land.[19] It follows that the failure to comply with section 2 will provide a defence to any claim for possession pursuant to a mortgage. A creditor in such circumstances may nevertheless have a right to claim repayment of the debt and, upon securing judgment, he may then seek to levy execution against the land. With regard to mortgages executed prior to September 26, 1989 and which fail to satisfy the formalities then applicable,[20] they could nevertheless result in the creation of a mortgage by reason of the doctrine of part performance and thus provide the foundation of a claim to possession.

Where a mortgage is provided to secure a surety's liability under a guarantee, the requirement for formality arises in relation to both the guarantee and mortgage. To be a valid contract of guarantee, it must be evidenced in writing so as

[16] *Samuel Keller (Holdings) Ltd v. Martins Bank Ltd* [1971] 1 W.L.R. 43; *Ashley Guarantee Plc v. Zacaria* [1993] 1 W.L.R. 62.
[17] *Goss v. Chilcott*, unreported, *The Times*, June 6, 1996; *Piggot's Case* (1614) 11 Co. Rep. 286.
[18] *Goss v. Chilcott, ante.*
[19] See *ante*, para. 5–07 and *United Bank of Kuwait v. Sahib* [1997] Ch. 107.
[20] Law of Property Act 1925, s.40(1).

to satisfy the requirements of the Statute of Frauds 1677.[21] Generally, if the formalities required by section 2 of the Property (Miscellaneous Provisions) Act 1989 have been complied with for the purposes of the supporting mortgage there should be no difficulty. However, errors falling foul of those provisions can be fatal to the validity of both guarantee and mortgage: for instance, the omission of the principal debtor's name.[22]

2. Registration

26–07   A failure to register a mortgage at the Land Registry does not affect its validity. However, it may affect the mortgagor's rights as against third parties[23] in the event of an attempt to secure vacant possession. A mortgage granted by a company over its property must be registered with the Registrar of Companies within 21 days. The failure to register does not give the mortgagor company a defence to a claim under the mortgage but merely renders the mortgage invalid as against any liquidator or creditor of the company.[24]

Bars to Claims for Possession

1. The terms of the mortgage including attornment clauses

26–08   The right to possession is created by the mortgage and both the time the right arises and the conditions required for its exercise are determined by construing the mortgage deed. Any claim for possession issued before the right to possession accrues under the terms of the mortgage will therefore be defective and vulnerable to attack on that basis. It was formerly common practice for mortgage deeds to contain an attornment clause whereby the mortgagor agreed to become the tenant of the mortgagee.[25] Such provisions rarely appear in modern mortgages. The advantage of such a provision was that the mortgagee would be able to distrain for non-payment and had access to procedures that were seen as more efficient. Some attornment clauses provide for a period of notice to quit to determine the tenancy whilst others provided that the mortgagee may exercise his rights without giving notice. Where a notice period is required, the right to possession will not arise before such notice has been given and expired. It follows a claim for possession commenced without the specified notice having expired will be defective.

The various statutory provisions giving tenants security of tenure do not alter the ability of a mortgagee where the mortgagor has attorned tenant to determine the tenancy and resort to his remedies *qua* mortgagee rather than lessor. The "tenancy" created by such a clause is not seen by the law as the real relationship between the parties and they are not treated as being lessor or lessee or, in the case of a mortgagee of residential premises, the same is not considered to be "let

---

[21] Statute of Frauds 1677, s.4.
[22] *State Bank of India v. Kaur*, unreported, *The Times*, April 22, 1995.
[23] See *ante*, para. 4–08.
[24] Companies Act 1985, s.395. See *ante*, para. 11–27 *et seq*.
[25] See Woodfall, *Law of Landlord and Tenant*, paras 6.078 to 6.081.

as a dwelling-house".[26] Provided the notional tenancy created in the attornment is determined in accordance with the provisions of the mortgage the fact that the mortgagor has attorned tenant will not act as a bar to a claim for possession.

2. Limitation

This is dealt with elsewhere in this work.[27]   **26–09**

NON EST FACTUM, INCLUDING FORGERY

1. Generally

Where an apparent signatory can establish that the signature on a contract or deed   **26–10**
(including a loan agreement or mortgage) is not his, either because it has literally been signed by a third party without his authority or because, despite the fact he physically signed the document, he can establish sufficient absence of consent for the law to treat the document as if it were not his, the transaction in question will be void (as opposed to voidable). In the context of a mortgage there may, where there was a loan agreement or guarantee separate from the legal charge, be two documents, either or both of which are challenged.

The fact that a successful plea of *non est factum* results in a finding that the transaction attacked was void can be particularly important for two reasons. First, it gives the defendant protection against the totality of the claimant's claim, even though the claimant may be an entirely innocent party to the void contract and notwithstanding that the wrongdoer may be a family member or joint owner with the innocent party or principal debtor. Where a third party, typically the principal debtor, forges a signature or otherwise secures a signature thereby giving rise to a successful plea of *non est factum*, it matters not that the other party to the contract (usually a bank) had no knowledge, whether actual or constructive, of those matters and was not in any way at fault.[28] Secondly, it gives protection against innocent third parties even when they purport to acquire an interest in the property for value. That aspect is particularly important since it is often many years before the dealings that are challenged are discovered and other transactions may have taken place in the intervening period. So where, following the initial void transaction, an innocent third party has relied on the void transaction, and for instance, acquired an interest in the property based on the belief that the void transaction was in fact genuine, the transaction will still not bind the purported signatory.

The law has long recognised the need to keep the plea of *non est factum* within narrow confines so as to ensure the confidence of those who, in the course of all manner of transactions regularly, rightly and of necessity, rely on signatures

---

[26] *Alliance Building Society v. Pinwill* [1958] Ch. 788; *Portman Building Society v. Young* [1951] 1 All E.R. 191; *Peckham Mutual Building Society v. Registe* (1981) 42 P. & C.R. 186.
[27] See *ante*, para. 18–27 *et seq.*
[28] *United Dominion Trust Ltd v. Western* [1976] Q.B. 513.

where they have no reason to question them.[29] Not surprisingly, given the extent to which the law in this area is seeking to strike a fair balance between two or more innocent parties whose interests are diametrically opposed, the principles underpinning the defences are narrowly defined and strictly applied, since, if the plea succeeds, the law is favouring the innocent party who, in a sense, would have been in the best position to avoid the difficulty in the first instance.

2. *Non est factum*—by forgery

26–11 A defence based on the allegation that the contract or deed was not signed by the defendant but by a third party forging his signature is a plea of *non est factum* in its simplest form, turning as it does on one finding of fact. Generally it will be necessary for such a defence to be supported by expert handwriting evidence or other forensic evidence showing that someone other than the defendant signed the document or that the signature or the signature of the defendant was not originally physically attached to that particular document. If a party to a document, whilst not signing himself, authorised the person who did sign to do so in his name and/or on his behalf he will of course be bound, notwithstanding the fact that the signature is not literally his. If an agent fails to read or understand the document signed, the principal is unlikely to be able to raise successfully a plea of *non est factum*. In such circumstances the named party would probably be found to have accepted the risk of his agents' actions.[30]

Where a forged signature relates to a mortgage and any moneys advanced under its terms comprised the funds for all or part of the purchase price for an interest in property which was conveyed into the name of the innocent party or which redeemed a binding prior mortgage by which the innocent party was bound, he cannot rely on the forgery to escape the mortgage and the mortgage debt entirely whilst at the same time claiming the benefit of the interest in his name. A claim by the victim of the forgery for a declaration setting aside the legal charge over the property will not be successful where the effect would be to leave the victim unjustly enriched by retaining property acquired with the mortgagee's money.[31]

Where property is in multiple ownership and one or more of the joint owners was a genuine signatory to a mortgage, equity will treat as done that which ought to have been done under the transaction. In those circumstances the transaction will be binding as far as possible against the interest of those who participated in it. Usually therefore, the beneficial interests of those who were parties to the transaction will be subject to an equitable charge to secure repayment of the money advanced.[32]

---

[29] See the dicta of Lord Reid in *Saunders v. Anglia Building Society* [1971] A.C. 1004, 1015G, and Donovan L.J. in *Muskham Finance Ltd v. Howard* [1963] 1 Q.B. 904, 912.

[30] *Norwich Building Society v. Steed* [1993] Ch. 116, *per* Scott L.J. at 127–8 (where a son's lack of care in ensuring his mother understood the nature and effect of a power of attorney he granted to her prevented him from relying upon her ignorance of that power when executing a transfer of his property). See also para. 26–15.

[31] See *post*, paras 26–44 and 26–46.

[32] *First National Securities v. Hegerty* [1985] Q.B. 850; *Ahmed v. Kendrick* (1988) 56 P. & C.R. 120.

3. *Non est factum*—where the defendant in fact signed the document

A plea of *non est factum* may be open to someone who, whilst intending to sign   **26–12**
a particular document or type of document and who actually does sign the
document in question, was actually misled into executing that deed or contract,
believing it to be of an essentially different nature.

(a) *The difference required*

In *Saunders v. Anglia Building Society*[33] the House of Lords considered, for the   **26–13**
purpose of a plea of *non est factum*, the necessary difference between the document actually signed and the document the defendant intended to sign. The
House of Lords did not draw a distinction, for these purposes, between the nature
and the content of the document. In order to establish the plea, it held that it is
necessary to show "a radical or fundamental difference between what [the
defendant] signed and what he thought he was signing".[34] An "all moneys
charge" has been found to be sufficiently different from a guarantee relating to
moneys borrowed to fund a particular purchase[35] and thus to permit a plea to be
raised.

(b) *Those under a disability*

Since the sixteenth century, the plea of *non est factum* has been extended to   **26–14**
protect those who are particularly vulnerable. Originally the extension was
understood to assist those who were forced to rely upon others to inform them of
the nature and content of a document they signed, being unable to read through
blindness or illiteracy. However, it is now clear that the defence can extend to
those who "are permanently or temporarily unable through no fault of their own
to have any real understanding of the purport of a particular document without
explanation, whether that be from defective education, illness or innate incapacity".[36] The extent of a defendant's disability was considered in *Lloyds Bank
Plc v. Waterhouse*,[37] where the Court of Appeal identified three crucial elements
to such a defence. First, the defendant must establish he is under a disability
which prevents him from having any real understanding without assistance.
Secondly, the defendant must establish that the document signed was sufficiently
different from that which he intended to sign. Thirdly, even those acting under a
disability are required to establish that they were not careless in failing to take
proper precautions to establish the significance of the document actually
signed.

[33] [1971] 1 A.C. 1004, affirming *sub nom. Gallie v. Lee* [1969] 2 Ch. 17.
[34] *ibid.*, *per* Lord Reid at 1017.
[35] *Lloyds Bank plc v. Waterhouse* [1993] 2 F.L.R. 97.
[36] *Saunders v. Anglia Building Society* [1971] 1 A.C. 1004, *per* Lord Reid at 1016 and *Norwich
    Building Society v. Steed, ante.*
[37] [1993] 2 F.L.R. 97.

(c) *Blank documents*

26–15   It follows, theoretically at least, that those who sign blank documents could potentially raise a successful plea of *non est factum*. However, in balancing the interests of the person signing such a document and those who may later rely on that signature, the court will have regard to how the defendant's signature came to be on a document, the content of which was not known or understood. It is a matter for anyone signing or authorising the signing of a document to consider what they need to know about its content and to what extent they should understand it properly before it is executed. The onus is clearly on those who sign blank documents to show that they have acted carefully and done all they prudently and reasonably could to protect their own interests.[38] For this reason, it is unlikely that those of full capacity signing blank documents, including loan agreements and mortgages, will be able to successfully rely on a plea of *non est factum*. It should be remembered that such a person is generally bound by his signature to a document which he has not read or which he is ignorant of its precise legal effect.[39]

It follows that a plea of *non est factum* may afford a defence in rare cases and should be borne in mind as having a potential significance where the mortgagor appears to suffer from a disability of some sort, or to have done so at the time of the transaction upon which reliance is made.

Vitiating Factors—Undue Influence, Misrepresentation, etc.

Part I: Undue Influence

26–16   During the 1990s there was a marked escalation in mortgage possession claims defended on the basis that the mortgagor had the right to set the mortgage and/or the underlying loan agreement aside as a result of a vitiating factor such as undue influence or misrepresentation. As a result the recent developments in this area and increased understanding of these defences to contractual claims generally have taken place against the background of mortgage transactions. Since the House of Lords is due to hear the appeals in *Royal Bank of Scotland v. Etridge (No. 2)*[40] in May 2001 and has granted leave to appeal in *Barclays Bank plc v. Colman*[41] the potential remains for further development and clarification. In the context of mortgages the position is often complicated by the fact that the wrongdoer, the perpetrator of the undue influence or misrepresentation, is not the mortgagor, or possibly, is not even a party to any aspect of the transaction but someone associated with the mortgagor who had an interest in the transaction proceeding. It follows that consideration of the various factors that can render a mortgage or the underlying loan agreement voidable involves two stages. First, it is necessary to identify the factor or wrong which would justify setting aside

---

[38] *per* Lord Reid at 1016; *Norwich Building Society v. Steed, ante.*
[39] *L'Estrange v. F. Graucob Ltd* [1934] 2 K.B. 394.
[40] *Royal Bank of Scotland v. Etridge (No. 2)* and combined appeals [1998] 4 All E.R. 705.
[41] [2000] 3 W.L.R. 405; petition to appeal allowed: [2000] 1 W.L.R. 2469.

the transaction. Secondly, it is necessary to ascertain whether that factor justifies the transaction being set aside as against the mortgagee, where the mortgagee is not the wrongdoer.

1. **Undue Influence**

The essence of undue influence is the absence of true consent to the contract by **26–17** a party to that contract because his agreement was obtained by the inappropriate use of influence over him. The defence exists both to prevent the wrongdoer taking the benefit of his wrongdoing and to protect those who are vulnerable against having advantage taken of them by another. Where one person has abused their position of influence or domination over another, thereby procuring the "victim" to enter into a transaction, that transaction may be voidable and the Court can set it aside. The principle has been described as a "fetter placed on the conscience of the recipient . . . and one that arises out of public policy and fair play".[42] It follows that when undue influence is raised as a defence, it is not the defendant's understanding of the agreement that is in question. Rather, it is the reasons for the defendant's acquiescence that are relevant. Unlike misrepresentation, the contracting party could understand the transaction correctly and yet be entering it as a result of undue influence rather than as a result of the exercise of their own free will. The defence should not however be understood as protecting those who act foolishly or without any regard for their own interests, or those who choose to take a financial risk in order to help those they care about. Further it should be noted that in practice, the actions of the wrongdoer in influencing the defending party are often alleged to involve elements of misrepresentation as well as pressure and influence.

2. **Establishing Undue Influence**

Undue influence can be established either as a matter of fact (actual undue **26–18** influence) or it may be presumed. Cotton L.J. described the two types of undue influence in *Allcard v. Skinner* as:

> "First, where the court has been satisfied that the gift was the result of influence expressly used by the donee for the purpose; second, where the relations between the donor and donee have at or shortly before the execution of the gift been such as to raise a presumption that the donee had influence over the donor . . . . The first class of cases may be considered as depending on the principle that no one shall be allowed to retain any benefit arising from his own fraud or wrongful act. In the second class of cases the court interferes, not on the ground that any wrongful act has in fact been committed by the donee, but on the ground of public policy, and to prevent the relations which existed between the parties and the influence arising therefrom being abused."[43]

---

[42] *Allcard v. Skinner* (1887) 36 Ch.D. 145.
[43] *ibid.*, at 171.

Thus, the focus of an allegation of actual undue influence will be upon the events that actually occurred, whereas presumed undue influence focuses on the relationship between the parties and the potential for abuse of that relationship.

(a) *Actual Undue Influence*

26–19   Actual undue influence has been described as a species of fraud.[44] In order to establish a defence based on actual undue influence, it is necessary to establish that the defendant entered into the particular transaction as a result of actual coercion, illegitimate pressure or such domination or control by the wrongdoer that the defendant's ability to make an independent decision was defeated. The defendant has the burden of proving that:

(a)   the wrongdoer has the capacity to influence the defendant;

(b)   that influence was exercised;

(c)   the exercise was undue; and

(d)   the exercise of that influence actually brought about the transaction.[45]

It is impossible to give an exhaustive definition of what may amount to undue influence.[46] The courts have repeatedly stressed the need for this jurisdiction to remain flexible so that its usefulness as an inhibitor of wrongful behaviour and a protection to the vulnerable is not fettered by exactly defined limits.[47] Nevertheless it is clear that not all actual influence, pressure or encouragement is undue influence. In *Royal Bank of Scotland v. Etridge (No. 2)*, Stuart-Smith L.J. said[48]:

"In our view the doctrine of undue influence should not be applied so as to shield persons from the consequences of external forces in the absence of some sort of fraud, victimisation or coercion practised by the alleged wrongdoer sufficient to affect his conscience. Influence which is undue must be recognised when it occurs for it cannot be further defined in advance."

The court had previously described the sort of substantial pressures many may be subjected to without being able to establish they had been a victim of undue influence:

"Legitimate commercial pressure brought by a creditor, however strong, coupled with proper feelings of family loyalty and a laudable desire to help

---

[44] *CIBC Mortgages Ltd v. Pitt* [1994] 1 A.C. 200.

[45] *Bank of Credit and Commercial International SA v. Aboody* [1990] 1 Q.B. 923, *per* Slade L.J. at 967.

[46] At first instance in *Royal Bank of Scotland v. Bennett* [1997] 1 F.L.R. 801, 822–826, Mr James Mumby Q.C. (sitting as a deputy judge of the Chancery Division) provided a detailed analysis of various ways the Courts had sought to define and describe incidents of actual undue influence.

[47] *Bank of Credit and Commerce International SA v. Aboody* [1990] 1 Q.B. 923.

[48] [1998] 4 All E.R. 705 at 746, para. 23.

a husband or son in financial difficulty, may be difficult to resist. They may be sufficient to induce a reluctant wife or mother to agree to charge her home by way of collateral security, particularly if they are accompanied by family pressure or emotional scenes. But they are not enough to justify the setting aside of the transaction unless they go beyond what is permissible and lead the complainant to execute the charge not because, however reluctantly, she is persuaded that it is the right thing to do, but because the wrongdoer's importunity has left her with no will of her own."[49]

It follows that the ability to establish that the defending mortgagor did not make the decision to enter the transaction himself but had lost the ability to exercise free will because of another's acts is central to a finding of actual undue influence.

Establishing such a proposition will require a detailed consideration of a **26–20** number of factors, including the circumstances surrounding the transaction, the relationship between the relevant parties (particularly when the transaction was concluded), any discussions or advice given leading up to the transaction and the reasons or motives of both the defendant and the alleged wrongdoer in wishing to bring about the traction in question. Whilst the nature of the transaction and the extent to which it is to the defendant's manifest disadvantage seems not to be a necessary element[50] of actual undue influence, it will be of highly significant evidential value in relation to a finding of actual undue influence if the defendant's acts have caused him manifest disadvantage. The causal link between the undue influence and entry into the transaction is critical; if the court concludes on the balance of probabilities that the transaction would have proceeded even without the undue influence, the court will not set the transaction aside.[51] By analogy with fraud, it appears to be sufficient to establish that the influence exercised was a significant reason for the entry into the transaction rather than the predominant or only reason.

(b) *Presumed Undue Influence*

By recognising that certain types of relationship will make some categories of **26–21** people particularly vulnerable to undue influence and give others the opportunity to take advantage of such relationships, the common law has developed a presumption of undue influence which will arise in certain situations. The evil that presumed undue influence focuses upon is subtly different to that addressed by actual undue influence. Presumed undue influence addresses the potential for abuse of relationships of trust, rather than a particular instance of undue influence. Hence it becomes the nature of the relationship and potential for abuse by one party of another for his own or a third party's advantage that is the primary

---

[49] *Royal Bank of Scotland v. Etridge (No. 2)*, *ante*, at 713, para. 10.
[50] *CIBC Mortgages Ltd v. Pitt*, *ante*, *per* Lord Browne-Wilkinson at 209; *Royal Bank of Scotland v. Etridge (No. 2)*, *ante*, at 713, paras 11–12.
[51] *BCCI SA v. Aboody*, *ante*, at 971.

factor which gives rise to the presumption rather than the actual cause of the entry into the particular transaction.

(i) The Categories of Presumed Undue Influence

26–22   There are two categories of cases involving presumed undue influence, most clearly classified by Lord Browne-Wilkinson in *Barclays Bank plc v. O'Brien*[52] as class 2A and class 2B, class 1 cases being those involving actual undue influence.

> *Class 2A:* Where there is a transaction between two people who are in a certain type of relationship, or where one party to such a relationship is induced to enter a transaction with a third party by the other party to the relationship, undue influence will be presumed;
> *Class 2B:* Where it is established that as between the particular defendant and the other contracting party, or the person who secured the defendant's entry into the transaction, there was actually a relationship such that the defendant "reposed trust and confidence" in the wrongdoer, undue influence will be presumed.

The difference is clear: class 2A cases require the defendant to adduce evidence of the existence of a certain relationship; class 2B cases require evidence of the reposing of trust and confidence outside a relationship which, *per se*, can give rise to the presumption of undue influence.

The relationships that give rise to a class 2A presumption of undue influence include that of parent and child,[53] guardian and ward,[54] solicitor and client,[55] doctor and patient[56] and religious adviser and follower or parishioner if role of adviser has been adopted.[57] Other relationships which are properly characterised as fiduciary in nature or confidential can similarly give rise to the presumption.[58] Where the necessary relationship is established and the transaction is occasioned in circumstances envisaged by Lord Browne-Wilkinson, once the defendant establishes the transaction was disadvantageous from his point of view, the presumption of undue influence will arise and it will be for the other party to the transaction to rebut that presumption. With regard to class 2B cases, the defendant has to prove the existence of a particular relationship in which he or she is dominated by, and dependant upon, the wrongdoer and/or has placed trust and confidence in the wrongdoer in relation to the subject matter of the transaction (*e.g.* financial matters). Thus class 2B presumed undue influence may arise in any

---

[52] [1994] A.C. 180 at 189.
[53] *Lancashire Loans Ltd v. Black* [1934] Ch. 380; *Wright v. Vanderplank* (1855) 2 K. & J. 1; *Archer v. Hudson* (1844) 7 Beav. 551.
[54] *Hylton v. Hylton* (1804) 2 Ves. Sen. 547; *Taylor v. Johnston* (1882) 19 Ch.D. 603; *Powell v. Powell* [1900] 1 Ch. 243.
[55] See Chitty, *Contracts* (28th ed., 1999), para. 7–055; *Wright v. Carter* [1903] 1 Ch. 27; *Demerara Bauxite v. Hubbard* [1923] A.C. 673; *McMaster v. Byrne* [1952] 1 All E.R. 1362.
[56] *Mitchell v. Homfray* (1881) 8 Q.B.D. 587; *Radcliffe v. Price* (1902) 18 T.L.R. 466.
[57] *Lyon v. Home* (1868) 6 L.R. Eq. 655; *Allcard v. Skinner* (1887) 36 Ch.D. 145.
[58] *Tate v. Williamson* (1866) 2 L.R. Ch. App. 55, 61.

relationship with the necessary characteristics and not just those of a family or domestic nature,[59] *e.g.* junior employees and their employers.[60]

(c) *Manifest Disadvantage*

Notwithstanding the absence in *Barclays Bank plc v. O'Brien*[61] of any require-   **26–23**
ment that the transaction in question should involve manifest disadvantage to the innocent party in order for undue influence to be presumed, the current position appears to be that before a presumption of undue influence can arise, the relevant transaction has to be shown to have been manifestly disadvantageous to the party allegedly influenced and that "manifest disadvantage" for these purposes is that which is clear and obvious and more than *de minimis*.[62] The conclusion that establishing manifest disadvantage is a prerequisite to raising a presumption of undue influence has been the subject of much criticism, however, pending the hearing of the petition to the House of Lords in *Barclays Bank Plc v. Coleman*[63] it must be treated as a necessary element.

In determining whether the disadvantage was manifest, the position is to be viewed objectively at the date upon which it was entered into; so, for example, where the charge created over the parties' matrimonial home was such that the moneys secured were not only limited to the proposed transaction but could also extend to further moneys which the husband could raise and secure without reference to the wife and thus subject the matrimonial home to a much greater risk than the wife could know of, manifest disadvantage was held to be "clear and obvious".[64] Cases where manifest disadvantage has been held to exist are where the transaction is particularly hazardous[65] or where the wife's exposure on the security given in support of a loan to a company in which she had an interest was disproportionate to her interest in that company.[66]

(d) *The Shifting Burden*

The effect of establishing presumed undue influence is that the onus of proof then   **26–24**
shifts to the other party to the transaction, to show that it was in fact entered into

---

[59] Relationships where sufficient trust and confidence has been found to have been reposed in the wrongdoer include that between lovers (*Massey v. Midland Bank plc* [1995] 1 All E.R. 929); close friends (*Banco Exterior v. Thomas* [1997] 1 W.L.R. 221); spouses (*Barclays Bank v. O'Brien, ante* (wife); *Barclays Bank plc v. Rivett* [1997] 29 H.L.R. 893 (husband)) and siblings (*Northern Rock Building Society v. Archer* (1998) 78 P. & C.R. 65).

[60] *Credit Lyonnaise Bank Netherland NV v. Burch* [1997] 2 All E.R. 144; *Steeples v. Lea* [1998] 1 F.L.R. 139.

[61] *Barclays Bank plc v. O'Brien, ante*, at 189; *Royal Bank of Scotland v. Etridge (No. 2), ante*, at 713–714, para. 11–3.

[62] *Barclays Bank plc v. Coleman* [2000] 3 W.L.R. 405. Leave to appeal to the House of Lords from this decision has been granted: [2000] 1 W.L.R. 2469.

[63] [2000] 3 W.L.R. 405.

[64] *ibid.*

[65] *Nightingale Finance Limited v. Scott* [1997] E.G.C.S. 161.

[66] *Goode Durrant Administration v. Biddulph* (1994) 26 H.L.R. 625 ($2\frac{1}{2}$% interest; exposure £300,000). In *Barclays Bank plc v. Sumner* [1996] E.G.C.S. 65, an unlimited exposure on a 50% holding was not considered disproportionate.

as a result of the exercise of "full, free and informed consent" in order to avoid a finding of undue influence.[67]

3. **Rebutting the Presumption of Undue Influence**

26–25   Evidence that the defendant acted independently and with a full appreciation of what he was doing will rebut a presumption of undue influence.[68] Given the nature of undue influence it is not enough to simply show that the defendant understood the transaction correctly, or indeed that when signing the defendant actually intended to sign the document that was executed.[69]

(a) *Independent Legal Advice*

The most common way of seeking to rebut the presumption is to establish that the defendant had the benefit of independent legal advice. The consideration of whether the defendant had the benefit of legal advice may arise when (1) establishing undue influence, and (2) considering whether to permit the right to the transaction to be set aside against the other contracting party, even if they were not the actual wrongdoer. At the first stage, its relevance will be as evidence to rebut the presumption of undue influence (or even possibly as part of the evidence to be considered in deciding whether any actual undue influence was the cause of the entry into the transaction). At that point, again the question of whether appropriate legal advice was given and its effect must be considered objectively by reference to what in fact occurred. At the second stage, the provision of legal advice will be relevant to the question whether, for instance, the claimant bank had constructive notice of the undue influence. Again, at that second stage the matter is to be considered only from the other contracting party's point of view and on the basis of what was properly known or is assumed to have been known by that party.

Often the advice given by a solicitor[70] to a client contemplating a loan agreement and/or mortgage will simply be to explain to the defendant the nature, effect and potential consequences of the transaction. However in *Royal Bank of Scotland v. Etridge (No. 2)*,[71] Stuart-Smith L.J. made it clear that:

> " . . . a solicitor who is asked to advise a client who may be subject to the undue influence of another 'takes upon himself no light nor easy task': see *Wright v. Carter* [1903] 1 Ch. 27 at 57, *per* Stirling L.J. How far he should go in probing the matter in order to satisfy himself that his client is able to make a free and informed decision and is not merely agreeing to do what the wrongdoer wants is a matter of professional judgment: see *Massey v. Midland Bank plc* [1995] 1 All E.R. 929 at 934, *per* Steyn L.J. It must

---

[67] *Zamet v. Hyman* [1961] 1 W.L.R. 1442 at 1444.

[68] *Inche Noriah v. Shaik Allie Bin Omar* [1929] A.C. 127 at 135.

[69] *Royal Bank of Scotland v. Etridge (No. 2)*, *ante*, at 714, para. 16–17; *Powell v. Powell* [1900] 1 Ch. 243, 247.

[70] Or a legal executive: see *Barclays Bank plc v. Coleman* [2000] 3 W.L.R. 405, currently under appeal to the House of Lords.

[71] [1998] 4 All E.R. 705 at 716. The appeal to the House of Lords is believed to be imminent.

depend on all the circumstances of the case. Independent advice may be desirable but it is not always necessary. It depends on the nature of the proposed transaction and the relationship between the parties. Where there is a real conflict of interest, and certainly where there is a possibility that he may be called on to advise the wife not to enter into the proposed transaction, a solicitor should decline to act if he is also acting (otherwise than in a purely ministerial capacity) for another party to the transaction."

It follows that in considering whether the independent legal advice was sufficient to rebut the presumption of undue influence, it will be relevant to consider what advice was given, whether it was stressed to the defendant that he/she must make his/her own decision about whether to enter the transaction and whether the solicitor satisfied himself as to why the transaction was being entered into and whether that was as a result of an independent and free decision so to do. Further, there will be occasions when it will be necessary for the advice to go further so as to identify the information that the defendant should ascertain before making a decision, or even so far as to make a recommendation whether or not the transaction should be entered into. The absence of independence in any sense on the part of the solicitor would clearly diminish the value of evidence of his involvement to rebut the presumption. Thus where the solicitor was advising the wife of a company director who was securing that company's borrowings against the jointly owned matrimonial home and the solicitor was also the company's secretary the bank was put on enquiry and could not avoid constructive notice of the company director's undue influence over his wife.[71a] If the entry into the transaction by the defendant was in accordance with the advice given by a solicitor and that advice was sufficient and independent, the presumption is very likely to be rebutted. A mortgagee will, notwithstanding a husband's undue influence on his wife, be able to rely upon security given by the wife if it can establish either (i) that on the basis of the facts as known to it at the relevant time there were no inquiries which it ought to have made (*i.e.* it was not put on inquiry); or (ii) that it made such inquiries as were reasonable in the circumstances and no further facts came to its knowledge as a result (*e.g.* that the mortgagor had been independently advised: see above); or (iii) that no further relevant facts would have come to its attention if it had made such inquiries as it ought reasonably to have made.[71b]

The position is rather more difficult in circumstances where the defendant was given independent legal advice and ignored or rejected it. In such circumstances there are good arguments that the presumption has been rebutted; however that argument will not always present itself. In some instances it can be argued that the ignoring of advice not to enter the transaction is actually an example of just how strong the undue influence was. In practice, a solicitor should withdraw if not satisfied that his client is exercising free will. Unless he does so, his client will (at a later stage) struggle to establish that the presumption should operate unless he can show that his solicitor had been negligent.

[71a] *National Westminster Bank v. Breeds* (unreported, February 1, 2001, Lawrence Collins J., Ch.D.).
[71b] *Bank of Scotland v. Bennett* [1999] 1 F.L.R. 1115 at 1135 *per* Chadwick L.J. CA.

PART II: MISREPRESENTATION AND OTHER VITIATING FACTORS

1. Misrepresentation

26–26   As with any other contract, if a defendant can establish that he was induced to enter a loan agreement and/or mortgage by a misrepresentation he may have a right to set that agreement aside.[72] In order to succeed the defendant will need to establish a misrepresentation of fact which was the effective cause of his entry into the contract. In the context of mortgages, the misrepresentation is most often about the circumstances in which liability will occur or the extent of that liability. If the defendant did not actually hear or understand the misrepresentation so that it was not operating on his mind in order to induce the decision to contract, it would not have been an effective cause.[73] The misrepresentation must still be effective at the time of entry into the transaction; if by that point the defendant is aware of the true position, the earlier misrepresentation does not give rise to a defence. Even if the defendant is unaware of the inaccuracy in the representation at the time of entry into the transaction, if it can be established that the defendant would in fact have entered the transaction even if the truth were known, a defence based on misrepresentation will fail.[74] In the normal course of events, a bank does not owe a proposed mortgagor a duty to explain the nature and effect of any proposed transaction that is being contemplated or to advise the taking of independent advice by that individual. However, if the bank chooses to do so and tenders an explanation, it must do so accurately[75] or bear the consequences of its failure. Very often the wrongdoer is not the party seeking to enforce the contract or even a party to the contract. In those circumstances it is necessary to consider whether any right to set aside the loan agreement or the mortgage can be exercised against the mortgagee. The same principles apply with regard to mortgages tainted by misrepresentation as with mortgages based on undue influence.

2. Other Vitiating Factors

26–27   Similarly, loan agreements and mortgages can also be challenged on the basis of a right to set them aside arising as a result of any other vitiating factor that provides a defence to a contractual claim. It follows that if a mortgagor can establish mistake or duress, a defence may arise depending on the ability to establish that any right to set the underlying agreement aside is effective as against the mortgagee, whether he is the wrongdoer or not.

---

[72] See Chitty, *Contracts* (28th ed., 1999), Chapter 6.
[73] *Horsfall v. Thomas* (1862) 1 H. & C. 90.
[74] *Industrial Properties Ltd v. Associated Electrical Industries Ltd* [1977] Q.B. 580; *Pan Atlantic Insurance Co. Ltd v. Pine Top Insurance Co. Ltd* [1995] 1 A.C. 501.
[75] *Barclays Bank plc v. Khaira* [1992] 1 W.L.R. 623.

PART III: EXERCISING THE RIGHT TO SET ASIDE

1. As against the mortgagee

Once a mortgagor has established that his entry into a transaction was brought **26–28**
about by a vitiating factor such as undue influence or misrepresentation, a right
to set aside the transaction will arise as between the mortgagor and the wrongdoer. If the mortgagee is, in fact or vicariously, the wrongdoer, the right to set
aside the transaction arises directly against the mortgagee.

2. Third Party Wrongdoer

Where the wrongdoer is a third party such as the mortgagor's husband, cohabitee **26–29**
or employer, the mortgagor will only succeed as against the mortgagee if it is
possible to establish the wrongdoer was acting as the mortgagee's agent or the
mortgagee had either actual or constructive notice of the vitiating factor.[76] It is
not surprising given the nature of the defences concerned that the common law
has developed principles that involve establishing some culpability on the part of
the third party before imposing the consequences on that third party of the
wrongdoer's actions. If not the wrongdoer itself, the mortgagee must be know-
ingly taking advantage of the wrongdoing or have conducted itself in a way that
justifies treating it as if it knew that it was taking advantage of the wrongdoing.
There are a number of ways in which the mortgagee's conscience can be
affected.

(a) *Agency*

Arguments based on agency (where for example, the wrongdoer is deemed to be **26–30**
the mortgagee's agent) have been largely discredited.[77] It is now widely recognised that at least in cases involving undue influence or misrepresentation as a
defence to a mortgage that it will rarely be necessary to resort to such arguments
now that well-developed concepts of actual and constructive notice have arisen
which are sufficient to protect the mortgagor in such situations. In light of the
disapproval of the artificiality that had crept into such cases before *Barclays Bank
plc v. O'Brien*, such an argument is only likely to succeed if supported by good
evidence of a genuine agency having existed.

PART IV: NOTICE

1. Actual Notice of the Vitiating Factor

The concept of actual notice speaks for itself and will of course be a question of **26–31**
fact. If it is possible to show that the mortgagee or its employee were actually

---

[76] *Barclays Bank plc v. O'Brien, ante*; *Royal Bank of Scotland v. Etridge, ante*, at 717, para. 27–8.
[77] *Barclays Bank plc v. O'Brien, ante*, at 194–5; *Royal Bank of Scotland v. Etridge, ante*, at 747, para.
27.

informed or observed for themselves that undue influence was being exercised in order to secure the mortgagor's entry into the loan agreement, the mortgagor's right to set the agreement aside will be effective against the mortgagee. Such cases are rare.

2. Constructive Notice of the Vitiating Factor

26–32 The courts have been heavily engaged in considering the ambit of constructive notice in the context of undue influence and misrepresentation defences to mortgagees' claims. The doctrine of constructive notice represents an attempt by the courts to ensure a fair allocation of the risk of the consequences of a third party's wrongdoing between the two innocent parties, namely the defendant mortgagor and the mortgagee. The starting point is that the mortgagee should be alert to indications that the mortgagor may have a right to set aside the transaction, for instance because it may have been secured by wrongdoing. If put on inquiry by such indications as are available to it, a mortgagee will be deemed to have constructive notice of that wrongdoing and would not be entitled to take the benefit of the transaction. If, having been initially put on inquiry, the mortgagee takes reasonable steps to inquire further and ensures that the risk of wrongdoing is largely dispelled, the mortgagee may avoid a finding of constructive notice.

The initial burden of establishing constructive notice lies with the mortgagor seeking to set aside the transaction.[78] In order to establish that the mortgagee had constructive notice of the undue influence alleged, the mortgagor has only to establish that the mortgagee knew enough about the transaction or the relationship between those involved to put it on inquiry that such a party was likely to have been introduced to or encouraged into the transaction by someone who might well be in a position to exercise undue influence. In addition, the mortgagee must be aware that the transaction was manifestly disadvantageous to the complainant party.[79]

It is essential that matters are considered from the mortgagee's point of view. It follows that only matters known to the mortgagee at the time of the transaction can be considered in determining whether the mortgagee had constructive notice.[80] A mortgagee who has knowledge that a wife is standing surety for or providing her interest in a property as security for her husband's debts, so that the transaction on its face is not to her advantage, is prima facie constructive notice that the wife's agreement to the surety contract or mortgage was secured by undue influence.[81] However, where on the basis of the mortgagee's information the transaction was a joint transaction for the benefit of both the defendant mortgagor and the wrongdoer, the mortgagee will not be on constructive notice.[82] A mortgagee is entitled to consider that a joint transaction is for the parties' joint

---

[78] *Barclays Bank plc v. Boulter & Boulter* [1999] 2 F.L.R. 986.
[79] *Barclays Bank plc v. Coleman* [2000] 3 W.L.R. 405. See *ante*, para. 26–23 *et seq.*
[80] *Britannia Building Society v. Pugh* [1997] 2 F.L.R. 7; *Royal Bank of Scotland v. Bennett* [1999] 1 F.L.R. 1115.
[81] *Barclays Bank plc v. O'Brien, ante.*
[82] *CIBC v. Pitt, ante.*

benefit and will only be found to have knowledge that the transaction is not for their joint benefit if it has actual knowledge to that effect.[83]

Where a mortgagee is initially put on inquiry, it is possible for it to avoid a **26–33** finding of constructive notice by taking reasonable steps to ensure that the mortgagor is aware of the risk or liability being incurred. In *Barclays Bank plc v. O'Brien*, Lord Browne-Wilkinson sought to describe what would constitute reasonable steps for a mortgagee seeking to avoid being fixed with constructive notice:

> "Normally the reasonable steps necessary to avoid being fixed with con-
> structive notice consist of making inquiry of the person who may have the
> earlier right (*i.e.* the wife) to see whether such right is asserted. It is plainly
> impossible to require of banks and other financial institutions that they
> should inquire of one spouse whether he or she has been unduly influenced
> or misled by the other. But in my judgment the creditor, in order to avoid
> being fixed with constructive notice, can reasonably be expected to take
> steps to bring home to the wife the risk she is running by standing as surety
> and to advise her to take independent advice. As to past transactions, it will
> depend on the facts of each case whether the steps taken by the creditor
> satisfy this test. However for the future in my judgment a creditor will have
> satisfied these requirements if it insists that the wife attend a private meeting
> (in the absence of the husband) with a representative of the creditor at which
> she is told of the extent of her liability as surety, warned of the risk she is
> running and urged to take independent legal advice. If these steps are taken
> in my judgment the creditor will have taken such reasonable steps as are
> necessary to preclude a subsequent claim that it had constructive notice of
> the wife's rights."[84]

Where the mortgagor's consent was treated almost as a formality by the mortgagee, mortgagees have been found to be on inquiry and to have constructive notice of the undue influence or misrepresentation. However, it has become apparent in the course of a large number of decisions made at first instance and in the Court of Appeal since *Barclays Bank plc v. O'Brien*, that in most cases the potential difficulties have not been addressed by the use of the private interviews but rather by the use of solicitors to certify the mortgagor's entry into the transaction. The circumstances in which a solicitor's involvement will avoid the mortgagee having constructive notice were considered in some depth in *Royal Bank of Scotland v. Etridge (No. 2)* and are currently the subject of a petition to the House of Lords.[85] A fundamental factor that underpins the Court of Appeal's approach to the involvement of a solicitor is that a mortgagee is obviously not entitled to inquire into exactly what passes between the solicitor and the mortgagor but is entitled to assume that the solicitor acted properly and

---

[83] *Halifax Mortgage Services Ltd v. Stepsky* [1996] 2 All E.R. 277—knowledge acquired by a solicitor while advising the mortgagor will not be imputed to the mortgagee even if the mortgagee instructed the solicitor.

[84] *Barclays Bank plc v. O'Brien, ante*, at 196–7.

[85] Due to be heard in May 2001.

professionally[86] and so gave sufficient advice and was sufficiently independent.[87] Further, as indicated above,[88] a solicitor advising someone who may be entering a transaction as a result of undue influence or something similar has a duty to address that and to ensure that the entry into the transaction is as a result of a free and informed decision or to withdraw from acting for that person. Where a potential mortgagor does not approach the mortgagee through a solicitor or appear to have a solicitor, the mortgagee can generally avoid a finding of constructive notice if it urges the mortgagor to take independent legal advice and, if advice is taken, receives confirmation from a solicitor that the transaction has been explained to the mortgagor.[89]

26–34   When giving advice to a potential mortgagor, a solicitor acts exclusively as that individual's solicitor regardless of who actually instructed or retained the solicitor in relation to that advice or the transaction as a whole.[90] In those circumstances the entitlement to make the assumption that a solicitor who did not withdraw acted properly, amounts to an assumption that the vitiating factor has been addressed. In the absence of express confirmation from a solicitor that he has undertaken the work he was instructed to do, a mortgagee is not entitled to assume that the mortgagor has been properly advised. So for instance, where a solicitor has simply witnessed the mortgagor's signature, the mortgagee will not avoid having constructive notice of undue influence.[91] However, it is not necessary for the confirmation to be full or detailed. Where the confirmation is inadequate, at most the mortgagee is put on inquiry as to whether the mortgagor has been properly advised and the mortgagor will only succeed in establishing the mortgagee had constructive notice if he was not properly advised *and* the mortgagee fails to make further inquiries or secure clearer confirmation.[92] Where a mortgagee is aware of material facts that would be relevant to the decision to enter the transaction and is aware that a solicitor does not have knowledge of those matters, the mortgagee will not be able simply to rely on the fact that a solicitor was instructed to advise and confirmed that he had so acted.[93] Where a solicitor instructed to advise the mortgagor acquires information in the course of that retainer, the mortgagee is not imputed with that knowledge, even if it was the mortgagee that instructed the solicitor.[94]

PART V: THE LOSS OF THE RIGHT TO SET ASIDE

26–35   Contracts obtained by undue influence, misrepresentation and duress are voidable rather than void *ab initio*. Where a contract is voidable, the innocent party

---

[86] *Royal Bank of Scotland v. Etridge, ante.*
[87] *Massey v. Midland Bank plc* [1995] 1 All E.R. 929; *Bank of Baroda v. Rayarel, ante*; *Royal Bank of Scotland v. Etridge, ante.*
[88] See para. 26–25.
[89] *Massey v. Midland Bank plc* [1995] 1 All E.R. 929; *Bank of Baroda v. Rayarel, ante*; *Royal Bank of Scotland v. Etridge, ante.*
[90] *Bank of Baroda v. Rayarel* [1975] 2 F.L.R. 376; *Royal Bank of Scotland v. Etridge, ante.*
[91] *Scottish Equitable Life plc v. Virdee* [1999] 1 F.L.R. 863.
[92] *Royal Bank of Scotland v. Etridge, ante.*
[93] *Royal Bank of Scotland v. Etridge, ante*, at 722; see also *Credit Lyonnaise Bank Nederland v. Burch, ante.*
[94] *Halifax Mortgage Services Ltd v. Stepsky* [1996] 2 All E.R. 277; *Royal Bank of Scotland v. Etridge, ante.*

to the contract has a choice of electing whether to rescind or affirm the contract. In determining whether the right to set aside a transaction is lost, the underlying test (as approved by Stuart-Smith L.J. in *Royal Bank of Scotland v. Etridge*[95] can be stated thus:

> "Upon whatever precise basis it is sought to uphold a transaction which was originally obtained by undue influence it is an essential ingredient that it would be inequitable to allow the influenced party to set aside the transaction."

1. **Affirmation**

If, after the defendant is free of the effects of the vitiating factor, a choice/election **26–36** is made to affirm the contract, the right to avoid/rescind such a contract may be lost.[96] In the case of a right to set aside based on misrepresentation, that would generally mean simply that the defendant knows that the representation made was false. The position is more complex where the vitiating factor is undue influence. In such circumstances, as a matter of principle, it is suggested that it should not be sufficient merely to establish the cessation of the pressure applied which initially secured the impugned transaction. Almost inevitably that particular pressure will end once the transaction has been completed. In order to be free of the undue influence so as to make an election, it is necessary for the innocent party to have moved out of the reach of the influential relationship. This necessarily involves the ending of the relationship between the two people or the changing of the nature of the relationship so that it is no longer possible for such influence to be exercised. Although it appears that it is not a rigid rule, generally a party will not be treated as having affirmed such a contract unless, with knowledge of both (1) the facts which give rise to the election, and (2) the existence of his right to elect, he unequivocally demonstrates to the other contracting party that he intends to proceed with the contract.[97] Affirmation may be by an express statement that the right to set aside is not being exercised or by reliance still being placed on the contract and the obligations arising thereunder. Alternatively, the affirmation may occur when the party with the right to set aside the contract continues to conduct himself in a manner that is consistent with the continued existence of the contract.

2. **Delay and Estoppel**

Delay in itself is not a bar to a claim to set aside a contract for undue influence **26–37** or misrepresentation.[98] Evidence of delay after the cessation of the influential

[95] [1998] 4 All E.R. 705, approving *Goldworthy v. Brickell* [1987] Ch. 378.
[96] *Hatch v. Hatch* (1804) 9 Ves. Jr. 292; *Allcard v. Skinner* (1887) 36 Ch.D. 145, 187, 191. See Chitty, *Contracts* (28th ed., 1999), paras 6–120 and 7–063.
[97] *Peyman v. Lanjani* [1985] 1 Ch. 457. See Chitty, *Contracts* (28th ed., 1999), paras 6–121 and 7–063.
[98] *Armstrong v. Jackson* [1917] 2 K.B. 822, 830; *Allcard v. Skinner, ante*, at 174, 191. Except where the misrepresentation is innocent: see *Leaf v. International Galleries* [1950] 2 K.B. 86; Chitty, *Contracts* (28th ed., 1999), para. 6–123.

relationship and with actual knowledge of both the facts that give rise to and of the existence of the possible right to set aside may be the basis of an inference that the party has subsequently acquiesced in the contract[99] so that affirmation would be made out. It is to be noted that the courts do not easily draw such an inference even when there is evidence that a mortgagor with actual knowledge of the possible right to set aside acts in a way that demonstrates an attitude inconsistent with the claim to set aside.[1] Delay coupled with some actions that can be construed as a representation that the contract is continuing will more readily result in an inference that the mortgagor is acquiescing in the continuation of the contract. Alternatively, if the mortgagee acts in reliance on a belief that the contract remains in place, the delay and actions of the mortgagor can form the basis of an estoppel barring any attempt by the mortgagor to set aside the contract.

3. *Restitutio in integrum*

26–38   Where a defendant has received a benefit under the transaction, the transaction can only be set aside if the defendant gives back that benefit. The setting aside of a transaction is a restitutionary remedy which can only be granted if both parties to the transaction are, *inter se*, put back into the position they were in prior to the transaction.[2] In the context of mortgages, it is often the case that the mortgagor is acting as surety for a principal debtor so that the mortgagor himself received no benefit. In those circumstances, the contract can be set aside without the money secured being repaid.

4. Mortgages of reversionary interests and expectancies

26–39   The courts have a general equitable jurisdiction to interfere and set aside mortgages of reversionary interests and expectancies (and the terms of redemption modified) if it is established that the mortgagor has been overreached.[3] This jurisdiction may also operate where the mortgagor is poor and ignorant or in weak health.[4] The onus of proof is on any person who acquires an expectancy to show that the bargain was not "catching" or extortionate.[5] Formerly undervalue was always a ground for setting aside such bargains, but section 174 of the Law of Property Act 1925 provides that no acquisition of a reversionary interest made in good faith is to be set aside merely on that ground. This section does not, however, in any way limit the general jurisdiction of the court to disallow and modify unconscionable agreements. Undervalue is still a material element in

---

[99] *Allcard v. Skinner, ante*, at 174–5, 187, 193; *Bullock v. Lloyds Bank Ltd* [1955] Ch. 317 at 327; *Re Pauling's Settlement Trusts* [1964] Ch. 303 at 353.

[1] *Bullock v. Lloyds Bank Ltd, ante*, at 327; *Re Pauling's Settlement Trusts, ante*, at 353.

[2] *Dunbar Bank plc v. Nadeem* [1998] 3 All E.R. 876; *Society of Lloyd's v. Khan* [1999] 1 F.L.R. 246. See Chitty, *Contracts* (28th ed., 1999), para. 7–064 and Goff & Jones, (5th ed., 1998), *The Law of Restitution*, pp. 65–67, 366 and 368.

[3] In the sense of having been overpowered, see *Croft v. Graham* (1863) 2 De G. J. & S. 155.

[4] *Bromley v. Smith* (1859) 26 Beav. 644; *Croft v. Graham, ante*; *Fry v. Lane* (1889) 40 Ch.D. 312; *Cresswell v. Potter* [1978] 1 W.L.R. 255.

[5] Re-enacting the provisions of the Sales of Reversions Act 1867.

considering whether the contract is oppressive and the section has done nothing to shift the onus of proof.[6] Here the fact that the "expectant" mortgagor has had independent advice will be important to rebut the presumption of overreaching. The court will, however, look into all the circumstances of the loan. The special jurisdiction of the court to reopen dealings with the expectancies will not, however, now be so often called into play owing to the extensive powers conferred on the court to interfere in cases where the Consumer Credit Act 1974 applies.

5. Control Under the Consumer Credit Act 1974

By reason of the 1974 Act the court now has a general and additional power to reopen extortionate[7] credit agreements[8] if the debtor or mortgagor is an "individual" as defined.[9] It is therefore possible that the case of *Cityland and Property (Holdings) Ltd v. Dabrah*[10] would not have been decided any differently in view of the court's power under section 139 of the 1974 Act.[11]   **26–40**

Finally, it must be remembered that in relatively few cases, where the mortgage is a "regulated agreement" within the meaning of section 189(1) of the Consumer Credit Act 1974, the mortgagor has an overriding right of redemption exercisable at any time.[12]

PART VI: THE EFFECT OF SETTING ASIDE A TRANSACTION

In circumstances where a party succeeds in setting aside a mortgage as against the mortgagee, a number of consequences flow. First, the successful party's beneficial interest will (subject to the matters raised below) be freed from the obligations that would otherwise be imposed upon it by the transaction that has been impeached. Secondly, in circumstances where the successful party is one of two registered proprietors and the transaction is binding on the other proprietor (for example, where the other proprietor is, in fact, the wrongdoer and has forged or otherwise obtained the successful party's signature to the transaction), the beneficial interest of the successful party remains freed from the obligations that would otherwise have been imposed upon it by the impeached transaction (again subject to the matters raised below) whilst the wrongdoer's beneficial interest in   **26–41**

---

[6] *Earl of Aylesford v. Morris* (1873) 8 Ch. App. 484.

[7] By virtue of s.138(1) a bargain is "extortionate" only if it requires payments which are "grossly exorbitant" or if it "otherwise grossly contravenes ordinary principles of fair dealing". For a recent case, see *Coldunell Ltd v. Gallon* [1986] Q.B. 1184.

[8] See *ante* para. 14–08.

[9] s.137(1) and s.189(1), the latter defining the "individual". The powers are contained in s.139(2). See also the similar powers of the court under the Insolvency Act 1986, s.244 in the case of companies and s.343 in the case of bankrupts.

[10] [1968] Ch. 166. In this case there was no provision for interest, but the payment of an extra sum as a "premium" representing 5% interest on the capital sum. The stipulation struck down as "unreasonable and oppressive". This case is difficult to reconcile with *Knightsbridge Estates Ltd v. Byrne* [1939] Ch. 441, see *ante*, pp. 296 *et seq.*

[11] Although it is unclear as to the extent to which the definition of "extortionate" differs from "unfair and unconscionably" see *e.g. Davis and Hedley Cheney v. Directloans Ltd* [1986] 1 W.L.R. 823 at 831.

[12] See *ante* chap. 14.

the property remains subject to the terms of the transaction which the wrongdoer himself has duly executed.[13] From the successful party's point of view this can have a number of consequences. First, the wrongdoer's execution of a mortgage or charge over his beneficial interest in the property will operate to sever any beneficial joint tenancy that may exist in relation to that property.[14] Secondly, the mortgagee is able to exercise all its remedies against the beneficial interest in the property that is properly charged to it. Such remedies obviously include taking possession of the property[15] and obtaining an order for sale.

PART VII: AN ORDER FOR SALE WHERE ONLY PART OF THE BENEFICIAL INTEREST STANDS CHARGED

26–42   An order for sale would, in such circumstances, require the mortgagee to invite the court to exercise its discretion under section 14 of the Trusts of Land and Appointment of Trustees Act 1996. In *The Mortgage Corporation v. Shaire*,[16] Neuberger J. concluded that the enactment of that Act had substantially altered the matters to which the court is now to have regard when exercising its discretion and that any authorities decided under section 30 of the Law of Property Act 1925 (which was repealed by the 1996 Act) should be treated with caution since they were "unlikely to be of great, let alone decisive, assistance".[17] Thus the approach previously adopted by the courts pursuant to which a sale of property would be ordered save other than in exceptional circumstances[18] is no longer good. Instead the court will have regard to all the circumstances of the case and the factors to which it is, by section 15 of the Act, directed to consider. Section 15 provides:

> "(1) The matters to which the Court is to have regard in determining an application for an order under section 14 include—
>
> > (a) The intentions of the person or persons (if any) who created the trust,
> > (b) The purposes for which the property subject to the trust is held,
> > (c) The welfare of any minor who occupies or might reasonably be expected to occupy any land subject to the trust at his home, and
> > (d) The interest of any secured creditor of any beneficiaries.
>
> (2) . . .
> (3) . . . the matters to which the court is to have regard also include the circumstances and wishes of any beneficiaries of full age and entitled to an interest in possession of the property subject to the trust or (in the

---

[13] *First National Securities v. Hegarty* [1985] Q.B. 850.
[14] *Ahmed v. Kendrick* (1988) 56 P. & C.R. 120.
[15] Possession will not be given of a dwelling-house to the mortgagee whilst a party enjoys an arguable defence to any claim (*e.g.* is asserting a defence of undue influence), particularly if the defendants are husband and wife: *Albany Home Loans Limited v. Massey* [1997] 2 All E.R. 609. However, once the strength of that defence has been determined, the usual considerations with regard to granting an order for possession apply.
[16] [2000] 1 F.L.R. 973.
[17] *ibid.*, at 991B–C.
[18] See *Re Citro* [1991] Ch. 142; *Lloyds Bank plc v. Byrne* [1993] 1 F.L.R. 369.

case of dispute) of the majority (according to the value of their combined interests)."[19]

Neuberger J. in *The Mortgage Corporation v. Shaire* held that the inclusion of section 15(1)(d) on an equal footing with sections 15(1)(a)–(c) removed the creditor's preferred status under section 30 of the Law of Property Act 1925, as typified in authorities such as *Lloyds Bank plc v. Byrne*.[20] Thus now, when considering whether a property held subject to a trust of land should be sold, the court will have regard to a number of factors, including those laid down in section 15. In *The Mortgage Corporation v. Shaire*, Neuberger J. further considered the mortgagee's commercial position and security if a sale was not ordered, the hardship that Mrs Shaire (who was, in effect, the innocent party by reason of the forging of her signature to a number of documents) would suffer in the event of an order for sale being made and what other property Mrs Shaire might be able to acquire in the event that a sale was sold and her equity realised.[21] Accordingly, a mortgagee which only enjoys security over part of the beneficial interest in a jointly-owned property cannot be certain that an order for sale will now be made in its favour; much depends on the overall circumstances of each particular case. In the event that the party whose interest is charged has been adjudged bankrupt, a mortgagee can rely on the provisions of the Insolvency Act 1986, which provide the court with a more limited discretion.[22]

PART VIII: THE EQUITY OF EXONERATION

Where, in such circumstances, the property is sold, it will become germane to **26–43** consider which liabilities fall to be deducted as against the interests of those beneficially entitled to share the net sale proceeds. If, for example, a portion of the secured indebtedness affects the totality of the beneficial interest in the property (*e.g.* funds were used to discharge an earlier valid mortgage) and a further portion does not (*e.g.* was advanced in reliance upon the husband's forged signature), how those liabilities are divided between those entitled to share the proceeds will have a profound effect. In the accounting exercise that follows upon a sale, the court will have regard to the equity of exoneration, which can best be demonstrated by reference to a decided case.

In *Re Pittortou (A Bankrupt)*[23] the husband took over the running of a restaurant on his own account, which had previously been run by certain members of his family. He and his wife executed a legal charge in favour of the bank, charging their then matrimonial home to secure any indebtedness to the bank on a bank account which he intended, amongst other things, to use for the purposes of the restaurant. In 1979 the matrimonial home was sold and a new home was purchased and registered in the joint names of the husband and wife, the legal

---

[19] Section 15(4) provides that "This section does not apply to an application if section 335A of the Insolvency Act 1986 (which . . . relates to applications by a trustee of a bankrupt) applies to it."

[20] [1993] 1 F.L.R. 369.

[21] In fact there was no evidence of this before the court but Neuberger J. clearly considered it to be significant: see [2000] 1 F.L.R. 973 at 993G–955C.

[22] See Insolvency Act 1986, s.335A and generally chap. 23.

[23] [1985] 1 W.L.R. 58.

charge on the earlier home was paid off, and a legal charge was executed on the new home by them to secure the bank account which was used both in regard to the conduct of the restaurant business and for payment of expenses in connection with the matrimonial home. In 1981, the husband left the wife and later there was a divorce. Following an act of bankruptcy on June 15, 1982 a receiving order was made on November 22, 1982 and on December 13, 1982 the husband was adjudicated bankrupt. The court held that although the position of the former wife was that of surety so far as her interest in the matrimonial home was concerned, her entitlement to have the secured indebtedness to the bank discharged so far as possible out of equitable interest of the husband depended on their presumed intention; that, since they had acted together in business and family affairs, it could not be presumed that they had intended that the payments out of the bank account should fall wholly on the husband's beneficial interest to the exoneration of the wife's interest; and that, accordingly, the payments made for the joint benefit of the household should be discharged out of the net proceeds of the sale of the house before division but the equity of exoneration should apply to payments made purely for business purposes and for the husband's sole benefit.

PART IX: LIMITATIONS TO THE RELEASE OF THE SUCCESSFUL PARTY'S INTEREST

1. Previous Mortgages—Subrogation & Imputed Consent

26–44   Where the owner of property is able to establish a right to set aside a mortgage over his property or that he is not bound because he was not a party to the contract and the money advanced was used wholly or partly to redeem an existing mortgage, the mortgagee will have some remedies.[24] Assuming that the earlier mortgage was valid, the owner will not be permitted to take the benefit of the redemption of that valid mortgage and escape the transaction that provided the funds for the redemption. The mortgagee whose money was used to redeem the original mortgage will be subrogated to the rights of the original mortgagee. Alternatively, the same result is achieved by the court imputing the owner's consent to a charge on the same terms and to the same extent as the original mortgage to which he actually consented.[25] It follows that although a mortgage may be set aside, the mortgagee may nevertheless be able to establish an equitable charge securing a sum equal to the redemption figure for the prior mortgage on the same terms as that mortgage.

2. Where the Mortgagor agreed to a more limited transaction

26–45   Where a right to set aside a mortgage is established on the basis that the terms of the loan agreement or mortgage were misrepresented, the right to set aside is not qualified or limited to a right to convert the loan agreement or mortgage to an agreement on the terms it was understood were being agreed to. So, for

---

[24] *Equity & Law Home Loans Ltd v. Prestridge* [1992] 1 W.L.R. 379.
[25] *ibid.*

instance, where the right to set aside arose as a result of a misrepresentation to the defendant that the liability secured by the charge was limited to £15,000, the mortgagee's contention that the original mortgage should be set aside on terms that a limited charge or mortgage be granted was rejected and the mortgage was simply set aside.[26] However, where the transaction consists of several distinct parts, for instance where separate advances were made at different times and the matters that give rise to the right to set aside only affect one distinct part of the transaction, the transaction can be severed so that the distinct part can be set aside and the rest survive.[27]

3. **Where the money advanced was used to purchase Property**

Where the money raised by the impugned transaction was used to acquire property or an interest in property, a defendant cannot seek both to set aside the transaction and retain the property acquired. The defendant will only be permitted to set aside the impugned mortgage if any benefit the defendant received is also given back to the mortgagee.[28] **26–46**

4. **Where at least two owners transact**

Where property is held subject to a trust of land with multiple registered owners, any two of those owners acting in their capacity as trustees can give a purchaser or mortgagee a valid receipt[29] so that as between the owners and a mortgagee, the mortgagee need not be concerned with the underlying beneficial ownership. Where there are a number of legal owners of a property, a transaction executed by at least two of them will be binding on all those with an interest in the property. So where two of three registered proprietors grant a mortgage, forging the third owner's signature, the mortgage will be enforceable against the property.[30] **26–47**

---

[26] *TSB Bank plc v. Camfield* [1995] 1 W.L.R. 430.

[27] *Barclays Bank plc v. Caplan* [1998] 1 F.L.R. 532.

[28] *Dunbar Bank plc v. Nadeem* [1998] 3 All E.R. 876. See Chitty, *Contracts* (28th ed., 1999), para. 7–064 and Goff & Jones, (5th ed., 1998); *The Law of Restitution*, pp. 65–67, 366 and 368.

[29] LPA 1925, s.27.

[30] *City of London Building Society v. Flegg* [1988] A.C. 54. The position was recently reviewed and reaffirmed by the Court of Appeal, particularly in light of the introduction of the Trusts of Land and the Appointment of Trustees Act 1996: *Sabherwal v. BMMSL*, unreported, December 17, 1999.

CHAPTER 27

COURT PROCEEDINGS

JURISDICTION

1. High Court; County Court

As a matter of jurisdiction,[1] proceedings by either party to a mortgage[2] can be **27–01** brought in the High Court or, if the claim satisfies the appropriate jurisdictional limits, in the county court. Both courts have concurrent jurisdiction in relation to (a) property wherever situated and which does not comprise a dwelling house[3] in whole or in part and (b) property which does comprise a dwelling house in whole or in part which is situated in Greater London.

(a) *Limitations to the jurisdiction of the High Court*

To this statement, there are a number of important and substantial exceptions. **27–02** First, the county court has exclusive jurisdiction in relation to a regulated agreement under the Consumer Credit Act 1974.[4] Secondly, in relation to possession proceedings in which there is no claim for sale or foreclosure[5] then unless part of the property is situated in Greater London, the proceedings must be brought in the county court if the claim is for possession of property comprising or including a dwelling house.[6] A claim with a value of less than £15,000 cannot be started in the High Court.[7] A claim with a value of less than £50,000 will generally be transferred to a county court[8] unless it is a claim for fraud or undue

---

[1] As opposed to practice which will differ markedly after October 15, 2001; see para. 27–07 discussing the provisions of CPR Part 55 which come into effect on October 15, 2001 and which make provision for where a claim is to be commenced. The effect of CPR Part 55 is to remove substantially all mortgage business from the High Court as a matter of practice, notwithstanding it retains jurisdiction.

[2] With regard to foreclosure proceedings, see also para. 27-07.

[3] A "dwelling house" includes any building or part of a building so used, and it does not matter that part of it is being used for business, trade or other non-residential purposes: County Courts Act 1984, s.21(8).

[4] Consumer Credit Act 1974, s.141.

[5] Such a claim must be a genuine claim. The mere addition of a claim for such relief does not bestow jurisdiction on the High Court (which it otherwise has: County Courts Act 1984, s.21(4)): *Trustees of Manchester Unity Life Insurance Collecting Society v. Sadler* [1974] 1 W.L.R. 770; *Frost Limited v. Green* [1978] 1 W.L.R. 949. The test is to identify the relief which the claimant genuinely seeks: *Trustees of Manchester ante.*

[6] County Courts Act 1984, s.30. In relation to proceedings begun on or after October 15, 2001, regard must be had to CPR Part 55: see *post*, para. 27–08.

[7] CPR, Part 7PD 2.1. See *ante*, n. 6.

[8] CPR Part 29PD 2.1. See *ante*, n. 6.

influence[9] or the circumstances are such that paragraph 7(5) of the High Court and County Courts Jurisdiction Order 1991 apply.[10] That Order and CPR Part 30.3[11] provide that when a court considers the question of transfer to or from a county court, it shall have regard to, *inter alia*, the importance of the action and whether it raises questions of general public interest; the complexity of the facts, legal issues, remedies and procedures involved and whether a transfer is more likely to result in a more speedy trial of claim. A claim for possession which the High Court cannot hear and determine (*i.e.* a claim for possession of a property including a dwelling house outside Greater London) cannot be transferred to the High Court.[12]

(a) *Unlimited jurisdiction of the County Court*

27–03 In addition to issues where the county court has exclusive jurisdiction (regulated mortgages under the Consumer Credit Act 1974 and possession proceedings involving a dwelling house outside Greater London) the county court has unlimited jurisdiction to hear and determine a claim of any value by a mortgagee for payment of principal and interest.[13] The county court also has an unlimited jurisdiction to make an order on an application by a person who is a trustee of land or has an interest in property subject to a trust of land under section 14 of the Trusts of Land and Appointment of Trustees Act 1996, s.14.[14]

(b) *Limitations to the jurisdiction of the County Court*

27–04 The county court has co-extensive jurisdiction with the High Court to hear and determine proceedings for foreclosure or redemption or any mortgage or for enforcing any charge or lien where the amount owing does not exceed the county court limit[15] or proceedings for relief against fraud or mistake, where the damage sustained does not exceed that limit.[16] The county court limit is currently £30,000.[17] This limit can be extended by a signed agreement by the parties to the proceedings or their legal representatives or agents in certain instances.[18] Where the original mortgage advance exceeded the county court limit but the amount owing had, at the date of the commencement of proceedings, been reduced below that limit, the county court has jurisdiction.[19]

---

[9] *ibid.*, para. 2.6.
[10] S.I. 1991 No. 724 (as amended).
[11] See generally CPR Part 30 and the Practice Direction thereto.
[12] *Yorkshire Bank v. Hall* [1999] 1 W.L.R. 1713.
[13] County Courts Act 1984, s.15(1) (as amended).
[14] High Court and County Courts Jurisdiction Order 1991, S.I. 1991 No. 724, art. 2(1)(p) (as inserted by S.I. 1996 No. 3141).
[15] *ibid.*, s.23(c).
[16] *ibid.*, s.23(g).
[17] High Court and County Courts Jurisdiction Order 1991, S.I. 1991 No. 724 (as amended).
[18] County Courts Act 1984, s.24.
[19] *Shields, Whitley and District Amalgamated Model Building Society v. Richards* (1901) 84 L.T. 587.

ALLOCATION OF BUSINESS

1. Part I: Until October 15, 2001

(a) *High Court: Assignment to the Chancery Division; district registries*

Section 61(1) of the Supreme Court Act 1981 provides for the assignment of all **27–05**
proceedings for the purposes of, *inter alia*, the redemption or foreclosure of
mortgages and the sale and distribution of the proceeds of property subject to any
lien or charge to the Chancery Division. CPR, Sched. 1, RSC Ord. 88, r. 2[20]
augments that provision and assigns to the Chancery Division any claim in which
there is a claim for (a) the payment of monies secured by mortgage of any real
or leasehold property or (b) delivery of possession (where before or after
foreclosure) to the mortgagee of any such property by the mortgagor or by any
other person who is or is alleged to be in possession of the property.

A claim begun in any other division which turns on the rights and remedies of
a mortgagor or mortgagee will be transferred to the Chancery Division.[21] A claim
for repayment is only a claim for the purposes of CPR, Schedule 1, RSC Ord. 88,
r. 2 if it is one in which the claimant is relying on the mortgage in order to found
the claim[22]; a claim for repayment due on an ordinary bank account (albeit one
secured on property) can be properly brought in the Queen's Bench
Division.[23]

A claim may not be issued out of a district registry unless it is a Chancery
district registry[24] and only then if the mortgaged property is situated in the
district of that registry.[25]

County Court CPR, Schedule 2, CCR Ord. 4, r. 3 provides that proceedings for **27–06**
the recovery of land, for the foreclosure or redemption of any mortgage or,
subject to Order 31, rule 4 (enforcement of a charging order by sale of the
property charged), for enforcing any charge or lien on land or for the recovery of
monies secured by a mortgage or charge on land may be commenced only in the
court for the district in which the land or any part of the land is situated.

2. Part II: After October 15, 2001

The Civil Procedure (Amendment) Rules 2001[26] and CPR Part 55 which is **27–07**
implemented thereby make provision for the allocation of possession claims[27]
between the High Court and county courts. A possession claim brought by a
mortgagee is subject to CPR Part 55.1–55.10 and CPR Part 55PD.[28]

[20] See Appendix IV.
[21] *Midland Bank v. Stamps* [1978] 1 W.L.R. 635.
[22] *National Westminster Bank plc v. Kitch* [1996] 1 W.L.R. 1316.
[23] *ibid.*
[24] These are Birmingham, Bristol, Cardiff, Leeds, Liverpool, Manchester, Newcastle upon Tyne and
    Preston: Chancery Guide, paragraph 12.1; CDPD 2.
[25] CPR, Sched. 1, RSC Ord. 88, r. 3.
[26] Brought into effect on October 15, 2001 by S.I. 2001 No. 256.
[27] A "possession claim" means a claim for the recovery of possession of land (including buildings
    or parts of building)": CPR Part 55.1(a).
[28] CPR Part 55.1–55.10 and CPR 55PD are to be found in Appendix IV.

(a) *Starting the claim: High Court v. County Court*

27–08   Except where the county court does not have jurisdiction, possession claims
should be brought in the country court for the district in which the land or any
part of it is situated.[29] Only exceptional circumstances will justify starting a claim
in the High Court[30] and these must be certified on the claim form and verified by
a statement of truth.[31] Such circumstances may include complicated disputes of
fact or points of general importance[31a]; they do not normally include the value of
the property or the amount of any financial claim although such factors may be
relevant.[31b] If a claimant starts a claim in the High Court and the court decides
that it should have been started in the county court, the Court will normally either
strike out or transfer it to the county court on its own initiative. There are real
sanctions in such circumstances: not only is there likely to be delay but the court
will normally disallow the costs of starting the claim in the High Court and of any
transfer.[31c] Clearly under CPR Part 55 the number of mortgage cases in the High
Court will fall dramatically.

(b) *Allocation within the High Court*

27–09   With effect from October 15, 2001, CPR, Sched. 1, RSC Ord. 88, rr. 1–5 and r. 7
are revoked.[32] Whilst CPR Part 55 does not make any express provision for the
allocation of business in the High Court to the Chancery Division, it is submitted
that as a matter of practice any business which justifies its commencement in the
High Court under the new regime should be commenced in the Chancery
Division. Moreover, section 61(1) of the Supreme Court Act 1981 provides for
the assignment of all proceedings for the purposes of, *inter alia*, the redemption
or foreclosure of mortgages and the sale and distribution of the proceeds of
property subject to any lien or charge to the Chancery Division.

COMMENCING A CLAIM

27–10   The consideration of how to commence a claim must, of necessity, fall into two
parts: a consideration of the existing procedure and a consideration of the new
procedure introduced by CPR Part 55 with effect from October 15, 2001.

3. Part I: The existing procedure current until October 15, 2001

27–11   The Civil Procedure Rules permit a claimant to use a Part 8 Claim Form where
(a) he seeks the court's decision on a question which is unlikely to involve a

---

[29] CPR Part 55PD, para. 1.2; CPR Part 55.3(1).
[30] CPR Part 55PD, para. 1.2.
[31] CPR Part 55.3(1).
[31a] *ibid.*, para. 1.3.
[31b] *ibid.*, para. 1.4.
[31c] *ibid.*, para. 1.2.
[32] S.I. 2001 No. 256, Sched. 3.

substantial dispute of fact or (b) any rule of practice direction requires or permits the use of a Part 8 Claim Form.[33]

(a) *High Court*

The Practice Direction to Part 8 requires proceedings in the High Court which are **27–12** "mortgage claims" under CPR, Schedule 1, RSC Ord. 88 to be begun by a Part 8 Claim Form.[34] However, if it is known that there is a dispute of fact (where, for example, a mortgagor is claiming that he or she is not bound by the mortgage purportedly executed by him or her because the signature is a forgery or was obtained by undue influence) an ordinary Part 7 Claim Form may be used.[35]

(i) *CPR, Schedule 1, RSC Ord. 88*[36]

A claim in which there is a claim for any of the following remedies: **27–13**

> "(a) payment of monies secured by mortgage;
> (b) sale of the mortgaged property;
> (c) foreclosure;
> (d) delivery of possession (whether before or after foreclosure or without foreclosure) to the mortgagee by the mortgagor or by any other person who is or is alleged to be in possession of the property;
> (e) redemption;
> (f) reconveyance of the property or its release from the security;
> (g) delivery of possession by the mortgagee"[37]

is a "mortgage claim"[38] and governed by the provisions of CPR, Sched. 1, RSC Ord. 88. The full text of that Order is contained in Appendix IV. In particular, it provides that a claim form by which a mortgage claim is begun shall be indorsed with or contain a statement showing where the property is situated and (if that property is outside Greater London) whether it consists of or includes part of a dwelling house.[39] A certificate must also be included that the claim is not one to which section 141 of the Consumer Credit Act 1974 applies.[40]

Furthermore, the order makes provision for the procedural requirements in the Chancery Division in the event that the defendant fails to acknowledge service,[41] for the evidence required in claims for delivery of possession or payment or monies secured by mortgage or both,[42] for the enforcement of a charging order by sale[43] and for the application by a party in whose favour a foreclosure order has been made for possession of the mortgaged property.[44]

---

[33] CPR, Part 8.1.
[34] CPR Part 8BPD, section A.
[35] The Chancery Guide, para. 21.3.
[36] See Appendix IV.
[37] CPR, Sched. 1, RSC Ord. 88, r. 1(1).
[38] *ibid.*, r. 1(3).
[39] *ibid.*, r. 3(2).
[40] *ibid.*
[41] *ibid.*, r. 4.
[42] *ibid.*, r. 5.
[43] *ibid.*, r. 5A.
[44] *ibid.*, r. 7.

(b) *County Court*

27–14   CPR Part 8BPD also requires proceedings commenced in the County Court to be begun by a Part 8 Claim if the claim includes a claim for the recovery of possession of land or, prior to April 26, 1999, would have been commenced by originating application and no other procedure is prescribed.[45] That Practice Direction also requires that the forms specified in CPR Part 4PD are to be used where the claimant intends to make a claim for or which includes the recovery of possession of land.[46] The specified forms are Form N5 (Summons for possession of property) and Form N120 (Particulars of claim for possession (mortgaged property)). Subject to some changes in terminology, these forms replicate those in use prior to the introduction of the Civil Procedure Rules. If the foregoing conditions are not met so as to require a claimant to use a Part 8 Claim Form and the matter is not one in which the court's decision is sought on a question which is unlikely to involve a substantial dispute of fact, the Part 7 procedure laid down in the Civil Procedure Rules should be followed.

(i) *CPR, Sched. 2, CCR Ord. 6*[47]

27–15   The provisions of this Order apply to mortgage claims generally[48] and claims for the possession of land comprising of or including a dwelling house in particular.[49] The order makes detailed provision as to the matters which must be included in the Particulars of Claim.

4. **Part II: the new procedure after October 15, 2001**

27–16   CPR Part 55.3 stipulates that the claim must be started in the county court for the district in which the land is situated (unless CPR Part 55.3(2) (claims in the High Court) applies) and that the claim form (N5, as amended in the light of CPR Part 55) and form of defence (N11M) must be in the form set out in CPR Part 55PD.[50]

27–17   An amended form of Particulars of Claim for possession (mortgaged residential premises) (N120) has also been produced to be used in conjunction with the claim form. All these forms together with the Notice of Issue (N206B) are set forth in Appendix IV in their current form as of July 18, 2001. The Particulars of Claim must be filed and served with the claim form.[51]

27–18   In addition to complying with the requirements of CPR Part 55 and its Practice Direction, the Particulars of Claim must also comply with the requirements of CPR Part 16.[52]

---

[45] CPR Part 8BPD, section B.1.
[46] CPR Part 8BPD, para. 8(2).
[47] See Appendix IV.
[48] CPR, Sched. 2, CCR Ord. 6, r. 5.
[49] CPR, Sched. 2, CCR Ord. 6, r. 5A.
[50] CPR Part 55PD, para. 1.5.
[51] CPR Part 55.4.
[52] *ibid.* See CPR 16.4.

PARTIES TO THE CLAIM

Obviously the parties to the mortgage should be joined as parties to any claim for **27–19** relief in connection with that mortgage. Consideration must be given to joining other parties, having regard to the relief claimed (*e.g.* sureties).

Where a mortgage of land consists of or includes a dwelling house, a "connected person"[53] to the mortgagor who is able, under the Family Law Act 1996 to meet the mortgagor's liabilities can apply to be joined prior to the final disposal of the matter and may be joined in a party to those proceedings if the court sees no special reason precluding joinder and is satisfied the connected person may be expected to assist in satisfying the mortgagor's liabilities to the mortgagee and that accordingly, that expectation may affect the outcome of the proceedings or that the expectation of the connected person's assistance should be considered by the Court when exercising its discretion under section 36 of the Administration of Justice Act 1970.[54]

PURSUING THE CLAIM UNDER CPR PART 55

Although the detailed procedural considerations and requirements of a posses- **27–20** sion claim are beyond the scope of this work and the substantive legal aspects concerning the various claims that may be brought and defended are considered elsewhere in the text, the changes effected by CPR 55 with regard to procedure after October 15, 2001 merit consideration.

1. The mortgagor's response

The mortgagor is not required to acknowledge service of the claim form and **27–21** Particulars of Claim.[55] His defence, however, must be in the prescribed form[56] and if one is not filed within 14 days, he is not precluded from taking part thereafter in the proceedings but the court may take his failure to file a defence into account when deciding what order should be made concerning costs.[57] CPR Part 12 (default judgments) do not apply to possession claims.[58]

2. The first hearing

A hearing date will be fixed by the court when the claim form is issued[59] which **27–22** will be not less than 28 days nor more than eight weeks from the date of issue.[60]

---

[53] A spouse, former spouse, co-habitants or former co-habitant.
[54] Family Law Act 1996, s.55(3).
[55] CPR Part 55.7(1).
[56] CPR Part 55.3(5).
[57] CPR Part 55.7(3).
[58] CPR Part 55.7(4).
[59] CPR Part 55.5(1).
[60] CPR Part 55.5(3).

At that hearing, the court may determine the claim or give case management directions.[61] If the claim is genuinely disputed on grounds which appear to be substantial, the claim will be allocated to either the fast track or the multi-track.[62]

3. Evidence

Unless the matter is allocated to the fast track or multi-track or the court orders otherwise, any fact that needs to be proved by evidence at a hearing at which the court decides the claim or gives case management directions may be proved by evidence in writing[63] and each party should wherever possible, include all the evidence he wishes to present in his verified statement of case.[63a] The Practice Direction requires the claimant's evidence to include the amount of any mortgage arrears and interest on those arrears, which should (if possible) be up to date to the date of the hearing (if necessary specifying a daily rate of arrears and interest).[63b] In addition the Practice Direction states that the defendant should give evidence of (1) the amount of any outstanding social security or housing benefit payments relevant to any mortgage arrears and (2) the status of any claims for social security or housing benefit about which a decision has not yet been made and (3) any applications to appeal or review a social security or housing benefit decision where that appeal or review has not yet been concluded.[63c] If the maker of the witness statement does not attend the hearing and the other party disputes material evidence contained in that statement, the court will normally adjourn the hearing so that oral evidence can be given.[63d] The Practice Direction specifically draws attention to the fact that pursuant to section 113 of the Land Registration Act 1925, office copies of the register and of documents filed at H.M. Land Registry (including original charges) are admissible in evidence to the same extent as the originals.[63e]

(a) *Fast or multi-track?*

27–23 When allocating to either of these tracks, the court is to have regard to the matters set out in CPR 26.8 (as modified by the relevant Practice Direction), the amount of any arrears of mortgage instalments, the importance to the defendant of retaining possession and the importance to the claimant of obtaining vacant

---

[61] CPR Part 55.8(1).

[62] CPR Part 55.5(2), (3).

[63] CPR Part 55.8(3).

[63a] CPR Part 55PD, para. 5.1.

[63b] CPR Part 55PD, para. 5.2. That paragraph further states that CPR Part 55.8(4) does not prevent such evidence being brought up to date orally or in writing on the day of the hearing if necessary.

[63c] CPR Part 55PD, para. 5.3.

[63d] *ibid.*, para. 5.4.

[63e] *ibid.*, para. 5.5.

possession.[64] The financial value of the property will not necessarily be the most important factor in deciding the track for a possession claim and the court may allocate a claim to the fast track notwithstanding the value of the property is in excess of £15,000.[64a]

Allocation to the small claims track is only possible by consent.[65]

4. Steps required of the mortgagee prior to the first hearing

In addition to the filing and service of a claim form and Particulars of Claim, **27–24** CPR 55 provides the following:

(1) If the mortgagee seeks possession of land which consists or of includes residential property, he must send a notice to the property addressed to "the occupiers" not less than 14 clear days[66] before the hearing stating that a possession claim for the property has started; providing details of both his name and address and that of the defendant and details of the court which issued the claim form and, furthermore, provide details of the hearing.[67] At the hearing the claimant must produce a copy of the notice and evidence that he has served it.[68]

(2) All witness statements must be filed and served at least two clear days before the hearing.[69] Thus, if that period includes a Saturday, Sunday, a Bank Holiday, Christmas Day or Good Friday, that day does not count.[70] So, if the hearing is on Tuesday, March 6, the evidence must be served on or before Thursday, March 1.

(3) If the claimant has effected service of the claim form and Particulars of Claim, he must produce at the hearing a copy of a certificate of service.[71]

(a) *Consumer Credit Act Claims Relating to the Recovery of Land*

Any application by the defendant for a time order under section 129 of the Consumer Credit Act 1924 may be made either in his defence or by application notice in the proceedings.[71a]

---

[64] CPR Part 55.9(1).
[64a] CPR Part 55PD, para. 6.1.
[65] CPR Part 55.5(2).
[66] CPR Part 2.8(2), *i.e.* not including the day on which the period begins or the day of the hearing.
[67] CPR Part 55.10.
[68] *ibid.*
[69] CPR Part 55.8(4); CPR Part 2.8(2).
[70] CPR Part 2.8(4).
[71] CPR Part 55.8(6).
[71a] CPR Part 55PD, para. 7.1.

COURT ORDERS

27–25 The contents of a foreclosure order nisi and order absolute are considered elsewhere.[72] The contents of many other orders, for example, an order for the taking of an account and the making of any inquiries that may be necessary, will require bespoke tailoring according to the circumstances of the case and reference may usefully be made to specialist texts.[73]

1. Orders for possession

27–26 The court will not, in general, make an order for possession against only one of two mortgagors in possession of the mortgaged property since such an order is of little benefit to the mortgagee, especially where the mortgagors are husband and wife. So where, for example, the mortgagors are husband and wife and the former admits the validity of the mortgage is against his beneficial interest in the mortgaged property and the latter disputes the validity as against her beneficial interest, the court will adjourn the mortgagee's proceedings for possession as against the husband with permission for the mortgagee to restore the same in the event that the wife leaves the mortgaged property or an order for possession is made against her.[74]

Where an order for possession is made against those in possession of the property, the following considerations apply.

(a) *High Court*

27–27 An order for immediate possession in favour of the mortgagee requires the mortgagor to deliver up vacant possession of the mortgaged premises[75] in accordance with the terms of the order. The order should, wherever practicable, express the last date for compliance as a calendar date and include the time of the day by which the possession must be delivered up.[76] The parties can agree to vary the specified date by an agreement contained in writing.[77] In the event that possession is not yielded up in accordance with the order, a writ of possession can be issued[78] without permission, except, *inter alia*,[79] where more than six years has elapsed since the date of the order[80] or the party entitled to enforce the order or the party against whom the order falls to be enforced has died.[81] If an application for permission is necessary, the application is made in accordance

---

[72] See *ante*, para. 16–98 *et seq.*
[73] *e.g. Atkin's Encyclopaedia of Court Forms* (1997) Vol. 28, Mortgages.
[74] *Albany Home Loans Limited v. Massey* [1997] 2 All E.R. 609.
[75] *National Union Life Insurance Society v. Preston* [1957] 1 W.L.R. 813.
[76] CPR Part 2.9(1).
[77] CPR Part 2.11.
[78] In accordance with CPR, Sched. 1, RSC Ord. 46 r. 6.
[79] See CPR, Sched. 1, RSC Ord. 46, r. 2.
[80] *ibid.*, r. 2(1)(a).
[81] *ibid.*, r. 2(1)(b). Applications for permission in this particular instance are dealt with without notice: CDPD 7—Mortgages and possession orders. See Appendix IV.

with CPR Part 23 and must be accompanied by a witness statement of evidence containing the prescribed information.[82]

A suspended order for possession will be in the prescribed form.[83] In the event   **27–28** that the conditions imposed by the court are not complied with, the mortgagee will have to apply to the Master at a further hearing on notice for permission to issue a writ of possession.[84] The application notice and the evidence upon which the applicant intends to rely must be served on each party in default not less than three clear days prior to the hearing[85] and must be lodged with the Masters' clerk at least one clear day before the hearing, having been indorsed with a certificate of service.[86]

(i) *Writ of restitution*

If, having obtained possession of the mortgaged property from the mortgagor   **27–29** under a writ of possession, the mortgagee is dispossessed by the mortgagor going back into possession, the court may permit a writ of restitution[87] to be issued.[88] The application for such a writ should be supported by evidence and is made without notice to the Master. The issue of a writ of restitution is the normal procedure; an application to commit the mortgagor for contempt of court is inappropriate.[89]

(b) *County Court*

An order for immediate possession will be in the prescribed form[90] as will a   **27–30** suspended order for possession.[91] In the event that the mortgagor does not deliver up possession of the mortgaged property in accordance with the terms of the order and the mortgagee wishes to enforce the order for possession, the mortgagee must file a request[92] certifying that the property has not been vacated in accordance with the order for possession and provide the prescribed details.[93] A warrant of possession will then be issued.[94] Permission is required to issue a warrant of possession where *inter alia*,[95] where more than six years has elapsed since the date of the order[96] or the party entitled to enforce the order or the party against whom the order falls to be enforced has died.[97]

---

[82] *ibid.*, r. 4.
[83] Chancery Masters' Practice Form, PF5: see Appendix IV.
[84] CPR, Sched. 1, RSC Ord. 46, r. 2(1)(d) applying r. 4.
[85] CDPD 7; Mortgages and possession orders. See Appendix IV.
[86] *ibid.* The certificate should be in the form contained in the Practice Direction.
[87] In Form No. 68.
[88] CPR, Sched. 1, RSC Ord. 46, r. 3.
[89] *Alliance Building Society v. Austin* [1951] 2 All E.R. 1068.
[90] Form N.29: see Appendix IV.
[91] Form N.31: see Appendix IV.
[92] In Form N325.
[93] CPR, Sched. 2, CCR Ord. 26, r. 17.
[94] In Form N49.
[95] See CPR, Sched. 2, RSC Ord. 26, r. 5.
[96] *ibid.*, r. 5(1)(a).
[97] *ibid.*, r. 5(1)(b).

(i) *Warrant of execution*

27–31 Such a warrant may be issued,[98] with the permission of the court, in aid of any warrant of possession.[99] The application is made without notice and must be supported by evidence of the wrongful re-entry into possession following the execution of the warrant of possession plus such further facts as would permit the issue of a writ of restitution in the High Court.[1]

On execution of a warrant of possession by the bailiff, a representative of the mortgagee should be in attendance in order to take possession of the property from the bailiff and secure it.

Setting aside an order or warrant An order for possession or any warrant for possession can be set aside even after the warrant has been executed if (a) the order giving rise to the warrant is set aside[2] or (b) the warrant has been obtained by fraud or (c) there has been an abuse of process or oppression in its execution.[3]

COSTS OF PROCEEDINGS AGAINST THE MORTGAGOR[4]

1. Recovery from the security

27–32 A mortgagee has an equitable right to obtain reimbursement from the security that he holds for those costs which he has reasonably and properly incurred in proceedings between the mortgagee and mortgagor and the mortgagor's surety[5] and the same are not usually within the discretion of the court unless misconduct is charged and proved.[6] Moreover, most well-drawn mortgages also make express provision for the mortgagee to add all and any costs that he has incurred to his security, often on an indemnity basis, thereby augmenting the equitable right. In the absence of special agreement, they are not a personal debt of the mortgagor.[7] In addition, at the conclusion of any proceedings, the court has a discretion to award costs in a party's favour.[8] Generally, the court will order costs to be paid by the unsuccessful party to the successful party[9] but, having regard to all the circumstances and in particular the parties' conduct,[10] the court may make a different order if justice so requires.[11]

---

[98] In Form N50.
[99] CPR, Sched. 2, CCR Ord. 26, r. 17(4).
[1] CPR, Sched. 2, CCR Ord. 26, r. 17(5).
[2] *Peabody Donation Fund Governors v. Haly* (1986) 19 H.L.R. 145.
[3] *Hammersmith & Fulham London Borough Council v. Hill* (1995) 27 H.L.R. 368.
[4] See also *ante*, paras 25–06 and 25–18.
[5] *Parker-Tweedale v. Dunbar Bank plc (No. 2)* [1991] Ch. 26; *Goomba Holdings Limited v. Minories Finance Limited (No. 2)* [1993] Ch. 171.
[6] *Charles v. Jones* (1886) 33 Ch. D. 80.
[7] *Frazer v. Jones* (1846) 5 Hare 475; *Sinfield v. Sweet* [1967] 1 W.L.R. 1489. See also para. 27–35.
[8] See generally CPR Part 44.3.
[9] CPR Part 44.3(2).
[10] CPR Part 44.3(5).
[11] CPR Part 44.3(6). *BCCI SA v. Ali (No. 3)* (1999) 149 N.L.J. 1734.

2. Interrelationship between the mortgagee's rights and the court's discretion

The following principles emerge.

27–33

(1) The court's exercise of its discretion under the Civil Procedure Rules remains a matter solely within its remit having regard to the appropriate circumstances of each case.

(2) However and generally speaking, an order for costs pursuant to the court's discretion should be made in such terms as reflects the mortgagee's contractual entitlement.[12]

(3) The court may deny a mortgagee the benefit of his equitable or contractual rights to add his costs to the security in circumstances where such an outcome would be appropriate.[13] A mortgagee's right to recover his costs by adding them to the mortgage security arises from the jurisdiction inherent in a court of equity to fix the terms on which the mortgagor may redeem the mortgaged security.[14] Accordingly, it follows that a court may disallow the mortgagee's costs if to permit them to be recovered from the mortgage debt would be inequitable as an exercise of its statutory discretion to award costs[15] or of its equitable discretion to fix the terms upon which the mortgagor can redeem the mortgaged security or both.[16]

(4) In order for a mortgagee to be deprived of his equitable or contractual right to add his costs to the security, the court should determine that issue specifically with reference to the mortgagee's specific rights; an adverse order for costs against a mortgagee will not be sufficient to deprive the mortgagee of his rights.[17]

3. Assessment of costs

The basis of the assessment of the mortgagee's costs (whether in the taking of an account or on a detailed assessment) should correspond to that contained in the mortgage deed[18] and, if the same is silent in that regard, the standard basis is the appropriate basis[19] unless the court, in the exercise of its discretion, considers that the mortgagee's costs of any litigation should be assessed on the indemnity basis. In practice, even if the mortgagee's costs are assessed on an indemnity basis, he will not necessarily recover all his costs. A mortgage deed will never be construed so as to require the payment by the mortgagor of all the mortgagee's costs, charges and expenses even if improperly or unreasonably incurred or

27–34

---

[12] *Goomba Holdings Limited v. Minories Finance Limited (No. 2)* [1993] Ch. 171: a contractual provision for costs on an indemnity basis was reflected in an order for taxation.

[13] See *ante*, paras 25–06 and 25–18.

[14] *Parker-Tweedale v. Dunbar Bank plc (No. 2)* [1991] Ch. 26; *Goomba Holdings Limited v. Minories Finance Limited (No. 2)* [1993] Ch. 171.

[15] Supreme Court Act 1981, s.51 (as amended); CPR Part 44.3.

[16] *Parker-Tweedale v. Dunbar Bank plc (No. 2)* [1991] Ch. 26; *Goomba Holdings Limited v. Minories Finance Limited (No. 2)* [1993] Ch. 171.

[17] *ibid.*

[18] *Goomba Holdings Limited v. Minories Finance Limited (No. 2)* [1993] Ch. 171.

[19] *Re Adelphi Hotel (Brighton) Limited* [1953] 1 W.L.R. 955.

improper or unreasonable in amount; an express provision to that effect would be open to serious question on public policy grounds[20] or under the provisions governing unfair contractual terms.

4. **Recovery from the mortgagor personally**

27–35   Generally, a mortgagor is not personally liable for the mortgagee's costs in the absence of special agreement to that effect,[21] most modern mortgages are drafted so as to impose that liability, however.

If the mortgagor raises a defence which fails and the mortgage security is insufficient to bear those costs, the mortgagor must pay the unsecured balance of those costs personally.[22] If the mortgagor brings a redemption action and then fails to redeem, he is liable personally to pay the costs of that action, which will be dismissed.[23]

[20] *Goomba Holdings Limited v. Minories Finance Limited (No. 2)* [1993] Ch. 171 at 187–188.
[21] *Frazer v. Jones* (1846) 5 Hare 475; *Sinfield v. Sweet* [1967] 1 W.L.R. 1489.
[22] *Liverpool Marine Credit Co. v. Wilson* (1872) 7 Ch. App. 507.
[23] *Mutual Life Assurance Society v. Langley* (1886) 32 Ch.D. 460.

Appendix I

PRECEDENTS

A: Legal Charges and Mortgages

1. Skeleton of Legal Charge or Mortgage

A–01   THIS [MORTGAGE]
             LEGAL CHARGE] is made   [date]

between
        [PARTIES[1]]

WHEREAS:—

        [RECITALS]

TESTATUM 1
NOW [receipt of advance *or*
        acknowledgement of existing debt]

THIS DEED WITNESSETH AS FOLLOWS:—
        [Borrower's covenant to pay principal and interest
        Reduction of interest on punctual payment

TESTATUM 2
        Demise, sub-demise or charge of mortgaged property
        Proviso for redemption or discharge
        Date on which mortgage money falls due
        Borrower's covenants

        Other operative clauses including lender's powers]

ATTESTATION CLAUSE

THE SCHEDULE(S)

2. Recitals

(a) Borrower's Title

A–02   (1) Borrowers' freehold title
The Borrower is seised for his own benefit of the property described in the
Schedule hereto ("the mortgaged property") for a legal estate in fee simple in
possession [subject as hereinafter mentioned but otherwise][2] free from
incumbrances

---

[1] The Borrower and Lender (not the Mortgagor and Mortgagee, to avoid errors in copying) may be
  defined with reference to their respective successors in title: (a) "the Borrower" shall where the
  context admits include persons deriving title under the Borrower or entitled to redeem this security;
  (b) "The Lender" shall where the context admits include persons deriving title under the
  Lender.
[2] Include these words if there are restrictive covenants or easements and list them in the
  Schedule.

(2) Borrower's leasehold title

The Borrower is possessed of the property described in the Schedule hereto ("the mortgaged property") for a legal estate for the residue of the term of years granted by the lease short particulars of which are set out in the said Schedule subject to the rent reserved and the covenants and conditions herein contained but otherwise free from incumbrances[3]

Where the Borrower has the capacity identified in recitals (3) to (7) below, omit the words "for his own benefit" but otherwise use recital (1) and continue after "incumbrances" as follows:

(3) Personal representatives[4-6]

as the personal representatives of [name of deceased] late of [address as in probate or letters of administration] [whose Will was proved by] [letters of administration to whose estate were granted to] the Borrowers on (date) [in] [out of] the [Principal] [name of district] Probate Registry

(4) Trustees of land solely in that capacity

as trustees of land

(5) Trustees of land beneficially entitled to the whole property

as trustees of land for themselves beneficially as [joint tenants] [tenants in common in equal shares] [part of their partnership property]

(6) Tenant for life

    (i) The said property is settled land the legal estate herein having been duly vested in the Borrower upon the trusts of the settlement by a Principal Vesting Deed [date] made between [parties] pursuant to the Settled Land Act 1925 and the Borrower accordingly has and can exercise the powers of a tenant for life under the said Act over the said property

    (ii) The Trustees are the trustees of the said settlement for the purpose of the said Act as stated in the said Vesting Deed

(b) Loan Agreement and Acknowledgment of Debt

(1) Loan agreement   **A–03**

The Lender has agreed with the Borrower to lend to him [the sum advanced] upon having the repayment thereof with interest thereon secured as appears herein below

(2) Acknowledgment of existing debt

The Borrower is indebted to the Lender in the sum of [amount of debt] and it has been agreed that in consideration of the Lender forbearing to enforce the immediate repayment thereof, repayment of the said debt with interest thereon shall be secured as appears herein below

---

[3] This form is suitable for an unincumbered lease where the whole of the property is mortgaged.

[4-6] If the property is being charged to raise money for administration, include in the recital of the loan agreement the phrase "which is required by the Borrowers as personal representatives as aforesaid for the purposes of administration."

(3) Loan agreement where building is to be financed: obligation to make further advances

    (i) The mortgaged property includes a dwelling-house now under construction and the Borrower has requested the Lender to lend him [total sum to be advanced] for the purpose of enabling him to complete the construction of the said dwelling-house which the Lender has agreed to do upon having the repayment thereof and of any other further advances which the Lender may agree to make to the Borrower with interest thereon secured as appears herein below

    (ii) Upon the treaty for the said loan it was agreed that the sum of [amount of initial advance] being part of the sum of [total sum to be advanced] aforesaid should be paid by the Lender to the Borrower on the execution of this deed and that the residue of the said [total sum to be advanced] should be paid as appears herein below

(4) Loan agreement where security extends to further advances but without obligation to make them

The Lender has agreed to lend to the Borrower the sum of [amount of initial advance] upon having the repayment thereof and of every other sum which may be advanced by the Lender to the Borrower with interest thereon secured as appears herein below

(5) Further security for loan already secured by legal charge on other land

    (i) By a legal charge ("the Mortgage") [date] between the parties to this deed certain property known as [address and brief description] was charged to the Lender to secure repayment of the sum of [amount advanced under the Mortgage] and interest at the rate of [   ] per cent. per annum thereon

    (ii) [Recite title of Borrower to subject-matter of further security]

    (iii) Upon the treaty for the advance of [amount advanced under the Mortgage] it was agreed that the repayment of the moneys made payable by it should be further secured by a mortgage of [description of property which is the subject-matter of the further security] [the property described in the Schedule hereto]

(6) Loan agreement where the borrower wishes to raise money for the purposes of the Settled Land Act 1925

The Borrower requires to raise the sum of [total sum to be advanced] for purposes authorised by section 71 of the Settled Land Act 1925 and the Lender has agreed to lend the same to the Borrower upon having the repayment thereof with interest at the rate hereinafter mentioned secured in a manner hereinafter appearing

(c) Subsisting Prior Mortgages

A–04 (1) Borrower's title—freehold property

The Borrower is seised of the property described in the First Schedule hereto ("the Mortgaged Property") for a legal estate in fee simple in possession subject (as mentioned in the said Schedule) to the [Legal Charge(s)] [Mortgage(s)] ("the

Prior Mortgage(s)") particulars of which are contained in the Second Schedule hereto

(2) Borrower's title—leasehold property
The Borrower is possessed of the property described in the First Schedule hereto ("the Mortgaged Property") for a legal estate for the residue of the term of years granted by the Lease mentioned in the said Schedule subject to the rent reserved and the covenants and conditions thereby contained and subject also as further mentioned in the said Schedule and to the [Legal Charge(s)] [Mortgage(s)] ("the Prior Mortgage(s)") particulars of which are contained in the Second Schedule hereto but otherwise free from incumbrances

(3) State of Mortgage debt
The principal sum of £[   ] remains owing on the security of the prior mortgage [but all interest thereon has been paid up to the date hereof] [together with the sum of £[   ] for interest thereon]
  Or:
There are now owing on the security of the prior mortgage the sum specified in the particulars contained in the Second Schedule hereto [but all interest thereon has been paid up to the date thereof] [together with the sums specified in the said particulars for interest thereon]

(d) Persons Joining In or Consenting

(1) Surety's agreement to act as such   **A–05**
The Surety has agreed to join in this deed as surety for the Borrower in manner hereinafter appearing

(2) Lessor's consent to charge of leasehold property
The consent of the Lessor (as required by the said lease) has been duly obtained by a consent in writing and dated [   ]

(3) Agreement of prior incumbrancer to postpone[7–8]
The [holder of the prior charge] has agreed to join in this deed for the purpose of postponing [the prior charge] to the security hereby created in manner hereinafter appearing

3. Testatum 1

NOW in pursuance of the said agreement and in consideration of   **A–06**
either [the sum of [amount advanced] now paid to the Borrower by the Lender the receipt of which the Borrower hereby acknowledges]
or
    [the forbearance of the Lender to enforce immediately the payment of the said debt of [amount of debt]]

[7–8] This is a suitable form where the spouse with the right of occupation under the Family Law Act 1996 agrees to postpone his or her charge to another security.

(a) Covenants to Pay

(1) Covenant to pay principal and interest
THIS DEED WITNESSETH AS FOLLOWS:

   The Borrower HEREBY COVENANTS with the Lender to pay to the Lender on [repayment date] the sum of [amount advanced] with interest thereon from the date hereof at the rate of [rate] per cent. per annum AND FURTHER if the said sum of [amount advanced] shall not be so paid to the Lender interest at the rate aforesaid by equal [interval] payments on [payment dates] in each year on the principal moneys for the time being remaining due on this security or on any order or judgment which may be recovered hereunder

Covenants for payment by instalments or lender's agreement to accept instalment payments (covenants (2) to (5))

(2) Covenant to pay by instalments where loan is interest-free
The Borrower HEREBY COVENANTS with the lender to pay to the Lender the said sum of £ [amount advanced] by equal [interval] instalments of £[amount of instalment] to be made on [payment dates] the first payment to be made on [first payment date] until the whole of the said sum of £[amount advanced] has been duly paid and satisfied [and no right to interest on the said sum shall be implied hereby]

(3) Flat rate system
If the Borrower shall pay to the Lender the said principal sum of £[amount advanced] with interest hereon at the rate [aforesaid][9] from the date hereof by the instalments at the times and in the manner set out herein, namely, by [number of instalments] equal [interval] instalments of £[aggregate amount of principal and interest] each the first instalment to be paid on the [date][10] and a subsequent instalment on every [payment dates] or within [   ][11] days after each such day and if

[there has been no breach of any provision contained in this deed or implied by law and on the part of the Borrower to be observed or performed (other than the covenant for payment of the mortgage money and interest contained in clause [number of clause])[12] of this deed][13]

[the power of sale applicable hereto (which notwithstanding this present provision shall be deemed to arise on [date])[14] shall not have become exercisable][15]

---

[9] If there is a provision for reduction of interest on punctual payment, replace "aforesaid" by the following: "[higher rate] reducing to [lower rate] as provided in clause [ ] hereof".

[10] This should be the date for repayment which is normally six months from the date of the mortgage deed.

[11] Usually 14 days.

[12] The number of the clause containing the borrower's covenant to repay principal and interest.

[13] This alternative should be used if the mortgage deed contains a clause excluding the operation of s.103 of LPA 1925. The author of *Hallett's Conveyancing Precedents* (1965) considers that it would be fairer to omit such a clause where the mortgage is of a dwelling-house and the borrower is in personal occupation (see p. 629, n. 3) but it is frequently found nowadays in building society mortgages.

[14] Usually 14 days.

[15] Should be used if s.103 of LPA 1925 has not been excluded.

then the Lender shall apply each such instalment in payment of the interest for the time being due on this security and subject thereto in reduction of the said principal moneys and shall accept payment of the said principal sum and the interest thereon by the instalments at the times and in the manner aforesaid.[16]

(4) Repayment by fixed instalments[17]
If the Borrower shall pay to the Lender on [first payment date] and thereafter every [interval] the sum of £[   ] on account of the principal sum due hereunder and also shall pay to the Lender on [dates as before] interest at the rate aforesaid on the principal moneys for the time being unpaid

[   ][18]

then the Lender shall accept payment of the said principal sum hereby secured and the interest thereon by the instalments at the times and in the manner aforesaid

(5) Repayment by equal instalments[19]
If the Borrower shall pay to the Lender on [first payment date] and thereafter for the next subsequent [number of instalments] [intervals] instalments of combined principal and interest of £[amount of instalment] each apportioned as to £[   ] to principal and as to the balance to interest

[   ][20]

then the Lender[21] . . .

The Borrower can covenant directly to pay by instalments and a provision can be inserted whereby the whole debt shall become immediately payable in the event of default

---

[16] No notice is required if the borrower wishes to exercise his right to pay off the mortgage on the contractual date for repayment: *Crickmore v. Freeston* (1871) 40 L.J.Ch. 137. It appears to be a settled rule of practice that once the borrower has failed to pay principal and interest on the legal redemption date, he must either give the lender six months' notice of his intention to pay off the mortgage, or pay six months' interest in lieu: *Fitzgerald's Trustee v. Mellersh* [1892] 1 Ch. 385 at 388; *Smith v. Smith* [1891] 3 Ch. 550 at 552. In the latter case it was said that there were recognised exceptions to the rule: see *Bovill v. Endle* [1896] 1 Ch. 648, where it was held that the rule does not apply where the lender takes proceedings to recover the mortgage money from the borrower or his estate and that going into possession is equivalent to taking proceedings. The mere fact that the mortgage is an instalment mortgage and contains a term precluding the lender from making immediate demand for payment or otherwise immediately enforcing his security does not displace the lender's right "to go into possession before the ink is dry on the mortgage" (*per* Harman J., *Four-Maids Ltd v. Dudley Marshall (Properties) Ltd* [1957] Ch. 317): see *Esso Petroleum Co. Ltd v. Alstonbridge Properties* [1975] 1 W.L.R. 1474 at 1483–1484 and *Western Bank v. Schindler* [1977] Ch. 1 at 10, CA.
[17] In the flat-rate system, the repayment is by fixed regular instalments in which the proportion of capital to interest increases throughout the mortgage period: but in the fixed-instalment system, the amount of the principal repaid is the same in every instalment and the interest decreases throughout the term.
[18] See nn. 12 or 14 above, depending on whether the operation of s.103 of LPA 1925 has been excluded.
[19] This form is suitable where the total sum to be repaid consists of the advance plus a lump sum representing interest at the agreed rate, not reducing over the period of the mortgage.
[20] See n. 16, (fixed-instalment system).
[21] Continue as for fixed-instalment system ((4) above).

in payment of any instalment. Such a clause is not a penalty.[22] In order to exercise his power of sale the Lender has to prove that the instalments are in arrears. If there is a direct covenant to repay by instalments and no redemption date is specified in the mortgage deed, the Borrower may not be able to redeem until the date of the final payment. In *De Borman v. Makkofaides*[23] it was held that, on the true construction of the special stipulations (*infra*), the principal outstanding did not not become due so long as the instalments were paid before the expiration of the stipulated notice period:

"3. The statutory power of sale shall be exercisable in any of the following events:

(a) If default is made in payment of the principal moneys for the time being owing on this security or any instalment thereof for one month after notice requiring payment thereof shall have been served on the borrower.

(b) If the borrower fails to observe any of his obligations hereunder after reasonable notice (not being less than one month) has been served on the borrower by the lender requiring him to perform the same.

(c) If the borrower commits any act of bankruptcy or if execution is levied against him or if distress is levied on the chattels of the borrower on the said property.

4. If the borrower shall pay to the lender the quarterly instalments hereinbefore referred to in repayment of the said sum of £18,000 the lender shall not (except as aforesaid) enforce the security hereby constituted."

The more usual form of a covenant for repayment by instalments is a covenant to repay at a fixed date with a proviso that if the specified instalments are paid on the payment dates or within a specified time-limit, the Lender will not require payment in any other manner.

(b) Proviso for Reduction of Interest Rate on Punctual Payment[24]

If the Borrower shall on [any] [every][25] day on which interest is hereby made payable or within [number of days] thereafter pay to the Lender interest on the principal moneys for the time being owing on this security at the rate of [reduced rate] per annum and if the power of sale applicable hereto[26] has not become exercisable[27] then the Lender will accept interest at such reduced rate for the [period][28] for which such interest shall be so paid to him.

---

[22] *Sterne v. Beck* (1863) 1 De G.J. & Sm. 595; *Wallingford v. Mutual Society* (1880) 5 App. Cas. 685, HL, *per* Lord Hatherley at 702; *Protector Endowment and Annuity Loan Co. v. Grice* (1880) 5 Q.B.D. 592, CA, *revsing* (1880) 5 Q.B.D. 121; *Cityland and Property (Holdings) Ltd v. Dabrah* [1968] Ch. 166 (provision that not only the whole debt but the whole of an added premium became due on default, held unreasonable on the facts).

[23] (1971) 220 E.G. 805.

[24] Unless an increase in the rate of interest in the event of the borrower's default is commercially justifiable and its dominant purpose is not to deter the borrower from acting in breach (see *Lonsdale Finance plc v. Bank of Zambia* [1996] Q.B. 752 where an increase of 1% p.a. was permitted), an increased rate is a penalty and void: see *Nicholls v. Maynard* (1747) 3 Atk. 519, following *Holles v. Wyse* (1693), *Higgins* (1689) 2 Vern. 134; *Strode v. Parker* (1694) 2 Vern. 316. Thus draftsman adopt the approach of allowing a discount for prompt payment in order to circumvent this restriction. See *Nicholls v. Maynard* (1747) 3 Atk. 519, following *Holles v. Wyse* (1693) 2 Vern. 289 (increase for non-punctual payment relievable in equity); *cf. Marquis of Hallifax v. Higgens* (1689) 2 Vern. 134; *Strode v. Parker* (1694) 2 Vern. 316. For the position where interest is omitted from the mortgage deed, see *ante*, pp. 437 *et seq.*

[25] If the word "every" is used, the right to reduction is terminated on the occasion of the first non-punctual payment: if "any," then it is lost for that period.

[26] See s.101 of LPA 1925.

[27] See s.103 of LPA 1925. The operation of this section is often excluded.

[28] Usually a quarter or half-year.

4. Testatum 2

(a) Form of Charge or Demise

(1) Charge of freeholds

A–07

The Borrower as [capacity][29] HEREBY CHARGES BY WAY OF LEGAL MORTGAGE[30] with [full] [limited] title guarantee All That the mortgaged property [(subject as stated in the Schedule hereto)[31]] with the payment to the Lender of the principal moneys interest and other money[32] hereby covenanted to be paid by the Borrower [or otherwise secured][33]

(2) Charge of leaseholds

The Borrower as [capacity][34] HEREBY CHARGES BY WAY OF LEGAL MORTGAGE[35] with [full] [limited] title guarantee All That the mortgaged property [[and all other (if any) the premises comprised in and demised by the Lease mentioned in the Schedule hereto][36]]

---

[29] *Conveyances prior to July 1995*: The covenants implied in a *conveyance* by a person conveying and being expressed to convey as a beneficial owner are the same as those implied in a *mortgage* by such a person. In a mortgage, however, they extend to persons from whom the mortgagor derives title, whether or not for value: see s.76(1)(*C*), (*D*) of, and Pts III, IV of Sched. 2 to LPA 1925. Hallett, *Conveyancing Precedents* (1965), at pp. 156–157 and 611, n. 16(ii) considers that the "beneficial owner" covenants are implied if the form of words in the text is used, whether or not the borrower actually is the beneficial owner as does Megarry and Wade, *The Law of Real Property* (6th ed., 2000), para. 5–056. In *Eastwood v. Ashton* [1915] A.C. 900 at 921, it was held that a purchaser could sue a vendor on the implied covenants for title as beneficial owner although the vendor's title had at the time of the case been extinguished by adverse possession. In *Pilkington v. Wood* [1953] 1 Ch. 770 at 777, Harman J. said, *obiter*, that it was a *sine qua non* that the covenantor must be, in fact, as well as being expressed to be, the beneficial owner. The learned editor of *Emmet on Title* (19th ed.), para. 14.003, considers that the words "conveys and is expressed to convey" ought to be construed as "expressly purports to convey," and that the views expressed in *Pilkington v. Wood* (and see also *Fay v. Miller, Wilkins & Co.* [1941] Ch. 360, CA: *Re Robertson's Application* [1969] 1 W.L.R. 109 at 112) are in conflict with the idea behind s.76 and with direct authority not cited in those cases. Nevertheless, the latest direct authority cited in support of the view expressed in Emmet is *Parker v. Judkin* [1931] 1 Ch. 475 and it may well be advisable to provide expressly that the "beneficial owner" covenants be implied. Hallett, *op. cit.* at p. 611 proposes the following: "Covenants by the Borrower with the Lender on the terms set forth in [Part III] [Parts III and IV] of the Second Schedule to the Law of Property Act 1925 shall be implied in this Legal Charge."

Conveyances after June 1995: The Law of Property (Miscellaneous Provisions) Act 1994 repeals (subject to limited saving and transitional provisions) LPA 1925, s.76. Under the 1994 Act a person disposing of property will do so subject to certain implied covenants if he does so expressly with "full title guarantee" or, to a lesser extent, "limited title guarantee": see LPA (MP) 1994, ss.1–6; Megarry and Wade, *The Law of Real Property* (6th ed., 2000), paras 5–066—5–071.

[30] See s.87 of LPA 1925 for the power, protections and remedies of a chargee by way of legal mortgage. The section refers to "a charge by deed expressed to be by way of legal mortgage." Such wording is unnecessary in a charge of registered land: *Cityland and Property (Holdings) Ltd v. Dabrah* [1968] Ch. 166 at 171, but Goff J. (as he then was) did not express any opinion as to the need for them in a charge of unregistered land.

[31] Include these words if the mortgaged property is subject to easements or restrictive covenants.

[32] See LPA 1925, Sched. 5, Form 1. The words "other money" apply to costs which the borrower has specifically covenanted to pay.

[33] The words "or otherwise secured" refer to moneys which may become due under the mortgage but which there is no specific covenant to pay.

[34] See n. 29 above.

[35] See n. 30 above.

[36] Omit these words if the mortgaged property is part only of the property originally demised.

(3) Mortgage of freeholds by demise

The Borrower as [capacity][37] HEREBY DEMISES unto the Lender with [full] [limited] title guarantee All That the mortgaged property to hold the same unto the Lender for the term[38] of [   ][39] years from the date hereof without impeachment of waste[40] [subject as is mentioned in the said Schedule][41] and subject also to the proviso for cesser on redemption contained herein[42] namely:

(4) Mortgage of leaseholds by sub-demise

The Borrower as [capacity][42a] HEREBY DEMISES unto the Lender with full [or limited] title guarantee All That the property described in the Schedule hereto and comprised in and demised by the Lease mentioned herein TO HOLD unto the Lender henceforth for all the residue of the term of years created by the Lease except the last 10 days thereof subject to the said rents covenants and conditions and subject also to the proviso for cesser on redemption contained herein namely:

(5) Second mortgage of freeholds by demise

As in (3) up to the word "years," then continue:

. . . and [one][43] day from the date hereof without impeachment of waste [subject as is mentioned in the said Schedule and] subject to the prior mortgage and to the principal moneys and interest thereby secured and also subject to the proviso for cesser on redemption contained herein namely:

(b) Provisos for cesser or discharge

A–08   (1) Discharge of legal charge

If the Borrower shall on [date][44] pay to the Lender the sum of £[amount of advance] with interest thereon from the date hereof at the said rate[45] the Lender will at the request and cost of the Borrower duly discharge this security[46]

---

[37] See nn. 29 and 30 above.

[38] The term granted is a legal term of years: s.1(1)(*b*), LPA 1925. S.149 of that Act makes it clear that entry is not required before it can take effect: *cf.* the position before 1926, see *Lewis v. Baker* [1905] 1 Ch. 46: *Re Moore and Hulm's Contract* [1912] 2 Ch. 105.

[39] The most usual length of term granted is 3,000 years from the date of the mortgage: but see the first specimen abstract to Sched. 6 to LPA 1925 (1000 years). There is no general rule as to the minimum length of the term; but see s.10(2) of the Trustee Act 1925 for a case where a minimum of 500 years is required.

[40] In accordance with the provisions of Pt. VII, Sched. I to LPA 1925. "Waste" means voluntary waste, that is, doing that which ought not to be done. For a discussion of waste, see Megarry and Wade, *Law of Real Property* (6th ed., 2000), paras 3–098—3–103.

[41] Include these words if the mortgaged property is subject to restrictive covenants or easements.

[42] The date mentioned in the proviso for cesser should be the same as the date for repayment in the covenant to repay.

[42a] See *ante*, nn. 29–30.

[43] Where there is a series of mortgages, each term is normally made one day longer than the mortgage term immediately prior to it, but this is not necessary: LPA 1925, s.149(5).

[44] The date specified should be the same date as that in the covenant for repayment.

[45] Insert before "rate" the word "reduced" if the deed contains a covenant for reduction of interest on punctual payment.

[46] This provision is not always included in a legal charge. The purpose of it is to make ascertainable the date when the right to foreclosure arises but in its absence it is normally accepted that the right arises on the date specified in the covenant for repayment.

(2) Proviso for cesser on redemption

PROVIDED that if the Borrower shall on [date][47] pay to the Lender the sum of £[amount of advance] with interest hereon from the date hereof at the said rate[48] the said term hereby granted shall absolutely cease and determine[49]

(c) Date on which Mortgage falls Due

The mortgage money shall become due and the statutory power of sale and of appointing a receiver shall arisé on [repayment date][50]

Borrower's Covenants and other Operative Clauses

(a) Covenants to Insure and Maintain the Security

(1) To [repair and][51] insure[52]   **A–09**

To keep the [mortgaged property][53] [buildings for the time being comprised in or subject to this security][54] insured against loss or damage by fire (and such other risks as the Lender from time to time in writing directs) [in the name of the Lender] [in the joint names of the Lender and the Borrower][55] to the full value thereof with some insurance office or underwriters approved by the Lender and duly and punctually to pay all premiums and other payments required for effecting and keeping up such insurance as and when the same shall become due and when required by the Lender to produce to him the policy or policies of such insurance and the receipt for each such payment

(2) To [repair and] insure, where the property charged is leasehold property and there are adequate repairing and insuring covenants in the lease

To keep the mortgaged property [in repair and] insured in accordance with the covenants in that behalf contained in the said Lease and to pay duly and

---

[47] See n. 44 above.

[48] See n. 45 above.

[49] See n. 45 above. The provision is normally included in a mortgage by demise or sub-demise, for the reason given in n. 46. The term ceases automatically on repayment, having become a satisfied term (LPA 1925, s.116) and merging in the reversion expectant on the term out of which it was created (*ibid.* s.5).

[50] Normally six months after the date of the mortgage deed. If there is no express provision, the power of sale *arises* when the mortgage money has become due (LPA 1925, s.101). In the absence of any term specifying that date, it is the date for repayment of the mortgage money or, if repayable by instalments, the date of the first instalment: see *Payne v. Cardiff R.D.C.* [1932] 1 K.B. 241. In the case of a mortgage for securing further advances, it is usual for the mortgage money to be deemed to have become due at the date for repayment of the initial advance.

[51] The obligation to keep in repair may be expressed in short form by inserting the following words: "in good and substantial repair (allowing the Lender to enter and view the state of repair of the same at all reasonable times without becoming liable as mortgagee in possession)". It is prudent for the lender to insert the non-accountability clause since, once a mortgagee has gone into possession he remains accountable, in the absence of some such provision, after he has gone out of possession: *Re Prytherch* (1889) 42 Ch.D. 590, at 599–560.

[52] Statutory powers relating to insurance are conferred on a mortgagee by deed, but they can be varied or extended, or displaced by contrary intention expressed in the deed: see LPA 1925, ss.101(1)(ii) and 108. A person interested is also given the right to have insurance moneys expended in reinstatement: Fire Prevention (Metropolis) Act 1774, s.83. In spite of its title, it is a general, not a local, Act, and it applies as between borrower and lender: *Sinnott v. Bowden* [1912] 2 Ch. 414; *Portavon Cinema Co. Ltd v. Price and Century Insurance Co. Ltd* [1939] 4 All E.R. 601 at 607.

[53] If defined or described in a Schedule.

[54] See *ante*, n. 51 if an obligation to repair is imposed.

[55] Neither phrase need be used.

punctually all premiums necessary for keeping up such insurance and to produce to the Lender on demand [the policy or policies of such insurance[56] and] the receipt for every such payment

(3) Application of insurance moneys[57]
All moneys received on any insurance whatsoever in respect of loss or damage by fire or otherwise to the mortgaged property or any part thereof shall if the Lender so requires be applied in making good the loss or damage or in or towards the discharge of the money for the time being owing thereon

(4) To repair buildings—long form
To keep the buildings for the time being comprised in this security in good condition and repair . . .

(5) To enter, inspect and execute repairs
Add to (4) after "repair" where lender is to be entitled to enter, inspect and execute repairs:

. . . and if the Borrower shall fail to do so the Lender may at any time thereafter enter upon the premises or any part thereof and execute such repairs as (in the opinion of the Lender) may be necessary or proper without thereby becoming liable as mortgagee in possession and the Borrower will on demand[58] repay to the Lender all the expenses thereby incurred by the Lender and will pay interest at the rate of [rate] per cent. per annum from the date of demand until repayment on any moneys not repaid on demand as aforesaid and all such expenses and interest shall be charged on the property hereby [mortgaged] [charged][59]

(6) To appoint a surveyor to survey the property
Add to (4) after "repair" where lender is to be entitled to appoint a surveyor to survey the property, numbering (4) as sub-clause (i):

(ii) For the purpose of ascertaining whether the said buildings are for the time being in good condition and repair the Lender may from time to

---

[56] If the policies are in the borrower's possession.

[57] It is important to include this covenant because otherwise the borrower would not be liable to apply moneys received under a policy, not effected under the mortgage, in making good or in discharge of the mortgage debt. In *Halifax Building Society v. Keighley* [1931] 2 K.B. 248 it was held that, where a borrower effects an insurance elsewhere independently, and a claim arises which is met by the two companies in their due proportions, the mortgagee has no claim to the proportion paid by the independent company.

It is not considered that the alternative way of dealing with this problem (*i.e.* a covenant not to insure in any other office) is a satisfactory protection for the mortgagee, as any breach of the covenant would normally come to light only when the claim had been made.

[58] This obligation may, alternatively, form part of a covenant for payment and charge of costs, charges and expenses: see *Encyclopedia of Forms and Precedents* (5th ed.) Vol. 28, forms 2.30, 2.36 at pp. 129, 134, respectively.

[59] The power given by this covenant should be cautiously exercised by the lender, as he will be liable, to the extent the repairs executed are not necessary or proper, as mortgagee in possession. He will be allowed the cost of necessary and proper repairs: see *Sandon v. Hooper* (1843) 6 Beav. 246: affd. (1844) 14 L.J.Ch. 120. Alternatively, where income-producing property is in disrepair, he could appoint a receiver and give him written directions as to the necessary or proper repairs, the cost of which the receiver must pay out of money received by him. For the power to appoint a receiver, see LPA 1925, s.101(1)(iii), and for the manner in which the receiver is to apply money received by him towards repairs, see s.109(8)(iii) of that Act.

time cause the same to be surveyed by a competent surveyor appointed by the Lender and such surveyor may without rendering the Lender liable as a mortgagee in possession at all reasonable times enter upon the said premises or any part thereof for the purpose of making a survey of the said buildings and the certificate of such surveyor shall be conclusive as to the state of repair and condition of the said buildings;

(iii) If the Borrower shall fail to do any repairs to the said buildings certified by any such surveyor as aforesaid to be necessary and proper the Lender may at any time thereafter enter upon the premises and execute the same without thereby becoming liable as mortgagee in possession;

(iv) On demand to repay to the Lender [the reasonable remuneration of any surveyor appointed by the Lender for making any such survey of the said buildings and] all expenses incurred by the Lender in the execution of such repairs as aforesaid and will pay interest at the rate of [rate] per cent. per annum from the date of demand until repayment on any moneys not repaid on demand as aforesaid all which moneys and interest shall be charged on the property hereby mortgaged.

(b) To Observe and Perform Conditions, etc.

(1) To observe and perform conditions (short form)[60] **A–10**
To observe and perform all covenants provisions and regulations affecting the mortgaged property

(2) The same (longer form)[61]
To observe and perform all restrictive and other covenants all building regulations and all restrictions conditions and stipulations (if any) for the time being affecting the mortgaged property or the mode of user or enjoyment of the same or any part thereof

(3) To pay outgoings, etc.
To pay all outgoings and to keep the mortgaged property free from any charges taking priority over the money hereby secured[62]

(4) Not to commit waste, etc.
Not to commit any waste upon or injure or in any manner or by any means lessen the value of the mortgaged property or any part thereof

---

[60] Some such clause as this is desirable so as to make the mortgagee's power of sale exercisable on breach of an obligation.

[61] See n. 60 above.

[62] Where a local authority has a charge in respect of the expense of executing works required to render a house fit for human habitation, or on premises of frontagers for expenses incurred in making up private streets, it has the same powers and remedies as if it were a mortgagee by deed having powers of sale and lease and of appointing a receiver. See the Housing Act 1985, ss.200, 229 (works executed pursuant to repair and improvement notices respectively); Highways Act 1980, s.212(3) where the powers arise by virtue of s.7 of the Local Land Charges Act 1975, pursuant to registration of the charge under s.5 thereof.

(c) In Respect of Building and Planning

A–11   (1) To erect a dwelling-house, where the purpose of the charge is to finance building

To proceed with and continue the erection of the said dwelling-house in a proper manner and with due diligence and to the satisfaction of the surveyor for the time being of the Lender within such time as shall be reasonably required by the Lender and to expend in the erection of the said dwelling-house

[the sum of £[amount to be spent]]

[the sum named in the contract dated [date] and made between [parties]].

(2) The same, including lender's power to re-enter and complete if the borrower fails to do so

To construct and complete the said dwelling-house at his own cost and before [date] in a proper and workmanlike manner fit for immediate habitation with proper drains sewers and conveniences and in accordance with the plans and specifications therefor and the byelaws and regulations applicable thereto (and to the satisfaction of [the surveyor for the time being of the Lender] [the surveyor or other proper officer of [the local authority]]) and to expend [continue as in (1) above]

If the Borrower shall fail to construct and complete the said dwelling-house as aforesaid in accordance with the covenant by him hereinbefore contained the Lender may at any time enter upon the mortgaged property and complete the same and may for that purpose use any plant or materials belonging to the Borrower and all expenses incurred by the Lender under this power shall be deemed to have been properly incurred under this security.[63]

(3) Authorised use of premises: Lender's powers on default

Not without the consent of the Lender and of the competent authority to use or suffer or permit the use of the mortgaged property[64] for any other purpose than its present use and if such consent is given by the competent authority to deliver a copy of the said consent to the Lender

And if the Borrower persists in such other use after a refusal of consent on the part of the Lender any and every power or remedy conferred on the Lender by the Law of Property Act 1925 (as varied and extended by this deed) shall become exercisable by the Lender

(4) To produce notices[65]

To produce to the Lender immediately on receipt any order direction requisition permission notice or other matter affecting or likely to affect the mortgaged property and served on the Borrower by any third party and [allow the Lender to

---

[63] If there is a charging clause (see (8) below) the costs and expenses may be made subject to it.
[64] "Suffer" is said to have a wider meaning than "permit" in that its meaning includes allowing something to be done which the covenantor is fully able to prevent: see *Barton v. Reed* [1932] 1 Ch. 362 at 375. To sell land, knowing that the purchaser intends to use it for some purpose other than the specified purpose is not to "permit" that use: see *Tophams v. Earl of Sefton* [1967] 1 A.C. 50.
[65] The very wide powers given to Ministers and authorities to serve notices requiring things to be done or requisitioning property make it advisable that all parties interested in the property should be fully aware of such notices.

make a copy thereof] [allow the Lender to retain the same but the Borrower shall be entitled to retain a copy thereof]

(5) To comply with statutory conditions
If at any time permission be obtained for any development of the mortgaged property within the provisions of the Town and Country Planning Act 1990 or any statutory amendment or replacement thereof or order made thereunder, to comply with all conditions subject to which permission is granted

(6) To comply with enforcement notices: lender's power to comply on default
To comply in all respects and at his own expense with the requirements of any valid enforcement notice or order made or served by a competent authority under or by virtue of the Town and Country Planning Act 1990 or any statutory amendment or replacement thereof or any order made thereunder requiring the discontinuance of or imposing conditions on the use of the mortgaged property or any part thereof or requiring the removal or alteration of any works or buildings thereon within the time specified therein (or within [period] from the date thereof whichever is the shorter)
    In the event of the Borrower failing to comply as covenanted hereinbefore with any such requirement as is mentioned herein the Lender may in so far as the same may be necessary to comply with such requirement enter upon the mortgaged property and execute any works and do anything thereon necessary to ensure such compliance upon giving the Borrower [number] days' notice in writing of the intention to do so and all costs and expenses incurred by the Lender under this power shall be deemed to have been properly incurred under this security

(7) Power of attorney
The Borrower hereby irrevocably appoints the Lender and the persons deriving title under him to be his attorney to apply for and procure on his behalf any licences permissions or other things from any competent authority necessary for the execution of the repairs and other works hereby authorised to be executed by the Lender on default of the Borrower

(8) Covenant to repay money properly paid under the security, costs charges and expenses
The Borrower will on demand repay to the Lender all money properly paid and all costs charges and expenses properly incurred hereunder by the Lender (as to such costs charges and expenses on a full indemnity basis)[66] together with interest thereon from the time of paying or incurring the same until repayment at the rate aforesaid and until so repaid such costs charges and expenses shall be charged upon the property for the time being subject to this security and shall be

---

[66] Unless this clause is included the costs charges and expenses do not constitute a debt for which the borrower can be sued: they are added to the security. In the absence of any contractual provision the costs in a mortgage action are recoverable by the lender on the standard basis. The view of the majority of commentators is that it is possible to contract that the costs should be recovered on an indemnity basis: see Hallett, *Conveyancing Precedents*, (1965), p. 613, n. 29(i) summarising the views up to 1965, and *Fisher and Lightwood's Law of Mortgage* (10th ed., 1988) p. 660 and cases there cited. Prideaux, *Precedents in Conveyancing* (25th ed.) Vol. 2, p. 443 suggests that such a provision might be considered harsh and unconscionable and thus be held invalid. See *Gomba Holdings UK Ltd v. Minories Finance Ltd (No. 2)* [1993] Ch. 171 at 187, CA.

added to the principal money hereby secured and interest thereon as aforesaid shall be charged upon the same property and shall be payable by equal [interval] payments on the respective dates hereinbefore appointed for payment of interest on the said principal money

(d) Modifications of Statutory Powers

A–12 (1) Retention of power to consolidate[67]
The restriction on the right of consolidating mortgage securities contained in section 93 of the Law of Property Act 1925 shall not apply to this [Mortgage] [Legal Charge]

(2) Borrower's covenant not to grant leases or accept surrenders without Lender's consent[68]
During the continuance of this security the Borrower shall not without the consent[69] in writing of the Lender grant or agree to grant any lease or tenancy of the mortgaged property or any part thereof or accept or agree to accept a surrender of any lease or tenancy

(3) Extension of Lender's leasing power
The statutory power of leasing conferred on the Lender shall be extended so as to authorise the Lender to grant leases and make agreements for leases for any term and at any rent with or without payment of a fine or premium [provided that any such fine or premium paid to the Lender shall be applied by the Lender as if it were money paid to the Lender on the exercise of the power of sale conferred or implied by this deed]

(4) Exclusion of section 103 of the Law of Property Act 1925 and extension of the powers of sale and of appointing a receiver
Section 103 of the Law of Property Act 1925 shall not apply to this security and the statutory powers of sale and appointing a receiver shall arise on [repayment date] and shall become exercisable by the Lender without notice to the Borrower immediately on the happening of any one or more of the following events:

> (i) if the Lender demands payment of any money repayable on demand and secured by this deed and it is not repaid immediately;
> (ii) if any payment of any money secured by this deed payable in any other manner or interest payable under it is not paid on the due date whether demanded or not;

---

[67] This clause need be inserted only where there is to be a series of charges of different properties in favour of the lender. It is advisable to register the right, if reserved, as a general equitable charge.

[68] It is advisable to frame the provision in this form rather than merely to exclude the exercise of the statutory powers by the borrower for, if that is done and the borrower grants a lease without the mortgagee's consent, it is a lease outside the statute and is not a breach of the terms of the mortgage: see *Iron Trades Employers Insurance Association Ltd v. Union Land and House Investors Ltd* [1937] Ch. 313.

[69] It is for the lessee to prove that the lender gave his consent and if he fails to do so, the lease does not bind the lender: *Taylor v. Ellis* [1960] Ch. 368. The provision sometimes found in the clause, that no intending lessee shall be concerned to inquire as to such consent, is best omitted, since, if it is included, the lender is estopped from denying that consent was given: *Lever Finance Ltd v. Needleman Property Trustee* [1956] Ch. 375. See also *post*, n. 76, para. A–14.

(iii) if the Borrower makes default in fulfilling or observing any of his obligations under this deed or any deed made by way of further assurance or supplemental to it;

(iv) if the powers of sale or appointing a receiver become exercisable under any other security given before or after this deed by the Borrower to the Lender or to any third party or if any money payable to the Borrower under any such other security is not paid within [14] days of the due date;

(v) if any distress or execution is levied or issued against any property of the Borrower or any steps are taken by any person to enforce any rights against the mortgaged property;

(vi) if the Borrower dies or is adjudicated bankrupt[70] or enters into any agreement or composition with his creditors or becomes of unsound mind or otherwise incapable of managing his affairs or being a company, is wound up or placed into liquidation or administration or enter into an agreement or composition with its creditors.

(5) Power to sell by instalment sale

The statutory power of sale is hereby modified so that any sale by the Lender may be in such form as to the manner thereof as to the method of payment of the purchase price and otherwise as the Lender may think fit.

(6) Covenant against registration[71]

No person or persons shall be registered under the Land Registration Acts 1925 to 1986 or any Act amending or reamending the same as proprietor or proprietors of the mortgaged property or any part thereof without the consent in writing of the Lender [and the costs incurred by the Lender of entering any caution against registration of the mortgaged property shall be deemed to be costs properly incurred by the Lender under this security][72]

(e) Surety Covenants

(1) Imposition of liability on the Surety[73]   **A–13**

The Surety hereby covenants with the Lender to jointly and severally perform and be bound by in accordance with the terms of this deed each and every

---

[70] A petitioner in bankruptcy must establish that the debtor cannot pay, or has no reasonable prospect of being able to pay: Insolvency Act 1986, s.267(2).

[71] This clause is very rarely required. Its purpose is to prevent the borrower from registering his title in H.M. Land Registry without the knowledge of the lender and obtaining a land certificate. It is unnecessary (i) if the land is already registered; (ii) when, as in the case of a first mortgage, the documents of title are handed over to the mortgagee; and (iii) if the mortgage is of unregistered freehold land or of a lease with more than 21 years to run which is protected by a deposit of title deeds and is executed after March 1998, since such mortgages trigger a requirement for compulsory registration of the underlying legal estate: LRA 1925, ss.123(2), 123A(1) inserted by the Land Registration Act 1997. A mortgage lender, will in such circumstances receive a charge certificate on completion of registration.

[72] When the clause is used, the words in brackets should be omitted if the mortgage deed contains a covenant to repay money properly paid, costs charges and expenses (see (8) para. A–11.

[73] Alternatively, the Borrower's obligation to make payment see *ante*, para. A–06 *et seq.* and to abide by all or certain specified covenants can be made expressly a joint and several obligation with the Surety, as appropriate, having to regard what the surety is able to covenant to do. In such circumstances, minor amendment of earlier precedents will be necessary.

obligation of the Borrower and without prejudice thereto to pay the Lender all and any sums due and owing to the Lender under the terms of this deed or due and owing by the Borrower, on demand.

(2) Where as between the Borrower and the Surety the Borrower is primarily liable[74]
As between the Borrower and the Surety the Borrower and the mortgaged property shall be primarily liable for the payment of the moneys hereby secured but this provision shall not prejudice the Lender in the exercise of any of his rights and remedies for enforcing this security

(3) Where as between the Surety and the Lender the Surety is a principal debtor
As in (2) up to "hereby secured" then continue as follows:

But as between the Surety and the Lender the Surety shall be treated as principal debtor for the moneys hereby secured And[75] the Surety shall not be released from liability hereunder by time given to the Borrower or any other variation of the provisions of this deed or by anything by reason of which but for this provision the Surety would have been released

Other Operative Clauses and Provisos

A–14   (1) Warranty that Borrower is in personal occupation
The Borrower HEREBY WARRANTS to the Lender that the Borrower is in personal occupation of the whole of the mortgaged property and that neither it nor any part of it is now let or agreed to be let[76]

(2) Freedom from accountability as mortgagee when out of possession
If the Lender shall enter into possession of the mortgaged property or part thereof he may from time to time at pleasure go out of such possession and shall not be liable to account as mortgagee in possession while in fact out of such possession PROVIDED that notice of such fact shall within [7] days after its happening be served on the Borrower[77]

---

[74] If this clause is used, the surety may in certain circumstances be released from his obligation. Thus if time is given to the borrower by way of a binding agreement for good consideration, the surety is released: *Rouse v. Bradford Banking Co.* [1894] A.C. 586 at 594. Although in general he is discharged by the creditor dealing with the principal debtor in a manner inconsistent with the contract the performance of which the surety had guaranteed, it has been held that he will not be discharged if there is a variation which is to his benefit or is insubstantial.

[75] This provision is effective to prevent waiver of the lender's rights against the surety by reason of a variation of the terms of the contract between the lender and the borrower.

[76] This clause reinforces the borrower's covenant not to lease or agree to lease without the lender's consent. If the warranty is given fraudulently and the tenant is a party, the lender is not bound by the tenancy granted: *Church of England Building Society v. Piskor* [1954] Ch. 553 at 614, and damages are available for breach of such warranty, whether or not the breach is fraudulent.

[77] The purpose of this clause is to prevent the lender being permanently liable to account on the footing of wilful default on the ground that, having gone into possession, he can never be held to go out: *Re Prytherch* (1889) 41 Ch.D. 590 at 599.

(3) Attornment clause[78]

The Borrower hereby attorns tenant to the Lender of the mortgaged property during the continuance of this security at the yearly rent of a peppercorn if demanded but nothing in this clause shall prevent the Lender from at any time entering on and taking possession of the mortgaged property and so determining the tenancy hereby created [after giving the Borrower or leaving upon the said property at least [7] days' notice in writing to quit][79]

(4) Lender's covenant to make further advances

The Lender HEREBY COVENANTS with the Borrower that he will from time to time advance to the Borrower[80] within [10] days after being so requested such further sums as the Borrower shall by notice in writing to the Lender request to be advanced not exceeding in the whole the sum of £[total amount of advances] including the sum of £[the initial advance] now advanced

PROVIDED ALWAYS that:

(i) the obligation of the Lender to make further advances shall only apply if and so long as the Borrower shall pay all interest payable hereunder within [14] days from the time hereby appointed for payment thereof and shall perform all his obligations under the covenants on his behalf herein contained or implied by statute (other than in regard to the payment of principal and interest);

(ii) no request shall be made as aforesaid for the payment [at any one time] [in any [3] month period] of a larger sum than £[ ] or [at any one time] a smaller sum than £[ ] and in either case the sum so requested shall be a multiple of £[100];

(iii) the aggregate amount of such advances shall not at any time exceed [three-quarters] of the sum for the time being certified in writing by a surveyor to be approved by the Lender and whose charges shall be paid by the Borrower as having been expended in material and labour for

---

[78] The original purpose of an attornment clause was to enable a lender to distrain for money due from the borrower and to obtain summary judgment. It is now invalid so far as it purports to confer a right of distress unless it is registered as a bill of sale (Bills of Sale Act 1878, s.6). In *Alliance Building Society v. Pinwill* [1958] Ch. 788 it was held that an attornment clause did not create the relationship of landlord and tenant so as to bring s.16 of the Rent Act 1957 (now s.5 of the Protection from Eviction Act 1977) into operation, and a similar decision was reached in *Steyning and Littlehampton Building Society v. Wilson* [1951] Ch. 1018 where an attornment clause relating to agricultural land was held not to create a tenancy within the Agricultural Holdings Act 1948. It is said, on the basis of the decision in *Regent Oil Co. Ltd v. J.A. Gregory (Hatch End) Ltd* [1966] Ch. 402 that an attornment clause enables restrictive covenants in the deed on the part of the borrower to be enforced against his successors in title. See *ante*, para. 3–36.

[79] There is no need to serve a notice terminating the tenancy but if it is provided that a notice should be served, proceedings cannot be begun until it has been served and the time limit has expired: *Woolwich Equitable Building Society v. Preston* [1938] Ch. 129; *Hinckley and Country Building Society v. Henny* [1953] 1 W.L.R. 352.

[80] It may be desired to make the covenant a personal covenant between the original lender and borrower, in which case the following proviso may be added:

(iv) the benefit of this covenant shall be personal to [name of borrower] and the burden of this covenant shall be personal to [name of lender] and such benefit and burden shall not pass to their respective personal representatives or any other persons respectively deriving title under them.

See Hallett, *Conveyancing Precedents* (1965), pp. 624–626 for other variations.

the construction of the said dwelling-house or works incidental thereto or [three-quarters] of the value of the said dwelling-house on the open market, which ever is the [less] [greater].[81]

(5) Proviso that debt shall not be called in for term certain[82]

If the Borrower shall comply with all his obligations hereunder the Lender shall not before the [   ] day of [   ][83] call in the said principal money hereby secured or any part thereof or take any other steps to enforce this security[84] PROVIDED nevertheless that the statutory power of sale shall as aforesaid be exercisable at any time after the said [date]

(6) Proviso restricting redemption for term certain[85]

The Borrower shall not be entitled to redeem this security during the period of [   ] years[86] from the date thereof unless the Lender shall have gone into possession or appointed a receiver of the mortgaged property or taken any other steps to enforce this security

(7) Proviso restricting dealings with equity

Not without the written consent of the Lender to convey assign transfer mortgage or otherwise howsoever dispose of the mortgaged property

(8) Lender's power (if lending on second mortgage) to settle and pass accounts

The Lender may settle and pass the accounts of any person in whom the First Mortgage may for the time being be vested and all accounts so settled and passed shall be conclusive in favour of the Lender and shall bind the Borrower

(9) Stipulation negativing Borrower's personal liability[87]

The Borrower shall not be liable personally for any of the principal money interest or other money secured by this deed

---

[81] The proviso will be used, *inter alia*, where there is a charge to secure present and future advances to finance building.

[82] At the earliest, the estimated date of completion of the building.

[83] This proviso does not affect the borrower's right to redeem on the contractual date. *Cromwell Property Investment Co. v. Western and Toovey* [1934] Ch. 322. s.10(2) of the Trustee Act 1925 authorises trustees lending on mortgage to contract that the principal shall not be called in for a period not exceeding 7 years.

[84] Where there is an obligation to make further advances.

[85] Even if there is a term restricting the lender from calling in the debt, the term must not be unduly long. Each case depends on its facts: see *Teevan v. Smith* (1882) 20 Ch.D. 724 at 729 (5 or 7 years considered reasonable; *Fairclough v. Swan Brewery Co.* [1912] A.C. 562, PC; *Knightsbridge Estates Trust v. Byrne* [1939] Ch. 441, CA, where a 40-year postponement was held not to be unreasonable, but at [1940] A.C. 613 the House of Lords decided the case independently of the Court of Appeal's reasoning, on the ground that the mortgage, being a debenture, could be made irredeemable. Ten years was held not unconscionable or unreasonable in *Multiservice Bookbinding L.A. v. Marden* [1979] Ch. 84. (See also *Davies v. Directloans Ltd* [1986] 1 W.L.R. 823).

[86] The same date as in the proviso not to call in.

[87] It is appropriate to include this clause if the borrowers are personal representatives or trustees with no beneficial interest in the mortgaged property.

Execution and Attestation Clauses[88]

(1) Non-corporate parties[89]   **A–14A**

Signed as a deed by [full name] in the presence of [witness's full name].[90]

(2) Corporate parties[91]

Signed as a deed by [company's name] acting by [name], a director and [name], [a director] [its secretary].[92]

The common seal of [company's name] was affixed in the presence of [director's name], a director and [name] its secretary.[93]

[SEAL]

---

[88] Taken from Land Registration Rule 1925, Sched. 3 as inserted by Land Registration Rules 1997, S.I. 1997 No. 3037.

[89] LP(MP)A 1989, s.1.

[90] The clause should be so laid out that the executing and attesting parties can sign consecutively beside their names.

[91] The clause should be so laid out that the signing and attesting parties can sign beside their representative names.

[92] Companies Act 1986, s.36A prescribes the formalities. A company may execute a deed under seal: s.36A(2).

[93] See n. 91.

B: Equitable Mortgages

NOTE

An equitable mortgage will arise if the interest to be mortgaged is purely equitable or a contract which satisfies section 2 of the Law of Property (Miscellaneous Provisions) Act 1989 is entered into. The long established practice of creating an equitable mortgage by the deposit of title deeds (with or without a memorandum of deposit which would otherwise fail to satisfy section 2) has not survived the 1989 Act: *United Bank of Kuwait Plc v. Sahib* [1997] Ch. 107.

To satisfy section 2, an equitable mortgage must be made in writing, signed by both parties and incorporate all the terms agreed.[94] Thus, after September 27, 1989 the principal attraction of an equitable mortgage of land (ease and informality of creation) is lost. Accordingly, if an equitable interest in land is required, the draftsman is referred to the preceding section and invited to amend (as appropriate) the forms of mortgage to create a legal charge.

---

[94] See *ante*, chap. 5.

1. Equitable Charge of Land[95]

I, [name, address, description] ("the Borrower") HEREBY CHARGE with [full]   **A–17**
[limited] title guarantee the [freehold] [leasehold] [freehold and leasehold] property described in the Schedule hereto with the payment to [name, address,
description] ("the Lender") on [date] of the sum of £[amount advanced] now
paid by the Lender to the Borrower (the receipt whereof the Borrower hereby
acknowledges) together with interest thereon at [rate] per cent. per annum from
the date hereof and also if the said sum of £[amount advanced] shall not be paid
on the date aforesaid with the payment on the [payment dates] in every year of
interest at the rate aforesaid on the principal money for the time being secured

Dated [date]

THE SCHEDULE
[particulars of property charged]

[Signature of borrower]

---

[95] If the charge is under hand only the chargee has the remedies of sale and appointment of a receiver
on application to the court, but is not entitled to possession or foreclosure. A chargee by deed has
the statutory powers of sale and appointment of a receiver.

C: Receipts: Surrenders and Releases

1. Skeleton Form of Receipt[96]on Discharge[97] of Mortgage

[I] [We] the [within named][98] [above named][98] Mortgagee(s) [(names) the Mort-   **A–20**
gagee(s) named in the Mortgage annexed][98] [identity of recipient as in forms (1)
to (9) on para. A–21].

HEREBY ACKNOWLEDGE that [I] [We] have this [date] received the sum of
£[amount] representing the [balance remaining owing in respect of the][99] principal money secured by the [within written] [above written] [annexed][1] [Legal
Charge] [Mortgage] and by a further charge dated [date][2] together with all
interest and costs the payment having been made by [identity of payer as in forms
(1) to (8), para. A–22] [the within named Borrower] [name, address, description]
[the person entitled to the immediate equity of redemption][3]

[EXECUTION AND ATTESTATION CLAUSE][4]

2. Recitals

(a) Identity of Recipient

(1) Original mortgagee, an individual   **A–21**
I, the within named mortgagee [name]

---

[96] The statutory form of receipt is form 2 of Sched. 3 to LPA 1925. S.115(5)(*F*) provides that a receipt
may be given in that form, with such variations and additions if any as are deemed expedient. LPA
1925, S.120 and Form 5, Sched. 4, s.120 provides that a statutory mortgage may be surrendered or
discharged by a receipt in that form with such variations or additions, if any, as circumstances may
require.

[97] s.115 sets out the requirements of a statutory receipt extinguishing a single mortgage of unregistered land. S.115(10) excludes the operation of the section in respect of a charge or incumbrance
registered under the Land Registration Act 1925.

[98] Alternatives arise from the provision in s.115(1) that the receipt may be written at the foot of,
indorsed on or annexed to a mortgage for all the money hereby secured. The same subsection also
provides that it must state the name of the person who pays the money and that it must be executed
by the person who is legally entitled to give a receipt for the mortgage money. In *Simpson v.
Geoghegan* [1934] W.N. 232 it was held that no seal is necessary: a document under hand is
sufficient. But if payment is to be made to the mortgagor's solicitor (or licensed conveyancer, see
Administration of Justice Act 1985, s.34(1)), he should produce a receipt under seal: see s.69 of
LPA 1925.

[99] Omit these words if no part of the principal has been repaid.

[1] See n. 9 above.

[2] This is a convenient way of referring to the further charge if there is only one such charge. If there
are more, it may be more convenient to refer to them in a Schedule.

[3] s.115(2) provides that, if by the receipt the money appears to have been paid by a person who is
not entitled to the immediate equity of redemption, the receipt shall operate as if the benefit of the
mortgage had by deed been transferred to him, unless: (a) it is otherwise expressly provided; or
(b) the mortgage is paid off out of capital money, or other money in the hands of a personal
representative or trustee properly applicable for the discharge of the mortgage, and it is not
expressly provided that the receipt is to operate as a transfer. A statutory receipt under the Building
Societies Act 1986 (Sched. 4, para. 2) cannot operate as a transfer, as there is no requirement under
that Act for the receipt to state the name of the payer; see *ante*, para. 8–35 *et seq.* S.115(3) provides
that the receipt does not operate as a transfer where there is no right to keep the mortgage alive.
That provision preserves the rule in *Otter v. Vaux* (1856) 6 De G.M. & G. 638 that a mortgagor
cannot keep a mortgage alive in his own favour so as to prejudice a subsequent incumbrancer.

[4] See *ante*, para. A–14A.

(2) Sole recipient, not the original mortgagee
I, [name, address, description]

(3) Personal representatives of mortgagee[5]
We [name, address, description of PR 1] and [name, address, description of PR 2] personal representatives of [name] late of [address, description] [whose will dated [date] was proved by us on [date] in the [Principal] [name of District] Probate Registry]

Or

[letters of administration to whose estate were granted to us on [date] out of the [Principal] [name of District] Probate Registry].

(4) Original corporate mortgagee
I, the within named mortgagee [name of company]

(5) A company other than the original mortgagee
I, [name of company] whose registered office is situated at [address of registered office]

(6) Duly-appointed liquidator
If the recipient is in liquidation, add to (4) or (5) above:

acting by [name, address, description] its duly appointed liquidator.[6]

(7) Survivor of joint beneficial mortgagees
I, the within named [name] the surviving mortgagee

(8) Original trustees of land
We, the within named mortgagees

(9) Trustees of land other than the original trustees
We [name, address, description of T1] and [name, address, description of T2]

---

[5] After stating the name of the person making payment, the receipt should continue: AND DECLARE that we have not previously hereto given or made any conveyance or assent in respect of any legal estate in the property comprised in the said [Legal Charge] [Mortgage] or in any part thereof AND ACKNOWLEDGE the right of the said [name of payer] to the production of the said [probate of the said Will] [letters of administration] (the possession of which is retained by us) and to delivery of copies thereof

[6] A suitable testimonium and attestation clause where the receipt is given by a corporate mortgagee in liquidation is: IN WITNESS whereof [name of company] acting by its liquidator [name] has caused its common seal to be affixed hereunto this [date] THE COMMON SEAL of [name of company] was affixed to this receipt by the direction of [name of liquidator] and in his presence Signed by the above named [name of liquidator] in the presence of [name of attesting witness]

(b) Identity of Payer

Insert after the words "payment having been made by":

(1) The original borrower, an individual
the within named borrower [name]

(2) Personal representatives of the original borrower
As in (2)(a)(3) replacing "us" by "them" and omitting the initial "We" and continue:

out of a fund properly applicable to the discharge of the said [Legal Charge]
[Mortgage][7]

(3) Original borrower, a body corporate
the within named borrower [name of company]

(4) Liquidator of original corporate borrower
the within named borrower [company name] acting by its duly appointed liquidator [name, address, description]

(5) Survivor of joint beneficial mortgagors
the within named [name] the surviving borrower

(6) Trustees
the within named [name of T1] and [name of T2] the present trustees of the
within mentioned [assent] [conveyance] [will] out of a fund properly applicable
to the discharge of the said [Legal Charge] [Mortgage][7]

(7) Trustees of settlement, named in the mortgage
the within named [name of T1] and [name of T2] the present trustees of the
settlement referred to in the [within mentioned] [above written] [annexed] Vesting [Deed] [Assent] dated [date] and made between [names of parties] out of
capital money properly applicable to the discharge of the said [Legal Charge]
[Mortgage]

(8) Trustees of settlement, not named in the mortgage
Replace the words preceding "the present trustees" by:

[name, address, description of T1] and [name, address, description of T2]

---

[7] See s.115(2) of LPA 1925 and the note to Form 2, Sched. 3. It is considered that, where the
statutory receipt is intended to extinguish the mortgage and the mortgagee is paid off out of capital
or other money in the hands of a personal representative or trustee, properly applicable to the
discharge of the mortgage, the receipt should state that the money is paid "out of a fund applicable
to the discharge of the mortgage." The payer should, having accepted a receipt in that form, be
estopped from denying the statement: but in any event the situation may be made plain by adding
the words "and this receipt shall not operate as a transfer."

3. Release and Surrender

(a) Part of Mortgaged Property[8]

A–23   THIS SURRENDER AND RELEASE[9] made [date] BETWEEN [name, address, description] (the "Lender")[10] of the one part and (name, address, description) (the "Borrower") of the other part

SUPPLEMENTAL to a [Legal Charge] [Mortgage] dated [date] and made between the Lender of the one part and the Borrower of the other part

WHEREAS

> (1) [recite state of mortgage debt]
> (2) The Lender has agreed with the Borrower for the consideration hereinafter appearing to execute the surrender and release of such part of the mortgaged property as is described in the First Schedule hereto

Now in pursuance of the said agreement and in consideration of the sum of £[amount] paid by the Borrower to the Lender (the receipt whereof the Lender hereby acknowledges) in reduction of the said mortgage debt[11]

THIS DEED WITNESSETH as follows:

With [full] [limited] title guarantee.[11a]

The Lender as Mortgagee HEREBY SURRENDERS AND RELEASES unto the Borrower ALL THAT the property described in the First Schedule hereto TO HOLD the same unto the Borrower discharged from all principal money and interest secured by and from all claims and liability under the said [Legal Charge] [Mortgage] [and to the intent that the term of years created by the said mortgage shall as respects the property hereby surrendered and released merge in the

---

[8] A statutory receipt is not available where only part of the mortgage money is being repaid: LPA 1925, s.115(1). A mortgage may be discharged by statutory receipt (before the conveyance) where the whole of the mortgaged property is being released so that the mortgagor can sell free from the mortgage: alternatively the mortgagee can join in the conveyance to surrender and release the property sold. See Hallett, *Conveyancing Precedents* (1965), precedents 48–51 at pp. 269–273.

[9] Although such a deed is often called a reconveyance (by contrast with a statutory receipt) there is nothing to reconvey where the mortgage was by way of legal charge, while if it was by demise or subdemise the term ceases on satisfaction. LPA 1925, s.116 provides as follows: "Without prejudice to the right of a tenant for life or other person having only a limited interest in the equity of redemption to require a mortgage to be kept alive by transfer or otherwise, a mortgage term shall, when the money secured by the mortgage has been discharged, become a satisfied term and cease."

[10] Or "the Mortgagee" if he is the original mortgagee and so referred to in the mortgage.

[11] It is a general rule that if payments are made and not specifically appropriated to either the principal or the interest of the mortgage, they are applied first in reduction or extinction of the interest: but the rule yields to a contrary intention expressed in the deed. See *Chase v. Box* (1702) Freem. Ch. 261: *Parr's Banking Co. v. Yates* [1898] 2 Q.B. 460 at 466, CA; *Wrigley v. Gill* [1906] 1 Ch. 165, CA.

[11a] See *post*, n. 27.

reversion immediately expectant hereon and be extinguished][12] PROVIDED ALWAYS that nothing herein contained shall prejudice or affect the security of the Lender under the said [Legal Charge] [Mortgage] in respect of property not surrendered or released for the payment to the Lender of so much of the said principal moneys as remains owing thereunder and the interest thereon

The Lender HEREBY ACKNOWLEDGES[13] the right of the Borrower to the production of the documents mentioned in the Second Schedule hereto (the possession of which is retained by the Lender) and to delivery of copies hereof

IN WITNESS whereof the parties[14] have hereunto set their respective hands [date]

[Execution and attestation clause as *per* para. A–14A]

THE FIRST SCHEDULE

[Description of the property released]

THE SECOND SCHEDULE

[Documents retained by lender]

(b) Whole of Mortgaged Property[15]

THIS SURRENDER AND RELEASE made [date]　　　　　　　　　　**A–24**
BETWEEN
　　　[parties as in previous precedent]

WITNESSETH that in consideration of the sum of £[amount] representing the [balance owing in respect of the][16] principal money secured by the within written [Legal Charge] [Mortgage] together with all interest and costs (the receipt whereof the Lender hereby acknowledges) the Lender with [full] [limited] title guarantee[17] HEREBY SURRENDERS AND RELEASES unto the Borrower ALL THAT the property mortgaged by the said [Legal Charge] [Mortgage] TO HOLD

---

[12] Include the words in brackets where the mortgage is by demise.
[13] This acknowledgment is for the benefit of a purchaser of the released property. The borrower cannot give it since he does not have them. The right to such acknowledgment is recognised: *Yates v. Plumbe* (1854) 2 Sm. & G. 174.
[14] Both parties should execute the deed.
[15] In a form suitable for indorsement on the original legal charge or mortgage.
[16] Omit these words if no part of the principal has been repaid.
[17] Title guarantee implies a covenant that he has not encumbered the property: Law of Property (Miscellaneous Provisions) Act 1994, s.3(3).

[*Continue as in previous precedent, including the words in round brackets if the mortgage is by demise, but omitting the proviso and acknowledgment for production*]

IN WITNESS, etc.

(c) Property Charged as Collateral security

A–25   THIS DEED OF RELEASE made [date]
BETWEEN [name, address, description] ("the Lender")
           [name, address, description] ("the Borrower")[18]
           [name, address, description] ("the Mortgagor")

WHEREAS

> (1) By a mortgage ("the Principal Mortgage") dated [date] and made between the Borrower and the Lender certain property was charged by way of legal mortgage with the payment to the Lender of the principal money interest and other moneys mentioned in the Principal Mortgage
>
> (2) By a mortgage ("the Collateral Mortgage") dated [date] and made between the Mortgagor and the Lender the property described in the Schedule hereto ("the Property") was charged by way of legal mortgage with the payments to the Lender of the moneys secured by the Principal Mortgage (and the Mortgagor covenanted with the Lender as security for the Borrower to pay the moneys secured by and to observe and perform the covenants and other conditions contained in the Principal Mortgage)[19]
>
> (3) The Lender being satisfied that the property comprised in the Principal Mortgage is a sufficient security for the moneys remaining due thereunder has agreed to release the Property from the Collateral Mortgage [and the Mortgagor from his covenants contained herein][19] [upon the payment of £[amount]][20]

[The Lender HEREBY ACKNOWLEDGES the receipt of £[amount] paid to him on [date] by [the Borrower] [the Mortgagor]][20]

The Lender with [full] [limited] title guarantee releases the Property to the Mortgagor freed and discharged from the Collateral Mortgage and all principal money interest and other moneys secured by it and from all claims and liability under it [and releases the Mortgagor from all moneys now or in the future payable under the Principal Mortgage and from all the covenants on the part of the Mortgagor contained therein [or in the Collateral Mortgage]][21]

IN WITNESS, etc.

[18] He needs to be a party only if he made the payment to the Lender.
[19] These words are included only if the Mortgagor has covenanted with the lender as surety for the borrower.
[20] Include if appropriate.
[21] See n. 29 above.

(d) Rights of Occupation under the Family Law Act 1996[22]

THIS DEED[23] OF RELEASE is made [date] **A–26**
BETWEEN [the spouse entitled to the charge—name, address, description]
["the Wife"] ["the Husband"] of the one part
and [the other spouse—name, address, description]
["the Husband"] ["the Wife"] of the other part

WHEREAS

(1) By a conveyance[24] dated [ ] and made between [names, addresses, descriptions of parties] the property described in the Schedule hereto ("the Property") was conveyed[24] to [name of purchaser] in fee simple (subject as mentioned in the Schedule but otherwise free from incumbrances)[25]

(2) The Wife[26] is entitled to a charge ("the Wife's charge") on the property by virtue of the Family Law Act 1996 and such charge is [registered under the Land Charges Act 1972 as a land charge class F under registration number [000] [protected by notice dated [date] at H.M. Land Registry][27]

(3) The Wife has agreed with the Husband to release the property from the Wife's rights of occupation in respect of the property and the Wife's charge

(4) In the negotiations leading up to the said agreement the Wife (as she hereby admits) has been advised independently by [name and address of solicitors] ("the Solicitor") as to the effect of this release as the Solicitor's endorsement hereon so warrants

NOW in pursuance of the said agreement the Wife with [full] [limited] title guarantee HEREBY RELEASES the property from the Wife's rights of occupation and from the Wife's charge to the intent that the Husband shall hold the property freed and discharged from the Wife's rights of occupation and the Wife's charge [and UNDERTAKES with the Husband to apply to H.M. Land Registry for the cancellation of the registration of the Wife's charge][28]

---

[22] Repealing the Matrimonial Homes Act 1983 with effect from October 1, 1997. The rights of occupation are set out in s.30 of the FLA 1996. The priority date of the charge is the latest of the three dates specified in s.31(3) of the 1996 Act. See also n. 30 below and *ante*, pp. 170–172 and para. 15–12 *et seq*.

[23] Family Law Act 1996, Sched. 4, para. 5(1) provides that a release may be in writing, and may apply to part only of the dwelling-house.

[24] Or "transfer," "transferred" as the case may be.

[25] Include if appropriate.

[26] In the remainder of this precedent the wife is treated as being entitled to the charge.

[27] The wife's matrimonial home rights are registrable, in the case of unregistered land, under s.2(7) of the Land Charges Act 1972 or in the case of registered land by notice (FLA 1996, s.31(10)(a)) provided the same amount to a charge on the legal estate: FLA 1996, s.31(13). Section 31(10)(b) provides the spouse's matrimonial home rights are not an overriding interest under LRA 1925, since if the spouse is in actual occupation and will not, in any situation, give rise to a caution: s.11. See para. 15–13.

[28] Land Charges Act 1972, s.16(1); Land Charges Rules 1974 (S.I. 1974 No. 1286); Land Registration (Matrimonial Homes Rights) Rules 1997, S.I. 1997 No. 1964.

I, [name and address of solicitors] warrant that I have advised [Wife's name] in the absence of any other person as to the effect of this deed and to potential liability under and by reason of this action.

[Signature of Solicitor]

IN WITNESS, etc.

THE SCHEDULE
(Description of property)

4. Legal Charge with Spouse Joining in to Postpone Charge to which he or she is Entitled under the Family Law Act 1996[29]

A–27   THIS LEGAL CHARGE is made [date]
BETWEEN [name, address, description] ("the Borrower")[30] of the first part
     and [name, address, description] ("the Lender")[30] of the second part
     and [name, address, description] (["the Wife"] ["the Husband"]) of the third part

WHEREAS

     (1) [as in recital (1) at para. A–26.]
     (2) [as in recital (2) at para. A–26.]
     (3) The Lender has agreed to lend to the Borrower the sum of £[the amount] upon having the repayment thereof with interest thereon at the rate hereinafter mentioned secured in the manner herein appearing such security to have priority to the Wife's Charge[31]
     (4) The Wife has agreed to join herein for the purpose of postponing the Wife's Charge to the security hereby created in manner hereinafter appearing
     (5) [as in recital (4) at para. A–26]

NOW in pursuance of the said agreement and in consideration of the sum of £[amount] paid by the Lender to the Borrower the receipt of which the Borrower hereby acknowledges
THIS DEED WITNESSETH as follows:

     (1) The Borrower HEREBY COVENANTS with the Lender to pay to the Lender on [date] the sum of £[amount advanced] with interest thereon from the date hereof at the rate of [rate] per cent. per annum and also if the said sum of £[amount advanced] shall not be so paid to the

---

[29] FLA 1996, Sched. 4, para. 5(1) provides that a spouse entitled by virtue of s.2 to a charge on an estate or interest of the other spouse may agree in writing that any other charge on or interest in that estate rank in priority to the charge to which that spouse is so entitled.
[30] Insert if necessary the reference to persons deriving title under these parties.
[31] See n. 36 above.

Lender (as well after as before any judgment) interest at the rate aforesaid by equal [interval] instalments on the [payment dates] in each year on the principal moneys or such part hereof as shall from time to time remain owing

(2) For the purpose of postponing the Wife's Charge to the security hereby created but not further or otherwise the Wife as with [full] [limited] title guarantee HEREBY RELEASES and the Borrower with [full] [limited] title guarantee HEREBY CHARGES BY WAY OF LEGAL MORTGAGE All That the property (subject as mentioned in the said Schedule) with the payment to the Lender of the principal moneys interest or other moneys hereby covenanted to be paid by the Borrower or otherwise hereby secured PROVIDED THAT if the Borrower shall on [date] pay to the Lender the said sum of £[amount advanced] thereon from the date hereof at the said rate the Lender will at the request and cost of the Borrower duly discharge this security. Nothing herein contained shall as between the Borrower and the Wife affect or prejudice any of the rights or remedies of the Wife under the Wife's Charge which shall remain in force subject to this Legal Charge and the postponement of the Wife's Charge shall be deemed to relate only to the moneys expressed to be secured by this deed and shall not in respect of any further moneys advanced by the Lender be deemed to confer on the Lender any like right of priority over the Wife's Charge.

IN WITNESS, etc.

[Solicitor's warranty as at para. A–26]

THE SCHEDULE
(description of property)

D: Transfers

1. Skeleton Form of Transfer[32]

THIS TRANSFER OF MORTGAGE made [date] A–28
BETWEEN[33]
[parties: either Lender (1), Transferee (2)
              or Lender (1), Borrower (2), Transferee (3)]
SUPPLEMENTAL TO[34] a [Legal Charge] [Mortgage] dated [date] between [name of Borrower] [the Borrower] of the one part and the Lender of the other part[35] affecting [short particulars of the mortgaged property].
WHEREAS
[recitals][36]
TESTATUM
[*in statutory form or in alternative form where there are recitals*].
IN WITNESS, etc.
    [To be executed and attested
    by the Lender, the Borrower (if a party)
    and the Transferee, if desired]

2. Further Charge(s)

(1) One further charge transferred A–29
SUPPLEMENTAL TO a legal Charge dated [date] and to a further charge dated [date] both made between [name of borrower] of the one part and [name of

---

[32] The skeleton is based on the statutory form (Form No. 1, Sched. 3 to LPA 1925). In that form there is no provision for the borrower to be made a party. s.95(1) of LPA 1925 provides that, where the borrower is entitled to redeem, he may require the lender, instead of reconveying or surrendering, and on the terms on which he would be bound to reconvey or surrender, to assign the mortgage debt, and convey the mortgaged property to any third person as the borrower directs, and the lender is bound to assign and convey accordingly notwithstanding any stipulation to the contrary.

  Although this is the usual case where the borrower is a party to a transfer, it is always advisable, if he is willing, that he should be made a party. This enables him to admit the state of the mortgage debt and interest and he is fixed with notice of the transfer. If he is not a party, the transferee should inquire from him as to the true state of the mortgage account between him and the lender. The transferee takes subject to the true state of the account (see *Matthews v. Wallwyn* (1798) 4 Ves. 118; *Chambers v. Godwin* (1804) 9 Ves. 254; *Dixon v. Winch* [1900] 1 Ch. 736; *Turner v. Smith* [1901] 1 Ch. 213; *De Lisle v. Union Bank of Scotland* [1914] 1 Ch. 22; *Parker v. Jackson* [1936] 2 All E.R. 281) though, in the absence of notice to the contrary he is entitled to rely on the receipt clause in the mortgage deed as showing that the original amount was in fact advanced: see *Bickerton v. Walker* (1885) 31 Ch.D. 151; *Powell v. Browne* (1907) 97 L.T. 854; and s.68(1) of LPA 1925. A lender is a "purchaser": s.205(1)(xxi).

[33] It is not always necessary to define the parties as including persons deriving title under them. Where there is a transfer of the whole mortgage debt and the borrower is not a party there is no need so to define the lender or the transferee. If the borrower joins in, both the borrower and the transferee should be so defined, to show that the admission by the borrower of the state of the mortgage debt is intended to bind persons taking under him and to benefit the transferee and persons taking under the transferee.

[34] See paras A–29 to A–30 for alternative forms.

[35] If there is a further charge or further charges insert here the following: "and to a further charge dated [date] and made between [parties]" or "and to the further charges referred to in the Schedule hereto."

[36] See para. A–30(1) *et seq.*

lender] of the other part and affecting [short particulars of the mortgaged property]

(2) Several further charges transferred
SUPPLEMENTAL to the Legal Charge and to the several Further Charges specified [herein] [or in the Schedule hereto]

3. Recitals

A–30 (1) State of mortgage debt[37]
There is now owing upon the security of the said Legal Charge (as the Borrower hereby admits) the principal sum of £[amount] [but all interest has been paid up to the date hereof] [together with the sum of £[amount of interest] for interest thereon]

(2) State of mortgage debt
If A–29 (1) or (2) are used, as above in A–30(1) except:

> (i) replacing the words "upon the security of the said Legal Charge" by the words "to the Lender"
> (ii) inserting the word "aggregate" before "principal"

(3) Agreement to transfer mortgage
The Transferee has agreed (at the request of the Borrower)[38] to pay to the Lender the sum of £[amount] upon having such transfer of the benefit of the [Legal Charge] [Mortgage] [and Further Charge(s)] as [is] [are] hereinafter contained

(4) Agreement by transferee to make further advance
The Transferee has at the request of the Borrower agreed to pay to the Lender the said sum of £[amount of principal owing] and to advance to the Borrower the further sum of £[amount of intended further advance] upon having such transfer of the benefit of the said [Legal Charge] [Mortgage] as is hereinafter contained and upon having the repayment of the aggregate sum of £[aggregate of principal owing and intended further advance] with interest at the rate hereinafter mentioned secured in manner hereinafter appearing

(a) Transferor's Title

(1) Transferee from original Lender
The benefit of the said [Legal Charge] [Mortgage] [and Further Charges] [is now] [remains] vested in the Lender[39]

---

[37] The recital of the state of the mortgage debt will bind the borrower (and his successors on title if "borrower" is appropriately defined.

[38] Omit these words if the transfer is not made at the borrower's request.

[39] It is not necessary to recite the immediate title of the transferor: *cf. Encyclopedia of Forms and Precedents*.

(2) Personal representatives of original Lender
[The Lenders proved the Will of the said [name of original mortgagee] in] [Letters of administration to the estate of the said (name of original mortgagee) were granted to the Lenders out of] the [Principal] [name of district] Probate Registry on [date]

(3) Personal representatives of transferee from original Lender
The benefit of the said [Legal Charge] [Mortgage] is vested in the Lenders as personal representatives of the late [name of transferee] and (*continue as in (2) inserting the name of the transferee as appropriate*)

(b) Personal Transfer[40] *by Representatives of a Mortgagee to Beneficiary*

(1) Death of deceased where original mortgagee, and title of personal   **A–31**
representatives
The [name of original lender] died on [date] and . . . (*Continue as in (2) or (3) above*)

(2) Death of deceased and his entitlement to the benefit of the mortgage
    (a) the [name of deceased] was at the date of his death hereinafter recited entitled to the benefit of the said [Legal Charge] [Mortgage]
    (b) the [name of deceased] died on [date] and . . . (*Continue as in (2) or (3) above*)

(3) Payment of debts by personal representatives
The personal representatives have duly paid and discharged all debts funeral and testamentary expenses and taxes payable out of the estate of the said [name]

(4) Beneficiary's entitlement
In the administration of the said estate the Beneficiary is entitled to have the [Legal Charge] [Mortgage] transferred to him and the personal representatives have agreed to make this transfer accordingly

(5) Recital where transfer is made to new trustees on their appointment
The Transferees have become jointly entitled in equity[41] to the benefit of the said [Legal Charge] [Mortgage]

4. Testatum Forms

(1) Testatum as in statutory form   **A–32**
WITNESSETH that in consideration of the sums of £[amount of principal] and £[amount of current interest] now paid by the Transferee to the Lender being the

---

[40] The personal representatives can, of course, assent rather than transfer.

[41] It is still usual to recite the fact that the transferees are jointly entitled in equity. Such a recital is a convenient method of indicating that the trustees are entitled to a transfer, without referring to any trusts: the recital itself is not notice of a trust (see *Re Harman and Uxbridge Railway* (1883) 24 Ch.D. 720 and *Carritt v. Real and Personal Advance Co.* (1889) 42 Ch.D. 263). Apart from this, the trusts are kept off the title by s.113(1) of LPA 1925 and, by virtue of that section, a purchaser who discovers the existence of a trust in the course of the examination of title no longer has to satisfy himself that the trustees have been properly appointed: *cf. Re Blaiberg and Abrahams' Contract* [1899] 2 Ch. 340.

respective amounts of the mortgage money and interest owing in respect of the said [Legal Charge] [Mortgage] (the receipt of which sums the Lender hereby acknowledges)[42] the Lender HEREBY CONVEYS AND TRANSFERS with [full] [limited] title guarantee to the Transferee the benefit of the said [Legal Charge] [Mortgage]

(2) Alternative form of testatum where agreements have been recited

Now in pursuance of the said agreement and in consideration of the sum of £[amount] now paid by the Transferee to the Lender (the receipt whereof the Lender hereby acknowledges) THIS DEED WITNESSETH that the Lender with [full] [limited] title guarantee HEREBY CONVEYS AND TRANSFERS to the Transferee the benefit of the said [Legal Charge] [Mortgage]

In (3) and (4) below, replace the words immediately following "THIS DEED WITNESSETH . . . " with the following clauses as necessary:

(3) Transfer made at Borrower's request
   (a) The Lender with [full] [limited] title guarantee by the direction of the Borrower directing as beneficial owner HEREBY CONVEYS AND TRANSFERS to the Transferee the benefit of the said [Legal Charge] [Mortgage]
   (b) The same covenants shall be implied in this Deed as would be implied therein if the Deed were a conveyance by way of mortgage made with full title guarantee by the Borrower

(4) Transfer made by personal representatives
   (a) In exercise of powers vested in them in this behalf enabling[43] the Lenders as personal representatives[44] of the said [name of original Lender or Transferee, as the case may be] deceased HEREBY CONVEY AND TRANSFER to the Transferee the benefit of the said [Legal Charge] [Mortgage]
   (b) The Lenders HEREBY DECLARE that they have not previously hereto given or made any conveyance or assent in respect of any legal estate in the mortgaged property or any part thereof[45]

---

[42] If the borrower is a party, the concluding words of the phrase in brackets should read "the Lender and the Borrower hereby acknowledge."

[43] Where the transfer is made on sale, the inclusion of these words enables reliance to be placed on s.17 of the Trustee Act 1925, which reads: "No purchaser or mortgagee, paying or advancing money on a sale or mortgage purporting to be made under any trust or power vested in trustees, shall be concerned to see that such money is wanted, or that no more than is wanted is raised, or otherwise as to the application thereof."
   By s.68(17) of that Act, "trustee" where the context admits includes a personal representative.

[44] Implying a covenant that they have not created an incumbrance.

[45] This clause is desirable since it protects a purchaser against any beneficiary who has taken an earlier assent without obtaining an indorsement on the grant of probate or letters of administration. s.36 of the Administration of Estates Act 1925 applies since the transfer is a conveyance. A transferee for value will obtain a good title against anyone except a previous purchaser provided that no notice of a previous assent or conveyance affecting the estate has been placed on or annexed to the probate or letters of administration. A personal representative making a false statement in regard to such matters is liable as if he had made a false statutory declaration.

    (c)   the Lenders HEREBY ACKNOWLEDGE the right of the Transferee to the production of [the probate of the said Will][46] [the said letters of administration] (the possession of which is retained by the Lenders) and to delivery of copies thereof

(5) Form of testatum, transfer on appointment of new trustees

Now in consideration of the premises THIS DEED WITNESSETH that the Lenders as Mortgagees HEREBY CONVEY AND TRANSFER with full [or limited] title guarantee to the Transferees the benefit of the said [Legal Charge] [Mortgage]

(6) Form of testatum, transferee making further advance

Now in pursuance of the said agreement and in consideration of the sum of £[amount of principal owing] now paid by the Transferee to the Lender (the receipt of which sum the Mortgagee hereby acknowledges) and of the sum of £[amount of further advance] now paid by the Transferee to the Borrower (the payment and receipt respectively of which sums of £[principal] and £[further advances] making together the aggregate sum of £[total of principal and further advance] the Borrower hereby acknowledges THIS DEED WITNESSETH AS FOLLOWS

    (a)   (Clause (a) of A32(3))
    (b)   (Clause (b) of A32(3))

Borrower's covenant to repay

    (c)   The Borrower HEREBY COVENANTS with the Transferee to pay to the Transferee on [date] the said aggregate sum of £[total, as above] being the outstanding principal sum of £[principal] together with the further advance of £[further advance] AND FURTHER if the said aggregate sum shall not be so paid to pay to the Transferee interest at the rate of [rate] per cent. per annum by equal [interval] instalments on the [payment dates] in every year on the principal moneys for the time being remaining due on this security [or under the said Legal Charge][47] or on any order or judgment which may be made or recovered hereafter

Charge

    (d)   The Borrower with full title guarantee HEREBY CHARGES BY WAY OF LEGAL MORTGAGE the premises contained in the said Legal

---

[46] Or "the documents mentioned in the Schedule hereto" if there are other documents retained by the personal representatives.

[47] To make it clear that the original legal charge is still subsisting. Since, by s.114(1)(*b*) of LPA 1925, the transferee has the benefit of the borrower's covenants with the lender, there is strictly no need for a covenant to pay the aggregate (rather than the further) sum: but in this way the borrower is made liable to the transferee as if he had taken a fresh mortgage.

Charge (subject as therein provided)[48] with the payment to the Transferee of the principal money and interest hereinbefore covenanted so to
be paid [and all other moneys secured by this Deed]

Covenants in Legal Charge to apply to the deed

(e) The covenants powers and provisions contained in the said Legal
Charge shall operate and take effect in like manner for protecting and
enforcing this security as if such covenants powers and provisions were
herein repeated.[49]

---

[48] These words may be included where the land is affected by easements or restrictive covenants, as
they limit liability on the covenants for title.
[49] This clause should be inserted if the legal charge contains provisions other than the covenant for
payment and the charge itself.

APPENDIX II

FORMS

Statutory Forms

Registered Land Forms

STATUTORY FORMS

B–01   **1. Law of Property Act 1925, Schedule 3**

(a) Form No. 1: Transfer of Mortgage (s.114)

This Transfer of Mortgage made the   day of   19   between *M.* of [&c.] of the one part and *T.* of [&c.], and to a Further Charge dated [&c.], and made between [&c.] affecting &c. (*here state short particulars of the mortgaged property*).

WITNESSETH that in consideration in the sums of £   and £   (for interest) now paid by *T.* to *M.*, being the respective amounts of the mortgage money and interest owing in respect of the said mortgage and further charge (the receipt of which sums *M.* hereby acknowledges) *M.*, as mortgagee, hereby conveys and transfers to *T.* the benefit of the said mortgage and further charge.

In witness, &c.

(b) Form No. 2: Receipt on Discharge of a Mortgage (s.115)

I, *A.B.* of [&c.] hereby acknowledge that I have this   day of   19   , received the sum of £   representing the [aggregate] [balance remaining owing in respect of the] principal money secured by the within [above] written [annexed] mortgage [and by a further charge dated, &c., *or otherwise as required*] together with all interest and costs, the payment having been made by *C.D.* of [&c.] and *E.F.* of [&c.]

As witness, &c.

Note.—If the persons are not entitled to the equity of redemption state that they are paying the money out of a fund applicable to the discharge of the mortgage.

2. Law of Property Act 1925, Schedule 4[1]

B–02   *(a) Form No. 1: Statutory Charge by Way of Legal Mortgage (s.117)*

This Legal Charge made by way of Statutory Mortgage the   day of   19   , between *A.* of [&c.] of the one part and *M.* of [&c.] of the other part Witnesseth that in consideration of the sum of £   now paid to *A.* by *M.* of

---

[1] Section 9 of the Law of Property (Miscellaneous Provisions) Act 1994 provides:
   "(1) Where a form set out in enactment, or in an instrument made under an enactment, included words which (in an appropriate case) would have resulted in the implication of a covenant by virtue of section 76 of the Law of Property Act 1925, the form shall be taken to authorise instead the use of the words 'with full title guarantee' or 'with limited title guarantee' or their Welsh equivalent given in section 8(4).
   (2) This applies in particular to the forms set out in Schedule 1 to the Settled Land Act 1925 and Schedules 4 and 5 to the Law of Property Act 1925."

which sum *A*. hereby acknowledges the receipt *A*. As Mortgagor and with full [or limited] title guarantee hereby charges by way of legal mortgage.

All That [&c.] with the payment of *M*. on the   day of   19   , of the principal sum of £   as the mortgage money with interest thereon at the rate of   per centum per annum.

Note.—Variations in this and the subsequent forms in this Schedule to be made, if required, for leasehold land or for giving effect to special arrangements. *M*. will be in the same position as if the Charge had been effected by a demise of freeholds or a subdemise of leaseholds.

(b) Form No. 2: Statutory Transfer, Mortgagor not Joining (s.118)

This Transfer of Mortgage made by way of statutory transfer the   day of   19   , between *M*. of [&c.] of the one part and *T*. of [&c.] of the other part supplemental to a legal charge made by way of statutory mortgage dated [&c.] and made [&c.] Witnesseth that in consideration of the sum of £   now paid to *M*. by *T*. (being the aggregate amount of £   mortgage money and £   interest due in respect of the said legal charge of which sum *M*. hereby acknowledges the receipt) *M*. as Mortgagee hereby conveys and transfers with full [or limited] title guarantee to *T*. the benefit of the said legal charge.

In witness, &c.

Note.—This and the next two forms also apply to a transfer of a statutory mortgage made before the commencement of this Act, which will then be referred to as a mortgage instead of a legal charge.

(c) Form No. 3: Statutory Transfer, a Covenantor Joining (s.118)

This Transfer of Mortgage made by way of statutory transfer the   day of   19   , between *A*. of [&c.] of the first part *B*. of [&c.] of the second part and *C*. of [&c.] of the third part Supplemental to a Legal Charge made by way of statutory mortgage dated [&c.] and made [&c.] Witnesseth that in consideration of the sum of £   now paid by *A*. to *C*. (being the mortgage money due in respect of the said Legal Charge to interest being now due or payable thereon of which sum *A*. hereby acknowledges the receipt) *A*. as Mortgagee with the concurrence of *B*. who joins herein as covenantor hereby conveys and transfers with full [or limited] title guarantee to *C*. the benefit of the said Legal Charge.

In witness, &c.

(d) Form No. 4: Statutory Transfer and Mortgage Combined (ss.117, 118)

This Transfer and Legal Charge is made by way of statutory transfer and mortgage the   day of   19   , between *A*. of [&c.] of the first part *B*. of [&c.] of the second part and *C*. of [&c.] of the third part Supplemental to a Legal Charge made by way of statutory mortgage dated [&c.] and made [&c.] Whereas a principal sum of £   only remains due in respect of the said Legal Charge as the mortgage money and no interest is now due thereon And Whereas *B*. is seised in fee simple of the land comprised in the said Legal Charge subject to that Charge.

Now this Deed Witnesseth as follows:

1. In consideration of the sum of £   now paid to A. by C. (the receipt and payment of which sum A. & B. hereby respectively acknowledge) A. as mortgagee hereby conveys and transfers with full [or limited] title guarantee to C. the benefit of the said Legal Charge.

2. For the consideration aforesaid B† as beneficial owner hereby charges by way of legal mortgage All the premises comprised in the said Legal Charge with the payment to C. on the   day of   19   of‡ the sum of £   as the mortgage money with interest thereon at the rate of   per centum per annum In Witness &c. [or in the case of a further advance after "acknowledge" at *insert* "and of the further sum of £   now paid by C. to B. of which sum B. hereby acknowledges the receipt" *also at † before* "as beneficial owner" *insert* "as mortgagor and" *as well where B. is not the original mortgagor. And after* "of" *at ‡ insert* "the sums of £   and £   making together"].

Note.—Variations to be made, as required, in case of the deed being by indorsement, or in respect of any other thing.

(e) Form No. 5: Receipt on Discharge of Statutory Legal Charge or Mortgage (s.120)

I *A.B.* of [&c.] hereby acknowledge that I have this   day of   19   received the sum of £   representing the [aggregate] [balance remaining owing in respect of the] mortgage money secured by the [annexed] within [above] written statutory legal charge [*or* statutory mortgage] [and by the further statutory charge dated [&c.] *or otherwise as required*] together with all interest and costs the payment having been made by *C.D.* of [&c.] and E.F. of [&c.]

As witness &c.

Note.—If the persons paying are not entitled to the equity of redemption state that they are paying the money out of a fund applicable to the discharge of the statutory legal charge or mortgage.

B–03

**Transfer of
charge**

HM Land Registry **TR3**

(If you need more room than is provided for in a panel, use continuation sheets CS and staple to this form)

1. Title Number(s) of the Property *(leave blank if not registered)*

2. Property

If this transfer is made under section 37 of the Land Registration Act 1925 following a not-yet-registered dealing with part only of the land in a title, or is made under rule 72 of the Land Registration Rules 1925, include a reference to the last preceding document of title containing a description of the property.

3. Date

4. Date of Transferor's charge

5. Transferor *(give full names and Company's Registered Number if any)*

6. Transferee **for entry on the register** *(Give full names and Company's Registered Number if any; for Scottish Co. Reg. Nos., use an SC prefix. For foreign companies give territory in which incorporated.)*

Unless otherwise arranged with Land Registry headquarters, a certified copy of the transferee's constitution (in English or Welsh) will be required if it is a body corporate but is not a company registered in England and Wales or Scotland under the Companies Acts.

7. Transferee's intended **address(es) for service in the U.K.** *(including postcode)* **for entry on the register**

8. The **Transferor transfers the charge referred to in panel 4 to the Transferee.**

9. Consideration *(Place "X" in the box that applies. State clearly the currency unit if other than sterling. If none of the boxes applies, insert an appropriate memorandum in the additional provisions panel.)*

☐   The Transferor has received from the Transferee for the charge the sum of *(in words and figures)*

☐   *(insert other receipt as appropriate)*

☐   The Transfer is not for money or anything which has a monetary value

10. The Transferor transfers with *(place "X" in the box which applies and add any modifications)*

☐   full title guarantee   ☐   limited title guarantee

11. Additional Provision(s) *Insert here any required or permitted statement, certificate or application and any agreed covenants, declarations, etc.*

12. *The Transferors and all other necessary parties should execute this transfer as a deed using the space below. Forms of execution are given in Schedule 3 to the Land Registration Rules 1925. If the transfer contains transferees' covenants or declarations or contains an application by them (e.g. for a restriction), it must also be executed by the Transferees.*

B–04

Transfer of a portfolio of charges

HM Land Registry **TR4**

(If you need more room than is provided for in a panel, use continuation sheets CS and staple to this form)

1. *List below the title number (leave blank if not yet registered) together with a brief description of the property. If this transfer is made under section 37 of the Land Registration Act 1925 following a not-yet-registered dealing with part only of the land in a title, or is made under rule 72 of the Land Registration Rules 1925, include a reference to the last preceding document of title containing a description of the property.*

Title Number   **Description of Property**   **Date of Transferor's charge**

2. Date

3. Transferor *(give full names and Company's Registered Number if any)*

4. Transferee **for entry on the register** *(Give full names and Company's Registered Number (if any); for Scottish Co. Reg. Nos., use an SC prefix. For foreign companies give territory in which incorporated.)*

Unless otherwise arranged with Land Registry headquarters, a certified copy of the transferee's constitution (in English or Welsh) will be required if it is a body corporate but is not a company registered in England and Wales or Scotland under the Companies Acts.

5. Transferee's intended **address(es) for service in the U.K.** *(including postcode)* **for entry on the register**

6. **The Transferor transfers the charges referred to in panel 1 to the Transferee.**

7. Consideration *(Place "X" in the box that applies. State clearly the currency unit if other than sterling. If none of the boxes applies, insert an appropriate memorandum in the additional provisions panel.)*

[ ]   The Transferor has received from the Transferee for the charges the sum of *(in words and figures)*

[ ]   *(insert other receipt as appropriate)*

[ ]   The Transfer is not for money or anything which has a monetary value

8. The Transferor transfers with (*place "X" in the box which applies and add any modifications*)

☐   full title guarantee   ☐   limited title guarantee

---

9. Additional Provision(s) *Insert here any required or permitted statement, certificate or application and any agreed covenants, declarations, etc.*

---

10. The Transferors and all other necessary parties should execute this transfer as a deed using the space below. *Forms of execution are given in Schedule 3 to the Land Registration Rules 1925. If the transfer contains transferees' covenants or declarations or contains an application by them (e.g. for a restriction), it must also be executed by the Transferees.*

B–05

| Cancellation of entries relating to a registered charge | HM Land Registry **DS1** |

*This form should be accompanied
by either Form AP1 or Form DS2*

(if you need more room than is provided for in a panel, use continuation sheet CS and staple to this form)

1. Title Number(s) of the Property

2. Property

3. Date

4. Date of charge

5. Lender

6. The Lender acknowledges that the property is no longer charged as security for the payment of sums due under the charge.

7. Date of Land Registry facility letter *(if any)*

8. *To be executed as a deed by the lender or in accordance with the above facility letter.*

B–06

**Release of part
of the land from a
registered charge**
*This form should be
accompanied by Form AP1*

HM Land Registry

DS3

(if you need more room than is provided for in a panel, use continuation sheet CS and staple to this form)

1. Title Number(s)

2. Property **released from the charge** *(insert address, including postcode, or other description of the property released from the charge)*   The property is defined *(place "X" in the box that applies and complete the statement)*   ☐   on the attached plan and shown *(state reference e.g. "edged red")*   ☐   on the filed plan(s) of the above title(s) and shown *(state reference e.g. "edged and numbered 1 in blue")*

3. Date

4. Date of charge

5. Lender

6. The Lender acknowledges that the property defined in panel 2 is no longer charged as security for the payment of sums due under the charge.

7. Date of Land Registry facility letter *(if any)*

8. Additional Provisions *Insert any agreed provisions as to rights granted or other matters.*

9. To be executed as a deed by the lender or in accordance with the above facility letter.

10. *Where the owners are joint proprietors, place "X" in the appropriate box.*

☐ The owners are holding the property on trust for themselves as joint tenants.

☐ The owners are holding the property on trust for themselves as tenants in common in equal shares.

☐ The owners are holding the property *(complete as necessary)*

11. The title is based on the title documents listed on Form DL which are all those which the applicant holds or has control of. *Place "X" in the appropriate box. If applicable complete the second statement; include any interests disclosed only by searches. Any interests disclosed by searches which do not affect the land being registered should be certified.*

☐ All rights, interests and claims affecting the property known to the applicant are disclosed in the title documents. There is no-one in adverse possession of the property or any part of it.

☐ In addition to the rights, interests and claims affecting the property disclosed in the title documents, the applicant only knows of the following:

12. Information in respect of a chargee or mortgagee

Do not give this information if a Land Registry MD reference is printed on the charge, unless the charge has been transferred. Full name and address within the U.K. (including postcode) for service of notices and correspondence of the present proprietor of each charge or mortgage to be registered. *Where the proprietor is a company include Company's Registered Number (if any); for Scottish Co. Reg. Nos., use an SC prefix. For foreign companies give territory in which incorporated.*

Unless otherwise arranged with Land Registry headquarters, the following documents are required:
(i) the original and a certified copy of any incorporated documents as defined in r. 139, Land Registration Rules 1925;
(ii) a certified copy of the chargee's constitution (in English or Welsh) if it is a body corporate but is not a company registered in England and Wales or Scotland under the Companies Acts.

13. *Place "X" in this box if you are NOT able to give this certificate* ☐

I/We have investigated or caused to be investigated the title in the usual way on the applicant's behalf on a transaction for value.

14. I/We confirm that we have authority to lodge this application and request the Registrar to complete the registration.

Signature of person
lodging this form _____ **Date** _____
(A form lodged by solicitors/licensed conveyancers must be signed in the firm's name)

N.B. Failure to complete the form honestly and with proper care may deprive the applicant of protection under the Land Registration Acts if, as a result, a mistake is made in the register. Any dealing with the land not lodged with this form must be lodged with the appropriate application form and will take priority from the day it is deemed to be delivered.

It would help the Registry if you could give the following information. The completion of this box is voluntary.
The property is

☐ a single residential property with vacant possession

It is a ☐ secondhand ☐ new ☐ newly converted

☐ flat/maisonette ☐ terraced house ☐ semi-detached house ☐ detached house

with ☐ no more than one ☐ two ☐ three ☐ four ☐ five or more bedrooms

☐ other residential
☐ non residential

B–07

Application to change the register	HM Land Registry **AP1**

(If you need more room than is provided for in a panel, use continuation sheet CS and staple to this form)

1. Administrative area(s) and postcode(s) *(if known)*

2. Title Number(s)	**Deposit No(s)** *(if any)*

3. This application affects *(place "X" in the box that applies)*

☐ the **whole** of the land in the title(s) *(go to panel 4)*

☐ **part** of the land in the title(s) *(if single property, give a brief description below)*

Property description

4. Application, Priority and Fees

Nature of applications numbered in priority order	Value £	Fees paid £	FOR OFFICIAL USE ONLY Record of fees paid
1.			
			Particulars of under/over payments
	TOTAL £		

Make cheques or postal orders payable to "H M Land Registry".

5. Documents lodged with this form *(number the documents in sequence; copies should also be be numbered and listed as separate documents)*

6. Application lodged by

Land Registry Key No.

Name

Address/DX No.

Reference

Telephone No.	Fax No.	FOR OFFICIAL USE ONLY Codes Dealing Status

7. Where the Registry is to deal with someone else

The Registry will send any land/charge certificate to the person named in panel 6 above and will, if necessary, contact that person. You can change this by placing "X" against one or more of the statements and completing the details below.

☐ Send any land/charge certificate to the person shown below

☐ Raise any requisitions or queries with the person shown below

☐ Issue to the person shown below the following document(s)

If you have placed "X" against any statement above, complete the following name and address details:

Name

Address/DX No.

Reference	Telephone No.

8. Address for service of the proprietor(s) of the land *Place "X" in the box that applies. Use U.K. address(es) only.*

☐   Enter the address(es) from the transfer/assent

☐   Enter the address(es), including postcode, as follows:

9. Information in respect of any new charge
Do not give this information if a Land Registry MD reference is printed on the charge, unless the charge has been transferred.
Full name and address within the U.K. (including postcode) for service of notices and correspondence of the person to be registered as proprietor of each charge. For a company include Company's Registered Number if any: for Scottish Co. Reg. Nos, use an SC prefix. For foreign companies give territory in which incorporated.

Unless otherwise arranged with Land Registry headquarters, the following documents are required:
  (i) the original and a certified copy of any incorporated documents as defined in r. 139, Land Registration Rules 1925:
  (ii) a certified copy of the chargee's constitution (in English or Welsh) if it is a body corporate but is not a company registered in England and Wales or Scotland under the Companies Acts.

10. Signature(s) of person(s)
  lodging this form .... **Date** ....
  (A form lodged by solicitors/licensed conveyancers must be signed in the firm's name)

Appendix III

STATUTORY ENACTMENTS

STATUTORY ENACTMENTS

C–01   1. County Courts Act 1984, sections 21, 23, 147(1) (as amended)

21. Actions for recovery of land and actions where title is in question

(1) A county court shall have jurisdiction to hear and determine any action for the recovery of land.

(2) A county court shall have jurisdiction to hear and determine any action in which the title to any hereditament[1] comes in question.

(3) Where a mortgage of land consists of or includes a dwelling-house and no part of the land is situated in Greater London then, subject to subsection (4), if a county court has jurisdiction by virtue of this section to hear and determine an action in which the mortgagee under that mortgage claims possession of the mortgaged property, no court other than a county court shall have jurisdiction to hear and determine that action.

(4) Subsection (3) shall not apply to an action for foreclosure or sale in which a claim for possession of the mortgaged property is also made.

(5) . . .

(6) . . . [2]

(7) In this section—

"dwelling-house" includes any building or part of a building which is used as a dwelling;

"mortgage" includes a charge and "mortgagor" and "mortgagee" shall be construed accordingly;

"mortgagor" and "mortgagee" includes any person deriving title under the original mortgagor or mortgagee.

(8) The fact that part of the premises comprised in a dwelling-house is used as a shop or office or for business, trade or professional purposes shall not prevent the dwelling-house from being a dwelling-house for the purposes of this section.

(9) This section does not apply to a mortgage securing an agreement which is a regulated agreement within the meaning of the Consumer Credit Act 1974.

23. Equity jurisdiction

A county court shall have all the jurisdiction of the High Court to hear and determine—

(a) . . .

(b) . . .

(c) proceedings for foreclosure or redemption of any mortgage or for enforcing any charge or lien, where the amount owing in respect of the mortgage, charge or lien does not exceed the County Court limit[3];

(d) . . .

---

[1] This includes both a corporeal and incorporeal hereditament, CCA 1984, s.147.

[2] Amended by High Court and County Courts Jurisdiction Order 1991 (S.I. 1991 No. 724) Art. 2(8) and Sch., Pt. 1.

[3] For purposes of s.23 this remains £30,000. County Courts Jurisdiction Order 1981 (S.I. 1981 No. 1123).

(e) ...
(f) ...
(g) ...

147. Interpretation

(1) In this Act, unless the context otherwise requires . . . "the County Court limit" means—

(a) in relation to any enactment contained in this Act for which a limit is for the time being specified by an Order under section 145, that limit,

(b) ...

(c) in relation to any enactment contained in this Act and not within paragraph (a) . . . the County Court limit for the time being specified by any other Order in Council or order defining the limit of a county court jurisdiction for the purposes of that enactment.[4]

2. Administration of Justice Act 1970, ss.36, 39

C–02

36. Additional powers of court in action by mortgagee for possession of dwelling-house

(1) Where the mortgagee under a mortgage of land which consists of or includes a dwelling-house brings an action in which he claims possession of the mortgaged property, not being an action for foreclosure in which a claim for possession of the mortgaged property is also made, the court may exercise any of the powers conferred on it by subsection (2) below if it appears to the court that in the event of its exercising the power the mortgagor is likely to be able within a reasonable period to pay any sums due under the mortgage or to remedy a default consisting of a breach of any other obligation rising under or by virtue of the mortgage.

(2) The court—

(a) may adjourn the proceedings, or

(b) on giving judgment, or making an order, for delivery of possession of the mortgaged property, or at any time before the execution of such judgment or order, may—
(i) stay or suspend execution of the judgment or order, or
(ii) postpone the date for delivery of possession, for such period or periods as the court thinks reasonable.

(3) Any such adjournment, stay, suspension[5] or postponement as is referred to in subsection (2) above may be made subject to such conditions with regard to payment by the mortgagor of any sum secured by the mortgage or the remedying of any default as the court thinks fit.

---

[4] Currently there are none.

[5] The court has no jurisdiction to order a stay or suspension of an order without defining or rendering ascertainable the period for which the order should be stayed or suspended: *Royal Trust Co. of Canada v. Markham* [1975] 1 W.L.R. 1416. See generally para. 16–84.

(4) The court may from time to time vary or revoke any condition imposed by virtue of this section.

(5) This section shall have effect in relation to such an action as is referred to in subsection (1) above begun before the date on which this section comes into force unless in that action judgment has been given, or an order made, for delivery of possession of the mortgaged property and that judgment or order was executed before that date.

(6) In the application of this section to Northern Ireland, "the court" means a judge of the High Court of Northern Ireland, and in subsection (1) the words from "not being" to "made" shall be omitted.

39. Interpretation of Part IV

(1) In this Part of the Act

"dwelling-house" includes any building or part thereof which is used as a dwelling;

"mortgage" includes a charge and "mortgagor" and "mortgagee" shall be construed accordingly;

"mortgagor" and "mortgagee" includes any person deriving title under the original mortgagor or mortgagee.

(2) The fact that part of the premises comprised in a dwelling-house is used as a shop or office or for business, trade or professional purposes shall not prevent the dwelling-house from being a dwelling-house for the purposes of this Part of this Act.

C–03   3. Administration of Justice Act 1973, s.8

8. Extension of powers of court in action by mortgagee of dwelling-house

(1) Where by a mortgage of land which consists of or includes a dwelling-house, or by any agreement between the mortgagee under such a mortgage and the mortgagor, the mortgagor is entitled or is to be permitted to pay the principal sum secured by instalments or otherwise to defer payment of it in whole or in part, but provision is also made for earlier payment in the event of any default by the mortgagor or of a demand by the mortgagee or otherwise, then for purposes of section 36 of the Administration of Justice Act 1970 (under which a court has power to delay giving a mortgagee possession of the mortgaged property so as to allow the mortgagor a reasonable time to pay any sums due under the mortgage) a court may treat as due under the mortgage on account of the principal sum secured and of interest on it only such amounts as the mortgagor would have expected to be required to pay if there have been no such provision for earlier payment.[6]

(2) A court shall not exercise by virtue of subsection (1) above the powers conferred by section 36 of the Administration of Justice Act 1970 unless it

---

[6] s.8(1) can apply only if: (i) the mortgage itself or some agreement made under it has the effect that the mortgagor was to be permitted to defer payment of the principal sum in whole or in part after it had become due; and (ii) the mortgage itself must make provision for earlier payment in the event of any default by the mortgagor or of a demand by the mortgagee or otherwise.

appears to the court not only that the mortgagor is likely to be able within a reasonable period to pay any amounts regarded (in accordance with subsection (1) above) as due on account of the principal sum secured, together with the interest on those amounts, but also that he is likely to be able by the end of that period to pay any further amounts that he would have expected to be required to pay by then on account of that sum and of interest on it if there had been no such provision as is referred to in subsection (1) above for earlier payment.

(3) When subsection (1) above would apply to an action in which a mortgagee only claimed possession of the mortgaged property, and the mortgagee brings an action for foreclosure (with or without also claiming possession of the property), then section 36 of the Administration of Justice Act 1970 together with subsections (1) and (2) above shall apply as they would apply if it were an action in which the mortgagee only claimed possession of the mortgaged property, except that—

(a) section 36(2)(b) shall apply only in relation to any claim for possession; and
(b) section 36(5) shall not apply.

(4) For purposes of this section the expressions "dwelling-house," "mortgage," "mortgagee" and "mortgagor" shall be construed in the same way as for the purposes of Part IV of the Administration of Justice Act 1970.

(5) This section shall have effect in relation to an action begun before the date on which this section comes into force if before that date judgment has not been given, nor an order made, in that action for delivery of possession of the mortgaged property and, where it is a question of subsection (3) above, an order nisi for foreclosure has not been made in that action.

(6) In the application of this section to Northern Ireland, subsection (3) shall be omitted.

APPENDIX IV

COURT RULES, FORMS AND PRECEDENTS

BEFORE OCTOBER 15, 2001[1]

AFTER OCTOBER 15, 2001

[1] The form of orders and Practice Forms will remain relevant after this date in appropriate cases.

1. RSC, Order 88—Mortgage Claims

Application and Interpretation

D–01   1.—(1) This order applies to any claim by a mortgagee or mortgagor or by any person having the right to foreclose or redeem any mortgage, being a claim in which there is a claim for any of the following remedies, namely—

    (a)   payment of moneys secured by the mortgage;

    (b)   sale of the mortgaged property;

    (c)   foreclosure;

    (d)   delivery of possession (whether before or after foreclosure or without foreclosure) to the mortgagee by the mortgagor or by any other person who is or is alleged to be in possession of the property;

    (e)   redemption;

    (f)   reconveyance of the property or its release from the security;

    (g)   delivery of possession by the mortgagee.

(2) In this order "mortgage" includes a legal and an equitable mortgage and a legal and an equitable charge, and references to a mortgagor, a mortgagee and mortgaged property shall be construed accordingly.

(3) A claim to which this order applies is referred to in this order as a mortgage claim.

(4) These rules apply to mortgage claims subject to the following provisions of this order.

Assignment of certain actions to Chancery Division

2. Without prejudice to section 61(1) of the Act (which provides for the assignment to the Chancery Division of proceedings for the purposes, among others, of the redemption or foreclosure of mortgages and the sale and distribution of the proceeds of property subject to any lien or charge) any claim in which there is a claim for—

(a) payment of moneys secured by a mortgage of any real or leasehold property; or

(b) delivery of possession (whether before or after foreclosure) to the mortgagee of any such property by the mortgagor or by any other person who is or is alleged to be in possession of the property, shall be assigned to the Chancery Division.

Commencement of claim

3.—(1) A claim form by which a mortgage claim is begun may not be issued out of a district registry, which is not a Chancery district registry, unless the mortgaged property is situated in the district of the registry.

(3) The claim form by which a mortgage claim is begun shall be indorsed with or contain a statement showing—

    (a)   where the mortgaged property is situated; and

(b) if the plaintiff claims possession of the mortgaged property and it is situated outside Greater London, whether the property consists of or includes a dwelling house, and a certificate that the claim is not one to which section 141 of the Consumer Credit Act 1974 applies.

Claim for possession: failure by a defendant to acknowledge service

4.—(1) Where in a mortgage claim in the Chancery Division being a claim in which the claimant is the mortgagee and claims delivery of possession or payment of moneys secured by the mortgage or both, any defendant fails to acknowledge service of the claim form, the following provisions of this rule shall apply, and references in those provisions to the defendant shall be construed as references to any such defendant.

(2) Not less than 4 clear days before the day fixed for the first hearing of the claim the claimant must serve on the defendant a copy of the notice of appointment for the hearing and a copy of the witness statement or affidavit in support of the claim.

(4) Where the hearing is adjourned, then, subject to any directions given by the court, the claimant must serve notice of the appointment for the adjourned hearing, together with a copy of any further witness statement or affidavit intended to be used at that hearing, on the defendant not less than 2 clear days before the day fixed for the hearing.

(5) Service under paragraph (2) or (4) and the manner in which it was effected, may be proved by a certificate signed by the claimant, if he sues in person, and otherwise by his solicitor.

The certificate may be indorsed on the witness statement or affidavit in support of the claim or, as the case may be, on any further witness statement or affidavit intended to be used at an adjourned hearing.

(6) A copy of any exhibit to a witness statement or affidavit need not accompany the copy of the witness statement or affidavit served under paragraph (2) or (4).

Claim in Chancery Division for possession or payment: evidence

5.—(1) The witness statement or affidavit in support of the claim (other than a claim to which rule 5A applies) to which this rule applies is begun must comply with the following provisions of this rule.

This rule applies to a mortgage claim in the Chancery Division in which the claimant is the mortgagee and claims delivery of possession or payment of moneys secured by the mortgage or both.

(2) The witness statement or affidavit must exhibit a true copy of the mortgage and the original mortgage or, in the case of a registered charge, the charge certificate must be produced at the hearing of the claim.

(2A) Unless the court otherwise directs the witness statement or affidavit may contain statements of information or belief with the sources and grounds thereof.

(3) Where the claimant claims delivery of possession the witness statement or affidavit must show the circumstances under which the right to possession arises and, except where the court in any case or class of case otherwise directs, the

state of the account between the mortgagor and mortgagee with particulars of—

(a) the amount of the advance;
(b) the amount of the periodic payments required to be made;
(c) the amount of any interest or instalments in arrear at the date of issue of the claim form and at the date of the witness statement or affidavit; and
(d) the amount remaining due under the mortgage.

(4) Where the claimant claims delivery of possession the witness statement or affidavit must—

(a) give particulars of every person who to the best of the claimant's knowledge is in possession of the mortgaged property; and
(b) state, in the case of a dwelling-house, whether—
    (i) a land charge of Class F has been registered, or a notice or caution registered under section 2(7) of the Matrimonial Homes Act 1967 or a notice registered under section 2(8) of the Matrimonial Homes Act 1983 has been entered, and, if so, on whose behalf; and
    (ii) he has served notice of the proceedings on the person on whose behalf the land charge is registered or the notice or caution entered.

(5) If the mortgage creates a tenancy other than a tenancy at will between the mortgagor and mortgagee, the witness statement or affidavit must show how and when the tenancy was determined and if by service of notice when the notice was duly served.

(6) Where the claimant claims payment of money secured by the mortgage the witness statement or affidavit must show how the claim is calculated including—

(a) the amount of the advance and the amount and dates of any periodic repayments and any interest claimed;
(b) the amount which would have to be paid (after taking into account any adjustment for early settlement) in order to redeem the mortgage at the date of commencement of the proceedings and at a stated date not more than 14 days after the date of commencement of the proceedings, specifying the amount of the solicitor's costs and administrative charges which would be payable;
(c) the dates between which a particular rate of interest applied, the number of days in that period, and the capital on which the interest was calculated.

(7) Where the claimant's claim includes a claim for interest to judgment, the witness statement or affidavit must state the amount of a day's interest.

Claim for the enforcement of charging order by sale

5A.—(1) This rule applies to a mortgage claim in the Chancery Division to enforce a charging order by sale of the property charged.

(2) The witness statement or affidavit in support of the claim must—

(a) identify the charging order sought to be enforced and the subject-matter of the charge;

(b) specify the amount in respect of which the charge was imposed and the balance outstanding at the date of the witness statement or affidavit;

(c) verify, so far as known, the debtor's title to the property charged;

(d) identify any prior incumbrancer on the property charged stating, so far as is known, the names and addresses of the incumbrancers and the amounts owing to them;

(e) set out the claimant's proposals as to the manner of sale of the property charged together with estimates of the gross price which would be obtained on a sale in that manner and of the costs of such a sale; and

(f) where the property charged consists of land in respect of which the claimant claims delivery of possession—

(i) give particulars of every person who to the best of the claimant's knowledge is in possession of the property charged or any part of it; and

(ii) state, in the case of a dwelling-house, whether a land charge of Class F has been registered, or a notice or caution pursuant to section 2(7) of the Matrimonial Homes Act 1967, or a notice pursuant to section 2(8) of the Matrimonial Homes Act 1983 has been entered and, if so, on whose behalf, and whether he has served notice of the proceedings on the person on whose behalf the land charge is registered or the notice or caution entered.

2. CCR Order 6, rr.5 and 5A

Mortgage claim

5.—(1) Where a claimant claims as mortgagee payment of moneys secured by **D–02** a mortgage of real or leasehold property or possession of such property, the particulars of claim shall contain the information required under this rule and, as the case may be, by rule 5A.

(2) Where there is more than one loan secured by the mortgage, the information required under the following paragraphs of this rule and under rule 5A shall be provided in respect of each loan agreement.

(3) The particulars shall state the date of the mortgage and identify the land sought to be recovered.

(4) Where possession of the property is claimed, the particulars of claim shall state whether or not the property consists of or includes a dwelling-house within the meaning of section 21 of the Act.

(5) The particulars shall state whether or not the loan which is secured by the mortgage is a regulated consumer credit agreement and, if so, specify the date on which any notice required by section 76 or section 87 of the Consumer Credit Act 1974 was given.

(6) The particulars shall show the state of account between the claimant and the defendant by including—

(a) the amount of the advance and of any periodic repayment and any payment of interest required to be made;

(b) the amount which would have to be paid (after taking into account any adjustment for early settlement) in order to redeem the mortgage at a stated date not more than 14 days after the commencement of proceedings specifying the amount of solicitor's costs and administrative charges which would be payable;

(c) where the loan which is secured by the mortgage is a regulated consumer credit agreement, the total amount outstanding under the terms of the mortgage;

(d) the rate of interest payable—

(i) at the commencement of the mortgage;

(ii) immediately before any arrears referred to in subparagraph (e) accrued; and

(iii) where it differs from that provided under (ii) above, at the commencement of the proceedings; and

(e) the amount of any interest or instalments in arrear at the commencement of the proceedings.

(7) The particulars of claim shall state any previous steps which the claimant has taken to recover the moneys secured by the mortgage or the mortgaged property and, in the case of court proceedings, state—

(a) the dates when proceedings were commenced and concluded; and

(b) the dates and terms of any orders made.

(8) In this rule "mortgage" includes a legal or equitable mortgage and a legal or equitable charge, and references to the mortgaged property and mortgagee shall be construed accordingly.

Mortgage claim—dwelling house

5A.—(1) This rule applies where a claimant claims as mortgagee possession of land which consists of or includes a dwelling-house and in such a case the particulars of claim shall be in the prescribed form.

(2) Where the claimant's claim is brought because of failure to make the periodic payments due, the particulars of claim shall—

(a) give details (whether by means of a schedule or otherwise) of all the payments which have been missed altogether;

(b) where a history of late or under-payments is relied upon, provide sufficient details to establish the claimant case;

(c) give details of any other payments required to be made as a term of the mortgage (such as for insurance premiums, legal costs, default interest, penalties, administrative or other charges) together with any other sums claimed stating the nature and amount of each such charge, whether any payment is in arrear and whether or not it is included in the amount of any periodic payment;

(d) give such relevant information as is known by the claimant about the defendant's circumstances and, in particular, whether (and, if so, what) payments on his behalf are made direct to the claimant by or under the Social Security Contributions and Benefits Act 1992.

(3) In a claim to which this rule applies, the claimant shall state in his particulars of claim whether there is any person on whom notice of the claim is required to be served in accordance with section 8(3) of the Matrimonial Homes Act 1983 and, if so, he shall state the name and address of that person and shall file a copy of the particulars of claim for service of that person.

(4) In this rule "mortgage" has the same meaning as in rule 5(8).

3. Claim Form and Witness Statement (High Court)

IN THE HIGH COURT OF JUSTICE   CLAIM NO   **D–03**

CHANCERY DIVISION[2]

BETWEEN:

[THE MORTGAGEE]

Claimant

and

[THE MORTGAGOR]

Defendant

INDORSEMENT[3]

The Claimant claims possession of the [freehold] [leasehold] property situate at and known as [address of property] and registered at HM Land Registry under title number [insert number] ("the property") pursuant to the terms of a legal mortgage pursuant to a deed dated [date] and made between the Claimant and the Defendant ("the mortgage"). The Defendant is in arrears with [his] payments under the terms of the mortgage, thereby entitling the Claimant to the relief sought.

The mortgaged property is situated [in Greater London] [in the district of the District Registry and comprises a dwelling house][4]

---

[2] A claim may not be issued out of a district registry which is not a Chancery registry unless the mortgage property is situated in the district of the registry: CPR, Sched. 1, RSC Ord. 88, r. 3(1). The Chancery district registries are Birmingham, Bristol, Cardiff, Leeds, Liverpool, Manchester, Newcastle upon Tyne and Preston: Chancery Guide, Chapter 12.

[3] CPR, Sched. 1, RSC Ord. 88 r. 3 stipulates that the claim form for a claim brought in the High Court shall contain an indorsement or statement in accordance with that rule. The following indorsement satisfies that rule, with the particulars necessary to give rise to the claim being set out in the accompanying witness statement which is required in support of the claim.

[4] CPR, Sched. 1, RSC Ord. 88 r. 3(3).

The claim is not one to which section 141 of the Consumer Credit Act 1974 applies.[5]

D–04 IN THE HIGH COURT OF JUSTICE   CLAIM NO

CHANCERY DIVISION

BETWEEN:

[THE MORTGAGEE]

Claimant

and

[THE MORTGAGOR]

Defendant

WITNESS STATEMENT

I, [NAME OF WITNESS] of [address], account manager with the [the mortgagee] STATE as follows:[6]

1. I am an accounts manager with the Claimant and am duly authorised to make this witness statement on the Claimant's behalf in these proceedings. I have day-to-day control of the account referred to in this statement and make this witness statement from facts and matters within my own knowledge and from my perusal of the relevant file and information contained therein pertaining to the Defendant's account referred to below. The facts and matters stated herein are true to the best of my information and belief.[7]

2. I make this statement in support of the Claimant's claim for possession of the property described below and for a money judgment.

3. There is now produced and shown to me marked "XY1" a true copy of a legal mortgage made by a deed and dated [date] between the Claimant and the Defendant ("the mortgage") pursuant to which the Defendant charged by way of legal mortgage the [freehold] [leasehold] property situate at and known as [address of property] and registered at HM Land Registry under title number [insert number] ("the property") to secure repayment of the monies advanced by the Claimant to the Defendant in the sum of £[insert sum] together with interest thereon and such other monies as are, from time to time, owed by the Defendant to the Claimant pursuant to the terms of the mortgage ("the mortgage debt").[8]

4. By clause 12 of the mortgage, it incorporated the Claimant's residential mortgagee terms from time to time in force ("the terms"). A true copy of the terms is now produced and shown to me and exhibited hereto marked "XY2".

---

[5] *ibid.*

[6] The evidence may be given by affidavit: see CPR, Sched. 1, RSC Ord. 88, r. 5(1).

[7] Statements of information and belief are permitted (CPR, Sched. 1, RSC Ord. 88 r. 5(2A)) but where something is outside the witness's actual knowledge and derived from the mortgagee's files, the better practice is specifically to state that to be the case at the appropriate juncture.

[8] The original mortgage or charge certificate must be produced at the hearing of the claim: CPR, Sched. 1, RSC Ord. 88 r. 5(2).

5. By clause 3 of the Terms, the Defendant covenanted with the Claimant that he would repay the mortgage debt with interest.

    (a) By such monthly payments made on the first day of each month as the Claimant shall from time to time require or

    (b) At once if the mortgage debt becoming due and payable pursuant to clause 7 of the Terms. Clause 7 provides that the mortgage debt becomes payable immediately by the Defendant to the Claimant if the monthly payments due pursuant to clause 3 were in arrears in a sum which exceeds in total the amount of three monthly repayments.

6. The Defendant is in default pursuant to the terms of the mortgage by reason of the arrears outstanding thereunder exceeding three monthly payments.

7. Pursuant to clause 9 of the Terms when the entirety of the mortgage debt has become due and immediately repayable in accordance with clause 7 of the Terms, the Claimant may exercise all or any of the following powers:

    (a) the statutory power sale pursuant to the Law of Property Act 1925 free from the restrictions or Terms imposed by section 103 of that Act;

    (b) to enter into possession of the property or any part thereof.

8. There is now produced and shown to me and exhibited hereto marked "XY3" a true copy of a Schedule detailing the payments which the Defendant has made, missed, [made late] and of other payments required under the terms of the mortgage.[9]

9. It can be seen from that exhibit that the state of account between the Claimant and the Defendant is accordingly as follows:

    (a) the amount of the advance was £[   ];

    (b) the amount of the periodic payments required to be made on a monthly basis are £[   ];

    (c) the amount of any interest or instalments in arrear at the date of the issue of the claim form herein were £[   ] and at the date of this witness statement are £[   ]; and

    (d) the amount remaining due under the mortgage is £[   ].[10]

10. To the best of the Claimant's knowledge, no one else is in possession of the mortgaged property[11] and no land charge of class F has been registered or a notice of caution registered under section 2(7) of the Matrimonial Homes Act 1967 or a notice registered under section 2(8) of the Matrimonial Homes Act 1983 has been entered.[12]

11. In addition to possession of the property the Claimant seeks a payment of money which is secured by the mortgage and the Court is referred to exhibit "XY2" which sets out the state of account of between the parties. The Court will see from that exhibit that the amount of advance is as described in paragraph 9 above and the dates of any periodic repayments and interest claimed are as set forth in the Schedule exhibited at "XY2".

12. There is now produced and shown to me and exhibited hereto marked "XY3" a true copy of a schedule detailing the Claimant's mortgage rates

---

[9] See CPR, Schedule 1, RSC Ord. 88 r. (6).

[10] See CPR, Sched. 1, RSC Ord 88 r. 5(3).

[11] See CPR, Sched. 1, RSC Ord. 88 r. 5(4)(a).

[12] If one has been entered the witness statement should state on whose behalf such an act has been done and that service of notice of the proceedings has been effected on that individual: *ibid.* r. 5(4)(b).

applicable to the Defendant's mortgage and the number of days in any period during which the stated rate of interest applied and the capital upon which that interest is calculated.[13]

13. In addition, I can confirm that the amount which would have to be paid by the Defendant (after taking into account any adjustment for early settlement) in order to redeem the mortgage on [insert date][14] is £[insert total amount], of which £[insert amount] represents solicitor's costs and administrative charges which would be payable.

14. In addition the Claimant seeks interest until judgment in this matter at the daily rate of £[insert amount].

15. The facts stated in this witness statement are true.

....

[SIGNATURE OF WITNESS]

4. **Particulars of Claim**

See precedent 20 below.

Chapter 21 Mortgage claims

D–05   21(1) In Greater London the High Court has concurrent jurisdiction with the county court in mortgage possession claims for dwelling-houses, and such claims are assigned to the Chancery Division. Lenders may take back bookings of such claims, timed at 12 an hour (or six a half-hour) and may book a whole day (or two whole days) at a time. This enables them to bring all their possession claims for Greater London at one time and place. This is not only beneficial to the lenders but is also likely to reduce the costs of the proceedings and therefore also benefit the borrowers.

(2) These claims are still subject to the special provisions of RSC Order 88. The effect of these is that not only is it impossible to obtain judgment in default, but it is also impossible to obtain judgment on a paper application. Even if (as is usually the case) the borrower fails to take any active part in the proceedings at all, judgment can only be obtained at a hearing of which notice has been given to the defendant.

(3) Claimants must use the Part 8 claim form. If there is a dispute of fact (*e.g.* where a mortgagor us claiming that he or she is not bound by a mortgage purportedly executed by him or her because the signature is a forgery or was obtained by undue influence) the court is likely to direct that the claim proceed as if it had been brought by a Part 7 claim form and will give appropriate case management directions.

(4) By rule 8.5 the claimant's evidence in support of the claim must be filed and served at the same time as the claim form. On the other hand RSC Order 88, rule 4(2) provides that in a case where a defendant has failed to acknowledge service the claimant must serve a notice of appointment upon him not less than four clear days before the day fixed for the first hearing of the claim together with a copy of the witness statement or affidavit in support of the claim. In order to

---

[13] CPR, Sched. 1, RSC Ord. 88 r. 5(6)(c).

[14] Being a stated date not more than 14 days after the commencement of these proceedings.

avoid unnecessary duplication of service of evidence and to reduce costs it will generally be considered sufficient if the claimant does not serve his or her evidence with the claim form but serves it with the notice of appointment; and this is so whether or not a defendant has acknowledged service. The court will usually fix a date for the hearing at the same time as it issues the claim form.

(5) RSC Order 88, rule 5(2) requires that in mortgage claims a copy of the mortgage must be exhibited to the witness statement or affidavit in support of the claim and that the original mortgage or charge certificate must be produced at the hearing.

(6) Most building society mortgages, or mortgages taken by companies which were previously building societies, now incorporate standard mortgage conditions and, in such cases, a copy of the relevant conditions must also be exhibited.

(7) Some standard forms of mortgage are now so abbreviated that they give no particulars of the amount of the advance, the term of the loan, the rate of interest or the amount of the instalments and instead all these matters are defined in the mortgage conditions by reference to the offer letter. Where the offer letter is thus, in effect, incorporated into the mortgage by reference, that letter should also be exhibited to the witness statement or affidavit.

(8) Many bank mortgages, although expressed in the usual bank "all monies" form, are also qualified by an offer letter or other side letter, providing for the repayment of the advance by instalments. In such cases the mortgage may be treated as an instalment mortgage for purposes of the Administration of Justice Acts 1970 and 1973. In these cases also, the relevant letter should be exhibited to the witness statement or affidavit in support.

(9) By RSC Order 88, rule 5(4) where there is a claim for payment of the mortgage debt, the evidence in support must state—

(1) the amount of the advance;
(2) the amount of the periodic payments required to be made;
(3) the amount of any interest or instalments in arrear at the date of issue of the claim form and at the date of the witness statement or affidavit;
(4) the amount remaining due under the mortgage.

(10) In claims for possession the requirements of RSC Order 88, rule 5(3) and (4) must be complied with strictly. In Order 88, rule 5(3) and (4) must be complied with strictly. In particular it is essential that particulars of every person who to the best of the claimant's knowledge is in occupation are given and no possession order will be made if with this requirement is not complied with. If someone other than the defendant is known to be in occupation a possession order will not be made unless this person has been given notice of the hearing. Although under CPR rule 8.5 a defendant who wishes to rely on written evidence is required to file and serve evidence in answer, the great majority of defendants are litigants in person and do not put in evidence but, if they take any active part of the proceedings, simply turn up at the hearing. The Master will consider their oral representations made at the hearing.

(11) Because defendants normally do not file acknowledgements of service or put in evidence but an oral hearing is nonetheless necessary in all cases, the Masters give no preliminary consideration to mortgage possession cases when the time for acknowledging service has expired. The claimant should therefore

take an appointment of sufficient length before the Master for the hearing of the claim as soon as the claim form has been served.

(12) Some points of detail relating to mortgages and possession claims are referred to in CPR rule 16.8 and in the PD supplementing Part 16.

Suspended possession orders

(13) A suspended possession order is an order under which a person is entitled to a remedy subject to the fulfilment of a condition for the purposes of RSC Order 46, rule 2(1)(d) (which remains in force), so that Order 46, rule 4 applies. Permission to issue execution should not be given without notice and it follows that an application for such permission must be made on notice.

(14) Suspended possession orders are made frequently in mortgagee possession claims by virtue of section 36 of the Administration of Justice Act 1970 and in such claims the defendant is often in default of acknowledging service of the claim form.

(15) Where a defendant has not acknowledged service no special directions as to service are needed, but a claimant requiring permission to issue execution on a suspended possession order when there has been a default in acknowledging service must send a copy of the application notice and of the witness statement in support of the application notice to each defendant in default at his or her last known address, so as to reach him not less than three clear days before the hearing, and lodge with the Master's Clerk, at least one day before the hearing, the witness statement in support of the application endorsed with a certificate by the claimant's solicitor in the form following or as near thereto as may be appropriate:

> "I certify that on day the day of 20 . . . a copy of the application notice herein dated together with a true copy of this document was sent by pre-paid letter post addressed to the defendant at [his/her] last known address. (signed) Claimant's solicitor".

No further proof of service should normally be required in default cases.

(16) The same principles apply and the same practice should be followed where permission to issue execution is required because six years or more have elapsed since the date of an unsuspended possession order or because there has been a change in the party liable to execution (see RSC Order 46, rule 2).

(17) Applications for permission to issue execution because of a change in the party entitled to execution or to issue a writ of restitution may be dealt with without notice.

(18) Rule 48.3 and paras. 1.3 and 1.4 of the PD supplementing Part 48 (Amount of costs where costs are payable under a contract) are of particular relevance to mortgage claims.

(19) In summary, where under a mortgage a mortgagee has a contractual right to his or her costs, the court's discretion in respect of costs under section 51 of the Supreme Court Act 1981 should be exercised so as to reflect that contractual right. The power of the court to disallow a mortgagee's costs sought to be added to the security stems not from section 51 but from the power of the courts of equity to fix the terms upon which redemption will be allowed. A decision by the court to refuse costs to a mortgagee litigant may be a decision in the exercise of

the court's discretion under section 51, or pursuant to its power to fix the terms upon which redemption will be allowed, or a decision as to the extent of the mortgagee's contractual right, in a given case, to add costs to his or her security, or any combination of these three things. A mortgagee is not to be deprived of a contractual or equitable right to add costs to his or her security without reference to the mortgagee's contractual or equitable rights to such costs and without a proper adjudication as to whether or not the mortgagee should be deprived of his or her costs.

(20) Outside Greater London the county courts have exclusive jurisdiction in mortgage possession cases.

6. Chancery Division Practice Direction

CDPD 7 Mortgages and possession orders

Mortgages

(i) RSC, O. 88, r.5(2) requires that in mortgage claims a copy of the mortgage must be exhibited to the witness statement or affidavit in support of the claim, and the original mortgage or charge certificate must be produced at the hearing.

(ii) Most building society mortgages now incorporate standard mortgage conditions, and in such cases a copy of the relevant conditions must also be exhibited.

(iii) Some standard forms of building society mortgage are now so abbreviated that they give no particulars of the amount of the advance, the term of the loan, the rate of interest or the amount of the instalments, but all these matters are defined in the mortgage conditions by reference to the offer letter. Where the offer letter is thus in effect incorporated into the mortgage by reference, that also should be exhibited to the witness statement or affidavit.

(iv) Many bank mortgages, although expressed in the usual bank "all monies" form, are also qualified by an offer letter or other side letter, providing for repayment of the advance by instalments. In *Governor and Company of the Bank of Scotland v. Grimes* [1985] 1 Q.B. 1179, it was held that in such cases the mortgage may be treated as an instalment mortgage for the purposes of Administration of Justice Act 1970, s.36 and Administration of Justice Act 1973, s.8. In these cases also the relevant letter should be exhibited to the witness statement or affidavit in support.

Suspended possession orders

(i) A suspended possession order is an order under which a person is entitled to a remedy subject to the fulfilment of a condition for the purposes of RSC, O. 46, r.2(1)(d), so that O. 46, r.4 accordingly applies. Permission to issue execution should not be given without notice and it follows that the court must therefore direct an application for such permission to be made upon notice (r.4(1)).

(ii) Suspended orders are made frequently in mortgagees' possession claims by virtue of s.36 of the Administration of Justice Act 1970 and in such claims the defendant is often in default of acknowledging service of the claim form.

(iii) Where a defendant has not acknowledged service no special directions as to service are needed but a claimant requiring permission to issue execution on a suspended possession order when there has been a default of acknowledging service must send a copy of the application notice and of the witness statement or affidavit in support of the application to each defendant in default at his last known address, so as to reach home not less than three clear days before the hearing, and will lodge with the Masters' clerk, at least one clear day before the hearing, the witness statement or affidavit in support of the application endorsed with a certificate by the claimant's solicitor in the form following or as near thereto as may be appropriate:

> "I certify that on the day of 20 . . . a copy of the application notice herein dated together with a true copy of the within document was sent by pre-paid letter post addressed to the defendant at [his] last known address being [insert address]. [signed] Claimant's Solicitor."

No further proof of service should normally be required in default cases.

(iv) The same principles apply and the same practice will be followed where leave to issue execution is required because six years or more have elapsed since the date of an unsuspended possession order or because there has been a change in the party liable to execution. (See RSC, O. 46, r.2.)

(v) Applications for permission to issue execution because of a change of the party entitled to execution or to issue a writ of restitution may be dealt with without notice.

7. **Civil Procedure Rules**

Types of claim in which Part 8 procedure may be followed

D–06   8.1—(1) The Part 8 procedure is the procedure set out in this Part.

(2) A claimant may use the Part 8 procedure where—

    (a)   he seeks the court's decision on a question which is unlikely to involve a substantial dispute of fact; or

    (b)   paragraph (6) applies.

(3) The court may at any stage order the claim to continue as if the claimant had not used the Part 8 procedure and, if it does so, the court may give any directions it considers appropriate.

(4) Paragraph (2) does not apply if a practice direction provides that the Part 8 procedure may not be used in relation to the type of claim in question.

(5) Where the claimant uses the Part 8 procedure he may not obtain default judgment under Part 12.

(6) A rule or practice direction may, in relation to a specified type of proceedings—

    (a)   require or permit the use of the Part 8 procedure; and

    (b)   disapply or modify any of the rules set out in this Part as they apply to those proceedings.

(Rule 8.9 provides for other modifications to the general rules where the Part 8 is being used.)

Contents of the claim form

8.2 Where the claimant uses the Part 8 procedure the claim form must state—

(a) that this Part applies;

(b)   (i) the question which the claimant wants the court to decide; or

       (ii) the remedy which the claimant is seeking and the legal basis for the claim to that remedy;

(c) if the claim is being made under an enactment, what that enactment is;

(d) if the claimant is claiming in a representative capacity, what that capacity is; and

(e) if the defendant is sued in a representative capacity, what that capacity is.

(Part 22 provides for the claim form to be verified by a statement of truth.)

Rule 7.5 provides for service of the claim form.)

(The costs practice direction sets out the information about a funding arrangement to be provided with the claim form where the claimant intends to seek to recover an additional liability.)

("Funding arrangement" and "additional liability" are defined in rule 43.2).

Issue of claim form without naming defendants

8.2A—(1) A practice direction may set out the circumstances in which a claim form may be issued under this Part without naming a defendant.

(2) The practice direction may set out those cases in which an application for permission must be made by application notice before the claim form is issued.[15]

(3) The application notice for permission—

(a) need not be served on any other person; and

(b) must be accompanied by a copy of the claim form that the applicant proposes to issue.

(4) Where the court gives permission it will give directions about the future management of the claim.

Acknowledgment of service

8.3—(1) The defendant must—

(a) file an acknowledgment of service in the relevant practice form not more than 14 days after service of the claim form; and

[15] Modified by The Civil Procedure (Amendment) Rules 2001 (S.I. 2001 No. 256).

    (b)　serve the acknowledgment of service on the claimant and any other party.

(2) The acknowledgment of service must state—

    (a)　whether the defendant contests the claim; and
    (b)　if the defendant seeks a different remedy from that set out in the claim form, what that remedy is.

(3) The following rules of Part 10 (acknowledgment of service) apply—

    (a)　rule 10.3(2) (exceptions to the period for filing an acknowledgment of service); and
    (b)　rule 10.5 (contents of acknowledgment of service).

(4) Part 11 (disputing the court's jurisdiction) applies subject to the modification that in rule 11(4)(a) and (5)(b) (time limit for application disputing court's jurisdiction) references to the period for filing a defence are treated as if they were references to a period of 14 days from the filing of an acknowledgment of service.
(The costs practice direction sets out the information about a funding arrangement to be provided with the acknowledgment of service where the defendant intends to seek to recover an additional liability.)
("Funding arrangement" and "additional liability" are defined in rule 43.2).

Consequence of not filing an acknowledgment of service

    8.4—(1) This rule applies where—

    (a)　defendant has failed to file an acknowledgment of service; and
    (b)　the time period for doing so has expired.

(2) The defendant may attend the hearing of the claim but may not take part in the hearing unless the court gives permission.

Filing and serving witness statements

    8.5—(1) The claimant must file any written evidence on which he intends to rely when he files his claim form.
    (2) The claimant's evidence must be served on the defendant with the claim form.
    (3) A defendant who wishes to rely on written evidence must file it when he files acknowledgement of service.
    (4) If he does so, he must also, at the same time, serve a copy of his evidence on the other parties.
    (5) The claimant may, within 14 days of service of the defendant's evidence on him, file further written evidence in reply.
    (6) If he does so, he must also, within the same time limit, serve a copy of his evidence on the other parties.
    (7) The claimant may rely on the matters set out in his claim form as evidence under this rule if the claim form is verified by a statement of truth.

Evidence—general

8.6—(1) No written evidence may be relied on at the hearing of the claim unless—

    (a) it has been served in accordance with rule 8.5; or
    (b) the court gives permission.

(2) The court may require or permit a party to give oral evidence at the hearing.

(3) The court may give directions requiring the attendance for cross-examination of a witness who has given written evidence.

(Rule 32.1 contains a general power for the court to control evidence.)

Part 20 claims

8.7 Where the Part 8 procedure is used, Part 20 (counterclaims, third party claims and other similar claims) applies except that a party may not make a Part 20 claim (as defined by rule 20.2) without the court's permission.

Procedure where defendant objects to use of the Part 8 procedure

8.8—(1) Where the defendant believes that the Part 8 procedure should not be used because—

    (a) there is a substantial dispute of fact; and
    (b) the use of the Part 8 procedure is not required or permitted by a rule or practice direction, he must state his reasons when he files his acknowledgement of service.

        (Rule 8.5 requires a defendant who wishes to rely on written evidence to file it when he files his acknowledgement of service.)

(2) When the court receives the acknowledgement of service and any written evidence it will give directions as to the future management of the case.

(Rule 8.1(3) allows the court to make an order that the claim continue as if the claimant had not used the Part 8 procedure.)

Modifications to the general rules

8.9 Where the Part 8 procedure is followed—

    (a) provision is made in this Part for the matters which must be stated in the claim form and the defendant is not required to file a defence and therefore—
        (i) Part 16 (statements of case) does not apply;
        (ii) Part 15 (defence) does not apply;
        (iii) any time limit in these Rules which prevents the parties from taking a step before a defence is filed does not apply;
        (iv) the requirement under rule 7.8 to serve on the defendant a form for defending the claim does not apply;

    (b) the claimant may not obtain judgment by request on an admission and therefore—

       (i) rules 14.4 to 14.7 do not apply;

      (ii) the requirement under rule 7.8 to serve on the defendant a form for admitting the claim does not apply; and

    (c) the claim shall be treated as allocated to the multi-track and therefore Part 26 does not apply.

8. **Form N5**

<table>
<tr>
<td rowspan="2">

Summons for possession of property
</td>
<td colspan="2">Claim No.</td>
</tr>
<tr>
<td colspan="2">

In the

                      County Court
</td>
</tr>
<tr>
<td>

Claimant's
full name
address
</td>
<td></td>
<td colspan="2">The court office is open from 10 am to 4 pm Monday to Friday

Telephone</td>
</tr>
<tr>
<td>

Name and
address for
service and
payment
(if different
from above)
Ref/Tel No.
</td>
<td></td>
<td colspan="2">

seal</td>
</tr>
<tr>
<td>

Defendant's
full name
(including
title e.g. Mr.
Mrs or Miss)
and address
</td>
<td></td>
<td colspan="2"></td>
</tr>
</table>

The claimant (your landlord or mortgage lender) is **claiming possession**

of [ ]

for the reasons given in the attached particulars of claim.

The claimant is also making a claim for money.
(details are given in particulars of claim)

WHAT THIS MEANS

- On the date set out below, the court will decide whether or not you have to leave, and if you have to leave, when.

WHAT SHOULD YOU DO

- **Get help and advice immediately** from a solicitor or any of the advice agencies on the attached list.
- Make sure the court knows as much about your circumstances as possible by:
  - **filling in the reply form** attached to this summons, and
  - **coming to the hearing**

(The notes on the back of this form give you more information about what you should do.)

The court will make its decision

on [   ] **at** [   ] **am/pm**

at [ ]

Court fee

Solicitor's costs

Total amount

Summons issued on

Important notes to help you

No one can evict you from your home unless the court lets them. The court will not make a decision before the date shown on the front of the form. In certain cases the court can:
- allow you a reasonable time to pay rent arrears or the amount borrowed and let you stay in the property;
- decide not to make a possession order;
- give you time to find somewhere else to live, or
- (for mortgage cases regulated by the Consumer Credit Act only) look at the original loan agreement and decide if it is fair.

But, the court cannot decide any of these things unless it knows about your circumstances. To make sure of this, fill in the reply form **and come to the hearing, even if you have reached agreement about repayment with your landlord or mortgage lender since the summons was issued.**

Filling in the reply form

- You must fill in the reply and make sure it reaches the court **within 14 days after the date of service.** The date of service will be 7 days after the court posted the summons to you. The postmark will tell you when this was.
- Fill in the reply form and take or send it to the court even if you cannot come to the hearing.
- If you need help to fill it in you can get it from
  - any county court;
  - any of the advice agencies on the attached list;
  - a solicitor.
- Keep the summons and a copy of your reply form. The court will send a copy of your completed reply to the claimant.

Disagreeing with the claim

- If you disagree with the claim it is even more important that you get help, fill in the reply form and come to the hearing. You may be able to get help with your legal costs. Ask about the legal aid scheme at any firm of solicitors showing the legal aid sign or at any advice agency. A leaflet about legal aid is available from any county court.

Registration of judgments

- If the court orders you to pay money to the claimant (a money judgment) and you do not pay, your name and address may be entered in the Register of County Court Judgments. **This may make it difficult for you to get credit.**
- If the money is paid in full within the time stated on the order, the order **will not be registered.**

- If you do not pay within the time stated on any order, **the order will be registered** when the claimant takes steps to enforce payment.

Interest on judgments

- If the money judgment entered against you is for more than £5000, the claimant may be entitled to interest on the total amount.

How to pay

- **PAYMENT(S) MUST BE MADE to the person named at the address for payment quoting their reference and the court claim number.**

- **DO NOT bring or send payments to the court. THEY WILL NOT BE ACCEPTED.**

- You should allow at least 4 days for your payments to reach the claimant or his representative. **Ask for a receipt.**

- Make sure that you keep records and can account for all payments made. Proof may be required if there is any disagreement. It is not safe to send cash unless you use registered post.

- A leaflet giving further advice about payment can be obtained from the court.

- If you need more information you should contact the claimant or his representative.

Certificate of Service

I certify that the summons of which this is a true copy was served by me on

by posting it to the Defendant on

at the address stated on the summons

                                                                Officer of the Court

I certify that the summons has not been served for the following reasons:

                                                                Officer of the Court

9. Form N120

Particulars of claim for possession (mortgaged property)	In the	
		County Court
	Claim No.	

Claimant

Defendant(s)

About the mortgage (legal charge)

Paragraph 1
Insert date of legal charge or mortgage. Give the address of the property charged. **If there is more than one loan agreement,** the details required in paragraphs 1–5 should be given for each of them (see note above).

1 A mortgage (legal charge) was agreed between the claimant(s) and the defendant(s) on

The property charged was

Paragraph 2
Delete the words in brackets to show whether the property is a dwelling-house or part of one.

2 The property is a (dwelling-house) (part of a dwelling-house).

Paragraph 3
Delete paragraph (a) if the loan is not secured by a regulated consumer credit agreement. If it is, give date notice of default was given to defendant and delete paragraph (b).

3 (a) The loan secured by the mortgage is a regulated consumer credit agreement.
Notice of default was given to the defendant(s) on

(b) The loan secured by the mortgage is not a regulated consumer credit agreement.

Paragraph 4(a)
Say what the amount of arrears outstanding is up to the date of issue of the claim. Give details of all payments missed. If a schedule of payments missed or not made on time is attached, say so. Say whether payments generally have been made regularly and on time giving sufficient detail to support your claim for possession.

4 The reason(s) the claimant is asking for possession is that the defendant(s) has(ve) not complied with the conditions which apply to the mortgage (legal charge) because:

(a) the agreed repayments of the loan and interest have not been made. Details are set out below.

Paragraph 4(b)
Delete this paragraph if the claim
for possession is for arrears of
repayments only. If not, give
details of any other failure to
comply with the agreed terms of
the loan.

(b)

Paragraph 5(a)
Give the amount loaned. But see
note to paragraph 1 if more than
one loan agreement.

5 (a) The amount loaned was

(b) The current terms of repayment are:

Paragraph 5(b)
Give the current terms of
repayment. Where appropriate,
give the amounts of any regular
instalments and (separately) any
interest which has to be paid.

Paragraph 5(c)
Give the amount required to pay
the mortgage in full. The date of
the calculation must not be more
than 14 days after the issue of the
summons. Also, give details of the
costs which the claimant would
incur if the mortgage were to be
paid in full.

(c) the amount required to pay the mortgage in full as at

would be   taking into account any

adjustment for early settlement. The solicitors and administrative costs
which would be involved if there were full settlement would

amount to

Paragraph 5(d)
Delete this paragraph if there are
no additional payments due under
the terms of the mortgage,
e.g. default interest, penalties,
insurance, costs of previous court
proceedings, etc. If there are
payments due, say how much
and what it is for. Indicate
whether or not they are included
in the amounts at paragraph 5(b).

(d) The following additional payments are also due under the terms
of the mortgage (legal charge):

| | | Included in paragraph 5(b) | |
		Yes	No
£	for	☐	☐
£	for	☐	☐
£	for	☐	☐

Paragraph 5(e)
Delete this paragraph if there are no additional payments listed at paragraph 5(d). If there are payments, give details of any payments which are in arrear and say by how much.

(e) Of the payments in paragraph 5(d), the following are in arrears:

arrears of £

arrears of £

arrears of £

Paragraph 5(f)
Delete this paragraph if the loan is not secured by a regulated consumer credit agreement. If it is, give the total amount of the loan outstanding.

(f) The total amount outstanding under the loan agreement secured by

the mortgage is

Paragraph 5(g)
Give the rates of interest which applied when the agreement was first made, the rate which applied immediately before the arrears now claimed occurred and the current rate, if different.

(g) Interest rates which have applied to the mortgage (legal charge) are as follows:

Date	%	Date	%

Paragraph 6
Give details of any steps already taken to recover arrears or repayment of money. If there have been previous court proceedings, give the date they were started and concluded and the terms of any order(s) made.

6   The following steps have already been taken to recover the money secured by the mortgage:

About the defendant(s)

Paragraph 7
Give what details you know of the defendant's financial and other circumstances. Say in particular whether the claimant is paid interest or arrears direct under Social Security regulations and if so, how much.

7   The following information is known about the defendant's circumstances:

Paragraph 8
Delete this paragraph if the property (land) being claimed does not include a dwelling-house. If it does, delete (a) or (b) as appropriate. Give the name of the person to be given notice under section 8(3) of the Matrimonial Homes Act 1983.

8　(a) There is no one who should be given notice of these proceedings because of a registered interest in the property.

(b) Notice of these proceedings will be given to

[   ] who has a

registered interest in the property.

What the court is being asked to do

Paragraph 9
Delete paragraphs (a)–(c) as appropriate.

9　The claimant is asking the court to make an order that the defendant(s):

(a) give the claimant possession of the property mentioned in paragraph 1;

(b) pay the oustanding arrears;

(c) pay the costs of making this application.

Paragraph 10
Delete if not applicable.

10　The claimant is also asking that judgment is entered against the defendant(s) for the total amount outstanding under the mortgage (legal charge).

Signed

(Solicitors for) Claimant

Date

Give an address where notices about this case can be sent to you

Postcode [   ]

10. **Chancery Masters' Practice**   **D–08**

Form PF5

Order for Possession of Mortgaged Property

IN THE HIGH COURT OF JUSTICE
CHANCERY DIVISION
Claim No.

Before   Master *[Sitting in Private]*

Claimant*

Defendant*

An Application by notice dated ( ) was made on (date)
by the [claimant] [defendant].

The Master heard   [counsel] [solicitor]   for [party]
[**The Master** read (documents)]

IT IS ORDERED that

(1)   [Unless the Defendant makes the payments set out in paragraph (2) below] the Defendant must within   days after being served with a copy of this Order personally/through the post give the Claimant possession of [Description of mortgaged property]

(2)   This Order is suspended, and is not to be enforced, if the Defendant makes the following payments to the Claimant at the time specified below:

   (a)   £   on or before

   (b)   £   on the   day of every month being in part his continuing monthly mortgage instalments and in the part the arrears until all the un paid instalments have been paid.

   or

   (c)   £   on   day of every month towards the arrears of mortgage instalments until they have been paid and all future monthly mortgage instalments as they become due on the   day of each month.

Note – Enforcing the Order – If the Defendant does not make any of the payments the Claimant may apply to the Master at a further hearing, notice of which has been given to the Defendant, for permission to make the Defendant leave the property.

Costs – The Claimant may add the cost of this Application to the Master to the amount payable under the mortgage.

---

*Where there is more than one claimant/defendant, the parties should be described as follows:

(1) AB
(2) CD
(3) EF Claimants
    and
(1) GH
(2) IJ
(3) KL Defendants

11. **Form N29**

Order for Possession
(mortgaged property)

Plaintiff

Defendant(s)

In the

County Court

Case No.	Always quote this	
Plaintiff's Ref.		
Defendant's Ref.		

seal

The court orders that the defendant(s) give the plaintiff possession of

on the

⁽¹⁾delete if no money judgment **⁽¹⁾The court adjudges** that the defendant(s) pay the plaintiff £   which is the amount currently outstanding under the mortgage, on the

Delete or insert any additional orders made **The court orders** that

Delete or complete as necessary **The court orders** that the plaintiff's costs of this action
be taxed by the court on scale   and   be added to the amount owing under the mortgage
assessed at the sum of £   be paid by the defendant(s) on or before the

Dated:

To the defendant(s)

This means that you must leave the property on the date stated above, unless you pay the whole amount owing on the mortgage by then.

If you do not leave the property, the plaintiff will be able to ask the court bailiff to evict you.

Payments should be made to the plaintiff at the place where you would normally pay your monthly repayments. If you need more information about making payments you should contact the plaintiff. The court cannot accept any payments.

Delete if no order for taxation The plaintiff's costs are to be taxed, that is looked at by the judge to decide if they are reasonable. You will be sent a copy of the plaintiff's bill and will be able to object to any amounts in it. The judge will decide if your objections are vaild.

Plaintiff's/Solicitor's address

──── Note ────

Delete if no money judgment or order for payment of costs

If you do not pay the money owed when it is due and the plaintiff takes steps to enforce payment, the order will be registered in the Register of County Court Judgments. **This may make it difficult for you to get credit**. Further information about registration is available in a leaflet which you can get from any county court office.

The court office at

is open between 10 am and 4 pm Monday to Friday. Address all communications to the Court Manager quoting the case number

N29 Order for possession (mortgaged property)

12. **Form N31**

Order for possession (Suspended)
(mortgaged property)

In the	
	County Court
Case No. *Always quote this*	
Plaintiff's Ref.	
Defendant's Ref.	

Plaintiff

Defendant(s)

Seal

The court orders that the defendant(s) give the plaintiff possession of

on the

(1)Delete if no money judgment (1)**The court adjudges** that the defendant(s) pay the plaintiff £   , which is the amount currently outstanding under the mortgage, on the

The court orders that the order (and judgment) be **suspended** and be not enforced so long as the defendant(s) pay to the plaintiff the arrears due under the mortgage of £   by the payments set out below **in addition to** the regular mortgage payments that fall due from time to time; and be discharged when those arrears have been paid.

Payments in respect of arrears

Complete and delete as necessary £   on or before the

£   per calendar month; the first such payment being made on or before the

(for   months and then £   per calendar month)

Delete or insert any additional orders made **The court orders** that

The court orders that the plaintiff's costs of this action

Complete and delete as necessary be taxed by the court on Scale   and   be added to the amount owing under the mortgage

assessed at the sum of £   be paid by the defendant(s) on or before the

Dated:

To the defendant(s)

This means that, unless you pay the arrears under the mortgage by at least the payments set out above **in addition to your normal payments**, you must leave the property on the date stated above.

If you do not make those payments or leave the property, the plaintiff will be able to ask the court bailiff to evict you.

Payments should be made to the plaintiff at the place where you would normally pay your monthly repayments. If you need more information about making payments you should contact the plaintiff. The court cannot accept any payments.

Delete if no order for taxation The plaintiff's costs are to be taxed, that is looked at by a judge to decide if they are reasonable. You will send a copy of the plaintiff's bill and will be able to object to any amounts in it. The judge will decide if your objections are valid.

Plaintiff's/Solicitor's address

—— Note ——
Delete if no money judgement or order for payment of costs

If you do not pay the money owed when it is due and the plaintiff takes steps to enforce payment, the order will be registered in the Register of County Court Judgments. **This may make it difficult for you to get credit.** Further information about registration is available in a leaflet which you can get from any county court office.

The court office at

is open between 10 am and 4 pm. When writing to the court, please address forms or letters to the Court Manager and quote the case number.

N31 Order for possession (possession suspended mortgaged property)

13. CPR Part 55.1–55.10: Possession Claims (Part II omitted)

D–11

Contents of this part

Interpretation

55.1 In this Part—

    (a) "a possession claim" means a claim for the recovery of possession of land (including buildings or parts of buildings);

    (b) "a possession claim against trespassers" means a claim for the recovery of land which the claimant alleges is occupied only by a person or persons who entered or remained on the land without the consent of a person entitled to possession of that land but does not include a claim against a tenant or sub-tenant whether his tenancy has been terminated or not;

    (c) "mortgage" includes a legal or equitable mortgage and a legal or equitable charge and "mortgagee" is to be interpreted accordingly; and

    (d) "the 1988 Act" means the Housing Act 1988.

Scope

55.2—(2) The procedure set out in this Section of this Part must be used where the claim includes—

    (a) a possession claim brought by a—
        (i) landlord (or former landlord);
        (ii) mortgagee; or
        (iii) licensor (or former licensor);

    (b) a possession claim against trespassers; or

    (c) a claim by a tenant seeking relief from forfeiture.

(2) This Section of this Part—

    (a)   is subject to any enactment or practice direction which sets out special provisions with regard to any particular category of claim; and

    (b)   does not apply where the claimant uses the procedure set out in Section II of this Part.

        (CCR Order 24, rule 10(1) provides that where an application for an interim possession order is made, unless otherwise provided, Part 55 does not apply.)

Starting the claim

55.3—(1) The claim must be started in the county court for the district in which the land is situated unless paragraph (2) applies or an enactment provides otherwise.

(2) The claim may be started in the High Court if the claimant files with his claim form a certificate stating the reasons for bringing the claim in that court verified by a statement of truth in accordance with rule 22.1(1).

(3) The practice direction refers to circumstances which may justify starting the claim in the High Court.

(4) Where, in a possession claim against trespassers, the claimant does not know the name of a person in occupation or possession of the land, the claim must be brought against "persons unknown" in addition to any named defendants.

(5) The claim form and form of defence sent with it must be in the forms set out in the relevant practice direction.

Particulars of claim

55.4 The particulars of claim must be filed and served with the claim form. (The relevant practice direction and Part 16 provide details about the contents of the particulars of claim.)

Hearing date

55.5—(1) The court will fix a date for the hearing when it issues the claim form.

(2) In a possession claim against trespassers the defendant must be served with the claim form, particulars of claim and any witness statements—

    (a)   in the case of residential property, not less than five days; and

    (b)   in the case of other land, not less than two days, before the hearing date.

(3) In all other possession claims—

    (a)   the hearing date will be not less than 28 days from the date of issue of the claim form;

    (b)   the standard period between the issue of the claim form and the hearing will be not more than eight weeks; and

(c) the defendant must be served with the claim form and particulars of claim not less than 21 days before the hearing date.

(Rule 3.1(2)(a) provides that the court may extend or shorten the time for compliance with any rule.)

Service of claims against trespassers

55.6 ...

Defendant's response

55.7—(1) An acknowledgment of service is not required and Part 10 does not apply.

(2) In a possession claim against trespassers rule 15.2 does not apply and the defendant need not file a defence.

(3) Where, in any other possession claim, the defendant does not file a defence within the time specified in rule 15.4, he may take part in any hearing but the court may take his failure to do so into account when deciding what order to make about costs.

(4) Part 12 (default judgment) does not apply in a claim to which this Part applies.

The hearing

55.8—(1) At the hearing fixed in accordance with rule 55.5(1) or at any adjournment of that hearing, the court may—

(a) decide the claim; or
(b) give case management directions.

(2) Where the claim is genuinely disputed on grounds which appear to be substantial, case management directions given under paragraph (1)(b) will include the allocation of the claim to a track or directions to enable it to be allocated.

(3) Except where—

(a) the claim is allocated to the fast track or the multi-track; or
(b) the court orders otherwise,

any fact that needs to be proved by the evidence of witnesses at a hearing referred to in paragraph (1) may be proved by evidence in writing.

(Rule 32.2(1) sets out the general rule about evidence. Rule 32.2(2) provides that rule 32.2(1) is subject to any provision to the contrary.)

(4) Subject to paragraph (5), all witness statements must be filed and served at least two days before the hearing.

(5) In a possession claim against trespassers all witness statements on which the claimant intends to rely must be filed and served with the claim form.

(6) Where the claimant serves the claim form and particulars of claim, he must produce at the hearing a certificate of service of those documents and rule 6.14(2)(a) does not apply.

Allocation

55.9—(1) When the court decides the track for a possession claim, the matters to which it shall have regard include—

   (a) the matters set out in rule 26.8 as modified by the relevant practice direction;

   (b) the amount of any arrears of rent or mortgage instalments;

   (c) the importance to the defendant of retaining possession of the land; and

   (d) the importance of vacant possession to the claimant.

(2) The court will only allocate possession claims to the small claims track if all the parties agree.

(3) Where a possession claim has been allocated to the small claims track the claim shall be treated, for the purposes of costs, as if it were proceeding on the fast track except that trial costs shall be in the discretion of the court and shall not exceed the amount that would be recoverable under rule 46.2 (amount of fast track costs) if the value of the claim were up to £3,000.

(4) Where all the parties agree the court may, when it allocates the claim, order that rule 27.14 (costs on the small claims track) applies and, where it does so, paragraph (3) does not apply.

Possession claims relating to mortgaged residential property

55.10—(1) This rule applies where a mortgagee seeks possession of land which consists of or includes residential property.

(2) Not less than 14 days before the hearing the claimant must send a notice to the property addressed to "the occupiers".

(3) The notice referred to in paragraph (2) must—

   (a) state that a possession claim for the property has started;

   (b) show the name and address of the claimant, the defendant and the court which issued the claim form; and

   (c) give details of the hearing.

(4) The claimant must produce at the hearing—

   (a) a copy of the notice; and

   (b) evidence that he has served it.

14. **CPR Part 55**

PRACTICE DIRECTION—POSSESSION CLAIMS

Section I—General Rules

55.3—Starting the Claim

1.1 Except where the county court does not have jurisdiction, possession claims should normally be brought in the county court. Only exceptional circumstances justify starting a claim in the High Court.

1.2 If a claimant starts a claim in the High Court and the court decides that it should have been started in the county court, the court will normally either strike the claim out or transfer it to the county court on its own initiative. This is likely to result in delay and the court will normally disallow the costs of starting the claim in the High Court and of any transfer.

1.3 Circumstances which may, in an appropriate case, justify starting a claim in the High Court are if—

(1) there are complicated disputes of fact;
(2) there are points of law of general importance; or
(3) the claim is against trespassers and there is a substantial risk of public disturbance or of serious harm to persons or property which properly require immediate determination.

1.4 The value of the property and the amount of any financial claim may be relevant circumstances, but these factors alone will not normally justify starting the claim in the High Court.

1.5 The claim form and defence must be in the forms annexed to this practice direction.

55.4—Particulars of claim

2.1 In a possession claim the particulars of claim must:

(1) identify the land to which the claim relates;
(2) state whether the claim relates to residential property;
(3) state the ground on which possession is claimed;
(4) give full details about any mortgage or tenancy agreement; and
(5) give details of every person who, to the best of the claimant's knowledge, is in possession of the property.

Residential property let on a tenancy

2.2 ...
2.3 ...
2.4 ...

Land subject to a mortgage

2.5 If the claim is a possession claim by a mortgagee, the particulars of claim must also set out:

(1) if the claim relates to residential property whether:

    (a) a land charge of Class F has been registered under section 2(7) of the Matrimonial Homes Act 1967;

    (b) a notice registered under section 2(8) or 8(3) of the Matrimonial Homes Act 1983 has been entered and on whose behalf; or

    (c) a notice under section 31(10) of the Family Law Act 1996 has been registered and on whose behalf; and

if so, that the claimant will serve notice of the claim on the persons on whose behalf the land charge is registered or the notice or caution entered.

(2) the state of the mortgage account by including;

    (a) the amount of;
        (i) the advance;
        (ii) any periodic repayment; and
        (iii) any payment of interest required to be made;

    (b) the amount which would have to be paid (after taking into account any adjustment for early settlement) in order to redeem the mortgage at a stated date not more than 14 days after the claim started specifying the amount of solicitor's costs and administration charges which would be payable;

    (c) if the loan which is secured by the mortgage is a regulated consumer credit agreement, the total amount outstanding under the terms of the mortgage; and

    (d) the rate of interest payable:

        (i) at the commencement of the mortgage;
        (ii) immediately before any arrears referred to in paragraph (3) accrued;
        (iii) at the commencement of the proceedings.

(3) if the claim is brought because of failure to pay the periodic payments when due:

    (a) in schedule form, the dates when the arrears arose, all amounts due, the dates and amounts of all payments made and a running total of the arrears;

    (b) give details of:

        (i) any other payments required to be made as a term of the mortgage (such as for insurance premiums, legal costs, default interest, penalties, administrative or other charges);

        (ii) any other sums claimed and stating the nature and amount of each such charge; and

        (iii) whether any of these payments is in arrears and whether or not it is included in the amount of any periodic payment.

(4) whether or not the loan which is secured by the mortgage is a regulated consumer credit agreement and, if so, specify the date on which any notice required by sections 76 or 87 of the Consumer Credit Act 1974 was given;

(5) if appropriate details that show the property is not one to which section 141 of the Consumer Credit Act 1974 applies;

(6) any relevant information about the defendant's circumstances, in particular:

   (a) whether the defendant is in receipt of social security benefits; and

   (b) whether any payments are made on his behalf directly to the claimant under the Social Security Contributions and Benefits Act 1992;

(7) give details of any tenancy entered into between the mortgagor and mortgagee (including any notices served); and

(8) state any previous steps which the claimant has taken to recover the money secured by the mortgage or the mortgaged property and, in the case of court proceedings, state:

   (a) the dates when the claim started and concluded; and

   (b) the dates and terms of any orders made.

Possession claim against trespassers

2.6 ...

55.5—Hearing Date

3.1 The court may exercise its powers under rules 3.1(2)(a) and (b) to shorten the time periods set out in rules 55.5(2) and (3).

3.2 Particular consideration should be given to the exercise of this power if:

   (1) the defendant, or a person for whom the defendant is responsible, has assaulted or threatened to assault:

      (a) the claimant;

      (b) a member of the claimant's staff; or

      (c) another resident in the locality;

   (2) there are reasonable grounds for fearing such an assault; or

   (3) the defendant, or a person for whom the defendant is responsible, has caused serious damage or threatened to cause serious damage to the property or to the home or property of another resident in the locality.

3.3 Where paragraph 3.2 applies but the case cannot be determined at the first hearing fixed under rule 55.5, the court will consider what steps are needed to finally determine the case as quickly as reasonably practicable.

55.6—Service in claims against trespassers

4.1 ...

55.8—The Hearing

5.1 Attention is drawn to rule 55.8(3). Each party should wherever possible include all the evidence he wishes to present in his statement of case, verified by a statement of truth.

5.2 If relevant the claimant's evidence should include the amount of any rent or mortgage arrears and interest on those arrears. These amounts should, if possible, be up to date to the date of the hearing (if necessary by specifying a daily rate of arrears and interest). However, rule 55.8(4) does not prevent such evidence being brought up to date orally or in writing on the day of the hearing if necessary.

5.3 If relevant the defendant should give evidence of:

(1) the amount of any outstanding social security or housing benefit payments relevant to rent or mortgage arrears; and

(2) the status of:

(a) any claims for social security or housing benefit about which a decision has not yet been made; and

(b) any applications to appeal or review a social security or housing benefit decision where that appeal or review has not yet concluded.

5.4 If:

(1) the maker of a witness statement does not attend a hearing; and

(2) the other party disputes material evidence contained in his statement,

the court will normally adjourn the hearing so that oral evidence can be given.

Evidence in mortgage possession claim

5.5 Attention is drawn to section 113 of the Land Registration Act 1925 which provides that office copies of the register and of documents filed in the Land Registry, including original charges, are admissible in evidence to the same extent as the originals.

55.9—Allocation

6.1 The financial value of the property will not necessarily be the most important factor in deciding the track for a possession claim and the court may direct a possession claim to be allocated to the fast track even though the value of the property is in excess of £15,000.

Consumer Credit Act Claims Relating to the Recovery of Land

7.1 Any application by the defendant for a time order under section 129 of the Consumer Credit Act 1974 may be made:

(1) in his defence; or

(2) by application notice in the proceedings.

15. Form N5 (as amended)

Claim form for possession of property

In the

Claim No.

Claimant
(name(s) and address(es))

SEAL

Defendant(s)
(name(s) and address(es))

The claimant is claiming possession of :

which (includes) (does not include) residential property. Full particulars of the claim are attached.
(The claimant is also making a claim for money).

This claim will be heard on: 20   at   am/pm

at

At the hearing
• The court will consider whether or not you must leave the property and, if so, when.
• It will take into account information the claimant provides and any you provide.

What you should do
• Get help and advice immediately from a solicitor or an advice agency.
• Help yourself and the court by **filling in the defence form** and **coming to the hearing** to make sure the court knows all the facts.

Defendant's name and address for service

Court fee	£
Solicitor's costs	£
Total amount	£

Issue date	

N5 Claim form for possession of property (10.01)   *Printed on behalf of The Court Service*

Claim No.	

Grounds for possession

The claim for possession is made on the following ground(s):

☐ rent arrears

☐ other breach of tenancy

☐ forfeiture of the lease

☐ mortgage arrears

☐ other breach of the mortgage

☐ trespass

☐ other *(please specify)* _____

Anti-social behaviour

The claimant is alleging:

☐ actual or threatened assault

☐ actual or threatened serious damage to the property

See full details in the attached particulars of claim

Does, or will, the claim include any issues under the Human Rights Act 1998?   ☐ Yes ☐ No

Statement of Truth

*(I believe)(The claimant believes) that the facts stated in this claim form are true.
* I am duly authorised by the claimant to sign this statement.

signed _____ date _____

*(Claimant)(Litigation friend *(where the claimant is a child or a patient)*)(Claimant's solicitor)
*delete as appropriate

Full name _____

Name of claimant's solicitor's firm _____

position or office held _____
                    (if signing on behalf of firm or company)

Claimant's or claimant's solicitor's address to which documents or payments should be sent if different from overleaf.		*if applicable*	
		Ref. no.	
		fax no.	
		DX no.	
		e-mail	
	Postcode	Tel. no.	

16. **Form N120 (as amended)**

**Particulars of claim
for possession**
(mortgaged residential
premises)

⌐In the   ⌐Claim No.

Claimant

Defendant

1.   The claimant has a right to possession of:

About the mortgage

2.   On   the claimant(s) and the defendant(s) entered into a mortgage of the
      above premises.

3.   To the best of the claimant's knowledge the following persons are in possession of the property:

[Delete (a) or (b) as appropriate]

4   (a) The agreement for the loan secured by the mortgage (or at least one of them) is a
          regulated consumer credit agreement. Notice of default was given to the defendant(s)
          on   20   .

      (b) The agreement for the loan secured by the mortgage is not (or none of them is) a regulated consumer
          credit agreement.

5.   The claimant is asking for possession on the following ground(s):

      (a) the defendant(s) (has)(have) not paid the agreed repayments of the loan and interest.
      Give details:

(b) because:

6.　(a) The amount loaned was £

(b) The current terms of repayment are: *(include any current periodic repayment and any current payment of interest)*

(c) The total amount required to pay the mortgage in full as at　　　　　　20　(not more than 14 days after the claim was issued) would be £　　　　　　taking into account any adjustment for early settlement. This includes £　　　　　　payable for solicitor's costs and administration charges.

(d) The following additional payments are also required under the terms of the mortgage:

　　£　　　　　　for　　　　　　[not] included in 6(c)

　　£　　　　　　for　　　　　　[not] included in 6(c)

　　£　　　　　　for　　　　　　[not] included in 6(c)

(e) Of the payments in paragraph 6(d), the following are in arrears:

　　　　　　arrears of £

　　　　　　arrears of £

　　　　　　arrears of £

[(f) The total amount outstanding under the regulated loan agreement secured by the mortgage is £　　　　　　]

(g) Interest rates which have been applied to the mortgage:

　　(i) at the start of the mortgage　　　　% p.a.

　　(ii) immediately before any arrears were accrued　　　　% p.a.

　　(iii) at the start of the claim　　　　% p.a.

7.   The following steps have already been taken to recover the money secured by the mortgage:

About the defendant(s)

8.   The following information is known about the defendant's circumstances:
(in particular say whether the defendant(s) (is)(are) in receipt of social security benefits and whether any payments are made directly to the claimant)

[Delete either (a) or (b) as appropriate]

9.   (a) There is no one who should be given notice of these proceedings because of a registered interest in the property under section 31(10) of the Family Law Act 1996 or section 2(8) or 8(3) of the Matrimonial Homes Act 1983 or section 2(7) of the Matrimonial Homes Act 1967.

(b) Notice of these proceedings will be given to   who has a registered interest in the property.

Tenancy

[Delete if inappropriate]

10.   A tenancy was entered into between the mortgagor and the mortgagee on
A notice was served on

What the court is being asked to do

11.   The claimant asks the court to order that the defendant(s):

(a) give the claimant possession of the premises;

(b) pay to the claimant the total amount outstanding under the mortgage.

Statement of Truth

*(I believe)(The claimant believes) that the facts stated in these particulars of claim are true.
* I am duly authorised by the claimant to sign this statement.

signed _____ date _____

*(Claimant)(Litigation friend *(where claimant is a child or a patient)*)(Claimant's solicitor)
delete as appropriate

Full name _____

Name of claimant's solicitor's firm _____

position or office held _____
                        (if signing on behalf of firm or company)

---

17. **Form N206B**

Notice of issue
(possession claim)

In the

Claim No.

Claimant

Defendant

Issue fee

Your claim was issued on

Seal

Date of hearing:
The claim will be heard on

20   at   am/pm

at

embargoed until 15 October 2001

Evidence
- If you intend to rely on any witness statements, you must file them in the court office and serve copies on all the other parties **no later than 2 clear working days before the hearing.**
- In a claim for possession against trespassers, any witness statements must be served with the claim form.

Hearing
At the hearing the court may:
- decide the claim;
- adjourn the claim to be heard on another day, or
- give case management directions and, in some cases, allocate the claim to a track.

Claimant's (solicitor's) address

Ref.

N206B Notice of issue (possession claim)

18. Notes for defendant—mortgaged residential premises

Notes for defendant - mortgaged residential premises

The claimant has asked the court to make an order that you give up possession of the premises mentioned in the claim form. You should note that no-one can evict you from the property unless the court says that they can; the court will not make a decision before the hearing date. What you do may affect the court's decision. You should therefore take action immediately. These notes explain in more detail what you can do.

You should:
- get help and advice immediately from a solicitor or advice agency (see 'Getting help' below);
- fill in the attached defence form and return it to the court within 14 days of receiving the claim form;
- attend the hearing, even if you have agreed about repayment of any arrears with your mortgage lender

What will happen at the hearing?

A judge will decide whether or not to make an order for possession. In making this decision, the judge will take account of the information provided by the claimant. The judge will also take account of any information you provide, such as details of your personal and financial circumstances, any proposal you have made to pay off any arrears, and any dispute you have about the amount owing. But the judge can only take the information into account if you provide it. Fill in these details on the defence form and attend the hearing. It is in your best interests to do both.

What kind of orders can the judge make?

The judge can:
- decide not to make an order
- make an order for possession but suspend it. This means that you will not have to give up possession so long as you can pay off any arrears in a reasonable time (the judge will decide how long) and pay the instalments as well;
- make a possession order for some future date to allow you time to move out or find somewhere else to live; or
- make an order that you give up possession a very short time ahead.
- if the loan agreement is 'regulated' (see paragraph 4 of the particulars of claim) the judge can make other orders which may help you.

Getting help

You should get help and advice immediately from a solicitor or an advice agency. This is particularly important whether or not you disagree with the claim. You may qualify for assistance from the Community Legal

N7 Notes for defendant - mortgaged residential premises (10.01)   *Printed on behalf of The Court Service*

Service Fund (CLSF) to *Community Legal Service* meet some or all of your legal costs. Ask about the CLSF at any county court office or any information or help point which displays this logo. Court staff can only help you complete the defence form and tell you about court procedures. **They cannot give legal advice.**

Replying to the claim

Although you should normally fill in the defence form and return it to the court within 14 days, the court will accept your defence at any time before, or even at, the hearing. You should note, however, that if you do return the form after the 14-day period, the court may order you to pay any costs caused by the delay.

Regulated consumer credit agreements

If you intend to apply to the court to consider or change the terms of your agreement, you should get advice immediately.

Paying any arrears

The court cannot accept payments. If you want to pay all or part of any arrears, send them to the claimant at the address for payment shown on the claim form, quoting the claimant's reference number, if one is given. Make sure you get receipts for all payments made. Proof may be required

if there is any disagreement. Make sure you include on your defence form details of any payments you have made since the claim was issued, saying how much was paid, to whom and when.

Enforcement of a possession order

Where the court makes a possession order, the claimant can ask a bailiff or sheriff to evict you if:

- you do not give up possession on the date given in the order for possession; or
- you do not make payments in accordance with the suspended order for possession.

If your circumstances change after the possession order is made, you may apply to the court for the order to be varied. Use application form N244, which is available from any court office. You may have to pay a fee to make the application.

Registration of judgments

If a county court makes a money judgment (e.g. for the balance due under the mortgage) your name and address will be entered in the Register of County Court Judgments if the claimant has to take steps to enforce the judgment. This may make it difficult for you to obtain credit.

19. Defence Form

Defence form
(mortgaged residential premises)

In the	Claim No.
	Claimant
	Defendant(s)
Date of hearing	

Personal details

1. Please give your:

    Forename(s)

    Surname

    Address *(if different from the address on the claim form)*

    post code

Disputing the claim

2. Do you agree with what is said about the property and the mortgage agreement in the particulars of claim? ☐ Yes ☐ No

    If No, set out your reasons below

3. Do you agree that there are arrears of mortgage repayments as stated in the particulars of claim? ☐ Yes ☐ No

    If No, state how much the arrears are: £_____ ☐ None

4. If the particulars of claim give any reasons for possession other than arrears of mortgage repayments, do you agree with what is said?   ☐ Yes   ☐ No

If No, give details below:

(Only answer these questions if the loan secured by the mortgage (or part of it) is a regulated consumer credit agreement)

5. Do you want the court to consider whether or not the terms of your original loan agreement are fair?   ☐ Yes   ☐ No

6. Do you intend to apply to the court for an order changing the terms of your loan agreement (a time order)?   ☐ Yes   ☐ No

Arrears

7. Have you paid any money to your mortgage lender since the claim was issued?   ☐ Yes   ☐ No

If Yes, state how much you have paid and when: £_____   date_____

8. Have you come to any agreement with your mortgage lender about repaying the arrears since the claim was issued?   ☐ Yes   ☐ No

I have agreed to pay £_____ each (week)(month).

9. If you have not reached an agreement with your mortgage lender, do you want the court to consider allowing you to pay the arrears by instalments?   ☐ Yes   ☐ No

10. How much can you afford to pay in addition to the current instalments?   £_____ per (week)(month)

About yourself

State benefits

11. Are you receiving Income Support?   ☐ Yes   ☐ No

12. Have you applied for Income Support?   ☐ Yes   ☐ No

If Yes, when did you apply?   _____

13. Does the Department of Social Security pay your mortgage   ☐ Yes   ☐ No
interest?

Dependants *(people you look after financially)*

14. Have you any dependant children?   ☐ Yes   ☐ No

If Yes, give the number in each age group below:

☐ under 11   ☐ 11-15   ☐ 16-17   ☐ 18 and over

Other dependants

15. Give details of any other dependants for whom you are
financially responsible:

Other residents

16. Give details of any other people living at the premises for
whom you are not financially responsible:

Money you receive

		Weekly	Monthly
17. Usual take-home pay or income if self-employed *including overtime, commission, bonuses*	£_____	☐	☐
Job Seekers allowance	£_____	☐	☐
Pension	£_____	☐	☐
Child benefit	£_____	☐	☐
Other benefits and allowances	£_____	☐	☐
Others living in my home give me	£_____	☐	☐
I am paid maintenance for myself (or children) of	£_____	☐	☐
Other income	£_____	☐	☐
Total income	£_____	☐	☐

Bank accounts and savings

18. Do you have a current bank or building society account?　　☐ Yes　　☐ No

If Yes, is it

☐ in credit? If so, by how much?　£_____

☐ overdrawn? If so, by how much? £_____

19. Do you have a savings or deposit account?　　☐ Yes　　☐ No

If Yes, what is the balance?　£_____

Money you pay out

20. Do you have to pay any court orders or fines?　　☐ Yes　　☐ No

Court	Claim/Case number	Balance owing	Instalments paid
		Total instalments paid £	per month

21. Give details if you are in arrears with any of the court payments or fines:

22. Do you have any loan or credit debts?　　☐ Yes　　☐ No

Loan/credit from	Balance owing	Instalments paid
	Total instalments paid £	per month

23. Give details if you are in arrears with any loan / credit repayments:

Regular expenses
(Do not include any payments made by other members of the household out of their own income)

24. What regular expenses do you have?
(List below)

		Weekly	Monthly
Council tax	£_____	☐	☐
Gas	£_____	☐	☐
Electricity	£_____	☐	☐
Water charges	£_____	☐	☐
TV rental & licence	£_____	☐	☐
Telephone	£_____	☐	☐
Credit repayments	£_____	☐	☐
Mail order	£_____	☐	☐
Housekeeping, food, school meals	£_____	☐	☐
Travelling expenses	£_____	☐	☐
Clothing	£_____	☐	☐
Maintenance payments	£_____	☐	☐
Other mortgages	£_____	☐	☐
Other	£_____	☐	☐
Total expenses	£_____	☐	☐

Priority debts

25. This section is for **arrears** only. **Do not** include regular expenses listed at Question 24.

		Weekly	Monthly
Council tax arrears	£_____	☐	☐
Water charges arrears	£_____	☐	☐
Gas account	£_____	☐	☐
Electricity account	£_____	☐	☐
Maintenance arrears	£_____	☐	☐
Others *(give details below)*			
	£_____	☐	☐
	£_____	☐	☐
	£_____	☐	☐

26. If an order for possession were to be made, would you have somewhere else to live? ☐ Yes ☐ No

If Yes, say when you would be able to move in: _____

27. Give details of any events or circumstances which have led to your being in arrears with your mortgage *(for example divorce, separation, redundancy, bereavement, illness, bankruptcy)*. If you believe you would suffer exceptional hardship by being ordered to leave the property immediately, say why.

Statement of Truth

*(I believe)(The defendant believes) that the facts stated in this defence form are true.
* I am duly authorised by the defendant to sign this statement.

signed_____ date _____
(Defendant)(Litigation friend(where defendant is a child or a patient)*)(Defendant's solicitor)
delete as appropriate

Full name _____

Name of defendant's solicitor's firm _____

position or office held _____
                         (if signing on behalf of firm or company)

20. **Particulars of Claim (County Court before and after October 15, 2001; High Court after October 15, 2001: Arrears of Periodic Payment)**

[DATE]

IN THE [   ] COUNTY COURT   CLAIM NO.   **D–35**

BETWEEN

[THE MORTGAGEE]

<u>Claimant</u>

and

[THE MORTGAGOR]

<u>Defendant</u>

PARTICULARS OF CLAIM[16]

1. By a legal mortgage pursuant to a deed dated [date] and made between the Claimant ("the mortgage"), the Defendant charged by way of legal mortgage the [freehold] [leasehold] property situate at and known as [address of property] and registered at HM Land Registry under title number [insert number] ("the property") to secure repayment of monies advanced by the Claimant to the Defendant in the sum of £[insert sum] together with interest thereon and such other monies as are, from time to time, owed by the Defendant to the Claimant ("the mortgage debt").

2. The mortgage incorporated the Claimant's Residential Mortgage Terms from time to time in force ("the Terms").

3. By clause 3 of the Terms, the Defendant covenanted with the Claimant that he would repay the mortgage debt with interest
   (a) By such monthly payments made on the first day of each month as the Claimant shall from time to time require or
   (b) At once if the mortgage debt becoming due and payable pursuant to clause 7 of the Terms. Clause 7 provides that the mortgage debt becomes payable immediately by the Defendant to the Claimant if the monthly payments due pursuant to clause 3 were in arrears in a sum which exceeds in total the amount of three monthly repayments.

4. The Defendant is in default pursuant to the terms of the mortgage by reason of the arrears outstanding thereunder exceeding three monthly payments.

5. Pursuant to clause 9 of the Terms when the entirety of the mortgage debt has become due and immediately repayable in accordance with clause 7 of the Terms, the Claimant may exercise all or any of the following powers:
   (a) the statutory power sale pursuant to the Law of Property Act 1925 free from the restricting or Terms imposed by section 103 of the Act;

---

[16] Form N120 may be more consistently used: see Precedents 9 or 16. If the claim is brought in the High Court, the Particulars should contain sufficient details to show s.141 of the Consumer Credit Act 1974 does not apply (CPR Part 55PD2.5(5)) the paragraphs addressing other matters under that Act should be deleted.

(b) to enter into possession of the property or any part thereof.

6. The Claimant seeks possession of the property.

7. The property comprises a dwelling house within section 21 of the County Courts Act 1984.

8. The loan secured upon the property is not a regulated consumer credit agreement pursuant to the Consumer Credit Act 1974.[17]

9. The state of account between the parties is as follows:

  (a) The amount of the advance was £[   ].

  (b) The monthly repayment required to be made is £[   ].

  (c) The amount which would have to be paid (after taking into account any adjustment for early settlement) in order to redeem the mortgage on [insert date][18] is £[insert total amount], of which £[insert amount] represents solicitor's costs and administrative charges which would be payable;

10. The rate of interest payable pursuant to clause 4 of the Term

  (a) At the commencement of the mortgage was [7%] per annum;

  (b) Immediately before any arrears referred to in the following sub-paragraph accrued was [6%] and, at the commencement of these proceedings was [$6\frac{1}{2}\%$];

11. The total amount of any interest or instalments in arrear at the commencement of these proceedings is £[insert amount].

12. The Claimant has not, prior to the commencement of these proceedings, taken any prior steps against the Defendant in respect of the property or the monies secured by the mortgage upon the property[19]

[13.(Before October 15, 2001) Attached to these Particulars of Claim is a Schedule detailing the payments which the Defendant has missed, [made late] and of other payments required under the terms of the mortgage.][20]

(After October 15, 2000) Attached to these Particulars of Claim is a Schedule detailing the dates the arrears arose, all amounts due, the dates and amounts of all payments made and a remaining total of the arrears. In addition the following details are provided in accordance with CPR Part 55PD 2.5(3)(b): [set out details].

14. No other relevant information is known by the Claimant about the Defendant's circumstances. No payments are made on his behalf direct to the Claimant by or under the Social Security Contribution and Benefits Act 1992.[21]

---

[17] If it is, the Particulars of Claim should so state and give the date on which any notice required by ss.76 and 87 of the Consumer Credit Act 1974 was given: CPR, Sched. 2, CPR Ord. 6 r. 5(5); CPR Part 55PD 2.5(4). In addition the Particulars of Claim should also state the total amount outstanding under the terms of the mortgage: *ibid.*, para. 2.2(c).

[18] Being a stated date not more than 14 days after the commencement of these proceedings *ibid.*, r. 5(6)(b); CPR Part 55PD 2.2(b).

[19] If any steps have been taken, they should be stated. If proceedings have been commenced, the date of commencement and conclusion should be stated together with the date and terms of any order: CPR, Sched. 2, CPR Ord. 6 r. 5(7); CPR Part 55PD 2.5(8).

[20] See CPR, Sched. 2, CPR Ord. 6 r. 5A(2)(b).

[21] If they are particulars of those payments must be provided: CPR, Sched. 2, CCR Ord. 6 r. 5A(2)(d); CPR Part 55PD 2.5(6).

15. (Before October 15, 2001) There is no person upon whom notice of this claim is required to be served in accordance with section 8(3) of the Matrimonial Homes Act 1983.[22]
   (1) Class F land charges under the Matrimonial Homes Act 1967, s.2 or
   (2) notice under ss.2(8) or 8(30 of the Matrimonial Homes Act 1983 or
   (3) notice under the Family Law Act 1996, s.31(10) has been entered or registered.[23]
16. (After October 15, 2001) No tenancy between the Claimant and the Defendant has been entered into.[24]

AND the Claimant claims:—

(1) Possession of the mortgaged property.
(2) Judgment in the sum of £[insert amount] being the monies due pursuant to the mortgage secured upon the property together with interest thereon pursuant to clause 4 of the Terms at the annual rate of [$6\frac{1}{2}\%$] giving a daily rate of accrual of £[insert amount] per day from [date of commencement of interest] until judgment or sooner payment.

[STATEMENT OF TRUTH]
[Solicitor's details]

---

[22] If there is the Particulars of Claim must state the name and address fo that person and a copy of them shall be filed for service upon that person. Although this Act has been repealed, its provisions were substantially re-enacted by Schedule 4 to the Family Law Act 1996. The Rules still refer to the former Act.

[23] If they have, details of who has entered or registered them must be given and the Claimant must state that notice of the claim will be served on them: CPR Part 55PD2.5(1).

[24] If one has, details must be provided: *ibid.*, para. 2.5(7).

INDEX

Abandoned premises,
possession proceedings, 16–24
Absolute owner,
See also **Owner.**
co-owners, 15–02, 15–02A
disabilities, persons subject to,
bankrupts, 15–02
minors 15–03–15–06. *See also* **Minors.**
generally, 15–01
married women 15–11. *See also* **Married women.**
mental disorder, persons suffering from,
15–07
minors. *See* **Minors.**
partners. *See* **Partners.**
Accord and satisfaction,
redemption out of court by, 18–36
Account,
allowances, mortgagee's, 25–02
building society, 8–24
contents, 25–02
costs,
exercising power of sale, 25–17
failure to accept proper tender, 25–07
foreclosure, 25–06–25–11
improvements, 25–16
joinder of parties, improper, 25–11
litigation, 25–18
maintenance of property, 25–14
management, 25–15
mortgage already paid off, 25–08
mortgage debt, in relation to,
25–12–25–17
oppressive conduct, 25–10
perfecting the security, 25–13
redemption, proceedings for,
25–06–25–11
security, in relation to, 25–12–25–17
untenable claims, 25–09
vexatious conduct, 25–10
current accounts, 25–04
foreclosure, 16–96
costs, 25–06–25–11
further advances, 25–03
future advances, 25–03
interest, 25–05
items, 25–02
judicial sale, 16–103
liability to account, 25–01
mortgagee in possession, liability of, 16–24,
16–31–16–35
basis of account, 16–33, 16–34
commission, 16–33
diligence, 16–34

Account—*cont.*
mortgagee in possession, liability of—*cont.*
duty, when arising, 16–32
extent of duty, 16–34
fair occupation rent, 16–34
generally, 16–31
gross negligence, 16–34
reasonable improvements, 16–34
rents, 16–35
speculation, 16–34
wilful default, 16–334
principal debt, 25–02
taking,
effect, 25–22
generally, 25–19
mortgagee in possession, 25–20
procedure, 25–21
Acknowledgment, 13–02
limitation. *See under* **Limitation.**
Action. *See* **Court proceedings.**
Administration,
by-passing moratorium, 23–18
dealing with charged property, 23–19
effect of application, 23–16
moratorium, 23–18
notice, 23–15
order, 23–17
presentation of petition, 23–16
procedure, 23–15
protection of creditors' interests, 23–20
Advances. *See* loans secured on land *under*
Building Society.
Advertising,
building society, 8–19
Advowsons, 6–08
Affirmation, 26–36
After-acquired goods, mortgage of,
bill of sale, 12–15
personal chattels, 12–15
Agency,
defences to claims by mortgagee, 26–30
receiver, appointment of, 16–46
Agreement,
consumer credit. *See* **Consumer credit.**
extrinsic evidence, 1–04
parol, 1–04
regulated. *See* **Regulated agreement.**
security, to create, 1–04
shams, 1–04
Agricultural charges,
See also **Agricultural mortgages.**
bankruptcy, 10–12
bill of sale, 10–12
creation, 10–07